Lecture Notes in Computer Science

Vol. 219: Advances in Cryptology – EUROCRYPT '85. Proceedings, 1985. Edited by F. Pichler. IX, 281 pages. 1986.

Vol. 220: RIMS Symposia on Software Science and Engineering II. Proceedings, 1983 and 1984. Edited by E. Goto, K. Araki and T. Yuasa. XI, 323 pages. 1986.

Vol. 221: Logic Programming '85. Proceedings, 1985. Edited by E. Wada. IX, 311 pages. 1986.

Vol. 222: Advances in Petri Nets 1985. Edited by G. Rozenberg. VI, 498 pages. 1986.

Vol. 223: Structure in Complexity Theory. Proceedings, 1986. Edited by A.L. Selman. VI, 401 pages. 1986.

Vol. 224: Current Trends in Concurrency. Overviews and Tutorials. Edited by J.W. de Bakker, W.-P. de Roever and G. Rozenberg. XII, 716 pages. 1986.

Vol. 225: Third International Conference on Logic Programming. Proceedings, 1986. Edited by E. Shapiro. IX, 720 pages. 1986.

Vol. 226: Automata, Languages and Programming. Proceedings, 1986. Edited by L. Kott. IX, 474 pages. 1986.

Vol. 227: VLSI Algorithms and Architectures – AWOC 86. Proceedings, 1986. Edited by F. Makedon, K. Mehlhorn, T. Papatheodorou and P. Spirakis. VIII, 328 pages. 1986.

Vol. 228: Applied Algebra, Algorithmics and Error-Correcting Codes. AAECC-2. Proceedings, 1984. Edited by A. Poli. VI, 265 pages. 1986.

Vol. 229: Algebraic Algorithms and Error-Correcting Codes. AAECC-3. Proceedings, 1985. Edited by J. Calmet. VII, 416 pages. 1986.

Vol. 230: 8th International Conference on Automated Deduction. Proceedings, 1986. Edited by J.H. Siekmann. X, 708 pages. 1986.

Vol. 231: R. Hausser, NEWCAT: Parsing Natural Language Using Left-Associative Grammar. II, 540 pages. 1986.

Vol. 232: Fundamentals of Artificial Intelligence. Edited by W. Bibel and Ph. Jorrand. VII, 313 pages. 1986.

Vol. 233: Mathematical Foundations of Computer Science 1986. Proceedings, 1986. Edited by J. Gruska, B. Rovan and J. Wiedermann. IX, 650 pages. 1986.

Vol. 234: Concepts in User Interfaces: A Reference Model for Command and Response Languages. By Members of IFIP Working Group 2.7. Edited by D. Beech. X, 116 pages. 1986.

Vol. 235: Accurate Scientific Computations. Proceedings, 1985. Edited by W.L. Miranker and R.A. Toupin. XIII, 205 pages. 1986.

Vol. 236: TEX for Scientific Documentation. Proceedings, 1986. Edited by J. Désarménien. VI, 204 pages. 1986.

Vol. 237: CONPAR 86. Proceedings, 1986. Edited by W. Händler, D. Haupt, R. Jeltsch, W. Juling and O. Lange. X, 418 pages. 1986.

Vol. 238: L. Naish, Negation and Control in Prolog. IX, 119 pages. 1986.

Vol. 239: Mathematical Foundations of Programming Semantics. Proceedings, 1985. Edited by A. Melton. VI, 395 pages. 1986.

Vol. 240: Category Theory and Computer Programming. Proceedings, 1985. Edited by D. Pitt, S. Abramsky, A. Poigné and D. Rydeheard. VII, 519 pages. 1986.

Vol. 241: Foundations of Software Technology and Theoretical Computer Science. Proceedings, 1986. Edited by K.V. Nori. XII, 519 pages. 1986.

Vol. 242: Combinators and Functional Programming Languages. Proceedings, 1985. Edited by G. Cousineau, P.-L. Curien and B. Robinet. V, 208 pages. 1986.

Vol. 243: ICDT '86. Proceedings, 1986. Edited by G. Ausiello and P. Atzeni. VI, 444 pages. 1986.

Vol. 244: Advanced Programming Environments. Proceedings, 1986. Edited by R. Conradi, T.M. Didriksen and D.H. Wanvik. VII, 604 pages. 1986

Vol. 245: H.F. de Groote, Lectures on the Complexity of Bilinear Problems. V, 135 pages. 1987.

Vol. 246: Graph-Theoretic Concepts in Computer Science. Proceedings, 1986. Edited by G. Tinhofer and G. Schmidt. VII, 307 pages. 1987.

Vol. 247: STACS 87. Proceedings, 1987. Edited by F.J. Brandenburg, G. Vidal-Naquet and M. Wirsing. X, 484 pages. 1987.

Vol. 248: Networking in Open Systems. Proceedings, 1986. Edited by G. Müller and R.P. Blanc. VI, 441 pages. 1987.

Vol. 249: TAPSOFT '87. Volume 1. Proceedings, 1987. Edited by H. Ehrig, R. Kowalski, G. Levi and U. Montanari. XIV, 289 pages. 1987.

Vol. 250: TAPSOFT '87. Volume 2. Proceedings, 1987. Edited by H. Ehrig, R. Kowalski, G. Levi and U. Montanari. XIV, 336 pages. 1987.

Vol. 251: V. Akman, Unobstructed Shortest Paths in Polyhedral Environments. VII, 103 pages. 1987.

Vol. 252: VDM '87. VDM – A Formal Method at Work. Proceedings, 1987. Edited by D. Bjørner, C.B. Jones, M. Mac an Airchinnigh and E.J. Neuhold. IX, 422 pages. 1987.

Vol. 253: J.D. Becker, I. Eisele (Eds.), WOPPLOT 86. Parallel Processing: Logic, Organization, and Technology. Proceedings, 1986. V, 226 pages. 1987.

Vol. 254: Petri Nets: Central Models and Their Properties. Advances in Petri Nets 1986, Part I. Proceedings, 1986. Edited by W. Brauer, W. Reisig and G. Rozenberg. X, 480 pages. 1987.

Vol. 255: Petri Nets: Applications and Relationships to Other Models of Concurrency. Advances in Petri Nets 1986, Part II. Proceedings, 1986. Edited by W. Brauer, W. Reisig and G. Rozenberg. X, 516 pages. 1987.

Vol. 256: Rewriting Techniques and Applications. Proceedings, 1987. Edited by P. Lescanne. VI, 285 pages. 1987.

Vol. 257: Database Machine Performance: Modeling Methodologies and Evaluation Strategies. Edited by F. Cesarini and S. Salza. X, 250 pages. 1987.

Vol. 258: PARLE, Parallel Architectures and Languages Europe. Volume I. Proceedings, 1987. Edited by J.W. de Bakker, A.J. Nijman and P.C. Treleaven. XII, 480 pages. 1987.

Vol. 259: PARLE, Parallel Architectures and Languages Europe. Volume II. Proceedings, 1987. Edited by J.W. de Bakker, A.J. Nijman and P.C. Treleaven. XII, 464 pages. 1987.

Vol. 260: D.C. Luckham, F.W. von Henke, B. Krieg-Brückner, O. Owe, ANNA, A Language for Annotating Ada Programs. V, 143 pages. 1987.

Vol. 261: J. Ch. Freytag, Translating Relational Queries into Iterative Programs. XI, 131 pages. 1987.

Vol. 262: A. Burns, A.M. Lister, A.J. Wellings, A Review of Ada Tasking. VIII, 141 pages. 1987.

Vol. 263: A.M. Odlyzko (Ed.), Advances in Cryptology – CRYPTO '86. Proceedings. XI, 489 pages. 1987.

Vol. 264: E. Wada (Ed.), Logic Programming '86. Proceedings, 1986. VI, 179 pages. 1987.

Vol. 265: K.P. Jantke (Ed.), Analogical and Inductive Inference. Proceedings, 1986. VI, 227 pages. 1987.

Vol. 266: G. Rozenberg (Ed.), Advances in Petri Nets 1987. VI, 451 pages. 1987.

Vol. 267: Th. Ottmann (Ed.), Automata, Languages and Programming. Proceedings, 1987. X, 565 pages. 1987.

Vol. 268: P.M. Pardalos, J.B. Rosen, Constrained Global Optimization: Algorithms and Applications. VII, 143 pages. 1987.

Vol. 269: A. Albrecht, H. Jung, K. Mehlhorn (Eds.), Parallel Algorithms and Architectures. Proceedings, 1987. Approx. 205 pages. 1987.

Lecture Notes in Computer Science

Edited by G. Goos and J. Hartmanis

324

M. P. Chytil L. Janiga V. Koubek (Eds.)

MFCS '88

Mathematical Foundations of Computer Science 1988

Proceedings of the 13th Symposium
Carlsbad, Czechoslovakia, August 29 – September 2, 1988

Springer-Verlag

Berlin Heidelberg New York London Paris Tokyo

Editors

Michal P. Chytil
Václav Koubek
Charles University
Malostranské nám. 25, CS-118 00 Prague 1, Czechoslovakia

Ladislav Janiga
Charles University
V Holešovičkách 2, CS-180 00 Prague 8, Czechoslovakia

CR Subject Classification (1987): D.3.3, F.1.2–3, F.3.2, F.4.1–3, G.2.2

ISBN 3-540-50110-X Springer-Verlag Berlin Heidelberg New York
ISBN 0-387-50110-X Springer-Verlag New York Berlin Heidelberg

Printing and binding: Druckhaus Beltz, Hemsbach/Bergstr.
2145/3140-543210

FOREWORD

This volume contains 11 invited papers and 42 short communications contributed for presentation at the 13th Symposium on Mathematical Foundations of Computer Science - MFCS'88, held at Carlsbad, Czechoslovakia, August 29 - September 2, 1988.

The contributions in these Proceedings were selected from 123 papers submitted in response to the call for papers. The following program committee members took part in the evaluation and the selection of submitted papers:
Franz-Josef Brandenburg (Passau), Michal Chytil (Praha), Aldo de Luca (Napoli), Peter van Emde Boas (Amsterdam), Rusinš Freivalds (Riga), Jozef Gruska (Bratislava), Juris Hartmanis (Ithaca), Matthew Hennessy (Brighton), Ker-I-Ko (Stony Brook), Vadim Kotov (Novosibirsk), Václav Koubek (Praha), Eugene L. Lawler (Berkeley), Antoni Mazurkiewicz (Warszawa), Dominique Perrin (Paris), Pavel Pudlák (Praha), Grzegorz Rozenberg (Leiden), Arto Salomaa (Turku), Andrzej Salwicki (Warszawa), James W. Thatcher (Yorktown Heights), Gerd Wechsung (Jena).

In evaluating the submitted papers, the following referees assisted the program committee members: I.J. Aalbersberg, L. Aceto, L. Banachowski, H. Barendregt, A. Bertoni, M. Bidoit, S.L. Bloom, A. Brandstädt, M. Broy, A. Carpi, A.K. Chandra, B.G. Cheblakov, L.A. Cherkasova, C. Choffrut, W.I. Chong, R. Cleaveland, C. de Felice, P. Degano, M. Dezani-Ciancaglini, P. Ďuriš, M. Fiby, A. Finkel, U. Goltz, S.S. Goncharov, M. Grabowski, P. Hájek, T. Harju, A. Hemmerling, H.J. Hoogeboom, R.R. Howell, J. Hromkovič, V.E. Itkin, M. Jantzen, J.P. Jouannaud, H. Jung, J. Karhumäki, A. Kelemenová, M. Kifer, H. Kirchner, P. Kleinschmidt, J.W. Klop, F. Kluźniak, R. Koymans, J. Krajíček, D. Kratsch, M. Křivánek, G.A. Kucherov, M. Latteux, M. Linna, G. Lischke, P. Materna, G. Mirkowska, T. Moriya, R. Motwani, H. Müller, V.A. Nepomniaschy, M. Nielsen, E. Ochmanski, E.R. Olderog, F.J. Oles, P. Padawitz, E. Pelz, W. Penczek, U. Petermann, A. Pitts, I. Prívara, A. Raghunathan, I.V. Ramakrishnan, J-L. Remy, A. Restivo, A. Rosenfeld, L.E. Rosier, K. Ruohonen, P. Ružička, M. Rycko, N. Sabadini, S.S. Safarov, K. Salomaa, P. Savický, H. Saran, S.G. Seduchyn, N.V. Shilov, L.

Staiger, P. Štěpánek, A. Stoughton, J. Šturc, K. Sutner, D.I. Sviridenko, A. Szalas, M. Takahashi, W. Thomas, J. Tiuryn, P. Turakainen, P. Urzyczyn, W. Tzeng, M. Vajteršic, G. Vidal-Naquet, W. Vogler, K. Voss, J. Vyskoč, E.G. Wagner, K.W. Wagner, T. Warnow, J. Wiedermann, M. Wirsing, S. Žák.

The symposium was organized by the Committee of Applied Cybernetics of the Czechoslovak Scientific and Technological Society in cooperation with the Faculty of Mathematics and Physics of Charles University, Prague, Computer Science Department of the Purkyně University, Brno, the Faculty of Natural Sciences of the Šafárik University, Košice, and the Faculty of Mathematics and Physics of Comenius University, Bratislava.

The organizing committee of MFCS'88 consisted of G. Andrejková, A. Goralčíková, J. Hromkovič, M. Chytil, L. Janiga - chairman, V. Koubek, J. Krajíček, B. Miniberger, J. Peterka, I. Peterková, Z. Renc, M. Zeithamlová, and J. Zlatuška.

As the editors of these Proceedings we wish to thank all those who submitted papers for consideration, and the program committee members with the referees for their meritorious work on evaluating the papers. Finally, the excellent cooperation of Springer-Verlag in the publication of this volume is highly appreciated.

Praha, May 1988

Michal P. Chytil, Ladislav Janiga, Václav Koubek

CONTENTS

INVITED LECTURES

COMMUNICATIONS

Sparse Sets, Tally Sets, and Polynomial Reducibilities*

Ronald V. Book

Department of Mathematics
University of California
Santa Barbara, Ca. 93106, U.S.A.

The properties of resource-bounded reducibilities have received a great deal of attention in the study of structural complexity theory. Recently, the properties of the corresponding reduction classes and degrees of sparse sets and of tally sets have been investigated. In some cases this has been done in the context of properties of reducibilities, which in other cases the motivation was quite different. There are some important examples of results about sparse sets and tally sets, and these include the following:

1. Efforts by P. Berman [12] and Fortune [17] relating to the Berman-Hartmanis conjecture [11] led Mahaney [27] to the result that $P = NP$ if and only if there is a sparse set that is NP-complete.
2. As reported by Berman and Hartmanis [11], A. Meyer observed that a set has polynomial-size circuits if and only if it is Turing reducible in polynomial time to some sparse set.
3. Results of Karp and Lipton [21], Long and Selman [28], and Balcázar, Book, and Schöning [7] culminated in results such as the equivalence of the following notions:
   a. the class $PSPACE$ is equal to the union (PH) of the classes in the polynomial-time hierarchy;
   b. there exists a sparse set S such that $PSPACE$ relativized to S is equal to PH relativized to S;
   c. for all sparse sets S, $PSPACE$ relativized to S is equal to PH relativized to S.

In the context of developing a structure theory for complexity classes and complexity-bounded reducibilities, one would like to develop intrinsic characterizations of reduction classes or degrees of a given set, i.e., for a set A characterize, in terms of properties other than reducibilities, the class of all sets B such that $B \leq_m^P A$, the class of all sets B such that $B \equiv_m^P A$, the class of all sets B such that $B \leq_T^P A$, etc. Similarly, one would like to develop intrinsic characterizations of the reducition classes of a class of sets, i.e., for a class $\mathcal{C}$ of sets characterize the class of all sets B such that for some $C \in \mathcal{C}$, $B \leq_m^P C$, the class of all sets B such that for some $C \in \mathcal{C}$, $B \equiv_m^P C$, etc.

The purpose of the present paper is to review a number of results having to do with resource-bounded reducibilities and the structure of the corresponding reduction classes and degrees for two

---

* Preparation of this paper was supported in part by the National Science Foundation under grant CCR-8611980.

specific classes, the class *SPARSE* of all sparse sets and the class *TALLY* of tally sets. Particular emphasis is placed on intrinsic characterizations of various classes in terms of *TALLY*.

In Section 3 the class of sets with small generalized Kolmogorov complexity is considered, and the characterization of this class as the class of sets that are p-isomorphic to tally sets is reviewed. In Section 4 the class of sets with self-producible circuits is considered, and the characterization of this class as the class of sets that are polynomial time Turing equivalent ($\equiv_T^P$) to tally sets is reviewed.

Based on the fact that the class of sets with polynomial-size circuits can be characterized as the class of sets that are polynomial time Turing (or truth-table) reducible to sparse (or tally) sets, one can consider the various classes of sets that can be specified as the reduction classes of *SPARSE* or of *TALLY* by the various polynomial-time truth-table reducibilities; in addition, one can consider the various classes that can be specified as the unions of the degrees of all sparse sets or of all tally sets with respect to those same reducibilities. The results of these efforts are reviewed in Section 5.

There has been a great deal of interest recently in classes specified by probabilistic machines and in the use of random oracle sets. Part of this interest stems from the "Random Oracle Hypothesis" of Bennett and Gill [10], while another part is due to the use of notions of probabilistic computation in the study of interactive proof systems. The subject of Section 6 is characterizations of complexity classes in terms of reduction classes of polynomial-time reducibilities for "almost every" tally set. Thus, the class $\{A \mid \text{for almost every tally set } T,\ A \leq_r T\}$ is studied instead of the class $\{A \mid \text{there is a tally set } T \text{ such that } A \leq_r T\}$. The characterizations (including those of the classes P and BPP) are similar to those studied previously.

2. Preliminaries

In this section we review some definitions and establish notation.

Throughout this paper we will consider the alphabet $\Sigma = \{0,1\}$. The length of a string x will be denoted by $|x|$. The cardinality of a set S will be denoted by $\|S\|$. For a set S, χ_S denotes the charcteristic function of S, and for $S \subseteq \Sigma^*$, $\overline{S} = \Sigma^* - S$.

For an oracle machine M, $L(M,A)$ denotes the set of strings accepted by M relative to oracle set A, and $L(M) = L(M,\emptyset)$ denotes the set of strings accepted by M when no oracle queries are made (or allowed). We assume that the reader is familiar with the well-studied complexity classes P, NP, and $PSPACE$ and with their relativizations. In particular, recall that set A is Turing-reducible to set B in polynomial time, written $A \leq_T^P B$, if and only if $A \in P(B)$.

We are particularly concerned with truth-table reducibilities that are computed in polynomial time. Recall the following definitions from [25]:

(i) set A is many-one reducible to set B, written $A \leq_m^P B$, if there is a function f that can be computed in polynomial time with the property that for all x, $x \in A$ if and only if $f(x) \in B$;

(ii) for every $k > 0$, set A is k-truth-table reducible to set B, written $A \leq_{k\text{-}tt}^P B$, if there exist polynomial time computable functions f and g such that for all x, $f(x)$ is a list of k strings, $g(x)$ is a truth-table with k variables, and $x \in A$ if and only if the truth-table $g(x)$ evaluates to **true** on the k-tuple $\langle \chi_B(y_1), \ldots, \chi_B(y_k) \rangle$ where $f(x) = \langle y_1, \ldots, y_k \rangle$;

(iii) set A is bounded truth-table reducible to set B, written $A \leq_{btt}^{P} B$, if there is an integer k such that $A \leq_{k-tt}^{P} B$;

(iv) set A is truth-table reducible to set B, written $A \leq_{tt}^{P} B$, if there exist polynomial time computable functions f and g such that for all x, $f(x)$ is a list of strings, $g(x)$ is a truth-table with the number of variables being equal to the number of strings in the list $f(x)$, and $x \in A$ if and only if the truth-table $g(x)$ evaluates to **true** on $\langle \chi_B(y_1), \ldots, \chi_B(y_k) \rangle$ where $f(x) = \langle y_1, \ldots, y_k \rangle$.

In the above we did not specify how a truth-table $g(x)$ with k variables is represented, because the representation does not matter as long as it evaluates each truth value in polynomial time (see [25] for several equivalent formulations). What is important to notice is that the polynomial-time truth-table reducibility is equivalent to non-adaptive polynomial-time Turing reducibility. In other words, in the above definitions (ii) and (iv), we may regard the truth-table evaluator g as a $(k+1)$-variable function, with the first variable x in Σ^* and the rest $b_1, \ldots, b_k$ in $\{0,1\}$. The function g is required to run in polynomial time and satisfy the condition that $g(x, b_1, \ldots, b_k) = 1$ if and only if the intended "truth-table" $g(x)$ evaluates to **true** on values $\langle b_1, \ldots, b_k \rangle$.

Recall that a set S is *sparse* if there is a polynomial q such that for all n, $\|S^{\leq n}\| \leq q(n)$. Let *SPARSE* denote the class of all sparse sets. Recall that a *tally* set is any subset of $\{0\}^*$. Let *TALLY* denote the class of all tally sets.

For background in structural complexity theory, see the monograph by Schöning [31] or the textbook by Balcázar, Díaz, and Gabarró [8].

3. Sets with small generalized Kolmogorov complexity

Kolmogorov complexity has arisen in a number of places in theoretical computer science and, in particular, in computational complexity theory (Li and Vitanyi [26] provide an interesting survey). The idea of the Kolmogorov complexity of finite strings provides a definition of the degree of randomness of a string. Informally, the Kolmogorov complexity of a finite string is the length of the shortest program that will generate the string; intuitively, it is a measure of the amount of information that the string contains. A string is considered to be "random" if the length of the shortest program that generates the strings is at least that of the string itself. A modification of the original idea has been developed: consider not only the length of a program but also, and simultaneously, the running time of the program. While Ko [22] and Sipser [34] used this modification in different settings, it was Hartmanis [19] who developed the formal definition. Hartmanis considered a variation on the basic concept by defining "a generalized, two-parameter version which measures how much and how fast a string can be compressed."

Given a universal Turing machine U and functions G and g, a string x is in the *generalized Kolmogorov class* $K_U[g(|x|), G(|x|)]$ if there is a string y of length at most $g(|x|)$ with the property that U will generate x on input y in at most $G(|x|)$ steps.

Balcázar and Book [6] modified the notion introduced by Hartmanis by considering sets of strings of "small generalized" Kolmogorov complexity by taking G to be a polynomial and g to be $\log n$.

Set A has *small generalized Kolmogorov complexity* if there exist constants c and k such that for all but finitely many $x \in A$, x is in $K[c \cdot \log |x|, |x|^k]$. The collection of all sets with small generalized Kolmogorov complexity will be denoted by **K[log,poly]**.

While Hartmanis considered properties of subsets of the *NP*-complete set *SAT* having small generalized Kolmogorov complexity, Balcázar and Book developed an intrinsic characterization of the class **K[log,poly]**.

A *polynomial semi-isomorphism* from set A to set B is a function f computable in polynomial time with the properties that:

(i) f witnesses the fact that $A \leq_m^P B$;

(ii) the restriction of f to A is a bijection from A to B whose inverse is computable in polynomial time.

Balcázar and Book showed that a set A is in **K[log,poly]** if and only if there exists a tally set T such that A is polynomial semi-isomorphic to T. This result formalizes the intuitive notion that sets with small generalized Kolmogorov complexity are not very powerful in terms of the information their strings encode. Allender and Rubinstein [1] strengthened this notion by improving the result of Balcázar and Book, showing that "semi-isomorphic" can be replaced by "isomorphic."

Sets A and B are *polynomially isomorphic (p-isomorphic)* if there is a bijection f witnessing $A \leq_m^P B$ such that f^{-1} is computable in polynomial time.

Theorem 3.1. *Any set A is in* **K[log,poly]** *if and only if there exists a tally set T such that A and T are p-isomorphic.*

Thus, when considering complexity classes (such as $P, NP, \Sigma_k^P, PH, PSPACE$) that are closed under p-isomorphism, **K[log,poly]** is essentially the same as the class of all tally sets. Hence, the class of tally sets provides an intrinsic characterization of the class of sets with small generalized Kolmogorov complexity (and the notion of small generalized Kolmogorov complexity provides a different way of viewing tally sets).

When we turn to reducibilities computed in polynomial time, there are two observations about tally sets that can be made immediately. If T is a tally set and M is an oracle machine that runs in time $p(n)$ for some polynomial p, then consider an oracle machine M' that on input x first queries the oracle for T about the strings $0, 00, 000, \ldots, 0^{p(|x|)}$ and constructs a table with the information obtained, and then simulates a computation of M on x using the table instead of querying the oracle. If $A = L(M,T)$, then M' witnesses $A \leq_{tt}^P T$ (whereas M witnesses $A \leq_T^P T$). In addition, the first part of the computation of M' on x can be considered to be the computation of an oracle transducer that relative to T computes the list of the strings in T of length at most $p(|x|)$. It is this latter property that was considered by Hartmanis and Hemachandra [20].

For any set A, let enum_A be the function that for each n and each input 0^n has as value a string encoding the set of all strings in A of length at most n. Set A is *self-p-printable* if there is a deterministic polynomial time-bounded oracle transducer that computes relative to A the function enum_A.

As observed above, every tally set is self-p-printable and, from the characterization of **K[log,poly]**, it is immediate that every set in **K[log,poly]** is self-p-printable.

It is clear that every self-p-printable set is sparse. Balcázar and Book observed that there are sparse sets that are not self-p-printable. From a result of Long [27], it is easy to see that there are sparse sets that are self-p-printable that are not in **K[log,poly]**. Thus, we have a difference between the class *TALLY* of all tally sets and the class *SPARSE* of all sparse sets that reflects properties of structural complexity.

4. Sets with self-producible circuits

The subject of this section is the class of sets with "self-producible" circuits, a special case of the class of sets with "polynomial-size circuits."

Let $A \subseteq \{0,1\}^*$. For each n, let C_n be a circuit that computes the characteristic function of the finite set $A^n = \{x \in A \mid |x| = n\}$. Set A has *polynomial-size circuits* if there exists a polynomial p such that for all n, $\|C_n\| \le p(n)$.

There are several intrinsic characterizations of the class of sets with polynomial-size circuits; several are of interest here.

Let *P*/poly denote the class of all sets A such that there exist $B \in P$ and a polynomial length-bounded function h: $\{0\}^* \to \{0,1\}^*$ with the property that for all x, $x \in A$ if and only if $\langle x, h(0^{|x|})\rangle \in B$.

If a set is in *P*/poly, then it can be recognized by a polynomial time-bounded machine that takes "advice." The string $h(0^{|x|})$ is considered to be additional information that is given, along with x, to a machine that witnesses $B \in P$.

From a variety of sources (A. Meyer, as reported by Berman and Hartmanis [11], for one part; Pippenger [30] for another; and Karp and Lipton [21] for still another) it is known that a set A has polynomial-size circuits if and only if it is in *P*/poly if and ony if there exists a sparse set S such that $A \le_T^P S$. Book and Ko [14] observed that in this intrinsic characterization of the class of sets with polynomial-size circuits, the notion of Turing reducibility can be replaced by that of truth-table reducibility, sparse sets can be replaced by tally sets, and both of these replacements can be done simultaneously. Thus, we have the following characterizations.

Theorem 4.1. *For any set A, the following are equivalent:*

(a) A has polynomial-size circuits;
(b) $A \in P/poly$;
(c) there exists a sparse set S such that $A \le_T^P S$;
(d) there exists a sparse set S such that $A \le_{tt}^P S$;
(e) there exists a tally set T such that $A \le_T^P T$;
(f) there exists a tally set T such that $A \le_{tt}^P T$.

In a very different context, Ko [22] defined the notion of "self-producible circuit."

A set A has *self-producible circuits* if there exist a set $B \in P$ and a polynomial length-bounded function h: $\{0\}^* \to \{0,1\}^*$ such that

(i) for every $x \in \{0,1\}^*$, $x \in A$ if and only if $\langle x, h(0^{|x|})\rangle \in B$, and
(ii) h can be computed relative to A by a deterministic polynomial time-bounded oracle transducer.

Observe that (i) says that $A \in P/poly$, while (ii) makes a finer distinction. It is clear that every self-p-printable set has self-producible circuits, and it is known that there exists a set with self-producible circuits that is not self-p-printable. Balcázar and Book [6] developed an intrinsic characterization of the class of sets with self-producible circuits by using tally sets.

Theorem 4.2. *Set A has self-producible circuits if and only if there exists a tally set T such that* $A \leq_T^P T$ *and* $T \leq_T^P A$.

Thus, when considering complexity classes (such as P, Δ_k^P, PH, or *PSPACE*) that are closed under $\leq_T^P$, the class of sets with self-producible circuits is essentially the same as the class of all tally sets. Hence, the class of tally sets provides an intrinsic characterization of the class of sets with self-producible circuits (and the notion of self-producible circuits provides a different way of viewing tally sets).

Let $\leq_r$ be any of the standard reducibilities, i.e., $r \in \{T, tt, btt, k-tt$ for any $k > 0, m\}$. For sets A and B, define $A \equiv_r^P B$ if $A \leq_r^P B$ and $B \leq_r^P A$. Using this notation, observe that Theorem 4.2 asserts that the class of sets with self-producible circuits is the class $\{A \mid$ for some $T \in TALLY, A \equiv_T^P T\}$. Classes of this form will be considered in Section 5.

Let *DEXT* be the class of sets accepted by deterministic machines that run in exponential time, and for any set A, let *DEXT(A)* be the class of sets accepted relative to A by deterministic oracle machines that run in exponential time. Balcázar, Díaz, and Gabarró [8] observed that if A has self-producible circuits, then *DEXT(A)* = *DEXT* implies that $A \in P$. This follows from the fact that if A has self-producible circuits, then there is some tally set T such that $T \equiv_T^P A$, and for every tally set T, *DEXT(T)* = *DEXT* implies that $T \in P$. But Book, Orponen, Russo, and Watanabe [16] showed the existence of a sparse set S such that *DEXT(S)* = *DEXT* and $S \notin P$. Hence, S does not have self-producible circuits but S has polynomial-size circuits since S is sparse. Thus we have the following result.

Theorem 4.3. *The class of sets with self-producible circuits is properly included in the class of sets with polynomial-size circuits.*

Using an entirely different technique, Long [27] has shown that there is a recursive sparse set S such that for all tally sets T, $T \not\equiv_T^P S$. Hence, there is a recursive set that witnesses the proper inclusion stated in Theorem 4.3.

5. Sets reducible to sparse sets or to tally sets

For any class C of sets and any of the standard reducibilities $\leq_r$ where $r \in \{T, tt, btt, k-tt$ for any $k > 0, m\}$, let $P_r(C) = \{A \mid$ for some $B \in C$, $A \leq_r^P B\}$. Expressed in this notation, Theorem 4.1 is the observation that P/poly = $P_T(SPARSE) = P_{tt}(SPARSE) = P_T(TALLY) = P_{tt}(TALLY)$. It is known [25] that for every two distinct α and β in $\{T, tt, btt, k-tt$ for any $k > 0, m\}$, the reducibilities $\leq_\alpha^P$ and $\leq_\beta^P$ are distinct. Furthermore, some of the distinctions can be made relative to a sparse set or even a tally set. Book and Ko [14] considered the possibility of making the distinctions relative to the class *SPARSE* or the class *TALLY*, and developed the following results about the class *SPARSE*.

Theorem 5.1.

(a) $P_{btt}(SPARSE) \neq P_{tt}(SPARSE)$.

(b) For every $k > 0$, $P_{k-tt}(SPARSE) \neq P_{(k+1)-tt}(SPARSE)$.

(c) $P_m(SPARSE) \neq P_{1-tt}(SPARSE)$.

Notice that part (a) asserts the existence of a set A such that for some sparse set S, $A \leq_{tt}^P S$, and not only is it the case that $A \not\leq_{btt}^P S$ but also for *every* sparse set S', $A \not\leq_{btt}^P S'$. Parts (b) and (c) can be interpreted similarly.

The situation with the class *TALLY* is quite different.

Theorem 5.2. $P_{btt}(TALLY) \neq P_{tt}(TALLY)$ *but* $P_m(TALLY) = P_{btt}(TALLY)$.

Part (b) of Theorem 5.1 is a formal statement verifying the intuitive notion that asking more questions provides more information: by increasing by just one at a time the number of nonadaptive questions asked of sparse oracle sets, one can obtain an infinite hierarchy of classes. Theorem 5.2 shows that this is not the case if tally sets are used as oracle sets since by possibly changing oracle sets, it is only necessary to ask one question of a tally oracle set to obtain the information obtained by any fixed number of questions.

Amir and Gasarch [4] and Beigel [9] have considered a type of "bounded" Turing reducibility: for any $k > 0$, consider $\leq_T^P$ restricted in such a way that only k oracle queries are made. Ko [24] has established results similar to Theorem 5.1 for this type of reducibility.

As noted above, $P_T(SPARSE) = P_{tt}(SPARSE) = P_T(TALLY) = P_{tt}(TALLY)$ so that the class *SPARSE* and the class *TALLY* do not help us to distinguish between $\leq_{tt}^P$ and $\leq_T^P$ by considering reduction classes. Tang and Book [35] studied this problem by investigating the relations $\equiv_r^P$ for $r \in \{T, tt, btt, k-tt \text{ for any } k > 0, m\}$. For any class C of sets and any of the standard reducibilities $\leq_r$, let $E_r^P(C) = \{A \mid \text{for some } B \in C, A \equiv_r^P B\}$. Using this notation, observe that from Theorem 3.1 we have $\mathbf{K}[\mathbf{log}, \mathbf{poly}] \subseteq E_m^P(TALLY)$; in fact, this inclusion is proper since every set in P is in $E_m^P(TALLY)$ but some sets in P are not in **K[log,poly]**, e.g., $\{0,1\}^* \notin \mathbf{K}[\mathbf{log}, \mathbf{poly}]$. Theorem 4.2 asserts that the class of sets with self-producible circuits is the class $E_T^P(TALLY)$; in addition the class *P-CLOSE* (the Boolean closure of $P \cup SPARSE$) studied by Schöning [32] is included in $E_{1-tt}^P(SPARSE)$. Tang and Book developed the following results.

Theorem 5.3.

(a) $E_{tt}^P(TALLY) \neq E_T^P(TALLY)$.

(b) $E_{btt}^P(TALLY) \neq E_{tt}^P(TALLY)$.

(c) $E_{btt}^P(SPARSE) \neq E_{tt}^P(SPARSE)$.

(d) For every $k > 0$, $E_{k-tt}^P(SPARSE) \neq E_{(k+1)-tt}^P(SPARSE)$.

(e) $E_m^P(SPARSE) \neq E_{1-tt}^P(SPARSE)$.

Using a result of Long [27], Tang and Book showed that for every reducibility $\leq_r$ considered here, $E_r^P(TALLY) \neq E_r^P(SPARSE)$. Since $E_T^P(TALLY) \subseteq E_T^P(SPARSE) \subseteq P_T(SPARSE) = P/\text{poly}$, this gives another proof of the fact that there are sets with polynomial size circuits that do not have self-producible circuits.

Tang and Book left a number of open questions, including the following:

(a) $E^P_m(TALLY) =? E^P_{1-tt}(TALLY)$;

(b) $E^P_m(TALLY) =? E^P_{btt}(TALLY)$;

(c) does there exist a $k > 0$ such that $E^P_{k-tt}(TALLY) = E^P_{(k+1)-tt}(TALLY)$?

Allender and Watanabe [2] showed that these three questions are equivalent in the sense given by the following result.

Theorem 5.4. *Either $E^P_m(TALLY) = E^P_{btt}(TALLY)$, or $E^P_m(TALLY) \neq E^P_{1-tt}(TALLY)$ and for every $k > 0$, $E^P_{k-tt}(TALLY) \neq E^P_{(k+1)-tt}(TALLY)$.*

In their proof Allender and Watanabe show that $E^P_m(TALLY) = E^P_{btt}(TALLY)$ if the following condition holds: For all length-increasing functions $f\colon \{0,1\}^* \to \{0\}^*$ computable in polynomial time, there exists a t such that for all $x \in \text{image}(f)$, $f^{-1}(x) \cap K[t \cdot \log n, n^t] \neq \emptyset$. Furthermore, if this condition does not hold, then $E^P_m(TALLY) \neq E^P_{1-tt}(TALLY)$ and for every $k > 0$, $E^P_{k-tt}(TALLY) \neq E^P_{(k+1)-tt}(TALLY)$. Thus, the notion of generalized Kolmogorov complexity appears once again, this time in a very different way from the way it was introduced.

The condition considered by Allender and Watanabe is equivalent to the following statement: for every honest function $f\colon \{0,1\}^* \to \{0\}^*$ computable in polynomial time is weakly invertible, that is, there is a function g such that g is computable in polynomial time and for all $x \in \text{image}(f)$, $f(g(x)) = x$. This statement asserts that a certain restricted type of one-way function fails to exist, so that Theorem 5.4 asserts that $E^P_m(TALLY) = E_{btt}(TALLY)$ if and only if this specific type of one-way function fails to exist.

Until this point all the reducibilities considered in this paper have been reducibilities computable in polynomial time. Now we turn to reducibilities computable in polynomial space. Assume that the query tape is a work tape so that it is subject to the space bound. If the length of each query is bounded by a polynomial in the size of the input and the (nonadaptive) truth-table reducibilities are such that the list of queries must be computed before any evaluation can be made, then only a polynomial number of queries can be made in any computation. Turing reducibilities computed by machines with these restrictions have been investigated in a different context [13,15].

For each $r \in \{T, tt, btt, k-tt \text{ for any } k > 0, m\}$ and each set A, the reduction class specified by deterministic machines of this type is denoted by $PQUERY_r(A)$, and for any class C of sets, $PQUERY_r(C)$ denotes $\bigcup_{A \in C} PQUERY_r(A)$. Similarly, for each r and each set A, $E^{PQ}_r(A)$ denotes $\{B \mid B \in PQUERY_r(A) \text{ and } A \in PQUERY_r(B)\}$, and for any class C of sets, $E^{PQ}_r(C)$ denotes $\bigcup_{A \in C} E^{PQ}_r(A)$.

The proofs of Theorems 5.1–5.3 can be trivially extended to apply to classes of the form $PQUERY_r(SPARSE)$, $PQUERY_r(TALLY)$, $E^{PQ}_r(SPARSE)$, and $E^{PQ}_r(TALLY)$. Of particular interest is the proof of Theorem 5.3(a) because it can be used to show that $E^P_T(TALLY) \not\subseteq E^{PQ}_{tt}(TALLY)$. This can be interpreted as showing that the potential additional computational power of space, as opposed to time, is not sufficient to overcome the power of Turing reductions computable in polynomial time over truth-table reductions computed in polynomial space when considering degrees of tally sets. Thus, the adaptive character of Turing reductions provides computational power that cannot be overcome by nonadaptive truth-table reductions even if the latter is provided with the potential additional computational power of space over time. But notice that this does not remain true if one considers only reduction classes since $P_T(TALLY) = P/\text{poly} \subseteq PSPACE/\text{poly} = PQUERY_{tt}(TALLY)$.

6. Characterizations by means of tally sets

In the previous sections we have reviewed three intrinsic characterizations of important classes of languages by using tally sets.

1. A set has small generalized Kolmogorov complexity if and only if it is p-isomorphic to a tally set.
2. A set has polynomial-size circuits if and only if it is Turing (or truth-table) reducible in polynomial time to a tally set.
3. A set has self-producible circuits if and only if it is Turing equivalent in polynomial time to a tally set.

In this section we consider some additional intrinsic characterizations involving tally sets. The machinery needed here is that of probabilistic machines and "random" oracles. We begin by reviewing the definition of the class *BPP*.

The class *BPP* (*bounded-error probabilistic polynomial time*) is the collection of all sets A with the property that there exists a probabilistic polynomial time-bounded machine M and a δ, $0 < \delta < 1/2$ such that for every x,

$$\text{Prob}[\,M \text{ accepts } x \text{ iff } x \in A] > \frac{1}{2} + \delta.$$

It is known that $P \subseteq BPP$ and that $\Sigma_2^P(BPP) = \Sigma_2^P$; the relationship between NP and BPP is not known.

Bennett and Gill [10] studied relations among relativized complexity classes by considering random oracles. They showed that for almost every set B, $P(B) \neq NP(B)$, and that for almost every set C, $P(C) = BPP(C)$. These results were developed in the formulation of the Random Oracle Hypothesis (ROH) which, when described informally, states that for two complexity classes, an inclusion relation holds between these two classes if and only if for almost every oracle set that same relation holds between these classes relativized to that oracle set. Ambos-Spies [3] developed a formalization of the ROH for classes included in the class *BPP*, and established the first nontrivial instance for which ROH holds. In the course of this work, Ambos-Spies developed two results that will be of interest here; he proved that for every set A,

a. $A \in P$ if and only if for almost every set B, $A \leq_m^P B$;
b. $A \in BPP$ if and only if for almost every set B, $A \leq_T^P B$.

In his study of probabilistic complexity classes and lowness, Schöning [33] defined the "*BP*" operator.

For language class $\mathcal{C}$, $BP\cdot\mathcal{C}$ is the collection of sets A such that for some $C \in \mathcal{C}$, some polynomial $p(n)$, and all x,

$$\Pr_{p(|x|)} [y : x \in A \text{ iff } \langle x, y\rangle \in C] > \frac{3}{4}.$$

It is not difficult to see that for every set A, $BPP(A) = BP\cdot P(A)$.

In the context of interactive proof systems, Babai [5] introduced the class AM ("Arthur-Melin") which can be characterized as $BP\cdot NP$. Goldwasser and Sipser [18] asked whether AM ($= BP\cdot NP$) is precisely $\{A \mid \text{for almost every set } B,\ A \in NP(B)\}$. More generally, Tang and Watanabe [37] asked whether for each integer k, $BP\cdot\Sigma_k^P$ can be characterized by means of oracle sets: is it the case that for every set A, $A \in BP\cdot\Sigma_k^P$ if and only if for almost every set B, $A \in \Sigma_k^P(B)$? The result (b) of Ambos-Spies noted above shows that the answer is "yes" in the case $k = 0$ since this is precisely $BP\cdot\Sigma_0^P = BP\cdot P = BPP$; however, the question is still open for each $k > 0$. In addition, Tang and Watanabe asked whether it is the case that for each k, $BP\cdot\Sigma_k^P(B) = \Sigma_k^P(B)$ for almost every set B. A result of Bennett and Gill [10] shows that the answer is "yes" for the case $k = 0$ since in that case we have $BP\cdot P(A) = BPP(A) = P(A)$ for almost every set B. Tang (in preparation) has shown that the answer is "yes" for all $k \geq 1$.

While Tang and Watanabe were not able to provide complete answers to the questions they posed, they did provide partial answers by considering tally sets as oracle sets.

Theorem 6.1. *For every integer $k \geq 0$,*

(a) for every set A, $A \in BP\cdot\Sigma_k^P$ if and only if for almost every tally set T, $A \in \Sigma_k^P(T)$;

(b) for every set A, $A \in PH$ if and only if for almost every tally set T, $A \in PH(T)$, if and only if for every tally set T, $A \in PH(T)$;

(c) for almost every tally set T, $BP\cdot\Sigma_k^P(T) = \Sigma_k^P(T)$.

Thus, parts (a) and (b) of Theorem 6.1 provide characterizations of the classes $BP\cdot\Sigma_k^P$ and Σ_k^P in terms of relativizations to tally sets.

Consider the characterizations of the classes P and BPP given by Ambos-Spies (a. and b. above). The measure used to define the notion of "almost all sets" is based on the Bernoulli independent testing sequence: the characteristic sequence of a random language is the sequence that results from tossing an unbiased coin infinitely often. Recall that for a set $S \subseteq \{0,1\}^*$, the ith bit in the characteristic sequence indicates whether the ith string in $\{0,1\}^*$ is in S. However, if we are considering only tally sets, then the characteristic sequence is considered differently: for a set $T \subseteq \{0\}^*$, the ith bit in the characteristic sequence indicates whether 0^i is in T.

Tang and Book [36] showed that by considering only tally sets as oracle sets one could still obtain the characterizations of P and BPP developed by Ambos-Spies. In addition, they considered reducibilities lying strictly between $\leq_m^P$ and $\leq_T^P$ in power and asked whether such reducibilities could be used to characterize classes lying between P and BPP; in each case, the answer was negative.

Theorem 6.2. *For every set A,*

(a) for almost every tally set T, $A \leq_T^P T$ if and only if for almost every tally set T, $A \leq_{tt}^P T$ if and only if $A \in BPP$;

(b) for almost every tally set T, $A \leq_{btt}^P T$ if and only if for almost every tally set T, $A \leq_m^P T$ if and only if $A \in P$.

Parts (a) and (b) of Theorem 6.2 provide additional characterizations of the classes BPP and P in terms of relativizations to tally sets.

As observed in Theorem 5.2, $P_m(TALLY) = P_{btt}(TALLY)$; in some sense Theorem 6.2(b) parallels this fact, even though $P_m(TALLY) \neq P$. But this does not assert that for every tally set T, $P_m(T) = P_{btt}(T)$; it is known that there is a fixed tally set T such that $P_m(T) \neq P_{1-tt}(T)$ and for every $k > 0$, $P_{k-tt}(T) \neq P_{(k+1)-tt}(T)$. In fact, it is the latter situation that is typical, as seen by the following result.

Theorem 6.3. *For almost every tally set T, $P_m(T) \neq P_{1-tt}(T)$ and for every $k > 0$, $P_{k-tt}(T) \neq P_{(k+1)-tt}(T)$. Hence, for almost every tally set T, $P_m(T) \neq P_{btt}(T)$.*

It follows from Theorem 6.3 that for every $k > 0$ and almost every tally set T, $E_m^P(T) \neq E_{1-tt}^P(T)$ and $E_{k-tt}^P(T) \neq E_{(k+1)-tt}^P(T)$. This means that for almost every tally set T, $E_m^P(T) \neq E_{btt}^P(T)$, while as noted in Section 5 it is not known whether $E_m^P(TALLY)$ is equal to $E_{btt}^P(TALLY)$.

Consider reducibilities computed by deterministic machines that operate in polynomial space. The situation where both the number of queries and the length of each query are bounded by polynomials was discussed in Section 5. In that context, we have the following results.

Theorem 6.4. *For every set A, the following are equivalent:*

(a) $A \in PSPACE$;

(b) for almost every tally set T, $A \in PQUERY_T(T)$;

(c) for almost every tally set T, $A \in PQUERY_m(T)$.

If the bound on the length of the queries is determined only by the running time of the machine (which is determined by the bound on the work space in the case of space-bounded machines), then denote the corresponding reducibility by $\leq_r^{PS}$ and the corresponding reduction class for each set B by $PSPACE_r(B)$ for each choice of $r \in \{T, tt, btt, k-tt \text{ for any } k > 0, m\}$. In this context Tang and Book showed that for every set A, $A \in PSPACE$ if and only if for almost all tally sets T, $A \leq_r^{PS} T$.

Just as in the case of polynomial time-bounded reducibilities, there exists a fixed tally set T such that $PSPACE_m(T) \neq PSPACE_{1-tt}(T)$ and for every $k > 0$, $PSPACE_{k-tt}(T) \neq PSPACE_{(k+1)-tt}(T)$, so that $PSPACE_m(T) \neq PSPACE_{btt}(T)$. This is the typical case since a result analogous to Theorem 6.3 holds, i.e., for almost every tally set T, $PSPACE_m(T) \neq PSPACE_{btt}(T)$.

References

1. E. Allender and R. Rubinstein, P-printable sets, *SIAM J. Comput.*, to appear.
2. E. Allender and O. Watanabe, Kolmogorov complexity and degrees of tally sets, *Proc. 3rd IEEE Conf. Structure in Complexity Theory*, 1988, to appear.
3. K. Ambos-Spies, Randomness, relativizations and polynomial reducibilities, *Proc. 1st Conf. Structure in Complexity Theory*, LNCS **223**, 1986, 23–34.
4. A. Amir and W. Gasarch, Polynomial terse sets, *Proc. 2nd IEEE Conf. Structure in Complexity Theory*, 1987, 22–27.
5. L. Babai, Trading group theory for randomness, *Proc. 17th ACM Symp. Theory of Computing*, 1985, 421–429.
6. J. Balcázar and R. Book, Sets with small generalized Kolmogorov complexity, *Acta Informatica* **23** (1986), 679–688.
7. J. Balcázar, R. Book, and U. Schöning, The polynomial-time hierarchy and sparse oracles, *J. Assoc. Comput. Mach.* **33** (1986), 603–617.
8. J. Balcázar, J. Díaz, and J. Gabarró, *Structural Complexity I*, Springer-Verlag, 1988.
9. R. Beigel, A structural theorem that depends quantitatively on the complexity of SAT, *Proc. 2nd IEEE Conf. Structure in Complexity Theory*, 1987, 28–32.
10. C. Bennett and J. Gill, Relative to a random oracle, $P^A \neq NP^A \neq \text{co}-NP^A$ with probability 1, *SIAM J. Comput.* **10** (1981), 96–113.
11. L. Berman and J. Hartmanis, On isomorphisms and density of NP and other complete sets, *SIAM J. Comput.* **6** (1977), 305–322.
12. P. Berman, Relationships between density and deterministic complexity of NP-complete languages, *Automata, Languages and Programming – 78*, LNCS **62**, 1978, 63–71.
13. R. Book, Bounded query machines: on NP and PSPACE, *Theoret. Comput. Sci.* **15** (1981), 27–39.
14. R. Book and K. Ko, On sets truth-table reducible to sparse sets, *SIAM J. Comput.* **17** (1988), to appear. Also see *Proc. 2nd IEEE Conf. Structure in Complexity Theory* 1987, 147–155.
15. R. Book and C. Wrathall, Bounded query machines: on NP( ) and NPQUERY( ), *Theoret. Comput. Sci.* **15** (1981), 41–50.
16. R. Book, P. Orponen, D. Russo, and O. Watanabe, Lowness properties in the exponent-time hierarcy, *SIAM J. Comput.* **17** (1988), to appear.
17. S. Fortune, A note on sparse complete sets, *SIAM J. Comput.* **8** (1979), 431–433.
18. S. Goldwasser and M. Sipser, Private coins in interactive proof systems, *Proc. 18th ACM Symp. Theory of Computing* 1986, 59–68.
19. J. Hartmanis, Generalized Kolmogorov complexity and the structure of feasible computations, *Proc. 24th IEEE Symp. Foundations of Computer Science* 1983, 439–445.
20. J. Hartmanis and L. Hemachandra, On sparse oracles separating feasible complexity classes, *STACS–86*, LNCS **210**, 1986, 321–333.
21. R. Karp and R. Lipton, Some connections between nonuniform and uniform complexity classes, *Proc. 12th ACM Symp. Theory of Computing* 1980, 302–309.
22. K. Ko, Continuous optimization problems and a polynomial hierarchy of real functions, *J. Complexity* **1** (1985), 210–231.
23. K. Ko, On the notion of infinite pseudo random sequences, *Theoret. Comput. Sci.* **48** (1988), 9–33.
24. K. Ko, Distinguishing reducibilities by sparse sets, *Proc. 3rd IEEE Conf. Structure in Complexity Theory*, 1988, to appear.
25. R. Ladner, M. Lynch, and A. Selman, A comparison of polynomial-time reducibilities, *Theoret. Comput. Sci.* **1** (1975), 103–123.

26. M. Li and P. Vitanyi, Two decades of applied Kolmogorov complexity, *Proc. 3rd IEEE Conf. Structure in Complexity Theory*, 1988, to appear.
27. T. Long, On restricting the size of oracles compared with restricting access to oracles, *SIAM J. Comput.* **14** (1985), 585–597.
28. T. Long and A. Selman, Relativizing complexity classes with sparse oracles, *J. Assoc. Comput. Mach.* **33** (1988), 618–627.
29. S. Mahaney, Sparse complete sets for NP: solution of a conjecture of Berman and Hartmanis, *J. Comput. Syst. Sci.* **23** (1982), 130–143.
30. N. Pippenger, On simultaneous resource bounds, *Proc. 20th IEEE Symp. Foundations of Computer Science*, 1979, 307–311.
31. U. Schöning, *Complexity and Structure*, LNCS **211**, 1986.
32. U. Schöning, Complete sets and closeness to complexity classes, *Math. Syst. Theory* **19** (1986), 29–41.
33. U. Schöning, Probabilistic complexity classes and lowness, *Proc. 2nd IEEE Conf. Structure in Complexity Theory* 1987, 2–8.
34. M. Sipser, A complexity theory approach to randomness, *Proc. 15th ACM Symp. Theory of Computing* 1983, 330–335.
35. S. Tang and R. Book, Separating polynomial-time Turing and truth-table reducibilities by tally sets, *Automata, Languages and Programming – 88*, LNCS, 1988, to appear.
36. S. Tang and R. Book, in preparation.
37. S. Tang and O. Watanabe, On tally relativizations of BP-complexity classes, *Proc. 3rd IEEE Conf. Structure in Complexity Theory*, 1988, to appear.

FUNCTIONAL PROGRAMMING AND COMBINATORY ALGEBRAS

Corrado Böhm[(1)]

Dipartimento di Matematica
Istituto "G. Castelnuovo"
Università degli Studi di Roma "La Sapienza"
P.le Aldo Moro 5 , I-00185 ROMA
BITNET address: boehm%vaxrma.infnet@iboinfn

KEYWORDS: Functional programming, algebraic programming, combinatory algebras, total recursive mappings on data structures, combinators and λ-terms in normal form.

Introduction

A kind of functional programming was first used in the programming language LISP [McC 60]. All data were expressed as hereditary finite sequences (lists) of atomic objects and functions on recursively defined lists were also expressed using the same data structure. λ-calculus notation was used to describe functions, but the full power of such a calculus was not exploited.

In a well known paper [Bac 78] Backus introduced a style of programming specially suitable for describing functions on finite sequences of atomic objects. This approach was very similar to the combinatory approach made in logic by Schönfinkel and Curry, as underlined in [Böh 82]. In all three cases it was a variablefree approach. In the years '70-'80 the discipline of structured programming has led to the development of programming languages where more and more a data discipline was superimposed. PASCAL and ML possess, in different ways, strongly typed data. In the same period of time, the fixpoint theory was used for the denotational semantics of programming languages. Since in the considered languages the WHILE construction occurs, the fixpoint theory of *partial* recursive functions was developed.

More recent functional languages like MIRANDA [Tur85] and the implementation of the G-machine [Joh 84] are constructed on techniques depending on the abstraction and on the reduction processes of combinators and λ-terms. The description of partial recursive functions through combinators requires to use the fixpoint combinator $\mathbf{Y}_c$ or some other equivalent device, with the actual drawback that no normal form

(1) This research has been supported by grants of Ministero della Pubblica Istruzione, Italia and of 'Projet stimulation' CEE.

representation is possible. On the other hand total recursive functions are describable by normal λ-terms or combinators only in a typed context.
This paper has an intermediate position. First, Church algebras are introduced allowing the combinatory expression of any element of the usual data structure (i.e. natural numbers, strings, linear lists, binary trees, trees and forests) in computer science. Second, normal combinators solving a special kind of recursive equations (called iterative equations) for functions from and to Church algebras are explicitly exhibited. Thirdly, Church algebras are shown to be isomorphically embeddable in some extensions, called *-algebras, where *any kind* of recursive definition for mappings is solvable.
Technically this paper is based on revisiting and combining the results of two previous papers: [BD 74] introducing a first version of Böhm trees and [BB 85] proposing solutions of iterative equations for mappings on absolutely free algebras, by means of second order typed λ-terms.
This intermediate approach (with the exclusion of the Church algebras presented for the first time here) has been successfully taught at least 4 times to graduate students in mathematics in my course of 'Theory and applications of computing machines'.
I do not claim that the proposed implementations are efficient nor that the analysis of the operating mode of our functions reflects the complexity features of wellknown algorithms. I claim only that the choice of the data structure and the idea of the algorithms are preserved by the formulation and consequently the understanding is facilitated.

1. Combinators as Functionals

Let us start with some examples of *functionals* as they are met in mathematics.

1.1. The partial derivatives of a function ($\partial/\partial x$ and $\partial/\partial y$)

Let $f(x,y) \equiv 2.x^2+3.y^2+4.x.y$.

Then $\partial/\partial x(f,x,y) = 4.x+4.y$ and $\partial/\partial y(f,x,y) = 6.y+4.x$.

The essential point in the previous example is that the argument of a functional may either be a function or a real number.

1.2. The operator of application

One of the simplest functionals is *appl* (apply) a binary operator defined by

$$\text{appl}(f,x) \equiv f(x)$$

which applies a function to an argument.

1.3. The family of compositors ($\Phi^n{}_m$)

Let m,n two nonnegative integers, and f a function of m arguments, g_i (i=1,...,m) m functions of n arguments, where constants are functions of 0 arguments.

In the recursive function theory (rft) a new function h of n argument is said to be defined by composition of f and $g_1,\ldots,g_m$ iff h is explicitly defined as

$$h(x_1,\ldots,x_n) = f(g_1(x_1,\ldots,x_n),\ldots,g_m(x_1,\ldots,x_n)).$$

Since h contains no trace of 'how' and 'from what' it is obtained[(2)], it is advisable to drop it and instead to explicitly define a family $\Phi^n{}_m$ of functionals called *compositors*, by

(1) $$\Phi^n{}_m(f,g_1,\ldots,g_m,x_1,\ldots,x_n) = f(g_1(x_1,\ldots,x_n),\ldots,g_m(x_1,\ldots,x_n))$$

$(m,n \geq 0)$

Before we leave rft let us introduce the family $U^n{}_i$ of *projectors* by

(2) $$U^n{}_i(x_1,\ldots,x_n) = x_i \qquad (0 < i \leq n).$$

We notice that, once a fixed number of functions is added to the projectors, following Parsons [Par 68], the family of "elementary functions" is obtained only by closing the former functions through a finite number of compositors.

Let us now go more deeply towards the notion of combinator.

1.4. Functions as functionals

The following crucial idea is due to Schönfinkel [Sch 24]: many-place functions can be reduced to one-place ones, provided that the idea of function is extended in such a way that functions can be argument as well as value of other functions. This is illustrated by the one to one correspondence

(3) $$f(x_1,\ldots,x_n) \leftrightarrow f(x_1)\ldots(x_n).$$

Relation (3) implies that a function of two variables may be conceived as a unary functional whose value is a unary function. This is reminiscent of the s-m-n theorem in rft or, more trivially, of the identification of add(1) with the successor function. In the following we will follow G. Jacopini's suggestion[(3)] and consider the l.h.s. of (3) as a syntactical shortening of the r.h.s. obtainable by the replacement

$$\text{")("} \rightarrow \text{","}.$$

The recursive definition of the domain $\mathbb{C}$ of the combinators

$$\mathbb{C} = \mathbb{C} \rightarrow \mathbb{C}$$

is a less obvious consequence of considering only unary functionals.

We will not enter this however fascinating world of recursive types [Cop 85].

A direct consequence of (3), also known as Curry principle, or currification, would be to consider "Data as Functionals" a theoretical justification of the recent activities in computer science developed under the title "Object Programming".

Another consequence of (3) is the loss of the notion of the arity of a function.

As a matter of fact a combinator may have any number of arguments.

---

(2) A philosophical reason for the success of combinatory logic and lambda-calculus in computer science is the replacement of objects and names with operators and variables respectively.

(3) Private communication.

In Sections 3-5 we will consider combinators, representing data, which will be applied to a suitable number of arguments to obtain the image of the originary datum under a given mapping. In order to compose mappings we simply have to apply the previous image to some other arguments, increasing indeed the total number of arguments of the originary combinator.

1.5.The combinatory algebra following [Bar 81]

Barendregt took as *basic combinators* two of the three combinators introduced by Schönfinkel, i. e. **K** and **S** , defined by the following *equalities*

(4) $\mathbf{K}(x, y) = x$

(5) $\mathbf{S}(x, y, z) = x(z, y(z))$

1.5.1 Definition. A *combinatory algebra* is a structure

$$\mathcal{C} \equiv (X, \mathrm{appl}, \mathbf{K}, \mathbf{S})$$

where Card(X) > 1 and (4) and (5) are valid in $\mathcal{C}$.

An alternate way is to represent combinators as closed λ-terms.

(4)' $\mathbf{K} = \lambda(x, y)\ x$

(5)' $\mathbf{S} = \lambda(x, y, z)\ x(z, y(z))$

Such a representation will be utilized later. Definition 1.5.1 employs a finite basis. It is also possible to use an infinite basis. An example of the latter is $\{\Phi^n{}_m, \mathbf{U}^n{}_i \mid n \geq i > 0, m \geq 0\}$ with the families of equations (1) and (2). Shönfinkel's basis is recovered by $\{\mathbf{I} = \Phi^0{}_0, \mathbf{S} = \Phi(\mathbf{I}), \mathbf{K} = \Phi^1{}_0\}$, where for simplicity $\Phi \equiv \Phi^1{}_2$.

Curry used also the basis

$\{\mathbf{K}, \mathbf{B} = \Phi^1{}_1, \mathbf{C} = \Phi(\Phi(\mathbf{S}), \mathbf{K}, \mathbf{K}(\mathbf{K})), \mathbf{W} = \Phi(\mathbf{I}, \mathbf{I})\}$.

It is easy to check that even projectors are superfluous. In fact

$$\mathbf{U}^n{}_i = \Phi^{i-1}{}_0(\Phi^{n-i}{}_0) \quad \text{and} \quad \Phi^{j+1}{}_0 = \Phi^1{}_1(\Phi^1{}_0, \Phi^j{}_0)^{(4)}.$$

We will next use an infinite basis especially useful to represent data structures which are absolutely free algebras.

2. A polynomial basis and reconstruction algorithm [BD 74] [CD 77]

In [BD 74] a first version of what Barendregt later called [Bar 77] Böhm tree was introduced. Revisiting that notion, I discovered that it encompasses a representation, via combinators, of absolutely free algebras, and related iterative functions. Therefore, we introduce the polynomial infinite basis $\{\pi^{m,n}{}_i \mid n \geq i > 0, m \geq 0\}$ defined by

(6) $\pi^{m,n}{}_i \equiv \lambda(y_1,\ldots,y_m,x_1,\ldots,x_n)\ x_i(y_1(x_1,\ldots,x_n),\ldots,y_m(x_1,\ldots,x_n))$.

Notice that

(7) $\pi^{m,n}{}_i = \Phi^n{}_{m+1}(\mathbf{I}, \mathbf{U}^n{}_i)$.

(4) More generally the following relation holds: $\Phi^{j+1}{}_m = \Phi^1{}_1(\Phi^1{}_m, \Phi^j{}_m)$.

Relation (6) and(7) may be also written, in a form which will be used later

(6*) $\pi^{m,n}{}_i\,(y_1,\ldots,y_m,x_1,\ldots,x_n) = x_i\,(y_1(x_1,\ldots,x_n),\ldots,y_m(x_1,\ldots,x_n))$

(7*) $\pi^{m,n}{}_i\,(y_1,\ldots,y_m,x_1,\ldots,x_n) = \Phi^n{}_m(x_i,y_1,\ldots,y_m,x_1,\ldots,x_n)$.

It is easy to verify that the $\pi^{m,n}{}_i$'s form a basis, since **I** ,**K** ,**S** can be expressed by

$$\mathbf{I} = \pi^{0,1}{}_1 \;,\; \mathbf{K} = \pi^{0,2}{}_1 \;,\; \mathbf{S} = \pi^{2,3}{}_1(\pi^{0,3}{}_3\,,\pi^{1,3}{}_2(\pi^{0,3}{}_3)).$$

Moreover also the Curry's basis can be expressed by

$$\mathbf{B} = \pi^{1,3}{}_1(\pi^{1,3}{}_2\,(\pi^{0,3}{}_3)) \;,\; \mathbf{C} = \pi^{2,3}{}_1(\pi^{0,3}{}_3,\pi^{0,3}{}_2)) \;,\; \mathbf{W} = \pi^{2,2}{}_1(\pi^{0,2}{}_2\,,\pi^{0,2}{}_2).$$

The combinatory algebra $\mathbb{C} \equiv (X, \text{appl}, \{\pi^{m,n}{}_i \mid n \geq i > 0,\ m \geq 0\})$, viewed *polynomially*, possesses some interesting subalgebras. Since the subalgebras to be defined will form a strictly inclusion chain, we will each time exhibit an element of the current algebra not belonging to the next sub-algebra. We begin with an element belonging to $\mathbb{C}$ not possessing normal form. To the right of the sign $\Rightarrow$ we will write, if it exists, the corresponding λ-term in normal form, otherwise we will write the application of terms in normal form.

$$\pi^{1,1}{}_1(\pi^{0,1}{}_1\,,\pi^{1,1}{}_1(\pi^{0,1}{}_1)) \Rightarrow (\lambda(x_1)x_1(x_1))(\lambda(x_1)x_1(x_1)).$$

(i) We call the next subalgebra of $\mathbb{C}$ Lukasiewicz algebra (L-algebra), because its elements can be written without parentheses [Luk 50]. The L-algebra is characterized by the fact that each $\pi^{m,n}{}_i$ has exactly m arguments. All the elements of this algebra possess normal form. An example is

$$\pi^{2,2}{}_1(\pi^{0,1}{}_1\,,\pi^{0,1}{}_1) \Rightarrow \lambda(x_1,x_2)x_1(x_1(x_2),x_1(x_2)).$$

(ii) The normal combinators algebra (LN-algebra) is the subalgebra of the L-algebra where each argument of $\pi^{m,n}{}_i$ (m>0) begins with $\pi^{m',n'}{}_{i'}$ where $n' \geq n$.

An example is

$$\pi^{1,1}{}_1(\pi^{0,2}{}_1) \Rightarrow \lambda(x_1)x_1(\lambda(x_2)x_1).$$

An important property of the elements of this algebra is that, once any element of LN is reduced to normal form, it is possible to reconstruct the term given initially by a linear algorithm (*reconstruction algorithm*). In other words any element of LN can be written in just one way. We are in presence of a term algebra, i.e an absolutely free algebra with a possibly infinite basis.

(iii) The *proper* combinators belong to the disjoint union of LNp-algebras for distinct p>0.

Each LNp-algebra is the subalgebra of the LN-algebra where n=p for all the basic elements $\pi^{m,n}{}_i$. An example is

$$\pi^{1,1}{}_1(\pi^{0,1}{}_1) \Rightarrow \lambda(x_1)x_1(x_1).$$

Notice that a LNp-algebra may still have an infinite basis, since inside this algebra there is no bounds for the value of m .

(iv) A Church p-algebra (LNpC-algebra) is a subalgebra of a LNp-algebra with a basis having exactly p elements. A LNpC-algebra is characterized by a finite function $\alpha:\{1,\ldots, p\} \to N$, giving for each basic combinator its arity.

$$\pi^{1,2}{}_1(\pi^{0,2}{}_2) \Rightarrow \lambda(x_1,x_2)x_1(x_2)\,, \text{ where } \alpha(1) = 1 \text{ and } \alpha(2) = 0$$

is an example of an element of a Church 2-algebra.

Any variable occurring in the closed λ-term, corresponding to any element of LNpC, has the same arity in each of its occurrencies.

This fact is the counterpart of the fact that term algebras with a finite number of constructors may be represented (together with the iterative functions mapping term algebras into term algebras) by second order typed λ-terms [BB 85].

The reconstruction algorithm

This algorithm, given a closed λ-term in *normal form*, will produce the corresponding element in LN. It can be viewed as a multilevel multivariable abstraction algorithm(5). The algorithm is sketched in [BD 74](6) and is based on a redenomination rule of bound variables rendering identical any two α-convertible normal terms. We specify the algorithm, to be executed left to right, on a given term, by means of the following rewriting rules for indices of variables :

(i) For every abstraction segment of variables like $\lambda(x_{j_1},\ldots,x_{j_n})$ the sequence $j_1,\ldots,j_n$ is to be rewritten as $p+1,\ldots,p+n$ and in the leftmost segment (of level 0) we must choose $p = 0$.

(ii) For any two segments

$$\lambda(x_{j_1},\ldots,x_{j_n}) \text{ and } \lambda(x_{k_1},\ldots,x_{k_{n'}})$$

lying on the same level (>0) of nested parentheses let p be the last value assigned to the index belonging to the segment located on the next lower level. Then we put

$$j_1 = k_1 = p+1.$$

The same obviously must be done if, on that level, there is just one segment.

Let now suppose that, by the rules just described, all the segments of the given term have been redenominated as well as the variables lying in the scope of all segments. To go on with the reconstruction algorithm we now need to apply the following rule uniformly to all variables.

(5) As Piperno pointed out privately to me some days ago, the Abdali's abstraction algorithm [Abd 76] uses an infinite basis containing the $\pi^{m,n}{}_i$ together with other combinators.

(6) Incidentally, the algoritm in [BD 74] is valid also for terms containing free variables. Unfortunately the definition of i is wrong. It has been corrected in the subsequent paper [BD 75] as follows:

$$i = \textbf{if } \exists\, \ell\ (1 \le \ell \le n)\colon j = j_\ell \textbf{ then } \ell \textbf{ else } n+j.$$

(iii) the variable x_i is to be rewritten as $\pi^{m,n}{}_i$ if it has m arguments and if it is in the scope of the nearest abstraction segment whose last abstracted variable has index n. As last stage of the algorithm we must erase all the abstraction segments and we may erase, if we wish it, all the remaining parentheses and commas (remember that a LN-algebra is still a L-algebra).

Example

$\lambda(x,y,z)\, y\,(x(y), \lambda\,(x,y)y(z,x), \lambda\,(y)y\,(x(\lambda\,(x)x))\,) \rightarrow$

$\rightarrow \lambda\,(x_1,x_2,x_3)\, x_2\,(\ x_1\,(x_2\,), \lambda\,(x,y)y\,(\,x_3,x)\,, \lambda\,(y)y\,(\,x_1\,(\,\lambda\,(x)x))\ \,) \rightarrow$

$\rightarrow \lambda\,(x_1,x_2,x_3)\, x_2\,(\ x_1\,(x_2\,), \lambda\,(x_4,x_5)\, x_5\,(x_3,x_4)\,, \lambda\,(x_4)\, x_4\,(\,x_1\,(\,\lambda\,(x_5)x_5))\,) \rightarrow$

$\rightarrow \pi^{3,3}{}_2\,(\,\pi^{1,3}{}_1\,(\pi^{0,3}{}_2)\,, \pi^{2,5}{}_5\,(\pi^{0,5}{}_3\,, \pi^{0,5}{}_4)\,, \pi^{1,4}{}_4(\pi^{1,4}{}_1(\pi^{0,5}{}_5))\,) \rightarrow$

$\rightarrow \pi^{3,3}{}_2\quad \pi^{1,3}{}_1\, \pi^{0,3}{}_2\quad \pi^{2,5}{}_5\, \pi^{0,5}{}_3\, \pi^{0,5}{}_4\quad \pi^{1,4}{}_4\, \pi^{1,4}{}_1\, \pi^{0,5}{}_5\,.$

3. Church algebras as data structures(7)

We give the name of Church p-algebras to the subalgebras of the combinatory algebra since Church [Chu 41] used combinators belonging to such algebras for numerals and for truth values.

The first proof that partial recursive functions are representable by λ-terms was carried out using fixpoints combinators such as $\mathbf{Y}_c$. If somebody is interested, as I am, in programs for total functions (as all the algorithms developed in Computer Science) fixpoint theory or fixpoint combinators are superfluous, when dealing with data structures that can accomodate themselves into Church algebras.

Notice that for every element $e \in$ LNnC holds

(8) $$e = \pi^{m,n}{}_i(e_1,\dots,e_m).$$

In order to simplify the notation, inside a given LNnC-algebra, we will write π_i instead of $\pi^{m,n}{}_i$.

Theorem (Main theorem for Church algebras)

$$e \in \text{LNnC} \quad \Rightarrow e(x_1,\dots,x_n) = e\,[x_1/\pi_1,\dots,x_n/\pi_n]^{(8)}.$$

Proof (by induction on the formation of the elements in LNnC)

As pointed out above there must be some nullary element in LNnC.

Let π_n be one of them. Then since $\pi_n \equiv \pi^{0,n}{}_n$ from (6*) we find that

$$\pi_n(x_1,\dots,x_n) = x_n = \pi_n\,[x_n/\pi_n] = \pi_n\,[x_1/\pi_1,\dots,x_n/\pi_n].$$

Let e be as in (8); we assume ,by induction, that

$$e_j(x_1,\dots,x_n) = e_j\,[x_1/\pi_1,\dots,x_n/\pi_n], \qquad j=1,\dots,m\,.$$

(7) The theorems of this section may be found, in a different context, in [BB 85].

(8) $E\,[x_1/t_1,\dots,x_n/t_n\,]$ is by definition the result of the simultaneously substituting x_1 for t_1 ,..., x_n for t_n, in E .

We have from (6*), where $y_1,\dots,y_m$ have been replaced by $e_1,\dots,e_m$,

$$e(x_1,\dots,x_n) = \pi_i(e_1,\dots,e_m)(x_1,\dots,x_n) = x_i(e_1(x_1,\dots,x_n),\dots,e_m(x_1,\dots,x_n)) =$$
$$= \pi_i[x_1/\pi_1,\dots,x_n/\pi_n](e_1[x_1/\pi_1,\dots,x_n/\pi_n],\dots,e_m[x_1/\pi_1,\dots,x_n/\pi_n])$$
$$= \pi_i(e_1,\dots,e_m)[x_1/\pi_1,\dots,x_n/\pi_n] = e[x_1/\pi_1,\dots,x_n/\pi_n].$$

❑

Corollary (fixpoint theorem for the elements of LNnC)

$$e \in \text{LNnC} \quad \Rightarrow \quad e(\pi_1,\dots,\pi_n) = e$$

Proof. Obvious.

❑

Theorem (Explicit solution of functional iterative equations)[9]

Let a function f (mapping a Church algebra LNnC into another arbitrary Church algebra) be iteratively defined by the following system:

(9) $$f(\pi^{m,n}{}_i(e_1,\dots,e_m)) = h_i(f(e_1),\dots,f(e_m)) \qquad i=1,\dots,n,$$

where $h_1,\dots,h_n$ are given combinators.

Then an explicit solution to f is

(10) $$f(e) = e(h_1,\dots,h_n).$$

Proof

Let e be as in (8). Utilizing an instance of (6*) once again we have

(12) $$e(h_1,\dots,h_n) = \pi^{m,n}{}_i(e_1,\dots,e_m)(h_1,\dots,h_n)$$
$$= h_i(e_1(h_1,\dots,h_n),\dots,e_m(h_1,\dots,h_n)).$$

Assuming (10), since e is an arbitrary element of LNnC, then

(13) $$f(e_j) = e_j(h_1,\dots,h_n) \qquad j=1,\dots,m$$

must also hold. The replacement of (13) and (10) in (12) will obviously satisfy (9).

❑

Remark If the image of LNnC onto f is again a Church algebra then any result possesses normal form and the correctness of results depends only on the correctness of the combinators h_i ($i=1,\dots,n$).

Data structures represented by Church algebras

The most important structures in computer science are:

N (natural numbers), L,N (finite sequences of natural numbers),

$U^{(n)}$(set of n elements,with the special case of boolean set with n=2)

$\Sigma_2{}^*$ (binary strings) T_2 (binary tree structures) F,T (tree and forest structures), etc. The structures with more than one support are heterogeneous algebras. Obviously the list is not exhaustive, since we could be interested in binary trees with nodes labeled with

(9) Since we are in a typeless context, unlike [BB 85], an actual distiction between heterogeneous and homogeneous algebras is not necessary. Consequently, we may treat heterogeneous algebras as homogeneous and introduce functions between algebras, rather than between supports of algebras.

naturals (T'_2,N), or with elements of some other algebra.

Examples

$(\{N\}, \{\pi^{1,2}_1 \equiv s : N \to N ; \pi^{0,2}_2 \equiv 0 : N\})$, $(\{U^{(2)}\}, \{\pi^{0,2}_1 \equiv \text{True} : U^{(2)} ; \pi^{0,2}_2 \equiv \text{False} : U^{(2)}\})$.

The predicate 'equal to zero' iteratively defined:

$P_{=0} (\pi^{0,2}_2) = \pi^{0,2}_1$; $P_{=0} (\pi^{1,2}_1 (n)) = \pi^{0,2}_2 = \mathbf{K} (\pi^{0,2}_2, P_{=0} (n))$.

Hence $P_{=0} (n) = n (\mathbf{K}(\pi^{0,2}_2), \pi^{0,2}_1)$.

$(\{\Sigma_2^*\}, \{\pi^{1,3}_1 \equiv s_0 : \Sigma_2^* \to \Sigma_2^* ; \pi^{1,3}_2 \equiv s_1 : \Sigma_2^* \to \Sigma_2^* ; \pi^{0,3}_3 \equiv \# : \Sigma_2^*\})$.

The function 'length of a binary string' $\ell : \Sigma_2^* \to N$.

$\ell (\pi^{1,3}_1 (\sigma)) = \pi^{1,2}_1 (\ell (\sigma))$; $\ell (\pi^{1,3}_2 (\sigma)) = \pi^{1,2}_1 (\ell (\sigma))$; $\ell (\pi^{0,3}_3) = \pi^{0,2}_2$.

Hence $\ell (\sigma) = \sigma (\pi^{1,2}_1, \pi^{1,2}_1, \pi^{0,2}_2)$.

It is interesting to observe that:

the combinator $\mathbf{S} \equiv \pi^{2,3}_1 (\pi^{0,3}_3 , \pi^{1,3}_2(\pi^{0,3}_3))$ is an element of a tree and forest structure;

$\mathbf{C} \equiv \pi^{2,3}_1 (\pi^{0,3}_3, \pi^{0,3}_2)$ is an element of a binary tree structure (with bit-marked leaves);

$\mathbf{B} \equiv \pi^{1,3}_1 (\pi^{1,3}_2(\pi^{0,3}_3)) \in \Sigma_2^*$; $\mathbf{W} \equiv \pi^{2,2}_1(\pi^{0,2}_2, \pi^{0,2}_2) \in T_2$. ❑

4. General recursion and *-algebras

Our aim is to find explicitly normal combinators not only representing solutions for iteratively defined mapping, but also for primitive recursive and more generally for any particular shape of the r.h.s. defining recursively a mapping from Church algebras to Church algebras .

Definition (*-algebras)(10)

Given any LNnC defined by the arity function a, i.e. with the basis

$$\{\pi^{a(i)}_i \mid i=1,\ldots,n\}$$

we defined a new subalgebra LNn* of LN (called *-algebra) generated by the basis

$$\{\pi^{*a(i)}_i \mid i=1,\ldots,n\}$$

where

(14) $$\pi^{*a(i)}_i(y_1,\ldots,y_{a(i)},x_1,\ldots,x_n) = x_i (y_1,\ldots,y_{a(i)},x_1,\ldots,x_n).$$

Theorem (Main theorem for *-algebras)

(i) The correspondence between LNnC and LNn* is one to one. More precisely, if we call e* the corresponding element of e in LNn* and we put

(15) $$x_i' \equiv \Phi^n_{a(i)} (x_i) \qquad i=1,\ldots,n$$

then we have

(16) $$e^* = e(\pi^{*a(1)}_1,\ldots,\pi^{*a(n)}_n)$$

(17) $$e^*(x_1',\ldots,x_n') = e (x_1,\ldots,x_n).$$

---

(10) In the special case of Church numerals the *-algebra was first introduced and employed by A. Berarducci in his master thesis (1983) to find a primitive recursion combinator in normal form.

(ii) Let $\mathbf{D}_n$ be the combinator defined by

(18) $\mathbf{D}_n(u_1,\ldots,u_n)(z) = z(u_1,\ldots,u_n)$,

and let the unknown combinator F* represent a mapping from a first *-algebra to a second one and satisfying the following system

(19) $F^*(\pi^{*a(i)}{}_i(e^*_1,\ldots,e^*_{a(i)})) = h^*_i(e^*_1,\ldots,e^*_{a(i)}, F^*)$

where the h^*_i 's are given combinators.

Then an explicit solution for F* is given by

(20) $F^*(e^*) = e^*(H_1(h^*_1),\ldots, H_n(h^*_n))$

or $F^* = \mathbf{D}_n(H_1(h^*_1),\ldots,H_n(h^*_n))$

where $H_i(t_i,y_1,\ldots,y_{a(i)},u_1,\ldots,u_n)=t_i(y_1,\ldots,y_{a(i)},\mathbf{D}_n(u_1,\ldots,u_n))$ $(i=1,\ldots,n)$.

Proof

(i) A *- algebra is obtained from a LNnC algebra simply by using $\pi^{*a(i)}{}_i$ instead of $\pi^{a(i)}{}_i$.
Then (16) comes from the application of the main theorem:

$$e(\pi^*_1,\ldots,\pi^*_n) = e[\pi^*_1/\pi_1,\ldots,\pi^*_n/\pi_n] = e^*.$$

From (14), where $y_1,\ldots,y_m$ have been replaced with $e^*_1,\ldots,e^*_m$, and $x_1,\ldots,x_n$ with $x_1',\ldots,x_n'$ and from (7*) and (15), it results

(21)
$$\begin{aligned}\pi^*_i(e^*_1,\ldots,e^*_{a(i)},x_1',\ldots,x_n') &= x_i'(e^*_1,\ldots,e^*_{a(i)},x_1',\ldots,x_n')\\ &= x_i(e^*_1(x_1',\ldots,x_n'),\ldots,e^*_{a(i)}(x_1',\ldots,x_n'))\\ &\qquad (i=1,\ldots,n).\end{aligned}$$

Let $\pi_n \equiv \pi^{0,n}{}_n$. Then, from definition(14) we have $\pi^*_n \equiv \pi^{*0,n}{}_n = \pi_n$ and $\pi^*_n(x_1',\ldots,x_n') = x_n = \pi_n(x_1,\ldots,x_n)$. Proceeding now by induction on (21), as in the proof of the previous main theorem, we obtain (17).

(ii) The proof is similar to the proof of last theorem:

(22)
$$\begin{aligned}e^*(H_1(h^*_1),\ldots,H_n(h^*_n)) &= \pi^*_i(e^*_1,\ldots,e^*_{a(i)})(H_1(h^*_1),\ldots,H_n(h^*_n)) =\\ &= H_i(h^*_1,e^*_1,\ldots,e^*_{a(i)},H_1(h^*_1),\ldots,H_n(h^*_n)) =\\ (\text{by def. of } H_i)\quad &= h^*_i(e^*_1,\ldots,e^*_{a(i)},\mathbf{D}_n(H_1(h^*_1),\ldots,H_n(h^*_n))) =\\ &= h^*_i(e^*_1,\ldots,e^*_{a(i)}, F^*) = F^*(e^*)\end{aligned}$$

❑

Corollary (Fixpoint theorem for the elements of *-algebras)

$$e^* \in LNn^* \quad \Rightarrow \quad e^*(\pi_1',\ldots,\pi_n') = e^*$$

Proof

Direct consequence of (17). ❑

Example:

The 'predecessor' function:

Transforming n into n*: $n^* = n(\pi^{*1,2}{}_1,\pi^{*0,2}{}_2)$.

System (19) for the predecessor p* becomes

$p^* (\pi^{*1,2}{}_1(n)) = n^* = \mathbf{K}(n^*,p^*) \qquad h^* = \mathbf{K}$

$p^* (\pi^{*0,2}{}_2) = \pi^{*0,2}{}_2$.

The explicit solution following (20) is

$p^* (n^*) = n^* (H\,\mathbf{K})\, \pi^{*0,2}{}_2$,

where $\quad H (t,y,u_1,u_2) = t\, y\, (D_2(u_1,u_2))$.

From (22) $\quad H (\mathbf{K},y,u_1,u_2) = H (\mathbf{K}) (y,u_1,u_2) = \mathbf{K} (y,D_2(u_1,u_2)) = y$,

hence $\quad H (\mathbf{K}) = \mathbf{U}^3{}_1$ and $p^*(n^*) = n^* (\mathbf{U}^3{}_1,\pi^{*0,2}{}_2)$.

From the fixpoint theorem $m^*(\Phi^2{}_1(\pi^{1,2}{}_1),\pi^{0,2}{}_2) = m\, (\pi^{1,2}{}_1,\pi^{0,2}{}_2) = m$;

hence $p(n) = n\, (\pi^{*1,2}{}_1,\pi^{*0,2}{}_2)\, (\mathbf{U}^3{}_1,\pi^{*0,2}{}_2)\, (\Phi^2{}_1(\pi^{1,2}{}_1),\pi^{0,2}{}_2)$. ❑

General remark on Church and *-algebras

Last theorem essentially states that the relation between LNnC and LNn* is an isomorph embedding of LNnC into LN. Obviously this it not the unique possible. Referring to (14) any other combinator different from π^*, but whose r.h.s. still beginning with ' $x_i\,(y_1$,' and containing all the variables of the l.h.s., could have been introduced equally well .

5. Parametric Church algebras

The last statement of section introduces the theme of parametric algebras. An algebra has a parametric support iff it is in the domain of some constructor but never in the codomain.

The combinatory counterpart of a parameter is the introduction of variables (free variables in λ-calculus). Deviating slightly from [BD 74] we can introduce for variables polynomial symbols $\pi^{m,n}{}_i$, with *nonpositive* index i as name of the variable and with m,n preserving their meanings.

We jump directly from the algebra of combinator forms to parametric Church subalgebras CnP, and will use for the new basis the polynomial symbol $\pi^{b(i),a(i),n}{}_i$, an extension of $\pi^{a(i),n}{}_i$, where b: $\{1,\dots,n\}\to N$ is the function assigning the number of parametric arguments to each basic combinator.

The definition of $\pi^{b(i),a(i),n}{}_i$ is the following

$$(23) \qquad \pi^{b(i),a(i),n}{}_i(z_1,\dots,z_{b(i)},y_1,\dots,y_{a(i)},x_1,\dots,x_n) = \\ = x_i\,(z_1,\dots,z_{b(i)},y_1(x_1,\dots,x_n),\dots,y_{a(i)}(x_1,\dots,x_n)) \qquad i=1,\dots,n.$$

Here z_j $(j=1,\dots,b(i))$ represents an element of a parametric set Z_j, element which may change each time we construct an element of CnP.

In other words, we have following inductive definition of CnP

(24) $\mathrm{CnP} \equiv \{\pi^{b(i),a(i),n}{}_i(z_1,\ldots,z_{b(i)},y_1,\ldots,y_{a(i)}) \mid$
$z_j \in Z_j, y_k \in \mathrm{CnP}, j=1,\ldots,b(i), k=1,\ldots,a(i), i=1,\ldots,n\}$.

Each parametric set Z_j belongs to a family $\mathcal{Z} \equiv \{ Z^1,\ldots,Z^p\}$, where p depends only on the CnP we are considering. In order for CnP to be a consistent extension of LNnC we use in (23) the following convention:

(25) If $Z_j = Z^h$ then $z_j \equiv \pi^{0,0,n}{}_{-h}$.

Theorem (Solution of functional iterative equations in CnP algebras)

Let a function f (mapping a Church algebra CnP into another arbitrary Church algebra) be iteratively defined by the following system:

(26) $f(\pi^{b,m,n}{}_i(z_1,\ldots,z_b,e_1,\ldots,e_m)) = h_i(z_1,\ldots,z_b,f(e_1),\ldots,f(e_m))$

where $i= 1,\ldots,n$, the z_j ($j=1,\ldots,b$) are defined in (25) and $h_1,\ldots,h_n$ are given combinators. Then an explicit solution for f is

(27) $f(e) = e(h_1,\ldots,h_n)$.

Proof. The same as for proving (10) from (9).

Examples

Pairs: $(\{Z_1,Z_2,D^2\}, \{\pi^{2,0,1}{}_1 \equiv \mathbf{D}_2 : Z_1 \times Z_2 \to D^2\})$;

Parametric lists: $(\{Z_1,L_{Z_1}\}, \{\pi^{1,1,2}{}_1 \equiv \mathrm{cons} : Z_1 \times L_{Z_1} \to L_{Z_1} ; \pi^{0,0,2}{}_1 \equiv \mathrm{nil} : L_{Z_1}\})$.

The function 'length of a parametric list' $\mathcal{L}: L_{Z_1} \to N$.

$\mathcal{L}(\pi^{1,1,2}{}_1(z_1,l)) = \pi^{1,2}{}_1(\mathcal{L}(l)) = \mathbf{K}(\pi^{1,2}{}_1,z_1,\mathcal{L}(l))$

$\mathcal{L}(\pi^{0,0,2}{}_2) = \pi^{0,2}{}_2$. Hence $\mathcal{L}(l) = l(\mathbf{K}(\pi^{1,2}{}_1),\pi^{0,2}{}_2)$. ❑

Extension to nonunary functions

A simple currification allows the extension of the explicit solution of iterative equation to the case of nonunary functions F of r+1 arguments, provided that the iterative definition involves only the last argument.

Corollary (solution for multivariables functions from LNnC or CnP algebras)

Let by definition

$$\pi^{0,m,n}{}_i \equiv \pi^{m,n}{}_i$$

Let a function F (mapping a Church algebra CnP into another arbitrary Church algebra) be iteratively defined by the following system:

$$F(w_1,\ldots,w_r,\pi^{b,m,n}{}_i(z_1,\ldots,z_b,e_1,\ldots,e_m)) =$$
$$= h_i(w_1,\ldots,w_r,z_1,\ldots,z_b,F(w_1,\ldots,w_r,e_1),\ldots,F(w_1,\ldots,w_r,e_m))$$

where $i= 1,\ldots,n$, the z_j ($j=1,\ldots,b$) are defined in (25) and $h_1,\ldots,h_n$ are given combinators and $w_1,\ldots,w_r$ are arbitrary ones, not depending on i.

Then an explicit solution for F is

(28) $F(w_1,\ldots,w_r,e) = e(h_1(w_1,\ldots,w_r),\ldots,h_n(w_1,\ldots,w_r))$.

Example

The function 'addition' add: $N \times N \to N$.

add $(w,\pi^{0,1,2}{}_1(n)) = \pi^{1,2}{}_1(\text{add}(w,n)) = \mathbf{K}(\pi^{1,2}{}_1,w,\text{add}(w,n))$; add $(w,\pi^{0,0,2}{}_2) = w = \mathbf{I}(w)$.

Hence: $\text{add}(w,n) = n\,(\mathbf{K}(\pi^{1,2}{}_1,w),\mathbf{I}(w)) = n(\pi^{1,2}{}_1,w)$.

We are now able to compute the function 'number of nodes of a binary tree'

nodes: $T_2 \to N$.

nodes $(\pi^{2,2}{}_1(t_1,t_2)) = \pi^{1,2}{}_1(\text{add}(\text{nodes}(t_1),\text{nodes}(t_2))) = \Phi^2{}_1(\pi^{1,2}{}_1,\text{add},\text{nodes}(t_1),\text{nodes}(t_2))$;

nodes $(\pi^{0,2}{}_2) = \pi^{0,2}{}_2$. Hence nodes $(t) = t\,(\Phi^2{}_1(\pi^{1,2}{}_1,\text{add}),\pi^{0,2}{}_2)$. ❑

Final remark

All the content of this section applies also to *-algebras providing a powerful tool to find explicit solutions to functions defined recursively, representing mappings from term data structures to other ones, provided that recursion is done for just one argument.

ACKNOWLEDGMENTS

I am grateful to Adolfo Piperno and Enrico Tronci for helpful discussions on the topics of this paper.

REFERENCES

[Abd 76] Abdali, S.K., An abstraction algorithm for combinatory logic, JSL 41, 1976

[Bac 78] Backus, J., Can programming be liberated from von Neumann style? A functional style and its algebra of programs, ACM Comm., 1978, vol.21, no.8, pp.613-641

[Bar 77] Barendregt, H.P., The type free lambda-calculus, in"Handbook of Mathematical Logic", Barwise (ed.), North Holland, 1981

[Bar 81] Barendregt, H.P., The lambda calculus, North Holland, 1981

[BB 85] Böhm, C. and Berarducci, A., Automatic synthesis of typed Λ-programs on term algebras, TCS 39 (1985), pp.135-154

[BD 74] Böhm, C. and Dezani-Ciancaglini, M., Combinatorial problems, combinator equations and normal forms, in: Lœckx (ed.) Progr,"Automata,Languages and Programming 2thColloquium", LNCS 14, 1974, pp. 185-199

[BD 75] Böhm, C. and Dezani-Ciancaglini, M., λ-terms as total or partial functions on normal forms, in "λ-Calculus and computer science theory", Böhm (ed.), LNCS 37 , Springer, 1975, pp.96-121

[Böh 82] Böhm, C., Combinatory foundation of functional programming, in"1982 ACM Symposium on Lisp and functional programming", 1982,Pittsburgh,Pen., pp. 29-36

[Chu 41] Church, A.,The calculi of lambda-conversion, Princeton Univ. Press, 1941

[CD 77] Coppo, M. and Dezani-Ciancaglini, M.,Tree and λ-terms in "Les Arbres an Algebre et Programmation" G.Jacobs (ed.), Debock, 1977, pp.91-120

[Cop 85] Coppo, M., A completeness theorem for recursively defined types, in "Automata,Languages and Programming 12th colloquium", LNCS 194, 1985, pp.120-128

[Joh 84] Johnsson,T., Effient compilation of lazy evaluation, in "Proceedings of the SIGPLAN '84 symposium on compiler construction", Montreal, 1984, pp.58-69

[McC 60] McCarthy, J., Recursive functions of symbolic expressions and their computation by machine, Comm.ACM 1960, vol.3, no. 4, pp184-195

[Par 68] Parsons,C, Hierarchies of primitive recursive functions, Zeits.f.Math.Logik und Grundlage d.Math, vol.14, 1968, pp.357-376

[Sch 24] Schönfinkel, M., Über die Bausteine der matematischen logik, Math. Annalen 92, 1924, pp..305-316

[Tur 85] Turner, D.A., Miranda: A non strict language with polymorphic types, in "Proceedings 1985 conference on functional programming languages and computer architecture", Nancy, 1985, pp.1-16

ON MODELS AND ALGEBRAS FOR CONCURRENT PROCESSES

Ludmila A. Cherkasova

Computing Center Siberian Division of the USSR Academy of Sciences

630090, Novosibirsk, USSR

Abstract

The paper consists of two parts. In the first part, three different groups of models for concurrent systems and processes are surveyed: 1) the models representing concurrency as nondeterministic interleaving of atomic actions; 2) the models representing concurrency as interleaving of multisets of actions; and 3) the models describing true concurrency. A number of algebras and algebraic calculi axiomatizing these models are discussed. Different equivalence relations introduced in these models are compared.

In the second part, the algebra of finite (generalized) processes AFP is introduced. The semantics of a process specified by a formula of AFP is characterized by a set of partial orders. The complete set of axioms and inference rules for deduction of partial and total properties of processes is presented.

In conclusion, the primitives of proposed algebra AFP are compared with those of CSP, and the directions of further developments are outlined.

1. Models, algebras and equivalence relations for concurrent processes

1.1. Models

Different models of concurrency have been proposed for the description of concurrent systems and processes and investigation of their behavioural properties. Depending on the representation of concurrency the models could be parted in the following three groups.

1) In such models as CCS [Mil180], TCSP [BHR84, Hoa85] and Process Algebra (PA) [BBK85], the concurrent execution of two processes is simulated by nondeterministic interleaving of their atomic actions (i.e. concurrency is simulated by sequential non-determinism). Therefore, concurrent execution of two atomic actions a and b could be defined by the following axiom: a || b = ab + ba (i.e. a precedes b, or b precedes a). However, if we consider the system with the actions a and b, which share a common resource (denote this situation by a mutex b), then the behaviour of such a system can be specified by the same axiom: a mutex b = ab + ba. Thus, the process a || b and a mutex b are indistinguishable in the models based on interleaving semantics. If behaviour of concurrent system and processes is characterized by sequencies of totally ordered actions, then the concurrency operator (or

relation) is not primitive:

concurrency = sequentiality + nondeterminism

2) In such models as MEIJE [AB84], SCCS [Mil83] and Algebra of Communicating Processes (ACP) [BK84], the concurrent execution of two processes is simulated by interleaving of multisets of their atomic actions. For example, the concurrent execution of two atomic actions a and b could be defined by the following axioms: $a \parallel b = ab + ba + a|b$, i.e. a precedes b, or b precedes a, or a and b occur at the same time (the last situation is denoted as co-occurrence, the so called contemporary occurrence). Thus, concurrency operator (or relation) is also not primitive in these models:

concurrency = sequentiality + nondeterminism + co-occurrence

3) The third group of concurrent models is based on the concept of process as partially ordered set of actions. Such models as Pomsets (partially ordered multisets) [Pr87], Occurrence Nets [Pet77, NPW81], Event Structures [NPW81], A-nets [KotCh84], Petri Nets [Rei85] are intended to describe true concurrency. The precedence relation on actions is defined as causal dependence of actions in these models. This relation induced some partial order on actions. Accordingly, two actions are concurrent if they are causally independent. Thus, the concurrent process the elements of which are partially ordered by the precedence relation can be explicitly represented by partially ordered set (poset) (see papers [Pr87, Pet77, GoRe83]). The behaviour of a concurrent nondeterministic process (or system) is described by a set of its "pure" concurrent subprocesses. Each process in such a set is a result of nondeterministic choice among conflict actions during a run of the system. However, often it is necessary and preferable to deal with conflicts on semantical level and to express the behaviour of a system with conflicts (or nondeterministic process) as some unique integral semantic object. By this reason, Event Structures, Occurrence Nets *) [NPW81] and A-nets generalize the posets by introducing the conflict relation [NPW81] or alternative relation [KotCh84]. Two actions a and b are alternative if the occurrence of a exludes the occurrence of b, and vice versa. The Petri Nets Theory gives more general models possessed suitable and various means for

---

*) Unfortunately, the term Occurrence Nets (O-nets) is used in the papers [Pet77, GoRe83] and [NPW81] to denote different objects: in the first case, the elements of the O-net are connected only by precedence and concurrency relations. In the second case O-nets are augmented by the conflict relation, and the forward conflict is allowed in the net structure.

adequate describing both concurrent nondeterministic processes and the wide class of concurrent systems.

1.2. Algebras

Among formal models proposed to specify concurrent systems and processes, algebraic calculi and process logics hold a special place. In these calculi, a process is specified by an algebraic (or logical) formula and the verification of process properties is accomplished by means of equivalences, axioms and inference rules. For a lack of space we consider here only algebraic calculi. All the calculi considered below have a similar basic core. They build up processes of atomic actions (some of which may communicate) using operators for specifying sequentiality, concurrency and nondeterminism. Depending of the semantics of concurrency operator the algebras could also be parted in the appropriate three groups.

1) CCS, TCSP and Process Algebra PA are the most well-known algebraic calculi for specifying concurrent processes with interleaving semantics. CCS and especially PA are the calculi which are not bound to a particular concrete model. They intend to serve as a basis for a family of concurrent models (of the first group), which could introduce new additional properties and identification of processes (with respect to CCS and PA), but cannot violate the presented ones.

However, in the Hoare's theory of CSP another strategy has been chosen: the set of basic operators, axioms and rules for TCSP is much more rich than the corresponding sets of CCS and PA. Only the most essential differencies are not identified. By this reason, TCSP operates with more transformations and equivalencies, than CCS and PA.

2) Such calculi as SCCS [Mil83], ACP [BK84] have been proposed for the axiomatization of the second group of concurrent models. The set of operators has been extended (w.r.t. CCS and PA) by introducing a new operator to adequately specify the contemporary occurrence (co-occurrence) of actions.

3) The elaboration of some suitable algebraic calculi for the third group of concurrent models is at the very beginning.

It should be noted that in literature the notion of process is used in two meanings: i) as a specification of "dynamic" object by means of some formalism, ii) as a behaviour (semantics) of specified dynamic object. These two meanings are different in some theories. Their identity is highly desirable in the elaboration of practical tools for the verification and synthesis of systems.

Algebras proposed for process specification could be (informally) called as: "descriptive" algebras and "analytical" ones. In the descriptive algebras, process specification provides a good insight into structural properties of designed concurrent systems. Analytical algebras contain sufficient support for the validation of behavioural properties. Desirable process algebra should be both descriptive and analytical.

In the paper [Pr87], a process is represented as a labelled partially ordered multiset (pomset), and the algebra of pomsets is proposed. However, the algebra is aimed more at development of a suitable and rich constructor for specifying concurrent systems and processes, than at proposing the tools for analysis and verification of behavioural properties of specified objects.

In the paper [BouCa87], an attempt to construct an algebra of Labelled Event Structures is undertaken. The algebra specifies the finite subclass of very "regular" event structures. For example, the following event structure N cannot be expressed by means of this algebra.

N:

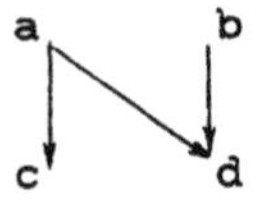

The precedence relation among actions is shown in the figure by the arcs connecting the actions. The non-connected elements are considered as concurrent.

It is more close to analytical algebraic calculus, because some congruence relation is introduced, and its axiomatization is proposed.

Different attempts to elaborate the "structure" algebra for Petri Nets are undertaken (i.e. the attempts to develop the descriptive algebra for the specification of Petri net structure). The most early works in this area are the papers [CamH74, LRC79] about COSY. COSY is a COncurrent SYstems notation which is based on the path expression notation [CamH74] and can be used for describing the "well-structured" subclasses of Petri Nets. COSY anticipates many of the features of CCS and CSP. Moreover, in the paper [Sh79], the problem of analysing (deducing) dynamic (behavioural) properties of process from their specification is considered.

In the paper [Kot78], a descriptive algebra for specifying Petri Nets has been proposed. This net algebra has continued further development of the COSY ideas. A Petri net can be specified by a formula of the proposed algebra. The net algebra provides a rich set of interesting formula equivalencies and transformations. Nevertheless, the net algebra has rather descriptive character than analytical one.

Other attempts to specify Petri Nets (more exactly: their special subclasses) with the help of CCS operators have been done in [GoM84, DDeNM87]. The concept of synchronized communication is a core of CCS. However, the Petri Net Theory provides more flexible synchronization mechanisms. By this reason, the proposed algebras are not very natural (adequate) for the net description.

As it had been noted above, the desirable process algebra should possess both descriptive and analytical abilities. Processes algebra AFP_1, proposed in [ChKot87] is intended to combine the mechanisms for the description of finite nondeterministic concurrent process and the derivation of their behavioural properties. The semantics of a process described by a formula of AFP_1 is defined as a set of partial orders. The second part of the paper is devoted to the main results obtained for AFP_1.

1.3. Equivalence relations

One of the purposes of algebraic calculi for concurrent systems and processes is to analyse and validate their behavioural properties, in particular, to determine, whether two processes specified by different algebraic formulae are (semantically) equal. To this end, a criterion for identifying processes is necessary. Such a criterion is partly determined by the semantics (model) of the theory. Depending on the purposes, the theory of concurrency is equipped with different semantics, giving a possibility to express a process equality on different levels.

Below we consider some equivalence relations, proposed for algebraic calculi based on the concurrent models of the first group (with interleaving semantics).

The notion of observational equivalence $\approx_0$ of processes has been proposed for CCS [Mil80] by Milner. The idea of this relation consists in the following: two processes are equivalent iff they have become equivalent after performing the same observable experiment (a sequence of actions). It is a very strong relation. For example, the processes $p_1 = ab + ac$ and $p_2 = a(b + c)$, the behaviours of which are represented by the following synchronization trees, are not observational equivalent.

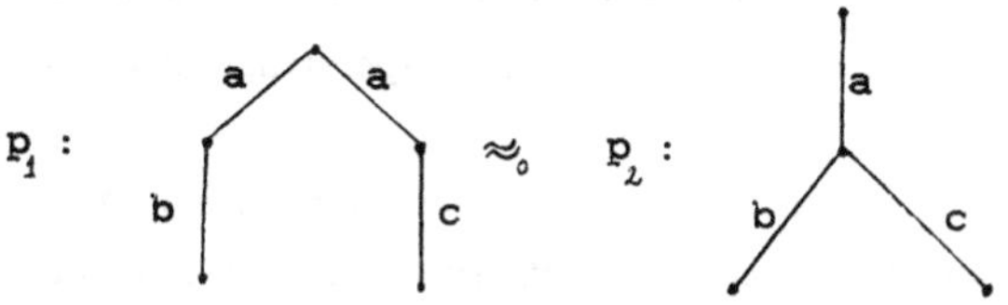

$a\,(b + c) \neq ab + ac$

However, the initial process behaviour could be changed (violated) if we replace one of its subprocesses by the equivalent one. In order that two processes be equivalent independently in whatever context they are replaced, Milner has introduced the notion $\approx_c$ of observational congruence ($A \approx_c B$ iff for any expression context $\mathcal{C}[\ ]$, $\mathcal{C}[A] \approx_0 \mathcal{C}[B]$), and has proposed axiomatization for it.

Another process equivalence relations have been considered by Hoare for CSP [Hoa82, BHR84]. The first equivalence relation is based on a notion of trace. Trace is a finite sequence of actions in which a process may be engaged up to a certain moment. Two processes are <u>trace equivalent</u> $\approx_T$, iff they generate the same set of traces. For example, the processes p and p mentioned above are trace equivalent. The trace equivalence is suitable for reasoning about potential communication sequences but is insensitive to deadlock. <u>Failure equivalence</u> $\approx_F$ compares semantics of two processes represented by the corresponding sets of failures. A failure is a pair (s, V) where s is a trace, and V is a set of actions the process is able to reject on the next step.

Comparing the various equivalences, we obtain the <u>following relationships</u>:

$\approx_C$ implies $\approx_O$ implies $\approx_F$ implies $\approx_T$

These equivalence relations have been proposed for the models of concurrency with interleaving semantics, in which atomic observations have been based on the sequencies of actions.

In order to introduce the equivalence relations reflecting essential differencies of processes defined by the concurrent models of the second and the third groups, we have to change the observation mechanism. Indeed, by using two new kinds of observations and according equivalence relations induced by such observations as sequences of multisets of actions ($\approx_M$) and partial ordering of actions ($\approx_{po}$), we are able to capture different information about the causal structure of processes.

The relationship between three equivalences which have been obtained in the [ADeNF87] are summarized in the following table:

Sequential Nondeterministic Processes:	$\approx_{po}$	=	$\approx_M$	=	$\approx_T$
Concurrent Deterministic Processes:	$\approx_{po}$	=	$\approx_M$	implies	$\approx_T$
Concurrent Nondeterministic Processes:	$\approx_{po}$	implies	$\approx_M$	implies	$\approx_T$

<u>Remark</u>. These equivalences are most weak ones for corresponding groups of concurrent models.

Hence, if we consider sequential nondeterministic processes the particular kind of observation is unimportant. On the other hand, when we deal with general concurrent nondeterministic processes, we have different semantics, depending on the chosen observation mechanisms.

More comprehensive results comparing some equivalences induced by the semantics of the first and the second groups of concurrent models can be found in [Po86].

2. Algebra AFP_1 of finite generalized concurrent processes

2.1. Syntax

Let $\mathfrak{A} = \{a, b, c, \ldots\}$ be a finite alphabet of action symbols (the action basis of a process) and $\overline{\mathfrak{A}} = \{\bar{a}, \bar{b}, \bar{c}, \ldots\}$ be dual to alphabet of the negated symbols denoting "non-actions", i.e. the symbols which point to the fact that the correspondent actions do not occur in a process. The special symbol δ denotes a "wrong" or "empty" action (deadlock, mistake, abort, etc.).

The basic operations are: $\|$ ("concurrency"), ∇ ("exclusive or", "alternative"), / ("succession"), v ("disjunction" or "union"), $\urcorner$ ("not occur").

Viewed intuitively, the formula $A \| B$ defines a process in which the subprocesses A and B occur concurrently. The operation ∇ is a modification of the exclusive or; the formula $(A \nabla B)$ defines a process in which if the subprocess A occurs then the actions of the subprocess B do not occur, and vice versa. The operation / is the only operation which orders actions in a process; the formula A / B defines a process in which all actions of the subprocess B can occur only if the subprocess A is completed. The operation $\urcorner$ is a modified negation: $\urcorner A$ means that the process A does not occur, i.e. no action of A occurs. The formula $A \vee B$ defines a process in which either the subprocess A or the subprocess B occurs.

A formula of AFP_1 in a basis $\mathfrak{A} \cup \overline{\mathfrak{A}} \cup \delta$ is defined as follows:

1) a, $\bar{a}$, δ, where $a \in \mathfrak{A}$, $\bar{a} \in \overline{\mathfrak{A}}$, are elementary formulae;
2) if A and B are formulae, then $A \| B$, $A \nabla B$, A / B, $A \vee B$, $\urcorner A$ are formulae.

2.2 Partial orders (basic notions and definitions)

The process defined by the AFP_1 formula will be characterized by a set of partial orders in the alphabet $\mathfrak{A} \cup \overline{\mathfrak{A}} \cup \delta$.

A partially ordered set (poset) is a pair $p = (V, <)$ consisting of

(i) a vertex set V, typically modelling process actions, i.e. $V \subseteq \mathfrak{A} \cup \overline{\mathfrak{A}} \cup \delta$;

(ii) a partial order $<$ over V, with $a < b$ typically interpreted as the action a necessarily preceding the action b in process.

Let us denote by $V^+ = \{x \in V \mid x \in \mathfrak{A}\}$ - the action subset of V, and $V^- = \{x \in V \mid x \in \overline{\mathfrak{A}}\}$ - non-action subset of V, i.e. $V = V^+ \cup V^-$ or $V = \{\delta\}$.

In this paper we will consider posets, which satisfy the following conditions:

1) action v and $\bar{v}$ do not occur in poset p both, i.e. either the action v occurs in p and occurs exactly once, or non-action $\bar{v}$ occurs in p;
2) if $\delta \in V$ then $V = \{\delta\}$;
3) partial order relation < over V is transitive and irreflexive;
4) $\forall\ \bar{v} \in V^-,\ \neg\exists\ x \in V: (x < \bar{v}) \vee (\bar{v} < x)$, i.e. all non-actions are incomparable.

Thus, poset p = (V, <) is either degenerate: $p = (\{\delta\}, \emptyset)$, or consists of two parts: "real" part, containing actions of V^+, and "imaginary" one, containing non-actions of V^-. Moreover, $< \cap (V^+ \times V^+) = <$, and $< \cap (V^- \times V^-) = \emptyset$.

Now we introduce the following poset operations: ⓪ (concatenation, succession), ⓥ (alternative), ⓘ (concurrency).

Let us define auxiliary regularization operation [ ] on wrong-constructed posets:

$$[p] = \begin{cases} p, & \text{if } p \text{ is a poset, satisfying the conditions 1)-4)} \\ (\{\delta\}, \emptyset), & \text{else.} \end{cases}$$

The concatenation p_1 ⓪ p_2 of two posets is defined as: $p = (V_1, <_1)$ ⓪ ⓪ $(V_2, <_2) = [(V_1 \cup V_2, <_1 \cup <_2 \cup (V_1^+ \times V_2^+))]$, i.e. in a new poset p every action of p_1 precedes every action of p_2, or if the constructed object does not satisfy the 1)-4) conditions, then $p = (\{\delta\}, \emptyset)$ is the degenerate poset.

Example. Let $p_1 = (\{a\}, \emptyset)$ and $p_2 = (\{b\}, \emptyset)$, then $p_3 = p_1$ ⓪ p_2 = $= (\{a, b\}, <_3)$, where $a <_3 b$, but $p_4 = p_3$ ⓪ $p_1 = (\{\delta\}, \emptyset)$.

The concurrency p_1 ⓘ p_2 of two posets is defined as: $p = (V_1, <_1)$ ⓘ ⓘ $(V_2, <_2) = [(V_1 \cup V_2, (<_1 \cup <_2)^*)]$, where $(<_1 \cup <_2)^*$ is transitive closure of relation $<_1 \cup <_2$.

Example. Let $p_1 = (\{a, c\}, <_1)$, where $a <_1 c$, and $p_2 = (\{b, c\}, <_2)$, where $b <_2 c$. Then $p_3 = p_1$ ⓘ $p_2 = (\{a, b, c\}, <_3)$, where $a <_3 c$, $b <_3 c$. Let us consider additionally: $p_4 = (\{a, c\}, <_4)$, where $c <_4 a$. Then p_4 ⓘ p_1 = $= (\{\delta\}, \emptyset)$.

The alternative p_1 ⓥ p_2 of two posets is defined as follows: p = $= (V_1, <_1)$ ⓥ $(V_2, <_2) = \{[(V_1 \cup \bar{V}_2, <_1)]\} \cup \{[(V_2 \cup \bar{V}_1, <_2)]\}$, where $\bar{V}$ = $= \{\bar{a} \mid \bar{a} \in V^-\} \cup \{\bar{a} \mid a \in V^+\}$. It should be noted that p_1 ⓥ p_2 is not a partial orders, but a set of two partial orders describing possible alternative computation (process realization), namely: if p_1 is realized, then actions of p_2 are not realized, and vice versa.

Example. Let $p_1 = (\{a\}, \emptyset)$, $p_2 = (\{b\}, \emptyset)$, then p_1 ⓥ p_2 = $= \{(\{a, \bar{b}\}, \emptyset)\} \cup \{(\{\bar{a}, b\}, \emptyset)\}$.

We extend the operation introduced above for sets of partial orders in the natural way. Let $P_1 = \bigcup_{i=1}^{n} \{p_i^1\}$ and $P_2 = \bigcup_{j=1}^{k} \{p_j^2\}$ be the sets of partial orders, then $P_1 \circ P_2 = \bigcup_{i=1}^{n} (\bigcup_{j=1}^{k} \{p_i^1 \circ p_j^2\})$, where $\circ \in \{ \oslash, \textcircled{$\|$}, \textcircled{$\triangledown$} \}$.

2.3. Semantics

Generalized concurrent process is characterized by the set of partial orders, associated with all possible (alternative) process realizations. Let us denote by C(A) the set of partial orders associated with formula A.

Semantics of AFP_1 formulae is defined as follows:

1) $C(a) = (\{a\}, \emptyset)$, $C(\bar{a}) = (\{\bar{a}\}, \emptyset)$, $C(\delta) = (\{\delta\}, \emptyset)$.
2) Let $\Phi = A \parallel B$, then $C(\Phi) = C(A) \textcircled{$\|$} C(B)$.
3) If $\Phi = A / B$, then $C(\Phi) = C(A) \oslash C(B)$.
4) Let $\Phi = A \triangledown B$, then $C(\Phi) = C(A) \textcircled{$\triangledown$} C(B)$.
5) If $\Phi = A \vee B$, then $C(\Phi) = C(A) \cup C(B)$.
6) Let $\Phi = \neg A$ and $\mathfrak{A}(A)$ be a set of symbols from joined alphabet $\mathfrak{A} \cup \bar{\mathfrak{A}}$, occuring in formula A, then $C(\Phi) = (\overline{\mathfrak{A}(A)}, \emptyset)$.

$N_1 = a \parallel b$	$C(N_1) = (\{a, b\}, \emptyset)$	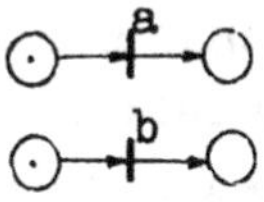
$N_2 = (a \parallel b) / c$	$C(N_2) = (\{a, b, c\}, <_2)$, where $a <_2 c$, $b <_2 c$	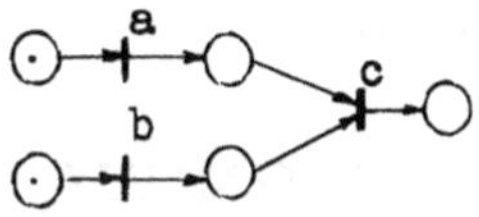
$N_3 = (a \triangledown b) / c$	$C(N_3) = \{(\{a, c, \bar{b}\}, <_3^1)$, $(\{b, c, \bar{a}\}, <_3^2)\}$, where $a <_3^1 c$, $b <_3^2 c$	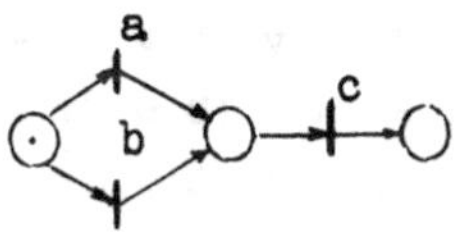
$N_4 = ((a \triangledown b) \parallel (b \triangledown c)) / d$	$C(N_4) = \{(\{a, c, d, \bar{b}\}, <_4^1)$, $(\{b, d, \bar{a}, \bar{c}\}, <_4^2)\}$, where $a <_4^1 d$, $c <_4^1 d$, $b <_4^2 d$.	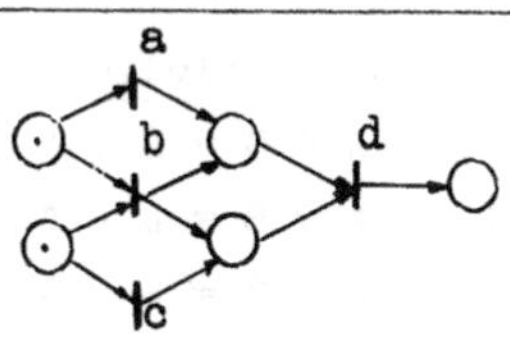

Figure 1.

On the left column of Figure 1 you can see the algebraic process specifications, on the right side, the corresponding process net representation is shown, and in the middle column, the process is characterized by the associated set of partial orders. For example, formula $N_2 = (a \parallel b) / c$ specifies a concurrent process, in which the action c occurs after concurrent execution of the actions a and b. The formula N_4 = $= ((a \triangledown b) \parallel (b \triangledown c)) / d$ specified generalized concurrent process consisting of two possible alternative realizations, one of them is defined by the poset in which the concurrent execution of the actions a and c precedes the occurence of the action d, and the action b is not realized, i.e. $\bar{b}$ holds; and the second process realization is characterized by the poset in which the action b occurs before the action d, and alternative to them actions a and c are not realized.

2.4. Axiomatization for AFP_1

Two processes specified by formulae A and B are equivalent $(A \approx_e B)$ iff $C(A) = C(B)$.

A context $\mathcal{C}[\ ]$ is an expession with zero or more "holes", to be filled by an expression. We write $\mathcal{C}[A]$ for the result of placing E in each "hole".

Two processes specified by formulae A and B are congruent $(A \approx_\omega B)$ iff $\mathcal{C}[A] \approx_e \mathcal{C}[B]$.

Now, we will propose the axiom system (denoted by Θ) corresponding to the congruence relation $\approx_\omega$ defined above.

The following axioms characterize the properties of the introduced operations:

1. Associativity

1.1. $A \parallel (B \parallel C) = (A \parallel B) \parallel C$

1.2. $A \triangledown (B \triangledown C) = (A \triangledown B) \triangledown C$

1.3. $A \vee (B \vee C) = (A \vee B) \vee C$

1.4. $A / (B / C) = (A / B) / C$

2. Commutativity

2.1. $A \parallel B = B \parallel A$

2.2. $A \triangledown B = B \triangledown A$

2.3. $A \vee B = B \vee A$

3. Distributivity

3.1. $(A \parallel B) / C = (A / C) \parallel (B / C)$

3.2. $A / (B \parallel C) = (A / B) \parallel (A / C)$

3.3. $(A \vee B) / C = (A / C) \vee (B / C)$

3.4. $A / (B \vee C) = (A / B) \vee (A / C)$,

3.5. $(A \vee B) \parallel C = (A \parallel C) \vee (B \parallel C)$,

3.6. $A \triangledown (B \parallel C) = (A \triangledown B) \parallel (A \triangledown C)$

4. Axioms for ∇ and $\neg$

4.1. $A \nabla B = (A \parallel \neg B) \vee (\neg A \parallel B)$

4.2. $\neg(A \parallel B) = \neg A \parallel \neg B$

4.3. $\neg(A \vee B) = \neg A \parallel \neg B$

4.4. $\neg(A / B) = \neg A \parallel \neg B$

4.5. $\neg a = \bar{a}$

4.6. $\neg \bar{a} = \bar{a}$

5. Structural properties

5.1. $\bar{a} / A = \bar{a} \parallel A$

5.2. $A / \bar{a} = \bar{a} \parallel A$

5.3. $A \parallel (A / B) = A / B$

5.4. $B \parallel (A / B) = A / B$

5.5. $A / B / C = (A / B) \parallel (B / C)$

5.6. $(A / B) \parallel (B / C) = (A / B) \parallel (B / C) \parallel (A / C)$

5.7. $A \parallel A = A$

5.8. $A \vee A = A$

6. Axioms for δ

6.1. $a \parallel \bar{a} = \delta$

6.2. $a / a = \delta$

6.3. $A \parallel \delta = \delta$

6.4. $\delta / A = \delta$

6.5. $A / \delta = \delta$

6.6. $\delta \vee A = A$

R e m a r k. The interpretation of $a \parallel \bar{a}$ and a / a as δ (the degenerate process) seems to be very natural. A careful reader will soon notice that to be completely precise we should actually introduce a whole family δ_a ($a \in \mathfrak{A}$) of degenerate processes and modify the axiomatization in a corresponding way. However, this is not essential and therefore we will not do that in this paper.

These axioms are easily proved to be sound, if equality is interpreted as congruence. In order to prove that the axiom set is complete we have to introduce a canonical form of AFP_1 formulae.

2.5. Canonical form of AFP_1 formulae

Let us denote by $\mathfrak{A}(A)$ the symbol set of the alphabet $\mathfrak{A}$, occuring in formula A (as a or $\bar{a}$). More exactly:

$\mathfrak{A}(a) = a$

$\mathfrak{A}(\bar{a}) = a$

$\mathfrak{A}(A \circ B) = \mathfrak{A}(A) \cup \mathfrak{A}(B)$, where $\circ \in \{/, \|, \nabla, v\}$

$\mathfrak{A}(\urcorner A) = \mathfrak{A}(A)$.

Let $\bar{\mathfrak{A}}(A)$ be dual to $\mathfrak{A}(A)$ alphabet: $\bar{\mathfrak{A}}(A) = \{\bar{a} \mid a \in \mathfrak{A}(A)\}$ and $\hat{\mathfrak{A}}(A) = \mathfrak{A}(A) \cup \bar{\mathfrak{A}}(A)$.

The formula Φ, containing only operations of concurrency and succession / over symbol of the joined alphabet $\mathfrak{A} \cup \bar{\mathfrak{A}}$, is called <u>$\|$-conjuctive term.</u>

$\|$-conjuctive term Φ is called <u>normal $\|$-conjucts</u>, if Φ has a form $\overset{n}{\underset{i=1}{\|}} A_i$ (where $\overset{n}{\underset{i=1}{\|}} A_i = A_1 \| A_2 \| \dots \| A_n$), and the <u>following requirements</u> are valid:

1) every formula A_i $(1 \leqslant i \leqslant n)$ has the following form:
   i) elementary formula a $(a \in \mathfrak{A})$ or $\bar{a}$ $(\bar{a} \in \bar{\mathfrak{A}})$, or
   ii) elementary succession a / b $(a \neq b)$;
2) for any formulae A_i and A_j $(1 \leqslant i \neq j \leqslant n)$ such, that $\mathfrak{A}(A_i) \cap \cap \mathfrak{A}(A_j) \neq \emptyset$, it should be, that A_i and A_j have a form of different elementary succession;
3) for any pair formulae $A_i = (a / b)$ and $A_j = (b / c)$ $(1 \leqslant i \neq j \leqslant n)$ there exists a term $A_k = (a / c)$, describing transitive closure of succession relation for actions a, b, c.

The formula Φ is in <u>canonical form</u> iff either $\Phi = \delta$ or $\Phi = \overset{n}{\underset{i=1}{\vee}} \Phi_i$, where Φ_i $(1 \leqslant i \leqslant n)$ is normal $\|$-conjucts, and any Φ_i and Φ_j $(1 \leqslant i \neq j \leqslant n)$ are different.

<u>Example</u>. Let $\Phi = (((a \| (a / b / c)) \nabla (d / e)) \| f$. The formula Φ has the following canonical normal form: $\Phi = ((a / b) \| (b / c) \| (a / c) \| f \| \| \bar{d} \| \bar{e}) \vee ((d / e) \| f \| \bar{a} \| \bar{b} \| \bar{c})$.

It should be noted that every normal $\|$-conjucts characterizes one of the possible alternative process realizations, and has a special form coinciding with partial order process representation.

Let $SAFP_1$ be the <u>class of structural processes</u>, specifiing by means of operations $\|$, / and ∇ over actions of the alphabet $\mathfrak{A}$.

We shall write $A =_\theta B$ to mean that the equation may be proved from 1-6 by normal equational reasoning.

<u>Theorem 1.</u>

Every formula A $(A \in SAFP_1)$ may be proved equal to a unique canonical form.

<u>Corollary 1.</u>

For any structural process formulae A and B $(A, B \in SAFP_1)$ the following statement is valid: $A \approx_\omega B \Leftrightarrow A =_\theta B$.

2.6. Deduction of partial and total properties

The formula of the introduced algebra specifies both processes and their properties. Two main classes of properties of generalized processes can be distinguished: the total and partial properties. The first properties are valid for any actual realization of process; the second ones are valid for a subset of possible realizations. The second class of properties emerges because of including alternative actions in generalized processes. Intuitively, the total properties correspond to the notion of validity of a model, the partial properties correspond to the notion of satisfiability.

Let us consider the process defined by the formula $(a \triangledown b) \parallel (c \triangledown d)$ and interpreted by the net form as shown in Figure 2.

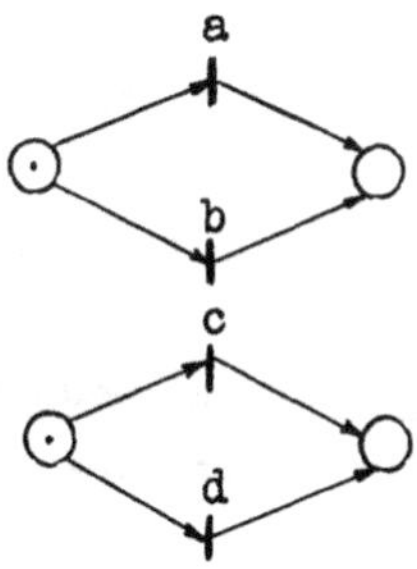

Figure 2.

The formula $(a \triangledown b)$ describes the total property of the process, namely the fact that its actions a and b are always alternative. The property described by the formula $(a \parallel c)$ is partial, as there exists realization of the process in which both a and c concurrently occur and there exists realization in which neither a nor c occurs.

Let us introduce some additional notions and definitions. We denote by $p' = p\upharpoonright_{V'}$, the projection of order p on the alphabet V', defined as follows:

$$p' = p\upharpoonright_{V'} = (V' \cap V, ((V' \cap V) \times (V' \cap V)) \cap <).$$

The projection $\upharpoonright$ is extended for sets of partial orders in the natural way: $(\{p_1\} \cup \{p_2\})\upharpoonright_V = \{p_1\upharpoonright_V\} \cup \{p_2\upharpoonright_V\}$.

A property Φ' is satisfiable (partial) for a process Φ (denotation: $\Phi \Vdash \Phi'$) iff

1) $C(\Phi) \neq (\{\delta\}, \emptyset)$, $C(\Phi') \neq (\{\delta\}, \emptyset)$ and $C(\Phi)\upharpoonright_{\hat{\alpha}(\Phi')} \supseteq C(\Phi')$, or
2) $C(\Phi) = (\{\delta\}, \emptyset)$.

Example. $(a \triangledown b) \parallel ((b \triangledown c) / d) \Vdash a \parallel c$.

In the following inference rules for the deduction of partial properties of process we suppose that for formulae A and B the condition $\alpha(A) \cap \alpha(B) = \emptyset$ is valid:

I. $A \circ B \Vdash A$ and $A \circ B \Vdash B$, where $\circ \in \{\parallel, /, \nabla\}$.

II. $A \circ B \Vdash A' \circ B'$, where $A \Vdash A'$ and $B \Vdash B'$, and $\circ \in \{\parallel, /, \nabla\}$.

Inference rules I, II in the case, when formula on the their left side has a form of normal -conjuct are valid without additional restrictions.

III. Let Φ be in a disjunctive normal form: $\Phi = \bigvee_{i=1}^{n} \Phi_i$

Then $\Phi = \bigvee_{i=1}^{n} \Phi_i \Vdash \bigvee_{i=1}^{k} \Phi_i'$, where $\forall i : 1 \leq i \leq k \leq n$: $\Phi_i \Vdash \Phi_i'$.

A formula Φ' is partially deduced from Φ iff there exists finite sequence: $\Phi \Vdash \Phi_1 \Vdash \Phi_2 \Vdash \ldots \Vdash \Phi'$ in which (for any i: $1 \leq i \leq n$) $\Phi_i \Vdash \Phi_{i+1}$ is an application of partial inference rules I-III or $\Phi_i =_\theta \Phi_{i+1}$

Theorem 2.

For any structural process formula $\Phi \in SAFP_1$ the following statement is valid: $\Phi \models\!\!\models \Phi' \iff \Phi \Vdash \Phi'$.

A property Φ' is valid (total) for a process Φ (denotation: $\Phi \models \Phi'$) iff

1) $C(\Phi) \neq (\{\delta\}, \emptyset)$, $C(\Phi') \neq (\{\delta\}, \emptyset)$ and $C(\Phi) \upharpoonright_{\hat{\mathfrak{A}}(\Phi')} = C(\Phi')$, or

2) $C(\Phi) = (\{\delta\}, \emptyset)$.

In the following inference rules for the deduction of total properties of process we suppose that for formulae A and B the condition $\mathfrak{A}(A) \cap \mathfrak{A}(B) = \emptyset$ is valid:

I. $A \circ B \vdash A$, $A \circ B \vdash B$, where $\circ \in \{\parallel, /\}$.

II. $A \circ B \vdash A' \circ B'$, where $A \vdash A'$, $B \vdash B'$ and $\circ \in \{\parallel, /, \nabla\}$.

Inference rules I, II in case, when formula on their left side has a form of normal $\parallel$-conjuct are valid without additional restrictions.

III. Let Φ be in a canonical form, i.e. $\Phi = \bigvee_{i=1}^{n} \Phi_i$.

If $\forall i : 1 \leq i \leq n$: $\Phi_i \vdash A_i$, then $\Phi \vdash \bigvee_{i=1}^{n} A_i$.

A formula Φ' is totally deduced from Φ iff there exists finite sequence: $\Phi \vdash \Phi_1 \vdash \Phi_2 \vdash \ldots \vdash \Phi'$ in which $\Phi_i \vdash \Phi_{i+1}$ $(1 \leq i \leq n)$ is an application of total inference rules I-III or $\Phi_i =_\theta \Phi_{i+1}$.

Theorem 3.

For any structural process formula $\Phi \in SAFP_1$ the following statement is valid: $\Phi \models \Phi' \iff \Phi \vdash \Phi'$.

CONCLUDING REMARKS

In this paper, we have proposed an algebra for specifying concurrent generalized processes and their properties. The algebra AFP_1 (in its specification part) seems to be close to CSP [Hoa85]. Both of the languages of AFP_1 and CSP are equipped with operation for sequential composition: the AFP_1 formula A / B defines sequential composition of two subprocesses A and B, the CSP formula a -> P represents sequential composition of the action a and the process P. Hoare uses two operators for choice: external choice $\square$ (which depends on the environment) and internal choice $\sqcap$ (the environment has no influence on choice in this case). We also have two operators for choice: alternative operation ∇ (it is slightly similar to $\square$) and disjunction $\vee$ (it corresponds to $\sqcap$). The concurrency operator $\|_A$ for CSP [Ol87] is similar to concurrency operator $\|$ for AFP_1, iff $A = \mathfrak{A}(B) \cap \mathfrak{A}(C)$ in a formula $B \| C$. In spite of this similarity, CSP and AFP_1 have different semantics for concurrency. The concurrent composition of two processes is simulated in CSP as interleaving. In our model, the concurrency is a basic relation. Both of the languages of CSP and AFP_1 are equipped with a constant for deadlock (called STOP in CSP and δ in AFP_1). However, they also have different semantics. If some semantical contradition is revealed in the AFP_1 formula, then this formula describes the degenerate (deadlock) process, i.e. the deadlock can not "occur" in the process after execution of some process actions. Thus, a process specified by AFP_1 formula is either δ (degenerate process),or it consists of completely "successful" realizations (executions).

Another definition of the process behaviour is possible by the same process specification. For example, the behaviour of the process $\Phi = (A \| B)$ may be defined as a maximal consistent prefix of behaviours of A and B, which does not contain any deadlocks. A new algebra, modified in this way, gives the possibility to specify and study the behaviour of more general systems and processes they generate.

Acknowledgements: I would like to thank especially V.E.Kotov for his help and work in this subject. I am also indebted to G.E.Mintz for his useful discussion about further improvement and development of AFP_1 (in Kazan). I am grateful to J.Gruska for his friendly support and attention to this work. I thank also T.Batireva for typing and helping in technical preparation of the paper.

REFERENCES

LNCS = Lecture Notes in Computer Science, Springer-Verlag.

[AB84] Austry D., Boudol G. Algebre de Processus et Synchronization. Theoret. Comput. Sci. Vol. 30, No 1, North Holland, Amsterdam,1984.

[ADeNF87] Aceto L., De Nicola R., Fantechi A. Testing Equivalences for Event Structures. LNCS, Vol. 280, p. 1-20, 1987.

[BBK85] Baeten J., Bergstra J., Klop J. An operational semantics for process algebra. Report CS-R8522 Centrum voor Wiskunde en Informatica, 1985.

[BHR84] Brookes S.D., Hoare C.A.R., Roscoe A.D. A Theory of Communicating Sequential Processes. Journal of ACM, Vol. 31, No 3, pp. 560-599, 1984.

[BK84] Bergstra J., Klop G. Process Algebra for Synchronous Communication. - Information and Control, Vol. 60, pp. 109-137, North Holland, Amsterdam, 1984.

[BouCa87] Boudol G., Castellani I. On the semantics of Concurrency: Partial Orders and Transition System. LNCS, Vol. 249, p. 123-137, 1987.

[CamH74] Campbell R.H., Haberman A.N. The Specification of Process Synchronization by Path Experissions. LNCS, Vol. 16, p. 89-102, 1974.

[ChKot88] Cherkasova L., Kotov V. Descriptive and Analytical process algebras. Will appear in proceedings of 9-th European workshop on Theory and Applications of Petri Nets.

[DDeNM87] Degano P., De Nicola R., Montanari U. CCS is an (Augmented) Contact-Free C/E Systems. LNCS, Vol. 280, p. 144-165, 1987.

[GoM84] Goltz U., Mycroft A. On the relationship of CCS and Petri Nets. LNCS, Vol. 172, p. 196-208, 1984.

[GoRe83] Goltz U., Mycroft A. Processes of Place-Transitions Nets. LNCS, Vol. 154, p. 264-177, 1983.

[Hoa82] Hoare C.A.R A model for Communicating Sequential Processes. Technical Monograph Prg-22, Computing Laboratory, University of Oxford, 1982.

[Hoa85] Hoare C.A.R. Communicating Seqiential Processes. Prentice Hall, 1985.

[Kot78] Kotov V.E. An algebra for parallelism based on Petri Nets. LNCS, Vol. 64, p. 39-55, 1978.

[KotCh84] Kotov V.E., Cherkasova L.A. On structural properties of generalized processes. LNCS, Vol. 188, p. 288-306, 1984.

[LTS79] Lauer P.E., Torrigiani P.R., Shields M.W. COSY - A System Specification Language Based on Paths and Processes. Acta Informatica, vol. 12, p. 109-158, 1979.

[Mil80] Milner R. Calculus of Communicating Systems. LNCS, Vol. 92, 1980.

[Mil83] Milner R. Calculi for Synchrony and Asynchrony Theoret. Comput. Sci. Vol. 25, North Holland, p. 267-310, 1983.

[NPW81] Nielsen M., Plotkin G., Winskel G. Petri Nets, Event Structures and Domains. Theoret. Comp. Sci. 13, p. 85-108, 1981.

[Ol87] Olderog E.R. TCSP: Theory of Communicating Sequential Processes. LNCS, Vol. 255, p. 441-465, 1987.

[Pet77] Petri C.A. Non-sequential Processes, GMD-ISF, Rep. 77-05, 1977.

[Po86] Pomello L. Some equivalenve notions for concurrent systems. An overview. LNCS, Vol. 222, p. 381-400, 1986.

[Pr87] Pratt V.R. Modelling Concurrency with Partial Orders. International Journal of Parallel Programming. Vol. 15, No 1, p. 33-71, 1987.

[Rei85] Reizig W. Petri Nets: An Introduction, Springer-Verlag, 1985.

[Sh79] Shields M.W. Adequate Path Expressions. LNCS, Vol. 70, p. 249-265, 1979.

String Matching with Constraints*.

Maxime Crochemore
Université de Paris-Nord
avenue J-B Clément
F - 93430 VILLETANEUSE

1. Introduction

Pattern recognition in a constantly growing field of research. Identification of pattern in images, for instance, is a first step towards their interpretation. More generally, all formal systems handling strings of symbols involve parsing phases to recognize certain patterns. Regular expressions is one of the techniques to specify simple patterns [26]. It leads to practicable algorithms available under most operating systems or edition tools especially with Unix.

String-matching is a particular case of pattern recognition. It consists in locating a word inside another word, called the text. Solutions to this problem can be divided into two families. In the first one the text is considered as fixed while the word is variable. This situation occurs when the text is a dictionary, for example. The basic solution of that sort is due to Weiner who introduced the notion of position trees [29]. It is a kind of index which as been improved in different ways (see [21], [5], [10]).

For the second family of solutions to string-matching, it is the word that is fixed. The two most famous and efficient string-matching algorithms of this family have been designed by Knuth, Morris & Pratt [18] and Boyer & Moore [7]. They have been subject to several studies, improvements or extensions (see [1], [11], [13-16], [22], [23], [25], [28]). A variation to the initial problem happens when approximate patterns are considered (see [20], [27]). String-matching is close to detection of repetitions in strings (see [3], [10], [17], [25]). In fact, the study of regularities in strings is a part of the analysis of string-matching algorithms.

In this paper, two string-matching algorithms belonging to the second family are presented. They respectively obey to time and space constraints. Both algorithms start by a first phase during which the word alone is processed. Then, the search is done during a second phase which essentially supports the contraints.

---

* This work has been supported by PRC Math.-Info.

One of the characteristics of the algorithm of [18] is that its second phase is sequential. This means that there is no need to memorize more than one character of the text at a time. After a character is read, if a new occurrence of the word has appeared, the algorithm outputs its position. However, the delay between the reading of two consecutive characters of the text depends on the length of the word. The first algorithm, presented in section 2 to 4, processes the text in real-time. The delay only depends on the size of the alphabet. Our algorithm heavily relies on properties of minimal automata recognizing the suffixes of a word. Previous solutions to real-time string-matching have been given by Galil [14] and Slisenko [25]. Our solution is close to Slisenko's one.

String-matching algorithms commonly achieve a linear time complexity by memorizing informations about the word which occupy linear space. So, during the preprocessing phase, they need dynamic memory space to be used at search phase. We present, in section 6, an algorithm which requires only constant additional memory space during all its phases [11]. It makes use of a deep theorem on words, recalled in section 5, known as the critical factorization theorem (see [19]). This algorithm shares the same constraints as the one in [15] but it is faster and simpler.

This discussion raises the question of whether there exists an efficient algorithm satisfying both time and space constraints simultaneously.

2. Failure functions

We consider a finite alphabet A. Let A^* be the set of words on the alphabet A. The empty word is denoted by ε. We denote by $|x|$ the length of the word x and thus $|\varepsilon| = 0$. Concatenation of two words u and v of A^* is noted uv and if $x = uv$ the pair (u, v) is said a **factorization** of x. The word u is called a **prefix** of x and v is called a **suffix** of x. A prefix of v is called a **factor** of x, and its position in x is $|u|$.

An automaton $\mathcal{A}$ is a sequence (Q, A, i, T, δ) where Q is the finite set of states, i the initial state, T the set of terminal states, and δ is the transition function. All the automata we consider here are deterministic. For $q \in Q$ and $a \in A$, $\delta(q, a)$ is the state reached from q by transition of letter a. The transition function extends to words and $\delta(q, x)$ denotes, if it exists, the state reached after reading the word x in the automaton from the state q. The automaton $\mathcal{A}$ recognizes the language $\{x \in A^* \,/\, \delta(q, x) \in T\}$.

A first solution to find occurrences of a word x inside a text t is to build a deterministic automaton for the language A^*x, such as $\mathcal{A}(x)$, the minimal automaton that recognizes A^*x. Then, when reading the text t in this automaton, the right end of an occurrence of x is found in t each time a terminal state is encountered. This method assumes that the transition function of the automaton $\mathcal{A}(x)$ is defined on every pair (state, letter). So, the size of $\mathcal{A}(x)$ is proportional to $|A|$, the number of letters in the alphabet. This solution is thus unrealizable for practical purposes. Failure function are used to cope with this problem.

Let $\mathcal{A} = (Q, A, i, T, \delta)$ be an automaton. Let ζ be a function from QxA to Q (so, ζ is a transition function), and let s be a funtion from Q into itself. We say that the pair (ζ, s) **represents** the transition δ if both conditions hold:

$$\delta \supseteq \zeta \quad \text{and} \quad \delta(q, a) = \delta(s(q), a)$$

whenever $\zeta(q, a)$ is not defined while $\delta(q, a)$ and $s(q)$ are. In this situation, the state $s(q)$ is a stand-in of state q. Function s is a default state function also called a **failure function.**

The first best example of failure function is given by the border of a word. A **border** of a nonempty word u is a word w which is both a proper prefix and suffix of u. The empty word is a border of any nonempty word. We designate by *border*(u) the longest border of u and call it "the" border of u. States of $\mathcal{A}(x)$ may be identified with prefixes of x. For u prefix of x and $a \in A$, let ζ be defined by

$$\zeta(u, a) = ua \quad \text{if } ua \text{ is a prefix of } x,$$

$$\zeta(\varepsilon, a) = \varepsilon \quad \text{if } a \text{ is not the first letter of } x.$$

Then the pair (ζ, *border*) represents the transition function δ of $\mathcal{A}(x)$, and may be implemented in size O(|x|). Morris and Pratt's string matching algorithm is based on that property and provides a linear algorithm to compute {*border*(u) / u prefix of x }.

Knuth, Morris and Pratt's string matching algorithm [18] works with another failure function f defined as follows. If u is a nonempty prefix of x,

$$f(u) = \text{longest border } w \text{ of } u \text{ such that, for all } a \in A,$$

$$wa \text{ and } ua \text{ are not both prefix of } x.$$

First note that $f(x)$ is *border*(x). Also note that $f(u)$ may be undefined on some prefix u of x. In that case it is always possible to define $f(u)$ as a new state on which all transitions go to the initial state of $\mathcal{A}(x)$. The function f is a failure function when associated to the transition ζ, if furthermore the following is added to the definition of ζ:

$$\zeta(u, a) = i$$

whenever ua is not a prefix of x and $f(u)$ is undefined. Then, (ζ, f) represents the transition δ of automaton $\mathcal{A}(x)$, as well as the pair (ζ, *border*) does.

Computing a transition with a representation (ζ, s) of the transition function δ of $\mathcal{A}(x)$ may be done by the schema in figure 1. This algorithm is subject to several variations. The failure functions usually considered insure that the algorithm stops. This technique save space but increases the time to compute a transition. Assuming the RAM model, computing a transition with (ζ, *border*) may take O(|x|). It is O(log(|x|)) in the worst case with the representation (ζ, f); the worst case is reached by prefixes of length |y|-2 of Fibonacci words y, inductively defined on the alphabet {a, b} by:

$$y_0 = \text{b}, \; y_1 = \text{a}, \; \text{and } y_{n+1} = y_n \, y_{n-1}, \text{ for } n>1$$

```
function TRANSITION (p, a);
        if (ζ (u, a) is defined) then
                return(ζ (u, a))
        else if (s(u) is defined) then
                return( TRANSITION(s(u), a)))
        else
                return(i)
end function.
```

figure 1. Computing a transition with a representation (ζ , s).

3. Suffix automata

The actual important part of the transition ζ considered in the preceding section for a representation of the transition δ of automaton $\mathcal{A}(x)$, defines the straightforward minimal automaton recognizing the prefixes of word x, providing all states of $\mathcal{A}(x)$ are terminal states. In order to improve the delay in the suggested above string-matching algorithm, another automaton will be used, say, the minimal automaton recognizing the suffixes of x.

Let $S(x)$ be the set of suffixes of x, and $F(x)$ be its set of factors:

$$S(x) = \{u \in A^*/ \exists y \in A^* \; x = yu\}$$

$$F(x) = \{u \in A^*/ \exists y ,z \in A^* \; x = yuz\}$$

We denote by $\mathcal{S}(x)$ the minimal (deterministic) automaton whose language is $S(x)$, and we call it the **suffix automaton** of x. Let $\mathcal{S}(x)$ be (Q, A, i, T, σ). The automaton is minimal among all deterministic automata recognizing $S(x)$ which implies that it does not have any sink state and the transition σ need not be defined on the whole set QxA. Its domain is denoted by $Dom(\sigma)$. Figure 2 gives the suffix automaton of *aabbabb*.

The main point about suffix automata, first noted by Blumer & al. is that their size is linear in the length of the given word. It has no more than $2|x|$ states and $3|x|$ transitions. The following proposition gives precise bounds on the number of states and transitions of the suffix automaton $\mathcal{S}(x)$ (see [10]).

Proposition 1. Let $x \in A^*$.

The number of states of $\mathcal{S}(x)$ satisfies $|x| + 1 \leq |Q| \leq 2|x| - 1$.

The number of transitions of $\mathcal{S}(x)$ satisfies $|x| \leq |Dom(\sigma)| \leq 3|x| - 4$.

Furthermore, for $|x| > 2$, $|Q| = 2|x| - 1$ iff $x \in ab^*$ and a, b are distinct letters

and, for $|x| > 3$, $|Dom(\sigma)| = 3|x| - 4$ iff $x \in ab^*c$ and a, b, c are distinct letters

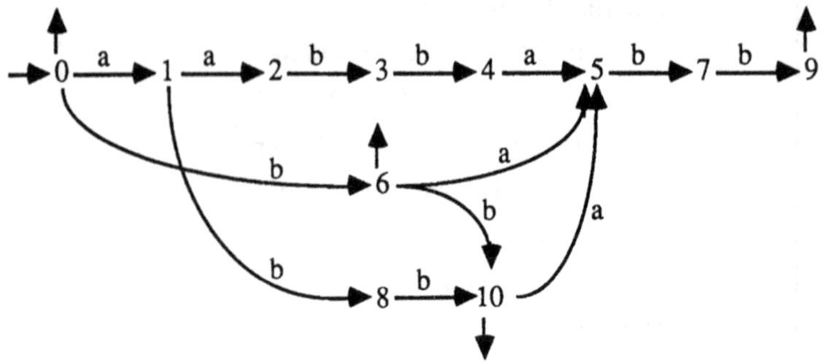

figure 2. Suffix automaton of *aabbabb*.

The construction of the suffix automaton $\mathcal{S}(x)$ can be done in time O(|x|) [5] [10]. It makes use of a failure function s defined on states of $\mathcal{S}(x)$. The set of states of $\mathcal{S}(x)$ identifies with the quotient sets

$$u^{-1}S(x) = \{w \in A^* \,/\, uw \in S(x)\}$$

for u running through factors of x. One may observe that two sets $u^{-1}S(x)$ and $v^{-1}S(x)$ are either disjoint or comparable. This allows to set $s(p)$ to the smallest quotient set strictly containing p (for p state of $\mathcal{S}(x)$). The function s is not defined at $S(x)$, the initial state of $\mathcal{S}(x)$. Let $\sigma(i, a)=i$ whenever it is not already defined. Then, the pair (σ, s) represents the complete transition function of an automaton $\mathcal{B}(x)$. Automata $\mathcal{A}(x)$ and $\mathcal{B}(x)$ are not equal in general, even when the latter has exactly $|x|+1$ states.

Construction of suffix automata is given in figure 3. The algorithm simultaneously builds the transition and the failure functions associated with $\mathcal{S}(x)$. It works sequentially on the input word and uses the function *length* defined on states of $\mathcal{S}(x)$ by

$$length(p) = \max\{\ |u| \in A^* \,/\, \sigma(i, u) = p\}.$$

The algorithm clearly shows that the number of states of the suffix automaton $\mathcal{S}(x)$ is less than twice the length of x, since at most two states are created at each pass in the main "while" loop. Automaton $\mathcal{S}(x)$ satisfies a less obvious property that is the key point to the real-time string-matching algorithm of the next section. It must be first observed that if two words u and v lead to the same state $\sigma(i, u)=\sigma(i, v)$ of $\mathcal{S}(x)$ one is a suffix of the other.

Proposition 2. Let u be a factor of x. Let w be the word defined as the longest suffix of u such that $\sigma(i, u) \neq \sigma(i, w)$. Let q be the state $\sigma(i, u)$ of $\mathcal{S}(x)$. Then

$$\sigma(i, w) = s(q) \text{ and } |w| = length(s(q)).$$

It can be shown that among all automata that recognize the factors of x, the suffix automata is the smallest automaton which satisfies the above proposition. Minimal factor automata, for instance, do not support in general the same property.

```
procedure suffix automaton ( x );
    create state initial;   length(initial) <-- 0;   last <-- initial;
    while (not end of x ) do
    {       a <-- next letter of x;
            p <-- last;   create state q;
            while (p ≠ initial  and  σ(p, a) undefined) do
            {       σ(p, a) <-- q;   p <-- s(p); }
            if (σ(p, a) undefined) then
            {       σ(initial, a) <-- q;   s(q) <-- initial; }
            else if ( length(p) + 1 = length(σ(p, a))) then
            {       s(q) <-- σ(p, a); }
            else
            {       create copy r  of σ(p, a) with same transitions;
                    length(r) <-- length(p) + 1;
                    s(σ(p, a)) <-- r;    s(q) <-- r;
                    σ(p, a) <-- r; }
            length(q) <-- length(last)+1;   last <-- q;
    }
end procedure
```

figure 3. Construction of transition and failure function of suffix automata.

Terminal states of suffix automata cannot be marked during their sequential construction. A final phase is necessary and is shown in figure 4.

```
function terminal states (𝒜 );
    Terminals <-- {last};
    q <-- last;
    while ( q ≠ initial ) do
    {       q <-- s(q);   Terminals <-- Terminals ∪ {q}; }
    return (Terminals);
end function
```

figure 4. Computation of terminal states of suffix automata.

4. Realtime algorithm

Suffix automata can be turned into transducers which sequentially output, for each factor of x, the position of its first occurrence in x [10]. The suffix transducer of x therefore behaves as an index which contains all the factors of the text x. We give another solution to string-matching which is to be applied when it is the pattern that must be preprocessed, that is, in the same situation as Knuth, Morris and Pratt's algorithm.

Let t be the text to be searched for the word x. We define the sequence $\{l_k / 0 \leq k \leq |t|\}$ by

$$l_k = \max\{ |w| / w \in F(x) \text{ and } w \in S(y) \text{ with } y \text{ prefix of length } k \text{ of } t \}.$$

Thus, the word x occurs in the text t at each position k-$|x|$ where l_k equals $|x|$, the length of x. The base of our string-matching algorithm is a sequential computation of the lengths l_k.

The sequential computation of the sequence of l_k's is possible with the representation (σ, s) introduced in the previous section. But, to achieve real-time, another representation (σ, r) has to be used. The optimisation introduced by the failure function r in relation to s parallels that of f in relation to *border* (section 2). For p state of $\mathcal{S}(x)$, let $Context(p)$ be $\{ a \in A / \sigma(p, a)$ is defined $\}$. Inside x, the set $Context(p)$ is the right context of length 1 of those words that reach state p. Then, for p state of $\mathcal{S}(x)$,

$$r(p) = s^j(p), \text{ for the smallest integer } j>0 \text{ such that}$$
$$Context(s^j(p)) \neq Context(p).$$

Function r is never defined at the initial state i of $\mathcal{S}(x)$. It may also be undefined at some other state. In both cases r could take, as value, a new state of $\mathcal{S}(x)$ on which all transitions by σ go to the initial state. Figure 5 gives tree-like pictures of failure functions s and r respectively, for the automaton $\mathcal{S}(aabbabb)$. One may note that r is undefined on states 1 and 6.

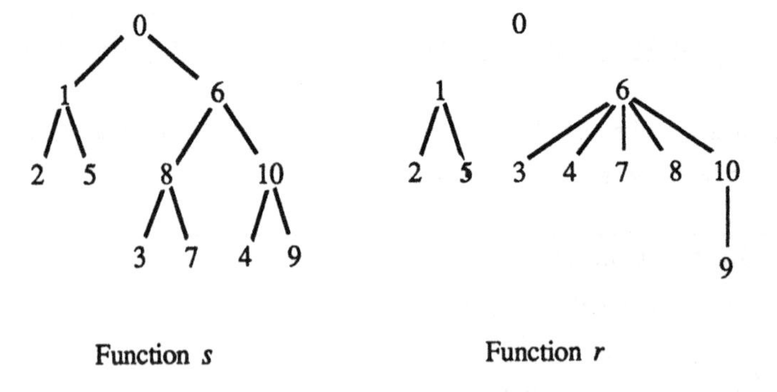

figure 5. Failure functions for *aabbabb*.

Figure 6 gives the string-matching algorithm. It reproduces, in a non-recursive version, the schema shown in figure 1. The successive values of variable l are those of the sequence $\{l_k\}$. Its computation relies on the property of function *length* given in proposition 2. Another consequence of proposition 2 is that *Context* increases in size when going from state p to its stand-in $s(p)$. And then, *Context* strictly grows going from p to $r(p)$ when it is defined. Therefore, the maximal length of the sequence $(r^j(p) \mid j \geq 0)$ is $|A|$, which shows that the internal "while" loop in procedure "match" takes a time $O(|A|)$ in the worst case. This means that the delay between two consecutive readings of letters of the text t is bounded by a constant. It is independent of the length of the word x.

Proposition 3. Procedure "match" finds all occurrences of a word x inside a text t in real-time and $O(|x|)$ space.

The preprocessing of x takes $O(|x|)$ time and $O(|x|)$ space. The total time complexity is linear in the sum of the lengths of the word x and the text t, $O(|x|+|t|)$. The algorithm needs $O(|x|)$ memory space.

```
procedure match ( x, t );
        position <-- 0;   l <-- 0;   q <-- initial;
        while (not end of text t ) do
        {       a <-- next letter of t;   position <-- position + 1;
                if ( σ (q, a) defined ) then
                {       l <-- l + 1;   q <-- σ (q, a); }
                else
                {       while ( q ≠ initial  and  σ (q, a) undefined ) do
                                q <-- r(q);
                        if (σ (q, a) undefined ) then
                        {       l <-- 0;   q <-- initial; }
                        else
                        {       l <-- length(q) + 1;   q <-- σ (q, a); }
                }
                if ( l = |x| ) then output(x occurs at position - |x|);
        }
end procedure
```

figure 6. Real-time string-matching algorithm

A distance between words is considered in [9]. It is called the **factor distance** and defined as

$$d(u, v) = |u| + |v| - 2.f(u, v)$$

where $f(u, v)$ is the maximal length of a common factor of the words u and v. A straightforward adaptation of the real-time algorithm provides a linear algorithm to compute the factor distance.

5. Critical factorization.

The second algorithm presented in this paper relies on a deep theorem on words, known as the critical factorization theorem.

Let x be a nonempty word. The ith letter of x is noted $x[i]$. We say that an integer p is a **period** of x if

$$x[i] = x[i+p]$$

whenever both sides are defined. In other terms, p is a period of x if two letters at distance p always coincide. We designate by $p(x)$ the smallest period of x and call it "the" period of x. One may verify that $p(x)$ equals $|x|-|border(x)|$.

Given a factorization (u,v) of x, the **repetition** at (u,v) is the minimal length of a nonempty word w such that

(i) w is a suffix of u or conversely u is a suffix of w, and

(ii) w is a prefix of v or conversely v is a prefix of w.

It is denoted by $r(u,v)$. One has always the inequalities $1 \leq r(u,v) \leq |x|$. More accurately, one may verify that

$$r(u,v) \leq p(x).$$

A factorization (u,v) of x such that $r(u,v) = p(x)$ is called a **critical factorization** of x. For instance, the word

$$x = abaabaa$$

has period 3. It has three critical factorizations, namely

(ab, aabaa), (abaa, baa), (abaab, aa).

The following result is due to Cesari, Vincent and Duval (see [19] for precise references).

Theorem (Critical Factorization Theorem). Each nonempty word has at least one critical factorization.

There exist several available proofs of this result. All of them lead to a more precise result asserting the existence of a critical factorization with a cutpoint in each factor of length equal to the period of x.

A weak version of the theorem occurs if one makes the additional assumption that the inequality

$$3\,p(x) \leq |x|$$

holds. Indeed, in this case, one may write

$$x = ywwz$$

where $|w| = p(x)$ and w is chosen minimal among its cyclic shifts. This means, by definition, that w is a Lyndon word (see [19]). One can prove that a Lyndon word is unbordered. Consequently the factorization

$$(yw,\ wz)$$

is critical. This version is the argument used in [15] to build a string-matching algorithm using restricted memory space.

The existence of a critical factorization may be proved by considering alphabetical orderings. Each order $\leq$ on the alphabet A extends to an **alphabetical ordering** (also noted $\leq$) on the set A^*. It is defined as usual by $x \leq y$ if either x is a prefix of y or

$$x = fag,\ \ y = fbh$$

with a,b two letters such that $a < b$.

Let $\leq$ be an alphabetical ordering on A^*. We denote by $\lesssim$ the alphabetical ordering obtained by reversing the order $\leq$ on A.

Theorem 4. Let x be a word on A. Let v (resp. v') be the maximal suffix of x according to the ordering $\leq$ (resp. $\lesssim$). Let $x = uv = u'v'$. Then, if $|u| \geq |u'|$, (u,v) is a critical factorization of x. Otherwise (u', v') is a critical factorization of x.

The critical factorization (u, v) the theorem provides is such that the length of u is less than the period of x. As an example, the theorem gives the factorization $(ab, aabaa)$ for the word $x = abaabaa$.

A consequence of theorem 4 is that the computation of a critical factorization relies on the localization of maximal suffixes. Several algorithms exist to solve this problem (see [6], [12], [24]). One is given in figure 6 as a function which returns the position of the maximal suffix of its input. It uses only constant extra memory space (five integers if $|x|$ is included) and its time linearity can be proved by showing that the sum $i+j+k$ strictly increases at each step of the "while" loop, from 2 up to $2|x|$ at most. The maximal number of letter comparisons is thus $2|x|$.

```
function maximal suffix (x);
        i <-- 0;  j <-- 1;  k <-- 1;  p <-- 1;
        while (j + k ≤ |x|) do
        {       a <-- x[i + k];  b <-- x[j + k];
                if ( a < b ) then
                {       i <-- j;  j <-- j + 1;  k <-- 1;  p <-- 1; }
                if ( a = b ) then
                {       if ( k ≠ p ) then { k <-- k + 1; }
                        else { j <-- j + p;  k <-- 1; }}
                if ( a > b ) then
                {       j <-- j + k;  k <-- 1;  p <-- j - i; }
        }
        return ( i );
end function
```

figure 7. Localization of a maximal suffix.

6. Constant-space algorithm

The algorithm presented in this section competes with those of [18] and [7]. It shares their efficiency in time, but requires only constant extra space while the others need linear space.

To find out the occurrences of a word x inside a text t, both algorithms of [18] and [7] search the text t from left to right. But the former scans the word x from left to right while the latter scans it in the reverse direction. The main feature of our algorithm is that it starts to scan the word x at a cutpoint of a critical factorization (u, v). It is conceptually divided into two phases. During the first phase, part v is first scanned from left to right. Then, when an occurrence of v is found in t, the second phase begins. The algorithm checks whether u occurs before the occurrence of v by scanning u from right to left. As far as we know, the algorithm in [15] was the first to proceed that way. It uses a factorization (u, v) of x which roughly satisfies: at most one prefix of$v$ is a cube.

The algorithm is described in figure 8. It assumes that (u, v) is a critical factorization of x such that $|u|$ is less than $p(x)$, the period of x. Such a factorization can be deduced from theorem 4 of section 5. We now explain the role of the variable l. After a mismatch is found or an occurrence of x is discovered, the word x is shifted to the right. When the shift is compatible with the period of x a prefix of x still matches the text t. The variable l memorizes the length of that prefix.

The correctness of procedure "match" in figure 8 relies on several properties of critical factorizations that are summarized below.

Proposition 5. Let (u, v) be a critical factorization of a word x of A^*.
(a) If yu is a prefix of x, $p(x)$ divides $|y|$.
(b) If w and yw are prefixes of x and $p(x) \leq |w|$, $p(x)$ divides $|y|$.
(c) If w is a prefix of v, z is a suffix of w and wz is a suffix of uw (in this situation w overlaps the cutpoint of the factorization), $p(x)$ divides $|z|$.

The time complexity of algorithm in figure 8 is linear in the length of the text. One can prove that comparisons done during the first phase strictly increase the value of $position+i$ which varies from $|u|+1$ to $|t|$ in the worst case. At the second phase, word x is shifted $p(x)$ places to the right. Since, by assumption, the length of u is less than $p(x)$, comparisons done during next second phases are done on different letters of t. Then at most $|t|$ comparisons are done for each phase.

Proposition 6. The maximum number of letter comparisons during a run of procedure "match" on inputs x and t is $2|t|$.

```
procedure match ( x, t );
    position <-- 0;   l <-- 0;
    while ( position + |x| ≤ |t| ) do
    {     i <-- max( |u|, l) + 1;
          while ( i ≤ |x| and x[i] = t[position + i] ) do
                i <-- i + 1;
          if ( i ≤ |x| ) then
          {     position <-- position + max(i-|u|, l-p(x)+1);
                l <-- 0; }
          else
          {     j <-- |u|;
                while ( j > s and x[j] = t[position +j] ) do
                      j <-- j - 1;
                if ( j = l ) then output(x occurs at position);
                position <-- position + p(x);
                l <-- |x| - p(x); }
    }
end procedure
```

figure 8. Constant-space string-matching algorithm.

The computation of the period $p(x)$ can be done in linear time by any of the classical methods, such as algorithm of [18]. But, those solutions need $O(|x|)$ memory space. In order to keep the extra memory space bounded, we propose another solution.

The full algorithm distinguishes two cases whether the period is small or not. As a consequence of property (a) of proposition 5, figure 9 shows a function which computes $p(x)$ or a lower bound of it. Now, if that function produces the exact period $p(x)$, the procedure "match" of figure 8 is applied. In the other situation one may observe that $p(x)$ is greater than half the length of x. A modified procedure "match" is applied in which variable l is eliminated and $|x|/2$ shifts are substituted to the $p(x)$ shifts of the original procedure. The assertion of proposition 6 remains true.

The entire string-matching algorithm, including the preprocessing of the x, is linear in the sum of the lengths of the word x and the text t. All steps of the process only require bounded extra space.

```
function small period (x);
        let (u, v) be a critical factorization of x computed with the help
        of function "maximal suffix";
        period p(v) is the final value of p in function "maximal suffix";
        if (|u|≤|x|/2 and u suffix of v[1]...v[p(v)]) then
                return (the period of x is p(v))
        else
                return (the period of x is greater than max(|u|,|v|))
end function
```

figure 9. Constant-space computation of small periods.

The above string-matching algorithm is linear in time and uses only constant memory space. However, we do not know of an algorithm computing the period of a word and satisfying the same time and space constraints.

7. References

[1] A.V. AHO & M.J. CORASICK, Efficient string matching : An aid to bibliographic search, *Comm. ACM* **18** (1975) 333-340.

[2] A.V. AHO, J.E. HOPCROFT & J.D. ULLMAN, *The design and analysis of computer algorithms*, Addison-Wesley, Reading, Mass., 1974.

[3] A. APOSTOLICO & F.P. PREPARATA, Optimal off-line detection of repetitionsin a string, *Theoret. Comput. Sci.* **22** (1983) 297-315.

[4] D.R. BEAN, A. EHRENFEUCHT & G.F. MCNULTY, Avoidable patterns in strings of symbols, *Pacific J. Math.* **85** (1979) 261-294.

[5] A. BLUMER, J. BLUMER, A. EHRENFEUCHT, D. HAUSSLER, M.T. CHEN & J. SEIFERAS, The smallest automaton recognizing the subwords of a text, *Theoret. Comput. Sci.* **40**, 1 (1985) 31-56.

[6] K.S. BOOTH, Lexicographically least circular substrings, *Inform. Process. Lett.* **10**, 4, 5 (1980) 240-242.

[7] R.S. BOYER & J.S. MOORE, A fast string searching algorithm, *Comm. ACM* **20** (1977) 762-772.

[8] Y. CESARI & M. VINCENT, Une caractérisation des mots périodiques, *C.R. Acad.Sc.* t.**286**, série A (1978) 1175.

[9] C. CHOFFRUT & M.P. SCHÜTZENBERGER, Counting with rationnal functions, to appear in *Theoret. Comput. Sci.* (1988).

[10] M. CROCHEMORE, Transducers and repetitions, *Theoret. Comput. Sci.* **45** (1986) 63-86.

[11] M. CROCHEMORE & D. PERRIN, Pattern matching in strings, to appear in *J. Assoc. Comput. Mach.* (1988).

[12] J.P. DUVAL, Factorizing Words over an Ordered Alphabet, *J. Algorithms* **4** (1983) 363-381.

[13] Z. GALIL, On improving the most case running time of the Boyer-Moore string-matching algorithm, *Comm. ACM* **22**, 9 (1979) 505-508.

[14] Z. GALIL, String Matching in real time, *J. Assoc. Comput. Mach.* **28**, 1 (1981) 134-149.

[15] Z. GALIL & J. SEIFERAS, Time Space Optimal String Matching, *J. Comput. Syst. Sci.* **26** (1983) 280-294.

[16] L.J. GUIBAS & A.M. ODLYSKO, A new proof of the linearity of the Boyer-Moore string searching algorithm, in: (Proc. 18 th Annual IEEE Symposium on Fundations of Computer Science (1977)) 189-195.

[17] R.M. KARP, R.E. MILLER & A.L. ROSENBERG, Rapid identification of repeated patterns in strings, trees, and arrays,in: (*ACM Symposium on Theory of Computing*, Vol. **4**, ACM, New York (1972)) 125-136.

[18] D.E. KNUTH, J.H. MORRIS & V.R. PRATT, Fast pattern matching in strings, *SIAM J. Comput.* **6**, 2 (1977) 323-350.

[19] LOTHAIRE, *Combinatorics on Words*, Addison-Wesley, Reading, Mass., 1982.

[20] G.M. LANDAU & U. VISHKIN, Efficient string matching with k differences, Technical Report 186, Courant Institute of Mathematical Sciences, New York University (1985).

[21] E.M. MCCREIGHT, A space-economical suffix tree construction algorithms, *J. Assoc. Comput: Mach.* **28**, 2 (1976) 262-272.

[22] R.L. RIVEST, On the worst-case behavior of string-searching algorithms, *SIAM J. Comput.* **6**, 4 (1977) 669-674.

[23] W. RYTTER, A correct preprocessing algorithm for Boyer-Moore string-searching, *SIAM J. Comput.* **9**, 3 (1980) 509-512.

[24] V. SHILOACH, Fast canonization of circular strings, *J. Algorithms* **2** (1981) 107-121.

[25] A.O. SLISENKO, Detection of periodicities and string-matching in real-time, *J. of Soviet Mathematics* **22**, 3 (1983) 1316-1387.

[26] K. THOMPSON, Regular expression search algorithm, *Comm. ACM* **11** (1968) 419-442.

[27] E. UKKONEN, Finding Approximate Patterns in Strings, *J.Algorithms* **6** (1985) 132-137.

[28] U. VISHKIN, Optimal parallel pattern matching in strings, in: (Proc. 12th ICALP, Lecture Notes in Computer Science **194**, Springer-Verlag (1985)) 497-508.

[29] P. WEINER, Linear pattern matching algorithms, *IEEE Symposium on Switching and Automata Theory*, Vol. **14**, IEEE, New York (1972)) 1-11.

Structure of Complexity Classes: Separations, Collapses, and Completeness

*Lane A. Hemachandra**
Department of Computer Science
Columbia University
New York, NY 10027, USA

Abstract

During the last few years, unprecedented progress has been made in structural complexity theory; class inclusions and relativized separations were discovered, and hierarchies collapsed. We survey this progress, highlighting the central role of counting techniques. We also present a new result whose proof demonstrates the power of combinatorial arguments: there is a relativized world in which UP has no Turing complete sets.

1 Introduction

Two years ago, the hunting season opened. Quickly, the strong exponential hierarchy fell, followed by the linear-space, logspace, and logspace oracle hierarchies. Soon the LBA problem, a venerable precursor of P =? NP, had been added to the game sack. Today, open season has been declared on P =? NP. Many reasonable men express confidence that P =? NP will be resolved within a decade—a view that only a few years ago would have been heretical.

In the first part of this paper, we survey some highlights of recent progress in structural complexity theory, and identify the reason for this sudden progress. For many years, NP was viewed as a mysterious black box. During the last few years, we have started to open that box. Counting and combinatorial techniques have been used to explore, and exploit, the strengths and weaknesses of nondeterministic computation.

We survey recent progress on collapsing hierarchies, establishing complexity class containments, and proving relativized separations and non-completeness results.

The second part of this paper—Section 3—presents a result that extends the use of counting arguments to a new area—proving Turing non-completeness. We show that there is a relativized world in which the cryptographic class UP, unique polynomial time, has no Turing complete sets. This extends a long line of research on completeness that has been pursued by Ambos-Spies, Hartmanis, Immerman, and Sipser [Sip82,HI85,HH86, Amb86]. The goal of this research is to understand the structure of complexity classes by determining which classes have complete sets under which reducibilities.

*Supported by NSF grant CCR-8809174 and a Hewlett-Packard Corporation equipment grant.

2 Recent Progress in Structural Complexity Theory

2.1 Collapsing Hierarchies and Class Containments

The most noteworthy recent progress in structural complexity theory is the sudden collapse of complexity hierarchies. The most surprising aspect of these collapses is the simplicity and elegance of the techniques used. The LBA problem, which remained open for twenty-five years, has a four-page resolution.

The key technique in these collapses has been the use of *census functions*—functions that count. Usually, census functions count the number of elements in prefixes of a set having certain properties. Census functions are not new; Mahaney's proof that NP has no sparse complete sets unless P = NP is based on the use of census information [Mah82].

We start by presenting two of the earlier of recent uses of census functions to explore class inclusions. The first shows the relationship between Turing reductions and truth-table reductions, and the second strengthens a long line of "small circuit [KL80]" results.

$P^{NP[\log]}$ indicates the class of languages accepted by polynomial-time Turing machines that make $\mathcal{O}(\log n)$ calls to an NP oracle. $P^{NP}_{truth-table}$ indicates the class of languages that are polynomial-time truth-table reducible to NP [LLS75].

Theorem 2.1 [Hem87c]
$P^{NP[\log]} = P^{NP}_{truth-table}$.

The proof simply uses binary search to find, in $\mathcal{O}(\log n)$ queries to NP, the number m of queries of the truth-table reduction that receive the answer "yes," and then uses one further NP query to guess and check which m queries are answered "yes" and determine if the truth-table system accepts.

Proof Sketch $S \leq^p_{\text{truth-table}}$ NP means there is a polynomial-time machine that answers "$x \in S$?" by making queries to SAT [GJ79], such that the queries asked of SAT are independent of the answers received [LLS75]. To prove the $\subseteq$ part, we have P perform binary search, using its NP oracle, to find the *number* of yes answers, and with one final query to the oracle have NP guess which queries receive yes answers and simulate the action of the truth-table reducer. The $\supseteq$ part it trivial—the truth-table reducer asks all queries that might be formed by any of the $n^{O(1)}$ possible sets of oracle answers of the run of $P^{NP[\log]}$. ∎

Detailed investigations of the interleaving of truth-table, oracle query, and boolean hierarchies can be found in [KSW86,AG87,Bei87].

The next example, due to Kadin, strengthens theorems of Karp, Lipton, Long, and Mahaney [KL80,Mah82,Lon82]. The Karp-Lipton "small circuits" theorem (so-called as the hypothesis is equivalent to "NP has small circuits") states:

Theorem 2.2 [KL80] If there is a sparse[1] set S such that $NP \subseteq P^S$, then $NP^{NP} = PH$, where PH is the polynomial hierarchy.

For the case of *simple* sparse sets, this was extended by Mahaney.

[1]A set A is sparse if it has only polynomially many elements of length at most n. That is, $(\exists k)(\forall n)$[there are at most $n^k + k$ elements of length $\leq n$ in A].

Theorem 2.3 [Mah82] If there is a sparse set $S \in \text{NP}$ such that $\text{NP} \subseteq \text{P}^S$, then $\text{P}^{\text{NP}} = \text{PH}$.

Kadin observed that Theorem 2.3 can be strengthened using census functions.

Theorem 2.4 [Kad87] If there is a sparse set $S \in \text{NP}$ such that $\text{NP} \subseteq \text{P}^S$, then $\text{P}^{\text{NP[log]}} = \text{PH}$.

Proof Sketch Let $census_S(1^i)$ equal the number of elements in S of length at most i. If there is a sparse set S as described in the theorem, then a P machine can make $\mathcal{O}(\log n)$ calls to an NP oracle to find—via binary search—$census_S(1^n)$. It is easy to see that, with $\mathcal{O}(\log n)$ NP queries to calculate the census function, and one further query (to guess exactly which strings are in S up to a certain length), $\text{P}^{\text{NP[log]}}$ can simulate P^S. So, using Theorem 2.3, $\text{PH} \subseteq \text{P}^{\text{NP}} \subseteq \text{P}^{(\text{P}^S)} \subseteq \text{P}^S \subseteq \text{P}^{\text{NP[log]}}$. ∎

The first hierarchy to fall under attack by census functions was the strong exponential hierarchy. Nondeterministic exponential time, NE, is defined as $\bigcup_{c>0} \text{NTIME}[2^{cn}]$. The following theorem states that the strong exponential hierarchy collapses.

Theorem 2.5 [Hem87c]
$\text{P}^{\text{NE}} = \text{E} \cup \text{NE} \cup \text{NP}^{\text{NE}} \cup \text{NP}^{\text{NP}^{\text{NE}}} \cup \cdots$.

This follows immediately from the lemma that $\text{P}^{\text{NE}} = \text{NP}^{\text{NE}}$. The collapse was first proven by a census argument that—level by level in the NP^{NE} computation tree—finds the number of yes answers to queries, and yields strengthenings of Theorem 2.5. Schöning and Wagner [SW88] developed the following elegant proof: consider an NP machine with an NE oracle A. The NP machine can query, for some k, at most n^k strings in A. Note, however, that P^{NE} can, by binary search, compute the function $census_A$, and thus simulate NP^{NE}.

The strong exponential hierarchy is a time hierarchy. However, the same techniques apply also to space hierarchies. The linear-space hierarchy, the logspace hierarchy, and the logspace hierarchy all collapsed under the application of census techniques [Tod87,LJK87,SW88]. These space results were strengthened by Szelepcsényi and Immerman [Sze87,Imm87].

Theorem 2.6 [Sze87,Imm87] For any space constructible $S(n) \geq \log n$, $\text{NSPACE}[S(n)] = \text{co} - \text{NSPACE}[S(n)]$.

The proof has been widely circulated. It uses *inductive counting*—iteratively counting the number of reachable configurations at each distance from the start of a co-NSPACE[$S(n)$] computation. In part, this comes full circle to the iterative use of census used to collapse the strong exponential hierarchy.

Inductive counting has since been used to show that the class of languages that logspace reduce to some context-free language, LOG(CFL), is closed under complement.

Theorem 2.7 [BCRT88]
LOG(CFL) = co-LOG(CFL).

A number of class containment results have been proven recently using the ability of nondeterministic machines to make extra copies of accepting paths. This approach has been used to evaluate the complexity of classes in the counting hierarchy—a hierarchy based on NP machines with altered acceptance mechanisms [CH86,GW, CGH*b]. More recently, this approach has been used to show that parity polynomial time is powerful enough to contain FewP—the subset of NP languages that are accepted by machines that never have many accepting paths.

Definition 2.8

1. **[PZ83]** (Parity Polynomial Time) $\oplus\mathrm{P} = \{L \mid$ there is a nondeterministic polynomial-time Turing machine N such that $x \in L$ if and only if $N(x)$ has an odd number of accepting paths$\}$.
2. **[All86]** $\mathrm{FewP} = \{L \mid$ there is a nondeterministic polynomial-time Turing machine N such that (1) $x \in L$ if and only if $N(x)$ has at least one accepting path and (2) $(\exists k)(\forall x)[N(x)$ has at most $|x|^k + k$ accepting paths$]\}$.
3. **[CH87]** Few is the class of all languages L such that there is a nondeterministic polynomial-time Turing machine N, a polynomial-time computable predicate $Q(\cdot,\cdot)$, and a polynomial $q(\cdot)$, such that (1) $x \in L$ if and only if $Q(x, ||N(x)||)$, and (2) $(\forall x)[||N(x)|| \leq q(|x|)]$, where $||N(x)||$ denotes the number of accepting paths of $N(x)$.

Theorem 2.9 [CH87] $\oplus\mathrm{P} \supseteq \mathrm{Few}$.

Corollary 2.10 [CH87] $\oplus\mathrm{P} \supseteq \mathrm{FewP}$.

A direct proof of the corollary is immediate. Given a FewP machine, N_i, that on inputs of length n never has more than $n^k + k$ accepting paths, we construct a new machine N, a nondeterministic machine with the parity acceptance mechanism, so that $N(x)$ has a path for each path of $N_i(x)$, and a path for each pair of paths of $N_i(x)$, ..., and a path for each $(n^k + k)$-tuple of paths of $N_i(x)$. Each path of $N(x)$ will accept if and only if all of the paths that it represents in $N_i(x)$ are accepting paths. Since $\sum_{1 \leq i \leq n^k+k} \binom{j}{i} = 2^j - 1$ is odd exactly when $j \neq 0$, it follows that $\mathrm{FewP} \subseteq \oplus\mathrm{P}$. The proof that $\mathrm{Few} \subseteq \oplus\mathrm{P}$ takes a bit more work, but follows the same lines.

2.2 Separations

The previous section described a number of collapsing hierarchies and class containments. Hierarchy separations, or even class separations, remain elusive. However, a number of hierarchies have been separated in relativized worlds. These include the boolean hierarchy, the counting hierarchy [CGH*b], and, most importantly, the polynomial hierarchy.

Definition 2.11

1. **Boolean Hierarchy [Wec85]** $\Sigma_0^{BH} = \mathrm{P}$. $\Sigma_1^{BH} = \mathrm{NP}$. $\Sigma_i^{BH} = \{L \mid (\exists L' \in \mathrm{NP})(\exists L'' \in \Sigma_{i-1}^{BH})[L = L' - L'']\}$, $i > 1$.
2. **Polynomial Hierarchy [Sto77]** $\Sigma_0^p = \mathrm{P}$. $\Sigma_1^p = \mathrm{NP}$. $\Sigma_i^p = \mathrm{NP}^{\Sigma_{i-1}^p}$, $i > 1$.

Theorem 2.12 [CGH*a]

1. There is a relativized world A in which $\Sigma_0^{BH}(A) \neq \Sigma_1^{BH}(A) \neq \cdots$.
2. For each k there is a relativized world A in which $\Sigma_0^{BH}(A) \neq \cdots \neq \Sigma_k^{BH}(A) = \Sigma_{k+1}^{BH}(A) = \cdots$.

Theorem 2.13 [Yao85,Ko88]

1. There is a relativized world A in which $\Sigma_0^p(A) \neq \Sigma_1^p(A) \neq \cdots$.
2. For each k there is a relativized world A in which $\Sigma_0^p(A) \neq \cdots \neq \Sigma_k^p(A) = \Sigma_{k+1}^p(A) = \cdots$.

Yao's and Ko's results exploit the connection between circuit theory and the theory of relativizations [FSS84].

The boolean hierarchy results are proven by exactly the approach we'll use in Section 3. An NP machine accepts, by definition, when *any* computation path accepts. This is an insensitive mechanism, and leaves NP open to relativized manipulation.

The crudeness of the acceptance mechanism of NP has also been used to show *robustness* [Sch85] results—results showing the difficulty of NP machines maintaining some computational invariant in all relativized worlds. The idea behind the proofs is that the crudeness of the acceptance mechanism tends to make NP machines oblivious to fine changes in the oracle. A representative result is that if a nondeterministic polynomial-time Turing machine N_i is categorical (i.e., has at most one accepting path on any input [Val76]) in every relativized world, then in every relativized world A, the language $L(N_i^A)$ is relatively simple. It falls into the second level of Schöning's [Sch83, Sch86] extended low hierarchy. The results below are from [HH87].

Theorem 2.14 (Robustly categorical machines accept simple languages)
$(\forall A)\,[N_i^A \text{ is categorical}] \Rightarrow (\forall A)\,[L(N_i^A) \in \mathrm{P}^{\mathrm{NP}\oplus A}]$.

Corollary 2.15 If $\mathrm{P} = \mathrm{NP}$ and N_i is robustly categorical (i.e., $(\forall A)\,[N_i^A$ is categorical]), then for every oracle A, $L(N_i^A) \in \mathrm{P}^A$.

Theorem 2.16 (Robustly complementary machines accept simple languages)
$(\forall A)\,[L(N_i^A) = \overline{L(N_j^A)}] \Rightarrow (\forall A)\,[L(N_i^A) \in \mathrm{P}^{\mathrm{NP}\oplus A}]$.

Corollary 2.17 [2] If $\mathrm{P} = \mathrm{NP}$ and N_i and N_j are robustly complementary (i.e., $(\forall A)\,[L(N_i^A) = \overline{L(N_j^A)}]$), then for every oracle A $L(N_i^A) \in \mathrm{P}^A$.

Theorem 2.18 (Machines robustly Σ^*-accepting on sparse oracles accept for transparent reasons)
$(\forall \text{ sparse } S)\,[L(N_i^S) = \Sigma^*] \Rightarrow (\forall \text{ sparse } S)\,(\exists f$ computable in $\mathrm{P}^{\mathrm{NP}\oplus S})\,(\forall x)[f(x)$ prints an accepting path of $N_i^S(x)]$.

Corollary 2.19 If $\mathrm{P} = \mathrm{NP}$ and N_i robustly accepts Σ^* on sparse oracles (i.e., $(\forall$ sparse $T)$ $[L(N_i^T) = \Sigma^*]$), then for every sparse oracle S, there is a function f computable in P^S so that on any input x, $f(x)$ prints an accepting path of $N_i^S(x)$.

Finally, we mention a lovely, combinatorially deep relativization of Torán [Tor88]. He has shown that there is an oracle A for which $\mathrm{NP}^A - \oplus\mathrm{P}^A \neq \emptyset$.

2.3 Completeness

The same obliviousness of NP machines that yielded the relativized separations mentioned in Section 2.2 has also led to proofs that some natural complexity classes may lack complete sets.

Complete languages have long been a useful tool in complexity theory. Much of our knowledge about NP comes from studying the NP-complete set SAT [Mah82,KL80,BH77]. Most common

[2] Manuel Blum and Russell Impagliazzo [BI87] independently proved Corollary 2.17 in their study of generic oracles. Tardos [Tar87] studies an analog where unbounded computational time is combined with restricted oracle access.

complexity classes—NP, coNP, PSPACE, etc.—have many-one complete sets that help us study them.

Sipser noted, however, that some classes may lack complete sets [Sip82]. His paper sparked much research into which classes have complete languages, and what strengths of completeness results (e.g., many-one or Turing) can be obtained. Of course, if P = PSPACE, then *all* classes between P and PSPACE have many-one complete languages. Thus, incompleteness results are typically displayed in relativized worlds [BGS75,Sip82].

Sipser showed that there are relativized worlds in which R and NP $\cap$ coNP lack many-one complete languages. Hartmanis and Hemachandra showed a relativized world in which UP—unique polynomial time (Section 3.1)—lacks many-one complete languages, and noted that if UP does have complete languages then UP has complete languages with an unusually simple form—the intersection of SAT with a set in P [HH86].

One way of strengthening the above theorems would be to show that these classes lack complete sets even with respect to reducibilities more flexible than many-one reductions, e.g., k-truth-table, positive truth-table, truth-table, and ultimately Turing reductions [LLS75]. Hartmanis and Immerman, exploiting an insightful characterization of Kowalczyk [Kow84], showed that NP $\cap$ coNP has many-one complete languages if and only if it has Turing complete languages [HI85]. An elegant generalization of their result by Ambos-Spies shows that for any class $\mathcal{C}$ closed under Turing reductions, $\mathcal{C}$ has Turing complete sets if and only if $\mathcal{C}$ has many-one complete sets [Amb86]. In particular, it follows from the result of Sipser [Sip82] that there is a relativized world A in which $NP^A \cap coNP^A$ lacks Turing complete sets [HI85, Amb86]. Similarly, since $P^{BPP} = BPP$ [Zac86], from [HH86]'s proof that BPP lacks many-one complete sets in some relativized worlds it follows that it also may lack Turing complete sets.

Theorem 2.20 There is a relativized world A in which BPP^A lacks Turing complete sets.

However, Ambos-Spies's result does not apply to UP or any other class not known to be closed under Turing reductions. Furthermore, the technique used to show that UP may lack many-one complete languages was an indirect proof via the contradiction of an enumeration condition that characterized the existence of many-one complete languages [HH86]—and does not generalize to the case of Turing completeness.

Section 3 constructs an oracle A for which UP^A contains no Turing complete sets. Our proof exploits the limited combinatorial control of nondeterministic machines to trivialize or corrupt candidates for Turing completeness. This approach extends our theme: the exploitation of the combinatorics of the nondeterministic acceptance mechanism.

It follows immediately from our proof that there is a relativized world A in which UP^A lacks complete languages under all reducibilities more restrictive than Turing reductions.

3 Does UP have Turing Complete Languages?

3.1 Definitions

Definition 3.1 [Val76]
(Unique Polynomial Time) UP = $\{L \mid$ there is a nondeterministic polynomial time Turing machine N such that $L = L(N)$, and for all x, the computation of $N(x)$ has at most one accepting path$\}$. We say that a machine N that for every input has at most one accepting path is *categorical.*

UP captures the power of uniqueness; UP is the class of problems that have (on some NP machine) unique witnesses. That is, if there is an NP machine N accepting L and for every input x the computation $N(x)$ has at most one accepting path (i.e., N is a categorical machine), then we say $L \in$ UP.

Recently, UP has come to play a crucial role in both cryptography and structural complexity theory. In cryptography, Grollmann and Selman have shown that one-way functions[3] exist if and only if P $\neq$ UP, and one-way functions whose range[4] is in P exist if and only if P $\neq$ UP $\bigcap$ coUP. Thus, we suspect that P $\neq$ UP because we suspect that one-way functions exist. In structural complexity theory, a conjecture that "P $\neq$ UP $\Longleftrightarrow$ there exist non-p-isomorphic NP-complete sets" was recently refuted in a relativized world [HH87].

[3] A function f is *honest* if $(\exists k)(\forall x)[|f(x)|^k + k \geq |x|]$ ([GS84], see also [Wat86]). A *one-way function* is a total, single-valued, one-to-one, honest, polynomial time computable function f such that f^{-1} (which will be a partial function if range(f) $\neq \Sigma^*$) is not computable in polynomial time [GS84].

[4] *Range*$(f) = \bigcup_{i \in \Sigma^*} f(i)$.

For background, we first define Turing reductions and completeness in the real (unrelativized) world.

Definition 3.2

1. $S_1 \leq_T^p S_2$ if $S_1 \subseteq \mathrm{P}^{S_2}$ [GJ79].
2. L is $\leq_T^p$-complete for UP if $L \in$ UP and every set in UP Turing reduces to L (i.e., $(\forall S \in \mathrm{UP})[S \leq_T^p L]$).

If we wish to discuss Turing completeness in relativized worlds, we must address the key question: are the Turing reductions allowed access to the oracle? Definitions 3.3.2 and 3.3.3 answer this question "yes" and "no," respectively.

Definition 3.3

1. $S_1 \leq_T^{p,A} S_2$ if $S_1 \subseteq \mathrm{P}^{S_2 \oplus A}$.
2. L is $\leq_T^{p,A}$-complete for UP^A if $[L \in \mathrm{UP}^A$ and $(\forall S \in \mathrm{UP}^A)[S \leq_T^{p,A} L]]$.
3. L is $\leq_T^p$-complete for UP^A if $[L \in \mathrm{UP}^A$ and $(\forall S \in \mathrm{UP}^A)[S \leq_T^p L]]$.

We suggest that Definition 3.3.2 above is the natural notion of relativized Turing completeness. Adopting it, we prove that there is a relativized world in which UP^A has no $\leq_T^{p,A}$-complete sets. However, for purposes of completeness results, the different notions of relativized Turing reductions stand or fall together.

Lemma 3.4 For any oracle A: [UP^A has $\leq_T^{p,A}$-complete sets if and only if UP^A has $\leq_T^p$-complete sets].

This is true since if B is $\leq_T^{p,A}$-complete for UP^A, then $B \oplus A$ is $\leq_T^p$-complete for UP^A. The analog of Lemma 3.4 for many-one reductions was proven by Sipser [Sip82].

The difference between Definitions 3.3.2 and 3.3.3 is exactly the difference between "full" (3.3.2) and "partial" (3.3.3) relativization discussed in [KMR86] and [Rog67, Section 9.3]. [KMR86] describes how this distinction has had a crucial effect on recent research asking if all NP-complete sets are polynomially isomorphic [Kur83,GJ86,HH87]. However, Lemma 3.4 indicates that in our study of Turing completeness, we need not be concerned with the distinction.

3.2 A Relativized World in Which UP Lacks Turing Complete Sets

This section sketches the construction of an oracle for which UP^A has no Turing complete sets. It follows immediately that UP^A lacks complete sets with respect to reductions more restrictive than $\leq_T^{p,A}$, such as truth-table reductions [LLS75], bounded truth-table reductions [LLS75], etc.

Theorem 3.5 There is a recursive oracle A such that UP^A contains no $\leq_T^{p,A}$-complete sets.

Corollary 3.6 There is a recursive oracle A such that UP^A contains no:

1. $\leq_T^p$-complete languages.
2. truth-table complete languages.
3. bounded truth-table complete languages.
4. [HH86] $\leq_m^p$ or $\leq_m^{p,A}$-complete languages.

Let $\{N_i\}$ be a standard enumeration of nondeterministic polynomial-time Turing machines and let $\{M_i\}$ be a standard enumeration of deterministic polynomial-time Turing machines. The idea of the proof is as follows. We wish to show that for no $L \in UP^A$ is $UP^A \subseteq P^L$, which suffices by Lemma 3.4. Each L in UP^A is, by definition, accepted by a *categorical* machine ($L = L(N_i^A)$, N_i^A categorical). Our goal is to show that for each i, either

1. N_i^A is not categorical, or
2. $(\exists \hat{L}_i)[\hat{L}_i \in UP^A \text{ and } \hat{L}_i \notin P^{L(N_i^A)}]$.

The second condition says that some UP^A language does not Turing reduce to $L(N_i^A)$. That is, every Turing reduction fails on some value. Thus it certainly suffices to show that for all i, either

1. N_i^A is not categorical or
2. (a) $(\forall j)(\exists x)[x \in \hat{L}_i \not\Leftrightarrow x \in L(M_j^{L(N_i^A)})]$, where $\hat{L}_i = \{1^n \mid (\exists k)[(n = (p_i)^k) \wedge (\exists y)[|y| = n \wedge y \in A]]\}$ and p_i is the ith prime, and
   (b) $\hat{L}_i \in UP^A$.

Note that we have specified $\hat{L}_i$.

Briefly put, for each $< i, j >$, we seek to find a way of extending the oracle to make N_i^A non-categorical. Failing this, we argue that we can choose our oracle in such a way as to determine the answers to all oracle queries made by M_j, and still have the flexibility to diagonalize against $\hat{L}_i$. The crucial step is a combinatorial argument that categorical machines which don't trivially accept must reject on an overwhelming number of oracle extensions.

Proof Sketch for Theorem 3.5

We wish to show that there is a relativized world A where UP^A has no Turing complete languages, i.e.,

$$(\forall L \in UP^A)(\exists L' \in UP^A)[L' \not\leq_T^{p,A} L].$$

By Lemma 3.4 it suffices to show that

$$(\forall L \in \mathrm{UP}^A)(\exists L' \in \mathrm{UP}^A)[L' \not\leq_T^p L].$$

Since each language in UP^A is accepted by at least one categorical machine, we can equivalently show that

$$(\forall i)[(N_i^A \text{ is noncategorical}) \vee (\exists \hat{L}_i \in \mathrm{UP}^A)[\hat{L}_i \not\leq_T^p L(N_i^A)]].$$

This says that:

$(\forall i)[(N_i^A$ is noncategorical$) \vee$
$(\exists \hat{L}_i \in \mathrm{UP}^A)[\hat{L}_i \notin \mathrm{P}^{L(N_i^A)}]]$. $\quad **$

Let requirement $R_{<i,j>}$ be
$R_{i,j}$: $(\exists x)[x \in \hat{L}_i \not\Leftrightarrow x \in L(M_j^{L(N_i^A)})]$, where $\hat{L}_i = \{1^n \mid (\exists k \ni n = p_i^k) \wedge (\exists y)[|y| = n \wedge y \in A]\}$, and p_i is the ith prime.

Note that we satisfy ($**$) if we can satisfy for all i the following, which simply (1) specifies the $\hat{L}_i$, (2) uses the fact that $\mathrm{P}^X = \bigcup_i L(M_i^X)$, where $\{M_i\}$ is a standard enumeration of polynomial machines and without loss of generality M_i runs in time $n^i + i$, and (3) notes that differing languages must differ on some specific element.

1. N_i^A is noncategorical, OR $\quad ***$
2. $(\forall j)[R_{i,j}$ is satisfied] and $(\hat{L}_i \in \mathrm{UP}^A)$.$****$

Our construction will go by stages. In stage $< i, j >$ we will either satisfy $R_{i,j}$ or know that N_i^A is noncategorical.

Initially set $A_{<i,j>} := \emptyset$. We'll have $A = \bigcup_{<i,j>} A_{<i,j>}$.

Stage $< i, j >$: If N_i^A has already been made noncategorical, skip this stage and set $A_{<i,j>} := A_{<i,j>-1}$. Otherwise, choose a huge integer n that is a power of the ith prime (i.e., so $(\exists k \ni n = p_i^k)$) and is much larger than any previously touched length.

A *legal* extension of $A_{<i,j>}$ will be one that does not touch any string shorter than n, and that adds strings to $A_{<i,j>}$ only at lengths that are powers of p_i.

If there is a legal extension $\hat{A}$ of $A_{<i,j>-1}$ such that for some $y \ni |y| \leq (n^j + j)^i + i$ we have that $N_i^{\hat{A}}(y)$ is noncategorical,[5] then choose two accepting paths of $N_i^{\hat{A}}(y)$ and set $A_{<i,j>}$ to be $A_{<i,j>-1}$ augmented to agree with $\hat{A}$ on all strings queried on those two paths and go to the next stage.

Otherwise, we've failed to make $N_i^{A_{<i,j>}}$ noncategorical, so we must try to satisfy requirement $R_{<i,j>}$. *Our goal is to fix the behavior of* $M_j^{L(N_i^A)}(1^n)$ *and yet have enough flexibility left to ensure that* $1^n \in \hat{L}_i$ *or* $1^n \notin \hat{L}_i$ *as we wish. Thus we can diagonalize to insure that* $R_{<i,j>}$ *is satisfied. Furthermore,* unless *we discover a way of making* N_i^A *noncategorical, we'll put only one string into* A *at each length* p_i^k *thus insuring that* $\hat{L}_i \in \mathrm{UP}^A$.

We simulate the behavior of $M_j^{L(N_i^{A_{<i,j>-1}})}(1^n)$, *and each time* M_j *makes an oracle query, we take action to control that query.*

We use T_l to indicate the set of strings of length n to which the lth query is oblivious. We'll eventually show that the T_l are all so huge that there must be at some string in $T_1 \cap T_2 \cap \cdots T_{n^j+j}$.

Action for the first query:

Run $M_j^{L(N_i^{A_{<i,j>-1}})}(1^n)$ until M_j asks its first oracle query, q_1.

Case 1: $N_i^{A_{<i,j>-1}}(q_1)$ accepts. Freeze the elements along the accepting path, and proceed to action for the second query. Set $T_1 = \{z \mid |z| = n$

[5]We *could* remove the bound on y's size, but this would make the construction nonrecursive.

and z has not just been frozen}.

Case 2: $N_i^{A_{<i,j>-1}}(q_1)$ rejects. We argue that there are a huge number of strings of length n that can be added to the oracle which will not change this rejection. Let $T_1 = \{z \mid n = |z|$ and the membership of element z in A has not yet been determined and $N_i^{A_{<i,j>-1} \cup \{z\}}(q_1)$ rejects}. Let $t_1 = ||T_1||$. By Lemma 3.7, $t_1 \geq 2^n - 8((n^j + j)^{2i} + i^2)$.

Action for the lth query:

At this point, we've already determined the answers to the first $l-1$ oracle queries. We proceed analogously to the action for the first query (except we respect—and use k of Lemma 3.7 to account for—strings frozen from case 1 of earlier queries, which causes the bounds on T_l to weaken slightly as l grows).

End of query sequence

Our goal was to fix the responses to the queries while leaving ourselves enough freedom to make $1^n \in \hat{L}_i$ or $1^n \notin \hat{L}_i$ as we like. We can now do that.

Each T_i is easily of size $\geq 2^n - n^{\log n}$. Thus, since each T_i is a subset of the set of length n strings, and since there are at most $n^j + j$ T_i's, there is some length n string $\hat{z}$ in $T_1 \cap T_2 \cap \cdots \cap T_{n^j+j}$. By the definition of the T_i's, adding this string to $A_{<i,j>-1}$ will have no effect on any of the oracle responses. That is, $M_j^{L(N_i^{A_{<i,j>-1}})}(1^n)$ accepts if and only if $M_j^{L(N_i^{A_{<i,j>-1}}) \cup \{\hat{z}\}}(1^n)$ accepts. If these do accept, choose $\hat{z} \notin A$. Thus, $1^n \notin \hat{L}_i$ but $1^n \in L(M_j^{L(N_i^A)})$, so requirement $R_{<i,j>}$ has been satisfied. On the other hand, if $M_j^{L(N_i^{A_{<i,j>-1}})}(1^n)$ rejects, choose $\hat{z} \in A$. Thus, $1^n \in \hat{L}_i$ but $1^n \notin L(M_j^{L(N_i^A)})$, so requirement $R_{<i,j>}$ has been satisfied.

End of Stage $<i,j>$

Note that if we never find a way of making N_i^A noncategorical, then $\hat{L}_i \in \mathrm{UP}^A$ (because the above procedure puts in only one string, $\hat{z}$, at each length important to $\hat{L}_i$) and $(\forall j)$[requirement $R_{<i,j>}$ is satisfied]. Thus $(* * **)$ is satisfied. On the other hand, if we do find a way of making N_i^A noncategorical, then $(* * *)$ is satisfied.[6] Thus we have met requirements that are, by the discussion following Corollary 3.6, sufficient to insure that UP^A has no $\leq_T^{p,A}$-complete languages. ∎

In the proof, we referred to the following lemma. Loosely, what the lemma says is that if a machine tries to be categorical on all possible oracle extensions and it rejects on the empty extension, then it must also reject on an overwhelmingly large proportion of extensions that add exactly one string.

Lemma 3.7 Let N_i^A be a nondeterministic Turing machine that runs in NTIME$[n^i + i]$. Suppose $N_i^A(x)$ rejects, A has no strings of length $|x|$, and k strings of length $|x|$ have been designated as forbidden from being added to the oracle A. Let $Rejectors_x = \{y \mid N_i^{A \cup \{y\}}(x)$ rejects and $|y| = |x|$ and y is not one of the k forbidden strings}. Then either $||Rejectors_x|| \geq 2^n - (k + 8(|x|^{2i} + i^2))$ or there exists a set S such that (1) $||S|| \leq 2$, (2) S contains no forbidden string, (3) $(\forall w \in S)[|w| = |x|]$, and (4) $N_i^{A \cup S}$ is noncategorical (in particular, it has more than one accepting path on input x).

Proof Sketch for Lemma 3.7

[6]In this case $\hat{L}_i$ may not be in UP^A, but since we have met condition $(* * *)$, we don't care if $\hat{L}_i$ is in UP^A.

Let $Acceptors_x = \{y \mid N_i^{A \bigcup \{y\}}(x)$ accepts and $|y| = |x|$ and y is not one of the k forbidden strings$\}$. Suppose there are $l + k$ strings in $Acceptors_x$, and thus at least l usable acceptors. Each acceptor v triggers exactly one accepting path (otherwise, set $S = \{v\}$ and we're done). For each pair of distinct acceptors v_q and v_r, we must have that v_q is queried on the unique path on which $N_i^{A \bigcup \{v_r\}}(x)$ accepts or v_r is queried on the unique path on which $N_i^{A \bigcup \{v_q\}}(x)$ accepts (otherwise $N_i^{A \bigcup \{v_q, v_r\}}(x)$ has two accepting paths so set $S = \{v_q, v_r\}$ and we're done). There are $\binom{l}{2}$ candidate *pairs* of elements of $Acceptors_x$, which each threaten to make the machine noncategorical when both are simultaneously added. Consider just the set of paths, $Paths$, that accept for some string added from $Acceptors_x$. Clearly $l/(n^i+i) \leq ||Paths|| \leq l$. Each element $v \in Acceptors$ kills the candidacy of at most $(n^i+i)+p_v$ pairs, where p_v is the number of occurrences of v along paths in $Paths$. So the total number of killed candidates is $\leq ((n^i+i)||Paths||)(n^i+i)+||Paths||(n^i+i) \leq l((n^i+i)^2+(n^i+i))$. To avoid the existence of a set S as described in the lemma, we thus must have $\binom{l}{2} \leq l((n^i+i)^2+(n^i+i))$. So easily we have $l \leq 8(n^{2i}+i^2)$. ∎

4 Conclusion

This paper surveyed recent progress in structural complexity theory, and suggested that counting arguments have played a crucial role in these advances. We proved, using counting techniques, that there is a relativized world in which UP has no Turing complete languages.

Many related open problems remain. How much further can counting techniques by pushed in obtaining complexity hierarchy collapses, class containments, and relativized separations? What techniques might be used to separate complexity classes?

This paper has surveyed just a few of the interesting recent uses of counting. A great variety of applications and discussions of counting in complexity can be found in [All85,CH88,Hem86, Hem87b,Hem87a,Sch88,Sim77,Wag86].

References

[AG87] A. Amir and W. Gasarch. Polynomial terse sets. In *Proceedings 2nd Structure in Complexity Theory Conference*, pages 22–27, 1987.

[All85] E. Allender. Invertible functions. 1985. Ph.D. thesis, Georgia Institute of Technology.

[All86] E. Allender. The complexity of sparse sets in P. In *Proceedings 1st Structure in Complexity Theory Conference*, pages 1–11, Springer-Verlag *Lecture Notes in Computer Science #223*, June 1986.

[Amb86] K. Ambos-Spies. A note on complete problems for complexity classes. *Information Processing Letters*, 23:227–230, 1986.

[BCRT88] A. Borodin, S. Cook, W. Ruzzo, and M. Tompa. Two applications of complementation via induction counting. In *Proceedings 3rd Structure in Complexity Theory Conference*, IEEE Computer Society Press, June 1988. To appear.

[Bei87] R. Beigel. *Bounded Queries to SAT and the Boolean Hierarchy*. Technical Report TR-7, Johns Hopkins Department of Computer Science, Baltimore, MD, June 1987.

[BGS75] T. Baker, J. Gill, and R. Solovay. Relativizations of the P=?NP question. *SIAM Journal on Computing*, 4(4):431–442, 1975.

[BH77] L. Berman and J. Hartmanis. On isomorphisms and density of NP and other complete sets. *SIAM Journal on Computing*, 6(2):305–322, 1977.

[BI87] M. Blum and R. Impagliazzo. Generic oracles and oracle classes. In *28th Annual IEEE Symposium on Foundations of Computer Science*, October 1987.

[Cai86] J. Cai. With probability one, a random oracle separates PSPACE from the polynomial-time hierarchy. In *18th ACM Symposium on Theory of Computing*, pages 21–29, 1986.

[CGH*a] J. Cai, T. Gundermann, J. Hartmanis, L. Hemachandra, V. Sewelson, K. Wagner, and G. Wechsung. The boolean hierarchy I: Structural properties. To appear in *SIAM Journal on Computing*.

[CGH*b] J. Cai, T. Gundermann, J. Hartmanis, L. Hemachandra, V. Sewelson, K. Wagner, and G. Wechsung. The boolean hierarchy II: Applications. To appear in *SIAM J. on Computing*.

[CH86] J. Cai and L. Hemachandra. The boolean hierarchy: Hardware over NP. In *Proceedings 1st Structure in Complexity Theory Conference*, pages 105–124, Springer-Verlag *Lecture Notes in Computer Science #223*, June 1986.

[CH87] J. Cai and L. Hemachandra. *On the Power of Parity Polynomial Time.* Technical Report CUCS 274-87, Columbia Computer Science Department, New York, NY, December 1987.

[CH88] J. Cai and L. Hemachandra. Enumerative counting is hard. In *Proceedings 3rd Structure in Complexity Theory Conference*, IEEE Computer Society Press, June 1988. To appear.

[FSS84] M. Furst, J. Saxe, and M. Sipser. Parity, circuits, and the polynomial-time hierarchy. *Mathematical Systems Theory*, 17:13–27, 1984.

[GJ79] M. Garey and D. Johnson. *Computers and Intractability: A Guide to the Theory of NP-Completeness.* W. H. Freeman and Company, 1979.

[GJ86] J. Goldsmith and D. Joseph. Three results on the polynomial isomorphism of complete sets. In *Proceedings 27th IEEE Symposium on Foundations of Computer Science*, pages 390–397, 1986.

[GS84] J. Grollmann and A. Selman. Complexity measures for public-key cryptosystems. In *Proceedings 25th IEEE Symposium on Foundations of Computer Science*, pages 495–503, 1984.

[GW] T. Gundermann and G. Wechsung. Counting classes with finite acceptance types. To appear.

[Hem86] L. Hemachandra. *Can P and NP Manufacture Randomness?* Technical Report TR86-795, Cornell Computer Science Department, Ithaca, NY, December 1986.

[Hem87a] L. Hemachandra. *Counting in Structural Complexity Theory.* PhD thesis, Cornell University, Ithaca, NY, May 1987. Available as Cornell Department of Computer Science Technical Report TR87-840.

[Hem87b] L. Hemachandra. On ranking. In *Proceedings 2nd Structure in Complexity Theory Conference*, pages 103–117, IEEE Computer Society Press, June 1987.

[Hem87c] L. Hemachandra. The strong exponential hierarchy collapses. In *19th ACM Symposium on Theory of Computing*, pages 110–122, May 1987.

[HH86] J. Hartmanis and L. Hemachandra. Complexity classes without machines: On complete languages for UP. In

Automata, Languages, and Programming (ICALP 1986), pages 123–135, Springer-Verlag *Lecture Notes in Computer Science #226*, July 1986. To appear in *Theoretical Computer Science*.

[HH87] J. Hartmanis and L. Hemachandra. One-way functions, robustness, and the non-isomorphism of NP-complete sets. In *Proceedings 2nd Structure in Complexity Theory Conference*, pages 160–174, IEEE Computer Society Press, June 1987.

[HI85] J. Hartmanis and N. Immerman. On complete problems for NP$\cap$coNP. In *Automata, Languages, and Programming (ICALP 1985)*, pages 250–259, Springer-Verlag *Lecture Notes in Computer Science #194*, 1985.

[Imm87] N. Immerman. *Nondeterministic Space is Closed under Complement.* Technical Report YALEU/DCS/TR 552, Yale University, Department of Computer Science, New Haven, CT, July 1987. To appear in STRUCTURES 1988.

[Kad87] J. Kadin. $P^{NP[\log n]}$ and sparse Turing-complete sets for NP. In *Proceedings 2nd Structure in Complexity Theory Conference*, pages 33–40, IEEE Computer Society Press, June 1987.

[KL80] R. Karp and R. Lipton. Some connections between nonuniform and uniform complexity classes. In *12th ACM Sym. on Theory of Computing*, pages 302–309, 1980.

[KMR86] S. Kurtz, S. Mahaney, and J. Royer. Collapsing degrees. In *Proceedings 27th IEEE Symposium on Foundations of Computer Science*, pages 380–389, 1986.

[Ko88] K. Ko. Relativized polynomial time hierarchies having exactly k levels. In *20th ACM Symposium on Theory of Computing*, ACM Press, May 1988.

[Kow84] W. Kowalczyk. Some connections between representability of complexity classes and the power of formal reasoning systems. In *Mathematical Foundations of Computer Science*, pages 364–369, Springer-Verlag *Lecture Notes in Computer Science #176*, 1984.

[KSW86] J. Köbler, U. Schöning, and K. Wagner. *The Difference and Truth-Table Hierarchies for NP.* Technical Report, Fachberichte Informatik, EWH Rheinland-Pfalz, Koblenz, West Germany, July 1986.

[Kur83] S. Kurtz. *A Relativized Failure of the Berman-Hartmanis Conjecture.* Technical Report TR83-001, University of Chicago Department of Computer Science, Chicago, IL, 1983.

[LJK87] K. Lange, B. Jenner, and B. Kirsig. The logarithmic alternation hierarchy collapses: $A\Sigma_2^L = A\Pi_2^L$. In *Automata, Languages, and Programming (ICALP 1987)*, Springer-Verlag *Lecture Notes in Computer Science*, 1987.

[LLS75] R. Ladner, N. Lynch, and A. Selman. A comparison of polynomial time reducibilities. *Theoretical Computer Science*, 1(2):103–124, 1975.

[Lon82] T. Long. A note on sparse oracles for NP. *Journal of Computer and System Sciences*, 24:224–232, 1982.

[Mah82] S. Mahaney. Sparse complete sets for NP: Solution of a conjecture of Berman and Hartmanis. *Journal of Computer and System Sciences*, 25(2):130–143, 1982.

[PZ83] C. Papadimitriou and S. Zachos. Two remarks on the power of counting. In *Proceedings 6th GI Conference on Theoretical Computer Science*, pages 269–276, Springer-Verlag Lecture Notes in Computer Science #145, 1983.

[Rog67] H. Rogers, Jr. *The Theory of Recursive Functions and Effective Computability.* McGraw-Hill, 1967.

[Sch83] U. Schöning. A low and a high hierarchy in NP. *Journal of Computer and System Sciences.*, 27:14–28, 1983.

[Sch85] U. Schöning. Robust algorithms: A different approach to oracles. *Theoretical Computer Science*, 40:57–66, 1985.

[Sch86] U. Schöning. *Complexity and Structure.* Springer Verlag *Lecture Notes in Computer Science #211*, 1986.

[Sch88] U. Schöning. The power of counting. In *Proceedings 3rd Structure in Complexity Theory Conference*, IEEE Computer Society Press, June 1988. To appear.

[Sim77] J. Simon. On the difference between one and many. In *Automata, Languages, and Programming (ICALP 1977)*, pages 480–491, Springer-Verlag *Lecture Notes in Computer Science #52*, 1977.

[Sip82] M. Sipser. On relativization and the existence of complete sets. In *Automata, Languages, and Programming (ICALP 1982)*, Springer-Verlag *Lecture Notes in Computer Science #140*, 1982.

[Sto77] L. Stockmeyer. The polynomial-time hierarchy. *Theoretical Computer Science*, 3:1–22, 1977.

[SW88] U. Schöning and K. Wagner. Collapsing oracle hierarchies, census functions, and logarithmically many queries. In *STACS 1988: 5th Annual Symposium on Theoretical Aspects of Computer Science*, Springer-Verlag *Lecture Notes in Computer Science*, February 1988.

[Sze87] R. Szelepcsényi. The method of forcing for nondeterministic automata. *Bulletin of the EATCS*, (33):96–99, 1987.

[Tar87] G. Tardos. Query complexity, or why is it difficult to separate $NP^A \cap coNP^A$ from P^A by random oracles A. July 1987. Manuscript.

[Tod87] S. Toda. Σ_2SPACE[n] is closed under complement. *Journal of Computer and System Sciences*, 35:145–152, 1987.

[Tor88] Jacobo Torán. *Structural Properties of the Counting Hierarchies.* PhD thesis, Universitat Politècnica de Catalunya, Barcelona, Spain, 1988.

[Val76] L. Valiant. The relative complexity of checking and evaluating. *Information Processing Letters*, 5:20–23, 1976.

[Wag86] K. Wagner. *Some Observations on the Connection Between Counting and Recursion.* Technical Report MIP-8611, Universität Passau, Fakultät für Mathematik und Informatik, June 1986.

[Wat86] Osamu Watanabe. On hard one-way functions (Abstract). *Bulletin of the European Association for Theoretical Computer Science*, June 1986.

[Wec85] G. Wechsung. On the boolean closure of NP. In *Proceedings of the 1985 International Conference on Fundamentals of Computation Theory*, pages 485–493, Lecture Notes in Computer Science, Springer-Verlag, 1985.

[Yao85] A. Yao. Separating the polynomial-time hierarchy by oracles. In *Proceedings 26th IEEE Symposium on Foundations of Computer Science*, pages 1–10, 1985.

[Zac86] S. Zachos. Probabilistic quantifiers, adversaries, and complexity classes: An overview. In *Proceedings 1st Structure in Complexity Theory Conference*, pages 383–400, IEEE Computer Society Press, June 1986.

INDUCTIVE SYNTACTICAL SYNTHESIS OF PROGRAMS FROM SAMPLE COMPUTATIONS

E.B.Kinber
Computing Centre
Latvian State University
226250, Riga, Rainis Blvd., 29. USSR

Designing or comprehending algorithms a human usually starts with considering a number of examples and then tries to generalize them. The goal of the researches in the inductive program synthesis is to understand and formalize this process, and to design eventually practical synthesizors.

Till the last time the inductive synthesis problems were studied basically on the recursive-theoretical level: given the sequence

$$f(0),\ f(1),\ \ldots,\ f(m),\ \ldots$$

of the values of a recursive function f, it is necessary to restore an algorithm computing f (see surveys [1,2,3]. Many good results are obtained in this area, but unfortunately, the research on this level has not given useful ideas for the construction of practical synthesizors.

A.Biermann and R.Krishnaswamy proposed in 1976 [4] a method of inductive synthesis from examples of full computation traces. This method does not put any significant restrictions on the class of synthesizable programs, what inevitably yields an exhaustive search. Furthermore, the presentation of full computation traces is inconvenient for the user.

For practical synthesizors the class of synthesizable programs should be apparently limited - we have to look for simple inductive synthesis models applicable to reasonable problems within which the synthesis is effective and the specification of samples is convenient for a user. Therefore, the process of synthesis can be split in two stages: the selection of a model appropriate for the given problem and the synthesis itself.

Here we give a survey of models of syntactical inductive synthesis. In this approach the input information is regarded as a string of characters without any semantics, and the synthesis is based on the detection of purely syntactical analogies in a sample computation. The required program is synthesized in a form of a grammar specifying all possible computation traces (sample computations). Since, to specify a program means actually to specify all its sample computations. Such a grammar can be considered as some nontraditional way for presenting a program scheme as a collection of all formal computation traces. Interpreting this program scheme we obtain a real program.

Of course, purely syntactical methods are restricted. For example, no syntactical algorithm is able to separate logical conditions from actions. For instance, an explanation of the sort-merge behaviour can start with

```
a(1) ≤ b(1)? yes; then a(1) → c(1);
a(2) ≤ b(1)? no;  then b(1) → c(2);
```

or with

```
a(1) ≤ b(1) Y; c(1): = a(1);
a(2) ≤ b(1) N; c(2): = b(1);
```

here the choice of a language is dependent of a user. Any syntactical synthesis method can hardly separate logical condition in this situation. On the other hand, the advantage of syntactical methods is that they do not depend on the language chosen by a user to explain the algorithm's behaviour. This advantage is quite important, since program synthesis systems should be oriented to nonprofessional users.

The first model of inductive syntactical synthesis was developed by J.M.Barzdin [5,6]. Formalizing the notion of dots he developed a model for syntactical synthesis of programs containing only FOR-loops - the dots expressions. The basic method in this model is that of identification in sample computations fragments of arithmetical progressions.

Within this model, given an arbitrary sufficiently long sample computation, a dots expression asymptotically equivalent to the required one is synthesizable in a polynomial (from the length of the input sample) time. Thus, for the following sample computation that explains the bubble-sort algorithm in a natural way:

```
          Input A: array (1 • • 4);
If A(1) ≤ A(2) then; else A(1) <-> A(2);
If A(2) ≤ A(3) then; else A(2) <-> A(3);
If A(3) ≤ A(4) then; else A(3) <-> A(4);
If A(1) ≤ A(2) then; else A(1) <-> A(2);
If A(2) ≤ A(3) then; else A(2) <-> A(3);
If A(1) ≤ A(2) then; else A(1) <-> A(2);
                Return A,
```

we obtain the dots expression

```
           Input A: array (1 • • k);
<<If A(1) ≤ A(2) then; else A(1) <-> A(2); ○○○
  If A(k-1) ≤A(k) then; else A(k-1) <-> A(k);> ○○○
 <If A(1) ≤ A(2) then; else A(1) <-> A(2); ○○○
```

If A(1) $\leqslant$ A(2) then; else A(1) <-> A(2); >>

Return A;.

From descriptions of this kind (sample computations) it is, evidently possible to restore the general algorithm. Therefore, a description of an algorithm by the sample computations can be considered as a program in some nontraditional programming language. How to define the semantics of such language? A usual way to define semantics of a language is to translate it to another language with the semantics known in advance. Since the intended language is that of examples, it is natural to define its semantics by means of inductive synthesis rules restoring general algorithms from their sample computations.

In order to realize these ideas in the possibly most general situation the language of the so-galled general regular expressions (g.r.e.) was developed in [7].

G.r.e.-s are regular expressions over an alphabet A = A'UN, where A' is a finite alphabet, a set $X = \{x, y, \ldots\}$ of variables, assignment operators x: = c, x: = y,y,x $\in$ X, c $\in$ N, and x: = x+1, x: = x-1 (the last two operators, for the sake of brevity, are denoted below by x^+ and x^-, respectively).

Examples of g.r.e.:

P_1: $(x:=0)(a\ x^+ x)^*$

P_2: $(x:=0, y:=0)(a\ x^+ x \cup b\ y^+ y)^*$

P_3: $(x:=0)((a\ x^+ x)^* (y:=x)(b\ y^+ y)^*)^*$.

Hand-written symbols here are not reflected explicitely in sample computations (as it will be seen below); they should be restored by a synthesizor.

To define sample computations of a given g.r.e. P we first define an *unfoldment* of P replacing every expression $(Q)^*$ by Q^r for some r, and then replacing every $U_1 \cup U_2 \cup \ldots \cup U_k$ by any U_i. Thus for P_1 we obtain an unfoldment

$\bar{P}_1$: $(x:=0)a\ x^+xa\ x^+xa\ x^+xa\ x^+xa\ x^+x$, for P_2

$\bar{P}_2$: $(x:=0, y:=0)\,a\ x^+xa\ x^+xb\ y^+ya\ x^+xb\ y^+yb\ y^+y$, for P_3

$\bar{P}_3$: $(x:=0, y:=0)\ a\ x^+xa\ x^+xa\ x^+xa\ x^+x\ (y:=x)\,b\ y^+yb\ y^+ya\ x^+x$
$(y:=x)\ b\ y^+yb\ y^+ya\ x^+x\ (y:=x)\,b\ y^+yb\ y^+yb\ y^+y$.

Now we enumerate all occurences of each variable in the unfoldment. For instance, for $\bar{P}_2$ we obtain

$$(x_{(1)}:=0,\ y_{(1)}:=0)\ a\ x^+_{(2)}x_{(3)}a\ x^+_{(4)}x_{(5)}b\ y^+_{(2)}y_{(3)}a\ x^+_{(6)}x_{(7)}$$
$$b\ y^+_{(4)}y_{(5)}b\ y^+_{(6)}y_{(7)}.$$

Now if $x_{(i)}$ is the left part in an operator $x_{(i)} = \mu$, then we set $v(x_{(i)}) = \mu$, otherwise

$$v(x_{(i)}) = v(x_{(i-1)})$$

$$v(x^+_{(i)}) = v(x_{(i-1)})+1$$

$$v(x^-_{(i)}) = v(x_{(i-1)})-1$$

Then deleting the brackets (,), the operators c: = c and the values of x^+, x^-, $x \in X$, we obtain a *value* of the g.r.e. P or a (formal) *sample computation* v = v(P).

Thus, for P_1 and P_2 one obtains

$v(P_1)$ = a1a2a3a4a5

$v(P_2)$ = a1a2a3a4b1b2a5b3b4b5

Cleene star and the union $\cup$ in our language correspond to the constructions

WHILE(P) DO(d)

and respectively,

CASE ($P_1 \to d_1$, $P_2 \to d_2$, ..., $P_k \to d_k$)

in traditional programming languages. "Neutral" iteration and union are chosen instead of the traditional WHILE and CASE constructions, since predicates are not separated from actions in formal sample computations, any purely syntactical synthesizer is hardly able to separate them as well. This separation can be made only when the program is interpreted in a certain way.

The g.r.e. are called below simply programs. Let *P* denote the class of all programs.

A version of a program for the standard sort-merge can look as follows:

```
(x: =1, y: = 1, z: =1)
Input: a,b,c: arrays;
(a(x) ≤ b(y)? suppose yes,
 then a(x)  -> c(z); x+ z+
∪ a(x) ≤ b(y)? suppose no,
 then b(y)  -> c(z); y+ z+)*
((a(x) = Λ , then (b(y)  -> c(z); y+ z+)*
     b(y) = Λ, then STOP)
∪ (b(y) = Λ , then (a(x)  -> c(z); x+ z+ )*
    a(y) = Λ , then STOP). Output: c.
```

Let V(P) denote the set of all sample computations of a program P. The set V(P) can apparently be considered as a free semantics of P.

Programs P_1, P_2 are called equivalent ($P_1 \equiv P_2$) iff $V(P_1) = V(P_2)$. Note that the equivalence of this kind is much more stronger than the functional equivalence of programs.

The question of the equivalence is quite important for g.r.e., since a synthesis algorithm usually tries to construct a program equivalent to the required one.

THEOREM 1. The inclusion problem is decidable for programs in *P*. (a weaker version of the theorem was proved in [7]).

COROLLARY 1. The equivalence problem is decidable for programs in *P*.

THEOREM 2. The class *P* is closed under the intersection and the difference.

A finite diagram (of the automaton type) can be naturally defined for every program. For example, the diagram

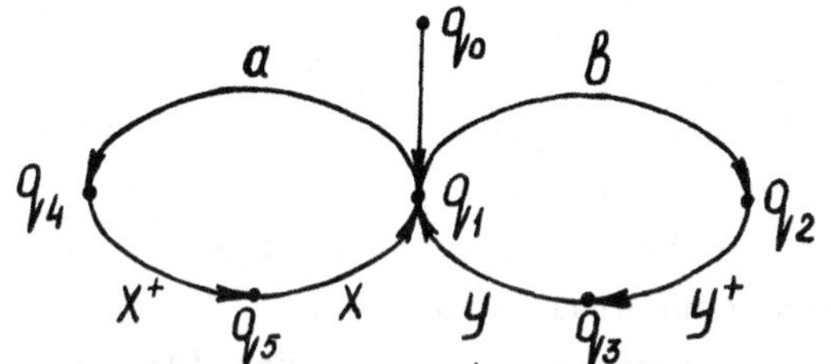

corresponds to $(x:=0, y:=0)(a\, x^+ x \cup b\, y^+ y)^*$.

The minimization means here the possibility, given a diagram D(P), to find a diagram D(P') with the minimal number of states such that V(P') $\rightleftharpoons$ V(P). The minimization problem is nontrivial, since infinitely many diagrams with the minimal number of states correspond to an arbitrary diagram in the general case.

THEOREM 3. The minimization problem for diagrams D(P), P $\in$ *P* is decidable.

It is quite clear that one (even very long) sample computation may be not sufficient for the correct synthesis of an arbitrary program in the general case. The more general problem is whether, given a g.r.e. P, one can find a finite set of sample computations that specifies P completely (otherwise no finite set of samples fits for the synthesis). In fact, we would like to define finite sets F(P) of sample computations of programs P such that

$$(F(P_1) = F(P_2)) \leftrightarrow (V(P_1) = V(P_2)).$$

This problem is open. It is solved positively in the case when programs have similar loop structures.

Since the problem of effective syntactical synthesis (even from finite sets of sample computations) can hardly be solved in the general case, we are interested to separate as wide as possible subclasses of *P* synthesizable from finite sets of samples (or one sample) in polynomial time.

First we consider the subclass of programs containing no symbol $\cup$. The point is that all partial recursive functions (p.r.f.) are expressible already in this subclass (in a very specific sense, since, in fact, no predicate is presented in programs). Therefore, the question of syntactical synthesis of programs for p.r.f. can be discussed. In order to investigate this question it will be convenient to change slightly the notion of sample computation taking into account explicitely also the values of symbols x^+ and x^- (i.e. results of x+1 and x-1). Let $\tilde{P}$ denote the subclass of such programs.

It is quite clear that any $P \in \tilde{P}$ is not synthesizable from an arbitrary (even very long) sample computation. For example, the sequence

1 2 3 4 5 6

can be a value of the program (more precisely, the fragment of a program) $(x^+)^*$, and a value of $(x^+x^+x^+)^*$ as well. No syntactical synthesizer evidently can make the right choice. Therefore we select the sublass of the so-called *canonical* programs in $\tilde{P}$ such that

(1) programs in the subclass are synthesizable from sample computations satisfying certain natural conditions,

(2) the subclass is universal (in a sense) for the class $\tilde{P}$.

To define the class of canonical programs we first define the collection of transformations over programs (many technical details are omitted). Let $P \in \tilde{P}$.

Π_1. If an expression $(R_1)^*(R_2)^*$ is in a subword of P and $R_1 \equiv R_2$ then to obtain $\Pi_1(P)$ replace $(R_1)^*(R_2)^*$ by $(R_1)^*$.

Π_2. If a subword $T(R)^*$ in P is equivalent to some expression $(R')^*T'$ then to obtain $\Pi_2(P)$ replace $T(R)^*$ by $(R')^*T'$.

Π_3. If $(R)^*S_1S_2(T_1T_2)^*$ is a subword of P, $R \equiv S_1T_1$, S_2 contains only assignments, and $S_2T_1 \equiv T_1S_2$, then to obtain $\Pi_3(P)$ replace $(R)^*S_1S_2(T_1T_2)^*$ by $(R)^*S_2(T_2T_1)^*T_2$.

(In other words, Π_2 and Π_3 "shift" loops to the left as far as possible).

Π_4. If $(R_1\ R_2\ \ldots\ R_k)^*$ is a subword of P and all R_i, $1 \leq i \leq k$, are equivalent then to obtain $\Pi_4(P)$ replace $(R_1R_2\ \ldots\ R_k)^*$ by $(R_1)^*$.

Π_5. If $S(R)^*$ or $(R)^*S$ is a subword of P and $S \equiv R$ then to obtain $\Pi_5(P)$ replace $S(R)^*$ ($R(S)^*$, respectively) by $(R)^*$.

Now let a constant $C \in N$ be fixed.

Π_6. If $R_1R_2\ \ldots\ R_C$ is a subword of P and all R_i, $1 \leq i \leq C$ are equivalent then to obtain $\Pi_6(P)$ replace $R_1R_2\ \ldots\ R_C$ by $(R_1)^*$.

Given a $C \in N$, we call a program P C-*canonical* iff no transformation $\Pi \in \{\Pi_1, \ldots \Pi_6\}$ is applicable to P. Let $\tilde{P}_C$ denote the class of all C-canonical programs.

For every Π_i the inverse transformation Π_i^{-1} evidently can be defined. The universality of a class $\tilde{P}_C$ means that any program $P \in \tilde{P}$ can be obtained from some C-canonical P' by a finite sequence of transformations Π_i, $1 \leq i \leq 6$. Canonical programs actually are programs where every sufficiently long uniform computation is induced by a loop, and all loops are "shifted" to the left as far as possible.

The synthesis of canonical programs is possible from "representative" sample computations reflecting the structure of the required program. The formal definition of a representative sample needs quite many technical details, so we restrict ourselves to an informal explanation (useful for a user, by the way): a sample computation is representative if different loops are unfolded in it "very different" numbers of times.

THEOREM 4. There exists a synthesis algorithm that, given an arbitrary representative sample computation of a C-canonical ($C \geq 2$) program P, constructs a program $P' \in \tilde{P}_C$ equivalent to P in a polynomial (on the length of the input sample) time.

Now we will consider some practically important models of the inductive synthesis (in fact, subclasses of *P*).

1. Iterative programs

We call a g.r.e. *iterative* if it does not contain symbols x^- and every x changes at most for 1 in each loop.

For example, the program for the standard sort-merge and the following program separating negative and nonnegative integers in an array a

```
        (i:=1) input: a; ((j:=1, m:=1, n:=1)
       (a(i,j) < 0? suppose yes,then
                    a(i,j)  -> b(i,m)  j+ m+
       U a(i,j) < 0? suppose no, then
                    a(i,j)  -> c(i,n)  j+ n+ )*
                    a(i,j)  = Λ , then  i+ )*
                    a(i,j)  = Λ , then STOP.
```

are iterative programs.

Like for programs in $\tilde{P}$, canonical programs and representative samples reflecting the structure of programs are defined. It must be noted that the above iterative programs for the sort-merge and for separating of negative and nonnegative integers are canonical.

Every iterative program can be easily transformed to an equivalent finite union of the so-called *indecomposable* programs containing the symbol $\cup$ only in loops.

THEOREM 5. There exists a synthesis algorithm that, given an arbitrary representative sample computation v of an indecomposable canonical iterative program P, an upper bound of the number of variables and constants in P, constructs a canonical iterative program P' equivalent to P in polynomial (on the length of the input sample) time.

For example, the iterative program for the sort-merge can be synthesized from the sample computation.

Input: a,b,c: arrays;

a(1)$\leq$b(1)? suppose yes, then a(1) $\to$ c(1);
a(2)$\leq$b(1)? suppose yes, then a(2) $\to$ c(2);
a(3)$\leq$b(1)? suppose yes, then a(3) $\to$ c(3);
a(4)$\leq$b(1)? suppose no, then b(1) $\to$ c(4);
a(4)$\leq$b(2)? suppose no, then b(2) $\to$ c(5);
a(4)$\leq$b(3)? suppose yes, then a(4) $\to$ c(6);

if a(5) = Λ , then
b(3) $\to$ c(7);
b(4) $\to$ c(8);
b(5) $\to$ c(9);
if b(6) = Λ , then STOP.

Output: c.

and a similar sample explaining the behaviour of the algorithm when the array b is exhausted before the array a.

As it was noted above, a syntactical synthesizer is not able to separate predicates and actions during the synthesis process in the general case. However, if the choice of possible logical conditions in loops is restricted and the synthesizer "knows" which logical conditions may occur in loops, then it is able to restore these conditions (predicates) and to synthesize eventually loops in a more convenient traditional form. For example, in the case of dots expressions the synthesizer "knows" that only FOR-loops may occur in programs. Of course, dots expression is a nontraditional form of programs oriented basically to the convenient inductive formalization of sample computations, however, dots expressions can be easily translated to FOR-loops in a traditional form.

We will consider some models, where the chòice of logical conditions in loops is restricted, and a synthesizer can use the according information.

2. WHILE-expressions containing interpreted functions ([8])

The logical conditions in programs in this model are predicates $x < y$, $x,y \in X \cup N$ (i.e. loops are actually of the type FOR), and programs can contain interpreted functions satisfying some natural conditions. For example, the following program computing the sum S(x) of the first x natural numbers can be written within this model:

Input: x; (z:=1, y:=1)
WHILE $(z \leq x)$ DO (y+z, obtain y; z^+)
Output: y.

Here loops in programs are presented in a traditional WHILE-form (instead of iteration in usual g.r.e.). The above program can be synthesized by the following sample computation explaining the algorithm computing S(x):

Input: 5;
[0+1, obtain 1;
1+2, obtain 3;
3+3, obtain 6;
6+4, obtain 10;
10+5, obtain 15;]
Output: 15.

Any effective syntactical synthesis from sample computations is hardly possible in this model. So samples are annotated by brackets [,] showing boundaries of loops in the required program. If samples have annotations of this kind, programs in this model are synthesizable in a polynomial time. The correctness of the synthesis algorithm is proved. Definitely, from the practical point of view more interesting is the case when annotations fix loop boundaries only approximately: in this case the synthesis algorithm becomes heuristic.

3. WHILE-expressions with logical conditions $(x_1 \leq y_1) \wedge (x_2 \leq y_2)$ ([8])

Loop conditions in this model contain only predicates $x \leq y$, $x,y \in X \cup N$, and their conjunctions. Note that values of logical conditions do not occur in sample computations (explaining the behaviour of a program) explicitely; of course, they are implicitely reflected in samples. One of the main synthesizer's goals is to restore these logical conditions.

For example,

(x:=0) WHILE $(x \leq y)$ DO (bxx^+)

is a program in this model.

Its value (sample computation) for y = 7 is

b0b1b2b3b4b5b6b7.

The program for the standard sort-merge can be the following:

Input: A: array (1 ... x_0), B: array (1 ... y_0),
C: array (1 ... x_0+y_0);
WHILE $((x \leq x_0) \wedge (y \leq y_0))$
DO (CASE : A(x) $\leq$ B(y)? Suppose yes,

then C(z): = A(x) $x^+ z^+$;
A(x) < B(y); Suppose no,
then C(z): = B(y) $y^+ z^+$;
WHILE ($x \leq x_0$) DO (C(z): = A(x) $x^+ z^+$)
WHILE ($y \leq y_0$) DO (C(z): = B(y) $y^+ z^+$)
Output: C.

This program apparently is more similar to any traditional form.

A synthesis algorithm is developed that, given a finite set of representative sample computations with annotations showing loop boundaries constructs the required program. The algorithm updates every input sample in a polynomial time. However, every new loop with a condition $(x_1 \leq y_1) \wedge (x_2 \leq y_2)$ actually doubles the number of samples necessary for the correct synthesis.

4. Inductive synthesis from partial sample computations

Sample computations necessary for the synthesis should be very long for very many algorithms. On the other hand, a sample computation can often be divided to fragments which contain similar sequences of actions. For algorithms of this kind it is quite natural to use for the synthesis only a partial sample computation sufficient for the program specification, and then to inform the synthesizer that the required program works further in the similar way.

A model of synthesis is developed that enables to synthesize programs from partial samples. This model combines tools convenient for the syntactical synthesis (say, iteration and union) with traditional programming tools as WHILE-statements. The polynomial-time synthesis from an arbitrary representative sample computation is possible within this model when values of variables in the sample computation are annotated by these variables.

For example, let us consider the following partial sample computation that explains the behaviour of a version of the well-known quicksort algorithm (the annotations are in brackets [,]):

Input: array K(1), K(2), ..., K(8 [=m]);
x_0:=1; y_0:= 8[=m]; x: = x_0; y: =y_0;
stack: =(1[=x_0], 8[=y] WHILE (¬Emp(stack)) DO
((x_0, y_0): = stack;
x: =1[=y_0]; y: = 8[=y_0];
K(1[=x]) ≤ K(8 [=y])?; suppose yes;
K(1[=x]) ≤ K(7[=y])?; suppose yes;
K(1[=x]) ≤ K(6[=4])?; suppose yes;
K(1[=x]) ≤ K(5[=y])?; suppose no;

```
        K(1[=x]) <-> K(5[=y]):
  K(2[=x]) ≤ K(5[=y])?; suppose yes;
  K(3[=x]) ≤ K(5[=y])?; suppose yes;
        K(4[=x]) <-> K(5[=y=x+1]);
  stack: =(5[=x+1], 8[=y0]); y0: =3[=x-1];
        x: =1[=x0]; y: =3[=y0]; P.
```

Here the special symbol P in the end of the sample computations means "to repeat the same actions for new values of variables". The given sample computation is, in fact, a linear representation of the explanation of the quicksort, given in [9]. This sample is sufficient for the synthesis (in polynomial time) of the following program:

```
  Input: array K(1), K(2), ..., K(m),
         x0: =1, y0: =m;
  stack: =(x0,y0) WHILE (¬Emp(stack)) DO((x0,y0): =stack);
     WHILE (x0 ≠ y0) DO ((x: =x0, y: =y0)
         WHILE (x ≠ y) DO
  ((K(x) ≤ K(y)?; suppose yes; y-)*
    K(x) ≤ K(y)?; suppose no;
        K(x) <-> K(y); x+
   (K(x) ≤ K(y)?; suppose yes; x+)*
    K(x) ≤ K(y)?; suppose no;
        K(x) <-> K(y); y-)
  stack: =(x+1, y0); y0: =x-1;))
```

All models discussed above can be easily translated to traditional programming languages if a certain interpretation of programs is specified. But that is not a subject of our paper.

The author is very grateful to J.M.Barzdin and A.N.Brazma for valuable discussions.

REFERENCES

1. Barzdin J.M. Inductive inference of automata, functions and programs. - Proc.Intern.Math. Congress, Vancouver, 1974, v.2, p.455-460.

2. Angluin D., Smith C.H. Inductive inference: theory and methods. - Computing Surveys, 1983, v.15, N 3, p.237-259.

3. Klette R., Wiehagen R. Research in the theory of inductive inference by GDR mathematicians - a survey. - Inform.Sci., 1980, v.22, p.149-169.

4. Biermann A.W., Krishnaswamy R. Constructing programs from example computations. - IEEE Trans. Soft.Eng. SE-2, 1976, p.141-153.

5. Barzdin J.M. An approach to the problem of inductive inference. In: "Applications of methods of math. logic"., Proc. of the 3-rd Conf. Tallin, 1983, p.16-28 (in Russian).

6. Barzdin J.M. Some rules of inductive inference and their use for program synthesis. - Inf. Processing 83, IFIP, North-Holland, 1983, p.333-338.

7. Brazma A.N., Kinber E.B. Generalized regular expressions - a language for synthesis of programs with branching in loops. - Theor.Com.Sci., 1986, v.46, p.175-195.

8. Barzdin J.M., Brazma A.N., Kinber E.B. Inductive synthesis: the state, problems, perspectives. - Kybernetika, Kiev, 1987, N 6, p.81-87(in Russian).

9. Knuth D.E. The art of computer programming, 1973, v.3, Addison-Wesley.

3-Dimensional Shortest Paths in the Presence of Polyhedral Obstacles

John H. Reif[†]
Computer Science Department
Duke University
Durham, NC 27706

James A. Storer[††]
Computer Science Department
Brandeis University
Waltham, MA 02254

Keywords: Mover's problem, minimal movement problem, shortest path, Euclidean space, robotics motion planning, Voronoi diagram, quadratic curves, theory of real closed fields.

Abstract: We consider the problem of finding a minimum length path between two points in 3-dimensional Euclidean space which avoids a set of (not necessarily convex) polyhedral obstacles; we let n denote the number of the obstacle edges and k denote the number of "islands" in the obstacle space. An island is defined to be a maximal convex obstacle surface such that for any two points contained in the interior of the island, a minimal length path between these two points is strictly contained in the interior of the island; for example, a set of i disconnected convex polyhedra forms a set of i islands, however, a single non-convex polyhedron will constitute more that one island. Prior to this work, the best known algorithm required double-exponential time. We present an algorithm that runs in $n^{k^{O(1)}}$ time and also one that runs in $O(n^{log(k)})$ space.

Introduction

The classical *mover's problem* is: Given a *source point* and a *destination point* along with a set of polyhedral *obstacles* in a $d \geq 2$ Euclidean space, can a given polyhedron (often referred to as a *sofa* or *piano)* be moved from the source point to the destination point without comming in contact with any of the obstacles. The *generalized mover's problem* allows the object to be moved to consist of a collection of polyhedra freely linked together at various vertices. Both the classical and generalized mover's problems have obvious applications to robotics mo-

† This work was partially supported by the Office of Naval Research grant number N000-14-80-C-0647 and was completed while this author was visiting the Laboratory for Computer Science at MIT.
†† This work was partially supported by NSF grant number DCR-8403244.

tion planning problems and have been of interest to researchers in this field for some time (see Lozano-Perez and Wesley [1979], and Lozano-Perez [1980]). Although the generalized mover's problem is PSPACE-hard (Reif [1979]), even for planar reachability of simple linkages (Hopcroft, Joseph, and Whitesides [1982b], Joseph and Plantinga [1985]), the classical mover's problem can be solved in polynomial time (Reif [1979], Schwartz and Sharir [1981,1982]). In addition, there has been much recent work pertaining to special cases and variations of both the generalized and classical mover's problems (e.g. Kedem and Sharir [1985], Leven and Sharir [1985], Hopcroft and Wilfong [1984,1984b], Bajaj [1984], O'Dunlaing, Sharir, and Yap [1983], Hopcroft, Joseph, and Whitesides [1982,1982b,1982c], Schwartz and Sharir [1981,1982]). The work mentioned above is concerned with the existence of a movement. In this paper, we consider the *minimal movement problem;* that is, determining the shortest possible movement, if one exists. We shall always assume 3-dimensional space to be Euclidean and will not bother to include the term "Euclidean" from this point on.

We restrict our attention to the 3-dimensional minimal movement problem where the object to be moved is a single point; that is, the *shortest path problem* 3-dimensional Euclidean space. Besides its relevance to computational geometry, this apparently simple problem is fundamental to more general versions of the minimal movement problem. One application of the efficient computation of minimal movement is to robotics. For example, consider a warehouse with a robot server that must repeatedly proceed from a source point (the service window) to various points in the warehouse (to retrieve objects).

Throughout this paper, we let n, the *size* of the obstacle space, denote the number of obstacle edges. An *island* is defined to be a maximal convex obstacle surface such that for any two points contained in the interior of the island, a minimal length path between these two points is strictly contained in the interior of the island; for example, a set of i disconnected polyhedra forms a set of i islands, however, a single non-convex polyhedra will constitute more that one island. Throughout this paper we let k denote the minimum number of islands into which the obstacle space can be decomposed. Note that k can easily be computed within the time bounds we use to solve the corresponding problems.

One of the inherent difficulties with computing shortest paths in three dimensional spaces is that although shortest paths are sequences of line segments that start and end on obstacle edges, they do not necessarily pass through obstacle vertices. Furthermore, the length of a minimal length path as well as the coordinates through which it passes may not be rational numbers. At best, one can only output a minimal path to within a given accuracy. However, it is also reasonable to consider the problem of testing whether a given rational length is achievable; Sharir and Schorr [1984] present a doubly exponential time algorithm to do this. Both Sharir and Schorr [1984] and Franklin and Akman [1984] give a polynomial time algorithm for the special case in 3-dimensions where the two points lie on the surface of a convex polyhedron. O'Rourke, Suri, and Booth [1984] generalize this work to obtain an algorithm for minimal movement on the surface of a non-convex polyhedron. Papadimitriou [1984] presents a fully polynomial approximation scheme for computing an approximate rational path, but this does not provide a test as to whether a given rational length is achievable. Franklin, Akman, and Verrilli [1984] consider generalizations of the Voronoi diagram that may be useful for algorithms relating to shortest path problems. However, prior to work presented in this paper, it has been an open problem as to whether an algorithm better than double-exponential time exists for the general 3-dimensional case. Canny and Reif [1987] have shown the problem to be NP-hard; hence, a single-exponential time algorithm is the best that can be reasonably expected. Here, we present an $n^{k^{O(1)}}$ time algorithm for finding the shortest path between two points (that avoids arbitrary polyhedral obstacles); this yields polynomial time when k is $O(1)$ and at most single-exponential time in general. In addition, this algorithm has an implementation that uses $n^{O(log(k))}$ space. Our algorithm for 3-dimensions employs the theory of real closed fields and works as follows. First, we show how to express a minimal length path as a formula. Second, we show how to rewrite this formula so that it is polynomial in length. Third, we show that the formula need only have $O(log(k))$ variables. Then, we can employ previously known algorithms for the theory of real closed fields. Our model of computation for our 3-space algorithm is the standard log-cost RAM†.

A 3-Dimensional Shortest Path Algorithm

In this section, we derive a single exponential time upper bound on the complexity of finding the shortest path between two points in a three dimensional obstacle space. Our approach will be to express paths as formulas in the theory of real closed fields.

Definition 1: A three dimensional *obstacle space* consists of a set of disjoint polyhedra. An *island* is defined to be a maximal convex obstacle surface such that for any two points contained in the interior of the island, a shortest path between these two points is strictly contained in the interior of the island; for example, a set of i disconnected polyhedra forms a set of i islands, however, a single non-convex polyhedra will constitute more that one island. ○

We use the following notation:

- n denotes the number of obstacle edges and k the minimum number of islands that can represent the space.
- $E = \{e_1 \cdots e_n\}$ denotes the set of obstacle edges; for convenience, we assume that obstacle edges are directed, so that we can talk about traversing an obstacle edge from its "start point" to its "end point".
- If edge $e=(u,v)$ has length l, then for $0 \leq \delta \leq 1$, let $e(x)$ denote the point

† See, for example, Aho, Hopcroft, and Ullman [1974].

on e of distance $x\delta$ from u (i.e., $e(0)=u$ and $e(1)=v$).

- $s=e_1(0)$ denotes the source vertex and $t=e_n(0)$ denotes the destination vertex†.

Without loss of generality, we always assume that s and t are vertices of some island. That is, if s and/or t are not on the surface of some island, islands consisting of single points can be created for them (such an island can be thought of as single edge of length 0). If s and/or t are on island surfaces but are not vertices, at most four new obstacle edges can be added to make s and/or t a vertex. For example, if s is in the interior of some face F, then pass two line segments through s to divide F into four faces. Note that the resulting polyhedron is not technically legal (since these new four faces will be co-planar), but this does not effect our construction.

Definition 2: A *direct* path in a three dimensional obstacle space is a straight line segment that does not intersect any island except at its endpoints. A *contact* path is a one dimensional curve which lies entirely on the surface of an island and has the property that is it a minimal length path between its endpoints. A *fundamental* path is on that consists of a direct path followed by a contact path. ○

Fact 1 (Sharir and Schorr [1984]): A contact path between two points a and b which lie on (possibly different) edges of an island consisting of $O(m)$ edges consists of a sequence of at most $O(m)$ straight line segments such that the endpoints of these line segments lie on the edges of the island. In addition, this contact path can be computed in time polynomial in m†.

Definition 3: A *normal* path is a sequence of (at most k) fundamental paths such that intersects each island in at most one contact path††. ○

Lemma 1: In a three dimensional obstacle space with k islands, if a shortest path between two points s and t has length l, then there is a normal path between s and t of length l.

Proof: This follows from the observation that the intersection of any minimal length path with an island must be a connected set. ○

An *open formula* $F(x_1 \cdots x_m)$ in the theory of real closed fields consists of a logical expression containing conjunctions, disjunctions, negations, and inequalities between rational polynomials in the variables $x_1 \cdots x_m$. A (partially quantified) formula in this theory is of the form $Q_1 x_{i_1} \cdots Q_r x_{i_r} F(x_1 \cdots x_m)$ where $r \leq m$; its *degree* is the maximum degree of any polynomial within the formula. Our approach is to show that for a given length l, we can describe by a formula (with re-

† Sharir and Schorr [1984] present an algorithm for computing the shortest path between two points on a convex polyhedron that works by "unfolding" the polyhedron and then computing shortest paths on flat surfaces. O'Rourke, Suri, and Booth [1984] generalize this work for a single non-convex polyhedron.
†† This definition is motivated by ideas from Reif and Sharir [1984].

latively short length and small number of quantifiers) the paths of length l between the source and destination. Once this has been done, we can make use of the following facts.

Fact 2 (Collins [1975])† Given a formula in the theory of real closed fields of length l, degree d, and v variables, satisfiability can be tested in time $(dl)^{2^{O(v)}}$. ○

Fact 3 (Ben-Or, Kozen, and Reif [1984]): Given a formula in the theory of real closed fields of length l, degree d, and v variables, satisfiability can be tested using space $(dl)^{O(v)}$. ○

We are now ready to state the main result of this section.

Theorem 1: Given two points s and t in a three dimensional obstacle space and a length l, in $n^{k^{O(1)}}$ time it is possible to determine whether there is a path between s and t of length l.

Proof: We first define the following predicates:

$D(i_1,i_2,\delta_1,\delta_2,l)$ is true if and only if there exists a direct path from $e_{i_1}(\delta_1)$ to $e_{i_2}(\delta_2)$ of length l.

$C(i_1,i_2,\delta_1,\delta_2,l)$ is true if and only if there exists a contact path from $e_{i_1}(\delta_1)$ to $e_{i_2}(\delta_2)$ of length l.

$N(i_1,i_2,\delta_1,\delta_2,l)$ is true if and only if there exists a normal path from $e_{i_1}(\delta_1)$ to $e_{i_2}(\delta_2)$ of length l.

A polynomial length formula for D can be constructed by checking for visibility and a polynomial length formula for C follows from Fact 1. A formula for N can be constructed as follows:

$$N^{(1)}(i_1,i_2,\delta_1,\delta_2,l) = \exists\, i_3\delta_3 l_1 l_2((l{=}l_1{+}l_2) \wedge D(i_1,i_3,\delta_1,\delta_3,l_1) \wedge C(i_3,i_2,\delta_3,\delta_2,l_2)$$

$$N^{(2j)}(i_1,i_2,\delta_1,\delta_2,l) = \exists\, i_3\delta_3 l_1 l_2((l{=}l_1{+}l_2) \wedge N^{(j)}(i_1,i_3,\delta_1,\delta_3,l_1) \wedge N^{(j)}(i_3,i_2,\delta_3$$

$$N = N^{(2^{\lceil \log_2(k) \rceil})}$$

As written above, the formula for N is not polynomial in length, due sub-formula duplication in the definition of $N^{(2j)}$. However, this duplication can be eliminated by the transformation that replaces the expression

$$f(\overline{a}) \wedge f(\overline{b})$$

† For slightly improved bounds, the reader can refer to Chistov & Grigor'ev [1985].

by the expression

$$\forall\overline{x}((\overline{x}=\overline{a} \vee x=\overline{b}) \rightarrow f(\overline{x}))$$

($\overline{a}$, $\overline{b}$, and $\overline{x}$ denote vectors of 5 variables). With this modification the above definition of $N^{(2i)}$ yields a a formula for N that has polynomial length, constant degree, and $O(log(k))$ variables. Hence, the theorem follows from Fact 2. ○

Corollary 1a: Within the time bounds stated by Theorem 1, the length of a path between s and t can be computed to within a polynomial number of bits of accuracy.

Proof: Given the test procedure provided by Theorem 1, these bits can be determined with binary search. ○

Corollary 1b: Given two points s and t in a three dimensional obstacle space and a length l, in $n^{O(log(k))}$ space it is possible to determine whether there is a path between s and t of length l.

Proof: Use Fact 3 instead of Fact 2.2 in the proof of Theorem 1. ○

References

C. Bajaj [1984]. "Reducibility among Geometric Location-Allocation Optimization Problems", Technical Report TR84-607, Computer Science Dept., Cornell University, Ithaca, NY.

M. Ben-Or, D. Kozen, and J. Reif [1984]. "The Complexity of Elementary Algebra and Geometry", *Proceedings* 16th *ACM Symposium on the Theory of Computing,* Washington, DC, 457-464.

J. Canny and J. H. Reif [1987]. "New Lower Bounds for Robot Motion Planning Problems", Proceedings 28th Annual IEEE Symposium on the Foundations of Computer Science, Los Angeles, CA, 49-60.

A. L. Chistov and D. Yu. Grigor'ev [1985]. "Complexity of Quantifier Elimination in the Theory of Algebraically Closed Fields", Technical Report, Institute of the Academy of Sciences, Leningrad, USSR.

G. E. Collins [1975]. "Quantifier Elimination for Real Closed Fields by Cylindric Algebraic Decomposition", *Proceedings Second GI Conference on Automata Theory and Formal Languages,* Springer-Verlag LNCS 35, Berlin, 134-183.

W. R. Franklin and V. Akman [1984]. "Minimal Paths Between Two Points

On/Around A Convex Polyhedron", Technical Report, Electrical, Computer, and Systems Engineering Dept., Rensselaer Polytechnic Institute, Troy, NY.

W. R. Franklin, V. Akman, and C. Verrilli [1984]. "Voronoi Diagrams with Barriers and on Polyhedra", Technical Report, Electrical, Computer, and Systems Engineering Dept., Rensselaer Polytechnic Institute, Troy, NY.

J. E. Hopcroft, D. A. Joseph, and S. H. Whitesides [1982]. "On the Movement of Robot Arms in 2-Dimensional Bounded Regions", Proceedings 23rd IEEE Symposium on Foundations of Computer Science", Chicago, IL, 280-289.

J. E. Hopcroft, D. A. Joseph, and S. H. Whitesides [1982b]. "Movement Problems for 2-Dimensional Linkages", Technical Report TR82-515, Computer Science Dept., Cornell University, Ithaca, NY.

J. E. Hopcroft, D. A. Joseph, and S. H. Whitesides [1982c]. "Determining Points of a Circular Region Reachable by Joints of a Robot Arm", Technical Report TR82-516, Computer Science Dept., Cornell University, Ithaca, NY.

J. E. Hopcroft and G. Wilfong [1984]. "On the Motion of Objects in Contact", Technical Report TR84-602, Computer Science Dept., Cornell University, Ithaca, NY.

J. E. Hopcroft and G. Wilfong [1984b]. "Reducing Multiple Object Motion Planning to Graph Searching", Technical Report TR84-616, Computer Science Dept., Cornell University, Ithaca, NY.

D. A. Joseph and W. H. Plantinga [1985]. "On the Complexity of Reachability and Motion Planning Questions", Proceedings First Annual Conference of Computational Geometry, Baltimore, MD, 62-66.

K. Kedem and M. Sharir [1985]. "An Efficient Algorithm for Planning Collision-Free Translational Motion of a Convex Polyhedral Object in 2-Dimensional Space Admidst Polygonal Obstacles", Proceedings First Annual Conference of Computational Geometry, Baltimore, MD, 75-80.

D. Leven and M. Sharir [1985]. "An Efficient and Simple Motion Planning Algorithm for a Ladder Moving in Two-Dimensional Space Admidst Polygonal Barriers", Proceedings First Annual Conference of Computational Geometry, Baltimore, MD, 221-227.

T. Lozano-Perez [1980]. "Automatic Planning of Manipulation Transfer Movements", AI Memo 606, Artificial Intelligence Laboratory, MIT, Cambridge, MA.

T. Lozano-Perez and M. A. Wesley [1979]. "An Algorithm for Planning Collision-Free Paths among Polyhedral Obstacles", *CACM* 22:10, 560-570.

C. O'Dunlaing, M. Sharir, and C. K. Yap [1983]. "Retraction: A New Approach to Motion Planning", *Proceedings* 15th *ACM Symposium on the Theory of Computing,* Boston, MA, 207-220.

J. O'Rourke, S. Suri, and H. Booth [1984]. "Shortest Paths on Polyhedral Surfaces", Technical Report, Dept. of Electrical Engineering and Computer Science, Johns Hopkins University.

C. H. Papadimitriou [1984]. "An Algorithm for Shortest Path Motion in Three Dimensions", Technical Report, Stanford University.

J. Reif [1979]. "Complexity of the Mover's Problem", *Proceedings* 20th *IEEE Symposium on Foundations of Computer Science",* San Juan, Puerto Rico, 421-427; also to appear in *Planning,* Geometry, and the Complexity of Robot Planning, ed. by J. Schwartz..

J. T. Schwartz and M. Sharir [1981]. "On the Piano Movers Problem 1: The Case of a 2-Dimensional Rigid Polygonal Body Moving Amidst Barriers", Technical Report TR39, Computer Science Dept., New York University, NY.

J. T. Schwartz and M. Sharir [1982]. "On the Piano Movers Problem 2: General Techniques for Computing Topological Properties of Real Algebraic Manifolds", Technical Report TR41, Computer Science Dept., New York University, NY.

M. Sharir and A. Schorr [1984]. "On Shortest Paths in Polyhedral Spaces", *Proceedings* 16th *ACM Symposium on the Theory of Computing,* Washington, DC, 144-153.

ROBUST ORACLE MACHINES

Uwe Schöning
EWH Koblenz, Informatik
Rheinau 3-4, D5400 Koblenz
W. Germany

Abstract. The notion of a robust oracle machine and an oracle set "helping" a robust oracle machine has been introduced for better understanding the nondeterministic "witness searching" process in NP problems. It is shown that straightforward modifications of the original notion are closely related with other concepts in structural complexity theory, such as "self-reducibility", "lowness", and "interactive proof systems".

0. Notation

We assume the reader is familar with the standard notions and results in (structural) complexity theory, like the definitions of the classes P and NP, and polynomial-time reducibility (see [BDG]). For a Turing machine M, we denote by L(M) the set accepted by M, and for an oracle Turing machine M, L(M,A) is the set accepted by M when using A as the oracle set. For a class of sets C, let co-C be the class of the complements of the sets in C. A probabilistic Turing machine is a nondeterministic Turing machine with a new acceptance definition: Each nondeterministic branch is assigned the same probability, and a probabilistic Turing machine "accepts" an input (in the probab. sense) if the probability for reaching an accepting state exceeds 1/2. A probabilistic Turing machine has bounded error if the acceptance probability is either $\geq 1/2 + \delta$ or $\leq 1/2 - \delta$, for all inputs x and a uniform constant $\delta>0$. The class of sets acceptable (in the probabilistic sense) by polynomial-time bounded-error probabilistic Turing machines is denoted by BPP (cf. [Gi]). It is known that each set in BPP has "polynomial-size circuits" (see [BG],[Sch1],[BDG]), and is included in the second level of the polynomial-time hierarchy ([Si],[La], cf. also [Sch1],[BDG]).
A probabilistic Turing machine with accepting, rejecting and neutral final states is zero-error, if for every x, Prob[M(x) accepts] $\cdot$Prob [M(x) rejects] = 0. The class of sets accepted (in the probabilistic sense) by polynomial-time, zero-error probabilistic Turing machines is denoted ZPP (for more discussion see [Gi],[Sch1],[BDG]). Note that ZPP = R $\cap$ co-R (R is defined in [AM], and is denoted VPP in [Gi]), and that ZPP, R and co-R are included in BPP.

1. Introduction and the Basic Result

When studying resource-bounded computational models and reducibilities, it is reasonable to look at the effect of restricting the oracle Turing machine model, either in the available computational resources, or in the access mechanism to the oracle, or restricting the class of allowed oracles such as sparse oracles - or combinations of the above restrictions. The idea of a robust oracle machine arose from such investigations on restricting oracle machines, but it has a different flavour since it addresses the behaviour of the oracle machine under every potential oracle.

Definition. An oracle machine M is robust if it always accepts the same set - independent of the oracle that is used.

Even if the oracle information is not allowed to affect the acceptance behaviour of the robust machine, it still might "help" the machine - in the sense of speeding up the computation.

Definition. An oracle set A (polynomially) helps a robust oracle machine M on a set S if there is a polynomial p such that, for all x in S, M on input x with oracle set A halts within $p(|x|)$ moves.

Within this chapter we will only consider the case $S = \Sigma^*$ (later we consider also the case $S = L(M,A)$). I.e. we are looking for situations where the machine M with an arbitrary oracle is running in exponential time, but when a particular oracle A is used, then M^A runs in polynomial time. First, we formalize the class of sets that can be "helped" in this sense, and then we prove that this class coincides with NP $\cap$ co-NP.

Definition. Let $P_{help}(A)$ be the class of languages that can be computed by some robust oracle machine M, such that A helps M (on Σ^*). For a class of sets **C**, let $P_{help}(\mathbf{C})$ be $\bigcup\{P_{help}(A) \mid A \text{ in } \mathbf{C}\}$. Finally, let $P_{help} = P_{help}(2^{\Sigma^*})$.

The definitions given here are from [Sch2] and [Ko1]. The following result is from [Sch2].

Theorem 1. $P_{help} = NP \cap co\text{-}NP$.

Proof. Let L = L(M,A) for a robust oracle machine M and an oracle set A that helps M on Σ^*. There is a polynomial p such that M on x using oracle A makes at most $p(|x|)$ steps. We can assume, on no computation, M asks the oracle for the same string twice. Let M' be a nondet. (non-oracle) machine which operates like M, but treats each oracle query as a nondeterministic guess. Further, M' shuts off each computation after $p(|x|)$ steps. Then, by robustness of M, it can be seen that M' witnesses both, $L \in NP$ and $\bar{L} \in NP$, hence $L \in NP \cap \text{co-NP}$.

Conversely, let L be in NP $\cap$ co-NP. Then there are two polynomial-time predicates B_1 and B_2 such that

$$L = \{ x \mid \exists y \;\; B_1(x,y) \} \text{ and } \bar{L} = \{ x \mid \exists z \;\; B_2(x,z) \} .$$

The range of the y's and z's is bounded by a polynomial p. By the fact that NP $\cap$ co-NP is included in $\bigcup_k \text{DTIME}(2^{n^k})$, there is an exponential-time deterministic machine M_L that accepts L. Then, the following oracle machine M robustly accepts L.

```
input x ;
w := e ;   (* the empty string *)
for i := 1 to p(|x|) do
   if (x,w0) ε ORACLE then w := w0
                       else w := w1 ;
if B1(x,w) is true then halt accepting ;
if B2(x,w) is true then halt rejecting ;
start the machine ML on input x ;
```

It should be clear that if this machine uses the following set A as the oracle, then it runs in polynomial time, hence A helps M (on Σ^*).

$$A = \{ (x,u) \mid \text{if } x \in L \text{ then } u \text{ is prefix of some string } y \text{ such that } B_1(x,y); \text{ otherwise } u \text{ is prefix of some string } z \text{ such that } B_2(x,z) \} .$$

#

Since the oracle set A can be seen to be in NP, we get the following

Corollary. $P_{help}(NP) = NP \cap \text{co-NP}$.

We donot claim that these results are particularly complicated and deep, but we think the theorem shows in a nice way what role the nondeterminism in the "witness search" process plays, because in the robust oracle machine model there is a clear separation between the computational part (the machine M) and the nondeterministic part (the helping oracle).

We want to point out that this is very much like the role of the "verifier" and the "prover" in the notion of interactive proof systems

[GMR], and indeed, we will later see that a probabilistic version of our model naturally leads to the notion of an interactive proof system.

We cite another result from [Sch2] which says that when the oracle space is restricted to languages in BPP, then the robust oracle machine accepts only languages in ZPP. (Notice that ZPP is included in NP $\cap$ co-NP = P_{help}, but the inclusion is not known to be proper). The ability of turning the bounded-error situation in the oracle to a zero-error situation in the set which the oracle machine accepts stems from the robustness condition on the oracle machine.

Theorem 2. $P_{help}(BPP) \subseteq ZPP$.

It is an open problem whether the inverse inclusion holds.

2. One-Sided Helping and Self-Helping

The robustness and helping notion as described so far helps understanding the nature of the P vs. NP $\cap$ co-NP problem. But very little is known about the P vs. NP $\cap$ co-NP question. Much more structural notions and results are known in the context of the P vs. NP problem (except a proof of "P$\neq$NP"), notions like completeness, self-reducibility, etc. have been studied extensively. Hence, in [Ko1] a modified, 1-sided version of robustness and helping is introduced which is a better tool for studying structural properties connected with the P vs. NP problem.

Definition. [Ko1] An oracle set A 1-helps a robust oracle machine M if A helps M on L(M,A) (which, by robustness, is the same as L(M,$\emptyset$)). Define $P_{1\text{-}help}(-)$ and $P_{1\text{-}help}$ analogously to $P_{help}(-)$ and P_{help}.

Modifying the proofs of Theorems 1 and 2 easily shows:

Theorem 3. $P_{1\text{-}help}$ = NP (and actually, $P_{1\text{-}help}(NP)$ = NP).

Theorem 4. $P_{1\text{-}help}(BPP) \subseteq R$.

This 1-sided definition has the advantage that for the NP sets the class of helpers coincides with the class of helpees. Every set in NP can be 1-helped by a set in NP, but it is not clear whether every set in NP can 1-help itself. We will later see that this is very closely related with the notion of self-reducibility (cf.[Ko2],[MP],[BBS],[Bal]).

If a set A does 1-help itself, more formally, if $A \in P_{1-help}(A)$, then we call A a self-1-helper. It is not at all clear whether every set in NP is a self-1-helper. In fact this would have some interesting consequences. But, e.g., the satisfiability problem, SAT, is a self-1-helper, as is demonstrated by the following algorithm (cf. [BDG,p.32]). (Hereby, G_a where $a \in \{0,1\}$ is the formula which results from G by fixing every occurence of the first variable in G to the constant a).

```
input F ;  (* F is a Boolean formula with n variables *)
G := F ;
for i := 1 to n do
   if G_0 ∈ ORACLE then begin
                           G := G_0 ;
                           a_i := 0
                        end
                   else begin
                           G := G_1 ;
                           a_i := 1
                        end ;
if F(a_1,...,a_n) ≡ TRUE then halt accepting
                        else start an exhaustive search algorithm to
                             determine whether F is satisfiable
                             or not ;
```

Theorem 3 says that all sets which can be 1-helped are in NP, and this is in particular true for all self-1-helpers. Although the graph non-isomorphism problem (i.e. the complement of the graph isomorphism problem) is not known to be in NP, it is "almost" a self-1-helper (and hence, "almost" in NP), as the following (probabilistic) algorithm shows.

```
input (G_1,G_2) ;(* two undirected, finite graphs *)
randomly choose i ∈ {1,2}, and randomly choose a permutation π
   of the vertices of G_i. Let the resulting graph  π(G_i) be H ;
if ( (G_1,H) ∈ ORACLE ) iff ( i=2 ))then halt accepting
   else start an exhaustive search algorithm to determine whether
        G_1 and G_2 are isomorphic or not ;
```

Clearly, this algorithms does not strictly fit in the definition of self-1-helping by two reasons: First, the algorithm is not deterministic, but acts probabilistically. Hence the outcome of the algorithm (accept or reject) is a random variable, and is not uniquely determined by the input and the oracle set, but also depends on the random choices.

This means secondly, that there is a small chance that the outcome of the machine is erroneous, hereby contradicting the robustness condition. But nevertheless, the properties of this machine come very close to a witness that graph non-isomorphism is a self-1-helper:

(1) There is an oracle A (namely Graph Non-Isomorphism itself) such that for any two non-isomorphic graphs as input, M always accepts (i.e. with probability 1), and does so in polynomial time (hence A 1-helps M). Further, in the case of two non-isomorphic graphs as input, even with "wrong" oracles, the machine does not make a mistake, just runs possibly in exponential time.

(2) If the input consists of two isomorphic graphs, then no matter what the oracle is, with probability at least 1/2 the machine answers correct (in exponential time), whereas with the remaining probability (at most 1/2) the algorithm erroneously accepts. (This is in conflict with the robustness condition, but observe, that by a standard iteration argument the machine M can be modified to a machine M' (which asks more oracle questions) and where the error probability is just 2^{-n} instead 1/2 - and all other stated properties are maintained.)

This notion could be made more formal (which we will not do here), and hereby it could be shown that Graph Non-Isomorphism is a "probabilistic self-1-helper", and hence, is "almost" in NP. Note that our treatment is actually a reformulation of the interactive proof protocol for the graph non-isomorphism problem presented in [GMW], with the additional aspect of <u>self</u>-helping. The notion of "almost-NP" is then captured by the class IP(2) = AM(2) (cf. [GS],[BHZ],[Bab] ,[Sch3],[Sch4]).
In [AFK] and in [TW] notions of "random self-reducibility" are developed, and in [TW] it is shown that graph isomorphism is random self-reducible according to their definition. The precise relationship to the above treatment is, to the author's knowledge, not yet clear.

(Deterministic) self-reducibility can be defined as follows.

<u>Definition</u>. A set A is <u>self-reducible</u> if there is a deterministic, polynomial-time oracle machine M such that A = L(M,A) and such that each "query tree" T(M,A,x) associated with an input x has polynomially bounded depth. The query tree T(M,A,x) is defined as follows: The root of this tree is labeled with x, and the subtrees below the root are the trees $T(M,A,y_1),\ldots,T(M,A,y_k)$ where $y_1,\ldots,y_k$ are all the strings queried by M on input x using oracle A. A set A is disjunctively (or d-) self-reducible if A is self-reducible via some machine M which has the additional property that M accepts whenever an answer to an oracle query is "yes".

Note that the condition on the depth of the tree prevents the machine, on input x, to query the oracle for x. In this case the tree would have an infinite branch.

A self-reducible set A can be considered as the "fixpoint" of the machine M, in fact, such fixpoints are unique:

<u>Proposition</u> [BBS] . If M is a self-reducing machine for both, A and B, then A = B.

This means, that we can henceforth drop the A in the notation and we write T(M,x) instead T(M,A,x).

Many sets in NP, like SAT, are self-reducible, in fact, d-self-reducible. On the other hand, every d-self-reducible set is in NP, and every self-reducible set is in PSPACE [Ko2]. It is not known whether every set in NP is (d-)self-reducible.

The following connection between self-reducibility and self-helping can be established.

<u>Theorem 5</u> [Ko1]. Each d-self-reducible set is a self-1-helper.

<u>Proof</u>. If A is a d-self-reducible set via some oracle machine M, then there is a function $f_M \in P(A)$ and a polynomial-time computable predicate B_M such that

$$A = \{ x \mid \exists y \; B_M(x,y) \} \qquad \text{(hence A is in NP)}$$

$$= \{ x \mid B_M(x, f_M(x)) \} \qquad \text{(A has "self-computable witnesses")}$$

Now, the following is a robust oracle machine accepting A.

<u>input</u> x ;
y := the result of simulating the machine which computes f_M on input x, but with the present ORACLE ;
<u>if</u> $B_M(x,y)$ is true <u>then</u> halt accepting
<u>else</u> start an exhaustive search algorithm to determine whether $x \in A$ or not ;

It can be seen that this machine is robust, accepts A, and if A is used as the ORACLE (in this case, $y = f_M(x)$), the machine halts within polynomial-time on inputs in A (hence A 1-helps this machine). #

In [Schn] it is shown that the graph isomorphism problem is many-one equivalent to extended graph isomorphism, which is a d-self-reducible problem. This does not imply that graph isomorphism is d-self-reducible because (d-)self-reducibility is not invariant under many-one equivalence. But the notion of self-1-helping is, hence it follows by Theorem 5 that graph isomorphism is a self-1-helper. This is an interesting dual result to the observations about graph non-isomorphism above.

Combining Theorems 4 and 5, we get

Corollary [Ko1]. Every set in $NP \cap BPP$ which is d-self-reducible or which is a self-1-helper is actually in R.

3. Weak Helpers and No-Helpers

We have seen that every set in NP can be 1-helped by some set in NP, and some sets in NP can even 1-help themselves. We will now consider the question whether there are sets that are not very helpful.

Definition [Ko1]. A set A is a no-(1-)helper if $P_{(1-)help}(A) = P$.

It is reasonable to suspect that sparse sets, i.e. sets which do not encode much information are no-helpers or no-1-helpers.

Definition. A set $A \subseteq \Sigma^*$ is sparse if for some polynomial p and for every n, $|A \cap \Sigma^n| \leq p(n)$. A set A is very sparse if for some constant k and for every n, $|A \cap \{ x \mid n \leq |x| < 2^n \}| \leq k$.

The following results are from [Ko1].

Theorem 6. Each very sparse set is a no-1-helper.

Proof. Let A = L(M,S) for a robust oracle machine M and a very sparse set S. Given the machine M, but without knowing S, there is only a polynomial number of potential oracle answers, hence computation paths, that have to be tried. An input x is in A if and only if at least one of these computations, within polynomial time, leads to acceptance. This gives a polynomial-time procedure to compute A, hence $A \in P$. #

By a straightforward diagonalization, very sparse set in EXPTIME - P can be constructed. This observation allows the following two conclusions.

Corollary. There exist no-1-helpers in EXPTIME - P.

Corollary. If every set in NP is polynomial-time Turing equivalent to a d-self-reducible set, then EXPTIME $\not\subseteq$ NP.

Proof. Let S be a very sparse set in EXPTIME - P. By way of a contradiction, assume that S is in NP. Then S is Turing equivalent to a d-self-reducible set B. Hence, by Theorem 5, $B \in P_{1\text{-help}}(B)$, and therefore $B \in P_{1\text{-help}}(S)$. This means, S 1-helps B. By Theorem 6, S is a no-1-helper, so B must be in P. But then also S is in P, because $S \in P(B)$. This is a contradiction. #

The last Corollary is a nice example of how a question of structural complexity theory (about d-self-reducibility of NP sets) relates to an open question about inclusion relationships of (standard) complexity classes.
There is another interesting link between the helping notion and the notion of "lowness".

Definition [Sch5]. For each $n \geq 0$, let $L_n = \{ A \in NP \mid \Sigma_n^P(A) \subseteq \Sigma_n^P \}$ and $H_n = \{ A \in NP \mid \Sigma_{n+1}^P \subseteq \Sigma_n^P(A) \}$. Define $LH = \bigcup_n L_n$ and $HH = \bigcup_n H_n$.

The hierarchy of classes $L_0 \subseteq L_1 \subseteq L_2 \subseteq \ldots$ is called the low hierarchy, and $H_0 \subseteq H_1 \subseteq H_2 \subseteq \ldots$ is the high hierachy. It can be shown [Sch5] that $L_0 = P$, $L_1 = NP \cap co\text{-}NP$, $H_0 = \{$ NP-complete sets under polynomial-time Turing reducibility $\}$, and $H_1 = \{$ NP-complete sets under polynomial-time strong nondeterministic Turing reducibility $\}$ (see [Lo]). The low and high hierarchies are disjoint if and only if the polynomial-time hierachy does not "collapse". More precisely, for each $n \geq 0$, $\Sigma_n^P \neq \Sigma_{n+1}^P$ implies $L_n \cap H_n = \emptyset$, and $\Sigma_n^P = \Sigma_{n+1}^P$ implies $L_n = H_n = NP$. Hence, if the polynomial hierarchy exists with infinitely many different levels, then $LH \cap HH = \emptyset$. In fact, in this case, $NP - (LH \cup HH)$ is non-empty [Sch5]. If a property of NP sets (like being sparse) implies membership in the low hierarchy (as shown in [KS]), then no NP-complete set (and more general, no set in HH) can have this property unless the polynomial-time hierarchy collapses. It is shown in [Sch3] that the graph isomorphism problem is a member of L_2, hence this problem cannot be NP-complete unless $\Sigma_2^P = \Sigma_3^P$. Further results about the low and the high hierarchies can be found in [Sch5],[KS],[Sch1],[Sch4].

In a sense, sets in LH are very "close" to P sets, and sets in HH are very "close" to NP-complete sets. This motivates the following definition. Call a set A a <u>weak-1-helper</u> if $P_{1\text{-help}}(A) \subseteq LH$.

<u>Theorem 7</u> [Sch6],[Ko1]. Every sparse set is a weak-1-helper.

<u>Proof</u>. We show that $P_{1\text{-help}}(\text{SPARSE})$ is included in L_2 where SPARSE denotes the class of sparse sets. Let $L \in \Sigma_2^p(A)$ where $A = L(M,S)$ for a robust oracle machine M and a sparse set S which 1-helps M. The set L has a quantifier characterization as

$$L = \{ x \mid \exists y \, \forall z \quad (x,y,z) \in L(M',A) \}$$

for some polynomial-time oracle machine M'. (As usual, we assume a polynomial length bound for the quantifications). Then L can be characterized as follows. (Hereby, the string w is intended to encode a polynomial size initial segment of the sparse set S).

$$L = \{ x \mid \exists w \, [\forall u \ (u \in A \Longrightarrow u \in L(M,w)) \text{ and } \exists y \ \forall z \ (x,y,z) \in L(M',L(M,w)) \,] \} .$$

It is not hard to see that these two characterizations of L are in fact equivalent. Furthermore, an analysis of the quantifier structure of the second characterization shows that L is in Σ_2^p, hence A is in L_2. #

The class $P_{1\text{-help}}(\text{SPARSE})$ has been investigated (under different names) in [Sch6] and in [Kä]. For example, the following equivalent characterization is from [Sch6]. A set A is in $P_{1\text{-help}}(\text{SPARSE})$ if and only if there is a polynomial-time computable predicate B and a sparse set S such that

$$A = \{ x \mid \exists y \ B(x,y) \} \qquad \text{(hence A is in NP)}$$
$$= \{ x \mid \exists y \in S \ B(x,y) \} \qquad \text{(only few witnesses suffice)}$$

Using this characterization,the following theorem is easily proved.

<u>Theorem 8</u> [Sch6]. The classes R, SPARSE ∩ NP, and APT ∩ NP (cf.[MP]) are included in $P_{1\text{-help}}(\text{SPARSE})$ (hence in L_2).

The inclusion SPARSE ∩ NP $\subseteq P_{1\text{-help}}(\text{SPARSE})$ can actually be improved to SPARSE ∩ NP $\subseteq P_{1\text{-help}}(\text{SPARSE} \cap \text{NP})$, that is, every sparse set in NP can be 1-helped by some sparse set in NP. But again, it is not clear whether every sparse set in NP can 1-help itself. If this would be the case, then, by Theorem 6, every very sparse set in NP is already in P. Notice that there are sparse sets in NP-P if and only if EXPTIME ≠ NEXPTIME [Ha].

4. Interactive Proof Systems

In chapter 2, using the graph isomorphism example, it was already argued that there is a close relationship between the 1-sided helping notion and interactive proof systems. Interactive proof systems have been introduced in [GMR] in terms of two Turing machines which interact by a common communication tape. Hereby, the prover machine has unrestricted computational power (i.e. it is somehow the "oracle"), and the verifier machine which is restricted to be a probabilistic, bounded-error and polynomial-time machine (such as in the definition of the class BPP). The aim of the prover is to convince the verifier that the current input string x is in a language L, whereas in case of inputs x not in L, no prover whatsoever (not only the present prover) should be able to "convince" the verifier (i.e. make the verifier accept the input). There are some nice examples of languages which can be "proved" in this interactive way, without knowing the membership of such languages in NP. Graph non-isomorphism is the most prominent example. The class of sets which can be interactively proved this way is denoted IP (for formal definitions see [GMR]). The inclusions $NP \cup BPP \subseteq IP \subseteq PSPACE$ can be shown.

By loosening the definition of $P_{1\text{-help}}$ a little bit - instead of deterministic computations we allow probabilistic computations with small error (hence non-robustness) probability - we can come up with a definition which is very close to the notion of interactive proof systems. Conceptually this is as the definitional step from P to BPP, therefore we use the notation $BPP_{1\text{-help}}$.

Definition. A set L is in $BPP_{1\text{-help}}(A)$ if there is a probabilistic, polynomial-time oracle machine M such that (1) and (2) hold for all x.

(1) if $x \in L$ then Prob[M on input x using oracle A accepts] $\geq 3/4$,

(2) if $x \notin L$ then for all oracles B,
Prob[M on input x using oracle B accepts] $\leq 1/4$.

As before, we analogously define $BPP_{1\text{-help}}(\mathbf{C})$ for a class of sets $\mathbf{C}$, and $BPP_{1\text{-help}} = BPP_{1\text{-help}}(2^{\Sigma^*})$.

The class $BPP_{1\text{-help}}$ does not seem to coincide exactly with IP, but with a generalization, called MIP, suggested in [FRS], which uses multiple provers, instead of a single prover. That is, the verifier has at each communication round the option to choose a prover. The provers do not know each others answers.

Theorem 9 [FRS]. $BPP_{1\text{-help}} = MIP$.

The class IP is clearly included in MIP, but MIP is not known to be included in PSPACE. (The problem here is the possibility of having the same oracle queries distributed in various places of the computation tree which corresponds to a $BPP_{1\text{-help}}$ computation. All these queries should be answered simultanously "yes" or "no" and cannot be treated independently. Therefore, the usual depth-first, polynomial-space evaluation of such computation trees does not work).

As in the case of the class $P_{1\text{-help}}$ it is interesting to consider the effect of restricting the oracle, or restricting the oracle access mechanism. Let $BPP_{1\text{-help,bounded-query}}$ be the variant of the class $BPP_{1\text{-help}}$ where the machine M is required to have, for each input x, only a polynomial number of different oracle queries in the computation tree. Here we can report the following result.

Theorem 10 [To]. $BPP_{1\text{-help,bounded-query}} = MA$.

The class MA is one of the classes introduced in [Bab] in terms of "Arthur-Merlin games".

5. Conclusion

This paper has (hopefully) demonstated how useful notions from structural complexity theory are, and how they can be intertwined with more standard issues, such as the inclusion relationship between various complexity classes. The notion of robustness and helping turned out to be particularly flexible to capture also "self-reducibility", "lowness", and "interactive proof systems".

Another continuation of the robustness idea is done in [HH] and [GB]. There robust properties are studied, that is, a property of an oracle machine which is maintained under each potential oracle. Accepting one particular language (as in the present paper) is just a special case. It is analyzed what price an oracle machine pays for having a property robustly.

References

[AFK] M. Abadi, J. Feigenbaum and J. Kilian, On hiding information from an oracle, Proc. 19th ACM STOC 1987, 195-203.

[AM] L. Adleman and K. Manders, Reducibility, randomness, and intractability, Proc. 9th ACM STOC, 1977, 151-163.

[Bab] L. Babai, Trading group theory for randomness, Proc. 17th ACM STOC, 1985, 421-429.

[Bal] J.L. Balcázar, Self-reducibility, Proc. 4th STACS, Lecture Notes in Computer Science 247, 136-147, Springer, 1985.

[BBS] J.L. Balcázar, R.V. Book and U. Schöning, Sparse sets, lowness and highness, Proc. MFCS 1984, Lect. Notes in Comput. Sci. 176, 185-193.
See also: SIAM Journal on Computing 15 (1986), 739-747.

[BDG] J.L. Balcázar, J. Diaz and J. Gabarro, Structural Complexity I, EATCS Monographs on Theor. Comput. Sci., Vol. 11, Springer, 1988.

[BHZ] R.B. Boppana, J. Hastad and S. Zachos, Does co-NP have short interactive proofs?, Inform. Proc. Letters 25 (1987), 127-132.

[FRS] L. Fortnow, J. Rompel and M. Sipser, On the power of multi-prover interactive protocols, 3rd Structure in Complexity Theory Conf., IEEE Comp. Society, 1988.

[GB] R. Gavaldá and J.L. Balcázar, Strong and robustly strong polynomial time reducibilities to sparse sets, manuscript, 1988.

[Gi] J. Gill, Computational complexity of probabilistic complexity classes, SIAM Journal on Computing 6 (1977), 675-695.

[GMR] S. Goldwasser, S. Micali and C. Rackoff, The knowledge complexity of interactive proof systems, Proc. 17th ACM STOC 1985, 291-304.

[GMW] O. Goldreich, S. Micali and A. Wigderson, Proofs that relase minimum knowledge, Proc. MFCS 1986, Lecture Notes in Comput. Sci. 233, 639-650, Springer, 1986.
Also: Proofs that yield nothing but their validity and a methodology of interactive proof systems, Proc. 17th ACM STOC 1985, 291-304.

[GS] S. Goldwasser and M. Sipser, Private coins versus public coins in interactive proof systems, 18th ACM STOC 1986, 59-68.

[Ha] J. Hartmanis, On sparse sets in NP - P, Inform. Proc. Letters 16 (1983), 55-60.

[HH] J. Hartmanis and L.A. Hemachandra, One-way functions, robustness, and non-isomorphism of NP-complete sets, Proc. 2nd Structure in Complexity Theory Conf., IEEE Computer Society, 1987, 160-174.

[Kä] J. Kämper, Non-uniform proof systems: a new framework to describe non-uniform and probabilistic complexity classes, Univ. Oldenburg, Techn. Report 3/87.

[Ko1] K. Ko, On helping by robust oracle machines, Proc. 2nd Structure in Complexity Theory Conf., IEEE Computer Society, 1987, 182-190.
Also: Theoret. Comput. Sci. 52 (1987), 15-36.

[Ko2] K. Ko, On self-reducibility and weak p-selectivity, Jounal of Computer and System Sciences 26 (1983), 209-221.

[KS] K. Ko and U. Schöning, On circuit-size complexity and the low hierarchy in NP, SIAM Journ. on Computing 14 (1985), 41-51.

[La] C. Lautemann, BPP and the polynomial hierachy, Inform. Proc. Letters 17 (1983), 215-217.

[Lo] T. Long, Strong nondeterministic polynomial-time reducibilities, Theor. Comput. Sci. 21 (1982), 1-25.

[MP] A. Meyer and M. Paterson, Whith what frequency are apparently intractable problems difficult?, Techn. Report 126, MIT, 1979.

[Sch1] U. Schöning, Complexity and Structure, Lecture Notes in Comput. Sci. 211, Springer, 1985.

[Sch2] U. Schöning, Robust algorithms:a different approach to oracles, Proc. ICALP 84, Lecture Notes in Computer Science 172, 448-453, 1984.
Also: Theor. Comput. Sci. 40 (1985), 57-66.

[Sch3] U. Schöning, Graph isomorphism is in the low hierarchy, Proc. STACS 87, Lect. Notes in Comput. Sci. 247, 114-124, Springer, 1987. (to appear in JCSS)

[Sch4] U. Schöning, Probabilistic complexity classes and lowness, Proc. 2nd Structure in Complexity Theory Conf., IEEE Computer Society, 1987, 2-8.

[Sch5] U. Schöning, A low and a high hierarchy within NP, Journ. of Comput. Syst. Sci. 27 (1983), 14-28.

[Sch6] U. Schöning, Netzwerkkomplexität, probabilistische Algorithmen und Relativierungen, Habilitationsschrift, Univ. Stuttgart, 1985.

[Schn] C.P. Schnorr, Optimal algorithms for self-reducible problems, Proc. 3rd ICALP 76, Edinburgh University Press 1976, 322-337.

[Si] M. Sipser, A complexity theoretic approach to randomness, Proc. 15th ACM STOC 1983, 330-335.

[To] J. Torán, personal communication, 1987.

[TW] M. Tompa and H. Woll, Random self-reducibility and zero knowledge interactive proofs of possession of information, Proc. 28th FOCS 87, IEEE Computer Soc., 1987, 472-482.

Recognizable Sets with Multiplicities in the Tropical Semiring

Imre Simon*
Instituto de Matemática e Estatística
Universidade de São Paulo
05508 São Paulo, SP, Brasil

Abstract

The last ten years saw the emergence of some results about recognizable subsets of a free monoid with multiplicities in the Min-Plus semiring. An interesting aspect of this theoretical body is that its discovery was motivated throughout by applications such as the finite power property, Eggan's classical star height problem and the measure of the nondeterministic complexity of finite automata. We review here these results, their applications and point out some open problems.

1 Introduction

One of the richest extensions of finite automaton theory is obtained by associating multiplicities to words, edges and states. Perhaps the most intuitive appearence of this concept is obtained by counting for every word the number of successful paths spelling it in a (nondeterministic) finite automaton. This is motivated by the formalization of ambiguity in a finite automaton and leads to the theory of recognizable subsets of a free monoid with multiplicities in the semiring of natural numbers. This theory leads, in turn, to the consideration of semigroups of matrices with coefficients in $\mathbb{N}$ and it encounters some classical results from algebra and analysis in the context of representation theory and (formal) power series (in noncommuting variables).

In finite automaton theory this approach was pioneered and vigorously pursued since the early sixties by the "French School" led by Marcel Paul

*This work was supported by FAPESP and CNPq

Schützenberger. A major step was undertaken by Samuel Eilenberg who sistematized both the formalism and the most important results in his seminal book, [12], published in 1974. In particular he explicited the machinery and this prompted the consideration of multiplicities in any semiring K. The two most important particular cases studied in Eilenberg's book are given by the boolean semiring (leading to classical finite automata) and the semiring of natural numbers (leading to the consideration of ambiguity in finite automata). More recent treatments of the subject can be found in [3,32].

In 1978 the author was led to the investigation of recognizable sets with multiplicities in another semiring, denoted $\mathcal{M}$, in [33,35]. This is just the semiring of the natural numbers extended with ∞ under the operations of taking minimums and addition. Such semiring, sometimes called the Min-Plus semiring, is important in operations research where it is used in problems of cost minimization [7]. Here, we shall call it the *tropical semiring*, a suggestion of Christian Choffrut.

Our purpose in this paper is to survey the emerging theory of recognizable subsets of a free monoid with multiplicities in the tropical semiring. We shall also point out, in our way, the applications of this theory to linguistic problems as well as to the capturing of the nondeterministic complexity of finite automata. We shall omit the proofs which can be found elsewhere.

2 The finite section and the limitedness problems

In this section we describe a problem from two different viewpoints.

Let K be a semiring and let M_nK denote the multiplicative monoid of $n \times n$ matrices with coefficients in K. Let S be a subset of M_nK. For $i,j \in [1,n]$ we define the (i,j)*-section* of S as being the set of cofficients (i,s,j), when s runs over S. A subset of K is called a *section* of S if it is an (i,j)-section for some i and j. Clearly, set S is finite if and only if every section of S is finite.

The *finite section problem* (for K) takes a finite subset X of M_nK and a pair (i,j) of indices as input. It consists of deciding whether or not the (i,j)-section of the subsemigroup of M_nK generated by X is finite.

Another, more restricted, problem is given by the *finite closure problem* (for K), which consists of deciding whether or not the subsemigroup of M_nK generated by a given finite set of matrices is finite or not. Clearly, whenever the finite section problem is decidable so is the finite closure problem. But the converse does not hold in general.

It turns out that the finite section problem is equivalent to the limitedness problem in automaton theory which we describe now.

Let $\mathcal{A}$ be a K-A-automaton, that is to say an automaton over the alphabet A with multiplicities in the semiring K. Then the behavior $||\mathcal{A}||$ of $\mathcal{A}$ is just a function $||\mathcal{A}||: A^* \to K$. We recall that, for a path c in $\mathcal{A}$, its label, denoted by $|c|$, is the product of letters of its edges and the multiplicity of c, denoted by $\|c\|$, is the product of multiplicities of its edges. The behavior of $\mathcal{A}$ associates to each word $s \in A^*$ the sum of multiplicities of all successful paths with label s. The family of behaviors of K-A-automata is denoted by $\mathrm{Rec}_K\, A^*$. Its elements are called recognizable K-subsets of A^*.

We say that a K-subset S, $S: X \to K$ is *limited* if its image XS is a finite subset of K. The *limitedness problem* (for K) consists of deciding whether or not the behavior of a given K-A-automaton is limited or not.

We shall be interested in the case when K is the tropical semiring $\mathcal{M}$. In this case, the operations of $\mathcal{M}$ being min and $+$, the multiplicity of a path is the sum of the multiplicities of its edges while the behavior of an $\mathcal{M}$-A-automaton $\mathcal{A}$ is given by

$$s||\mathcal{A}|| = \min\{\ \|c\|\ |\ c \text{ is a successful path with label } |c| = s\,\}.$$

Thus, in particular, the behavior of $\mathcal{A}$ is limited if and only if there is a natural m, such that for every $s \in A^*$, either $s||\mathcal{A}|| = \infty$ or $s||\mathcal{A}|| \leq m$. A successful path with label s and multiplicity $s||\mathcal{A}||$ is called *victorious*. Further details about our notation can be found in [12,36].

Using a standard construction which associates a subsemigroup of $M_n K$ to every K-A-automaton $\mathcal{A}$ it can be shown that for every semiring K the finite section problem is decidable if and only if the limitedness problem is decidable.

These problems were considered in [28] where their decidability for the semiring of natural numbers was shown. Indeed, in this case, under certain connectivity hypothesis, the finite section problem is equivalent to the finite closure problem whose decidability also follows from work of G. Jacob [22]. Related work can be found in [6,40].

For the tropical semiring these questions were addressed in 1978 in [33,35], where we proved that every torsion subsemigroup of $M_n\mathcal{M}$ is locally finite, a Schur-type result. At the same time it was shown that the finite closure problem for the tropical semiring is decidable.

The limitedness problem for the tropical semiring was raised in [9]. It was shown to be decidable in a memorable paper by Kosaburo Hashiguchi,

[17], in 1982. The solution is very complicated and difficult to visualize and this led to further research to find other proofs of this result.

The first attempt in this direction was completed by Hashiguchi himself [16] in 1986. He obtained an improved proof accompanied by a new characterization of the limited recognizable $\mathcal{M}$-subsets of A^*. Unortunately, Hashiguchi's proofs are not completely satisfactory. This is because his method conduces to a bound, say B, such that $\|\mathcal{A}\|$ is limited if and only if the image $A^*\|\mathcal{A}\|$ is contained in the set $Y = [0, B] \cup \infty$. The algorithm then consists of checking whether or not the inverse image $Y\|\mathcal{A}\|^{-1}$ of Y is everything or not. This can be done because for every $y \in \mathcal{M}$, the set $y\|\mathcal{A}\|^{-1}$ is a recognizable subset of A^* which can be computed. Thus, the algorithm neeeds the construction of $B+2$ automata which is just impossible in practice because of the exponential bounds B furnished by the proof.

The second attempt to find an alternate proof of Hashiguchi's theorem was completed by Hing Leung [26] in 1987. Leung visualized the finite section problem as a question of convergence using the one-point compactification of the tropical semiring equiped with the discrete topology. Let us denote by ω the point at infinity and by $\mathcal{T}$ the resulting semiring.

Thus, $\mathcal{T}$ has elements $\mathbb{N} \cup \{\omega, \infty\}$ totally ordered by $0 < 1 < 2 < \cdots < \omega < \infty$. The operations of $\mathcal{T}$ are $\min(a, b)$ and $a+b$, where $a+b = \max(a, b)$ if a or b does not belong to $\mathbb{N}$. A sequence a_n converges to a if and only if either $a_n = a$ for every sufficiently large n or $a = \omega$ and, for every $m \in \mathbb{N} \cup \{\infty\}$, there exists $p \in \mathbb{N}$ for which $m \notin \{a_n \mid n > p\}$.

The topology of $\mathcal{T}$ extends naturally to $M_n\mathcal{T}$ where matrix multiplication results a continuous function. Thus, $M_n\mathcal{T}$ becomes a topological semigroup and the topological closure of any subsemigroup is again a subsemigroup of $M_n\mathcal{T}$.

Leung's solution consists of an algorithm which decides whether or not ω belongs to the (i, j)-section of the topological closure of the subsemigroup of $M_n\mathcal{T}$ generated by a given finite subset of $M_n\mathcal{T}$. This clearly solves the finite section problem. His algorithm is easy to state and can be computed for examples with small n.

Finally, I also attempted to find an alternate proof for Hashiguchi's theorem. Unfortunately my proof, initiated in 1986, is still incomplete but it will be essentially another proof of correctness of Hing Leung's algorithm, obtained independently.

Maybe a word on one of the main differences among the three approaches is in order. All these proofs are built around some Ramsey-type result which serves as a stopping rule for the algorithms. Hashiguchi uses the weakest possible Ramsey type result: the pigeon-hole principle. Leung uses a powerful theorem of T. C. Brown about locally finite semigroups [5,33,39]. My own proof uses a new Ramsey-type result, developed in [38,34], from which Brown's theorem follows easily.

We close this section by stating the algorithm for deciding the finite section problem for the tropical semiring.

Initially we consider another semiring, denoted by $\mathcal{R}$, which has elements $\{0, 1, \omega, \infty\}$ totally ordered by

$$0 < 1 < \omega < \infty.$$

The operations of $\mathcal{R}$ are min and max for addition and multiplication respectively.

Let us consider an idempotent element e of $M_n\mathcal{R}$. The position (i,j) of e is said to be *blind* if $(i,e,j) = 1$ and there is no $k \in [1,n]$ such that $(k,e,k) = 0$ and $(i,e,k),(k,e,j) \in \{0,1\}$. This is equivalent to saying that $(i,e'^3,j) = 3$, where e' is the matrix e considered as an element of $M_n\mathcal{T}$. It can be shown that position (i,j) of e is blind if and only if the (i,j)-section of the cyclic subsemigroup of $M_n\mathcal{T}$ generated by e' is infinite. To record this situation we make the following definition.

The *perforation* of e is another idempotent matrix in $M_n\mathcal{R}$, denoted $e^\#$, given by

$$(i,e^\#,j) = \begin{cases} \omega & \text{if } (i,j) \text{ is blind} \\ (i,e,j) & \text{otherwise.} \end{cases}$$

A subset Y of $M_n\mathcal{R}$ is *closed under perforation* if the perforation of every idempotent in Y is also in Y.

The semirings $\mathcal{T}$ and $\mathcal{R}$ are related by the function $\Psi\colon \mathcal{T} \to \mathcal{R}$, given by

$$x\Psi = \begin{cases} x & \text{if } x \in \mathcal{R} \\ 1 & \text{otherwise.} \end{cases}$$

Function Ψ extends naturally to $M_n\mathcal{T}$ but we warn the reader that it is not continuous.

Having defined this much notation we can state the promised algorithm. Let X be a finite subset of $M_n\mathcal{M}$. Let Y be the least subsemigroup of $M_n\mathcal{R}$ closed under perforation which contains $X\Psi$. Hing Leung [26] showed that the (i,j)-section of the subsemigroup of $M_n\mathcal{M}$ generated by X is finite if and only if the (i,j)-section of Y contains ω.

Since $\mathcal{R}$ is a finite semiring, Y is finite and can be computed by starting with $X\Psi$ and alternately closing it under product and perforation. This yields an algorithm to decide the finite section problem for the tropical semiring.

A word about the complexity of this problem. Leung [26] has shown that the finite section problem for the tropical semiring is PSPACE-hard. Later he proved [25] that the algorithm converges after a polynomial number of closures under product and perforation. It follows that it has polynomial space complexity; hence, the limitedness problem is PSPACE-complete.

3 Applications to linguistic problems

The initial motivation for both the finite closure and the finite section problems came from linguistic considerations.

The original linguistic problem to be solved was posed by John Brzozowski in 1966 during the seventh SWAT (now FOCS) Conference. It asked for an algorithm to decide whether or not a given recognizable subset of A^* possessed the finite power property. Recall that a subset X of A^* has the finite power property if there exists a natural m for which

$$X^* = (1 \cup X)^m.$$

This problem was shown decidable independently by K. Hashiguchi and the author in 1978 [15,35], while in [20] it is shown that the problem becomes undecidable for context-free languaages. See also [27].

Hashiguchi's solution (see also [37,31]) is very short and he works directly on the automaton recognizing X. His method is based on an ingenious idea built around a double recurrence.

On the other hand, the author reduced the finite power property to the finite closure problem for the tropical semiring. The basic idea of the reduction is simple and we illustrate it by an example in Figure 1. Let $\mathcal{A}$ be a finite automaton recognizing X and let $\mathcal{B}$ be the automaton recognizing X^*, obtained by the standard construction. Let q be the initial (and only final) state of $\mathcal{B}$. We transform $\mathcal{B}$ into an $\mathcal{M}$-A-automaton by assigning multiplicity 1 to every edge with terminus in q and multiplicity 0 to the remaining edges of $\mathcal{B}$ (on the Figure multiplicity 0 is omitted). Clearly, for every $s \in A^*$, we have

$$s\|\mathcal{B}\| = \begin{cases} \min\{\, m \mid s \in X^m \,\} & \text{if } s \in X^* \\ \infty & \text{otherwise.} \end{cases}$$

It follows that X has the finite power property if and only if $\|\mathcal{B}\|$ is limited.

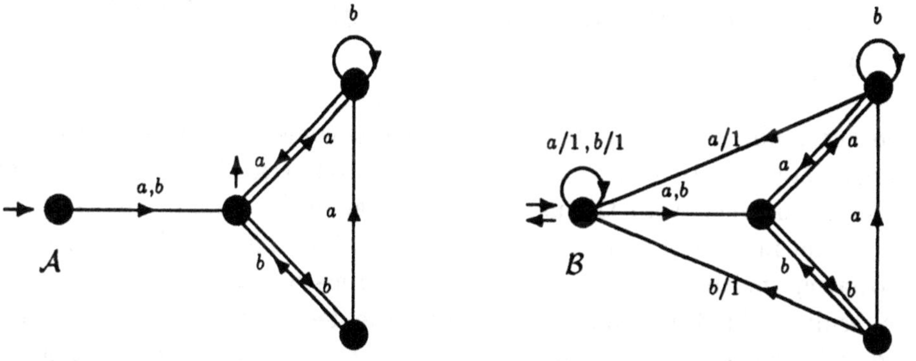

Figure 1: A set $X = |\mathcal{A}|$ with the finite power property: $X^* = (1 \cup X)^4$.

Let S be the standard submonoid of $M_n\mathcal{M}$ associated to $\mathcal{B}$. It turns out that in the particular case of this construction, due to the restricted way of assigning multiplicities to the edges of $\mathcal{B}$, the (q,q)-section of S is finite if and only if S itself is finite. Hence, X has the finite power property if and only if the monoid S is finite.

Hashiguchi extended this idea and developed an algorithm to decide whether a given set belongs to the closure of a given finite family of sets under a given subset of the rational operations. More precisely, let X be a recognizable subset of A^*, let F be a finite family of recognizable subsets of A^*, and let ρ be a subset of the operations in $\{\cup, ., *\}$ (the rational operations). The algorithm decides whether or not the set X belongs to the closure of F under ρ. For instance, X has the finite power property if and only if X^* belongs to the closure of $\{X\}$ under union and concatenation. This algorithm uses, in a very significant way, the finite section problem for the tropical semiring. Actually, we are unaware of any other proof which avoids the finite section problem. For more details consult [19,30].

Building on this idea, Hashiguchi, in a veritable "tour de force", solved last year the entire star-height problem in [14] after a partial solution he obtained in [18] in 1982. More precisely, he developed an algorithm to compute the star-height of a given recognizable set. It is worth recalling that this classical problem, formulated by Eggan [11] in 1963, remained open for 24 years in spite of the many attempts to solve it. Unfortunately, the ideas in this deep paper are too complex to be reported here.

4 The nondeterministic complexity of finite automata

Another application of the tropical semiring is connected to the capture of the nondeterministic complexity of a finite automaton. The idea here is to associate to every word the minimum number of "decisions" necessary to spell it out in a given nondeterministic automaton. This can be realized by associating multiplicity 1 to every nondeterministic edge. The behavior of the resulting $\mathcal{M}$-A-automaton is precisely the desired series. This idea, for Turing Machines, first appeared in [23] and was later considered for finite automata by J. Goldstine, C. Kintala and D. Wotschke [24].

More precisely, let $\mathcal{A} = (Q, I, T)$ be a (not necessarily deterministic) finite automaton over the alphabet A. We say that edge (p, a, q) of $\mathcal{A}$ is *deterministic* if there are no other edges (p, a, r) in $\mathcal{A}$, with $r \neq q$.

We convert $\mathcal{A}$ into an $\mathcal{M}$-A-automaton by defining the multiplicity of (p, a, q) in $Q \times A \times Q$:

$$(p,a,q)E = \begin{cases} 0 & \text{if } (p,a,q) \text{ is a deterministic edge} \\ 1 & \text{if } (p,a,q) \text{ is not a deterministic edge} \\ \infty & \text{if } (p,a,q) \text{ is not an edge of } \mathcal{A}. \end{cases}$$

The behavior $\|\mathcal{A}\|$ of $\mathcal{A}$ ($\|\mathcal{A}\|\colon A^* \to \mathcal{M}$) is called the *nondeterministic complexity* of the finite automaton $\mathcal{A}$. Thus, $s\|\mathcal{A}\|$ is the minimum number of nondeterministic edges needed to spell s from I to T.

An important aspect of the nondeterministic complexity of automaton $\mathcal{A}$ is the assymptotic behavior of the coefficients in $\|\mathcal{A}\|$. This can be measured by the function sh defined as follows. Let $F\colon A^* \to \mathcal{M}$ be an $\mathcal{M}$-subset of A^*. For F and for $m \geq 0$, we define

$$\mathrm{sh}(F, m) = \min\{\, |s| \mid s \in A^*,\, m \leq sF < \infty \,\}.$$

Thus, $\mathrm{sh}(F, m)$ is the minimum length needed to achieve a finite coefficient which exceeds m. Note that if F is limited then $\mathrm{sh}(F, m)$ is undefined for sufficiently large m and if F is unlimited then $\mathrm{sh}(F, m)$ is always defined and unbounded. In particular, we use the function $\mathrm{sh}(\|\mathcal{A}\|, m)$ to measure the assymptotic behavior of the nondeterministic complexity of automaton $\mathcal{A}$.

It was shown in [36] that the nondeterministic complexity $\|\mathcal{A}_p\|$ of automaton $\mathcal{A}_p$, shown in Figure 2, satisfies

$$\mathrm{sh}(\|\mathcal{A}_p\|, m) \in \Theta(m^p).$$

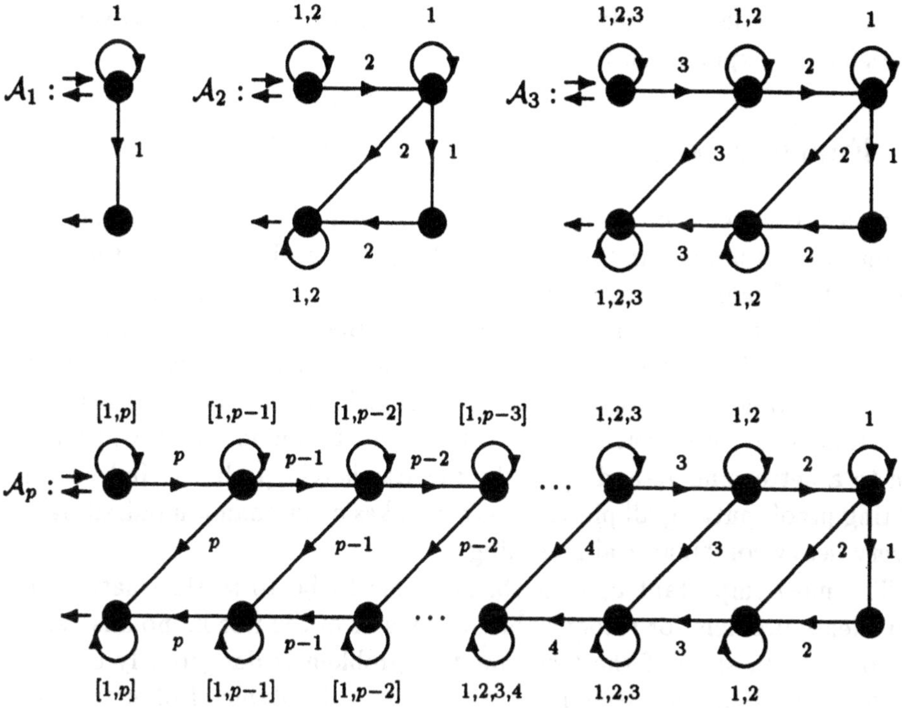

Figure 2: Automata $\mathcal{A}_p$

Inspired by this fact we define, for every p, the family $\mathcal{H}_p$ of $\mathcal{M}$-subsets in $\mathrm{Rec}_{\mathcal{M}}\, A^*$ for which sh grows not faster than a p-degree polynomial. More precisely, we put

$$\mathcal{H}_p = \{\, F \in \mathrm{Rec}_{\mathcal{M}}\, A^* \mid \mathrm{sh}(F, m) \in O(m^p) \,\}.$$

In particular, $\mathcal{H}_0$ results to be the family of limited recognizable $\mathcal{M}$-subsets of A^*.

Using a characterization of limited recognizable subsets of A^* obtained by Hashiguchi in [16] one can prove that the families $\mathcal{H}_p$ exhaust $\mathrm{Rec}_{\mathcal{M}}\, A^*$. In other words, the families $\mathcal{H}_p$ form a proper hierarchy of the recognizable $\mathcal{M}$-subsets of A^*. More details can be found in [36].

We mention that the aluded characterization of Hashiguchi is done in terms of the star-height of rational expressions which do not use unions. Further, the existence of such an expression of height p implies pertinence to $\mathcal{H}_p$. Also, it can be shown that the algorithm of the previous section applied to the automaton $\mathcal{A}_p$ converges with exactly p closures under perforation. These facts hardly happen by coincidence but we do not yet have a satisfactory explanation for them.

5 Further research

We close this paper mentioning some open problems. The first challenge is to obtain a deeper understanding of the existing results. This is needed because the proofs of many of the reported results are utterly intricate and rely on very elaborated combinatorial arguments. Better and more informative proofs have to be found! A brilliant example in this direction is given by the introduction of the topology on the tropical semiring done by Leung. I hope that many other such simplifications will be found which will finally lead to a better understanding of the the star-height problem. Indeed, the existing proof, putting all pieces together, takes more than a hundred pages of very heavy combinatorial reasoning.

The most important open problem seems to be to settle whether the equivalence problem for recognizable $\mathcal{M}$-subsets of the free monoid is decidable or not. In spite of the fact that this problem is dangerously close to known undecidable problems I believe that it is decidable. I offer two (admittedly unrelated) facts to support my belief. Indeed, the same problem is decidable for the semiring $\mathbb{N}$ [12, page 143]; on the other hand, the basic tool [12, page 156] to prove undecidability results related to $M_n\mathbb{N}$ cannot be used for the tropical semiring. This is so because it is easy to see that every finitely generated subsemigroup of $M_n\mathcal{M}$ has polynomial growth function, i.e. for every $f\colon A^* \to M_n\mathcal{M}$, A finite, $|A^m f| \in O(m^{n^2})$. Thus, $M_n\mathcal{M}$ does not contain free subsemigroups generated by at least two letters.

Another open problem is to characterize the classes $\mathcal{H}_p$ in the hierarchy of the previous section. In particular, are there decision procedures for each of those classes? I vagely believe and strongly hope that the p-th family in the hierarchy is intimately related to the family of sets of star height p.

Another problem: I conjecture that the complexity of every recognizable $\mathcal{M}$-subset is basically a polynomial. More precisely, for every recognizable $\mathcal{M}$-subset F of A^* there exists p such that $\mathrm{sh}(F, m) \in \Theta(m^p)$.

Still another one: in [9] Choffrut embedded $\mathcal{M}$ in some other semirings of interest such as the semiring K of the recognizable subsets of $\{a\}^*$. Mascle showed in [29] that the Schur-type result of [35] extends to this semiring. He also showed that the finite closure problem remains decidable. However, let us take an excursion to the theory of recognizable rational relations [2,10,21,8,4]. Recently it was proved [13] that it is undecidable whether a rational subset of $A^* \times \{ a \}^*$ is recognizable or not. This was made even more precise in [1] where "tight bounds" are given for the decidability of related questions. But a construction of Choffrut [9,8] can be used to reduce the above question to the finite section problem for the semiring K. Hence, the finite section problem for K is undecidable. A similar argument can be used to show that the equivalence problem for K-recognizable sets is also undecidable. These facts motivate further investigations to try to make more precise the transition of the finite section problem from decidable to undecidable when extending the tropical semiring. In particular, what happens for the semiring $(Z \cup \{ \infty \}, \min, +)$, where Z is the ring of integers?

A final question: can one characterize the family of victorious paths of $\mathcal{M}$-A-automata, seen as subsets of the free monoid generated by the edge set? These sets seem to be peculiar, whatever that means, and more information on them could well clarify the problems we addressed in this paper.

References

[1] I. J. Aalbersberg and H. J. Hoogeboom. Decision problems for regular trace languages. In T. Ottman, editor, *Automata, Languages and Programming*, pages 250–259, Springer-Verlag, Berlin, 1987.

[2] J. Berstel. *Transductions and Context-Free Languages.* B. G. Teubner, Stuttgart, 1979.

[3] J. Berstel and C. Reutenauer. *Les Séries Rationnelles et leurs Langages.* Masson, Paris, 1984.

[4] J. Berstel and J. Sakarovitch. Recent results in the theory o rational sets. In J. Gruska, B. Rovan, and J. Wiedermann, editors, *Mathematical Foundations of Computer Science 1986*, pages 15–28, Springer-Verlag, Berlin, 1986. Lecture Notes in Computer Science, 233.

[5] T. C. Brown. An interesting combinatorial method in the theory of locally finite semigroups. *Pacific J. Math.*, 36:285–289, 1971.

[6] T. H. Chan and O. Ibarra. On the finite-valuedness problem for sequential machines. *Theoretical Comput. Sci.*, 23:95–101, 1983.

[7] P. Chemouil, G. Cohen, J. P. Quadrat, and M. Viot, editors. *Algebres Exotiques et Systemes a Evenements Discrets.* Institut National de Recherche en Informatique et en Automatique, Le Chesnay, 1987.

[8] C. Choffrut. *Free Partially Commutative Monoids.* Technical Report RT-MAP-8504, Instituto de Matemática e Estatística da Universidade de São Paulo, 1985.

[9] C. Choffrut. *Series Rationelles d'Image Finie.* Technical Report 79-6, Laboratoire d'Informatique Théorique et Programmation, Paris, 1979.

[10] C. Choffrut. Sur les transductions reconnaissables. *R.A.I.R.O. Informatique théorique*, 12:203–212, 1978.

[11] L. C. Eggan. Transition graphs and the star height of regular events. *Michigan Math. J.*, 10:385–397, 1963.

[12] S. Eilenberg. *Automata, Languages, and Machines, Volume A.* Academic Press, New York, NY, 1974.

[13] A. Gibbons and W. Rytter. On the decidability of some problems about rational subsets of the free partially commutative monoids. 1987. manuscript.

[14] K. Hashiguchi. Algorithms for determining relative star height and star height. 1987. Manuscript.

[15] K. Hashiguchi. A decision procedure for the order of regular events. *Theoretical Comput. Sci.*, 8:69–72, 1979.

[16] K. Hashiguchi. Improved limitedness theorems on finite automata with distance functions. 1986. Manuscript.

[17] K. Hashiguchi. Limitedness theorem on finite automata with distance functions. *J. Comput. Syst. Sci.*, 24:233–244, 1982.

[18] K. Hashiguchi. Regular languages of star height one. *Information and Control*, 53:199–210, 1982.

[19] K. Hashiguchi. Representation theorems on regular languages. *J. Comput. Syst. Sci.*, 27:101–115, 1983.

[20] C. E. Hughes and S. M. Selkow. The finite power property for context-free languages. *Theoretical Comput. Sci.*, 15:111–114, 1981.

[21] O. Ibarra. The unsolvability of the equivalenc problem for ϵ-free NGSM's with unitary input (output) alphabet and applications. *SIAM J. Comput.*, 7:524–532, 1978.

[22] G. Jacob. La finitude des representations lineaires de semi-groupes est decidable. *J. Algebra*, 52:437–459, 1978.

[23] C. M. R. Kintala and P. Fischer. Computations with a restricted number of nondeterministic steps. In *Proc. of the Ninth Annual ACM Symposium on Theory of Computing*, pages 178–185, Association for Computing Machinery, New York, 1977.

[24] C. M. R. Kintala and D. Wotschke. Amounts of nondeterminism in finite automata. *Acta Inf.*, 13:199–204, 1980.

[25] H. Leung. 1987. Private communication.

[26] H. Leung. *An Algebraic Method for Solving Decision Problems in Finite Automata Theory.* PhD thesis, Department of Computer Science, The Pennsylvania State University, 1987.

[27] M. Linna. Finite power property of regular languages. In M. Nivat, editor, *Automata, Languages and Programming*, pages 87–98, North-Holland Pu. Co., Amsterdam, 1973.

[28] A. Mandel and I. Simon. On finite semigroups of matrices. *Theoretical Comput. Sci.*, 5:101–111, 1977.

[29] J. Mascle. Torsion matrix semigroups and recognizable transductions. In L. Kott, editor, *Automata, Languages and Programming*, pages 244–253, Springer-Verlag, Berlin, 1986. Lecture Notes in Computer Science, 226.

[30] J. E. Pin. *Langages Rationells et Reconnaissables.* Technical Report 85-60, Laboratoire d'Informatique Théorique et Programmation, Paris, 1985.

[31] A. Salomaa. *Jewels of Formal Language Theory.* Computer Science Press, Rockville,MD, 1981.

[32] A. Salomaa and M. Soittola. *Automata-Theoretic Aspects of Formal Power Series.* Springer-Verlag, New York, 1978.

[33] I. Simon. Caracterização de conjuntos racionais limitados. 1987. Tese de Livre-Docência, Instituto de Matemática e Estatística da Universidade de São Paulo.

[34] I. Simon. *Factorization Forests of Finite Height.* Technical Report 87-73, Laboratoire d'Informatique Théorique et Programmation, Paris, 1987.

[35] I. Simon. Limited subsets of a free monoid. In *Proc. 19th Annual Symposium on Foundations of Computer Science*, pages 143–150, Institute of Electrical and Electronics Engineers, Piscataway, N.J., 1978.

[36] I. Simon. *The Nondeterministic Complexity of a Finite Automaton.* Technical Report RT-MAP-8703, Instituto de Matemática e Estatística da Universidade de São Paulo, 1987.

[37] I. Simon. On Brzozowski's problem: $(1 \cup A)^m = A^*$. In M. Fontet and I. Guessarian, editors, *Seminaire d'Informatique Théorique, annee 1979-1980*, pages 67–72, Laboratoire d'Informatique Théorique et Programmation, Paris, 1980.

[38] I. Simon. Word Ramsey theorems. In B. Bollobás, editor, *Graph Theory and Combinatorics*, pages 283–291, Academic Press, London, 1984.

[39] H. Straubing. The Burnside problem for semigroups of matrices. In L. J. Cummings, editor, *Combinatorics on Words, Progress and Perspectives*, pages 279–295, Academic Press, New York, NY, 1983.

[40] A. Weber and H. Seidl. *On Finitely Generated Monoids of Matrices with Entries in* $\mathbb{N}$. Technical Report 9/87, Fachbereich Informatik, Universität Frankfurt, 1987.

Reusable Specification Components*

Martin Wirsing, Rolf Hennicker, Ruth Breu

Universität Passau Postfach 2640 D-8390 Passau

Abstract
An approach to the formal description of reusable software components is presented which is based on the algebraic specification of abstract data types. A reusable component consists of a tree of algebraic specifications where a specification is a child of another specification if it is an implementation. Every node of the tree is a structured specification. In contrast to other approaches to software reusability these trees are considered as objects of the language and can be constructed and manipulated by operators of the language.

*This research has been partially sponsored by the ESPRIT project DRAGON

1. Introduction

The idea of reusing software is motivated by the aim of reducing the cost for developing software and of increasing its reliability. Early examples of reusable software systems are program libraries such as the SAC-system for algebraic computation or SPSS for solving statistical problems.
One may distinguish two different approaches to software reuse: the design of highly generic modules of general nature which are put together for particular applications, and the generalization of particular applications in order to reuse them for a similar problem area.

A common problem for both approaches is the abstract description of reusable components; it is central for the identification and the correct use of such components. A formal specification is the only form of specification which can serve as a basis for a correctness proof; it can be processed automatically (at least for the syntactic aspects and several semantic conditions) and it establishes a degree of confidence in functionality of the component which is particularly important if a component has to be modified before being reused.

Abstract data types describe objects by their sorts (names of carrier sets), the names of the basic relevant functions and their characteristic properties; thus abstract data types provide a semantic model for components. [Goguen 84] proposes the algebraic specification language OBJ as well-suited for the design of reusable software systems. A component is specified as an interface of a structured abstract data type and may be parameterized by other components. Combination of components is possible by instantiation using appropriate fitting morphisms. [Gaudel, Moineau 88] consider reusability as a relation between two specifications, one being reusable for the other. In ACT II [Ehrig, Weber 86] a component is a parameterized module consisting of two equational specifications: an interface specification and an implementation specification. Similarly, in Larch [Guttag et al. 85] a component consists of a pair: an "abstract" interface specification and an implementation; but the implementation is written in a conventional programming language.
For describing large components two levels of abstraction may not be enough; in the approach of [Matsumoto 84] a component consists of four parts at four different levels of abstraction: a requirement specification, a design specification, a source program and the object code. A consequent development of the multi-level concept is the object-oriented approach of [Meyer 87a]. It is based on abstract data type descriptions in the language Eiffel [Meyer 87b]. A reusable component is represented by a graph of specifications in which two specifications are connected either by the "is-a-relation" (which corresponds to the implementation relation of abstract data types) or by the "client relation" (which roughly corresponds to the parameter part of interfaces).

In our approach (which has been informally presented in [Wirsing 88]) a reusable component consists of a tree of algebraic specifications where a specification is a child of another specification if it is an implementation. Hence the tree may also be seen as a "top-down" program development tree where each node of the tree is an instance of a certain level of abstraction of the program with the root being the most "abstract" formal specification and the leaves representing the "concrete" implementations. Every node of the tree is itself a structured specification. In contrast to other approaches these trees are considered as objects of the language and can be constructed and manipulated by the operators of the language. That way modifications of components can be done consistently for all nodes of the tree. For the description of structured specifications the algebraic specification language ASL (cf. [Sannella, Wirsing 83], [Wirsing 86]) is used.

In section 2 the syntax and semantics of ASL is briefly summarized. In particular, the semantic domain SPEC for algebraic specifications is defined and a simple implementation relation for specifications is introduced.
Based on these definitions in section 3 a partially ordered domain RC for reusable components is defined and it is shown that all operators for specifications can be extended to monotonic operations on reusable components. Finally in section 4, the syntax and semantics of the language for reusable components is defined.

2. Structured algebraic specifications

Algebraic specifications provide a basis for describing data structures in an implementation independent way. For reusability these descriptions need to be given in a structured way. We base our approach on syntax and semantics of a language for structured algebraic specifications. In particular, we use here the specification language ASL (cf. [Sannella, Wirsing 83], [Wirsing 86]). More generally, any specification language would be appropriate if it satisfies the following two properties:

- it admits a partially ordered domain as semantics the ordering of which can be considered as notion of implementation,
- all specification building operations are monotonic.

In the following we present such a partially ordered domain and two specification building operators. Moreover, some simple examples for structured specifications (using also other operators of ASL) and implementations are given.
We assume the reader to be familiar with notations for algebraic specifications such as S-sorted signature $\Sigma = <S,F>$, Σ-term algebra $T(\Sigma)$ or $T(\Sigma,X)$, resp., class $Alg(\Sigma)$ of all isomorphism classes of Σ-algebras, the Σ-reduct $A|_\Sigma$ of a Σ'-algebra A with $\Sigma \subseteq \Sigma'$ (see e.g. [Ehrig, Mahr 85], [Wirsing 86]).

ASL is a strongly typed higher order language. It contains constructs for building signatures, sets of terms and sets of formulas as well as five specification building operators, one of them forming *basic* non-structured *specifications* by giving a signature and a set of axioms and another one building the *sum of two specifications*. A third operation allows to restrict the interpretation of a specification to those models which are *reachable* on certain sorts with certain functions. Hence reachability implies an induction principle for (the models of) specifications.

Syntax

<spec expr> ::= <basic spec> | <sum> | <reach> | ...

<basic spec>::= **signature** <signature> **axioms** <set of axioms>

<sum>::= <spec expr> + <spec expr>

<reach>::= **reachable** <spec expr> **on** <set of sorts> **with** <set of function symbols>

To each expression of the language a unique mode **m** is associated. For example specification expressions are of mode **spec**, expressions for set of sorts are of mode **setsort**.
The semantics of an algebraic specification is determined by its signature and the class of all models. The domain DOM[**spec**] $=_{def}$ SPEC for algebraic specifications is given as follows.

Definition 2.1 Let SIG be a given set of signatures.

$$SPEC =_{def} \{<\Sigma,C> : \Sigma \in SIG \text{ and } C \subseteq Alg(\Sigma)\}$$

For each sp$\in$ SPEC, we denote its first component (its signature) by sig(sp) and its second component (its class of models) by Mod(sp).

If all signatures in SIG are formed by elements from a universal set of sorts and a universal set of function names and if, moreover, $Alg(\Sigma)$ is restricted to isomorphism classes of countable algebras, then SPEC forms a set ([Sannella, Wirsing 83], [Wirsing 86]).

All specification building operations of ASL have operations on SPEC as semantic counterparts. E.g. there exist functions

$+: SPEC \times SPEC \to SPEC$ and

reach: $SPEC \times SETSORT \times SETOPN \to SPEC$

defined by

$$<\Sigma1,C1> + <\Sigma2,C2> =_{def} <\Sigma1 \cup \Sigma2, \{ A \in Alg(\Sigma1 \cup \Sigma2) : A|_{\Sigma1} \in C1 \text{ and } A|_{\Sigma2} \in C2 \}>,$$

$$reach(<\Sigma,C>,S,F) =_{def} \begin{cases} <\Sigma, \{A \in C : A \text{ is reachable on } S \text{ with } F\}> & \text{if } S \subseteq sorts(\Sigma) \text{ and } F \subseteq opns(\Sigma) \\ \bot_{SPEC} & \text{otherwise} \end{cases}$$

For the definition of reachability of algebras see [Wirsing 86].

The semantics of ASL is given by a semantic function M from the set of ASL-expressions into a partially ordered domain. In particular, for specification expressions we have

M: <spec expr>$\to$ SPEC.

Then the semantics of basic specifications and sum are given as follows.

Semantics

$M[$ **signature** Σ **axioms** $E] =_{def} < M[\Sigma], \{ A \in Alg(M[\Sigma]) : A \models M[E] \} >$
if Σ is of mode **sig** and E is of mode **formulas**,

$M[SP + SP'] =_{def} M[SP] + M[SP']$
if SP and SP′ are of mode **spec**,

M[**reachable** SP **on** S **with** F] $=_{def}$ reach(M[SP],M[S],M[F])
if SP is of mode **spec**, S is of mode **setsort** and F is of mode **setopn**.

For simplicity here the semantic function M associates to every expression of mode **m** an object of the domain DOM[**m**]. In general the syntax of expressions comprises for each mode **m** also identifiers of this mode. Then the semantic function M associates to every expression E of mode **m** a function M[E]: ENV$\to$DOM[**m**], where ENV denotes the set of *environments* of the identifiers. For example, $M[T + T'](\rho) =_{def} M[T](\rho) + M[T'](\rho)$.
For the definition of the complete syntax and semantics of ASL we refer to [Sannella, Wirsing 83] and [Wirsing 86].

As a first example, we consider the following specification NAT of natural numbers. The "reachable"- operator indicates that "zero" and "succ" are both constructors.

Example 2.2

```
spec NAT ≡
  reachable
    signature <  { nat },
                 { zero: → nat,
                   succ: nat → nat } >
    axioms       { zero ≠ succ(x),
                   succ(x) = succ(y) ⇒ x = y }
  on nat with    { zero, succ }
```

The specification NAT admits exactly the isomorphism class of the standard model IN as models. By NAT1 we will denote in the following an extension of NAT which comprises the usual standard operators on natural numbers such as +, *, <, ... ◊

For writing structured specifications it is convenient to use a derived operator "**enrich . by .**" defined by

enrich SP **by sorts** S **opns** F **axioms** E $=_{def}$

SP + **signature** < (**sorts sig** SP)∪S, (**opns sig** SP)∪F >

axioms E

where **sig, sorts** and **spec** denote the operations for selecting the signature (of a specification), the sorts and the function symbols (of a signature).

This is illustrated by the following three specifications of loose sets, sequences and trees of natural numbers.

Example 2.3
The specification SETNAT is a loose specification of finite sets of natural numbers:

```
spec SETNAT ≡
   reachable
     enrich BOOL  + NAT  by
       sorts     { set }
       opns      { empty: → set,
                   add: nat, set → set,
                   . ∈ .: nat, set → bool }
       axioms  { x ∈ empty = false,
                   x ∈ add(x,s) = true,
                   x ≠ y  ⇒ x ∈ add(y,s) = (x ∈ s) }
   on  set  with { empty, add }
```

The function "∈ " is a boolean function; it has objects of sort bool as results. Therefore SET needs a specification BOOL of truth values as given specification.

Sequences of natural numbers are described by the following specification SEQNAT.

```
spec SEQNAT ≡
   reachable
     enrich NAT by
       sorts     { seq }
       opns      { empty: → seq,
                   append: nat, seq → seq,
                   first: seq → nat,
                   rest: seq → seq }
       axioms  { first(append(x, s)) = x,
                   rest(append(x, s)) = s }
   on seq with  { empty, append }
```

The specification TREENAT has two constructors: the constant "empty" for the empty tree and the function symbol "node" which allows to combine two given trees together with a label of sort nat. Trees can be decomposed using the function symbols left, label and right.

```
spec TREENAT ≡
   reachable
     enrich NAT1 by
       sorts     { tree }
       opns      { empty: → tree,
                   node: tree, nat, tree → tree,
                   left, right: tree → tree,
                   label: tree → nat }
       axioms  { left(node(t1,x,t2)) = t1,
                   right(node(t1, x, t2)) = t2,
                   label(node(t1, x, t2)) = x }
   on tree with {empty, node }
```

The ordering between specifications is given by a simple implementation relation, the *refinement* relation: a specification SP´ is a refinement of SP, if its signature contains more sorts and/or function symbols and if its model class is included in the one of SP.

Definition 2.4 For $<\Sigma,C>$, $<\Sigma',C'> \in$ SPEC,

$$<\Sigma,C> \text{ ~~~> } <\Sigma',C'> \text{ iff } \Sigma \subseteq \Sigma' \text{ and } C'|_\Sigma \subseteq C, \text{ where } C'|_\Sigma = [\, A|_\Sigma : A \in C \,].$$

We write also SP ~~~> SP´ if M[SP](ρ) ~~~> M[SP´](ρ) for all environments ρ.

The relation ~~~> is obviously a partial ordering on SPEC. All specification building operations of ASL are monotonic w.r.t. ~~~>. This holds in particular for "+" and "reach".

Lemma 2.5 For any sp1, sp1´, sp2, sp2´ ∈ SPEC, S∈SETSORT, F∈SETOPN,
(1) sp1~~~>sp1´ and sp2~~~>sp2´ implies sp1+sp2~~~>sp1´+sp2´,
(2) sp1~~~>sp1´ implies reach(sp1,S,F)~~~>reach(sp1´,S,F).

Moreover, the sum-operator yields exactly the least upper bound of two specifications.

Lemma 2.6 For any two sp1, sp2 ∈ SPEC, sp1+sp2 is the least upper bound of sp1 and sp2 w.r.t. ~~~>.

Proof: Obviously, spi~~~>sp1+sp2 for i=1,2. Thus sp1+sp2 is an upper bound of sp1 and sp2. To show that it is the least upper bound, let sp´ be any specification with sp1~~~>sp´ and sp2~~~>sp´.
(i) sig(spi)⊆sig(sp´) holds for i=1,2 and therefore we have sig(sp1+sp2) = sig(sp1)∪sig(sp2) ⊆sig(sp´).
(ii) Let A∈Mod(sp´). By assumption we have $A|_{sig(spi)} \in$ Mod(spi) for i=1,2. Hence $A|_{sig(sp1+sp2)} \in$ Mod(sp1+sp2).
Properties (i) and (ii) imply that sp1+sp2 ~~~> sp´. ◊

In the following example we give three simple implementations of loose sets: sequences, array-pointers and ordered trees. For their specification two other derived operators for renaming and forgetting symbols are used (cf. [Sannella, Wirsing 83]).

Example 2.7
The following specification is an implementation of SETNAT by sequences:

```
spec SETNATbySEQNAT ≡
   rename
     enrich SEQNAT + BOOL by
       opns    { .∈ .: nat, seq→ bool }
       axioms { x ∈ empty = false,
                x ∈ append(x, s) = true,
                x ≠ y  ⇒ x ∈ append(y, s) = (x ∈ s) }
   by [ set / seq, add / append ]
```

Sequences may be implemented by arrays with pointers. In the following specification sequences are represented by pairs <a,p> consisting of an array a and a pointer p which indicates the component of the last entry. Appending a natural number x to a sequence is implemented by putting x into the next free component of the array. The empty sequence is represented by the pair <empty_array,zero>. For the implementation a specification ARRAYNAT is assumed as already given. ARRAYNAT describes dynamic arrays of natural numbers. The entry of an element x into an array a at index p is performed by the operation "put". Accessing to a component of an array is performed by the operation "get". For the indices of the components again natural numbers are used. The ARRAYNAT-operation "delete" deletes the entry of an array-component.

```
spec SETNATbySEQNATbyARRAYNAT ≡
  rename
    enrich ARRAYNAT by
      sorts   { seq }
      opns    { <.,.>: array, nat → seq,
                pointer: seq → integer,
                select_array: seq → array,
                empty: → seq,
                append: nat, seq → seq,
                first: seq → nat,
                rest: seq → seq,
                .∈.: nat, seq→ bool     }
      axioms { pointer(<a,p>) = p,
                select_array(<a,p>) = a,
                < select_array(s), pointer(s) > = s,
                empty = < empty_array, 0 >,
                append(x,s) = < put(select_array(s),pointer(s)+1,x), pointer(s)+1 >,
                first(s) = get(select_array(s),pointer(s)),
                rest(s) = < delete(select_array(s),pointer(s)),pointer(s)-1 >,
                x ∈ < empty_array,p > = false,
                x ∈ < put(a,i,y),p > = eq(x,y) or (x ∈ <a,p-1>) }
  by [ set / seq, add / append ]
```

One can prove that SETNATbySEQNATbyARRAYNAT is an implementation of SETNATby-SEQNAT. Note that the former is a concrete specification describing (the denotational semantics of) a machine level program.
By the transitivity of the implementation relation this implies that SETNATbySEQNATby-ARRAYNAT is also an implementation of SETNAT; i.e. SETNAT ~~~> SETNATbySEQNAT ~~~> SETNATbySEQNATbyARRAYNAT.

An alternative implementation is the implementation of sets by ordered trees.

The following specification ORDTREENAT0 adds two function symbols to the specification of trees: the function symbol "put" extends an ordered tree by one element in such a way that the order is preserved. The function symbol "∈" determines for ordered trees whether an element is a node of the tree or not.

```
spec ORDTREENAT0 ≡
  enrich TREENAT by
    opns   {  put: nat, tree: → tree,
                . ∈ .: nat, set → bool }
    axioms{  put(x,empty) = node(empty, x, empty),
              put(x, node(t1, y, t2) ) =
                  if x<y
                     then node(put(x,t1),y,t2)
                     else if y<x
                            then node(t1,y,put(x,t2))
                           else node(t1, y, t2) fi
                  fi,
              x ∈ empty = false,
              x ∈ node(t1, y, t2) =
                 if x<y
                    then x ∈ t1
                    else if y<x then x ∈ t2
                                    else true fi
                 fi  }
```

The function put yields, applied to ordered trees, also ordered trees, whereas the constructor "node" does not preserve the order. Therefore, when dealing with ordered trees it may be "dangerous" to give access to "node". Using the operator **forget** which just "forgets" the function "node" from the models of ORDTREENAT0 and the operator **restrict** which restricts the resultant structures to the subalgebras which are generated by the remaining constructors (empty and put for tree), we obtain a specification for ordered trees:

spec ORDTREENAT ≡
  restrict
    forget { node } **from** ORDTREENAT0

The specification SETNAT can be implemented by ordered trees if "tree" is renamed into "set", "put" is renamed into "add":

SETNAT ~~~> SETNATbyORDTREENAT

where

spec SETNATbyORDTREENAT ≡ **rename** ORDTREENAT **by** [set / tree, add / put]

◊

3. A domain for reusable components

In this section a partially ordered domain for reusable components is constructed and the basic operations for reusable components are defined. It is shown that all monotonic operations for algebraic specifications can be extended to monotonic operations on reusable components.
Informally, the semantics of a reusable component is an equivalence class of trees. The nodes of the trees are objects of a partially ordered domain and two consecutive nodes are related by the ordering of the domain. In our particular application to software development, the nodes will be objects of the domain SPEC for algebraic specifications and the nodes are related by ~~~>. Hence such trees may be seen as (the semantics of) a top down program development tree where the root represents the most abstract description of a problem and the leaves are different concrete implementations. (In the terminology of [Parnass 76] such trees are program families where the root describes the most common properties of the programs under consideration.)

For the construction of the domain RC for reusable components we proceed as follows:
At first the set SPECTREE of finite, unordered trees of SPEC-objects is defined where each father node is related to its children nodes by the ordering ~~~>. Then the ordering ~~~> is extended to trees of SPEC-objects yielding a quasi ordering $\leq_{SPECTREE}$ on SPECTREE. In a next step some basic operations for SPECTREE-objects are defined and all operations for algebraic specifications are extended to monotonic operations on SPECTREE. Finally, the quasi ordering $\leq_{SPECTREE}$ gives rise to an equivalence relation (t1 ~ t2 iff t1 $\leq_{SPECTREE}$ t2 and t2 $\leq_{SPECTREE}$ t1) such that factorization wrt. ~ yields the partially ordered domain RC for reusable components. From the definition of RC it follows immediately that all monotonic operations on SPECTREE are compatible with the equivalence relation and hence induce monotonic operations on RC. In particular, all operations for algebraic specifications induce monotonic operations for reusable components.

Definition 3.1 The set SPECTREE is the least set with the following properties:

(0) $\perp_{SPECTREE} \in$ SPECTREE

(1) <sp, Ø> ∈ SPECTREE for all sp ∈ SPEC \ $\{\perp_{SPEC}\}$

(2) If $<sp_1, s_1>, \ldots, <sp_n, s_n> \in$ SPECTREE, sp ∈ SPEC \ $\{\perp_{SPEC}\}$
and sp ~~~> sp_i for i = 1,...,n, then $< sp, \{<sp_1, s_1>, \ldots, <sp_n, s_n>\} > \in$ SPECTREE.

◊

Remark 3.2 An equivalent definition of SPECTREE can be given constructively :

$$\text{SPECTREE} = (\cup_{i \in \mathbb{N}} \text{SPECTREE}_i) \cup \{\perp_{SPECTREE}\}$$

where

$$\text{SPECTREE}_0 = \{<sp, \emptyset> \mid sp \in \text{SPEC} \setminus \{\perp_{SPEC}\}\},$$

$$\text{SPECTREE}_{i+1} = \text{SPECTREE}_i \cup \{\langle sp, s\rangle \mid sp \in \text{SPEC} \setminus \{\bot_{\text{SPEC}}\},\ s \text{ is a finite subset of } \text{SPECTREE}_i \text{ such that for all } \langle sp', s'\rangle \in s \text{ holds: } sp \rightsquigarrow sp' \}. \quad \Diamond$$

Each pair <sp, s> ∈ SPECTREE is a finite, unordered tree where the nodes are objects of the semantic domain SPEC for algebraic specifications. For each tree <sp, s> ∈ SPECTREE the nodes increase (wrt. ~~~>) with the depth of the tree. The *root* of <sp, s> is the SPEC-object sp and s is the set of *sons*. If s = Ø the tree consists only of one node sp. Since s is a set, SPECTREE-objects are independent of the order and of the number of occurrences of sons, i.e.

$$\langle sp, s \cup s'\rangle = \langle sp, s' \cup s\rangle \text{ and } \langle sp, s \cup s\rangle = \langle sp, s\rangle.$$

In the following, objects of SPECTREE are often picturally represented by their tree representation, e.g. $\langle sp, \{\langle sp_1, \emptyset\rangle, \langle sp_2, \{\langle sp_{21}, \emptyset\rangle\}\rangle\}\rangle$ is represented by the tree

The ordering ~~~> on the domain for algebraic specifications induces a quasi ordering $\leq_{\text{SPECTREE}}$ on SPECTREE with least element $\bot_{\text{SPECTREE}}$. Informally, $t \leq_{\text{SPECTREE}} t'$ holds if t´ is a refinement of t. In particular, $\langle sp, \emptyset\rangle \leq_{\text{SPECTREE}} \langle sp', s\rangle$ whenever sp ~~~> sp´. Formally, the relation $\leq_{\text{SPECTREE}}$ is defined as follows.

Definition 3.3 For all t, t´ ∈ SPECTREE:

$t \leq_{\text{SPECTREE}} t'$ iff

$t = \bot_{\text{SPECTREE}}$ or

(t = <sp, s>, t´ = <sp´, s´>, sp ~~~> sp´ and there exists a map $\phi: s \rightarrow s'$, such that for all $r \in s$: $r \leq_{\text{SPECTREE}} \phi(r)$) ◊

Example 3.4 If sp ~~~> sp´, sp_1 ~~~> sp_1', sp_{11} ~~~> sp_{11}' and sp_2 ~~~> sp_2' then

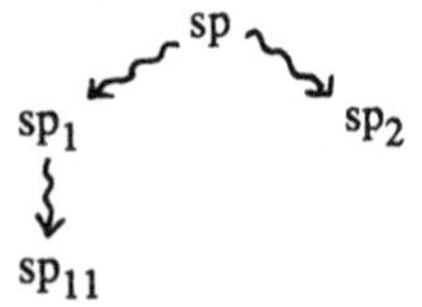

$\leq_{\text{SPECTREE}}$

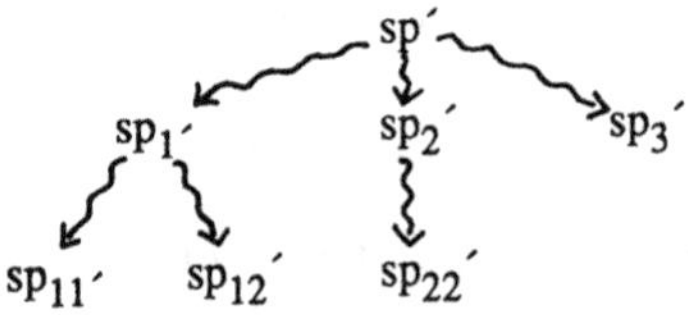

◊

Fact 3.5 The relation $\leq_{\text{SPECTREE}}$ is reflexive and transitive but not antisymmetric.

Example 3.6

If t =

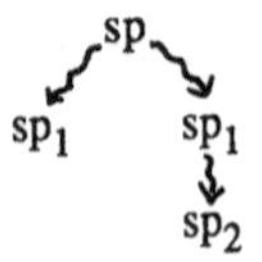

and t´ =

then $t \leq_{\text{SPECTREE}} t'$ and $t' \leq_{\text{SPECTREE}} t$ but $t \neq t'$.

Similarly, if $t = \overset{sp}{\underset{sp_1 \quad sp_2}{\swarrow \searrow}}$, $t' = \overset{sp}{\underset{sp_2}{\downarrow}}$ and $sp_1 \rightsquigarrow sp_2$,

then $t \leq_{SPECTREE} t'$ and $t' \leq_{SPECTREE} t$ but $t \neq t'$. ◊

From the definition of $\leq_{SPECTREE}$ follows immediately that the function

$$\text{root: SPECTREE} \rightarrow \text{SPEC}$$

which determines the root of a tree is monotonic. "root" is defined by

$$\text{root}(\bot_{SPECTREE}) =_{def} \bot_{SPEC} ,$$

$$\text{root}(<sp, s>) =_{def} sp.$$

For the construction of SPECTREE-objects the following operation "implement" is introduced:

$$\text{implement: SPEC x } \mathcal{P}_{fin}(\text{SPECTREE}) \rightarrow \text{SPECTREE}$$

$$\text{implement}(sp, s) =_{def} \begin{cases} <sp, s> & \text{if } sp \neq \bot_{SPEC} \text{ and } sp \rightsquigarrow \text{root}(r) \text{ for all } r \in s \\ \bot_{SPECTREE} & \text{otherwise.} \end{cases}$$

Here $\mathcal{P}_{fin}(\text{SPECTREE})$ denotes the set of finite subsets of SPECTREE. On $\mathcal{P}_{fin}(\text{SPECTREE})$ the following quasi ordering is defined (cf. definition 3.3):

$$s \leq_{\mathcal{P}_{fin}(SPECTREE)} s' \text{ iff there exists a map } \phi: s \rightarrow s', \text{ such that for all } r \in s :$$

$$r \leq_{SPECTREE} \phi(r).$$

Fact 3.7 The operation "implement" is monotonic in the second argument.
Moreover, "implement" is monotonic for first arguments with result $\neq \bot_{SPECTREE}$, i.e.
for all $sp, sp' \in SPEC, s \in \mathcal{P}_{fin}(\text{SPECTREE})$ the following holds:

If $sp \rightsquigarrow sp'$ and $\text{implement}(sp', s) \neq \bot_{SPECTREE}$

then $\text{implement}(sp, s) \leq_{SPECTREE} \text{implement}(sp', s)$. ◊

In the next step all operations for algebraic specifications are extended to monotonic operations on SPECTREE. For that purpose the following general construction is used:

Definition 3.8 Let PO be a partially ordered set and f: SPEC x PO $\rightarrow$ SPEC a monotonic function. The function

$$f^*: \text{SPECTREE x PO} \rightarrow \text{SPECTREE}$$

is defined recursively on the structure of SPECTREE-objects:

$$f^*(\bot_{SPECTREE}, p) =_{def} \bot_{SPECTREE} ,$$

$$f^*(<sp, \emptyset>, p) =_{def} \begin{cases} <f(sp,p), \emptyset> & \text{if } f(sp,p) \neq \bot_{SPEC} \\ \bot_{SPECTREE} & \text{otherwise,} \end{cases}$$

$$f^*(<sp, \{t_1,...,t_n\}>, p) =_{def} \begin{cases} <f(sp, p), \{f^*(t_1,p),...,f^*(t_n,p)\}> & \text{if } f(sp,p) \neq \bot_{SPEC} \\ \bot_{SPECTREE} & \text{otherwise.} \end{cases}$$

◊

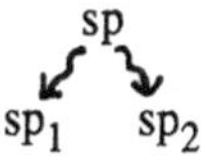

Proposition 3.9
Under the assumptions of definition 3.8 the function f^*: SPECTREE x PO $\rightarrow$ SPECTREE is well-defined and monotonic.

Proof:
(1) Well-definedness of f^*:

Obviously $f^*(\perp_{SPECTREE}, p)$ and $f^*(<sp, \emptyset>, p)$ are objects of SPECTREE.

Now assume that $f^*(t_i,p) \in$ SPECTREE for i = 1,…,n.

If $f(sp,p) = \perp_{SPEC}$ then $f^*(<sp, \{t_1,\ldots,t_n\}>, p) = \perp_{SPECTREE} \in$ SPECTREE.

Otherwise, since sp~~~>root(t_i) for i = 1,…,n, the monotonicity of f implies f(sp,p)~~~>f(root(t_i),p). Since f(root(t_i),p) = root($f^*(t_i,p)$) one obtains

$<f(sp, p), \{f^*(t_1,p),\ldots,f^*(t_n,p)\}> \in$ SPECTREE.

(2) Monotonicity of f^*:

Let t, t´ $\in$ SPECTREE and $t \leq_{SPECTREE} t'$. W.l.o.g. $t' = <sp', \{t_1',\ldots,t_k'\}>$.

Case 0: $t = \perp_{SPECTREE}$.

Then obviously $f^*(t,p) \leq_{SPECTREE} f^*(t',p)$.

Case 1: $t = <sp, \emptyset>$.

Then sp~~~>sp´ and the monotonicity of f implies f(sp,p)~~~>f(sp´,p).

If $f(sp,p) = \perp_{SPEC}$ then $f^*(t,p) = \perp_{SPECTREE} \leq_{SPECTREE} f^*(t',p)$.

If $f(sp,p) \neq \perp_{SPEC}$ then $f(sp',p) \neq \perp_{SPEC}$. Hence $f^*(t,p) = <f(sp,p), \emptyset>$ and $f^*(t',p) = <f(sp', p), \{f^*(t_1',p),\ldots,f^*(t_k',p)\}>$. Then $f^*(t,p) \leq_{SPECTREE} f^*(t',p)$ by definition of $\leq_{SPECTREE}$.

Case 2: $t = <sp, \{t_1,\ldots,t_n\}>$.

Then sp~~~>sp´ and for each t_i there exists a t_j' such that $t_i \leq_{SPECTREE} t_j'$. From the monotonicity of f and from the induction hypothesis follows that f(sp,p)~~~>f(sp´,p) and $f^*(t_i,p) \leq_{SPECTREE} f^*(t_j',p)$.

If $f(sp,p) = \perp_{SPEC}$ then (as in case 1) $f^*(t,p) = \perp_{SPECTREE} \leq_{SPECTREE} f^*(t',p)$.

If $f(sp,p) \neq \perp_{SPEC}$ then $f(sp',p) \neq \perp_{SPEC}$ and hence

$f^*(t, p) = <f(sp, p), \{f^*(t_1,p),\ldots,f^*(t_n,p)\}>$,

$f^*(t',p) = <f(sp', p), \{f^*(t_1',p),\ldots,f^*(t_k',p)\}>$.

Then the assumptions and the definition of $\leq_{SPECTREE}$ imply that

$f^*(t,p) \leq_{SPECTREE} f^*(t',p)$.

The monotonicity of f^* in the second argument follows simply from the monotonicity of f in its second argument. ◊

Corollary 3.10 By the construction of definition 3.8 the specification building operations of ASL (admitting only one SPEC-argument) can be extended to monotonic operations on SPECTREE.

E.g.

reach*: SPECTREE x SETSORT x SETOPN $\rightarrow$ SPECTREE,

$reach^*(\perp_{SPECTREE}, S,F) =_{def} \perp_{SPECTREE}$,

$$reach^*(<sp, \emptyset>, S,F) =_{def} \begin{cases} <reach(sp,S,F), \emptyset> & \text{if } reach(sp,S,F) \neq \perp_{SPEC} \\ \perp_{SPECTREE} & \text{otherwise,} \end{cases}$$

$$\text{reach}^*(\langle sp, \{t_1,\ldots,t_n\}\rangle, S, F) =_{def}$$

$$\begin{cases} \langle \text{reach}(sp,S,F), \{\text{reach}^*(t_1,S,F),\ldots,\text{reach}^*(t_n,S,F)\}\rangle & \text{if reach}(sp,S,F) \neq \bot_{SPEC} \\ \bot_{SPECTREE} & \text{otherwise.} \end{cases}$$

◊

It is possible to generalize this construction to operations of the form

$$f: SPEC \times \ldots \times SPEC \times PO \to SPEC$$

yielding an extension

$$f^*: SPECTREE \times \ldots \times SPECTREE \times PO \to SPECTREE.$$

For simplicity in the following it is directly shown how the "+" - operator for specifications can be extended to an operation "+*" which constructs the sum of two SPECTREE-objects.

Definition 3.11 The operation

$$+^*: SPECTREE \times SPECTREE \to SPECTREE$$

is recursively defined on the structure of SPECTREE-objects:

$$\bot_{SPECTREE} +^* t =_{def} t +^* \bot_{SPECTREE} =_{def} t,$$

$$\langle sp, s\rangle +^* \langle sp', s'\rangle =_{def} \langle sp + sp', \cup_{r\in s}\{r +^* \langle sp',s'\rangle\} \cup \cup_{r'\in s'}\{\langle sp,s\rangle +^* r'\}\rangle$$

◊

Fact 3.12 The operation +* is well-defined and monotonic in both arguments. (Proof by induction on the structure of the arguments.) ◊

Example 3.13

If t = 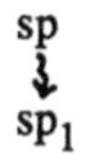

and t′ = 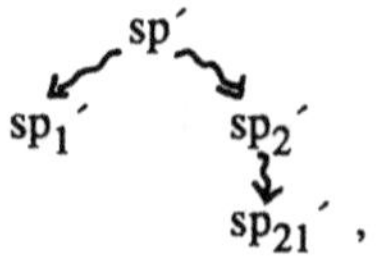

,

then t +* t′ =

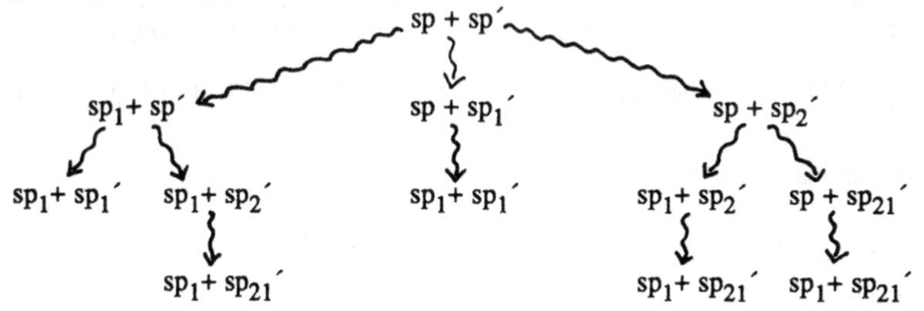

◊

The sum of two trees t and t′ consists of all combinations of nodes of t and t′ such that the order of t and t′ is respected. Obviously, t +* t′ is a refinement of t and t′, i.e. $t \leq_{SPECTREE} (t +^* t')$ and $t' \leq_{SPECTREE} (t +^* t')$ holds. If one is interested in the coarsest refinement of t and t′ one can construct a least upper bound of t and t′.

Proposition 3.14 The operation

$$\text{lub: SPECTREE} \times \text{SPECTREE} \rightarrow \text{SPECTREE}$$

$$\text{lub}(\bot_{\text{SPECTREE}}, t) =_{def} \text{lub}(t, \bot_{\text{SPECTREE}}) =_{def} t$$

$$\text{lub}(<sp, s>, <sp', s'>) =_{def} <sp + sp', \cup_{r \in s}\{r +^* <sp',\emptyset>\} \cup \cup_{r' \in s'}\{<sp,\emptyset> +^* r'\}>$$

is well-defined and monotonic.
Moreover, lub(t, t') is a least upper bound of t and t' (wrt. $\leq_{\text{SPECTREE}}$). ◊

(Note that least upper bounds wrt. $\leq_{\text{SPECTREE}}$ are not uniquely determined since $\leq_{\text{SPECTREE}}$ is not antisymmetric.)

Both binary operations "+*" and "lub" have been defined in a <u>non-strict</u> way ($\bot +^* t \neq \bot$, $\text{lub}(\bot, t) \neq \bot$) in order to get upper bounds; obviously the strict versions of these operations are monotonic as well.
Informally, lub(t, t') is simply obtained by adding the root sp' of t' to each node of t (yielding the tree $t1 = t +^* <sp', \emptyset>$), by adding the root sp of t to each node of t' (yielding the tree $t2 = <sp, \emptyset> +^* t'$) and finally by putting t1 and t2 together by identification of their roots.

Example 3.15 Let t and t' be as in example 3.13.

lub(t, t') =

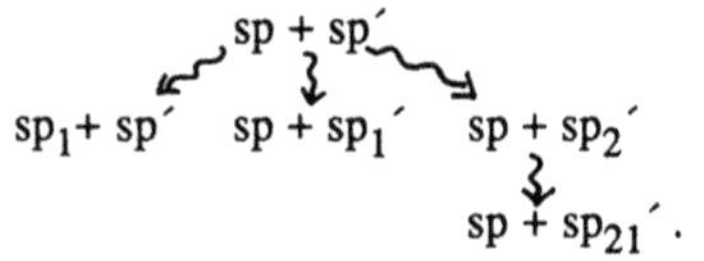

◊

For showing that lub(t, t') is a least upper bound of t and t' the following lemma is used:

Lemma 3.16
Let $t, t' \in$ SPECTREE and $sp \in \text{SPEC} \setminus \{\bot_{\text{SPEC}}\}$ such that $t \leq_{\text{SPECTREE}} t'$ and sp~~~>root(t').
Then

$$t +^* <sp, \emptyset> \leq_{\text{SPECTREE}} t'.$$

<u>Proof:</u>
The proof is straightforward by induction on the structure of t. It is based on the following consequence of the least upper bound property of the "+" - operation for SPEC-objects (cf. lemma 2.6):
If $sp_1, sp_2, sp_3 \in$ SPEC, such that sp_1 ~~~> sp_3 and sp_2 ~~~> sp_3, then $sp_1 + sp_2$ ~~~> sp_3.

◊

By means of the lemma 3.16 and proposition 3.14 can be proved:

<u>Proof of proposition 3.14:</u>

(1) Well-definedness of lub:

We have to show that sp + sp' ~~~> root(r +* <sp',∅>) for all $r \in s$ and

sp + sp'~~~>root(<sp,∅> +* r') for all $r' \in s'$.

Since root(r +* <sp',∅>) = root(r) + sp' and sp~~~>root(r) for all $r \in s$, the monotonicity of +* implies sp + sp'~~~>root(r) + sp' and hence sp + sp'~~~>root(r +* <sp',∅>) for all $r \in s$.

Analogously one shows that sp + sp'~~~>root(<sp,∅> +* r') for all $r' \in s'$.

(2) The monotonicity of lub follows directly from the "least upper bound" property.

(3) Least upper bound:

Obviously lub(t, t') is an upper bound of t and t'.

Now let t = <sp, s>, t' = <sp', s'> and t'' = <sp'', s''>, such that t'' is an upper bound of t and

t', i.e. $t \leq_{SPECTREE} t''$ and $t' \leq_{SPECTREE} t''$. We have to show that $lub(t, t') \leq_{SPECTREE} t''$. Since t'' is an upper bound of t and t', $sp \sim\!\sim\!\sim\!> sp''$ and $sp' \sim\!\sim\!\sim\!> sp''$. Hence $sp + sp' \sim\!\sim\!\sim\!> sp''$ (by lemma 2.6).

Moreover, there exist maps $\phi: s \rightarrow s''$ and $\phi': s' \rightarrow s''$ such that $r \leq_{SPECTREE} \phi(r)$ for all $r \in s$ and $r' \leq_{SPECTREE} \phi'(r')$ for all $r' \in s'$. Since $sp'' \sim\!\sim\!\sim\!> root(\phi(r))$ and $sp'' \sim\!\sim\!\sim\!> root(\phi'(r'))$ for all $r \in s$ and $r' \in s'$ lemma 3.16 implies $r +^* \langle sp'',\emptyset\rangle \leq_{SPECTREE} \phi(r)$ and $r' +^* \langle sp'',\emptyset\rangle \leq_{SPECTREE} \phi'(r')$ for all $r \in s$ and $r' \in s'$.

Since $sp \sim\!\sim\!\sim\!> sp''$ and $sp' \sim\!\sim\!\sim\!> sp''$, $\langle sp,\emptyset\rangle \leq_{SPECTREE} \langle sp'',\emptyset\rangle$ and $\langle sp',\emptyset\rangle \leq_{SPECTREE} \langle sp'',\emptyset\rangle$. Then the monotonicity of $+^*$ implies

$r +^* \langle sp',\emptyset\rangle \leq_{SPECTREE} r +^* \langle sp'',\emptyset\rangle$ and $r' +^* \langle sp,\emptyset\rangle \leq_{SPECTREE} r' +^* \langle sp'',\emptyset\rangle$ for all $r \in s$ and $r' \in s'$. Now by transitivity of $\leq_{SPECTREE}$ one obtains

$r +^* \langle sp',\emptyset\rangle \leq_{SPECTREE} \phi(r)$ and $r' +^* \langle sp,\emptyset\rangle \leq_{SPECTREE} \phi'(r')$ for all $r \in s$ and $r' \in s'$.

Then by definition of lub (and commutativity of $+^*$) $lub(t, t') \leq_{SPECTREE} t''$, i.e. $lub(t, t')$ is a least upper bound of t and t'. ◊

In the last step of this section the partially ordered domain RC for reusable components is constructed. It consists of all equivalence classes of SPECTREE-objects, where for all $t, t' \in$ SPECTREE the equivalence relation ~ is defined by:

$$t \sim t' \text{ iff } t \leq_{SPECTREE} t' \text{ and } t' \leq_{SPECTREE} t.$$

Definition 3.17

(1) The set RC is defined by factorization of SPECTREE wrt. the equivalence relation ~, i.e.

$$RC =_{def} SPECTREE/\sim \; = \{[\,t\,] \mid t \in SPECTREE\}$$

([t] denotes the equivalence class of t wrt. ~.)

(2) For all $[\,t\,], [\,t'\,] \in RC$:

$$[\,t\,] \leq_{RC} [\,t'\,] \text{ iff } t \leq_{SPECTREE} t'.$$ ◊

Obviously $\leq_{RC}$ defines a partial ordering on RC. Moreover, RC together with the ordering $\leq_{RC}$ has the following property:

Fact 3.18 $(RC, \leq_{RC})$ is an upper semilattice with least element $[\,\bot_{SPECTREE}\,]$.
For $[\,t\,], [\,t'\,] \in RC$ the least upper bound is defined by $[\,lub(t, t')\,]$. ◊

The next proposition says that all monotonic operations on SPECTREE are compatible with the equivalence relation ~ and hence induce monotonic operations on RC:

Proposition 3.19

Let PO be a partially ordered set and f^*: SPECTREE x … x SPECTREE x PO → SPECTREE a monotonic function. Then the function

$$f_{RC}: RC \times \ldots \times RC \times PO \rightarrow RC,$$

$$f_{RC}([t_1],\ldots,[t_n],p) =_{def} [f(t_1,\ldots,t_n,p)]$$ is well-defined and monotonic.

<u>Proof:</u>
The well-definedness and the monotonicity of f_{RC} follow directly from the monotonicity of f^*. ◊

Corollary 3.20 All specification building operations "f" of ASL induce monotonic operations "f_{RC}" on RC.
E.g.

$+_{RC}$: RC x RC → RC, [t] $+_{RC}$ [t′] = [t +* t′] and

$reach_{RC}$: RC x SETSORT x SETOPN → RC, $reach_{RC}$([t], S,O) $=_{def}$ [reach*(t,S,O)] .

Proof By corollary 3.10 and proposition 3.19. ◊

Finally, the characteristic tree operations "root" and "implement" for determining the root of a tree respectively for constructing SPECTREE-objects induce corresponding operations on RC.

Fact 3.21
(1) The operation $root_{RC}$: RC → SPEC, $root_{RC}$([t]) $=_{def}$ root(t)
is well-defined and monotonic.

(2) The operation $implement_{RC}$: SPEC x $\mathcal{P}_{fin}$(RC) → RC,

$implement_{RC}$(sp, {$[t_1]$, ...,$[t_n]$}) $=_{def}$ [implement(sp, {t_1,...,t_n})] (n≥0)

is well-defined and monotonic in the second argument.
Moreover, "$implement_{RC}$" is monotonic for all first arguments with result $\neq \perp_{SPECTREE}$.

Here $\mathcal{P}_{fin}$(RC) denotes the set of finite subsets of RC. On $\mathcal{P}_{fin}$(RC) the following quasi ordering is defined:

$s \leq_{\mathcal{P}_{fin}(RC)} s'$ iff there exists a map ϕ: s → s′, such that for all r ∈ s : $r \leq_{RC} \phi(r)$

(cf. the definition of $\leq_{\mathcal{P}_{fin}(SPECTREE)}$ before fact 3.7) ◊

4. A language for reusable components

In this section the language ASL for algebraic specifications (cf. section 2) is extended to the description of reusable components. For that purpose a new mode **rc** for reusable components is introduced. The semantics of **rc** is the domain RC of section 3:

DOM[**rc**] $=_{def}$ RC.

Expressions of mode **rc** can be built by the extension of the specification building operations of ASL to reusable components. For the construction of components an operation **implement** ... **by** is defined which combines a set of already given components together with a specification which is the root of the new component. The constructs for components correspond exactly to the operations on RC defined in section 3.

Syntax

<rc expr> :: = <implement> | <rc sum> | <rc reachable> | ...

<implement> :: = **implement** <spec expr> **by** { {<rc expr>{,<rc expr>}*} }

<rc sum> :: = <rc expr> $+_{rc}$ <rc expr>

<rc reachable> :: = **reachable**$_{rc}$ <rc expr> **on** <set of sorts> **with** <set of function symbols>

For describing the root of a component the syntax of specification expressions (i.e. expressions of mode **spec**) is extended by expressions of the form

root <rc expr>.

Derived operations

If a component is constructed by the **implement**-operation and the set of children components is empty, then the following abbreviation is used:

rc SP $=_{def}$ **implement** SP **by** {}.

The derived operations for algebraic specifications can be extended to derived operations for reusable components, for example

enrich$_{rc}$ T **by sorts** S **opns** F **axioms** E $=_{def}$
T $+_{rc}$ **rc(signature** <(**sorts sig root** T) $\cup$ S ; (**opns sig root** T) $\cup$F> **axioms** E)

Semantics

M[**implement** SP **by** {$T_1,\ldots,T_n$}] $=_{def}$ implement$_{RC}$(M[SP], {M[T_1],...,M[T_n]})
if SP is of mode **spec** and $T_1,\ldots,T_n$ are of mode **rc**,

M[T $+_{rc}$ T′] $=_{def}$ M[T] $+_{RC}$ M[T′] if T and T′ are of mode **rc**,

M[**reachable**$_{rc}$ T **on** S **with** F] $=_{def}$ reach$_{RC}$(M[T], M[S], M[F])
if T is of mode **rc**, S is of mode **setsort** and F is of mode **setopn**,

M[**root** T] $=_{def}$ root(M[T]) if T is of mode **rc**.

The **implement**-operation constructs trees of specifications where children nodes are implementations of their father node.

Example 4.1 From example 2.7 one obtains the following component for finite sets of natural numbers. The root is an abstract description of properties of finite sets of natural numbers whereas the leaves are different "concrete" implementations by ordered trees and by arrays of natural numbers.

RC-SETNAT $=_{def}$ **implement** SETNAT **by**
{ **rc** SETNATbyORDTREENAT,
implement SETNATbySEQNAT **by**
{**rc** SETNATbySEQNATbyARRAYNAT}}

Picturally, RC-SETNAT can be represented by the following tree of specifications:

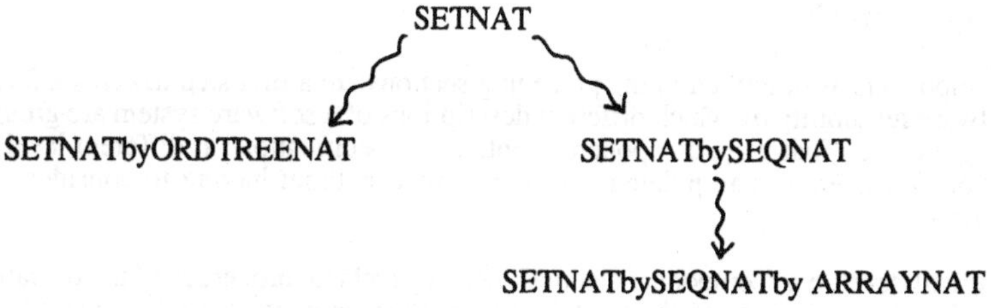

The application of the operations such as **reachable**$_{rc}$ or **enrich**$_{rc}$ modifies a component T by simultaneous application of the corresponding ASL-operation to all nodes of T, i.e. the application of a single operator changes a component consistently at all levels of abstraction. For **enrich**$_{rc}$ this property can be expressed formally by the following (semantical) identity.

Proposition 4.2
For SP of mode **spec**, $T_1,\ldots,T_n$ of mode **rc**, S of mode **setsort**, F of mode **setopn** the following holds:

reachable$_{rc}$ (**implement** SP **by** $\{T_1,\ldots,T_n\}$) **on** S **with** F =
  implement (**reachable** SP **on** S **with** F) **by**
    {**reachable**$_{rc}$ T_1 **on** S **with** F ,..., **reachable**$_{rc}$ T_n **on** S **with** F }

enrich$_{rc}$ (**implement** SP **by** $\{T_1,\ldots,T_n\}$) **by** Δ =
  implement (**enrich** SP **by** Δ) **by**
    {**enrich**$_{rc}$ T_1 **by** Δ,..., **enrich**$_{rc}$ T_n **by** Δ }

where Δ = **sorts** S **opns** F **axioms** E.

Proof Obvious from the definition of the semantics. ◊

Example 4.3 The component RC-SETNAT is enriched by functions computing the union and the cardinality of sets:

enrich$_{rc}$ RC-SETNAT **by** Δ

where

Δ = **opns** { union : set, set → set,
  card : set → nat }
axioms { union(empty, s) = s,
  union(add(x,s1),s2) = add(x,union(s1, s2)),
  card(empty) = zero,
  card(add(x, s)) = **if** x ∈ s **then** card(s)
    else succ(card(s)) **fi** }.

Then (by proposition 4.2) the enrichment Δ distributes over all specifications of the component RC-SETNAT, i.e. **enrich**$_{rc}$ RC-SETNAT **by** Δ =

enrich SETNAT **by** Δ

enrich SETNATbyORDTREENAT **by** Δ **enrich** SETNATbySEQNAT **by** Δ

enrich SETNATbySEQNATbyARRAYNAT **by** Δ
◊

5. Concluding remarks

Specification components as described in the preceding sections are a first step towards a formal approach to software reusability by which different descriptions of a software system are grouped together to a single object.That way, components containing specifications at different levels of abstraction can be consistently manipulated and transformed without having to consider each specification separatly.

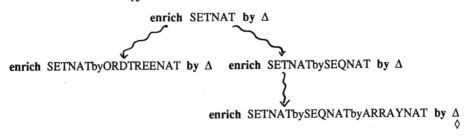

In a next step we will develop a "component algebra", i.e. the algebraic properties of the operations for components. For the extensions of the specification building operators (such as reach*, +*) many properties are consequences of the properties of the corresponding operators on specifications and thus in many cases they can be derived from the equations of "module algebra" [Bergstra et al. 86].

The partial order of the domain RC of components and the monotonicity of the operations induce a parameterization mechanism for components: a parameterized component is a monotonic function from RC into RC; the $\lambda\pi$-calculus as introduced by [Feijs et al. 88] provides a mathematical foundation for dealing with parameter constraints.

Finally, using parameterized specifications and components the approach of [Sannella, Tarlecki 87] for documenting implementation decisions can be integrated in our framework (cf.[Wirsing 88]).

References

[Bergstra et al. 86] J.A. Bergstra, J. Heering, P. Klint: Module algebra. Math. Centrum Amsterdam, Report CS-R8615.

[Ehrig, Mahr 85] H. Ehrig, B. Mahr: Fundamentals of algebraic specification 1. EATCS Monographs on Theor. Comp. Science, Vol. 6, Springer Verlag, 1985.

[Ehrig, Weber 86] H. Ehrig, H. Weber: Programming in the large with algebraic module specifications. In: H.J. Kugler (ed.): Information Processing 86. Amsterdam: North-Holland, 1986, 675-684.

[Feijs et al. 88] L.M.G. Feijs, H.B.M. Jonkers, C.P.J. Koymans, G.R. Renardel de Lavalette: The calculus $\lambda\pi$.To appear in: J.A. Bergstra, M. Wirsing(eds.): Algebraic methods: theory, tools and applications. Springer Lecture Notes in Computer Science, 1988.

[Gaudel, Moineau 88] M.C. Gaudel, Th. Moineau: A theory of software reusability. In: H. Ganzinger (ed.): ESOP '88. Springer Lecture Notes in Computer Science 300, 1988, 115-130.

[Goguen 84] J.A. Goguen: Parameterized programming. IEEE Trans. on Software Engineering, Vol. SE-10, No. 5, 1984, 528-543.

[Guttag et al. 85] J.V. Guttag, J.J. Horning, J.M. Wing: Larch in five easy pieces. Digital Systems Research Center, Tech. Report 5, 1985.

[Matsumoto 84] Y. Matsumoto: Some experiences in promoting reusable software. IEEE Trans. on Software Engineering, Vol. SE-10, No. 5, 1984, 502-513.

[Meyer 87a] B. Meyer: Reusability: the case for object-oriented design. IEEE Software, March 1987.

[Meyer 87b] B. Meyer: Eiffel: programming for reusability and extendibility. Sigplan Notices 22, 1987.

[Parnass 76] D.L. Parnass: On the design and development of program families. IEEE Trans. on Software Engineering, Vol. SE-2, No. 1, 1976, 1-9.

[Sannella, Tarlecki 87] D.T. Sannella, A. Tarlecki: Towards formal development of programs from algebraic specifications: implementations revisited. In H. Ehrig et al. (eds.): TAPSOFT 87. Springer Lecture Notes in Computer Science 249, 1987, 96-110.

[Sannella, Wirsing 83] D.T. Sannella, M. Wirsing: A kernel language for algebraic specifications and implementation. In: Marek Karpinski (ed.): Proc. FCT 83, Found. of Computation Theory, Borgholm, August 1983. Springer Lecture Notes in Computer Science 158, 1983, 413-427.

[Wirsing 86] M. Wirsing: Structured algebraic specifications: a kernel language. Theoretical Computer Science 42, 1986, 123-249.

[Wirsing 88] M. Wirsing: Algebraic description of reusable software components. In: E. Milgrom, P. Wodon (eds.): COMP EURO 88. IEEE Computer Society, 834, Computer Society Press, 1988, 300-312.

Comparing Interconnection Networks

by

Burkhard Monien
Fachbereich Mathematik/Informatik
Universität Paderborn
4790 Paderborn
Federal Republic of Germany

Hal Sudborough
Computer Science Program, MP 31
University of Texas at Dallas
Richardson, Texas 75083-0688
U.S.A.

Abstract

We review results on embedding network and program structures into popular parallel computer structures. Such embeddings can be viewed as high level descriptions of efficient methods to simulate an algorithm designed for one type of architecture on a different network structure and/or techniques to distribute data/program variables to achieve optimum use of all available processors.

I. Common Network and Algorithm Structures

Various parallel computer architectures have gained favor and are in use today. Other structures included here are often used as program/data structures. Typical measurements to compare topologies of networks (graphs) include their diameter, namely the maximum distance between any pair of nodes, and their maximum node degree, i.e. the maximum number of edges incident to a node. These properties are important, as (a) a network's diameter measures how much distance exists between processors and hence gives a lower bound on communication time and (b) a network's maximum node degree describes the largest number of connections made to an individual processor.

Binary Hypercubes The binary hypercube of dimension n, denoted by Q(n), is the graph whose nodes are all binary strings of length n and whose edges connect those binary strings which differ in exactly one position.

Clearly, a binary hypercube Q(n) has 2^n nodes and, as each node is connected to n edges, a total of $n2^{n-1}$ edges. It is also easily seen that the diameter of the hypercube Q(n) is n, which is the logarithm of the number of its nodes. An illustration of Q(4) is shown in Figure 1.

Binary Trees The complete binary tree of height n, denoted by B(n), is the graph whose nodes are all binary strings of length at most n and whose edges connect each string x of length i ($0 \leq i < n$) with the strings xa, a in {0,1}, of length i+1. The node e, where e is the empty string, is the *root* of B(n) and a node x is at level i, $i \geq 0$, in B(n) if x is a string of length i. A binary tree is a connected subgraph of B(n), for some $n \geq 0$. A variation of a complete binary tree allows for double roots, denoted by DRB(n), i.e. its nodes are all binary strings of length at most n plus one new node e' (called the *alternate root*), where e represents the empty string, obtained from B(n) by simply inserting e' into the edge connecting e with the node 1. (The new node e' thus has two neighbors: the root e and the node 1.) See Figure 2 for an illustration of DRB(2).

Clearly, B(n) has $2^{n+1}-1$ nodes and $2^{n+1}-2$ edges. It is also easily seen that the diameter of B(n) is 2n, which is O(log N), where N is the number of its nodes, and the maximum node degree is 3.

Meshes The d-dimensional mesh of dimensions $a_1, a_2, \ldots, a_d$, denoted by $[a_1 \times a_2 \times \ldots \times a_d]$, is the graph whose nodes are all d-tuples of positive integers $(z_1, z_2, \ldots, z_d)$, where $1 \leq z_i \leq a_i$, for all i ($1 \leq i \leq d$), and whose edges connect d-tuples which differ in exactly one coordinate by one.

Clearly, $[a_1 \times a_2 \times \ldots \times a_d]$ has $a_1 \times a_2 \times \ldots \times a_d$ nodes. Its diameter is $(a_1-1)+(a_2-1)+ \ldots +(a_d-1)$ and maximum node degree is 2d, if each a_i is at least three.

Pyramids The pyramid of height n, denoted by P(n), is the graph whose nodes are all triples of nonnegative integers (i,x,y), where $0 \le i \le n$ and $1 \le x,y \le 2^i$, and whose edges connect (i,x,y) with the vertices in { (i+1,u,v) ¦ u in {2x,2x-1} and v in {2y,2y+1} } as well as with all vertices (i,a,b) such that (x,y) and (a,b) are adjacent nodes in the mesh [2^i x 2^i], for all i ($0 \le i < n$) and all x,y ($1 \le x,y \le 2^i$).

P(n) has $1+4+4^2+...+4^n$ nodes. Its diameter is 2n-1 and it has maximum node degree 9. An illustration of P(2) is shown in Figure 3.

X-trees The X-tree of height n, denoted by X(n), is the graph whose nodes are all binary strings of length at most n and whose edges connect each string x of length i ($0 \le i < n$) with the strings xa, a in {0,1}, of length i+1 and, when binary(x) < 2^i-1, connects x with successor(x), where binary(x) is the integer x represents in binary notation and successor(x) denotes the unique binary string of length i such that binary(successor(x)) = binary(x)+1. (For completeness let binary(e)=0, where e is the empty string.)

X(n) has $2^{n+1}-1$ nodes and $2^{n+2}-n-4$ edges. Its diameter is 2n-1 and it has maximum node degree 5. An illustration of X(2) is shown in Figure 4.

Mesh-of-Trees The mesh-of-trees of dimension n, denoted by MT(n), is the graph whose nodes are all pairs (x,y), where x and y are binary strings of length at most n, with at least one of x,y of length exactly n, and whose edges connect, when x is of length less than n, (x,y) with (xa,y), and, when y is of length less than n, (x,y) with (x,ya), where a is in {0,1}.

MT(n) has $2^{n+1}(2^{n+1}-2^{n-1}-1)$ nodes and $2^{n+2}(2^n-1)$ edges. Its diameter is 4n and it has maximum node degree 3. An illustration of MT(2) is shown in Figure 5.

Butterflies The butterfly network of dimension n, denoted by BF(n), is the graph whose nodes are all pairs (i,x), where i is a nonnegative integer ($0 \le i < n$) and x is a binary string of length n and whose edges connect (i,x) with both (i+1(mod n),x) and with (i+1(mod n),x¦i+1), where x¦i+1 denotes the binary string which is identical to x except in the (i+1)-th bit.

BF(n) has $n2^n$ nodes and $n2^{n+1}$ edges, for all n>2. Its diameter is n + floor(n/2) and it has maximum node degree 4. An illustration of BF(3) is shown in Figure 6.

Cube connected cycles The cube connected cycle network of dimension n, denoted by CCC(n), is the graph whose nodes are all pairs (i,x), where i is a nonnegative integer ($0 \le i < n$) and x is a binary string of length n and whose edges connect (i,x) with both (i+1(mod n),x) and with (i,x¦i+1), where x¦i+1 denotes the binary string which is identical to x except in the (i+1)-th bit.

CCC(n) has $n2^n$ nodes and $3n2^{n-1}$ edges, for all n>2. Its diameter is 2n + floor(n/2) and it has maximum node degree 3. An illustration of CCC(3) is shown in Figure 7.

Shuffle-Exchange Networks The shuffle-exchange network of dimension n, denoted by SE(n), is the graph whose nodes are all binary strings of length n and whose edges connect each string xa, where x is a binary string of length n-1 and a is in {0,1}, with the string xb, where b≠a is a symbol in {0,1}, and with the string ax. (An edge connecting xa with xb, a≠b, is called an *exchange* edge and an edge connecting xa with ax is called a *shuffle* edge.)

SE(n) has 2^n nodes. Its diameter is 2n-1 and it has maximum node degree 3. An illustration of SE(3) is shown in Figure 8.

DeBrujn Networks The DeBrujn network of dimension n, denoted by DB(n), is the graph whose nodes are all binary strings of length n and whose edges connect each string xa, where x is a binary string of length n-1 and a is in {0,1}, with the string bx, where b≠a is a symbol in {0,1}, and with the string ax. (An edge connecting xa with bx, a≠b, is called a *shufflexchange* edge and an edge connecting xa with ax is called a *shuffle* edge.)

DB(n) has 2^n nodes and $2(2^n-1)$ edges. Its diameter is n and it has maximum node degree 4. An illustration of DB(3) is shown in Figure 9.

II. Measuring the Quality of Embeddings

Let G and H be finite undirected graphs. An *embedding* of G into H is a one-to-one mapping f from the nodes of G to the nodes of H. G is called the *guest* graph and H is called the *host* graph of the embedding f. The *dilation* of the embedding f is the maximum distance in the host between the images of adjacent guest nodes, i.e. max{ $distance_H(f(x),f(y))$ | (x,y) is an edge in G }, where $distance_H(a,b)$ denotes the length of the shortest path in H between the nodes a and b. The *expansion* of the embedding f is the ratio of the number of nodes in the host graph to the number of nodes in the guest, i.e. |nodes(H)|/|nodes(G)|. When hosts are chosen from a collection C and no graph K in C satisfies |nodes(G)| $\leq$ |nodes(K)| < |nodes(H)|, then H is called an *optimal* host in C for G. If there is a unique optimal host graph H in C for G, then H is called the *optimum* host in C for G. We shall sometimes augment an embedding of G in H by a routing of G's edges, i.e. a mapping r of G's edges to paths in H. The *edge congestion* of such a routing r of G's edges, is the maximum, over all edges e in H, of the number of edges in G mapped to a path in H which includes e. That is, it is the maximum over all edges e in H of the number of edges of G routed through e.

III. Embedding into Binary Hypercubes

As a binary hypercube has a regular structure and its diameter and number of connections at each node is logarithmic in its size, it is a popular architecture in the design of parallel computer networks. Several papers discuss the ability of binary hypercubes to simulate other network and algorithm structures. The following is a survey of some of this work:

A. Binary Trees

The complete binary tree B(n), which has $2^{n+1}-1$ nodes, can be embedded into the hypercube Q(n+1), which has 2^{n+1} nodes, with dilation 2. In fact, B(n) can be embedded into Q(n) in such a way that exactly one of its edges connects nodes assigned to positions at distance 2 in the hypercube and all others connect nodes at distance 1 [BhCLR], [BhI], [Hav], [Ne]. To see this observe that the double rooted binary tree DRB(n) is a subgraph of Q(n). This can be seen by a simple inductive argument. Observe that DRB(1) is a subgraph of Q(2). Now assume that DRB(n) is embedded in Q(n+1) by a dilation 1 embedding f. Consider the positions assigned in the hypercube for the root e, the alternate root e', and the neighbors of these two nodes: 0 and 1. These four nodes form a chain of length 4, say 0, e, e', 1. As it is a dilation 1 embedding the successive positions they are mapped to must differ in exactly one bit position, say the first differ in the i-th bit, the next differ in the j-th bit, and the last differ in the k-th bit, where $1 \leq i,j,k \leq n+1$. Then consider the embedding f' of DRB(n) into Q(n+1) such that f'(0)=f(e) and, in addition, whenever x and y are neighbors in DRB(n) and f(x) and f(y) differ in the i-th (j-th, k-th) bit, then f'(x) and f'(y) differ in the j-th (k-th, i-th) bit, respectively. This embedding is illustrated in Figure 10(a). The reader can then verify that f'(e)=f(e') and f'(e')=f(1), as f(0) and f(e) differ in the i-th bit, f(e) and f(e') differ in the j-th bit, and f(e') and f(1) differ in the k-th bit (i may be equal to k). A dilation 1 embedding g of DRB(n+1) is then obtained by the following assignments: g(e)=f(e'), g(e')=f'(e), g(0)=f(e), g(1)=f'(e'), and, for all strings x over {0,1} of length at least 2, if x=10y, then g(x)=f(1y), if x=11y, then g(x)=f'(1y), if x=00y, then g(x)=f(0y), and, if x=01y, then g(x)=f'(0y). This embedding is illustrated in Figure 10(b).

Note that an inorder numbering of the nodes of a complete binary tree of height n also describes a dilation 2 embedding [BhCLR]. This is illustrated in Figure 11. Dilation 1 is not possible, as it is known that the complete binary tree B(n) is not a subgraph of Q(n+1), for all n>1. The argument is straightforward. Both binary trees and hypercubes are bipartite graphs, i.e. their nodes can be assigned two colors, say black and white, so that adjacent nodes do not receive the same color. Such a two coloring of B(n), for n>1, must result in $2^n+2^{n-2}+... > 2^n$ nodes receiving the same color, as all nodes at the same level must receive the same color and so must all nodes at odd (even) levels. Similarly, Q(n+1) is bipartite and any two coloration of its nodes results in all nodes with an even number of occurrences of the bit 1 getting the same color and similarly with those with an odd number of occurrences of the bit 1. Thus any two coloration of Q(n+1) has exactly 2^n nodes in each color class. So, B(n) cannot be a subgraph of Q(n+1), as it has too many nodes in the same color class. Note that dilation 2 embeddings are possible, as we've seen, as they allow nodes in the same color class of B(n) to change color classes in Q(n+1).

Embeddings of arbitrary binary trees into hypercubes with small dilation have also been described. The principal technique is the use of an appropriate bisection theorem, i.e. a result describing a set of edges in the tree whose deletion results in two collections of subtrees, each having half of the total number of nodes. Bhatt, Chung, Leighton, and Rosenberg [BhCLR] described a dilation 10 embedding with small expansion (small here means roughly 4). An alternative construction was described by Monien and Sudborough [MoS2], giving a dilation 5 embedding with expansion 1. They showed also that, if all binary trees of size at most 2^{15} can be embedded into a binary hypercube with dilation 3, then *all* binary trees can be embedded with dilation three. (It is, as yet, unknown whether the set of all binary trees with at most 2^{15} nodes can be embedded in a binary hypercube with dilation 3.)

Other embeddings of trees into hypercubes include results about caterpillars and refinements of caterpillars. A *caterpillar* is a tree in which there is a simple path P such that every vertex is either included in P or is adjacent to a node in P. (The edges connecting nodes in P to adjacent nodes are called *legs.*) A tree T is a refinement of a caterpillar if it is possible to obtain T from some caterpillar by the addition of degree two nodes into some number of the caterpillar's legs. For example, caterpillars and refinements of caterpillars are known to be subgraphs of hypercubes [MoSpUW], [HavL].

B. Meshes

Any mesh whose dimensions are a power of 2 is a subgraph of its optimum hypercube. That is, for all n>0, if $n = n_1+n_2+...n_k$, then $[2^{n_1} \times 2^{n_2} \times ... 2^{n_k}]$ is a subgraph of Q(n). This is easily seen by induction on n. For example, this means that Q(4) contains as a subgraph the meshes [2 x 8], [4 x 4], [4 x 2 x 2], and Q(4) is, of course, identical to the mesh [2 x 2 x 2 x 2]. It follows from this that many meshes whose dimensions are not all a power of two are also subgraphs of their optimum hypercubes. For example, the mesh [7 x 7] with 49 points is a subgraph of the mesh [8 x 8] and, therefore, of its optimum hypercube Q(6). The general statement is that a d-dimensional mesh $[a_1 \times a_2 \times ... \times a_d]$ is a subgraph of its optimum hypercube if and only if ceiling(log a_1)+ceiling(log a_2)+ ...+ceiling(log a_d) = ceiling(log a_1+log a_2+...+log a_d) [BrS], [ChC], [Gr].

That this condition is necessary is easily seen. For example, suppose we have a dilation 1 embedding f of a 2-dimensional mesh [m x n] in its optimum hypercube, i.e. the hypercube Q(t), for t = ceiling($\log_2$(m x n)). Call, for any s, nodes (i,s) and (i+1,s) *column-adjacent nodes in the i-th row* and (s,i) and (s,i+1) *row-adjacent nodes in the i-th column.* First, observe that any dilation 1 embedding must map all column-adjacent nodes in the same row and all row-adjacent nodes in the same column to hypercube nodes that differ in the same bit position. For instance, let f map (i,s) to 0^t and (i+1,s) to $0^{k-1}10^{t-k}$, i.e. hypercube nodes that differ in just the k-th bit. Let f map (i,s+1) to $0^{p-1}10^{t-p}$, for some p, which (without any loss of generality) we assume is greater than k. Then, the mesh node (i+1,s+1), which is a neighbor of both (i+1,s) and (i,s+1) must map to the cube node $0^{k-1}10^{p-k-1}10^{t-p}$, as f is a dilation 1 embedding. Therefore, (i,s+1) and (i+1,s+1) also map to hypercube nodes that differ in just the k-th bit. The general statement follows. Secondly, observe that row-adjacent nodes in the same column and column-adjacent nodes in the same row cannot be mapped to hypercube nodes that differ in the same position, as each row and column intersect and this would result in mesh nodes being mapped to the same hypercube node. So, if f is a dilation 1 embedding of the mesh [m x n] into its optimum hypercube Q(t), then there must be (a) at least ceiling($\log_2$m) bits in the binary strings denoting hypercube positions that are altered for column-adjacent nodes in the m-rows and (b) at least ceiling($\log_2 n$) bits, distinct from those described in (a), for the row-adjacent nodes in the n-columns. This is only possible, if t $\geq$ ceiling($\log_2 m$)+ceiling($\log_2 n$).

It is known that every 2-dimensional mesh can be embedded into its optimum hypercube with dilation 2 [Ch]. This is optimum, as the preceding paragraph shows many 2-dimensional meshes are not subgraphs of their optimum hypercubes. An earlier technique [BeMS] for embedding a [m x n] mesh into its optimum hypercube actually did so by embedding with dilation 2 into the mesh [$2^{m'}$ x p], where m'=ceiling($\log_2 m$) and p is determined by the technique. (As the latter mesh has a power of two rows, it is a subgraph of a hypercube.) For example, the mesh [5 x 50] by this technique is embedded with dilation 2 in the mesh [8 x 32]. The latter mesh is a subgraph of the optimum hypercube Q(8) for the [5 x 50] mesh. The embedding of a [m x n] mesh into a mesh [$2^{m'}$ x p], where m'=ceiling($\log_2 m$) is done via the construction of tiles. A *(m,2^i)-tile*, for any i>0 and any m ($2^{i-1} \leq m \leq 2^i$), is an embedding of a [m,2^i] mesh into a [2^i,m] mesh such that rows of the original mesh are embedded as horizontal chains, i.e. the nodes in the first (last) column of the original [m,2^i] mesh are embedded into the first (last, respectively) columns of the host [2^i,m] mesh. (In particular, the embedding that simply rotates the original mesh and maps rows to columns with dilation 1 is not satisfactory.) A recursive construction of (m,2^i) tiles, for all i>0, is described and it is shown that each constructed tile describes a dilation 2 embedding. (An example of the (5,8)-tile constructed is shown in Figure 16.)

For a mesh [m x n] one performs the embedding into [$2^{m'}$ x p], for some p, by taking the (m,$2^{m'}$)-tile T and chaining it together in the form T-T^R-T-T^R-formed by a vertical reflection of T [BeMS]. Although this technique falls short of embedding every 2-dimensional mesh into its optimum hypercube, it does describe a dilation 2 embedding for a large number. As indicated, moreover, a new technique embeds all 2-dimensional meshes with dilation 2 into their optimum hypercubes [Ch]. This technique is similar to the one just described, but does not embed meshes into meshes. Instead it embeds a mesh into the optimum hypercube directly (using binary reflected gray codes) and uses the additional edges available in a cube.

These techniques have also been investigated for their ability to embed multi-dimensional meshes into their optimum hypercubes. The technique of embedding meshes into meshes (using explicitly constructed dilation 2 tiles) results in a method to embed d-dimensional tiles with dilation at most d into hypercubes. Under certain conditions (described in [BeMS]) the technique is guaranteed to embed a d-dimensional mesh into its optimum hypercube. As this condition is not satisfied by a large number of d-dimensional meshes, the general question of embedding multi-dimensional meshes into their optimum hypercubes is still open. The technique used to show that all 2-dimensional meshes can be embedded with dilation 2 into their optimum hypercube has also been extended to the multi-dimensional case [Ch].

Lower bounds have also been derived. Let dilation(d) denote the maximum, over all d-dimensional meshes M, of the minimum dilation possible in any embedding of M into its optimum hypercube. As indicated in the previous paragraphs, it is known that dilation(2)=2. Exact values of dilation(d), for d>2, are not known. However, it is known that dilation(d) must grow at least as fast as some constant multiple of d/log d [BeMS]. Thus, embeddings of d-dimensional meshes into optimum hypercubes must accept increasingly large dilation as the number of dimensions grow.

C. Pyramids

The pyramid P(k), for all k>0, can be embedded into its optimum hypercube, Q(2k+1), with dilation 2 and edge congestion 2 [MaLS]. The embedding is described recursively. A dilation 2, edge congestion 2 embedding of P(1) into Q(3) is shown in Figure 12. Define the following invariant property, for the sake of induction: P(k) can be embedded into Q(2k+1) by an embedding f_k which:

(a) has dilation 2 and edge congestion 2,
(b) maps the apex of the pyramid P(k) to a hypercube node, called the *standard apex position*, which has an unassigned neighbor, called the *alternate apex*

position such that at most one edge is routed through the edge connecting the standard and alternate apex positions, and

(c) the embedding g_k that agrees with f_k on every node of P(k) except the apex and maps the apex to the alternate instead of the standard apex position also satisfies conditions (a)-(b), where the role of the standard and alternate apex positions are reversed.

Embed the nodes and edges of P(k+1) into Q(2k+3) by the embedding f_{k+1} which is defined as follows:

(1) View Q(2k+3) as partitioned into four copies of Q(2k+1), which we refer to as the quadrants of Q(2k+3). The four quadrants are defined by the sets of nodes in Q(2k+3) that begin with the prefixes 00, 01, 10, and 11, respectively,

(2) Embed a copy of P(k) into each of the four quadrants, where the copies embedded in the 10 and 11 quadrants are mapped by f_k and the copies embedded in the 00 and 01 quadrants are mapped by g_k, i.e. the apexes of the copies of P(k) embedded in the 00 and 01 quadrants are placed at the alternate apex positions, and

(3) Place the apex of P(k+1) in the apex position of the 00 quadrant and then route the edges of P(k+1) as shown in Figure 13.

It is easily seen that conditions (a)-(c) are satisfied by f_{k+1}. Note that the edges connecting corresponding nodes in the four copies of the pyramid P(k), while not explicitly shown in Figure 13, connect nodes assigned to corresponding hypercube positions (hence are neighbors in the embedding). Furthermore these edges connect nodes assigned to distinct quadrants and are not used for other edges in the embedding. Thus f_{k+1} is a dilation 2, edge congestion 2 embedding of the pyramid P(k+1) into its optimum hypercube.

Earlier dilation 3, edge congestion 2 and dilation 2, edge congestion 3 embeddings of pyramids into their optimum hypercubes were described [LaW], [LaW2]. (The authors also conjectured that no embedding could achieve dilation 2 and edge congestion 2 simultaneously [LaW2].) The pyramids P(1), P(2), and P(3) have maximum node degrees of 5, 7, and 9, respectively, while their optimum hypercubes, namely Q(3), Q(5), and Q(7), have maximum node degree 3, 5, and 7, respectively. Therefore, edge congestion 2 is necessary for any embedding of these pyramids into their optimum hypercubes. It is unknown, as yet, whether there exists a dilation 2, edge congestion 1 embedding of P(k) into Q(2k+1), for k>3. It seems likely that edge congestion 1 embeddings of pyramids into hypercubes are possible if one embeds into larger than optimum hypercubes. On the other hand, any embedding of a pyramid into a hypercube must have dilation at least 2, as pyramids have odd length cycles.

D. X-trees

There is a dilation 2, edge congestion 2 embedding of X(k) into Q(k+1), for all k>0. The embedding strategy is similar to that used for embedding complete binary trees and pyramids and is easily defined recursively. In particular, we assume for an inductive hypothesis that there is a dilation 2, edge congestion 2 embedding of X(k) into P(k+1) such that the root of the X-tree is assigned to a hypercube position that has an unassigned neighbor and that there is one edge routed through the edge connecting the position of the root and this neighbor. Such an embedding of X(1) into Q(2) is shown in Figure 14(a). Let f_k denote such a dilation 2, edge congestion 2 embedding of X(k) into Q(k+1). An appropriate embedding f_{k+1} of X(k+1) into Q(k+2) is defined by the following:

(1) Embed a copy of X(k) into each of two copies of Q(k+1) by f_k,

(2) Place a new node, the root of X(k+1), into the unassigned position adjacent to the position of the root in the embedding f_k of one of the two copies, and

(3) Route the edges as shown in Figure 14(b).

Note that edges connecting nodes in copies of X(k) will connect nodes assigned to corresponding positions in each of the two copies of Q(k+1). So, these edges connect nodes placed at distance 1 in the hypercube and they also have edge congestion 1.

E. Mesh of Trees

A dilation 2 embedding of MT(n) into Q(2n+2) is easily described using a dilation 2 embedding of the complete binary tree B(n) into Q(n+1) and the observation that MT(n) is a product of two such trees. For example, take the dilation 2 embedding f_n of B(n) into Q(n+1) given by the inorder numbering of nodes (using binary notation). Then define the embedding g_n of the mesh of trees MT(n) into Q(2n+2) by $g_n(x,y) = f_n(x)f_n(y)$. The embedding g_2 of MT(2) into Q(6) is shown in Figure 15.

F. Butterflies and Cube Connected Cycles

The butterfly BF(n) can be embedded with dilation 1 into its optimum hypercube Q(n+ceiling($\log_2 n$)), i.e. BF(n) is a subgraph of Q(n+ceiling($\log_2 n$)) [HeR]. Moreover, there is a linear time algorithm to map the nodes of BF(n) to the corresponding hypercube nodes defined by this embedding. Using this embedding of the butterfly and the observation that CCC(n) can be embedded in BF(n) with dilation 2, it follows that CCC(n) can be embedded into its optimum hypercube Q(n+ceiling($\log_2 n$)) with dilation 2.

G. Shuffle-Exchange and DeBrujn Networks

It remains open whether either of these networks can be embedded into a hypercube with O(1) dilation and O(1) expansion. As the Shuffle-Exchange network can be embedded with dilation 2 into the DeBrujn network, a positive resolution of both questions can be obtained by an appropriate embedding of the DeBrujn graph.

H. Complexity Issues

Hypercube Embedding Problem
Instance: A finite undirected graph G and positive integers k and n.
Question: Does there exist a dilation k embedding of G into Q(n)?

This problem is known [KrVC] to be NP-complete even when k=1 (by a reduction from the 3-partition problem [GaJ]). In fact, the construction used in this reduction builds a disconnected nonplanar graph, so the complexity of the problem is currently open for several interesting families of graphs, for example: trees, planar and connected graphs.

IV. Embeddings into Binary Trees

A simple path can be embedded into its optimum complete binary tree with dilation 3 [Se]. An outerplanar graph with maximum vertex degree d can be embedded into a binary tree with dilation 3·ceiling($\log_2 2d$) [HoR]. For any n>0, the X-tree X(n) can be embedded in the complete binary tree B(n) with dilation O(log n) = O(log log N), where N is the number of vertices in the X-tree [BhCHLR].

It is known to be NP-complete to decide, given a graph G and a positive integer k, whether G can be embedded into a binary tree with dilation k [Mo]. In fact, it is NP-complete even for trees. On the other hand, for each fixed bound k on the amount of dilation, there is a polynomial algorithm (using dynamic programming), which when given a graph G, decides if G can be embedded with dilation at most k in a binary tree [MaSS]. It is easily established, using the respective diameters of a guest graph and the intended binary tree host, that many graphs cannot be embedded into a complete binary tree with O(1) dilation. Complete ternary trees require c(log log n) dilation [HoMR], for some c>0, and a dilation O(log log n) embedding exists [Ell1].

V. Embeddings into Meshes

Embedding meshes into meshes is an interesting issue. Every 2-dimensional mesh can be embedded into either its optimum square 2-D mesh or the next-larger-size square 2-D mesh with dilation at most 3 [Ell2]. The technique uses *squeezing* and *folding*, which were described in an earlier paper [AlR]. Examples of these operations are shown in Figure 16. In fact, a similar squeezing operation was used, via the recursive construction of tiles, as described earlier, to embed a mesh M into a mesh M' in which M' is a subgraph of M's optimum hypercube [BeMS].

Embeddings into meshes of complete binary trees, meshes of trees, planar graphs, shuffle-exchange networks, and other structures have also been described in work on VLSI [Ull]. For example, complete binary trees are embedded into meshes by the well known H-tree construction and with (better dilation) by a modified H-tree construction, as described in [Ull]. Embeddings of general network structures into meshes are described by separator theorems, such as the $O(n^{1/2})$ planar separator theorem, and the recursive construction of a network layout based on separator results [Ull].

The problem of, given a finite undirected graph G and positive integers k and d, deciding whether G can be embedded with dilation at most k into a d-dimensional mesh is known [BhCo] to be NP-complete (by a reduction from 1-in-3 3SAT [GaJ]) even when the graph G is a binary tree, k=1, and d=2. There are also interesting upper and lower bound results on embeddings of meshes into meshes of a different number of dimensions, the routing of messages between the processors in such a simulation [KoA], [RaTK], and results about embeddings of meshes with "wrap around edges" (called *toruses*) [MaT].

VI. Embeddings into Butterfly and Cube Connected Cycle Networks

The complete binary tree $B(n+\text{floor}(\log_2 n))$ can be embedded into the butterfly network Q(n+3) with dilation 4 [BhCHLR]. This shows that an n-vertex X-trees, for example, can be embedded into a butterfly network with dilation O(log log n) and O(1) expansion, via an embedding of X-trees into complete binary trees [BhCHLR]. The paper also shows that, there is a constant c>0, such that for any nontree planar graph G whose smallest 1/3:2/3 separator is of size S(n) and in which F(G) is the largest number of vertices in any face (of a planar embedding) , any embedding of G into a butterfly must have dilation at least $[c\cdot\log S(n)]/F(G)$.

In particular, as a 2-dimensional mesh is planar, has a $n^{1/2}$ separator, and has 4 nodes per face, any embedding of 2-D meshes into a butterfly must have dilation at least $c\cdot\log n$, for some constant c>0. This is proportional to the butterfly's diameter and hence a random placement in fact achieves this dilation.

VII. Concluding Remarks

Not much is known about embeddings into shuffle-exchange or DeBrujn networks. For example, can arbitrary binary trees be embedded with O(1) dilation and O(1) expansion in shuffle-exchange graphs? Clearly, the complete binary tree B(n) is a subgraph of the DeBrujn network DB(n), as the DeBrujn graph DB(n) can be viewed as a complete binary tree (with an added node adjacent to the root) together with edges forming another complete binary tree added on. (See Figure 9.) The DeBrujn graph DB(n) can also be embedded with dilation 2 in the shuffle-exchange SE(n), as the shufflexchange edge of the DeBrujn can be simulated by a consecutive shuffle edge and exchange edge of the shuffle-exchange graph. Thus, the complete binary tree B(n) can be embedded with dilation 2 in the shuffle-exchange network SE(n).

There is a wealth of results about embedding graphs into simple paths, i.e. linear layouts. In linear layouts dilation is customarily called *bandwidth* and edge congestion is called *cutwidth*. The interested reader should consult some of the literature sources [ChiCDG], [Chu], [ChuLR], [ChuMST], [ElST], [FeL], [GuS], [MaPS], [MaS], [MaS2], [Mi], [MiS], [MoSu1], [MoSu3], [MoSu4], [Si], [Su], [Ya], [Ya2]. We are guilty of a possibly unavoidable (certainly unintentional) sin of not including all relevant references about embedding problems. Hopefully, some of these omissions will be forgiven by referring interested readers to the following sources for additional work: [AnBR], [BeS], [Bi], [CyKVC], [Gr], [HasLN], [Hav], [HavL], [HoJ], [Ne], [SaS], [Wu].

References

[AlR] R. Aleliunas, A. L. Rosenberg, "On Embedding Rectangular Grids in Square Grids", IEEE Trans. on Computers, C-31,9 (1982), pp. 907-913.

[AnBR] F.N. Annexstein, M. Baumslag, A. L. Rosenberg, "Group Action Graphs and

Parallel Architectures", manuscript, Computer and Info. Sci., University of Massachusetts, Amherst, Massachussets 01003, U.S.A., 1987.

[BeS] B. Becker, H. U. Simon, "How Robust is the n-Cube?" Proc. 27th IEEE Symp. Foundations of Computer Sci., Oct. 1986, pp 283-291.

[BetMS] S. Bettayeb, Z. Miller, I. H. Sudborough, "Embedding Grids into Hypercubes", Proc. of Aegean Workshop On Computing, Springer Verlag's Lecture Notes in Computer Science, to appear, 1988.

[BhCLR] S. Bhatt, F. Chung, T. Leighton, A. Rosenberg, "Optimal Simulation of Tree Machines", Proc. 27th Annual IEEE Symp. Foundations of Computer Sci., Oct. 1986, pp. 274-282.

[BhCHLR] S. Bhatt, F. Chung, J.-W. Hong, T. Leighton, A. Rosenberg, "Optimal Simulations by Butterfly Networks", Proc. 20th Annual ACM Theory of Computing Symp., 1988, pp. 192-204.

[BhCo] S. Bhatt, S. S. Cosmadakis, "The Complexity of Minimizing Wire Lengths for VLSI Layouts", Info. Processing Letters 25 (1987).

[BhI] S. N. Bhatt, I. C. F. Ipsen, "How to Embed Trees in Hypercubes", Research Report YALEU/DCS/RR-443, Yale Univeristy, Dept. of Computer Science, 1985.

[Bi] D. Bienstock, "On Embedding Graphs in Trees", manuscript, Bell Communications Research, Morristown, New Jersey 07060, U.S.A., 1988.

[BrS] J. E. Brandenburg, D. S. Scott, "Embeddings of Communication Trees and Grids into Hypercubes", Intel Scientific Computers Report, #280182-001, 1985.

[Ch] M. Y. Chan, "Dilation 2 Embedding of Grids into Hypercubes", Tech. Report, Computer Science Program, Univ. Texas at Dallas, 1988.

[ChC] M. Y. Chan, F. Y. L. Chin, "On Embedding Rectangular Grids in Hypercubes", to appear in IEEE Trans. on Computers

[ChS] T. F. Chan, Y. Saad, "Multigrid Algorithms on the Hypercube Multiprocessor", IEEE Trans. on Comp., Vol c-35, No. 11, Nov. 1986, pp. 969-977.

[ChiCDG] P.Z. Chinn, J. Chvatalova, A.K. Dewdney, N.E. Gibbs, "The Bandwidth Problem for Graphs and Matrices - A Survey", J. Graph Theory, 6 (1982), pp. 223-254.

[Chu] F.R.K. Chung, "Labelings of Graphs", A chapter in Selected Topics in Graph Theory, III, (eds. L. Beinike and R. Wilson).

[ChuLR] F.R.K. Chung, F. T. Leighton, A.L. Rosenberg, "A Graph Layout Problem with Applications to VLSI Design", manuscript, 1985.

[ChuMST] M.-J. Chung, F. Makedon, I. H. Sudborough, J. Turner, "Polynomial Algorithms for the Min-Cut Linear Arrangement Problem on Degree Restricted Trees", SIAM J. Computing 14,1 (1985), pp. 158-177.

[CyKVC] G. Cybenko, D. W. Krumme, K.N. Venkataraman, A. Couch, "Heterogeneous Processes on Homogeneous Processors", manuscript, Dept. of Computer Sci., Tufts University, Medford, Massachusetts 02155 U.S.A., 1986.

[Ell1] J. A. Ellis, "Embedding Graphs in Lines, Trees, and Grids", Ph.D. Thesis, Northwestern Univ., Evanston, Illinois, U.S.A. (1984).

[Ell2] J. A. Ellis, "Embedding Rectangular grids into Square Grids", Proc. of Aegean Workshop On Computing, Springer Verlag's Lecture Notes in Computer Science, to appear, 1988.

[ElST] J. A. Ellis, I. H. Sudborough, J. Turner, "Graph Separation and Searching", manuscript, Computer Science Program, University of Victoria, P. O. Box 1700, Victoria, B.C. V8W 2Y2, Canada (1987).

[FeL] M. R. Fellows, M.A. Langston, "Layout Permutation Problems and Well-Partially-Ordered Sets", manuscript, Department of Computer Science, Washington State University, Pullman, Washington, 99164-1210 U.S.A., 1988.

[GaJ] M. R. Garey, D. S. Johnson, Computers and Intractability: A Guide to the Theory of NP-Completeness, W. H. Freeman and Co., San Francisco, 1979.

[Gr] D. S. Greenberg, "Optimum Expansion Embeddings of Meshes in Hypercube", Technical Report YALEU/CSD/RR-535, Yale University, Dept. of Computer Science.

[GuS] E. Gurari, I. H. Sudborough, "Improved dynamic programming algorithms for bandwidth minimization and the min cut linear arrangement problem" J. Algorithms, 5 (1984), pp. 531-546.

[HasLN] J. Hastad, T. Leighton, M. Newman, "Reconfiguring a Hypercube in the Presence of Faults", Proc. 19th Annual ACM Symp. Theory of Computing, May 25-27, 1987.

[Hav] I. Havel, "On Hamiltonian Circuits and Spanning Trees of Hypercubes", Cas. Pest. Mat. (in Czech.), 109 (1984), pp. 135-152.

[HavL] I. Havel, P. Liebl, "One Legged Caterpillars Span Hypercubes", J. Graph Theory, 10 (1986), pp. 69-76.

[HeR] L.S. Heath, A. L. Rosenberg, "An Optimal Mapping of the FFT Algorithm onto the Hypercube Architecture", COINS Tech. Report 87-19, Computer and Info. Sci., University of Massachusetts, Amherst, Massachussets 01003, U.S.A., 1987.

[HoJ] C.-T. Ho, S. L. Johnson, "On the Embedding of Arbitrary Meshes in Boolean Cubes with Expansion Two Dilation Two", Proc. 1987 International Conference on Parallel Processing, pp. 188-191.

[HoR] J. W. Hong, A. L. Rosenberg, " Graphs that are Almost Binary Trees", SIAM J. Computing 11,2 (1982), pp. 227-242.

[HoMR] J. W. Hong, K. Mehlhorn, A. Rosenberg, "Cost Trade-offs in Graph Embeddings with Applications", J. ACM, 30,4 (1983), pp. 709-728.

[KoA] S. R. Kosaraju, M. J. Atallah, "Optimal Simulations Between Mesh-Connected Arrays of Processors", Proc. 1986 ACM Theory of Computing Symp., pp. 264-272.

[KrVC] D. W. Krumme, K.N. Venkataraman, G. Cybenko, "Hypercube Embedding is NP-complete", Proc. of Hypercube Conf., SIAM, Knoxville, Tennessee, Sept., 1985.

[LaW] T.-H. Lai, W. White, "Embedding Pyramids into Hypercubes", OSU-CISRC-11/87-TR41, Dept. of Computer and Info. Sci., The Ohio State Univ., Columbus, Ohio, 43210, U.S.A., 1988.

[LaW2] T.-H. Lai, W. White, "Mapping Multiple Pyramids into Hypercubes Using

Unit Expansion", manuscript, Dept. of Computer and Info. Sci., The Ohio State Univ., Columbus, Ohio, 43210, U.S.A., 1988.

[MaT] Y. E. Ma, L. Tao, "Embeddings among Toruses and Meshes", Proc. of the 1987 Int. Conf. on Parallel Processing, August, 1987, pp. 178-187.

[MaLS] F. Makedon, T. Leighton, I. H. Sudborough, "Simulating Pyramid Machines with a Hypercube", manuscript, Computer Science Program, University of Texas at Dallas, Richardson, Texas 75083-0688, U.S.A., 1988.

[MaPS] F. Makedon, C. H. Papadimitriou, I.H. Sudborough, "Topological Bandwidth", SIAM J. Alg. and Discrete Meth. 6 (1985), pp. 418-444.

[MaS] F. Makedon, I.H. Sudborough, "Minimizing Width in Linear Layouts", Springer Verlag's Lecture Notes in Computer Science, Vol. 154 (1985), pp. 478-490; to appear in Discrete Applied Math.

[MaS2] F. Makedon, I. H. Sudborough, "Graph Layout Problems", Surveys in Computer Science (ed. H. Maurer), Bibliographisches Insitut, Zurich, 1984, pp. 145-192

[MaSS] F. Makedon, C. G. Simonson, I. H. Sudborough, "On the complexity of tree embedding problems", manuscript, Computer Science Program, University of Texas at Dallas, Richardson, Texas, 75083-0688, U.S.A., 1988.

[Mi] Z. Miller, "A Linear Algorithm for Topological Bandwidth in Degree 3 Trees", to appear in SIAM J. Computing.

[MiS] Z. Miller, I. H. Sudborough, "A Polynomial Algorithm for Recognizing Small Cutwidth in Hypergraphs", Proc. of Aegean Workshop On Computing, Springer Verlag's Lecture Notes in Computer Science, vol. 227 (1986), pp. 252-260.

[Mo] B. Monien, "The Problem of Embedding Trees into Binary Trees is NP-Complete", manuscript (1984).

[MoSpUW] B. Monien, G. Spenner, W. Unger, and G. Wechsung, "On the Edge Length of Embedding Caterpillars into Various Networks", manuscript, Dept. of Math. and Computer Science, Univ. Paderborn, Paderborn, W. Germany, 1988.

[MoSu1] B. Monien, I. H. Sudborough, "Min Cut is NP-complete for Edge Weighted Trees", to appear in Theoretical Computer Science.

[MoSu2] B. Monien, I. H. Sudborough, "Simulating Binary Trees on Hypercubes", Proc. of Aegean Workshop On Computing, Springer Verlag's Lecture Notes in Computer Science, to appear, 1988.

[MoSu3] B. Monien, I. H. Sudborough, "Bandwidth constrained NP complete problems", Theoretical Computer Science 41 (1985), pp. 141-167.

[MoSu4] B. Monien, I. H. Sudborough, "On eliminating nondeterminism from Turing machines that use less than logarithm worktape space", Theoretical Computer Science 21 (1982), pp. 237-253.

[Ne] L. Nebesky, "On Cubes and Dichotomic Trees", Cas. Pest. Mat. (in Czech.), 99 (1974), pp. 164-167.

[RaTK] S. Rajasekaran, T. Tsantilas, D. Krisanc, "Optimal Routing Algorithms for Mesh-Connected Processor Arrays", Proc. of Aegean Workshop On Computing Springer Verlag's Lecture Notes in Computer Science, to appear, 1988.

[SaS] Y. Saad and M. H. Schultz, "Data Communication in Hypercubes", Yale University Research Reprot RR-428, October 1985.

[Se] M. Sekanina, "On an Ordering of the Set of Vertices of a Connected Graph", Publications Faculty Science, Univ. Brno 412 (1960), pp. 137-142.

[Si] C. G. Simonson, "A Variation on the Min Cut Linear Arrangement Problem", to appear in Math. Systems Theory.

[Su] I. H. Sudborough, "Bandwidth constraints on problems complete for polynomial time", Theoretical Computer Science, 26 (1983), pp. 25-52.

[Ull] J. D. Ullman, Computational Aspects of VLSI, Computer Science Press, 11 Taft Court, Rockville, Maryland 20850, U.S.A., 1984.

[Wu] A. Y. Wu, "Embedding of Tree Networks into Hypercubes", J. of Parallel and Distributed Computing, 2,3 (1985), pp. 238-249.

[Ya] M. Yannakakis, "A Polynomial Algorithm for the Min Cut Linear Arrangement of Trees", J. ACM, 32,4 (1985), pp. 950-959.

[Ya2] M. A. Yannakakis, "Linear and Book Embeddings of Graphs", Proc. of Aegean Workshop On Computing, Springer Verlag's Lecture Notes in Computer Science, vol. 227 (1986), pp. 226-235.

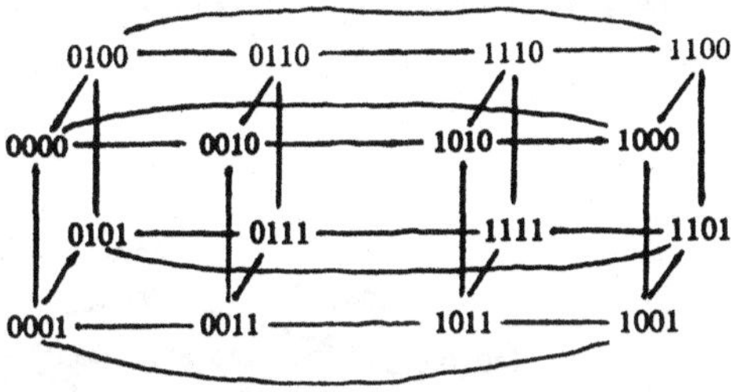

Figure 1. The hypercube, Q(4), of dimension 4.

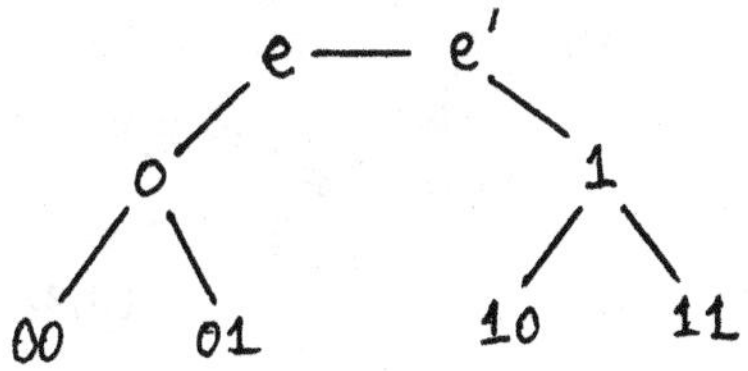

Figure 2. The double rooted complete binary tree of height 2, DRB(2).

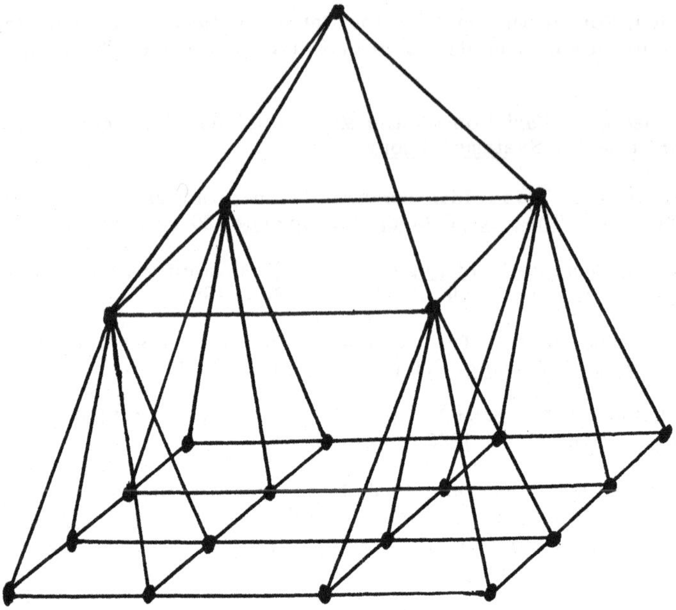

<u>Figure</u> 3. The pyramid of height 2, P(2).

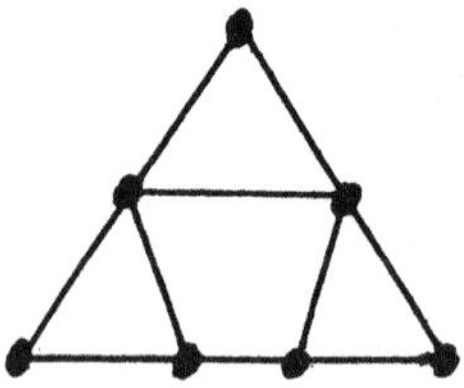

<u>Figure</u> 4. The X-tree of height 2, X(2).

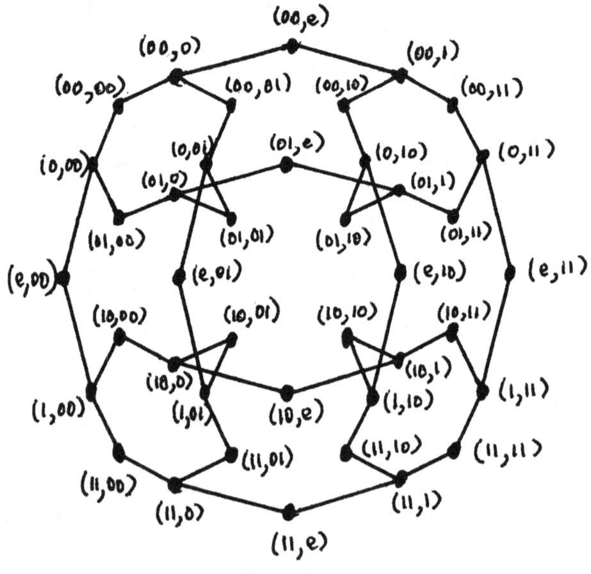

<u>Figure</u> 5. The mesh-of-trees of dimension 2, MT(2).

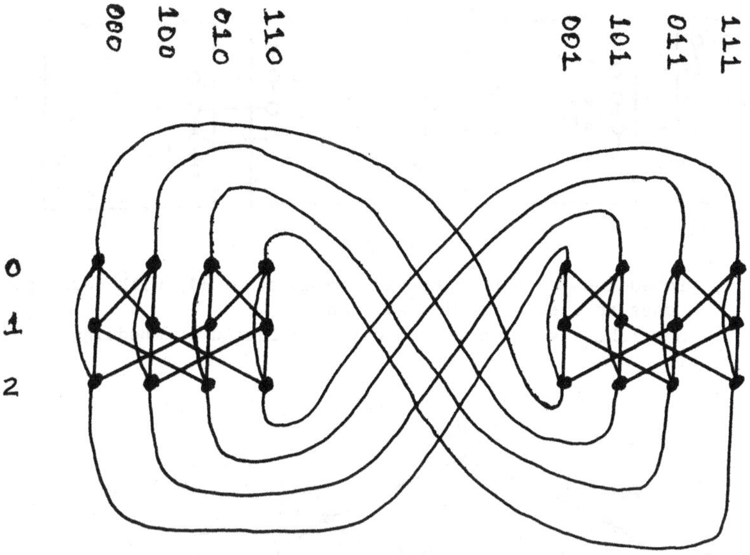

Figure 6. The butterfly of dimension 3, BF(3).

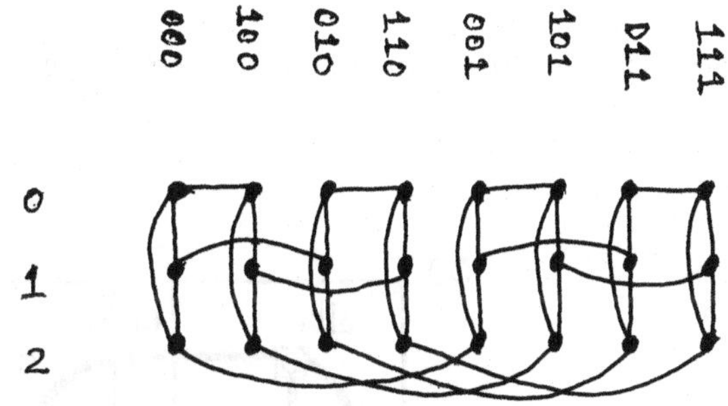

Figure 7. The cube connected cycles of dimension three, CCC(3).

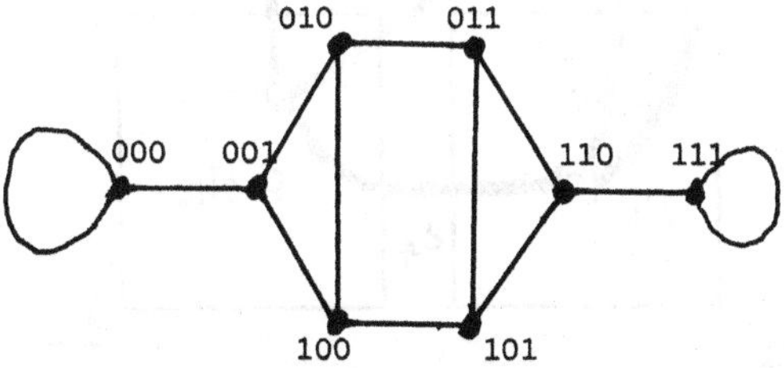

Figure 8. The shuffle-exchange network of dimension three, SE(3).

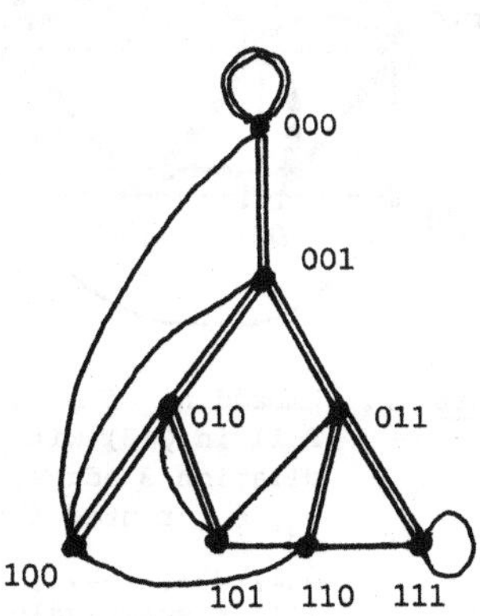

Figure 9. The DeBrujn network, DB(3).

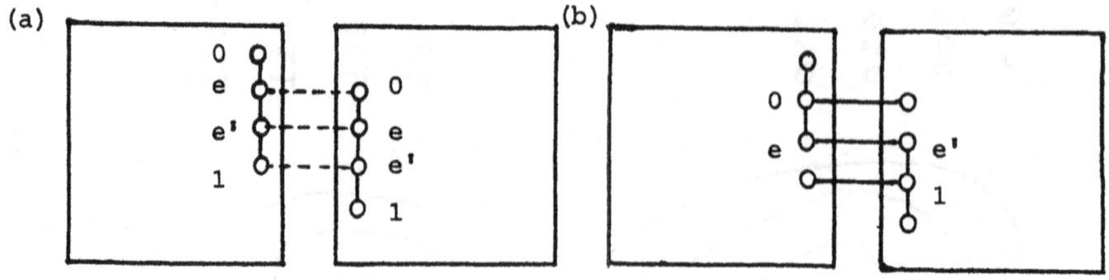

Figure 10. (a) Embeddings of B(n) into two copies of Q(n+1) with corresponding nodes shifted as indicated, and
(b) new labelings of nodes to obtain dilation 1 embedding of B(n+1).

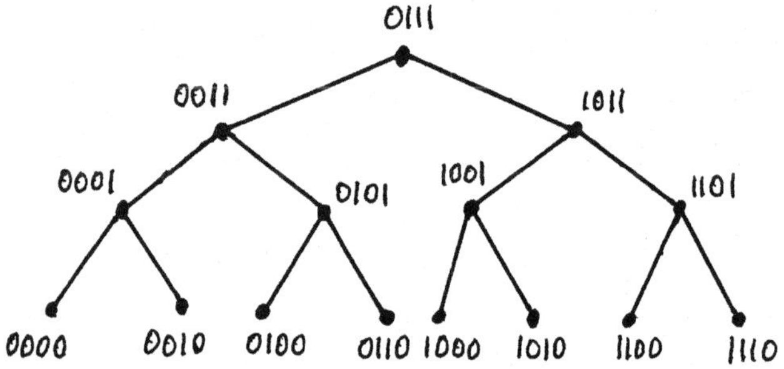

Figure 11. In-order labeling gives dilation 2 embedding

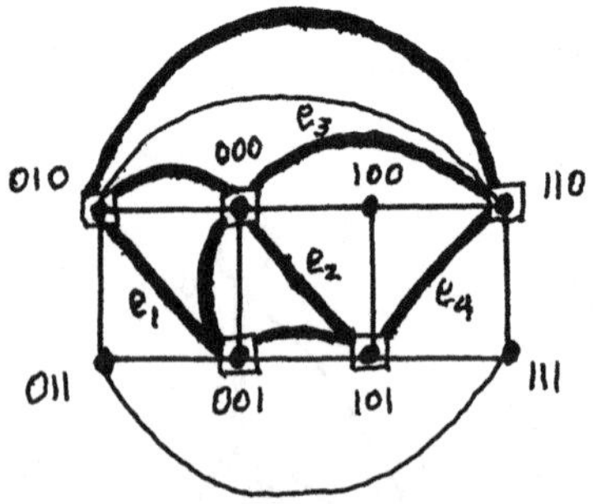

Figure 12. Embedding of pyramid P(1) in Q(3) with dilation 3 edges: e_1, e_2 e_3, e_4 routed through 011, 001, 100, and 111, respectively.

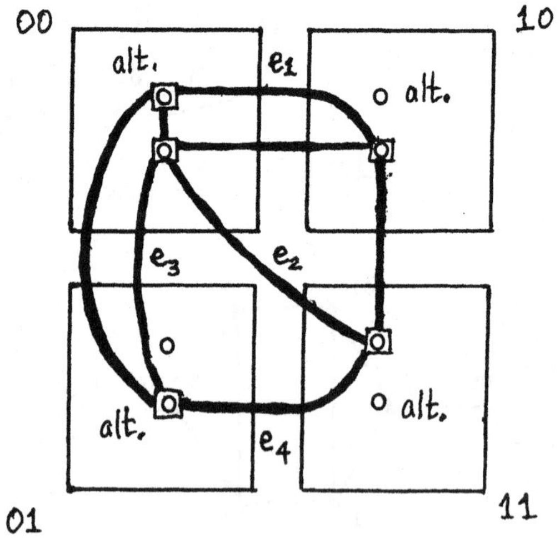

Figure 13. Dilation 2 edges: e_1, e_2, e_3, e_4 are routed through 10-alt., 10-apex, 01-apex, and 11-alt., resp.

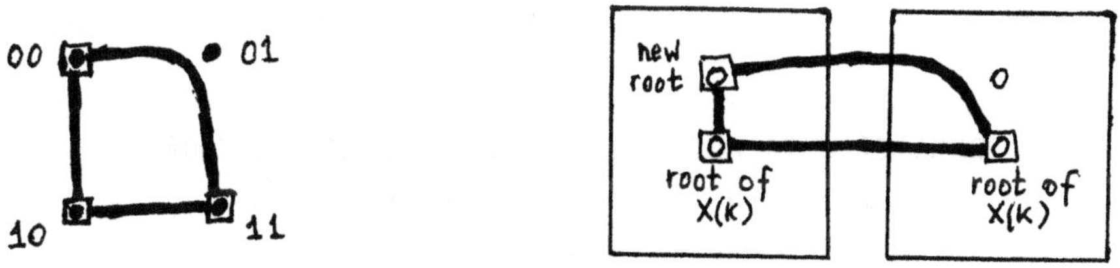

Figure 14. (a) A dilation 2, edge congestion 1 embedding of the X-tree X(1), into the hypercube Q(2), and
(b) Embedding of two copies of X(k) into Q(k+1) with dilation 2 and edge congestion 2, the placement of a new root and the routing of edges, and the resulting dilation 2, edge congestion two embedding of X(k+1) into Q(k+2).

(e,00) --> 011000	(e,01) --> 011010	(e,10) --> 011100	(e,11) --> 011110
(0,00) --> 001000	(0,01) --> 001010	(0,10) --> 001100	(0,11) --> 001110
(1,00) --> 101000	(1,01) --> 101010	(1,10) --> 101100	(1,11) --> 101110
(00,00)--> 000000	(00,01)--> 000010	(00,10)--> 000100	(00,11)--> 000110
(01,00)--> 010000	(01,01)--> 010010	(01,10)--> 010100	(01,11)--> 010110
(10,00)--> 100000	(10,01)--> 100010	(10,10)--> 100100	(10,11)--> 100110
(11,00)--> 110000	(11,01)--> 110010	(11,10)--> 110100	(11,11)--> 110110
(00,e) --> 000011	(01,e) --> 010011	(10,e) --> 100011	(11,e) --> 110011
(00,0) --> 000001	(01,0) --> 010001	(10,0) --> 100001	(11,0) --> 110001
(00,1) --> 000101	(01,1) --> 010101	(10,1) --> 100101	(11,1) --> 110101

Figure 15. A dilation 2 embedding of the mesh-of-trees of height 2, MT(2), into the hypercube of dimension 6, Q(6).

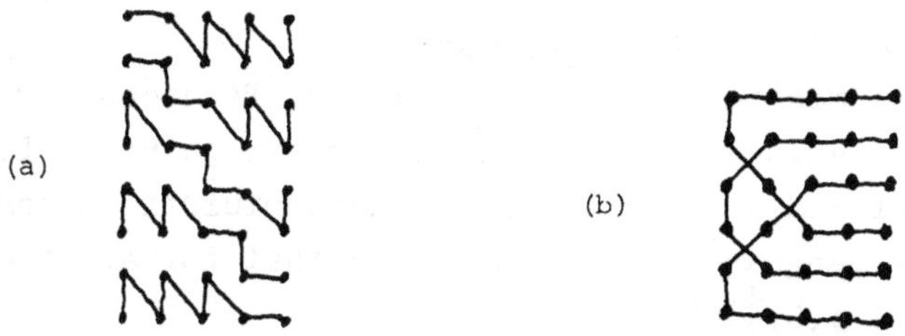

Figure 16. (a) the "squeezing" technique is illustrated by a copy of the (5,8)-tile, and
(b) the "folding" of the mesh [3 x 10] into the mesh [6 x 5].

PROBABILISTIC AUTOMATA COMPLEXITY OF LANGUAGES DEPENDS ON LANGUAGE STRUCTURE AND ERROR PROBABILITY

Farid M. Ablayev
Department of Theoretical Cybernetics
Kazan University Lenina str. 18
420000 Kazan, USSR

Abstract. New lower bound of complexity for probabilistic automata with error bounded probability was proved. It depends on the language structure and on error probability of recognition. It is shown that for languages which are "rich" with formulated property a new lower bound of probabilistic complexity is more precise than that of Rabin's lower bound. In addition with the help of a new lower bound we improve the hierarchy of complexity of probabilistic automata depending on error probability previously shown by the author.

1. INTRODUCTION

Probabilistic automata or shortly PA which accept a language with e-isolated cut point $\frac{1}{2}$ corresponds to a PA which computes with $(\frac{1}{2}-e)$ bounded error probability. Rabin [1] proved that PA with isolated cut point can accept only regular languages, i.e. can do no more than deterministic automata (shortly DA). But as PA compute with some error probability it is expected that PA require a smaller number of states than any DA recognizing the same language.

Let P(L,e) be the minimal number of states of PA necessary for accepting the regular language L with e-isolated cut point $\frac{1}{2}$. Let D(L) denote the number of states of the minimal deterministic automaton accepting the regular language L. It is evident that for arbitrary regular language L and $e \in (0,\frac{1}{2})$ holds:

1. $P(L,e) \leq D(L)$
2. $P(L,\frac{1}{2}) = D(L)$

For arbitrary regular language L and $e \in (0,\frac{1}{2}]$ from Rabin's reduction theorem [1] published in 1963 we have

$$P(L,e) \geqslant \frac{\log D(L)}{\log(1+1/e)} + 1 .$$

This Rabin's lower bound of complexity for PA shows what is the maximum economy of complexity we can expect using a PA inside a DA. The first example of the language which is recognized by PA with isolated cut points requiring a fewer number of states than any DA recognizing this language was given in [1] . The problem presented by M.Rabin in [1] was to improve if possible the lower bound of probabilistic complexity.

Six years ago R.Freivald [2] constructed the sequence of regular languages $\overline{V} = \{V_t\}$ over a single letter alphabet such that

$$D(V_t) \geqslant e^{at(\ln t)+o(t(\ln t))}$$

for some $a > 0$ and

$$P(V_t,\frac{1}{4}) \leqslant t^2 \ln t .$$

Pokrovskaya [3] presented a set of regular languages W over a single letter alphabet such that holds for the greater majority of languages V from W

$$P(V,e)=D(V)$$

for arbitrary $e \in (0,\frac{1}{2}]$.

So on the one hand there are languages for which PA gives "nearly" the maximum economy of complexity and on the other hand there are languages for which PA does not have any advantages. In [4] we presented two examples of languages over two letter alphabet with the following properties:

(i) the deterministic complexity of these languages (the number of states of the minimal automaton accepting them) is nearly the same,

(ii) the probabilistic complexity of these languages is rather different.

These examples of languages show that the probabilistic complexity of languages does not depend on their deterministic complexity.

The question arises why for some languages PA are much more effective than others? The case of finite automata is a particular one of the general problem[5] . Why are probabilistic algorithms more effective sometimes? in this paper we formulate a certain property F of the structure of regular languages in the terms of property of states of DA representing them. It is proved (Theorem 1) that the probabilistic complexity of arbitrary regular language L depends upon the power of F-subset of states of DA representing L and upon required error probability. From theorem 1 it follows that in the case when a "great majority" of states of DA representing L form F-set we have:

$$P(L,e) \geqslant D(L)^{\alpha(e)}$$

where $\alpha(e)$ depends on e, $0 \leqslant \alpha(e) \leqslant 1$ and $\alpha(\frac{1}{2})=1$, $\alpha(0)=0$. In this case PA do not have much advantage over DA. Or in other words our lower bound of P(L,e) is more precise than Rabin's universal lower bound. In the case when the power of F-set of states of DA representing L is"rather lower" than D(L) then Rabin's universal lower bound is better than our lower bound of P(L,e).

In addition as our new lower bound for P(L,e) is more precise than in [4] and holds for all $e \in (0,\frac{1}{2}]$ it means that we have improved the infinite hierarchy of complexity of PA depending on degree of isolation of cut point previously shown by the author [4].

2. DEFINITIONS.

The set of all words over the alphabet X is denoted by X^*. The length of a word v is denoted by /v/. The number of elements of finite set Q is denoted by /Q/. In this paper a finite deterministic automaton over the alphabet X is a system

$$A = (X,S,s_0,\delta,F)$$

where S is a finite set of states, $s_0 \in S$ initial state, $F \subseteq S$ set of final states, $\delta : S \times X \to S$ transition function. A word v is accepted by A if and only if $\delta(s_0,v) \in F$. The language L accepted by A consists of all words accepted by A.

Let $R \subset X^*$ be the ordered finite set, $R = \{r_1, r_2, \dots, r_t\}$. For all states $s \in S$ define t-tuple of 0 and 1

$z^R(s) = (z_1,z_2,\dots,z_t)$ as follows

$$z_i = \begin{cases} 1, & \text{if } \delta(s,r_i) \in F \\ 0, & \text{otherwise} \end{cases}$$

Definition. Subset $S' = \{s_1,s_2,\dots,s_d\}$ of the set of states S of automaton A is called F-set (full set) if there is a finite set of words R such that (i) set $z(S',R) = \{z^R(s_2),\dots,z^R(s_d)\}$ consists of all binary t-tuples,

(ii) $s \neq s'$ implies $z^R(s) \neq z^R(s')$.

Note that if A is a minimal automaton then two arbitrary states $s,s' \in S$ are F-set.

A probabilistic automaton is given by a list:

$$B = (X, C, \{M(x) : x \in X\}, m_0, \vartheta, F),$$

where C is the ordered finite set of states, $F \subseteq C$ set of final states, ϑ is a /C/-dimensional column whose i-th component is equal to 1 if $s_i \in F$ and to 0 if $s_i \notin F$. For each $x \in X$ M(x) is a stochastic /S/× /S/ matrix whose component is the transition probability of B. For each word $v \in X^*$ $v = x_1 x_2 \ldots x_n$ we define $M(x) = M(x_1)M(x_2)\ldots M(x_n)$, $m(v) = m_0 M(v)$, $\vartheta(v) = M(v)\vartheta$. Let $m_a(v)$, $\vartheta_a(v)$ denote components of m(v) and $\vartheta(v)$ respectively, corresponding to the state $a \in C$. We define the function $p : X^* \to [0,1]$ in the following way: for $V \in X^*$ $p(v) = m(v)\vartheta$. The set of words $\{v \in X^* : p(v) > \frac{1}{2}\}$ is called the language accepted by PA B with cut point $\frac{1}{2}$. Cut point $\frac{1}{2}$ is said e-isolated, $0 < e \leq \frac{1}{2}$, if for all words $v \in X^*$ $p(v) \geq \frac{1}{2} + e$, or $p(v) \leq \frac{1}{2} - e$ holds.

3. LOWER BOUND OF COMPLEXITY FOR PA.

Theorem 1. For arbitrary regular language $L \subseteq X^*$, for $e \in [0, \frac{1}{2}]$ holds

$$P(L,e) \geq d^{(1-h(\Delta))},$$

where $\Delta = \frac{1}{2} + e$ - error probability, d - power of F-subset of the set of states of DA representing language L, $h(\Delta) =$

$= -\Delta \log \Delta - (1-\Delta)\log(1-\Delta)$.

Sketch of proof. We use the information approach which was first used for probabilistic algorithms in [6] . Let $S' = \{s_1, s_2, \ldots, s_d\}$ be an arbitrary F-subset of S of DA A representing L. Let $R = \{r_1, r_2, \ldots, r_t\}$ be a set of words corresponding to S' (see definition). Let $G = \{u_1, u_2, \ldots, u_d\}$ be a set of words such that $\delta(s_0, u_i) = s_i$ for $1 \leq i \leq d$. Let P be the probability distribution on G suah that for all $u \in G$ holds $P(u) = 1/d$. Let $\pi = (\pi_1, \pi_2, \ldots, \pi_t)$ be the random vector such that for each $u \in G$ corresponds a $\pi(u) = (\pi_1(u), \pi_2(u), \ldots, \pi_t(u))$, where

$$\pi_i(u) = \begin{cases} 1, & \text{if } ur_i \in L \\ 0, & \text{otherwise} \end{cases},$$

$r_i \in R, i \in \{1, 2, \ldots, t\}$.

Let B be a PA representing L with e-isolated cut point $\frac{1}{2}$. Let θ be a random number, $\theta \in C$ such that

$$P(\theta = a \,/\, \pi = \sigma) = m_a(u)$$

where the word $u \in G$ corresponds to the value σ of the random vector π.

On the one hand from the definition of quantity of information we have

$$I(\pi;\theta) = H(\theta) - H(\theta/\pi) \leqslant H(\theta) \leqslant \log/C/ .$$

And on the other hand we have

$$I(\pi;\theta) = H(\pi) - H(\pi/\theta) .$$

Thus

$$/C/ \geqslant 2^{H(\pi) - H(\pi/\theta)} .$$

From the definition of a random vector π we have

$$H(\pi) = t = \log d .$$

In order to prove the theorem we must prove that

$$H(\pi/\theta) \leqslant h(\Delta)t = h(\Delta)\log d .$$

From the definition of π we have

$$H(\pi/\theta) \leqslant \sum_{i-1}^{t} H(\pi_i/\theta) .$$

In order to prove that

$$H(\pi_i/\theta) \leqslant h(\Delta)$$

for all $i \in \{1,2,\dots,t\}$ let η_r, $r \in R$ be a random number of 0 and 1 such that

$$P(\eta_r = 1/\theta = a) = \vartheta_a(r) .$$

Than we have

$$H(\pi_i/\theta) = H(\pi_i/\theta, \eta_r) \leqslant H(\pi_i/\eta_r) .$$

As this unequality holds for all $r \in R$ than we have

$$H(\pi_i/\theta) \leqslant H(\pi_i/\eta_{r_i}) .$$

From the condition of the theorem we have $P(\pi_i=1) = P(\pi_i=0) = \frac{1}{2}$.

From these equations and the definition of entropy H we obtain

$$H(\pi_i/\eta_{r_i}) \leqslant h(\Delta) . \quad \square$$

4. Examples.

Let $l \geqslant 1$, $n=2^{2^l}$ - are integers, $X=\{0,1\}$. We define bin(r) as an integer corresponding to a binary word $r \in X^*$. Let $//r//=\mathrm{bin}(r)+1$.

Example 1. Let $t=\log(\log n)^2$. Let $W_n \subset X^*$ denote the language $\{v:\ v=ur\}$, where $/u/=2^t$, $/r/=t$ and it is required that the $//r//$-th letter of the word u equals 1.

Let A be a DA, representing W_n and $s(u)=\delta(s_0,u)$. Then the subset $S'=\{s(u):/u/=2^t\}$ is the F-subset of the set of states of A and $/S'/> n^{\log n}$. Thus from theorem 1 we have that for all $e \in (0,\frac{1}{2}]$ holds

$$P(W_n,e) \geq n^{(1-h(\Delta))\log n} .$$

It is easy to see that

$$D(W_n) = O(n^{\log n}) .$$

So from Rabin's lower bound we have

$$P(W_n,e) \geq \frac{(\log n)^2}{\log(1+1/e)} + 1 .$$

<u>Example 2</u>. Let V_n denote the language $\{v: v=ww\}$ where $/w/=n$.

Let A be a DA representing V_n. From the definition of the language V_n follows that the power of the arbitrary F-subset of the set of the states of A is not more than 2 . Thus from theorem 1 we have that for all $e \in (0,\frac{1}{2}]$ holds

$$P(V_n,e) \geq 2^{(1 - h(\Delta))} .$$

On the other hand we have that

$$D(V_n) \geq 2^n .$$

So from Rabin's lower bound we obtain

$$P(V_n,e) \geq \frac{n}{\log(1+1/e)} + 1 .$$

<u>Theorem 2</u>.[4] For arbitrary $e \in (0,\frac{1}{2})$ holds

$$P(V_n,e) \precsim n^4/\log n .$$

<u>5. HIERARCHY</u>.

Let $X=\{0,1\}$, $k \geq 2$ be an even number and $n=2^k+k$. Let L_k denote the language $\{v \in X^*: v=ur\}$ where $/u/=2^k$, $/r/=k$ and it is required that the $//r//$-th letter of the word u equals 1.

<u>Theorem 3</u>. [4] For arbitrary $e \in (0,\frac{1}{2}]$ holds

$$P(L_k,e) \precsim n(2^n/n)^{f(e)} ,$$

where $f(e)=3/2 - 1/(2e+1)$.

From theorem 1 it follows that for the language L_k and arbitrary $e \in (0,\frac{1}{2})$ holds

$$P(L_k,e) \gtrsim (2^n/n)^{1-h(\Delta)} ,$$

where $\Delta = \frac{1}{2} + e$.

Theorem 4. There exists an infinite sequence of numbers $0 < e_1 < e_2 < \dots < \frac{1}{2}$ such that for each $i \geq 1$ holds

$$P(L_k,e_i) \,/\, P(L_k,e_{i+1}) \to 0, \text{ when } k \to \infty .$$

The proff of theorem 4 results from the statement of theorem 3, the lower bound of $P(L_k,e)$ and the following properties of functions $f(e)$ and $g(e) = 1 - h(\Delta)$

(i) for each $e \in (0,\frac{1}{2})$ holds $g(e) < f(e)$,

(ii) for each $e \in (0,\frac{1}{2})$ there exists e', $e' \in (0,\frac{1}{2})$, such that $e < e'$ and $f(e) < g(e')$.

6.CONCLUSION.

1. The deterministic complexity of the language V_n is higher than that of the language W_n but the W_n probabilistically is more complex than V_n. Thus probabilistic complexity of languages does not depend upon deterministic complexity, but on the structure of language.

2. Theorem 1 gives precise value of complexity for the language W_n when $e=\frac{1}{2}$.

3. As the lower bound of theorem 1 and Rabin's lower bound are independent then we can state

Theorem 5. Foe arbitrary regular language L, for $e \in (0,\frac{1}{2}]$ holds

$$P(L,e) \geq \max \left\{ d^{(1-h(\Delta))}, (\log D(L))/\log(1+1/e))+1 \right\},$$

where $\Delta=\frac{1}{2}+e$ - error probability, d - power of F-subset of the set of states of DA representing L, $h(\Delta)=-\Delta\log\Delta -(1-\Delta)\log(1-\Delta)$.

REFERENCES.

1. M.O.Rabin, Probabilistic automata, Information and Control, 1963, v.6, No.3, 230-245.

2. R.Frievald, On growing the number of states in determinisation of finite probabilistic automata, Avtomatika and vichislitelnaya technika, 1982, No.3, 39-42.

3. I.Pokrovskaya, Some bounds of the number of states of probabilistic automata recognizing regular languages, Problemy kebernetiky, 1979, No.36, 181-194.

4. F.M.Ablayev, The complexity of probabilistic automata with isolated cut point, Theoretical Computer science (to be published).

5. F.M.Ablayev, R.Freivald, Why sometimes probabilistic algorithms can be more effective, Lecture Notes in Computer Science, v.233, MFCS-1986, 1986, 1-14.

6. R.Freivald, I.Ikannicks, On some advantages of nondeterminate machines over probabilistic ones, Izvestiya VUZ Mathematica, 1977, No.21, 118-123.

BREADTH-FIRST PHRASE STRUCTURE GRAMMARS AND QUEUE AUTOMATA (0)

E. Allevi, A. Cherubini (1) and S. Crespi Reghizzi (2)
(1) Dipartimento di Matematica, (2) Dipartimento di Elettronica
Politecnico, Piazza Leonardo da Vinci 32, 20133 Milano, Italy

1. INTRODUCTION

We define and develop a theory of breadth-first (BF) phrase-structure grammars. Their novelty comes from a different application of rewriting rules to derivations: the least recently produced nonterminal symbol must be rewritten first. In other words nonterminals in a sentential form are inserted and rewritten by a FIFO discipline.

The naturally corresponding recognizer is then a queue automaton, a class of devices equipped with a FIFO memory tape, investigated by Brandenburg [2],[3]; Vauquelin and Franchi Zannettacci [6]. However the idea of BF grammars is original, and corresponds to automata making a restricted use of states (for type 2 grammars). Ayers's [1] automata can operate on two ends of the tape: the grammatical characterization is in term of ordered type 1 grammars.

BF grammars of type 0 and 1 have the same generative capacity of their classical counterparts, and correspond to unrestricted queue automata and to linearly bounded queue automata respectively.

Type 2 BF grammars (or Breadth-first Context-Free) are essentially different from context-free grammars (e.g. they generate the anagrams on three letters but not the palindromes). BCF languages are recognized by a queue automaton with a single state essentially, and display an interesting "pumping lemma", which allows us to obtain some language family comparisons.

2. PRELIMINAIRES

Def. 1 . A breadth-first grammar, or BF-grammar, is a 4-tuple $G = (V_N, \Sigma, P, S)$ where V_N (nonterminal) and Σ (terminal) are disjoint finite alphabets, the axiom $S \in V_N$, and P is a finite set of productions $\alpha \to x\beta$

(0) Work supported by a grant of Ministero Pubblica Istruzione (60%)

with $\alpha \in V_N^+$, $x \in \Sigma^*$, $\beta \in V_N^*$. The empty word is noted ε. Elements of V_N are denoted by upper case latin letters, the words in $(V_N \cup \Sigma)^*$ are denoted by u,v,...,z and the words in V_N^* are denoted by lower case Greek letters.

Def. 2 . Let u, v be two strings and $G = (V_N, \Sigma, P, S)$. v <u>immediately derives</u> from u, $u \Rightarrow v$, iff: $u = x\beta\gamma$, $x \in \Sigma^*$; $v = xy\gamma\delta$, $y \in \Sigma^*$ and $(\beta \to y\delta) \in P$.

The reflexive and transitive and the transitive closure and r applications of $\Rightarrow$ are written $\Rightarrow^*$, $\Rightarrow^+$ and $\Rightarrow^r$ resp.

Def. 3 . The <u>language generated</u> by G, a BF grammar, is $L(G) = \{x \mid x \in \Sigma^*, S \Rightarrow^* x\}$. The class of languages generated by BF-grammars (BF languages) is called L_{BF}. Allowance of productions of the form $\alpha \to \beta$, $\alpha, \beta \in (\Sigma \cup V_N)^*$ would not enlarge the family of languages and is not considered.

Def. 4. For i=0,1,2,3, G is called of <u>type</u> i if productions in P have the following form i):

0) No restrictions

1) $\alpha \to x\beta$ and $|\alpha| \leq |x\beta|$, with the possible exception of the production $S \to \varepsilon$ whose occurence in P implies, however, that S does not occur on the right side of any production in P.

2) $A \to x\alpha$ $(x \in \Sigma^*)$ (also called <u>B</u>readth-<u>F</u>irst <u>C</u>ontext-<u>F</u>ree).

3) $A \to xB$ or $A \to x$ $(x \in \Sigma^*)$

Clearly type 3 BF-languages coincide with regular languages.

Example 1. The type 2 grammar $G_1 = (\{S,A,B,C\}, \{a,b,c\}, \{S \to ABCS, A \to A, A \to a, B \to B, B \to b, C \to C, C \to c, S \to \varepsilon\}, S)$ generates the language $L_1 = L(G_1)$ of the words which are anagrams of $(abc)^*$.

Example 2. The type 2 grammar $G_2 = (\{S,A,B\}, \{a,b\}, \{S \to AB, A \to aAA, A \to a, B \to bB, B \to b\}, S)$ generates $L_2 = \{a^{n_1}ba^{n_2}b...a^{n_i}ba^{n_{i+1}}ba^* \mid i \geq 1, n_1 = 1, \forall i\ 0 \leq n_{i+1} \leq 2n_i\}$.

Example 3. The type 1 grammar $G_3 = (\{S,T,A,B,Q,R\}, \{a,b,c\}, \{S \to aTQ, S \to bTR, TR \to aTRA, TR \to bTRB, TQ \to aTQA, TQ \to bTQB, A \to A, B \to B, T \to c, QA \to aQ, QB \to bQ, RA \to aR, RB \to bR, Q \to a, R \to b\})$ generates palindromes, $L_3 = L(G_3) = \{ucu^R \mid u \in \{a,b\}^*\}$

Next we present the basic definitions of queue automata

A queue recognizer has a memory operating with a FIFO policy. It is provided with an unidirectional input tape and with one queue, that is unbounded memory tape having a reading head positioned at the beginning of the string written in the queue, and a writing head at the end. In a move, the automaton reads a symbol from both input and memory tapes, and writes a finite string at the end of the queue; the heads can hold or advance, but only in one and the same direction. This point of view is formalized in the following definitions.

Def. 5 . A <u>Nondeterministic Queue Automaton</u> M - shortly a FIFO automaton - is a 7-uple $(Q,\Sigma,\Gamma,\partial,q_0,S,F)$ where:

- Q,Σ,Γ are finite sets of internal states, input and memory alphabets resp.;
- ∂ is a (possibly partial) transition mapping
  $\partial : Q \times \Sigma \times \Gamma \rightarrow PF(Q \times \{Hold, Shift\} \times [\{Hold, Shift\} \times \Gamma^*])$
  (where PF(E) is the set of finite subsets of a set E)
- $q_0 \in Q$ is the initial state
- $S \in \Gamma$ is the initial memory symbol
- $F \subseteq Q$ is the set of final states.

Intuitively $(q',D_0,\langle D_1,\alpha\rangle) \in \partial(q,a,A)$ indicates the following move: M goes from state q to state q' reading a from the input and A from the queue. M advances the input head if D_0=Shift, and the trailing head if D_1= Shift. M writes α onto the queue and advances the leading head by $|\alpha|$ positions

Def. 6 . A <u>configuration</u> of a FIFO automaton M is a 3-uple $c=\langle q,x,g\rangle$ where: $q \in Q$, $x \in \Sigma^*$, $g \in \Gamma^*$. A configuration c_0 is said <u>initial</u> if $q=q_0$ and $g=S$. Let $c=\langle q,ax,Ag\rangle$ $(x\in\Sigma^*, g\in\Gamma^*, A\in\Gamma)$ be a configuration of M, and let $(q',D_0,\langle D_1,\alpha\rangle) \in\partial(q,a,A)$, where $D_0,D_1\in\{Hold,Shift\}$, $\alpha\in\Gamma^*$. Let x',g' be the strings:

$$x' = \begin{cases} ax & \text{if } D_0 = Hold \\ x & \text{if } D_0 = Shift \end{cases} \qquad g' = \begin{cases} Ag\alpha & \text{if } D_1 = Hold \\ g\alpha & \text{if } D_1 = Shift. \end{cases}$$

The <u>move</u> $c \vdash_M c'$ (or $c \vdash c'$) is defined by putting $c'=\langle q',x',g'\rangle$. A string x is <u>accepted</u> by M if $c_0 \vdash_M^* c_F$ where c_0 is an initial configuration, and $c_F= \langle q_F,\varepsilon,g\rangle$ with $q_F\in F$. The <u>language</u> L(M) <u>accepted</u> by M is then: $L(M)=\{x\in\Sigma \mid c_0 \vdash_M^* c_F\}$.

Def. 7. FIFO = $\{L \mid \exists$ a FIFO automaton M: $L = L(M)\}$

Def. 8. A FIFO-automaton M operates in <u>real-time</u> if every move shifts the input tape by one position..

Statement 1. *Let* L *be a BF-language, then* L *belongs to* FIFO.

Hint. It is simple to construct an recognizer M of L(G), G a BF-grammar. Every production $\alpha\rightarrow x\beta$ $(\alpha\in V_N^+, x\in\Sigma^*, \beta\in V_N^*)$ of G corresponds to a chain of moves which, starting in the state q, reads x from the input, α from the queue, writes β onto the queue and returns to state q. Finitely many intermediate states are needed in order to memorize the scanned prefixes of x and α.

3. <u>MAIN RESULTS</u>

As a characterization of the class of languages generated by BF-grammars

Lemma 1. *Let* M *a queue automaton. There exists a BF-grammar* G *of type 0 such that* L(G) = L(M).

Hence we have the following

Theorem 1. The family of type 0 BF languages is equivalent to the family of the recursively enumerable languages.

For type 1 BF grammars we prove the equivalence to context sensitive grammars. Since productions of type 1 BF-grammars are length increasing we have

Lemma 2 Every language generated by a BF-grammar of type 1 is linear bounded (with respect to space).

Hence every language generated by a type 1 BF-grammar is context sensitive.

Theorem 2. The family of type 1 BF languages is equivalent to the family of the context sensitive languages.

Proof. Let L be generated by a type 1 grammar $G = (V_N, \Sigma, P, S)$ with ε-free productions of the following forms:

$$A \to BC \tag{1}$$

$$AB \to CD \tag{2}$$

$$A \to a \tag{3}$$

Let $u, v \in (\Sigma \cup V_N)^*$ and $u \Rightarrow^G v$, thus $u = u_1 \alpha u_2$, $v = u_1 \beta u_2$ and $\alpha \to \beta$ is in P. We outline the construction of a type 1 BF grammar $G' = (V_N', \Sigma, P', S)$ such that $L = L(G')$. In a BF-grammar the strings derived from the axiom belong to $\Sigma^* V_N^*$, we suppose that V_N' contains a primed copy Σ' of Σ and, for every $u \in (\Sigma \cup V_N)^*$ and we denote $u' = h(u)$ where $h(a) = a'$ for $a \in \Sigma$ and $h(A) = A$ for $A \in V_N$. Three cases occur depending on the form of the production applied in the derivation $u \Rightarrow^G v$.

Case (1): we include into P' the following productions

$$a' \to a' \ \forall a \in \Sigma;\ A \to A', A' \to A \ \forall A \in V_N;\ A \to B'C' \text{ if } (A \to BC) \in P \tag{4}$$

Case (2): we include into P' the productions

$$AB \to C'D' \text{ if } (AB \to CD) \in P \tag{5}$$

Case (3): we add to P' the productions

$$A \to a' \text{ if } (A \to a) \in P \tag{6}$$

In any case, we have $u' \Rightarrow^{(+,G')} v'$. Hence we have proved that $S \Rightarrow^{(+,G')} w'$ iff $S \Rightarrow^G w$.

To derive a from a', we introduce new nonterminals and productions:

$$\begin{array}{ll} S' \to A''B' \text{ if } (S \to AB) \in P & A'' \to A'' \ \forall A \in V_N \\ S' \to a \text{ if } (S \to a) \in P & a''b' \to ab'' \ \forall a, b \in \Sigma \\ A'' \to a'' \text{ if } (A \to a) \in P & a'' \to a,\ a'' \to a'' \ \forall a \in \Sigma \\ A'' \to B''C' \text{ if } (A \to BC) \in P & \end{array} \tag{7}$$

(Notice that simply introducing a production of the type $a' \to a$ would not do, since a permutation of the string could result). The effect of the new productions is to doubly prime the leftmost nonterminal of w in order to orderly derive the next terminal. Hence, if we consider the grammar $G' = (V_N', \Sigma, P', S')$ where $V_N' = V_N \cup V_N' \cup V_N'' \cup \Sigma' \cup \Sigma'' \cup S'$ and P' is formed by productions (4), (5), (6), (7), for every $w \in L$ we obtain $w \in L(G')$.

Conversely, let $S' \Rightarrow^{(+,G')} u'$ where $u' = x_1 a'' \alpha_1 x_2' \alpha_2 \ldots x_n' \alpha_n$, $x_1 \in \Sigma^*$, $a'' \in \Sigma''$ or $a'' \in V_N''$, $\alpha_i \in V_N^*$, $x_i' \in \Sigma^*$ and suppose, e.g., $a'' \in \Sigma''$, thus $u' \Rightarrow^{G'} x_1 \alpha_1 x_2' \alpha_2 \ldots x_n' \alpha_n a''$

$\Rightarrow^{\theta'} x_1 x_2' \alpha_2 ... x_n' \alpha_n a'' y_1' \beta_1' \Rightarrow^{\theta'} x_1 \alpha_2 ... a'' y_1' \beta_1' x_2' \Rightarrow^{\theta'} ... \Rightarrow^{\theta'} x_1 a'' y_1' \beta_1' y_2' \beta_2' ... y_n' \beta_n' \Rightarrow^{(+,G')}$ $x_1 a'' y_1' \beta_1 y_2' \beta_2 ... y_n' \beta_n$ where $\alpha_i \rightarrow y_i' \beta_i'$ is a production of G'. Hence, if we consider $u = x_1 a \alpha_1 x_2 \alpha_2 ... x_n \alpha_n$ where x_i and a are the non marked copies of x_i' and a" resp., we have $u \Rightarrow^{(+,\theta)} x_1 a y_1 \beta_1 y_2 \beta_2 ... y_n \beta_n$, since, if $\alpha_i \rightarrow y_i' \beta_i'$ is in P', $\alpha_i \rightarrow y_i \beta_i$ is in P. Analogously we proceed when $a'' \in V_N''$. Hence L(G) = L(G').

Since a real-time automaton can only write a linear memory space, we have

Statement 2. The family of languages recognized by a real time queue automaton is strictly contained within the family of type 1 BF languages.

Palindromes (ex.3) are not recognized by a real time queue automaton [3].

Type 2 BF-grammar properties are studied here with more detail since they notable differ from the properties of context-free grammars.

Let L(G), G a type 2 BF grammar; for every $w \in L(G)$ we construct the syntax tree, with nodes labeled by terminals, nonterminals or ε, in this way.

Let $S \Rightarrow w_1 \Rightarrow ... \Rightarrow w_r \Rightarrow w$ with $w_i \in (V_N \cup \Sigma)^+$, $w \in \Sigma^*$. The root of the tree has label S. For i=1,2,...,r let $w_i = xA_i\beta_i$ $(x \in \Sigma^*, A_i \in V_N, \beta_i \in V_N^*)$ and $A_i \rightarrow x_i \alpha_i$ the production such that $w_{i+1} = x x_i \beta_i \alpha_i$ $(x_i \in \Sigma^*, \alpha_i \in V_N^*)$. Thus we can assume that, for each $j \leq i$ every symbol in w_j is a label of some node, hence there is a node labeled by A_i. Suppose that $x_i = a_1 ... a_r$, $\alpha = B_1 ... B_s$ $(a_1, ..., a_r \in \Sigma,\ B_1, ..., B_s \in V_N)$, then append to the node labeled A_i the arcs $(A_i, a_1), ..., (A_i, a_r), (A_i, B_1), ..., (A_i, B_s)$ from left to right. The leaves are labeled by terminals or ε and w is the set of terminals ordered breadth-first, left to right.

It is convenient to define a derivation by levels:

Def. 9. Let u_i, u_{i+1} be two elements of $\Sigma^* V_N^*$. u_{i+1} <u>derive by level</u> from u_i $(u_i \Rightarrow^{(Lev)} u_{i+1})$ if $u_0 = S$, $u_i = x\beta$ with $|\beta| = r$ and $u_i \Rightarrow^r u_{i+1}$ and analogously if v_i is a substring of u_i, v_{i+1} is a derivation by level of v_i if $v_i = y\delta$, $|\delta| = s$ and $v_i \Rightarrow^s v_{i+1}$. Obviously v_{i+1} is a substring of u_{i+1}.

Closures (transitive and reflexive, transitive) and r applications of $\Rightarrow^{(Lev)}$ are denoted by $\Rightarrow^{(*,Lev)}$, $\Rightarrow^{(+,Lev)}$, $\Rightarrow^{(r,Lev)}$ resp. The relation $\Rightarrow^{(Lev)}$ is contained in $\Rightarrow^*$ and clearly $L(G) = \{x \in \Sigma^* \mid S \Rightarrow^{(*,Lev)} x\}$.

By an argument identical to the one of context free grammar (e.g. see [5], Th. 6.2 ,p.55), we have

Lemma 3. For every BCF-grammar $G_\perp$ *there is an* ε*-free BCF-grammar* G_1*, such that* $L(G_1) = L(G) \setminus \{\varepsilon\}$. *If* $\varepsilon \in L(G)$, *there is a BCF-grammar* $G' = (V_N', \Sigma, P', S')$ *such that* $L(G') = L(G)$, *the only production in* G' *with* ε *as the right side is* $S' \rightarrow \varepsilon$ *and* S' *does not occur on the right side of any production in* G'.

Theorem 3. *For every BCF-grammar* G *such that* $\varepsilon \notin L(G)$, *there is an equivalent grammar whose productions are either of the form* $A \to \alpha$ *where* $\alpha \in V_N^+$ *with* $|\alpha| \le 2$ *or* $A \to a$ *and* a *is a terminal (called BCF normal form).*

Proof. By Lemma 1 we may assume that the given grammar $G=(V_N, \Sigma, P, S)$ is ε-free . From G we construct a normal form grammar G" as follows :

1. Replace each production $p: A \to x\alpha$ where $x = a_1 ... a_r$ $(r \ge 1)$, $a_i \in \Sigma$, $\alpha \in V_N^*$, by the productions $p': A \to A'_1 ... A'_r \alpha$; $p'_i: A'_i \to a_i$, $1 \le i \le r$ where A'_i are new nonterminals.

Let $G' = (V_N', \Sigma, P', S)$ be the grammar thus obtained. Clearly G and G' are equivalent since generation of each terminal is delayed in G' by one step and G' contains only productions of the forms

$$A \to a \text{ or } A \to \alpha, \text{ with } \alpha \in V_N^*. \qquad (8)$$

2. Consider now a grammar $G = (V_N, \Sigma, P, S)$ having only productions of forms (8). Let $k(G) = \max_{(A \to \alpha) \in P}\{|\alpha|\}$. Inductively we construct from G an equivalent grammar $G'=(V_N', \Sigma, P', S)$ such that $k(G') = k(G)-1$ until k=2. Replace each production $p \in P$ of the form $A \to B_1 ... B_{k-1} B_k$ by productions

$$p': \begin{cases} A \to B'_1 ... B'_{k-2}\, C'_p \\ C'_p \to B_{k-1}\, B_k \\ B'_i \to B_i, \quad 1 \le i \le k-2 \end{cases}$$

where primed symbols are new.

Replace each production $q \in P$ of the form $A \to D_1 ... D_r$, $r<k$ by the productions

$$q': \quad A \to D'_1 ... D'_r, \quad D'_i \to D_i, \quad 1 \le i \le r.$$

Then let $P' = \{A \to a \mid (A \to a) \in P\} \cup \{p'\} \cup \{q'\}$ and $V_N' = V_N \cup \{$new nonterminals created at this step$\}$. Then G and G' are equivalent. In fact, let $x\alpha, y\beta$ two elements of $\Sigma^* V_N^*$ such that $x\alpha \Rightarrow^{(Lev, G)} y\beta$, we prove that $x\alpha \Rightarrow^{(+, G')} y\beta$. Let $\alpha = A_1 A_2 ... A_r$; since $x\alpha \Rightarrow^{(Lev)} y\beta$ there exist r productions of P $A_i \to x_i \alpha_i$ $(i=1,...,r; x_i \in \Sigma^*; \alpha_i \in V_N^*)$ such that $y\beta = x x_1 ... x_r \alpha_1 ... \alpha_r$. Moreover by hypothesis (8) on G, it is either $x_i = \varepsilon$ or $\alpha_i = \varepsilon$.

Now for every i such that $x_i = \varepsilon$, we use the productions of P' $A_i \to \alpha'_i$ with $\alpha'_i = B'_{i,1} B'_{i,2} ... B'_{i,k-2}\, C'_i$ if $\alpha_i = B_{i,1} B_{i,2} ... B_{i,k-1} B_{i,k}$ $(r \ge k)$ or $\alpha'_i = D'_{i,1} D'_{i,2} ... D'_{i,r}$ if $\alpha_i = D_{i,1} D_{i,2} ... D_{i,r}$ $(r<k)$ and we have $x\alpha \Rightarrow^{(+, G')} x x_1 ... x_r \alpha'_1 ... \alpha'_r$ then using the productions $B'_{i,h} \to B_{i,h}$, $C'_i \to B_{i,k-1}\, B_{i,k}$, or $D'_{i,j} \to D_{i,j}$ we obtain $x x_1 ... x_r \alpha'_1 ... \alpha'_r \Rightarrow^{(+, G')} x x_1 ... x_r \alpha_1 ... \alpha_r = y\beta$. Then $x\alpha \Rightarrow^{(+, G')} y\beta$ and $L(G) \subseteq L(G')$.

Conversely suppose that $S \Rightarrow^{(*, Lev, G')} x\alpha \Rightarrow^{(Lev, G')} y\beta \Rightarrow^{(Lev, G')} z\gamma$, where $x\alpha \in \Sigma^* V_N^*$, $y\beta \in \Sigma^* V_N^*$, $z\gamma \in \Sigma^* V_N^*$. Then the following cases are possible

1) In the derivation $x\alpha \Rightarrow^{(*, G')} y\beta$ only productions are used of the form $A_i \to a_i$ which are also in P, hence $x\alpha \Rightarrow^{(+, G)} y\beta$.

2) Either some production p' or some production q' are used in the derivation $x\alpha \Rightarrow^{(2, Lev, G')} y\beta$. By using the corrisponding productions p or q and we obtain $x\alpha \Rightarrow^{(+, G)} y\beta$, hence $L(G') \subseteq L(G)$.

By definition obviously every BCF language is letter-equivalent to a context-free language. Thus from well known results it follows :

Statement 3. *For every BCF language, the set* $\Psi(L)$ *is semilinear* (where Ψ is the Parikh mapping). *A language over a unary alphabet is a BCF language if and only if it is regular.*

The family of languages generated by BCF-grammars is called L_{BCF}.

Statement 4. L_{BCF} *is closed under union, (possible erasing) homomorphisms and reverse homomorphisms.*

Consider the operator π: $\pi(v)=\{w|w$ is a permutation of $v\}$ mapping a string onto all permutations. Then let $\pi(L)=\{\pi(x)|x\in L\}$.

Statement 5. *The family* L_{BCF} *is closed with respect to* π.

Hint. Let $L=L(G)$. Then add to P the productions $A\rightarrow A$ for each $A\in V_N$. Clearly the grammar thus obtained generates $\pi(L)$.

Statement 6. *Let L be a language in* L_{BCF}, *then L is recognized by a queue automaton with a constant (independent of G) number of states* .

The first part of this statement follows from Statement 1. Here we provide a construction for an automaton with 3 states.

Hint. Let $G=(V_N,\Sigma,P,S)$ be a normal form BCF-grammar, we may construct a FIFO automaton $M=(\{q_0,q_1,q_f\},\Sigma,\partial,q_0,S,\{q_f\})$ as follows

$\partial(q_0,a,S)=(q_0,Shift,<Shift,\perp>)$ if $S\rightarrow a$ is in P

$\partial(q_0,a,S)=(q_0,Hold,<Shift,\alpha\perp>)$ $\forall$ $a\in\Sigma$ if $S\rightarrow\alpha$ is in P

$\partial(q_0,a,A)=(q_0,Shift,<Shift,\varepsilon>)$ if $A\rightarrow a$ is in P

$\partial(q_0,a,A)=(q_0,Hold,<Shift,\alpha>)$ $\forall$ $a\in\Sigma$ if $A\rightarrow\alpha$ is in P

$\partial(q_0,a,\perp)=(q_1,Hold,<Shift,\perp>)$ $\forall$ $a\in\Sigma$

$\partial(q_0,\perp,\perp)=(q_1,Hold,<Shift,\perp>)$

$\partial(q_1,a,A)=(q_0,Shift,<Shift,\varepsilon>)$ if $A\rightarrow a$ is in P

$\partial(q_1,a,A)=(q_0,Hold,<Shift,\alpha>)$ $\forall$ $a\in\Sigma$ if $A\rightarrow\alpha$

$\partial(q_1,\perp,\perp)=(q_f,Shift,<Shift,\perp>)$.

The proof follows by induction.

Now we prove a periodicity property for L_{BCF}. First we introduce some operations on ordered sets of strings.

Def. 10. Let $x,y\in\Sigma^*$ and let $x=x_1x_2...x_r$, $y=y_1y_2...y_s$ $(x_i,y_j\in\Sigma^*,1\le i\le r,1\le j\le s)$ be two decompositions, to be denoted by $\underline{x}=<x_1,x_2,...,x_r>$, $\underline{y}=<y_1,y_2,...,y_s>$ and called marked strings. The <u>marked merge</u> of $\underline{x}$, $\underline{y}$, $m(\underline{x},\underline{y})$, is defined by

$m(\underline{x},\underline{y})=<x_1y_1,...,x_r\,y_r,\ y_{r+1},...,\ y_s>$ if $r\le s$ (and similarly if $r>s$).

Moreover $m(\underline{x},\underline{y})$ indicates the element $x_1y_1x_2y_2...x_ry_ry_{r+1}...y_s$ of Σ^*. The concatenation is defined on marked strings by $\underline{x}\,\underline{y}=<x_1,...,x_r,y_1,...,y_s>$. Since m is associative it is possible to define $m(\underline{x},\underline{y},\underline{z})=m(m(\underline{x},\underline{y}),\underline{z})=m(\underline{x},m(\underline{y},\underline{z}))$.

Theorem 4. *Let* L *be a language of* L_{BCF}. *There exist two constants* p *and* q *depending only on* L, *such that for every word* t *of* L, *with* $|t|>p$ *the following properties hold:*

(i) *There exist* $u,x,y,w,z,v \in \Sigma^*$ *and finite decompositions* $\underline{u}, \underline{x}, \underline{y}, \underline{w}, \underline{z}, \underline{v}$ *such that* $t=m(\underline{u},\underline{x}\ m(\underline{y},\underline{w},\underline{z}),\underline{v})$.

(ii) $|x\ m(\underline{y},\underline{w},\underline{z})|<q$, $xyz\neq\varepsilon$

(iii) $m(\underline{u},\underline{x}\ m(\underline{y},\underline{x}\ m(\underline{y},\underline{w},\underline{z}),\underline{z}),\underline{v}) \in L$.

Proof. Let $v \in L$ such that $S \Rightarrow^{(r,Lev)} v$, then there exists an integer $k=k(r)$ such that $|v|<k$. Let $t \in L$ and suppose $|t|>k(|V_N|)$, then

$$S \Rightarrow^{(n,Lev)} t, \qquad (9)$$

where $n>|V_N|$, and in the syntax tree of t there is a path containing more than $|V_N|$ nodes, hence two occurrences of a nonterminal A. Denote the higher (lower) occurrence A' (A"). First we show that we can always assume that there exist two elements A' and A" such that the subtree rooted in A' bifurcates before A", i.e. if $A' \Rightarrow^{(s,Lev)} x\alpha A''\beta$ is the derivation induced by (9), $|x\alpha\beta|>0$. By contradiction, assume that $\forall$ A', A", where A" is a son of A', the derivation induced by (8) is $A' \Rightarrow^{+} A''$, then the tree obtained erasing every path [A', A"] generates t', a permutation of t. Then $S \Rightarrow^{(m,Lev)} t'$, with $m\leq|V_N|$, a contradiction, being $|t'|>k(|V_N|)$. Hence, we may consider the tree T_1 rooted in A', and we may suppose that T_1 contains at most n-1 nodes. Denote by $d_1^T(A)$ and by $d_1^N(A)$ the string of terminals and of nonterminals resp., such that $A \Rightarrow^{(Lev)} d_1^T(A)d_1^N(A)$ is the derivation induced by (8). Similarly, we can write $A \Rightarrow^{(2,Lev)} d_1^T(A)d_2^T(A)d_2^N(A)$ where $d_2(A)=d_1^T(d_1^N(A))$ and $d_2^N=d_1^N(d_1^N(A))$.

Now suppose that A" has distance s from A', then

$$A(=A') \Rightarrow^{(s,Lev)} d_1^T(A)d_2^T(A) \ldots d_s^T(A)d_s^N(A) \qquad (10)$$

where $d_s^N(A)=\alpha A\beta$, $x=d_1^T(A)d_2^T(A)\ldots d_s^T(A)$. The elements α,β belong to V_N^* and, if $x=\varepsilon$, it is $\alpha\beta\in V_N^+$. Then we have $d_{s+1}^T(A)=d_1^T(\alpha)w_1d_1^T(\beta)$ and $d_{s+1}^N(A)= d_1^N(\alpha)\alpha_1d_1^N(\beta)$ where $A\Rightarrow^{(Lev)} w_1\alpha_1$ is the derivation of A" induced by (9). Let

$$\alpha \Rightarrow^{(i,Lev)} d_1^T(\alpha)d_2^T(\alpha)\ldots d_i^T(\alpha)=y$$
$$\beta \Rightarrow^{(j,Lev)} d_1^T(\beta)d_2^T(\beta)\ldots d_j^T(\beta)=z \qquad (11)$$
$$A(=A'') \Rightarrow^{(h,Lev)} w_1w_2\ldots w_h=w$$

Let $\underline{x}=\langle d_1^T(A),d_2^T(A),\ldots,d_s^T(A)\rangle$, $\underline{y}=\langle d_1^T(\alpha),d_2^T(\alpha),\ldots,d_i^T(\alpha)\rangle$, $\underline{z}=\langle d_1^T(\beta),d_2^T(\beta),\ldots, d_j^T(\beta)\rangle$ and $\underline{w}=\langle w_1,w_2,\ldots,w_h\rangle$, then it is $\alpha A\beta \Rightarrow^{(+,Lev)} m(\underline{y},\underline{w},\underline{z})$ and $A=A' \Rightarrow^{(+,Lev)} x\ m(\underline{y},\underline{w},\underline{z})$. From the hypothesis on T_1 it follows that $|x\ m(\underline{y},\underline{w},\underline{z})|\leq k(n-1)$.

Now, being A=A' a label of the syntax tree T, it is $S \Rightarrow^* u'\gamma A\mu$, $u'\in\Sigma^*$, $\gamma,\mu\in V_N^*$ and $\mu \Rightarrow^{(1,Lev)} d_1^T(\mu)\ldots d_1^T(\mu)$, $\gamma \Rightarrow^{(r,Lev)} d_1^T(\gamma)\ldots d_r^T(\gamma)$. Then, putting $\underline{u}=\langle u'd_1^T(\gamma),d_2^T(\gamma),\ldots,d_r^T(\gamma)\rangle$, $\underline{v}=\langle d_1^T(\mu),\ldots,d_1^T(\mu)\rangle$, we have $S\Rightarrow^{+} m(\underline{u},\underline{x}\ m(\underline{y},\underline{w},\underline{z}),\underline{v})$, hence $t=m(\underline{u},\underline{x}\ m(\underline{y},\underline{w},\underline{z}),\underline{v})$. Replacing the third relation of (11) by (10), it is $\alpha A\beta \Rightarrow^{+} m(\underline{y},\underline{x}\ m(\underline{y},\underline{w},\underline{z}),\underline{z})$ and $S \Rightarrow^{+} m(\underline{u},\underline{x}\ m(\underline{y},\underline{x}\ m(\underline{y},\underline{w},\underline{z}),\underline{z}),\underline{v})$, whence $m(\underline{u},\underline{x}\ m(\underline{y},\underline{x}\ m(\underline{y},\underline{w},\underline{z}),\underline{z}),\underline{v}) \in L$.

Fact 1. *The class* L_3 *of regular languages is contained in* L_{BCF}

Fact 2. $\mathcal{L}_{BCF}$ *and the class of context free languages* $\mathcal{L}_2$ *are incomparable.*

In fact the language L_1 of Ex.1 belongs to $\mathcal{L}_{BCF}$ but is obviously not context free. Conversely the context free language $L = \{a^n b^n | n \geq 0\}$ is not in $\mathcal{L}_{BCF}$, using Th.4.

Remark 1. If we consider extended BCF-grammars which allow also productions with regular expressions on the right side, we can generate a class of languages wider than $\mathcal{L}_{BCF}$. For instance the grammar $G=(\{A,B\},\{a,b\}, \{S\to(aB)^*, B\to b\}, S)$ generates the language $\{a^n b^n | n \geq 0\}$ which is not in $\mathcal{L}_{BCF}$. The string a^2b^2 is intuitively obtained by the derivation $S \Rightarrow a^2B^2 \Rightarrow a^2bB \Rightarrow a^2bb$.

Since the languages generated by extended BCF-grammars are also semilinear, it follows that their family is strictly included by the type 1 BF family.

Fact 3. Copy $=\{u\hat{u} | u\in\{a,b\}^*\} \notin \mathcal{L}_{BCF}$.

Immediate since $\{a^n b^n\}=h(\text{Copy})$

Fact 4. $\mathcal{L}_{BCF}$ *is not closed with respect to the intersection with regular languages.*

In fact $L = \{a^*b^*\} \cap L_3$ where L_3 is the language of anagrams on two letters. $\{a^*b^*\}$ is a regular language, clearly $L_3 \in \mathcal{L}_{BCF}$ and $L \notin \mathcal{L}_{BCF}$.

Fact 5. The class of languages recognized by a real time FIFO-automaton is not contained in $\mathcal{L}_{BCF}$.

In fact $\{a^n b^n\}$ is easily recognized by a Real Time FIFO-automaton.

Aknowledgment: C.Citrini and D.Mandrioli were actively present along this investigation.

REFERENCES

[1] Ayers K., "Deque automata and a subfamily of context-sensitive languages which contains all semilinear bounded languages", Theor.Comp.Sci. 40 (1985), 163-174.

[2] Brandenburg F.J.,"Multiple equality sets and Post machines",J.Comput.System Sci., 21, 1980, 293-316.

[3] Brandenburg F.J.,"Intersections of some families of languages", Proc 13 ICALP, Lecture Notes in Computer Science 226, 1986, 61-68.

[4] Cherubini A., Citrini C. and Mandrioli D., Quasi Real Time FIFO automata, Rapp. int. n. 87035, Dip. Elettronica, Politecnico di Milano, 1987.

[5] Salomaa A, Formal Languages, Academic Press, 1973.

[6] Vauquelin B., Franchi Zannettacci P., "Automates à file", Theoretical Comp. Sci., 11, 1980, 221-225

[7] Vollmar R.,"Ueber einen Automaten mit Pufferspeicherung", Computing 5 (1970), 57-70.

IMPLEMENTING ABSTRACT DATA STRUCTURES IN HARDWARE

Frank Bauernöppel, Hermann Jung
Humboldt-Universität zu Berlin, Sektion Mathematik
P.O. Box 1297, Berlin 1086, German Democratic Republic

0. INTRODUCTION

Despite of the many models of higly parallel computers, the classical von Neumann architecture will still dominate in the near future for general purpose computing. It is common practice to accelerate sequential computers by replacing software by fast hardware devices like arithmetic co-processors. But there is a growing number of standard problems that can be solved by a special hardware much more efficiently.

In this paper we consider the case of abstract data structures. This concept provides the user with a set of procedures for manipulating the data but hides implementation details. In order to apply this concept for designing special hardware, we also have to redesign the data structures involved.

We demonstrate this approach for heaps supporting *Insert*, *Min*, *DelMin*, and *Delete* operations. Typically, an intermixed sequence of N such operations costs $O(N \cdot \log N)$ sequential time. We show, how to implement heaps on a model of very moderate parallel computation, namely a PRAM with $O(\log N)$ processors and $O(\log N)$ global memory without read or write conflicts. This implementation runs in $O(N)$ time, e.g. the speed-up is optimal.

Previously, heaps supporting Push (*Insert*) and Pop (*DelMin*) operations have been studied in [MeSi]. Another important data structures are search trees. Parallel insertions resp. deletions in 2-3 trees are studied in [PVW].

1. HEAPS

A **heap** is an abstract data structure supporting at least the following operations on a multiset H of keys drawn from an ordered keyset:

Insert(key): Add the given key to the heap;
Min: Return minimum key of the heap;
DelMin: Delete minimum key from the heap.

Additional operations are provided by several implementations of heaps. Typically, these operations assume that the internal position i of the key to be manipulated is known. This is due to the fact that heaps do not support an operation for efficiently finding a certain key. Examples of additional operations are:

DecKey(i,Δ): Replace the key at position i by key−Δ (Δ>0);

Delete(i): Delete the key at position i from the heap.

For efficient sequential implementations of heaps and its applications cf. [Fl], [Wi], [AHU], [Vu], [TaFr], [SlTa], [Meh],[Br], [Em], and [EKZ]. The fastest implementations achieve the following running time bounds per heap operation:

1. *Worst Case Running Time Bounds:* (cf. [AHU], [Vu])
   $O(1)$ for *Min*;
   $O(\log N)$ for *Insert*, *DelMin*, *DecKey*, and *Delete*.
2. *Amortized Running Time Bounds:* (cf. [TaFr])
   $O(1)$ for *Min*, *Insert*, and *DecKey*;
   $O(\log N)$ for *DelMin* and *Delete*.

There is a wide range of applications of heaps. We only mention three typical examples here:

1. *Sorting:*
   Insert N keys into an empty heap and reextract them in ascending order by N *DelMin* operations.
2. *Minimum spanning tree:*
   Compute for a given graph G=(V,E) with predescribed non-negative edge lengths a spanning tree of minimum total length.
3. *Single Source Shortest Paths:*
   Compute for a given graph G=(V,E) with predescribed non-negative edge lengths the distances (lengths of shortest paths) from one source vertex to every vertex of V.

For a detailed discussion of efficient, heap-oriented algorithms solving 2. and 3 the reader is referred to [TaFr]. The algorithms in that paper use $O(|V|)$ *Insert* and *Delete* operations and $O(|E|)$ *DecKey* operations. Thus, they achieve a running time bound of $O(|E|+|V|\cdot\log|V|)$.

In the sequel we describe how to overcome the logarithmic worst-case running time for *Insert* and *Delete* by using more processors working in one heap. As a consequence, running time of the three algorithms described above will decrease to $O(N)$ resp. $O(|E|+|V|)$.

As in the sequential implementations, we assume that the heap-operations are invoked one after another but we do not know these operations in advance (on-line computation). After a constant number of elementary steps the parallel heap will answer a query and will be ready for the next operation.

We will use a comparison based model of computation (comparison is the only operation between keys). There is a well known lower bound of $\Theta(N \cdot \log N)$ for sorting N keys in this model. Thus, we cannot succeed with $o(\log N)$ processors. The implementation below will meet this lower bound.

2. Global Structure of Parallel Heaps

The heap contains a set of **items**. An item i consists of:

- a tag field *state*(i), marking i as **full**, **empty**, or **watched**;
- if state(i)=full: a key field key(i), containing the key;
- if state(i)=watched: P(i), an identifier of the processor watching item i (cf. below).

Like in some sequential implementations, the items of the heap are stored in a linear array, indexed by natural numbers. This array is considered to be an **implicit binary tree** by setting: An item i has two **sons**, namely item $2 \cdot i$ and $2 \cdot i+1$.

The keys in the heap are ordered in the following way (**heap order**): If item j is a descendant of item i in the tree, both items are full, and no processor is performing a *swap*-primitive (cf. below) at i, then key(i) ≤ key(j).

The tree structure divides the heap into **layers**: Layer l consists of items 2^l to $2^{l+1}-1$.

In addition to the implicit binary tree, there are two unordered linear lists for each layer l. One list contains the indices of the empty items in this layer, the other list contains the indices of the full items in it. Thus, we can find any full or empty item in a given layer in constant time.

The heads of all these lists are stored in two arrays indexed by the layers. We keep two pointers e and f pointing to the first non-empty list of empty items (uppermost layer) and f points to the last non-empty list of full items (downmost layer) respectively.

Note that we can neither build nor store huge lists of empty items beforehand. To avoid this problem, we insert an item to the corresponding list of empty items only if its father becomes non-empty. On the other hand, an item can be removed from this list as soon as its father gets empty again.

The processors work in a pipeline-like manner, starting at the root of the heap and walking downwards to the leaves (downmost non-empty items). There is a global clock pulse, synchronizing all activities.

Each clock pulse is divided into three phases:

<u>Phase 0</u>: One (formerly inactive) processor starts his job at the root of the heap.

<u>Phase 1</u>: All active processors move from their current position (item) to an appropriate son.

<u>Phase 2</u>: All active processors move from their current position (item) to an appropriate son.

Whenever a processor reaches a leaf, it gets inactive. By induction it is clear that at the beginning of phase 1 (2) all active processors are located at even (odd) layers.

Now we proceed by describing the possible jobs for a processor (processor primitives). The implementation of heap-operations using these primitives is described afterwards.

3. Processor-Primitives

There are two primitives for each processor P: *sink* and *swap*. *Sink* tries to insert a new key into the subtree rooted at the current position while *swap* rebuilds heap-order when an insertion took place. Phase 1 or 2 of a processor P is described now:

```
PROCEDURE sink(i,j,key):
  { P is located at item i, an ancestor of item j and tries to insert
    the key at target position j }
BEGIN
  IF current heap-operation deletes the key transported by P THEN
    release this key and get inactive;
  ELSIF state(i)=watched and P(i)=P THEN { P arrived }
    key(i):=key;
    state(i):=full;
    start swap(i) in the same phase;
  ELSE
    IF state(i)=full and key < key(i) THEN {preserve heap-order}
      exchange key and key(i);
    END;
    GOTO the son i' of i in direction j and perform
         sink( i', j, key ) in the next phase;
  END;
END sink;

PROCEDURE swap(i):
  { P is located at a full item i and tries to rebuild  heap-order
    between i and its sons }
BEGIN
  IF the current heap operation deletes key(i) THEN get inactive;
  ELSIF both sons of i are empty {i is a leaf} THEN get inactive;
  ELSE
    IF one son of i say j is watched THEN
      exchange the contents of i and j;
    ELSE
      let j be a full son of minimum key among the full sons of i;
```

```
      IF key(j) < key(i) THEN exchange key(j) and key(i) END;
    END;
    GOTO j and perform swap(j) in the next phase;
  END;
END swap;
```

Whenever a processor alters the tag field state(i) of an item i, a corresponding update is made in the lists of full resp. empty items. If neccessary, the e or f pointer is updated too. There are two more procedures using these lists and pointers:

GetEmpty: return an empty item in (uppermost possible) layer e;

GetFull: return a full item in (downmost possible) layer f.

4. HEAP-OPERATIONS

Now we show, how to implement *Min*, *Insert*, and *Delete* using the processor primitives described above. Note that *DelMin* is equivalent to *Delete*(1) and *DecKey*(i,Δ) can be implemented as the sequence *Delete*(i); *Insert*(key(i)-Δ) without loss of efficiency. Phase 0 of a newly activated processor P is described in dependence of the current heap-operation:

```
PROCEDURE Delete(i):
BEGIN
  state(i) := watched;
  P(i) := P;
  j := GetEmpty;
  k := GetFull;
  IF i < j THEN
    IF  i < k THEN
      state(k) := empty;
      sink( 1, i, key(k) ); < in phase 1 >
    ELSE
      state(i) := empty;
    END;
  ELSE < j < i >
    state(i) := empty;
    state(j) := watched;
    P(j) := P;
    IF j < k THEN
      state(k) := empty;
      sink( 1, j, key(k) ); < in phase 1 >
    ELSE
      state(j) := empty;
    END;
  END;
END Delete;

PROCEDURE Insert(key):
BEGIN
  i := GetEmpty;
  state(i) := watched;
  P(i) := P;
  sink( 1, i, key ); < in phase 1 >
```

```
END Insert;


PROCEDURE Min:
BEGIN
  RETURN value of key(1);
  get inactive;
END Min;
```

Note that the root is always full and never out of heap-order at the end of each clock pulse (if the heap is not empty at all). Thus, key(1) is correctly a minimum key among all keys in the heap.
In the next section we will show that the heap is balanced in some sense. It will follow that O(log N) processors are sufficient for manipulating N keys.

5. Depth and Size Analysis

Firstly, we prove some usefull inequalities between the following parameters (taken at the end of a clock pulse):

d: Maximum depth of a non-empty item in the heap;

e: Minimum depth of an empty item in the heap; and

f: Maximum depth of a full item in the heap.

For technical reasons, we assume $d > 6$ in the sequel. For lower values of d we can handle all keys individually. The following facts can be easily proved:

Fact 1: There are at most l watched items in layers 1 to l.

This is because processor P(i) watching an item i is always located at an ancestor of i, and each layer contains no more than one processor at a time.

Fact 2: In layer e-1 there are at least $2^{e-1}-(e-1)$ items full.

This follows since layer e-1 contains 2^{e-1} items at all, no empty items (by definition of e) and at most e-1 watched items (by Fact 1). By a similar argument follows:

Fact 3: In layer f+1 there are at least $2^{f+1}-(f+1)$ items empty.

Now we are ready to prove:

<u>Lemma 1:</u> $d \le f + 1$.

Proof: Let i be a downmost non-empty item (layer d). If i is full, $f=d$ and the lemma holds. Otherwise, i is watched. When i became watched, it must have been an uppermost empty item one step ago. Thus, when i became watched, layer $d-1$ contained at least $2^{d-1}-(d-1)$ full items (by Fact 2). Consequently, layer $d-1$ contains now (e.g. at most d steps later) at least $2^{d-1}-2\cdot d+1 > 0$ full items.

■

<u>Lemma 2:</u> $e \le f + 1$.

Proof: This follows immediately from Fact 3.

■

<u>Lemma 3:</u> $f \le e + 1$.

Proof: (By induction on the number of computational steps.) Firstly, we observe that e can decrease only if $f<e$ previously. (Then a *Delete* causes a decrease of e to at most f. In addition, f may decrease to $f-1$.) Thus, we can restrict to the case when f increases. Let us assume that a first watched item at layer f becomes full. Then, like in lemma 1, this layer f must have been the uppermost layer containing empty items at most d steps ago. Hence, layer $f-1$ contained at that moment at least $2^{f-1}-(f-1) \ge 2^{d-2}-d > d$ full items. From the observation above follows $e \ge f-1$.

■

From the inequalities above we get insigth into the dynamic structure of a parallel heap. $e \ge f-1 \ge d-2$ means:

<u>Theorem:</u> A parallel heap of depth d contains $O(2^d)$ keys.

Furthermore, it follows that in one step the values of pointers e and f can change by constants only. This enables us to update these values in constant time.

6. Conclusions

We have proposed a method for maintaining heaps with $O(\log N)$ processors in constant time per operation. This results in an optimal worst-case running time bound of $O(N)$ for an intermixed on-line sequence of N *Min*, *Insert*, and *Delete* Operations. Moreover, this bound

is tight in the class of comparison based computations.
From the algorithms described follows that neither read nor write conflicts occur. If we allocate one processor per layer and transmit only the processor jobs from layer to layer, we get an alternative implementation with a simple interconnection scheme: Each processor is connected to the two processors at adjacent layers and has its own local memory (its layer and the lists of empty resp. full items). Furthermore each processor must have access to the small global memory containing the two arrays of list heads and the e and f pointer.

7. Open Problems

Although the kind of parallelism used in our model is very moderate, one can think of even more restricted models like processors with a bounded degree interconnection network and no global memory. This approach has been taken in [MeSi] for heaps supporting *Min*, *Insert*, and *DelMin* when N is known beforehand, but this restriction can be dropped [BaJu]. It is open whether the general *Delete* can be implemented in that model.
Another interesting problem is whether one can design a more processor efficient heap if the keys are drawn from a bounded domain (as in the sequential $O($ log log N $)$ priority queue [Em], [EKZ])
The situation for search trees is somewhat different. Constant query time is not to be expected in exclusive-read exclusive-write models since a key to be searched cannot be distributed among many processors in constant time. In [PVW] multiple insertions resp. deletions in 2-3 trees are considered. The general case of intermixed sequences is still open.

8. Acknowledgements

We thank F. Meyer auf der Heide for pointing out independent work in this area and helpful comments on an earlier draft of this paper.

9. References

AHU Aho,A.V.; Hopcroft,J.E.; Ullman,J.D.; "The Design and Analysis of Computer Algorithms"; Addison-Wesley; Reading MA; 1974

BaJu Bauernöppel, F.; Jung, H.; Implementing Heaps on A Chain of Processors; submitted

Br Brown, M.R.; "Implementation and Analysis of Binomial Queue Algorithms"; SIAM J.Comp. 7(1978), 298-319

EKZ Emde Boas, P.v.; Kaas, R.; Zijlstra, E.; "Design And Implementation of An Efficient Priority Queue"; Math. Systems Theory 10(1977), 99-127

Em Emde Boas, P.v.; "Preserving Order in A Forest in Less Than Logarithmic Time"; Inf.Proc.Letters 6(1977), 80-82

Fl Floyd, F.W.; "Algorithm 245: Treesort 3"; Comm. ACM 7(1964), 12, 701

Meh Mehlhorn, K; "Data Structures And Algorithms, Part 1: Sorting And Searching"; Springer; 1984

MeSi Meyer auf der Heide, F.; Simons, B; "Data Structures on Parallel Machines with Few Processors"; IBM Comp.Sci. Research Report RJ 5240 (54240) 8/18/86

PVW Paul, W.; Vishkin, U; Wagener, H; "Parallel Computation on 2-3 Trees"; ICALP 1983; Springer Lecture Notesin Computer Science

SlTa Sleator, D.D.; Tarjan, R.E.; "Self-Adjusting Heaps"; SIAM J.Comp. 15(1986), 1, 52-69

TaFr Tarjan, R.E.; Fredman, M.L.; "Fibonacci Heaps and Their Uses in Improved Network Optimization Algorithms"; J. ACM 34(1987), 3, 596-615

Vu Vuillemin, J.; "A Data Structure for Manipulating Priority Queues"; Comm. ACM 21(1978), 4, 309-315

Wi Williams, J.W.; "Algorithm 232: Heapsort"; Comm. ACM 7(1964), 6, 347-348

Distribution of Sequential Processes

J. Beauquier

L.R.I., Université de Paris-Sud, 91405 Orsay Cedex, France

A. Petit

L.I.F.O., Université d'Orléans, 45067 Orléans Cedex 2, France

and

L.R.I., Université de Paris-Sud, 91405 Orsay Cedex, France

ABSTRACT

We present a solution to the distribution problem, in a particular framework: how to transform a set of sequential processes into a set of respectively equivalent concurrent processes? The models of systems are finite automata in the non-distributed case and some collection of finite automata with synchronization in the distributed case. The concurrency criterion is commutativity.

I INTRODUCTION

In this paper we present a solution to the distribution problem, in a particular framework: how a set of sequential processes can be transformed into a set of concurrent processes, such that the concurrent executions be equivalent to sequential ones. The model (cf [AN], [BN], [Pr]) that we choose for a non-distributed system is a finite automaton. Each letter of the automaton's alphabet is considered as an elementary task; a word is then a sequence of elementary tasks and the language accepted by the finite automaton is the set of correct sequential processes. The equivalence rule between sequential and concurrent processes is the rule of commutativity. Let A be a finite automaton and let L be the language accepted by A. If f=uvw is a word of L and if for any x commutatively equivalent to v (x is a permutation of v) uxw is in L, then we say that the elementary tasks corresponding to the letters of v can be performed concurrently, without changing the result of the computation. This approach is quite classical and can be found, for instance, in [CD], [CP] or [St]. The problem considered here is the distribution of computations on a single processor over m processors. In the papers considering the distribution problem ([Pr], [St]...) there is no unicity on the choice of the model of distributed system. However all the proposed models can be represented as elements of sub-classes of Petri nets. The models that we use (and that we will define later) are very simple devices: some collections of finite automata with synchronization. So a distributed process is viewed as a set of sequential processes which are executed independently from each other, but need to synchronize themselves sometimes.

The distribution problem is, given a finite automaton A recognizing a language L, to find a "distributed system" which accepts the same language L and such that, if two tasks can be performed concurrently in A, they are performed by two different processors in the "distributed system".

Some results have been obtained by Prinoth ([Pr]) which gives a solution for only cycle-free finite automata. Starke ([St]) proposes a solution for general finite automata but he allows an arbitrary finite number of data units to be memorized for a synchronization. We propose in this paper a solution, for general finite automata, in which only one data unit has to be memorized for a synchronization, yielding much simpler machines than Starke'ones.

The distribution problem can also be viewed, in terms of trace languages, as the fact to find a recognizer of the set of all linearizations of the traces of a recognizable trace language. In this sense the paper of Zielonka [Zi], on asynchronous automata, can be considered of a solution to the distribution problem. However this very nice result on trace monoids theory doesn't seem very useful to resolve, in practice, the distribution of computations on a single processor over several processors. For instance, in a asynchronous automaton even an elementary task need the cooperation of several processors to be executed. We think that an elementary task has, by definition, to be executed by a single processor as in our models that we will now define.

II PRELIMINARIES

For any integer t we will note by [t] the set $\{1,2,\ldots,t\}$.

For any word w of Σ^+ we will note by $w^{(i)}$ the ith letter of w.

We assume that the reader is familiar with the classical notions of finite automata theory ([Ha], [HU]).

A system in the non-distributed case is a deterministic finite automaton $A=\langle\Sigma,Q,q_0,\delta,F\rangle$, where Σ is a finite input alphabet, Q a finite set of states, δ a partial mapping of $Q\times\Sigma$ into Q (classically extended to $Q\times\Sigma^*$) and $F\subseteq Q$ the set of final states. We denote by L(A) the language recognized (or accepted) by A.

A process in A is a word f in L(A): $f=x_1x_2\ldots x_n$. Each x_i represents an elementary task. So a word in L(A) can be viewed as a sequence of elementary tasks executed by a single processor.

The set of concurrent tasks is given by a symmetric and irreflexive relation $\theta \subseteq \Sigma\times\Sigma$ called concurrency relation. Two tasks are concurrent if $(a,b)\in\theta$. We will note by $\bar{\theta}$ the no-concurrency relation defined by $(a,b)\in\bar{\theta}$ iff $(a,b)\notin\theta$. We say that a language L over Σ is θ-closed iff for every words f, g of Σ^* and every letters a, b of Σ such that $(a,b)\in\theta$ we have fabg in L iff fbag is in L.

The next easily proved proposition gives an algorithm to decide whether a language L is θ-closed for some concurrency relation θ. It gives also the finest concurrency relation for which a language is closed. We will say that a finite automaton A is θ-minimal iff for any state q in Q and for any letters a, b in Σ such that (a, b) is in θ we have $\delta(q,ab)=\delta(q,ba)$.

<u>Proposition 1</u> : Let L be a recognizable language over Σ and θ a concurrency relation on Σ. If L=L(A) for some θ-minimal automaton then L is θ-closed. Conversely, if L is θ-closed then its minimal automaton is θ-minimal.

We will now define our first model for distributed systems. A synchronized automaton (S.A.) is a collection of finite automata, which execute their computations independently from each other and synchronize themselves at the end of these computations to accept or refuse the word.

<u>Definition 2</u> : A synchronized automaton Π with t components over an alphabet Σ is a (t+2)-tuple $\langle A_1,A_2,\ldots,A_t,q_0,T\rangle$ where

i) $\forall i\in[t]$ $A_i=\langle\Sigma_i,Q_i,q_{0,i},\delta_i\rangle$ is a deterministic finite automaton

ii) $q_0=(q_{0,1},q_{0,2},\ldots,q_{0,t})$ is the initial t-tuple of Π

iii) $T\subseteq Q_1\times Q_2\times\ldots\times Q_t$ is the set of final t-tuples of Π

iv) $(\Sigma_1,\Sigma_2,\ldots,\Sigma_t)$ is a disjoint partition of Σ

A word f of Σ^* is recognized by the synchronized automaton Π iff for any i in [t] there exists a state q_i of Q_i such that $\delta_i(q_{0,i},f_i)=q_i$ (where f_i is the projection of f over Σ_i) and $(q_1,q_2,\ldots,q_t)$ is in T.

The language recognized by Π, noted by $L(\Pi)$, is the set of words recognized by Π. A S.A. Π induces, in a quite natural way, a concurrency relation θ_π defined by : $(a,b)\in\theta_\pi$ iff there exists $i\neq j$ such that a is in Σ_i and b in Σ_j. One can easily prove the following proposition on $L(\Pi)$:

<u>Proposition 3</u> : Let Π be a synchronized automaton. Then $L(\Pi)$ is a θ_π-closed recognizable language over Σ^*.

With these notion of S.A. the distribution problem can be reformulated as follows:

<u>The distribution problem</u> (on a synchronized automaton) : Let L be a recognizable language of Σ^*, θ-closed for some concurrency relation θ. Is it possible to find a S.A. Δ such that L(Δ)=L and $\theta_\Delta=\theta$?

We can remark that the concurrency relation induced by a S.A. Δ verifies $\overline{\theta_\Delta}$ is transitive. So we can not expect to have a complete answer to the distribution problem on a S.A.. Nevertheless we will see that in the particular case where $\overline{\theta}$ is transitive we can solve the distribution problem on a S.A..

III THE DISTRIBUTION PROBLEM ON A SYNCHRONIZED AUTOMATON

To state the results concerning the distribution problem on a S.A., we need the concept of θ-partition for some concurrency relation θ. A disjoint partition $(\Sigma_1,\Sigma_2,\ldots,\Sigma_p)$ of an alphabet Σ is a θ-partition iff for any a in Σ_i and b in Σ_j such that $i\neq j$, (a,b) belongs to θ. One can easily prove the next proposition, which gives us a characterization of the θ-partition of a given alphabet Σ.

<u>Proposition 4</u> : Let Σ be a finite alphabet and let θ be a concurrency relation on Σ. Then $(\Sigma_1,\Sigma_2,\ldots,\Sigma_p)$ is a θ-partition of Σ iff $(\Sigma_1,\Sigma_2,\ldots,\Sigma_p)$ is a disjoint partition of Σ such that each Σ_i is the union of connected components of $\overline{\theta}$.

<u>Remark 5</u> : Let L be a θ-closed recognizable language on Σ^* and let $(\Sigma_1,\Sigma_2,\ldots,\Sigma_p)$ be a θ-partition of Σ. Each letter of Σ_i commutes with each letter of Σ_j, so for any f_i of Σ_i^*, $f_1f_2\ldots f_p$ belongs to L implies that every word of the shuffle of $f_1,f_2,\ldots,f_p$ belongs to L.

We can now give the main result on the distribution problem on a S.A..

<u>Proposition 6</u> : Let Σ be a finite alphabet, θ a concurrency relation on Σ, L a θ-closed recognizable language on Σ^* and $(\Sigma_1,\Sigma_2,\ldots,\Sigma_p)$ a θ-partition on Σ. Then there exists a synchronized automaton $\Pi=\langle A_1,A_2,\ldots,A_p,q'_0,T\rangle$ such that $L(\Pi)=L$ and the alphabet of each A_i is Σ_i.

Let $A=\langle\Sigma,Q,q_0,\delta,F\rangle$ be a deterministic finite automaton recognizing the language L. In order to prove the result, we need to introduce the following notations and definitions:

$\forall i\in[p],\ \forall q\in Q\quad L_i^{\langle q\rangle}=\{\, f\in\Sigma_i^* \ /\ \delta(q_0,f)=q\,\}$

$L_0^{\langle q_1,q_2,\ldots,q_p\rangle}=\{\,(f_1,f_2,\ldots,f_p)\in L_1^{\langle q_1\rangle}\times L_2^{\langle q_2\rangle}\times\ldots\times L_p^{\langle q_p\rangle}\ /\ f_1f_2\ldots f_p\in L\,\}$

We will say that a p-tuple $(q_1,q_2,\ldots,q_p)$ of Q^p is valid iff $L_0^{\langle q_1,q_2,\ldots,q_p\rangle}\neq\emptyset$.

We also need to prove the following lemma:

<u>Lemma 7</u> : Let $(q_1, q_2, \ldots, q_p)$ be a valid p-tuple, then
$L_o^{<q_1, q_2, \ldots, q_p>} = L_1^{<q_1>} \times L_2^{<q_2>} \times \ldots \times L_p^{<q_p>}$

Proof of the lemma : $(q_1, q_2, \ldots, q_p)$ is valid so, for any i, there exists a word f_i of $L_i^{<q_i>}$ such that $f_1 f_2 \ldots f_p$ belongs to L. Let be $(g_1, g_2, \ldots, g_p)$ in $L_1^{<q_1>} \times L_2^{<q_2>} \times \ldots \times L_p^{<q_p>}$. We will prove that $(g_1, g_2, \ldots, g_p)$ belongs to $L_o^{<q_1, q_2, \ldots, q_p>}$, i.e. that $g_1 g_2 \ldots g_p$ belongs to L.
A is deterministic, f_1 belongs to $L_1^{<q_1>}$ and $f_1 f_2 \ldots f_p$ to L, so
$\exists\ q_f \in F \ /\ \delta(q_o, f_1) = q_1$ and $\delta(q_1, f_2 \ldots f_p) = q_f$
but, by hypothesis, we have $\delta(q_o, g_1) = q_1$, so $g_1 f_2 \ldots f_p$ belongs to L. This implies (remark 5) that $f_2 g_1 f_3 \ldots f_p$ belongs to L i.e
$\exists\ q'_f \in F \ /\ \delta(q_o, f_2) = q_2$ and $\delta(q_2, g_1 f_3 \ldots f_p) = q'_f$
But, by hypothesis, we have $\delta(q_o, g_2) = q_2$, so $g_2 g_1 f_3 \ldots f_p$ belongs to L and thus (remark 5) $g_1 g_2 f_3 \ldots f_p$ belongs to L. We then prove by a trivial induction that $g_1 g_2 \ldots g_p$ belongs to L and the lemma 7 is proved.
We can now construct the S.A. Π of the proposition 6. Let A_i be the projection of the automaton A on Σ_i: $A_i = \langle \Sigma_i, Q, q_o, \delta_i, F \rangle$, where δ_i is the restriction of δ on $Q \times \Sigma_i$ and let be T the set of valid p-tuples $(q_1, q_2, \ldots, q_p)$ of Q^p. The remark 5 and the lemma 7 involve that the language recognized by $\langle A_1, A_2, \ldots, A_p, (q_o, q_o, \ldots, q_o), T \rangle$ is equal to L and that achieves the proof of the proposition 6.
To conclude on the distribution problem on a S.A. we have to compare the concurrency relations θ and θ_π.

<u>Proposition 8</u> : θ_π is included in θ and the equality holds iff $\bar{\theta}$ is transitive and the Σ_i are the connected components of $\bar{\theta}$.

The inclusion $\theta_\pi \subseteq \theta$ is always true by definition of a θ-partition. If $\bar{\theta}$ is not transitive, one can find three letters a,b,c of Σ such that $(a,b) \in \bar{\theta}$, $(b,c) \in \bar{\theta}$ and $(a,c) \in \theta$. So a,b and c are in the same connected component of $\bar{\theta}$ and then in the same Σ_i. So we would have $(a,c) \in \theta_\pi$ but $(a,c) \notin \bar{\theta}$. Likewise, if one of the Σ_i is the union of at most two connected components of $\bar{\theta}$, one can find two letters a and b in Σ such that $(a,b) \in \theta_\pi$ and $(a,b) \notin \bar{\theta}$. The proposition 8 is so proved.
So we give an answer to the distribution problem on a S.A., only in the particular case where $\bar{\theta}$ is transitive (we can note that it is the case when L is commutatively closed i.e. when $\theta = \Sigma \times \Sigma$).
Nevertheless, these results will help us to give a complete answer to the distribution problem on a more complicated machine than a synchronized automaton, a generalized synchronized automaton, that we will define now.

IV DEFINITION OF A GENERALIZED SYNCHRONIZED AUTOMATON

The unique synchronization in a synchronized automaton is performed at the end of a computation, when it is decided whether or not the computations executed on each of the components are compatible, i.e. if the t-tuple of the reached states is final or not. It seems natural to introduce a new type of automaton, for which the synchronizations could not only be performed at the end of a computation but also in the middle of the computation.

So, we define a generalized synchronized automaton (G.S.A.) as a collection of synchronized automata the computations of which are linked through states of synchronization.

We will say that some synchronized automata $\Pi_1, \Pi_2, \ldots, \Pi_t$ are compatible if there exist an alphabet Σ containing the alphabet of each Π_i and a concurrency relation θ on Σ containing each related concurrency relation θ_{π_i}.

<u>Definition 9</u> : A generalized synchronized automaton is a 6-tuple $\langle C, S, s_o, F, \delta_c, \delta_s \rangle$ where

i) C is a finite set $\{\Pi_1, \Pi_2, \ldots, \Pi_p\}$ of compatible synchronized automata. The alphabet of each Π_i is Σ_i.

ii) S is a finite set of states : the synchronization states.

iii) $s_o \in S$ is the initial state.

iv) $F \subseteq S$ is the set of final states.

v) δ_c is a function of $S \times \Sigma$ (where $\Sigma = \cup\, \Sigma_i$) in 2^{Q_o} (where Q_o is the set of initial states of each S.A. of C). δ_c is called choice function.

vi) δ_s is a function of $T = \cup\, T_i$ (where T_i is the set of final t-tuples of the S.A. Π_i) in S. δ_s is called synchronization function.

Intuitively, a computation in a G.S.A. is performed in the following way: from s_o we enter by the choice function δ_c in a S.A. able to do the first task and then we execute the following tasks in this S.A.. If we arrive in a final t-tuple we can go out of this S.A. by the synchronization function δ_s and start again from the reached synchronization state. A word f of Σ^* will be recognized by the G.S.A. iff all the possible computations of this word in the G.S.A. lead to a final synchronization state.

To define properly the acceptance way of a G.S.A. Γ we have to introduce, for a word f of Σ^+ with $\Sigma = \cup\, \Sigma_i$, the concept of $(\Sigma_1, \Sigma_2, \ldots, \Sigma_p)$ decomposition of f accepted by the G.S.A. Γ.

Definition 10 : A decomposition $(f_1, f_2, \ldots, f_t)$ of f is a $(\Sigma_1, \Sigma_2, \ldots, \Sigma_p)$ decomposition of f iff

i) $f = f_1 f_2 \ldots f_t$.

ii) $\forall i \in [t]\ \exists j(i) \in [p]$ such that $f_i \in \Sigma^+_{j(i)}$.

This $(\Sigma_1, \Sigma_2, \ldots, \Sigma_p)$ decomposition is accepted by the G.S.A. Γ iff

i) $\forall\ i \in [t]\ f_i \in L(\Pi_{n(i)})$ for some S.A. $\Pi_{n(i)}$ of C. The computation of f_i leads to the final t-uple $t_{n(i)}$ of $\Pi_{n(i)}$.

ii) the initial state $q^{(o)}{}_{n(1)}$ of $\Pi_{n(1)}$ belongs to $\delta_c(s_o, f_1{}^{(1)})$.

iii) $\forall\ i \in [t-1]$ the initial state $q^{(o)}{}_{n(i+1)}$ of $\Pi_{n(i+1)}$ belongs to $\delta_c(\delta_m(t_{n(i)}), f_{i+1}{}^{(1)})$.

iv) $\delta_m(t_{n(t)})$ belongs to F.

A word f of Σ^+ will be recognized by the G.S.A. Γ iff all the possible $(\Sigma_1, \Sigma_2, \ldots, \Sigma_p)$ decomposition of f are accepted by Γ.

Definition 11 : A word f of Σ^+ is recognized by the G.S.A. Γ iff for any $(\Sigma_1, \Sigma_2, \ldots, \Sigma_p)$ decomposition $(f_1, f_2, \ldots, f_t)$ of f, $(f_1, f_2, \ldots, f_t)$ is accepted by Γ.

$L(\Gamma)$ is the set of words recognized by Γ. If s_o belongs to F we will say that the empty word ϵ belongs to $L(\Gamma)$.
As does a S.A., a G.S.A. Γ induces a concurrency relation θ_Γ on Σ defined by $(a,b) \in \theta_\Gamma$ iff there exists a S.A. Π_i of C such that (a,b) belongs to θ_{π_i}, the concurrency relation induced by Π_i. The S.A. of C being compatible, if $(a,b) \in \theta_\Gamma$ then for any S.A. Π of C, the alphabet of which contains a and b, we have $(a,b) \in \theta_\Gamma$.

Remark : in the general case $L(\Gamma)$ is not θ_Γ-closed but we can algorithmically decide if $L(\Gamma)$ is θ_Γ-closed or not.

V THE DISTRIBUTION PROBLEM ON A GENERALIZED SYNCHRONIZED AUTOMATON

To state the result concerning the distribution problem on a G.S.A., we need a technical result from the proof of the proposition 6. This proposition give us the construction of a S.A. $\Pi = \langle A_1, A_2, \ldots, A_p, (q_o, q_o, \ldots, q_o), T\rangle$ from a deterministic finite automaton $A = \langle \Sigma, Q, q_o, \delta, F\rangle$ recognizing a θ-closed language L, for some concurrency relation θ on Σ and from a θ-partition $(\Sigma_1, \Sigma_2, \ldots, \Sigma_p)$ of Σ. We will need, when A is chosen θ-minimal (it's always possible from the proposition 1), the relation between the set of final p-tuples T of the S.A. Π and the set of final states F of A.

Proposition 12 : For any final p-tuple $(q_1,q_2,\dots,q_p)$ of T there exists a unique state of F, noted $F_\pi(q_1,q_2,\dots,q_p)$, such that for any p-tuple $(f_1,f_2,\dots,f_p)$ of $L_o^{(q_1,q_2,\dots,q_p)}$ and for any word f of the shuffle of $(f_1,f_2,\dots,f_p)$ we have $\delta(q_o,f)= F_\pi(q_1,q_2,\dots,q_p)$.

The proof of this proposition follows exactly the proof of the lemma 7, by using the fact that $(\Sigma_1,\Sigma_2,\dots,\Sigma_p)$ is a θ-partition and A is θ-minimal. Thus we have, for any words f of Σ_i* and g of Σ_j* (with $i\neq j$), for any state q of Q and for any word h of the shuffle of f and g, $\delta(q,fg)=\delta(q,h)$ and this proposition can easily be proved.
We can now prove the result concerning the distribution problem on a G.S.A..

Proposition 13 : Let be Σ a finite alphabet, θ a concurrency relation on Σ and L a recognizable θ-closed language of Σ*. Then there exists a G.S.A. Π, such that L(Π)=L and $\theta_\pi=\theta$.

Let $A=\langle\Sigma,Q,q_{\langle o\rangle},\delta,F\rangle$ be a θ-minimal deterministic automaton recognizing the language L (proposition 1). Let S be the set of subsets Σ_i of Σ such that $\bar\theta\cap\Sigma_i\times\Sigma_i$ is transitive and S' the set of the largest elements of S for the inclusion.
We are not interested in the set Σ' of S' such that $\bar\theta\cap(\Sigma'\times\Sigma') = \Sigma'\times\Sigma'$ so we define S~ as the set of the elements Σ' of S' such that $\bar\theta\cap(\Sigma'\times\Sigma')\neq\Sigma'\times\Sigma'$. Finaly in order to have a partition of Σ we define S" as the union of S~ and of all the singletons {x} such that for any Σ' of S~ we have $x\in\Sigma'$ (it is clear that such a letter x verifies $\theta\cap(\{x\}\times\Sigma) = \emptyset$).
So, by construction, S" is a partition of Σ.
For any couple (q,q') of Q×Q and any Σ' of S" we define $L_{q,q',\Sigma'}$ as the set $\{ w\in\Sigma'^* / \delta(q,w)=q' \}$ if there exists a letter x belonging to a $\Sigma''\neq\Sigma'$ such that $\delta(q',x)$ is in Q or if q' is in F. In the other cases $L_{q,q',\Sigma'}$ is the empty set. We note $L_{q,\Sigma'}$ the union, for q' in Q, of the $L_{q,q',\Sigma'}$. $L_{q,\Sigma'}$ is recognized by the automaton $A_{q,\Sigma'}=\langle\Sigma',Q,\{q\},\delta_{\Sigma'},F_{\Sigma'}\rangle$ where $\delta_{\Sigma'}$ is the restriction of δ to Q×Σ' and $F_{\Sigma'} = F \cup \{ q'\in Q / x\in\Sigma''\neq\Sigma' \;\delta(q',x)\in Q \}$. A is θ-minimal so $A_{q,\Sigma'}$ is also θ-minimal and then (proposition 1) $L_{q,\Sigma'}$ is a θ-closed (and thus a $(\theta\cap\Sigma'\times\Sigma')$-closed) recognizable language. Moreover $\bar\theta\cap\Sigma'\times\Sigma'$ is transitive so we can construct, from the $(\theta\cap\Sigma'\times\Sigma')$-minimal automaton $A_{q,\Sigma'}$ a S.A. $\Pi_{q,\Sigma'}=\langle\dots,T_{q,\Sigma'}\rangle$ recognizing the language $L_{q,\Sigma'}$, such that the related concurrency relation $\theta_{\pi_{q,\Sigma'}}=\theta\cap\Sigma'\times\Sigma'$ (propositions 6 and 8).
The S.A. $\Pi_{q,\Sigma'}$ are, by construction, compatible and we can build, from these S.A., a G.S.A. Γ in a quite simple and natural way: $\Gamma=\langle C,Q,q_{\langle o\rangle},F,\delta_c,\delta_m\rangle$ with :
$C=\{ \Pi_{q,\Sigma'} / q\in Q \text{ and } \Sigma'\in S" \}$.
$\delta_c(q,a)$ is the set of initial t-tuples of the $\Pi_{q,\Sigma'}$ for Σ' in S" such that $L(\Pi_{q,\Sigma'})\cap a\Sigma^*\neq\emptyset$.

$\delta_*(t_{q,x'})$ is, for $t_{q,x'}$ in $T_{q,x'}$, equal to $F_{\pi q,x'}(t_{q,x'})$ (with the notations of the proposition 12).
The equality of the languages L and $L(\Gamma)$ results of the construction of the G.S.A. and of the proposition 12. One can see [BP] for further details.
To achieve the proof of the proposition 13 we have to compare the concurrency relation θ_Γ and θ. By definition, the concurrency relation θ_Γ is equal to the smallest relation containing all the θ_Π, for Π in C. Then θ_Γ is included in θ. Conversely, let a and b be in Σ, such that (a,b) belongs to θ. There exists an element of S" containing a and b so (a,b) is in θ_Γ and the reverse inclusion is proved. That completes the proof of the proposition 13.

VI CONCLUSION

The results of the paper easily allow to obtain a policy to distribute a set of sequential computations over m different processors. The different sequences of elementary tasks corresponding to the different runs of a program are classicaly represented by a finite automaton. The commutation relations can be computed from the interference relations (Bernstein's relations) of the elementary tasks. Then, a S.A. or a G.S.A. is constructed. If case of a S.A. (i.e. if $\bar{\theta}$ is transitive), each component of the S.A. is related with a processor or, in other words, each maximal clique of $\bar{\theta}$ is related with a processor (a clique of $\bar{\theta}$ is a subset Σ' of Σ such that $\bar{\theta} \cap \Sigma' \times \Sigma' = \Sigma' \times \Sigma'$). The instruction set (elementary tasks) of the ith processor is so equal to (or more exactly contains) the tasks corresponding to the alphabet of the ith component of the S.A.. And an elementary task, corresponding to a letter red by the ith component, is to be executed on the ith processor. If a G.S.A. is to be constructed, we propose two different ways to relate the processors with the components of the S.A. constituing this G.S.A.. In the first solution we will use the fact that those S.A. read in turn the letters. So after a passage through a synchronization state, each component of the concerned S.A. is related with a processor. An alternative solution is to relate, at the beginning of the computation, each of the maximal cliques of $\bar{\theta}$ with a processor. Then we can show that the alphabet of two distinct components of a S.A. of the constructed G.S.A. are always contain in two different maximal cliques of $\bar{\theta}$. So distinct components are automatically related with distinct processors.

As we just have seen the number of needed processors is, in all cases, at most equal to the number of maximal cliques of $\bar{\theta}$. Nevertheless if we have less processors we can, even if it means to reduce the concurrency relation θ, apply our results. On the other hand if we have more processors than connected components we can, by duplicating the same properly selected components (of a S.A.), prove similar results which permit the use of every processor.

An implicit assumption maid up to now is that, for each maximal clique of $\bar{\theta}$, there exists a processor able to execute the corresponding tasks. If it is not the case (i.e. if the processors are specialized) we can, under the hypothesis that different non-concurrent tasks can always be executed by a same processor, use our results by reducing the concurrency relation θ (which is necessary in view of the tasks able to be executed by the different processors).
A by-product of our results is a solution of the reconfiguration problem [Pr]. A set of distributed computations over m processors being given, we want to obtain a policy to distribute the same computations over m' (m'≠m) processors. But it is straightforward to reconstruct an equivalent finite automaton from a S.A. or a G.S.A.. Now, as we just explain, a new S.A. or G.S.A., with m' components, can be built and thus the reconfiguration problem is solved.

VII BIBLIOGRAPHY

[AN] ARNOLD A. and M. NIVAT, Controlling behaviour of systems, some basic concepts and some applications, Lecture Notes in Computer Science 88, p.113-122,(1980).

[BN] BEAUQUIER J. and M. NIVAT, Application of formal language theory to problems of security and synchronization, in Formal language theory (R. Book ed.), Academic Press, p. 407-454 (1980).

[BP] BEAUQUIER J. and A.PETIT, Distribution of sequential processes, rapports internes n°87-5 L.I.F.O. Université d'Orléans and n°379 L.R.I. Université d'Orsay (France).

[CD] COFFMAN E.G. and P.J. DENNING, Operating Systems Theory, Prentice Hall (1973).

[CP] CORI R. and D. PERRIN, Sur la reconnaissabilite dans les monoides partiellement commutatifs, R.A.I.R.O. Informatique Theorique, Vol. 19-1, p. 21-32 (1983).

[Ha] HARRISON M., Introduction to Formal Language Theory, Addison Wesley.

[HU] HOPCROFT J.E. and J.D ULLMAN, Formal languages and their relation to automata, Addison Wesley (1969).

[Pr] PRINOTH R., Construction of distributed systems from cycle-free finite automata, Lecture Notes in Computer Science 66, p. 199- 220 (1985).

[St] STARKE P.H., Multiprocessor systems and their concurrency, Journal of Information Processing and Cybernetics (EIK), Vol.20 (1984).

[Zi] ZIELONKA W., Notes on finite asynchronous automata, R.A.I.R.O. Informatique théorique et applications, Vol. 21-2, p. 99-135 (1987)

AUTOMATA AND RATIONAL EXPRESSIONS ON PLANAR GRAPHS[1]

Francis Bossut, Max Dauchet and Bruno Warin
U.A. 369 C.N.R.S.
LIFL, Université de Lille I, UFR d'IEEA, Bat. M3
59655 VILLENEUVE D'ASCQ Cedex FRANCE

Abstract. We study languages (i.e. sets) of planar directed acyclic graphs (pdags). These pdags are constructed by parallel composition and serial composition of letters and pdags on a doubly ranked alphabet. Our purpose is to introduce an algorithmic process (generalization of Kamimura and Slutzki's parallel automata) for accepting pdag languages and a specification of these languages by means of well-suited rational expressions. So our main result is a Kleene-like theorem proving the equivalence between rationality and automaton-definability.

1. Introduction

Directed Acyclic Graphs (dags) are for instance used for unification algorithms (Martelli & Montanari, 1982), to model parallelism (Degano & Montanari, 1985; Grabowsky, 1981; Ochmanski, 1985; Winkowski, 1979), relational data bases, program schemes or to study the complexity of computations (Claus, Ehrig and Rozenberg, 1979; Ehrig, Pfender and Schneider, 1983). Planar dags (pdags) specially model derivations of phrase-structure grammars (Kamimura & Slutzki, 1981). Graph languages have been studied from a categorical point of view (Ehrig, 1979) and Courcelle (1987) have recently studied a notion of recognizability for graph languages.

Our purpose is to introduce an algorithmic process (automata) for accepting pdag languages and a specification of these languages by means of well-suited rational expressions. So our main result is a Kleene-like theorem proving the equivalence between rationality and automaton-definability. For a class of non-planar but very particular dags, such a result is obtained by Ochmanski (1985).

From the automaton point of view, our approach is closely related to Kamimura & Slutzki's work (1981, 1982) but we generalize their pdags. Let us point out that our automaton definability is only algorithmic, it can't be studied as recognizability in the algebraic sense (Courcelle, 1988) because we consider as initial or final controls non bounded sequences of states.

Concerning rationality, we consider the closure of an alphabet of vertices (or nodes) under serial composition (denoted "."), parallel asynchronous composition (denoted &) and their iterations. With these two basic operations, magmoïd (Arnold & Dauchet, 1978, 1979) becomes our implicit framework.

Two important facts might be pointed out. The first one concerns the class of graphs, the second one the nature of Kleene's theorem.
1) our class is between the dags accepted by Kamimura & Slutzki's automata and the general class of graph studied from an algebraic point of view by Courcelle. The class defined by Kamimura & Slutzki is too narrow to lead to a "rational definition": it is not closed under parallel composition. Kamimura & Slutzki only study single rooted pdags when our pdags have a non-bounded number of roots and are

1 : Supported by PRC (Programme de Recherche Coordonnées) mathématique et informatique

generally non connected. Thus new problems arise about determinism, rational control of roots, connected sub-pdags. On the other hand, the general point of view of Courcelle and Ehrig does not permit an practical definition of automaton.

2) our Kleene-like theorem is not an extension of general results à la Eilenberg. It is, as for Ochmanski, a somewhat difficult and technical result, which establishes the adequation between the specification and the algorithmic points of view. The proof of this theorem underlines the importance of connectivity (we use the decomposition of pdags in connected components).

2. Pdags and pdag automata - Definitions

We will assume that the reader is familiar with the rudiments of tree language theory (Engelfriet, 1975; Thatcher, 1973) and dag automaton à la Kamimura & Slutzki (1981, 1982). We consider labelled, directed, acyclic, ordered and planar graphs that we call pdags. Our labels are symbols from a finite doubly ranked alphabet $\Sigma = \cup \Sigma_{i,j}$. We suppose $i \geq 1$ and $j \geq 1$. A symbol $\sigma \in \Sigma_{i,j}$ has head-rank i and tail-rank j.

we also denote it:

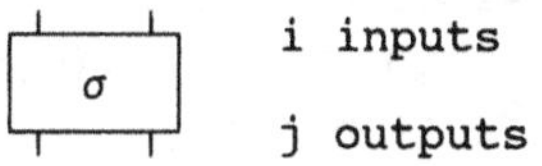

We connect pdags in series by means of a binary operator denoted "." (or omitted) and we connect pdags in parallel by means of a binary operator denoted "θ". We introduce a special pdag denoted "e" $\in \Sigma$ that allows to define neutral elements for serial composition. Formally, pdag algebra is defined inductively as follows:

2.1. Definition. Let Σ be a finite doubly ranked alphabet and a new symbol **e** of head-rank and tail-rank 1.

The set **DP(Σ)** of pdags over Σ and its subsets $\mathbf{DP(\Sigma)_{i,j}}$ of pdags of head-rank i and tail-rank j, are defined inductively as follows:

(i) $e \in DP(\Sigma)_{1,1}$, if $a \in \Sigma_{i,j}$ then $a \in DP(\Sigma)_{i,j}$,

(ii) Let $d \in DP(\Sigma)_{i,j}$ and $d' \in DP(\Sigma)_{i',j'}$
$(d\theta d') \in DP(\Sigma)_{k,l}$ with $k=i+i'$ and $l=j+j'$,
$(d.d')$ is defined if $j=i'$ and $(d.d') \in DP(\Sigma)_{i,j'}$,

(iii) $DP(\Sigma)$ is the union of all the $DP(\Sigma)_{i,j}$ for $i,j \geq 1$.

Two expressions are equivalent if and only if they are equivalent with respect to the congruence relation generated by these axioms:

(i) associativity of θ and .

(ii) e is a neutral element.
We note for $p>0$, $e_p = e\theta...e\theta e$, p times,
then for all $\delta \in DP(\Sigma)_{p,q}$, $e_p.\delta=\delta$ and $\delta.e_q=\delta$

(iii) If d.d' and f.f' are defined then $(d.d')\theta(f.f')=(d\theta f).(d'\theta f')$.

2.2. Proposition. Two expressions d and f are equivalent if and only if they denote the same pdag.

Example. Let Σ be such that $\Sigma_{11} = \{a\}$, $\Sigma_{12} = \{b\}$ and $\Sigma_{21} = \{c\}$. The expression $b.(a\theta e).(e\theta b).(c\theta a).c$ is equivalent to $b.(a\theta b).(c\theta a).c$. And they are equivalent to:

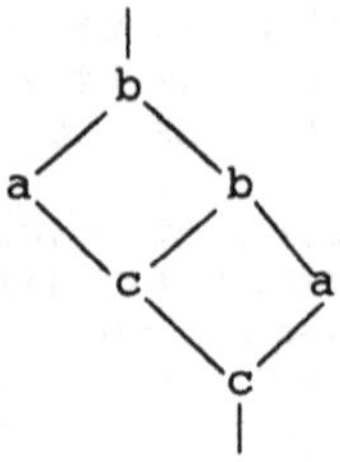

Remark. We identify an expression with its class, i.e. with the pdag that this class represents.

Basic operators extended to sets. Let A, B be two sets of pdags then:

$A.B = \{\delta.\delta' / \delta \in A \text{ and } \delta' \in B\}$; $A\theta B = \{\delta\theta\delta' / \delta \in A \text{ and } \delta' \in B\}$

$A^* = A \,.\, A^* \cup \{ e_p \,/\, p \in N \}$; $A^\theta = \{\delta_1\theta\delta_2\theta\ldots\theta\delta_n / \delta_i \in A,\ n>0\}$

A (finite) top-down pdag automaton M is a system <Σ,Q,T,B,R> where:

.**Σ** is a finite doubly ranked alphabet.

.**Q** is a finite set of states. For every state q,

tail-rank(q)=head-rank(q)=1

.**T and B** are two recognizable word languages over Q in the usual sense, with θ identified to the word concatenation. **T** is called the top control and **B** is the bottom control.

.**R** is a finite set of rules of the form:

$$(p_1\theta p_2\theta\ldots\theta p_m).\sigma \vdash \sigma.(q_1\theta q_2\theta\ldots\theta q_n)$$

with $\sigma \in \Sigma_{m,n}$, $p_1,\ldots p_m, q_1\ldots q_n \in Q$.

Remark about notation. Q^θ denotes the set of words over Q, usualy denoted by Q^*. So, a word abc... is denoted by aθbθc...

Elementary move. We define the binary relation $\vdash R-$ between pdags over Σ ∪ Q as follows: $\delta \vdash R- \delta'$ if and only if δ' is obtained from δ by replacing, in δ, exactly one occurrence of the left-hand side of a rule of R by its right-hand side. $\vdash R^*-$ denotes the reflexive and transitive closure of $\vdash R-$.

Pdag language accepted by a top-down automaton. A pdag δ is accepted by M iff, for some $q_1\theta\ldots\theta q_m \in T$ and $q'_1\theta\ldots\theta q'_n \in B$:

$$(q_1\theta\ldots\theta q_m).\delta \vdash R{*}- \delta.(q'_1\theta\ldots\theta q'_n)$$

L(M) denotes the pdag language accepted by M. We obtain a **bottom-up automaton** by reversing the direction of the elementary move and exchanging the role played by B and T. A pdag language P is said to be **automaton-definable** if and only if P = L(M) for pdag automaton M. The family of automaton-definable languages is denoted by **AD** (**A**utomaton-**D**efinable).

2.3. Example

Let Σ be { 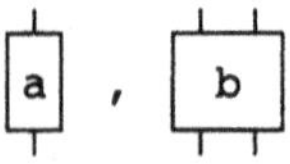 } and δ be 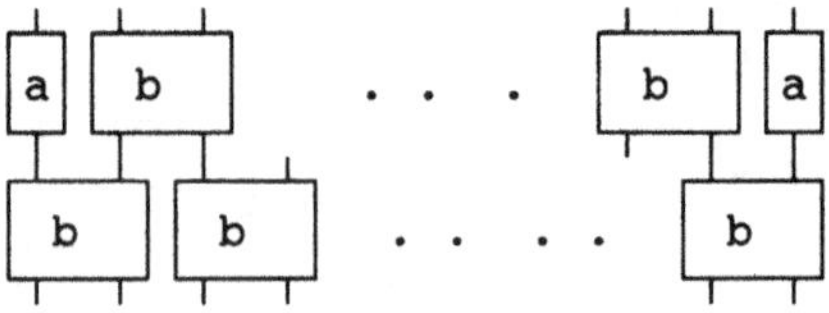

Then the "set of walls" W = {δ' ∈ DP(Σ)/ δ'= δ.δ...δ } is accepted by the automaton M = <Σ,Q,B,T,R> where

$Q = \{ q_L, q_R, q_1, q_2, q_{L'}, q_{R'} \}$; $B = T = q_L \,\theta\, (q_1 \,\theta\, q_2)^\theta \,\theta\, q_R$

$R = q_L.a \vdash a.q_{L'}$; $(q_{L'}\theta q_2).b \vdash b.(q_L\theta q_1)$

$q_R.a \vdash a.q_{R'}$; $(q_1\theta q_{R'}).b \vdash b.(q_2\theta q_R)$; $(q_1\theta q_2).b \vdash b.(q_2\theta q_1)$

For instance we have the accepting computation:

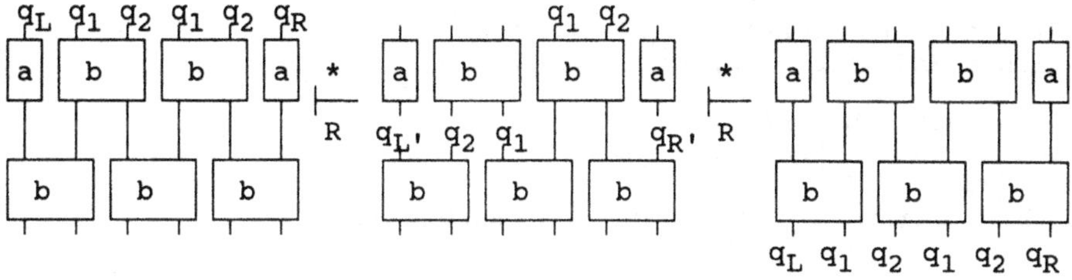

3. PROPERTIES OF PDAG AUTOMATA

3.0. Preliminaries.

1-Let $A = <\Sigma,K,K_0,K_F,\mu>$ be a finite word automaton. K denotes the set of states of A, K_0 and K_F denote the subsets of initial and final states, respectively. μ denotes the set of transitions, they are of the form k.x —> x.k' also denoted (k,x,k') with $x \in \Sigma$, k and $k' \in K$. For every k and $k' \in K$, let us define

$P_{k,k'} = \{ m \in (K x \Sigma x K)^* \mid m=(k,x_1,k_1).(k_1,x_2,k_2)...(k_{n-1},x_n,k') \}$.

2-Let Σ be a product of sets : Σ_1 x Σ_2 x .... x Σ_n.
Let us denote by $\pi_{\Sigma i}$ the morphism from Σ^* to $\Sigma_i{}^*$ defined by :

$$\forall\ (x_1,x_2,\ldots,x_n) \in \Sigma \quad \pi_{\Sigma i}((x_1,x_2,\ldots,x_n)) = x_i$$

3.1. Discussion about top and bottom control. Kamimura & Slutzki's pdags have a single root. So, the top-control does not arise and bottom control is not introduced either. We study unconnected pdags and then we introduce controls B and T to check the relationships between connected components.

3.1.1. Definition. A pdag automaton is said to be without bottom control iff its bottom control B is the set of all the words over $Q_f \subset Q$. Qf is said to be the set of final states of the automaton. A corresponding definition can easily be stated for top control.

The following proposition states that top control **and** bottom control have the same power as top **or** bottom control.

3.1.2. Proposition. For every pdag automaton M, we can construct a pdag automaton M' without bottom control (or top control) that accepts the same pdag language.

Proof. We give a construction that suppresses bottom control for a top-down automaton.

Let M be the pdag automaton $<\Sigma,Q,T,B,R>$. We construct a pdag automaton $M'=<\Sigma,Q',T',B',R'>$ without bottom control as follows:

Let $A = <Q,K,K_0,K_F,\mu>$ be a finite word automaton which accepts B in the usual sense. Then we define

. $Q' = K \times Q \times K$.   . $B' = \mu^{\theta}$.
. $T' = \{ m \in P_{k,k'} \mid k \in K_0,\ k' \in K_F$ and $\pi_Q(m) \in T \}$.
. $R' = \{ m.a \vdash a.m' \mid \pi_Q(m).a \vdash a.\pi_Q(m') \in R$
with m and $m' \in P_{k,k'}$ for some $k,k' \}$

It is obvious that $L(M) \subset L(M')$.
Finally, let us sketch the proof that $L(M') \subset L(M)$:
let δ be a pdag of $L(M')$.

Then there exists $m_i \in T$ and $m_f \in \mu^{\theta}$ such that:

$$m_i.\delta \vdash_{R'}^{*} \delta.m_f$$

So m_i and m_f belong to the same $P_{k,k'}$, moreover k belongs to K_0 and k' to K_F, therefore $\pi_Q(m_f)$ belongs to B.
Finally $\pi_Q(m_i).\delta \vdash_R^{*} \delta.\pi_Q(m_f)$ and $\delta \in L(M)$. ∎

3.2. Connectivity on pdags. In the study of rationality, we shall find out the importance of considering the pdag connected components. Top-down automaton C presented below enables us to solve some problems dealing with connectivity.

Definitions. We shall say that an edge of δ is a **right-hand edge** (respectively a **left-hand edge**) if and only if this edge is the rightmost input (respectively leftmost) of a connected subgraph δ'' of δ such that $\delta = \delta . (e_n \,\theta\, \delta'' \,\theta\, e_p)$ where e_0 denotes the absence of e.

Automaton C. $C = < \Sigma, H, T, B, P_{co} >$ where
$H = \{ l, c, r, \# \}$, $T = H^{\theta}$, $B = \#^{\theta}$,
P_{co} is the union, for all letters x of Σ, of the rules of the following forms:

i) $(l \,\theta\, c^{\theta}).x \vdash x.((l \,\theta\, c^{\theta} \,\theta\, r + \#)^{\theta} \,\theta l\, \theta\, c^{\theta})$
ii) $c^{\theta} .x \vdash x.(c^{\theta} + c^{\theta} \,\theta\, r \,\theta\, (l \,\theta\, c^{\theta} \,\theta\, r + \#)^{\theta} \,\theta\, g \,\theta\, c^{\theta})$
iii) $(c^{\theta} \,\theta\, r).x \vdash x.(c^{\theta} \,\theta\, r \,\theta\, (l \,\theta\, c^{\theta} \,\theta\, r + \#)^{\theta})$
iv) $(\# + l \,\theta\, c^{\theta} \,\theta\, r).x \vdash x.(\# + l \,\theta\, c^{\theta} \,\theta\, r)^{\theta}$

Properties of automaton C. The properties that result from the behaviour of automaton C can be introduced by the following accepting computation:

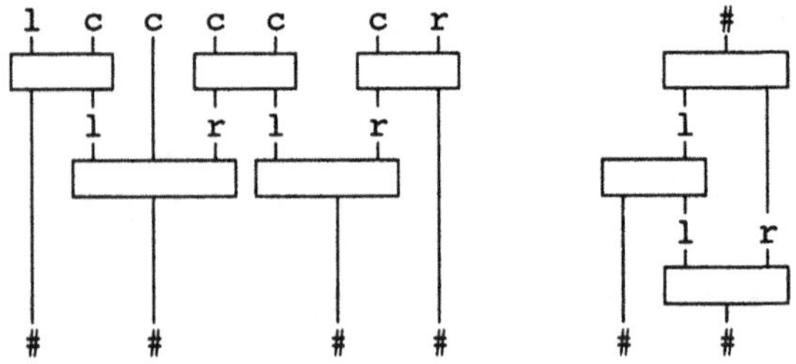

We observe that the rules have been elaborated so that:
. state **r** (resp. **l**) "walks along" right-hand (resp. left-hand) edges;
. state **#** "walks along" right-hand and left-hand edges;
. state **c** "walks along" the ones that are neither right-hand nor left-hand edges.

The following properties are easy to verify
Property 1 : $L(C) = DP(\Sigma)$;
Considering the top control $l \,\theta\, c^{\theta} \,\theta\, r + \#$, we obtain:

Property 2 : The subset of DP(Σ) connected pdags denoted **CO(Σ)** is automaton-definable.

If we restrict automaton-definability to connected graphs, the following proposition states that we can consider automata without controls.

Proposition 3.2.1. For any automaton-definable pdag language G, there is a pdag automaton $M = <\Sigma,Q,QI^{\theta},QF^{\theta},R>$ where QI and QF are subsets of Q, which accepts **among the connected pdags** the ones belonging to G.

Construction. According to proposition 3.1.2., there exists an automaton $M_1=<\Sigma, Q_1,T_1,QF_1{}^{\theta},R_1>$ where QF_1 is a subset of Q_1 such that $L(M_1)= G$.
Let us consider a word automaton $A = <Q_1,V,V_i,V_f,\mu>$ which recognizes (word) language T_1. We denote by μ_i transitions of μ beginning by an element of V_i, μ_f transitions ending by an element of V_f, and μ_{if} intersection of μ_i and μ_f.
Then, the searched automaton is the following:

$M = < \Sigma,Q,QI^{\theta},QF^{\theta},R >$ where
- $Q = V \times Q_1 \times V \times H$
- $QI = \mu_i \times \{l\} \cup \mu_f \times \{r\} \cup \mu_{if} \times \{\#\} \cup \mu \times \{c\}$
- $QF = V \times QF_1 \times V \times \{\#\}$
- A rule $w.\delta \vdash \delta.w'$ belongs to R if and only if

.its projection on Q_1 belongs to R_1;
.its projection on H belongs to P_{co};
.the projections of w and w' on $V \times Q_1 \times V$ belongs to the same $P_{vi,vj}$.

Proof. For δ accepted by M, there exists w_i belonging to QI^{θ} and w_f to QF^{θ} such that $w_i.\delta \vdash_R^* \delta.w_f$. If we suppose δ connected, then:

- $\pi_H(w_i)$ is a word of $l \ \theta \ c^{\theta} \ \theta \ r + \#$,
- $\pi_{VxQ1xV}(w_i)$ and $\pi_{VxQ1xV}(w_f)$ belong to a same $P_{v,v'}$

So $\pi_{Q1}(w_i)$ is a word of T_1, and therefore δ is a connected pdag of G ∎

4. Rationality on pdags

We attempt, as in the case of word or tree languages to describe the automaton-definable pdag languages by "rational expressions". Such a project requires the introduction of new concepts: many-sorted letters and an asynchronous parallel composition operator.

Definitions. A **many-sorted doubly ranked alphabet (Σ,S)** is a finite subset of $S^*x\Sigma xS^*$, where Σ is a finite set of labels, and S a finite set of sorts. A triplet (s,a,s') belonging to (Σ,S) will be noted

$$a^{s}_{s'}$$; s is called the coarity and s' the arity of $a^{s}_{s'}$

With such a many-sorted alphabet (Σ,S), we construct by serial and parallel composition a set of graphs that are still planar, acyclic, ordered, directed but whose nodes and edges are labelled. Arity and coarity definitions are extended in a canonical way to this new class of graphs denoted **DP(Σ,S)**. We also extend the algebraic frame, in such manner that:

- the serial composition operator respects arity and coarity;
- we introduce a new set of symbols $\{e_s,\ s \in S\}$, arity and coarity of e_s are s; for $w = s_1 s_2 \dots s_n$ in S^+, we denote by e_w the parallel composition of e_{s1} , $e_{s2} \dots e_{sn}$.
- for every pdag δ, the arity of which is w, $\delta . e_w = \delta$, and for every pdag δ, the coarity of which is w , $e_w . \delta = \delta$.

Example. The pdag of fig. 1 can be written:

$$a^{s_1}_{s_1 s_0} . \left[a^{s_1}_{s_1 s_0} \ \Theta \ a^{s_0}_{s_1 s_0} \right] . \left[b^{s_1 s_0}_{s_1} \Theta \ b^{s_1 s_0}_{s_0} \right] . b^{s_1 s_0}_{s_1}$$

Notation. Henceforth, we shall denote by τ the subset $\{e_w / w \in S^+\}$.

4.1. Rational expressions on (Σ,S). The set of rational expressions on (Σ,S), denoted by Exp(Σ,S), is recursively defined by:

. if $x \in (\Sigma,S)$ then $x \in Exp(\Sigma,S)$

. if $exp, exp' \in Exp(\Sigma,S)$ then

$(exp + exp')$, $(exp\ .\ exp')$, $(exp\ \&\ exp')$, exp^*, $exp^\&$ $\in Exp(\Sigma,S)$

So, with the (Σ,S) letters, we construct a set of well-formed expressions. In order to give a "meaning" to these expressions, we must interpret them.

We call **&** the mapping that associates the set

$$(E \ \Theta \ E') \cup (E \ \Theta \ \tau) \cup (\tau \ \Theta \ E')$$

to a pair of subsets E,E' of DP(Σ,S).And **&** superscript the one that associates $(E \cup \tau)^\Theta$ to a subset E of DP(Σ,S).

Operator & simulates an **asynchronous** parallel composition for it doesn't require simultaneous presence of elements belonging to the concerned subsets.

The interpretation of pdag rational expressions. To each rational expression is associated a subset of DP(Σ,S) by the following interpretation function $I : Exp(\Sigma,S) \longrightarrow 2^{DP(\Sigma,S)}$ recursively defined by:

. if $x \in (\Sigma,S)$ then $I(x) = \{x\}$

. if $exp, exp' \in Exp(\Sigma,S)$ then

$I(exp+exp') = I(exp) \cup I(exp')$; $I(exp.exp') = I(exp).I(exp')$;

$I(exp^*) = [I(exp)]^*$; $I(exp\&exp') = I(exp)\ \&\ I(exp')$;

$I(exp^\&) = [I(exp)]^\&$

Notation. For any subset E of D(Σ,S), and any expressions exp, exp' of Exp(Σ,S), we write $exp \equiv E$ if $I(exp) = E$ and $exp \equiv exp'$ if $I(exp) = I(exp')$. We shall use a particular morphism Φ from **DP(Σ,S)** to **DP(Σ)** that erases edge's sorts.

4.2. Rational pdag-languages. A **rational language of pdags** is given by a triplet (T,exp,B) where T, B are rational word languages of S^*, and exp is a rational expression of Exp(Σ,S). A pdag δ belongs to

(T,exp,B) if and only if there exists a pdag δ' of I(exp) the coarity and arity of which belong respectively to T and B such that $\Phi(\delta')=\delta$.

Example. The rational language:

$$\left[s_0 , \left[a \begin{matrix} s_0 \\ \\ s_0 s_1 \end{matrix} . \left[\left[a \begin{matrix} s_0 \\ \\ s_0 s \end{matrix} + a \begin{matrix} s_1 \\ \\ s s_1 \end{matrix} \right]^{\&} \right]^{*} . \left[\left[b \begin{matrix} s_0 s \\ \\ s_0 \end{matrix} + b \begin{matrix} s s_1 \\ \\ s_1 \end{matrix} \right]^{\&} \right]^{*} . b \begin{matrix} s_0 s_1 \\ \\ s_1 \end{matrix} \right] , s_1 \right]$$

represents the set of pdags that have the figure 2 pattern.

The set of rational pdag-languages on Σ will be denoted by **Rat(Σ)** or more simply **Rat** if there is no ambiguity.

4.3. A Kleene like theorem in pdags. In the string case, it is well known that any recognizable language is rational and conversely. We are going to show that our definitions leads to a comparable result in pdags. First, we present lemmas and definitions to prove theorem 4.3.7.

Lemma 4.3.1. If exp $\in$ Exp(Σ,S) and $\delta \in$ I(exp) then:

$$\delta = \delta_1 \ominus \delta_2 \ominus \ldots \ominus \delta_n \Longrightarrow \{\delta_1\} \,\&\, \{\delta_2\} \,\&\ldots\&\, \{\delta_n\} \subset I(exp)$$

Corollary. Each δ_i belongs to I(exp).

Definitions. We denote by **CO(Σ,S)** the subset of **DP(Σ,S)** of connected pdags. Given exp belonging to Exp(Σ,S), we call:

C(exp) = I(exp) $\cap$ CO(Σ,S)
C_l(exp) = { $\delta \in$ CO(Σ,S) / $\exists\ \delta' \in$ DP(Σ,S) : $\delta \ominus \delta' \in$ I(exp) }
C_r(exp) = { $\delta \in$ CO(Σ,S) / $\exists\ \delta' \in$ DP(Σ,S) : $\delta' \ominus \delta \in$ I(exp) }
C_c(exp) = { $\delta \in$ CO(Σ,S) / $\exists\ \delta',\delta'' \in$ DP(Σ,S) : $\delta' \ominus \delta \ominus \delta'' \in$ I(exp) }

Lemma 4.3.2. For exp rational expression, we denote by **Ω(exp)** the set:

$$C(exp) \cup (C_l(exp) \ominus \tau) \cup (\tau \ominus C_r(exp)) \cup (\tau \ominus C_c(exp) \ominus \tau)$$

then, for every rational expression exp: **$exp^* \equiv \Omega(exp)^*$** .

Lemma 4.3.3. We can also establish that:

$$C_r(exp^*) = ((\tau \ominus C_c(exp) \ominus \tau) \cup (\tau \ominus C_r(exp)))^* \cap CO(\Sigma,S)$$
$$C_l(exp^*) = ((\tau \ominus C_c(exp) \ominus \tau) \cup (C_l(exp) \ominus \tau))^* \cap CO(\Sigma,S)$$
$$C_c(exp^*) = (\tau \ominus C_c(exp) \ominus \tau)^* \cap CO(\Sigma,S)$$

Definition 4.3.4. We shall say that a subset E of DP(Σ,S) is **(Σ,S)-automaton-definable** if and only if there exists a pdag automaton M = <Σ,QxS,T,B,R> such that:

1 . L(M) = Φ(E)
2 . for every rule w.a $\vdash$ a.w' of R, $a\begin{matrix}\pi_S(w)\\ \\ \pi_S(w')\end{matrix}$ belongs to (Σ,S).

Lemma 4.3.5. For every $E \subset CO(\Sigma,S)$:

E is (Σ,S)-automaton-definable $\Longrightarrow$ $(E^{\&})^*$ is (Σ,S)-automaton-definable

Proof.
Step 1: Let $M_1 = <\Sigma,Q_1,T_1,B_1,R_1>$ be an automaton that verifies points 1, 2 of definition 4.3.4 for E. We apply successively to this automaton the transformations seen in 3.1 (suppression of bottom control) and in 3.5 (supression of top control). Then we obtain an automaton $M_2 = <\Sigma,Q_2,QI^{\Theta},QF^{\Theta},R_2>$ that verifies points 1, 2 of definition 4.3.4 for set E^{Θ}.
Step 2: Let us consider a finite substitution s that transforms an initial state (in QI) into a final state (in QF) without altering its projection on S.
So automaton $M = <\Sigma,Q,(QI \cup QF)^{\Theta},QF^{\Theta},R>$ where

$$R = \{ w.a \vdash a.s(w') \ / \ w.a \vdash a.w' \in R_2 \}$$

verifies the points 1,2 of definition 4.3.4 for $(E^{\&})^*$.

As a matter of fact:

- M verifies point 2 : obvious.
- $\Phi((E^{\&})^*) \subset L(M)$: obvious.
- On the other hand , we give only an intuitive argument and leave out formal details. Given a pdag δ ($\notin \tau$) accepted by M, then there exists w_i ($\in QI^{\Theta}$) and w_f ($\in QF^{\Theta}$) such that $w_i.\delta \vdash R^* - \delta.w_f$. Here we admit necessarily a substring v_1 of w_i is such that $\pi_H(v_1) \in (1 \ \theta \ c^{\theta} \ \theta \ r + \#)$. Let us consider pdag δ_1 accepted from v_1 until final states or initial states resulting from substitution s. It is easy to check that δ_1 belongs to $\Phi(E)$. So δ can be written as the serial composition of a pdag of $\Phi(E^{\&})$ and a pdag δ' of L(M). We can repeat this splitting on δ' and so we conclude that δ belongs to $\Phi((E^{\&})^*)$. ∎

After this sequence of lemmas, we can state the main lemma:

Lemma 4.3.6. For every exp belonging to $Exp(\Sigma,S)$, I(exp), C(exp), C_L(exp), C_r(exp) and C_c(exp) are (Σ,S)-automaton-definable.

Proof. By induction on the construction of rational expressions,

Kleene-like theorem 4.3.7. For any doubly ranked alphabet Σ, the class RAT of rational languages is exactly the class AD of automaton-definable sets.

Proof.
- The automaton's states can be simulated by sorts in a many sorted alphabet and so AD $\subset$ RAT.
- Conversely: given a rational language (A,exp,Z), we know that I(exp) is (Σ,S)-automaton-definable by lemma 4.3.6.
Let $M = <\Sigma,Q,T,B,R>$ be an automaton which verifies points 1,2 of the definition 4.3.4 for I(exp). Then, if we restrict its top and bottom controls in the following way:

T become $T' = \{ w \in T \ / \ \pi_S(w) \in A \}$ and

B become $B' = \{ w \in B \ / \ \pi_S(w) \in Z \}$

then this new automaton will accept all the pdags of (A,exp,Z) and only these ones.█

Figures.

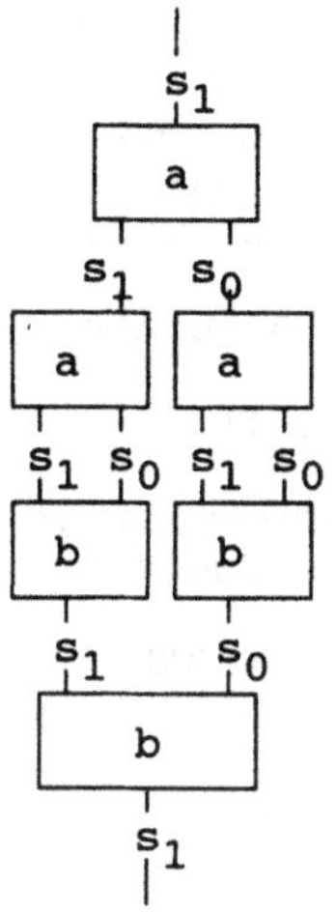

figure 1

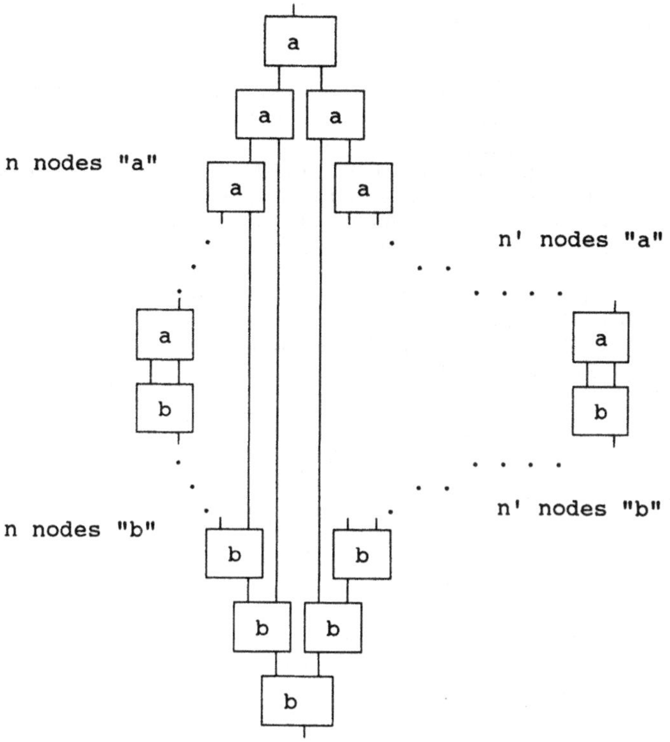

figure 2

REFERENCES

ARNOLD,A. and DAUCHET,M. (1978), Théorie des Magmoides (I), RAIRO Informatique Théorique 12-3, 235-257.

ARNOLD,A. and DAUCHET,M. (1979), Théorie des Magmoides (II), RAIRO Informatique Théorique 13-2, 135-154.

BOSSUT,F. and WARIN.B.(1986), "Rationalité et reconnaissabilité dans des Graphes Acycliques", Doctorat, Université de Lille I.

CLAUS,V., EHRIG,H., ROZENBERG,G.Ed. (1979), "Graph Grammars and their Applications to Computer Sciences and Biology", L.N.C.S. 73.

COURCELLE,B. (1987), Recognizability and Second-Order Definability for Sets of Finite Graphs, Technical Report n° I-8634, University of Bordeaux.

COURCELLE,B. (1988), On recognizable sets and tree automata, To appear in Proceedings of the Colloquium on Resolution Equations in Algebraic Structures, Austin

DEGANO,P. and MONTANARI,V. (1985), Specification Languages for Distribued Systems, TAPSOFT'85-L.N.C.S. 185, 29-51.

EHRIG,H., PFENDER,M., SCHNEIDER,H,J.,Ed. (1983), "Graph Grammars and their Applications to Computer Sciences", L.N.C.S. 153.
EILENBERG,S. and WRIGHT,J.B. (1967), Automata and tree grammars, Inf. and Control 11, 217-231.
ENGELFRIET,J. (1975), Bottom-up and Top-down tree transformations -a comparison, Math Syst Theory 9, 193-231.
GRABOWSKY,J. (1981), On Partial Languages, Fund. Informaticae 4, 427-498.
KAMIMURA,T. and SLUTZKI,G. (1981), Parallel and Two-way Automata on Directed Ordered Acyclic Graphs, Information and Control 49, 10-15.
KAMIMURA,T. and SLUTZKI,G. (1982), Transductions of Dags and Trees, Math. SysT. Theory 15, 225-249.
MARTELLI and MONTANARI,V. (1982), An Efficient Unification Algorithm, Transactions on Programming Languages and Syst., 256-282.
OCHMANSKI,E. (1985), Regular Behaviour of Concurrent Systems, Bull. EATCS 27.
THATCHER,J.W. (1973), Tree automata: Informal Survey, In Currents in the Theory of Computing (A.V,Aho,Ed.), Prentice-Hall, Englewood Cliffs, 143-172.
WINKOWSKI,J. (1979), An Algebraic Approach to Concurrence, MFCS 79-L.N.C.S. 74, 523-532.

ON MAXIMAL PREFIX SETS OF WORDS

Véronique BRUYERE
Université de l'Etat, Faculté des Sciences
15,avenue Maistriau, B-7000-Mons (Belgium)

ABSTRACT

In his paper [6], Schützenberger proved that two finite subsets of words are maximal prefix if their product is maximal prefix, provided this product is finite and unambiguous. The finiteness condition is necessary; however, the authors in [1] wonder whether the unambiguity hypothesis is also necessary. We answer positively by giving an example of a finite maximal prefix and ambiguous product of which the two factors are not maximal prefix. We also give a generalized version of the Schützenberger theorem where the finiteness condition is weakened.

INTRODUCTION

A set X of words over an alphabet is called prefix if no element of X appears in the beginning of another word of X. The set X is said to be maximal prefix if it is prefix and is not properly contained in any other prefix set over the same alphabet.

It is rather easy to prove that maximal prefix sets are closed under the catenation product; but the converse is not so immediate. Schützenberger [6] has proved the converse under two restrictive conditions: the two factors X and Y of a maximal prefix product XY are also maximal prefix, provided this product is finite and unambiguous (unambiguous means that each word w in the product XY has only one factorization $w=xy$ with $x\in X$ and $y\in Y$).
Such a maximal prefix and unambiguous product appears in the proof of a well-known Schützenberger result [7] about the codes with finite deciphering delay.

Simple examples show that the Schützenberger theorem over maximal prefix products is no longer true for infinite products. However, the authors in [1] say that it is not known whether the hypothesis of unambiguity is necessary.

In this paper, we study the two conditions - unambiguity and finiteness - under which the sets X and Y are maximal prefix if their product XY is maximal prefix.
We first show that the hypothesis of unambiguity is necessary: we present an example of a finite maximal prefix product that is ambiguous such that its two factors are not maximal prefix sets. The size of the counterexample is impressive: the set Y is composed of 39 words and the product XY of 94 words ! Two theorems try to explain such a behaviour, and describe the form of X and Y.
Then, we prove that the finiteness condition can be weakened. Indeed, it turns out that the examples showing the necessity of the finiteness

hypothesis are all of the same kind. If the sets X and Y are in a certain manner infinite, the Schützenberger theorem remains true.

BASIC DEFINITIONS

We use the basic definitions and notations of [1].
We denote by A an *alphabet*, by A^* the *free monoid* generated by A. The *empty word* is denoted by 1. A^+ is the *free semigroup* $A^*\setminus\{1\}$. The *length* $|w|$ of a word w is the number of its letters.
Several operations can be defined on subsets of words $X,Y\subset A^*$:

Union :	$X+Y = \{w\in A^* \mid w\in X \text{ or } w\in Y\}$
Minus :	$X-Y = \{w\in A^* \mid w\in X \text{ and } w\notin Y\}$
Catenation product :	$XY = \{xy \mid x\in X \text{ and } y\in Y\}$
Star :	$X^* = \{x_1x_2\ldots x_n \mid n\in\mathbb{N},\ x_i\in X,\ 1\leq i\leq n\}$.

Let $u,v\in A^*$, the word u is a *(proper) left factor* of v if

$$\exists w\in A^*\ (\in A^+) : uw=v.$$

This relation defines a partial order on A^*, denoted by $u \leq (<) v$.
Let $X\subset A^*$, the set of the proper left factors of its elements is denoted by XA^-.

A set $X\subset A^*$ is said to be *prefix* if

$$\forall x,x'\in X : x\leq x' \Rightarrow x=x'.$$

X is *maximal prefix* if it is prefix and not properly contained in another prefix subset of A^*.
It can be shown [1] that

PROPOSITION 1. *Let $X\subset A^*$ be a prefix set. Then X is maximal prefix iff*

$$\forall w\in A^* : w \in XA^- + X + XA^+.$$

♦

PRODUCTS AND MAXIMAL PREFIX SETS

Maximal prefix sets are closed under the catenation product: if $X,Y\subset A^*$ are maximal prefix sets, then their product XY is again maximal prefix.
Schützenberger [6] has proved the converse under two additional conditions: the sets X,Y must be finite and their product unambiguous.
Recall that a product XY is qualified *unambiguous* if

$$\forall x,x'\in X,\ \forall y,y'\in Y : xy=x'y' \Rightarrow x=x',\ y=y'.$$

Otherwise, it is said to be *ambiguous*.
This result is stated as follows (a proof can be found in [1]) :

THEOREM 2 (Schützenberger). *Let $X,Y\subset A^*$ be such that the product XY is unambiguous and finite. If XY is maximal prefix, then X and Y are maximal prefix.*

♦

The finiteness condition of theorem 2 is necessary. For instance, over the alphabet {a,b}, $X=a^*$ is not prefix, Y={b} is not maximal prefix, however the product $XY=a^*b$ is unambiguous and maximal prefix.

On the other hand, the authors in [1] wonder whether the hypothesis of unambiguity is necessary.
We will first answer, by constructing a counterexample and comment its form and size. Then, we will go back to the finiteness condition. We will show that this condition can be weakened in theorem 2.

Before, let us discard some trivial cases of maximal prefix products. We will not consider trivial products XY that are either empty or with one factor (X or Y) equal to {1}.
The problem of a one-letter alphabet is also easy to solve. Indeed, if a product $XY \subset \{a\}^*$ is maximal prefix, then it is composed of a unique word a^n where n>0. Consequently, XY is finite and unambiguous and by theorem 2, X and Y are maximal prefix. It comes that over a one-letter alphabet, a product XY is maximal prefix if and only if X and Y are maximal prefix. In what follows, we will consider the alphabet A to be composed of at least two letters.

THE UNAMBIGUITY CONDITION

The following counterexample shows that the unambiguity hypothesis of theorem 2 is necessary. The set X and Y are defined over the alphabet {a,b}, X is equal to {1,ab,ababa}, Y and XY are represented respectively by the leaves of the following trees (the root is the empty word, each node is associated with a word that is equal to the label of the path from the root to this node)

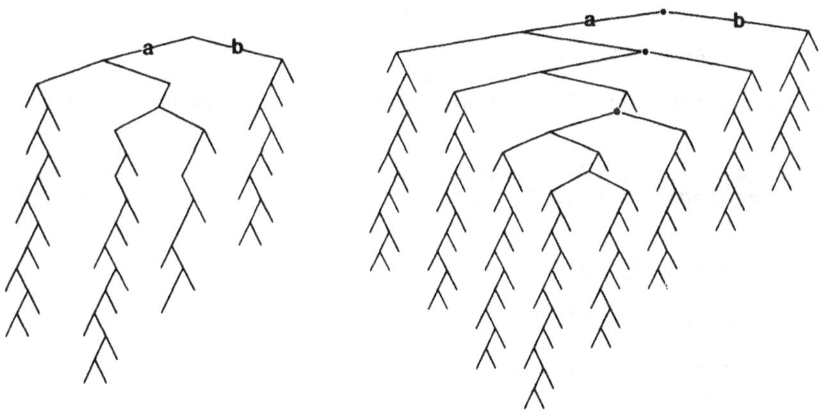

X is clearly not prefix, Y is not maximal prefix (for instance Y + {abb} is again prefix) but the product XY is ambiguous, finite and maximal prefix.
Notice the size of Y, although X has only 3 words. Notice also that Y lacks 7 words to be maximal prefix : abaaa, abaabaa, abababaa, ababaabaabab, ababaabab, ababab and abb. The following results explain such a behaviour.

First, let us show that if XY is an ambiguous product which is finite and prefix, then Y is prefix but not maximal prefix (as observed in the example).

PROPOSITION 3. Let $X,Y \subset A^*$. *If XY is ambiguous, finite and prefix, then Y is prefix but not maximal prefix.*

Proof:

It is easy to show that Y is prefix.
As the product XY is ambiguous,

$$\exists x,x' \in X,\ \exists y,y' \in Y,\ \exists t \in A^+ : x=x't \text{ and } xy = x'y'.$$

For every $i \geq 0$ and t' $1<t' \leq t$, the word $y=t^i t'$ does not belong to Y. Otherwise,

$$x'y = x't^i t' < x't^{i+1}t' = xy$$

which is in contradiction with the hypothesis XY prefix. So, as Y is finite, Y is not maximal prefix by proposition 1.

♦

Let us denote by Y' the smallest maximal prefix set containing Y. If we add the maximal prefix condition to XY in the preceding result, the words xz where $x \in X$ and $z \in Y'-Y$ must satisfy the following relation by proposition 1 :

$$xz \in (XY)A^- + XY + XYA^+.$$

In fact, $xz \in (XY)A^- + XY$ because Y' is of minimal size and the alphabet has at least two letters.
Moreover, as XY is finite, we can choose x such that no word in X has x as proper left factor. Then, for this x, there exist $x' \in X$, $y' \in Y$ such that

$$xz \leq x'y' \quad \text{and} \quad x' < x.$$

Let $t \in A^+$ be defined by $x't=x$. Some results can be proved about this word t:

PROPOSITION 4. Let $X,Y \subset A^*$ *such that the product XY is ambiguous, finite and maximal prefix. Let Y' be the smallest maximal prefix set containing Y. If*

$$\exists x,x' \in X,\ \exists z \in Y'-Y,\ \exists y' \in Y : xz \leq x'y'$$

$$\textit{and} \quad x=x't \quad \textit{with } t \in A^+,$$

then there exists $z' \in Y'-Y$ *distinct from z such that* $Y' \cap t^*A^- = \{z'\}$.

Proof :

As Y' is a finite maximal prefix set, by proposition 1, there exists a unique word $z' \in Y'$ such that $Y' \cap t^*A^- = \{z'\}$. This word z' does not belong to Y (cfr proposition 3). Suppose now that z'=z:

$$\exists t' \in A^*,\ \exists i \in \mathbb{N} : z=t^i t' \quad \text{with } 1<t' \leq t.$$

Then, $xz = x't^{i+1}t' \leqslant x'y'$. Consequently, $t^{i+1}t' \leqslant y'$ and $y' \in zA^*$, which is impossible.

♦

The previous result shows that $Y'-Y$ contains two distinct words with one of the form t^it'. We can go further :

THEOREM 5. *Let* $X,Y \subset A^*$ *such that the product is ambiguous and finite. If* XY *is maximal prefix, then*

$$card(Y'-Y) \geqslant 4 \text{ and } card(X) \geqslant 3$$

where $Y' \subset A^*$ *is the smallest maximal prefix set containing* Y.

We will only give here the main ideas of the proof. For more details, the reader should consult [2].
The techniques used in the proof are based on the propositions 3 and 4, and on a well-known result on conjugate words, the Fine and Wilf theorem [4] and a corollary. Recall that two words $x,y \in A^*$ are *conjugate* if $\exists z \in A^*$ such that $xz=zy$.
We just mention the last three results; the proofs can be found in [5].

PROPOSITION 6. *Let* $x,y \in A^*$ *be two conjugate words. Then, there exist* $u,v \in A^*$ *such that* $x=uv$, $y=vu$, $z \in u(vu)^*$.

♦

THEOREM 7 (Fine and Wilf). *Let* $x,y \in A^*$. *Let* $n=|x|$, $m=|y|$. *If two powers* x^p *and* y^q *of* x *and* y *have a common left factor of length at least equal to* $n+m-gcd(n,m)$, *then* x *and* y *are powers of the same word.*

♦

COROLLARY 8. *Let* $x,y \in A^*$. *If* $xy=yx$, *then* x *and* y *are powers of the same word.*

♦

Proof of theorem 5:

We denote by Z the set $Y'-Y$, by z any of its the words. We know that $card(Z)$ is non nul by proposition 3.
We have also observed that for every $x \in X$ and $z \in Z$, $xz \in (XY)A^- + XY$. Since XY is a finite maximal prefix set, there are words $x_1,x_2 \in X$ of maximal length, $t_1 \in A^+$ and $y_2 \in Y$ such that

$$x_1=x_2t_1$$
$$x_1z_{i_0} \leqslant x_2y_2 \quad \text{for some word } z_{i_0} \in Z.$$

By result 4, there exists a word $z_1 \neq z_{i_0}$ such that $Z \cap t_1{}^*A^- = \{z_1\}$. It follows that $card(Z) \geqslant 2$.

XY being maximal prefix, x_1z_1 belongs to $(XY)A^- + XY$. As x_1 is of maximal length,

$$\exists x_3 \in X, \exists y_3 \in Y, \exists t_2 \in A^+ : x_1=x_3t_2 \quad \text{and} \quad x_1z_1 \leqslant x_3y_3.$$

The word x_3 is distinct from x_2 by proposition 4 and it is a proper left factor of x_2 by maximality of $|x_2|$:

$$\exists t_3 \in A^+ : x_2=x_3t_3 \quad \text{and} \quad t_2=t_3t_1.$$

So $card(X) \geqslant 3$.
Proposition 4 shows that there exists $z_2 \neq z_1$ such that

$Z \cap t_2{}^*A^- = \{z_2\}$.
Let us now study the word t_3. Let z_3 be the unique word belonging to $Z \cap t_3{}^*A^-$. A combinatorial study using the results 4, 6-8 show that z_3 is distinct from z_1 and z_2. Thus, card(Z)$\geqslant$3.

Consider the subsets $(t_2t_1)^*A^-$ and $(t_1t_2)^*A^-$. If card(Z)=3, it can be proved that their intersection with Y is nonempty, using the preceding results. Then, $(t_2t_1)^*A^-$ and $(t_1t_2)^*A^-$ have respectively the words y_{12} and y_{21} of Y. As XY is prefix

$$x_1y_{12} = x_3y_{21} \quad \text{and} \quad t_2y_{12} = y_{21}$$
$$x_1y_{21} = x_2y_{12} \quad \text{and} \quad t_1y_{21} = y_{12}$$

So, $y_{12} = t_1y_{21} = t_1t_2y_{12}$, which is impossible. It follows that card(Z)$\geqslant$4.

By considering the proposed counterexample, one can observe that

t_1=aba, t_2=ababa, t_3=ab,
z_1=abaabaa, z_2=ababaabab, z_3=ababab,
ababaabaabab $\in Z \cap (t_2t_1)^*A^-$.

But other words belong to Z : abb, abaaa, ababaaa.
However, this example is of minimal size in the sense of card(Z), because the following theorem shows that card(Z)$\geqslant$7 if the set X has exactly three words. Again, we will only give the main ideas of the proof; a more detailled version is presented in [3].

THEOREM 9. Let $X,Y \subset A^*$ *such that the product* XY *is ambiguous and finite. If* XY *is maximal prefix and card(X)=3, then card(Y'-Y)$\geqslant$7, where* $Y' \subset A^*$ *is the smallest maximal prefix set containing Y.*

Proof :

We know by theorem 5 that card(Y'-Y)$\geqslant$4. We use the notations and results of the proof of theorem 5.
Suppose that card(X)=3. Thus, $X=\{x_1,x_2,x_3\}$. As

$$x_3z_{i_0}\ ,\ x_3z_1,\ x_2z_3 \in (XY)A^- + XY\ ,$$

we have $x_2<x_3z_{i_0}$, $x_2<x_3z_1$ and by proposition 4, $x_1<x_2z_3$.
Thus, $t_3<z_{i_0}$ and one of the sets $(t_1t_2)^*A^-$, $(t_2t_1)^*A^-$ intersects Z in the word z_4 distinct from z_1, z_2, z_3. Moreover, the form of words t_1 and t_3 can be described : if $|t_3|\leqslant|t_1|$, then $t_1 \in t_3{}^*A^-$ and if $|t_1|<|t_3|$, then $t_3 \in t_1{}^*A^-$.
In the rest of the proof, we will suppose that $|t_3|\leqslant|t_1|$, the arguments being similar in the other case.

As $t_1 \in t_3{}^*A^-$, the word t_1 has the form $t_3{}^k t'$ where $k\geqslant1$ and $1<t'<t_3$. Let us consider the subsets

$$U_j = t_3{}^j(t'^*A^-) \qquad j=0,\ldots,k.$$

As Y' is maximal prefix,

$$\forall j \quad U_j \cap Y' = \{u_j\} \qquad \text{for some word } u_j \in A^+.$$

Suppose every u_j belongs to Y. As XY is prefix, $x_3u_1=x_2u_0$, thus $u_1=t_3u_0$. Similarly, $x_3u_2=x_2u_1$ and then

$$u_2=t_3u_1=t_3{}^2u_0,\ \ldots\ ,\ x_3u_k=x_2u_{k-1} \text{ and } u_k=t_3{}^ku_0.$$

So, $x_2u_k = x_2t_3{}^ku_0 < x_2t_3{}^kt'u_0 = x_1u_0$, in contradiction with the XY prefix hypothesis. Consequently, one of the word u_j we denote by z_5, belongs to Z. By combinatorial arguments using the results 4,6-8, we check that

$$\forall j \quad 0 \leqslant j \leqslant k : u_j \notin \{z_1, z_2, z_3, z_4\}.$$

We can deduct that z_5 is distinct from z_m $1 \leqslant m \leqslant 4$ and card(Z)$\geqslant$5.

By the same technique, it is possible to construct two other new words z_6 and z_7 of Z, showing that card(Z)$\geqslant$7 as announced in the proposition. z_6 is one of the words v_j with $t_3 = t't''$ and

$$\{v_j\} = Y' \cap t_3{}^j(t''^*A^-) \qquad j=0,\ldots,k+1.$$

Let W_j be the subsets

$$t_3{}^j[(t't_2)^*A^-], \; 0 \leqslant j \leqslant k$$

and W_{k+1} be equal to $(t_2t')^*A^-$. z_7 is one of the words w_j such that $\{w_j\} = W_j \cap Y'$, $0 \leqslant j \leqslant k+1$.

♦

For the proposed counterexample, we have $z_5 = u_1$ = abaaa, $z_6 = v_1$ = abb, $z_7 = w_2$ = ababaaa.

THE FINITENESS CONDITION

Counterexamples to the finiteness hypothesis of Schützenberger theorem 5 are all of the same kind. Indeed, this condition can be weakened. A proof, given by Schützenberger [7] about the finite deciphering delay of codes, suggests to us how to proceed, because an unambiguous maximal prefix product -not always finite- appears in this proof.
A generalized version of theorem 5 is stated as follow :

<u>*THEOREM 10.*</u> *Let* $X,Y \subset A^*$ *such that*

a) $\exists x_0 \in X : x_0A^+ \cap X = \emptyset$

b) $\forall x \in X, \exists n \in \mathbb{N} : Y \cap R_x{}^nA^* = \emptyset$, *where* $R_x = \{w \in A^+ : x \in A^*w\}$.

If XY is unambiguous and maximal prefix, then X and Y are maximal prefix.

In the proof, we will show that X is prefix. The conclusion follows by use of the following proposition [1]:

<u>*PROPOSITION 11.*</u> *Let* $X,Y \subset A^*$.*If XY is maximal prefix and X is prefix, then X and Y are maximal prefix.*

♦

Proof of theorem 10 :

As XY is prefix, Y is prefix too. Suppose Y is not maximal prefix. Let Y' be the smallest maximal prefix set including Y. Let us denote the set Y'-Y by Z, and any of its elements by z. As before, for every $z \in Z$ and $x \in X$, $xz \in (XY)A^- + XY$.

Let $x_0 \in X$ be the word of hypothesis a). Let us show by induction on n that

$\forall n>0,\ \exists z_n \in Z,\ \exists y_n \in Y,\ \exists x_n \in X,$
$\exists t_1, t_2, \ldots, t_n \in A^+,\ \exists z_n' \in A^*, \exists a \in A$:

$$x_0 = x_n t_n, \quad z_n = z_n' a, \quad x_0 z_n \leqslant x_n y_n, \quad t_{n-1} \ldots t_2 t_1 \leqslant z_n'.$$

If n=1, it is immediate (condition a).
Let n be a fixed nonnegative integer and assume that the induction hypothesis is satisfied for this n.
By definition of Y'and as $|A| \geqslant 2$, there exists a word $y \in Y$ such that $y \in z_n' A^+$.
Consider the word $t_n y$. As Y' is a maximal prefix set,

$$t_n y \in Y'A^- + Y' + Y'A^+,$$

but $t_n y \notin YA^- + Y + YA^+$,

otherwise, suppose that there exists $y' \in Y$ such that $t_n y \leqslant y'$ (the conclusion is similar in the case $y' < t_n y$). Then, $x_0 y = x_n t_n y \leqslant x_n y'$. As XY is prefix and unambiguous, $x_0 = x_n$ and $y = y'$. It is impossible.
So, there exists $z_{n+1} \in Z$ such that $t_n y A^* \cap z_{n+1} A^* \neq \emptyset$.
Moreover, $t_n z_n' < z_{n+1}$ because Y' prefix.
Consider the word $x_0 z_{n+1}$. It belongs to $(XY)A^- + XY$:

$$\exists x_{n+1} y_{n+1} \in XY,\ \exists t_{n+1} \in A^+ : x_0 z_{n+1} \leqslant x_{n+1} y_{n+1} \text{ and } x_0 = x_{n+1} t_{n+1}.$$

Then $t_n t_{n-1} \ldots t_1 \leqslant t_n z_n' \leqslant z_{n+1}' < z_{n+1}$.
This concludes the proof by induction.
It then follows that

$$\forall n\ R_{x_0}{}^n A^* \cap Y \neq \emptyset$$

because in the result by induction, $t_n t_{n-1} \ldots t_1 A^* \in Y$. This contradicts the hypothesis b). So, Y is maximal prefix.

Suppose X is not prefix : there exist $x, x' \in X$ and $t \in A^+$ such that $xt = x'$. We have $Y \cap t^* A^- = \emptyset$.
For every $n \geqslant 0$, consider the word t^n. As $Y \cap t^* A^- = \emptyset$ and Y is maximal prefix, t^n belongs to YA^-, i.e.

$$\exists u_n \in A^+ : t^n u_n \in Y.$$

This leads to a contradiction with the hypothesis b), since $t \in R_{x'}$. So, X is prefix and then maximal prefix by proposition 11.

♦

Examples of sets $X, Y \subset A^*$ satisfying conditions a) and b) exist: over the alphabet {a,b},

$X = a^* b$, $Y = \{a, b\}$

$X = \{a, b\}$, Y as proposed by Schützenberger in [7]: let w be the infinite word $aba^2b^2a^3b^3 \ldots a^n b^n \ldots$ and P the set of the left factors of w, Y is defined as PA-P. In fact, such a set Y satisfies the condition b) for every x in A^*.

The two conditions are necessary because for the first one, we have the counterexample, $X = a^*$, $Y = \{b\}$ and for the second one, $X = \{1, a\}$, $Y = (a^2)^* b$.

REFERENCES

1. J. BERSTEL and D. PERRIN, "Theory of codes", Academic Press, Orlando, 1985.

2. V. BRUYERE, Maximal prefix products, *Semigroup Forum* **36** (1987), 147-157.

3. V. BRUYERE, Answer to a question about maximal prefix sets of words, submitted to *Theor. Comp. Science*.

4. N.J. FINE and H.S. WILF, Uniqueness theorems for periodic functions, *Proc. Amer. Math. Soc.* **16** (1965), 109-114.

5. M. LOTHAIRE, "Combinatorics on words", Reading, Massachusetts, Addison-Wesley, 1983.

6. M.P. SCHUTZENBERGER, Sur certains sous-monoïdes libres, *Bull. Soc. Math. France* **93** (1965), 209-223.

7. M.P. SCHUTZENBERGER, On a question concerning certain free submonoids, *J. Combinatorial Theory* **1** (1966), 437-442.

Infinite Behaviour of Deterministic Petri Nets

Heino Carstensen

Universität Hamburg, Fachbereich Informatik
Rothenbaumchaussee 67/69, D-2000 Hamburg 13

1 Introduction

Petri nets have turned out to be an adequate tool for modelling, designing, and analysing concurrent systems. Many concurrent systems are designed to run without explicit termination, e. g. operating systems. This leads to the investigation of infinite behaviour, especially of Petri nets. For the infinite behaviour we consider definitions which were given by [Landweber 69] for finite automata.

The cooperation of distributed actions can be sufficiently modelled by Petri nets, because concurrency is a fundamental element of the net theory. The actions will be represented by the transitions of the net. In Petri nets a transition always causes the same changing in any situation it appears. But often this is too strict, because it is not possible to model actions which may appear in different situations and cause different changes. On behalf of this labelled Petri nets were introduced, in which actions are represented by the label of transitions, i. e. several transitions may have the same label.

The problem in a labelled Petri net is that two or more transitions with the same label might be activated. There is no way to determine which transition will follow. This phenomenon causes severe problems, e. g. for labelled Petri nets it is undecidable if two given nets have the same behaviour.

Real systems mostly have the property that the changes resulting from an action are determined by the action and the situation in which it appears. This leads us to deterministic Petri nets. Here in any possible situation all activated transitions have different labels, hence every sequence of actions determines the corresponding sequence of transitions.

In the following section we will give necessary definitions and results concerning languages of labelled Petri nets and infinite behaviour of finite automata and nets. Then deterministic Petri nets will be compared with nondeterministic nets for finite behaviour. The fourth section investigates the infinite behaviour of deterministic nets with specifications on the markings. Whereas in the fifth section the infinite behaviour is defined on transitions which must appear. Finally the power of several classes of infinite behaviour of deterministic Petri nets is compared and an overall hierarchy is established.

2 Basic definitions and results

In this section we want to give the formal definition of Petri nets and some notations which will be used later. Finally we will define the infinite behaviour of Petri nets.

First some mathematical notations will be needed.

Definition 1 The positive integers are denoted by $\mathbb{N}^+$ and $\mathbb{N} = \{0\} \cup \mathbb{N}^+$. The cardinality of $\mathbb{N}$ is ω, i. e. $|\mathbb{N}| = \omega$. The quantors $\exists$ and $\forall$ will be extended to $\underset{\infty}{\exists}$ and $\underset{\infty}{\forall}$, there are infinitely many and for all but infinitely many. Let A be a set and p a predicate, then $\underset{\infty}{\exists}\, a \in A : p(a)$ means $|\{a \in A \mid p(a)\}| = \omega$. And $\underset{\infty}{\forall}$ is defined by $\left(\underset{\infty}{\forall}\, a \in A : \neg p(a)\right) \Leftrightarrow \left(\neg \underset{\infty}{\exists}\, a \in A : p(a)\right)$.

With the lemma of Dickson [Dickson 13], i. e., in every infinite sequence of vectors over positive integers there is an increasing infinite subsequence, it is easy to show the following technical lemma.

Lemma 1 *Let $A \subseteq (\mathbb{N}^k)^*$, $k \in \mathbb{N}^+$, be an infinite set of sequences of vectors, if*
a) there is $q \in \mathbb{N}$ with $\forall w \in A : \forall i, j \in \mathbb{N}, i < |w|, j \leq k : |w(i)(j) - w(i+1)(j)| \leq q$ and
b) there is a vector $x \in \mathbb{N}^k$ with $\forall w \in A/\{\lambda\} : w(1) = x$,
then it exists an $n \in \mathbb{N}$, so that for every sequence $v \in A$ with $|v| \geq n$: $\exists i, j \in \mathbb{N}^+, i < j \leq n : v(i) \leq v(j)$.

Definition 2 A *labelled Petri net* $N = (S, T; F, W, h, m_0)$ is given by two finite and disjunct sets, the set of *places* S, and the set of *transitions* T, a *flow relation* $F \subseteq (S \times T) \cup (T \times S)$, a *weight function* $W : F \to \mathbb{N}^+$, a *labelling function* $h : T \to (X \cup \{\lambda\})$, where X is a given finite alphabet and λ the empty word, and an *initial marking* $m_0 : S \to \mathbb{N}$. A net N is called λ-free if $h : T \to X$. A *marking* m of N is a mapping $m : S \to \mathbb{N}$, and it is given by a vector over $\mathbb{N}^S$.

The dynamic behaviour of a Petri net is described by the firing rule.

Definition 3 Let N be a Petri net. A transition $t \in T$ is *activated* by a marking $m \in \mathbb{N}^S$, written $m\ (t\rangle$, if on every input place s of t, $(s,t) \in F$, there are at least $W(s,t)$ tokens, i. e. $\forall s \in S : (s,t) \in F \Rightarrow W(s,t) \le m(s)$. An activated transition may fire and it produces a *follower marking* m', $m\ (t\rangle\ m'$, by subtracting $W(s,t)$ tokens from every input place and adding $W(s',t)$ tokens on every output place s' of t, $(t,s') \in F$.
A sequence $v = t_1 t_2 \ldots t_n$ of transitions is called *firing sequence* from m, if it exists a sequence of markings $\delta(v,m) = m_1 m_2 \ldots m_{n+1}$ with $m = m_1\ (t_1\rangle\ m_2\ (t_2\rangle \ldots (t_n\rangle\ m_{n+1} = m'$, written $m\ (v\rangle\ m'$. The sequence $\delta(v,m)$ is the *corresponding marking sequence* of v starting from m, if it starts from the initial marking, it is defined: $\delta_0(v) = \delta(v, m_0)$. For an arbitrary sequence α, $\alpha(i)$ denotes the ith element of α and $\alpha[i]$ the prefix of length i of α, i. e. $\alpha[i] = \alpha(1)\ldots\alpha(i)$.

Definition 4 Let N be a Petri net, then $\mathrm{F}(N) = \{v \in T^* \mid m_0\ (v\rangle\}$ is the *set of firing sequences* and $\mathrm{L}(N) = \{h(v) \in X^* \mid v \in \mathrm{F}(N)\}$ the *set of words* or the *language* of N. For the infinite behaviour we define: $\mathrm{F}_\omega(N) = \{v \in T^\omega \mid \forall i \in \mathbb{N}^+ : v[i] \in \mathrm{F}(N)\}$ is the *set of infinite firing sequences* and $\mathrm{L}_\omega(N) = \{h(v) \in X^\omega \mid v \in \mathrm{F}_\omega(N)\}$ the *set of infinite words* or ω*-language* of N. The *class* of all ω-languages of λ-free Petri nets will be denoted by $\mathcal{L}_\omega$, i. e. $\mathcal{L}_\omega = \{\mathrm{L}_\omega(N) \mid N \text{ is a } \lambda\text{-free Petri net}\}$, and $\mathcal{L}_{\omega\lambda}$ if arbitrary Petri nets are assumed.

To define infinite behaviours (languages) of finite automata [Landweber 69] introduces five levels of successful ω-sequences with respect to sets of states of the automaton. A word is called successful if the corresponding sequence of states fulfills certain properties. The individual levels were called i-successful, for $i \in \{1, 1', 2, 2', 3\}$. We will introduce an additional definition for 4-successful.

For the present we will define i-successful sequences independently of automata or Petri nets.

Definition 5 Let Y be a finite or an infinite set and $\mathcal{A} = \{A_1, A_2, \ldots, A_k\} \subseteq \wp(Y)$, with $A_i \neq \emptyset$, $1 \le i \le k$, a finite nonempty set of *anchorsets*, then an infinite sequence $\alpha \in Y^\omega$ is called
1-*successful* for $\mathcal{A}$, if $\exists A \in \mathcal{A}$: $\exists\, i \in \mathbb{N}^+$: $\alpha(i) \in A$, 1′-*successful* for $\mathcal{A}$, if $\exists A \in \mathcal{A}$: $\forall\, i \in \mathbb{N}^+$: $\alpha(i) \in A$,
2-*successful* for $\mathcal{A}$, if $\exists A \in \mathcal{A}$: $\underset{\infty}{\exists}\, i \in \mathbb{N}^+$: $\alpha(i) \in A$, 2′-*successful* for $\mathcal{A}$, if $\exists A \in \mathcal{A}$: $\underset{\infty}{\forall}\, i \in \mathbb{N}^+$: $\alpha(i) \in A$,
3-*successful* for $\mathcal{A}$, if $\exists A \in \mathcal{A}$: $\underset{\infty}{\forall}\, i \in \mathbb{N}^+$: $\alpha(i) \in A$ and $\forall a \in A$: $\underset{\infty}{\exists}\, i \in \mathbb{N}^+$: $\alpha(i) = a$.
4-*successful* for $\mathcal{A}$, if $\exists A \in \mathcal{A}$: $\forall a \in A$: $\underset{\infty}{\exists}\, i \in \mathbb{N}^+$: $\alpha(i) = a$.

Definition 6 Let N be a Petri net and $\mathcal{D} = \{D_1, D_2, \ldots, D_k\}$, $k \in \mathbb{N}^+$, a set of finite anchorsets of markings, $D_i \subseteq \mathbb{N}^S$. The *terminal language* of the net N and the anchorset D_1 is $\mathrm{L}_0(N, D_1) = \{h(v) \in X^* \mid v \in \mathrm{F}(N) \text{ and } \delta_0(v)(|v|) \in D_1\}$. For $i \in \{1, 1', 2, 2', 3, 4\}$ the *i-successful language* or the *i-behaviour* of $(N, \mathcal{D})$ is a language over infinite words: $\mathrm{L}^i_\omega(N, \mathcal{D}) = \{h(v) \in X^\omega \mid v \in \mathrm{F}_\omega(N) \text{ and } \delta_0(v) \text{ is } i\text{-successful for } \mathcal{D}\}$. The corresponding *classes of languages* are $\mathcal{L}_0$ or $\mathcal{L}^i_\omega$. Let $\mathcal{L}_1$ be a class of languages of finite words then we define $\mathcal{KC}_\omega(\mathcal{L}_1) := \left\{ \bigcup_{i=1}^{k} A_i B_i^\omega \mid A_i, B_i \in \mathcal{L}_1, k \in \mathbb{N}^+ \right\}$ to be the ω*-Kleene-Closure* of $\mathcal{L}_1$.

For the finite automaton it exists a similar definition of i-successful behaviour, but instead of markings we have to consider states. The classes of i-successful regular languages will be written as $\mathcal{R}^i_\omega$, they were introduced and investigated in [McNaughton 66], [Landweber 69], and [Hossley 72]. The following inclusions hold for nondeterministic noncomplete finite automata. Similar results were shown for push-down automata and Turing machines, where the anchorsets are defined for states of the finite control [Cohen, Gold 77].

Theorem 1

$$\mathcal{R}^{1'}_\omega \subset \mathcal{R}^1_\omega = \mathcal{R}^{2'}_\omega \subset \mathcal{R}^2_\omega = \mathcal{R}^3_\omega = \mathcal{KC}_\omega(\mathcal{R})$$

The integration of the 4-successful class causes no problems, it is easy to show that $\mathcal{R}^2_\omega = \mathcal{R}^4_\omega$.

For Petri nets we get quite different inclusions [Valk 83], [Carstensen, Valk 85].

Lemma 2

$$\begin{array}{ccccccccccc} \mathcal{L}_\omega & \subset & \mathcal{L}^1_\omega & & & & & & & & \\ \cup & & \cup & & & & & & & & \\ \mathcal{L}^{1'}_\omega & \subset & \mathcal{L}^{2'}_\omega & \subset & \mathcal{L}^3_\omega & \subset & \mathcal{L}^2_\omega & \subset & \mathcal{L}^4_\omega & \subset & \mathcal{KC}_\omega(\mathcal{L}_0) \end{array}$$

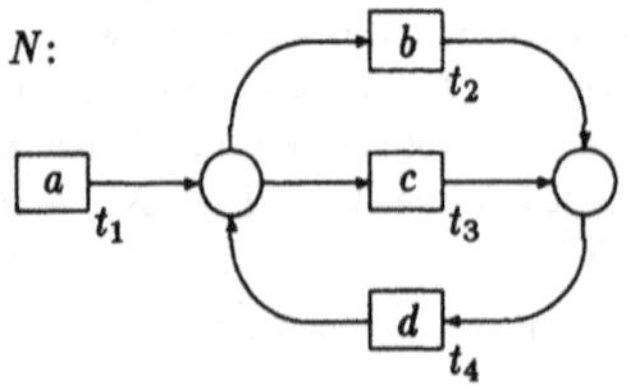

Figure 1: Petri net for the proof of lemma 5

Definition 7 Let N be a Petri net and $\mathcal{E} = \{E_1, E_2, \ldots, E_k\}$, $k \in \mathbb{N}^+$, a set of anchorsets of transitions, $E_i \subseteq T$. For $i \in \{1, 1', 2, 2', 3, 4\}$ the *transitional i-behaviour* of $(N, \mathcal{E})$ is given by $\mathrm{K}^i_\omega(N, \mathcal{E}) = \{h(v) \in X^\omega \mid v \in \mathrm{F}_\omega(N) \text{ and } v \text{ is } i\text{-successful for } \mathcal{E}\}$.
The corresponding *classes of languages* are $\mathcal{K}^i_\omega$.

In [Carstensen, Valk 85] it was shown:

Lemma 3

$$\mathcal{K}^{1'}_\omega \subset \mathcal{K}^1_\omega = \mathcal{K}^{2'}_\omega \subset \mathcal{K}^2_\omega = \mathcal{K}^3_\omega = \mathcal{K}^4_\omega$$

Lemma 4

$$\mathcal{K}^1_\omega = \mathcal{L}_\omega$$

There are no further inclusions between the classes $\mathcal{K}^i_\omega$ *and* $\mathcal{L}^i_\omega$.

The proofs are given in [Valk 83], but one proof is not correct. The language which should be a counter example for $\mathcal{K}^1_\omega \not\subseteq \mathcal{L}^1_\omega$ is no counter example, but the mentioned idea leads to another example. We will give the proof here, since in the deterministic case we will refer to it.

Lemma 5

$$\mathcal{K}^1_\omega \not\subseteq \mathcal{L}^1_\omega$$

Proof: Take the net N in figure 1 with the language $L = \mathrm{K}^1_\omega(N, \{\{t_3\}\})$.

For every $n \in \mathbb{N}^+$ the word $a^n c b^{n-1} d^n (b^n d^n)^\omega$ is element of L. The language L cannot be described by a net N' without anchorsets, otherwise also a^ω is in the language of N', i. e. $L \notin \mathcal{L}_\omega$.

Suppose there is a net N' and a set of anchorsets $\mathcal{D}'$ with $L = \mathrm{L}^1_\omega(N', \mathcal{D}')$. Then $L = \mathrm{L}^1_\omega(N', \{D'\})$ for $D' = \{m \mid \exists D \in \mathcal{D}': m \in D\}$, since only an arbitrary marking of the anchorsets must be reached.

For all $d' \in D'$ we can determine the length, so that in a sequence consisting only of transitions labelled with a, starting from d', two markings must be in the relation greater or equal, i. e. $len(d') = \min\left\{ l \in \mathbb{N}^+ \;\middle|\; \begin{array}{l} \forall v \in T^*, h(v) \in a^*, |v| \geq l: \\ \exists i, j \in \mathbb{N}^+, i < j \leq l : \delta(v, d')(i) \leq \delta(v, d')(j) \end{array} \right\}$. Let $len = \max\{len(d') \mid d' \in D'\}$.

Since the anchorset is finite, two different words of the described form must reach the same marking in D'. Let this be the words $v = a^i c b^{i-1} d^i (b^i d^i)^\omega$ and $w = a^j c b^{j-1} d^j (b^j d^j)^\omega$, with $i, j \in \mathbb{N}^+$ and $j - i > len$. Then for a marking $d' \in D'$ partitions $v_1 v_2 = v$ and $w_1 w_2 = w$ exist with $m_0 \; (v_1\rangle \; d' \; (v_2\rangle$ and $m_0 \; (w_1\rangle \; d' \; (w_2\rangle$.

If $h(w_1) \in a^*$ and w_2 starts with at least len transitions labelled with a, then also a^ω would be 1-successful. Otherwise the word $h(v_1 w_2)$ is 1-successful. Both words are not in the language L, hence we have a contradiction.

Theorem 2 *The figure 2 shows all inclusions between the mentioned classes. There are no more inclusions between these classes with the exception of those resulting from transitivity.*

In [Carstensen 82] it was shown that every transitional 2-behaviour can be described as the ω-language of a λ-net. Note it was settled that an infinite sequence of λ-transitions is mapped on the empty word, i. e. it is no word of an ω-language. The proof uses the fact that only finitely many λ-transitions may follow each other, hence at least one other transition must appear infinitely often. With a transformation of the net one can ensure that this also holds for a certain transition.

Theorem 3

$$\mathcal{K}^2_\omega \subset \mathcal{L}_{\omega\lambda}$$

With the same ideas as for Petri net languages of finite words it could be shown that this inclusion is proper.

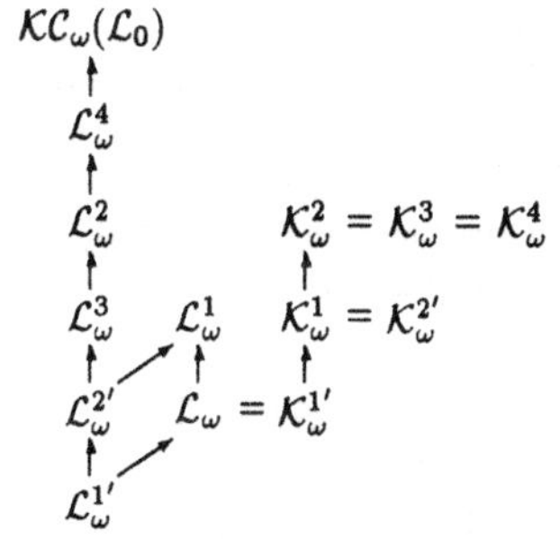

Figure 2: Hierarchy of the i-behaviours of Petri nets

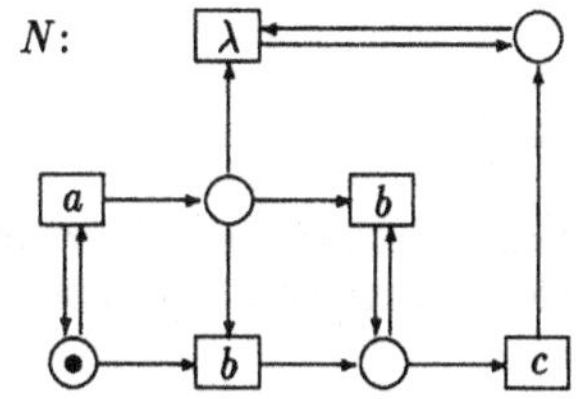

Figure 3: A deterministic net for the proof of lemma 6

3 Comparing deterministic and nondeterministic Petri nets

The deterministic Petri nets were introduced in [Vidal–Naquet 81] and the classes of languages of these nets were compared with the known classes.

Definition 8 Let N be a Petri net, N is called *deterministic*, if
$\forall t, t' \in T : \forall m \in R(N, m_0) : [(m\ (t\rangle \text{ and } m\ (t'\rangle\ ) \Rightarrow (h(t) \neq h(t') \text{ or } t = t')]$.
A λ-net N is called *deterministic*, if
$\forall t, t' \in T : \forall m \in R(N, m_0) : [(m\ (t\rangle \text{ and } m\ (t'\rangle\ ) \Rightarrow [(h(t) \neq h(t') \text{ or } t = t') \text{ and } (h(t) = \lambda \Rightarrow t = t')]]$.
The classes of languages of deterministic Petri nets will be denoted by $\mathcal{L}_{\text{dt}}$, $\mathcal{L}_{\text{0dt}}$, $\mathcal{L}_{\lambda\text{dt}}$, $\mathcal{L}_{0\lambda\text{dt}}$, $\mathcal{L}_{\omega\text{dt}}$, $\mathcal{L}_{\omega\lambda\text{dt}}$, $\mathcal{L}^i_{\omega\text{dt}}$, $\mathcal{L}^i_{\omega\lambda\text{dt}}$, $\mathcal{K}^i_{\omega\text{dt}}$, and $\mathcal{K}^i_{\omega\lambda\text{dt}}$, .

In deterministic nets between two transitions not labelled by λ only a certain number of λ-transitions may appear. Hence it is not difficult to transform an arbitrary net into a λ-free net by introducing new transitions for every possibility of sequences of λ-transitions ending with a labelled transition.

Theorem 4

$$\mathcal{L}_{\text{dt}} = \mathcal{L}_{\lambda\text{dt}}$$

In [Vidal–Naquet 82] this equality was also claimed for deterministic Petri nets with terminal markings, i. e. $\mathcal{L}_{\text{0dt}} = \mathcal{L}_{0\lambda\text{dt}}$. But this is not correct, since in a λ-net unbounded many λ-transitions may appear at the end of a firing sequence.

Lemma 6

$$\mathcal{L}_{\text{0dt}} \subset \mathcal{L}_{0\lambda\text{dt}}$$

Proof: We only have to show the inequality of the classes. Consider the language $L = \{a^n b^m c \mid n, m \in \mathbb{N}^+ : n \geq m\}$. The net in figure 3 shows that $L = \mathrm{L}_0(N, \{(0,0,0,1)\})$. N is deterministic, since the λ-transition may appear only at the end of firing sequences, hence $L \in \mathcal{L}_{0\lambda\text{dt}}$.
Suppose $L \in \mathcal{L}_{\text{0dt}}$, i. e., there is a λ-free Petri net N' and a finite anchorset D', with $L = \mathrm{L}_0(N', D')$. Every word $a^n b^n c$, $n \in \mathbb{N}^+$, is a word of L with a unique firing sequence in N'. Lemma 1 ensures that there is a $n \in \mathbb{N}^+$ with two markings m_1 and m_2 so that

m_0 $(a^q\rangle$ m_1 $(a^r\rangle$ m_2 $(b^n c\rangle$ d, for $d \in D'$, $q, r \in \mathbb{N}^+ : q + r = n$ and $m_1 \leq m_2$. (We only consider names of firing sequences since in deterministic nets the corresponding firing sequence is determined.)
For all $i \in \mathbb{N}^+$ the sequence $a^q (a^r)^i b^n c$ must lead to a terminal marking. There are only finitely many terminal markings, hence for all i it must be the same marking, i. e., the sequence a^r may not change the marking in the net N'. Hence it holds for a marking m, m_0 $(a^q\rangle$ m $(a^r\rangle$ m. But now the subsequence a^r may be omitted and it follows m_0 $(a^q b^n c\rangle$ d, $d \in D$, i. e. $a^q b^n c \in \mathrm{L}_0(N', D')$. This is a contradiction to the definition of L since $q < n$.

The next lemma was originally proved in [Vidal–Naquet 82]:

Lemma 7 *$\mathcal{L}_{\mathrm{dt}}$, $\mathcal{L}_{0\lambda\mathrm{dt}}$, and $\mathcal{L}_{0\lambda\mathrm{dt}}$ are not closed under union.*

Proof: In [Carstensen 87] it was shown for some $L1, L2 \in \mathcal{L}_{\mathrm{dt}}$ that $L1 \cup L2 =$
$L = \{w_1 w_2 \mid w_1 \in \{a, b\}^*, w_2 \in c^* \text{ and } [(|w_2|_c \leq |w_1|_a) \vee (|w_2|_c \leq |w_1|_b))\} \notin \mathcal{L}_{\mathrm{dt}}$. The same was shown for some $L1', L2' \in \mathcal{L}_{0\mathrm{dt}}$ that $L1' \cup L2' =$
$L' = \{w_1 w_2 \mid w_1 \in \{a, b\}^*, w_2 \in c^* \text{ and } (|w_2|_c = |w_1|_a) \vee (|w_2|_c = |w_1|_b)\} \notin \mathcal{L}_{0\mathrm{dt}}$.

Other closure properties of deterministic nets were studied in [Pelz 87]. These classes are not closed under most operations, with exception of the intersection.

4 *i*-behaviour of deterministic nets

Before the infinite behaviour, i. e. the (transitional) i-behaviour, of deterministic nets will be investigated, we will have a look on the corresponding classes for deterministic finite automata ([Hossley 72] and [Cohen, Gold 78]).

Theorem 5 *For $i \in \{1, 1', 2', 3\}$: $\mathcal{R}^i_{\omega\mathrm{dt}} = \mathcal{R}^i_\omega$ and $\mathcal{R}^2_{\omega\mathrm{dt}} \subset \mathcal{R}^2_\omega$*

In the case of noncomplete automata the following results hold:

Theorem 6

$$\begin{array}{ccccc} & & \mathcal{R}^2_{\omega\mathrm{dt}} & \subset & \mathcal{R}^3_{\omega\mathrm{dt}} \\ & & \cup & & \cup \\ \mathcal{R}^{1'}_{\omega\mathrm{dt}} & \subset & \mathcal{R}^1_{\omega\mathrm{dt}} & \subset & \mathcal{R}^{2'}_{\omega\mathrm{dt}} \end{array}$$

The classes of the 1- and of the 1′-behaviour are again incomparable if the automata must not only be deterministic but also complete, the other relationships will not change.

Corresponding investigations were made in [Cohen, Gold 78] for deterministic push-down automata. Here nondeterminism is of course more powerful than determinism, but there were the same relationships as shown in theorem 6. The classes of the 1- and of the 1′-behaviour are incomparable if only "continuable" push-down automata are allowed. This means that for every infinite input there is a computation in the push-down automata.

For the infinite behaviour of Petri nets we can show that λ-transitions can be eliminated. The same ideas with which $\mathcal{L}_{\lambda\mathrm{dt}} = \mathcal{L}_{\mathrm{dt}}$ was proved can also be applied here. The phenomenon that arbitrarily many λ-transitions may follow each other can only happen at the end of a firing sequence, but an infinite sequence never ends.

Theorem 7

$$\mathcal{L}_{\omega\lambda\mathrm{dt}} = \mathcal{L}_{\omega\mathrm{dt}}, \quad \mathcal{L}^i_{\omega\lambda\mathrm{dt}} = \mathcal{L}^i_{\omega\mathrm{dt}}, \quad \mathcal{K}^i_{\omega\lambda\mathrm{dt}} = \mathcal{K}^i_{\omega\mathrm{dt}}$$

This theorem allows us to restrict our investigations of ω-behaviour of deterministic Petri nets on λ-free nets.

Lemma 8 *For $i \in \{1, 2, 2', 3, 4\}$: $\mathcal{L}^i_{\omega\mathrm{dt}}$ is not closed under union.*

Proof: Consider the language L' of the proof of lemma 7. For all $i \in \{1, 2, 2', 3, 4\}$ the language $L'.d^\omega$ can be described as the union of two deterministic i-behaviours. If the classes $\mathcal{L}^i_{\omega\mathrm{dt}}$ would be closed under union, one could show that L' is a deterministic language of a net with terminal markings.

This shows that nondeterminism is more powerful, with the exception of the 1′-behaviour.

Theorem 8

$$\text{a) } \mathcal{L}^{1'}_{\omega\mathrm{dt}} = \mathcal{L}^{1'}_\omega, \quad \text{b) } \textit{For } i \in \{1, 2, 2', 3, 4\} : \mathcal{L}^i_{\omega\mathrm{dt}} \subset \mathcal{L}^i_\omega$$

Proof: a) The classes of 1′-behaviours of nets and finite automata are equivalent. It is easy to see that a deterministic automaton corresponds to a deterministic Petri net.
b) The classes $\mathcal{L}^i_\omega$ are closed under finite union, not so the classes $\mathcal{L}^i_{\omega dt}$.

The following inclusions are valid between the classes of deterministic behaviours of nets:

Lemma 9

$$\text{a) } \mathcal{L}^{1'}_{\omega dt} \subseteq \mathcal{L}_{\omega dt}, \quad \text{b) } \mathcal{L}^{1'}_{\omega dt} \subseteq \mathcal{L}^{2}_{\omega dt}, \quad \text{c) } \mathcal{L}^{1'}_{\omega dt} \subseteq \mathcal{L}^{2'}_{\omega dt}, \quad \text{d) } \mathcal{L}_{\omega dt} \subseteq \mathcal{L}^{1}_{\omega dt}, \quad \text{e) } \mathcal{L}^{2'}_{\omega dt} \subseteq \mathcal{L}^{3}_{\omega dt}$$

$$\text{f) } \mathcal{L}^{1'}_{\omega dt} \subseteq \mathcal{L}_{\omega dt}, \quad \text{g) } \mathcal{L}^{2}_{\omega dt} \subseteq \mathcal{KC}_\omega(\mathcal{L}_{0dt}), \quad \text{h) } \mathcal{L}^{3}_{\omega dt} \subseteq \mathcal{KC}_\omega(\mathcal{L}_{0dt})$$

Proof: a) – c) Obviously the 1′-behaviour of a deterministic finite automaton is also the ω-language or the i-behaviour of a deterministic Petri net.
d) Choose the set with the initial marking as the anchorset, then $\mathrm{L}_\omega(N) = \mathrm{L}^1_\omega(N, m_0)$.
e) Let $L = \mathrm{L}^{2'}_\omega(N, \mathcal{D})$, then $L = \mathrm{L}^3_\omega(N, \{D' \mid \exists D \in \mathcal{D}: \emptyset \neq D' \subseteq D\})$.
f) Let $L = \mathrm{L}^2_\omega(N, \mathcal{D})$, then $L = \mathrm{L}^4_\omega(N, \{\{d\} \mid \exists D \in \mathcal{D}: d \in D\})$.
g) $\mathcal{KC}_\omega(\mathcal{L}_{0dt})$ is closed under finite union by its definition. Hence it is sufficient to consider a language of the form $L = \mathrm{L}^2_\omega(N, \{\{d\}\})$. Then $L = A.B^\omega$ with $A = \mathrm{L}_0(N, \{d\})$ and $B = \mathrm{L}_0(N_d, \{d\})$, where N_d is the net N with the new initial marking d. If d can be reached in N then N_d is deterministic, too. Otherwise the language L is empty and can easily be represented. Hence $L \in \mathcal{KC}_\omega(\mathcal{L}_{0dt})$.
h) Again we only have to consider a language of the form $L = \mathrm{L}^3_\omega(N, \{D\})$. Let $d \in D$, the language L can be written as $L = A.B^\omega$, where $A = \mathrm{L}_0(N, \{d\})$ and B is the set of all words of firing sequences starting and ending in d, visiting every marking of D. The language B is the behaviour of a finite automaton, hence it is also the terminal language of a deterministic net. Thus $L \in \mathcal{KC}_\omega(\mathcal{L}_{0dt})$.

In the following we will show that there are no more inclusions between these classes. The question if the class $\mathcal{L}^4_{\omega dt}$ is not in $\mathcal{KC}_\omega(\mathcal{L}_{0dt})$ will remain a conjecture. First we will look at cases which are similar to the nondeterministic case. In several proofs it will be shown that a behaviour cannot even be represented by a nondeterministic net.

The next lemmata will show that the hierarchy is splitted in more branches than in the nondeterministic case.

Lemma 10

$$\text{a) } \mathcal{L}_{\omega dt} \not\subseteq \mathcal{KC}_\omega(\mathcal{L}_{0dt}), \quad \text{b) } \mathcal{L}_{\omega dt} \not\subseteq \mathcal{L}^4_{\omega dt}, \quad \text{c) } \mathcal{L}^1_{\omega dt} \not\subseteq \mathcal{L}_{\omega dt}, \quad \text{d) } \mathcal{L}^2_{\omega dt} \not\subseteq \mathcal{L}^1_{\omega dt}, \quad \text{e) } \mathcal{L}^2_{\omega dt} \not\subseteq \mathcal{L}^3_{\omega dt},$$

$$\text{f) } \mathcal{L}^3_{\omega dt} \not\subseteq \mathcal{L}^{2'}_{\omega dt}, \quad \text{g) } \mathcal{L}^4_{\omega dt} \not\subseteq \mathcal{L}^2_{\omega dt}$$

Proof: a), b) By theorem 2 it holds $\mathcal{L}^4_\omega \subseteq \mathcal{KC}_\omega(\mathcal{L}_{0dt})$. Additionally [Valk 83] proved that $\mathcal{L}_\omega \not\subseteq \mathcal{KC}_\omega(\mathcal{L}_0)$ with a language having a not semilinear Parikh image. He used a net for this language which was deterministic.
c) It is easy to see that the language $L = a^*bc^\omega$ can be described as the 1-behaviour of a deterministic finite automaton, hence $L \in \mathcal{L}^1_{\omega dt}$. If there would be a net N' with $L = \mathrm{L}_\omega(N')$, then also a^ω would be a possible word in N'.
d), e) We may use the corresponding proof in [Valk 83], since the considered language $L = \{w \in \{a,b\}^\omega \mid \overset{\infty}{\exists} i \in \mathbb{N}^+: |w[i]|_a = |w[i]|_b \text{ and } \forall j \in \mathbb{N}^+ |w[j]|_a \geq |w[j]|_b\}$ has a deterministic net. Thus it holds $L \in \mathcal{L}^2_{\omega dt}$, $L \notin \mathcal{L}^1_\omega$, and $L \notin \mathcal{L}^3_\omega$.
f) In [Valk 83] it was shown that for the language $L = (a^*b)^\omega$ that $L \notin \mathcal{L}^1_\omega$. With $\mathcal{L}^{2'}_\omega \subseteq \mathcal{L}^1_\omega$, L cannot be element of $\mathcal{L}^{2'}_\omega$. But L is the 3-behaviour of a finite automaton, thus $L \in \mathcal{L}^3_\omega$.
g) In [Carstensen 87] the inequality was shown for the nondeterministic case with a deterministic net.

The following lemmata show differences to the nondeterministic case, where we had inclusions.

Lemma 11

$$\text{a) } \mathcal{L}^{2'}_{\omega dt} \not\subseteq \mathcal{L}^1_{\omega dt}, \quad \text{b) } \mathcal{L}^{2'}_{\omega dt} \not\subseteq \mathcal{L}^4_{\omega dt}$$

Proof: Take net N from figure 4 and the anchorset $D = \{(0),(1)\}$. Let $L = \mathrm{L}^{2'}_{\omega dt}(N, \{D\})$, i. e. $L = \{w \in \{a,b\}^* \mid \forall i \in \mathbb{N}^+: |w[i]|_a \geq |w[i]|_b \text{ and } |w|_a = |w|_b\}.(ab)^\omega$. The word $w = (ab)^\omega$ is element of L.
a) Suppose $L \in \mathcal{L}^1_{\omega dt}$, i. e. $L = \mathrm{L}^1_\omega(N', \mathcal{D}')$. For w a partition $w = w_1\, w_2$ must exist with $m_0\ (w_1\rangle\ d\ (w_2\rangle$, where $d \in D'$ for a $D' \in \mathcal{D}'$. But also the word $w_1\, a^n b^n\, w_2$ is element of L for all $n \in \mathbb{N}$. Hence the word $w_1 a^\omega$ must be 1-successful, too, since a corresponding firing sequence is possible and a marking of $\mathcal{D}$ will be reached. This is a contradiction to the definition of L.

N: 

Figure 4: Petri net for the proof of lemma 11

b) Suppose $L \in \mathcal{L}^4_{\omega dt}$, i. e. $L = \mathrm{L}^4_\omega(N', \mathcal{D}')$. For $w \in L$ there must be a partition $w = w_1 w_2 w_3$ and an anchorset $D \in \mathcal{D}'$, $D = \{d_1, d_2, \ldots, d_k\}$, so that $m_0 \ \langle w_1 \rangle \ d_1 \ \langle w_2 \rangle \ d_k \ \langle w_3 \rangle$ and in w_2 all markings of D will be reached, thus $w_2 = v_1 v_2 \ldots v_{k-1}$ with $d_1 \ \langle v_1 \rangle \ d_2 \ \langle v_2 \rangle \ldots \ \langle v_{k-1} \rangle \ d_k$. Also the sequence $w' = w_1 w_2 aabbw_3$ is element of L, thus also for this sequence there must be a partition and an anchorset, as described above, i. e. $m_0 \ \langle w'_1 \rangle \ d'_1 \ \langle w'_2 \rangle \ d'_{k'} \ \langle w'_3 \rangle$, where in w'_2 all markings of some $D' \in \mathcal{D}'$ will be reached at least once. Without loss of generality we may demand that $w'_1 > w_1 w_2$.
If $D \neq D'$, we start this consideration again with the sequence $w'' = w'_1 w'_2 aabbw'_3$. There are only finitely many anchorsets, hence some time two anchorsets must be the same. Let this be the set D''. Then $v = \underbrace{abab\ldots}_{v_1} v_2 \, aabb \underbrace{\ldots}_{v_3} v_4 \underbrace{\ldots}_{v_5}$ with $m_0 \ \langle v_1 \rangle \ d_1 \ \langle v_2 \rangle \ d_k \ \langle aabbv_3 \rangle \ d_1 \ \langle v_4 \rangle \ d_k \ \langle v_5 \rangle$, in v_2 and v_4 all markings of D'' will be reached. But then also $v_1(v_2 aabbv_3)^\omega$ would be 4-successful. This is a contradiction to the definition of L.

5 Transitional i-behaviour of deterministic nets

Just as for the i-behaviour the classes of the transitional i-behaviour of deterministic nets will be compared. We will see that fewer inclusions are valid than in the nondeterministic case. But the relationships among the classes will be the same as for deterministic noncomplete automata or deterministic push-down automata.

First we will compare the deterministic case with the unrestricted case.

Lemma 12 *For all $i \in \{1, 1', 2, 2', 3, 4\}$: $\mathcal{K}^i_{\omega dt}$ is not closed under union.*

Proof: Similar as in the proof of lemma 8 this problem can be reduced to the proof for the languages of finite words. Take the language L from the proof of lemma 7. For all $i \in \{1, 1', 2, 2', 3, 4\}$ the language $L.d^\omega$ can be described as the union of two transitional i-behaviours. Remember that L includes all prefixes of itself. If there would be a net N' with $L.d^\omega$ as its transitional i-behaviour, L could be described as the finite behaviour of a deterministic net.

With this lemma it is obvious, that the transitional i-behaviour is more powerful in the nondeterministic case.

Lemma 13 *For all $i \in \{1, 1', 2, 2', 3, 4\}$: $\mathcal{K}^i_{\omega dt} \subset \mathcal{K}^i_\omega$*

Comparing the classes of transitional i-behaviour we start with inclusions which were already shown in the nondeterministic case. The proofs are often more complicate, since the deterministic transitional i-behaviours are not closed under union. In general it is not sufficient to look at only one anchorset.

Lemma 14

$$\mathcal{L}_{\omega dt} = \mathcal{K}^{1'}_{\omega dt}$$

Proof: 1) For $L \in \mathcal{L}_{\omega dt}$: Let $L = \mathrm{L}_\omega(N)$, then $L = \mathrm{K}^{1'}_\omega(N, \{T\})$.
2) For $L \in \mathcal{K}^{1'}_{\omega dt}$: Let $L = \mathrm{K}^{1'}_\omega(N, \mathcal{E})$. Build a new net N' in the following way: The places consist of the old places S, and a place $s_{\tilde{\mathcal{E}}}$ for each set $\tilde{\mathcal{E}}$ with $\emptyset \neq \tilde{\mathcal{E}} \subseteq \mathcal{E}$. These new places will act as some kind of a finite control of the N', showing from which anchorsets the transitions of a firing sequence may be chosen, so that a 1'-successful continuation is still possible. At the initial marking on the places of S there lies the old marking and on $s_\mathcal{E}$ one token. The transitions consist of copies of the old transitions, which only differ with respect to the new places. For each place $s_{\tilde{\mathcal{E}}}$ take a set of transitions $T_{\tilde{\mathcal{E}}} = \{t_{\tilde{\mathcal{E}}} \mid \exists E \in \tilde{\mathcal{E}} : t \in E\}$. For each transition $t_{\tilde{\mathcal{E}}} \in T_{\tilde{\mathcal{E}}}$ construct the set $\tilde{\mathcal{E}}'(t) = \{E \mid E \in \tilde{\mathcal{E}} \wedge t \in E\}$. If this set is empty, eliminate the transition from N'. Every transition $t_{\tilde{\mathcal{E}}} \in T_{\tilde{\mathcal{E}}}$ has the place $s_{\tilde{\mathcal{E}}}$ as a precondition and it puts a token on $s_{\tilde{\mathcal{E}}'(t)}$.
It is easy to see that a firing sequence v is possible, iff there is at least one anchorset, so that v consists of copies of transitions from this anchorset. The net N' is deterministic, since at any time exactly one place $s_{\tilde{\mathcal{E}}}$ is marked and hence always only one set of copies of the original transitions is activated.

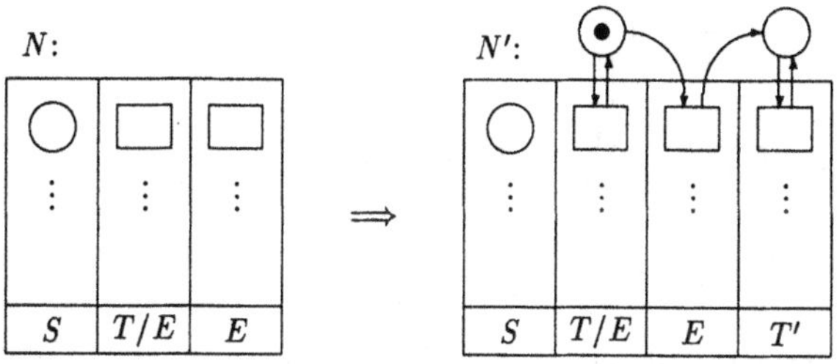

Figure 5: Transformation for the proof of lemma 15 e), f)

Lemma 15

$$\text{a) } \mathcal{L}_{\omega\text{dt}} \subseteq \mathcal{K}^1_{\omega\text{dt}}, \quad \text{b) } \mathcal{K}^{2'}_{\omega\text{dt}} \subseteq \mathcal{K}^3_{\omega\text{dt}}, \quad \text{c) } \mathcal{K}^4_{\omega\text{dt}} \subseteq \mathcal{K}^3_{\omega\text{dt}}, \quad \text{d) } \mathcal{K}^2_{\omega\text{dt}} \subseteq \mathcal{K}^4_{\omega\text{dt}},$$

$$\text{e) } \mathcal{K}^1_{\omega\text{dt}} \subseteq \mathcal{K}^{2'}_{\omega\text{dt}}, \quad \text{f) } \mathcal{K}^1_{\omega\text{dt}} \subseteq \mathcal{K}^2_{\omega\text{dt}}$$

Proof: a) Let $L = \mathrm{L}_\omega(N)$, then $L = \mathrm{K}^1_\omega(N, \{T\})$.

b) Let $L = \mathrm{K}^{2'}_\omega(N, \mathcal{E})$, then $L = \mathrm{K}^3_\omega(N, \{E' \mid \exists E \in \mathcal{E}: \emptyset \neq E' \subseteq E\})$, i. e., the set of the transitions appearing infinitely often must be a subset of an original anchorset.

c) Let $L = \mathrm{K}^4_\omega(N, \mathcal{E})$, then $L = \mathrm{K}^3_\omega(N, \{E' \mid \exists E \in \mathcal{E}: E \subseteq E'\})$, i. e., an original anchorset is subset of the transitions appearing infinitely often.

d) Let $L = \mathrm{K}^2_\omega(N, \mathcal{E})$, it holds $L = \mathrm{K}^2_\omega(N, \{\{t \mid \exists E' \in \mathcal{E}: t \in E\}\})$. Then $L = \mathrm{K}^4(N, \{\{t\} \mid t \in E\})$, i. e., at least one transition of E appears infinitely often.

e), f) Let $L = \mathrm{K}^1_\omega(N, \mathcal{E})$, then $L = \mathrm{K}^1_\omega(N, \{\{t \mid \exists E' \in \mathcal{E}: t \in E'\}\})$, since for the transitional i-behaviour it is sufficient that only some transition of some anchorset will be fired once. Construct a net N' according to the figure 5, where T' consists of copies of the original transitions, which have the same behaviour with respect to the places of S. Then $L = \mathrm{L}^i_\omega(N, \{T'\})$ for $i \in \{2, 2'\}$.

Lemma 16

$$\mathcal{K}^4_{\omega\text{dt}} \subseteq \mathcal{K}^2_{\omega\text{dt}}$$

Proof: Let $L \in \mathcal{K}^4_{\omega\text{dt}}$, i. e. $L = \mathrm{K}^4_\omega(N, \{E_1, E_2, \ldots, E_k\})$. Construct the net N' from N in the following way. We use similar ideas as in the proof of lemma 14 ($\mathcal{K}^{1'}_{\omega\text{dt}} \subseteq \mathcal{L}_{\omega\text{dt}}$).

For the places in N' take all places of N and additionally for each subset of transitions, which is no anchorset, a new place $s_{\hat{T}}$, $\hat{T} \in \wp(T)/\mathcal{E}$. As the transitions take for every place $s_{\hat{T}}$ copies of the transitions T, these sets will be denoted by $T_{\hat{T}} = \{t_1^{\hat{T}}, t_2^{\hat{T}}, \ldots, t_n^{\hat{T}}\}$. Transition $t_i^{\hat{T}}$ acts like the original transition t_i with respect to the places of S. Additionally it takes a token from place $s_{\hat{T}}$ and puts one on $s_{\hat{T}'}$, where $\hat{T}' = \hat{T} \cup \{t_i\}$, if $\hat{T} \cup \{t_i\} \notin \mathcal{E}$ and $\hat{T}' = \emptyset$ otherwise. The initial marking remains unchanged on the places of S and a token will be on $s_\emptyset$.

In N' and N the same words are possible, since always exactly one of the places $s_{\hat{T}}$ contains a token, hence exactly the transitions of the set $T_{\hat{T}}$ are activated. These are copies of transitions from N. This also shows that N' is deterministic.

A token on place $s_{\hat{T}}$ means that copies of all transitions from $\hat{T}$ have fired after the last time $s_\emptyset$ was marked. Between two markings, in which $s_\emptyset$ has a token, the copies of all transitions of an anchorset must have fired. Since there are only finitely many different anchorsets, we only have to ensure that infinitely often on $s_\emptyset$ lies a token, to get the language L. This will be indicated by the firing of transitions of the set $T_\emptyset$, hence $L = \mathrm{K}^2_\omega(N', \{T_\emptyset\})$.

The following lemmata show nonexisting inclusions. As far as possible we will use examples of [Valk 83] and [Carstensen, Valk 85].

Lemma 17

$$\text{a) } \mathcal{K}^1_{\omega\text{dt}} \not\subseteq \mathcal{L}_{\omega\text{dt}}, \quad \text{b) } \mathcal{K}^2_{\omega\text{dt}} \not\subseteq \mathcal{K}^{2'}_{\omega\text{dt}}, \quad \text{c) } \mathcal{K}^{2'}_{\omega\text{dt}} \not\subseteq \mathcal{K}^2_{\omega\text{dt}}$$

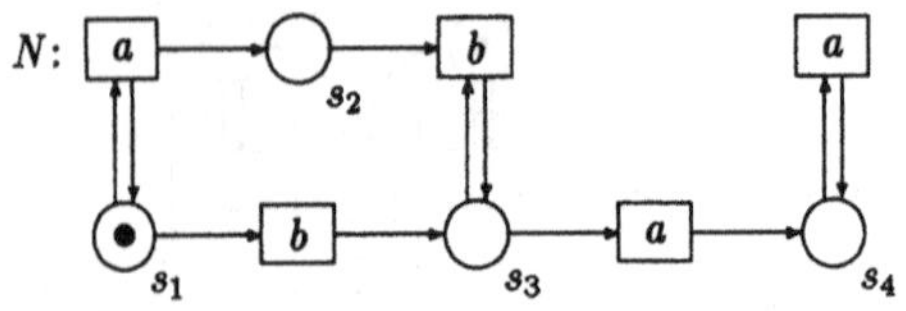

Figure 6: Petri net for the proof of lemma 18 a), b), c)

Proof: a) The language $L = a^*b^\omega$ is the 1-behaviour of a deterministic finite automaton, hence it is also the transitional 1-behaviour of a deterministic net. But $a^*b^\omega \notin \mathcal{L}_\omega$, because otherwise also a^ω would be possible.
b) The language $L = (a^*b)^\omega$ is the 2-behaviour of a deterministic finite automaton, hence it is also the transitional 2-behaviour of a deterministic net. But in [Valk 83] it was shown that $a^*b^\omega \notin \mathcal{L}_\omega$.
c) Consider the language $L = \{a,b\}^*.b^\omega$. For a net N with two transitions t_1 and t_2, $h(t_1) = a$ and $h(t_2) = b$, without places it holds: N is deterministic and $L = \mathrm{K}^{2'}_\omega(N, \{\{t_2\}\})$.
Suppose $L \in \mathcal{K}^2_{\omega\mathrm{dt}}$, then there is a net N', so that $L = \mathrm{K}^2_\omega(N', \mathcal{E}')$ and hence also $L = \mathrm{K}^2_\omega(N', E')$ for $E' = \{t \mid \exists E \in \mathcal{E}' : t \in E\}$. Starting from the initial marking m_0 we build a sequence of markings $\mu = m_0, m_1, m_2, \ldots \infty$ in the following way:
The sequence $w = b^\omega$ is 2-successful, i. e., there is a partition of $w = w_1 w_2$, so that some transition of E' appears in $w_1 \in b^+$. Then let m_1 be defined by $m_0\ (w_1\rangle\ m_1$. Now consider the sequence $w_1 ab^\omega \in L$. The marking m_2 is defined by $m_0\ (w_1\rangle\ m_1\ (aw_2\rangle\ m_2$, where some transition of E' appears in $w_2 \in b^+$. For each m_i consider the sequence $m_0\ (w_1\rangle\ m_1\ (aw_2\rangle\ \ldots\ m_{i-1}\ (aw_i\rangle\ m_i$, where some transition of E' appears in $w_i \in b^+$.
By the lemma of Dickson [Dickson 13] there must be two markings m_i and m_j in μ, with $i, j \in \mathbb{N}^+$, $i < j$ and $m_i \le m_j$, i. e. $m_0 \underbrace{(w_1\rangle \ldots m_i}_{v_1} \underbrace{(aw_{i+1}\rangle \ldots m_j}_{v_2}$, $m_i \le m_j$. Then also the sequence $v = v_1(v_2)^\omega$ is possible and 2-successful, since a transition of E' appears in w_{i+1}. But $h(v) \notin L$, because a appears infinitely often.

6 The hierarchy of deterministic (transitional) i-behaviour

In this section the relationship between the classes of the transitional i-behaviour and the i-behaviour, $\mathcal{L}^i_{\omega\mathrm{dt}}$, will be investigated and a hierarchy for all deterministic classes will be established. We will see that there are no further inclusions, just like in the nondeterministic case. Again we will use ideas of proof for the nondeterministic cases, but we have to inspect more cases.

Lemma 18

$$\text{a) } \mathcal{L}^1_{\omega\mathrm{dt}} \not\subseteq \mathcal{K}^3_{\omega\mathrm{dt}}, \quad \text{b) } \mathcal{L}^{2'}_{\omega\mathrm{dt}} \not\subseteq \mathcal{K}^3_{\omega\mathrm{dt}}, \quad \text{c) } \mathcal{L}^2_{\omega\mathrm{dt}} \not\subseteq \mathcal{K}^3_{\omega\mathrm{dt}}, \quad \text{d) } \mathcal{K}^1_{\omega\mathrm{dt}} \not\subseteq \mathcal{L}^1_{\omega\mathrm{dt}}$$

Proof: a), b), c) In [Valk 83] it was shown that the language $L = \{a^i b^i a^\omega \mid i \in \mathbb{N}^+\}$ is not a transitional 2-behaviour, i. e. $L \notin \mathcal{K}^2_\omega = \mathcal{K}^3_\omega$, hence more than ever $L \notin \mathcal{K}^3_{\omega\mathrm{dt}}$. In figure 6 a deterministic net N is given so that for $D = \{0,0,0,1\}$ it holds: $L = \mathrm{L}^1_\omega(N, \{D\}) = \mathrm{L}^{2'}_\omega(N, \{D\}) = \mathrm{L}^2_\omega(N, \{D\})$.
d) The net for the nondeterministic case in the proof of lemma 5 is deterministic.

Now we are able to establish the hierarchy.

Theorem 9 *The figure 7 shows all inclusions between the deterministic i-behaviour. The nonexistence of the inclusion between $\mathcal{L}^4_{\omega\mathrm{dt}}$ and $\mathcal{KC}_\omega(\mathcal{L}_{0\mathrm{dt}})$ can only be suggested.*

7 Conclusions

The infinite behaviour of deterministic Petri nets was investigated. The power of several definitions of infinite behaviour (i-behaviour and transitional i-behaviour) was compared with each other and with the nondeterministic case. It not only turned out that deterministic nets are less powerful than nondeterministic nets, but also that between the several classes of behaviours of nets there are less inclusions than in the

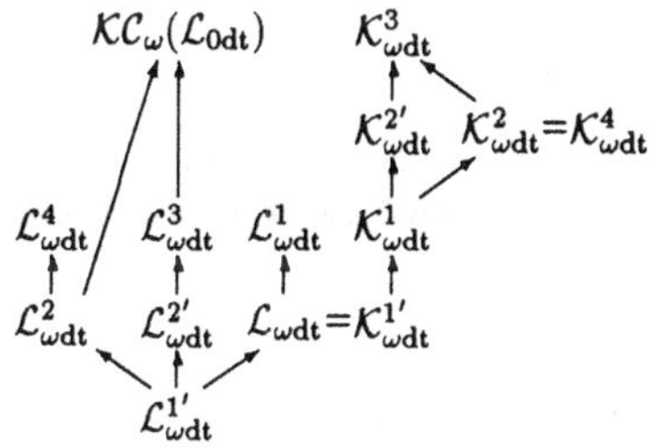

Figure 7: Hierarchy of the deterministic i-behaviour

nondeterministic case. Also the influence of λ-transitions was investigated. The power of infinite behaviours of deterministic nets is not increased if λ-transitions are allowed. In contrast it was shown that nets with these transitions are more powerful for finite behaviour with terminal markings, as well as for infinite behaviour of nondeterministic nets. An open problem for the hierarchy is the problem if $\mathcal{L}^4_{\omega dt} \subseteq \mathcal{KC}_\omega(\mathcal{L}_{0dt})$. I suggest that this inclusion does not hold.

References

[Carstensen 82] H. Carstensen: *Fairneß bei Petrinetzen mit unendlichem Verhalten*; Universität Hamburg, Fachbereich Informatik, Bericht Nr. 93, IFI–HH–B–93/82, 1982.

[Carstensen 87] H. Carstensen: *Fairneß bei nebenläufigen Systemen – Eine Untersuchung am Modell der Petrinetze*; Universität Hamburg, Fachbereich Informatik, Bericht Nr. 126, FBI–HH–B–126/87, 1987.

[Carstensen, Valk 85] H. Carstensen, R. Valk: *Infinite Behaviour and Fairness in Petri Nets*; In G. Rozenberg (ed.): *Advances in Petri Nets 1984*; Lecture Notes in Computer Science 188, (pp. 83 – 100), Springer, Berlin 1985.

[Cohen, Gold 77] R. S. Cohen, A. Y. Gold: *Theory of ω–Languages*, Part I: *Characterization of ω–Context-Free Languages*, Part II: *A Study of Various Models of ω–Type Generation and Recognition*; Journal of Computer and System Sciences 15, (pp. 169 – 208), 1977.

[Cohen, Gold 78] R. S. Cohen, A. Y. Gold: *ω-Computations on Deterministic Pushdown Machines*; Journal of Computer and System Sciences 16, (pp. 275 – 300), 1978.

[Dickson 13] L. E. Dickson: *Finiteness of the Odd Perfect and Primitive Abundant Numbers with n Distinct Prime Factors*; American Journal of Mathematics 35, (pp. 413 – 422), 1913.

[Hossley 72] R. Hossley: *Finite Tree Automata and ω–automata*; Project MAC, M. I. T., Technical Report 102, 1972.

[Landweber 69] L. H. Landweber: *Decision Problems for ω–Automata*; Mathematical System Theory 3, (pp. 376 – 384), 1969.

[McNaughton 66] R. McNaughton: *Testing and Generating Infinite Sequences by a Finite Automaton*; Information and Control 9, (pp. 521 – 530), 1966.

[Pelz 87] E. Pelz: *Closure Properties of Deterministic Petri Nets*; STACS 87, Proceedings, Lecture Notes in Computer Science 247, (pp. 371 – 382), Springer, Berlin 1987.

[Valk 83] R. Valk: *Infinite Behaviour of Petri Nets*; Theoretical Computer Science 25, (pp. 311 – 341), 1983.

[Vidal–Naquet 82] G. Vidal–Naquet: *Deterministic Languages of Petri Nets*; in *Application and Theory of Petri Nets*, Informatik Fachberichte 52, (pp. 198 – 202), Springer, Berlin 1982.

[Vidal–Naquet 81] G. Vidal–Naquet: *Réseaux de Petri déterministes*; Thèse d'Etat, Université de Paris VI, 1981.

TESTING ISOMORPHISM OF OUTERPLANAR GRAPHS IN PARALLEL

Bogdan S. Chlebus Krzysztof Diks Tomasz Radzik
Uniwersytet Warszawski, Instytut Informatyki
PKiN, VIIIp, 00-901 Warszawa, Poland

Abstract. It is shown that isomorphism of two outerplanar graphs with n vertices can be verified on CRCW PRAM in time $O(\log n)$ using n processors. This improves the previous results of Ruzzo [R] and Miller & Reif [MR] concerning parallel isomorphism of trees.

1.Introduction.

The problem of verifying graph isomorphism has for a long time drawn attention of many researchers. The sequential complexity of the problem is not even known to be polynomial. The isomorphism of certain special classes of graphs has been investigated, and efficient sequential algorithms have been developed (cf. Garey & Johnson [GJ]).

The first parallel isomorphism algorithm for a class of graphs was given by Ruzzo [R] who showed that isomorphism of trees of degree at most $\log n$ could be done in $O(\log n)$ time. This result was improved by Miller & Reif [MR] who exhibited a 0-sided randomized algorithm for testing isomorphism of trees using $O(n/\log n)$ processors, and a deterministic $O(\log n)$ time algorithm using $O(n^2 \log n)$ processors. Miller & Reif [MR] also developed a $O(\log^3 n)$ time PRAM algorithm testing isomorphism of any planar graphs.

The main result of this paper is exhibiting a deterministic parallel algorithm on ARBITRARY CRCW PRAM ([V]) testing isomorphism of outerplanar graphs in time $O(\log n)$ using n processors. Since the outerplanar graphs comprise the class of trees, this improves the previous results of Ruzzo [R] and Miller & Reif [MR].

Our approach to the isomorphism problem for outerplanar graphs is the following. First we introduce a suitable linear encoding of the graphs, which determines them uniquely up to isomorphism, and then develop an algorithm for an efficient construction of such encodings.

Thus the test for isomorphism is reduced to comparing two strings.

2. Codes

2.1 Trees

A *tree* T is a connected acyclic graph. A tree in which one vertex is distinguished as a root is a *rooted* tree. Given a rooted tree T, the notation V_T denotes the set of vertices, r_T - the root, T_v - the subtree of T rooted at v, $size_T(v)$ - the number of vertices in T_v. We omit the subscript "T" when the tree is clear from context.

An *ordered tree* D is a rooted tree with a fixed order on sons of each vertex $w \in V_D$. For an ordered tree D the *bracket structure* of a vertex is defined as follows: $bs_D(w)=()$ for a leaf w, and $bs_D(w)=(bs_D(v_1)bs_D(v_2)...bs_D(v_k))$ for w having k consecutive sons $v_1,v_2,...,v_k$. A *bracket structure of an ordered tree* D is the bracket structure of its root. The bracket structure can serve as a linear code of an ordered tree. We use the notation $code_{TREE}(D)= bs(D)= bs_D(r_D)$ for an ordered tree D. The code for T_v is often referred to as the code of v.

When considering ordering on strings we mean the following one. Let b_1 and b_2 be two strings of symbols from a linearly ordered alphabet; set $b_1 < b_2$ iff $length(b_1) < length(b_2)$ or these lengths are equal and b_1 precedes lexicographically b_2.

Fixing orders on siblings in a rooted tree T gives an ordered tree D called an *ordering of T*. D is a *canonical ordering of T* iff for each vertex w with the consequtive sons $v_1,v_2,..,v_k$ in D, the relation $bs_D(v_1) \le bs_D(v_2) \le .. \le bs_D(v_k)$ holds. It can be verified by induction on heights of trees that two rooted trees T_1 and T_2 are isomorphic iff $bs(D_1)=bs(D_2)$ for any canonical orderings D_1 and D_2 of T_1 and T_2, respectively . Define $code_{TREE}(T)$, for a rooted tree T, to be the bracket structure of any of its canonical orderings D. It follows that function $code_{TREE}$ provides a sound method of encoding for the class of rooted trees. Let T be a tree and let c_1 and c_2 be its centres (they may be equal). Selecting c_1 and c_2 as the roots of T we obtain two rooted trees T_1 and T_2, respectively. Define $code_{TREE}(T) = \min \{ code_{TREE}(T_1), code_{TREE}(T_2) \}$ as a code for the (non-rooted) tree T.

A *labeled* tree (of any kind) is a tree in which some of the vertices have attached labels. Codes for such trees are obtained as defined before with the following modification: for each labeled vertex v its label enclosed in the cubic brackets '{' and '}' is inserted just before the rightmost bracket of the code of T_v.

2.2 Certain special trees

2.2.1 C-trees

A *c-tree* T is a labeled tree in which for each vertex the set of edges incident to it is cyclically ordered. Suppose first that T is rooted. T can be converted into an ordered tree by selecting a son of each vertex v (if there is any) as the first element in the (unique) linear ordering on the set of sons of v, which is compatible with the cyclical ordering in T. We consider k ordered trees $T_1,...,T_k$ defined in this way, where k is the degree od r_T. Let $v_1,...,v_k$ be the sons of r_T. Tree T_i, for $1 \le i \le k$, is determined by selecting a son of each vertex as follows:

(1) if v is r_T then v_i is selected;

(2) if $v \ne r_T$ then the first vertex on the cycle after the one being the father of v in the rooted tree T is selected (if there is any). Define

$$\text{code}^{C}_{\text{TREE}}(T) = \min_{1 \le i \le k} \text{code}_{\text{TREE}}(T_i).$$

Observe that codes of T_i are cyclical shifts of each other modulo the outermost brackets which remain intact. If T is not rooted, select the centres of T as the possible roots, construct two corresponding codes as defined above, and select the smaller one as code of T.

2.2.2 P-trees

A *p-tree* is a rooted labeled tree in which the labeled vertices have (linearly) ordered sons. A word that reads the same backwards as forwards is a *palindrome*. Two p-trees T_1 and T_2 are *p-isomorphic* iff there exists a bijection h from V_{T_1} onto V_{T_2} which preserves the root, the father function, the labels, and, for each labeled vertex $w \in V_{T_1}$, the following holds: if $\langle v_1,v_2,...,v_k\rangle$ and $\langle u_1,u_2,...,u_k\rangle$ are the ordered sequences of the sons of w and h(w) respectively, then :

a) $\langle h(v_1),h(v_2),...,h(v_k)\rangle$ is equal to $\langle u_1,u_2,...,u_k\rangle$, if label(w) is not a palindrome, and

b) $\langle h(v_1),h(v_2),...,h(v_k)\rangle$ is equal either to $\langle u_1,u_2,...,u_k\rangle$ or $\langle u_k,u_{k-1},...,u_1\rangle$, if label(w) is a palindrome.

Let T be a p-tree. Define its *canonical p-ordering* D by induction on the height of T as follows. If T is a one-vertex tree then D is T. Suppose that T consists of the root r_T and k subtrees with their respective canonical p-orderings $D_1,...,D_k$, listed in the order if r_T is labeled. There are the following cases:

(1) r_T is not labeled: order $D_1,...,D_k$ nondecreasingly with respect to $\text{code}_{\text{TREE}}(D_1),...,\text{code}_{\text{TREE}}(D_k)$;

(2) r_T is labeled by a palindrome: select either the ordering $D_1,...,D_k$ or its reverse depending on whether the string

$code_{TREE}(D_1)\ldots code_{TREE}(D_k)$ is smaller then its reverse or not.
Define

$$code^{P}_{TREE}(T) = code_{TREE}(D).$$

Observe that $code^{P}_{TREE}(T_1) = code^{P}_{TREE}(T_2)$ iff T_1 and T_2 are p-isomorphic.

2.3 Outerplanar graphs

In this section we describe encoding of outerplanar graphs, i.e., graphs which have planar embedding such that all vertices belong to the unbounded region (cf. Harary [H]). The method is to associate with a graph certain trees and construct encoding employing the previous codes for trees. This in turn will enable us to use the algorithms testing isomorphism of trees also in the general case of outerplanar graphs. For the reason of convenience we use a certain characterization of planarity and outerplanarity by means of *abstract embeddings* instead of the usual embeddings in the plane.

An *embedded graph* H is a graph together with fixed cyclic orders for all sets of edges incident to one common vertex, that is, $H = \langle G_H, \{\rho_v : v \in V_H\} \rangle$ where $G_H = \langle V_H, E_H \rangle$ is an underlying graph and ρ_v is a cyclic permutation on $E^v_H = \{e \in E_H : v \text{ is incident to } e\}$. Let $\tilde{E}_H$ be the set of darts of H, i.e., all ordered pairs $\langle v,w \rangle$ for which $\{v,w\} \in E_H$. Associate with H the permutation σ_H on $\tilde{E}_H$ defined as follows: $\sigma_H(\langle w,v \rangle) = \langle v,s \rangle$, where $\{v,s\} = \rho_v(\{v,w\})$. The cycles of σ_H are *regions* of H. We say that a vertex v *belongs to a region* r if r contains $\langle v,w \rangle$ for some w. A vertex may belong to many regions. Two embedded graphs are *isomorphic* if there exists a bijection between their sets of vertices which preserves all orders on adjacent edges, i.e., it preserves all ρ_v (or, equivalently, it preserves σ). An *embedding* H_G of a graph G is an embedded graph for which G is the underlying graph.

A biconnected embedded graph H is *planar* if either $|V_H| = 2$ or $|V_H| > 2$ and no region contains two opposite darts $\langle v,w \rangle$ and $\langle w,v \rangle$ for some $v,w \in V_H$. An embedded graph H is *planar* if all its biconnected components are planar. H is *outerplanar* if it is planar and has for each connected component B the region r such that each $v \in V_B$ belongs to r (note that r may contain two opposite darts since B need not be biconnected). A graph G is *planar* (*outerplanar*) if it has an planar (outerplanar) embedding. These definitions of planarity are equivalent to the standard definitions based on embeddings in the plane (cf. Harary [H], MacLane [M]). It is clear that two graphs G_1 and G_2 are isomorphic iff there are two isomorphic embeddings H_1 and H_2 of G_1 and G_2, respectively. The above statement holds true if we substitute "graphs" for "planar graphs" ("outerplanar graphs") and "embeddings" for "planar embeddings" ("outerplanar embeddings"), respectively. In the sequel the term "vertex" will refer to graphs and "node" to trees.

Let G be a connected outerplanar graph. Consider the following graph T_G reflecting the connections between the biconnected components (blocks) of G. The *nodes* of T_G are the blocks and articulation points of G (for these two kinds of nodes we use the terms "block nodes" and "articulation nodes"). The *edges* of T_G are pairs {a,B} where a is an articulation point of G belonging to B.

Fact 1. T_G is a tree. □

The tree T_G has exactly one centre since each maximal simple path in T_G has an even length. Let us assume we have two encodings: $code^V_{OP}$ for outerplanar graphs with one distinguished vertex, and $code^B_{OP}$ for outerplanar graphs with one distinguished block, such that any two codes from these two classes are always distinct. Then we can define the encoding for connected outerplanar graphs as follows:

$$code_{OP}(G) = \begin{cases} code^V_{OP}(G_u) & \text{if u, an articulation point of G, is the centre of } T_G\text{, and } G_u \text{ is G with u as a distinguished vertex,} \\ code^B_{OP}(G_B) & \text{if B, a block of G, is the centre of } T_G\text{, and } G_B \text{ is G with B as a distinguished block.} \end{cases}$$

If G is not connected, let $code_{OP}(G_1) \leq \ldots \leq code_{OP}(G_k)$ be the codes of the connected components $G_1,\ldots,G_k$ of G. Define $code_{OP}(G)$ as the string $code_{OP}(G_1)\ldots code_{OP}(G_k)$. Therefore it remains to define $code^V_{OP}$ and $code^B_{OP}$. First we describe the encoding for biconnected outerplanar graphs.

2.3.1 Biconnected outerplanar graphs

Let B be a biconnected outerplanar graph with $m \geq 3$ vertices. B has exactly two different outerplanar embeddings B_{e_1} and B_{e_2}, one being the mirror reflection of the other. Let B_e be one of these embeddings. B_e may be viewed as a convex polygon with added non-intersecting diagonals; the vertices of this polygon correspond to the vertices of B_e, the sides and the diagonals correspond to the edges of B_e. B_e determines a cyclic order on the vertices of B by the region r containing all the vertices. Fix a linear order on edges incident to a vertex v as this very linear order consistent with the cyclic order in the plane where the first edge is the edge {v,w} for which {v,w} belongs to r. Let B^*_e be the (embedded) graph dual to B_e with the following modification: the vertex corresponding to unbounded region in B_e of degree m is split into m nodes, each of degree one.

Fact 2. B_e^* is a c-tree. □

Define

$$code_{BOP}(B) = \min \{ code^C_{TREE}(B^*_{e_1}), code^C_{TREE}(B^*_{e_2}) \}.$$

This very embedding of B which determines the above code will be referred to as the *canonical embedding*. To encode properly the biconnected outerplanar graphs that are blocks of some outerplanar graph, the positions of articulation points should be taken into account.

2.3.2. Biconnected outerplanar graphs with some marked vertices and one distinguished vertex distinct from the marked ones.

Let B be a graph of this kind. The marked vertices and the distinguished one will be articulation points when B will be a block of some graph. Let B_e^* be as defined above. For each marked or distinguished vertex v in B create a node a_v and add it to B_e^* as a leaf as follows: If the number of edges incident to v is even, then let {v,w} and {v,u} be two consecutive middle edges in B_e among edges incident to v, which are determined by order imposed by B_e on the edges incident to v. Let r be the region in B_e between these edges (i. e., the region comprising {w,v} and {v,u}) and let a_r be the node in B_e^* corresponding to r. Attach a_v to a_r between branches corresponding to {v,w} and {v,u}. If the number of edges incident to v is odd, let {v,w} be the middle one and let $\{a_s,a_t\}$ be the edge in B_e^* corresponding to {v,w} with a_s corresponding to the region determined by {v,w}. Create an additonal node b on the edge $\{a_s,a_t\}$ and attach a_v to it after $\{b,a_s\}$. It may happen that w is a distinguished vertex too and {v,w} is its middle edge. In such a situation one additional node b can serve as both the vertices, and a_w is attached to b after $\{b, a_t\}$.

Set the node corresponding to the distinguished vertex in B as the root in B_e^* and attach an empty label to each node a_v corresponding to a marked vertex v. Thus we obtain a rooted c-tree which uniquely determines B_e. The code for B is defined as follows:

$$code^1_{BOP}(B) = \min \{ code^C_{TREE}(B^*_{e_1}), code^C_{TREE}(B^*_{e_2}) \},$$

where B_{e_1} and B_{e_2} are two embeddings of B.

Lemma 3. The following statements are equivalent:

(1) $B^*_{e_1}$ is isomorphic to $B^*_{e_2}$;

(2) $code^C_{TREE}(B^*_{e_1}) = code^C_{TREE}(B^*_{e_2})$

(3) $\mathrm{code}^{C}_{TREE}(B^{*}_{e_1})$ is a palindrome.

Proof. Observe that $\mathrm{code}^{C}_{TREE}(B^{*}_{e_1})$ is a reversed copy of $\mathrm{code}^{C}_{TREE}(B^{*}_{e_2})$, what follows from the symmetry of the construction of B^{*}_{e}. □

2.3.3. Biconnected outerplanar graphs with some labeled vertices.

This encoding will handle this very block B of an outerplanar graph for which no vertex was distinguished (that is, the centre of T_G), and labels will be the codes of maximal connected subgraphs obtained after removing B. They will be attached to the appropriate articulation points incident to B.

Let B be a biconnected outerplanar graph with some labeled vertices, and let B_e be an outerplanar embedding of B. We define B^{*}_{e} as in the previous case, but instead of empty labels the given labels are attached to the appropriate nodes. B^{*}_{e} is a c-tree. Set

$$\mathrm{code}^{2}_{BOP}(B) = \min \{ \mathrm{code}^{C}_{TREE}(B^{*}_{e_1}), \mathrm{code}^{C}_{TREE}(B^{*}_{e_2}) \},$$

where B_{e_1}, B_{e_2} are two outerplanar embeddings of B.

2.3.4 Outerplanar graphs with one distinguished vertex or one distinguished block.

In this subsection we define $\mathrm{code}^{V}_{OP}(G)$ and $\mathrm{code}^{B}_{OP}(G)$ considered in the beginning of the section.

First consider the case when G is a connected outerplanar graph with a distinguished vertex u. Let T_G be as defined at the beginning of the section. If u is not an articulation point in G, then the new articulation node a_u and the edge (a_u, B_u) are added to T_G, where B_u is the block containing u. After this modification there is always a node a_u in T_G corresponding to the distinguished vertex u. Set a_u as the root of T_G. For each block B distinguish the vertex corresponding to the father of B in T_G, and mark all the remaining articulation points in B. Finally label each block-node B with $\mathrm{code}^{1}_{BOP}(B)$. For each block-node B in T_G fix the order of its sons, i.e., articulation nodes corresponding to articulation points in B, according to the canonical outerplanar embedding of B. Now T_G becomes a p-tree. Observe that two such p-trees T_{G_1} and T_{G_2} are p-isomorphic iff G_1 and G_2 are isomorphic. Hence we can set

$$\mathrm{code}^{V}_{OP}(G) = \mathrm{code}^{P}_{TREE}(T_G)$$

as the encoding for outerplanar graphs with one distinguished vertex.

Now consider the second case when G is a connected outerplanar graph with a distinguished block B. Denote by $G \setminus B$ the graph obtained from G by removing all the edges from B and then all the isolated vertices. Convert B into B' by labeling each articulation point u with

$code^{V}_{OP}(H_u)$, where H_u is this connected component of $G \setminus B$ which contains u, and u is the distinguished vertex in H_u. Define the encoding for outerplanar graphs with one distinguished block as follows:

$$code^{B}_{OP}(G) = code^{2}_{BOP}(B').$$

Observe that no string can serve as both $code^{V}_{OP}$ and $code^{B}_{OP}$. This is because only in strings of the form $code^{V}_{OP}$ all sons of the root are labeled, i.e., only strings $code^{V}_{OP}$ are of the form ((..(..)).. (..(..))). In a string of the form $code^{B}_{OP}$ there must be on the first level at least two sub-bracket structures of the form ((..)..(..)).

This completes the description of encoding of outerplanar graphs. The following theorem follows from the preceding considerations.

Theorem 4. Two outerplanar graphs G_1 and G_2 are isomorphic iff $code_{OP}(G_1) = code_{OP}(G_2)$. □

3. Algorithms

Algorithms of this section are based on the following facts:

Fact 5: Two strings of length n can be compared in constant time on COMMON using n processors. □

Fact 6: The centre of any tree with n vertices can be found in O(logn) time using n processors. □

Proofs of the above facts are in the full version of the paper.

3.1 Isomorphism of rooted trees

Let T be a rooted tree with *n* vertices. Assume that T as an input to the algorithm is given in the form of an array containing values of the father function. The code of T can be found in the natural manner by computing codes of all vertices, going from leaves up to the root. This is the idea of sequential solutions of the tree isomorphism problem ([AHU]) but its straightforward parallel implementation fails for trees which are not balanced.

The first part of the algorithm transforms T into an ordered tree D in which for each vertex v its sons are ordered with respect to the lengths of their codes. Then the bracket structure of D is constructed. Let us call this bracket structure the *initial approximation code*. Employing the Euler Tour Technique [TV] one can find the *initial approximation code* in O(log*n*) time using O(*n*) processors.

Clearly the initial approximation code and the exact code may be different, namely there may be sibling vertices of the same size. The second part of the algorithm handles such vertices. Let *a family* denote a set of all sibling vertices of the same size, provided this set contains at least two vertices. To obtain the canonical ordering we must sort vertices of each family according to their codes in T, considering families in the bottom-up order. Actually all sortings are performed on the approximation code, thus "to sort a family" means to sort lexicographically an appropriate sequences of substrings in the approximation code.

The efficient implementation of the scheme follows from the following fact.

Lemma 7. Any path from a leaf to the root crosses at most log n families.

Proof. Let a path go through vertices $v_1, v_2, \ldots, v_k$, which belong to some families. Observe that the code of a vertex v_{i+1} is at least twice as long as the code of v_i. □

In the first part of the algorithm the initial approximation code has been computed and put in the table $C[1..2n]$. There is one processor associated with each entry of the table as well as with each vertex of the tree. Let the *table* processors be the processors actually performing sortings, while the *vertex* processors are responsible for a correct and efficient scheduling of individual sortings. A sorting procedure for a given family is initiated as soon as all its descendant families have been sorted. Such synchronization is achieved in the following way. For each family its leftmost member is distinguished. Using the doubling technique along the paths to the root, for each distinguished vertex the distinguished vertex of the next family is found. We obtain a forest F with vertices being the distinguished vertices of T. Each distinguished vertex v corresponds to one sorting. Vertex v initializes its sorting when it has received messages from all its sons in F that their sortings have already been completed. This is being performed in the way the OR function can be computed on the concurrent-write PRAM . Namely, after O(1) steps the processor p_v associated with v writes 0 to x[v]. Then each processor associated with such a son w of v in F that the sorting corresponding to w has not been accomplished yet writes 1 to x[v]. If x[v] remains 0 then the processor p_v starts the sorting corresponding to v by putting sorting parameters to a special location par[v]. If the sequence to be sorted is $\langle C[i+1]\ C[i+2]\ldots C[i+k]\rangle$, $\langle C[i+k+1]\ C[i+k+2]\ldots C[i+2k]\rangle, \ldots,$ $\langle C[i+(s-1)k+1]\ C[i+(s-1)k+2]\ldots C[i+sk]\rangle$, then the parameters designated for the appropriate table processors are $i+1$, k and s . In the next step after initializing par[v] all table processors which are to take part in the sorting corresponding to v read the sorting parameters and begin the sorting procedure. To get to know where to look for the parameters of the next sorting each table processor scans its path in F while subsequent sortings follow.

Lemma 8. The time needed for sorting is $O(\log n)$.

Proof. Let $v_1, v_2, \ldots, v_m$ be the path in F such that v_1 is a leaf, v_m is a root, the sorting for v_{i+1}, $i = 1, 2, \ldots, m-1$, is initiated as soon as the sorting for v_i has been accomplished and the completion of the sorting corresponding to v_m terminates the whole algorithm. Let s_i and k_i, for $i = 1, 2, \ldots, m$, be the number of strings and the length of one string in the sorting corresponding to v_i. Since $s_i k_i < k_{i+1}$ for $i = 1,2,\ldots,m-1$ and $s_m k_m < 2n$, we have $k_1 s_1 s_2 \ldots s_m < 2n$.

As a sorting procedure we can employ the parallel mergesort of Cole [C] taking $O(\log s)$ steps for a sequence of length s. Because two strings of length k can be compared in $O(1)$ time on k processors. Hence s strings of length k can be sorted lexicographically in $O(\log s)$ time with ks processors. Thus the time needed for sortings is bounded by the following sum:

$$\sum_{i=1}^{m} c \log s_i = c \log(s_1 s_2 \ldots s_m) < c \log 2n = O(\log n),$$

for some constant c. □

It completes the proof of the following theorem.

Theorem 9. The isomorphism of two rooted trees with n vertices can be checked in $O(\log n)$ time on CRCW PRAM with n processors. □

3.2 Isomorphism of outerplanar graphs

To be able to verify if two outerplanar graphs are isomorphic, it is enough to be able to construct $\text{code}_{OP}(G)$. To this end the algorithm from the previous section can be used with the following extentions.

First consider the remaining cases of trees. To handle the non-rooted trees it is enough to be able to find the centre of a tree. To form the code of a labeled tree each vertex must compute the positions of its brackets and of the beginning of its label (if there is any). This computations can be done in a logarithmic time using Euler Tour Technique. To put quickly labels in proper places of the code we assume that one processor is associated with each position q of each label l. This processor knows the vertex to which l belongs and the offset of q in l. While finding the code of a c-tree the algorithm of Apostolico, Iliopoulos & Paige [AIP] can be used as a procedure selecting the least lexicographic representation of a cyclic string. To construct the encoding code^{P}_{TREE}, the modifications are straightforward.

Now consider the case when the inputs are outerplanar graphs. The input graph can be divided into blocks, and for each block its outerplanar embedding can be found in logarithmic time with the linear number of processors using the algorithms of Tarjan & Vishkin [TV] and Diks [D]. The algorithm of Diks [D] recognizes the outerplanar graphs, and if a given graph turns out to be outerplanar then the algorithm produces its outerplanar embedding. To build B_e^* we must identify the regions of B_e, that is, to identify the cycles of the σ_{B_e} permutation of the $O(m)$ darts of B_e. Having $O(\log m)$ time and m processors the direct doubling technique is sufficient to this end. Since the size of B_e^* is $O(m)$, $code_{BOP}(B)$ can be found by m processors in $O(\log m)$ time. These codes should be combined as was described while defining $code_{OP}(G)$ using the algorithms constructing codes for trees. Therefore we have proved the following:

Main theorem. There is an algorithm for (ARBITRARY) CRCW PRAM to test isomorphism of two outerplanar graphs with n vertices in time $O(\log n)$ using n processors.

References

[AHU] A. V. Aho, J. E. Hopcroft, & J. D. Ullman, "The Design and Analysis of Computer Algorithms", Addison-Wesley, Reading, MA, 1974.

[AIP] A. Apostolico, C. S. Iliopoulos & R. Paige, An $O(n \log n)$ cost parallel algorithm for the single function coarsest partition problem, *in* Proc. of the International Workshop on Parallel Algorithms and Architectures, Suhl (GDR) May 1987, ed. A. Albrecht, H. Jung and K. Mehlhorn, Akademie-Verlag, Berlin, 1987.

[C] R. Cole, Parallel mergesort, Proc. of the *27th* IEEE Symp. on Foundations of Computer Science, Toronto (Canada), 1987, pp. 511-516.

[D] K. Diks, Parallel recognition of outerplanar graphs, *in* Proc. of the International Workshop on Parallel Algorithms and Architectures, Suhl (GDR) May 1987, ed. A. Albrecht, H. Jung and K. Mehlhorn, Akademie-Verlag, Berlin, 1987, pp. 105-113.

[GJ] M. R. Garey & D. S. Johnson, "Computers and Intractability: a Guide to the Theory of NP-Completeness", Freeman, San Francisco, CA, 1979.

[H] F. Harary, "Graph Theory", Addison-Wesley, Reading, MA, 1969.

[M] S. MacLane, A structural characterization of planar combinatorial graphs, Duke Math. J. 3 (1937), 340-472.

[MR] G. L. Miller & J. H. Reif, Parallel tree contraction and its application, Proc. *26th* IEEE Symp. on Foundations of Computer Science, 1985, pp. 478-489.

[R] W. L. Ruzzo, On uniform circuit complexity, J. Computer System Sci. 22 (1981).

[TV] R. Tarjan & U. Vishkin, An efficient parallel biconnectivity algorithm, SIAM J. Comput. 14 (1985), 862-874.

[V] U. Vishkin, Synchronous parallel computations - a survey, Technical Report #71, Computer Science Department, New York University, New York, 1984.

EFFICIENT SIMULATIONS BETWEEN CONCURRENT-READ CONCURRENT-WRITE PRAM MODELS

B. S. Chlebus†, K. Diks†, T. Hagerup‡, T. Radzik†

† Instytut Informatyki, Uniwersytet Warszawski
PKIN, p. 850, 00-901 Warszawa, Poland.

‡ FB Informatik, Universität des Saarlandes
D-6600 Saarbrücken, West Germany.

Abstract. We give several simple and efficient algorithms for simulations of stronger CRCW PRAMs on weaker ones. The models that we consider are the well-known PRIORITY, ARBITRARY and COMMON PRAMs, and COLLISION and COLLISION$^+$, defined by the property that a special collision symbol is stored in each memory cell into which more than one processor attempts to write, or more than one value is attempted to be written, respectively, in a given step. Our results are the following, where n denotes the number of processors of the simulated PRAM :

1) A O(1)-time simulation between any pair of models, provided that the simulating machine has $\Theta(n \log n)$ processors;

2) Two n-processor simulations: of PRIORITY on ARBITRARY with $O(\log\log n)$ slowdown, and of PRIORITY on COLLISION$^+$ with $O((\log\log n)^2)$ slowdown.

1. Introduction

The Parallel Random Access Machine (PRAM) has been generally accepted as the model of a synchronized parallel computer with a shared global memory (cf. [G,FW]). Various PRAMs have been introduced, differing in whether they allow read/write conflicts, i. e., attempts by several processors to access the same memory cell in the same step of computation. In this paper we consider only concurrent-read concurrent-write (CRCW) PRAMs, i. e., PRAMs that allow simultaneous reading from as well as simultaneous writing to each cell by arbitrary sets of processors. Simultaneous writing is not immediately logically meaningful, and further stipulations concerning the write conflict resolution rule employed are needed. Of interest to us are the following models:

ARBITRARY [SV]: If several processors simultaneously attempt to write to the same cell, then one of them succeeds and writes its value, but there is no rule assumed to govern the process of selection of this processor.

COLLISION [FRW1]: Whenever two or more procesors simultaneously attempt to write to the same cell, a special collision symbol is written in the cell.

COLLISION^{+} : Whenever at least two distinct values are attempted to be written to the same cell , a special collision symbol is written in the cell.

COMMON [K]: If two or more processors simultaneously attempt to write to the same cell, they must be writing the same value, which then gets stored in the cell.

PRIORITY [G]: If several processors simultaneously attempt to write to the same cell, then the lowest-numbered processor writes its value to the cell.

Much effort has been devoted to determining the relative power of these various models. Some relations are obvious: for instance, ARBITRARY is stronger then COLLISION^{+} in the sense that one step of an n-processor COLLISION^{+} can be simulated by O(1) steps of an n-processor ARBITRARY. If we express such a fact by "$\text{COLLISION}^{+} \leq$ ARBITRARY", then the following relations are easy to verify:

$$\text{COLLISION} \leq \text{COLLISION}^{+} \leq \text{ARBITRARY} \leq \text{PRIORITY}$$
$$\text{COMMON} \leq \text{COLLISION}^{+}$$

Grolmusz and Ragde [GR] proved that COMMON is not comparable in the sense of this relation '≤' with COLLISION. Kučera [K] showed that if the simulated machine uses n processors and the simulating one is allowed to use n^2 processors, then any of the considered models can be simulated on an arbitrary weaker one with only a constant slowdown (actually Kučera [K] did not consider COLLISION*s* and ARBITRARY, but the statement holds true also for these models). However, a brutal squaring of the number of involved processors is seldom acceptable in efficient algorithms, and later work has concentrated mainly on the case when the machines have the same number of processors. We continue this line of research.

A number of lower-bound type results are known concerning relationships between pairs of various CRCW PRAM models. Fich, Meyer auf der Heide, and Wigderson [FMW] proved an $\Omega(\log\log\log n)$ lower bound for a problem on COMMON that needs only O(1) steps on COLLISION. This lower bound was later improved to $\Omega(\sqrt{\log n})$ by Ragde, Szemeredi, Steiger, and Wigderson [RSSW]. Grolmusz and Ragde [GR] demonstrated a lower bound of $\Omega(\log\log\log n)$ on COLLISION for a problem that can be done in O(1) steps on ARBITRARY, and showed that COMMON and COLLISION are incomparable, i.e., that is not possible to simulate one step of one of these models by O(1) steps of the other one. Assuming certain additional restrictions on either the size of the shared memory or the way the input is stored, further separation results have been proved (cf. [FRW1, FRW2, GR, LY]).

As regards the simulation-type results between n-processor models, one should first note that the simulation problem can be reduced to sorting and hence solved in all cases with a logarithmic slowdown. The only previous sub-logarithmic result known to the authors is a simulation with slowdown $O(\log n/\log\log n)$ of PRIORITY on COMMON developed by Fich, Ragde, and Wigderson [FRW2].

In this paper we contribute a number of efficient algorithms simulating stronger CRCW PRAMs on weaker ones. We concentrate on the time and number of processors as measures of complexity. The size of the simulating memory can be bounded by $O(nm)$, where m is the size of the simulated memory. Some additional assumptions concerning existence of sufficient amount of initialized "clear" space are needed to make the simulations designed for COLLISION^{+} work also on COLLISION.

First we show that any of the considered models can simulate all the other n-processor PRAMs in a step-by-step manner with O(1) slowdown provided it has $O(n \log n)$ processors at its disposal. This is an improvement of the result of Kučera [K] who used n^2 processors to the same effect.

Next we show that, as far as $O((\log\log n)^k)$-time simulations are concerned for a fixed k, all the considered models except COMMON are equivalent. More precisely, PRIORITY can be deterministically simulated step by step on COLLISION^{+} with $O((\log\log n)^2)$ slowdown. These are the first-ever announced simulations between different n-processor PRAMs to achieve a slowdown which is polynoomial in loglog n. It also shows that the $\Omega(\sqrt{\log n})$ lower bound between COMMON and COLLISION (cf. [RSSW]) cannot be proved for any pair of CRCW models which does not include COMMON, and therefore that the most significant gap in computing power is between COMMON and the remaining CRCW PRAMs.

The following are the presented n-processor simulations: the first one is a simulation of PRIORITY on ARBITRARY with $O(\log\log n)$ slowdown, the next is a simulation of PRIORITY on COLLISION$^+$ with slowdown $O((\log\log n))^2$.

2. A general outline of the simulations.

In this section we describe the general setting of our simulations of PRIORITY and ARBITRARY on weaker models. Let M_1 be the simulated machine and M_2 the simulating one, both machines having n processors. Let $Q_1, Q_2,\ldots, Q_n$ and $P_1, P_2,\ldots,P_n$ be the processors of M_1 and M_2, respectively. Machine M_2 simulates M_1 step by step. In each step of M_2, except for writing steps, processor P_i performs the action of Q_i

Let us concentrate on a writing step. In each such step processors P_1, $P_2,\ldots,P_n$ are partitioned into disjoint groups depending on the memory cells to which the Q_i's intend to write. Let $m_1, m_2,\ldots,m_k$ be these memory cells and $S_1, S_2,\ldots,S_k$ the corresponding groups of processors ($P_i \in S_l$ iff Q_i writes to m_l). If the simulated machine is PRIORITY, we are to choose from each S_l, $l = 1,2,\ldots,k$, the lowest-numbered processor, which may then proceed to do the actual writing. If the simulated machine is ARBITRARY, any single processor from S_l, $l = 1,2,\ldots,k$, will do. These problems can be generalized as follows.

<u>The Select-One Problem</u>

S is a nonempty set of processors containing indices from the interval of integers $I = a + [1..n]$, i.e., $I = \{a+1,a+2,\ldots,a+n\}$. Select a single processor from S (arbitrarily). The pair (S,I) is an instance of the problem, and n is its size. Only processors from S are available to solve the problem.

<u>The Find-First Problem</u>

All as above except that the processor with the smallest index is to be selected.

<u>Remark</u>: The parameter a was introduced only for convenience in the description of the algorithms. Initially $a = 0$. We distinguish between "the number of a processor" and "the index of a processor". The *number* of a processor is its real number which identifies it among all the

processors. The *index* of a processor may change during computations. Initially, before each simulated step, the index of a processor is equal to its number.

2.1. Proposition. If $T_1(n)$ ($T_2(n)$, resp.) is the time that machine M needs to solve the Find_First (Select_One, resp.) problem then one step of an n-processor PRIORITY (ARBITRARY, resp.) can be simulated by M in time $O(T_1(n))$ ($O(T_2(n))$, resp.) . □

3. Constant time simulation of PRIORITY on COMMON

In this section we show that the Find_First problem can be solved in constant time on COMMON, and hence on $COLLISION^+$ and ARBITRARY, provided that each processor $P_i \in S$ has additionally $h = \lceil \log n \rceil - 1$ auxiliary processors $P_{i,1}, P_{i,2}, \dots, P_{i,h}$ (take $P_{i,0} = P_i$). Thus it is possible to simulate PRIORITY on all of these models in constant time.

Let T be a complete binary tree with height h+1 and with leaves numbered from left to right by consecutive integers from the respective interval I (see the definition of the Find_First problem). A leaf v_i (i.e., having number i) is *distinguished* if processor P_i (i.e., with index i) is in S. The algorithm is based on the following simple lemma.

3.1 Lemma. P_i is the processor with the smallest index iff for each ancestor w of v_i such that w is the right son of its father, the (left) brother of w is not an ancestor of any distinguished leaf. □

Let $v_{i,j}$ be the j-th ancestor of leaf v_i. More precisely $v_{i,0} = v_i$, $v_{i,1}$ is the father of $v_{i,0}$, $v_{i,2}$ the father of $v_{i,1}$, and so on. For each $P_i \in S$ and $0 \le j \le h$, processor $P_{i,j}$ is associated with vertex $v_{i,j}$. For $v \in T$, let M(v) denote the memory cell corresponding to vertex v. The array R is to store the result of computation.

All processors $P_{i,j}$ such that $P_i \in S$ and $0 \le j \le h$ perform concurrently the following algorithm.

```
begin
(0)   R(i) := 1;
(1)   M(brother(v_i,j)) := 0;
(2)   M(v_i,j) := 1;
(3)   if  v_i,j is the right son  and  M(brother(v_i,j)) = 1  then
                R(i) := 0;
end
```

Observe that after termination of this algorithm, for each processor $P_i \in S$, the following equivalence holds: $R(i) = 1$ iff P_i is the first processor in S. This follows directly from the lemma 3.1. Therefore we have proved:

3.2. Theorem. One step of a PRIORITY with n processors can be simulated in constant time on a COMMON with $O(n \log n)$ processors. □

4. Simulation of PRIORITY on ARBITRARY

In this section we describe a solution of the Find_First problem on ARBITRARY. If the size n of the problem is not greater than 2, then the computation is straightforward. For $n > 2$ our algorithm can be described recursively as follows.

<u>begin</u>

(1) Partition the set S into $q = \lceil \sqrt{n} \rceil$ subsets $S_0, S_1, \ldots, S_{q-1}$ such that S_l, for $l = 0, \ldots, q-1$, contains processors with indices from the interval $I_l = a + l \cdot q + [1..q]$, where $I = a + [1..n]$.

(2) Select an arbitrary processor P_l from each nonempty subset S. Let S' be the set of elements from S except processor P_l. Change the index of each selected processor P_l to l and create from these processors a new set T.

(3) For each nonempty subset S'_l solve simultaneously the local subproblems (S'_l, I_l) as well as the global one $(T, J=[1..q])$.

(4) Let S_j be the the first nonempty subset given by the solution of the global problem. If S contains only one processor P_j then set this processor as the one having the smallest index among all the processors in S. Otherwise select the processor with the smallest index among P_j and the processor with the smallest index in S'_j.

<u>end</u>

Each of the above steps except the recursive step (3) can be done on ARBITRARY in constant time. (In fact only step 2 uses simultaneous writing). The complexity of the algorithm depends on the depth of the recursion $D(n)$. Each subproblem has size at most $\lceil \sqrt{n} \rceil$; hence $D(n) \le D(\lceil \sqrt{n} \rceil) + O(1)$ and $D(n) = O(\log\log n)$. This proves the following theorem.

4.1 Theorem. One step of an n-processor PRIORITY can be simulated by $O(\log\log n)$ steps of an n-processor ARBITRARY. □

5. Simulation of PRIORITY on COLLISION$^+$

First we describe a solution of the Select_One problem. Then by some modifications we obtain an algorithm which solves the Find_First problem. The idea of the simulation on COLLISION$^+$ is a reduction of the number of processors in S by a factor of $1/\log n$ followed by an application of the constant-time algorithm from section 3. The processors eliminated during the reduction will serve as the auxiliary processors in the latter algorithm. The elimination is done by repeating $\log\log n$ times an algorithm solving the Partition problem, i.e., reducing the number of processors by at least a half.

<u>The Partition Problem</u>

Given a nonempty set S of processors, indexed with distinct numbers from an interval $I = a + [1..n]$, partition S into two disjoint subsets A and B such that $|A| \le |B|$, and if $|S| > 1$ then $|A| > 0$. Only the processors from S are available to carry out the computation. An instance of the problem is defined as (S,I), and its size as n.

We describe below the algorithm solving the partition problem on COLLISION.

<u>begin</u>
    <u>if</u> $n \le 2$ <u>then</u>
        <u>if</u> $|S| = 1$ <u>then</u>
(1)   the only element of S is allocated to B
        <u>else</u> { $|S| = 2$ }
(2)   allocate the processor with a smaller index to A and the other one to B
    <u>else</u> {$n > 2$} <u>begin</u>
(3)   divide S into $q = \lceil\sqrt{n}\,\rceil$ subsets $S_0, S_1, \ldots, S_{q-1}$, such that S_l contains the processors with indices in the interval $I_l = a + l \cdot q + [1..q]$;
(4)   remove the processor from each one-element subset S_l, change its index to l and place it in a new set T;
(5)   for each nonempty subset S_l solve recursively the Partition problem (S_l, I_l), and solve $(T, J = [1..q])$ if T is not empty.
    <u>end</u>
<u>end</u>

Observe that $|A| \le |B|$ since each element in A has a partner in B (see step 2), and that this partnership function is an injection from A into B. If $|S| \ge 2$ then by induction A is not empty because there is at least one subproblem in step 5 with at least two elements. Steps

(1)-(4) can be performed on COLLISION in constant time. The recursion depth is O(loglog n) as in the algorithm of the previous section, hence the following fact is true.

5.1 Lemma. Partition problems of size n can be solved on COLLISION in O(loglog n) time. □

Executing loglog n times the above algorithm (after each execution we continue with the set A of processors) we can reduce the initial set S to a subset S' ≤ S such that $|S'| \le \lceil |S|/\log n \rceil$. If $|S'| > 1$ we now want to apply the algorithm of section 3 (which works on COLLISION$^+$). To this end it is necessary for each processor from S' to collect log n additional processors. This can be done by a modification of step 2 of the above algorithm. Let us assume that in this step processor x is allocated to A and processor y to B. Processor x then takes over all additional processors gathered until that moment by processor y (including processor y itself). After loglog n iterations of the partition algorithm, each processor of S' has collected log n additional processors, provided that $|S'| > 1$. Applying now the algorithm of section 3, we can select the processor from S' with smallest index. Observe that it need not be the first processor in the initial set S. The first processor is lost when it is the only element placed in T on some level of the recursion. Thus we have a solution for the Select_One problem in the case of ARBITRARY, what is summed up as follows.

5.2 Proposition. The simulation of one step of an n-processor ARBITRARY can be done on an n-processor COLLISION$^+$ in time O((loglog n)^2). □

Next we describe how to improve the above solution to be able to handle the simulation of PRIORITY. To this end we maintain during the whole reduction process a function M: S --> S such that the following invariant:

(*) if processor x is the first one among the processors which are still active (not eliminated) then M(x) is the first processor in S.

Initially M(x) = x for each processor in S. To preserve the above invariant we add step 6 to the partition algorithm.

(6) Restore the original indices of processors from T, i.e., as before the recursive call. If T contains only one processor z then for each processor $x \in$ A, if the index of M(z) is smaller than M(x), then let M(x) := M(z).

After applying of the algorithm of section 3 to set S' (of the surviving processors) the first processor in S', say x, informs $M(x)$ that it is the first one in S.

The above arguments prove the following theorem.

5.3 Theorem. One step of an n-processor PRIORITY can be simulated by an n-processor COLLISION^{+} in $O((\log\log n)^2)$ time. □

References

[FMW] F. E. Fich, F. Meyer auf der Heide, and A. Wigderson, Lower bounds for parallel random-access machines with unbounded shared memory, Advances in Computing Research, 1986.

[FRW1] F. E. Fich, P. L. Ragde, and A. Wigderson, Relations between concurrent-write models of parallel computation, *in* Proceedings, *3rd* Annual ACM Symposium on Principles of Distributed Computing, 1984, pp. 179-189 (to appear in SIAM J. Computing)

[FRW2] F. E. Fich, P. L. Ragde, and A. Wigderson, Simulations among concurrent-write PRAMs, manuscript, 1986, to appear in Algorithmica.

[FW] S. Fortune, and J. Wyllie, Parallelism in random access machines, *in* Proceedings, *10th* Annual ACM Symposium on Theory of Computing, San Diego, Calif., 1978, pp. 114-118.

[G] L. Goldschlager, A universal interconnection pattern for parallel computers, J. ACM 29 (1982), 1073-1086.

[GR] V. Grolmusz, and P. L. Ragde, Incomparability in parallel computation, *in* Proceedings, *28th* Annual IEEE Symposium on Foundations of Computer Science, 1987, pp. 89-98.

[K] L. Kučera, Parallel computation and conflicts in memory access, Information Processing Letters 14 (1982), 93-96.

[LY] M. Li, and Y. Yesha, New lower bounds for parallel computation, *in* Proceedings, *18th* Annual ACM Symposium on Theory of Computing, 1986, pp. 177-187.

[RSSW] P. L. Radge, A. Szemerédi, W. Steiger, and A. Widgerson, The parallel complexity of element distinctness is $\Omega(\sqrt{\log n})$, manuscript, 1986. (submitted to SIAM J. of Discrete Mathematics).

[SV] Y. Shiloach, and U. Vishkin, An $O(\log n)$ parallel connectivity algorithm, J. Algorithms 3 (1982), 57-63.

MULTIPLE PROPOSITIONAL DYNAMIC LOGIC OF PARALLEL PROGRAMS

- Extended Abstract -

Ryszard Danecki
Institute of Mathematics, Polish Acad. of Sci.
Mielżyńskiego 27/29, 61-725 Poznań, Poland

The paper presents a variant of Propositional Dynamic Logic (PDL) of parallel programs. Formulae are interpreted in multiple structures which are Cartesian products of standard PDL structures with atomic programs and atomic formulae defined coordinatewise. This provides a natural description of parallelism with shared memory. A class of semantics for this logic is defined and the satisfiability problem investigated. As the main result we present a decision procedure for the problem of whether or not a given formula is satisfied in a multiple structure in which one coordinate is unknown and all remaining are equal to a given finite structure. If two coordinates are unknown the problem is undecidable. As a consequence a new upper bound for the satisfiability problem of Boolean PDL [Ab80] is obtained. Our result can be also interpreted as a generalization of the decidability of PDL with interleaving programs to the case where programs are synchronized by means of shared variables ranging over a finite domain.

Our approach can be briefly described as follows. We extend the syntax of classical PDL of [FL79] by relativizing all atomic programs and atomic formulae to natural numbers (called coordinates or processors) and by adding cobegin..//..coend program forming functor which can be nested and combined freely with standard sequential operations. The semantics is based on the following intuitions. We assume that a single PDL structure describes a processor with local memory. It provides the information how memory states (i. e. processor states) change when atomic programs A, B, ... are executed, and defines the truth values of predicates P, Q, ... for all states. In consequence, a Cartesian product of PDL structures describes a system of independent processors with local memories. Now, atomic programs have the form A(1), A(2), ..., B(1), B(2), ... which means: perform A at the processor no. 1, perform A at the processor no. 2, and so on. Atomic formulae have the form P(1), P(2), ..., Q(1), Q(2), ... where P(1) means: the predicate P is true for the current state of the processor no. 1, and so on. The meaning of compound programs and formulae constructed from these atoms is defined according to standard rules of PDL. For example, the sequential program $a = A(1);P(2)?;B(1)$ means: perform A at the processor no. 1, test if P is true for the current state of the processor no. 2, perform B at the processor no. 1. So, the formula $[a]P(2)$ saying "after any successful execution of a, P(2) is true" is universally valid, while $[a]P(1)$ is not. Of course, the meaning of parallel composition of programs cannot be inferred from the classical PDL. Here we follow the ideas of Salwicki and Müldner [SM81] (see [MS87] Chapter 7 for systematic presentation) and define the class of simple regular semantics of parallel programs. This generalizes the notions of simple MAX and ARB semantics of [MS87]. Our main result - the decidability of the degenerated satisfiability problem - holds for Multiple PDL with any simple regular semantics.

MULTIPLE PDL

The syntax of Multiple PDL of parallel programs is defined as follows. There are two countable sets $ProgSymb = \{A, B, \dots\}$, and $PredSymb = \{P, Q, \dots\}$ of program and predicate symbols, respectively. For any natural number i, expressions A(i), B(i), ... are atomic programs, and P(i), Q(i), ... are atomic formulae. If p, q are formulae and a, b are programs (atomic or not), then $\neg p$, p&q, $\langle a \rangle p$ are formulae and $a;b$, $a \cup b$, a^*, p?, a//b are programs.

By a standard PDL structure we mean a triple $M = (U, \models, \prec\succ)$, where U is a nonempty set of states, $\models \subseteq PredSymb \times U$ is a satisfiability relation and $\prec\succ \subseteq U \times ProgSymb \times U$ is a relation definig meaning of every program symbol. We write "$u \models P$ in M" instead of $(u, P) \in \models$, and "$u \prec A \succ v$ in M" instead of $(u, A, v) \in \prec\succ$. Intuitively, $u \models P$ means that P is true at state u of M and $u \prec A \succ v$ means that there is an execution of A which started with the state u ends with the state v. A multiple PDL structure $\underline{M} = M_0 \times M_1 \times \dots$ is a Cartesian product of an infinite sequence of standard PDL structures $M_i = (U_i, \models_i, \prec\succ_i)$. Formally, $\underline{M} = (\underline{U}, \models, \prec\succ)$ where $\underline{U} = U_0 \times U_1 \times \dots$, and $\models$, $\prec\succ$ are defined for atomic formulae P(i), ..., and atomic programs A(i), ... as follows. For any $\underline{u}, \underline{v} \in \underline{U}$

with $\underline{u}=u_0u_1\dots$, $\underline{v}=v_0v_1\dots$, $\underline{u}\models P(i)$ in $\underline{M}$ iff $u_i\models_i P$ in M_i, $\underline{u}\langle A(i)\rangle\underline{v}$ in $\underline{M}$ iff $u_i\langle A\rangle_i v_i$ in M_i and $u_j=v_j$ for all $j\neq i$. In other words, P(i) is true at $\underline{u}$ in $\underline{M}$ iff P is true at the i-th coordinate of $\underline{u}$. To execute A(i) in $\underline{M}$ means to execute A at the i-th coordinate of $\underline{M}$.

In a very broad sense, a semantics of programs is any mapping ρ which to every multiple structure $\underline{M}$ and every program a assigns a binary relation $\rho(\underline{M}, a)\subseteq\underline{U}\times\underline{U}$, where $\underline{U}$ is the universe of $\underline{M}$. The satisfiability relation $\models$ for atomic formulae is defined in every multiple structure $\underline{M}$. If a semantics of programs ρ is already chosen, the satisfiability relation can be extended to arbitrary formulae as follows: $\underline{u}\models\neg p$ in $\underline{M}$ iff not $\underline{u}\models p$ in $\underline{M}$, $\underline{u}\models p\&q$ in $\underline{M}$ iff $\underline{u}\models p$ and $\underline{u}\models q$ in $\underline{M}$, $\underline{u}\models\langle a\rangle p$ in $\underline{M}$ iff there is $\underline{v}\in\underline{U}$ such that $(\underline{u}, \underline{v})\in\rho(\underline{M}, a)$ and $\underline{v}\models p$ in $\underline{M}$. In this way a semantics of programs ρ is extended to a semantics of formulae. A formula p is satisfiable in the semantics ρ if $\underline{u}\models p$ in $\underline{M}$ for some $\underline{M}$ and $\underline{u}\in\underline{U}$, where $\models$ is as above. A tautology is a formula whose negation is not satisfiable. $PM\text{-}PDL_\rho$ will stand for all tautologies of the semantics ρ .

We say that the semantics ρ is normal if for all multiple structures and all programs the following conditions hold. $\rho(\underline{M}, A(i)) = \langle A(i)\rangle$ in $\underline{M}$ for any atomic program A(i), $\rho(\underline{M}, a;b)=\rho(\underline{M}, a)\bullet\rho(\underline{M},b)$ (superposition of relations), $\rho(\underline{M}, a\cup b) = \rho(\underline{M}, a)\cup\rho(\underline{M}, b)$ (union) $\rho(\underline{M}, a^*)=\rho(\underline{M}, a)^*$ (reflexive, transitive closure), $\rho(\underline{M}, p?) = \{(\underline{u}, \underline{u}) : \underline{u}\models p \text{ in } \underline{M}\}$. As we see any two normal semantics must be identical on sequential programs. The set of tautologies of the normal semantics which do not contain parallel composition // will be called Multiple PDL of sequential programs (M-PDL).

SIMPLE REGULAR SEMANTICS

We begin with defining the set of elementary (i. e. indivisible) actions. Within the PDL framework this is usually the set of all atomic programs and tests, i. e. programs of the form p?, where p is any formula. The assumption that arbitrary tests are elementary actions is somehow counterintuitive especially when time dependences in parallel programs are considered. So, we shall assume that in PM-PDL only atomic formulae can be tested. The notion of a simple semantics (cf. [MS87]) is based on the following two assumptions. (1) Any two elementary actions have the same execution times, and in consequence can be performed in a single step. (2) Parallel programs are executed in steps where at aech step a number of elementary actions can be performed simultaneously. In other words, a simple semantics assigns to every program a set of execution sequences, every of which describes one possible course of computations. An execution sequence $C_1C_2 \ldots C_n$ means: first perform simultaneously all elementary actions from the set C_1, then all elementary actions from C_2, and so on. We say that a simple semantics is regular if for every program the corresponding set of execution sequences is a regular language.

Systematically this can be described as follows. Suppose we are given a mapping which to every PM-PDL program a assigns a finite automaton Aut(a) over a finite alphabet consisting of finite sets of elementary actions. The language recognized by Aut(a) will be denoted by ExecSeq(a) and called the set of all execution sequences of the program a. The semantics ρ corresponding to the mapping $a \longmapsto$ Aut(a) is defined as follows. For any program a, a multiple structure $\underline{M}=(\underline{U}, \models, \langle\rangle)$, and $\underline{u}, \underline{v} \in \underline{U}$, $(\underline{u}, \underline{v}) \in \rho(\underline{M}, a)$ iff there exist a sequence $C_1C_2 \ldots C_n \in \mathrm{ExecSeq}(a)$ and $\underline{w}_0, \underline{w}_1, \ldots, \underline{w}_n \in \underline{U}$ such that $\underline{w}_0 = \underline{u}$, $\underline{w}_n = \underline{v}$ and $\underline{w}_{i-1} \langle C_i \rangle \underline{w}_i$ in $\underline{M}$ for all $i = 1, \ldots, n$. Here $\underline{w}_{i-1} \langle C_i \rangle \underline{w}_i$ means that $\underline{w}_i$ is obtained from $\underline{w}_{i-1}$ by a simultaneous execution of all elementary actions contained in C_i. Namely, if C is a set of elementary actions, $\underline{M}=(\underline{U}, \models, \langle\rangle) = M_0 \times M_1 \times \ldots$ is a multiple structure with $M_i = (U_i, \models_i, \langle\rangle_i)$, then by definition for any $\underline{u}, \underline{v} \in \underline{U}$, $\underline{u} = u_0u_1 \ldots$, $\underline{v} = v_0v_1 \ldots$, $\underline{u} \langle C \rangle \underline{v}$ in $\underline{M}$ iff the following three conditions hold: (1) For any atomic program $A(i) \in C$ involving the i-th coordinate, $u_i \langle A \rangle_i v_i$ in M_i, (2) For any test $P(i)? \in C$ involving the i-th coordinate $u_i = v_i$ and $u_i \models_i P$ in M_i, (3) For any coordinate j such that there is no elementary action in C involving j, $u_j = v_j$.

Every semantics ρ which can be defined in the above way will be called simple regular. We shall always assume that the mapping $a \longmapsto$ Aut(a) is effectively computable in time polynomial on the size of Aut(a).

SIMPLE ARB AND MAX SEMANTICS

It is very natural to explain the meaning of parallel programs in terms of place/transition systems (Petri nets). If the systems are finite and the capacity of places is bounded, this usually leads to simple regular semantics. Good examples of such an approach are ARB and MAX semantics for cobegin..//..coend programs proposed by Salwicki and Muldner [SM81, MS87] . Below we show how their ideas can be applied to PM-PDL. Our task is to present mappings $a \longmapsto Aut(a)$ which - according to the previous section - define corresponding semantics for PM-PDL. This will be done by constructing for every program a place/transition system which together with a firing strategy can be converted into a finite automaton.

The place/transition system corresponding to a program a in both ARB and MAX semantics is defined as follows. First, the syntactical tree T of the program a is constructed. In such a tree interior nodes are labelled with ;, $\cup$, $*$ or // and leaves with elementary actions, i. e. atomic programs A(i) or tests P(i)?. With every node α of T we associate two places. At figures (cf. Fig. 1 or 2) these places are denoted by black dots laying left and right of α . In the text the left place will be denoted by $\bullet\alpha$ and the right by $\alpha\bullet$. Places are connected by transitions according to rules depicted at the Fig. 1. For example, if these rules are applied to the program a = =(A(1)//B(2));A(1), the resulting place/transition system is as at the Fig. 2. For simplicity transitions of the form $\bullet\!\!\longrightarrow\!\!\!|\!\!\longrightarrow\!\!\bullet$ are represented by single arrows $\bullet\!\!\longrightarrow\!\!\bullet$, and $\bullet$—A(i)$\longrightarrow\bullet$ stands for $\bullet\!\!\longrightarrow\!\!\!|\!\!\longrightarrow\!\!\bullet$ with additional label A(i). Similarly for $\bullet$—P(i)?$\longrightarrow\bullet$.

At any place we can put at most one token. A token at $\bullet\alpha$ means that the program corresponding to the node α is ready for execution, and a token at $\alpha\bullet$ means that such an execution has just ended. (The program corresponding to α is the program described by the subtree of T with the root α .) Thus, to begin the whole program a we put a token at the place $\bullet\lambda$ where λ is the root of T, and the execution of a ends when a token appears at $\lambda\bullet$. The only difference between ARB and MAX semantics is in the firing strategy. The ARB allows arbitrary conflict-free sets of enabled transitions to be executed simultaneously in a single step, while MAX allows only maximal conflict-free sets of enabled transitions. As usual, a transition is enabled if tokens appear at all its input places. Firing (executing) a transi-

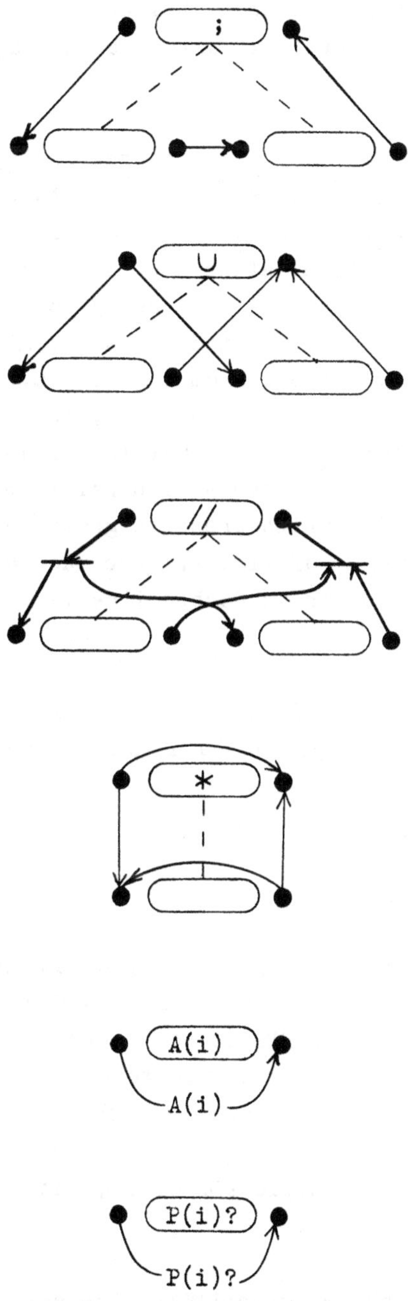

Fig. 1

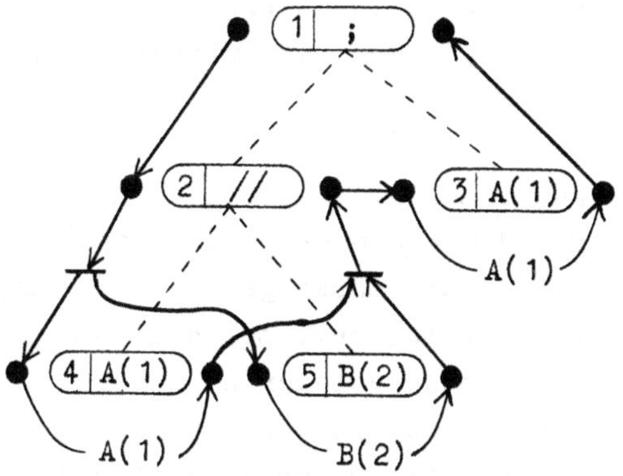

Fig. 2

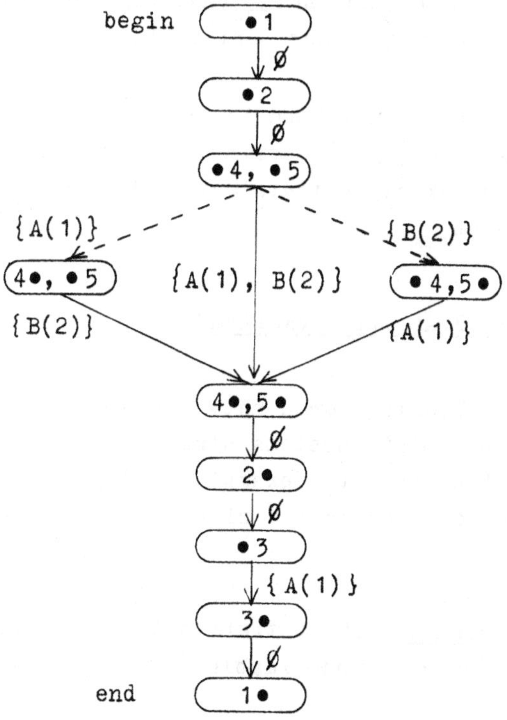

Fig. 3

tion means removing tokens from input places and putting one token at every output place. A set of transitions is conflict-free iff no two of them have an input place in common, and no two are labelled with elementary actions involving the same coordinate (exclusive access to processors).

Now the finite automata $Aut_{arb}(a)$ and $Aut_{max}(a)$ corresponding to ARB and MAX are defined as follows. In both cases the set of states consists of all markings of the place/transition system for a. The marking with the only token at $\bullet\lambda$ is the initial state and the marking with the only token at $\lambda\bullet$ is the final state. If a marking s' can be obtained from s by firing (according to adopted strategy) a set of transitions labelled with elementary actions from the set C, then there is a transition (s, C, s') in the automaton. Thus, the only difference between $Aut_{arb}(a)$ and $Aut_{max}(a)$ is that the transition relation of the latter is contained in the transition relation of the former. This can be seen at the Fig. 3 which presents graphs of $Aut_{arb}(a)$ and $Aut_{max}(a)$ for the program a of Fig. 2. Here the max automaton does not contain the transitions drawn in dashed lines.

It is not hard to see that the mappings $a \longmapsto Aut_{arb}(a)$ and $a \longmapsto Aut_{max}(a)$ define two different normal semantics for PM-PDL. There exists a tautology of $PM\text{-}PDL_{arb}$ whose negation is a tautology of $PM\text{-}PDL_{max}$.

SATISFIABILITY PROBLEMS

Looking for a natural model of communicating parallel programs we often obtain systems strong enough to express the Post Correspondence Problem (cf. for example [Pe85]). The Multiple PDL is no exception. Two coordinates and simple sequential programs are enough to define PCP. (The proofs of theorems stated below can be found in [Da] .)

Theorem 1 The satisfiability problem for Multiple PDL of sequential programs is undecidable.

Now consider the following degenerated satisfiability problem. Input: A formula p and a finite PDL structure M. Question: Does there exist a PDL structure M_0 such that p is satisfied in the multiple structure $\underline{M} = M_0 \times M \times M \times M \times \ldots$ (all coordinates but the first are equal to M).

Theorem 2 The degenerated satisfiability problem is decidable for Multiple PDL of parallel programs with any (effectively defined) simple regular semantics. For simple ARB and MAX semantics the procedure runs in time $\exp(c|M|^k \cdot \exp 3|p|)$ and for sequential Multiple PDL in time $\exp(c \cdot |p| \cdot \log|p| \cdot |M|^k)$. Here $|p|$ is the length of the formula, $|M|$ is the cardinality of the universe of M, k is the number of coordinates involved, c is a constant.

The proof of this theorem (see [Da]) follows the tree automata technique introduced for PDL by Streett [St82] . The degenerated satisfiability problem is reduced to the emptiness problem for special tree automata of [Ra70] . In the reduction we unwind the multiple structure according to its first coordinate. The unwinding procedure for standard PDL produces a tree whose nodes correspond to single nodes of the initial structure. In the multiple case one node of the tree corresponds to the set of nodes of the form $\{w\} \times U \times U \times \ldots$ where w is a single node in M_0 and U is the universe of M. Since M is finite and only a finite number of coordinates appear in the formula, the result of such an unwinding can be coded in a tree using only a finite set of labels. The rest is analogous to the standard PDL case.

A RELATION TO BOOLEAN PDL

Consider a PDL structure B which "simulates" a Boolean variable. More specifically, let X be a predicate symbol, $\uparrow X$, $\downarrow X$ two program symbols. The universe of B has two states, the one with X true and the one with X false. After any execution of $\uparrow X$ (resp. $\downarrow X$) X is true (false). All other predicate symbols are in B always fals and the relations of other program symbols are empty. Multiple structures of the form $\underline{M} = M_0 \times B \times B \times B \times \ldots$, where M_0 is any PDL structure and B is as above, are just the Boolean PDL structures of [Ab80] . Here atomic formulae X(1), X(2), ... are just the Boolean variables, and programs $\uparrow X(1)$, $\downarrow X(1)$, $\uparrow X(2)$, ... set their values.

Abrahamson [Ab80] has proved that the satisfiability problem for Boolean PDL belongs to $\mathrm{NTIME}(c^{n3^k})$ for some c, and does not belong to $\mathrm{DTIME}(d^{n2^k})$ for some $d > 1$, where n is the length of the formula tested and k is the number of Boolean variables it contains.

The lower bound for Boolean PDL is also a lower bound for the degenerated satisfiability problem for Multiple PDL of sequential programs. On the other hand, the sequential part of Theorem 2 gives also a new upper bound for Boolean PDL.

Theorem 3 The satisfiability problem for Boolean PDL belongs to DTIME($2^{c \cdot n \cdot \log n \cdot 2^k}$), where k is the number of Boolean variables and n is the length of the formula tested.

References

[Ab80] K. R. Abrahamson, Decidability and Expressiveness of Logics of Processes, Ph. D. Thesis, Technical Report 80-08-01, August 1980, University of Washington, Seattle.

[Da] R. Danecki, Multiple Propositional Dynamic Logic of Parallel Programs, Fundamenta Informaticae, to appear.

[FL79] M. J. Fisher, R. E. Ladner, Propositional Dynamic Logic of Regular Programs, JCSS 18:2 (1979), pp. 194-211.

[MS87] G. Mirkowska, A. Salwicki, Algorithmic Logic, PWN-Polish Scientific Publishers and D. Reidel Publishing Company 1987.

[Pe85] D. Peleg, Concurrent Dynamic Logic, Proc. STOC'85, pp. 232-239.

[SM81] A. Salwicki, T. Müldner, On the Algorithmic Properties of Concurrent Programs, in Logic of Programs, Proc., LNCS 125, pp. 169-197, Springer 1981.

[St82] R. S. Streett, Propositional Dynamic Logic of Looping and Converse is elementarily decidable, Information and Control 54 (1982) pp. 121-141.

[Ra70] M. O. Rabin, Weakly definable relations and special automata, in: Math. Logic and Found. of Set Theory (Y. Bar-Hillel ed.), pp. 1-23, North-Holland 1970.

THE STEINER TREE PROBLEM AND HOMOGENEOUS SETS

A. D'Atri †, *M. Moscarini* ‡, *A. Sassano* ‡

† Dpt. Ingegneria Elettrica, Università dell'Aquila, I-67100 L'Aquila, Italy
‡ IASI-CNR, Viale Manzoni 30, I-00185 Roma, Italy

ABSTRACT The Steiner tree problem has been extensively studied in the literature because of its various applications (e.g., network design, circuit layout and database query answering). The main result in the paper states that an instance of this problem on a graph G is polynomially reducible to an instance of the same problem on an induced subgraph of G whenever G contains a *homogeneous set* of nodes (i.e., a set of two or more nodes such that every remaining node in G is adjacent either to all or to none of its nodes). This result allows, in particular, to solve in polynomial time the Steiner tree problem on a new class of graphs, called *homogeneous graphs*, defined in terms of homogeneous sets, that properly contains some classes of graphs on which the problem is polynomially solvable. A polynomial algorithm to recognize homogeneous graphs is also given.

1. INTRODUCTION

A *homogeneous set* [6] (also called *nontrivial partitive set* in [4] and *module* in [9]) H in a graph $G = (V, E)$ is a proper subset of V such that H contains two or more nodes and every remaining node in G is adjacent to either all or none of the nodes of H. A homogeneous set H is said to be *maximal* if there is no homogeneous set properly containing H.

The *reduction* of a connected graph G with respect to a subset $S \subset V$ is the graph G' obtained by replacing S with a single node v_S having the same neighbors as S.

Homogeneous graphs are recursively defined in terms of reduction of their two connected components with respect to maximal homogeneous sets.

This new class of graphs extends the class of *distance hereditary graphs* [1,3,7], by generalizing the concept of "twin nodes" (i.e., nodes having the same closed or open neighborhood) to the concept of homogeneous set of nodes.

Similarly to distance hereditary graphs, also homogeneous graphs have structural properties with interesting implications from the algorithmic point of view. In particular, we consider the *cardinality Steiner problem* (*CSP*) on a connected graph $G = (V, E)$ with *terminal* nodes $T \subseteq V$, i.e., the problem of finding a minimum subset $S \subseteq V$ containing T such that S induces a connected subgraph of G.

Such a problem has been extensively studied in the literature with respect to its computational complexity [8]; in particular, it has been proved that it is polynomially solvable in strongly

---

This work has been partially supported by MPI National projects on "Design and Analysis of Algorithms" and on "Formal Aspects of Databases".

chordal, permutation, series parallel and distance hereditary graphs. On the other hand, it is NP-hard for chordal, planar, bipartite and comparability graphs.

In this paper we show that *CSP* is polynomially solvable in homogeneous graphs. The main idea underlying the algorithm is that of recursively reducing a homogeneous graph to a family of trees, in which *CSP* is easily solvable, and, then, recovering the optimal solution of the original problem.

The paper is organized as follows. In Section 2 we provide several properties of homogeneous sets and a polynomial algorithm to find all the maximal homogeneous sets in a connected graph. In Section 3 we discuss some properties of the reduction of a graph with respect to its homogeneous sets and introduce the class of homogeneous graphs, providing a polynomial algorithm to recognize such a class. In Section 4 we show that if *CSP* is polinomially solvable in a reduction G' of a graph G with respect to a homogeneous set, then it is also polinomially solvable in G. As a consequence we provide a polynomial algorithm to solve *CSP* in homogeneous graphs. Finally, in the conclusions we discuss how the results in the paper allow to extend every class in which *CSP* is polynomially solvable (as the classes cited above) to a larger class in which the same problem is also polynomially solvable.

2. HOMOGENEOUS SETS

We shall use standard terminology from graph theory [5]. In particular, we shall consider finite, simple, loopless, undirected graphs $G = (V, E)$, where V is the node set and E is the edge set. Furthermore, for the sake of simplicity, we shall consider connected graphs (unless specified otherwise), even if the definitions and results in the paper can be suitably extended to unconnected graphs.

Let S and T be a pair of subsets of V. We denote: with $\overline{G}$ the *complement* of G, with $\langle S\rangle_G$ (or simply $\langle S\rangle$, whenever no ambiguity arises) the subgraph of G induced by S, with $N_T(S)$ the *neighborhood of S in T*, that is the set of nodes in $T - S$ adjacent to some node in S (for simplicity we shall use v instead of $\{v\}$ and, if $V = T$, we shall omit V when no confusion arises). A proper subset H of V is *homogeneous* in G if it contains at least two nodes and for every $v \in H$, $N(v) - H = N(H)$.

The property of being homogeneous is not hereditary, namely, proper nontrivial subsets of a homogeneous set can be non homogeneous. Furthermore, nondisjoint homogeneous sets satisfy the following properties:

Theorem 2.1. *Let H_1 and H_2 be two nondisjoint homogeneous sets in a graph, we have that:*
(i) If $|H_1 \cap H_2| \geq 2$ then $H_1 \cap H_2$ is homogeneous.
(ii) If $H_1 \cup H_2 = V$ then $V - (H_1 \cap H_2)$ is homogeneous.
(iii) $H_1 \cup H_2$ is homogeneous if and only if $H_1 \cup H_2 \neq V$.

Proof. *Proof of (i)* Since H_1 and H_2 are homogeneous, the nodes in $H_1 \cap H_2$ have the same neighbors in both $V - H_1$ and $V - H_2$ and, hence, also in $(V - H_1) \cup (V - H_2) = V - (H_1 \cap H_2)$; this implies that $H_1 \cap H_2$ is homogeneous.

Proof of (ii). Since $H_1 \cup H_2 = V$ we have that $H_1 \not\subseteq H_2$ and $H_2 \not\subseteq H_1$ (otherwise H_1 or H_2 would coincide with V); furthermore there exists a node in $H_1 - H_2$ adjacent to every node in H_2 and a node in $H_2 - H_1$ adjacent to every node in H_1; this implies that every node in $V - (H_1 \cap H_2)$ is adjacent to every node in $H_1 \cap H_2$ and, hence, $V - (H_1 \cap H_2)$ is a homogeneous set in G.

Proof of (iii). Necessity trivially follows from the definition of homogeneous set. In order to prove the sufficiency, let $v \in H_1 \cap H_2$. Since G is connected $N(H_1 \cup H_2) \neq \emptyset$ and since H_1 and H_2 are homogeneous, every node in $H_1 \cup H_2$ must have the same set of adjacent nodes as v in $N(H_1 \cup H_2)$. □

Let H be a homogeneous set in G; H is *minimal* if no proper subset of it is homogeneous and H is *maximal* if no proper superset of it is homogeneous. We denote by $\mathcal{H}_G$ the family of all maximal homogeneous sets in G. Furthermore, we say that two nodes $u, v \in V$, are ***homogeneable*** if there exists a homogeneous set containing both; if u and v are homogeneable, we denote by H_{uv} the minimum homogeneous set containing both u and v (i.e., the homogeneous set containing u and v such that no proper subset of it, containing both nodes, is homogeneous). Observe that, by (i) of Theorem 2.1, if u and v are homogeneable then H_{uv} is unique and it needs not to be a minimal homogeneous set.

In the following theorem we prove some useful properties of maximal and minimal homogeneous sets.

Theorem 2.2. *Let $G = (V, E)$ be a graph, we have that:*

(i) Maximal homogeneous sets in G are pairwise disjoint if and only if the complement $\overline{G}$ of G has at most two connected components.

(ii) Every two minimal homogeneous sets in G cannot share more than one node.

(iii) For every minimal homogeneous set H in G, if $|H| > 2$ then $\langle H \rangle$ is connected and disjoint from the remaining minimal homogeneous sets in G.

Proof. *Proof of (i) Necessity.* Suppose that maximal homogeneous sets in G are pairwise disjoint and the graph $\overline{G}$ has three or more connected components. Let $K_1, \ldots, K_m$, $m \geq 3$, be the node sets of such components. Evidently, for every $i = 1, \ldots, m$, $V - K_i$ is homogeneous; we will prove that it is also maximal. In fact, if $V - K_i$ is not maximal then for some i, $1 \leq i \leq m$, there exists a maximal homogeneous set H such that $H \supset V - K_i$ and hence $H \cap K_i \neq \emptyset$. Since H is homogeneous no node in $K_i - H$ can be adjacent in $\overline{G}$ to a node in H; therefore, $\langle K_i \rangle_{\overline{G}}$ is not connected (contradiction). Consider, now, the node sets K_1, K_2 and K_3 and the two maximal homogeneous sets $V - K_1$ and $V - K_2$; we have that $(V - K_1) \cap (V - K_2)$ contains K_3 and, hence, is not empty (contradiction).

Sufficiency. Let us suppose, by contradiction, that H_1 and H_2 are two maximal homogeneous sets whose intersection is not empty. Due to (iii) in Theorem 2.1 and to the maximality of H_1 and H_2, we have $H_1 \cup H_2 = V$. Therefore, since H_1 and H_2 are homogeneous, we have that every node in $H_1 - H_2$ is adjacent to every node in H_2 and, analogously, every node in $H_2 - H_1$ is adjacent to every node in H_1; moreover, since $V - (H_1 \cap H_2)$ is homogeneous, every node in $H_1 \cap H_2$ is adjacent to every node in $V - (H_1 \cap H_2)$. This implies that nodes in $H_1 - H_2$, $H_2 - H_1$ and $H_1 \cap H_2$ belong to at least three distinct components in $\overline{G}$.

Proof of (ii) Trivially follows from (i) of Theorem 2.1.

Proof of (iii) Let H be a minimal homogeneous set in G and suppose, by contradiction, that $|H| > 2$ and $\langle H \rangle$ is not connected. For every connected component $\langle H' \rangle$ of $\langle H \rangle$ we have $N(H') = N(H)$. Let $\langle H^* \rangle$ be the largest connected component of $\langle H \rangle$. Now, if $|H^*| \geq 2$ then H^* is homogeneous (contradiction), otherwise every connected component of $\langle H \rangle$ has a single node and, hence, every pair of nodes in H is homogeneous (contradiction).

In order to prove the second part of (iii), let us suppose, by contradiction, that there exists a pair H_1 and H_2 of minimal homogeneous sets such that $|H_1| > 2$ and $H_1 \cap H_2 = \{u\}$ (by (ii) the intersection contains at most one node). We will show that H_1 cannot be minimal by proving that every node in $H_1 - \{u\}$ is adjacent to u (hence, $H_1 - \{u\}$ is also homogeneous). In fact, since $|H_1| > 2$, $\langle H_1 \rangle$ is connected; let us consider any node $v \in H_2 - \{u\}$ and a node $w \in H_1 - \{u\}$ adjacent to u; since H_2 is homogeneous, we have that v is adjacent to w. Let, now, z be any node in $H_1 - \{u\}$ distinct from w; since H_1 is homogeneous and w is adjacent to v then z is adjacent to v; now, since H_2 is homogeneous and v is adjacent to z then u is adjacent to z. Therefore, every node in $H_1 - \{u\}$ is adjacent to u and H_1 is not minimal. □

From the above theorem we deduce the following characterization of the family of maximal homogeneous sets in a graph.

Theorem 2.3. *Let $G = (V, E)$ be a graph, we have that:*

(i) If $\overline{G}$ is connected, the family $\mathcal{H}_G$ is composed by the sets of nodes H such that no two nodes $u \in H$ and $v \in V - H$ are homogeneable.

(ii) If $\overline{G}$ is not connected, $\mathcal{H}_G$ is composed by the nontrivial sets $V - K_i$, where K_i is the node set of the i-th connected component of $\overline{G}$.

Proof. *Proof of (i)* Denote by $\mathcal{H}'$ the family of the homogeneous sets H such that no two nodes $u \in H$ and $v \in V - H$ are homogeneable. Suppose, by contradiction, that $\overline{G}$ is connected and $\mathcal{H}' \neq \mathcal{H}_G$. It follows that either there exists a maximal homogeneous set not belonging to $\mathcal{H}'$ or there exists an element in $\mathcal{H}'$ which is not maximal.

In the first case, let H be a maximal homogeneous set such that there exist two nodes $u \in H$ and $v \in V - H$ that are homogeneable. Now, since H is maximal there exists a maximal homogeneous set, distinct from H, containing H_{uv} and hence having a non empty intersection with H. But, since $\overline{G}$ is connected, the latter property contradicts (i) of Theorem 2.2.

In the second case, let H be an element of $\mathcal{H}'$ which is not maximal. Let H' be the maximal homogeneous set containing H (by (i) in Theorem 2.2 we have that H' is unique) and let v be a node in $H' - H$. Consider a node $u \in H$, evidently $H_{uv} \subseteq H'$ and hence u and v are homogeneable, contradicting the hypothesis that $H \in \mathcal{H}'$.

Proof of (ii) Let $K_1, \ldots, K_m$, $m \geq 2$, be the node sets of the connected components of $\overline{G}$, and $\mathcal{H}'$ be the family $\{V - K_i : i = 1, \ldots, m, |V - K_i| > 1\}$. As shown in the proof of (i) in Theorem 2.2, every element of $\mathcal{H}'$ is a maximal homogeneous set and, hence, $\mathcal{H}' \subseteq \mathcal{H}_G$.

If for some i, $1 \leq i \leq m$, $|V - K_i| = 1$ then it is easy to see that $m = 2$; furthermore, either both connected components of $\overline{G}$ have only one node and $\mathcal{H}_G$ is empty or one of them has at least two nodes and it is the unique element in $\mathcal{H}_G$. In both cases $\mathcal{H}' = \mathcal{H}_G$.

Therefore, consider the case in which for every i, $i = 1,\dots,m$, $|V - K_i| > 1$ and let us suppose, by contradiction, that there exists a maximal homogeneous set H not belonging to $\mathcal{H}'$. Since $V - K_i$ is homogeneous, for each $i = 1,\dots,m$, $H \cap K_i \neq \emptyset$. Since H is homogeneous there exists a node $w \in V - H$ adjacent in G to every node in H. Without loss of generality suppose that $w \in K_1$. Since w is adjacent in G to every node in $H \cap K_1$, $\langle K_1 \rangle_{\overline{G}}$ cannot be connected (contradiction). □

We close this section with an algorithm which, given a graph G, produces the family $\mathcal{H}_G$ of its maximal homogeneous sets. The algorithm uses the procedure HUV which, given a pair of nodes $u, v \in V$, either outputs the set H_{uv}, if u and v are homogeneable, or concludes that no homogeneous set contains $\{u, v\}$ (by setting the boolean variable *succeeds* to *false*). The procedure HUV will be described later.

```
procedure MAXHOM(input: G; output: ℋ_G);

begin
    let K_1,...,K_m be the connected components of Ḡ;
    ℋ_G := ∅;
    if m > 1
    then for i := 1 to m
         do if |V − K_i| > 1 then ℋ_G := ℋ_G ∪ {V − K_i}
    else for each v ∈ V
         do begin
              S := {v};
              for each u ∈ V − S
              do begin
                   HUV(G, u, v, H_uv, succeeds);
                   if succeeds then S := S ∪ H_uv
              end;
              if S ≠ {v} then ℋ_G := ℋ_G ∪ {S}
         end
end;
```

Theorem 2.4. *Given a graph $G = (V, E)$ the procedure MAXHOM computes, in the variable $\mathcal{H}_G$, the family of all the maximal homogeneous sets of G.*

Proof. If $\overline{G}$ is not connected, the correctness of the algorithm follows from (ii) in Theorem 2.3. If, on the other hand, $\overline{G}$ is connected, suppose that the set S, computed in the inner do-loop of the procedure MAXHOM starting from a node v, properly contains $\{v\}$. By (i) of Theorem 2.2 and (iii) of Theorem 2.1, we have that S is homogeneous. Furthermore, for every $u \in V - S$, v and u are not homogeneable. This implies that, for every $w \in S$ and for every $u \in V - S$, w and u are not homogeneable. In fact, again by (i) of Theorem 2.2 and (iii) of Theorem 2.1, if for a node $w \in S$ we have that w and u are homogeneable then, since $H_{vu} \subseteq S \cup H_{wu}$, v and u should also be homogeneable. Therefore, by (i) in Theorem 2.3, S is maximal.

Conversely, suppose, by contradiction, that there exists a maximal homogeneous set H that is not contained in $\mathcal{H}_G$ when the procedure stops. Let v and u be two nodes in H; we have that the set u and v are homogeneable. Consequently, the set S, produced by the inner do-loop, starting from the node v, belongs to $\mathcal{H}_G$ and, hence, is maximal. Since $H \cap S \neq \emptyset$ and $H \neq S$, we contradict (i) of Theorem 2.2. □

We describe now the procedure HUV and we prove its correctness. The procedure receives in input a graph $G = (V, E)$ and a pair of nodes $u, v \in V$ and it produces, if u and v are homogeneable, the set H_{uv}. The procedure stops with the boolean variable *succeeds* set to ***true*** if and only if u and v are homogeneable.

```
procedure HUV(input: G, u, v; output: H_uv, succeeds);

begin
    succeeds := false;
    S^0 := {u, v};
    if N(u) = N(v)
    then begin
        succeeds := true;
        H_uv := S^0
    end
    else if N(u) ∩ N(v) ≠ ∅
        then begin
            h := 0;
            while {w ∈ N(S^h) : N(w) ⊉ S^h} ≠ ∅
            do begin
                S^{h+1} := S^h ∪ {w ∈ N(S^h) : N(w) ⊉ S^h};
                h := h + 1
            end;
            if S^h ≠ V
            then begin
                succeeds := true;
                H_uv := S^h
            end
        end
end;
```

Theorem 2.5. *Given a graph $G = (V, E)$ and two nodes $u, v \in V$, the procedure HUV stops with the variable succeeds set to true if and only if the nodes u and v are homogeneable.*

Proof. *Sufficiency.* Suppose, by contradiction, that u and v are homogeneable and the algorithm stops with the boolean variable *succeeds* set to *false*. In this case the set S^h produced by the while-statement must be equal to V. Since $S^0 \subseteq H_{uv} \subset S^h$, there exists an index $k \leq h$ such that $S^{k-1} \subseteq H_{uv}$ and there exists a node $\overline{w}$ in $S^k - H_{uv}$ and, hence in $S^k - S^{k-1} = \{w \in N(S^{k-1}) : N(w) \not\supseteq S^{k-1}\}$. Then $\overline{w}$ is a node in $N(H_{uv})$ not adjacent to at least one node in H_{uv} and a contradiction arises.

Necessity. Suppose, now, that the algorithm stops with the boolean variable *succeeds* set to ***true***. In this case either $N(u) = N(v)$ or the set S^h produced by the while-statement is different from V. In the first case $H_{uv} = S^0$. In the second case $N(S^h) \neq \emptyset$ (due to the fact that G is connected) and $\{w \in N(S^h) : N(w) \not\supseteq S^h\} = \emptyset$; then we have that $2 \leq |S^h| < |V|$ and each node in $N(S^h)$ is adjacent to each node in S^h; hence, S^h is homogeneous. Suppose that $H_{uv} \neq S^h$, it follows that $S_0 \subseteq H_{uv} \subset S^h$. Consequently, there exists an index $k \leq h$ such that $S^{k-1} \subset H_{uv}$ and there exists a node $w \in S^k - H_{uv}$ not adjacent to every node of S^{k-1} and hence H_{uv} cannot be homogeneous which is a contradiction. □

Remark 2.1. *It is easy to see that the procedure HUV requires polynomial time, and, since the procedure MAXHOM requires no more than $|V|^2)$ calls of the procedure HUV, we have that the overall complexity of the procedure MAXHOM is also polynomial.* □

3. REDUCTION AND HOMOGENEOUS GRAPHS

The *reduction* of G with respect to $S \subseteq V$ is the graph $G_S = (V_S, E_S)$ where $V_S = (V - S) \cup \{v_S\}$ and $E_S = (E - \{(v, v') | v \in S\}) \cup \{(v_S, v) | v \in N(S)\}$. It is easy to see that the following properties hold.

Proposition 3.1. *Let G be a graph and S_1 and S_2 be two disjoint sets of nodes in G. We have $(G_{S_1})_{S_2} = (G_{S_2})_{S_1}$.*

Proposition 3.2. *Let G be a graph and H a homogeneous set in G. There exists an induced subgraph of G isomorphic to G_H.*

Proof. Let v be a node in H. We will prove that the subgraph of G induced by $V - H \cup \{v\}$ is isomorphic to G_H. It is sufficient to consider the bijection f that associates to each node in $V - H$ the node itself and to the node v the node v_H. By definition of reduction and homogeneous set, (u, w) is an edge of $\langle V - H \cup \{v\} \rangle$ if and only if $(f(u), f(w))$ is in E_H. □

Lemma 3.1. *Let G be a graph and H and H' be homogeneous sets in G such that $H' \not\subseteq H$.*
(i) If $H' \cap H = \emptyset$ then H' is homogeneous in G_H.
(ii) If $H' \cap H \neq \emptyset$ then $H' - H \cup \{v_H\}$ is homogeneous in G_H if and only if $H \cup H' \neq V$.

Proof. *Proof of (i).* If $N(H') \cap H = \emptyset$ the statement trivially follows. Conversely, the nodes in $N(H') \cap H$ are replaced in G_H by the node v_H. Since v_H is adjacent to every node $u \in H'$ then H' is homogeneous in G_H.

Proof of (ii). In order to prove the sufficiency, we note that if $H \cup H' \neq V$ then, by (iii) in Theorem 2.1, $H \cup H'$ is homogeneous in G and, by definition of reduction, $H' - H \cup \{v_H\}$ is homogeneous in G_H.

In order to prove the necessity, let us suppose, by contradiction, that $H \cup H' = V$; in this case $H' - H \cup \{v_H\} = V_H$ and a contradiction arises. □

Consider, now, the procedure HOMSTRUCT.

```
procedure HOMSTRUCT(input: G; output: G_ℋ);

begin
    MAXHOM(G, ℋ_G);
    if there exists a maximal homogeneous set H in ℋ_G
    then begin
        G := G_H;
        HOMSTRUCT(G, G_ℋ)
    end
    else G_ℋ := G
end;
```

Theorem 3.1. *Let G be a graph such that $\overline{G}$ is not connected. The graph $G_{\mathcal{H}}$ computed by the procedure HOMSTRUCT with input G is composed by a single edge.*

Proof. If G has no maximal homogeneous set it is easy to see that, due to (ii) in Theorem 2.3, G and, hence, $G_{\mathcal{H}}$ are composed by a single edge. On the other hand, if G has a maximal homogeneous set, suppose that the procedure HOMSTRUCT selects the maximal homogeneous set H; by (ii) in Theorem 2.3 we have that $H = V - K$, where K is the node set of a connected component of $\overline{G}$. Again by (ii) in Theorem 2.3, if K has at least two nodes then it becomes the unique maximal homogeneous set in the graph G_H. Therefore, after at most two recursive calls, we obtain a graph composed by a single edge. □

The following corollary trivially follows (by (i) in Theorem 2.2 and by Proposition 3.1 if $\overline{G}$ is connected, and by Theorem 3.1 if $\overline{G}$ is not connected).

Corollary 3.1. *Let G be a graph. The graph $G_{\mathcal{H}}$ computed by the procedure HOMSTRUCT is unique up to an isomorphism.*

We call *homogeneous structure* of G a graph $G_{\mathcal{H}}$ produced by the procedure HOMSTRUCT applied to the graph G. Since the set $\mathcal{H}_G$ can be computed in polynomial time, and each call of the procedure HOMSTRUCT reduces the cardinality of the node set by at least one, the homogeneous structure of a graph can be computed in polynomial time.

We are now ready to introduce the (recursive) definition of homogeneous graph.

Definition. *A graph G is a homogeneous graph if either it is a tree or the homogeneous structure of each 2-connected component of G is a homogeneous graph.* □

From this definition it follows, by Theorem 3.1, that:

Corollary 3.2. *Let G be a graph. If $\overline{G}$ is not connected then G is a homogeneous graph.*

Furthermore, by the polynomiality of the procedure HOMSTRUCT it follows:

Proposition 3.3. *The recursive procedure RECOGNIZE decides in polynomial time whether a graph is homogeneous.*

Observe that the boolean variable *succeeds* is set to *false* if and only if a 2-connected component with no homogeneous set is found.

```
procedure RECOGNIZE(input: G; output: succeeds);

    procedure HOMGRAPH(input: G)

    begin {HOMGRAPH}
        for each 2-connected component C of G
        do begin
            HOMSTRUCT(C, C_ℵ);
            if C = C_ℵ
            then succeeds := false
            else HOMGRAPH(C_ℵ)
        end
    end; {HOMGRAPH}

begin {RECOGNIZE}
    succeeds := true;
    HOMGRAPH(G)
end; {RECOGNIZE}
```

4. THE CARDINALITY STEINER PROBLEM

The *cardinality Steiner problem* on G with *terminal* nodes T, denoted $CSP(G, T)$, is the problem of finding a *Steiner set* S for T (i.e., a subset S of V containing T such that $\langle S\rangle$ is connected) with minimum cardinality. In the following we assume that $\langle T\rangle$ is not connected; in fact in this case T is trivially the unique solution of $CSP(G,T)$.

The cardinality Steiner problem on a graph $G = (V, E)$ with terminal nodes T is reducible in polynomial time to the cardinality Steiner problem on the reduction $G_H = (V_H, E_H)$ of G with respect to a homogeneous set H with terminal nodes T_H, where T_H is defined as:

$$T_H = \begin{cases} T, & \text{if } H \cap T = \emptyset; \\ (T - H) \cup \{v_H\}, & \text{otherwise.} \end{cases} \tag{4.1}$$

In fact, the following theorem provides a transformation that maps a solution S_H of $CSP(G_H, T_H)$ in a solution S of $CSP(G,T)$ in polynomial time.

Theorem 4.1. *Let G be a graph, T a subset of its nodes and H a homogeneous set in G. If S_H is a solution of $CSP(G_H, T_H)$ then the set*

$$S = \begin{cases} S_H, & \text{if } v_H \notin S_H; \\ (S_H - \{v_H\}) \cup Z, & \text{otherwise} \end{cases} \tag{4.2}$$

is a solution of $CSP(G,T)$ with Z defined as follows:

$$Z = \begin{cases} H \cap T, & \text{if } H \cap T \neq \emptyset \text{ and } T \not\subseteq H; \\ T \cup \{w\}, \text{ for some } w \in N(H), & \text{if } T \subseteq H; \\ \{v\}, \text{ for some } v \in H, & \text{if } H \cap T = \emptyset. \end{cases}$$

Proof. The following three cases arise.

case 1) $v_H \notin S_H$. Let us suppose, by contradiction, that S_H is not a solution of $CSP(G,T)$. Since $v_H \notin T_H$, from the definition of T_H it follows that

$$H \cap T = \emptyset \tag{4.3}$$

and, hence, S_H is a Steiner set for T in G. Let S' be a solution of $CSP(G,T)$; we have that $|S'| < |S_H|$ and, hence,

$$S' \cap H \neq \emptyset \tag{4.4}$$

(otherwise S' would be also a solution of $CSP(G_H,T_H)$ and a contradiction would arise).
By (4.3) and the definition of T_H, we have that the set of nodes $(S' - H) \cup \{v_H\}$ is also a Steiner set for T_H in G_H. Furthermore, by (4.4) we have that

$$|(S' - H) \cup \{v_H\}| \leq |S'| < |S_H|$$

contradicting the optimality of S_H.

case 2) $v_H \in S_H$ and $H \cap T \neq \emptyset$. In this case, by definition of T_H, we have that $v_H \in T_H$.

If $T \subseteq H$ we have that $S_H = \{v_H\}$ and, moreover, since $\langle T \rangle$ is not connected, the solution of $CSP(G,T)$ must contain at least one node not in T. But, since H is homogeneous, $\langle T \cup \{w\} \rangle$, for any w adjacent to H, is connected; hence, $T \cup \{w\}$ is a solution of $CSP(G,T)$.

If $T \not\subseteq H$ then $(S_H - \{v_H\}) \cup (H \cap T)$ is a Steiner set for T in G; in fact, $\langle S_H \rangle$ is connected and contains a node w adjacent to v_H and, hence, to each node in $H \cap T$. Let us suppose, by contradiction, that the set of nodes $(S_H - \{v_H\}) \cup (H \cap T)$ is not a solution of $CSP(G,T)$.

Let S' be a solution of $CSP(G,T)$; we have that:

$$|S'| < |(S_H - \{v_H\}) \cup (H \cap T)|$$

By definition of T_H we have that $S'' = S' - (H \cap T) \cup \{v_H\}$ is a Steiner set for T_H in G_H. Consequently, since $|H \cap T| \geq 1$, we have that

$$|S''| \leq |S'| < |(S_H - \{v_H\}) \cup (H \cap T)| \leq |S_H|$$

and a contradiction arises.

case 3) $v_H \in S_H$ and $H \cap T = \emptyset$. Since by Proposition 3.2, for every v in H, $(S_H - \{v_H\}) \cup \{v\}$ induces a connected subgraph in G then it is a Steiner set for T in G.

Let us suppose, by contradiction, that $(S_H - \{v_H\}) \cup \{v\}$ is not a solution of $CSP(G,T)$, for any $v \in H$. Let S' be a solution of $CSP(G,T)$; we have that:

$$|S'| < |(S_H - \{v_H\}) \cup \{v\}| = |S_H|, \qquad \forall v \in H \tag{4.5}$$

If $S' \cap H = \emptyset$ then S' is a solution of $CSP(G_H,T_H)$ and (4.5) is contradicted. On the contrary, if $S' \cap H \neq \emptyset$, the set $S'' = (S' - H) \cup \{v_H\}$ is a Steiner set in G_H such that $|S''| \leq |S'| < |S_H|$ which is also a contradiction. □

The previous theorem provides a criterion to obtain from a solution of the problem $CSP(G_H, T_H)$ a solution of the problem $CSP(G,T)$. If we apply recursively this theorem we can obtain a solution of $CSP(G,T)$ from a solution of $CSP(G_{\mathcal{H}}, T_{\mathcal{H}})$, where $G_{\mathcal{H}}$ is the homogeneous structure of G and $T_{\mathcal{H}}$ is the set of terminal nodes of $G_{\mathcal{H}}$ obtained by applying (4.1) at each reduction step.

The function EXPANSION recovers a solution of $CSP(G,T)$ from a solution of $CSP(G_{\mathcal{H}}, T_{\mathcal{H}})$ by recursively applying (4.2) ($Term(v_H)$ denotes the set of terminal nodes in H when the graph is reduced with respect to H).

```
function EXPANSION(input: S,T);

    begin
        while there is v_H ∈ S − V
        do begin
            if Term(v_H) ≠ ∅
            then if T ≠ {v_H}
                then S := (S − {v_H}) ∪ Term(v_H)
                else for some w ∈ N(H) do S := (S − {v_H}) ∪ Term(v_H) ∪ {w}
            else for some w ∈ H do S := (S − {v_H}) ∪ {w};
            T := (T − {v_H}) ∪ Term(v_H)
        end;
        EXPANSION:=S
    end;
```

Since, by (i) in Theorem 2.2 and (ii) in Theorem 2.3, the number of homogeneous sets in a graph is linear in the number of nodes, then it is easy to prove the following corollary.

Corollary 4.1. *Given a solution of the Steiner problem $CSP(G_{\mathcal{H}}, T_{\mathcal{H}})$, the function EXPANSION produces in polynomial time a solution of $CSP(G,T)$.*

Corollary 4.1 allows to derive the following important properties of homogeneous sets of nodes in a graph.

Remark 4.1. *CSP is solvable in polynomial time in every graph that can be recursively reduced to a simpler graph in which CSP is polynomiallly solvable.* □

In fact, the solution of the original problem can be recovered, by using Theorem 4.1, from the solutions of the derived problems on the graphs in the family.

On the other hand, Corollary 4.1 provides a sharper definition of the boundary between polynomiality and NP-hardness for *CSP*.

Remark 4.2. *Given any class of graphs G for which CSP is NP-hard, we have that CSP is also NP-hard for the class of graphs whose members are the homogeneous structures of G.* □

For example, since it is easy to see that the homogeneous structure of a comparability graph is a uniquely partially orderable graph [4] and *CSP* is NP-hard for comparability graphs [8], we have that:

Remark 4.3. *CSP is NP-hard for uniquely partially orderable graphs.* □

Another consequence of the previous theorem is that, if the graph is homogeneous then we are guaranteed that a recursive use of the procedure DECOMPOSE decomposes the graph into a family of trees where *CSP* is trivially solvable.

```
procedure STEINER(input: G = (V, E), T; output: S);

    procedure DECOMPOSE(input: G, T)

    begin {DECOMPOSE}
    Step 1: for every cutpoint v ∈ V − T
          do if there exists a Steiner set for T in ⟨V − {v}⟩
              then T := T ∪ {v};
    Step 2: for every 2-connected component C of G
          do begin
          Step 2.1: for every maximal homogeneous set H in C
              do begin
                  C := C_H;
                  Term(v_H) := H ∩ T;
                  if H ∩ T ≠ ∅ then T := (T − H) ∪ {v_H}
              end;
          Step 2.2: if C is a tree
              then begin
                  let S_C be the solution of CSP(C, T);
                  S := S ∪ EXPANSION(S_C, T)
              end
              else DECOMPOSE(C, T)
          end
    end; {DECOMPOSE}

begin {STEINER}
    S := T;
    DECOMPOSE(G, T)
end; {STEINER}
```

Theorem 4.2. *Given a hom-graph G and a subset T of its nodes, the procedure STEINER provides a solution of $CSP(G, T)$ in polynomial time.*

Proof. The procedure DECOMPOSE starts by adding to the set of terminal nodes the nodes that are cutpoints in the graph and whose removal disconnects the original set of terminal nodes (*Step 1*). Successively (*Step 2*), it computes the homogeneous structure of each 2-connected component C of G by reducing C with respect to each maximal homogeneous set H and by storing in $Term(v_H)$ the set of terminal nodes in H (*Step 2.1*). Then (*Step 2.2*), if $C_{\mathcal{H}}$ is a tree, the procedure DECOMPOSE computes a solution of the cardinality Steiner problem for $C_{\mathcal{H}}$ and invokes the procedure EXPANSION, if $C_{\mathcal{H}}$ contains at least a cycle then the procedure DECOMPOSE recursively calls itself.

As observed above, the procedure STEINER converges if G is homogeneous, since, by definition, it can be always decomposed in a family of trees.

In order to prove that the procedure STEINER requires a polynomial number of elementary steps, observe that *Step 2.1* and *Step 2.2* can be performed in polynomial time by Remark 2.1 and Corollary 4.1, respectively and that finding a cutpoint and checking the connectivity (*Step 1*) can be also done in polynomial time. □

5. CONCLUDING REMARKS

We introduced a new class of graphs (that can be recognized in polynomial time) defined in terms of homogeneous sets of nodes, and we proved that the cardinality Steiner problem is solvable in polynomial time for this class of graphs.

This polynomiality result is based on Theorem 4.1 that shows that if the cardinality Steiner problem is polynomially solvable in the reduction of a graph with respect to one of its homogeneous sets then it is also polynomially solvable in the graph.

Therefore, given any class $\mathcal{G}$ of graphs for which the cardinality Steiner problem is polynomially solvable, we can obtain a larger class of graphs for which the cardinality Steiner problem is also polynomially solvable. This new class can be defined by substituting in the definition of homogeneous graph the requirement that G is a tree with the requirement that G belongs to $\mathcal{G}$.

REFERENCES

[1] H.J. Bandelt and H.M. Mulder, Distance - hereditary graphs, *Journal of Combinatorial Theory (B)* **41** (1986), 182–208.
[2] D.G. Corneil, H. Lerchs and L. Stewart Burlingham, Complement reducible graphs, *Discrete Applied Mathematics* **3** (1981), 163–174.
[3] A. D'Atri and M. Moscarini, Distance-hereditary graphs, Steiner trees and connected domination, *SIAM J. on Computing* **17** (1988).
[4] M.C. Golumbic, "Algorithmic graph theory and perfect graphs", Academic Press, New York, 1980.
[5] F. Harary, "Graph Theory", Addison-Wesley, Reading, Massachusetts, 1969.
[6] R.B. Hayward, Weakly triangulated graphs, *Journal of Combinatorial Theory (B)*.**39** (1985), 200–208.
[7] E. Howorka, A characterization of distance-hereditary graphs, *Quart. J. Math. Oxford (2)* **28** (1977), 417–420.
[8] Johnson, D.S., The NP-Completeness Column: An Ongoing Guide, *Journal of Algorithms* **6** (1985), 434–451.
[9] Spinrad, J., On comparability and permutation graphs, *SIAM J. on Computing* **14** (1985), 658–670.

TERMINATION OF REWRITING IS UNDECIDABLE IN THE ONE-RULE CASE †

Max Dauchet

LIFL (UA 369, CNRS), Université de Lille-Flandres-Artois

UFR d'IEEA, 59655 VILLENEUVE D'ASCQ Cedex FRANCE

ABSTRACT: It is well known that it is undecidable whether a term rewriting system is terminating. We prove in this paper that the property remains undecidable if the system has only one rule.

I. Introduction.

A rewrite system (also called term rewriting system) terminates iff no infinite derivations are possible. It is well known that termination (also called uniform termination) is, in general, an undecidable property (see, for example, Huet,G., Lankfork,D.S. (1978) [4]). Then a lot of works have been devoted to introduce methods for proving that particular systems of rewrite rules are terminating - or non-terminating - programs (see Dershowitz,N. (1985, 1987) [2]) for a survey of termination of rewriting).

Classical proofs of undecidability of termination simulate Turing machines with rewrite systems, the number of rules of which depends on the number of machine transition. Lipton,R., Snyder,L. (1977) [7] asserts that *three* rules suffice for undecidability. Dershowitz,N. (1985, 1987) [2] gives a new coding of Turing machines by *two* rules-rewrite systems, which leaves open the termination problem of the *one* rule case only (Jouannaud, J.P. (1987) [6]).

This paper is devoted to prove that termination is undecidable, even in the *one* rule case.

In the next section, we present our construction and the precise result. In section III, we present a detailed proof.

Let us recall that a rule is left-linear if no variable occurs more than once on the left-hand side of the rule; a rule is right-linear if no variable occurs

† The preparation of this paper was supported in part by the "GRECO de Programmation" and the PRC "Mathématiques et Informatique".

more than once on the right-hand side of the rule. A rule is *linear* if it is both left- and right-linear. In this paper, we need a non-linear rule to simulate a Turing machine. So, our construction leaves open the following problems:

Does termination is decidable in the one-*linear*-rule case?

Does termination is decidable in the *one-rule semi-Thue* system case? (asemi-Thue system can be viewed as a rewrite system over words, consisting of monadic (hence, linear) terms). R.V.Book (1985, 1987) [1] expects the word problem is decidable in the one-rule Thue systems case; by the same way, we suggest that one should attempt to show that the first question above (and hence, the second one) get positive answer.

In this paper, we assume that the reader is familiar with the basic notions of rewrite systems (see, for example, Dershowitz,N. (1985, 1987) [2] and Huet,G.,Oppen,D.C. (1980) [5]).

II.Construction.

A/Turing machine: notations.

Let M be a Turing machine, with a single tape. States are denoted q, q_1, q_i, q', ...q'_i... and so on. Letters of the tape alphabet Γ are denoted by first letters of the greek alphabet α, β, γ, α', ..., α_1,..., α_i,..., α'_i.... Without lack of generality, we suppose that the non-blank portion of tape is always enclosed between special symbols $\#_l$ and $\#_r$.

An *instantaneous description* (I.D.) *D* of *M is denoted*

$$M\ (\ \alpha_m\ldots\alpha_1\#_l,\ q,\ \delta,\ \beta_1\ldots\beta_n\#_r\ )$$

which means that M is in state q, the head scans the symbol δ, with non-blank left portion of tape $\#_l\alpha_1\ldots\alpha_m$ (from the left end to the symbol preceding the read head) and right portion $\beta_1\ldots\beta_n\#_r$ (from the symbol following the read head). If a non-blank portion is empty, we denote it \$.

(q,α,β,q',L) denotes the *left-moving M-instruction* signifying "if M is in state q reading the symbol α, then replace on the tape α with the symbol β, move left and go into state q' ". *Right-moving instructions* are defined by the same way.

To increase the non-blank portion of the tape, there are *special-left moving instructions* of the form $(q,\#_l,\#_l\beta,q',L)$, signifying "if M is in state q reading the symbol $\#_l$, then insert the symbol β, move left to position the head on $\#_l$ again, and go into state q' " Special-right moving instructions are defined by the same way.

Obviously, moving instructions such as $(q,\#_l,\beta,q',L)$ are forbiden. Without lack of generality, we do not considere "standing" instructions.

B/Rewrite rules: notations.

For any term, x, x^*, $\mathbf{x}$, y, $\mathbf{x}$, z, z', z'', $x_1,\ldots,$ x_n, ...x', ...x'_i, ...y'_j... denote variables.

Let us define the ranked alphabet Σ, on which the rewrite rule R_M is defined:

- Each state symbol and tape symbol of M will be a constant of Σ.
- V and # are binary operators.
- \$ is a special constant which is used like NIL.
- The 5-ary operator D will get the left-context $\alpha_m \ldots \alpha_1 \#_1$ as first son, the current state as second son, the scanned type symbol as third son, the right-context as forth son, and, as fifth son, a term which denotes the next rule used in a M-computation and which "computes" by overlaping the corresponding next I.D.
- The 6-ary operator T is the root of the last son of D. Its four first sons will be matched by M-instructions.

C/The rule R_M

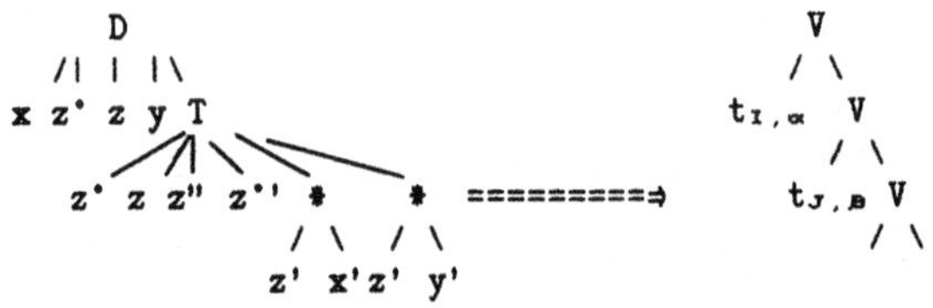

For every M-instruction I, J, ... K and tape symbols $\alpha, \beta, \ldots \chi$, with terms $t_{I,\alpha}$ defined after

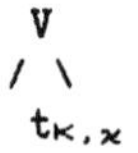

If I is a right-moving instruction (q, λ, μ, q', R) then, for every tape symbol α

$t_{I,\alpha}$ =

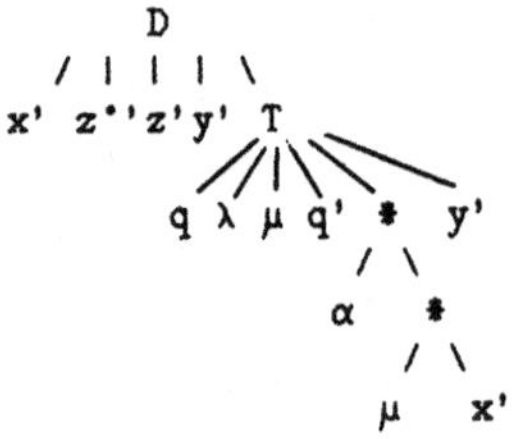

If I is a left-moving instruction (q, λ, μ, q', L) then, for every tape symbol α

$t_{I,\alpha}$ =

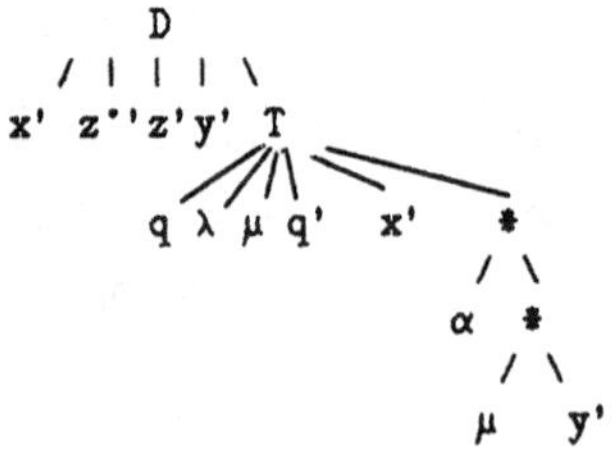

If I is a special right-moving instruction $(q, \#_r, \mu\#_r, q', R)$ then, for only the tape symbol $\alpha = \#_r$

$t_{I,\alpha}$ =

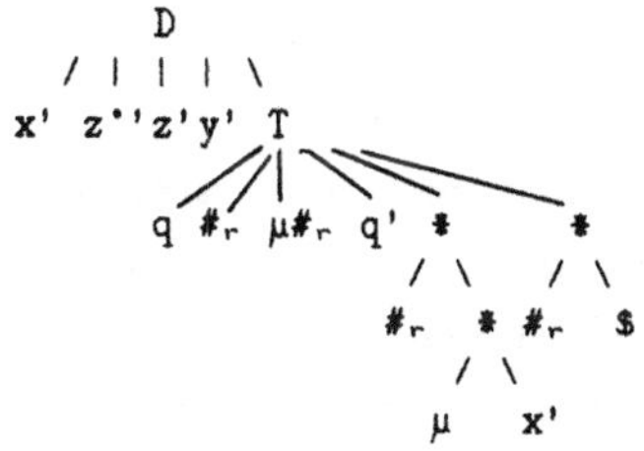

If I is a special left-moving instruction $(q, \#_l, \#_l\mu, q', L)$ then, for only the tape symbol $\alpha = \#_l$

$t_{I,\alpha}$ =

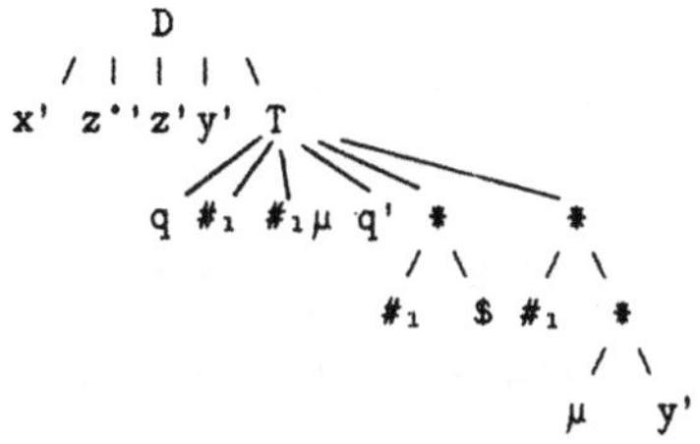

F/ The result.

<u>Theorem</u> :

$\mathcal{M}$ halts for all input tapes if and only if R_M terminates for all initial term.

Proof: see section III for a detailed proof. Nevertheless, it is easy to get an intuitive idea of this proof, which is sometimes tedious but always follows classical ways. The simulation lemma of section III checks the idea of the construction: if we unify the left-hand side of the rule with some subterm $t_{I,\alpha}$ of the right-hand side, we simulate a step of Turing machine using the instruction I. The two last lemmas are devoted to prove that there is no "perverse" infinite R_M-derivation, i.e. no infinite derivation which does note simulate infinite $\mathcal{M}$-computation. König's lemma is then our main tool.

<u>Corollary</u> :

It is undecidable if one-rule rewrite systems terminate.

Proof: Since it is undecidable if a Turing machine halts uniformly, it is also undecidable if R_M systems terminate. ·

III. Proof of the theorem.

A/Preliminaries.

Remark: According to most of the papers, we considere rewriting of *closed* terms, i.e. terms without variables. Nevertheless, terms might also contain variables, but for the purpose of this paper, these are treated as constants. So, in the following, we considere closed initial terms.

Let an *instantaneous description of M*

$$\Delta = M\,(\,\alpha_m \ldots \alpha_1 \#_1,\ q,\ \delta,\ \beta_1 \ldots \beta_n \#_r\,)$$

Let us denote $\alpha_m \ldots \alpha_1 \#_1$ its *left-context* and $\beta_1 \ldots \beta_n \#_r$ its *right-context*.
The left context will be identified to the term

```
      *
     / \
    αm
        
        *
       / \
      α1  *
         / \
        #1  $
```

which is also denoted $\alpha_m \ldots \alpha_1 \#_1$ or

$*(\alpha_m, *(\ldots . *(\alpha_1, *(\#_1, \$)) \ldots)$

More generally, we said that a term is a *left-list* if it is $ or if it is of the form $*(\alpha, *(\beta, *(\ldots\ldots *(\chi, *(\#_1, \$)) \ldots)))$. A *right-list* is defined by the same way, where $\#_1$ is replaced with $\#_r$.

B/Let us name LEFT the left-hand side of R_M and RIGHT its right-hand side. Let us abbreviate the form of RIGHT with $V(t_{I,\alpha}, \ldots, t_{K,\chi})$ or

```
        V
      /..|..\
  tI,α.....tK,χ
```

Our rule LEFT → RIGHT applies to a term t if a subterm s of t matches LEFT with some substitution S of (closed) terms for variables appearing in LEFT (i.e. s = LEFT.S, also denoted S(LEFT)). We write t ⇒ u to indicate that the term t *rewrites* in this way to the term u. So, t= t'.LEFT.S ⇒ u= t'.RIGHT.S. Such a substitution S is decomposed as follows (we use mnemonic names). Using notations of the definition of R_M (section II C/), let us name OLC (i.e. Old Left Context), the term substituted by S to the variable x. We note S: x ----> OLC. By the same way, S can be decomposed in three sub-substitutions, that we denote OLD, NEW and AUX-part.

OLD-part: x----> OLC
z°---> OST (Old STate)
z----> OSC (Old SCanned symbol)
y----> ORC (i.e.Old Right Context)

NEW-part: x'---> NLC (New Left Context)
z°'--> NST (New STate)
z'---> NSC (New SCanned symbol)
y'---> NRC (New Right Context)

AUX-part: z"---> RWR (ReWRited symbol (or string for special instructions))

We denote OLD= <OLC,OST,OSC,ORC> etc...

Remark: Only NEW occurs in RIGHT. Hence, RIGHT.S=RIGHT.NEW=RIGHT<NLC,NST,NSC,NRC>

If we considere a substitution S', we note OLD',OLC',.... the corresponding components.

A *derivation* is a sequence of rewrites; if t ⇒..⇒u in zero or more steps, abbreviated t *⇒ u, then we say that u is *derivable* from t.

Let us consider a derivation step where LEFT *overlaps* RIGHT, i.e. LEFT is unified with a non-variable subterm t of RIGHT. Then, considering occurences of D, LEFT is necessarily unified with some $t_{J,\beta}$ of RIGHT. Such a derivation step will be sometimes denoted J,β⇒ or J⇒.

By the same way, we will sometimes denote J|- a computation step of a Turing machine *M* using the instruction J of *M*.

The following lemma illustrates the main idea leading to the construction of R_M.

<u>Simulation lemma:</u>

Let J be the right instruction (q,λ,μ,q',R).

The following M-computation step exists

$M(\ \alpha_m\ldots\alpha_1\#_1,\ q,\ \lambda,\ \beta_1\ldots\beta_n\#_r\ )\ J|-\ M(\ \mu\alpha_m\ldots\alpha_1\#_1,\ q',\ \beta_1,\beta_2\ldots\beta_n\#_r\ )$

if and only if the following R_M-derivation step exists for some u:

$RIGHT\langle\alpha_m\ldots\alpha_1\#_1,q,\ \lambda,\ \beta_1\ldots\beta_n\#_r\rangle\ J\ \Rightarrow\ u.RIGHT\langle\mu\alpha_m\ldots\alpha_1\#_1,\ q',\ \beta_1,\ \beta_2\ldots\beta_n\#_r\rangle.$

The corresponding results holds by the same way when J is a left instruction or a special instruction.

Proof: The R_M-derivation above exists iff, for some tape symbol α, the term $t_{J,\alpha}\langle\alpha_m\ldots\alpha_1\#_1,q,\lambda,\beta_1\ldots\beta_n\#_r\rangle$ matchs LEFT with a substitution S such that the NEW-part of S is $\langle\mu\alpha_m\ldots\alpha_1\#_1,q',\beta_1,\beta_2\ldots\beta_n\#_r\rangle$

Let us compute S:

$z'' = \mu$

$x= \alpha_m\ldots\alpha_1\#_1$, $z^{\circ}= q$, $z= \lambda$, $y= \beta_1\ldots\beta_n\#_r$,

$x'= \mu\alpha_m\ldots\alpha_1\#_1$, $z^{\circ\prime}= q'$, $z'= \alpha= \beta_1$, $y'=\beta_2\ldots\beta_n\#_r$.

We obtain the wished NEW-part and remark that $\alpha= \beta_1$.

We leave to the reader the proof of the other cases (left instructions, special right instructions and special left instructions).

<u>Corollary:</u>

If there is some infinite M-computation, then there is some infinite R_M-derivation.

Proof: using the "only part" of our simulation lemma, it is easy to construct by induction such an infinite derivation.

Now, our aim is to use the "if" part of the simulation lemma to prove the reciprocity of that corollary and hence to establish the result which is the goal of this paper. But we must prove that there is no "perverse" infinite R_M-derivation, i.e. no infinite derivation which does note simulate infinite *M*-computation. This is the reason why we introduce the following definition and lemmas. It is obvious that the two lemmas below lead to the conclusion.

Definition:

An infinite R_M-derivation is *a good infinite derivation* if it is the inductive limit of *good finit derivations* (gfd) defined as follows

- For every (closed) substitution σ, RIGHT.σ is a 0 step-gfd, called *of type* $\langle\emptyset\rangle$ or $\langle\emptyset\rangle$-gfd.
- A n+1 step-gfd of type $\langle I_1,\ldots. I_n, I_{n+1}\rangle$ is

  $\text{RIGHT}.\sigma_0 \overset{*}{\Rightarrow} u_n(\text{RIGHT}.\sigma_n)=u_{n+1}(\text{LEFT}.\sigma_{n+1})\ I_{n+1}\Rightarrow u_{n+1}(\text{RIGHT}.\sigma_{n+1})$

with $\text{RIGHT}.\sigma_0 \overset{*}{\Rightarrow} u_n(\text{RIGHT}.\sigma_n)$ is a $\langle I_1,\ldots. I_n\rangle$-gfd and at the last step, the left-hand side LEFT of R_M overlaps the right-hand side RIGHT of the occurence of R_M in the nth step.

Unformaly, theses gfd are closely related to the derived pair of Guttag,J.V.,Kapur,D.,Musser,D.R.(1983). We can draw as follows *a good infinite derivation* $\langle I_1,\ldots. I_n, I_{n+1}\rangle$

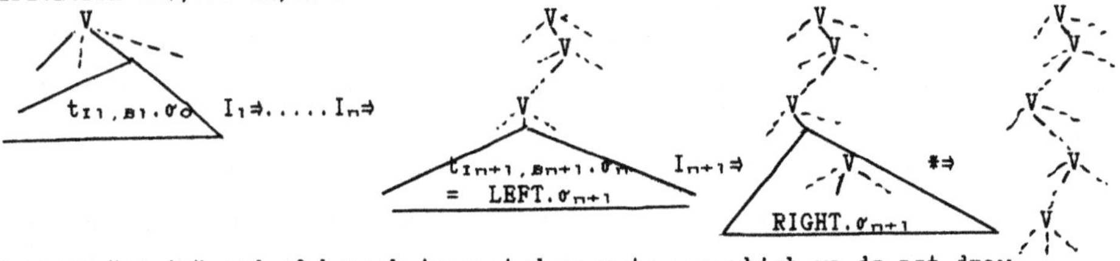

At every "empty" end of branch is rooted some $t_{I,B}.\sigma$ which we do not draw.

<u>Lemma:</u> *From every good infinite* R_M*-derivation, we can deduce some infinite M-computation.*

Proof: We use notations of the definition for the good infinite R_M-derivation GID that we consider.

First part: Let us suppose that σ_0 simulates an instantaneous description, i.e. that it substitutes to x' a term which is a left-list (see section III A/), to z'' a constant which is a state, to z' a constant which is a tape symbol and to y' a term which is a right-list. Then, we easily deduce from the simulation lemma that there is an infinite *M*-computation

$$\sigma_0\ I_1\Rightarrow \sigma_1\ \ldots\ldots\ \sigma_n\ I_n\Rightarrow \sigma_{n+1}\ I_{n+1}\Rightarrow\ldots.$$

Second part: If σ_o does note simulate an instantaneous description, let us deduce from it a substitution σ'_o which simulates an instantaneous description.

Construction of σ'_o:

Let us denote σ_o = <t,u,v,w>. Intuitively, we "extract of t by the following way, the term t' which is, starting from the root, its bigger subterm of left-context type" : NODE = root of t;

While (NODE=# and first son of NODE is a tape symbol) do NODE=second son of NODE;

substitute $\#_1$ to NODE

We deduce a right-list w' of w by the same way.

Now consider σ'_o = <t',u,v,w'>. As $t_{I1,B1}.\sigma_o$ is unified with LEFT at the first step of GID, u is necessarily a state and v a tape-symbol. So σ'_o simulates an instantaneous description.

Eventually, *we must verify that all the derivation steps of GID remain possible when we start from $t_{I1,B1}.\sigma'_o$ instead of $t_{I1,B1}.\sigma_o$*. We use two facts to check this property:

- At the first step, t matchs the variable x of LEFT. As x only occurs once in LEFT, we can substitute t' to t without break any subterms-equality constraint.

- At every step, unification only scans "left-context part t' " of t; indeed, otherwise unification would scratch. So, no step is affected when we substitute t' to t.

<u>Lemma:</u> *We can pull a good infinite derivation out every infinite derivation.*

Proof: (Let us recall the sub-term order defined on closed terms by $t \leqslant u$ iff $u=t.\sigma$ for some substitution σ).

For every term t, let us denote V[t] the number of occences of V that we can reach, starting from the root and meeting only occurences of V along the corresponding branch.

Consider an infinite R_M-derivation starting from an initial term θ. Choose a mimimal subterm τ of θ, such that an infinite sub derivation starts from τ (perhaps $\theta=\tau$). The root of τ is an occurence of D. Subterms of τ rooted to other occurences of D are only derived a finite number of step; so we can cut off an initial finite subderivation and consider that the infinite derivation is outermost (i.e. only outermost occurences of LEFT -hence of D- are derived). In such a derivation, if t_n denotes the nth derived term, V[t_n] strictly increases. We deduce of König's lemma that we get an infinite branch only labeled with V. Eventually, we considere only the steps growing this infinite branch and we obtain a good infinite computation.

REFERENCES

[1] R.V. Book, Thue Systems as Rewriting Systems, in: J.P. Jouannaud, ed., *Proceedings of the First International Conference on Rewriting Techniques and Applications, Dijon, France. Springer Lec. Notes Comp. Sci.***202** **(1985)** 63-94. Revised version: *J. Symbolic Computation*,3 (1987) 39-68.

[2] N. Dershowitz, Termination, in: J.P. Jouannaud, ed., *Proceedings of the First International Conference on Rewriting Techniques and Applications, Dijon, France. Springer Lec. Notes Comp. Sci.***202** (1985) 180-224. Revised version: Termination of rewriting. *J.Symbolic Computation*, 3 (1987) 69-116.

[3] J.V. Guttag, D. Kapur and D.R. Musser, On proving uniform termination and restricted termination of rewriting systems. *SIAM J.Comput.*12 (1983) 187-214.

[4] G. Huet, D.S. Lankfork, *On the uniform halting problem for term rewriting systems.* Rapport Laboria 283 (1978), INRIA, Le Chesnay, France.

[5] G. Huet and D.C. Oppen, Equations and rewrite rules:A survey, in: R.V. Book, ed., *Formal Language Theory: Perspectives and Open Problems*, 1980, pp. 349-405. New York: Academic Press.

[6] J.P. Jouannaud, Editorial of *J. Symbolic Computation*, 3, 1-2, 1987, 1-2.

[7] R. Lipton and L. Snyder, On the halting of tree replacement systems. *Proceedings of the Conference on Theoretical Computer Science*, University of Waterloo, Waterloo, Canada, (1977), 43-46.

Local Checking of Trace Synchronizability

Volker Diekert
Walter Vogler
Institut für Informatik
Technische Universität München
Arcisstr. 21
D-8000 München 2

Extended Abstract

Abstract

Trace theory has been developed to describe the behaviour of concurrent systems. For a modular approach synchronization of traces is of special interest. We characterize those trace monoids for which synchronization can be described locally.

§1 Introduction

Free partially commutative monoids were introduced by Cartier/Foata [CaFo69] in order to treat some combinatorial problems. Independently Mazurkiewicz introduced them to describe the behaviour of concurrent systems. (See [Mazu77], [Mazu87] for a detailed explanation.) He called the elements of these monoids traces. In particular, trace theory was successfully applied to Petri nets.

In this paper we investigate the synchronization of traces. The synchronization operator was suggested to build up trace languages in a modular fashion. It is especially useful, since it directly corresponds to a synchronization operator of Petri nets. The definition of trace synchronization is global in character, it would be desirable to have a "local" description instead. (We will give a precise meaning to this in section 2.) In fact it was conjectured in [AaRo86] that such a local description is always possible. Unfortunately it turns out that this is false in general. Our main result in section 4 gives a simple graph-theoretic characterization of those trace monoids for which synchronization can be described locally.

The complexity of this graph-theoretic property is not known. It is in NP but we do not know whether it is complete or not. Slight variations of the problem are NP-complete, but for a restricted class of graphs we give a polynomial time algorithm in section 5.

In this paper we use the language of category theory, because it is convenient to express our results. For the notions we use we refer the reader to [MacL70] or any other book on categories. However our main result in section 4 can be understood without any knowledge of category theory.

§2 Synchronization of Traces

In this section we introduce traces and synchronization of them. For this we need some terminology about graphs.

An undirected graph $G = (X, E)$ consists of a finite set X of vertices and some edge-set $E \subseteq \binom{X}{2} = \{\{x, y\} \mid x, y \in X, x \neq y\}$, i.e. it does not have loops or multiple edges. A morphism $h : (X, E) \to (X', E')$ of undirected graphs is a mapping $X \to X'$ such that $\{h(x), h(y)\} \in E$ for all $\{x, y\} \in E$. Note that in particular $h(x) \neq h(y)$ for all edges $\{x, y\} \in E$. A directed graph $G = (X, E)$ consists of a finite set X of vertices and some set $E \subseteq X \times X \setminus \{(x, x) \mid x \in X\}$ of (directed) edges. A cycle in a graph is a sequence $x_1, \ldots, x_n$ of vertices such that $\{x_i, x_j\} \in E$ ($(x_i, x_j) \in E$ resp.) for $j - 1 \equiv i \bmod n$. A chord of a cycle is an edge $\{x_j, x_k\}$ with $k \notin \{j+1, j-1\}$ mod n, (a directed edge (x_j, x_k) with $k \not\equiv j + 1 \bmod n$, respectively). For undirected graphs $G_1 = (X_1, E_1)$, $G_2 = (X_2, E_2)$ we define their complex product $G_1 * G_2 = (X, E)$ by $X = X_1 \dot\cup X_2$, $E = E_1 \dot\cup E_2 \dot\cup \{\{x, y\} \mid x \in X_1, y \in X_2\}$.

A concurrent alphabet (X, D) consists of a finite set X of actions and a reflexive symmetric relation D, the dependency relation. Its complement $X \times X \setminus D$, denoted by I, is called independency relation, which is irreflexive and symmetric. The idea is to describe the behaviour of a system by sequences of actions, but if some independent actions x and y can occur then xy and yx really describe the same behaviour. Thus we define $\equiv$ to be the least congruence relation on $X^* \times X^*$ with $xy \equiv yx$ for all $(x, y) \in I$, and denote by $[w]$ the congruence class of $w \in X^*$. The set of traces over some concurrent alphabet (X, D) is defined as $\Theta(X, D) := \{[w] \mid w \in X^*\}$. This set is a monoid under the multiplication $[v] \cdot [w] := [vw]$ with neutral element $[\varepsilon]$. These monoids are usually called free partially commutative and were first studied by Cartier/Foata in [CaFo69]. We will call them trace monoids for simplification. Any subset of a trace monoid is called a trace language. For a trace $t = [w]$ we define the alphabet of t, *alph*(t), by the alphabet of w, i.e. the set of letters occuring in w.

Concurrent alphabets and traces can be related to graphs in the following way: For a concurrent alphabet (X, D) its dependency graph is the undirected graph $(X, \{\{x, y\} \mid (x, y) \in D, x \neq y\})$. Each trace t is identified with its dependency graph *dep*(t), a directed graph defined inductively as follows: *dep*(ε) is the empty graph, for a trace t and a letter $x \in X$ *dep*(tx) is obtained from *dep*(t) by adding a new vertex labelled x and edges from old vertices with labels dependent to x to this new vertex. We can identify a trace with its dependency graph. We define the union and the intersection of two concurrent alphabets as $(X_1, D_1) \cup (X_2, D_2) := (X_1 \cup X_2, D_1 \cup D_2)$ and $(X_1, D_1) \cap (X_2, D_2) := (X_1 \cap X_2, D_1 \cap D_2)$. For $X' \subseteq X$ the projection $p : X^* \to X'^*$ simply eliminates all symbols of $w \in X^*$ that do not belong to X'. We can extend this projection to a mapping $p : \Theta(X, D) \to \Theta(X', D')$ if $X' \subseteq X$, $D' \subseteq D$ by setting $p([w]) = [p(w)]$.

Now we can define the synchronization of two trace languages, which enables us to build up trace languages in a modular way: Let $C_1 = (X_1, D_1)$, $C_2 = (X_2, D_2)$ be two concurrent alphabets, C their union, C' their intersection, $p_i : \Theta(C) \to \Theta(C_i)$, $p'_i : \Theta(C_i) \to \Theta(C')$, $i = 1, 2$, the corresponding projections. For trace languages L_1, L_2 over C_1, C_2 resp., we define their synchronization $L_1 \parallel L_2$ as a trace language over C by $L_1 \parallel L_2 := \{t \in \Theta(C) \mid p_1(t) \in L_1,\ p_2(t) \in L_2\}$.

This definition has a global character. We have to check all $t \in \Theta(C)$ to find $L_1 \parallel L_2$. It would be much nicer to have a local condition, namely to check for all pairs $(t_1, t_2) \in L_1 \times L_2$ whether $p'_1(t_1) = p'_2(t_2)$ and construct $L_1 \parallel L_2$ from those pairs which fulfill this condition. In fact it was conjectured in [AaRo86, Thm. 5.1] that there is a bijection from $L_1 \parallel L_2$ onto $\{(t_1, t_2) \in L_1 \times L_2 \mid p'_1(t_1) = p'_2(t_2)\}$. Unfortunately this is not true in general. (For an example see below.) In §4 we shall give a precise characterization of those C_1, C_2 where there is such a bijection.

Remark: The mistake in [AaRo86] vanishes if one is willing to renounce some concurrency. For example, it is always true that we have a bijection from $L_1 \parallel L_2$ onto the set $\{(t_1, t_2) \in L_1 \times L_2 \mid \exists w_1 \in t_1,\ w_2 \in t_2 : p'_1(w_1) = p'_2(w_2) \text{ in } X'^*\}$. (This follows from Corollary 4.3 below.)

As it was pointed out by one of the anonymous referees this is also a local description of $L_1 \parallel L_2$, and it holds in every case. But it has the disadvantage that we have to work with words, i.e. we have to consider all the representatives of the traces involved.

§3 A categorial approach to the general embedding theorem

Some results of this paragraph may also be found in [Fisch86] where the ideas have been developed in collaboration with the first author.

For a graph $G = (X, E)$ we define $\Theta(G) := \Theta(X, D)$ where $D = \{(x, y) \in X \times X \mid \{x, y\} \in E \text{ or } x = y\}$. We will give a functorial meaning to Θ in the following way.

Let $h : G \to G'$ be a morphism of undirected graphs $G = (X, E)$, $G' = (X', E')$. Define a morphism of monoids in the opposite direction $\Theta(h) : \Theta(G') \to \Theta(G)$ by $\Theta(h)(y) := [\prod_{x \in h^{-1}(y)} x]$ (= product over all elements in $h^{-1}(y)$) for $y \in X'$. Since there is no edge between x_1, x_2 for any x_1, $x_2 \in h^{-1}(y)$ this mapping $\Theta(h)$ is well-defined.

Remark 3.1:
The construction above defines a contravariant functor Θ from the category of undirected graphs to the category of trace monoids. Of course, if one uses the independence graphs (which are the complements of the dependence graphs), one can define a covariant functor to trace-monoids in an obvious way. But this functor yields only letter-to-letter mappings. It is therefore not possible to derive the following results on embeddings.

Let in the following $\hookrightarrow$ denote an injective, $\twoheadrightarrow$ a surjective mapping. Directly from the definition of Θ we obtain

Proposition 3.2:
Let G_1, G_2 be undirected graphs and $M_i = \Theta(G_i)$, $i = 1, 2$. Then the functor Θ applied to the canonical injection

$$G_i \hookrightarrow \underset{\text{(disjoint union)}}{G_1 \sqcup G_2} \hookrightarrow \underset{\text{(complex product)}}{G_1 * G_2}, \quad i = 1, 2,$$

yields the canonical projections

$$\underset{\text{(free product)}}{M_1 * M_2} \twoheadrightarrow \underset{\text{(direct product)}}{M_1 \times M_2} \twoheadrightarrow M_i, \quad i = 1, 2.$$

□

Another basic property of our functor is the following:

Lemma 3.3:
Let $h : G \to G'$ be a morphism of undirected graphs. Then for all vertices x of G and all traces $t' \in \Theta(G')$ we have $x \in alph(\Theta(h)(t'))$ if and only if $h(x) \in alph(t')$. □

Theorem 3.4:
Let $h : G \to G'$ be a morphism of undirected graphs and $\Theta(h) : \Theta(G') \to \Theta(G), y \to \prod_{x \in h^{-1}(y)} x$ be the morphism of monoids defined above. Then we have:

i) The mapping h is injective if and only if $\Theta(h)$ is a surjective homomorphism.
ii) The morphism h is surjective on vertices and edges if and only if $\Theta(h)$ is an embedding of monoids.

Proof: The only part in the proof of 3.4 which requires non-trivial arguments is to show that if h is surjective on edges and vertices then $\Theta(h) : \Theta(G') \to \Theta(G)$ is injective. Since there is a mistake in the proof of [Fisch86] for this part, we give a correct proof here. For simplification of the notation we define $H := \Theta(h)$.

We need some elementary combinatorics on traces. For a trace t let $min(t)$ denote the labels of minimal elements in the dependency graph $dep(t)$ of t. Since the minimal elements commute, the set $min(t)$ defines a trace by the product of its elements and we may write $t = min(t) \cdot s$ for some trace s. (In fact, $min(t)$ is the first factor in the so-called Foata-normal-form of the trace t.)

Lemma 3.5:
Let $h : G \to G'$ be surjective on edges and vertices. Then for all letters $y \in X'$ and all traces $t' \in \Theta(G')$ it holds: $y \in min(t')$ if and only if $h^{-1}(y) \subseteq min(\Theta(h)(t'))$.

Proof of 3.5: Clearly, $y \in min(t')$ implies $h^{-1}(y) \subseteq min(H(t'))$. For the other direction assume $y \notin min(t')$. Since h is surjective on vertices, $h^{-1}(y)$ is not empty. If $y \notin alph(t')$ then it follows from Lemma 3.3 that $h^{-1}(y)$ is no subset of $alph(H(t'))$. Otherwise we may write $t' = uxvyw$ where $y \notin alph(uxv)$ and x is dependent to y. Since h is surjective on edges there are dependent letters p, $q \in X$ such that $h(p) = x$ and $h(q) = y$. Therefore we have $H(t') = H(ux)H(vyw)$, $p \in alph(H(ux))$, $q \notin alph(H(ux))$, by Lemma 3.3, and p, q are dependent. It is easily verified that this implies $q \notin min(H(t'))$. Hence, $h^{-1}(y)$ is not a subset of $min(H(t'))$. □

We now return to the proof of 3.4.
Let $h : G \to G'$ be surjective on edges and vertices, and $H := \Theta(h)$. Let t', $t'' \in \Theta(G')$ be traces such that $H(t') = H(t'')$. By Lemma 3.5 we have $min(t') = min(t'')$. Since trace monoids are cancellative, see [CaFo69, Cor. 1.3], it follows by induction that $t' = t''$, hence the result. □

Corollary 3.6: (General Embedding Theorem) Let $G = \bigcup_{i=1}^{n} G_i$ be a union of undirected graphs G_i and let $\tilde{G}$ denote the disjoint union of G_i, $i = 1, \ldots, n$. Then the functor Θ applied to the canonical diagram

$$\begin{array}{ccl} G_i & \overset{j_i}{\hookrightarrow} & \tilde{G} \quad (= \dot{\bigcup}_{i=1}^{n} G_i \ \text{, disjoint union}) \\ & \searrow^{k_i} & \downarrow \pi \\ & & G \end{array}$$

yields the following diagram of free partially commutative monoids.

$$\begin{array}{ccl} \Theta(G_i) & \overset{p_i}{\twoheadleftarrow} & \prod_{i=1}^{n} \Theta(G_i) \quad (= \text{direct product}) \\ & \nwarrow^{q_i} & \uparrow \varphi \\ & & \Theta(G) \end{array}$$

where p_i, q_i are the natural projections and φ is a canonical embedding. □

Since every graph may be covered by cliques and cliques correspond to free monoids, we obtain as a special case the following well-known embedding theorem, see [ClLa85, Lemma 3.1] or [CoPe85, Prop. 1.1].

Corollary 3.7: Every trace monoid is effectively embeddable in a direct product of free monoids. □

Consider a graph G which is the union of two subgraphs, $G = G_1 \cup G_2$, and let $G' = G_1 \cap G_2$. Then G may be viewed as the push-out in the diagram:

$$\begin{array}{ccc} G & \longleftarrow & G_2 \\ \uparrow & & \uparrow \\ G_1 & \longleftarrow & G' \end{array}$$

The dual categorial construct of a push-out is a pull-back. In the category of monoids the pull-back is given by a fibered product. Let M_1, M_2 be monoids and $p_i' : M_i \to M'$ be projections onto a third monoid M'. Then the fibered product of M_1 and M_2 over M' is defined by $M_1 \times_{M'} M_2 := \{(m_1, m_2) \in M_1 \times M_2 \mid p_1'(m_1) = p_2'(m_2)\}$. Now, for $M = \Theta(G)$, $M_i = \Theta(G_i)$, $M' = \Theta(G')$, $i = 1, 2$, at first glance, one might expect that M is the fibered product $M_1 \times_{M'} M_2$. This need not be the case, as we see in the next section.

§4 Synchronization of trace monoids and fibered products.

Let (X_1, D_1), (X_2, D_2) be concurrent alphabets, set $X := X_1 \cup X_2$, $D := D_1 \cup D_2$, $X' = X_1 \cap X_2$, $D' := D_1 \cap D_2$. Let $M = \Theta(X, D)$, $M_i = \Theta(X_i, D_i)$, $M' = \Theta(X', D')$ be the associated trace monoids and G, G_i, G' be the corresponding dependency graphs, $i = 1, 2$. We colour edges in G as follows: An edge is coloured blue if it belongs to G_1 but not to G_2, yellow if it belongs to G_2 but not to G_1, and green if it belongs to G'. Thus each edge in G has exactly one colour.

Recall, by definition of the synchronization of trace languages, we have $M = M_1 \parallel M_2$. Since $G = G_1 \cup G_2$ the functoriality of Θ yields a canonical morphism

$$\varphi : M_1 \parallel M_2 \longrightarrow M_1 \times_{M'} M_2.$$

Since $M_1 \times_{M'} M_2$ is a subset of $M_1 \times M_2$, this morphism is always injective by the general embedding theorem.

Theorem 4.1:
Let as above $M_1 \parallel M_2 = M(X_1 \cup X_2, D_1 \cup D_2)$, $M' = M(X_1 \cap X_2, D_1 \cap D_2)$, $M_1 \times_{M'} M_2 = \{(t_1, t_2) \in M_1 \times M_2 \mid p_1'(t_1) = p_2'(t_2) \text{ in } M'\}$, and $\varphi : M_1 \parallel M_2 \to M_1 \times_{M'} M_2$, $t \mapsto (p_1(t), p_2(t))$. Then the following assertions are equivalent:

i) The canonical embedding

$$\varphi : M_1 \parallel M_2 \hookrightarrow M_1 \times_{M'} M_2$$

is an isomorphism.

ii) Every cycle in G which contains some blue edge and some yellow edge has a chord.

Proof: Let $\tilde{M}$ be the set of isomorphism classes of finite directed labelled graphs (V, E, λ) where V is a finite set of vertices, $E \subseteq V \times V$ is the set of edges, $\lambda : V \to X$ is the labelling function to X and the following condition is satisfied:

We have $(\lambda(x), \lambda(y)) \in D$ if and only if $(x,y) \in E$ or $(y,x) \in E$ or $x = y$. The set $\tilde{M}$ forms a monoid with the multiplication $[V_1, E_1, \lambda_1] \cdot [V_2, E_2, \lambda_2] = [V_1 \dot{\cup} V_2, E_1 \dot{\cup} E_2 \dot{\cup} \{(x_1, x_2) \in V_1 \times V_2 \mid (\lambda(x_1), \lambda(x_2)) \in D\}, \lambda_1 \dot{\cup} \lambda_2]$ and unit element $1 = [\emptyset, \emptyset, \emptyset]$. Note that $\tilde{M}$ contains all dependency graphs of traces from M, but it contains also graphs with cycles.

Similarly to the above we colour the edges of an element $[V, E, \lambda] \in \tilde{M}$. An edge $(x,y) \in E$ is coloured blue, (yellow, green resp.) if $(\lambda(x), \lambda(y)) \in D_1 \setminus D_2$ ($(\lambda(x), \lambda(y)) \in D_2 \setminus D_1$, $(\lambda(x), \lambda(y)) \in D_1 \cap D_2$ resp.). Let $\tilde{\tilde{M}}$ be the submonoid of $\tilde{M}$ consisting of elements $[V, E, \lambda]$ such that neither the restriction of $[V, E, \lambda]$ to the blue and green edges nor the restriction of $[V, E, \lambda]$ to the yellow and green edges contains a directed cycle. Restricting an element of $\tilde{\tilde{M}}$ to the subgraph induced by the vertices with label in X_i we obtain a trace of M_i $i = 1, 2$.

Obviously these two graphs coincide on the subgraph induced by the vertices with labels in X', therefore we obtain a homomorphism from $\tilde{\tilde{M}}$ to the fibered product $M_1 \times_{M'} M_2$. One sees easily that this mapping is a bijection. Hence we identify $M_1 \times_{M'} M_2$ and $\tilde{\tilde{M}}$. The image $\varphi(M)$ in $M_1 \times_{M'} M_2$ then is exactly the submonoid of acyclic graphs.

i) $\Rightarrow$ *ii)*: Assume $(x_1, \ldots, x_n)$ is a chordless cycle in G with blue and yellow edges. We may assume that (x_i, x_{i+1}) is blue for some $i \neq n$ and (x_n, x_1) is yellow. Then this cycle yields a directed labelled graph:

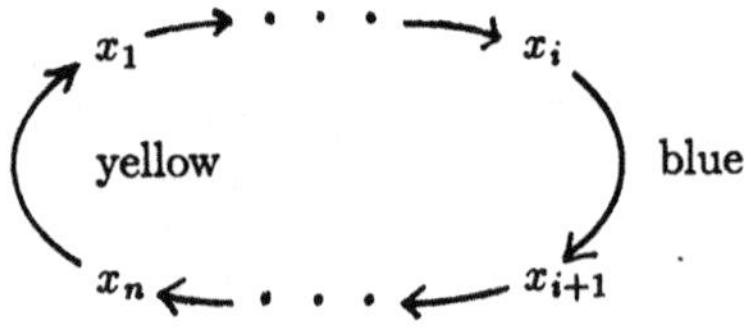

which belongs to $M_1 \times_{M'} M_2$ but not to $\varphi(M)$.
(Note that this cycle corresponds to $(p_1(x_1 \ldots x_n), p_2(x_{i+1} \ldots x_n x_1 \ldots x_i)) \in M_1 \times_{M'} M_2 \setminus \varphi(M)$.)
Hence φ is not surjective.

ii) $\Rightarrow$ *i)*: Assume φ is not an isomorphism, i.e. it is not surjective (see above). Then there is a graph $[V, E, \lambda] \in \tilde{M}$ which contains a directed cycle but the restriction to the blue and green and to the yellow and green edges does not. Then every cycle in $[V, E, \lambda]$ contains necessarily blue and yellow edges. Let $(x_1, \ldots, x_n)$ be such a cycle of minimal length in $[V, E, \lambda]$. Since for an edge (x,y) of $[V, E, \lambda]$ the pair (y,x) is not an edge, we have $n \geq 3$. Assume that $\lambda(x_i) = \lambda(x_j)$ for different i, j; since $n \geq 3$ we may assume $i + 1 \not\equiv j \mod n$. By definition of $\tilde{M}$ we either have $(x_{i+1}, x_j) \in E$ or $(x_j, x_{i+1}) \in E$ and find a shorter cycle in both cases, a contradiction. Thus all the labels $\lambda(x_1), \ldots, \lambda(x_n)$ are different and $(\lambda(x_1), \ldots, \lambda(x_n))$ is a chordless cycle in G with blue and yellow edges. □

Example 4.2:

Consider

G

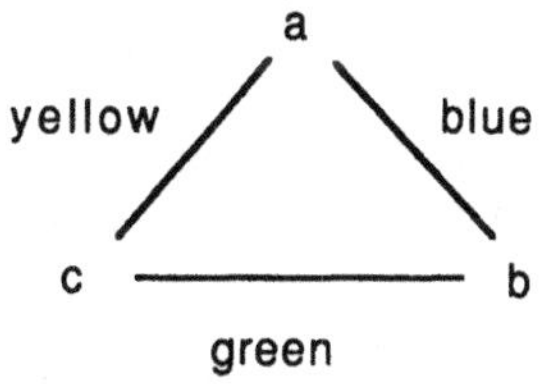

G_1

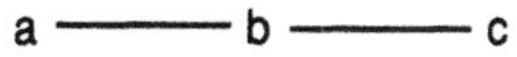

G_2

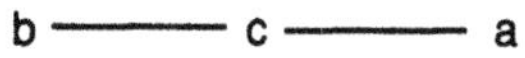

Then $\varphi : M_1 \parallel M_2 \to M_1 \times_{M'} M_2$ is not surjective. We have $([abc], [bca]) \in M_1 \times_{M'} M_2$, but $([abc], [bca]) \notin \varphi(M)$.

Corollary 4.3: Let with the above notation M' be a free monoid. Then $\varphi : M_1 \parallel M_2 \to M_1 \times_{M'} M_2$ is an isomorphism.

Proof: Let $(x_1, \ldots, x_n)$ be a cycle in G with some blue edge $(x_i, x_{i+1}), 1 \le i \le n-1$ and some yellow edge (x_n, x_1). Then there is an index $j \in \{1, \ldots, i\}$ and an index $k \in \{i+1, \ldots, n\}$ such that $x_j, x_k \in X'$. Since M' is free, we obtain a chord (x_j, x_k). □

Remark 4.4: It is possible to generalize Theorem 4.1 to the synchronization of $M_1 \parallel \ldots \parallel M_n$ with $n \geq 2$ and a corresponding generalization of a fibered product. This will be shown in the full version, [DieVo88], of this extended abstract. For example every trace monoid is the synchronization $X_1^* \parallel \ldots \parallel X_n^*$ where the X_i, $1 \le i \le n$ correspond to a covering of cliques. In this case, we obtain a characterization where all quasi-reconstructable tuples of words $(w_1, \ldots, w_n) \in X_1^* \times \ldots \times X_n^*$ are reconstructable (in the sense of [CoMe85]).

§5 Algorithms

For lack of space we give no proofs in this section. They will appear in [DieVo88].

In the following we call a graph with a colouring of its edges with blue, yellow and green a three-coloured graph. We denote the respective edge sets with E_{blue}, E_{yellow}, E_{green} and write edges $\{x, y\}$ as xy henceforth.

Theorem 4.1 raises the following graph theoretic problem:

(*1) Given a three-coloured graph. Is there a chordless cycle containing some blue edge and some yellow edge?

We can also formulate the following polynomially equivalent problem:

(*2) Given a graph and two edges e_1, e_2. Is there a chordless cycle containing e_1 and e_2?

We do not know whether these problems are NP-complete (obviously they are in NP). On the one hand we can give some NP-complete variations of the above problems:

Theorem 5.1 The following problems are NP-complete:
a) [due to K.-J. Lange] Given a directed three-coloured graph. Is there a chordless directed cycle containing some blue and some yellow edge?
b) Given a three-coloured graph. Is there a chordless cycle with some blue and some yellow edges, but no green edges? □

On the other hand if the number of green edges is bounded logarithmically in the number of vertices we can give a polynomial algorithm that answers (*1). First we will deal with the case that there are no green edges at all.

In the following we call a chordless cycle with some blue and some yellow edge a forbidden cycle.

Algorithm 5.2:

function forbidden_cycle_1 (G: three-coloured graph || G has no green edge):boolean;

begin define a graph H with vertex set $V_{\text{blue}} \dot{\cup} V_{\text{yellow}}$, where $V_i = \{X \mid X$ is a connected component of $(V(G), E_i)\}$, and edge set $\{XY \mid X \in V_{\text{blue}}, Y \in V_{\text{yellow}}, X \cap Y \neq \emptyset\}$;
H contains a cycle or there are $X \in V_{\text{blue}}, Y \in V_{\text{yellow}}$ with $| X \cap Y | \geq 2$
end

Theorem 5.3:
Given a three-coloured graph G without green edges. Then forbidden_cycle_1 answers (*1) in polynomial time. □

Now we come to an algorithm that handles any three-coloured graph:
For $x_1, \ldots, x_n \in V(G)$ let $G - \{x_1, \ldots, x_n\}$ be defined in the obvious way as the graph obtained from G by deleting $x_1, \ldots, x_n$ and their incident edges. For an edge xy that does not lie on a triangle let G/xy be defined in the obvious way as the graph obtained from G by contracting xy, i.e. eliminating xy and identifying x and y. Since xy does not lie on a triangle it is obvious how to colour the edges of G/xy using the colouring of G.

Algorithm 5.4:

function forbidden_cycle (G: three-coloured graph):boolean;

if there is some green edge xy
then there is some v with ($vx \in E_{\text{yellow}}$ and $vy \in E_{\text{blue}}$) or ($vx \in E_{\text{blue}}$ and $vy \in E_{\text{yellow}}$)
or forbidden_cycle ($G - \{x\}$)
or forbidden_cycle ($G - \{y\}$)
or forbidden_cycle ($(G - \{v \mid (x, v, y)$ is a triangle $\})/xy$)
else forbidden_cycle_1(G)

Theorem 5.5:
Algorithm 5.5 solves (*1) in time exponential in $min(|V|, |E_{\text{green}}|)$ and polynomial in $|V|$. □

Corollary 5.6 Problem (*1) can be solved in polynomial time if the number of green edges is bounded logarithmically in the number of vertices (in particular, if it is bounded by some constant). □

Acknowledgement: We would like to thank Christian Choffrut and the anonymous referees for valuable comments. Special thanks are due to Harald Hadwiger for having typed the manuscript.

References

[AaRo86] Aalbersberg, I.J., Rozenberg, G.: Theory of Traces, University of Leiden, Report 86-16 (1986), Vakgroep Informatica.

[CaFo69] Cartier, P., Foata, D.: Problèmes combinatoires de commutation et réarrangements. Lect. Not. in Math., No. 85, Springer: 1969

[CoMe85] Cori, R., Métivier, Y.: Recognizable subsets of some partially abelian monoids. Theor. Comp. Sci., Vol. 35, 241-254, (1985)

[CoPe85] Cori, R., Perrin, D.: Automates et Commutations Partielles. R.A.I.R.O., Informatique theoriques 19 , No. 1, (1985), p. 21-32

[ClLa85] Clerbout, M., Latteux, M.: Partial Commutations and Faithful Rational Transductions, Theoret. Comp. Sci. 35 (1985), p. 241-254

[DieVo88] Diekert, V., Vogler, W.: On the Synchronization of Traces and Petri Nets: submitted.

[Fisch86] Fischer, W.: Über erkennbare und rationale Mengen in freien partiell kommutativen Monoiden, Diplomarbeit Universität Hamburg 1986, available as Report FBI-HH-B-121/86

[MacL70] MacLane, S.: Categories. For the working mathematician. Graduate Texts in Mathematics, Springer: 1970

[Mazu77] Mazurkiewicz, A.: Concurrent Program Schemes and Their Interpretations. DAIMI Rep. PB 78, Aarhus University, Aarhus (1977)

[Mazu87] Mazurkiewicz, A.: Trace Theory, in: Brauer,Reisig,Rozenberg (Eds.): Petri Nets, Applications and Relationship to Other Models of Concurrency, Bad Honnef 1986, LNCS 255, p.279-324 (1987)

EDGE SEPARATORS FOR PLANAR GRAPHS AND THEIR APPLICATIONS

Krzystof DIKS* / Hristo N.DJIDJEV** / Ondrej SÝKORA*** / Imrich VRŤO***

* Institute of Informatics,Warsaw University,PKiN,00901 Warsaw,Poland

** Centre of Informatics and Computer Technology,Bulgarian Academy of Sciences, Acad. Bonchev str. bl. 25-A, 1113 Sofia, Bulgaria

***Institute of Technical Cybernetics, Slovak Academy of Sciences, Dúbravská 9, 842 37 Bratislava, Czechoslovakia

ABSTRACT

We show that every planar graph with n vertices and a maximal degree k has an $O(\sqrt{kn})$-edge separator. This improves known results about edge separators of graphs with vertex degree bounded by a constant. We show that any n vertex tree of a maximal degree k can be divided into two parts of $\leq n/2$ vertices by removing $O(k \log n/\log k)$ edges. The sizes of both separators are existentially optimal. We apply the edge separator to average cost efficient embeddings of planar graphs of degree k into binary trees, meshes and hypercubes.

1. INTRODUCTION

One basic technique in the design of efficient algorithms on planar graphs is "divide and conquer". For planar graphs one uses the fact that there exists a small subset of vertices (edges) which separates the graph into roughly equal pieces.

Formally, we say a graph G with n vertices has an f(n)-vertex separator if there exists a partition of the vertices into three sets A,B and C such that $|C| \leq f(n)$, $|A| \leq 2n/3$, $|B| \leq 2n/3$ and no edge exists between A and B. It is known that each tree has a 1-vertex separator. Heath [H] proved that each outerplanar graph has a 2-vertex separator. Lipton and Tarjan [LTa] showed that planar graphs have $\sqrt{8n}$-vertex separators. Djidjev [Da] improved this to $\sqrt{6n}$-vertex separators. The last improvement with $f(n) = 7\sqrt{n}/3$ was achieved by Gazit [Ga]. Vertex separators of planar graphs were extended for graphs of genus g by Djidjev [Dc] with $f(n) = \sqrt{6(2g+1)n}$ and an O(n) time algorithm for finding $O(\sqrt{(g+1)n})$-vertex separators was proposed [Db]. Independently,

Gilbert, Hutchinson and Tarjan [GHT] proved a $6\sqrt{(g+1)n}$-vertex separator theorem. Gazit and Miller [GM] constructed a parallel algorithm for finding $O(\sqrt{n})$-vertex separators. Applications of vertex separators are reported in [Gi,LRT,LTb,RH,Ri].

We say a graph G with n vertices has an f(n)-edge separator if there exist a partition of the vertices into two sets A, B and a set of edges C such that $|A| \leq 2n/3$, $|B| \leq 2n/3$, $|C| \leq f(n)$ and every edge between A and B belongs to C. The edge separator has applications to graph layouts for VLSI [Lt,Ls,Va]. However, only graphs with vertex degrees bounded by a constant were studied in those applications. E.g. Leiserson [Ls] and Valiant [Va] used an $O(\sqrt{n})$-edge separator for planar graphs with n vertices (a direct corollary of the $O(\sqrt{n})$-vertex separator of planar graphs). On the other hand, note that general planar graphs have O(n)-edge separators which can not be improved in the worst case. E.g. a star of degree n-1 requires an n/3-edge separator. Thus, it seems that edge separators (unlike vertex separators) depend on the degree of the graph. In this paper we prove this intuition precisely showing that n-vertex planar graphs of degree k have $O(\sqrt{kn})$-edge separators. We show that this upper bound is existentially optimal, i.e. there exists a planar graph which requires an $\Omega(\sqrt{kn})$-edge separator. The separator can be found in O(n) time. We show then that any n vertex tree of a maximal degree k can be divided into two subforests of $\leq n/2$ vertices by removing $O(k\log n/\log k)$ edges. This bound is proved to be existentially optimal. Finally, we apply the $O(\sqrt{kn})$-edge separator to embedding of planar graphs of degree k in binary trees with the average cost $\Theta(\log k)$. This radically improves the former best results O(k) by Lipton and Tarjan [LTb]. The above edge separator is also applied to average cost efficient embedding of planar graphs of degree k into meshes and hypercubes.

Our paper concentrates on worst case edge separators. That is, we find a relatively small edge separator when the minimal separator is relatively large. The opposite approach is to look for efficient algorithms which find the minimal separator for planar graphs. Rao [Ra] proposed an algorithm which finds a nearly optimal (up to O(log n) factor) separator for every planar graph in polynomial time. In comparison with Rao's result, our algorithm is faster (runs in linear time) and finds better edge separators for the class of n-vertex planar graphs of degree k with $\Omega(\sqrt{kn/\log n})$-minimal edge separators.

2. PLANAR GRAPHS

Before introducing the main proposition of this section we state the following lemma which we shall essentially apply.

LEMMA 2.1. [LTa]: Let G be an n-vertex planar graph. Suppose G has a breadth first search spanning tree of radius r. Then there exists a partition of the vertices of G into three sets A,B,C such that no edge joins a vertex in A with a vertex in B, $|A|, |B| \leq 2n/3$, $|C| \leq 2r+1$, and C contains the root of the tree.

THEOREM 2.1. Let $G = (V,E)$ be an n-vertex planar graph with maximal degree of its vertices k. Then G has edge separator of size $3\sqrt{2km} \approx 4.243\sqrt{km}$, where $|E| = m$.

Proof: Let G be connected. Suppose that there exists a breadth first search spanning tree of radius r and let t be the root of the tree. According to Lemma 2.1. there exists a $(2r+1)$-vertex separator including t.

If there holds $r < \lceil\sqrt{m/(2k)}\rceil$ then by removing of the edges which are incident to the vertices from the vertex separator one obtains an edge separator of size:

$$(2\lceil\sqrt{m/(2k)}\rceil -2+1)k \leq (\sqrt{2m/k} + 1)k \leq (\sqrt{2}+1)\sqrt{mk} .$$

If there holds $r \geq \lceil\sqrt{m/(2k)}\rceil$ then let us set $r_0 = \lceil\sqrt{m/(2k)}\rceil$. Divide the vertices of G into levels: U_i, $i=0,1,2,\ldots,r$, according to their distance from the vertex t and denote $L_i = \{(u,v) \in E: u \in U_{i-1}, v \in U_i\}$, $i=1,2,\ldots,r$. Following [Vea], define $\mathcal{L}_s = \{L_i : i = s \pmod{r_0}\}$. We can assume $r_0 \geq 2$. Otherwise $m \leq 2k$ and we have a trivial separator of size $m = \sqrt{m}\cdot\sqrt{m} \leq \sqrt{2km}$.

As $|\bigcup_{s=0}^{r_0-1} \mathcal{L}_s| \leq m$ and $\mathcal{L}_i \cap \mathcal{L}_j = \emptyset$ for $i \neq j$, there exists s_0 such that $|\mathcal{L}_{s_0}| \leq m/r_0$. By removing of the edges from $\mathcal{L}_{s_0}$ the graph G is partitioned into q mutually not connected subgraphs $G_i = (V_i, E_i)$, $i = 1,2,\ldots,q$, such that G_i is the subgraph of G, induced by the set of vertices $V_1 = \bigcup_{j=0}^{s_0-1} U_j$, $V_i = \bigcup_{j=s_0+(i-2)r_0}^{s_0+(i-1)r_0-1} U_j$, for $2 \leq i \leq q-1$ and

$$V_q = \bigcup_{j=s_0+(q-2)r_0}^{r} U_j .$$

If $|V_i| \leq n/3$ for $i=1,2,\ldots,q$, we find minimal j such that $\sum_{l=1}^{j} V_l \geq n/3$. The sets $A = \bigcup_{l=1}^{j} V_l$, $B = V-A$ give the required partition.

Let $C = \mathcal{L}_{s_0}$, then $|C| \leq m/r_0 \leq \sqrt{2km}$.

If there exists V_i such that $n/3 \leq |V_i| \leq 2n/3$, then let us set $A = V_i$, $B = V-V_i$, $C = \mathcal{L}_{s_0}$.

If there exists V_i such that $|V_i| > 2n/3$, then we add a new vertex z and connect it by edges to all vertices from the set $U_{s_0+(i-2)r_0}$. One gets a $(|V_i|+1)$-vertex planar graph. Trivially there exists a breadth-first search spanning tree of the graph rooted at z which is of radius r_0. Therefore the graph has $(2r_0+1)$-vertex separator according to Lemma 2.1, including z. Delete from the graph edges incident to the vertex z. All edges incident to the vertex separator create an edge separator of the graph G_i of size $\leq 2r_0k$ (the edges incident to the vertex z are not included). Hence there is a number of at least q+1 subgraphs each of not more than 2n/3 vertices. For these subgraphs we apply the above argument and we get the required partition by an $(m/r_0 + 2r_0k)$ -edge separator.

Since $r_0 = \lceil\sqrt{m/(2k)}\rceil$ then

$$C \leq m/\lceil\sqrt{m/(2k)}\rceil + 2\lceil\sqrt{m/(2k)}\rceil k \leq 2\sqrt{2km} + 2k \leq 3\sqrt{2km}.$$

Let G be not connected. If all connected components have $\leq n/3$ vertices, then we can get a separator and a partition using the above method. If one of the components has number of vertices from the interval $[n/3, 2n/3]$, then we put the vertices of the component in A and the other vertices in B. If there exists a component with more than 2n/3 vertices then we apply the connected graph separator to this component. □

According to the fact that $m \leq 3n-6$ the following corollary holds.

COROLLARY 2.1. G has an edge separator of size $3\sqrt{6kn} \approx 7.348\sqrt{kn}$.

REMARK 2.1. By more careful analysis of the arguments in the proof one can get edge separators of size $(2+\sqrt{7})\sqrt{kn} \approx 4.646\sqrt{kn}$ and $(\sqrt{2} + \sqrt{14}/2)\sqrt{(k+5)n} \approx 3.285\sqrt{(k+5)n}$.

REMARK 2.2. In the time of preparing the last version of this paper we found out that from the following theorem of Miller [Mi] we can derive an $2\sqrt{2n(k+1)}$ -edge separator.

THEOREM 2.2. [Mi] If G is an embedded 2-connected planar graph, $\#$ is an assignment of nonnegative weights to the vertices, edges and faces of G which sums to 1, and no face has weight $> 2/3$ then there exists a simple cycle weighted separator of size $2\sqrt{2\lfloor d/2\rfloor n}$, where d is the maximum face size. Further this cycle is constructible in linear sequential time or polylogarithmic parallel time with polynomial number of processors.

The following theorem shows that the edge separator in Theorem 2.1 can be improved at most by a constant in the worst case.

THEOREM 2.3. For arbitrary $k > 0$ such that $k \equiv 0 \pmod 4$ there exists an infinite sequence of planar graphs $G_i = (V_i, E_i)$, $|V_i| = n_i$, of degree k whose minimal edge separators are of sizes at least $\sqrt{kn_i}/9$.

Sketch of proof. The sequence of graphs can be constructed in the following way. Let us consider a mesh of size ixi. Replace each edge by k/4 new edges and on each edge place exactly one new vertex. We get a graph G_i of degree k and of $n_i = i^2 + (i-1)ik/2$ vertices.

By applying the method of Leighton [Lt, Lemma 3] we can derive for these graphs the above lower bounds. □

For some applications it can be useful to have an edge separator which separates a graph into two subgraphs whose numbers of vertices differ at most by one.

COROLLARY 2.2. The vertices of any n-vertex planar graph of degree k can be partitioned into sets A and B so that $|A|, |B| \leq \lceil n/2 \rceil$ and each edge connecting A and B is from a set of edges C such that:
$|C| \leq 9(2+\sqrt{6})\sqrt{kn} \approx 40.045\sqrt{kn}$.

The proof of Corollary 2.2 follows the method used in Corollary 3 of [LTa].

REMARK 2.3. This constant can be substantially reduced by combining techniques presented in [Vea, Veb] and the separator from Remark 2.2.

It is evident that an $O(\sqrt{nk})$-edge separator can be found in a linear time. The algorithm follows the construction from the proof of Theorem 2.1. It is based on the representation of a planar embedding of a graph described in [LTa]. The algorithm essentially utilizes the fact that for graphs with a spanning tree of radius r a $(2r+1)$-vertex separator can be found in a linear time [LTa]. Similarly a linear algorithm can be derived for finding the partition from Corollary 2.2.

3. OUTERPLANAR GRAPHS AND TREES.

As any n vertex outerplanar graph of degree k has a 2-vertex separator |H|, this yields a 2k-edge separator. By simple analysis we are able to improve this to a k-edge separator. Interesting is to state the size of an edge separator in the case of division the outerplanar graph into two subgraphs of not more than $\lceil n/2 \rceil$ vertices each. According to the above mentioned method [LTa, Corollary 3] we can get an $O(k\log(n/k))$-edge separator.

We do not know whether this upper bound is optimal in the worst case but we can improve this in the case of trees as shown in the theorem below. First we state a lemma.

LEMMA 3.1. Let T be an n-vertex tree and p be an integer $1 \le p \le n/2$. Then one of the following cases holds.

1. T can be separated into two subgraphs T_1, T_2 such that $|T_1| = n-p$, $|T_2| = p$ by deleting an edge.
2. T can be separated into three subgraphs T_1, T_2, T_3 such that $|T_1| \le n-p$, $|T_2| \le p$, $|T_3| \le n/l$, whereby T_3 is a tree, by deleting of at most l edges, $l \ge 3$.

Proof. It is easy to find a vertex $v \in T$ by deleting of which T is separated into trees $G_1, G_2, \dots, G_r$, $r \ge 2$, whereby $n-p \ge |G_1| \ge |G_2| \ge \dots \ge |G_r|$, $p \le |G_2|$, where $|G_i|$ denotes the number of vertices of G_i.

If $r = 2$ then the first case holds.

If $r = 3$ then we delete the edge joining v with G_3 and one of the edges joining v with G_1, G_2 according to whether $|G_2| < p$ or $|G_1| < n-p$.

Let $r \ge 4$. Denote $|G_i| = n_i$, $i=1,2,\dots,r$. Let l be the smallest integer such that $l \ge 3$ and $n_l \ge n_{l+1} + \dots + n_r = n'_l$. Then $n_i < n_{i+1} + \dots + n_r = n'_i$, for $3 \le i \le l-1$. We prove by induction that the set $n_1, n_2, \dots, n_j$, for any j, $2 \le j \le l-1$ can be divided into two sets A^*, B^* such that

$$N_1 = \sum_{i \in A^*} n_i \le n-p, \quad N_2 = \sum_{i \in B^*} n_i \le p.$$

The case j=2 is trivial. Let the claim be true for some $j \le l-2$. Then either $N_1 + n_{j+1} \le n-p$ or $N_2 + n_{j+1} \le p$. Otherwise

$$n-1 = N_1 + N_2 + n_{j+1} + n'_{j+1} \ge N_1 + N_2 + 2n_{j+1} > n.$$

Therefore there exists a partition of the set $\{n_1, n_2, \dots, n_{l-1}\}$ into two sets A^*, B^* such that $N_1 = \sum_{i \in A^*} n_i \le n-p$, $N_2 = \sum_{i \in B^*} n_i \le p$.

Then either $N_1 + n'_l \le n-p$ or $N_2 + n'_l \le p$. Otherwise a contradiction as above will arise. Thus we divided the set $\{1,2,\dots,r\} - \{l\}$ into two sets A,B such that

$\sum_{i \in A} n_i \le n-p$, $\sum_{i \in B} n_i \le p$. Moreover A or B contains the set $\{l+1,\dots,r\}$ and $l\, n_l \le l\, n_{l-1} = (l-1) n_{l-1} + n_{l-1} \le (n_1 + \dots + n_{l-1}) + n_l + n'_l = n-1$.

According to the construction of the sets A,B, $1 \in A$, $2 \in B$. Assume that $\{l+1,\dots,r\} \subset B$. Now delete all edges joining v with G_i, for $i \in A$ and $i = l$. Clearly, the number of these edges is at most $l-1$. Let T_1 be $\bigcup_{i \in A} G_i$, T_2 be a graph induced by $\bigcup_{i \in B} G_i \cup \{v\}$ and $T_3 = G_l$. Evidently $|T_1| \leq n-p$ and $|T_2| \leq p+1$. If $|T_2| = p+1$ then we separate a leaf u of T_2 by deleting of one edge and add u to T_1. If $\{l+1,\dots,r\} \subset A$ the argument is similar. □

<u>THEOREM 3.1.</u> For any n vertex tree T of degree k and any p such that $1 \leq p \leq n/2$ there exists a partition A,B of the set of the vertices of T such that $|A| = n-p$, $|B| = p$ and any edge connecting a vertex in A with a vertex in B belongs to a set C of $\leq k\log n/\log k$ edges.

<u>Proof.</u> For k=2 the theorem is obviously true. The set C can be found applying the following recursive procedure. (The set C is empty at the beginning .)

```
procedure  SEPARATE (T,p)
begin
   if T is a star graph then
     C = C ∪ {any p edges of T};  stop;
   fi;
   if the case 1. of Lemma 3.1 holds then
     C = C∪{the edge found in the case 1.
     of Lemma 3.1};  stop;
   fi
   if the case 2. of Lemma 3.1 holds then
      C = C∪{l edges found in the case 2.
      of Lemma 3.1};
      SEPARATE (T3, min { p-|T2|, n-p-|T1|});
   fi
end
```

Now we prove that the size of C also satisfies the theorem.

Let $k \geq 3$ and $c(n,k)$ denotes the maximum size of a set C found by the algorithm when applied on any n vertex tree of degree at most k for arbitrary p. We prove by induction on n that

$$c(n,k) \leq k\log n/\log k.$$

Trivially $c(k+1,k) \leq k/2 < k\log(k+1)/\log k$. Assume that the claim is true for all j such that $k+1 \leq j \leq n-1$. Then

$$c(n,k) \leq \max\{l+c(|T_3|,k):\ 3 \leq l \leq k\} \leq \max\{l+c(\lfloor n/l \rfloor,k):\ 3 \leq l \leq k\} \leq$$
$$\leq \max\{l+k\log(n/l)/\log k\ :\ 3 \leq l \leq k\} = k\log n/\log k + \max\{\log l(l/\log l - k/\log k):\ 3 \leq l \leq k\} = k\log n/\log k.\ \square$$

The following theorem claims that the edge separator in Theorem

3.1 for $p = \lfloor n/2 \rfloor$ can be improved only by a constant in the worst case.

THEOREM 3.2. For arbitrary $k \geq 3$ there exists an infinite sequence of trees $T_i = (V_i, E_i)$, $|V_i| = n_i$, of degree k whose minimal edge separators dividing the vertices of T_i into two subforests of at most $\lceil n/2 \rceil$ vertices are of sizes $\Omega(k \log n_i / \log k)$.

The theorem can be proved using the method of Rosenberg [Ro]. Note that for odd k the sequence T_i is the set of all complete (k-1)-ary trees.

4. APPLICATIONS

A large variety of computational problems can be mathematically formulated as graph embedding problems. For instance, problems concerning representation of some kind of data structure by another kind of data structure e.g. [LTb], adaptation of the interconnection structure of a parallel algorithm differing from the interconnection architecture of the used parallel computer e.g. [BS], and laying out circuits in standard formats e.g. [Ls, Va].

Let $G_1 = (V_1, E_1)$ and $G_2 = (V_2, E_2)$ be undirected graphs with $|V_1| = |V_2|$, $|E_1| > 0$. An embedding of G_1 in G_2 is a bijection $\varphi : V_1 \to V_2$. The average cost of the embedding is

$$ACOST(\varphi) = (1/|E_1|) \sum_{(u,v) \in E_1} d_2(\varphi(u), \varphi(v)).$$

where $d_2(x,y)$ denotes the distance between x and y in G_2.

Lipton and Tarjan [LTa] proved that every planar graph of degree k can be embedded in a binary tree so that the average cost is $O(k)$. Using our $O(\sqrt{kn})$-edge separator, we substantially improve this result.

THEOREM 4.1. Every planar graph of degree k can be embedded in a binary tree with the average cost $O(\log k)$.

Proof: Let G be an n-vertex planar graph of degree k. Define an embedding of the vertices of G in the vertices of a binary tree T by using the following recursive procedure. If G has one vertex v, embed v in a tree of one vertex, the image of v. Otherwise, apply Corollary 2.2 to find a partition A,B and a set of edges C. Let $|A| = \lfloor n/2 \rfloor$ and $|C| \leq c\sqrt{kn}$. Let v be a vertex in A. Embed the subgraph G_1 induced by $A - \{v\}$ in a binary tree T_1 by the method recursively. Embed the subgraph G_2 of G induced by B in a binary tree T_2. Let T consists of a root (the image of v) with two children: the root of T_1 and the root of T_2.

Let $h(n)$ be the maximum depth of a tree T of n vertices produced by this algorithm. Then

$h(n) \leq h(\lceil n/2 \rceil) + 1.$

From this it follows $h(n) \leq \log n$.

Let us define: $s(G) = \sum_{(u,v)\in G} d_2(\varphi(u), \varphi(w))$. Then

$s(G) = 0$, for $n = 1$

$s(G) \leq s(G_1) + s(G_2) + 2c\sqrt{kn}\log n + k\log n.$

This follows from the fact that for every edge $(u,w)\in G$ belonging neither to G_1, nor to G_2, it holds:

$d_2(\varphi(u), \varphi(w)) \leq 2 \log n$, if $(u,w)\in C$;

$d_2(\varphi(u), \varphi(w)) \leq \log n$, if this edge is incident to the vertex v.

If $s(n)$ is the maximum value of $s(G)$ for all n-vertex planar graphs G of degree k, then:

$s(n) \leq 6n\log n$, for $k < n \leq 2k$; otherwise

$s(n) \leq s(\lceil n/2 \rceil - 1) + s(\lfloor n/2 \rfloor) + 2c\sqrt{kn}\log n + k\log n.$

A direct solution of this recurrence relation gives

$s(n) = O(n \log k - \sqrt{kn}\log n).$

Since G is connected and G has at least n-1 edges

$ACOST(\varphi) = O(\log k)$. □

By induction on the height of the complete (k-1)-ary tree, we are able to prove the following theorem.

<u>THEOREM 4.2.</u> Average cost of embedding of the complete (k-1)-ary tree into any binary tree is $\Omega(\log k)$.

The same result trivially holds for outerplanar graphs although in this case even $WCOST(\varphi) = \max_{(u,v)\in E_1} d_2(\varphi(u), \varphi(v))$ is of $\Theta(\log k)$ [HR,Mo].

<u>REMARK 4.1.</u> We are able to apply the above method to embedding n-vertex planar graphs of degree k into paths, square meshes, d-dimensional meshes and hypercubes with corresponding average costs $\Theta(\sqrt{kn})$, $O(\sqrt{k}\log(n/k))$, $\Theta(d\ k^{1/d})$, $k \gg d$, $O(\log k)$. The first of these results is a generalisation of the result [DEL] that embedding of n vertex square mesh into path is of $\Theta(\sqrt{n})$. In case of outerplanar graphs we can improve the first two results to $O(k\log(n/k))$ and $\Theta(\sqrt{k})$ respectively. Note that n vertex trees of degree k can be embedded into path with average cost $\Theta(k\log n/\log k)$ [J,S].

Other application of our results could be that of estimating the cutwidth [H,Y] of certain classes of graphs. From Theorem 2.1 one easily obtains the following estimation.

<u>THEOREM 4.3.</u> The cutwidth of any planar n-vertex graph of degree k is

$O(\sqrt{kn})$.

This theorem improves the $O(k\sqrt{n})$ results mentioned in [H,Y]. The following theorem is evident.

THEOREM 4.4. The graphs defined in Theorem 2.3 require $\Omega(\sqrt{kn_i})$ cutwidth.

5. CONCLUSION

We have investigated edge separators for planar graphs, outerplanar graphs and trees of given degree and applied them for efficient average cost embeddings. The details of proofs will appear in a journal version.

The results of the paper evoke some open question:

5.1. Improving of constant factors in the upper and lower bounds for separators.

5.2. We conjecture that the edge separator which divides any planar graphs into two halves is of size at most n. We know a graph requiring n-edge separator.

5.3. Finding efficient edge separators for graphs of genus g.

5.4. We conjecture that Theorem 3.1 holds also for outerplanar graphs.

5.5. It is interesting to study separators dividing planar graphs into two parts of p and n-p vertices $1 \leq p \leq n/2$.

5.6. Are the upper bounds in Remark 4.1. optimal ?

5.7. Studying WCOST(φ) for graphs mentioned in Theorem 4.1 and Remark 4.1.

5.8. Is it possible to embed planar graphs of degree k in some constant number of pages with cutwidth $O(\sqrt{kn})$? See [H,Y].

REFERENCES

[BS] F.Berman,L.Snyder, On mapping parallel algorithms into parallel architectures, J. of Parallel and Distributed Computing, Vol.4, 1987, pp. 439-458.

[Da] H.N.Djidjev, On the problem of partitioning planar graphs, SIAM J. Alg. Disc. Meth., Vol. 3, No. 2, 1982, pp.229-240.

[Db] H.N.Djidjev, A linear algorithm for partitioning graphs of fixed genus, SERDICA, Vol. 11, 1985, 369-387.

[Dc] H.N.Djidjev, A separator theorem for graphs of fixed genus, SERDICA, Vol. 11, 1985, pp. 319-329.

[DEL] R.A.De Millo, S.C.Eisenstat, R.J.Lipton, Preserving average proximity in arrays, Comm. ACM, 21, 1978 , pp. 228-230.

[Ga] H.Gazit, An improved algorithm for separating planar graphs, manuscript.

[GHT] J.R.Gilbert, J.P.Hutchinson, R.E.Tarjan, A separator theorem for graphs of bounded genus, Journal of Algorithms, No.5, 1984, pp. 391-398.

[Gi] J.R.Gilbert, Graph separator theorem and sparse Gaussian elimination, Ph.D. thesis, Stanford University, 1980.

[GM] H.Gazit, G.L.Miller, A parallel algorithm for finding a separator for planar graphs. In: Proc. 28-th Foundations of Computer Science, IEEE, 1987, 238-248.

[H] L.S.Heath, Embedding outerplanar graphs in small books, SIAM J. Alg. Disc. Meth., Vol.8, No.2, 1987, pp. 198-218.

[HR] J.Hong, A.L.Rosenberg, Graphs that are almost binary trees, SIAM J. Comput., Vol. 11, No. 2, 1982, pp. 227-242.

[J] M.A.Jordanskij, Minimal numberings of tree vertices, Probl. Kib., Vol. 31, 1976, pp.109-133 (in Russian).

[JV] D.B.Johnson, S.M. Venkatesan, Partition of planar flows in networks. In: Proc. 24-th Ann. Symp. on Theory of Computing, ACM, New York, 1983, pp. 259-263.

[LRT] R.J.Lipton, D.J.Rose, R.E.Tarjan, Generalized nested dissection, SIAM J.Numer. Anal., 16, 1979, 346-358.

[Ls] C.E.Leiserson, Area efficient graph layout (for VLSI), In: Proc. 21-st Foundations of Computer Science, IEEE, Syracuse, 1980, pp. 270-281.

[Lt] F.T.Leighton, A layout strategy which is provably good, In: Proc. 23-rd Foundations of Computer Science, IEEE, San Francisco, 1982, pp. 85-98.

[LTa] R.J.Lipton, R.E.Tarjan, A separator theorem for planar graphs, SIAM J. Appl. Math., Vol. 36, No. 2, 1979, pp. 177-189.

[LTb] R.J.Lipton, R.E.Tarjan, Applications of a planar separator theorem, SIAM J.Computing, Vol. 9, No.3, 1980, pp. 615-627.

[Ml] G.L.Miller, Finding small simple cycle-separators for 2-connected planar graphs, J. of Comp. and System Science, Vol. 32, 1986, pp. 265 - 279.

[Mo] B.Monien, The complexity of embedding graphs into binary trees, In: FCT'85, LNCS 199, pp. 300-309.

[Mt] S.Mitchel, Linear algorithm to recognize outerplanar and maximal outerplanar graphs, IPL, Vol. 9, No.5, 1979, pp.229-232.

[Ra] S.Rao, Finding near optimal separators in planar graphs, In: Proc. 28-th Foundations of Computer Science. IEEE, 1987, pp. 225-237.

[RH] S.S.Ravi, H.B.Hunt, An application of the planar separator theorem to counting problem, IPL, Vol. 25, No.6, 1987, pp.317-322.

[Ri] D.Richards, Finding short cycles in planar graphs using separators, J. of Algorithms, Vol. 7, 1986, pp. 382-394.

[Ro] A.L.Rosenberg, A hypergraph model for fault-tolerant VLSI processor arrays, IEEE Trans. on Computers, C-34, No. 6, 1985, pp. 578-584.

[S] M.A.Scheidwasser, On the length and the width of embeddings of graphs in meshes, Probl. Kib., Vol. 29, 1974, pp.63-102 (in Russian).

[Va] J.G.Valiant, Universality consideration in VLSI circuits, IEEE Trans. on Computers, C-30, No.2, 1981, pp. 135-140.

[Vea] S.M.Venkatesan, Improved constants for some separator theorems, J. of Algorithms, to appear.

[Veb] S.M.Venkatesan, On separating a planar graph into two halves, Submitted to SIAM J. of Discrete Mathematics.

[Y] M.Yannakakis, Linear and book embeddings of graphs, in: Proc. Aegean Workshop on Computing, July 8-11, 1986, Lecture Notes in Computer Science, Vol. 227, Springer-Verlag, Berlin, 1986.

A Fast Parallel Algorithm for Eigenvalue Problem of Jacobi Matrices

M. A. Frumkin*)

1. Introduction. As parallel, vector and systolic computers come in programming practice we must revize complexity theory of algorithms. Conterpart of time complexity of an algorithm for parallel computer is the depth of the algorithm. The class of problems which have polynomial algorithms with depth bounded by a k degree polynomial on logarithm of size of problem S. Cook defined as NC^k [1] and he defined $NC = \bigcup_k NC^k$. Such problems as matrix multiplication, matrix inversion, polynomial multiplication and division, GCD of polynomials, resultant of two polynomials of one variable are in NC. Such problems as maximum network flow and linear programming are P-complete and are not in NC if $NC \neq P$. About perfect matching in bipartite graph and GCD of two integers it is not known neither they are in NC nor they are P-complete [1,3].

In the paper we show that approximation of eigenvalues of Jacobi matrix is in NC^5. Using the algorithm we construct a fast parallel algorithm for expansion of a vector by a set of orthogonal polynomials defined by a second order linear recurrence.

2. A recursive method for isolation of roots of polynomials. All parallel algorithms of the paper are based on a method for isolation of roots of solutions of a second order linear reccurence

$$x_i(t) = (a_i - t)\, x_{i-1}(t) - u_i x_{i-2}(t), \quad \text{with } u_i > 0$$
$$x_1 = a_0 - t\ ,\ x_0 = 1. \tag{2.1}$$

It is well known that roots of $x_i(t)$ are real and intermit roots of $x_{i-1}(t)$. Let $\{x_i(t)\}$ and $\{y_i(t)\}$ be solutions of the recurrence of type (2.1). We shall prove a property of isolation of roots of

*)Institute of Problems of Cybernetics, Acad. of Sci of the USSR

polynomial

$$z_{n,k}(t) = \det \begin{vmatrix} x_n(t) & y_{k-1}(t) \\ x_{n-1}(t) & y_k(t) \end{vmatrix} \qquad (2.2)$$

by roots of $x_n, x_{n-1}, y_{k-1}, y_k$.

Lemma 2.3. Let $\{x_n(t)\}$ be a solution of (2.1). Then $\arg(x_n(t), x_{n-1}(t))$ strictly increase.

Proof. It is sufficient to prove that

$$d_n = \det \begin{vmatrix} x_n & x_n' \\ x_{n-1} & x_{n-1}' \end{vmatrix} > 0.$$

Initial conditions shows that $d_1=1$. Diffirentiation of (2.1) shows that $x_n' = -x_{n-1} + (a_n - t)x_{n-1}' - u_n x_{n-2}'$, consequently

$$\begin{vmatrix} x_n & x_n' + x_{n-1} \\ x_{n-1} & x_{n-1}' \end{vmatrix} = \begin{vmatrix} a_n - t & -u_n \\ 1 & 0 \end{vmatrix} \begin{vmatrix} x_{n-1} & x_{n-1}' \\ x_{n-2} & x_{n-2}' \end{vmatrix}$$

Then

$$d_n = x_{n-1}^2 + \det \begin{vmatrix} a_n - t & -u_n \\ 1 & 0 \end{vmatrix} \begin{vmatrix} x_{n-1} & x_{n-1}' \\ x_{n-2} & x_{n-2}' \end{vmatrix} = x_{n-1}^2 + u_n d_{n-1}.$$

and induction on n shows that $d_n > 0$.

Theorem 2.4. Let $\{x_n(t)\}$ and $\{y_n(t)\}$ be two solutions of (2.1) with different a_k and u_k and let $\{z_n(t)\}$ be as in (2.2). Let $t_1 < \ldots < t_{2(n+k+1)}$ be all roots of polynomials $x_n, x_{n-1}, y_{k-1}, y_k$ in increasing order. Then every interval $(-\infty, t_1], \ldots$ $\ldots, [t_{2i}, t_{2i+1}], \ldots, [t_{2(n+k+1)}, \infty)$ contains exactly one root of polynomial $z_{n,k}(t)$ and intervals $[t_{2i-1}, t_{2i}]$ do not contain a root of the polynomial.

Proof. Set $X(t) = (x_n(t), x_{n-1}(t))^T$, $Y(t) = (y_{k-1}(t), y_k(t))^T$. Lemma 2.3 shows that $\arg(X(t))$ strictly increase and $\arg(Y(t))$ strictly decrease so $\phi(t) = \arg(X(t)) - \arg(Y(t))$ strictly increase.

Roots of $z_{n,k}(t)$ coinside with values of t such that $X(t)$ and $Y(t)$ are collinear and hence $\phi(t)$ is a multiple of π. If $t=-\infty$ then $X(t)$ and $Y(t)$ are situated in the first quadrant near x and y axes correspondingly and rotate in positive and negative directions as t increase. Continuty arguments shows that $\phi(t)$ must receive 0 before X(t) and Y(t) leave the first quadrant that is before t path over t_1. After that vectors X(t) and Y(t) will be situate in neighbour quadrants so $z_{n,k}(t)$ does not equal 0. It may happen only when X(t) and Y(t) turn out in opposite quadrants, that is after t path over t_2. Similar considerations show that intervals $[t_j, t_{j+1}]$ which contain roots of $z_{n,k}(t)$ intermit intervals which does not contain ones.

If we know roots of polynomials $x_n, x_{n-1}, y_{k-1}, y_k$ and ends t_0 and $t_{2(n+k)-1}$ of an interval that contains all roots of $z_{n,k}(t)$ then the roots may be refined by bisection method. But it has linear convergence speed and it may be necessary up to $O(\log(\max((t_{2i+1}-t_{2i})/e))$ iterations. On the other hand Newton's method has a quadratic convergence speed but it converges only in a neighbour of a root. For convergence of Newton's method it is sufficently to take as initial approximation an end of an interval which contains one root and which does not contain a root of the second derivation. Hence we estimate radius of neigbourhood in which the second derivation does not contain a change of the sign in terms of distance from the root to ends of the interval. Then we shall show that the neighbourhood may be localized in $O(\log\log^2 M/e)$ iterations. In the neigbourhood Newton's method finds the root in $O(\log\log M/e)$ iterations.

Lemma 2.5. Let ε be the distance from a root s_1 of N degree polynomial z(t) to ends of an interval which does not contain other roots of the polynomial. Then neigbourhood of s_1 with radius ε/C_N^2 does not contain roots of the second derivation other then s_1.

Proof. Double differentiation of $z(t) = \prod (t-s_i)$ shows that $z''(t) = 2z(t) \prod_{i<j} 1/(t-s_i)(t-s_j)$. Let $z''(y)=0$, $z(y)\neq 0$, $r=|y-s_1|$ and let s_2 be a root nearest to y after s_1. Then

$$\sum_{i<j} \frac{1}{(y-s_i)(y-s_j)} = 0 \text{ and } |y-s_1| = \frac{-1}{\sum_{\substack{i<j \\ (i,j)\neq(1,2)}} (y-s_2)/(y-s_i)(y-s_j)}$$

Thus

$$r=|y-s_1| \geq 1/\sum_{\substack{i<j\\(i,j)\neq(1,2)}} 1/|y-s_i| \geq 1/\sum 1/(\varepsilon-r)\geq(\varepsilon-r)/(C_N^2-1)$$

Inequality $r\geq(\varepsilon-r)/(C_N^2-1)$ implies the assertion of the lemma.

If ε is a distance from the root s to the ends of the interval in which s is located and the length of the interval is $O(\varepsilon)$ then in 2log N iterations we can locate a neighbourhood of s in which the second derivation does not change the sign.

Lemma 2.6. Let M be the length of interval in which the root s is located. Using $O((\log\log M/\varepsilon)^2)$ iterations we can locate the root within interval of length 2ε.

Proof. In order to locate the root in short interval we shall use the following superexpontiation algorithm (SE for short). Let s is in the right half of the interval $I_0=(a,b)$ and m_0 is maximal integer such that s is in interval

$$I_1=(b-(b-a)/2^{2^{m_0}}, b).$$

If s is in right half of I_1 then repeat the same procedure with I_1. Let s is in the left half of I_k then

$$|I_{j+1}| = |I_j|/2^{2^{m_j}}, \quad |I_j|/2^{2^{m_j+1}} < \varepsilon, \quad \varepsilon < |I_k| \leq 2\varepsilon$$

Consequently

$$|I_{j+1}| = |I_j|^{1/2}|I_j|^{1/2}/2^{2^{m_j}} < (|I_j|\varepsilon)^{1/2},$$

Using $|I_j| \leq 2^{2^{1-j}}\varepsilon$ as a step of induction we see that

$$|I_{j+1}| < (2^{2^{1-j}}\varepsilon^2)^{1/2} < 2^{2^{1-j-1}}\varepsilon.$$

Thus $k, m_j \leq l=\log\log M/\varepsilon$ and the lemma follows.

Using the two lemmas we can construct an algorithm for roots refinement of a polynomial $z_{n,k}$ represented as in (2.2) if roots of $x_n, x_{n-1}, y_{k-1}, y_n$ and ends t_0 and $t_{2(n+k)-1}$ of the interval that include all roots of $z_{n.k}$ are known. The algorithm is a combination of SE algorithm from lemma 2.6, bisection method and Newton's method. Let $N=k+n=\deg z_{n,k}(t)$.

Algorithm SEBN($t_0, t_{2N-1}, x_n, x_{n-1}, y_{k-1}, y_k, z_{n,k}, e$).

Step 1. Sort roots of the polynomials $x_n, x_{n-1}, y_{k-1}, y_k$ in increasing order and return a sequence $t_0 < t_1 \leq \ldots < t_{2N-1}$.

Step 2. For $i=0,1,\ldots,N-1$ do steps 3-5 in parallel.

Step 3. Apply SE to intervals (t_{2i}, t_{2i+1}) and return intervals (v_{2i}, v_{2i+1}).

Step 4. By bisection algorithm make C_N^2-fold reduction of intrevals (v_{2i}, v_{2i+1}) and return (w_{2i}, w_{2i+1}).

Step 5. By Newton's method with precision e find root s_i in interval (w_{2i}, w_{2i+1}).

Theorem 2.7. In assumptions of theorem 2.4 let $M = \max\{t_{2i+1} - t_{2i}\}$, then roots of polynomial $z_N(t)$ with precision e may be found with depth $O(\log^2 N(\log N + \log\log^2 M/e))$ in time $O(N \log^2 N(\log N + \log\log^2 M/e))$.

Proof. Convergence of SEBN follows from 2.5 and 2.6 and we have to estimate complexity of the algorithm only.

Depth of the step 1 is $O(\log N)$ and its time complexity is $O(N \log N)$ if we use AKS algorithm.

For execution of iterations of steps 3-4 we have to evaluate polynomial $z_{n,k}(t)$ in N points and for Newton's iteration of step 5 evaluate the derivation in N points too. Fast algorithm for multiplication of Vandermonde matrix by a vector give us a tool for execution of iteration in time $O(N\log^2 N)$ and with depth $O(\log^2 N)$. So we shall estimate numbers of iterations of steps 3-5.

Lemma 2.6 shows that the number of iterations of step 3 is $O(\log\log^2 M/e)$.

Number of iterations of step 4 is $O(\log N)$ and number of iterations of step 5 is $O(\log\log M/e)$ as bisection method and Newton's method have linear and quadratic convergency speeds correspondingly. Multiplication of time and space of one iteration by the numbers of iterations gives us assertion of the theorem.

3. Application to tridiagonal matrices. We shall apply results of section 2 to characteristic polynomial of a tridiagonal matrix

$$J = \begin{vmatrix} a_1 & b_1 & & & \\ c_2 & a_2 & b_2 & & \\ & & & & \\ & & c_{n-1} & a_{n-1} & b_{n-1} \\ & & & c_n & b_n \end{vmatrix}$$

Let B_i and C_j be upper left and lower right minors of $A = J-tI$ of orders i and j correspondingly. Expansions of B_i and C_j by i-th and (n-j)-th columns shows that $\{B_i\}$ and $\{C_j\}$ are solutions of (2.1) with $u_i = c_i b_{i-1}$ and $u_j = c_{n-j} b_{n-j-1}$ correspondigly.

Lemma 3.1. Characteristic polynomial of J may be expressed as follows

$$\det\ A = \det \begin{vmatrix} B_k & u_k B_{k-1} \\ C_{n-k-1} & C_{n-k} \end{vmatrix}$$

Proof. An expansion of det A by k-th column yeilds det A = $= -B_{k-2}C_{n-k}b_{k-1}c_k + B_{k-1}(a_k - t)C_{n-k} - b_k c_{k+1} B_{k-1} C_{n-k-1}$. If we note that $B_k = -B_{k-2}b_{k-1}c_k + B_{k-1}(a_k - t)$ then lemma follows.

In order to apply 2.7 and get consistent system of relations for recursive isolation of roots of pricipal minors of A we shall execute all computations for four submatrices.

Let A[i], i=1,...,4 be the minors of A defined as follows:

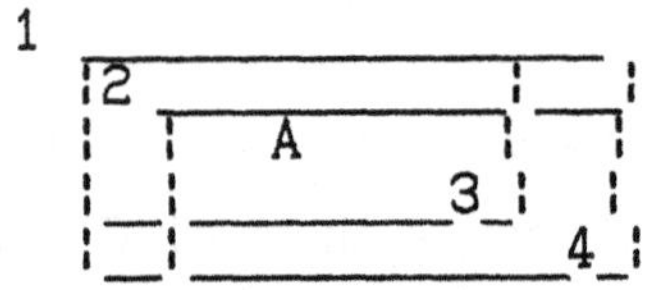

A[1] - (1,3), A[3] - (2,3)
A[2] - (1,4), A[4] - (2,4)

Lemma 3.2. Following identities are true

$$A[1] = \det \begin{vmatrix} B[2] & u_k\ B[1] \\ C[3] & C[1] \end{vmatrix} \qquad A[2] = \det \begin{vmatrix} B[2] & u_k\ B[1] \\ C[4] & C[2] \end{vmatrix}$$
$$A[3] = \det \begin{vmatrix} B[4] & u_k\ B[3] \\ C[3] & C[1] \end{vmatrix} \qquad A[4] = \det \begin{vmatrix} B[4] & u_k\ B[3] \\ C[4] & C[2] \end{vmatrix} \qquad (3.3)$$

Proof follows from 2 directly. If $u_i > 0$, i=1,...,N that is J is a Jacobi matrix then lemma 3.3 shows that the theorem 2.4 gives essentially more concise partition of the spectrum of Jacobi matrix then Cauchy's theorem [2].

Let A_j^i be the submatrix of order 2^i of A arranged in rows and columns with indices $j*2^i+1,\dots,(j+1)*2^i$. Then the following algorithm computes eigenvelues of matrix J of order $N=2^l$.

Standard estimations of spectral radius of tridiagonal matrix [2] shows that

$$t_0 = \min_{1\le i\le n} (|a_i|-|c_i|-|b_i|) \text{ and } t_\infty = \min_{1\le i\le n} (|a_i|+|c_i|+|b_i|)$$

are bounds of the spectrum.

Algorithm EIGVAL(A,e).

Step 1. for i=1 to l do steps 2-4.

Step 2. par j=0 to $2^{(l-i)}-1$ do step 3-4.

Step 3. set $k=j*2^i$;

$$A_j^i[1]=A_{2j}^{i-1}[2]A_{2j+1}^{i-1}[1]-u_kA_{2j}^{i-1}[1]A_{2j+1}^{i-1}[3];$$

$$A_j^i[2]=A_{2j}^{i-1}[2]A_{2j+1}^{i-1}[2]-u_kA_{2j}^{i-1}[1]A_{2j+1}^{i-1}[4];$$

$$A_j^i[3]=A_{2j}^{i-1}[4]A_{2j+1}^{i-1}[1]-u_kA_{2j}^{i-1}[3]A_{2j+1}^{i-1}[3];$$

$$A_j^i[4]=A_{2j}^{i-1}[4]A_{2j+1}^{i-1}[2]-u_kA_{2j}^{i-1}[3]A_{2j+1}^{i-1}[4];$$

Step 4.

$$\mathrm{SEBN}(t_0,t_\infty,A_{2*j}^{i-1}[2],A_{2*j+1}^{i-1}[3],A_{2*j}^{i-1}[1],A_{2*j+1}^{i-1}[1],A_j^i[1],e);$$

$$\mathrm{SEBN}(t_0,t_\infty,A_{2*j}^{i-1}[2],A_{2*j+1}^{i-1}[4],A_{2*j}^{i-1}[1],A_{2*j+1}^{i-1}[2],A_j^i[2],e);$$

$$\mathrm{SEBN}(t_0,t_\infty,A_{2*j}^{i-1}[4],A_{2*j+1}^{i-1}[3],A_{2*j}^{i-1}[3],A_{2*j+1}^{i-1}[1],A_j^i[3],e);$$

$$\mathrm{SEBN}(t_0,t_\infty,A_{2*j}^{i-1}[4],A_{2*j+1}^{i-1}[4],A_{2*j}^{i-1}[3],A_{2*j+1}^{i-1}[2],A_j^i[4],e);$$

Theorem 3.4. Algorithm EIGVAL finds approximations with precision e of eigenvalues of Jacobi matrix. Depth of the algorithm is $O(\log^3 N(\log N + \log\log^2 M/e))$ and its time complexity is $O(N \log^3 N(\log N + \log\log^2 M/e))$.

Proof. Steps 3 and 4 may be executed in parallel for all $i=0,\dots,2^{l-i}-1$.

If on step 3 we use a fast algorithm for mutiplication of polynomials then depth of the step is $O(i)$ and its time compliexity is $O(i2^i)$. Theorem 2.7 implies that depth of the step 4 is $O(i^2(i+\log\log^2 M/e))$ and its time complexity is

$O(2^i i^2(i+\log\log^2 M/e))$. Hence if i is fixed then total depth of steps 2-4 is $O(i^2(i+\log\log^2 M/e))$ and total time complexity is $O(N\, i^2(i+\log\log^2 M/e))$. Assertion follows if we sum the estimates for $i=1,\dots,\log N$.

4. Expansion by orthogonal polynomials. Orthogonal polynomials are a solution of a system of three term equations [2]:

$$tx_i = b_i x_{i+1} + a_i x_i + c_i x_{i-1} \quad \text{where } b_i c_{i+1} > 0,\ i \le 0 \qquad (4.1)$$
$$x_0 = 1,\ x_{-1} = 0$$

Set $X_N(t) = (x_0(t), x_1(t), \dots, x_{N-1}(t))^T$ Then we can rewrite (4.1) in the following form

$$\begin{vmatrix} & \begin{vmatrix} 0 \\ \\ 1 \end{vmatrix} \end{vmatrix} \ \ \begin{vmatrix} A \end{vmatrix} \ X_{N+1}(t) = 0.$$

where J and A are as above. If t_k is a root of $x_N(t)$ then t_k is eigenvalue of J and $X_N(t_k)$ is corresponding eigenvector of J.

The matrix J is sum of direct sum of two Jacobi matrices of half order and of a rank one matrix: $J=J_1 \oplus J_2 - pq^T$. Let U diagonalize $J_1 \oplus J_2$ that is $U(J_1 \oplus J_2)U^{-1} = D_1 \oplus D_2 - Upq^T U^{-1} = D_1 \oplus D_2 - vw^T$.

If Z diagonalize $D_1 \oplus D_2 - vw^T$ then then UZ diagonalize J. Let z^j be j-th column of Z. It is an eigenvector of $D_1 \oplus D_2 - vw^T$ hence

$$(D_1 \oplus D_2) z^j - (w^T z^j) v = t_j z^j,\quad d_i z_i^j - (w^T z^j) v_i = t_j z_i^j,$$

$$z_i^j = \frac{w^T z^j}{d_i - t_j} v_i = \frac{h_j v_i}{d_i - t_j}.$$

That is

$$Z = \left| \frac{h_j v_i}{d_i - t_j} \right|$$

is production of a Cauchy matrix and two diagonal matrices. Fast algorithm for multiplication of Cauchy matrix by a vector has depth $O(\log^2 N)$ and time complexity $O(N \log^2 N)$. This implies the following assertion.

Theorem 4.2. If $t_1,\dots,t_N$ are roots of orthogonal polynomial $x_N(t)$ then expansion of a vector by a vectors $X_{N-1}(t_k)$ may be computed with depth $O(\log^3 N)$ and time $O(N \log^3 N)$.

This result together with theorem 3.4 shows that expansion of a vector by a system of orthogonal polynomials may be computed with depth $O(\log^3 N(\log N + \log\log^2 M/e))$ and time $O(N \log^3 N(\log N + \log\log^2 M/e))$ without preprocessing of (4.1).

References

1. Cook S.A. The taxonomy of problems with fast parallel algorithms. Inf. and Control, v. 64, 1985, 2-22.
2. Parlett B.N. The symmetric eigenvalue problem. Prentice-Hall, 1980.
3. Reif J.H. Logarithmic depth circuits for algebraic functions. SIAM J. on Computing, v. 15, No.1, 1986, pp. 231-242.
4. Vichirco V.I. An algorithm for some sum of reciprocals. Zap. Nauchn. Semin. LOMI, v. 137, Leningrad, 1984, pp. 3-6 (In Russian).

STRONG AND ROBUSTLY STRONG POLYNOMIAL TIME REDUCIBILITIES TO SPARSE SETS

Ricard Gavaldà and José L. Balcázar
Facultat d'Informàtica U.P.C.
08028 Barcelona, Spain

Abstract. Reducibility defined by oracle strong nondeterministic machines is studied. Two definitions of relativized strength are presented and separated. The corresponding reduction classes of the sparse sets are characterized in terms of nonuniform complexity classes. An oracle-restricted positive relativization of the probabilistic class ZPP is developed.

1. Introduction

In the study of complexity classes defined by sequential models of computation, several classes have been identified by considering bounded amounts of the main resources. In particular, the class P can be defined this way and is sometimes considered to capture the essence of "feasibility". Another possibility is the study of models that take advantage of parallel computation: among them, the boolean circuits are clearly a prominent, well studied model.

In order to study the problems solved by boolean circuits of feasible (i.e. polynomial) size, the nonuniform complexity classes are defined. So, Pippenger (1979) shows that the nonuniform class corresponding to the uniform class P (and denoted by Karp and Lipton (1980) as $P/poly$) is precisely the class of sets with polynomial size circuits. Yap (1983) and Schöning (1984) study the class corresponding to NP, namely $NP/poly$, and characterize such sets as the range of polynomial size circuits with many outputs (generators). We study here the model corresponding to another important complexity class: $NP \cap coNP$.

Inspired by the work of Long (1982) on strong nondeterministic machines, we propose a model of strong generators, and study its relationship with $(NP \cap coNP)/poly$. It turns out that the two classes seem not to be exactly equivalent, and therefore we engage in a deeper study of their differences and relationships.

Thus we focus on the two concepts of "strength" for nondeterministic oracle machines used in the literature: that which depends of the oracle set and that which is "robust" against changes on the oracle set. References that use these definitions are, respectively, Long (1982) and Book, Long, and Selman (1985). We obtain two forms of reducibility, show that their zero degrees coincide, and then separate them in the class of the recursive sets. We then consider their relativizations to sparse sets, and we see that, due to an overlooked hypothesis, the very general theorem of Schöning (1984) can be applied only to one of these two reducibilities. (A complete restatement of this theorem can be found in the preliminaries.) Thus a characterization of $(NP \cap coNP)/poly$ in terms of sparse oracles is obtained.

However, this class does not seem to correspond exactly to the polynomial size strong generators, which are instead characterized as $(NP/poly) \cap (coNP/poly)$. Our conclusion is that the appropriate nonuniform generalization of $NP \cap coNP$ is thus this class, and not $(NP \cap coNP)/poly$, which seems the most natural one.

Finally, since sets in ZPP can be considered as well tractable, we have studied relativizations of this class, restricted in an analogous manner to a certain degree of robustness. The interest of the obtained class is justified by the fact shown here that the class yields an oracle-restricted positive relativization of the equality $P \stackrel{?}{=} ZPP$.

2. Preliminaries

We assume that the reader is familiar with basic concepts of complexity theory, such as the classes P, NP, PSPACE, and the polynomial time hierarchy.

Besides the standard Turing machines with final, accepting states, we consider also machines having three kinds of computations: those that accept the input, those that reject the input, and those that are "undefined" in the sense that they stop without answer. For a machine M and an oracle set B, $M^B(x)$ denotes the set of possible computations of M with oracle B and input x, and $L(M, B)$ the set of accepted inputs.

Other notations are either adjacent to an appropriate reference, or are standard and can be found in textbooks like Garey and Johnson (1979), Hopcroft and Ullman (1979), or Balcázar, Díaz, and Gabarró (1988).

Our notation for nonuniform classes follows Karp and Lipton (1980). In particular, all our complexity classes are of the form $C/poly$, for a complexity class C. Two kinds of known results about these classes will be used here: the connection with classes relativized to sparse oracles and the equivalence with certain types of boolean circuits.

Generalizing previous results, Schöning (1984) presents a result which allows to relate, in an almost "mechanical" way, nonuniform "advice" classes to sparse relativizations. A somewhat informal argument, however, makes the result applicable only to complexity classes defined by oracle-independent conditions on the machines, as being polynomially clocked and the like. In order to apply this result to the machines we deal with here, an implicit hypothesis has to be remarked. Thus, we reformulate here this result. The proof is essentially the same, and will be omitted.

Let us start with some definitions. Let C be a relativizable complexity class; we assume that for each set in C there is a "type C" machine to witness it.

We say that C is *good* if and only if for every oracle machine N of type C and oracle machine M of type P (i.e. polynomial time clocked) with output, the machine that simulates M and then simulates N under the empty oracle on the output of M is also of type C.

We say that C is *oracle-resistant* if and only if for every oracle machine N of type C, the (non oracle) machine that on input $\langle x, y\rangle$ simulates N on input x using as oracle the set encoded by y is also of type C.

Informally, "goodness" means that the class is "closed under composition with P machines", which allows to perform some preprocessing on the input without exceeding the computational power of the class; while "oracle-resistance" means that the fact that a machine behaves as a type C machine does not really depend of the oracle used, which allows to "get rid of" the oracle remaining again within the class.

1. Theorem (Schöning 1984). Let C be a good, oracle-resistant class such that type C machines make queries polynomially bounded on the length of the input. Then

$$C(\emptyset)/poly = \bigcup\{C(S) : S \text{ sparse}\}$$

The proof is as in Schöning (1984). It can be seen that the inclusion left to right only requires goodness, but that in the converse inclusion the additional property of oracle-resistance is needed as well. In fact, we will present below a class to which the theorem does not seem to apply, since it is good but not oracle-resistant.

The result is of course applicable to the classes in the polynomial time hierarchy, and to PSPACE.

2. Proposition. P, NP, PSPACE, and all the classes in the polynomial time hierarchy are good, oracle-resistant, and accepted by machines making polynomially bounded queries.

Finally, it should be noticed that nonuniform complexity classes frequently can be characterized by very natural computational models. In particular, $P/poly$ is the class of sets accepted by polynomial size boolean circuits; see Pippenger (1979). By using circuits with many outputs, Yap (1983) proposes to consider circuits as generators instead of as acceptors, considering the sets that are the range of a family of polynomially bounded circuits, and relates this class to $NP/poly$. Schöning (1984) completes the relationship by establishing a characterization of $NP/poly$. In section 5 below we present a "strong" version of these generators, and give a characterization in the framework of our discussion about the classes $NP/poly \cap coNP/poly$ and $(NP \cap coNP)/poly$.

3. Strong machines and robustly strong machines

In this section we present the strong nondeterministic machines, and two versions of the oracle strong nondeterministic machines. Strong machines were introduced by Long (1982), who studied extensively the strong nondeterministic Turing reducibility, based on previous work by Adleman and Manders (1977). Robustly strong machines have been used by Book, Long, and Selman (1985) to obtain positive relativizations of the equality $P \stackrel{?}{=} NP \cap coNP$, and later by Long and Selman (1986) to obtain oracle-restricted positive relativizations of the same equality, as discussed below.

3. Definition. A (non oracle) nondeterministic Turing machine is *strong* if and only if for every input x:

1. there is a defined computation in $M(x)$, and
2. there is an accepting computation in $M(x)$ if and only if there is no rejecting computation in $M(x)$.

Besides their theoretical importance to define reducibilities, strong machines are attractive since they are nondeterministic but not inconsistent: they do not give contradictory answers.

The following fact is clear: by switching accepting and rejecting states on a strong machine, a new strong machine is obtained which accepts the complement of the originally accepted language. This allows to characterize the class of sets accepted by strong machines in polynomial time.

4. Proposition (Long, 1982). A is accepted in polynomial time by a strong machine if and only if $A \in NP \cap coNP$.

Consider now strong polynomial time nondeterministic machines which have access to an oracle set. At least two interpretations of the word "strong" are possible; we present both, and define their corresponding polynomial time reducibilities.

5. Definition. M is *strong under oracle* B if and only if for every input x:

1. there is a defined computation in $M^B(x)$, and

2. there is an accepting computation in $M^B(x)$ if and only if there is no rejecting computation in $M^B(x)$.

The corresponding reducibility is denoted $\leq^{SN}$.

6. Definition. A set A is *SN-reducible* to a set B ($A \leq^{SN} B$) if and only if $A = L(M, B)$ for a polynomial time machine M which is strong under B.

The notation of Long (1982) for this reducibility is $\leq_T^{SN}$; other versions, more restricted, are defined as well, like $\leq_{tt}^{SN}$. Long shows that all of these reducibilities are different among them and from $\leq_T^P$ and $\leq_T^{NP}$, and that the power of $\leq_T^{SN}$ is intermediate between $\leq_T^P$ and $\leq_T^{NP}$.

As mentioned, a second interpretation of the concept of strong nondeterministic oracle machine has been used in the literature; it requires the machine to be strong no matter the oracle it uses. We call these machines "robustly strong", and define the corresponding reducibility.

7. Definition. M is *robustly strong* if and only if for every oracle A, M is strong under A.

8. Definition. A set A is *RS-reducible* to a set B ($A \leq^{RS} B$) if and only if $A = L(M, B)$ for a polynomial time machine M which is robustly strong.

It is clear that $\leq_T^P$ implies $\leq^{RS}$ and that $\leq^{RS}$ implies $\leq^{SN}$. The following theorem shows another basic relationship.

9. Theorem. For any two sets A and B:

(i) $A \leq^{SN} B$ and $B \in NP \cap coNP \Rightarrow A \in NP \cap coNP$.

(ii) $A \leq^{RS} B$ and $B \in NP \cap coNP \Rightarrow A \in NP \cap coNP$.

The proof for $\leq^{SN}$ can be found in Long (1982) and the other is similar. An interesting consequence is that the zero degree of both reducibilities is exactly $NP \cap coNP$.

These two reducibilities, however, do not coincide in general: our main result in this section shows that $\leq^{RS}$ differs essentially from all the reducibilities of Long, above $NP \cap coNP$. We prove first that it differs from $\leq^{SN}$. Intuitively, the difference is due to the fact that plain strong machines may expect the adequate oracle and exploit its structure in order to be strong, while robustly strong machines must maintain their "coherence" by themselves, expecting no "a priori" particular property of the oracle.

10. Theorem. For every recursive set $A \notin NP \cap coNP$, there is a recursive set B such that $A \leq^{SN} B$ but $A \not\leq^{RS} B$.

Proof. Let A be fixed. We construct B such that, for all word x,

$$x \in A \iff \exists y(|y| = |x| \text{ and } \langle x, y, 1\rangle \in B) \iff \forall z(|z| = |x| \Rightarrow \langle x, z, 0\rangle \notin B)$$

which guarantees that $A \leq^{SN} B$, using the natural procedure.

We construct B so that $A \not\leq^{RS} B$ by diagonalization over all the machines that could reduce A to B. At stage n, and using the initial segment B_{n-1} constructed so far, we search for the minimum word x that satisfies:

(1) it does not interfere with previous stages, and

(2) the machine M_n with oracle B_{n-1} and input x is not strong, or

(3) $M_n(x)$ accepts and $x \notin A$, or

(4) $M_n(x)$ rejects and $x \in A$.

When found, x is used to extend B_{n-1} to B_n, in a way that preserves the condition stated above. It is easy to see that, by conditions (1) to (4), x witnesses that $A \not\leq^{RS} B$ via M_n.

We prove now that the witness x must exist at each stage. Otherwise, if conditions (2) to (4) are false for all x, M_n is correctly RS-reducing A to B_{n-1}. But, since B_{n-1} is finite, A must be in $NP \cap coNP$, which contradicts the hypothesis. ∎

We use a result from Long (1982) to show that $\leq^{RS}$ also differs from $\leq_{tt}^{SN}$.

11. Theorem. For every recursive set $A \notin NP \cap coNP$, there is a recursive set B such that $A \leq^{RS} B$ but $A \not\leq_{tt}^{SN} B$.

Proof. Given A, Long shows that there is a B such that $A \leq_T^P B$ and $A \not\leq_{tt}^{SN} B$. Since $\leq_T^P$ implies $\leq^{RS}$, the same B satisfies the statement of the theorem. ∎

4. Nonuniform classes defined by strong machines

We characterize in this section the nonuniform classes corresponding to the reduction class of the sparse sets, using the reducibilities defined in the previous section. We start with the class corresponding to the robustly strong reducibility.

12. Theorem. $\{A : \exists S(S \text{ sparse and } A \leq^{RS} S)\} = (NP \cap coNP)/poly$

Proof. (Sketch.) It is enough to prove that this class satisfies the hypothesis required to apply theorem 1. Both are reasonably straightforward. Robust strength is required for the property of the class being oracle-resistant. ∎

However, when we want to characterize in a similar manner the class

$$\{A : \exists S(S \text{ sparse and } A \leq^{SN} S)\}$$

some problems arise. Indeed, it is not difficult to see that if there is an oracle B under which a given machine M is not strong, then the machine that is given as input a pair formed by x and an initial segment of B is not strong (in the non-oracle sense). Thus, this class is not oracle-resistant and Schöning's theorem does not apply.

Anyway, a characterization in the style of the advice classes (although not properly an advice class) is obtained in the remaining of this section, preceded by a result that amounts, roughly speaking, to "factor out" sparse oracles from complementary machines.

13. Theorem.

$$\{A : \exists S(S \text{ sparse and } A \leq^{SN} S)\} = \bigcup\{NP(S) : S \text{ sparse }\} \cap \bigcup\{coNP(S) : S \text{ sparse }\}$$

Proof. (Sketch.) Inclusion left to right is immediate. For the converse, form the join of the two sparse oracles involved and design a machine that chooses nondeterministically among the two machines involved, using for each one the corresponding part of the oracle. This machine can be shown to be strong. ∎

The nonuniform-like class characterization is as follows:

14. Theorem. $\{A : \exists S(S \text{ sparse and } A \leq^{SN} S)\} = (NP/poly) \cap (coNP/poly)$

Proof. Follows from the previous result by two applications of theorem 1, since both NP and $coNP$ belong to the polynomial time hierarchy. ∎

To end this section, we note the interesting (although not surprising) fact that tally sets can be substituted for the sparse sets in all the characterizations given.

15. Proposition.

(i) $A \leq^{SN} S$ for some sparse $S \iff A \leq^{SN} T$ for some tally T.

(ii) $A \leq^{RS} S$ for some sparse $S \iff A \leq^{RS} T$ for some tally T.

The proof follows standard techniques; see Hartmanis (1983).

5. Strong generators

As previously indicated, we present here a nonuniform model corresponding to the SN-reducibility to sparse oracles. It is similar to the small generators described by Yap (1983) and Schöning (1984).

16. Definition. A set A has *polynomial size strong generators* if and only if there is a polynomial p such that for every n, a circuit C_n and an integer e_n exist for which

1) C_n has at most $p(n)$ gates
2) C_n has e_n inputs
3) C_n has $n+1$ outputs, plus one additional output "domain indicator". Only "valid outputs" are considered, and these are those that appear under an input for which the domain indicator evaluates to 1.
4) for every $x \in \Sigma^n$

$$x \in A \iff \exists y(|y| = e_n \text{ and } C_n(y) = 1x) \iff \forall z(|z| = e_n \Rightarrow C_n(z) \neq 0x)$$

Notice that from 1 and 2 it follows that $e_n \leq p(n)$.

Those circuits are very similar to the generators studied in Yap (1983) and Schöning (1984), the difference being that a "strength" condition has been added. Indeed, condition 4 is analogous to the condition imposed to the nondeterministic machines in order to consider them strong. Intuitively, if C_n is a family of strong generators for A then for each n every word of length n appears as output of C_n if the appropriate input is chosen, and moreover C_n correctly indicates whether this output word is in A or in $\overline{A}$. The reader is advised to compare this model with the generators of Yap (1983) and Schöning (1984).

Our main result in this section is a characterization of the reduction class of the sparse sets under the SN-reducibility.

17. Theorem. A set A has polynomial size strong generators if and only if $A \leq^{SN} S$ for some sparse set S.

Proof. (Sketch.) Given A with polynomial size strong generators, it is an easy task to obtain standard generators for both A and $\overline{A}$. By the results in Yap (1983), both sets are in $NP/poly$, and therefore in $NP(S)$, resp. $NP(S')$, for some sparse set S, resp. S', by theorem 1. It only remains to apply theorem 13 to obtain the implication left to right.

For the converse, follow backwards the same argument, using the converse of Yap's result —which appears in Schöning (1984)—, to obtain generators for both A and $\overline{A}$, and combine the generators into a family of strong generators. ∎

Generators can be viewed also as acceptors with nondeterministic gates in a standard manner. It is easy to see that this view can be adapted as well to the strong generator model. In this case, for every word there is an extension of values of the nondeterministic gates which yields a valid output, and this output always correctly determines membership to A of the input word.

6. An oracle-restricted positive relativization of ZPP

Positive relativizations have appeared in several previous papers; see Book, Long, and Selman (1984) and the references there. A positive relativization of a pair of classes C and D is a restricted way of relativizing both classes, such that the restriction is meaningless for the unrelativized case, and such that the unrelativized classes coincide if and only if their restrictions coincide in every relativization.

A different sort of positive relativization has been developed in Long and Selman (1986) and in Balcázar, Book, and Schöning (1986). In it, an additional condition is imposed to the class of oracles, sometimes substituting the restriction on the oracle machines. As examples of this kind of oracle-restricted positive relativizations, we state some results from these references.

18. Theorem. The polynomial time hierarchy equals $PSPACE$ if and only if for every sparse set S, the polynomial time hierarchy relative to S equals $PSPACE(S)$; and the polynomial time hierarchy differs from $PSPACE$ if and only if for every sparse set S, the polynomial time hierarchy relative to S differs from $PSPACE(S)$.

19. Theorem. $P = NP$ if and only if for every tally set T, $P(T) = NP(T)$.

20. Theorem. $P = NP \cap coNP$ if and only if for every tally set T, $P(T)$ equals the class of sets $L(M,T)$ where M is robustly strong.

By restricting probabilistic machines so that certain functions describing machine's behavior are computable by certain probabilistic models, Russo (1985) has obtained (in joint work with S. Zachos) positive relativizations of ZPP and other probabilistic classes, defined by Gill (1977). Here we present a different view, by exhibiting an oracle-restricted positive relativization of ZPP. It is based on the following definition.

21. Definition. A nondeterministic machine M is *robustly* ZPP if and only if for every oracle set A and input x, either more than half the computations accept and no computation rejects, or more than half the computations reject and no computation accepts.

The main result of this section is as follows.

22. Theorem. $P = ZPP$ if and only if for every tally set T, $P(T)$ equals the class of sets $L(M,T)$ where M is robustly ZPP.

The only nontrivial part of the proof is to show that if $P = ZPP$ then robustly ZPP machines can be simulated in deterministic polynomial time. The idea is that the condition of robust-ZPP-ness implies that a machine which is given part of the oracle as input is also a ZPP machine. Then a $P(T)$ machine can be constructed that first scans the oracle to construct a table recording the accesible part of it, then simulates the ZPP machine that incorporates the oracle as part of the input. For similar proofs see Long and Selman (1986).

The result is also true for a slightly more general (but very technical) class of oracles: those with "self-producible circuits". These sets are characterized in terms of tally sets in Balcázar and Book (1986), and the generalization of theorem 22 to them is immediate from this characterization.

7. Conclusions

Motivated by the question of finding a nonuniform analog of the class $NP \cap coNP$, two versions of strong nondeterministic reducibilities have been defined and compared, and differences have been found at arbitrary height within the class of recursive sets. The corresponding reduction classes of the sparse sets have been characterized in different manners. Strangely enough, the class corresponding more naturally to a nonuniform model of computation is the one that is not properly a nonuniform class in the sense of Karp and Lipton (1980), and is also the one for which the very general technique of Schöning (1984) for dealing with this kind of classes fails.

More precisely, the reduction classes of sparse sets under both reducibilities turn out to be, respectively, $(NP/poly) \cap (coNP/poly)$ and $(NP \cap coNP)/poly$. There seems to be more than a syntactic difference between these classes. It is not difficult to see that the second class is included in the first, and that they are equal if $NP = coNP$; it would be interesting to know what the consequences of equality can be.

As shown by Long and Selman (1986), the reduction class of the tally sets under the robustly strong machines yields an oracle-restricted positive relativization of the equality $P \stackrel{?}{=} NP \cap coNP$. Motivated by this fact, we have shown that a natural analogous condition yields an oracle-restricted positive relativization of the equality $P \stackrel{?}{=} ZPP$. What is the reason that such an apparently natural condition does not yield a natural nonuniform model? The answer is not known yet, but surely more insight has been gained from the comparison between both reducibilities.

The reader may have noticed that we have not shown that robustly strong polynomial time reducibility differs from plain polynomial time reducibility. Such a question has been addressed in Book, Long, and Selman (1985), where positive relativizations of $P \stackrel{?}{=} NP \cap coNP$ were investigated. The separation has been left there as an important open problem; moreover, if two additional technical conditions are imposed (confluence and maturity), then a positive relativization is obtained.

An important step forward has been obtained by Hemachandra (1987), who shows — theorem 5.3— that the reduction class of any recursive set A under $\leq^{RS}$ is always included in the class $P(A \oplus SAT)$. It follows that:

— if $\leq^{RS}$ equals $\leq^P_T$, then $P = NP \cap coNP$, and

— if $\leq^{RS}$ differs from $\leq^P_T$ anywhere in the recursive sets, then $P \neq NP$, since if $P = NP$ then $P(A \oplus SAT) = P(A)$ and therefore $\leq^P_T$ and $\leq^{RS}$ must coincide.

So, although robustly strong machines are not exactly a positive relativization of anything, proving equality or inequality with deterministic machines would have important consequences.

Still another work intimately related to the present one has been reported by Kämper (1987) and by Kadin (1987). The former studies a concept of "proof systems" that allows to show lowness properties of classes similar to the ones that we study here. The latter shows that if the boolean hierarchy over NP collapses then the polynomial time hierarchy collapses; actually, although not explicitly mentioned, his argument can be decomposed into the lowness of a class similar to ours, and the proof that the collapse of the boolean hierarchy implies membership of SAT in such a low class. See Schöning (1983) for the concepts of lowness and highness, and the reason that lowness of SAT implies the collapse of the polynomial time hierarchy.

8. References

L. Adleman, K. Manders: "Reducibility, randomness, and intractability". 9th ACM STOC (1977), 151–163.

J.L. Balcázar, R. Book: "Sets with small generalized Kolmogorov complexity". *Acta Informatica* 23 (1986), 679–688.

J.L. Balcázar, R. Book, U. Schöning: "The polynomial time hierarchy and sparse oracles". *J. ACM* 33 (1986), 603–617.

J.L. Balcázar, J. Díaz, J. Gabarró: *Structural Complexity I.* Springer-Verlag 1988.

R. Book, T. Long, A. Selman: "Qualitative relativizations of complexity classes". *J. Comp. Sys. Sci.* 30 (1985), 395–413.

R. Book, T. Long, A. Selman: "Quantitative relativizations of complexity classes". *SIAM J. Comp.* 13 (1984), 461–487.

M. Garey, D. Johnson: *Computers and intractability: a guide to the theory of NP-completeness.* Freeman 1979.

J. Gill: "Computational complexity of probabilistic Turing machines". *SIAM J. Comp.* 6 (1977), 675–695.

J. Hartmanis: "On sparse sets in $NP - P$". *Inf. Proc. Lett.* 16 (1983), 55–60.

L. Hemachandra: "Counting in Structural Complexity Theory". Ph.D. dissertation, Cornell University, Tech. Rep. 87-830 (1987).

J. Hopcroft, J. Ullman: *Introduction to automata theory, languages, and computation.* Addison-Wesley 1979.

R. Karp, R. Lipton: "Some connections between nonuniform and uniform complexity classes". 12th ACM STOC (1980), 302–309.

J. Kadin: "The polynomial time hierarchy collapses if the boolean hierarchy collapses". Cornell Univ. Tech. Rep. 87-843 (1987).

J. Kämper: "Non-uniform proof systems: a new framework to describe non-uniform and probabilistic complexity classes". Univ. Oldenburg Tech. Rep. 3/87 (1987).

T. Long: "Strong nondeterministic polynomial time reducibilities". *Theor. Comp. Sci.* 21 (1982), 1-25.

T. Long, A. Selman: "Relativizing complexity classes with sparse oracles". *J. ACM* 33 (1986), 618–628.

N. Pippenger: "On simultaneous resource bounds". 20th IEEE FOCS (1979), 307–311.

D. Russo: "Structural properties of complexity classes". Ph.D. dissertation, Univ. California Santa Barbara (1985).

U. Schöning: "A low and a high hierarchy within NP^{+}". *J. Comp. Sys. Sci.* 27 (1983), 14–28.

U. Schöning: "On small generators". *Theor. Comp. Sci.* 34 (1984), 337–341.

L. Stockmeyer: "The polynomial time hierarchy". *Theor. Comp. Sci.* 3 (1977), 1–22.

C. Yap: "Some consequences of nonuniform conditions on uniform classes". *Theor. Comp. Sci.* 27 (1983), 287–300.

CONTEXT-FREE-LIKE FORMS FOR THE PHRASE-STRUCTURE GRAMMARS

Viliam Geffert
University of P.J.Šafárik
Department of Theoretical Cybernetics
Nám.Feb.Víťazstva 9
04154 Košice, Czechoslovakia

ABSTRACT: Some new normal forms for the phrase-structure grammars are presented. Each phrase-structure grammar can be replaced by an equivalent grammar with all of the rules context-free, of the form $S \to v$, where S is the initial symbol, and either two extra rules $AB \to \varepsilon$, $CD \to \varepsilon$, or two extra rules $AB \to \varepsilon$, $CC \to \varepsilon$, or two extra rules $AA \to \varepsilon$, $BBB \to \varepsilon$, or even a single extra rule $ABBBA \to \varepsilon$, or a single extra rule $ABC \to \varepsilon$.

1. INTRODUCTION

Problems concerning normal forms of various devices generating or recognizing languages have turned out to be of crucial importance in the development of formal language theory. Normal form should enable a simpler manipulation and should be a basis for deeper understanding of the given class of devices while preserving its generative (or computational) power. In spite of the fact, that much research has been done on the comparison of many different models of grammars and automata, the central position of context-free languages (and grammars) remains. A similar characterization of recursively enumerable languages would also be useful.

We are going to establish that each recursively enumerable language can be generated by a grammar using only context-free rules of the form $S \to v$ (rewriting only the initial symbol), but two extra non-context-free rules $AB \to \varepsilon$, $CD \to \varepsilon$. Clearly, S,A,B,C,D are the only nonterminal symbols used by this type of grammar. Then we shall show some additional normal forms.

2. A VARIANT OF POST CORRESPONDENCE PROBLEM

Before passing to main results, we need to define the main notions.

(The reader is assumed to be familiar with the basic definitions and notations of the formal language theory.) We begin with the definition of a g-system, introduced by Rovan (Ro) in order to unify the theory of grammars.

Definition: A generative system (g-system, for short) is a 4-tuple $G=(N,T,P,S)$, where N and T are finite alphabets of nonterminal and terminal symbols, S in N is an initial symbol, and P represents a binary relation over $V^*\times V^*$ (where $V=N\cup T$). P is given in the form of 1-a-transducer (Gi) from V^* to V^*, i.e. $P=(K,V,V,H,q_I,q_F)$, where K is a finite set of states, q_I,q_F in K are initial and final states, respectively, and H is a finite subset of $K\times V\times V^*\times K$ (the set of transitions, or edges).
$u\in V^+$ is said to directly generate $v\in V^*$, written $u\Rightarrow v$, if P is able to rewrite u to v, i.e. there exists a path of transitions

$$(q_I,s_1,v_1,q_1)(q_1,s_2,v_2,q_2)\dots(q_{n-1},s_n,v_n,q_F)\in H^+,$$

such that $s_1\dots s_n=u$, and $v_1\dots v_n=v$. Finally, a language generated by G is $L(G)=\{w\in T^*;\ S\Rightarrow^* w\}$, where $\Rightarrow^*$ denotes the reflexive transitive closure of the relation $\Rightarrow$.

As is usual, G is said to be of time complexity $T(n)$ if, for each $w\in L(G)$ of length at most n, there exists a derivation of at most $T(n)$ steps generating w. Similarly, G is of space complexity $S(n)$ if there is some derivation of w in which each sentential form is of length at most $S(n)$.

It can be easily seen that g-system is a generalization of the notion of grammar. (We could use the classical definition of the phrase-structure grammar as a starting-point as well, but g-systems give us a more natural correspondence between various types of devices and the phrase-structure grammars in normal form.)

Definition: Let $\Sigma_L=\{a_1,\dots a_{n_L}\}$ be an alphabet. An Extended Post Correspondence (EPC, for short) is

$$P=(\ \{(u_1,v_1),\dots(u_r,v_r)\}\ ,\ (z_{a_1},\dots z_{a_{n_L}})\ )\ ,$$

where $u_i,v_i,z_a\in\{0,1\}^*$ for each $i=1,\dots r$, $a\in\Sigma_L$. The language represented by P in Σ_L, written L(P) is the set:

$$L(P)=\{x_1\dots x_n\in\Sigma_L^*;\ \exists s_1,\dots s_l\in\{1,\dots r\},\ l\geq 1 \text{ such that } v_{s_1}\dots v_{s_l}=u_{s_1}\dots u_{s_l}z_{x_1}\dots z_{x_n}\}\ .$$

Note, that the classical Post Correspondence Problem is to determine whether or not $\varepsilon \in L(P)$, where P is an EPC for $\Sigma_L = \emptyset$ (i.e. $L(P) \subseteq \emptyset^* = \{\varepsilon\}$).

Theorem 1: For each recursively enumerable language L there exists an Extended Post Correspondence P such that L(P)=L.

The proof is based on the fact that g-systems are capable of generating any recursively enumerable language. The construction of EPC for a given language L is similar to the construction of classical Post Correspondence Problem imitating the computation of a Turing machine (and its halting problem). (Po) But, instead of Turing machine, we shall rather simulate the derivation of a word by a g-system generating the language L. (The proof is also very strongly related to the representation described in (Ge1).)

We also obtain the correspondence between time/space complexity of g-system and EPC: If $w \in L(G)=L(P)$ is generated by a derivation $S = w_0 \Rightarrow_G w_1 \Rightarrow_G \dots \Rightarrow_G w_k = w$, then we can find a solution of P for w of length $l \leq c.\sum_{i=0}^{k} |w_i| \in O(\sum |w_i|)$.

3. THE MAIN RESULTS

We can now state the main theorem. The proof is based on the representation by an extended Post correspondence: We have shown that for each rec.e. language L there exists an EPC $P = (\{(u_1,v_1),..(u_r,v_r)\}, (z_{a_1},..z_{a_{n_L}}))$ such that L=L(P), i.e. $w=x_1..x_n \in \Sigma_L^*$ is a word in L if and only if there exist $s_1,..s_l \in \{1,..r\}$, $l \geq 1$ such that

$$v_{s_1} \dots v_{s_l} = u_{s_1} \dots u_{s_l} z_{x_1} \dots z_{x_n} .$$

Since $u_i, v_i, z_a \in \{0,1\}^*$ for each i=1,..r, $a \in \Sigma_L$, we can use the following way of generating $w=x_1 \dots x_n$:

1st stage: $S \Rightarrow z'^R_{x_n} S x_n \Rightarrow z'^R_{x_n} z'^R_{x_{n-1}} S x_{n-1} x_n \Rightarrow \dots$

$\Rightarrow z'^R_{x_n} \dots z'^R_{x_1} S x_1 \dots x_n \Rightarrow$

$\Rightarrow z'^R_{x_n} \dots z'^R_{x_1} A x_1 \dots x_n \Rightarrow$

2nd stage: $\Rightarrow z'^R_{x_n} \dots z'^R_{x_1} u'^R_{s_l} A v''_{s_l} x_1 \dots x_n \Rightarrow$

$$\Rightarrow z'^R_{x_n}\ldots z'^R_{x_1}u'^R_{s_1}u'^R_{s_{l-1}}Av''_{s_{l-1}}v''_{s_1}x_1\ldots x_n \Rightarrow \ldots$$

$$\ldots\ldots\ldots\ldots$$

$$\Rightarrow z'^R_{x_n}\ldots z'^R_{x_1}u'^R_{s_1}\ldots u'^R_{s_2}Av''_{s_2}\ldots v''_{s_1}x_1\ldots x_n \Rightarrow$$

$$\Rightarrow z'^R_{x_n}\ldots z'^R_{x_1}u'^R_{s_1}\ldots u'^R_{s_1}v''_{s_1}\ldots v''_{s_1}x_1\ldots x_n\ ,$$

where z'_{x_i}, u'_{s_j}, v''_{s_j} denote strings over some new alphabets $\{0',1'\}$, and $\{0'',1''\}$ corresponding to z_{x_i}, u_{s_j}, v_{s_j}, respectively. (Similarly, φ',φ'' will be notations for strings in $\{0',1'\}^*$, and $\{0'',1''\}^*$, respectively, corresponding to $\varphi\in\{0,1\}^*$.)

Note that, the only thing we should be able to do in the 1st stage of derivation is to rewrite the symbol S to $z'^R_x Sx$, for each $x\in\Sigma_L$ (and also to A in the last step). Similarly, the 2nd stage will be just repeated rewriting of A to $u'^R_s Av''_s$, for each $s\in\{1,..r\}$ (and to $u'^R_s v''_s$ in the last step). It should be clear that, for the first two stages, we need context-free rules only.

3rd stage: $z'^R_{x_n}\ldots z'^R_{x_1}u'^R_{s_1}\ldots u'^R_{s_1}v''_{s_1}\ldots v''_{s_1}x_1\ldots x_n =$

$$= (u_{s_1}\ldots u_{s_1}z_{x_1}\ldots z_{x_n})'^R(v_{s_1}\ldots v_{s_1})''x_1\ldots x_n =$$

$$= \varphi'^R_1\varphi''_2 x_1\ldots x_n \Rightarrow^* x_1\ldots x_n$$

/if and only if $\varphi_1 = \varphi_2$

The 3rd stage of derivation is just a cancellation of substrings $0'0''$, and $1'1''$ (by rules $0'0''\rightarrow\varepsilon$, $1'1''\rightarrow\varepsilon$). It now follows easily that $\varphi'^R_1\varphi''_2 w \Rightarrow^* w$ if and only if $\varphi_1=\varphi_2$.

It is obvious that this type of rewriting generate exactly the language L(P), and we can now construct a phrase-structure grammar with six nonterminal symbols, namely $S,A,0',0'',1',1''$ and with only two non-context-free rules $0'0''\rightarrow\varepsilon$, $1'1''\rightarrow\varepsilon$, for each rec.e. language L.

We cannot detail here a long technical proof showing that the symbol A can be eliminated and replaced everywhere by S. The only thing causing problems is that we can now use a 2nd stage rule (i.e. $S\rightarrow u'^R_s Sv''_s$, for some $s=1,..r$) before applying the last rule of the 1st stage ($S\rightarrow z'^R_{x_1}Sx_1$). It can be shown that if we violate the correct ordering, then we shall not be able to derive a terminal string in the 3rd stage of the derivation, because the Extended Post Correspondence P, constructed in Theorem 1, has some "good" technical properties such that the condition $\varphi_1 = \varphi_2$ cannot be satisfied in this case. We are now ready for the main theorem:

Theorem 2: Each recursively enumerable language L can be generated by a phrase-structure grammar with five nonterminal symbols, using only context-free rules of the form $S \to v$, where S is the initial nonterminal, but two extra rules $AB \to \varepsilon$, $CD \to \varepsilon$.

It can be easily seen that several known results are simple consequences of this theorem. For example, any rec.e. set can be recognized by a nondeterministic 1-state machine with two 1-turn pushdown stores. We also obtain that each rec.e. language L can be expressed in the form $L=p(L_1)$, where L_1 is a deterministic linear language, and p is a cancellation of well-balanced parentheses subwords over alphabet of two pairs of parentheses. We can use a cancellation of a palindrome prefix over two-letter alphabet as well. If we restrict p to be a polynomially-bounded cancellation then we shall obtain a characterization of the class of NP-languages by deterministic linear (and hence also by context-free) languages. Now we shall consider a number of other normal forms:

Theorem 3: Each recursively enumerable language L can be generated by a phrase-structure grammar using only context-free rules of the form $S \to v$, where S is the initial symbol, and

a) either two extra rules $AB \to \varepsilon$, $CC \to \varepsilon$,
b) or two extra rules $AA \to \varepsilon$, $BBB \to \varepsilon$,
c) or a single extra rule $ABBBA \to \varepsilon$,
d) or a single extra rule $ABC \to \varepsilon$.

In all cases, no additional nonterminal symbols not mentioned here are used.

We have shown various normal forms, but constructions can be given uniformly, by the transformations for putting the grammar exhibited in Theorem 2 into these forms. To give an idea, we shall briefly show the construction for the case d):

Firstly, we are going to encode the symbols 0',1',0",1" by symbols A,B,C. Define a homomorphism $h: \{0',1',0'',1''\}^* \to \{A,B,C\}^*$ by

$$h(0') = AB, \qquad h(0'') = C,$$
$$h(1') = A, \qquad h(1'') = BC.$$

But then we have to modify also the grammar G of Theorem 2, which gives $G'=(\{S,A,B,C\},\Sigma_L,P',S)$, where

$$P' = \{S\to h(z_x'^R)Sx;\ x\in\Sigma_L\} \cup \qquad \text{/instead of } S\to z_x'^R Sx$$
$$\cup\ \{S\to h(u_s'^R)Sh(v_s'');\ s=1,..r\} \cup \qquad \text{/instead of } S\to u_s'^R S v_s''$$
$$\cup\ \{S\to h(u_s'^R)h(v_s'');\ s=1,..r\} \cup \qquad \text{/instead of } S\to u_s'^R v_s''$$
$$\cup\ \{ABC\to\varepsilon\} \qquad \text{/instead of } 0'0''\to\varepsilon,\ 1'1''\to\varepsilon.$$

The first two stages of derivation in G, i.e. $S \Rightarrow_G^* \varphi_1'^R\varphi_2''w$ will correspond to $S \Rightarrow_{G'}^* h(\varphi_1'^R)h(\varphi_2'')w$. The rule $ABC\to\varepsilon$ is not applicable until the symbol S is annihilated: The sentential form is in $\{AB,A\}^*S\{C,BC\}^*\Sigma_L^*$, since the corresponding sentential form in G is in $\{0',1'\}^*S\{0'',1''\}^*\Sigma_L^*$. Therefore, there are no substrings of the form ABC.

The 3rd stage of derivation: Let $\varphi_1'^R\varphi_2''w$ be a sentential form derivable from S in G, where $\varphi_1,\varphi_2\in\{0,1\}^*$, $w\in\Sigma_L^*$. In G', this corresponds to $h(\varphi_1'^R)h(\varphi_2'')w \in \{AB,A\}^*\{C,BC\}^*\Sigma_L^*$, so also here the only place we can modify is at the frontier between $h(\varphi_1'^R)$ and $h(\varphi_2'')$, by rule $ABC\to\varepsilon$. The cancellation of substrings 0'0", 1'1" in G will correspond to the cancellation of ABC. Thus, if $\varphi_1=\varphi_2$, then $\varphi_1'^R\varphi_2''w \Rightarrow_G^* w$, and also $h(\varphi_1'^R)h(\varphi_2'')w \Rightarrow_{G'}^* w$.

On the other hand, if $\varphi_1\neq\varphi_2$, and hence the derivation in G is blocked, since we shall obtain different symbols at the frontier, i.e. $\varphi_1'^R\varphi_2''w \Rightarrow_G^* \psi_1'^R1'0''\psi_2''w$, or $\varphi_1'^R\varphi_2''w \Rightarrow_G^* \psi_1'^R0'1''\psi_2''w$, then the corresponding derivation in G' will produce the sentential form $h(\psi_1'^R)ACh(\psi_2'')w \in \{AB,A\}^*AC\{C,BC\}^*\Sigma_L^*$, or $h(\psi_1'^R)ABBCh(\psi_2'')w \in \{AB,A\}^*ABBC\{C,BC\}^*\Sigma_L^*$, respectively. Therefore, neither here can we derive a terminal string, the derivation cannot continue, since there are no substrings of the form ABC, or S.

4. TIME AND SPACE COMPLEXITY

Let L be a language generated by some g-system G. By Theorem 1, we can construct an extended Post correspondence P such that L(P)=L(G). If a word $w=x_1..x_n\in L(G)$ is generated by a derivation $S = w_0 \Rightarrow_G \ldots \ldots \Rightarrow_G w_k = w$, then there exists a solution of P for w, i.e. there exist $s_1,..s_l\in\{1,..r\}$, $l\geq1$, satisfying

$$v_{s_1}\ldots v_{s_l} = u_{s_1}\ldots u_{s_l}z_{x_1}\ldots z_{x_n}$$

such that $1 \leq c \cdot \sum_{i=0}^{k} |w_i|$. It can be shown that the simulation of EPC P by a phrase-structure grammar of Theorem 2 is linear, requiring at most $O(\sum |w_i|)$ steps. The space complexity is also bounded by $O(\sum |w_i|)$. All grammars of Theorem 3 simulate the grammar of Theorem 2. Each nonterminal symbol is encoded by a string of fixed length, similarly, each derivation step is imitated by a constant number of steps. Thus all these grammars have the same time and space bound $O(\sum |w_i|)$.

In order to establish our normal forms, we could use the classical definition of the phrase-structure grammar as well, instead of introducing a notion of a g-system. However, an iterated rewriting of the sentential form by a nondeterministic finite-state transducer (i.e. g-system) makes manipulation much more easier and mentally simpler. For example, if a language L is recognized by a k-pushdown nondeterministic automaton A of time complexity $T_A(n)$ and space complexity $S_A(n)$, then L is also generated by a g-system G of the same time and space complexity (for each k). From this we shall obtain a phrase-structure grammar in normal form with the time and space complexity bounded by $\sum_{t=0}^{T_A(n)} p_t$, where p_t is the number of symbols saved onto pushdowns of A at time t. The proof is quite intuitive: Let $x_1..x_n$ be an input of A. To determine the computational history of A at any given time we need to know three things; the state q it is in, what has been scanned on the input tape, i.e. $x_1..x_i$, and what is on its pushdown stores, i.e. strings $A_j\beta_j$ (with the symbol A_j on top, for each j=1,..k). In g-system this will correspond to the sentential form

$$x_1 \ldots x_i q A_1 \beta_1 B A_2 \beta_2 B \ldots A_k \beta_k B \ ,$$

where B is a new symbol, used as a bottom-of-the-stack marker. A move by a particular transition $(q', \gamma_1, \ldots, \gamma_k) \in \delta(q, a, A_1, \ldots, A_k)$ (the automaton changes its state from q to q' and replaces the topmost symbol A_j by the string γ_j on its j-th pushdown (for each j=1,..k), providing the input head scans the symbol a) will be imitated by rewriting the above sentential form to

$$x_1 \ldots x_i a q' \gamma_1 \beta_1 B \gamma_2 \beta_2 B \ldots \gamma_k \beta_k B \ .$$

(Where $a = x_{i+1}$, or $a = \varepsilon$.)

The following edges in G are needed:

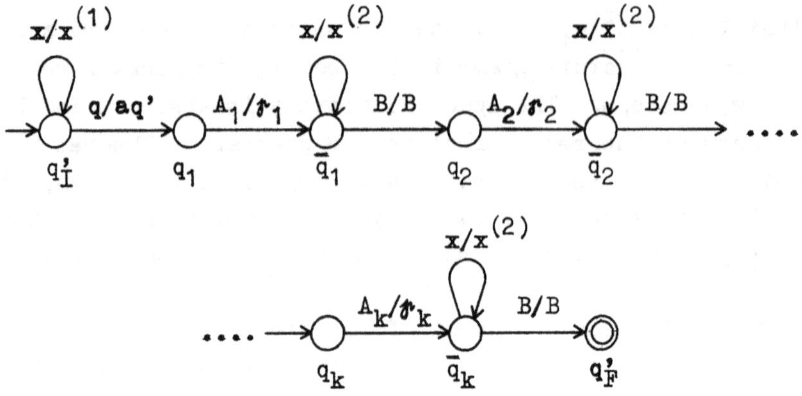

(1) - for each $x \in \Sigma_L$
(2) - for each $x \neq B$

(For each transition of A, we use new distinct states $q_1, \ldots q_k$, $\bar{q}_1, \ldots \bar{q}_k$, so the only states shared by different paths are q'_I, and q'_F.) The derivation will be initiated by rewriting S to $q_I(Z_I B)^k$, which corresponds to the initial computational history of A, and terminated by a path of edges from q'_I to q'_F erasing $q_F B^k$. (q_I, q_F, and Z_I denote the initial and final state of A, and its initial pushdown symbol, respectively.) It should be clear that A and G represent the same language, and that their time and space complexities are asymptotically equal.

Since k tapes can be easily replaced by 2k pushdowns, it follows immediately that k-tape nondeterministic Turing machine can be replaced by a phrase-structure grammar in normal form of time complexity $O(T_A(n) \cdot S_A(n)) \subseteq O(T_A^2(n))$. This simulation can be extended up to the multihead multidimensional multitape machines, to L-systems with interactions, and so forth.

ACKNOWLEDGEMENT This work was performed as a part of the SPZV I-1-5/08 grant. I would like to give a special thank to Branislav Rovan for several helpful discussions, suggestions, and comments concerning this work.

REFERENCES

(Ge1): Geffert V., A representation of recursively enumerable languages by two homomorphisms and a quotient, to appear in Theoretical Computer Science

(Ge2): Geffert V.,Grammars with context dependency restricted to synchronization,Proceeding of MFCS'86,LNCS 233,Springer,1986, 370-378

(Gi): Ginsburg S.,Algebraic and automata-theoretic properties of formal languages,North-Holland,Amsterdam,1975

(Ha): Harrison M.A.,Introduction to formal language theory,Addison-Wesley,1978

(Po): Post E.L.,A variant of a recursively unsolvable problem,Bulletin of the American Math.Soc.,52,pp.264-268,1946

(RoSa): Rozenberg G.,Salomaa A.,The mathematical theory of L-systems, Academic Press,New York,1980

(Ro): Rovan B.,A framework for studying grammars,Proceeding of MFCS'81,LNCS 118,Springer,1981,473-482

ON THE EXPRESSIVE STRENGTH OF THE FINITELY TYPED LAMBDA - TERMS

Andreas Goerdt
Universität Duisburg
Fachbereich Mathematik
Fachgebiet Praktische Informatik
Lotharstraße 63
D-4100 Duisburg 1
West-Germany

ABSTRACT

In the setting of the language of finitely typed λ-terms with if-then else and fixpoints we investigate the question: In which respect do higher types bear on the expressive strength of programming languages?

We restrict attention to the set of closed λ-terms of first-order type, the set of programs. (Terms of first-order type have type $i \to \ldots \to i \to i$, i for individuals, they have subterms of arbitrary types.) The set of programs can be naturally classified into an infinite syntactic hierarchy: A program is in the n'th level of this hierarchy, i. e. a level-n-program, if n is an upper bound on the functional level of its subterms.

Using a novel diagonalization technique over a class of finite interpretations, such that the set of cardinalities of the interpretations of this class has no finite upper bound, we show: Level-(n +1)-programs define more functions (in the sense of the theory of program schemes) than level-n-programs. Using reductions to already established hierarchies KfTiUr 87 shows: Level-(n+2)-programs define more functions than level-n-programs.

INTRODUCTION

The investigation of the expressive power of higher types in programming languages can at least be traced back to In 76, DaFeIn 78, Da 82. The approach in these papers is algebraically oriented. In particular the notion of equivalence of programs employed is related to the notion of formal equivalence [La 74] and the authors obtained hierarchy results for higher types under this notion of equivalence. The definition of formal equivalence is based on the infinite tree representing the structure of possible procedure calls of the program in question. It lead to the investigation of tree and string languages which can be defined with higher type concepts [DaGo 86, En 83, EnSch 77, En Sch 78]. Only the paper KfTiUr 87 investigates higher types in programming languages under the usual notion of equivalence of program schemes, i. e. two program schemes are equivalent if they have the same semantics in all first-order interpretations of the underlying signature, and states the result mentioned above.

From KfUr 85, theorem 2.5, it follows: If the desired hierarchy result holds, then it must already hold if we restrict attention to any class of finite interpretations with equality, such that there is a natural number N, such that the set of cardinalities of the substructures generated by N individuals is not bounded. Otherwise level-1-programs are universal, assuming equality is available.

We consider a class of finite enumerated structures [Lei 87]: For $m > 0$ the interpretation $\mathcal{I}_m$ is given by: Set of individuals $I_m = \{0, \dots, m\}$, successor operation NEXT ($\mathcal{I}_m(\text{NEXT})(m) = m$, $\mathcal{I}_m(\text{NEXT}): I_m \to I_m$ is the semantics of NEXT in $\mathcal{I}_m$), constants MIN, MAX and prove the result: There is a level-$(n+1)$-program Q, such that there is no level-n-program, which is semantically equivalent to Q in all interpretations $\mathcal{I}_m$, which implies the hierarchy result above. We can even glue the interpretations together, which gives the hierarchy result for a single interpretation.

Our proof is based on the following ideas: We define an indexing of the level-n-programs of type $i \to i$ with natural numbers. ψ_k is the program with index k. Then we construct a level-$(n+1)$-program Q of type $i \to i$ such that for $m > k$:

$$\mathcal{I}_m(Q)(k) = \begin{cases} \mathcal{I}_m(\psi_k)(k) & \text{if } \mathcal{I}_m(\psi_k)(k) \text{ is defined} \\ \text{any other defined value} & \text{otherwise.} \end{cases}$$

Assuming Q is a level-n-program, we get the known contradiction, as then $P(y) =$ if $Q(y) = \text{MAX}$ then MIN else NEXT(Q(y)) fi is a total level-n-program.

The definition of Q relies on the following observations (for the time being we assume $n = 1$): Let $D_m = (D_m^\tau | \tau \text{ type})$ the continuous type structure of finite cpo's over I_m. The computation of a recursive definition θ in a level-1-program corresponds to the computation of the supremum of the chain $(\theta^n(\bot))_{n \in \mathbb{N}}$ in D_m^τ, τ first-order type. The maximum chain length in D_m^τ is bounded by m^i for a suitable i independent of m. Hence the depth of nested recursive calls is bounded by this number -

actually a greater nesting depth entails nontermination.

Level-2-programs have parameters of type $i \to i$, i. e. parameters standing for functions $I_m \to I_m$, which allows them to count up to m^m in I_m. The level-2-program Q over I_m applied to an index k of a level-1-program simulates the computation of ψ_k applied to k over I_m and counts the depth of nested recursive calls, reacting appropriately when it gets too large. We must choose the indices large enough such that, if $k \in I_m$, then $m^m >$ the maximum terminating recursion depth of ψ_k. This is possible because of the above bound on the recursion depth.

As the <u>one</u> program Q has to simulate <u>all</u> level-1-programs, we must be able to encode arbitrary types of level-1-programs in Q, i. e. Q must be able to represent arbitrary long parameter lists of terms of type i.

One could imagine that Q simulates the computation of ψ_k only on counters. But we do not know the exact complexity of terms occurring in computations of level-1-programs and accordingly we do not know whether the counting power of Q is sufficient.

Instead, our Q simulates directly the computation of the level-1-program indexed by the input. We represent arbitrary long lists of parameters by one parameter of type $i \to i$: The parameter list $(t_0, \ldots, t_n)$ corresponds to the function $(0 \to t_0, \ldots, n \to t_n)$. We have to make sure, that the indices of the level-1-programs are large enough to allow for this representation in interpretations containing the index .

In section 1 we give our basic definitions and introduce systems of recursive equations equivalent to λ-terms. In section 2 we diagonalize over level-1-programs with a level-2-program. In section 3 we point out the additional problems for higher levels and introduce a new normalform, which allows us to diagonalize with a level-(n + 1)-program over all level-n-programs. We treat details of the diagonalization only for n = 2.

1 BASIC DEFINITIONS AND RESULTS

The family of types, $Type = (Type^n | n \in \mathbb{N})$ is defined by: $i \in Type^0$ (base type), if $\tau \in Type^n$, $\rho \in Type^m$ then $(\tau \to \rho) \in Type^k$, $k = \max\{n+1, m\}$. level $\tau = n$ iff $\tau \in Type^n$. $\to$ associates to the right. $\tau \in Type^n$ can be uniquely decomposed as $\tau = \tau_1 \to \ldots \to \tau_{m-1} \to \tau_m \to i$, $n = \max\{\text{level } \tau_j\} + 1$.

$Var = (Var^\tau | \tau \in Type)$ is a family of variables. The family of finitely typed λ-terms, $Term = (Term^\tau | \tau \in Type)$, is defined by:

$Var^\tau \subseteq Term^\tau$, MIN, MAX $\in Term^i$, NEXT $\in Term^{i \to i}$,
if $t \in Term^{\tau \to \rho}$, $s \in Term^\tau$, then $t(s) \in Term^\rho$,

if $t \in Term^{\tau}$, $F \in Var^{\tau}$, then $\mu F.t \in Term^{\tau}$ (fixpoint),
if $t \in Term^{\rho}$, $y \in Var^{\tau}$, then $\lambda y.t \in Term^{\tau \to \rho}$,
if $t_1, t_2 \in Term^{i}$, $s, r \in Term^{\tau}$, then if $t_1 = t_2$ then s else r fi $\in Term^{\tau}$.

For a first order interpretation $\mathcal{I} = (I, NEXT, MIN, MAX)$, I a set of individuals, NEXT: $I \to I$, a total function, MIN, MAX constants, the (denotational) semantics of t under the assignment of its free variables μ, $\mathcal{I}(t)(\mu)$, is as usual [Pl 77]. For $m > 0$ the interpretation $\mathcal{I}_m$ is as in the introduction. The type structure of cpo's of continuous functions, starting with the flat cpo $D^{i}_{m} = I_m \cup \{\bot\}$, $D_m = (D^{\tau}_{m} | \tau \in Type)$, is as usual.

As the authors of KfTiUr 87 we prefer to use recursive equations instead of λ-terms (both notations are equivalent with respect to their expressive strength): Fnam = $(Fnam^{\tau} | \tau \in Type)$ is a subfamily of Var, the family of function names, analogously for Par = $(Par^{\tau} | \tau \in Type)$, the family of (formal) parameters. The family of functional programs Prog = $(Prog^{\tau} | \tau$ first-order type) consists of deterministic systems of equations

$$F_1(\bar{y}_1) = t_1(\bar{y}_1, F_1, \ldots, F_k), \quad \ldots \quad , F_k(\bar{y}_k) = t_k(\bar{y}_k, F_1, \ldots, F_k)$$

with type of the program = type F_1. The t_j are from $Term^{i}$ without fixpoints or abstractions. Their variables are indicated in the brackets. $F_j(\bar{y}_j) = F_j(y_{j_1}) \ldots (y_{j_m})$ is of **type** i. P is a level-n-program iff for each function name F in P level $F \leq n$. (<u>Not</u>: P is a level-n-program if level (type P) $\leq n$, type P is always a first-order type.) Given an interpretation $\mathcal{I}$, the sematics of programs is defined by the call-by-name (or OI, outermost-innermost) reduction strategy [Pl 77]. This definition is equivalent to the denotational semantics defined with the help of the simultaneous minimal fixpoint.

As mentioned in the introduction we need a bound on the chain length (i. e. a bound on the maximum number of different elements in a chain) in D_m. A computation reveals: Let D, C be two finite cpo's, then the chain length in the function space $\{f: D \to C \mid f \text{ continuous}\}$ is bounded by card C · card D + 1. The chain length in $D^{\tau_1}_{m} \times \ldots \times D^{\tau_k}_{m}$ (in such a cpo the simultaneous fixpoint necessary for the denotational semantics of a program is computed) is bounded by m^m if the τ_j are types of level ≤ 1 and $m \geq$ a constant depending on these types. For types of level ≤ 2 we get the bound $(m^m)^{(m^m)}$, and so on for higher levels.

Restricting attention to defined values ($\neq \bot$) we can in the interpretation $\mathcal{I}_m$ simulate logical connectives, even quantifiers (everything is finite). The "macro" NEXT1: $(i \to i) \to (i \to i)$ in $\mathcal{I}_m$ simulates the successor operation to the base m, which allows counting up to m^m in a level-2-program. MAX1, MIN1: $i \to i$ define the maximal and minimal value w. r. t. NEXT1, MAX1(y) = MAX, MIN1(y) = MIN. The macro NEXT2: $((i \to i) \to (i \to i)) \to ((i \to i) \to (i \to i))$ can be defined similarly as NEXT1 and using NEXT1. It allows counting up to $(m^m)^{(m^m)}$ in the interpretation I_m by level-3-programs. The NEXT functions can be extended to any level, which gives exponentially increasing counting power if the level of programs goes up. We can define a level-1-macro PAIR:$i \to i \to i$ having the semantics

$$I_m(\text{PAIR})(k)(l) = \begin{cases} \langle k, l\rangle & \text{if } \langle k, l\rangle \leq m \quad (\langle\ \rangle \text{ the pairing function}) \\ m & \text{otherwise,} \end{cases}$$

FST, SND:$i \to i$ describe the inverse functions. The level-1-program PR:$i \to i \to i \to i$ with the semantics

$$I_m(\text{PR})(k)(n)(r) = \begin{cases} n_k & \text{if } n = \langle n_1, \ldots, n_r\rangle \quad r \geq k \\ m & \text{if } r < k \end{cases}$$

can be defined with FST and SND.

2 LEVEL 2 IS MORE POWERFUL THAN LEVEL 1

To make the intended diagonalization process easier, we introduce a normalform for level-1-programs.

2.1 Definition and theorem

(a) A level-1-program is in Chomsky normalform if its equations, with $\bar{y} = (y_1, \ldots, y_n)$ for a suitable n, y_j of type i, have the structure:

1) $F(\bar{y})$ = if $H_1(\bar{y}) = H_2(\bar{y})$ then $G(\bar{y})$ else $H(\bar{y})$ fi
2) $F(\bar{y}) = G(\bar{y})$
3) $F(\bar{y}) = G(H_1(\bar{y})), \ldots, H_m(\bar{y}))$
4) $F(\bar{y}) = y_j$
5) $F(y_1) = \text{NEXT}(y_1)$
6) $F(y_1)$=MIN, $F(y_1)$ = MAX.

(b) Inductively on the right hand side of equations we can transform every level-1-program into an equivalent program in Chomsky normalform.

2.2 Indexing level-1-programs in Chomsky normalform

Let P be a level-1-program in normalform of type $i \to i$. Its equations are given by: $F_1(y_1) = t_1, \ldots, F_k(\bar{y}_k) = t_k$. The index of P, $\ulcorner P \urcorner \in \mathbb{N}$ is given by $\ulcorner P \urcorner = \langle k, \ulcorner t_1 \urcorner, \ldots, \ulcorner t_k \urcorner\rangle$. The function symbols are encoded by $\ulcorner F_i \urcorner = i$. The right hand sides of P are encoded as (numbering from 2.1):

1) $\langle 1, \ulcorner H_1 \urcorner, \ulcorner H_2 \urcorner, \ulcorner G \urcorner, \ulcorner H \urcorner\rangle$ $(H_1, H_2, G, H \in \{F_1, \ldots, F_k\})$

2) <2 , $\ulcorner G \urcorner$>, 3) <3, $\ulcorner G \urcorner$, m, <$\ulcorner H_1 \urcorner$, ..., $\ulcorner H_m \urcorner$>> 4) <4, j>

5) < 5, 1>, 6) < 6, 1> and < 6, 2>

W. l. o. g. we can assume that the index of a program, i, is larger than the length of its longest argument list and that for $m \geq i$ m^m is a bound for its terminating recursion depth (cf. explanations in section 1). Let ψ_k be the program having index k.

2.3 Diagonalization

(a) The level-2-program Q (cf. introduct.) of type $i \to i$ is defined with the help of the functions EVAL, EVAL1, ..., EVAL6: $(i\to i)\to i\to i\to (i\to i)\to i$. The idea is: Q calls EVAL which in turn calls the EVALj, which simulate our six types of equations in level-1-programs in Chomsky normalform. Assume in evaluating the program ψ_k applied to k the term $F_1(k_1, F_2(k_2))$ occurs, then EVAL generates in its place the term EVAL(C)(k)(1)(P) with C standing for the counter of recursion depth, k remembering the index of the actual program to be simulated, 1 encoding the outermost symbol F_1, and P encoding the parameterlist of F_1. It is

P = λy. if y = 0 then k_1 (We use 0 and MIN interchangeably.)
else if y = 1 then EVAL(C')(k)(2)(P') — For F_2.
else Dummy
fi
fi.

P' = λy.if y=0 then k_2 else Dummy fi encodes the parameter list k_2 of F_2.

It is Q(y) = EVAL(MIN1)(y)(1)(CONNECT(MIN1)(0)(y)) — (1: For F_1, the starting function of each program.)

The parameter list is generated by CONNECT: $(i \to i) \to i \to i \to (i \to i)$ with

$$\text{CONNECT}(y_1)(y_{0_1})(y_{0_2})(y_{0_3}) = \text{if } y_{0_3} = y_{0_1} \text{ then } y_{0_2} \text{ else } y_1(y_{0_3}) \text{ fi}$$

The function EVAL is given by:

EVAL(C)(k)(j)(P) = if $\forall y. C(y) \geq$ MAX1(y)
then MIN
else EVAL1(NEXT1(C))(k)(PR(j)(SND k)(FST k))(P)

(SND k: Encoding ψ_k's right hand sides. FST k: Number of equations of ψ_k.)

In case the recursion depth is too large, EVAL results in MIN. Otherwise it computes the index of the right hand side belonging to F_j and hands it over to the first of the functions EVAL1, ..., EVAL6, which simulate the right hand sides of equations. For example EVAL1 looks like:

```
EVAL1(C)(k)(j)(P) = if FST j = 1
                      then ┌if EVAL(C)(k)(SND j)(P)=EVAL(C)(k)(THRD j)(P)
   Representation of the   │ then
   right hand side         │   EVAL(C)(k)(FOURTH j)(P)
   of the type-1)-equa-    │ else
   tion belonging to j.    │   EVAL(C)(k)(FIFTH j)(P)
                           └fi
                      else EVAL2(C)(k)(j)(P)
                    fi
```

SND, THRD, FOURTH,... are the appropriate projections.

The other types of equations can be treated similarly. Details can be found in the full version of this paper [Go 88].

(b) The level-2-program Q has the semantics as stated in the introduction. Assuming we have a level-1-program having the same semantics as Q in the interpretations I_m, we get the contradiction as specified in the introduction. Hence level 2 is more powerful than level 1.

3 LEVEL N + 1 IS MORE POWERFUL THAN LEVEL N

To us the main difference between level-1-programs and level-n-programs for $n \geq 2$ is, that in level-n-programs "half-filled" parameter lists can occur. That means: With $F: (i \to i \to i) \to i$, $G: i \to i \to i \to i$, $t: i$, we can have the term F(G(t)) in computations. The parameter list of G is only half-filled. Note that this in level-1-programs cannot happen because there parameters are always of type i, hence their parameter lists must be totally filled. As in section 2 we want the diagonalizing program Q to encode parameter lists as functions. Hence in simulation Q would generate for the above term something looking roughly like

F(λy.if y = 0 then G(λy.if y = 0 then t else Dummy fi) else Dummy fi)

The term F(G(t)) can reduce to F'(G(t)(s)) for s:i, $F': (i \to i) \to i$. Simulating this reduction in our encoding is (at least directly) not possible, because this would entail for a function EVALj standing at the position of F to have access to G's parameter list, λy.if y = 0 then t else Dummy fi, which is not possible.

A second problem in connection with half filled parameter lists is: Let $F: (i \to i) \to (i \to i)$, $G: i \to i \to i$, t:i, then F(G(t))(s) of type i can reduce to G(t)(s) by a projection. We cannot expect Q to encode all parameters of a level-n-computation-term in one function, instead Q collects parameters in different functions iff their levels are different. The above terms become

F(λy.if y = 0 then G(λy.if y = 0 then t else Dummy fi)else Dummy fi)
(λy.if y = 0 then s else Dummy fi)

and

G(λy.if $y = 0$ then t else(if $y = 1$ then s else Dummy fi) fi)

That is in the encoding G must be able to connect functions representing two parts of a parameter list of the same level into one. This would make it necessary to have two G's with different types - one to use before the connection of the parameter lists, one after.

Fortunately our Chomsky normalform for higher types allows us to get around these problems. To begin with we can restrict attention to a normalized type structure Ntype $=(\mathrm{Ntype}^n \mid n \in \mathbb{N})$ with, $i \in \mathrm{Ntype}^0$ and if $\tau_1,\ldots,\tau_m \in \mathrm{Ntype}^n$, $m \geq 1$, then $\tau_1 \to \ldots \to \tau_m \in \mathrm{Ntype}^{n+1}$. This type structure is important to us: Let $F: \tau$, $\tau \in \mathrm{Ntype}^3$ then F applied to its parameters looks like $F(t_{2_1})\ldots(t_{2_k})(t_{1_1})\ldots(t_{1_m})(t_{0_1})\ldots(t_{0_n})$ where the t_{i_j} are <u>all</u> parameters of level i. As we want Q to represent parameters of different levels by different functions, half applied parameter lists are only worrying if not all parameters of the same level are supplied. Ntype makes at least sure that if not all parameters of level n are supplied, then the level-m-parameter lists are totally filled for $m > n$ and not present at all for $m < n$. (The type structure in Da 82 is more restricted than ours in that the second clause reads: $\tau_1 \times \ldots \times \tau_{m-1} \to \tau_m$ is a type of level $n+1$. As in terms the parameters for $\tau \times \ldots \times \tau_{m-1}$ must be supplied <u>together</u> no half-filled parameter lists of the same level can occur. In programs according to Damm's types subterms of level-m-terms have a level $\geq m$. The semantic strength of Damm's types is unknown.)

Moreover, our Chomsky normalform will ensure, that half-filled parameter lists of the same level can only occur as the first parameter of symbols LIFT being declared as functions such that $\mathrm{LIFT}(t_1)(t_2) \Rightarrow t_1$, level t_1 = level t_2. The term with a half filled parameter list $\mathrm{LIFT}(t_1)$ lifts t_1 from level n to level $n+1$. type LIFT $= \tau \to \tau \to \tau$.

<u>3.1 Definition and theorem</u>

(a) A level-n-program is in Chomsky normalform, if all its types are from Ntype and the equations have the following structure. In writing $G(\bar{t}_k)\ldots(\bar{t}_0)$, $\bar{t}_k$ are <u>all</u> (note the type structure is Ntype) parameters of level k, $\bar{t}_0$ all of level 0.

1.1) $F(\bar{y}_k)\ldots(\bar{y}_0) = \text{if } H_1(\bar{y}_k)\ldots(\bar{y}_0) = H_2(\bar{y}_k)\ldots(\bar{y}_0) \text{ then } G(\bar{y}_k)\ldots(\bar{y}_0) \text{ else } H(\bar{y}_k)\ldots(\bar{y}_0) \text{ fi}$

2.1) $F(\bar{y}_k)\ldots(\bar{y}_0) = G(\bar{y}_k)\ldots(\bar{y}_0)$

3.0) $F(\bar{y}_k)\ldots(\bar{y}_0) = G(\bar{y}_k)\ldots(\bar{y}_1)(H_1(\bar{y}_k)\ldots(\bar{y}_0), \ldots, H_m(\bar{y}_k)\ldots(\bar{y}_0))$

3.1) " $= G(\bar{y}_k)\ldots(\bar{y}_2)(H_1(\bar{y}_k)\ldots(\bar{y}_1), \ldots, H_m(\bar{y}_k)\ldots(\bar{y}_1))(\bar{y}_0)$

.
.
.

3.k) " $= G(H_1(\bar{y}_k), \ldots, H_m(\bar{y}_k))(\bar{y}_{k-1})\ldots(\bar{y}_1)(\bar{y}_0)$

4.1) $F(\bar{y}_k)\dots(\bar{y}_0) = y_{k_j}(\bar{y}_{k-1})\dots(\bar{y}_0)$ where $\bar{y}_k = (y_{k_1},\dots,y_{k_m})$

5.1) $F(y_0) = NEXT(y_0)$

6.1) $F(y_0) = MAX$, 6.2) $F(y_0) = MIN$

7.1) $F(\bar{y}_k)\dots(\bar{y}_0) = G(\bar{y}_{k-1})\dots(\bar{y}_0)$

In the following equations half filled parameter lists of the same level occur, hence arguments are lifted to a higher level,

8.1) $F(\bar{y}_k)\dots(\bar{y}_0) = G(\bar{y}_k)\dots(\bar{y}_1, LIFT^i(y_{0_1}))(\bar{y}_0)$ $\bar{y}_0 = (y_{0_1},\dots,y_{0_m})$

8.2) " $= G(\bar{y}_k)\dots(\bar{y}_2, LIFT^\tau(y_{1_1}))(\bar{y}_1)(\bar{y}_0)$ $\bar{y}_1 = (y_{1_1},\dots,y_{1_m})$, type $y_{1_1} = \tau$

⋮

8.k) " $= G(\bar{y}_k, LIFT^\tau(y_{(k-1)_1}))(\bar{y}_{k-1})\dots(\bar{y}_0)$ $\bar{y}_{k-1} = (y_{(k-1)_1},\dots,y_{(k-1)_m})$, type $y_{(k-1)_1} = \tau$

$LIFT^\tau: \tau \to \tau \to \tau$

$LIFT^\tau(y_{k_1}, y_{k_2})(\bar{y}_{k-1})\dots(\bar{y}_0) = y_{k_1}(\bar{y}_{k-1})\dots(\bar{y}_0)$

9.1) $F(\bar{y}_k)\dots(\bar{y}_0) = G(H_1,\dots,H_m)(\bar{y}_k)\dots(\bar{y}_0)$

(b) A level-n-program can be transformed into a semantically equivalent level-n-program in Chomsky normalform. In the proof we have at first to transform a given program such, that all its types are normalized (this can be done by lifting the parameters to the appropriate levels and by introducing dummy parameters when these lifted parameters are invoked (see LIFT above)). The transformation into Chomsky normalform afterwards proceeds inductively on the right hand sides of equations.

3.2 Indexing of level-n-programs

Let the level-n-program P of type $i \to i$ in Chomsky normalform be given by the equations: $F_1(y_1) = t_1,\dots,F_k(\bar{y}_k) = t_k$ (the $\bar{y}_i$ are all parameters of F_i). It is $\ulcorner P \urcorner = \langle k, \ulcorner t_1 \urcorner,\dots,\ulcorner t_k \urcorner\rangle$. $\ulcorner F_i \urcorner = \langle i, \text{level } F_i\rangle$.

Referring to the equations as numbered in 3.1, the right hand sides are encoded by:

1.1) $\langle\langle 1,1\rangle, \ulcorner H_1 \urcorner, \ulcorner H_2 \urcorner, \ulcorner G \urcorner, \ulcorner H \urcorner\rangle$

2.1) As in 2.2.

3.0) $\langle\langle 3, 0\rangle, \ulcorner G \urcorner, m, \langle\ulcorner H_1 \urcorner,\dots,\ulcorner H_m \urcorner\rangle\rangle$

3.1) $\langle\langle 3, 1\rangle, \ulcorner G \urcorner, m, \langle\ulcorner H_1 \urcorner,\dots,\ulcorner H_m \urcorner\rangle\rangle$

⋮

3.k) $\langle\langle 3, k\rangle, \ulcorner G \urcorner, m, \langle\ulcorner H_1 \urcorner,\dots,\ulcorner H_m \urcorner\rangle\rangle$

4.1) $\langle\langle 4, 1, k\rangle, j\rangle$

Analogously.

⋮

8.1) $\langle\langle 8, 1\rangle, \ulcorner LIFT^i \urcorner, n\rangle$, length $\bar{y}_1 = n$

⋮

8.k) $\langle\langle 8, k\rangle, \ulcorner LIFT^\tau \urcorner, n\rangle$, length $\bar{y}_k = n$

9.1) $\langle\langle 9, 1\rangle, \ulcorner G \urcorner, m, \langle\ulcorner H_1 \urcorner,\dots,\ulcorner H_m \urcorner\rangle\rangle$.

In 3.3 we present some details of our diagonalization process for higher levels. We restrict attention to diagonalizing with a level-3-program over all level-2-programs. For higher levels we can proceed analogously.

3.3 Diagonalization of level 3 over level 2

We proceed as in 2.3 using the functions

$$\text{EVAL, EVAL1.1}, \ldots, \text{EVAL9.1} : \underbrace{((i \to i) \to (i \to i))}_{\text{Counter of recursion depth.}} \to i \to i \to \underbrace{(i \to (i \to i) \to i)}_{\text{List of the level-1-parameters}} \to \underbrace{(i \to i)}_{\text{List of the level-0-parameters.}} \to i$$

- Index of the current symbol or right hand side.
- Index of the level-2-program to be simulated.

Note: The type is a level-3-type. Each single level-1-parameter expects a list of level-0-parameters as arguments, encoded with the type $i \to i$, hence it has the type $(i \to i) \to i$.

It is $\text{EVAL}(C)(k)(j)(P_1)(P_0) = \text{if} \, \forall y_1 . y_0 . C(y_1)(y_0) \geq \text{MAX}$
then MIN
else $\text{EVAL1.1}(\text{NEXT2}(C))(k)(\text{PRO})(P_1)(P_0)$
fi ,
with PRO = PR(j)(SND(k))(FST(k)), comment cf. 2.3.

We define some examples of the EVALi.j (numbering from 3.1).

$\text{EVAL3.1}(C)(k)(j)(P_1)(P_0) = \text{if FST(FST } j) = 3 \text{ and SND(FST } j) = 1$
then EVAL(C)(k)(THRD j)
$(\text{CON1}(C)(k)(\text{FOURTH } j)(\text{FIFTH } j)(P_1))(P_0)$
else $\text{EVAL 3.2}(C)(k)(j)(P_1)(P_0)$
fi

The function CON1 constructs the level-1-parameter list which is needed to simulate a function of type 3.1.

$\text{EVAL8.1}(C)(k)(j)(P_1)(P_0) = \text{if FST(FST } j) = 8 \text{ and SND(FST } j) = 1$
then EVAL(C)(k)(SND j)
$(\text{CONNECT}(\text{THRD } j)(P_1)(\text{LIFT}^i(P_0(0))))(P_0)$
else $\text{EVAL8.2}(C)(k)(j)(P_1)(P_0)$
fi

and $\text{LIFT}^i : i \to ((i \to i) \to i)$ with $\text{LIFT}^i(y_0)(y_1) = y_0$. This is a LIFT^i different from the LIFT^i in the Chomsky normalform. CONNECT attaches its third argument to the list specified as second argument at the position specified by the first argument. We encode a level-1-parameter by a term of type $(i \to i) \to i$. These parameters are lifted by $\text{LIFT}^{(i \to i) \to i}$ having type

$$((i \to i) \to i) \to \underbrace{(i \to (i \to i) \to i)}_{\text{Level-1-parameter list.}} \to \underbrace{(i \to i)}_{\text{Level-0-parameter list.}} \to i$$

As to higher types: Let $\text{Countertype}_1 = i \to i$ and $\text{Countertype}_{n+1} = \text{Countertype}_n \to \text{Countertype}_n$. Moreover let $T_1 = (i \to i) \to i$ and $T_{n+1} = (i \to T_n) \to T_{n-1}$. The $i \to T_n$ serves to encode a parameter list of level n. It is level $T_n = n+1$. The function EVAL to diagonalize over all level-n-programs has the type: $\text{Countertype}_n \to i \to i \to T_n$ which is a level-(n+1)-type.

REFERENCES

Da 82 W. Damm, The OI- and IO-hierarchies, Theoretical Computer Science, vol. 20, pp 95 - 207, 1982.

DaFeIn 78 W. Damm, E. Fehr, K. Indermark, Higher type recursion and self application as control structures, in Formal Description of Programming Concepts, ed. Neuhold, pp 461 - 478,1978.

En 83 J. Engelfriet, Iterated pushdown-automata and complexity classes, Proc. 15th STOC, pp 365 - 373, 1983.

EnSch77/78 J. Engelfriet, E. M. Schmidt, IO and OI, J. Comp. and System Sciences, vol 15, pp328 - 353 1977,/vol 16, pp 67 - 99,1978

DaGo 86 W. Damm, A. Goerdt, An automata-theoretic characterization of the OI-hierarchy, Information and Control, vol 71, pp 1-32, 1986.

Go 88 A. Goerdt, On the expressive strength of the finitely typed lambda-terms, Technical report, University of Duisburg, 1988.

In 76 K. Indermark, Schemes with recursion on higher types, Proc. 5th MFCS, LNCS 45, Springer-Verlag, pp 352 - 358, 1976.

Kf Ur 85 A. J. Kfoury, P. Urzyczyn, Necessary and sufficient conditions for the universality of programming formalisms, Acta Informatica, vol 22, pp 347 - 377, 1985.

KfTiUr 87 A. Kfoury, J. Tiuryn, P. Urzyczyn, The hierarchy of functional programs, Proc. LICS 1987, pp 225 - 235, 1987.

La 74 H. Langmaack, On procedures as open subroutines, Acta informatica, vol 2, pp 311 - 333, 1973 and vol 3 pp 227 - 241, 1974.

Lei 87 D. Leivant, Characterization of complexity classes in higher order logic, Proc. of the 2nd annual conference Structure in Complexity, pp 203 - 217, 1987.

Pl 77 G. Plotkin, LCF considered as a programming language, Theoretical Computer Science, vol 5, pp 223 - 255, 1977.

HOARE CALCULI FOR HIGHER-TYPE CONTROL STRUCTURES AND THEIR COMPLETENESS IN THE SENSE OF COOK

Andreas Goerdt
Universität Duisburg
Fachbereich Mathematik
Fachgebiet Praktische Informatik
Lotharstraße 63
D-4100 Duisburg 1
West-Germany

ABSTRACT

We show that the Hoare Calculus for the language of finitely typed λ-terms, introduced in Go 85, is complete in the sense of Cook, i. e. complete for expressive interpretations, if the first-order theory of the interpretation is supplied as oracle. This is the classical notion of completeness for Hoare Calculi [Ap 81] . In Go 85 completeness in the sense of Cook was only proved with respect to Herbrand definable interpretations, which is much easier because of the characterizations in Ur 83, and amounts essentially to completeness for arithmetic and finite interpretations.

The completeness result above implies that we get - in a uniform manner as demonstrated in Go 87 - Hoare Calculi which are complete in the sense of Cook for imperative languages with control structures ranging from normal recursive procedures with local variables (i. e. variables declared by new x) to recursive procedures and functions of higher type (without global variables [Cl 79]). No such calculi were known for languages with higher type procedures and functions, hence we solve positively a question in TrHaMe 83.

INTRODUCTION

One research topic in Hoare Logic is the construction of Hoare Calculi which are complete in the sense of Cook for languages within the bounds of Cl 79, where it was shown that for languages with higher type procedures and unrestricted use of local variables no calculi complete in the sense of Cook can exist. For a discussion of the notion of completeness in the sense of Cook see FeLe 86, Cl 84. The construction of calculi complete in the sense of Cook for languages involving higher type concepts (in particular Clarke's language L_4, a language with higher type procedures without global variables [Cl 79]) raised some interest in the literature [Cl 79, DaJo 83, dBMeKl 81, ErNaOg 82, GeClHa 84, GeClHa 86, Ha 83, La 83, Ol 84] but only the calculus for Clarke's L_4 introduced in GeClHa 84, GeClHa 86 is complete in the sense of Cook.

In the present paper we show that the Hoare Calculus for the language of finitely typed λ-terms, a language capturing the essentials of higher-type concepts, is complete in the sense of Cook. That is we have been able to remove the assumption of the interpretation being Herbrand definable (every individual is addressable by a simple expression) from the proof in Go 85. This is important as the idea of Hoare Calculi is to capture the meaning of control structures totally independent of the interpretation.

With the calculus for λ-terms being complete in the sense of Cook, the application of this calculus to imperative languages [Go 87] yields in a uniform manner Hoare Calculi which are complete in the sense of Cook for all languages considered in the papers above (except of Ha 83). This shows that as far as Hoare Calculi are concerned the essence of these languages is captured by the language of typed λ-terms. Moreover the simple syntactic structure of λ-terms makes a completeness proof on the level of λ-terms easier to understand.

The idea of our completeness proof: The expressiveness assumption, which we assume to hold for the interpretation in question, in the context of λ-terms says: The semantics of every closed λ-term of first-order type (that is a type $\tau_1 \to \dots \to \tau_n \to \rho$, τ_i, ρ base types, such a term has of course subterms of arbitrary types) is expressible by a first-order predicate over the interpretation. As usual in Hoare Logic the completeness proof proceeds inductively on the syntax of terms. Hence it is crucial that the right intermediate assertions making statements about (possibly open) subterms, which are generally of higher type, exist, and that the corresponding formulae can be derived. We introduce a so called <u>family of strongest assertions</u> which has the right properties for the induction and restrict attention in the inductive proof totally to assertions from this family. This part of the proof is based on ideas from Go 85. What follows is the actual novelty of this paper.

For uniformaly locally finite interpretations (that means for each n there is a finite bound on the cardinality of the substructures generated by arbitrary n individuals) the existence of such a family follows by finite methods. Otherwise we need among others "interpreter predicates" which describe the following function (suitably encoded in the interpretation): Input: index of a λ-term t of first-order type and arguments for this term. Output: the semantics of t applied to its arguments. The indexing of λ-terms over not uniformly locally finite interpretations is based on the following representation of natural numbers in the interpretation [ClGeHa 83]: The distance between a finite set of individuals S and another individual j, that is the minimum number of operations necessary to generate j from S, is either undefined (if j cannot be generated from S) or a natural number. As the interpretation is not uniformly locally finite, there is an N such that the distances between individuals $i_1,\dots,i_N$ and another individual j are not bounded. We represent natural numbers by these distances.

The existence of the interpreter predicates follows from the following <u>key lemma</u> (also observed in Hu 87): If the interpretation is expressive

w. r. t. λ-terms, then first-order predicates can define any computable function over the interpretation (i. e. any function definable by Friedman's effective definitional scheme, Sh 75, Sh 85, KfUr 85). As the function we want to be described by the interpreter predicates is computable, Church's thesis for arbitrary structures and the key lemma entail the existence of the interpreter predicates.

The essential difference between the completeness proof presented here and the proof in GeClHa 86 for a related situation: The authors reduce the question of completeness of their calculus to the question of the existence of interpreter predicates (as we do - though the reductions are different because the calculi are different). To prove the existence of the interpreter predicates they construct (complex) interpreter programs in their programming language, showing the desired behaviour and apply the expressiveness assumption. Note that for us it is sufficient to see that the functions described by the interpreter programs are computable, which is obvious.

In section 1 we give some basic definitions and indicate a proof of the key lemma. In section 2 we present the ideas of our proof for Herbrand definable finite interpretations (the simplest case). In section 3 we show how these ideas can be extended to the general case of expressive interpretations.

1 BASIC DEFINITIONS AND RESULTS

To begin with we recall the Hoare Calculus for the language of finitely typed λ-terms as defined in Go 85. The base types are ind and bv (individuals and Boolean values). We are given a signature of operation and relation symbols over these types. For our proof it is vital, that = is in the signature, as operation symbol of type (indind, bv) and as relation symbol of type indind and bvbv. In λ-terms only the operation symbols occur, whereas in predicates and assertions operation and relation symbols occur. We are given a fixed interpretation $I = (I^{ind}, I^{bv}, \psi_{Ops}, \psi_{Rel})$ with I^{ind} a set of individuals and $I^{bv} = \{tt, ff\}$ the set of Boolean values, ψ_{Ops}, ψ_{Rel} interpretations of the operation and relation symbols as usual. The set of types, Type, over ind, bv is given by: ind, bv $\in$ Type, if $\tau, \rho \in$ Type, then $(\tau \to \rho) \in$ Type. Let $D = (D^{\tau} | \tau \in Type)$ be the type structure of cpo's of continuous functions over $I^{ind} \cup \{\bot\}$ and $I^{bv} \cup \{\bot\}$. Term $= (Term^{\tau} | \tau \in Type)$ is the family of finitely typed λ-terms with if-then-else and fixpoints (cf. LS 84). Let always t, s, r $\in$ Term. With μ an assignment of variables occurring in terms, $\mathcal{T}(t)(\mu)$ is the (denotational) semantics of t in I under μ. Let Pred be the set of two-sorted first-order predicates over sorts ind and bv and the signature above. $\pi \models p$ is the usual notion of validity of predicates in I, π is an assignment of individual variables.

A Hoare Calculus relies on two formal languages, the set of programs, here given by the λ-terms, and a set of assertions, denoting properties of programs. In our case we have a typed family of assertions, Ass $= (Ass^{\tau} | \tau \in Type)$ given by (motivation cf. Go 85):

If $p \varepsilon$ Pred, u an individual variable of base type $\tau(\tau \varepsilon \{ind, bv\})$, then $(p)_u \varepsilon Ass^{\tau}$

if $p \varepsilon Ass^{\tau}$, $q \varepsilon Ass^{\rho}$, then $(p, q) \varepsilon Ass^{\tau \to \rho}$,

if $p, q \varepsilon Ass^{\tau}$, τ no base type, then $p \wedge q$, $\forall u.p \varepsilon Ass^{\tau}$.

Let always p, q ε Ass. The semantics of $p \varepsilon Ass^{\tau}$ is the set $A(p)(\pi) \subseteq D^{\tau}$ of cpo elements satisfying p. It is given by:

$c \varepsilon A((p)_u)(\pi) \Leftrightarrow$ if $c \neq \bot$ then $\pi[c/u] \models p$ ($\pi[c/u]$ the variant as usual.),

$c \varepsilon A((p, q))(\pi) \Leftrightarrow c(A(p)(\pi)) \subseteq A(q)(\pi)$,

$c \varepsilon A(p \wedge q)(\pi) \Leftrightarrow c \varepsilon A(p)(\pi) \cap A(q)(\pi)$, analogously for $\forall u.p \varepsilon$ Ass.

The formulae of our calculus are sequents like $y_1\ p_1, \ldots, y_n\ p_n \to t\ p$, where the y_i are the free variables occurring in t and p_i, p are assertions of the appropriate types. $y_i\ p_i$ is an assumption for the free variable y_i of t. The semantics of formulae is given by

$\mu, \pi \models y_1\ p_1, \ldots, y_n\ p_n \to t\ p$ iff for all k $\mu(y_k) \varepsilon A(p_k)(\pi)$ implies $\mathcal{T}(t)(\mu) \varepsilon A(p)(\pi)$. Saying, if all assumptions hold, the conclusion holds. E. g. the formula $y\ (false)_u \to \lambda z.y + z\ ((true)_u, (false)_u)$ is valid (the operation symbols are interpreted as strict functions).

The calculus has one rule for each syntactic construct of λ-terms:

Application rule

$$\frac{A \to t\ (p, q) \quad B \to s\ p}{A \cup B \to t(s)\ q}$$

Abstraction rule

$$\frac{A, y\ p \to t\ q}{A \to \lambda y.t\ (p, q)} \quad \text{if } y \text{ not in } A$$

Fixpoint rule

$$\frac{A \to t\ (p, p)}{A \to fix(t)\ p}$$

if-then-else-rule

$$\frac{A \to r\ (p)_u \quad B \to s\ (q_1)_v \quad C \to t\ (q_2)_v}{A \cup B \cup C \to \text{if } r \text{ then } s \text{ else } t \text{ fi } (q)_v}$$

with $q = (p[tt/u] \wedge q_1) \vee (p[ff/u] \wedge q_2)$ v not free in p. We only allow s and t of base type which is no semantic restriction.

As to the soundness of the fixpoint rule it is important that all sets $A(p)(\pi)$ are closed under least upper bounds of ω-chains, hence admissable for Scott's induction.

The calculus has some further "logical" rules:

And-rule

$$\frac{A \to t\ p \quad B \to t\ q}{A \cup B \to t\ p \wedge q}$$

Universal quantifier rule

$$\frac{A \to t\ p}{A \to t\ \forall u.p} \quad \text{if } u \text{ not free in } A$$

Implication rule

$$\frac{A \to t\ p \quad impl(p, q)}{A \to t\ q}$$

The soundness of these rules is clear, knowing that impl(p, q) stands for a first-order predicate whose validity implies $A(p)(\pi) \subseteq A(q)(\pi)$ for all π. It is defined in Go 85.

Theproof of our key lemma formulated in the introduction: If I is uniformly locally finite (cf. introduction) the claim is 2.11(a) from Kf 83. Otherwise we apply theorem 1.4 from KfUr 85, use the NEXT function from Ur 83 and proceed similarly as in the proof of theorem 2.5 in KfUr 85, applying the expressivenes assumption and using the fact that predicates allow for existential quantification.

In the rest of this paper we indicate a proof of

1.1 Theorem

If I is expressive w. r. t. the language of λ-terms, then any valid formula t p, t a closed term of first-order type is derivable.

Let in the following I expressive and t p valid. In explaining our proof we assume that t is of type ind → ind.

2 COMPLETENESS FOR HERBRAND DEFINABLE FINITE INTERPRETATIONS

Let I Herbrand definable and finite. The above result follows if we are able to derive the formula t Sa(t). Sa(t) is the strongest assertion of t. It gives us complete information about the behaviour of t:

$$Sa(t) = (Sa(d_0), Sa(d_0')) \wedge \dots \wedge (Sa(d_n), Sa(d_n'))$$

where $D^{ind} = \{d_0, \dots, d_n\}$ and $\mathcal{I}(t)(d_i) = d_i'$ and

$$Sa(d\ ) = \begin{cases} (false)_v & \text{if } d = \bot \\ (v = d)_v & \text{otherwise} \end{cases}$$

is the strongest assertion of d. (Distinguish strongest assertions for elements from D and for terms.)

Inductively on t we show t Sa(t) is derivable. In the induction we restrict attention to assertions from the following family of strongest assertions $Sa = (Sa^\tau \mid \tau \in Type)$:

2.1 Family of strongest assertions

It is $Sa^\tau = \{ Sa(d) \mid d \in D^\tau\}$. For τ base type, $d \in D^\tau$, Sa(d) is already defined. If $\tau = \rho \to \sigma$, $d \in D^\tau$; then

$$Sa(d) = (Sa(d_0), Sa(d(d_0))) \wedge \dots \wedge (Sa(d_n), Sa(d(d_n))$$

with $D^\rho = \{d_0, \dots, d_n\}$. Sa(d) reflects all argument-value pairs belonging to d. For $p \in Sa$ it is $D(p) \in D$ uniquely determined by $Sa(D(p)) = p$.

2.2 Inductive argument to prove 1.1

The induction hypothesis of our induction on the syntax of terms reads: Let $p_i \in Sa$, $d_i = D(p_i)$, fr $s \subseteq \{y_1, \dots, y_n\}$, $q = Sa(\mathcal{I}(s)(\mu[d_1/y_1, \dots, d_n/y_n]))$ then

$$y_1\ p_1, \dots, y_n\ p_n \to s\ q$$

is derivable. This implies that t Sa(t) is derivable.

In the induction we proceed by case distinction on the syntax of s. E.g. let $s = r_1(r_2)$ an application. Let $A = y_1\ p_1, \dots, y_n\ p_n$, d_i as above and $q_i = Sa(\mathcal{I}(r_i)(\mu[d_1/y_1, \dots, d_n/y_n]))$, let q as above. We can derive:

$A \to r_1\ q_1$, $A \to r_2\ q_2$ — Derivable by ind. hyp.

Impl.rule: $A \to r_1\ (q_2, q)$ — Application rule

$A \to r_1(r_2)\ q$

The application of the implication rule is admissable because the structure of strongest assertions implies, that $\models impl(q_1,(q_2, q))$, in fact q_1 has the form $\ldots\wedge(q_2, q)\wedge\ldots$. We see that it is useful for strongest assertions to contain <u>all</u> argument-value pairs of the element in question. This allows the implication rule to extract the necessary information.

The remaining cases of syntactic structure of s can be treated similarly.

3 COMPLETENESS FOR EXPRESSIVE INTERPRETATIONS

We show the derivability of t p if our interpretation I is expressive.

Some technical consideration proves that it is sufficient to show the following theorem:

3.1 Theorem

The formula $y\ (inp = u)_{inp} \rightarrow t(y)\quad q$ is derivable, where q (an assertion of base type) is up to equivalence specified by $Max(A(q)(\pi)) = \mathcal{T}(t(y))(\mu[\pi(u)/y])$. q is the strongest assertion of t(y) under the assumption $y\ (inp = u)_{inp}$. Under the assignment π the assumption $y\ (inp = u)_{inp}$ binds y to $\pi(u)$. The assumption is used to make the input value y available to assertions by binding y to u.

In defining a family of strongest assertions analogously to section 2 we encouter problems not present before: Not every individual need be addressable by a predicate, hence not every cpo-element need be addressable by an assertion. There can be infinitely many arguments to functions, that means that we cannot capture all argument-value pairs by a finite conjunction. For infinite I on higher types we have continuum many arguments (or even more). So simple indexing techniques do not allow us to proceed as in section 2.

In 2.1 we define the strongest assertion Sa(d) for any element of D. But in fact it is not necessary to take account of all of D to prove 3.1. The validity of the formula in 3.1 depends on the infinite computation tree of the term t(y) defined by the call-by-name reduction strategy. In deriving an assertion for t(y) the calculus must in some way or other gain information about this computation tree. Variables occurring in this computation tree are never bound to arbitrary elements of D but only to terms from the type structure of computation terms defined in 3.2. Also subterms of higher type in the computation tree are "finally" applied to one of these computation terms.

3.2 Definition

(a) The type structure of computation terms $CT = (CT^{\tau} | \tau \in Type)$ is given by $CT^{\tau} = \{s \in Term^{\tau} | fr\ s \subseteq \{y\}\}$. Note that CT is closed under application. Hence it is a reasonable type structure. CT depends on our fixed term t(y) through the free variable y.

(b) $\sim^{\tau} \subseteq CT^{\tau} \times CT^{\tau}$ is defined by: τ base type, then $t \sim^{\tau} s$ iff $\mathcal{T}(t) = \mathcal{T}(s)$. τ higher type, then $t \sim^{\tau} s$ iff for all $s_1 \in CT\ t(s_1) \sim s(s_1)$. Two terms are equivalent if they cannot be distinguished by applying them to computation terms. Hence a computation of t cannot distinguish two equivalent terms.

Instead of defining a strongest assertion for each $d \in D$ as in 2.1, we define strongest assertions only for classes $CT^{\tau}/\sim^{\tau}$. We have at most denumerably many of such classes. If s is of type $\rho \to \sigma$, Sa(s), the strongest assertion of s will be the conjunction of all argument-value pairs (Sa(r), (Sa(s(r)) for r ranging over $CT^{\rho}/\sim^{\rho}$. If there are infinitely many such classes in $CT^{\rho}/\sim^{\rho}$ this conjunction will be expressed by a universal quantifier and an appropriate indexing. Here the interpreter predicates mentioned in the introduction come in.

If I is unformly locally finite, we can be sure that each $CT^{\tau}/\sim^{\tau}$ consists only of finitely many classes, because the cardinalities of substructures of I being generated by one element, corresponding to y, are finitely bounded. We then can proceed as in section 2.

Let in the sequel I not uniformly locally finite. Let N be such that the cardinalities of substructures of I generated by N individuals are not finitely bounded.

3.3 Definition

(a) Let $dist(i_1,\dots,i_N,j) = dist(\bar{i}, j) \in \mathbb{N}$ be the distance of j from $i_1,\dots,i_N$, i. e. the minimum number of steps to generate j from $\bar{i}$, if this number is defined at all. dist is surjective by the choice of N. Hence any natural number can be encoded in I.

(b) Let $\psi^{\tau}: I^{N+1} \to CT^{\tau}$ be an effective indexing of CT^{τ}. The n'th term in an effective listing of CT^{τ} is indexed by $(\bar{i}, j)$ with $dist(\bar{i}, j) = n$. A term equal to $\perp$ is indexed by the undefined distance.

3.4 Definition and theorem

As the above indexing is effective the expressiveness assumption (!) and the key lemma (cf. introduction) imply the existence of the predicates with the semantics specified as follows:

(1) $APP^{\tau\rho}(\bar{x}, \bar{y}, \bar{z})$ describes the application $CT^{\tau\to\rho} \times CT^{\tau} \to CT^{\rho}$ on the indices of computation terms ($\bar{x}, \bar{y}, \bar{z}$ are N + 1 tuples).

(2) For each closed term t from CT we have a predicate giving us an index just of t, $IND_t(\bar{x})$.

(3) For τ base type we have interpreter predicates $INTER^{\tau}(\bar{x},u,outp)$ with (annotations: $\bar{x}$ = Index; u = Input value for y)

$$\models INTER^{\tau}(\bar{i},j,k) \text{ iff } \mathcal{I}(\psi^{\tau}(\bar{i}))(\mu[j/y]) = k.$$

$INTER^{\tau}$ computes the semantics of a term from CT^{τ} applied to its argument y given an index of the term. Note that terms in CT have only y as free variable. Here y is assigned the value j.

To represent the possibly infinite conjunction of argument-value pairs by a universal quantifier over assertions, we introduce universal assertions.

3.5 Universal assertions

For τ base type the universal assertion of type τ is given by

$$U^{\tau}(\bar{z}, u) = (INTER^{\tau}(\bar{z}, u, outp))_{outp \in Ass^{\tau}}.$$

With $\bar{z}$ assuming all possible values $U^{\tau}(\bar{z}, u)$ captures all computation terms of type τ .

For τ = ind $\to$ind it is

$$U^{\tau}(\bar{z}, u) = \forall y_1 . (U^{ind}(\bar{y}_1, u), (\exists \bar{w}. APP^{indind}(\bar{z}, \bar{y}_1, \bar{w}) \wedge INTER(\bar{w}, u, at))_{at}$$

Conjunction of all argument computation terms.

$U^{\tau}(\bar{z},u)$ captures all computation terms if $\bar{z}$ assumes all its values. For higher types we proceed analogously.

3.6 Family of strongest assertions

(a) The strongest assertions of type $\tau = \tau_1 \to \tau_2 \to \dots \to \tau_n \to \rho$, ρ base type have the form

$$\forall y_1 . (U^{\tau_1}(\bar{y}_1, u), \forall \bar{y}_2 . (U^{\tau_2}(\bar{y}_2, u), \dots, \forall \bar{y}_n . (U^{\tau_n}(\bar{y}_n, u), p') \dots))$$

such that p' for each assignment of individual variables determines exactly one element from $CT^{\tau}/\sim^{\tau}$. That is expressed by the condition: For each π there exists a $t \in CT_{\tau}$ such that for all argument indices $\bar{i}_1, \dots, \bar{i}_n$ all actual arguments j (this is the value for u corresponding to the free variable of our computation terms y) holds:

$$d \in A(p')(\pi[\bar{i}_1/\bar{y}_1, \dots, \bar{i}_n/\bar{y}_n, j/u]) \text{ iff } d \sqsubseteq 7(t(\psi^{\tau_1}(\bar{i}_1)) \dots (\psi^{\tau_n}(\bar{i}_n)))(\mu[j/y])$$

A term from CT.

Sa =($Sa^{\tau} | \tau \in$ Type) is the family of strongest assertions. Let for $p \in Sa$ $Term(p,\pi) \in CT_{\tau}$ be a representative of the uniquely determined class from $CT^{\tau}/\sim^{\tau}$ belonging to p under π .(This class is given by the t above.) For p, q with $Term(p,\pi) \sim Term(q,\pi)$ p and q are under π equivalent with respect to the notion of implication, impl, for assertions.

3.7 Theorem

Let r an arbitrary λ-term with free variables $y'_1, \dots, y'_n$. Let $p_1, \dots, p_n \in$ Sa, let $q \in$ Sa with

$$Term(q,\pi) \sim \lambda y'_1, \dots, y'_n . r(Term(p_1, \pi)) \dots (Term(p_n, \pi)) \in CT$$

for all π . Such a q is unique up to equivalence and exists as follows inductively on n. For n = 0 apply 3.4(2). The formula $y'_1\ p_1, \dots, y'_n\ p_n \to r\ \ q$ is derivable in our calculus. The proof proceeds inductively on the syntax of r as in 2.2. For r = t(y) theorem 3.1 follows. Though in the induction terms not from CT occur, the fact that we bind their free variables to assertions from Sa implies that we can "consider" them as terms from CT.

REFERENCES

Ap 81 Apt, K. R., Ten years of Hoare's Logic, a survey, part I, ACM TOPLAS vol 3, 1981, 431 - 483.

Cl 79 Clarke E. M., Programming languages for which it is impossible to obtain good Hoare-like axioms, JACM vol 26, 1979, 129 - 147.

CL 84 Clarke, E. M., The characterization problem for Hoare Logic, Report no CS-84-109, Carnegie Mellon University, 1984.

ClGeHa 83 Clarke, E. M., German, S. M., Halpern, J., Effective axiomatizations of Hoare Logics, JACM vol 30, 1983, 612 - 636.

DaJo 83 Damm, W., Josko, B., A sound and relatively*complete Hoare Logic for a language with higher type procedures, Acta Informatica vol 20, 1983, 59 - 101.

dBMeKl 81 de Bakker, J. W., Meyer, J.-J. Ch., Klop, J. W., Correctness of programs with function procedures, Logics of Programs 1981, LNCS vol 134, 1982, 94 - 112.

ErNaOg 82 Ernst, G. W., Navlakha, J. K., Ogden, W. F., Verification of programs with procedure type parameters, Acta Informatica vol 18, 1982, 149 - 169.

FeLe 86 Fernando, T., Leivant, D., Skinny and fleshy failures of relative completeness, 14th POPL, 1986.

GeClHa 84 German, S. M.,Clarke, E. M., Halpern, J. Y., Reasoning about procedures as parameters, Logics of programs 1983, LNCS vol 164, 1984, 206 - 220.

GeClHa 86 -, True relative completeness of a Hoare Calculus for L_4, LICS 1986, 1986.

Go 85 Goerdt, A.,A Hoare Calculus for functions defined by recursion on higher types, Logics of programs 1985, LNCS vol 193, 1985, 106 - 117.

Go 87 -, Hoare Logic for Lambda-Terms as a basis of Hoare Logic for imperative languages, LICS 1987, 1987, 293 - 299.

Ha 83 Halpern, J. Y., A good Hoare axiom system for an Algol-like language, 11th POPL, 1983, 262 - 271.

Hu 87 Hungar, H., A characterization of expressive interpretations, Report no 8705, Institut für Informatik und Praktische Mathematik, Christian-Albrechts-Universität Kiel, 1987.

Kf 83 Kfoury, A. J., Definability by programs in first-order structures, TCS vol 25, 1983, 1 - 66.

KfUr 85 Kfoury, A. J., Urzyczyn, P., Necessary and sufficient conditions for the universality of programming formalisms, Acta Informatica vol 22, 1985, 347 - 377.

La 83 Langmaack, H., Aspects of programs with finite modes, FCT 1983, LNCS 158, 1983, 241 - 254.

LS 84 Loeckx, J., Sieber, K., The foundations of program verification, Teubner Verlag, Wiley & Sons, 1984.

Ol 84 Olderog, E. R., Correctness of programs with Pascal-like procedures without global variables, TCS vol 30, 1984, 49-90.

Sh 75 Shepherdson, J. C., Computation over abstract structures: serial and parallel procedures and Friedman's effective definitional schemes, Logic Colloquium 1973, North Holland, 1975, 445 - 531.

Sh 85 Shepherdson, J. C., Algorithmic procedures, generalized Turing Algorithms, and elementary recursion theory, Harvey Friedman's research on the foundations of mathematics, North Holland ,1985, 285 - 308.

TrHaMe 83 Trakhtenbrot, B. A., Halpern, J. Y., Meyer, A. R., From denotational to operational semantics for Algol-like languages: an overview, Logics of Programs 1983, LNCS 164, 1984, 473 - 500.

Ur 83 Urcyczyn, P., A necessary and sufficient condition in order that a Herbrand interpretation be expressive relative to recursive programs, Information and Control vol 56, 1983, 212 - 219.

Acknowledgement

I should like to thank Jurek Tiuryn for valuable hints and motivating me to carry out the research presented here.

ON REPRESENTING CCS PROGRAMS BY FINITE PETRI NETS

Ursula Goltz, GMD–F1P
Postfach 1240
D–5205 St. Augustin 1

Abstract A non–interleaving semantics for a subset of CCS using finite place/transition–systems is presented. Straightforward constructions on nets for CCS operations are given. When restricting the language appropriately (no restriction and relabelling, only *guarded choice*), these operations yield a net semantics with a clear distinction of concurrency and nondeterminism. It is shown that the usual interleaving semantics is retrievable from the net semantics. Partial order semantics and equivalence notions for labelled P/T–systems are discussed. This shows how the intuitive causal dependencies in a CCS program are represented via the net semantics.

1. Introduction

A lot of research is recently devoted to the non–interleaving semantics of CCS and CSP–like languages, aiming at a clear destinction of nondeterminism and concurrency. A rather complete list of references of this field is given in [Ol]. Most of these approaches are based on Petri nets which offer a well–established theory for the representation of concurrency.

A first attempt for a semantics of CCS using Petri nets was presented in [Ci] where a subset of CCS (only bounded parallelism) was considered. In [GoMy], acyclic Petri nets called *occurrence nets* were used to model full CCS. This work was similar to and inspired by Winskel's semantics using *event structures* [Wi1, Wi3] and uses constructions for occurrence nets from [Wi2]. Both occurrence nets and event structures represent simple recursive constructs like $\mu x(a.x)$ by infinite objects. It was observed in [GoMy] that many recursive CCS programs have natural representations as finite nets and it was tried to generate them by folding the infinite representations.

All approaches so far gave a net semantics to (parts of) CCS in a *denotational* style by defining CCS–like operations for nets. Next, [DDM1], [Ol] and [DDM2] presented an *operational* net semantics for full CCS (or extendable to full CCS), based on Plotkin–style transition rules. These approaches generate *one–safe nets* (places will never carry more than one token) and some recursive expressions (like $\mu x(a.x)$) are represented by finite (cyclic) nets. [Ol] and [DDM2] succede to fully preserve concurrency in the modelling of choice and recursion and thus improve the approach of [DDM1]. An attempt for a denotational semantics with one–safe nets is made in [GlVa]. Unfortunately, it is not clear how to solve recursive equations in this framework to obtain finite representations when possible.

However, all approaches using one–safe nets must yield infinite nets in case of unboundedly growing parallelism. Consider the CCS program $P = \mu x(a.x|b.nil)$. In [Ol] (and other approaches using one–safe nets) it is represented by the infinite net

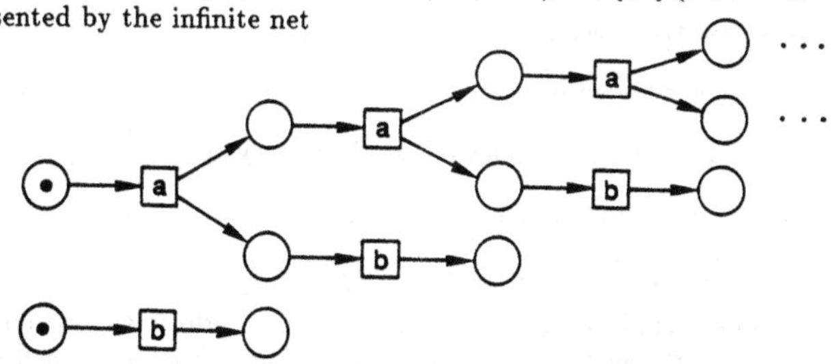

As observed in [GoMy], the following representation of P as a finite net may be given.

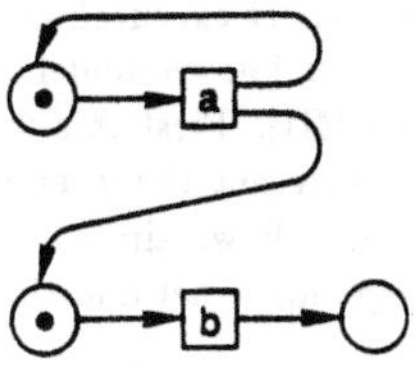

The growth of parallelism will now be represented by arbitrarily large numbers of tokens on places. Unfolding this net into an acyclic net obviously gives the infinite net above.

In this paper, composition operators for CCS-programs are investigated with the aim of generating systematically Petri net representations with finite net structure for CCS-programs, as in the above example. This uses the full power of Petri nets which lies in the representation of infinite behaviours by a finite static structure (the net structure) together with the rule for the "token game". However it is not possible to treat full CCS in this way, as stated in [GoMy], since CCS is Turing powerful and finite place/transition-system are not. Still it seems worthwhile to construct net representations with a finite net structure whenever this is possible. For example, analysis methods based on S-invariants may only be applied when CCS-programs are represented as finite nets. On the other hand, a severe drawback in net theory is the lack of compositionality. What is missing is a calculus for constructing nets inductively by means of composition operators similar as in CCS and CSP, thus allowing for inductive proof techniques. This would also generate a subclass of well-structured nets which are easier to analyse ([Ko], [BRS], [Cz]). Giving a net semantics to subsets of CCS may be seen as a step in this direction, if composition operators for nets are explicitly defined, in contrast to the operational approaches mentioned above.

In this paper, we will in particular investigate a looping construct which generates net structures with cycles. This construction was first defined in [Go1] and is also used in [Tau1, Tau2], but for TCSP without parallelism inside recursion. Here it will be shown that CCS may be restricted such that this rather simple construction allows to model recursion, even in case of recursively generated parallelism. We will exclude restriction and relabelling. However, it turns out that this is not yet sufficient, because initial parallelism in sum components may not be handled. We restrict the sum operation to *guarded choice* (operands must be prefixed), as in programming notations like 78-CSP or *Occam*. Thus we obtain a compositional net semantics using finite place/transition-systems for a subclass of CCS. It is shown that the usual interleaving semantics may be retrieved from the net semantics.

Finally, partial order semantics and equivalence notions for labelled nets are discussed. This allows to derive more abstract partial order semantics for CCS from semantics based on Petri nets.

2. Syntax and interleaving semantics of a subset of CCS

We start by recalling the syntax of (pure) CCS without restriction and relabelling.
We assume a set *Act* of *action names*, denoted by $a, b, \ldots$ with the following structure:
$Act := \Lambda \cup \{\tau\}$; $\Lambda := \Delta \cup \bar{\Delta}$ where Δ is a set of *names*, $\bar{\Delta} := \{\bar{a} | a \in \Delta\}$ *(conames)*, the mapping $a \mapsto \bar{a}$ is a bijection, extended by $\bar{\bar{a}} = a$.

Completementary actions a and $\bar{a}$ are those which will be allowed to communicate in a parallel composition. The result of a communication will then be an internal action not participating in any further communication. Internal actions have the special name τ.

We also assume a set *Var* of *variables*, denoted by $x, y, \cdots$.

The set *CCS* of *CCS terms* is then defined by the following production system.

$$P ::= \underline{nil} \mid x \mid a.P \mid P|Q \mid P + Q \mid \mu x P \quad \text{where } a \in Act, x \in Var.$$

CCS terms without free occurrences of variables are called *CCS programs.*

The intuitive meaning of the operators is as follows. *nil* is not able to perform any action. $a.P$ performs a and then behaves like P. In $P|Q, P$ and Q are executed concurrently (usually modelled by arbitrary interleaving); complementary actions may be performed jointly as a τ-action. $P+Q$ behaves like P or like Q, depending on whether the initially executed action is one of P or of Q.

Next we will introduce the well-known model of labelled transition systems together with Park's notion of bisimulation equivalence [Pa,Mil]. First this will be used to give the interleaving semantics of CCS in the usual style. Later we will represent the interleaving semantics of nets also as transition systems. This allows to state the consistency result we aim at as follows. We associate transition systems with both the CCS expression and the corresponding net and show that they are bisimulation equivalent.

Definition $\mathcal{A} = (St, \rightarrow; q_o)$ is called a *(labelled) transition system* iff

- St is a set (of *states*),
- $\rightarrow \subseteq St \times Act \times St$ (*transition relation*),
- $q_o \in St$ (*initial state*).

An element $(p, a, q) \in \rightarrow$ will be written $p \xrightarrow{a} q$.

Two transition systems $\mathcal{A}_i = (St_i, \rightarrow_i; q_i)$, i=i,2, are *bisimular* ($\mathcal{A}_1 \approx \mathcal{A}_2$) if there exists a *bisimulation* R between $\mathcal{A}_1$ and $\mathcal{A}_2$, i.e. a relation $R \subseteq St_1 \times St_2$ with $(q_1, q_2) \in R$ and, for all $(p, q) \in R$,

- $p \xrightarrow{a}_1 p' \Rightarrow \exists q'$ with $q \xrightarrow{a}_2 q'$ and $(p', q') \in R$,
- $q \xrightarrow{a}_2 q' \Rightarrow \exists p'$ with $p \xrightarrow{a}_1 p'$ and $(p', q') \in R$.

With these notions, we can now give the usual operational interleaving semantics to the language defined above by associating, with each term P, a transition system $\mathcal{A}(P) = (CCS, \rightarrow; P)$ where $\rightarrow$ is given in the following table (independently of P). For explanation see [Mil] or [Ol].

prefixing	$a.P \xrightarrow{a} P$		
parallel composition	$\dfrac{P \xrightarrow{a} P'}{P\|Q \xrightarrow{a} P'\|Q}$	$\dfrac{Q \xrightarrow{a} Q'}{P\|Q \xrightarrow{a} P\|Q'}$	$\dfrac{P \xrightarrow{a} P' \; Q \xrightarrow{\bar{a}} Q'}{P\|Q \xrightarrow{\tau} P'\|Q'}$
sum	$\dfrac{P \xrightarrow{a} P'}{P+Q \xrightarrow{a} P'}$	$\dfrac{Q \xrightarrow{a} Q'}{P+Q \xrightarrow{a} Q'}$	
recursion	$\dfrac{P[\mu x P/x] \xrightarrow{a} P'}{\mu x P \xrightarrow{a} P'}$	where $[\ldots]$ denotes substitution as usual	

We derive the usual strong bisimulation equivalence for CCS terms (neglecting the distinction of internal and visible actions).

We define two CCS programs P, Q to be *(interleaving) equivalent* ($P \sim Q$) iff $\mathcal{A}(P) \approx \mathcal{A}(Q)$. As usual ([Mil]), $\sim$ is extended to CCS terms by defining, for arbitrary terms P, Q with free variables $x_1, \cdots, x_n$,

$$P \sim Q \text{ iff, for all } P_1, \ldots, P_n, \; P[P_1/x_1, \ldots, P_n/x_n] \sim Q[P_1/x_1, \ldots, P_n/x_n].$$

3. Place/transition–systems

As explained in the introduction, we need to allow arbitrarily many tokens on places to be able to model unbounded parallelism with finite nets. This is possible in place/transition–systems with infinite place capacities (often called Petri nets). For basic notions see [Re]. To be able to represent multipel occurrences of action names in CCS terms, we label the transitions by elements of *Act.*

Variables will be represented by associating elements of *Var* with certain places.

For the definition of composition operators, we distinguish *initial places* in the nets. When considering the behaviour of nets, the initial places will carry the initial marking. Recursion may cause ingoing arcs to initial places, as in the net for $\mu x(a.x|b.nil)$ shown in the introduction.

We will allow arc weights (multiple arcs) since these will arise naturally from the recursion construction.

Definition $N = (S, T; I, L)$ is called a *(labelled) place/transition–system (P/T–system)* iff

- S is a set (of *places*),
- $T \subseteq \mathbb{N}_+^S \times Act \times \mathbb{N}_+^S$ (*transitions*),

- $I \subseteq S$ *(initial places)*,
- $L : N^o --> Var$

($N^o \subseteq S$ denotes the places which are not contained in any transition preset.)

In this definition, we slightly deviate from the usual notation for nets. This turns out to be more convenient for defining composition operators. We write labelled transitions in the form *(preset, action name, postset)*. The usual notation with an explicit flow relation F may easily be derived.

The pre- and postsets of transitions are multisets over S, since we consider arc weights. $\mathbb{N}^S_+$ denotes the non-empty multisets over S (we exclude transitions with empty pre- or postset). $^\bullet t$ and $t^\bullet$ will denote the pre- and postset of t, respectively. For $t \in T$, $l(t) := pr_2(t)$ denotes the *label of t.*

Variables may only be attached to places without outgoing arcs. This corresponds to the tail recursion of CCS.

The *dynamic behaviour* of place/transition–systems may be described by defining, for any marking $M \in \mathbb{N}^S$, which transitions are enabled by M and which transitions may be executed independently in one *step.* We allow transitions to occur concurrently with themselves; this is necessary to be able to fully preserve the intuitive concurrency of CCS programs with unbounded parallelism in finite net representations. Hence steps are multisets over T.

Definition Let $N = (S, T; I, L)$, $G \in \mathbb{N}^T_+$, $M, M' \in \mathbb{N}^S$.

G is called a *step from M to M'* ($M[G\rangle M'$) iff

- for all $s \in S, M(s) \geq \sum_{t \in T} {}^\bullet t(s) \cdot G(t)$ (M *enables* G) and
- for all $s \in S, M'(s) = M(s) - \sum_{t \in T} {}^\bullet t(s) \cdot G(t) + \sum_{t \in T} t^\bullet(s) \cdot G(t)$.

For the comparison with the usual CCS–semantics, we associate now an interleaving semantics with P/T–systems by considering only occurrences of single transitions (steps $M[\{t\}\rangle M'$). Furthermore, we abstract from actual transitions but rather consider labels since we want to compare behaviours with respect to actions. We write $M[a\rangle M'$ if there exists a transition t with $M[\{t\}\rangle M'$ and $l(t) = a$. This leads to the following description of the *interleaving semantics of a (labelled) net* N by a transition system $\mathcal{A}(N)$:

$$\mathcal{A}(N) := (\mathbb{N}^S, \rightarrow; I) \text{ where } M \xrightarrow{a} M' \text{ iff } M[a\rangle M'.$$

4. Composition of place/transition–systems

In this section, composition operations for P/T–systems will be defined which correspond to the CCS operations introduced in section 2. We apply name overloading, using the same names for the net operations as on the syntactic level.

In the definition of the net operations, we will use the following notations for multisets. For $M, M' \in \mathbb{N}^S, M + M'$ denotes the *multiset union* of M and M' : $(M + M')(s) = M(s) + M'(s)$. For $M \in \mathbb{N}^S, M' \in \mathbb{N}^{S'}$ and $S \cap S' = \emptyset, M \cup M' \in \mathbb{N}^{S \cup S'}$ denotes the *composition* of M and M', obtained as the union of the graphs of M and M'. $O_S \in \mathbb{N}^S$ denotes the *empty multiset* over S. When defining the net operations, we will however use usual set notation for the pre– and postsets of transitions when no multiplicities occur.

We start by defining a very simple net called *nil.*

Definition $nil := (\{s\}, \emptyset; \{s\}, \emptyset)$, graphically  .

A very similar net serves for introducing *variables.*

Definition For $x \in Var$, let $x := (\{s\}, \emptyset; \{s\}, \{(s, x)\})$, graphically 

.

The next operation will introduce action occurrences in a net, corresponding to *prefixing* in CCS.

Definition For $a \in Act, N = (S, T; I, L)$, let $a.N := (S \uplus \{s\}, T \cup \{(\{s\}, a, I)\}; \{s\}, L)$.

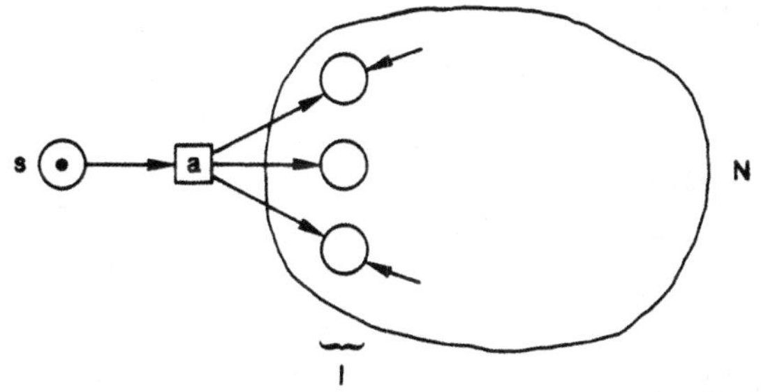

Note that names of places in nets have no significance since we do not distinguish isomorphic nets.

Parallel composition of two nets N_1 and N_2 is simply modelled by the disjoint union of N_1 and N_2, enlarged by τ–transitions for all syntactically possible communications.

Definition Let $N_i = (S_i, T_i; I_i, L_i)$, i = 1,2, w.l.o.g. $S_1 \cap S_2 = \emptyset$.

Then $N_1|N_2$ is defined by
$N_1|N_2 := (S_1 \cup S_2, T_1' \cup T_2' \cup T; I_1 \cup I_2, L_1 \cup L_2)$ where

$$T_1' := \{{}^\bullet t \cup O_{S_2}, l(t), t^\bullet \cup O_{S_2} | t \in T_1\},$$

$$T_2' := \{{}^\bullet t \cup O_{S_1}, l(t), t^\bullet \cup O_{S_1} | t \in T_2\},$$

$$T := \{({}^\bullet t_1 \cup {}^\bullet t_2, \tau, t_1^\bullet \cup t_2^\bullet) \mid t_1 \in T_1,\ t_2 \in T_2,\ l(t_1) = \overline{l(t_2)}\}.$$

Sum

The sum of two nets should behave either like the first or like the second component. This is achieved by a construction based on building the cartesian product of the initial places of the two nets ([Wi2], [GoMy]). This ensures that initial parallelism in the components is fully preserved. However this does not allow to treat nets with ingoing arcs at initially marked places [Wi2]. Furthermore, it is not clear how to define the sum for terms like $x + y$. Hence we define $+$ only for a special class of nets. We call a P/T–system $N = (S, T; I, L)$ *in normal form* if $I = {}^\circ N$ (${}^\circ N \subseteq S$ denotes the set of places without ingoing arcs). We call a variable x *guarded in* N if $L^{-1}(x) \cap {}^\circ N = \emptyset$. N is called *well-formed* if all variables are guarded in N.

The restricted language considered in the next section will ensure that operands of $+$ generate always well-formed nets in normal form. Actually, the construction reduces to a much simpler form (gluing together the single initial places) for guarded choice. Still, we give the general definition here, since we will use it for the counter-example at the end of this section.

Definition Let $N_i = (S_i, T_i; I_i, L_i)$, i = 1,2, w.l.o.g. $S_1 \cap S_2 = \emptyset$.

Let N_1 and N_2 be well-formed and in normal form. Then $N_1 + N_2$ is defined by

$$N_1 + N_2 := (S_1' \cup S_2' \cup I, T_1' \cup T_2'; I, L_1 \cup L_2)$$

where $I := I_1 \times I_2,\ S_1' := S_1 \setminus I_1,\ S_2' := S_2 \setminus I_2$,

$$T_1' := \{(({}^\bullet t)', l(t), t^\bullet \cup O_{S_2' \cup I}) \mid t \in T_1,\ ({}^\bullet t)'(s) = \begin{cases} {}^\bullet t(pr_1(s)) & \text{iff} \quad s \in I, \\ {}^\bullet t(s) & \text{iff} \quad s \in S_1', \\ 0 & \text{otherwise} \end{cases} \},$$

$$T_2' := \{(({}^\bullet t)', l(t), t^\bullet \cup O_{S_1' \cup I}) \mid t \in T_2,\ ({}^\bullet t)'(s) = \begin{cases} {}^\bullet t(pr_2(s)) & \text{iff} \quad s \in I, \\ {}^\bullet t(s) & \text{iff} \quad s \in S_2', \\ 0 & \text{otherwise} \end{cases} \}.$$

For example, let N_1 = 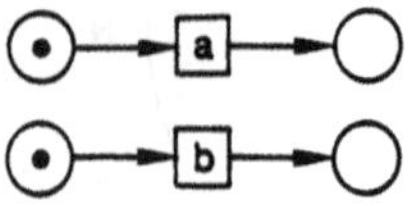

and N_2 = 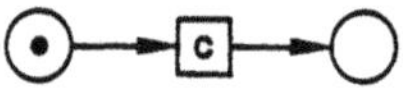

Then $N_1 + N_2$ = 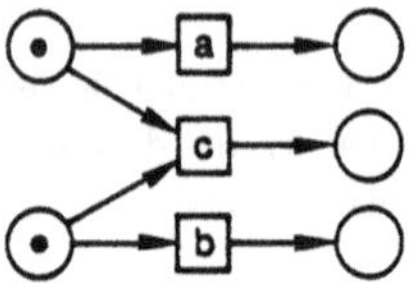

Recursion

Essentially, $\mu x N$ will be obtained from the P/T–system N by removing all places labelled by x and replacing each of them by arcs to all initial places of N (note that only places without outgoing arcs may carry variables). For this construction, we will require that N is well-formed.

However, this is not sufficient to capture the intended behaviour, since new communication possibilities may arise when recursion generates parallelism. Hence we need to first add all syntactically possible communications for recursion.

Definition Let $N = (S, T; I, L)$.

The *(syntactical) completion* of $N, V(N)$, is defined by
$V(N) := (S, T \cup T'; I, L)$ where

$T' := \{({}^\bullet t_1 +^\bullet t_2, \tau, t_1^\bullet + t_2^\bullet) | t_1, t_2 \in T, l(t_1) = \overline{l(t_2)}\}$.

Now we may implement recursion as explained above, using the complete version $V(N)$ instead of N.

Definition Let N be a P/T–system, let be N well-formed.

Let $V(N) = (S, T; I, L)$.
Then $\mu x N := (S', T'; I, L\lceil S')$ where $\lceil$ denotes restriction,
$S' := S \setminus L^{-1}(x)$,
$T' := \{({}^\bullet t\lceil S', l(t), (t^\bullet + \sum_{s \in L^{-1}(x)} t^\bullet(s) \cdot I)\lceil S') \mid t \in T\}$.

The definition of T' needs some explanation. All transitions of T are adopted with the following modification. $t^\bullet$ is changed by adding the appropriate arcs to initial places, depending on the number of x–labelled places in $t^\bullet$.

Note that all operations we have introduced preserve finiteness of P/T–systems (a P/T–system is *finite* if $S \cup T$ is finite). This attempt of representing of recursive expressions by finite structures was inspired by [Mi2] where similar constructions are presented for the sequential case.

However, it is not possible to obtain a correct semantics for the sublanguage of CCS defined in section 2 with these natural and rather simple operations.

Consider the CCS program $P = \mu x((a.nil|b.x) + c.nil)$. The corresponding P/T–system would be

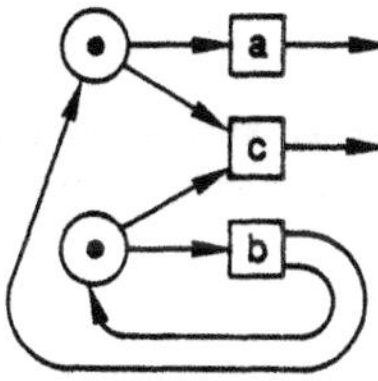

Now consider the following derivation (using the rules given in section 2).

$$\mu x((a.nil|b.x) + c.nil) \xrightarrow{b} a.nil|\mu x((a.nil|b.x) + c.nil)$$

$$\overset{\text{with the "inner" } a}{\longrightarrow} a.nil|nil|b.\mu x((a.nil|b.x) + c.nil)$$

Next only a or b is possible.
Trying to simulate this in the net, we have to fire b and then a and reach a marking where c is enabled.

The problem lies in the initial parallelism of + components inside recursion. No correct representation is possible in this case without representing some actions in the CCS expression by more than one transition. It is unclear whether any finite net for P with a precise representation of the (intuitive) partially ordered behaviour may be given.

We will show next that the language may be restricted in a natural way to avoid the problem. Then the simple construction considered here does indeed model recursion correctly.

5. CCS with guarded choice

In this section, we consider a restricted language where operands of + are prefixed.
Let the set $RCCS \subseteq CCS$ be defined by the following production system.

$$P ::= nil \mid x \mid a.P \mid P|Q \mid a.P + b.Q \mid \mu x P$$
$$x \in Var, a, b \in Act, \text{ P is well–formed in } \mu x P$$

A variable x is *guarded* in a term P if all free occurrences of x are in the scope of a prefixing operator $a.(\ldots)$. P is *well-formed* if all variables are guarded in P.

The restriction to guarded variables in recursion is necessary for the net construction for recursion. (The restriction to binary choice has no significance.)

As before, the *interleaving semantics* of a term P is given by the transition system $\mathcal{A}(P) = (RCCS, \rightarrow; P)$. $\rightarrow$ is defined by the table in section 2, observing that $\rightarrow$ does not lead outside $RCCS$.

The *net semantics* of a term $P \in RCCS$ is obtained by interpreting the syntactical operations in P by the corresponding net operations, yielding a finite P/T–system $N(P)$. If P is a program (no free variables) then $N(P)$ is a usual P/T–system without any variables at places.

We will now show that the given net semantics is correct in the sense that the usual interleaving semantics may be retrieved in the net. Formally, we will show that $\mathcal{A}(P)$ and $\mathcal{A}(N(P))$ are bisimular.

We will prove this result by induction on the structure of P. For the inductive step, it turns out that we need a more general hypothesis to handle recursion. We observe that recursion generates multiplicities of the initial marking.
This leads to comparing $\underbrace{P|\cdots|P}_{k\ times}$ with the transition system $\mathcal{A}(V(N(P)), k) = (\mathbb{N}^S, \rightarrow; k\cdot I)$ where $M \xrightarrow{a} M'$ iff $M[a\rangle M'$ as before, and $k \cdot I$ denotes the marking with k tokens on each initial place.

$V(\ldots)$ adds possible communications as for recursion.

Since we will have to consider expressions containing free variables, we need to refine the notion of bisimulation slightly by considering unguarded variables. For this, we need the following representation of terms: Any $P \in RCCS$ may be written as $\widetilde{P}\,\underbrace{|x|\cdots|x}_{m\ times}$ such that x is guarded in $\widetilde{P}$, using only commutativity and associativity of $|$ and that nil is neutral for $|$. m is unique and $\widetilde{P}$ is unique up to these operations. m

will be denoted by $P(x)$ and $P \setminus x$ will denote an arbitrary representative for $\tilde{P}$. (Here and in the sequel we use the convention that $\underbrace{P|\ldots|P}_{m} = nil$ for $m = 0$.)

Correspondingly, we use the following notations for markings of P/T-systems. For a given marking M and $x \in Var, M(x)$ denotes the total number of tokens on x-labelled places and $M \setminus x$ denotes the marking obtained by removing all tokens from x-labelled places.

Theorem Let $P \in RCCS$.

There exist bisimulations R_k between $\mathcal{A}(V(N(P)), k)$ and $\mathcal{A}(\underbrace{P|\ldots|P}_{k})$, for all $k \in I\!N$, with

$(M,Q) \in R_k \Rightarrow \forall x \in Var : M(x) = Q(x)$ and $(M,Q) \in R_k, (M',Q') \in R_{k'} \Rightarrow (M + M', Q|Q') \in R_{k+k'}$.

Proof by induction on the structure of P.

We show here only the construction of the bisimulations R_k for the case that P is a recursive term $\mu x P'$ (the full proof is given in [Go2]).

$$\text{So let } P = \mu x P', \quad V(N(P')) = (S', T'; I, L), \quad V(N(P)) = (S, T; I, L\lceil S).$$

By the induction hypothesis, there exists, for each $m \in I\!N$, a bisimulation R'_m between $\mathcal{A}(V(N(P')), m)$ and $\mathcal{A}(\underbrace{P'|\ldots|P'}_{m})$.

For each $k \in I\!N$, we now define the bisimulation R_k between $\mathcal{A}(V(N(P)), k)$ and $\mathcal{A}(\underbrace{P|\ldots|P}_{k})$ inductively as follows.

We define relations $R^i_k, i \geq 0$, by

$$R^o_k := R'_k$$

$$R^{i+1}_k := \{(M,Q) \mid M = M' \setminus x + M'', Q = (Q' \setminus x)|Q'', (M',Q') \in R^i_k, (M'',Q'') \in R'_{M'(x)}\}.$$

Then $R_k := \bigcup_{i \in I\!N} \hat{R}^i_k$ where $\hat{R}^i_k := \{\hat{M}, \hat{Q})|(M,Q) \in R^i_k, M(x) = 0, \hat{M} := M\lceil S, \hat{Q} \sim Q[P/x]\}$. ∎

This theorem implies the consistency result, using that $\mathcal{A}(V(N), 1) \approx \mathcal{A}(N)$.

Corollary For $P \in RCCS$, $\mathcal{A}(N(P)) \approx \mathcal{A}(P)$.

6. Partial order semantics of P/T-systems

In this section we investigate how the intuitive causal dependencies in a CCS program are expressible via the net semantics.

In [DDM2], a C/E-system semantics for CCS is presented, and it is shown that the intuitive parallelism of CCS programs is fully preserved in this semantics. For this, a *step transition system* semantics for CCS is given, where not only single occurrences of actions but rather multisets of actions are considered in the transition relation. A similar result could be shown for our approach (the bisimulation relations R_k, constructed in the proof of the theorem in section 5, are even step bisimulations).

This shows that the intuitive parallelism in CCS programs is not restricted in our net semantics. However, step semantics do not fully reflect the causality structure of CCS programs or nets. For example, $P_1 = a.nil|b.nil$ and $P_2 = (a.nil|b.nil) + (a.b.nil)$ are identified in step semantics ([BoCa]). A semantics fully capturing the intuitive causalities in CCS programs is obtained by adopting an approach based on *partial orders*.

C.A. Petri has suggested to represent the behaviour of non-sequential systems by means of partial orders [Pe]. For nets, this was formalised by defining *processes* of systems as mappings from a particular kind of nets, called *causal nets* (or *occurrence nets*), to the system (see e.g. [Re]).

Causal nets are acyclic nets with only unbranched places. We write causal nets as $K = (B, E)$ where $E \subseteq \mathcal{P}_+(B) \times Act \times \mathcal{P}_+(B)$ (*events*). (Since we will be interested in the partial order of action occurrences, we consider causal nets with events labelled by elements of Act). We require that K is *founded* (every element has only finitely many predecessors). Corresponding to the notations for P/T-systems, ${}^\bullet e$ and $e^\bullet$ denote the pre- and postset of $e \in E$, respectively; ${}^\circ K$ denotes the initial conditions of K.

Furthermore we use the following notation.

Let X, Y be sets, $f : X \to Y$.
For $A \in \mathbb{N}^X$, let $f(A) \in \mathbb{N}^Y$ be defined by $f(A)(y) := \sum_{x \in f^{-1}(y)} A(x)$ (the *multiset image of* A).

Using these notations, we obtain the following reformulation of the notion of process for P/T-systems of [GoRe]. We consider P/T-systems without variables (as obtained for CCS programs) and with arbitrary initial marking, M_o.

Definition Let $N = (S, T; M_o)$ be a P/T-system.
Let $K = (B, E)$ be a causal net, $p : B \cup E \to S \cup T$ with $\forall x \in B \cup E : p(x) \in S \Leftrightarrow x \in B$ and $\forall e \in E : pr_2(p(e)) = pr_2(e)$ (labels are respected).
Then p is called a *process of* N iff

- $p({}^\circ K)$ is a marking reachable from M_o in N and
- $\forall e \in E : p({}^\bullet e) = {}^\bullet p(e)$ and $p(e^\bullet) = p(e)^\bullet$.

The possible partial orders of action occurrences in a P/T-system (*pomsets* over *Act*) may now easily be derived from its set of processes. The use of pomsets (or *partial words*) for describing net semantics was proposed by [Gra].

The notion of process for P/T-systems has provoked some criticism in the sense that it is not "abstract enough" (see e.g. [Be]).The problem is that the causal dependencies in processes sometimes show which of the "indistinguishable" tokens on a place has been chosen for firing a transition. However, it turns out that this property allows in our approach to derive a precise representation of causalities in CCS programs from the P/T-system semantics.

Example

Let $P = \mu x(a.(x|b.x))$. $N(P) =$

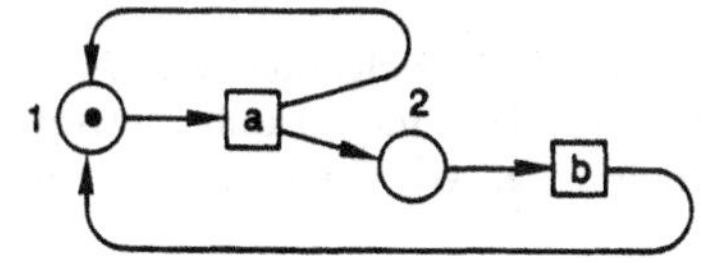

Consider the processes

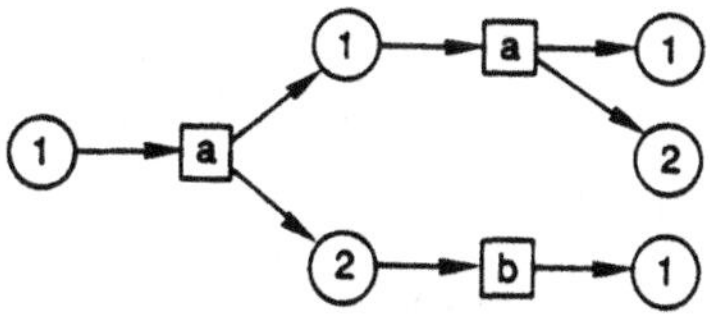

and

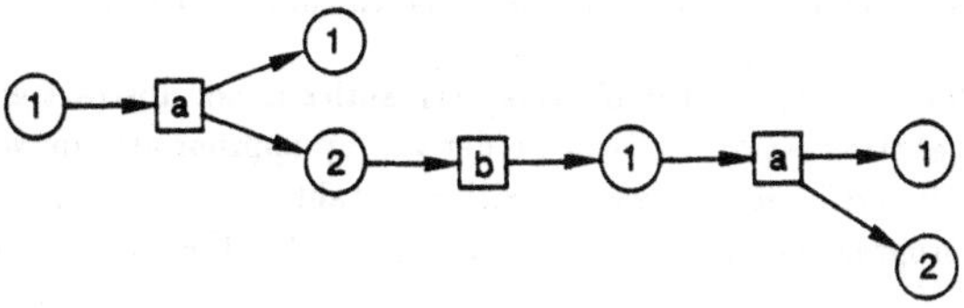

The corresponding pomsets are

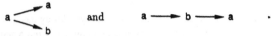

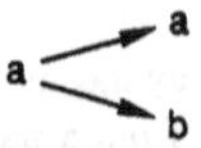

and $a \to b \to a$.

This corresponds to two derivation possibilities for the sequence *aba* in CCS, which differ in their intuitive causality structure:

$$P \xrightarrow{a} P \mid b.P \xrightarrow{b} P \mid P \cdots.$$

Next there are two possibilities of executing a, in the left or in the right component of $P|P$. Only in the left component, a may be executed independently of b (intuitively).

We have demonstrated so far that the pomset semantics does indeed represent the causal dependencies in a net and, via the net semantics, in a CCS program. However, for labelled nets, the set of all pomsets of a given system does not show where conflicts are resolved. The nets for $P_1 = a.(b.nil + c.nil)$ and $P_2 = a.b.nil + a.c.nil$ are indistinguishable in pomset semantics. Pomset semantics may be seen as a *linear time* semantics in the terminology of interleaving semantics. The usual transition system of CCS is a *branching time* semantics where choices are explicitly represented.

A very precise "branching time" semantics for nets is given by the notion of *unfolding*. Unfolding a net yields a tree–like structure where choices are represented by branched places. Processes may be retrieved from this representation as "paths" in this "tree".

The unfolding of a one–safe net was defined inductively by Winskel [Wi3], a similar definition is given in [GlVa]. The generalisation to P/T–systems has not yet been formalised. It should be consistent with the process definition as presented above.

Similar as for processes, we may abstract from conditions in unfoldings. We then obtain *event structures* [Wi3] where the events are labelled by elements of *Act*. As synchronisation trees they give a very precise semantics, for example distinguishing expressions like P and $P + P$. An equivalence notion is needed to obtain a more abstract semantics. So we finally suggest a semantics lying between the pomset semantics and the event structure semantics which does exhibit choice but still identifies expressions like P and $P + P$. It is based on transition systems labelled by partial orders as in [BoCa] and was introduced similar as here in [GlVa].

With a P/T–system $N = (S, T; M_o)$, we associate the *partial order transition system*, $\mathcal{A}_p(N) = (\mathbb{N}^S, \to; M_o)$ where, for $M, M' \in \mathbb{N}^S$,

$M \xrightarrow{u} M' :\Leftrightarrow$ there exists a (finite) process $p : K \to N$
with $p({}^\circ K) = M, p(K^\circ) = M'$ and u is the pomset derived from p.

This yields an equivalence notion for nets based on partial orders by defining a *partial order bisimulation* $\approx_p$ in the canonical way.

It must be left for further investigations which partial order semantics and equivalence notions are adequate for nets. Many problems may already be treated by interleaving semantics or by step semantics. There is certainly a tradeoff between the precision of the semantics and their complexity in proofs.

7. Discussion

We conclude by evaluating the results of this paper under two aspects.

- What is gained for developing a partial order semantics for full CCS?

- What are the consequences for the development of a compositional calculus of nets?

A criticism against Petri net semantics for CCS is that the obtained semantics is not abstract enough [He]. In section 6, we discussed how a more abstract semantics can be derived by appropriate equivalence notions for nets. This problem needs further investigation. However, with a suitable equivalence notion, it would be possible to associate with a CCS program not just one particular net but rather an equivalence class of nets. This would unify different approaches based on different net models since these equivalence classes would combine representations as one–safe nets ([DDM2]) with occurrence net representations and, if possible, finite representations as constructed here.

For a compositional calculus of nets, the insights on the interplay of concurrency, choice and recursion will help to find appropriate composition operators. We have investigated a simple looping construct. It turned out that it is possible to model recursion with this simple construction when the +–operator is simplified. The restriction to guarded choice seems natural (it is satisfied in languges like *"concrete" CSP* or *Occam*).

The parallel composition operators of CCS is less attractive in our framework since we are not able to enforce communication by restriction. However, the parallel composition operator of TCSP as considered in [Ol] can not be modelled in finite nets.

Example

Consider $P = \mu x(a.b.(x\|_{\{b\}}x)$ where $\|_{\{b\}}$ denotes parallel composition with enforced communication for b. P may be represented by the infinite net

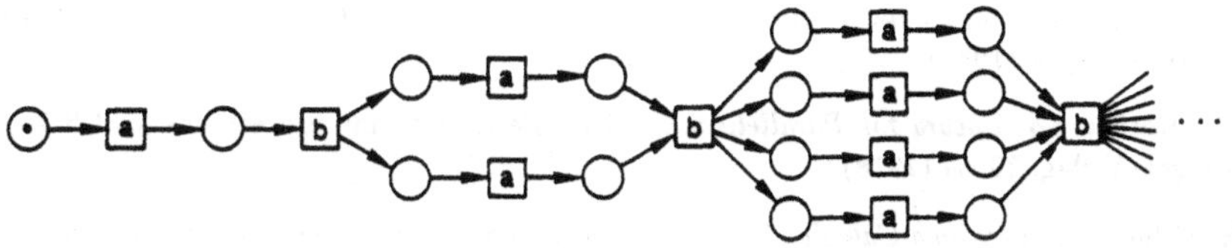

This causality structure can not be represented in a finite net.

A simple modification of the CCS parallel composition operator would be to force actions to communicate when they have a syntactical correspondent. However this has the effect that the associativity of | is lost.

Acknowledgements

Dirk Taubner has contributed to this paper by many critical and helpful remarks. Wolfgang Reisig helped me by many patient discussions and critical remarks. Thanks to Gertrud Jacobs for the careful preparation of the manuscript and to Elisabeth Münch for the beautiful drawings.

References

[**Be**] E. Best: *In Quest of a Morphism,* Petri Net Newsletter 18, 14–18 (1984).

[**BoCa**] G. Boudol, I. Castellani: *On the Semantics of Concurrency: Partial Orders and Transition Systems,* in: proceedings TAPSOFT '87, Vol. 1, LNCS 249, Springer–Verlag (1987).

[**BRS**] G. Boudol, G. Roucairol, R. de Simone: *Petri Nets and Algebraic Calculi of Processes,* INRIA, Rapports de Recherche No. 292 (1984).

[**Ci**] F. de Cindio, et al.: *Milner's Communicating Systems and Petri Nets,* in: selected papers from the 3rd European Workshop on Application and Theory of Petri Nets, Springer Informatik Fachberichte 66 (1983).

[**Cz**] L. Czaja: *Making Nets Abstract and Structured,* Advances in Petri Nets 85, LNCS 222, Springer–Verlag, 181–202 (1986).

[**DDM1**] P. Degano, R. De Nicola, U. Montanari: *A New Operational Semantics for CCS based on Condition/Event Systems*", nota interna B4-42, Dept. of Computer Science, Univ. Pisa (1986).

[**DDM2**] P. Degano, R. De Nicola, U. Montanari: *A Distributed Operational Semantics for CCS Based on Condition/Event Systems,* Nota Interna B4-21, Istituto di Elibaratione dell 'Informazione, C.N.R, Pisa (1987).

[**GlVa**] R.J. van Glabbeek, F.W. Vaandrager: *Petri Net Models for Algebraic Theories of Concurrency,* in: proceedings PARLE, Vol. II, LNCS 259, Springer-Verlag (1987).

[**GoMy**] U. Goltz, A. Mycroft: *On the Relationship of CCS and Petri Nets,* in: proceedings ICALP 84, LNCS 172, Springer-Verlag (1984).

[**GoRe**] U. Goltz, W. Reisig: *"The Non-sequential Behaviour of Petri Nets,* in: Information and Control, Vol. 57, Nos. 2-3, (1983).

[**Gra**] J. Grabowski: *On Partial Languages,* Fundamenta Informaticae IV.2, 427-498 (1981).

[**He**] M. Hennessy: *Axiomatising Finite Concurrent Processes,* University of Sussex, Computer Science, Report No. 4/84 (1987).

[**Ko**] V.E. Kotov: *An Algebra for Parallelism based on Petri Nets,* in: proceedings MFCS 78, LNCS 64, Springer-Verlag, 39-54 (1978).

[**Mi1**] R. Milner: *Lectures on a Calculus for Communicating Systems,* in: Seminar on Concurrency, Carnegie-Mellon Univ., Pittsburgh 1984, LNCS 197, Springer-Verlag (1985).

[**Ol**] E.-R. Olderog: *Operational Petri Net Semantics for CCSP,* in: Advances in Petri Nets 1987, LNCS 266, Springer-Verlag (1987).

[**Pa**] D. Park: *Concurrency and Automata on Infinite Sequences,* in: proceedings 5th GI Conf. on Theoretical Computer Science, LNCS 104, Springer-Verlag (1981).

[**Pe**] C.A. Petri: *Non-Sequential Processes,* Internal Report 74-07, GMD, Institut für Informationssystemforschung (1977).

[**Re**] W. Reisig: *Petri Nets,* EATCS Monographs on Theoretical Computer Science Vol. 4, Springer-Verlag (1985).

[**Tau1**] D. Taubner: *Theoretical CSP and Formal Languages,* report TUM-I8706, TU München, Institut fü Informatik (1987)

[**Tau2**] D. Taubner: *A Step Failures Consistent Transition of Regular TCSP to Finite and Safe Petri Nets,* manuscript (1987)

[**Wi1**] G. Winskel: *Event Structure Semantics for CCS and Related Languages,* in: proceedings ICALP 82, LNCS 224, Springer-Verlag (1982).

[**Wi2**] G. Winskel: *A New Definition of Morphism on Petri Nets,* in: proceedings 1st STACS, LNCS 166, Springer-Verlag (1984)

[**Wi3**] G. Winskel: *Event Structures,* in: Petri Nets: Applications and Relationships to Other Models of Concurrency, LNCS 255, Springer-Verlag (1987).

A Taxonomy of Fairness and Temporal Logic Problems for Petri Nets*

Rodney R. Howell, Louis E. Rosier
Dept. of Computer Sciences
The University of Texas at Austin
Austin, TX 78712

Hsu-Chun Yen
Dept. of Computer Science
Iowa State University
Ames, IA 50011

1 Introduction

In the specification and analysis of concurrent systems, some notion of fairness is often necessary to exclude from consideration certain computations which prevent particular events from occurring, even though these events may be possible infinitely often. Many definitions of fairness have been proposed (see, e.g., [1,2,3,4,7,12,13,18]), and each has its merit in particular applications. Several versions of fairness have been defined (or adapted) for Petri nets [1,2,3,4,18], a powerful formalism often employed to model concurrent systems [17]. Decidability issues concerning fairness in Petri nets were considered in [2,3,21]. One problem examined in these papers is the fair nontermination problem; i.e., for a certain definition of fairness, does there exist an infinite fair computation? Though the decidablity of a number of these problems has been determined, only a few rough complexity bounds have been given for those known to be decidable [3]. In [8], we examined the complexity of the fair nontermination problem for conflict-free Petri nets with respect to several definitions of fairness. In this paper, we extend this study to general Petri nets, examining the 24 versions of fairness presented in [1,2,3,4,7,12,13,18]. The results of this study are summarized in a table in Section 5.

In the study of Petri nets, a scarcity of knowledge concerning computational complexity is by no means unique to the fair nontermination problem. For example, the precise complexity of the reachability problem has remained elusive for many years. For this problem, the most efficient algorithm is not primitive recursive [11,15], whereas the best known lower bound is exponential space [14]. We show in this paper that there is a close relationship between the reachability problem and several of the fair nontermination problems. In particular, we show several of these problems to be equivalent to reachability; i.e., their complexities are equivalent to that of reachability with respect to PTIME many-one reductions. (Throughout this paper, we will use the word "equivalent" in this sense when referring to decision problems.) Thus, to determine the precise complexity of any of these problems (modulo PTIME reductions), it is sufficient to consider only the reachability problem. For examples of other (more classical) problems known to be equivalent to reachability, see [17].

Clearly, since some versions of the fair nontermination problem have been shown to be undecidable [2,3], not all versions are equivalent to reachability. Rather, one of the main points of this paper is that most versions are either highly undecidable (in particular, complete for Σ_1^1 — the first level of the analytical hierarchy), equivalent to reachability, or equivalent to boundedness (i.e., exponential space complete with respect to PTIME many-one reductions). In some sense, it is easier to show problems to be highly undecidable or equivalent to boundedness than it is to show equivalence to reachability. The reason for this is that highly undecidable problems and exponential space complete problems as a whole are fairly well understood. The reachability problem, however, is not well understood, as is evidenced by the lack of knowledge concerning its complexity. Hence, as a way to overcome this difficulty, we develop in this

*This work was supported in part by U. S. Office of Naval Research Grant No. N00014-86-K-0763 and National Science Foundation Grant No. CCR-8711579.

paper a framework based upon temporal logic for reducing fair nontermination problems to the reachability problem.

The remainder of the paper is organized as follows. In Section 2, we give the basic definitions of Petri nets and temporal logic. In Section 3, we develop the logics that are later used to show various types of fair nontermination problems to be equivalent to reachability. In Section 4, we examine the fair nontermination problem for the 24 types of fairness. In most cases, we are able to show the problems to be either highly undecidable, equivalent to reachability, or equivalent to boundedness. We conclude in Section 5 with a summary of our results and a discussion of open problems. No detailed proofs are given in this paper. The interested reader should consult [10].

2 Definitions

A *Petri Net* (PN, for short) is a tuple (P,T,φ,μ_0), where P is a finite set of *places*, T is a finite set of *transitions*, φ is a *flow function* $\varphi : (P \times T) \cup (T \times P) \rightarrow N$, and μ_0 is the *initial marking* $\mu_0 : P \rightarrow N$, where N is the set of natural numbers. A *marking* is a mapping $\mu : P \rightarrow N$. We often establish an order on the places, $p_1,\ldots,p_k$, and designate a marking μ as a vector in N^k, where the ith component represents $\mu(p_i)$. A transition $t \in T$ is *enabled* at a marking μ iff for every $p \in P$, $\varphi(p,t) \leq \mu(p)$. A transition t may *fire* at a marking μ if t is enabled at μ. We then write $\mu \xrightarrow{t} \mu'$, where $\mu'(p) = \mu(p) - \varphi(p,t) + \varphi(t,p)$ for all $p \in P$. A sequence of transitions $\sigma = t_1 \ldots t_n$ is a *firing sequence* from μ_0 iff $\mu_0 \xrightarrow{t_1} \mu_1 \xrightarrow{t_2} \ldots \xrightarrow{t_n} \mu_n$ for some sequence of markings $\mu_1,\ldots,\mu_n$. We also write $\mu_0 \xrightarrow{\sigma} \mu_n$, and denote $t_1 \ldots t_j$ by $\sigma[j]$ for $1 \leq j \leq n$. We extend these notions to infinite firing sequences in the obvious way.

For a PN $\mathcal{P} = (P,T,\varphi,\mu_0)$, the *reachability set* of $\mathcal{P}$ is the set $R(\mathcal{P}) = \{\mu \mid \mu_0 \xrightarrow{\sigma} \mu \text{ for some } \sigma\}$. Given a marking μ of $\mathcal{P}$, the *reachability problem* (RP) is to determine whether $\mu \in R(\mathcal{P})$. The *boundedness problem* (BP) is to determine whether $R(\mathcal{P})$ is finite. Throughout this paper, we will define several fairness properties for firing sequences. Given a fairness property x, the *nontermination problem with respect to x* (NTP^x) is to determine whether there is an infinite firing sequence σ in $\mathcal{P}$ that satisfies x.

A *labeled Petri net* is a triple $\mathcal{P}=(\mathcal{P}_1,\Sigma,h)$, where $\mathcal{P}_1=(P,T,\varphi,\mu_0)$ is a PN, Σ is a finite set of labels, and $h : T \rightarrow \Sigma \cup \{\epsilon\}$ is a labeling function. We also extend $h : T^* \rightarrow \Sigma^*$ by $h(\epsilon)=\epsilon$ and $h(\sigma t)=h(\sigma)h(t)$. Given a marking μ of $\mathcal{P}$, we define the *terminal language of $\mathcal{P}$ with respect to μ* as $L^t(\mathcal{P},\mu) = \{h(\sigma) \mid \mu_0 \xrightarrow{\sigma} \mu\}$.

Let $\mathcal{N}$ denote the set of all PNs, $\mathcal{T}^*$ denote all finite firing sequences of nets in $\mathcal{N}$, $\mathcal{T}^\omega$ denote all infinite firing sequences of nets in $\mathcal{N}$, and $\mathcal{T}^\infty = \mathcal{T}^* \cup \mathcal{T}^\omega$. A *predicate* is a partial function $q : \mathcal{N} \times \mathcal{T}^\infty \times N \rightarrow$ {true, false}. For $\mathcal{P} \in \mathcal{N}$, σ a (finite or infinite) firing sequence of $\mathcal{P}$, and $n \in N$, we say $<\mathcal{P},\sigma,n> \models q$ iff $q(\mathcal{P},\sigma,n) =$ true. A *well-formed formula* (wff) is either a predicate or of the form $\neg f$, $f \wedge g$, $\mathbf{X}f$, or $f\ \mathbf{U}\ g$, where f and g are wffs. For a firing sequence σ of $\mathcal{P}$ and wffs f and g, we say:

- $<\mathcal{P},\sigma,n> \models \neg f$ iff not $(<\mathcal{P},\sigma,n> \models f)$;
- $<\mathcal{P},\sigma,n> \models \mathbf{X}f$ iff $<\mathcal{P},\sigma,n+1> \models f$;
- $<\mathcal{P},\sigma,n> \models f\ \mathbf{U}\ g$ iff $\exists\, r > n$ such that $<\mathcal{P},\sigma,r> \models g$ and $\forall\, s, n < s < r, <\mathcal{P},\sigma,s> \models f$;
- $<\mathcal{P},\sigma,n> \models f \wedge g$ iff $<\mathcal{P},\sigma,n> \models f$ and $<\mathcal{P},\sigma,n> \models g$.

We also use the following abbreviations: $f \vee g \equiv \neg(\neg f \wedge \neg g)$; $f \supset g \equiv \neg f \vee g$; $\mathbf{F}f \equiv \text{true}\ \mathbf{U}\ f$; $\mathbf{G}f \equiv \neg\mathbf{F}\neg f$.

We say that $\mathcal{P}$ is a *(finite) model* for f iff there is an infinite (finite, respectively) firing sequence σ in $\mathcal{P}$ such that $<\mathcal{P},\sigma,0> \models f$. Let $\mathcal{F}$ be a set of wffs. The *(finite) model checking problem with respect to $\mathcal{F}$*, denoted $MCP(\mathcal{F})$ ($FMCP(\mathcal{F})$, respectively), is to determine whether a given PN $\mathcal{P}$ is a (finite) model for a given formula $f \in \mathcal{F}$. Let Q be a set of predicates. We then define

- $\mathcal{L}(Q) = \{f \mid f \text{ is a wff using predicates from } Q\}$;

- $\tilde{\mathcal{L}}$(Q,F,X) = {f | f is a wff using predicates from Q and the operators **F**, **X**, $\wedge, \vee$, and $\neg$, such that $\neg$ is used only on predicates}; and

- $\mathcal{L}^\infty$(Q) = {**GF**f | f is a Boolean combination of predicates from Q}.

For a PN $\mathcal{P}$=(P,T,φ,μ_0), a wff f, and a natural number n, we define the *model language of* $\mathcal{P}$ *with respect to f and n* as $L^m(\mathcal{P}$,f,n) = {σ | σ is finite and $<\mathcal{P},\sigma$,n$>\models$ f}. A set $\mathcal{F}$ of wffs is said to be *RP-decidable* iff for all f $\in \mathcal{F}, \mathcal{P} \in \mathcal{N}$, we can construct in PTIME a labeled PN $\mathcal{P}'=(\mathcal{P}_1',\Sigma$,h), $\mathcal{P}_1'=(P',T',\varphi',\mu_0')$, $P'=p_1,...,p_k$, and a marking μ' on $p_1,...,p_{k-1}$ such that for all n $\in$ N, $L^m(\mathcal{P}$,f,n) = $L^t(\mathcal{P}',(\mu'$,n)). We will refer to p_k as the *marker*.

3 A temporal logic for Petri nets

In this section, we will present a temporal logic for reasoning about Petri nets such that if $\mathcal{F}$ is the set of all wffs in the logic, then FMCP($\mathcal{F}$) $\equiv_{PTIME}$ RP. The logic will be $\tilde{\mathcal{L}}$(Q,F,X) for a set Q of predicates to be defined later. Even though FMCP($\tilde{\mathcal{L}}$(Q,F,X)) is no harder than RP, Q will contain a sufficient variety of predicates to provide a powerful mechanism for showing fair nontermination problems to be equivalent to RP. Furthermore, certain restrictions of the logic provide interesting extensions to the results shown in [8]. The first extension we show is that MCP($\tilde{\mathcal{L}}$(Q',F,X)) $\equiv_{PTIME}$ RP, where Q' is the set of predicates from the logic developed in [8]. The second extension is that MCP($\mathcal{L}^\infty$(Q')) $\equiv_{PTIME}$ RP. Both of these extensions may be considered refinements of the main result of this section — that FMCP($\tilde{\mathcal{L}}$(Q,F,X)) $\equiv_{PTIME}$ RP. All of these logics will be used in the next section to show various fair nontermination problems to be equivalent to RP. The main result of this section may therefore be viewed as an umbrella under which a number of the subsequent results in this paper are derived.

In order to show that FMCP($\tilde{\mathcal{L}}$(Q,F,X)) $\leq_{PTIME}$ RP, we first show that the reduction holds for any RP-decidable set of predicates whose negations are also RP-decidable. We will then define Q and show that both Q and $\tilde{Q}$ = {$\neg$q | q $\in$ Q} are RP-decidable. We first state the following lemma, which follows immediately from the definition of the terminal language of a labeled PN.

Lemma 3.1: Given a labeled PN $\mathcal{P}=(\mathcal{P}_1,\Sigma$,h) and a marking μ, $L^t(\mathcal{P},\mu) \neq \emptyset$ iff $\mu \in R(\mathcal{P}_1)$.

We can now give the following lemma, relating the FMCP to the RP.

Lemma 3.2: For a set of wffs $\mathcal{F}$, if $\mathcal{F}$ is RP-decidable, then FMCP($\mathcal{F}$) $\leq_{PTIME}$ RP.

Proof. Given an RP-decidable set $\mathcal{F}$ of wffs, let f $\in \mathcal{F}$, and let $\mathcal{P}$ be an arbitrary PN. Since $\mathcal{F}$ is RP-decidable, we can construct in PTIME a labeled PN $\mathcal{P}'=(\mathcal{P}_1',\Sigma$,h) and a marking μ such that $L^t(\mathcal{P}',\mu)$ = $L^m(\mathcal{P}$,f,0). Then $\mathcal{P}$ is a finite model for f iff $L^m(\mathcal{P}$,f,0) $\neq \emptyset$ iff $L^t(\mathcal{P}',\mu) \neq \emptyset$ iff $\mu \in R(\mathcal{P}_1')$ (from Lemma 3.1). Therefore, FMCP($\mathcal{F}$) $\leq_{PTIME}$ RP.

□

The following theorem now gives a framework for defining our set of predicates.

Theorem 3.1: If a set of predicates Q is RP-decidable and $\tilde{Q}$={$\neg$q | q $\in$ Q} is RP-decidable, then FMCP($\tilde{\mathcal{L}}$(Q,F,X)) $\leq_{PTIME}$ RP.

The proof of the above theorem involves showing that for any f $\in \tilde{\mathcal{L}}$(Q,F,X) and any PN $\mathcal{P}$, we can construct in PTIME a labeled PN $\mathcal{P}'$ and a submarking μ such that for all n$\in$N, $L^t(\mathcal{P}',(\mu$,n)) = $L^m(\mathcal{P}$,f,n). The theorem then follows from Lemma 3.2.

We are now ready to define our predicates. For a PN $\mathcal{P}$ = (P,T,φ,μ_0), p $\in$ P, t $\in$ T, c,n $\in$ N, and a <u>finite</u> firing sequence σ, let:

- $<\mathcal{P},\sigma$,n$>\models$ ge(p,c) iff $\mu_0 \overset{\sigma[n]}{\rightarrow} \mu$ and $\mu(p) \geq c$;

- $<\mathcal{P},\sigma$,n$>\models$ fi(t) iff t is the (n+1)st transition in σ;

- $<\mathcal{P},\sigma,n>\models$ lp(p) iff $\mu_0 \stackrel{\sigma[n]}{\rightarrow} \mu_1, \mu_0 \stackrel{\sigma}{\rightarrow} \mu_2$, and $\mu_1(p) \leq \mu_2(p)$;
- $<\mathcal{P},\sigma,n>\models$ zl(p) iff $\mu_0 \stackrel{\sigma[n]}{\rightarrow} \mu_1, \mu_0 \stackrel{\sigma}{\rightarrow} \mu_2$, and $\mu_1(p) = \mu_2(p)$;
- $<\mathcal{P},\sigma,n>\models$ co(μ) iff $\mu_0 \stackrel{\sigma[n]}{\rightarrow} \mu_1$ and there is a $\mu_2 \in R(P,T,\varphi,\mu_1)$ such that $\mu_2 \geq \mu$.

Let Q be the set of all of the above predicates for all places p, transitions t, and markings μ, and let $\tilde{Q} = \{q \mid \neg q \in Q\}$. We wish to show that FMCP($\tilde{\mathcal{L}}$(Q,F,X)) $\leq_{PTIME}$ RP. From Theorem 3.1, we need only show that Q and $\tilde{Q}$ are RP-decidable. For most elements of Q $\cup$ $\tilde{Q}$, this is straightforward. The main difficulty lies with $\neg$co(μ). In showing $\neg$co(μ) to be RP-decidable, we construct a PN that will in some sense produce all markings from which no marking greater than or equal to μ can be reached. In order to construct such a PN, we first construct a modified Turing machine (TM) that accomplishes the same purpose. This modified TM will be such that using Lipton's construction [14], we can transform it to a PN. Having done this, we can show the main result of this section, that FMCP($\tilde{\mathcal{L}}$(Q,F,X)) is equivalent to RP. From this result we will subsequently derive two refinements concerning logics developed in [8]; these refinements will be given in Theorems 3.3 and 3.4. We will then use Theorem 3.2 and its refinements in Section 4 to show seven fair nontermination problems to be equivalent to RP. The reason we can use a finite model checking problem to encode a fair nontermination problem is that $\tilde{\mathcal{L}}$(Q,F,X) has the power to express certain loops which may be iterated to produce an infinite "fair" path. Thus, Theorem 3.2 is an umbrella under which powerful machinery is developed for proving certain fair nontermination problems to be equivalent to RP.

Theorem 3.2: FMCP($\tilde{\mathcal{L}}$(Q,F,X)) $\equiv_{PTIME}$ RP.

Let Q′ be the set of predicates ge(p,c) and fi(t) extended to infinite firing sequences, and let $\tilde{Q}' = \{\neg q \mid q \in Q'\}$. MCP($\tilde{\mathcal{L}}$(Q′,F,X)) was shown in [8] to be NP-complete for conflict-free PNs. (The logic in [8] also included predicates asserting that a transition t is enabled; this assertion and its negation can clearly be encoded in $\tilde{\mathcal{L}}$(Q′,F,X).) Although $\tilde{\mathcal{L}}$(Q′,F,X) can only express loops in which the repeated markings are explicitly stated, this is sufficient to encode several of the types of fairness given by Landweber [12] and Carstensen and Valk [4]. The following theorem states that MCP($\tilde{\mathcal{L}}$(Q′,F,X)) for general PNs is equivalent to reachability.

Theorem 3.3: MCP($\tilde{\mathcal{L}}$(Q′,F,X)) $\equiv_{PTIME}$ RP.

One question left open in [8] was whether MCP($\mathcal{L}^{\infty}$(Q′)) is decidable for conflict-free PNs. In Theorem 3.4, we give a positive answer to this question by showing the problem with respect to general PNs to be equivalent to RP. Again, Theorem 3.4 may be viewed as a refinement of Theorem 3.2.

Theorem 3.4: MCP($\mathcal{L}^{\infty}$(Q′)) $\equiv_{PTIME}$ RP.

4 The fair nontermination problem

In this section, we examine the complexities of 24 fair nontermination problems. The machinery developed in Section 3 may be used to prove Theorems 4.2, 4.6, and 4.12, where a total of seven of these problems are shown to be equivalent to RP. Particularly in the latter two theorems, this machinery provides for very succinct reductions to RP, whereas "brute force" reductions are much longer and considerably more tedious. In the remainder of the theorems in this section, most of the problems we study are either equivalent to BP or Σ_1^1-complete. The results of this section are summarized in a table in Section 5.

The first notions of fairness we consider were defined in Landweber [12], and Carstensen and Valk [4]. These definitions of fairness are such that a fair firing sequence must visit certain *predefined* markings or transitions infinitely often. It is worth mentioning that the notion of "enabledness" does not play any role in these definitions (other than the fact that the definitions deal with firing sequences). Given an infinite firing sequence $\sigma = t_1t_2...$, we define $\inf^M(\sigma)$ ($\inf^T(\sigma)$) to be the set of markings (transitions) that occur infinitely often in σ (i.e., $\inf^M(\sigma) = \{\mu \mid$ there are infinitely many i such that $\mu_0 \stackrel{\sigma[i]}{\rightarrow} \mu\}$ and $\inf^T(\sigma)=\{t_i \mid t_i$ occurs infinitely often in $\sigma\}$). Let $\mathcal{A}$ be a finite set of finite nonempty sets of markings. An infinite firing sequence $\sigma = t_1t_2...$ is said to be

- M1-fair iff $\exists$ A $\in \mathcal{A}$, $\exists$ i $\in$ N : $\mu_0 \stackrel{\sigma[i]}{\rightarrow} \mu \in$ A (i.e., some marking reached by σ is in A).
- M1′-fair iff $\exists$ A $\in \mathcal{A}$, $\forall$ i $\in$ N : $\mu_0 \stackrel{\sigma[i]}{\rightarrow} \mu_i \in$ A (i.e., every marking reached by σ is in A).
- M2-fair iff $\exists$ A $\in \mathcal{A}$, $\inf^M(\sigma) \cap A \neq \emptyset$ (i.e., some marking reached infinitely often by σ is in A).
- M2′-fair iff $\exists$ A $\in \mathcal{A}$, $\inf^M(\sigma) \neq \emptyset$ and $\inf^M(\sigma) \subseteq A$ (i.e., σ reaches some marking infinitely often and every marking reached infinitely often by σ is in A).
- M3-fair iff $\exists$ A $\in \mathcal{A}$, $\inf^M(\sigma)$=A (i.e., the set of markings reached infinitely often by σ is an element of $\mathcal{A}$).
- M3′-fair iff $\exists$ A $\in \mathcal{A}$, A $\subseteq \inf^M(\sigma)$ (i.e., every marking in A is reached infinitely often by σ).

Similarly, let $\mathcal{A}$ be a finite set of nonempty subsets of transitions. σ is said to be:

- T1-fair iff $\exists$ A $\in \mathcal{A}$, $\exists$ i $\in N^+$: $t_i \in$ A.
- T1′-fair iff $\exists$ A $\in \mathcal{A}$, $\forall$ i $\in N^+$: $t_i \in$ A.
- T2-fair iff $\exists$ A $\in \mathcal{A}$, $\inf^T(\sigma) \cap A \neq \emptyset$.
- T2′-fair iff $\exists$ A $\in \mathcal{A}$, $\inf^T(\sigma) \subseteq$ A.
- T3-fair iff $\exists$ A $\in \mathcal{A}$, $\inf^T(\sigma)$=A.
- T3′-fair iff $\exists$ A $\in \mathcal{A}$, A $\subseteq \inf^T(\sigma)$.

We will now investigate the complexity of the nontermination problems with respect to each of the above fairness constraints. The first theorem gives an exception to our general classification scheme due to the fact that for M1′-fairness the entire allowable reachability set is given as input to the problem. The proof is basically the same as the one used in [8] with respect to conflict-free PNs.

Theorem 4.1: $NTP^{M1'}$ is NLOGSPACE-complete.

To show the following theorem, we make use of the temporal logic results given in Theorems 3.3 and 3.4. This machinery makes the proof very succinct; however, this particular theorem is not exceedingly difficult to prove without using these results. The real power of our logic will be exploited in Theorems 4.6 and 4.12.

Theorem 4.2: $NTP^x \equiv_{PTIME}$ RP, for x $\in$ {M1, M2, M2′, M3, M3′}.

We now turn our attention to the 6 transition-related types of fairness. The NTP^x, for x $\in$ {T1, T1′, T2, T2′, T3, T3′}, has been shown to be decidable in [21]. However, no complexity analysis was given there. In what follows, we show that these problems are equivalent to the BP. The proofs require showing the fact that if an infinite x-fair computation exists, then there must be a short "witness" to this fact. The proof of such a fact, generally speaking, is based on the method that Rackoff used in the complexity analysis of the BP in [19] (see also [20]).

Theorem 4.3: $NTP^x \equiv_{PTIME}$ BP, for x $\in$ {T1, T1′, T2, T2′, T3, T3′}.

We now examine the NTP with respect to several notions of fairness in which the constraints are imposed in an implicit fashion, instead of by an explicit listing the markings and/or transitions that a "fair" firing sequence must visit. We will first examine three types introduced by Lehman, Pnueli, and Stavi [13] and two extensions given by Carstensen [3]. (See also Carstensen and Valk [4].) Given a Petri net $\mathcal{P}$ and a set of subsets of transitions $\mathcal{T}$, an infinite firing sequence σ is said to be:

- *impartial* iff every transition in $\mathcal{P}$ occurs infinitely often in σ.
- *just* iff every transition that is enabled almost everywhere in σ occurs infinitely often in σ.
- *fair* iff every transition that is enabled infinitely often in σ occurs infinitely often in σ.
- *fdp with respect to* $\mathcal{T}$ (fdp-$\mathcal{T}$) iff for every T $\in \mathcal{T}$, if almost everywhere in σ some t in T is enabled, then some t′ in T occurs infinitely often in σ. (Here, fdp stands for finite delay property.)
- *fair with respect to* $\mathcal{T}$ (fair-$\mathcal{T}$) iff for every T $\in \mathcal{T}$, if some t in T is enabled infinitely often in σ, then some t′ in T occurs infinitely often in σ.

The following theorem is shown using the technique described above regarding Theorem 4.3.

Theorem 4.4: $\text{NTP}^{imp} \equiv_{PTIME}$ BP.

At this time, we do not know whether either NTP^{just} or $\text{NTP}^{fdp-\mathcal{T}}$ is decidable. The main difficulty, we feel, is due to the fact that these fairness properties are nonmonotonic in the sense that the existence of a just (fdp-$\mathcal{T}$, respectively) firing sequence starting in μ by no means guarantees a just (fdp-$\mathcal{T}$) firing sequence starting in any μ', where $\mu' \geq \mu$. At the same time, we are unable to enforce zero-testing using either of these properties. However, we are able to show the next three theorems regarding these problems.

Theorem 4.5: RP $\leq_{PTIME}$ $\text{NTP}^{fdp-\mathcal{T}}$ even if $\mathcal{T} = \{\{\text{t}\}\}$ for some transition t.

In [3], Carstensen showed that $\text{NTP}^{fdp-\mathcal{T}}$ is decidable if $|\mathcal{T}| = 1$. We are able to improve upon this result by showing the problem to be equivalent to RP. In this proof, as opposed to Theorem 4.2, the real power of the machinery developed in Section 3 is exploited. Without the umbrella of Theorem 3.2 and its subsequent refinement in Theorem 3.4, this proof would have been much longer and considerably more tedious. As it is, we are able to give a very succinct proof of an unobvious theorem.

Theorem 4.6: $\text{NTP}^{fdp-\mathcal{T}} \equiv_{PTIME}$ RP if $|\mathcal{T}| = 1$.

Proof. From Theorem 4.5, we need only show that $\text{NTP}^{fdp-\mathcal{T}} \leq_{PTIME}$ RP if $|\mathcal{T}| = 1$. Let $\mathcal{P} = (\text{P},\text{T},\varphi,\mu_0)$ be an arbitrary PN, T′ $\subseteq$ T, and $\mathcal{T} = \{\text{T}'\}$. An infinite firing sequence σ is fdp with respect to $\mathcal{T}$ iff

$$<\mathcal{P},\sigma,0> \models \mathbf{GF}[(\textstyle\bigwedge_{t\in T'} \neg(\bigwedge_{p\in P} \text{ge}(\text{p},\varphi(\text{p},\text{t})))) \vee (\bigvee_{t\in T'} \text{fi}(\text{t}))].$$

Thus, from Theorem 3.4, $\text{NTP}^{fdp-\mathcal{T}} \leq_{PTIME}$ RP if $|\mathcal{T}| = 1$.

□

The following theorem gives a lower bound for NTP^{just}.

Theorem 4.7: RP $\leq_{PTIME}$ NTP^{just}.

In [3], Carstensen showed the NTP^{fair} and the $\text{NTP}^{fair-\mathcal{T}}$ to be undecidable. In what follows, we improve this result by showing both to be complete for Σ_1^1 — thè first level of the analytical hierarchy. We will later use these results to show a third version to be Σ_1^1-complete. The reason these problems are so highly undecidable is that the associated fairness constraints can enforce not only zero-testing, but also unbounded nondeterminism (see also [3,5]).

Theorem 4.8: $\text{NTP}^{fair-\mathcal{T}}$ is Σ_1^1-hard even if $\mathcal{T}$ contains only singleton sets.

Theorem 4.9: NTP^{fair} and $\text{NTP}^{fair-\mathcal{T}}$ are Σ_1^1-complete.

In [3], Carstensen also considered fairness for bounded PNs. Given a PN $\mathcal{P}$, we say an infinite firing sequence σ is *bd-fair* if $\mathcal{P}$ is bounded and σ is fair. Although $\text{NTP}^{bd-fair}$ is clearly decidable and as hard as BP, no tighter bounds have been given for the problem. We now show the problem to be nonprimitive recursive. The idea is to use a bounded PN to generate a potentially very large number (see [9,16]), and to use this number to bound the succeeding computation. In this fashion, a counter machine with a nonprimitive recursive time bound may be simulated using a strategy similar to Carstensen's [3].

Theorem 4.10: $\text{NTP}^{bd-fair}$ is not primitive recursive.

In [1], Best extended the definition of fairness using the notions of *i (∞) -enabledness.* A transition t is said to be i-enabled (or ∞-enabled if i = ∞) at a marking μ if there is a firing sequence σ no longer than i transitions such that $\mu \xrightarrow{\sigma} \mu'$, and t is enabled at μ'. For $1 \leq i \leq \infty$, an infinite computation σ is said to be *i-fair* iff for every transition t, if t is i-enabled in infinitely many markings in σ, then t occurs infinitely often. (Note that "0-fairness" coincides with "fairness" as defined in [13]. Also, an equivalent definition for ∞-fairness was given in Queille and Sifakis [18].) We can show that NTP^{i-fair}, $0 \leq i < \infty$, is Σ_1^1-complete, but that $NTP^{\infty-fair}$ is equivalent to RP.

Theorem 4.11: For every i, $0 \leq i < \infty$, NTP^{i-fair} is Σ_1^1-complete.

The following theorem is the last which uses the machinery developed in Section 3. In this theorem, we can use Theorem 3.2 directly to give a succinct reduction to RP. As in Theorem 4.6, a direct reduction to RP would have been much more tedious.

Theorem 4.12: $NTP^{\infty-fair} \equiv_{PTIME}$ RP.

Queille and Sifakis [18] have extended fairness in two other ways, namely, *fair choice from states*, and *fair reachability of predicates.* Applying these notions of fairness to Petri nets, we have that for a PN $\mathcal{P}$ = (P,T,φ,μ_0), an infinite firing sequence σ satisfies:

- *fair choice from states* (state-fair, for short) iff for any marking μ reached infinitely often by σ, every transition enabled at μ is executed infinitely often from μ in σ.

- *fair reachability of predicates* (pred-fair, for short) iff for any (finite or infinite) set of markings M, if there are infinitely many i such that $\mu_0 \xrightarrow{\sigma[i]} \mu_i \xrightarrow{\sigma_i'} \mu_i' \in M$ for some σ_i', then there must be infinitely many j such that $\mu_0 \xrightarrow{\sigma[j]} \mu_j \in M$.

At this time, we are unable to establish tight bounds for either $NTP^{state-fair}$ or $NTP^{pred-fair}$. $NTP^{state-fair}$ seems to be related to the problem of finding a *home state*, that is, a marking that is reachable from any reachable marking (see [6], where a decision procedure was given to determine whether a given marking is a home state). Because the definition of pred-fair is quantified over all sets of markings, it appears to be a very difficult problem. The next three theorems give the bounds we are able to derive for these two problems.

Theorem 4.13: $NTP^{state-fair}$ is decidable.

The above theorem follows from the fact that in an unbounded PN there is a firing sequence in which no marking is reached infinitely often. Thus, a decision procedure merely decides whether the PN is bounded, and if so, searches for a state-fair firing sequence in the (finite) reachability graph. We now define the following problem, which will be used in giving our lower bound for $NTP^{state-fair}$.

- **BRP:**
  Instance: Given a bounded Petri net $\mathcal{P}$ and a marking μ,
  Question: Is $\mu \in R(\mathcal{P})$?

The following two theorems can now be shown by straightforward reductions.

Theorem 4.14: BRP $\leq_{PTIME}$ $NTP^{state-fair}$.

Theorem 4.15: RP $\leq_{PTIME}$ $NTP^{pred-fair}$.

Finally, we examine *equifairness* as defined by Francez [7]. Given a Petri net $\mathcal{P}$ and an infinite firing sequence σ, σ is said to be *equifair* iff there exist infinitely many i's such that all transitions occur the same number of times in $\sigma[i]$. Using a strategy similar to that of Rackoff [19], we can show the following theorem.

Theorem 4.16: $NTP^{equifair} \equiv_{PTIME}$ BP.

5 Conclusion

We have exhibited a temporal logic powerful enough to express certain fairness constraints, yet whose FMCP is equivalent to the reachability problem for PNs. This logic was instrumental in showing seven fair nontermination problems to be equivalent to RP. In developing this logic, we were able to answer a question left open in [8], namely, is there a decision procedure for $\mathcal{L}^{\infty}(Q')$? We were able to give a positive answer to this question and show that the problem is equivalent to reachability. One question that remains open is whether there is a decision procedure for $\tilde{\mathcal{L}}(Q',\mathbf{GF})$; i.e., wffs including predicates from Q' and the operators **GF**, $\wedge, \vee$, and $\neg$, where $\neg$ is allowed only on predicates.

The following table summarizes the fairness results of this paper.

NTP	complexity	NTP	complexity	NTP	complexity	NTP	complexity
M1	RP	T1	BP	imp	BP	fair-$\mathcal{T}$	Σ_1^1
M1′	NL	T1′	BP	just	≥RP	i-fair	Σ_1^1
M2	RP	T2	BP	fair	Σ_1^1	∞-fair	RP
M2′	RP	T2′	BP	bd-fair	NPR	state-fair	D, ≥BRP
M3	RP	T3	BP	fdp-$\mathcal{T}$	≥RP	pred-fair	≥RP
M3′	RP	T3′	BP	fdp-T	RP	equifair	BP

- ≥BRP: as hard as the BRP,
- ≥RP: as hard as the RP,
- NPR: decidable, but not primitive recursive,
- D: decidable,
- fdp-T: fdp-$\mathcal{T}$ with $|\mathcal{T}| = 1$.

Most of the problems examined have been shown to be either equivalent to boundedness, equivalent to reachability, or Σ_1^1-complete. Two exceptions to this general rule are $\mathrm{NTP}^{M1'}$ and $\mathrm{NTP}^{bd-fair}$. $\mathrm{NTP}^{M1'}$ can be decided in nondeterministic logspace because the entire allowable reachability set is explicitly given as input. Using the fact that bounded PNs can generate very large numbers, we were able to show that $\mathrm{NTP}^{bd-fair}$ is not primitive recursive. Aside from the fact that the precise complexity of RP is still unknown, the precise complexities of four of the fair nontermination problems we have examined remain open. Two of these, NTP^{just} and $\mathrm{NTP}^{fdp-\mathcal{T}}$ are particularly interesting because they are related to the open temporal logic question mentioned above; i.e., they are both expressible in $\tilde{\mathcal{L}}(Q',\mathbf{GF})$.

Acknowledgment: We would like to thank Prof. H. Carstensen for his suggestions and encouraging comments. In particular, we thank him for suggesting that model checking with respect to general PNs might be decidable for $\tilde{\mathcal{L}}(Q',\mathbf{F},\mathbf{X})$. We would also like to thank the referees for their helpful comments.

References

[1] E. Best. Fairness and conspiracies. *Information Processing Letters*, 18:215–220, 1984. Addendum, Vol. 19, page 162, 1984.

[2] G. Brams. *Reseaux de Petri: Theorie et Pratique – Tome 1: Theorie et Analyse*. Masson, Paris, 1983.

[3] H. Carstensen. Decidability questions for fairness in Petri nets. In *Proceedings of the 4th Symposium on Theoretical Aspects of Computer Science*, pages 396–407, 1987. LNCS 247.

[4] H. Carstensen and R. Valk. Infinite behaviour and fairness in Petri nets. In *Advances in Petri Nets 1984*, pages 83–100, Springer-Verlag, 1985. LNCS 188.

[5] A. Chandra. Computable nondeterministic functions. In *Proceedings of the 19th IEEE Symposium on the Foundations of Computer Science*, pages 127–131, 1978.

[6] D. Escrig. A collection of algorithms to decide liveness and other related properties of a place transition system. Unpublished manuscript.

[7] N. Francez. *Fairness*. Springer-Verlag, 1986.

[8] R. Howell and L. Rosier. On questions of fairness and temporal logic for conflict-free Petri nets. In *Proceedings of the 8th European Workshop on Applications and Theory of Petri Nets*, pages 197–214, 1987.

[9] R. Howell, L. Rosier, D. Huynh, and H. Yen. Some complexity bounds for problems concerning finite and 2-dimensional vector addition systems with states. *Theoret. Comp. Sci.*, 46:107–140, 1986.

[10] R. Howell, L. Rosier, and H. Yen. *A Taxonomy of Fairness and Temporal Logic Problems for Petri Nets*. Technical Report 88-03, Department of Computer Sciences, The University of Texas at Austin, Austin, Texas 78712, 1988.

[11] R. Kosaraju. Decidability of reachability in vector addition systems. In *Proceedings of the 14th Annual ACM Symposium on Theory of Computing*, pages 267–280, 1982.

[12] L. Landweber. Decision problems for ω-automata. *Math. Syst. Theory*, 3:376–384, 1969.

[13] D. Lehman, A. Pnueli, and J. Stavi. Impartiality, justice, and fairness: the ethics of concurrent termination. In *Proceedings of the 8th International Colloquium on Automata, Languages, and Programming*, pages 264–277, 1981. LNCS 115.

[14] R. Lipton. *The Reachability Problem Requires Exponential Space*. Technical Report 62, Yale University, Dept. of CS., Jan. 1976.

[15] E. Mayr. An algorithm for the general Petri net reachability problem. *SIAM J. Comput.*, 13(3):441–460, 1984. A preliminary version of this paper was presented at the *13th Annual Symposium on Theory of Computing*, 1981.

[16] H. Müller. The reachability problem for VAS. In *Advances in Petri Nets*, pages 376–391, Springer-Verlag, 1985. LNCS 188.

[17] J. Peterson. *Petri Net Theory and the Modeling of Systems*. Prentice Hall, Englewood Cliffs, NJ, 1981.

[18] J. Queille and J. Sifakis. Fairness and related properties in transition systems — a temporal logic to deal with fairness. *Acta Informatica*, 19:195–220, 1983.

[19] C. Rackoff. The covering and boundedness problems for vector addition systems. *Theoret. Comp. Sci.*, 6:223–231, 1978.

[20] L. Rosier and H. Yen. A multiparameter analysis of the boundedness problem for vector addition systems. *J. of Computer and System Sciences*, 32(1):105–135, 1986.

[21] R. Valk and M. Jantzen. The residue of vector sets with applications to decidability problems in Petri nets. *Acta Informatica*, 21:643–674, 1985.

BRANCHING PROGRAMS AS A TOOL FOR
PROVING LOWER BOUNDS ON VLSI COMPUTATIONS
AND OPTIMAL ALGORITHMS FOR SYSTOLIC ARRAYS +

Juraj Hromkovič, Juraj Procházka
Department of Theoretical Cybernetics, Comenius University
842 15 Bratislava, Czechoslovakia

Abstract. The branching programs that were studied as a nonuniform computing model providing lower bounds on the space of deterministic sequential computations are considered. It is shown that branching programs can provide lower bounds on the general model of VLSI computations - multilective circuits, and that one-time-only branching programs provide lower bounds on the area of the basic model of VLSI computations. Using this technique we obtain new lower bounds on area complexity of VLSI computations.

Another technique is introduced to prove time and area optimality of some algebraic algorithms for one-dimensional systolic arrays. A new efficient algorithm on two-way systolic array is developed for GCD problem.

1. INTRODUCTION AND DEFINITIONS

This paper is divided into three parts. The first one relates the branching programs as a tool for proving lower bounds on the space complexity of sequential computations to the general model of VLSI computations - multilective VLSI circuits. Considering one-time-only branching programs we obtain a stronger relation to the VLSI circuits. Using this new lower bound proof technique for VLSI computations several lower bounds for language recognition on VLSI circuits are established. Further, the nonexistence of the area simulation of multilective VLSI circuits by VLSI circuits is proved.

The second part of this paper is devoted to the development of another technique for proving lower bounds on the time and area of two-way one-dimensional systolic arrays. Applying this technique one can prove both the time and the area optimality of some algorithms solving algebraic problems on this parallel computing model.

A new efficient algorithm for computing GCD of two polynomials on one-dimensional

+ This work was supported by the ŠPZV I-1-5/8 grant and the ŠPZV III-8-1/10 grant.

systolic arrays is presented in the third part. This algorithm has some advantages over the original algorithm of Brent and Kung |4|.

Now, let us give the basic definitions for VLSI computing models. At first we give the formal definition of the basic model of VLSI circuit (for a more detailed definition see Hromkovič |8,9|).

Definition 1.1 Let $X=\{x_1,\dots,x_n\}$, $Y=\{y_1,\dots,y_m\}$ be sets of Boolean variables. A <u>problem instance P</u> from the input variables X to the output variables Y is a set of Boolean functions $\{f_1,\dots,f_m\}$ such that f_i: $\{0,1\}^{|X|}\to\{0,1\}$ and $y_i = f_i(x_1,\dots,x_n)$ for $i=1,\dots,m$. The positive integer n is called the <u>size</u> of P.

Definition 1.2 A <u>problem</u> is an infinite sequence of problem instances, where each two instances in the sequence have a different size parameter n.

As an example of a problem the recognition of a language $L \subseteq \{0,1\}^*$ can be considered. To see this fact we associate with each language $L \subseteq \{0,1\}^*$ the infinite sequence of Boolean functions $\{h_i^L\}_{i=1}^{\infty}$, where $h_i^L : \{0,1\}^i \to \{0,1\}$ and $h_i^L(x_1,\dots,x_i)=1$ iff $x_1x_2\dots x_i \in L \cap \{0,1\}^i$. So, the i-th problem instance is the Boolean function h_i^L.

Definition 1.3 A <u>4-graph</u> is a directed graph $G=(V,E)$ with the property that, for each $v \in V$, the sum of output edges from v and input edges to v is bounded by 4.

Definition 1.4 A <u>VLSI graph</u> M_G is a 4-graph G embeded in the lattice in such a way that each square of the lattice has one of the following contents:

(a) a vertex of the graph,

(b) one directed line going in the horizontal or in the vertical direction (this line is a part of an edge of the graph),

(c) one broken line coming in the lattice square in one of two vertical (horizontal) directions and outgoing in one of two horizontal (vertical) directions,

(d) two crossing lines, one going in the horizontal direction, the other one in the vertical direction (this depicts the place of two crossing edges without any vertex of the embeding of the directed graph in the plane),

(e) the empty content.

Definition 1.5 The <u>area complexity of a VLSI graph</u> is the area of a minimal rectangle involving all non-empty squares of the lattice. The <u>area complexity of a 4-graph G</u> is the minimum of the area complexities of all VLSI graphs that are embedings of G in the lattice.

Definition 1.6 A VLSI circuit is a 6-tuple $R = (M_G, P, p, X, Y, r)$, where:

(1) M_G is a VLSI graph that is the embeding of a 4-graph $G=(V,E)$ in the lattice.

(2) P is a finite, nonempty set (called processor set) of functions from $\{0,1\}^i$ to $\{0,1\}^j$, where $i+j \leq 4$, $i,j \in \{0,1,2,3,4\}$.

(3) $X = \{x_1,\dots,x_n\}$ is the set of input variables .

(4) $Y = \{y_1,\dots,y_m\}$ is the set of output variables .

(5) r is a function (called I/O function) from $X \cup Y$ to $V \times N$ such that for all $x,y \in X \cup Y$, $x \neq y$ implies $r(x) \neq r(y)$, and if $(v,t)=r(x)$ for an $x \in X$ (Y), then v is called the input processor (output processor), and v has indegree (outdegree) zero and outdegree (indegree) at most three.

(6) p is a function from V to P such that:
   (i) For each $v \in V$ which is not an input or output processor, if v has the indegree i and the outdegre j then $p(v)=f_v$, where f_v: $\{0,1\}^i \rightarrow \{0,1\}^j$.
   (ii) For each input vertex $v \in V$, $p(v)=f_v$, where f_v: $\{0,1\} \rightarrow \{0,1\}^j$ and j is the outdegree of v.
   (iii) For each output vertex $v \in V$, $p(v)=f_v$, where f_v: $\{0,1\}^i \rightarrow \{0,1\}$ and i is the indegree of v.

The computation of a VLSI circuit can be defined as follows. Let $R=(M_G,P,p,X,Y,r)$ with $G=(V,E)$ be a VLSI circuit, and let $v_1,\dots,v_m$ be a fixed order of all vertices in V. Let $e_{i1},\dots,e_{ij_i}$, for $j_i \in \{1,2,3,4\}$, be the sequence of all input edges of v_i from E for all v_i´s that are not input processors, and let e_{i1} be the input edge of v_i not in E if v_i is an input processor. For each time unit t one can associate a Boolean value a^t_{ik} to each e_{ik} , $i=1,\dots,m$, $k \in \{1,\dots,j_i\}$. In the time unit t=0 all input edges from E have the value 0 . For all $x \in X$, if $r(x)=(v_i,0)$ then e_{i1} has the value of the input variable x , if for all x assigned to v_i $r(x)=(v_i,t')$ for $t' \neq 0$ then e_{i1} has the value 0 . Clearly, knowing the values of all input edges in the time unit t we obtain the input values in the time unit t+1 as the output values of all processors (vertices) with given inputs. The input edge of an input processor v has in the time unit t either the value 0 (if no input variable is coming in v in the time unit t) or the value of an input variable coming in v in the time unit t . We define a state s_t of R in the time unit t as the sequence $a^t_{11},\dots,a^t_{1j_1},a^t_{21},\dots,a^t_{2j_2},\dots,a^t_{m1},\dots,a^t_{mj_m}$ of the values of the input edges $e_{11},\dots,e_{1j_1},e_{21},\dots,e_{2j_2},\dots,e_{m1},\dots,e_{mj_m}$. A computation of R on an input is a sequence of states $s_0,s_1,\dots,s_t,s_{t+1},\dots$ such that , for each t, s_t is the state of R working on the given input in the time unit t . Taking the output values from the output processors in the time unit determined by r one can associate exactly one problem instance to R .

Definition 1.7 The time complexity $T(R)$ of a VLSI circuit $R=(M_G,P,p,X,Y,r)$ is $\max\{t \mid (v,t)=r(y) \text{ for a } y\in Y\}$.

In the case that we have an infinite sequence of VLSI circuits solving a problem we can consider the area and time complexity as functions of the size of the problem. Considering an infinite sequence of VLSI circuits $\mathcal{R}$ let $T_{\mathcal{R}}(n)$ ($A_{\mathcal{R}}(n)$) denote the function from positive integers to positive integers called the time (area) complexity of $\mathcal{R}$.

Now, let us define the area and time complexity of a problem.

Definition 1.8 Let $\mathcal{P} = \{P_i\}_{i=1}^{\infty}$ be a problem, and let n_i be the size of the problem instance P_i for any $i=1,2,\ldots$. Let, for $i=1,2,\ldots$, R_i be a circuit solving P_i with minimal area (time) complexity. We say that the **area**(time) complexity of $\mathcal{P}$ is the function $A_{\mathcal{P}}$ ($T_{\mathcal{P}}$) from $\{n_i \mid i=1,2,\ldots\}$ to positive integers defined by $A_{\mathcal{P}}(n_i)=A(R_i)$ ($T_{\mathcal{P}}(n_i)=T(R_i)$) for all positive integers i .

We have defined the basic model of VLSI circuits here. Now, we give the definition of a possible generalization of this model in an informal way.

A multilective VLSI circuit $R=(M_G,P,p,X,Y,r)$ can obtain each input variable several times. So, for each input variable x, $r(x)$ is a set of pairs (v,t) instead of one pair ($r(x)$ and $r(y)$ are disjoint for different $x,y\in X\cup Y$).

2. BRANCHING PROGRAMS FOR PARALLEL COMPUTATIONS

The branching programs represents a tool for proving lower bounds on the space complexity of sequential computations (see Pudlák at al. |20| for details), and they were studied in several papers |1-3,5,6,11,16,17,20,21,24-27|. We define m-MP (m branching programs) as a generalization of branching programs (BP) and we show the relation between VLSI circuits and branching programs by the use of m-BP.

Definition 2.1 Let $X=\{x_1,\ldots,x_n\}$ be a set of Boolean variables. The m-branching programs, m-BP, for X and a positive integer $m\leq n$, is an acyclic directed graph with the following properties:

1. there is exactly one source,
2. every node has outdegree 2^k for a $k\in\{0,1,\ldots,m\}$,
3. every node v is labelled by a set $\{x_{i_1},\ldots x_{i_r}\}\subseteq X$ for $r\leq m$, each edge e leading from v is labelled by $l(e)=(k_1,\ldots,k_r)$, $k_i\in\{0,1\}$ for $i\in\{1,\ldots,r\}$, and $l(e)\neq l(e')$ for different e and e' leading from v ,
4. every sink is labelled by 0 or 1 .

Definition 2.2 Let U be an m-BP for $X=\{x_1,\ldots,x_n\}$. Given an input

$a=(a_1,\ldots,a_n) \in \{0,1\}^n$, U computes a function value $f_U(a)$ in the following way. The computation starts at the source. If the computation has reached a node v labelled by $x_{i_1},\ldots,x_{i_r}$ then the computation proceeds via the edge labelled by $l(a_{i_1},\ldots,a_{i_r})$. Once the computation reaches a sink, the computation ends and $f_U(a)$ is defined to be the label of that sink. The length of U is the length of the longest path in U, and the complexity of U, c(U) is the number of nodes in U.

It is easy to see that 1-branching programs are the orifinal BP as defined in |16,20|, and that each Boolean function can be computed by an m-BP of length n/m and complexity $O(2^n)$. Let, for each Boolean function f, c(f) be the complexity of the minimal BP computing f . Using a simulation of multilective VLSI circuits by m-BPs we are able to prove the following results.

Theorem 2.3 Let R be a multilective VLSI circuit computing a Boolean function f. Then $3A(R) + \log_2 T(R) \geq \log_2(c(f))$.

It is very hard to prove a nontrivial lower bound on c(f) for a given Boolean function f . The highest known lower bound on a Boolean function sequence $\mathcal{P}=\{f_i\}_{i=1}^{\infty}$ is $(n^2/\log_2 n)$ due to Nečiporuk |17|. So, using BP we are able to give only logarithmic lower bound on the area and $\log_2 T(R)$ of multilective VLSI circuits solving $\mathcal{P}$. So, we shall introduce a special technique for proving lower bounds on VLSI circuits that will be more successful for proving specific lower bounds on non-uniform sequence of VLSI circuits.

Definition 2.4 Let m be a positive integer. Let U be an m-BP. If, for each path $v_1,\ldots,v_k$ of vertices in U and each $i \neq j$, $l(v_i) \cap l(v_j) \neq \emptyset$ then we say that U is one-time-only m-BP, shortly $m\text{-BP}_1$. Let $c_1(f)$, for a Boolean function f, denote the complexity of the minimal 1-BP_1 (BP_1) computing f .

Theorem 2.5 Let R be a VLSI circuit computing a Boolean function f . Then $A(R) \geq \log_2(c_1(f))/4 - \log_2 n$.

Using the lower bound obtained for a specific language in Babai at al.|1| we can establishe the following result by applying Theorem 2.5 .

Theorem 2.6 There is no area efficient simulation of multilective VLSI circuits by VLSI circuits .

3. LOWER BOUNDS ON ONE-DIMENSIONAL SYSTOLIC ARRAYS

Now, we shall consider a special model for VLSI computations - so called one-dimensional systolic arrays that is the simplest type of VLSI circuits from the point of view of the topology. The one-dimensional systolic array is usually defined as a sequence of connected processors working over finite alphabet. The another (more formal) possibility is used in |10| -- the one-dimensional systolic array is a VLSI circuit whose graph can be obtained by a special embeding of 4-graphs in the vertices of a tree with the degree of vertices bounded by 2. In the following we shall consider the first type of definition (that is suitable for symbolic computations that will investigate in what follows) which means that we cannot use the pipeling technique in order to decrease the computational complexity. I.e, our assumption is that each input (output) variable is assigned to one processor as opposed to the second approach, where each variable over a finite alphabet is considered as a constant-length sequence of Boolean variables and each of the Boolean variables in the sequence can be assigned to another processor.

It is known that one-dimensional systolic arrays can solve any problem, i.e. this topological restriction on VLSI circuits does not decrease their power in the total sence. On the other hand it is clear (see |10|) that some problems require more area and time to be solved on one-dimensional systolic arrays than on the general model of VLSI circuits. The aim of this section is to find a technique for proving that some problems in symbolic a algebraic computations have the nice property that they can be solved in optimal area by one-dimensional systolic arrays. Further, we prove that the area-optimal algorithms on one-dimensional systolic arrays |4,13,14| working in time proportional to the area are time-optimal in the class of one-dimensional systolic array algorithms.

To obtain these results we introduce a new technique for proving lower bounds on the area of VLSI circuits and on the time of one-dimensional systolic arrays.

Let, for a positive integer k, $\Sigma = \{a_1,\dots,a_k\}$ be a set of symbols. In what follows we shall consider variables over Σ, and k-valued functions of n variables from Σ^n to Σ. Now, the problem instance of the size n is a set of k-valued functions of n variables.

Lemma 3.1 Let $P = \{f_1, f_2, \dots, f_m\}$ be a problem instance with the set of input variables $X = \{x_1,\dots,x_n\}$. Let there are r positive integers $1 \leq i_1, i_2, \dots, i_r \leq m$ such that each of functions $f_{i_1},\dots,f_{i_r}$ depends on at least $s+1$ input variables. Let there be at least $k^{r'}$ different suboutputs given by $f_{i_1},\dots,f_{i_r}$. Then, for each VLSI circuit R working over alphabet Σ and solving P, $\underline{A(R) \geq \min\{r' + (2/3)s - n, s/3\}}$.

Lemma 3.2 Let P and X have the same meaning as in Lemma 3.1. Let there be an $i \in \{1,\dots,m\}$ that f_i depends on all variables in an $X_1 \subseteq X$, and let, for each $j \in \{1,\dots,m\}$, f_j depends on at least one variable in X_1. Then, for each one-dimensional systolic array R without useless processors solving P, $T(R) \geq A(R)/6$.

There are several one-dimensional systolic arrays presented in |4,13,14,19| that are working simultaneously in linear area and in linear time. We conjecture that they are optimal according to the area in the class of all VLSI circuits, and that they are time-optimal in the class of one-dimensional systolic arrays. Using the lower bound technique introduced in the previous two lemmas we are able to prove such optimality result for the multiplication of two integers (polynomials).

4. SYSTOLIC SYSTEM FOR POLYNOMIAL GCD COMPUTATION

4.1 Introduction Brent, Kung already in 1982 constructed systolic system computing polynomial GCD over finite field, see |4|.

1, There are two kinds of linear systems concerning the way, data travel through the system, one-way and two-way linear systolic systems (1-LSS and 2-LSS). Brent-Kung systolic system computing polynomial GCD is 1-LSS. In this section we construct 2-LSS computing GCD. This systolic system has nearly half of processors of Brent-Kung system. That means, a utilization of processors in 2-LSS presented here is more effective.
2. 2-LSS computing GCD, presented here is also extended for polynomials over unique factorization domain (UFD). The advantage of the extension to UFD is obvious. We can compute, e.g. GCD of integer polynomials. Futher not only integer polynomials but there is recurent possibility for computation GCD of multivariate polynomials.

4.2 Sequential algorithm for polynomial GCD

Collins in his ingenious algorithm (see |28| or |30|) had solved GCD problem for polynomials over UFD. We present here modified version of Collins algorithm, that is simpler and more convenient for systolization. For more details and the proof of correctness see |18|.

```
Algorithm CM (Modified Collins algorithm)
Input : Polynomials u, v  such that  u≠Ø  and  v≠Ø  ;
Output : GCD(u,v) .
function  CM(u,v);
begin  d:=GCD(cont(u),cont(v));  (% cont(u) is GCD of polyn coeff. (uØ,...,um) %)
        u:=pp(u);  v:=pp(v);  (% pp(u)  is  u/cont(u) %)
        a:=1;  repeat  R(u,v,a) until  v=Ø;  CM:= d*pp(u)
end;
procedure  R(u,v,a);           (% pseudodivision of  u, v  %)
begin  M:= deg(u);
        while  deg(u)  ≧ deg(v)  do
                begin mp:=deg(u); np:=deg(v);
                      u:=lc(v)*u - lc(u)*v*x^(mp-np);
                      u:=u*lc(v)^(mp-deg(u)-1)     (% lc(u) is leading coeff. %)
                end;
        u:=u/a; a':=lc(v)^(M-deg(u)); a:=a'; u:=:v  (% ':=:' exchanges values %)
end.
```

4.3 Two way LSS for polynomial GCD computation Our systolic system named PC-system is derived from the above mentioned sequentia algorithm. We present the formal description of PC-system.

4.3.1 Processor The processor of PC-system (see Fig.1) is constructed without loss of generality (w.l.g.) as a processor with memory registers.

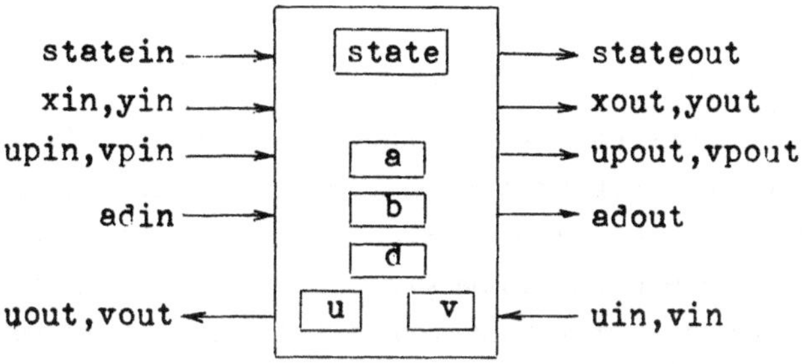

Fig.1 Processor of PC-system

4.3.2 Program of PC-system processor

```
begin    xout:=xin; yout:=yin;
case     statein of
initial: begin  xout:=uin; yout:=vin;
           if  (uin=0)  or  ((vin≠0)  and  (d>=0))  then
             begin  stateout:=reduceU; d:=d-1; upout:=uin;
             if  state≠reduceU  then
                begin vpout:=vin div a; adout :=1; a:=b; b:=vpout end
             else begin vpout:=vin; adout:=1; b:=b*vin end
          else begin  stateout:=reduceV; d:=d+1; vpout:=vin;
                if  state≠reduceV then
                  begin upout:=uin div a; adout:=a; a:=b; b:=upout  end
                else begin upout:=uin; adout:=1; b:=b*uin  end
                end;
          state:=stateout; xout:=upout; xout:=upout; yout:=vpout
        end  (% initial%) ;
reduceU: begin stateout:=reduceU; v:=vin div adin; vpout:=v;
         uout:=yin*uin - xin*v; vout:=vpin; adout:=adin
         end  (% reduceU %);
reduceV: begin stateout:=reduceV; u:=uin div adin; upout:=u;
          vout:=xin*vin - yin*u; uout:=upin; adout:=adin
         end  (% reduceV %)
end  (% case %)
end  (% program %) .
```

We do not have other kind of processors in PC-system. For the proper functioning of PC-system, the memory register of the first processor (see Fig. 2) must be initilized in the first step as a:=1; b:=1; d:=deg(U)-deg(v); state:=initial. Input and output timing (see Fig.2) determines for each processor when to receive input from outside and when to put output to outside enviroment (see |29|).

PC-system computing GCD of two polynomials U, V from D|x|, where D is UFD,

$$U = u_m x^m + u_{m-1} x^{m-1} + \dots + u_1 x + u_0 \qquad deg(u)=m ,$$

$$V = v_n x^n + v_{n-1} x^{n-1} + \dots + v_1 x + v_0 \qquad deg(v)=n ,$$

is constructed from (max(m,n)+2) processors (because different pairs of coefficients of U,V enter different processors as we see from formal description of PC-system). Let m>=n (w.l.g.), then PC-system can be described by communication graph (see Fig.2). A communication graph is an abstraction of a systolic system showing main aspects of interprocessors communication and main aspects of input-output communication. For more details see Gruska |29|.

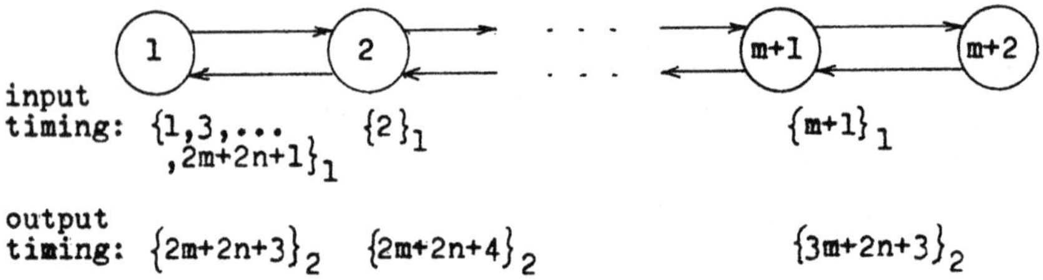

Fig.2 Communication graph of PC-system

Analyzing the proces of computation GCD of two polynomials U,V (using similar GCD-preserving transformation as Brent, Kung in |4|) we can derive that the time complexity of this computation (that is the number of steps between input and output of the first pair of coefficients) is $2*(m+n+1)$. Time complexity is the same as in Brent, Kung |4|, but the number of processors is about one half comparing with |4|.

ACNOWLEDGEMENT We are indebted to J o z e f G r u s k a for several valuable advices, hints and the time he spent with us to discuss the systolization of the GCD algorithm.

REFERENCES

1. BABAI,L - HAJNAL,P. - SZEMERÉDI,E. - TURÁN,G.: A lower bound for read-once only

Brancinching programs. JCSS 35 (1987), 153-162.

2. BOLLOBÁS,B.: Extremal Graph Theory. Academic Press, New York 1987.
3. BORODIN,A. - DOLEV,D. - FICH,F.E. - Paul,W.: Bounds for width two branching programs. Proc. 15th ACM STOC, ACM 1983, 87-93.
4. BRENT,R.P. - KUNG,H.T.: Systolic VLSI arrays for linear-time GCD computation. In: VLSI´83 (F.Anceau and E.J.Aas Eds.), North-Holland, Amsterdam 1983, 145-154.
5. CHANDRA,A.K. - FURST,M.L. - LIPTON,R.J.: Multiparty protocols. In: Proc. 15th ACM STOC, ACM 1983, 94-99.
6. FTÁČNIK,M. - HROMKOVIČ,J.: Nonlinear lower bound for real-time branching programs. Computers AI 4 (1985), No.3, 353-359.
7. GEDDES,K.O.: Algebraic algorithms for symbolic computation -- Chapt.2, Research report, University of Waterloo, Computer Science Department 1981.
8. HROMKOVIČ,J.: Lower bound technique for VLSI algorithms. In Proc. IMYCS´86, Hungarian Academy of Sciences, Budapest 1986, 9-19.
9. HROMKOVIČ,J.: Some complexity aspects of VLSI computations. Part 1. A framework for the study of information transfer in VLSI circuits. Computers AI 7, No.3, to appear.
10. HROMKOVIČ,J.: Some complexity aspects of VLSI computations. Part 2. Topology of circuits and information transfer. Computers AI 7, No.4, to appear.
11. JUKNA,S.P.: Lower bounds on the complexity of local circuits. In: 12th MFCS´86, Lecture Notes in Computer Science 233, Springer-Verlag 1986, 440-448.
12. KATRIŇÁK,T. - GAVALEC,M. - GEDEONOVÁ,E. - SMÍTAL,J.: Algebra a teoretická aritmetika. ALFA - SNTL 1985 (in Slovak).
13. KUNG,H.T.: Use of VLSI in algebraic computation: Some suggestions. In: Proc. SYMSAC´81, ACM 1981, 218-222.
14. KUNG,H.T.: Let´s design algorithms for VLSI systems. CMU Computer Science Dept., Technical report, 1979.
15. LIPSON,J.D.: Elements of Algebra and Algebraic Computing. Addison-Wesley 1981.
16. MASEK,W.: A fast algorithm for the String editing problem and decision graph complexity. M.Sc. Thesis, MIT, May 1976.
17. NEČIPORUK,E.I.: On a Boolean function. Soviet Math. Dokl. 7 (1966), 999-1000.
18. PROCHÁZKA,J.: Zložitosť algebraických výpočtov na niektorých modeloch počítačov. Dissertation thesis, VUSEIAR Bratislava, 1986 (in Slovak).
19. PROCHÁZKA,J.: The polynomial GCD-algorithm implemented in a systolic architecture. Acta Math. Com. Univ. XLVIII-XLIX (1986), 325-333.
20. PUDLÁK,P. - ŽÁK,S.: Space complexity of computations. Unpublished manuscript, 1982.
21. PUDLÁK,P.: A lower bound on complexity of branching programs. In Proc. 11th MFCS´84, Lecture Notes in Computer Science 176, Springer-Verlag 1984, 480-489.
22. THOMPSON,C.D.: A Complexity Theory for VLSI. Doct. dissertation, CMU-CS-80-140, Computer Science Dept., Carnegie-Mellon University, Pittsburg, August 1980.
23. ULLMAN,J.D.: Computational Aspects of VLSI. Comp. Science Press 1984.
24. WEGENER,I.: On the complexity of Branching programs and Decision trees for Qlique functions. Universität Frankfurt, Fachbereich Informatik, Int. Rept. 5/84, 1984.
25. WEGENER,I.: Time-space trade-offs for Branching programs. JCSS 32 (1986), 91-96.
26. WEGENER,I.: Optimal decision trees and one-time-only branching programs for symetric Boolean functions. Information and Control 62 (1984), 129-143.
27. ŽÁK,S.: An exponential lower bound for one-time only branching programs. In: Proc. 11th MFCS´84, Lecture Notes in Computer Science 176, Springer-Verlag 1984, 562-566.

28. COLLINS,G.E.: Subresultants and reduced polynomial remainder sequences. JACM 14 (1967), 128-142.

29. GRUSKA,J.: Tvorba paralelných výpočtových sietí. Research report, Institute of Technical Cybernetics of the Slovak Academy of Sciences, Bratislava 1985 (in Slovak).

30. KNUTH,D.E.: The art of computer programming. Vol.2: Seminumerical algorithms. Second ed., Addison-Wesley, Reading, 1981.

TWO LOWER BOUNDS FOR CIRCUITS OVER THE BASIS (&, V, ¬)

(Preliminary Report)

Stasys P. Jukna

Institute of Mathematics and Cybernetics
Lithuanian Academy of Sciences
232600 Vilnius, Akademijos, 4
Lithuanian SSR, U.S.S.R.

ABSTRACT *A general approximation technique to get lower bounds for the complexity of combinational circuits over an arbitrary algebras of operations is presented. The technique generalizes recent methods for monotone circuits and yields some new results. This report contains an* $\exp(\Omega(\log^2 n))$ *lower bound for the complexity of realization of non-monotone Boolean functions by circuits over the basis* (&,V,¬) *computing sufficiently many prime implicants , and of three-valued functions by circuits over some incomplete three-valued extensions of* (&,V,¬).

INTRODUCTION

The general idea of approximation technique in the theory of lower bounds for Boolean circuits is to approximate the circuits by more restricted ones. Various refinements of such an approach have already been used in a great many of lower bounds proofs. At present we have three main refinements. These are :

- *probabilistic approximations*, by Furst,Saxe and Sipser [5], Ajtai [1], Hastad [7], Yao [17], Hajnal et al. [6] , etc.
- *functional approximations*, by Andreev [3,4], Razborov [13-15], Alon and Boppana [2], Paterson [12], Smolensky [16], Ugol'nikov [19], etc. ;
- *topological approximations*, [8-10].

The aim of this report is to develope the functional approximation technique in order to obtain lower bounds for circuits over an arbitrary algebras of operations. The technique generalizes the methods of [2-4,12-16] and yields some new results.

The first result concerns Boolean circuits over the basis (&,V,¬) with ¬ -gates on the top of circuit. Any such circuit S computes some Boolean function f_S and also some disjunctive normal form (DNF for short) D_S of f_S (see Section 3 for details). A circuit S is called to be a *δ-circuit* ($0 \le \delta \le 1$) iff

$$| D_S \cap \mathrm{Imp}(f_S) | \ge | \mathrm{Imp}(f_S) |^{\delta} - 1 ,$$

where Imp(f) denotes the set of all prime implicants of f of minimal length ; S is **-circuit* if $D_S = \mathrm{Imp}(f_S)$. For $\delta \in [0,1] \cup \{*\}$ and a Boolean function f , let $C_\delta(f)$ denote the minimum number of gates in a δ-circuit computing f ; in case of monotone basis $\langle \&, \vee \rangle$ we will write $C_\delta^+(f)$. Notice that $C_\delta(f) \le C_\gamma(f) \le C_*(f)$ for any $0 \le \delta \le \gamma \le 1$, and that $C_0(f) = C(f)$ is the usual combinational complexity of f . Moreover, if f is monotone then $C_\delta^+(f) = C_\gamma^+(f) = C^+(f)$ since $Imp(f_S) \subseteq D_S$ for any monotone S .

These functionals have been considered by many authors. Probably, the first non-trivial result in this direction is an exponential trade-off between $*$-circuits and (monotone) 1-circuits proved by Okol'nishnikova in [11]. Namelly, she proved the bound $C_*(f_n) \ge exp(\Omega(n^{1/4})$ for a single sequence of monotone canonical functions f_n such that $C_1^+(f_n) \le 2n$. (A function f is *canonical* if $Imp(f)$ coincides with the set $PI(f)$ of all prime implicants of f). Latter, Andreev [3,4], Razborov [13,14] and Alon and Boppana [2] have considered the functional $C^+(f)$ and obtained super-polynomial (up to $exp(\Omega(n^{1/3-o(1)}))$ in [4]) lower bounds for some sequences of monotone canonical functions f_n with $\cup f_n^{-1}(1) \in NP$. These bounds hold also for $C_1(f_n)$. This is becouse any minimal circuit over $\langle \&, \vee, \neg \rangle$ computing a *positive* DNF (i.e. a DNF without negations) has no *null-chains*. However, it is known [8-10,13,14] that the presence of null-chains may substantialy reduce the circuit size. For example, in [13] a sequence of montone canonical functions f_n is given such that $C^+(f_n) \ge n^{\Omega(\log n)}$ and $C_\delta(f_n) \le n^{O(1)}$ for some $0 \le \delta < 1$. Thus we need a technique to prove lower bounds for *non-positive* DNFs, and, in particular, for $C_\delta(f)$ with a *non-monotone* f .

Such a technique is described in Section 1. In Section 2 the technique is demonstrated by a general lower bound on the complexity of realization of sets by circuits over basises consisting of so-called $\exists$-operations. This general bound yield all the known bounds [2,3,13,14] and some new lower bounds. In Section 3 a sequence of non-monotone Boolean functions π_n is given and it is proved that for any constant $\delta \in (0,1]$ it holds that

$$n^{\Omega(\ln n)} \le C_\delta(\pi_n) \le n^{\ln n} .$$

In section 4 we prove that circuits over some three-valued extensions of $\langle \&, \vee, \neg \rangle$ require super-polynomial number of gates to compute a single sequence of three-valued functions.

1. Circuits and Metric Criterions of Their Complexity

Fix some $n \ge 1$ and let F be a collection of n-ary operations $f : \mathfrak{A}^n \longrightarrow \mathfrak{A}$ over some set $\mathfrak{A}$. A *circuit over the algebra* $(\mathfrak{A}; F)$ *with input* $\mathfrak{B} \subseteq \mathfrak{A}$ is an ordered sequence $S = \langle s_1,\dots,s_t \rangle \subseteq \mathfrak{A}$ such that $\forall\, i = 1,\dots,t$ $\quad s_i = f(b_1,\dots,b_n)$ for some $f \in F$ and $b_1,\dots,b_n$

$\in \mathfrak{H} \cup \{s_1,\dots,s_{i-1}\}$. The number t of elements in S is the *size* of S. We say S *computes* a vector $A \in \mathfrak{A}^k$ iff $A \subseteq \mathfrak{H} \cup S$. (Here and in what follows we shall often identify a vector with the set of its elements). The *circuit-size complexity* of $A \in \mathfrak{A}^k$ *over an algebra* $(\mathfrak{A};F)$ *with respect to* $\mathfrak{H} \subseteq \mathfrak{A}$, denoted by $L_F(A,\mathfrak{H})$, is the size of a minimal circuit over $(\mathfrak{A};F)$ with input $\mathfrak{H}$, computing A. Notice that $L_F(A,\mathfrak{H}) = 0$ for any $A \subseteq \mathfrak{H}$.

We say an algebra $(\mathfrak{B};G)$ is a *Q-image* of an algebra $(\mathfrak{A};F)$, where $Q \subseteq \mathfrak{A}\times\mathfrak{B}$, iff for each $f \in F$ there is some $g \in G$ such that for all vectors $A = (a_1,\dots,a_n) \in \mathfrak{A}^n$ and $B = (b_1,\dots,b_n) \in \mathfrak{B}^n$ we have that $\{(a_i,b_i) : i=1,\dots,n\} \subseteq Q$ implies $(f(A),g(B)) \in Q$. For $\mathfrak{H} \subseteq \mathfrak{A}$, put $Q(\mathfrak{H}) = \{ b\in\mathfrak{B} : (a,b)\in Q$ for some $a\in\mathfrak{H} \}$.

THEOREM 1. *If* $(\mathfrak{B};G)$ *is a Q-image of* $(\mathfrak{A};F)$ *then for any* $a\in\mathfrak{A}$ *and* $\mathfrak{H} \subseteq \mathfrak{A}$ *we have :*

$$L_F(a,\mathfrak{H}) \geq \inf_{b\in Q(a)} L_G(b,Q(\mathfrak{H})) .$$

Proof : straightforward. ∎

For numbers $k,m \geq 1$, let $\mathfrak{A}_{k,m}$ denote the set of all $k\times m$-matrices over $\mathfrak{A}$. Thus, e.g., $\mathfrak{A}_{k,1} = \mathfrak{A}^k$, the k-th cartesian degree of $\mathfrak{A}$. A *semimetric* over $\mathfrak{A}$ is a functional

$$\rho : \bigcup_{k\geq 1} (\mathfrak{A}^k\times\mathfrak{A}^k) \longrightarrow R_+$$

satisfying the usual "triangle rule": $\rho(x,y) \leq \rho(x,z) + \rho(z,y)$.
For $A \in \mathfrak{A}^k$ and a subset $\mathfrak{B} \subseteq \mathfrak{A}$, put $\rho(A,\mathfrak{B}) = \inf\{\rho(A,B): B\in\mathfrak{B}^k \}$.
For a $k\times m$-matrix A, let $\underline{A}$ denote the vector $(A_1,\dots,A_k) \in \mathfrak{A}^{km}$, where A_i stands for the i-th row of A. Given a vector of operations $\underline{f} = (f_1,\dots,f_k) \in F^k$ and a matrix $A \in \mathfrak{A}_{k,m}$, we denote by $\underline{f}(A)$ the vector $(f_1(A_1),\dots,f_k(A_k)) \in \mathfrak{A}^k$. Put $\underline{f}(\mathfrak{B}) = \{ \underline{f}(B) : B \in \mathfrak{B}_{k,n} \}$ and define the "one-step-closure" $F(\mathfrak{B})$ of $\mathfrak{B} \subseteq \mathfrak{A}$ by $F(\mathfrak{B}) = \bigcup \{ f(\mathfrak{B}) : f \in F \}$. A semimetric ρ is called to be *F-contractible on* $\mathfrak{B} \subseteq \mathfrak{A}$ iff for any $A\in\mathfrak{A}_{k,n}$ and $\underline{f} \in F^k$ it holds

$$\rho(\underline{f}(A),\underline{f}(\mathfrak{B})) \leq \rho(\underline{A},\mathfrak{B}).$$

The following theorem generalizes the standard approach of proving circuit-size lower bound - demonstrating that a certain amount of progress must be made, and that no step makes more than δ progress, for some small δ.

THEOREM 2. *Let* $(\mathfrak{A};F)$ *be an algebra,* $A\in\mathfrak{A}^k$ *be a vector and* $\mathfrak{H} \subseteq \mathfrak{A}$. *Then for any subset* $\mathfrak{B} \subseteq \mathfrak{A}$ *and any F-contractible on* $\mathfrak{B}$ *semimetric* ρ *we have that*

$$L_F(A,\mathfrak{H}) \geq \rho(A,\mathfrak{B})\,\delta^{-1} - 1 ,$$

where $\delta = \sup \{ \rho(C,\mathfrak{B}) : C \in (\mathfrak{H} \cup F(\mathfrak{B}))^m,\ m\geq 1 \}$.

Proof: We proceed by induction on $t = L_F(A,\mathfrak{H})$. If $t = 0$ then $A \subseteq \mathfrak{H}$, and hence $\rho(A,\mathfrak{B}) \le \delta$. For the induction step assume that $A = \underline{f}(C)$ for some $\underline{f} \in F^k$ and $C \in \mathfrak{U}_{k,n}$ with $L_F(\underline{C},\mathfrak{H}) \le t-1$. By the triangle rule we have, for any $B \in \mathfrak{U}_{k,n}$, that

$$\rho(A,\mathfrak{B}) = \rho(\underline{f}(C),\mathfrak{B}) \le \rho(\underline{f}(C),\underline{f}(B)) + \rho(\underline{f}(B),\mathfrak{B}) .$$

Since ρ is F-contractible on $\mathfrak{B}$, we have by the induction hypothesis that for *some* $B \in \mathfrak{B}_{k,n}$ $\rho(\underline{f}(C),\underline{f}(B)) \le \rho(\underline{C},\mathfrak{B}) \le t\delta$. Therefore, $\rho(A,\mathfrak{B}) \le t\delta + \rho(\underline{f}(B),\mathfrak{B}) \le t\delta + \delta = (t+1)\delta$. ∎

Let us now introduce an algebraic definition of contractible semimetrics, generalizing the methods of [2-4,12-18].

Let $(\mathfrak{U};\bullet)$ be a semigroup with a unit element 1, and let $\ll \subseteq \mathfrak{U}^2$ be some reflexive and transitive relation. A triple $\mathfrak{S} = (\mathfrak{E},\bullet,\ll)$, is an *approximation structure* iff $\bullet$ is monotone with respect to $\ll$ and $1 \in \mathfrak{E} \subseteq \mathfrak{U}$. Define "linear covers" $Cov_t(\mathfrak{E})$ of $\mathfrak{E}$ by :
$Cov_{t+1}(\mathfrak{E}) = \{ a\bullet b : a \in Cov_t(\mathfrak{E}) \text{ and } b \in \mathfrak{E} \}$ where $Cov_0(\mathfrak{E}) = \{1\}$.

A structure induces the following natural *measure of accurancy* $\rho(A,B)$ (with which a vector A is approximated by a vector B) : $\rho(A,B)$ is the minimum number $m \ge 0$ for which $Cov_m(\mathfrak{E})$ contains an element e such that $(\forall i)$ $a_i \ll b_i\bullet e$. Notice that $\rho(x,x) = 0$, since $\ll$ is reflexive, but $\rho(x,y) \ne \rho(y,x)$ on the whole.

A structure $\mathfrak{S} = (\mathfrak{E},\bullet,\ll)$ is *compatible with an algebra* $(\mathfrak{U};F)$ iff each operation $f \in F$ is both "$\ll$-*monotone*" and "$(\bullet,\ll)$-*idempotent*", i.e. if for any $A,B \in \mathfrak{U}^n$ and $c \in \mathfrak{U}$: $a_1 \ll b_1,\dots, a_n \ll b_n$ implies $f(A) \ll f(B)$, and $f(A\bullet c) \ll f(A)\bullet c$, where $A\bullet c = (a_1\bullet c,\dots,a_n\bullet c)$.

LEMMA 1. *Let $\mathfrak{S}$ be an approximation structure and let ρ be the induced measure of accurancy. If $\mathfrak{S}$ is compatible with an algebra $(\mathfrak{U};F)$ then ρ is a semimetric F-contractible on any subset $\mathfrak{B} \subseteq \mathfrak{U}$.*

Proof : Since $\ll$ is transitive and reflexive and $\bullet$ is monotone with respect to $\ll$, we have that ρ is a semimetric. To show that ρ is F-contractive on a subset $\mathfrak{B} \subseteq \mathfrak{U}$, let $f \in F$ and $A \in \mathfrak{U}_{k,n}$ with $\rho(\underline{A},\mathfrak{B}) = \rho(\underline{A},\underline{B}) = m$ for some $B \in \mathfrak{B}_{k,n}$, i.e. $a_i \ll b_i\bullet e$ for some $e \in Cov_m(\mathfrak{E})$ and all $i = 1,\dots,nk$. Since $\mathfrak{S}$ is compatible with $(\mathfrak{U};F)$, we have :

$$\forall j=1,\dots k \qquad f_j(A_j) \ll f_j(B_j\bullet e) \ll f_j(B_j)\bullet e .$$

Therefore, $\rho(\underline{f}(A),\underline{f}(\mathfrak{B})) \le m = \rho(\underline{A},\mathfrak{B})$. ∎

Given a subsets $\mathfrak{B},\mathfrak{C} \subseteq \mathfrak{U}$ and a pair of semimetrics ρ_0 and ρ_1, we shall write $[\rho_0,\rho_1](\mathfrak{C},\mathfrak{B}) \le d$ if for any $c \in \mathfrak{C}$ there exists an $b \in \mathfrak{B}$ such that $\rho_0(c,b) \le d$ and $\rho_1(b,c) \le d$.

THEOREM 3. *Let $(\mathfrak{U};F)$ be an algebra, $a \in \mathfrak{U}$ and $\mathfrak{B},\mathfrak{H} \subseteq \mathfrak{U}$. Let also*

ρ_0 and ρ_1 be a pair of accurancy measures induced by a pair of approximation structures $\mathfrak{S}_0$ and $\mathfrak{S}_1$. If these structures both are compatible with $(\mathfrak{A};F)$ *and* $[\rho_0,\rho_1](\mathfrak{B} \cup F(\mathfrak{B}),\mathfrak{B}) \le d$ $(d>0)$ *then*

$$L_F(a,\mathfrak{B}) \ \ge \ d^{-1} \inf_{b\in\mathfrak{B}} \max \{ \rho_0(a,b),\ \rho_1(b,a) \} .$$

Proof : Follows directly from Theorem 2 and Lemma 1 . ∎

2. The General Lower Bound

Let E be some finite set, $|E| \ge 2$ and $n \ge 1$. *Points* are elements of E^n and *figures* are elements of the power set $P(E^n)$ of E^n. Fix some element $* \in E$ and define the *weight* $N(x)$ of a point x by $N(x) = |\{i : x(i) \ne * \}|$, where $x(i)$ is the i-th coordinate of x. We say x *covers* y ($x \angle_* y$ for short) if $\forall i$ $y(i) \in \{x(i),*\}$. Hence, if $x \angle_* y$ then $N(x) \ge N(y)$. Thus, for any distinguished point $*\in E$, $(E^n, \angle_*)$ is an upper semilattice with the maximal element $\underline{*} = (*,\dots,*)$ and the *join* $\sup(x,y)$ defined as the (unique) point z of minimal weight such that $\{x,y\} \angle_* z$. For a point x and figures X,Y we shall write $x \angle_* Y$ if $x \angle_* y$ for some $y\in Y$, and $X \angle_* Y$ if $x \angle_* Y$ for all $x\in X$. For a figure X, set $X^\nabla = \{ x\in E^n : x \angle_* X \}$ and $\lfloor X \rfloor = \{ x\in X : \forall y\in X \ (x \angle_* y \Rightarrow y = x) \}$

An operation $f : P(E^n)^m \dashrightarrow P(E^n)$ is an $\exists$-*operation* if there is a system $\Omega_f \subseteq P(\{1,\dots,m\})$ such that for any point x and figures $X_1,\dots,X_m$ it holds that

$$x \angle_* f(X_1,\dots,X_n) \quad \text{iff} \quad (\exists \omega \in\Omega_f)(\forall i \in\omega) \quad x \angle_* X_i .$$

Let $\mathfrak{F}$ denote the set of all $\exists$-operations. Notice that, for example, the union $\cup$ and the *concatenation* $\odot$, given by

$$X\odot Y = \lfloor \{ x\in E^n : x \angle_* X \text{ and } x \angle_* Y \} \rfloor ,$$

both are $\exists$-operations with $\Omega_\cup = \{\{1\},\{2\}\}$ and $\Omega_\odot = \{\{1,2\}\}$.

Lemma 2. *For any* $F \subseteq \mathfrak{F}$ *and* $\mathfrak{A} \subseteq P(E^n)$ *containing* E^n, *the structure* $(\mathfrak{A},\cup,\angle_*)$ *is an approximation structure compatible with the algebra of figures* $(P(E^n);F)$.

To apply Theorem 3, we shall make use of the concept of closed figure similar to that of closed system of sets introducd in [2,13]. Let $p\ge1$ and $r\ge2$ be numbers to be choosen later, and let E^n_p denote the set of all points of weight at most p. The *closure* of a figure $X\subseteq E^n_p$, denoted by $X^\circledast$, is the smallest figure $Y\supseteq X$ such that for any r (not necessarily distinct) points $x_1,\dots,x_r$ of Y, the figure Y contains all the points $y\in E^n_p$ such that $y \angle_* \sup(x_i,x_j)$ for all $1\le i<j\le r$. A figure X is *closed* if $X^\circledast = X$. Let $\mathfrak{B}_{p,r}$ denote the set of all closed figures.

LEMMA 3. *For any figure* $X \subseteq E^n_p$ *it holds that*

(i) $\left| \lfloor X^{\circledast} \rfloor - X^{\nabla} \right| \le 2r^p$ *and*

(ii) if X *is closed then* $\left| \lfloor X \rfloor \cap E^n_k \right| \le (r-1)^k$ *for any* $0 \le k \le p$.

Proof: Similar to that of lemmas 2.3 and 2.5 in [2]. ∎

For an m-ary ∃-operation f and a sequence of figures $\underline{X} = (X_1, \ldots X_m)$, set

$$f[\underline{X}] = \bigcup_{\omega \in \Omega_f} \bigcap_{i \in \omega} X_i .$$

Notice that $f[\underline{X}] \subseteq f(\underline{X})$ but $f[\underline{X}] \ne f(\underline{X})$ in general. For example, $\cup[X,Y] = X \cup Y$ but $\odot[X,Y] = X \cap Y \ne X \odot Y$ on the whole. Moreover, if $f \in \mathfrak{F}$ and all $X_i \subseteq E^n_p$ then $f[\underline{X}] \subseteq E^n_p$ whereas $\neg(f(\underline{X}) \subseteq E^n_p)$ in general.

Given a collection of ∃-operations F, let $\mathfrak{G}^0_{p,r}$ and $\mathfrak{G}^1_{p,r}$ denote the sets of all figures of the form $f(\underline{X})^{\nabla} - (f[\underline{X}]^{\circledast})^{\nabla}$ and, respectively, of the form $(f[\underline{X}]^{\circledast})^{\nabla} - f(\underline{X})^{\nabla}$, where $f \in F$ and $X_i \in \mathfrak{B}_{p,r}$. Let ρ_0 and ρ_1 be the measures of accurancy induced by the structures $(\mathfrak{G}^0_{p,r}, \cup, \angle_*)$ and $(\mathfrak{G}^1_{p,r}, \cup, \angle_*)$. Fix the following collection of "singular" figures

$$\mathfrak{S}_0 = \{\emptyset\} \cup \{ \{x\} : x \in E^n \text{ and } N(x) \le 1 \}$$

It is easy to see that then for any $p \ge 1$ and $r \ge 2$, it holds that

$$[\rho_0, \rho_1](\mathfrak{S}_0 \cup F(\mathfrak{B}_{p,r}), \mathfrak{B}_{p,r}) \le 1 .$$

Therefore, by Theorem 3 and Lemma 2 we have, for any figure X, that

$$L_F(X, \mathfrak{S}_0) \ge \inf_{Y \in \mathfrak{B}_{p,r}} \max \{ \rho_0(X,Y), \rho_1(Y,X) \} \qquad (1)$$

To bound ρ_0 and ρ_1, let us introduce some auxiliary parameters. For figures X and Y, set $R(X) = \min \{ N(x) : x \in X \}$, $\gamma_X(Y) = |\{ x \in \lfloor X \rfloor : x \angle_* Y \}|$, and for $k \ge 0$, put $\gamma_X(k) = \max \{ \gamma_X(\{y\}) : y \in E^n \text{ and } N(y) = k \}$. A figure X is *r-disjoint* if $\gamma_X(t) \le \gamma_X(s)(3r-3)^{s-t}$ for all $0 \le s \le t$.

THEOREM 4. *Let* X *be a figure,* $\mathfrak{S}$ *be a collection of figures,* $1 \le p \le R(X)$, $r \ge 2$ *and* $0 \le \varepsilon \le (|E|-1)^{-1}$. *Let also* F *be a collection of ∃-operations of arity at most* m *and let* $\ell = \lceil (p+1)/m \rceil$. *Then for any r-disjoint figure* Y *and for any figure* Z *such that* $Y \angle_* X \angle_* Z$, *it holds that*

$$L_F(X, \mathfrak{S}) \ge \min \left\{ \frac{\gamma_Y(0)}{2m(r-1)^{\ell} \gamma_Y(\ell)} , \frac{1 - \gamma_Z(0)\, \varepsilon^{R(Z)}}{2r^p(1 - \varepsilon^p)^r} \right\} - \delta_F(\mathfrak{S})$$

where

$$\delta_F(\mathfrak{S}) = \sum_{W \in \mathfrak{S}} L_F(W, \mathfrak{S}_0).$$

Proof : By (1) it is sufficient to prove that for any closed figure B

$\in \mathfrak{B}$, it holds that $\rho_0(X,B) \ge u$ or $\rho_1(B,X) \ge v$ (or both), where u and v stand for the first and second expression in $\min(...)$. There are two possible cases, depending on B.

Case 1 : $\underline{*} \notin B$. Then $\rho_0(X,B) \ge \rho_0(Y,B) \ge u$.

The first inequality holds for any $Y \angle_* X$. The idea of proof of the second one is analogous to that of Theorem 4.3 in [2]. By the definition of ρ_0, there exist $t \le \rho_0(Y,B)$ figures $U_1,\dots,U_t$ in $\mathfrak{C}^{0}_{p,r}$ such that $\lfloor Y \rfloor \subseteq (B \cup U_1 \cup \dots \cup U_t)^{\nabla}$. Hence, $\rho_0(Y,B) \ge (\gamma_Y(0) - \gamma_Y(B))/\max \gamma_Y(U_i)$. Since $\underline{*} \notin B$, we have that $N(x) \ge 1$ for all $x \in B$, and since Y is r-disjoint, we have by Lemma 3(ii) that

$$\gamma_Y(B) \le \sum_{k=1}^{p} (r-1)^k \gamma_Y(k) \le \frac{1}{2} \gamma_Y(0)$$

To bound $\gamma_Y(U_i)$, recall that $U_i = f(\underline{W})^{\nabla} - (f[\underline{W}]^{\circledcirc})^{\nabla}$ for some $f \in F$ and some sequence of closed figures $\underline{W} = (W_1,\dots,W_m)$. If $x \in U_i^{\nabla}$ then there is some $\omega \in \Omega_f$ so that, for any $j \in \omega$, the point x covers some point y_j of $\lfloor W_j \rfloor$. Moreover, as no point of $f[\underline{W}]^{\circledcirc}$ is covered by x, we have that $x \angle_* \bigcap_{k \in \omega'} W_k$ for *no* $\omega' \in \Omega_f$. Let z be the point of minimal weight which covers all the points y_j, $j \in \omega$. If $N(z) \le p$ then, since figures W_j are closed, the point z is in $\bigcap_{k \in \omega} W_k$, which is impossible since $x \angle_* z$. Thus $N(z) \ge p+1$ and so $N(y_j) \ge \lceil N(z)/|\omega| \rceil \ge \ell$ for some $j \in \omega$. Therefore, if $x \in U_i^{\nabla}$ then x covers some point of $\lfloor W_1 \rfloor \cup \dots \cup \lfloor W_m \rfloor$ of weight at least ℓ. Hence, by Lemma 3(ii) we have that

$$\gamma_Y(U_i) \le \sum_{k=\ell}^{p} m(r-1)^k \gamma_Y(k) \le m(r-1)^{\ell} \gamma_Y(\ell).$$

Case 2 : $\underline{*} \in B$. Then $\rho_1(B,X) \ge v$.

Indeed, by the definition of ρ_1, there exist $t \le \rho_1(B,X)$ figures $D_1,\dots,D_t \in \mathfrak{C}^{1}_{p,r}$ such that $B^{\nabla} \subseteq (X \cup D_1 \cup \dots \cup D_t)^{\nabla}$. Let $x \in (E-\{*\})^n$ be a random point in which each $x(i) \in E-\{*\}$ appears independently with probability ε $(0 \le \varepsilon \le (|E|-1)^{-1})$. Then $\mathrm{Prob}\{ x \angle_* B \} = 1$, since $\underline{*} \in B$, and $\xi_0 = \mathrm{Prob}\{ x \angle_* X \} \le \mathrm{Prob}\{ x \angle_* Z \} \le \gamma_Z(0)\, \varepsilon^{R(C)}$. Hence $t \ge (1 - \xi_0)/\xi$ where $\xi = \max \mathrm{Prob}\{ x \angle_* D_i \}$. By Lemma 3(i), $\xi \le 2r^p \eta^r$ where $\eta = \max \{ \mathrm{Prob}(\neg(x \angle_* y)) : y \in E^n_p \}$. It remains to observe that $\eta \le 1 - \varepsilon^p$. ∎

3. The Complexity of Disjunctive Normal Forms

Fix some alphabet of Boolean variables $\{u_1,\dots,u_n\}$, and let $E^n = \{*,0,1\}$. We identify a monomial $\&_{i \in I} u_i^{\sigma_i}$ with the point $x \in E^n$ such that $\forall j=1,\dots,n$, $x(j)=\sigma_j$ if $j \in I$ and $x(j)=*$ otherwise. So, *DNFs are figures over* E^n. A DNF $X \subseteq E^n$ *realizes* a Boolean function $f(u_1,\dots,u_n)$ iff $f^{-1}(1) = X^{\nabla} \cap \{0,1\}^n$. Let $Imp(f)$ denote the set of all prime implicants of minimal length of f, i.e. $x \in Imp(f)$ iff x is a prime implicant of f and $N(x) \le N(y)$ for any other prime implicant y of f.

For $\delta \in [0,1]$ and a Boolean function f, let $D(f,\delta)$ denote the set of all DNFs X realizing f and such that $|X \cap Imp(f)| \ge |Imp(f)|^{\delta} - 1$.

LEMMA 4. *For any Boolean function* f *and* $\delta \in [0,1]$ *it holds that*

$$C_{\delta}(f) \ge \min_{A \in D(f,\delta)} L_{\{\cup,\odot\}}(X,\mathfrak{F}_0) .$$

Proof: Take $Q = \{ (f,X) : X \text{ realizes } f \}$ and apply Theorem 1. ∎

EXAMPLE 1. Let q be a prime number such that $s = [\frac{1}{12} \ln q] \ge 1$, and let $GF(q)$ be the Galois field of order q with the addition $+$. Fix an element $e \ne 0$ of $GF(q)$ and consider the following Boolean function $\pi_n(U)$ of $n = q^2$ variables $U = \{u_{a,b} : a,b \in GF(q) \}$. Given a quadratic $q \times q$-matrix $\mathcal{A} = (\alpha_{a,b})$ with $\alpha_{a,b} \in \{0,1\}$, let $\pi_n(\mathcal{A}) = 1$ iff there is a polynomial p of degree at most $s-1$ over $GF(q)$ such that for all $a \in GF(q)$, $\alpha_{a,p(a)} = 1$ and $\alpha_{a,p(a)+e} = 0$. Notice that π_n is non-monotone: $\pi_n(\mathcal{A}) = 0$ if $\mathcal{A}$ contains more than $n-q$ or less than q ones. Set $Y_n = Imp(\pi_n)$, and let $Z_n = \{ K^{+}_{p_1} \& K^{-}_{p_2} :$ p_1 and p_2 are polynomials of degree atmost $s-1$ $\}$, where a monomial K^{+}_{p} (K^{-}_{p}) consists of all the literals $u_{a,p(a)}$ (resp., $\bar{u}_{a,p(a)\oplus e}$), $a \in GF(q)$. Notice that $Y_n \subseteq Z_n$ and $X_n \not\prec_{*} Z_n$ for any DNF X_n realizing π_n. Moreover $R(Y_n) = R(Z_n) = 2q$, $\gamma_{Y_n}(0) = |Y_n| = q^s$, $\gamma_{Z_n}(0) = q^{2s}$ and $\gamma_{Y_n}(k) \le q^{s-[(k+1)/2]}$ for all $k \ge 1$. Since $\cup$ and $\odot$ both are $\exists$-operations, Theorem 4 implies the following

COROLLARY 1. *For any DNF* X_n *with* $\lfloor X_n \rfloor = Y_n$ *we have that*

$$L_{\{\cup,\odot\}}(X_n,\mathfrak{F}_0) \ge n^{\Omega(\ln n)}.$$

Proof : Take $r = [q^{1/3}]$, $p = [\frac{1}{2} \ln r]$ and $\varepsilon = ((\ln r)^2/r)^{1/p}$ and apply Theorem 4 ∎

Since Y_n realizes π_n, Lemma 4 and Corollary 1 yield

COROLLARY 2. *For any constant* $\delta \in (0,1]$ *it holds that*

$$n^{\Omega(\ln n)} \le C_{\delta}(\pi_n) \le n^{\varepsilon \ln n} , \qquad \varepsilon \le 1/47.$$

Therefore, we have that either $C(\pi_n) \ge n^{\Omega(\ln n)}$ or *all* the minimal circuits for π_n compute DNFs X_n such that $|X_n \cap Y_n| \le |Y_n|^{o(1)}$.

4. THE COMPLEXITY OF THREE-VALUED FUNCTIONS

Let $E_3 = \{0,1,2\}$ and let $\mathfrak{B}^n_3$ denote the set of all n-ary three-valued predicates $f : E^n_3 \longrightarrow \{0,1\}$.

Probably, the first non-trivial lower bound for circuits over an incomplete three-valued basises has been proved by Tkachev in [18]. He considers circuits over the algebra $(\mathfrak{P}_3^n; \wedge , \oplus)$ with input $H_0 = \{\nu_1,\dots,\nu_n\}$, where $\mathfrak{P}_3^n$ is the set of all three-valued functions $f: E_3^n \longrightarrow E_3$, $x\wedge y = \min(x,y)$, $x\oplus y = xy (\mathrm{mod}\ 2)$ and $\nu_i : E_3^n \longrightarrow E_3$ is the i-th projection, i.e. for $\sigma\in E_3^n$, $\nu_i(\sigma) = \sigma(i)$, the i-th coordinate of σ. In [18] the bound

$$L_{\{\wedge,\oplus\}}(t_n,H_0) \geq 2\binom{n}{n/2} - 1$$

is proved for the sequence of three-valued predicates $t_n \in \mathfrak{B}_3^n$ given by : $t_n(\sigma) = 1$ iff $\sigma\in\{1,2\}^n$ and $|\{i : \sigma(i)=1\}| \geq n/2 +1$.
Set $x\vee y = \max(x,y)$ and $H = \{\iota_1,\dots,\iota_n,\eta_1,\dots,\eta_n\}$ where for $\sigma\in E_3^n$

$$\iota_i(\sigma) = \begin{cases} 1 & \text{if } \sigma(i)=1, \\ 0 & \text{otherwise,} \end{cases} \quad \text{and} \quad \eta_i(\sigma) = \begin{cases} 1 & \text{if } \sigma(i)=2, \\ 0 & \text{otherwise.} \end{cases}$$

Notice that the predicate t_n has polynomial-size circuits over the algebra $(\mathfrak{B}_3^n ; \vee , \oplus)$ even with input H :

$$L_{\{\vee,\oplus\}}(t_n,H) \leq O(n^{5.3}) .$$

This follows from the representation

$$t_n(\sigma) = \xi_1(\sigma)\oplus\xi_2(\sigma)\oplus \dots \oplus\xi_n\oplus \mathrm{MAJ}_n(\iota_1(\sigma),\dots,\iota_n(\sigma)),$$

where $\xi_i(\sigma) = \iota_i(\sigma) \vee \eta_i(\sigma)$, and from the result of Valiant [20] that the monotone Boolean formula-size complexity of Boolean majority function MAJ_n is $O(n^{5.3})$.

In this section we demonstrate Theorem 4 by a super-polynomial lower bound for $L_{\{\vee,\oplus\}}(\cdot,H)$. To do this, let $0\in E_3$ be the distinguished element of E_3 (i.e. 0 plays a role of $*$), and let $\preceq_0$ be the corresponding order relation on E_3^n. Identify a predicate $f\in\mathfrak{B}_3^n$ with the figure $X_f = f^{-1}(1) \subseteq E_3^n$.

LEMMA 5. *For any predicate* $f \in \mathfrak{B}_3^n$ *it holds that*

$$L_{\{\vee,\oplus\}}(f,H) \geq L_{\{\cup,\odot\}}(X_f,\mathfrak{H}_0).$$

Proof. Define $Q \subseteq \mathfrak{B}_3^n \times P(E_3^n)$ by $Q = \{(f,Y) : X_f= \{x\in E_3^n : x \preceq_0 Y \}\}$. Then $Q(H) \subseteq \mathfrak{H}_0$ and the algebra of figures $(P(E_3^n); \cup, \odot)$ is Q-image of $(\mathfrak{B}_3^n; \vee, \oplus)$. It remains to apply Theorem 1. ■

EXAMPLE 2. Let us consider the following three-valued extention $\Pi_n\in\mathfrak{B}_3^n$ of π_n (see Example 1).For a quadratic $q\times q$-matrix $M = (m_{a,b})$ with $m_{a,b}\in E_3$, let $\Pi_n(M) = 1$ iff there is a polynomial p of degree at most s-1 over GF(q) such that $\forall a\in GF(q)$ $m_{a,p(a)}=1$ and $m_{a,p(a)+e}=2$.
Lemma 5 and Corollary 1 directly yield the following bound.

COROLLARY 3: $n^{\Omega(\ln n)} \leq L_{\{\vee,\oplus\}}(\Pi_n,H) \leq n^{C\ln n}$, $C\leq 1/47$.

Obviously we are just begining to understand the power of functional (as well as probabilistic and topological) approximations in lower bounds proofs. The two examples given in this note, as well as examples is [2-4,13,14], all concern the standard algebra of DNFs. Of course, Theorems 1-3 admit further applications. For example, one may consider more subtle representations of Boolean functions such as the algebra of prime implicants, etc. Besides, a suitable combination of functional, probabilistic and topological approximation techniques may help.

REFERENCES

[1] M. Ajtai, Σ^1_1-formulae on finite structures. *Ann.of Pure and Appl.logic*, 24 (1984), pp. 1-48.

[2] N. Alon and R.B. Boppana, The monotone circuit complexity of Boolean functions, *Combinatorica*, 7, N.1 (1987), pp. 1-22.

[3] A.E. Andreev, On one method of obtaining lower bounds of individual monotone function complexity, *Doklady Akad. Nauk SSSR*, 282 (1985), pp. 1033-1037.

[4] A.E. Andreev, On one method of obtaining effective lower bounds of monotone complexity, *Algebra i Logika*, 26,N.1(1987),pp. 3-21.

[5] M. Furst, J.B. Saxe and M. Sipser, Parity, circuits and the polynomial time hierarchy , *Proc. 22nd FOCS* (1981),pp.260-270.

[6] A. Hajnal, W. Maass, P. Pudlak, M. Szegedy and G. Turan, Threshold circuits of bounded depth, *Proc. 28th FOCS* (1987), 99-110.

[7] J. Hastad, Almost optimal lower bounds for small depth circuits, *Proc. 18th STOC* (1986), pp. 6-20.

[8] S.P. Jukna, Lower bounds on the complexity of local circuits, *Lect. Notes in Comput. Sci*. 233 (Springer-Berlin, 1986),440-448.

[9] S.P. Jukna, Entropy of contact circuits and lower bounds on their complexity, *Theoret. Comput.Sci.*, 57, N.1 (1988).

[10] S.P. Jukna, On one entropic method of obtaining lower bounds on the complexity of Boolean functions, *Doklady Akad. Nauk SSSR*, 298, N.3 (1988), pp. 556-559.

[11] E.A. Okol'nishnikova, On the influence of one type of restrictions to the complexity of combinational circuits, *Discrete Analysis* , 36 (Novosibirsk, 1981), pp. 46-58.

[12] M.S. Paterson, Bonded-depth circuits over {⊕,&}, Preprint, 1986.

[13] A.A. Razbororov, Lower bounds for the monotone complexity of some Boolean functions, *Doklady Akad. Nauk SSSR*, 281 (1985), pp. 798-801.

[14] A.A. Razborov, A lower bound on the monotone network complexity of the logical permanent, *Mat. Zametki*, 37, N.6 (1985)

[15] A.A.Razborov, Lower bounds for the size of bounded-depth circuits over the basis { ⊕ ,&}, Preprint (Moscow, 1986).

[16] R. Smolensky, Algebraic methods in the theory of lower bounds for Boolean circuit complexity, *Proc. 19th STOC* (1987), pp.77-87.

[17] A. Yao, Lower bounds by probabilistic arguments, *Proc. 24th FOCS* (1983), pp. 420-428.

[18] G.A. Tkachev, On the complexity of one sequence of functions of k-valued logic, *Vestnik MGU*, Ser.2, N.1 (1977), pp. 45-57.

[19] A.B. Ugol'nikov, On the complexity of realization of Boolean functions by circuits over the basis with median and implication *Vestnik MGU*, Ser.1, N.4 (1987), pp. 76-78.

[20] L.G. Valiant, Short monotone formulae for the majority function, *Journal of Algorithms*, v. 5 (1984), pp. 363-366.

POSITIVE / NEGATIVE

CONDITIONAL REWRITING

Stéphane Kaplan[1,2,3]

Abstract :
This paper introduces positive/negative conditional term rewriting systems, with rules of the generic form :

$$u = v \wedge u' \neq v' \;\Rightarrow\; \lambda \rightarrow \rho\,,$$

as they often appear in algebraic specifications. We consider the algebraic semantics of such systems (viewed as sets of axioms). They do not in general have initial models ; however, we show that they admit *quasi-initial models*, that are in some sense extremal within the class of all models. We then introduce the subclass of *reducing* rewrite systems, constrained by the condition : $\lambda > \rho, u, v, u', v'$ (for some reduction ordering >). For such systems, we show that an optimal *rewrite relation* $\rightarrow$ may be defined, and constructed as a "limit". We prove the total validity of an interpreter that computes the normal forms of terms for $\rightarrow$. It is then shown that when $\rightarrow$ is confluent, the algebra of normal forms is a quasi-initial model. We state a general result about the converse. Lastly, we present a complete critical-pair criterion à la Knuth-Bendix to check for the confluence of reducing systems.

1. Introduction : positive/negative conditional TRS

The field of term rewriting systems has seen important developments during the last decade. One crucial aspect of rewriting is that it provides a natural, operational interpretation of algebraic specifications. Strong connections are known to exist between the two domains – from the algebraic, operational and logical points of view.

Originally, term rewriting systems were limited to *equational* rules, i.e. formulae of the form : $\lambda \rightarrow \rho$. These rules are not, however, expressive enough to simulate the algebraic specifications one tends to write naturally. More recently, attention has been devoted to *positive conditional* rules, of the generic form : $u = v \Rightarrow \lambda \rightarrow \rho$. In this paper, we further generalize the class of rules under consideration, introducing *positive/negative conditional* rules of the form :

$$u = v \wedge \bar{u} \neq \bar{v} \;\Rightarrow\; \lambda \rightarrow \rho.$$

These correspond exactly to the axioms used, naturally, when writing algebraic specifications. In spite of their obvious importance, this class of rules has not been studied so far, perhaps for the following reasons :

- They do not exhibit a straightforward algebraic behaviour. This is to be contrasted with the cases of equational and positive conditional systems, which have initial algebra semantics. In the positive/negative case, as shown below, the specifications do not admit, in general, an initial model. However, we show that they admit what we call *quasi-initial* models, having interesting algebraic properties ; among them, that there exists a privileged model that precisely captures the intuition of the specifier. Moreover, under favourable circumstances, this model may be described by rewriting.

1 Computer Science Department, Hebrew University, Givat Ram, Jerusalem (Israel) - *kaplan@humus.bitnet*
2 L.R.I., Bât. 490, Université des Sciences, F-91405 Orsay Cedex (France) - *kaplan@lri.lri.fr*
3 Computer Science Department, Bar-Ilan University, Ramat-Gan (Israel) - *kaplan@bimacs.bitnet*

- *positive/negative* systems are at least as complicated as positive ones, about which not much was known until recently. However, we feel that recent results about positive systems have implications for positive/negative ones. In particular, we systematically use in this paper the notion of *reducing* systems, satisfying the condition :

$$\lambda > \rho, \quad u, v, \overline{u}, \overline{v}.$$

(for some reduction ordering >). Intuitively, this means that the complexity of a computation decreases monotonically along the rewrite sequences, as well as along the "recursive calls" to evaluate u, v, $\overline{u}$ and $\overline{v}$. Reducing systems are shown to have various interesting properties. In particular, they may be assigned a minimal semantics (which is not necessarily the case for non-reducing systems), closely connected to the algebraic notion of quasi-initial models.

Note that an inequation "$\overline{u} \neq \overline{v}$" cannot be replaced by an expression such as "$\neg$Eq($\overline{u}$,$\overline{v}$)" or even "notEq($\overline{u}$,$\overline{v}$)", for defined predicates (or boolean functions) 'Eq' or 'notEq'. This is because definitions by predicate generate semi-decidable specifications (cf. e.g. [BBTW 81], [Kaplan 82]), whereas inequations allow to define co-semi-decidable specifications.

The paper is organized as follows :

- Section 1 introduces general definitions.
- Section 2 deals with the algebraic aspects of positive/negative systems ; it is shown that such specifications do not admit in general an initial model. Quasi-initial models are introduced as a natural extension of the notion of initial model, and general results about the existence and completeness of quasi-initial models are presented.
- Section 3 considers positive/negative rewriting. It is proved that in the case of reducing systems, there exists a minimal rewrite relation. This relation may be constructed as a (non-monotonic) limit, and is decidable. We show the total correctness of a universal interpreter to compute it. When the relation is known to be confluent, the normal form algebra is a quasi-initial model. A converse result is also stated, establishing a strong link between the algebraic and the operational aspects of such systems.
- Lastly, section 4 considers the confluence of reducing systems. A general critical pair theorem à la Knuth-Bendix is proved.

In sections 2 to 4, only the most interesting proofs are presented. The remaining proofs are to be found in the appendices.

We assume that the reader has basic knowledge about term rewriting systems and algebraic specifications. We refer to the papers [HO 80], [Klop 87], and to [ADJ 78], [EM 85], as general introductions to the former and to the latter fields, respectively.

Throughout this paper, a signature Σ is given, together with a set of variables X. T_Σ stands for the set of ground terms on Σ, and $T_\Sigma(X)$ for the set of terms with variables on Σ and X.

Definition 1.1:

• a *positive/negative conditional term rewriting system* (P/N CTRS) is a finite set of formulae of the form :

$$r : (\wedge_{i=1}^{n} u_i = v_i) \wedge (\wedge_{j=1}^{m} \bar{u}_j \neq \bar{v}_j) \ \Rightarrow \ \lambda \rightarrow \rho,$$

where λ, ρ, the u_i, the v_i, the $\bar{u}_j$ and the $\bar{v}_j$ are in $T_\Sigma(X)$ and satisfy :

$$Var(\lambda) \ \supseteq \ Var(\rho),\ Var(u_i),\ Var(v_i),\ Var(\bar{u}_j),\ Var(\bar{v}_j).$$

• a *reducing* P/N CTRS is a P/N CTRS such that there exists a reduction ordering '>' that satisfies, for any ground substitution σ :

$$\lambda\sigma \ > \ \rho\sigma,\ u_i\sigma,\ v_i\sigma,\ \bar{u}_j\sigma,\ \bar{v}_j\sigma.$$

Thus, a P/N CTRS is simply a collection of equational clauses with a distinguished, oriented positive literal.

We recall that a reduction ordering is a partial ordering on the set of ground terms, that is *well-founded* and satisfies the following *monotonicity* property :

if $t > t'$, *then* $f(\ldots , t , \ldots) > f(\ldots , t' , \ldots)$

The case n = m = 0 corresponds to classical, unconditional term rewriting systems (TRS) [HO 80], [Klop 87], while the case m = 0 and n > 0 corresponds to classical *positive* conditional term rewriting systems (or simply "conditional TRS" - CTRS) [Kaplan 84a], [RZ 84,85], [Ganzinger 86].

The condition on the variables is in order to avoid rules with more variables in the premise than in the left-hand side ; equation solving is needed in order to apply such rules. Thus, they fall outside the scope of rewriting, which should be a "direct" process.

The condition '$\lambda > \rho$' is often assumed for classical TRS to ensure termination. The condition '$\lambda > u_i, v_i$', has been introduced in [Kaplan 84b] and further developed in [JW 86], [Ganziger 86]. This proved to be very fruitful for classical CTRS, for reasons that are recalled hereafter. We will demonstrate that for our generalization to P/N CTRS, is even more useful (even "necessary" for defining the semantics of the rewriting).

Examples :

• Algebraic specifications are often written in the following way :

$p(x) = 0 \ \Rightarrow \ f(x) \rightarrow e_1(x)$

$p(x) \neq 0 \ \Rightarrow \ f(x) \rightarrow e_2(x),$

which is more natural than the version :

$zerop?(x) = True \quad \Rightarrow \ f(x) \rightarrow e_1(x)$

$zerop?(x) = False \quad \Rightarrow \ f(x) \rightarrow e_2(x),$

that one needs to use when restricted to strictly positive CTRS.

• The following system, inspired by the work of [BBK 87] on *priority rewrite rules* :

$EQ(x,x) \ \rightarrow \ True$

$x \neq y \ \Rightarrow \ EQ(x,y) \ \rightarrow \ False,$

specifies in an elegant and generic way an equality predicate above any (canonical) specification. Note that many interesting case of priority rewrite rules may be modelized by P/N CTRS.

We are now going to consider the algebraic, and then the operational semantics, of P/N systems.

2. Algebraic semantics

In this chapter, we address the question of the *algebraic* semantics of P/N systems, i.e. the class of their models. Rigorously, we have to consider P/N conditional *axioms*, that are like non-oriented P/N conditional rules (each '$\rightarrow$' sign being replaced by an '=' sign). The satisfiability of a P/N axiom is defined as for positive conditional axioms.

A crucial difficulty is that, as opposed to the case of equations or strictly positive conditional axioms, *P/N axioms do not necessarily admit an initial model.* For instance, the system :

$$\{ \ a \neq b \ \Rightarrow \ a = c \ \}$$

(which *algebraically* equivalent to : $a=b \vee a=c$, but not *operationally* - cf. hereafter), admits as finitely generated models :

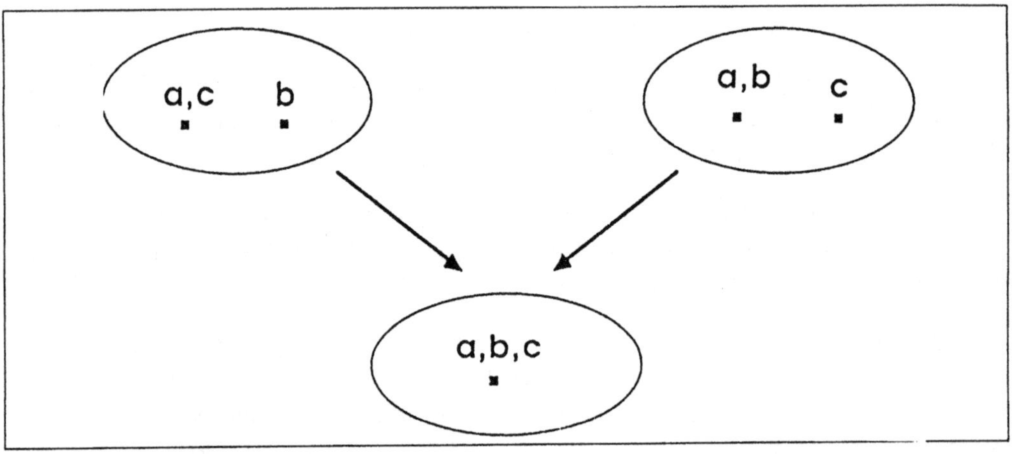

and thus no initial model. In this case, what is the algebraic semantics of a P/N system ?

To answer this question, let E be a given P/N system. Consider the following classical ordering between the models (up to an isomorphism) of E :

$$M \leq M' \quad \textit{iff} \quad \text{there exists a unique morphism } \phi \text{ from M into M'}.$$

We say that a model is *quasi-initial* if it is minimal for '$\leq$'.

Theorem 2.1 :

(1) The models of E admit a non-empty class of quasi-initial models.

(2) The quasi-initial models are finitely generated.

(3) For any E-model M, there exists a quasi-initial model Q such that $Q \leq M$.

Proof of theorem 2.1 : cf. Appendix 1

Pictorially :

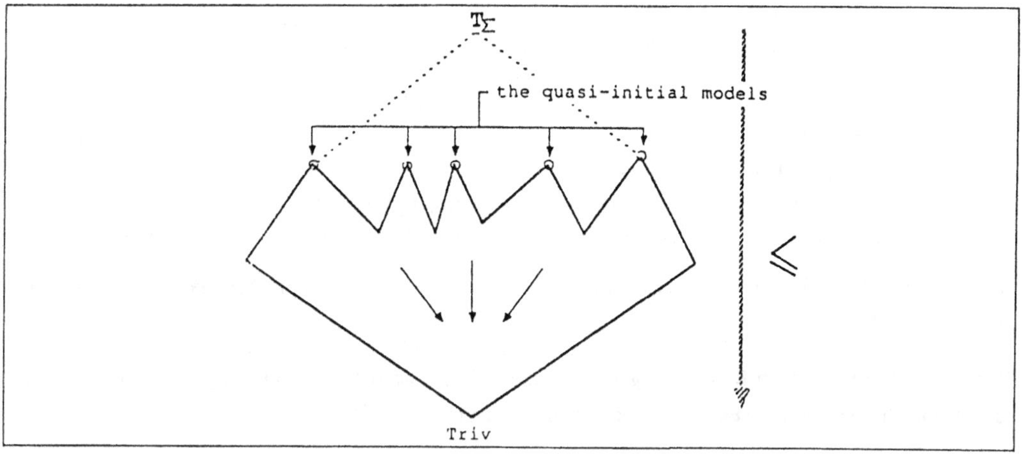

The quasi-initial models are the peaks of the class of the E-models.

We shall consider the semantics of a P/N system to be precisely the class of its quasi-initial models. We show in section 3 that, under favourable circumstances, the quasi-initial models are obtained as the normal-form algebra of the system, interpreted as a CTRS in "every possible fashion". In the case of the above example, there are two quasi-initial models, corresponding to the two (*reducing*) systems :

$$a \neq b \;\Rightarrow\; a \rightarrow c \qquad \textit{and} \qquad a \neq c \;\Rightarrow\; a \rightarrow b.$$

A converse result may also be stated.

3. Operational semantics

In this section, we consider how P/N *rewrite rules* work, i.e. the operational semantics of P/N systems. As before, one difficulty with P/N systems stems from the fact that there is no smallest precongruence ("rewrite *relation*") satisfying the rules. For instance, for the system :

$$\mathbf{S}_1 : \; \{\; a \neq b \;\Rightarrow\; a \rightarrow c \;\},$$

the two relations :

$$R_1 : \{\, a \rightarrow c \,\} \qquad \textit{and} \qquad R_2 : \{\, a \rightarrow b \,\}$$

are minimal, "satisfy" $\mathbf{S}_1$, but are incomparable.

We draw the attention of the reader to the following point. A system such as $\mathbf{S}_1$ is equivalent, from an algebraic point of view, to {a=b ∨ a=c }, and thus to {a≠c ⇒ a→b}. However, when a specifier writes $\mathbf{S}_1$, he adds an information, from the operational point of view, that does not exist under the form {a=b ∨ a=c}. For instance, a definition such as {p(x)≠0 ⇒ f(x)→*exp*} should certainly not be operationally understood as {p(x)=0 ∨ f(x)=*exp*}, nor as {f(x)=*exp* ⇒ p(x)→0} ! Our treatment of positive/negative systems therefore has to take into account this additive information.

We now have the following result :

Definition and property 3.1

Given a reducing P/N system, there exists a well-defined, unique precongruence $\rightarrow_R$ on T_Σ such that :

$t \rightarrow_R t'$ *iff*

there exists a context K[X], a substitution σ,

a rule r : $(\wedge_{i=1}^{n} u_i = v_i) \wedge (\wedge_{j=1}^{m} \bar{u}_j \neq \bar{v}_j) \Rightarrow \lambda \rightarrow \rho$ of R

such that :

$t = K[\lambda\sigma]$, $t' = K[\rho\sigma]$

$\forall i \in [1..n]$, $u_i\sigma \downarrow_R v_i\sigma$ and $\forall j \in [1..m]$, $\bar{u}_j\sigma \not\downarrow_R \bar{v}_j\sigma$

As usual, $p \downarrow_R p'$ iff there exists a q such that $p \xrightarrow{*}_R q$, $p' \xrightarrow{*}_R q$, and $p \not\downarrow_R p'$ iff there exists no such q such that $p \xrightarrow{*}_R q$, $p' \xrightarrow{*}_R q$.

With the previous system R = S_1, $\rightarrow_R$ is the relation R_1. The second relation R_2 does not satisfy the statement : "$t \rightarrow t'$ *iff* there exists a rule r ..." with t = a and t' = b.

Note :

The rewrite relation is defined on ground terms. It is easily extended to terms with variables, by having the variables play the role of constants. However, the resulting relation is *not* closed under substitution, i.e. $t \rightarrow_R t'$ does not imply $t\sigma \rightarrow_R t'\sigma$ (as opposed to the case of equational, or positive conditional rules). This justifies our consideration of rewriting on T_Σ mainly.

Proof of property 3.1

In order to prove property 3.1, we provide an explicit construction for $\rightarrow_R$. To this effect, we define the following sequence of binary relations :

- $\rightarrow_0 \ = \varnothing$
- $\rightarrow_{k+1} \ = \{(t,t')$ | there exists a context K[X], a substitution σ and a rule r

  that satisfy : $t = K[\lambda\sigma]$, $t' = K[\rho\sigma]$

  $\forall i \in [1..n]$, $NF_{\rightarrow_k}(u_i\sigma) \cap NF_{\rightarrow_k}(v_i\sigma) \neq \varnothing$

  $\forall j \in [1..m]$, $NF_{\rightarrow_k}(\bar{u}_j\sigma) \cap NF_{\rightarrow_k}(\bar{v}_j\sigma) = \varnothing \}$

Here, '$NF_{\rightarrow_k}(t)$' stands for the set of the normal forms of t for $\rightarrow_k$. The next lemma ensures that this is meaningful :

Lemma 3.2

Given a reducing P/N CTRS R, for any term t, for any k≥0, each set $NF_{\rightarrow_k}(t)$ is well-defined, finite and computable.

Proof of lemma 3.2

- This is obvious for k = 0.
- We assume that the property holds for a given k and prove it for k+1. Let us define the ordering :

  $t >^{st} t'$ *iff* $t \triangleright t'$ or t' is a strict subterm of t.

$>^{st}$ is well-founded [JK 84]. We establish the desired property by $>^{st}$-induction [Huet 77], as most of the proofs in this paper. To this effect, consider the predicate :

$$P(t) \ : \ NF_{\rightarrow_{k+1}} \text{ is well-defined, finite and computable.}$$

We assume that, for a given t,

$$\forall\tau,\ t >^{st} \tau \ \Rightarrow\ P(\tau)\ ,$$

and we prove that P(t). This will show that P(t) holds for *any* t.

Given t as above, and a "matching triple" (K,σ,r), the sets $NF_{\rightarrow_k}(u_i\sigma)$, $NF_{\rightarrow_k}(v_i\sigma)$, $NF_{\rightarrow_k}(\overline{u}_j\sigma)$, $NF_{\rightarrow_k}(\overline{v}_j\sigma)$ are well-defined, finite and computable, by the hypothesis *on k*. Thus one may decide whether $t \rightarrow_{k+1} t'$ or not. If this is the case, due to the fact that $t >^{st} t'$, we have that $NF_{\rightarrow_{k+1}}(t')$ is well-defined, finite and computable ; this is then also the case for $NF_{\rightarrow_{k+1}}(t)$. □ lemma 3.2

This establishes that each relation $\rightarrow_k$ is well-defined.

We then have the next lemma :

Lemma 3.3 :
Given a reducing P/N CTRS R, for any t, there exists an integer $\psi(t)$ such that :

for any t',

either $\forall k \geq \psi(t),\ t \rightarrow_k t'$

or $\forall k \geq \psi(t),\ t \not\rightarrow_k t'$

Example :

Consider the system : $S_2 = \{\ a(0) \rightarrow \alpha,\ even?(n) = T \wedge a(n) \neq \alpha \ \Rightarrow\ a(s(n)) \rightarrow \alpha,$
$even?(n) = T \wedge a(n) = \alpha \ \Rightarrow\ a(s(s(n))) \rightarrow \alpha\ \}$

We have :

$$\rightarrow_k \ = \ \{\ a(0) \rightarrow T\ ,\ a(2) \rightarrow T, \ldots ,\ a(2k\text{-}2) \rightarrow T,$$
$$a(2k\text{-}1) \rightarrow \alpha\ ,\ a(2k+1) \rightarrow \alpha\ ,\ a(2k+3) \rightarrow \alpha, \ldots\ \}.$$

We can thus adopt : $\psi(a(n)) = n/2+1$.

Proof of lemma 3.3 :

As before, we proceed by $>^{st}$-induction. Consider the predicate :

$$P(t) \ \textit{iff}\ \exists\psi(t),\ \forall t',\ \textit{either}\ \ \forall k{\geq}\psi(t), t{\rightarrow_k}t'$$
$$\textit{or}\ \ \forall k{\geq}\psi(t), t{\not\rightarrow_k}t'$$

(i.e. : the redexes of t are "stable" after some index $\psi(t)$). Suppose that, for a given t, $\tau >^{st} t$ implies that $P(\tau)$ holds. If (K,σ,r) is a matching triple for t, we have :

$$t >^{st} u_i\sigma,\ v_i\sigma,\ \overline{u}_j\sigma,\ \overline{v}_j\sigma.$$

Thus : $P(u_i\sigma)$, $P(v_i\sigma)$, $P(\overline{u}_j\sigma)$ and $P(\overline{v}_j\sigma)$. Let :

$$\psi \ = \ Sup_{K,\sigma,r}\ Sup_{i,j}\{\ \psi(u_i\sigma), \psi(v_i\sigma), \psi(\overline{u}_j\sigma), \psi(\overline{v}_j\sigma)\ \}$$

Then $\psi(t) = \psi$ shows that P(t). Thus, P(t) holds for *any* t. □ lemma 3.3

We finally define '$\rightarrow_R$' by :

$$t \rightarrow_R t' \quad \textit{iff} \quad t \rightarrow_k t' \text{ for } k{\geq}\psi(t).$$

It is left to the reader to check that $\rightarrow_R$ satisfies definition 3.1.

Example :
With the previous system $\mathbf{S}_2$, we have as "limit" :

$$\rightarrow_R \;=\; \{\, a(0) \rightarrow \alpha\,,\, a(2) \rightarrow \alpha\,,\, \ldots\,,\, a(2n) \rightarrow \alpha\,,\, \ldots \,\}.$$

Lastly, the uniqueness of a relation satisfying the property of 3.1 is proved by $>^{st}$-induction, using the predicate :

$$P(t) : \;\forall \tau\, (\, t\, s\, \tau \;\Leftrightarrow\; t \rightarrow_R \tau\,)$$

for another possible relation 's' ■ property 3.1

Note :
For strictly *positive* CTRS, as shown in [Kaplan 84a], the functional ∂ that associates to a finitely terminating and finitely branching precongruence $\rightarrow\, = \,\rightarrow_k$ the precongruence $\rightarrow_{k+1}$ as above, is shown to be continuous on the lattice of the precongruences ordered by inclusion. The least fixpoint of ∂ is the rewrite relation $\rightarrow_R$. It is constructed as l.u.b. of the $(\rightarrow_k)_{k\geq 0}$, starting with *any* $\rightarrow_0$. However, even for *reducing* positive/negative systems, the sequence $(\rightarrow_k)_{k\geq 0}$ is in general non-monotonic, as shown by the system $\mathbf{S}_2$ above. However, lemma 3.3 ensures the existence of a "limit" $\rightarrow_R$. The choice of $\rightarrow_0$ matters for $\rightarrow_R$; for instance, with the reducing system $\mathbf{S}_1$,

- starting with $\rightarrow_0 = \emptyset$ gives as a limit : $\{\, c \rightarrow d \,\}$
- starting with $\rightarrow_0 = \{\, a \rightarrow b \,\}$ gives as a limit : $\{\, a \rightarrow b \,\}$ (which is not satisfactory).

For non-reducing systems, there may even be no "limit" to the sequence, as shown by the next example :

Let $\mathbf{S}_3 \;=\; \{\; a \neq b \;\Rightarrow\; c \rightarrow d\;,\;\; c \neq d \;\Rightarrow\; a \rightarrow b \;\}$
Then :

$$\rightarrow_0 \;=\; \emptyset, \qquad \rightarrow_1 \;=\; \{\, c \rightarrow d\,,\, a \rightarrow b \,\},$$
$$\rightarrow_2 \;=\; \emptyset, \qquad \rightarrow_3 \;=\; \{\, c \rightarrow d\,,\, a \rightarrow b \,\}, \quad \ldots$$

All these points demonstrate the utility of *reducing* systems. This is even more striking for P/N systems than for strictly positive systems, since in the latter case $\rightarrow_R$ is always definable while this is not so in the former. On the other hand, this does not seem to be too drastic a restriction : the systems that one would write naturally are reducing in general. Lastly, notice that reducing systems are *finitely terminating*.

Consider now the following nondeterministic procedure :

function F(t)
  choose a rule r : $(\wedge_{i=1}^{n} u_i{=}v_i) \wedge (\wedge_{j=1}^{m} \overline{u}_j{\neq}\overline{v}_j) \;\Rightarrow\; \lambda \rightarrow \rho$ in R
  such that $t = K[\lambda\sigma]$ **and**
    $\forall i \in [1..n],\; F(u_i\sigma) \cap F(v_i\sigma) \neq \emptyset$,
    $\forall j \in [1..m],\; F(\overline{u}_j\sigma) \cap F(\overline{v}_j\sigma) = \emptyset$
   then return(F(K[ρσ]))
  when-no-other-choice return(t)
end function

Here, computing the intersection of $F(u_i\sigma)$ and $F(v_i\sigma)$ (resp. $F(\overline{u}_j\sigma)$ and $F(\overline{v}_j\sigma)$) means that, after finding a possible match σ, one recursively performs *all* the non-deterministic computations of the F's ; this produces *sets* of results that are compared two by two. Note that this may be improved when $\rightarrow_R$ is known to be confluent (cf. theorem 3.4). We then have the following correctness result :

Theorem 3.4

(1) For a reducing P/N system R, the function 'F' computes in a totally correct fashion the normal forms of t for $\rightarrow_R$.

(2) Let R a reducing P/N system such that $\rightarrow_R$ is confluent. Then 'F' is still totally correct if instead of comparing the *sets* $F(u_i\sigma)$ and $F(v_i\sigma)$ (resp. $F(\overline{u}_j\sigma)$ and $F(\overline{v}_j\sigma)$), one checks whether :

$$F(u_i\sigma) = F(v_i\sigma) \quad \text{and} \quad F(\overline{u}_j\sigma) \neq F(\overline{v}_j\sigma)) \quad (\forall i,j)$$

for *any* execution of the recursive calls.

Total correctness means that all parallel branches eventually terminate, and that the set of results computed this way is the set of the normal forms of t.

Proof :

(1) Consider the predicate :

$P(t)$: $F(t)$ computes the set $NF_R(t)$ in a totally correct fashion.

Let t such that $\tau >^{st} t \Rightarrow P(\tau)$. Let (K,σ,r) be a matching triple for t ; we have :

$$t >^{st} u_i\sigma,\ v_i\sigma,\ \overline{u}_j\sigma,\ \overline{v}_j\sigma,$$

and F computes correctly the set of the normal form of these terms. Let :

$$\psi = \mathrm{Sup}\ (\ \psi(t)\ ,\ \mathrm{Sup}_{K,\sigma,r}\ \mathrm{Sup}_{i,j}\ \{\psi(u_i\sigma), \psi(v_i\sigma), \psi(\overline{u}_j\sigma)\ , \psi(\overline{v}_j\sigma)\ \}\ )$$

Then the normal forms $\rightarrow_R$ and for $\rightarrow_\psi$ coincide on t and the $u_i\sigma$, $v_i\sigma$, $\overline{u}_j\sigma$, $\overline{v}_j\sigma$. This implies the (total) correctness of F on t, i.e. P(t). □

(2) The second point follows from the fact that when $\rightarrow_R$ is confluent, each *set* $F(u_i\sigma)$, etc... is actually a singleton. ■

We then have the fundamental result :

Theorem 3.5

Given a *reducing* P/N CTRS R such that $\rightarrow_R$ is confluent, the algebra Q_R of the normal forms for $\rightarrow_R$ of the terms of T_Σ is a quasi-initial model of R.

Proof : cf. Appendix 2

This result states the connection between the algebraic and the operational aspects of P/N systems : the algebra of normal forms, which may be computed by the above procedure, provides one *peak* in the class of the models of R (considered canonically as a set of P/N axioms).

Having shown that rewriting determines quasi-initial models, we now examine the converse. To this effect, we associate to any P/N axiom in *premise form* :

$$(\wedge_{i=1}^{n} u_i{=}v_i) \wedge (\wedge_{j=1}^{m} \overline{u}_j{\neq}\overline{v}_j) \Rightarrow \lambda = \rho$$

its *disjunctive form* :

$$(\wedge_{i=1}^{n} u_i=v_i) \Rightarrow \lambda=\rho \vee (\vee_{j=1}^{m} \bar{u}_j=\bar{v}_j).$$

Conversely, to any disjunctive form : $\wedge_{i=1}^{n} u_i=v_i \Rightarrow \vee_{k=1}^{p} a_k=b_k$, one may associate p distinct P/N axioms in premise form.

Similarly, to a finite family of P/N axioms, we can associate a family of disjunctive form axioms, to which we can in turn associate a family of P/N *premise form* rewriting systems (choosing the orientation in the premises). For instance :

$\{ a \neq b \Rightarrow c \to d \}$	-->	$\{ a = b \vee c = d \}$	-->	$\{ a \neq b \Rightarrow c \to d \}$
				$\{ c \neq d \Rightarrow a \to b \}$
←-- P/N CTRS --→		←-- disjunctive form --→		←-- family of P/N CTRS --→

For axioms having variables, we take as disjunctive normal form the family of all the ground instances of the disjunctive form of the axiom, and then only consider the possible P/N CTRS. For instance, to the system :

$$S_5 \;=\; \{\, a(x) \neq b(x) \;\Rightarrow\; c(x) \to d(x) \,\}$$

may be associated :

$$a(0) \neq b(0) \quad\Rightarrow\quad c(0) \to d(0)$$
$$c(s(0)) \neq d(s(0)) \quad\Rightarrow\quad a(s(0)) \to b(s(0))$$
$$a(s(s(0))) \neq b(s(s(0))) \quad\Rightarrow\quad c(s(s(0))) \to d(s(s(0)))$$
$$c(s(s(s(0)))) \neq d(s(s(s(0)))) \quad\Rightarrow\quad a(s(s(s(0)))) \to b(s(s(s(0))))$$

...

Theorem 3.6
Given a family of P/N axioms E in disjunctive form, such that for any premise form rewriting system R of it, R is reducing and $\to_R$ is confluent. Then the family of the Q_R obtained this way coincides with the family of quasi-initial models.

Proof : cf. Appendix 3

Intuitively, this states that all the quasi-initial models may be obtained by rewriting (provided that the premise form systems are all reducing and confluent). The theorem is mainly interesting as a converse of theorem 3.5. Notice that its hypothesis is fulfilled for instance by the above systems S_1 and S_5.

For example, as announced before, the quasi-initial models of $\{a = b \vee c = d\}$ are obtained as normal form algebras of $\{a \neq b \Rightarrow c \to d\}$ and $\{c \neq d \Rightarrow a \to b\}$.

4. Confluence results

In this section, we address the question of the *confluence* of *reducing* P/N systems, by providing a criterion *à la* Knuth-Bendix.

To introduce our results, consider the following example :

$even?(x) = T \;\Rightarrow odd?(x) \to F,$

$even?(x) \neq T \;\Rightarrow odd?(x) \to T,$

(the predicate 'even?' having been defined previously). We notice that, with the traditional approach, <T,F> is a critical pair [deduced from the term 'odd?(x)']. However, this critical pair may be obtained only under the condition even?(x)=T∧even?(x)≠T, which is never realized; we say that even?(x)=T∧even?(x)≠T ⇒ <T,F> is a *contextual critical pair*, the context of which 'even?(x)=T∧even?(x)=F' is not "satisfiable". Such pairs need not of course be considered when checking for confluence.

Definition 4.1

- Given a reducing system R and two rules in R :

$$r_1 : (\wedge_{i=1}^{n_1} u_{1,i} = v_{1,i}) \wedge (\wedge_{j=1}^{m_1} \bar{u}_{1,j} \neq \bar{v}_{1,j}) \Rightarrow \lambda_1 \to \rho_1$$

and

$$r_2 : (\wedge_{i=1}^{n_2} u_{2,i} = v_{2,i}) \wedge (\wedge_{j=1}^{m_2} \bar{u}_{2,j} \neq \bar{v}_{2,j}) \Rightarrow \lambda_2 \to \rho_2$$

such that $\lambda_{1|\omega}$ and λ_2 are unifiable, ω being a non variable occurrence of λ_1. Let μ be their most general unifier. The formula :

$$((\wedge_{i=1}^{m_1} u_{1,i} = v_{1,i}) \wedge (\wedge_{i=1}^{m_2} u_{2,i} = v_{2,i}) \wedge (\wedge_{j=1}^{m_1} \bar{u}_{1,j} \neq \bar{v}_{1,j}) \wedge (\wedge_{j=1}^{m_2} \bar{u}_{2,j} \neq \bar{v}_{2,j}))\mu$$

$$\Rightarrow \langle \lambda_1\mu[\omega \leftarrow \rho_2\mu] \, , \rho_1\mu \rangle$$

is called a *contextual critical pair* [abbreviated CCP] with associated *critical context*:

$$((\wedge_{i=1}^{m_1} u_{1,i} = v_{1,i}) \wedge (\wedge_{i=1}^{m_2} u_{2,i} = v_{2,i}) \wedge (\wedge_{j=1}^{m_1} \bar{u}_{1,j} \neq \bar{v}_{1,j}) \wedge (\wedge_{j=1}^{m_2} \bar{u}_{2,j} \neq \bar{v}_{2,j}))\mu$$

From now on, we abbreviate the premises of r_1 and r_2 by P_1 and P_2 when no confusion arises. The critical context is then $P_1\mu \wedge P_2\mu$.

For a positive/negative clause $C : (\wedge_{i=1}^{n} a_i = b_i) \wedge (\wedge_{j=1}^{m} \bar{a}_j \neq \bar{b}_j)$, we write $(C)\downarrow_R$ whenever : $a_i \downarrow_R b_i$ and $\bar{a}_j \not\downarrow_R \bar{b}_j$ $(\forall i,j)$.

We then have the result :

Theorem 4.2

[Knuth-Bendix theorem for reducing positive/negative conditional TRS]

Given a reducing system R,

$\to_R$ is locally confluent (and thus confluent) on T_Σ *iff*

for any contextual critical pair $C \Rightarrow \langle t,t' \rangle$, for any substitution $\zeta : X \to T_\Sigma$,

if $(C\zeta)\downarrow_R$, **then** $t\zeta \downarrow_R t'\zeta$.

Proof : cf. Appendix 4

This result extends the classical Knuth-Bendix criterion for equational systems (cf. [Huet 77]) and for conditional systems (cf. [Kaplan 84b], [JW 86], [Ganziger 86]), to the framework of positive/negative systems.

CONCLUSION

We defined in this paper a rigorous basis for the treatment of positive/negative conditional rules. Our approach manages to preserve the coherence between the algebraic and the operational aspects of such systems, in spite of the non-existence of *one* "optimal" model. We assign precise semantics to the information contained in a formula such as $a \neq b \Rightarrow c \rightarrow d$, which is certainly relevant to a specifier but disappears in the algebraic formulation $a=b \vee c=d$.

For these purposes, the notion of reducing systems appears essential. It allows one to define proper semantics for such systems, which is not possible for certain non-reducing systems. The correctness of a universal interpreter was proved. For confluent reducing systems, normal form algebras are quasi-initial models and conversely, under favorable circumstances, the quasi-initial models are obtained by normal form algebras. Lastly, a critical pair criterion is obtained, to check for the confluence of these systems.

On the whole, positive/negative conditional reducing systems do not appear, within our approach, to be more intractable *in practice* than the positive systems studied for instance in [Kaplan 84b,87], [JW 86], [RZ 84,85], [Ganziger 86], etc. (though their mathematical semantics are more complex).

As a direction for future research, the connection between negative conditional rewriting and logic programming with failure ([BH 86], [ABW 87], [Lifshitz 86]) should be examined. The previous works have been extended by [Przymusinski 86], which relies on the notions of locally stratified programs and perfect models; these concepts bear close resemblance respectively to our reducing systems and to our quasi-initial models. Przymusinski's systems are constrained to conditions interpretable into $\lambda\sigma > \bar{u}_j\sigma, \bar{v}_j\sigma$ (though not necessarily $\lambda\sigma > u_i\sigma, v_i\sigma$). However, they manipulate boolean predicates (instead of equations between terms in our case), and via outermost reduction strategies.

As already mentioned, we make use the partial information stated by a specifier, when writing a formula $a \neq b \Rightarrow c \rightarrow d$ instead of $a=b \vee c=d$. It might also be interesting to examine the latter form, which concerns properties that hold in *all* the quasi-initial models. However, we believe that the first approach, which is the one developed in this paper, is more natural as a specification method and as a high-level programming paradigm.

ACKNOWLEDGEMENTS :

I thank Nachum Dershowitz, Krzysztof Apt and Jan-Willem Klop for fruitful discussion and comments.

The research reported on here has been partially supported by the METEOR Esprit Contract.

REFERENCES

[ABW 87] **K. Apt, H. Blair, A. Walker,** *Towards a theory of declarative knowledge*, I.B.M. T.J. Watson Research Center Report, submitted for publication (1987)

[ADJ 78] **J.A. Goguen, J.W. Thatcher, E.G. Wagner,** *An Initial Algebra Approach to the Specification, Correctness, and Implementation of Abstract Data Types,* Current Trends in Programming Methodology, Vol. 4, Ed. Yeh R., Prentice-Hall, pp. 80-149 (1978)

[BBK 87] **J. Baeten, J. Bergstra, J.W. Klop,** *Term rewriting systems with priority*, Proc. of the RTA'87 Conf., LNCS 256, Springer Verlag (1987)

[BBWT 81] **J. Bergstra, M. Broy, M. Wirsing, J. Tucker,** *On the power of algebraic specifications*, Proc. of the MFCS'81 Conference, LNCS 118 (1981)

[BH 86] **N. Bidoit, R. Hull,** *Positivism vs. Minimalism in Deductive Data Bases*, Proc. of the ACM SIGACT-SIGMOD Symposium on Principle of Data Base Systems, Cambridge (1986)

[Dershowitz 85] **N. Dershowitz,** *Termination*, Proc. of the 1st Conf. on Rewriting Techniques and Applications, LNCS 202, Dijon - France (1985)

[EM 85] **H. Ehrig, B. Mahr,** *Fundamentals of algebraic specifications. I : Equations and initial semantics*, EATCS monographs on Theoretical Computer Science, Springer Verlag (1985)

[Ganziger 86] **H. Ganziger,** *Ground term confluence in parametric conditional equational specifications*, Proc. of the STACS'87 Conf., LNCS 252, Springer Verlag (1987)

[Huet 77] **G. Huet,** *Confluent reductions : abstract properties and applications to term rewriting systems*, Proc. of the 18th FOCS Conf., Providence (1978)

[HO 80] **G. Huet, D.C. Oppen,** *Equations and rewrite rules : a survey*, Formal languages : Perspective and open problems, R. Book Ed., Academic Press (1980)

[JK 84] **J.-P. Jouannaud, C. Kirchner,** *Completion of a set of rules modulo a set of equations*, Proc. of the 11th POPL Conf. (1984)

[JW 86] **J.-P. Jouannaud, B. Waldmann,** *Reductive conditional term rewriting systems*, Proc. of the 3rd TC2 Working Conf. on the formal Description of Programming Concepts, North-Holland Pub. Company (1986)

[Kaplan 82] **S. Kaplan,** *Specifications of abstract data types: the power of several classes of axioms with semi-decidable congruence*, Proc. of the AFCET Mathematics for Computer Science Conf., Paris (1982)

[Kaplan 84a] **S. Kaplan,** *Conditional rewrite rules*, TCS **33** (1984)

[Kaplan 84b] **S. Kaplan,** *Fair conditional term rewrite systems*, Report 194, University of Paris-South (1984)

[Kaplan 87] **S. Kaplan,** *Simplifying conditional term rewriting systems*, to appear in the Journal of Symbolic Computation (1987)

[Klop 87] **J.W. Klop,** *Term rewriting systems : a tutorial*, Bulletin of the EATCS, **32**, pp. 143-183 (1987)

[Lifschitz 86] **V. Lifschitz,** *On the declarative semantics of logic programs with negation*, Workshop on the Foundations of Deductive Data Bases and Logic Programming, Washington D.C. (1986)

[Przymusinski 86] **T.C. Przymusinski,** *On the semantics of stratified deductive databases*, Workshop on the Foundations of Deductive Data Bases and Logic Programming, Washington D.C. (1986)

[RZ 84] **J.L. Rémy, H. Zhang,** *REVEUR4 : a system for validating conditional algebraic specifications of abstract data types*, Proc. of the 6th ECAI Conf. (1984)

[RZ 85] **J.L. Rémy, H. Zhang,** *Contextual rewriting*, Proc. of the 1st RTA Conf., LNCS 202, Springer Verlag (1985)

Appendix 1 : Proof of theorem 2.1

(1) We show that the class of the E-models is inductive. Let $(M_i)_{i\in I}$ be an decreasing chain for '≤'. Let M_∞ be the "limit" defined as the set of chains $(t_i)_{i\in I}$ with :

- $t_i \in M_i$
- $t_{i+1} = \phi_i(t_i)$, where f_i is the unique morphism from M_i to M_{i+1}.

Let $\overline{M}_\infty$ be the finitely generated part of M_∞. Then $\overline{M}_\infty$ is an inf of $(M_i)_{i\in I}$: inj$\circ\pi_i$ (where 'inj' is the canonical injection $\overline{M}_\infty \to M_\infty$, and '$\pi_i$' is the projection $M_\infty \to M_i$) is a morphism from $\overline{M}_\infty$ into M_i, and it is unique.

Via Zorn's lemma, the class of the E-models admits a minimal element, which is quasi-initial by construction. □

(2) This comes from the fact that for any model M, there exists a unique morphism from its finitely generated part Gen(M) into M. □

(3) For a given E-model M, let Gen_M be the class of the E-models N such that Gen(M) ≤ N. Then, similarly, Gen_M is inductive ; any minimal element Q of Gen_M is quasi-initial, and satisfies Q ≤ M.

■

Appendix 2 : Proof of theorem 3.5

Firstly, Q_R is considered as an algebra by letting :

$$f^{Q_R}[NF_{\to_R}(t_1),\ldots,NF_{\to_R}(t_n)] \quad =_{def} \quad NF_{\to_R}[f(t_1,\ldots,t_n)].$$

The confluence of $\to_R$ ensures the well-definedness of each f^{Q_R}.

Since Q_R is known to be a R-model, we simply have to prove its minimality. By *reductio ad absurdum*, we suppose that there exists an R-model M and a morphism $\phi : M \to Q_R$. We may suppose that M is finitely generated. If ϕ is not an isomorphism, there exist τ and τ' in M such that $\tau \neq \tau'$ and $\phi(\tau) = \phi(\tau')$. We have :

$$\tau = t^M \quad \text{and} \quad \tau = t'^M,$$

for two terms t and t'. Since there is a unique morphism from T_Σ into Q_R, it coincides with $\phi \circ (\,)^M$. Thus : $t\downarrow_R = t'\downarrow_R = \alpha$. One shows by $>^{st}$-induction that if $u \to_R v$, then $u^M = v^M$. Thus, $t^M = \alpha^M = t'^M$, which contradicts $\tau \neq \tau'$. ■

Appendix 3 : Proof of theorem 3.6

It is sufficient to show that any (finitely generated) quasi-initial model M is isomorphic to some Q_R. So, for any ground instance of the disjunctive form of an axiom of E :

$$\wedge_{i=1}^{n} u_i\sigma = v_i\sigma \Rightarrow \lambda = \rho \vee (\vee_{j=1}^{m} \bar{u}_j\sigma = \bar{v}_j\sigma),$$

one chooses one of the literals of the disjunction that is valid in M, say : $\bar{u}_{j_0}\sigma = \bar{v}_{j_0}\sigma$. Then one considers the rule :

$$\wedge_{i=1}^{n} u_i\sigma = v_i\sigma \wedge \lambda \neq \rho \wedge (\wedge_{j\neq j_0} \bar{u}_j\sigma \neq \bar{v}_j\sigma) \Rightarrow \bar{u}_{j_0}\sigma \to \bar{v}_{j_0}\sigma$$

(up to the orientation). We assume, as in the theorem, that the orientations may be globally chosen such that the resulting system R is reducing and confluent. Consider the reduction ordering > associated to R. We show by $>^{st}$-induction that for any term t, $M \models t^M = NF_{\to_R}(t)$.

Assume that this holds for any τ such that $t >^{st} \tau$. If t is irreducible for $\rightarrow_R$, there is nothing to prove. Otherwise, we suppose that $t \rightarrow_R t' \rightarrow_R^* NF_{\rightarrow_R}(t)$. Then, since $t >^{st} t'$, $M \models t'^M = NF_{\rightarrow_R}(t') = NF_{\rightarrow_R}(t)$. Now, by construction of the rules of R, $M \models t = t'$.

Then, the application ϕ from Q_I into M defined by : $\phi(NF_{\rightarrow_R}(t)) = t^M$ is well-defined. It is a morphism, and is unique since Q_I is finitely generated. So, it is an isomorphism. ■

Appendix 4 : Proof of theorem 4.2

We prove by $>^{st}$-induction that, under the assumptions of the theorem, for any term τ such that $\tau \rightarrow_R^* \tau_1, \tau_2$, then $\tau_1 \downarrow_R \tau_2$. We assume that this holds for any τ such that $t >^{st} \tau$, and prove that this is also true for t. We suppose that $t \rightarrow_{r_1} \overline{t}_1 \rightarrow_R^* t_1$ and $t \rightarrow_{r_2} \overline{t}_2 \rightarrow_R^* t_2$. Since $t >^{st} \overline{t}_1, \overline{t}_2$, it is sufficient to prove that $\overline{t}_1 \downarrow_R \overline{t}_2$. Let us denote by ω_1 and ω_2 the occurrences of the term t where the rules r_1 and r_2 apply, and σ_1 and σ_2 the respective matching substitutions. As usual, there are three cases to consider.

(1) ω_1 and ω_2 are *orthogonal* (i.e. no one is on the path from the root of t to the other). Then :

$$\overline{t}_1 \rightarrow_{r_2} t[\omega_1 \leftarrow \rho\sigma_1, \omega_2 \leftarrow \rho\sigma_2] \quad \text{and} \quad \overline{t}_2 \rightarrow_{r_1} t[\omega_1 \leftarrow \rho\sigma_1, \omega_2 \leftarrow \rho\sigma_2].$$

(2) ω_1 is between the root of t and ω_2, so that ω_2 is a *not* the occurrence of a variable of $\lambda\sigma_1$. Then $\sigma = \sigma_1 \cup \sigma_2$ is a unifier of $\lambda_{1|\omega}$ and λ_2 (with $\omega = \omega_1 - \omega_2$). Thus, we have : $\sigma = \mu\zeta$ for a certain substitution ζ. Now, since $(P_1\sigma_1)\downarrow_R$ and $(P_2\sigma_2)\downarrow_R$, this implies that $((P_1 \wedge P_2)\mu\zeta)\downarrow_R$. The hypothesis of the theorem yields : $\overline{t1} \downarrow_R \overline{t2}$.

(3) ω_1 is between the root of t and ω_2, so that ω_2 is the occurrence of a variable x of $\lambda\sigma_1$. Then $t_{|\omega_1} \rightarrow_{r_2} \lambda_1\sigma_1[\omega \leftarrow \rho_2\sigma_2] \rightarrow_{r_2}^* \lambda_1\sigma_1[x \leftarrow \rho_2\sigma_2]$. Let $\sigma'_1 = \sigma \cup \{x \leftarrow \rho_2\sigma_2\}$. We are going to show that $(P_1\sigma'_1)\downarrow_R$. Then, it will be possible to apply r_1 to $\lambda_1\sigma'_1$, yielding $t_{2|\omega_1} \rightarrow_R^* \rho_1\sigma'_1 = t'$. On the other hand, it is clear that $t_{1|\omega_1} \rightarrow_R^* t'$, which terminates the proof.

Proof that $(P_1\sigma'_1)\downarrow_R$:

Let $P_1 = (\wedge_i a_i = b_i) \wedge (\wedge_j \overline{a}_j \neq \overline{b}_j)$. Then :

- For any i, we have : $a_i\sigma'_1 \; {}_R^*\!\!\leftarrow a_i\sigma_1 \rightarrow_R^* b_i\sigma_1 \rightarrow^* b_i\sigma'_1$. Now, one may apply the $>^{st}$-induction hypothesis, since $t >^{st} a_i\sigma_1$, $b_i\sigma_1$. This gives : $a_i\sigma'_1 \downarrow_R b_i\sigma'_1$.
- For any j, we have : $\overline{a}_j\sigma_1 \rightarrow_R^* \overline{a}_j\sigma'_1$, $\overline{b}_j\sigma_1 \rightarrow_R^* \overline{b}_j\sigma'_1$. We derive that : $\overline{a}_j\sigma'_1 \not\downarrow_R \overline{b}_j\sigma'_1$, since otherwise, one would have : $\overline{a}_j\sigma_1 \downarrow_R \overline{b}_j\sigma_1$.

This terminates the proof of theorem 4.2 ■

ON THE COMPUTATIONAL COMPLEXITY OF CODES IN GRAPHS

JAN KRATOCHVÍL and MIRKO KŘIVÁNEK*
Charles University, Prague

Abstract. This paper links to continuing research of the first author on codes in graphs [7-11]. Here codes are studied from the point of view of their computational complexity. It is shown that the problem of perfect code recognition is *NP*-complete even when restricted to k-regular graphs (k≥4) or to 3-regular planar graphs. On the other hand in the case of trees and graphs of bounded tree-width an optimal $\Theta(n)$ algorithm is developed. Some optimization problems are also investigated.

II. Introduction. The theory of self-correcting codes belongs to thoroughly investigated parts of applied combinatorics. Special attention was paid to the most effective codes, so-called perfect codes. Such codes were shown to be fairly rare, namely in the case of the classical Hamming metrics [2,14]. The classical concept of perfect codes was generalized by Biggs [3] to perfect codes in graphs. However, Biggs and others [6,14] studied only distance regular graphs for which a strong necessary condition for the existence of perfect codes was derived [3].

Perfect codes in general graphs (and their cartesian powers) were studied in [7,9,10,11]. On the other hand within the context of domination theory the notion of t-codes coincides with the $2t$-packings and perfect codes with efficient independent dominating sets, c.f.[1,12]. Though one can easily construct general graphs containing perfect codes , still typical graphs do not contain perfect codes. For example for every fixed $p, 0<p<1$, the random graph $G_{n,p}$ almost surely does not contain a 1-perfect code [8]. In subsequent sections computational problems concerning codes in a variety of graph families will be discussed.

II. Background. Through-out this paper we shall use the following notation and conventions :

a) notation from graph theory is standard [4],

b) due to space limitation , figures are preferred in the proof of Theorem 8 (all figures are listed in the Appendix). In this respect a mapping $\Phi_C : V(G) \to \{\circ, \otimes, \bullet\}$, where

$$\Phi_C(u) = \begin{cases} \bullet & \text{if } u \in C \\ \otimes & \text{if } u \text{ is covered by C and } u \notin C \\ \circ & \text{if } u \text{ is uncovered by C in G,} \end{cases}$$

will be widely used. The reader is encouraged to follow this notation in his own pictures while going through the proofs. Also the labels from our figures are referred to in the text without stating it explicitlly. All omitted proofs and technical details will appear in forthcomming full paper.

c) *NP*-completeness terminology is that of [5].

We start with some necessary definitions :

Let G be a graph (undirected, without loops and multiple edges).

*Partially supported by IMA, University of Minnesota, with funds provided by National Science Foundation.

The set $C \subset V(G)$ is said to be a

$$t\text{-code} \Leftrightarrow (\forall\, u,v \in C)\ d(u,v) \geq 2t+1$$

$$t\text{-perfect code} \Leftrightarrow (\forall\, u \in V(G))(\exists!\ c \in C)\ d(u,c) \leq t$$

In the sequel we shall deal with 1-codes and 1-perfect codes only usually dropping out the prefix "1-". Thus C is a code iff the sets of neighboring vertices of each $u \in C$ are pair-wise disjoint, while C is a perfect code iff these sets form a partition of $V(G)$. Let C be a perfect code in $G - v$. Then the vertex v is called uncovered by C in G if $d(v,C) > 1$. First we shall be interested in the following optimization decision problems :

1. **PERFECT CODE (PC) :**
   INSTANCE : A graph G;
   QUESTION : Does G contain a perfect code?;

1a. **PCvC :**
   INSTANCE : A graph G, a specified vertex v;
   QUESTION : Does G contain a perfect code C such that $v \in C$?;

1b. **PCvNC:**
   INSTANCE : A graph G, a specified vertex v;
   QUESTION : Does G contain a perfect code C such that $v \notin C$?;

1c. **PCvU :**
   INSTANCE : A graph G, a specified vertex v;
   QUESTION : Is there a perfect code in $G - v$ such that v is uncovered by C in G?;

2. **PERFECT CODE COMPLETION (PCC):**
   INSTANCE : A graph G, non-negative integer k;
   QUESTION : Is there a sequence of at most k changes (will be specified latter) that transforms G into a graph having a perfect code?;

2a. **PCC-VERTEX ADDITION (VA):**
   INSTANCE : A graph G, non-negative integer k;
   QUESTION : see 2 where change ≡ vertex addition with some of its incident edges;

2b. **PCC-VERTEX DELETION (VD):**
   INSTANCE : A graph G, non-negative integer k;
   QUESTION : see 2 where change ≡ vertex deletion;

2c. **PCC-EDGE ADDITION (EA):**
   INSTANCE : A graph G, non-negative integer k;
   QUESTION : see 2 where change ≡ edge addition;

2d. **PCC-EDGE DELETION (EA):**
   INSTANCE : A graph G, non-negative integer k;
   QUESTION : see 2 where change ≡ edge deletion;

2e. **PCC-MIXED (VDEAD):**
   INSTANCE : A graph G, non-negative integer k;
   QUESTION : see 2 where change ≡ vertex deletion and/or edge addition and/or edge deletion;

3. **DEFECT:**
   INSTANCE : A graph G, non-negative integer k;
   QUESTION : Does it hold that $def(G) \stackrel{def}{=} \min\{j;$ there exists a code in G such that exactly j vertices are left uncovered$\} \leq k$?;

Suppose that $VA(G), VD(G), EA(G), ED(G), VDEAD(G)$ denote the minimum number of changes required in corresponding computational problems in 2a-2e.

Now, we shall present *NP*-completeness results for problems 1-3. Their proofs originate in the following fundamental theorem :

THEOREM 1. *The problem* **PC** *is NP-complete in connected graphs.*□

The proof is postponed to section III. As it is customary with the *NP*-completeness proofs we omit trivial verification of membership in class *NP*. Our polynomial transformations start in the following preliminary assertion:

PROPOSITION. *The two following problems are NP-complete :*
(I) **kRkP** *: INSTANCE : A Finite set of elements* $X = \{x_1, x_2, \ldots, x_{kq}\}$, *(*$k \geq 3$*, q is a positive integer), and a collection* $\mathcal{C}$ *of k-element subsets of X such that each element of X appear in exactly k subsets.*

QUESTION : is there a subcollection $\mathcal{C}' \subseteq \mathcal{C}$ *such that* $\mathcal{C}'$ *forms a partition of X ?;*

(II) **13p3S** *: INSTANCE : A formula in conjunctive normal form with the set of clauses C over the set of variables X such that :*

(i) $|c| = 3$ *for each clause c of C,*

(ii) The bipartite graph $G = (C \cup X, E)$, *where* $E = \{\{x,c\};$ *either* $x \in c$ *or* $\neg x \in c \}$, *is planar;*

QUESTION : Is there a satisfying truth assignement for C such that each clause in C has exactly one **true**-*literal ?* □

THEOREM 2. *The problems* **PCvC, PCvNC, PCvU** *are NP-complete in connected graphs.*□

THEOREM 3. $VA(G) \leq 1$ *for all graphs G.*□

COROLLARY. *The problem* **VA** *is NP-complete for* $k = 0$. *On the other hand it becomes trivial for* $k \geq 1$.□

THEOREM 4. $EA(G) = def(G)$.□

THEOREM 5.

(i) The problems **VD, EA, ED, VDEAD** *are NP-complete in connected graphs for every fixed* $k \geq 0$.

(ii) The problem **DEFECT** *is NP-complete in connected graphs for every fixed* $k \geq 0$.

(iii) There is no polynomial approximation algorithm for problems **VD, EA, ED, VDEAD** *in connected graphs.*□

For the problem of computing defect in "perfect-code-free" graphs we have another refinement.

THEOREM 6. *The problem* **DEFECT** *is NP-complete in connected graphs for* $k = cn$, *where* $n = \mathrm{card}(V(G))$ *and* $c = 1 - \frac{1}{r}$, *r is an arbitrary positive integer.*

Proof. We use the polynomial transformation from the problem **PCvU**. Given a connected graph G we choose an arbitrary vertex $v \in G$ and construct G' as follows

$$V(G') = V(G) \cup \bigcup_{i=1}^{m} (\{u_i\} \cup \bigcup_{j=1}^{k} \{u_{ij}\}),$$

$$E(G') = E(G) \cup \bigcup_{i=1}^{m} (\{\{v,u_i\}\} \cup \bigcup_{j=1}^{k} \{\{u_i,u_{ij}\}\}).$$

Now $def(G') \geq (k-1)(m-1)$ and the equality holds iff G contains a perfect code not covering a vertex v. Let us put $k=2r$, $m = (r-1)n+2r^2-r$. For $n' \stackrel{\mathrm{def}}{=} \mathrm{card}(V(G'))$ we have

$$cn' = (1-\tfrac{1}{r})(n+[(r-1)n+(2r-1)r](2r+1)).$$

Consequently $(k-1)(m-1) = (2r-1)(r-1)(n+2r+1)$.□

III. Regular graphs. This section is devoted to the problem **PC** considered for k-regular graphs. The investigations of codes in graphs are interesting both from practical and theoretical points of view. See [5] for the discussion of formally very similar problems on dominating sets. The main result of this section is read as the following

THEOREM 7. *The problem* **PC** *is NP-complete even when restricted to k-regular graphs,* $k \geq 4$.

Proof. The proof is technically complicated and thus divided in several steps. In each step one auxilliary graph is introduced. Graph G_1 has

$$V(G_1) = \bigcup_{i=1}^{k} (\{a_i,b_i,c_i\} \cup \bigcup_{j=1}^{k-1} \{x_{ij}\}) \text{ and}$$

$$E(G_1) = \bigcup_{i=1}^{k} (\{\{a_i,b_i\}\} \cup \bigcup_{j=1}^{k-1} \{\{b_i,x_{ij}\},\{x_{ij},c_i\}\}) \cup \{\{x_{ij},x_{rs}\}; i+j \equiv r+s \bmod k\}.$$

Now we proceed to the definition of a graph G_2.

$$V(G_2) = \bigcup_{i=1}^{k} \{c_i,d_i,e_i\} \cup \{u,v\}.$$

The set $E(G_2)$ depends on the parity of k. If k is even then

$$E(G_2) = \bigcup_{i=1}^{k/2} \{\{c_i,u\},\{d_i,u\},\{c_{i+k/2},v\},\{d_{i+k/2},v\}\} \cup$$

$$\cup \bigcup_{1\le i,j\le k/2} \{d_i,e_j\},\{d_{i+k/2},e_{j+k/2}\}\} \cup$$

$$\cup \bigcup_{1\le i\ne j\le k/2} \{\{d_i,d_{k+1-j}\},\{e_i,e_{k+1-j}\}\}$$

else

$$E(G_2)=\bigcup_{i=1}^{(k-1)/2}\{\{c_i,u\},\{d_i,u\},\{c_{k+1-i},v\},\{d_{k+1-i},v\}\} \cup$$

$$\cup \bigcup_{1\le i,j\le(k-1)} \{\{d_i,e_j\},\{d_{k+1-i},e_{k+1-j}\}\} \cup$$

$$\cup_{1\le i\ne j\le(k-1)/2}\{\{d_i,d_{k+1-j}\},\{e_i,e_{k+1-j}\}\} \cup \{\{c_{(k+1)/2},v\},\{u,d_{(k+1)/2}\}\}$$

$$\cup \bigcup_{i=1}^{(k-1)/2}\{\{d_{(k+1)/2},e_i\},\{d_{(k+1)/2},d_{k+1-i}\},\{e_{(k+1)/2},e_i\},\{e_{(k+1)/2},e_{k+1-i}\}\}.$$

Further we need graph $G_3 = (V(G_1) \cup V(G_2),E(G_1) \cup E(G_2))$ supposing that $V(G_1) \cap V(G_2) = \{c_i\,;i=1,\dots,k\}$. Concerning graph G_3 we have a simple observation :

LEMMA 7.1. *Let C be a code in G_3 covering all vertices of degree k. Then exactly one of the two following cases occurs :*
(i) $\Phi_C(a_i) = \otimes$, $\Phi_C(e_i) = \circ$, $i=1,\dots,k$;
(ii) $\Phi_C(a_i) = \circ$, $\Phi_C(e_i) = \otimes$, $i=1,\dots,k$.□

Finally k-regular graph $G_{\mathfrak{M}}$ is introduced for an instance of **kRkP** for $\mathfrak{M} = (M,\mathcal{T})$, where $\mathcal{T} \subset \binom{M}{k}$ and $\mathrm{card}(\{T;\ m \in T \in \mathcal{T}\}) = k,\ \forall\ m \in M$.

First we denote by G_T a graph which is isomorphic to G_3 in such a way that its vertices a_i are renamed by vertices from T. Similarly the vertices e_i are renamed as e^m_T, $m \in T$. Moreover $V(G_T) \cap V(G_{T'}) = T \cap T'$ for $T \ne T' \in \mathcal{T}$, and $M' = \{m';\ m \in M\}$. Further "new" vertices $\{f^m_T, g^m_T\ ;\ m \in T \in \mathcal{T}\}$ have to be considered. Finally we put

$$V(G_{\mathfrak{M}}) = \bigcup_{T\in\mathcal{T}} V(G_T) \cup M' \cup \bigcup_{m\in M,\, m\in T} \{f^m_T, g^m_T\},$$

$$E(G_{\mathfrak{M}}) = \bigcup_{T\in\mathcal{T}} E(G_T) \cup \bigcup_{m\in M}\left[\ \bigcup_{T\ni m} \{\{m',f^m_T\},\{g^m_T,e^m_T\}\} \cup \bigcup_{\substack{T\cap T'\ni m\\ T\ne T'}} \{\{f^m_T,g^m_{T'}\}\}\right].$$

Obviously, $G_{\mathfrak{M}}$ is a k-regular graph. Therefore the proof of Theorem 7 will be concluded by the following lemma

LEMMA 7.2. $G_{\mathfrak{M}}$ *contains a perfect code iff there is a partition of* $\mathfrak{M}$ *into k-tuples, i.e. there exists* $\mathcal{T}' \subset \mathcal{T}$ *such that* $\mathrm{card}(\{T; m \in t \in \mathcal{T}'\}) = 1,\ \forall\ m \in M$.

Proof. Let C be a perfect code in $G_{\mathbf{M}}$. Then $C \cap V(G_T)$ is a code in G_T that covers all vertices of degree k for every k-tuple T. Using Lemma 7.1 we obtain that

$$\mathcal{T}' = \{T;\ C \cap V(G_T) \text{ is a code of type (i) from Lemma 7.1}\}$$

is a partition of the system $\mathbf{M}$.

Conversely, let there is a partition $\mathcal{T}'$ of $\mathbf{M}$. Let C_T (C'_T, resp.) be a code of type (i) (type (ii), resp.) covering all vertices of degree k in G_T. Then

$$C = \bigcup_{T\in\mathcal{T}'} C_T \cup \bigcup_{T\notin\mathcal{T}'} C'_T \cup \bigcup_{m\in T\in\mathcal{T}'} \{f_T^m, g_T^m\}$$

is a perfect code in $G_{\mathbf{M}}$. □

By virtue of Lemma 7.2 the polynomial transformation **kRkP** $\propto$ **PC** in k-regular graphs is established. Both Theorem 7 and Theorem 1 are proved. □

IV. 3-regular planar graphs. It is easy to see that the result of the previous section holds also for 3-regular graphs. However our aim is to go one step further. In particular we place the requirement of planarity on input instances. After a lot of technical difficulties we are able to prove :

THEOREM 8. *The problem* **PC** *is NP-complete in 3-regular planar graphs.*

Proof. As in the proof of Theorem 7 the proof will be divided in several steps. We shall need several special graphs.

Two graphs $H_{x,k}$; $H'_{x,k}$ are visualized on Figures 1 and 2, where $k_1(x),\ldots,k_n(x)$, $n=n(x)$, denote all clauses containing a variable x such that $k_j(x)$ preserves the counter-clockwise orientation determined by the planar representation of G (for a given formula F, c.f. Proposition (*II*)).

Similarly $x_1(x), x_2(x), x_3(x)$ denote variables occuring in a clause k under counter-clockwise orientation determined by the planar representation of G . We have the following lemma

LEMMA 8.1. *Let* C *be a code that covers all vertices of degree* 3 *in* $H_{x,k}$ ($H'_{x,k}$, *resp.*). *Then* $\Phi_C(L_x^{k_i(x)}), \Phi_C(P_x^{k_i(x)}) \in \{\bullet, \otimes\}$ *and moreover provided* $\Phi_C(L_x^{k_i(x)}) \neq \Phi_C(P_x^{k_i(x)})$ *it holds either*

(*I*) $\Phi_C(L_x^{k_i(x)}) = \bullet$, $\Phi_C(P_x^{k_i(x)}) = \otimes$, $\Phi_C(P_k^{x_i(k)}) = \bullet$, $\Phi_C(L_k^{x_i(k)}) = \otimes$,

($\Phi_C(L_x^{k_i(x)}) = \bullet$, $\Phi_C(P_x^{k_i(x)}) = \otimes$, $\Phi_C(P_k^{x_i(k)}) = \Phi_C(L_k^{x_i(k)}) = \circ$, *resp.*)

or

(*II*) $\Phi_C(L_x^{k_i(x)}) = \otimes$, $\Phi_C(P_x^{k_i(x)}) = \bullet$, $\Phi_C(P_k^{x_i(k)}) = \Phi_C(L_k^{x_i(k)}) = \circ$,

($\Phi_C(L_x^{k_i(x)}) = \otimes$, $\Phi_C(P_x^{k_i(x)}) = \Phi_C(P_k^{x_i(k)}) = \bullet$, $\Phi_C(L_k^{x_i(k)}) = \otimes$, *resp.*)

□

Now, our aim is to present a polynomial transformation from 13p3S to PC considered for 3-regular planar graphs. Let F constitute an instance of 13p3S. Let G be a planar representation of this instance. For each variable x we put

$$V(H_x) = \bigcup_{i=1}^{n(x)} \{L_x^{k_i(x)}; P_x^{k_i(x)}; S_i; Z_i\},$$

$$E(H_x) = \bigcup_{i=1}^{n(x)} \{\{P_x^{k_i(x)}, S_i\}, \{P_x^{k_i(x)}, Z_{i-1}\}, \{L_x^{k_i(x)}, S_i\}, \{L_x^{k_i(x)}, Z_i\}, \{S_i, Z_{n+1-i}\}\}.$$

Further, for every clause we construct a graph H_k, see Figure 3.

Finally we put

$$V(H_F) = \bigcup_{x} V(H_x) \cup \bigcup_{k} V(H_k) \cup \bigcup_{x\in k} V(H_{x,k}) \cup \bigcup_{\neg x\in k} V(H'_{x,k})$$

$$E(H_F) = \bigcup_{x} E(H_x) \cup \bigcup_{k} E(H_k) \cup \bigcup_{x\in k} E(H_{x,k}) \cup \bigcup_{\neg x\in k} E(H'_{x,k}).$$

Obviously, graph H_F is planar and 3-regular.

The proof of Theorem 8 is concluded by Lemma 8.2 with the aid of Lemma 8.1 :

LEMMA 8.2. *Graph H_F contains a perfect code iff the clause F is one-in-three satisfiable (i.e., there exists a* **true/false** *valuation of variables such that in each clause exactly one variable receives value* **true**). □□

As a concluding remark of this section we conjecture that our *NP*-completeness result could be strengthened to 3-regular planar bipartite graphs.

V. Trees. In this section we outline a recursive procedure *DEF* for computing the defect in (rooted) trees.

procedure $DEF(T$: tree; t: root, $x \in \{\circledast, \bullet, \circ\})$: **integer** $\cup\ \infty$;
  case x **of**
    $\bullet$: DEF := **if** $V(T) = \{t\}$ **then** 0 **else** $\sum_{u\in pre(t)} (DEF(T_u, u, \circ) - 1)$;
    $\circ$: DEF := **if** $V(T) = \{t\}$ **then** ∞ **else**

$$\sum_{u\in pre(t)} \min\{DEF(T_u, u, \circ), DEF(T_u, u, \circledast)\} + 1;$$

    $\circledast$: DEF := **if** $V(T) = \{t\}$ **then** 1 **else if**
      $(\exists\ u \neq v \in pre(t)\ \&\ DEF(T_u, u, \circ) = DEF(T_u, u, \circledast) = DEF(T_v, v, \circ) = DEF(T_v, v, \circledast) = \infty)$
      then ∞ **else if**
        $(\exists\ u \in pre(t) : DEF(T_u, u, \circ) = DEF(T_u, u, \circledast) = \infty)$
        then

$$DEF(T_u, u, \bullet) + \sum_{u\neq v\in pre(t)} \min\{DEF(T_v, v, \circ), DEF(T_v, v, \circledast)\}$$

else

$$\sum_{u\in pre(t)} \min\{DEF(T_u,u,\circ),DEF(T_u,u,\otimes)\}+$$

$$+\ \min_{u\in pre(t)}\{DEF(T_u,u,\bullet)-\min\{DEF(T_u,u,\circ),DEF(T_u,u,\otimes)\}\};$$

endprocedure.

Having this procedure the defect in a given tree T is given by

$$\min_{x\in\{\bullet,\circ,\otimes\}} DEF(T,t_o,x).$$

It remains to explain the notation used in the outlined procedure :

(i) t_o is a root of a given tree T;

(ii) $pre(t) \overset{def}{=} \{x;\ d(x,t_o)=d(t,t_o)+d(x,t)=d(t,t_o)+1\}$;

(iii) $T_u \overset{def}{=} T|\{x;\ d(x,t_o)=d(x,u)+d(u,t_o)\}$.

By a careful time and correctness analysis in amortized complexity fashion [15] we are able to prove the following

THEOREM 9. *Procedure DEF computes defect in trees and takes $\Theta(n)$ time.*□

A similar result holds for graphs of bounded tree-width [13].The details will appear elsewhere.

REFERENCES

[1] R.B.Allan,R.Laskar,S.Hedetniemi:*A note on total domination.* Discrete Math.49(1984),7-13.

[2] M.R.Best:*A contribution to the nonexistence of perfect codes.*Mat Centrum Amsterdam,1982.

[3] N.Biggs:*Perfect codes in graphs.*J.Combin.Theory ser.B, 15(1973), 289-296.

[4] B.Bollobás:*Graph theory:an introductory course.*Springer-Verlag, New York,1979.

[5] M.R.Garey,D.S.Johnson:*Computers and Intractability : a guide to the theory of NP-completeness.*W.H.Freeman,San francisco,1979.

[6] P.Hammond,D.H.Smith:*Perfect codes in the graphs* O_k,J.Combin. Theory ser.B,19(1975),239-255.

[7] J.Kratochvíl:*Perfect codes in graphs and their powers (in Czech)* PhD Thesis, Charles University,1987.

[8] J.Kratochvíl,J.Matoušek,J.Malý:*On the existence of perfect codes in random graphs* (submitted).

[9] J.Kratochvíl:*Perfect codes over graphs.*J.Combin.Theory Ser.B, 40(1986),224-228.

[10] J.Kratochvíl:*1-perfect codes over self-complementary graphs.* Comment.Math.Univ.Carolin.,26(1985),589-595.

[11] J.Kratochvíl:*Perfect codes in general graphs.*Proc.7th Hungarian colloq.on Combinatorics, Eger, 1987 (to appear).

[12] A.Meir,J.W.Moon:*Relations between packing and covering numbers of a tree.*Pacific J.Math.61(1975),225-233.

[13] N.Robertson,P.D.Seymour:*Graph minors III. Planar tree-width.* J.Combin.Theory Ser.B, 36(1984),49-64.

[14] D.H.Smith:*Perfect codes in* O_k *and* $L(O_k)$. Glasgow Math.J.,21(1980) 169-172.

[15] R.E.Tarjan:*Data structures and network algorithms.* SIAM, Philadelphia,1983.

[16] A.Tietväväinen:*On the nonexistence of perfect codes over finite fields.* SIAM J.Appl.Math.,24(1973),86-96.

Appendix.

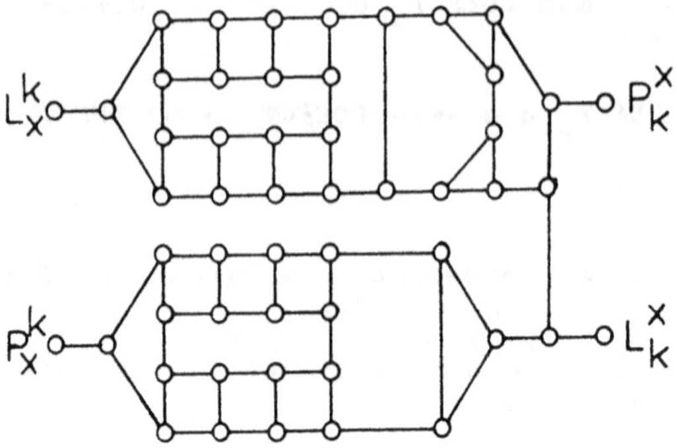

Figure 1.

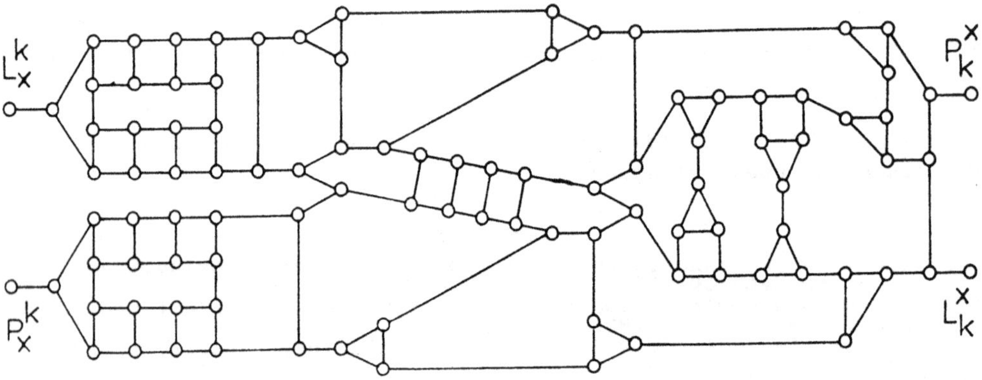

Figure 2.

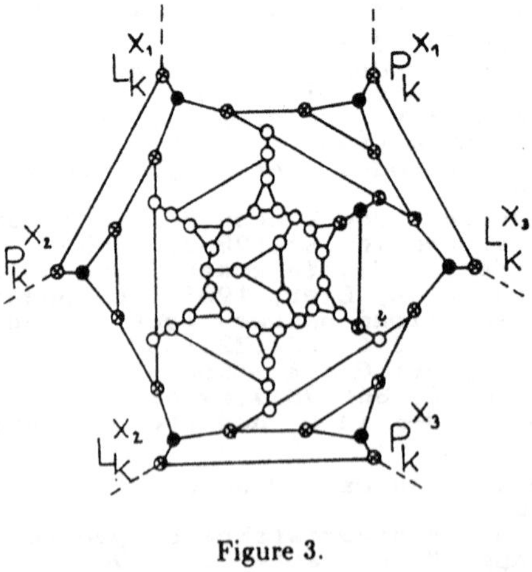

Figure 3.

SEPARATING THE ERASER TURING MACHINE CLASSES

L_e , NL_e , co-NL_e AND P_e

Matthias Krause

Sektion Mathematik
Humboldt Universität Berlin

DDR-1086 Berlin, PF

Christoph Meinel
Stephan Waack

Karl-Weierstraß-Institut für Mathematik
Akademie der Wissenschaften der DDR
DDR-1086 Berlin, PF 1304

INTRODUCTION

One of the most important problems in complexity theory is that for separating complexity classes such as L , NL or P (or to prove their coincidence). Recently the following approach proves to be quite successful. One describes the complexity classes under consideration by means of Boolean circuits or branching programs [SV81], [Ba86], [Me86] and proves lower bounds for Boolean circuits or branching programs with certain resources constraints. In the case of Boolean circuits f.e. lower bounds were obtained for monotone circuits [Ra85], [An85] or for bounded depth circuits [Ya85], [Ha86]. In the case of branching programs in [A&86], [KW86], [Kr87] exponential lower bounds were obtained for read-once-only branching programs.

In the following we investigate read-once-only Ω-branching programs which generalize the concept of read-once-only branching programs. Briefly speaking, Ω-branching programs are branching programs some of whose nodes are equipped with devices for performing Boolean functions $\omega \in \Omega$ from a set $\Omega \subseteq \mathbb{B}_2$ of 2-argument Boolean functions. If $\mathcal{P}_{\Omega\text{-}BP}$ denotes the class of languages acceptable by polynomial size Ω-branching programs then we have

$$\begin{array}{ccccccc} & & \mathcal{P}_{\{\vee\}\text{-}BP} & & & & \\ & & \| & & & & \\ \mathcal{P}_{BP} = \mathcal{L} & \subseteq & \mathcal{NL} & \subseteq & \mathcal{P} = \mathcal{P}_{\{\vee,\wedge\}\text{-}BP} & & \text{[Me88]} . \\ & & \| & & & & \\ & & \mathcal{P}_{\{\wedge\}\text{-}BP} & & & & \end{array}$$

Hence lower bounds for branching programs, disjunctive $\{\vee\}$-branching programs, or conjunctive $\{\wedge\}$-branching programs would essentially contribute to a separation of these classes. In the following we start with a separation of the corresponding read-once-only classes. We prove (Theorem 2) that

$$\begin{array}{ccccc} & & \mathcal{P}_{\{\wedge\}\text{-}BP1} & & \\ & \subsetneq & & \subsetneq & \\ \mathcal{P}_{BP1} & & \nparallel & & \mathcal{P}_{\{\vee,\wedge\}\text{-}BP1} \; (= \mathcal{P}_{\{\vee,\wedge\}\text{-}BP}) , \\ & \subsetneq & & \subsetneq & \\ & & \mathcal{P}_{\{\wedge\}\text{-}BP1} & & \end{array}$$

However these separation results are especially interesting since the classes $\mathcal{P}_{BP1}$, $\mathcal{P}_{\{\vee\}\text{-}BP1}$, $\mathcal{P}_{\{\wedge\}\text{-}BP1}$ *and* $\mathcal{P}_{\{\vee,\wedge\}\text{-}BP1}$ correspond to the nonuniform logarithmic space bounded eraser Turing machine classes $\mathcal{L}_e$, $\mathcal{NL}_e$, $co\text{-}\mathcal{NL}_e$ and $\mathcal{P}_e = \mathcal{P}$ (Theorem 1). Hence the separation result of Theorem 2 yields

$$\begin{array}{ccccc} & & \mathcal{NL}_e & & \\ & \subsetneq & & \subsetneq & \\ \mathcal{L}_e & & \nparallel & & \mathcal{P}_e \; (= \mathcal{P}) , \\ & \subsetneq & & \subsetneq & \\ & & co\text{-}\mathcal{NL}_e & & \end{array}$$

Since up to now only $\mathcal{L}_e = \mathcal{P}_{BP1}$ has been separated by exponential lower bounds we have done further steps on the stony way of separating larger and larger complexity classes by means of exponential lower bounds with $\mathcal{L}_e \subsetneq \mathcal{NL}_e$, $\mathcal{L}_e \subsetneq co\text{-}\mathcal{NL}_e$ and $\mathcal{NL}_e \subsetneq \mathcal{P}_e$, $co\text{-}\mathcal{NL}_e \subsetneq \mathcal{P}_e$. On the other hand we obtain $\mathcal{NL}_e \subsetneq \mathcal{NL}$ and $co\text{-}\mathcal{NL}_e \subsetneq co\text{-}\mathcal{NL} = \mathcal{NL}$ as a corollary of $\mathcal{NL}_e \neq co\text{-}\mathcal{NL}_e$ and of Immerman's result $\mathcal{NL} = co\text{-}\mathcal{NL}$ [Im87]. This shows that the eraser concept causes proper restrictions of the computational power not only in the deterministic case but also in the nondeterminstic and in the co-nondeterministic cases. Similarly we obtain $\mathcal{P}_{\{\vee\}-BP1} \underset{\neq}{\subset} \mathcal{P}_{\{\vee\}-BP}$ and $\mathcal{P}_{\{\wedge\}-BP1} \underset{\neq}{\subset} \mathcal{P}_{\{\wedge\}-BP} = \mathcal{P}_{\{\vee\}-BP}$ which proves that read-once-only disjunctive and read-once-only conjunctive branching programs are less powerful than those not assumed to be read-once-only.

The paper is organized as follows. In Section 1 we introduce eraser Ω-Turing machines and read-once-only branching programs and relate these two concepts (Theorem 1). In Section 2 we prove an exponential lower bound (Lemma 1) and a polynomial upper bound (Lemma 2) for the problem of deciding whether a given Boolean matrix is a permutation matrix. Finally, in Section 3 we use these bounds for separating the above-mentioned eraser Turing machine classes (Theorem 2).

1. Eraser Ω-Turing machines and read-once-only Ω-branching programs

In [A&86] Ajtai et.al. introduced the eraser Turing machine model and related the class of languages accepted by (nonuniform) logarithmic space bounded eraser Turing machines to the class of languages accepted by polynomial size read-once-only-branching programs. In the following section we investigate logarithmic space bounded deterministic, nondeterministic, co-nondeterministic and alternating eraser Turing machines. These machines are usual deterministic, nondeterministic, co-nondeterministic and alternating Turing machines with the property that each computation path depends on every input bit at most once. (In the case of deterministic eraser Turing machines we can think that if an input bit has been read it is erased.) Let us denote by L_e, NL_e , $co\text{-}NL_e$ and P_e the classes of languages acceptable by logarithmic space bounded deterministic, nondeterministic, co-nondeterministic and alternating eraser Turing machines, respectively. Following [Me88] we can relate these classes to the classes of languages accepted by polynomial size disjunctive, conjunctive, and alternating read-once-only-branching programs, respectively. Unifying this approach we consider eraser Ω-Turing machines and read-once-only Ω-branching programs for an arbitrary set of 2-valued Boolean functions $\Omega \subseteq \mathbb{B}_2$.

Let M be a nondeterministic 1-tape Turing machine with a read-only input tape all of whose computation paths are assumed to be finite. M is called an *Ω-Turing machine* if the nonterminal states are labelled by Boolean functions chosen from the set $\Omega \cup \{id\}$ and if the terminal states are labelled by Boolean constants. The *configurations* of M are five-tuples giving M's current state, its label from $\Omega \cup \{id\} \cup \{0,1\}$, the working tape content and the positions of the input and working heads. A configuration c' is a direct successor of a configuration c on an input $w \in \{0,1\}^*$ if c' is reachable from c in one step by means of the next-move relation of M under w. For each value of the input bit read in c the number of direct successors of c equals the arity of the Boolean function assigned to the state of c. Let c_0 be the initial configuration. *Terminalconfigurations* are these whose states are terminal and therefore labelled by Boolean constants.

A *computation* of an Ω-Turing machine M on an input $w \in \{0,1\}^*$ can be described by means of the *computation tree* T(M,w) of M on w. Its root is the tuple (c_0,w). The nodes of T(M,w) are the tuples (c,w) such that the sons of (c,w) are exactly the tuples (c',w) with direct successors c' of c. The leaves of T(M,w) are built from terminal configurations. Generally we assume our Ω-Turing machines to halt on every input, i.e. all computations trees T(M,w), $w \in \{0,1\}^*$, are assumed to be finite.

By means of the Boolean functions $\omega \in \Omega \cup \{id\}$ included in the configurations c of the nodes (c,w) of T(M,w) the Boolean values included in the leaves of T(M,w) extend to Boolean values associated with all nodes of T(M,w). If the root of T(M,w) gets the value 1 or 0 then T(M,w) is called *accepting* or *rejecting*, respectively. M *accepts* or *rejects* $w \in \{0,1\}^*$ if its computation tree T(M,w) is accepting or rejecting.

An Ω-Turing machine M is called an *eraser Ω-Turing machine* if each path in the computation tree T(M,w) of M on $w \in \{0,1\}^n$ from the root to a leaf contains for all $i \le n$ at most one configuration properly depending on the i-th input bit. Indeed, eraser Ω-Turing machines generalize the concept of eraser Turing machines introduced in [A&86] which erase an input bit after having read it.

An eraser Ω-Turing machine M is called s(n) *space bounded* if for all $w \in \{0,1\}^*$ the configurations included in the nodes of T(M,w) consume at most space $s(|w|)$. Of special interest in our further considerations are the classes $L_e(\Omega)$ consisting of all languages acceptable by logarithmic space bounded eraser Ω-Turing machines.

PROPOSITION 1:

(i) $L_e(\emptyset) = L_e$

(ii) $L_e(\{\vee\}) = NL_e$

(iii) $L_e(\{\wedge\}) = co\text{-}NL_e$

(iv) $L_e(\{\wedge,\vee\}) = AL_e = P_e$. ∎

In order to define read-once-only Ω-branching programs we recall the definition of a branching program. *A branching program* P is a directed acyclic graph where each node has outdegree 2 or 0 . Nodes with outdegree 0 are called *sinks* and are labelled by Boolean constants. The remaining nodes are labelled by Boolean variables taken from a set $X = \{x_1,...,x_n\}$. There is a dis- tinguished node, called the *source*, which has indegree 0 . A branching program *computes* an n-argument Boolean function as follows: Starting in the source, the value of the variable labelling the current node is tested. If this is 0 (1) the next node tested is the left (right) successor to the current node. The path from the starting node to a sink traced in this way is called a *computaion path*. The branching program P *accepts* $A \subseteq \{0,1\}^n$ if for all $w \in \{0,1\}^n$ the computation path under w halts at a sink labelled $\chi_A(w)$, where χ_A denotes the characteristic function of A . The natural *complexity measure* for a branching program is the number of non-sink nodes.

An *Ω-branching program* P is a branching program some of whose nodes are equipped with devices for performing Boolean functions $\omega \in \Omega$ from a set $\Omega \subseteq \mathbb{B}_2$ of 2-argument Boolean functions. Formally, this can be described by labelling some of the non-sink nodes of P by Boolean functions $\omega \in \Omega$ instead of Boolean variables. The Boolean values assigned to the sinks of P extend to Boolean values associated with all nodes of P in the following way: if both successor nodes v_0 , v_1 of a node v of P carry the Boolean values δ_0 , δ_1 and if v is labelled by a Boolean variable x_i we associate with v the value δ_0 or δ_1 iff $x_i = 0$ or $x_i = 1$. If v is labelled by a Boolean function ω then we associate with v the value $\omega(\delta_0,\delta_1)$. P is said to *accept* (*reject*) an input $w \in$

$\{0,1\}^n$ if the source of P associates with 1 (0) under w . An Ω-branching program is said to be *read-once-only* if every variable x_i , $1 \le i \le n$, is tested at most once on every computation path. By $\mathcal{P}_{\Omega\text{-}BP1}$ we denote the class of all languages $A \subseteq \{0,1\}^*$ whose restrictions $A^n = A \cap \{0,1\}^n$ will be accepted by read-once-only Ω-branching programs of polynomial size in n .

In order to relate eraser Ω-Turing machine classes , $\Omega \subseteq \mathbb{B}_2$, and read-once-only Ω-branching program classes we have to consider the nonuniform counterpart $\mathcal{L}_e(\Omega) = L_e(\Omega)/poly$ of the class $L_e(\Omega)$ consisting of languages $A \subseteq \{0,1\}^*$ for which there exists a polynomial length-restricted advice $\alpha : \mathbb{N} \longrightarrow \{0,1\}^*$ and a logarithmic space bounded eraser Ω-Turing machine M such that M accepts $w\#\alpha(|w|)$ iff $w \in A$.

THEOREM 1: The classes of languages acceptable by nonuniform (*log* n) space bounded eraser Ω-Turing machines, $\Omega \subseteq \mathbb{B}_2$, coincides with those of all languages acceptable by polynomial size read-once-only Ω-branching programs

$$\mathcal{L}_e(\Omega) = \mathcal{P}_{\Omega\text{-}BP1} .$$

PROOF: The proof can be obtained by similar arguments as of [A&86] and [Me88]. ∎

Proposition 1 and Theorem 1 together yield

COROLLARY:

(i) $\mathcal{P}_{BP1} = \mathcal{L}_e$;

(ii) $\mathcal{P}_{\{\vee\}\text{-}BP1} = \mathcal{NL}_e$;

(iii) $\mathcal{P}_{\{\wedge\}\text{-}BP1} = co\text{-}\mathcal{NL}_e$;

(iv) $\mathcal{P}_{\{\vee,\wedge\}\text{-}BP1} = \mathcal{P}_e$. ∎

Let us only remark that it is not difficult to show that the class $\mathcal{P}_e$ coincides with the class $\mathcal{P}$ of languages nonuniformly acceptable by polynomial time bounded Turing machines

$$\mathcal{P}_e = \mathcal{P} .$$

2. THE LOWER AND THE UPPER BOUND

In the following section we review our $exp(\Omega(n))$ lower bound for the size of disjunctive read-once-only branching programs which decide whether a given Boolean $n \times n$ matrix is a permutation matrix (Lemma 1). Additionally, we give conjunctive read-once-only branching programs of size $O(n^2)$ which perform this task (Lemma 2).

Let $F = \{f_n\}$ be the sequence of Boolean functions f_n defined on the set of Boolean $n \times n$ matrices A with

$f_n(A) = 1$ iff A is a permutation matrix, i.e. A contains exactly one 1 in every row and in every column.

Recall, that there is a 1-1 correspondence between $n \times n$ permutation matrices and n-permutations $\sigma \in S_n$

$$\sigma \longmapsto A^{\sigma} = (a_{ij}) \quad \text{with} \quad a_{ij} = \begin{cases} 1 & \text{if } j = \sigma(i) \\ 0 & \text{otherwise} . \end{cases}$$

LEMMA 1: Every disjunctive read-once-only-branching program which computes f_n is of size $2^{\Omega(n)}$. ■

COROLLARY: Every conjunctive read-once-only branching program which computes $\neg f_n$ is of size $2^{\Omega(n)}$. ■

PROOF: For every conjunctive read-once-only branching program computing $\neg f_n$ we obtain an disjunctive read-once-only branching program of equal size computing $\neg(\neg f_n) = f_n$ if we replace the conjunctive $\wedge$-nodes by disjunctive $\vee$-nodes, the 1-sinks by 0-sinks and the 0-sinks by 1-sinks. Hence, Lemma 1 implies the corollary. ■

LEMMA 2: f_n can be computed by means of a conjunctive read-once-only branching program of size $O(n^2)$. ■

In analogy with the Corollary of Lemma 1 we obtain the following corollary to Lemma 2 .

COROLLARY: $\neg f_n$ can be computed by means of a disjunctive read-once-only branching program of size $O(n^2)$. ■

3. THE SEPARATION RESULT

Due to the lower and the upper bound proved in section 2 for the problems $F = \{f_n\}$ and $\neg F = \{\neg f_n\}$ of deciding whether a given matrix is a permutation matrix we can separate the eraser Turing machine classes $\mathcal{L}_e$, $\mathcal{NL}_e$, $co\text{-}\mathcal{NL}_e$ and $\mathcal{P}_e = \mathcal{P}$ from each other.

PROPOSITION 2:

(i) $\mathcal{P}_{BP1} \neq \mathcal{P}_{\{\vee\}\text{-}BP1}$;

(ii) $\mathcal{P}_{BP1} \neq \mathcal{P}_{\{\wedge\}\text{-}BP1}$;

(iii) $\mathcal{P}_{\{\vee\}\text{-}BP1} \neq \mathcal{P}_{\{\wedge\}\text{-}BP1}$;

(iv) $\mathcal{P}_{\{\vee\}\text{-}BP1}, \mathcal{P}_{\{\wedge\}\text{-}BP1} \neq \mathcal{P}_{\{\vee,\wedge\}\text{-}BP1}$.

PROOF: Trivially, we have

$$\mathcal{P}_{BP1} \subseteq \mathcal{P}_{\{\vee\}\text{-}BP1}, \quad \mathcal{P}_{\{\wedge\}\text{-}BP1} \subseteq \mathcal{P}_{\{\vee,\wedge\}\text{-}BP1}$$

(i) is a consequence of Lemma 1 and Lemma 2 of Section 2 : Due to the corollary of Lemma 1 it holds

$$\{\neg f_n\} \notin \mathcal{P}_{\{\wedge\}\text{-}BP1}$$

and, therefore,

$$\{\neg f_n\} \notin \mathcal{P}_{BP1} .$$

Whereas the corollary of Lemma 2 implies

$$\{\neg f_n\} \in \mathcal{P}_{\{\vee\}\text{-}BP1} .$$

(ii) and (iii) can be obtained analogously to (i) if one regards $\{f_n\}$ instead of $\{\neg f_n\}$, or $\{f_n\}$ and $\{\neg f_n\}$ simultaneously, respectively.

Finally, (iv) is a consequence of (iii) . ■

COROLLARY:

(i) $\mathcal{P}_{\{v\}\text{-BP1}} \underset{\neq}{\subset} \mathcal{P}_{\{v\}\text{-BP}}$;

(ii) $\mathcal{P}_{\{\wedge\}\text{-BP1}} \underset{\neq}{\subset} \mathcal{P}_{\{\wedge\}\text{-BP}}$.

PROOF: (i) and (ii) follow immediately from Proposition 2 (iii) and from $\mathcal{P}_{\{v\}\text{-BP}} = \mathcal{P}_{\{\wedge\}\text{-BP}}$ [Me88]. ■

Altogether, Proposition 2 and the Corollary of Proposition 1 yield:

THEOREM 2:

(i) $\mathcal{L}_e \neq \mathcal{NL}_e$;

(ii) $\mathcal{L}_e \neq co\text{-}\mathcal{NL}_e$;

(iii) $\mathcal{NL}_e \neq co\text{-}\mathcal{NL}_e$;

(iv) $\mathcal{NL}_e$, $co\text{-}\mathcal{NL}_e \neq \mathcal{P}_e = \mathcal{P}$. ■

REFERENCES:

[A&86] M.Ajtai, L.Babai, P.Hajnal, J.Komlos, P.Pudlak, V.Rödl, E.Szemeredi, G.Turan: Two lower bounds for branching programs, Proc. 18th ACM Symp. on Theory of Computing, 30-38

[An85] A.E.Andreev: On a method of obtaining lower bounds for the complexity of individual montone functions, Dokl. Akad. Nauk SSSR 282/5, 1033-1037

[Ba86] D.A.Barrington: Bounded-width polynomial size branching programs recognize exactly those languages in NC^1, Proc. 18th ACM Symp. on Theory of Computing, 1-5

[BC80] A.Borodin, S.Cook: A time-space tradeoff for sorting on a general sequential model of computation, Proc. 12th ACM Symp. on Theory of Computing 1980, 294-301

[Ha86] J.Hastad: Improved lower bounds for small depth circuits, Proc. 18th ACM Symp. on Theory of Computing,

[Im87] N.Immerman: Nondeterministic space is closed under complement, Techn. Report 552, Yale Univ., 1987

[KL80] R.M.Karp, R.J.Lipton: Some connections between non-uniform and uniform complexity classes, Proc. 12th ACM Symp. on Theory of Computing, 1980,302-309

[Kr87] M.Krause: Exponential lower bounds on the complexity of local and real-time branching programs, to appear in EIK 24 (1988),3

[KW87] K.Kriegel, S.Waack: Exponential lower bounds for real-time branching programs, Proc. Fundamentals of Computation Theory'87, Kazan, LNCS 278, 263-267

[Me86] Ch.Meinel: p-projection reducibility and the complexity classes *L*(nonuniform) and *NL*(nonuniform), Proc. 12th MFCS, Bratislava, LNCS 233, 527-535; revised and extended version in EIK 23 (1987), 10/11, 545-558

[Me88] Ch.Meinel: The power of polynomial size Ω-branching programs, Proc. STAC'88, Bourdeaux, LNCS 294, 81-90

[Ra85] A.A.Razborov: A lower bound for the monotone network complexity of the logical permanent, Matem. Zametki 37/6

[We87] I.Wegener: The Complexity of Boolean functions, Teubner, Stuttgart, 1987

[Ya85] A.C.Yao: Separating the poynomial-time hierarchy by oracles, Proc. 26th IEEE Symp. on Foundations of Computer Science, 1-10

Compositional Proofs by Partial Specification of Processes

Kim G. Larsen
Department of Mathematics and Computer Science
Aalborg University Centre
9000 Aalborg, Denmark

Bent Thomsen
Department of Computing
Imperial College of Science and Technology
London SW7 2BZ, England

Abstract

The purpose of this paper is to present and illustrate a new compositional proof method for non-deterministic and concurrent systems; i.e. a method which allows factoring the correctness proof of a system into similar but smaller proofs of correctness of subsystems.
Our method is an extension of the well established notion of bisimulation [Par81,Mil83]; it is based on a concept of partial processes which may be related through a notion of partial bisimulation. Compared with existing methods our method has the distinct advantage of leading to simple and intuitive subspecifications without complicating the underlying theory unduly.
The method is motivated and its use illustrated through the verification of a simple scheduler.

Introduction

For the verification of larger systems it is essential that the proof method used is compositional in order to avoid a combinatorial explosion of the verification. That is, the method must allow us to decompose the problem of correctness for a concurrent system with respect to a given specification into similar problems for the components of the system with respect to suitable subspecifications. The purpose of this paper is to present and illustrate such a compositional proof method for concurrent systems.

In recent years several equivalences between nondeterministic and concurrent processes have been proposed in order to capture various extensional aspects of processes. As such, the proposed equivalences are useful for relating process descriptions at different levels of abstraction, and may be used as the notion of correctness of a system SYS with respect to a specification $SPEC$. That is, to prove SYS correct with respect to $SPEC$ simply consists in proving $SYS \equiv SPEC$, where $\equiv$ is the equivalence under consideration. Provided $\equiv$ is a *congruence* with respect to the various process constructing operations we may give a ***compositional proof*** of $SYS \equiv SPEC$. First we view SYS as being some combination of n components $SYS_1 \ldots SYS_n$, i.e. $SYS \equiv C[SYS_1, \ldots, SYS_n]$. Then, for each component SYS_i, we must find a suitable subspecification $SPEC_i$ and prove their equivalence (congruence), that is $SYS_i \equiv SPEC_i$. Finally, we must prove that the subspecifications — when combined — will entail the global specification: $C[SPEC_1, \ldots, SPEC_n] \equiv SPEC$. Combining these three steps $SYS \equiv SPEC$ will follow due to the congruence property of $\equiv$.

Though this approach nicely factors the proof it often becomes unnecessarily complicated. Due to the behavioural constraints that the components impose on each other, only very minor parts of their behaviour need be accessible in the total system SYS. However, the subspecifications satisfying $SYS_i \equiv SPEC_i$ must describe *all* behavioural aspects of the components including the behaviour which is inaccessible. Hence, the subspecifications may be unduly complicated and unintuitive.

Our method is an extension of the well established notion of bisimulation [Par81,Mil83] and is developed specifically in order to make it possible to obtain ***simple*** subspecifications by relaxing condition $SYS_i \equiv SPEC_i$. An alternative compositional proof methodology also leading to simple subspecifications has been

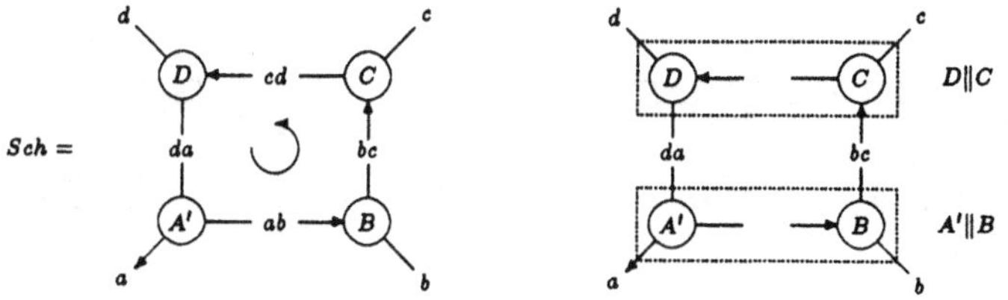

Figure 1: A simple scheduler and a decomposition of it.

developed in [Lar85,Lar86] and its use in verification is illustrated in [LarMil87]. Here the conditions of $SYS_i \equiv SPEC_i$ are relaxed by parameterizing the equivalence in question with information of the behavioural constraints imposed by the other subsystems. However, an explicit "calculation" of this information is required. Our new technique has the additional advantage of *not* requirering any such calculations, while still leading to simple subspecifications. Obviously, the definition of the subspecifications will be highly influenced by one's intuition of the behavioural constraints between subsystems — indeed, the better intuition you have, the simpler a subspecification you are likely to write down — but you are at no time required to *formalize* this intuition. Making the extra effort of a formalization may though in certain cases turn out to bring valuable new insight.

In our new method, $SYS_i \equiv SPEC_i$ is relaxed by allowing specifications to be *partial.* Partial specifications may be related through a notion of *partial bisimulation* and the induced implementation ordering. For total specifications (i.e. ordinary processes) the notion of partial bisimulation degenerates to the standard notion of bisimulation [Par81,Mil83]. Our method is in the spirit of that of Koymans and Mulder [KoyMul85]. However, their method was developed as part of a verification of the Alternating Bit Protocol and has yet to be studied in general terms.

In this paper we give a full presentation of our method and illustrate its use in the verification of a simple scheduler. In section 1 the simple scheduler is presented and the shortcomings of the standard notion of bisimulation in compositional proofs is demonstrated. Based on these shortcomings requirements to our new method are formulated. Sections 2-5 introduce the notion of partial bisimulation and it is proved that the induced implementation ordering fulfils our requirements. Section 2 and section 4 may be viewed as a short introduction to CCS. For a thorough introduction to CCS readers are advised to consult [Mil80,Mil83]. Finally, in section 6 we apply our results in a verification of the simple scheduler.

1 A Simple Scheduler

We consider a simple scheduler consisting of 4 cyclic cells A, B, C and D displayed in figure 1. Intuitively the purpose of the scheduler is to act as a sequentializer in a system where we want four agents to perform their tasks repeatedly. The scheduler will ensure that the agents perform in rotation by repeatedly signalizing to the surrounding system via the channels a, b, c and d in sequence. A more elaborate scheduler may be found in [Mil80].

In the above scheduler a typical cell X has the behaviour: $X \Leftarrow pred.X'$, $X' \Leftarrow x.X''$ and $X'' \Leftarrow \overline{succ}.X$. We obtain A, B, C and D by the renamings: $A \Leftarrow X[da/pred, a/x, ab/succ]$, $B \Leftarrow X[ab/pred, b/x, bc/succ]$, $C \Leftarrow X[bc/pred, c/x, cd/succ]$, $D \Leftarrow X[cd/pred, d/x, da/succ]$. The scheduler Sch is then defined as: $Sch \Leftarrow (A'\|B\|C\|D)$ where $P\|Q$ is the restricted parallel composition in CCS [Mil80], i.e. $P\|Q = (P\,|\,Q)\backslash I$, where $I = sort(P) \cap sort(Q)$. Note, that $\|$ is associative in our case, since no two ports are identically named.

We want to prove that Sch is *bisimulation equivalent* to the specification: $Spec \Leftarrow a.\tau.b.\tau.c.\tau.d.\tau.Spec$. We may prove this equivalence directly by exhibiting a bisimulation containing the pair $(Spec, Sch)$. However, we prefer to give a compositional proof in order to demonstrate our techniques. Thus, we decompose Sch into the two subsystems $A'\|B$ and $D\|C$ as indicated in figure 1. The two subsystems will obviously communicate

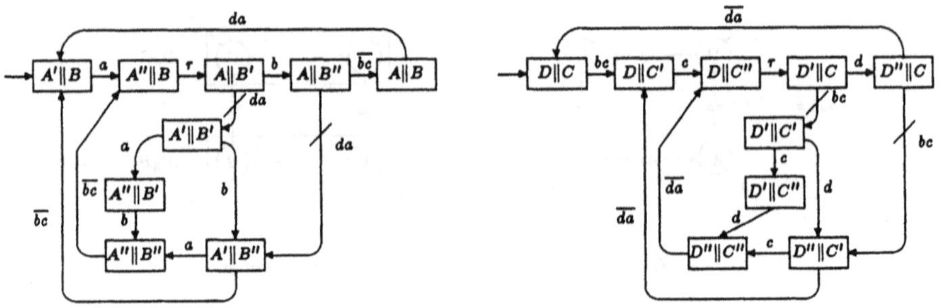

Figure 2: The behaviour of $A'\|B$ and $D\|C$

over the ports *da* and *bc*, and it is intuitively clear that the interaction between the two subsystems will consist of a simple alternation of *bc* and *da*, starting with *bc*.

We may now complete the correctness proof by finding subspecifications $A'B$ and DC satisfying :

$$A'B \sim A'\|B \text{ and } DC \sim D\|C \text{ and } (A'B)\|(DC) \sim Spec \tag{1}$$

From the congruence–property of $\sim$ we may then conclude $Sch \sim Spec$ as desired.

Obviously — in order to reduce our proof obligations — we want the subspecifications $A'B$ and DC to be as simple as possible and a first guess would probably yield: $A'B \Leftarrow a.\tau.b.\overline{bc}.da.A'B$ and $DC \Leftarrow bc.c.\tau.d.\overline{da}.DC$ Unfortunately, these subspecifications are far too simple for (1) to hold. In fact, no simple subspecifications $A'B$ and DC which satisfy the equivalences in (1) exist, as may be seen from the display of the full behaviours of $A'\|B$ and $D\|C$ shown in figure 2.

As previously mentioned the interactions between the two subsystems are subject to certain restrictions. As a consequence not all of their potential behaviour will be accessible in the total system. In particular, in an execution of the total system the overcrossed derivations (marked $\not\rightarrow$) will never be examined. It follows that approximately 50% of the two subsystems potential behaviour is never realized. However, any subspecifications satisfying the equivalences of (1) must also cover the inaccessible behaviour, and will therefore necessarily be unduly complicated and certainly not intuitive.

Obviously, the defect of the foregoing strategy is that the conditions in (1) are too strong since they do not in any way take into consideration — neither explicitly nor implicitly — the restrictions imposed by the two subcomponents on one another. One way of reflecting these restrictions would be to allow the use of some kind of *partial specifications*, in order that only the accessible part of a subsystem needs to be specified. In the present example it seems natural — in light of our initial guess — to specify $A'\|B$ and $D\|C$ partially as follows:

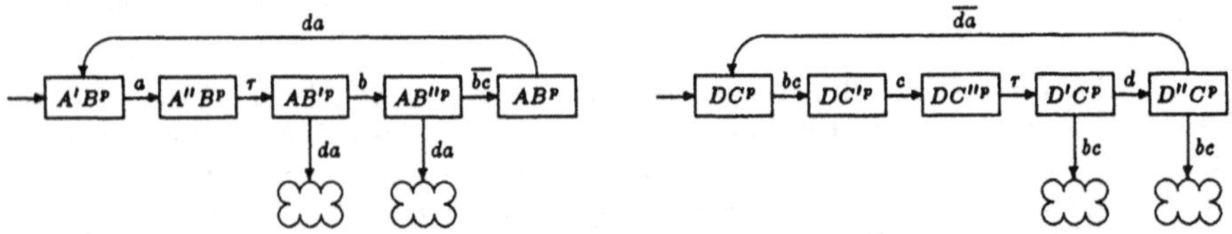

Figure 3: Partial behaviour of $A'\|B$ and $D\|C$.

Here ☁ should be thought of as an area where any behaviour may be encountered. Intuitively, we may view a partial specification S — so far a diagram with possible occurrences of ☁ — as defining a set of (concrete) processes: namely, all the processes being equivalent to some "instance" of S. This naturally induces an ordering on partial specifications given by $S \lhd T$ iff "all instances of S are equivalent to some instance of T". In case S is totally specified (i.e. a concrete process), $S \lhd T$ then becomes "S is equivalent to some instance of T". If T also is totally specified $S \lhd T$ simply degenerates to $S \sim T$.

The conditions of (1) may then be replaced by the weaker conditions: $A'\|B \lhd A'B^p$ and $D\|C \lhd DC^p$. We must now prove that the partial subspecifications — when combined — entail the global specification: $A'B^p\|DC^p \lhd Spec$. Obviously this requires a suitable extension of the parallel composition (and all other process constructions) to partial specifications. In particular, we want $\lhd$ to be transitive and substitutive with respect to the various process constructions, since this will enable us to conclude: $Sch = A'\|B\|C\|D \lhd Spec$ and — since both Sch and $Spec$ are totally specified — $Sch \sim Spec$.

In the following sections we shall develop a formal theory of partial specifications satisfying the above requirements.

2 Processes and Bisimulation

We take the approach of many recent researchers, especially R. Milner (see e.g. [Mil80,Mil83]), by defining the semantics of concurrent systems by the set of experiments they offer to an observer. I.e. we use the model of *labeled transition systems* [Plo81] as a mean of expressing the operational semantics of concurrent systems.

Let Pr be a set of processes and Act a set of actions which processes may perform. A derivation relation $\longrightarrow \subseteq Pr \times Act \times Pr$ defines the dynamic change of processes as they perform actions. For $(p, a, q) \in \longrightarrow$ we normally write $p \stackrel{a}{\longrightarrow} q$ which may be interpreted as: " the process p can perform an action a and by doing so become the process q". We use the usual abbreviations as e.g. $p \stackrel{a}{\longrightarrow}$ for $\exists q \in Pr.p \stackrel{a}{\longrightarrow} q$ and $p \stackrel{a}{\not\longrightarrow}$ for $\neg\exists q \in Pr.p \stackrel{a}{\longrightarrow} q$. The triple $\mathcal{P} = (Pr, Act, \longrightarrow)$ constitutes the transition system of processes. Based on the operational semantics given by the transition system, several equivalences and preorders have been proposed in order to capture various aspects of the observational behaviour of processes. One of these is the equivalence induced by the notion of bisimulation [Par81,Mil83].

Definition 2.1 *A* bisimulation *R is a binary relation on Pr such that whenever pRq and $a \in Act$ then:*

(i) Whenever $p \stackrel{a}{\longrightarrow} p'$, then $q \stackrel{a}{\longrightarrow} q'$ for some q' with $p'Rq'$

(ii) Whenever $q \stackrel{a}{\longrightarrow} q'$, then $p \stackrel{a}{\longrightarrow} p'$ for some p' with $p'Rq'$

Two processes p and q are said to be bisimulation equivalent iff there exists a bisimulation R containing (p, q). In this case we write $p \sim q$.

Now for $R \subseteq Pr^2$ we can define $\mathcal{B}(R)$ as the set of pairs (p, q) satisfying for all $a \in Act$ the clauses (i) and (ii) above. From this definition it follows immediately that R is a bisimulation just in case $R \subseteq \mathcal{B}(R)$. Also, $\mathcal{B}$ is easily seen to be a monotone endofunction on the complete lattice of binary relations (over Pr) under subset inclusion. Standard fixed point results, due to Tarski [Tar55], yield that a maximal fixed point for $\mathcal{B}$ exists and is defined as $\bigcup\{R \mid R \subseteq \mathcal{B}(R)\}$. This maximal fixed point actually equals $\sim$. Moreover, $\sim$ is an equivalence relation and even a congruence with respect to the usual CCS process constructions [Mil80] and indeed any natural process construction [Sim85,Lar86].

3 Partial Processes and Partial Bisimulation

We may now concentrate on the formalization of partial specifications. So far partial specifications have been presented as diagrams with possible occurrences of ☁ , the intuition of ☁ being that any behaviour may be encountered in this area. However, we want an *operational semantics* for $\mathcal{E}3$ and for partial specifications in general in order to facilitate the necessary extension of process constructions. In addition — and perhaps more important — this enables the definition of $\triangleleft$ to be based directly upon an operational semantics yielding an efficient and elegant proof technique similar to that of bisimulation.

As a first step towards an operational semantics of partial specifications we introduce a distinguished *indeterminate action* $*$, and with it the possibility of *indeterminate moves* or transitions, $p \xrightarrow{*} q$, of processes. An indeterminate transition, $p \xrightarrow{*} q$, is to be determined each time the process p is activated; i.e. whenever the execution is at p, $p \xrightarrow{*} q$ may be instantiated to any (proper) transition of the form $p \xrightarrow{a} q$ $(a \in Act)$ or — alternatively — $p \xrightarrow{*} q$ may give rise to *no* proper transition at all.

In a sense, indeterminate transitions represent one-step approximations of the unknown behaviour area $\mathcal{E}3$. In fact, we may think of $\mathcal{E}3$ as being specified recursively as $\mathcal{E}3 \Leftarrow *.\mathcal{E}3$, since the first action of an unknown behaviour — if indeed such an action exists — could be any action at all, and obviously the behaviour to be encountered after the first step remains unknown.

Formally, we introduce a system of *partial processes* as a labeled transition system $\mathbb{P} = (PPr, Act_*, \longrightarrow)$, where $Act_* = Act \cup \{*\}$ with $*$ being a distinguished action symbol not a member of Act; and $\longrightarrow \subseteq PPr \times Act_* \times PPr$.

To define the *implementation ordering*, $\triangleleft$, between partial processes let us introduce two new "proper" transition relations, $\longrightarrow_{may}, \longrightarrow_{must} \subseteq PPr \times Act \times PPr$, defined as follows:

$$p \xrightarrow{a}_{may} p' \;\Leftrightarrow^{\Delta}\; p \xrightarrow{a} p' \text{ or } p \xrightarrow{*} p'$$
$$p \xrightarrow{a}_{must} p' \;\Leftrightarrow^{\Delta}\; p \xrightarrow{a} p'$$

From the intuition of indeterminate transitions we may interpret $p \xrightarrow{a}_{may} p'$ as "p may be able to perform the action a and become p'", and similarly $p \xrightarrow{a}_{must} p'$ as "p must be able to perform the action a and become p'". Note that $p \xrightarrow{a}_{must} p'$ implies $p \xrightarrow{a}_{may} p'$.

Now, $p \triangleleft q$ should express that p is an implementation or a refinement of q. As such we expect that any behavioural aspect which p *may* realize should also be realisable by its specification q. Dually, the behavioural aspects which are already determined by q (by the determined transitions) should remain being determined in p. Using the new transition relations $\longrightarrow_{may}$ and $\longrightarrow_{must}$, this may be formalized by the following notion of partial bisimulation:

Definition 3.1 *A* partial bisimulation *R is a binary relation on PPr such that whenever pRq and $a \in Act$ then the following holds:*

(i) Whenever $p \xrightarrow{a}_{may} p'$, then $q \xrightarrow{a}_{may} q'$ for some q' with $p'Rq'$

(ii) Whenever $q \xrightarrow{a}_{must} q'$, then $p \xrightarrow{a}_{must} p'$ for some p' with $p'Rq'$

p is said to implement *q if there exists a partial bisimulation R containing (p,q). We write $p \triangleleft q$ in this case.*

Now for $R \subseteq PPr^2$ we can define $\mathbb{B}(R)$ as the set of all pairs (p,q) satisfying for all $a \in Act$ the clauses (i) and (ii) above. Then R is a partial bisimulation just in case $R \subseteq \mathbb{B}(R)$. Moreover, $\mathbb{B}$ is easily seen to be a monotone endofunction on the complete lattice of binary relations over PPr (under subset inclusion), and standard fixed point results yield that $\mathbb{B}$ has a maximal fixed point, which actually equals $\triangleleft$.

Example 3.2 *Let $\mathcal{U} \Leftarrow *.\mathcal{U}$. Then $p \triangleleft \mathcal{U}$ for all partial processes p, since $\{(p,\mathcal{U}) \mid p \in PPr\}$ is a partial bisimulation ($\mathcal{U}$ may be able to do any action, but there is no action $\mathcal{U}$ must be able to do).*

The above definition of $\lhd$ is perhaps somewhat far from our original intuition in section 1, where $p \lhd q$ was informally defined as "all instances of p are equivalent to some instance of q". However, based on a (denotational) semantics of partial processes in terms of the instances they define, our original intuition of $\lhd$ may be formalized directly and proved equivalent to the above definition of $\lhd$ in terms of partial bisimulations. In fact we do so in [LarTho88]. In the present paper, however, we use the definition of $\lhd$ in terms of partial bisimulations due to the efficient proof technique it induces.

The relation $\lhd$ enjoys many pleasant properties and fulfils our requirements to an implementation ordering as may be seen from the following:

Proposition 3.3 $\lhd$ *is a preorder*

PROOF: Since $Id = \{(p,p) \mid p \in PPr\}$ is easily seen to be a partial bisimulation $\lhd$ is reflexive. Composition of partial bisimulations are easily seen to be partial bisimulations and therefore $\lhd$ is transitive. □

The relationship between $\lhd$ and $\sim$ is of particular interest: as expected $\sim$ is stronger than $\lhd$, and $\lhd$ degenerates to $\sim$ for total processes.

Proposition 3.4 *If* $p \sim q$ *then* $p \lhd q$ *and* $q \lhd p$

PROOF: From definition of $\mathcal{B}$ and $\mathcal{PB}$ it is easy to see that $\mathcal{B}(R) \subseteq \mathcal{PB}(R)$ for all $R \subseteq PPr^2$. Since $\mathcal{B}(R)$ obviously is symmetric also $R^{-1} \subseteq \mathcal{B}(R^{-1}) \subseteq \mathcal{PB}(R^{-1})$, which yields the second result. □

Definition 3.5 p *is* total *iff* $q \overset{*}{\not\rightarrow}$ *whenever* q *is a derivative of* p.

Note how this definition resembles that of being stable in [Mil80], where the ability to perform τ-actions (internal actions) is investigated.

Proposition 3.6 *if* p *and* q *are total and* $p \lhd q$ *then* $p \sim q$.

PROOF: If $p \lhd q$ then there exists a relation R such that $R \subseteq \mathcal{PB}(R)$ and $(p,q) \in \mathcal{PB}(R)$. Let $SR = (Der(p) \times Der(q)) \cap R$ where $Der(p) = \{p' \mid \exists p_0 \ldots p_{n-2}.\ \exists a_0 \ldots a_{n-1}.p \xrightarrow{a_0} p_0 \xrightarrow{a_1} \ldots \xrightarrow{a_{n-2}} p_{n-2} \xrightarrow{a_{n-1}} p'\}$. SR is easily verified to be a partial bisimulation concerning p and q and their derivatives only. If a process p is total $p \xrightarrow{a}_{must}$ and $p \xrightarrow{a}_{may}$ both degenerate to $p \xrightarrow{a}$ since $p \overset{*}{\not\rightarrow}$. From this one may deduce that $SR \subseteq \mathcal{PB}(SR) = \mathcal{B}(SR)$ showing that SR is a bisimulation containing (p,q) which yields $p \sim q$ proving the proposition. □

4 Process Construction

So far processes have been described as objects with no internal structure. In practice, however, processes are often combined of smaller processes; e.g. the Simple Scheduler is the parallel combination of 4 cyclic cells. In this section we shall describe some process constructions and their operational semantics. In particular, we introduce a general static process construction replacing all the static constructs of CCS.

Dynamic Operations

The two fundamental dynamic process constructions are prefixing and nondeterminism. Let $a \in Act$ and $p \in Pr$ then there is a process $a.p \in Pr$. Prefixing has the operational semantics: $a.p \xrightarrow{a} p$ for all $a \in Act$. For $p_1, p_2 \in Pr$ there is a process $p_1 + p_2 \in Pr$ with the operational semantics $p_1 + p_2 \xrightarrow{a} p$ iff $p_1 \xrightarrow{a} p$ or $p_2 \xrightarrow{a} p$. This means that $p_1 + p_2$ nondeterministicly chooses to follow the actions of either p_1 or p_2. Together with the process $nil \in Pr$ which represents inaction these constitute the dynamic operations. Bisimulation equivalence $\sim$ has been shown [Mil80] to be a congruence with respect to these process constructions, i.e. they are preserving $\sim$.

Static Operations

Instead of giving a number of static operations such as parallel composition, renaming and restriction as in CCS [Mil80] or synchronous parallel composition as in SCCS [Mil83], we give one general process construction which may be instantiated to give all the above mentioned operations (in the spirit of Peter Aczel [Acz84]). Let $f : Act_0^n \hookrightarrow Act$ be an n-ary partial function, where $Act_0 = Act \cup \{0\}$, 0 being a distinguished no-action symbol not in *Act*. We introduce an n-ary process construction $(\ldots)[f]$ with the following operational semantics:

$$\frac{[(p_i \xrightarrow{a_i} p_i') \vee (p_i = p_i' \;\&\; a_i = 0)]_{i \leq n}}{(p_1 \ldots p_n)[f] \xrightarrow{a} (p_1' \ldots p_n')[f]} \quad f(a_1 \ldots a_n) \simeq a$$

Here $f(a_1 \ldots a_n) \simeq a$ means true if $f(a_1 \ldots a_n)$ is defined and a is instantiated to the value of $f(a_1 \ldots a_n)$; otherwise $f(a_1 \ldots a_n) \simeq a$ is false. The premises of the above rule intuitively say that a component process p_i either contributes an action a_i or remains inactive (indicated by $a_i = 0$), in any action of the combined process.

To see that the above process construction is indeed general we observe that if we instantiate f to an identity function on a subset B of *Act* we obtain the restriction operation $\lceil B$ known from SCCS [Mil83]. If we instantiate f to an endofunction $\Phi : Act \rightarrow Act$ we obtain a renaming operation. If *Act* has an abelian group structure with composition operation $\cdot$ we obtain the synchronous communication operator $\times$ from SCCS by instantiating f to $\cdot$. The asynchronous parallel operator $|$ from CCS is obtained by instantiating f to a function satisfying: $f(a, \overline{a}) = \tau$, $f(a, 0) = a = f(0, a)$ for all $a \in Act$ and f undefined for all other combinations of $(a, b) \in Act_0^2$. Also the communication operator $\|$ known from CSP [HBR81] can be obtained by instantiating f to a function satisfying: $f(a, a) = a$ for all $a \in Act$ and f undefined for all other combinations of $(a, b) \in Act_0^2$. This shows the generality of the process construction. We may now give *one* simple proof of the congruence property of $\sim$.

Proposition 4.1 *$\sim$ is preserved by the process construction* $(\ldots)[f]$

PROOF: The relation $R = \{((p_1 \ldots p_n)[f], (q_1 \ldots q_n)[f]) \mid \forall i. p_i \sim q_i\}$ is a bisimulation. The arguments for this are similar but simpler than the arguments given in the following proposition 5.2 showing $\lhd$ is preserved by $(\ldots)[f]$'s extension to *PPr*. □

5 Partial Process Constructions

We may now extend the process constructions prefixing, nondeterminism and the general $(\ldots)[f]$ to constructions upon partial processes. The extensions must cater for the indeterminate nature of $*$-actions , and should preferably imply substitutiveness of $\lhd$ wrt. all the extended constructions.

Dynamic Operations

The dynamic operations are trivially extended to partial processes i.e. let $b \in Act_*$ and $p \in PPr$ then there is a process $b.p \in PPr$ with the operational semantics: $b.p \xrightarrow{b} p$ for all $b \in Act_*$. Let $p_1, p_2 \in PPr$ then there is a process $p_1 + p_2 \in PPr$ with the operational semantics: $p_1 + p_2 \xrightarrow{a} p$ iff $p_1 \xrightarrow{a} p$ or $p_2 \xrightarrow{a} p$. Also $nil \in PPr$.

Proposition 5.1 *Prefixing and nondeterminism preserves* $\lhd$

PROOF: The relations $R_1 = \{(b.p, b.q) \mid p \lhd q, b \in Act_*\} \cup \lhd$ and $R_2 = \{(p_1 + p_2, q_1 + q_2) \mid p_i \lhd q_i\} \cup \lhd$ are both partial bisimulations. □

Static Operations

The extension of the general process construction $(\ldots)[f]$ to a construction upon partial processes is done by extending $f : Act_0^n \hookrightarrow Act$ uniquely to a function $\overline{f} : (Act_*)_0^n \hookrightarrow Act_*$ satisfying

$$\overline{f}(b_1 \ldots b_n) = \begin{cases} * & \exists i \leq n. b_i = * \\ f(b_1 \ldots b_n) & otherwise \end{cases}$$

That is f extended in such a way that it becomes strict wrt. $*$ in all arguments separately.

The operational semantics is then given by

$$\frac{[(p_i \xrightarrow{b_i} p_i') \vee (p_i = p_i' \ \& \ b_i = 0)]_{i \leq n}}{(p_1 \ldots p_n)[\overline{f}] \xrightarrow{b} (p_1' \ldots p_n')[\overline{f}]} \quad \overline{f}(b_1 \ldots b_n) \simeq b$$

Again $\overline{f}(b_1 \ldots b_n) \simeq b$ yields true if $\overline{f}(b_1 \ldots b_n)$ is defined and b is instantiated to the value of $\overline{f}(b_1 \ldots b_n)$ and false otherwise.

Remember that the extension $\overline{f}$ of f is strict with respect to the $*$-action in all arguments separately. Hence, when a subprocess p_i in $(p_1 \ldots p_n)[\overline{f}]$ contributes an $*$-action the combined process has to perform an $*$-action as well. Obviously, given the simple "flat" structure of our action set, where actions are either totally indeterminate ($*$) or totally determined ($a \in Act$), this seems the only sensible choice. However, it clearly leads to loss of information as can be seen from the following example: the partial process $(*.nil)\backslash c$ can be shown to have the derivation $(*.nil)\backslash c \xrightarrow{*} nil\backslash c$ from the above rule and $*.nil \xrightarrow{*} nil$. Thus $(*.nil)\backslash c \xrightarrow{a}_{may} nil\backslash c$ for any action $a \in Act$ and in particular $(*.nil)\backslash c \xrightarrow{c}_{may} nil\backslash c$. Even though this statement is valid — since it merely states that something *might* be possible — the fact that we are forced to make the statement clearly indicates a loss of information, since we *know* that $(*.nil)\backslash c$ will never be able to perform a c–action in any execution.

To repair this situation, it seems that we need to refine our action set in order to accommodate for partial actions other than $*$. In the present example we could do with a partial action $*\backslash c$, which may be instantiated to any total action but c. Thus assuming an information ordering $\sqsubseteq$ on actions we would expect: $* \sqsubseteq *\backslash c \sqsubseteq a$ for all a but c. Then the partial process $(*.nil)\backslash c$ should have the derivation: $(*.nil)\backslash c \xrightarrow{*\backslash c} nil\backslash c$ and hence $(*.nil)\backslash c \xrightarrow{a}_{may} nil\backslash c$ for all actions a but c. We believe that this refinement may be obtained as an instance of the more general theory developed in [Tho87], where preorders on processes are induced by preorders on actions. We pursue this possibility in [LarTho88]. In the present paper, however, we prefer to stay with the simpler "flat" structure on actions, since it leads to a simpler, yet adequate, theory.

We can now show that $\lhd$ is indeed preserved by the extended construct, under the technical assumption that no partial process is able to perform all actions in Act.

Proposition 5.2 *$\lhd$ is preserved by the process construction* $(\ldots)[f]$.

PROOF: For simplicity and clarity we shall deal only with the case when f is a unary function $Act_0 \hookrightarrow Act$. The extension of the proof to functions of arbitrary arity is straightforward and left for the reader.

To prove the proposition we show that the relation $R = \{(p[\overline{f}], q[\overline{f}]) \mid p \lhd q\}$ is a partial bisimulation, i.e. $R \subseteq \mathcal{B}(R)$. This will follow almost directly from the following two easily established lemmas, which relate derivatives of combined processes to derivatives of components. (We extend the relations $\longrightarrow_{may}$ and $\longrightarrow_{must}$ to allow for the no–action symbol 0 by defining $p \xrightarrow{0}_{may} p' \Leftrightarrow^{\Delta} p = p'$ and likewise for $\longrightarrow_{must}$)

$$\textbf{(A)} \quad p[\overline{f}] \xrightarrow{a}_{may} r \Leftrightarrow \exists p'.\exists b \in Act_0. \, p \xrightarrow{b}_{may} p' \ \& \ f(b) \simeq a \ \& \ r = p'[\overline{f}] \text{ or } \exists p'. \, p \xrightarrow{*} p' \ \& \ r = p'[\overline{f}]$$

$$\textbf{(B)} \quad p[\overline{f}] \xrightarrow{a}_{must} r \Leftrightarrow \exists p'.\exists b \in Act_0. \, p \xrightarrow{b}_{must} p' \ \& \ f(b) \simeq a \ \& \ r = p'[\overline{f}]$$

Given (A) and (B) the only non–trivial part in the proof of R being a partial bisimulation is to find a matching $\longrightarrow_{may}$–derivative for $q[\overline{f}]$ when $p[\overline{f}] \stackrel{a}{\longrightarrow}_{may} r$, because $p \stackrel{*}{\longrightarrow} p'$ and $r = p'[\overline{f}]$ for some p'. However, $p \stackrel{*}{\longrightarrow} p'$ implies $p \stackrel{b}{\longrightarrow}_{may} p'$ for all $b \in Act$. Since $p \lhd q$ it follows for all $b \in Act$ that $q \stackrel{b}{\longrightarrow}_{may} q_b$ for some q_b with $p' \lhd q_b$. Now let $c \in Act$ such that $q \stackrel{c}{\not\longrightarrow}$ (such an action exists due to our technical assumption). Then $q \stackrel{c}{\longrightarrow}_{may} q_c$ implies $q \stackrel{*}{\longrightarrow} q_c$ and therefore $q[\overline{f}] \stackrel{*}{\longrightarrow} q_c[\overline{f}]$. Thus, $q[\overline{f}] \stackrel{a}{\longrightarrow}_{may} q_c[\overline{f}]$ is a matching move since $p' \lhd q_c$. □

6 Proving the Simple Scheduler

We now show how to use our compositional proof method for proving the correctness of the simple scheduler introduced earlier. The proof consists of several tasks. First we prove that $A'\|B \lhd A'B^p$ and that $D\|C \lhd DC^p$. By the precongruence property of $\lhd$ (proposition 5.1 and 5.2) we may conclude that $Sch = A'\|B\|C\|D \lhd A'B^p\|DC^p$. Secondly we prove that $A'B^p\|DC^p \lhd Spec$. Then by transitivity (proposition 3.3) it follows that $Sch \lhd Spec$. Since both Sch and $Spec$ are concrete (i.e. they can not perform any $*$-actions) it follows by proposition 3.6 that $Sch \sim Spec$ which is the desired result.

To prove $A'\|B \lhd A'B^p$ we may substitute the process $\mathcal{U} \Leftarrow *.\mathcal{U}$ for ☁ in figure 3. Then it is easily seen from figure 2 and figure 3 that the relation

$$R_1 = \{(A'\|B, A'B^p), (A''\|B, A''B^p), (A\|B', AB'^p), (A''\|B, A''B^p), (A\|B, AB^p)\} \cup \ \{(p, \mathcal{U}) \mid \text{p is any agent}\}$$

is a partial bisimulation, showing $A'\|B \lhd A'B^p$.

Note that the above partial bisimulation does not depend on the inaccessible part of $A'\|B$. The relation R_1 can be viewed as consisting of two parts, where the second part is a totally general part, acting as a closure operation in order to cover the inaccessible behaviour of the implementation. This closuring resembles to some extend the notion of bisimulation upto '$\sim$', investigated in [Mil83].

It is easily seen from figure 3, with the process $\mathcal{U} \Leftarrow *.\mathcal{U}$ substituted for ☁ , and figure 2 that the relation

$$R_2 = \{(D\|C, DC^p), (D\|C', DC'^p), (D\|C'', DC''^p), (D'\|C, D'C^p), (D''\|C, D''C^p)\} \cup \ \{(p, \mathcal{U}) \mid \text{p is any agent}\}$$

is a partial bisimulation, showing $D\|C \lhd DC^p$.

To see that $A'B^p\|DC^p \lhd Spec$ one may easily verify that the relation

$$\begin{aligned} R_3 \ = \ & \{(A'B^p\|DC^p, Spec), (A''B^p\|DC^p, \tau.b.\tau.c.\tau.d.\tau.Spec), (AB'^p\|DC^p, b.\tau.c.\tau.d.\tau.Spec), \\ & (AB''^p\|DC^p, \tau.c.\tau.d.\tau.Spec), (AB^p\|DC'^p, c.\tau.d.\tau.Spec), (AB^p\|DC''^p, \tau.d.\tau.Spec), \\ & (AB^p\|D'C^p, d.\tau.Spec), (AB^p\|D''C^p, \tau.Spec)\} \end{aligned}$$

is a partial bisimulation.

7 Concluding Remarks

The proof method presented in this paper supports compositional verification of concurrent systems and has the distinct advantage of leading to simple subspecifications. At the same time the underlying theory is only slightly more complicated than the existing one for bisimulation equivalence.

Even though we believe correctness proofs have been made significantly simpler with this new proof method, it is still imperative that automatic tools are available if larger systems are to be tackled. Fortunately, the induced implementation ordering, $\lhd$, is polynomial–time decidable, and is as such amenable to mechanical assistance. Based directly on the operational definition of partial bisimulation a decision procedure has been implemented in PROLOG, and the resulting system has been used to automatically carry out the above verification of the simple scheduler. Moreover, complete axiomatizations of the implementation–ordering,

$\triangleleft$, for various process calculi (regular behaviours and finite behaviours) have been given in [Tho87], thus enabling correctness proofs to be carried out algebraically.

Future work includes a closer study of the relationship between our new method and the existing methods in [KoyMul85] and [Lar85,LarMil87], in particular with respect to expressibility and applicability. It would be interesting to see how the explicit representation of behavioural constraints in terms of parameterizing the equivalence — which is the approach taken in [Lar85,LarMil87] — formally relates to the present approach, where the representation is implicitly given in terms of partial specifications.

In [Tho87] the Concurrent Alternating Bit Protocol has been verified using the compositional proof method of this paper, and it compares favourable with the correctness proof of both [KoyMul85] and [LarMil87]. However, a fair comparison of the applicability of the various methods obviously requires the verification of many more — and in particular larger — systems.

Acknowledgement

The first author would like to thank the people in the Computer Science Department at Edinburgh University for many helpful comments and discussions.

References

[Acz84] P. Aczel: *A Simple Version of SCCS and Its Semantics*, Unpublished notes, Edinburgh 1984.

[HBR81] C.A.R. Hoare, S.D. Brookes & A.W. Roscoe: *A Theory of Communicating Processes*, Technical Report PRG-16, Programming Research Group, University of Oxford 1981.

[Hen85] M. Hennessy & R. Milner: *Algebraic Laws for Nondeterminism and Concurrency*, Journal of the Association for Computing Machinery pp. 137-161, 1985.

[KoyMul85] C. P. Koymans & J. C. Mulder: *A Modular Approach to Protocol Verification Using Process Algebra*, Logic Group Preprint Series No. 6, University of Utrecht 1985.

[Lar85] K. G. Larsen: *Context Dependent Bisimulation Between Processes*, in proceedings of ICALP 85, LNCS 194, Springer Verlag 1985. Full version in TCS 49 (1987).

[Lar86] K. G. Larsen: *Context Dependent Bisimulation Between Processes*, Ph. D. Thesis, Edinburgh University 1986.

[LarMil87] K. G. Larsen & R. Milner: *Verifying a Protocol Using Relativized Bisimulation*, in proceedings of ICALP 87, LNCS 267, Springer-Verlag 1987.

[LarTho88] K. G. Larsen & B. Thomsen: *A Modal Process Logic*, to appear in proceedings of LICS 88.

[Mil80] R. Milner: *A Calculus of Communicating Systems*, LNCS 92, Springer-Verlag, 1980.

[Mil83] R. Milner: *Calculi for Synchrony and Asynchrony*, Theoretical Computer Science 25 (1983) pp 269-310, North Holland.

[Par81] D. Park: *Concurrency and Automata on Infinite Sequences*, LNCS 104, Springer-Verlag, 1981.

[Plo81] G. Plotkin: *A Structural Approach to Operational Semantics*, DAIMI FN-19 Aarhus University Computer Science Department 1981.

[Sim85] R. de Simone: *Higher-level Synchronising Devises in MEIJE-SCCS*, TCS 37 (1985) p. 245-267.

[Tar55] A. Tarski: *A Lattice-Theoretical Fixpoint Theorem and Its Applications*, Pacific Journal of Math. 5, 1955.

[Tho87] B. Thomsen: *An Extended Bisimulation Induced by a Preorder on Actions*, M. Sc. Thesis, Aalborg University Centre 1987.

INTRODUCING NEGATIVE INFORMATION IN RELATIONAL DATABASES

D. Laurent
LIFO, University of Orléans
BP 6749, 45067 Orléans Cedex 2
France

N. Spyratos
LRI, University of Paris-Sud
91405 Orsay
France

ABSTRACT – Traditionally, databases are used in order to deal with positive information such as "John's address is Paris". We propose here to study another kind of information, called *negative information* such as "John's address is *not* Paris".

We define set-theoretic semantics for relational databases in which negative information may be recorded. We also present an axiomatization for deductive query answering in the presence of positive information, negative information, and functional dependencies. Our model does *not* make use of the closed world assumption.

1. INTRODUCTION

In the relational model of data one views the database as a collection of relations, where each relation is a set of tuples over some domains of values. One notable feature of the relational model is the absence of semantics: a tuple in a relation represents a relationship between certain values, but from the mere syntactic definition of the relation, we know nothing about the nature of the relationship.

One approach in order to remedy this deficiency of the relational model is proposed in [S], where tuples are seen as strings of uninterpreted symbols. Interpretations for these symbols are provided using subsets of an underlying population of objects, and set containment provides the basic inference mechanism. Let us explain the approach informally, using an example.

Consider the following (very small) database, containing only two tuples

AGE	*SITUATION*
young	*unemployed*

SITUATION	*SEX*
unemployed	*female*

The tuple *young unemployed* can be seen as a string of two uninterpreted symbols, *young* and *unemployed*. Now, think of a possible world, and let W be the set of all individuals in that world. Moreover, let $I(young)$ be the set of all individuals of W that are young, and let $I(unemployed)$ be the set of all individuals of W that are unemployed. Call $I(young)$ the interpretation of the symbol *young*, and $I(unemployed)$ the interpretation of the symbol *unemployed*. Clearly, the intersection $I(young) \cap I(unemployed)$ is the set of all individuals of W that are both young and unemployed. It is precisely this intersection that we define to be the interpretation of the tuple *young unemployed*. That is,

$$I(young\ \ unemployed) = I(young) \cap I(unemployed).$$

In other words, the interpretation of a tuple is the intersection of the interpretations of its constituent symbols.

This kind of set-theoretic semantics for tuples allows for a very intuitive notion of truth. Namely, a tuple t is called *true* in I iff $I(t)$ is nonempty. Thus, for example, the (atomic) tuple *young* is true iff $I(young)$ is nonempty, that is, iff there is at least one individual in W which is young. Similarly, the tuple *unemployed* is true in I iff there is an individual in W which is unemployed. Finally, the tuple *young unemployed* is true in I iff there is an individual in W which is both young and unemployed.

The set-theoretic semantics just introduced allows for a very natural notion of inference through set-containment. To see this, consider the following question:

Assuming that *young unemployed* is true in I
and that *unemployed female* is true in I
can we infer that *young unemployed female* is true in I ?

If we recall the definition of truth given earlier, then we can reformulate this question as follows:

Assuming that $I(young) \cap I(unemployed) \neq \emptyset$ (1)
and that $I(unemployed) \cap I(female) \neq \emptyset$ (2)
can we infer that $I(young) \cap I(unemployed) \cap I(female) \neq \emptyset$? (3)

Clearly, the answer depends on the interpretation I, and the following diagram shows a configuration where the answer is no.

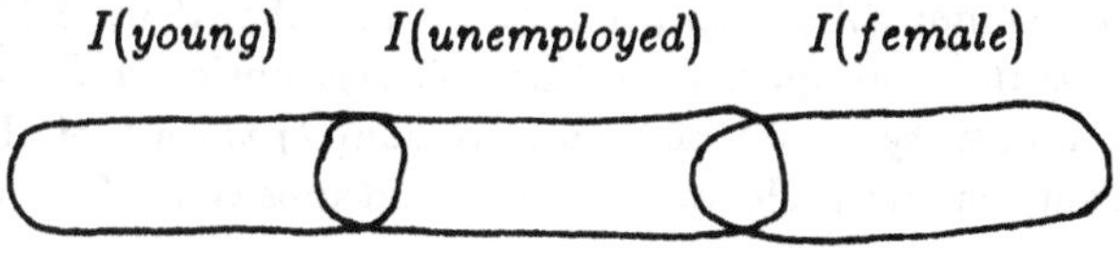

However, if we impose constraints on the interpretation I, for instance, if we require that

$$I(unemployed) \subseteq I(young) \tag{4}$$

(meaning that all unemployed individuals are young) or

$$I(unemployed) \subseteq I(female) \tag{5}$$

(meaning that all unemployed individuals are female) then the answer is yes. Roughly speaking, we can summarize our example as follows:

[(1) and (2)] does *not* imply (3)

whereas

[(1) and (2)] and [(4) or (5)] implies (3).

It turns out that constraints such as (4) and (5) provide the right interpretations for functional dependencies and other semantic constraints (see [S]).

We have seen so far the basic ingredients of the model introduced in [S], known as the *partition model.* The partition model has been used to study variants of the weak instance assumption [CKS], as well as to derive algorithms for (deductive) query and update processing [Le, SL1, SL2]. Moreover in [La1, La2, LaS1] the model has been used in order to deal with incomplete information. In this paper we use the partition model in order to provide semantics for databases containing negative informations such as:

"No old individual can be unemployed".

Clearly, such an information must be interpreted in our possible world W in the following way: the interpretation of the tuple *old unemployed* must be empty. That is, each interpretation I in our world W must satisfy:

$$I(old\ \ unemployed) = \emptyset \qquad \text{and so} \qquad I(old) \cap I(unemployed) = \emptyset.$$

The paper is organized as follows. In Section 2 we give formal definitions of the following concepts: database, interpretation, truth, model and semantic implication. In Section 3, we present a sound and complete axiomatazition for deducing positive *and* negative tuples from a given database. Finally Section 4 contains some concluding remarks and suggestions for further work. Throughout the paper, we assume some familiarity with the basic relational terminology.

2. THE MODEL

We shall consider separately the syntax and the semantics of our model. The syntactic part is essentially the relational model. The semantic part is a formalization of the concepts already explained in the introduction.

2.1. Syntax

We begin with a finite, nonempty set $U = \{A_1, \ldots, A_n\}$. The set U is called the *universe* and the A_i's are called the *attributes*. Each attribute A_i is associated with a countably infinite set of symbols (or values) called the *domain* of A_i and denoted by $dom(A_i)$.

We assume that $U \cap dom(A_i)$ is empty for all i, and that $dom(A_i) \cap dom(A_j) = \emptyset$ for $i \neq j$ (we shall discuss the consequences of this last assumption in Section 4). A *relation scheme* over U is a nonempty subset of U; we call $sch(U)$ the set of all relation schemes over U and a relation scheme is denoted by the juxtaposition of its attributes (in any order).

A *tuple* t over a relation scheme R is a function defined on R such that $t(A_i)$ is in $dom(A_i)$, for all A_i in R. We denote by $dom(R)$ the set of all tuples over R. Clearly $dom(R)$ is the cartesian product of the domains of all the attributes in R. If t is a tuple over $R = A_1 \ldots A_n$, and if $t(A_j) = a_j$, $j = 1, \ldots, n$, then we denote the tuple t as $a_1 \ldots a_n$.

Note that tuples of the form xx', where x and x' are symbols from the same attribute domain, are not possible. This follows from our earlier assumption that all attribute domains are mutually disjoint sets.

In order to be able to model negative information, we introduce the concept of a *negative tuple*. That is, for every relation scheme R and for every tuple t over R, t is associated with a symbol $\neg t$. We refer to t as a *positive tuple* and to the associated symbol $\neg t$ as a *negative tuple*. In the sequel, by the term tuple, we mean positive or negative tuple. For example, if ab is a positive tuple over AB, then $\neg ab$ is the associated negative tuple over AB.

Definition 2.1. *A database over U is a pair $D = (\delta, F)$ such that*

(1) δ is a function assigning to every relation scheme R a finite set of tuples over R, and

(2) F is a set of ordered pairs (X, Y) such that X and Y are subsets of U.

Every pair (X, Y) in F is called a functional dependency and is denoted as $X \rightarrow Y$. ◇

Example 2.1.

Consider a universe of three attributes, say $U = \{A, B, C\}$, and let $dom(A) = \{a_1, a_2, \ldots\}$, $dom(B) = \{b_1, b_2, \ldots\}$, $dom(C) = \{c_1, c_2, \ldots\}$.

Define a function δ on relation schemes over U as follows:

$$\delta(AB) = \{a_1b_1, a_2b_1, \neg a_3b_3\},$$
$$\delta(BC) = \{b_1c_1, b_1c_2\},$$
$$\delta(R) = \emptyset \quad \text{for all} \quad R \quad \text{different than} \quad AB \quad \text{and} \quad BC.$$

Let F be the set $\{A \rightarrow B, BC \rightarrow A\}$. The database (δ, F) just defined is shown in Figure 2.1(b). The function δ is represented by two tables, with schemes AB and BC as headers and the corresponding tuples as rows. Clearly, the convention used here is that relation schemes that are assigned empty relations are not represented. ◇

$U = \{A, B, C\}, dom(A) = \{a_1, a_2, \ldots\}, dom(B) = \{b_1, b_2, \ldots\}, dom(C) = \{c_1, c_2, \ldots\}$

(a) I: $a_1 \rightarrow \{1,3\}$ $\quad a_2 \rightarrow \{2,4\}$ $\quad b_1 \rightarrow \{1,2,3,4\}$
$b_2 \rightarrow \{5,6\}$ $\quad c_1 \rightarrow \{3\}$ $\quad c_2 \rightarrow \{1\}$
$x \rightarrow \emptyset$, for every x different than $a_1, a_2, b_1, b_2, c_1, c_2$.

(b)

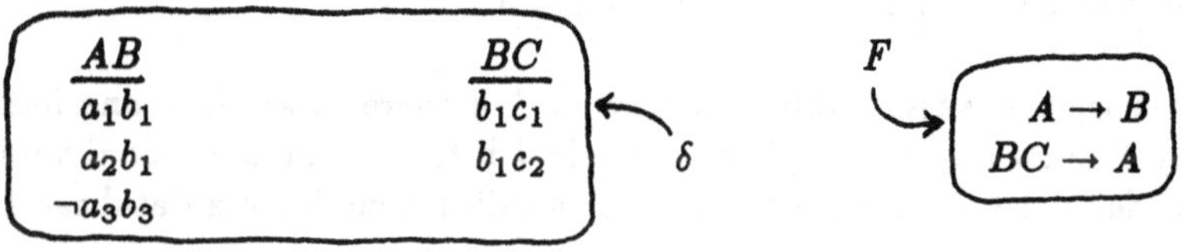

FIGURE 2.1 – An interpretation I of $U = \{A, B, C\}$, and a database $D = (\delta, F)$ over U, for which I is a model.

2.2. Semantics

We assume that the "real world" consists of a countably infinite set of objects, and we identify these objects with the positive integers. Let ω be the set of all positive integers, and let $2^\omega = \{\tau | \tau \subseteq \omega\}$ be the set of all subsets of ω. The set 2^ω is the semantic domain in which tuples and dependencies receive their interpretation. Throughout our discussions, we consider fixed the universe of attributes $U = \{A_1, A_2, ..., A_n\}$, and the associated domains $dom(A_i)$. For notational convenience, we denote by $SYMBOLS$ the union of all attribute domains, and by $TUPLES$ the union of all domains. That is:

$$SYMBOLS = \bigcup_{A \in U} dom(A) \quad \text{and} \quad TUPLES = \bigcup_{R \in sch(U)} dom(R).$$

Clearly, $SYMBOLS$ is a subset of $TUPLES$.

Definition 2.2. *An interpretation of U is a function I from SYMBOLS into 2^ω such that*

$$\forall A \in U, \forall a, a' \in dom(A), [a \neq a' \Rightarrow I(a) \cap I(a') = \emptyset]. \qquad \diamond$$

Thus the basic property of an interpretation is that *different* symbols of the *same* domain are assigned disjoint sets of integers. In Figure 2.1(a) we see a function I satisfying this property. The intuitive motivation behind this definition is that an attribute value, say a, is a (atomic) property, and $I(a)$ is a set of objects having property a. Furthermore, an object cannot have two different properties a, a' of the same "type"; hence $I(a) \cap I(a') = \emptyset$ (we shall discuss the consequences of this restriction in Section 4).

Given an interpretation I, we extend it from $SYMBOLS$ to $TUPLES$ as follows:

$$\forall R \in sch(U), \forall a_1 a_2 ... a_k \in dom(R), I(a_1 a_2 ... a_k) = I(a_1) \cap \ldots \cap I(a_k).$$

The intuitive motivation for this extension is that a tuple, say ab, is the conjunction of the (atomic) properties a and b. Accordingly, $I(ab)$ is the set of objects having both properties a and b; hence we have $I(ab) = I(a) \cap I(b)$. Notice that the basic property of an interpretation is satisfied by the extension, namely:

$$\forall R \in sch(U), \forall t, t' \in dom(R), [t \neq t' \Rightarrow I(t) \cap I(t') = \emptyset].$$

Our definition of an interpretation suggests an intuitive notion of truth.

Definition 2.3. *Let I be an interpretation. We say that:*

- *a positive tuple t is true in I if* $I(t) \neq \emptyset$,
- *a negative tuple t is true in I if* $I(t) = \emptyset$. $\diamond$

That is, a positive tuple t is true in I if there is *at least one* individual having property t and a negative tuple t is true in I if there is *no* individual having property t. We now define when an interpretation I is called a model of a database D.

Definition 2.4. *Let $D = (\delta, F)$ be a database over U. An interpretation I of U is called a model of D if*

(1) $\forall R \in sch(U), \forall t \in \delta(R), t$ *is true in* I,

(2) $\forall (X \to Y) \in F, \forall x \in dom(X), \forall y \in dom(Y), [I(x) \cap I(y) \neq \emptyset \Rightarrow I(x) \subseteq I(y)]$. $\diamond$

Roughly speaking, we say that I is a model of D if

(1) every tuple appearing in D is true in I,

(2) I satisfies every functional dependency $X \to Y$ in F in the sense that the set $\{(x, y) | x \in dom(X), y \in dom(Y), I(x) \cap I(y) \neq \emptyset\}$ is a function.

In Figure 2.1 we see an interpretation I and a database (δ, F). We can easily verify that I is a model of (δ, F), as follows:

(1) The tuples appearing in the database are a_1b_1, a_2b_1, b_1c_1, b_1c_2, and $\neg a_3b_3$. The first three tuples receive non-empty interpretations under I, and the last one is interpreted by the empty set.

(2) For $A \rightarrow B$: the only true positive tuples over AB with respect to I are a_1b_1, a_2b_1, and we have $I(a_1) \subseteq I(b_1)$ and $I(a_2) \subseteq I(b_1)$. Thus $A \rightarrow B$ is satisfied.
For $BC \rightarrow A$: the only true positive tuples over ABC with respect to I are $a_1b_1c_1$ and $a_1b_1c_2$, and we have $I(b_1c_1) \subseteq I(a_1)$ and $I(b_1c_2) \subseteq I(a_1)$. Thus $BC \rightarrow A$ is also satisfied. ◇

Having defined the concepts of interpretation, truth, and model, we can now define the concept of consistency. A database D is called *consistent* iff D possesses at least one model; and otherwise D is called *inconsistent*.

Now, given a consistent database D and a model I of D, all tuples appearing in the database are true in I (by definition). However, it may happen that some tuples that do not appear explicitely in the database are also true in I. For example, in the database of Figure 2.1, tuples $a_1b_1c_1$, $a_1b_1c_2$ fall into this category, as $I(a_1b_1c_1) = \{3\}$ and $I(a_1b_1c_2) = \{4\}$. (Note, however, that tuples $a_2b_1c_1$, $a_2b_1c_2$ are not true in that interpretation.)

Definition 2.5. *Let $D = (\delta, F)$ be a database over universe U. Let t be any tuple. We say that D implies t, denoted $D \models t$, if t is true in every model of D.* ◇

Clearly, D implies all tuples appearing in D (by definition). For example, in Figure 2.1, $D \models a_1b_1$, a_2b_1, b_1c_1, b_1c_2 and $\neg a_3b_3$.

On the other hand, D does not imply the tuples $a_2b_1c_1$, $a_2b_1c_2$, as they are false in the model I shown in Figure 2.1(a). Notice that D does not imply the tuples $a_1b_1c_1$, $a_1b_1c_2$ either. Indeed, although these tuples are true in the model I of Figure 2.1, we can find a model I' of D in which these tuples are false. Indeed, define I' such that:

$$I'(a_1) = \{2,4\}, \quad I'(a_2) = \{1,3\}, \quad \text{and} \quad I'(x) = I(x) \quad \text{for all} \quad x \neq a_1, a_2.$$

Then I' is a model of D falsifying $a_1b_1c_1$, $a_1b_1c_2$ (and, moreover, verifying $a_2b_1c_1$, $a_2b_1c_2$).

At this point of the presentation, an important remark is in order, concerning "closed worlds". First, let us note that if a positive tuple t contains a symbol *not* appearing in D, then D does *not* imply t (as, in this case, we can always find a model of D in which t is false). On the other hand, a positive tuple built exclusively from symbols appearing in D may not be implied by D.

For example, suppose that ab and bc are the only tuples in D, and that there are no functional dependencies. Then one can easily see that the tuple abc is not implied by D (consider the model: $I(a) = \{1,2\}$, $I(b) = \{2,3\}$, $I(c) = \{3,4\}$), althought it is built from symbols appearing in D. If the dependency $A \rightarrow C$ is given then abc is no longer implied by D, but if the dependency $B \rightarrow C$ is given, then abc *is* implied by D. ◇

So we can summarize our discussion as follows:

(1) Given a database D, positive tuples outside D are of two kinds: those that are not implied by D and those that may be implied by D, given appropriate functional dependencies.
(2) No assumption of any kind (such as the "closed world assumption" of Reiter [R]) is necessary in our model.

3. QUERY PROCESSING

By *querying* a database $D = (\delta, F)$ we mean giving a tuple t (positive or negative) and asking whether D implies t. Clearly, in order to process queries, we need a mechanism for solving the following inference problem: given a database D and a tuple t, decide whether $D \models t$. Before we present such a mechanism, we need some restrictions on the functional dependencies in F on one hand and some additional notation on the other hand.

We shall assume that each dependency in F has a single attribute on the right hand side and that F is closed under Armstrong's axioms. The reader is referred to [M] for details about these axioms and to [Le] as regards the differencies between our notion of functional dependency and the one defined in the relational model.

We denote positive tuples by small letters and the associated relation schemes by the corresponding capital letters. For example, if x denotes a tuple, then x is assumed to be defined over relation scheme X. Moreover, given tuples x and y we denote by xy the *join* of x and y. For example, if $x = a$ and $y = b$, then xy denotes the tuple ab; similarly, if $x = ab$ and $y = bc$, then xy denotes the tuple abc. With these conventions in mind, let us consider the following rules, or axioms:

*A*1	$xy \vdash x$
*A*2	$\neg x \vdash \neg xy$
*A*3	$xy\ ,\ yz\ ,\ Y \rightarrow X \text{ or } Y \rightarrow Z \vdash xyz$
*A*4	$xy\ ,\ y \neq y'\ ,\ X \rightarrow Y \vdash \neg xy'$
*A*5	$\neg xyz\ ,\ xy\ ,\ Y \rightarrow X \text{ or } Y \rightarrow Z \vdash \neg yz$

Given a database D and a tuple t (positive or negative), we say that D *derives* t, denoted by $D \vdash t$, iff, starting from tuples recorded in D, we can generate t by application of the axioms *A*1 to *A*5 above. The following theorem says that D implies t iff D derives t, thus providing a syntactic characterization of semantic implication.

Theorem 3.1. *$D \models t$ iff $D \vdash t$ for every consistent database $D = (\delta, F)$ and for every tuple t (positive or negative).* ◇

Proof (sketch): Because of a lack of place, we omit the easy proof of the soundness of axioms *A*1 to *A*5 and we only give the guide lines of the proof of the completeness. The reader is referred to [LaS2] for the complete proof.
Given $D = (\delta, F)$, we consider $D_P = (\delta_P, F)$ where for any R in $sch(U)$, δ_P consists in the *positive* tuples from $\delta(R)$. Then the following Lemma holds.

Lemma 3.1. $D \models t$ iff $D_P \models t$ for any positive tuple t. ◇

Thus the completeness of axioms *A*1 to *A*5 is shown in the following way:

- First, we prove that $D \models t$ if $D \vdash t$ for any positive tuple t. This proof is based on Lemma 3.1. and on results obtained in [SL1].
- Then we prove that $D \models t$ if $D \vdash t$ for any negative tuple t. We proceed by contradiction: if t is a negative tuple such that $D \not\vdash t$ then we show that D has a model m in which $m(t) \neq \emptyset$ (and thus t is not true in m). Let us note that this part of the proof explicitely requires the set F to be closed under Armstrong's axioms. ◇

Example 3.1.

Consider the following consistent database:

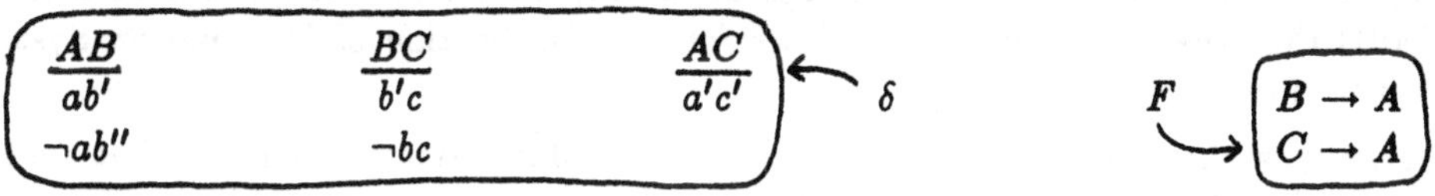

FIGURE 3.1 – A database $D = (\delta, F)$ containing negative information.

Here are three examples of derivations, using axioms $A1$ to $A5$:

(i) $D \vdash ac$, because

$A3$: $ab', b'c, B \rightarrow A \vdash ab'c$

$A1$: $ab'c \vdash ac$.

(ii) $D \vdash \neg b''c$, because

$A2$: $\neg ab'' \vdash \neg ab''c$

$A5$: $\neg ab''c, ac, C \rightarrow A \vdash \neg b''c$.

(iii) $D \vdash \neg ab'c'$, because

$A4$: $a'c', C \rightarrow A \vdash \neg ac'$

$A2$: $\neg ac' \vdash \neg ab'c'$. ◇

We believe that the axiomatization that we have just seen is an important step towards query processing in the presence of negative information and functional dependencies. However, what is needed here is efficient algorithms for applying the axioms and for testing database consistency (see [LaS2]).

4. CONCLUDING REMARKS

We have seen a set-theoretic interpretation of the relational model, that allows for a natural interpretation of (positive and negative) tuples as well as inference of tuples in a common framework. Although no closed world assumption is necessary, it may very well be that our axiomatization yields the same results as these obtained under open world assumption. We are currently investigating this possibility.

In the set-theoretic interpretation that we have used, we have required that attribute values in the same domain be interpreted by disjoint sets. This requirement which allows for a natural interpretation of functional dependencies, has an important consequence on the expressive power of the model. Namely, our set-theoretic semantics is not adequate in the case where two different attributes have the *same* domain. Indeed, if a tuple ab is in the database, where a and b belong to the *same* domain, then we must have, at the same time, $I(a) \cap I(b) = \emptyset$, because a and b are in the same domain *and* $I(a) \cap I(b) \neq \emptyset$, because ab is in the database. We are currently investigating appropriate extensions of our model in order to deal with this difficulty.

One must note that, when considering an Information Storage and Retrieval System (or, for short i.s.r.) as defined in [MP], the above mentioned restriction about domains of attributes is also assumed. Moreover, in such a system, any object *must* be associated with a value for each attribute, which is not the case in our approach. Thus, the problem of negative information in an i.s.r. may be treated in a very simple way, namely by complementation with respect to the set of objects that are of interest. So, even if partition semantics seems to be closely related to i.s.r. semantics, we present here a more general approach. Moreover, as regards incomplete information, it has been shown in [LaS1] that the partition model allows for a generalization of Information Systems defined by Lipski in [L].

Finally, we have studied queries such as: "Give all tuples over scheme R that are true in the database" but queries with selection conditions (see [La2]) can also be treated in the present framework. Moreover, the set-theoretic semantics that we have used seems to be adapted also for the processing of updates. We are currently working in these directions.

REFERENCES

[CKS] S. S. Cosmadakis, P. C. Kanellakis, N. Spyratos, "Partition Semantics for Relations", Proc. ACM PODS 1985, *JCSS*, 33-2, 1986.

[La1] D. Laurent, "Information Incomplète Explicite dans le Modèle Partitionnel de Bases de Données", In 2ᵉ Journées Bases de Données Avancées, Giens (France), *INRIA Ed.*, 1986.

[La2] D. Laurent, "La Logique des Partitions : Application à l'Information Disjonctive dans les Bases de Données", Thèse de 3ᵉ cycle, Univ. of Orléans, Jan. 1987.

[LaS1] D. Laurent, N. Spyratos, "Partition Semantics for Incomplete Information in Relational Databases", ACM-SIGMOD, Int. Conf. 1988.

[LaS2] D. Laurent, N. Spyratos, "Introducing Negative Information in Relational Databases", rep. *LIFO n°*87-7, Dec. 1987.

[Le] Ch. Lecluse, "Une Sémantique Ensembliste pour les Bases de Données. Application au Modèle Relationnel", Thèse de 3ᵉ cycle, Univ. of Paris-Sud, March 1987.

[L] W. Lipski Jr, "On Semantic Issues Connected with Incomplete Information Databases", *ACM TODS*, 4-3, 1979.

[M] D. Maier, "The Theory of Relational Databases", *Pitman*, 1983.

[MP] W. Marek, Z. Pawlak, "Information Storage and Retrieval Systems: Mathematical Foundations", *Theoretical Computer Science*, 1, 1976.

[R] R. Reiter, "Towards a Logical Reconstruction of Relational Database Theory", In "On Conceptual Modelling" (M. L. Brodie, J. Mylopoulos, J. W. Schmidt).

[S] N. Spyratos, "The Partition Model: a Deductive Database Model", *ACM TODS*, 1987.

[SL1] N. Spyratos, Ch. Lecluse, "Incorporating Functional Dependencies in Deductive Query Answering", Proc. International Conference on Data Engeneering, Los Angeles, Feb. 1987.

[SL2] N. Spyratos, Ch. Lecluse, "The Semantics of Queries and Updates in Relational Databases", rep. *INRIA n°*561, Aug. 1986.

On Positive Occur-Checks in Unification*

Philippe Le Chenadec
INRIA B.P. 105 78153 Le Chesnay Cedex France

Abstract

We address the problem of structuring the so-called positive occur-checks preventing unifiability. We introduce the notions of *elementary* and *derived* occur-checks. There exists a finite basis of elementary occur-checks for a given unification problem, obtained by a linearization process. Linearization gives unification problems that possess a *single* positive occur-check, necessarily elementary. We prove soundness and completeness of an equational deduction system well-suited for cyclic equations (= positive occur-checks), or, more generally, for reasoning about unification. Finally, up to permutation, there exists a *minimum* equational deduction associated to a given elementary positive occur-check. We give a deterministic algorithm computing this deduction, thus exhibiting the sequential nature of these occur-checks. This classification problem was encountered while dealing with higher-order unification. Besides insights in the nature of unification and its complexity, this technical analysis should also be of interest in symbolic debugging for systems where unification is involved. The minimum deduction appears to be a fundamental tool in the study of higher-order unification.

1 Introduction

Let $\mathcal{E}$ be a unification problem, i.e. a set of equations on some free algebra of terms. Classically, unification iterates a simplification step followed by a substitution building step. If simplification does not fail while $\mathcal{E}$ is not unifiable, there exists a so-called positive occur-check: an equation derived from $\mathcal{E}$ of the form $\phi = C[\phi]$, $C[\phi]$ a non-variable term. In concrete terms, unification computes a unification graph $\mathcal{G}_{\mathcal{E}}$ [8,10]. Positive occur-checks correspond to cycles in $\mathcal{G}_{\mathcal{E}}$. We study the structure of these cycles, in relation to the input equations.

In a first step, it is wise to consider the simplest case. Also, we try to incrementally remove cycles, by forgetting some input equations and/or by *linearizing* the set $\mathcal{E}$: if the variable ϕ possesses at least two distinct occurrences in $\mathcal{E}$, one of them is replaced with a fresh variable. Hence, a good definition for an "elementary positive occur-check" is a set of equations that possesses at least one positive occur-check, but such that removing one equation or linearizing one variable yields a unifiable set of equations. The first result of this paper establishes that, under this definition, the positive occur-check is *unique*. Hence an exhaustive search on the input $\mathcal{E}$ will produce all the elementary or primitive cycles of $\mathcal{E}$. We also address the problem of equational deductions for reasoning about these occur-checks. We introduce a sound and complete equational deduction system, in natural deduction style [12], interesting in its own right, for reasoning about equations that are valid in the "model" $\mathcal{G}_{\mathcal{E}}$. Next we establish a normalisation result for some deductions, called path deductions, of the form $\mathcal{D} \vdash \phi = C[\psi]$, ϕ, ψ variables. More precisely, we are interested in equations associated to paths in $\mathcal{G}_{\mathcal{E}}$, here the path goes from the vertex of ϕ to the vertex of ψ, as precised by the displayed occurrence of ψ in $C[\psi]$. We obtain a syntactical characterization of the normal deductions for such cyclic equations. Finally, the main result of the paper is the existence of a

*Part of this research was supported by the Office of Naval Research under contract N00014-84-K-0415 and by the Defense Advanced Research Projects Agency (DOD), ARPA Order No. 5404, monitored by the Office of Naval Research under the same contract. The views and conclusions contained in this document are those of the author and should not be interpreted as representing the official policies, either expressed or implied, of DARPA or the U.S. Government.

Figure 1: Unification Graphs for $\mathcal{E}_0$, $\mathcal{E}_1$ and $\mathcal{E}_2$

minimum deduction $\mathcal{D}_c \vdash \phi = C[\phi]$ associated to an elementary positive occur-check c, the existence proof is constructive and establishes the sequential nature of occur-checks: the set of variable occurrences involved in the occur-check is linearly ordered.

Let us see some examples. The simplest one is $\mathcal{E}_0 : \ \phi = f(\phi, \psi)$ (cf. Fig. 1). We have one cycle, the minimum deduction reduces to the axiom $\mathcal{E}_0$. Adding $\phi = f(\theta, \theta)$ defines $\mathcal{E}_1$ with two cycles, one primitive, $\mathcal{E}_0$, the other one derived: it owes its existence to the primitive cycle. The example $\mathcal{E}_3$ also defines a unique elementary cycle: $\phi = f(\psi, \psi)$, $\phi = f(\theta, f(\theta, \omega))$. Here, the minimum deduction will be something like:

$$(trans)\ \dfrac{(simpl)\ \dfrac{\phi = f(\theta, f(\theta,\omega)) \quad \phi = f(\psi,\psi)}{\theta = \psi} \qquad (simpl)\ \dfrac{\phi = f(\psi,\psi) \quad \phi = f(\theta, f(\theta,\omega))}{\psi = f(\theta,\omega)}}{\theta = f(\theta,\omega)}$$

Our next example C will be used throughout the paper, it contains a unique cycle, which is primitive:

$$\psi = \mu \to a, \quad \psi = \nu \to b, \quad \psi = (c \to ((\beta \to d) \to e)) \to f$$

$$\theta = \nu \to g, \quad \theta = \lambda \to h, \quad \theta = (i \to (j \to \gamma)) \to k$$

$$\omega = \phi \to l, \quad \omega = \lambda \to m$$

$$\phi = \beta \to n, \quad \mu = (o \to \gamma) \to p, \quad \lambda = q \to (\alpha \to \alpha)$$

The use of an infixed arrow as function symbol reveals the origin of the problem: it arose while studying instances of higher-order unification in connection with the full-fledged problem of type inference for Girard's higher-order polymorphic λ-calculus F_ω and its extension, the Calculus of Constructions [5,1]. Higher-order unification is undecidable already at order 2 [6,7]. However, the unification problems involved in type inference possess a shallow first-order structure, given by the constants and the head variables of a unification problem, with the property that this shallow structure is disjoint from the stripped terms. Also, a natural idea is that a regular structure underlies this search tree, as positive occur-checks are closely related to regular trees [2]. A first step towards this goal is the separability result of section 3. To such elementary occur-checks is canonically associated a finite automaton recognizing derived sets of equations [9], where the notion of derivation is borrowed from higher-order unification [7]. The next step is to ensure that the first-order cyclic equations (with infinite solutions) are solved by type lifting: some first-order variables become functional, e.g., a cyclic equation $x = f(x, y)$ becomes $X(z) = f(X(t), y)$. Notice that this latter equation has a trivial solution $X = \lambda x.x$ and $z = f(t, y)$. Type lifting is handled through the equational deductions. Checking on the minimum deduction, lifted to functional equations, that the associated higher-order equation is protected in the way mentionned above is a necessary condition for these functional equations to possess solutions.

The paper is organized as follows. Section 2 establishes some basic results on unification, relating occurrences of variables in the unification graph to occurrences of variables in the input. Section 3 establishes the separability result mentionned above. Section 4 proves the soundness and completeness of the equational

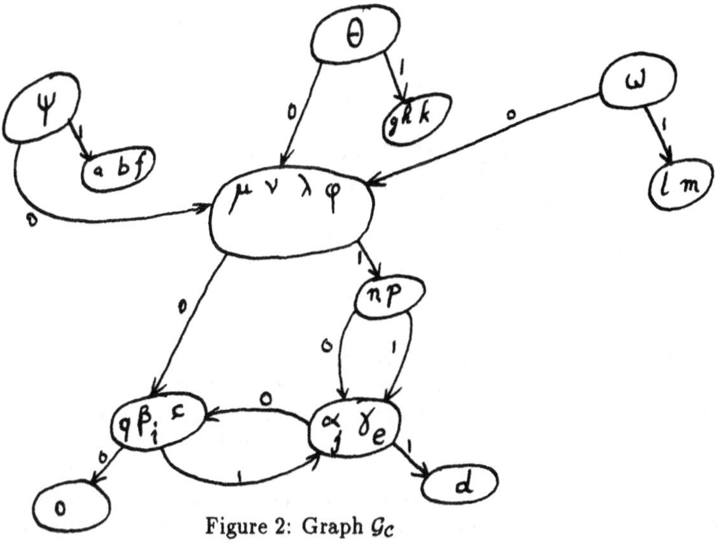

Figure 2: Graph $\mathcal{G}_C$

system and introduces reduced forms for the deductions. As far as we know, a detailed study of this kind of equational reasoning does not appear in the literature. Section 5, the heart of the paper, proves the unicity of the minimal deduction by providing a deterministic algorithm that finds such a deduction. The results being somewhat tricky and technical, we sketch the proofs. They will appear in some journal. We try here to give some intuition of the results and why they are important.

2 First-Order Unification

Throughout the paper, terms in $\mathcal{T}$ are built up over a single binary infix function symbol, denoted by an arrow $\rightarrow$ and a denumerable set of variables $\mathcal{S}$. By the well-known bijective correspondance between k-ary and binary trees, the general case is reducible to this one. A unification problem is a set $\mathcal{E}$ of equations of the form $\phi = \tau$, $\phi \in \mathcal{S}$, $\tau \in \mathcal{T}$. The equation is strict when $\tau \in \mathcal{S}$. The equality generated by the strict equations is noted $=_s$. We use the context notation: $C[\phi]$ denotes a term with a specified occurrence of ϕ. This occurrence is denoted O_C. Two contexts $C_1[\_]$, $C_2[\_]$ are equivalent iff $O_{C_1} = O_{C_2}$. This is noted $C_1[\_] \sim C_2[\_]$. The subterm of τ at occurrence O is denoted τ/O. The size of a term is its number of occurrences of the binary function symbol. We assume known the theory of regular trees [2,8].

Lemma 2.1 *Any set of equations $\mathcal{E}$ has a most general unifier, mapping variables to regular trees.*

Proof. See Theorem 4.9.2, p.141 of [2]: notice that we have only one function symbol and no constants. □
This theorem tells us nothing about the fine structure of the substitution. A useful tool here is Huet's version of first-order unification [8]. This algorithm computes an equivalence relation on terms, then it checks that the "subterm" relation computed is acyclic. The relation is represented by a graph $\mathcal{G}_\mathcal{E} = (V^\mathcal{E}, E^\mathcal{E})$, whose vertices are congruence classes of terms and egdes encode the subtree relation by labels 0 (resp. 1) for left (resp. right) sons. Initially, each term is represented as a labeled directed acyclic graph (dag), where only the leaves (variables) are shared. The input equations define a binary relation on vertices. Unification iteratively computes the downward closure of this relation. The graph at iteration i is noted $G_i = (V^i, E^i)$.

Let $G = (V, E)$ be a unification graph. The vertex of a subterm is denoted $V(\tau)$. A path $p = v_0, \ldots, v_n$, $n > 0$, is a sequence of vertices such that there exists an edge from v_i to v_{i+1}. It can be represented by a

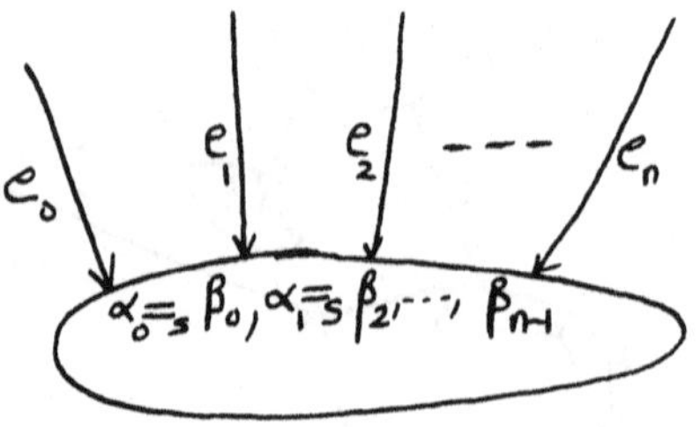

Figure 3: A Chain between two co-incident edges.

pair $p = (v_0, O)$, v_0 a vertex and O an occurrence in Σ^*, $\Sigma = \{0,1\}$. The source (resp. target) of p is the vertex v_0 (resp. v_n) (resp. for edges). A cycle c is a path such that $v_0 = v_n$ and $v_i \neq v_j$, $0 \leq i < j < n$. For a term τ in a vertex v of $c = (v, O)$, the occurrence $O(\tau, c)$ is the prefix of O such that the subterm $\tau/O(\tau, c)$ is a variable. A vertex is non-empty iff it contains some variable. Each cycle c is non-empty: it contains at least one vertex with a term τ. The term $\tau/O(\tau, c)$ is a variable in some vertex of the cycle. Hence, a cycle corresponds to a positive occur-check. A vertex v is a predecessor (resp. ancestor) of a vertex v' if there is an edge (resp. path) from v to v', resp. successor (resp. descendant). A vertex v is initial if v is not the target of any edge. Let e be an edge from v to v', labeled 0 (resp. 1), $\phi \in v'$ occurs by e iff there exists a subterm $\phi \to \tau \in v$ (resp. $\tau \to \phi$). We now give some properties relating the local structure of the graphs to occurrences of variables in $\mathcal{E}$.

Lemma 2.2 *Let $\mathcal{E}$ be a set of equations and i be some iteration. Let v be an initial vertex of V^i, for all $\phi, \psi \in v$ we have $\phi =_s \psi$. Let v be a non-initial vertex of V^i, then for all $\phi \in v$ there exists $\psi \in v$ such that $\phi =_s \psi$ and ψ occurs by some edge incident to v.*

This lemma is proved by induction on the iterations. A vertex is shared iff it is the target of two distinct edges. Notice that if v is shared, ϕ can occur by distinct edges.

Proposition 2.3 *Let $\mathcal{E}$ be a set of equations and i be some iteration, then:*

1. *For all edges e in E^i incident to a non-empty vertex v, there exists a variable $\phi \in v$ that occurs by e.*
2. *For all vertices v in V^i and for all pairs (e, e') of distinct edges in E^i incident to v, there exists a sequence of pairs (ϕ_j, ψ_j) of variables in v, $j = 0, \ldots, n-1$, and a sequence of edges e_k incident to v, $k = 0, \ldots, n$, $e_0 = e$, $e_n = e'$, such that $\phi_j =_s \psi_j$, ϕ_j occurs by e_j and ψ_j occurs by e_{j+1}.*

The two propositions are simultaneously proved by induction on the iterations. A weak consequence of the second part of this Proposition can be termed the unique incident edge property for empty vertices: shared vertices are non-empty. The chains are described in Fig. 3, they play a central rôle in section 5.

3 Elementary Cyclic Sets of Equations

To a set $\mathcal{E}$ of equations we associate its directed graph $\mathcal{G}_{\mathcal{E}} = (V^{\mathcal{E}}, E^{\mathcal{E}})$. We consider "subgraphs" $\mathcal{G}_E$ for $E \subseteq \mathcal{E}$ that separate the cycles in $\mathcal{G}_{\mathcal{E}}$.

Definition 3.1 *The set E' is a one-step linearization of a set E of equations iff E' is equal to E where some occurrence of a variable that occurs at least twice in E has been uniquely renamed. The set E' is a linearization of E iff there is a non-void sequence of one-step linearizations from E to E'. An elementary cyclic set E of a set of equations $\mathcal{E}$ is a linearization of some subset of $\mathcal{E}$ such that:*

1. *$\mathcal{G}_E$ contains at least one cycle,*

2. *the graph $\mathcal{G}_{E'}$ is cycle-free for every linearization E' of E,*
3. *the graph $\mathcal{G}_{E'}$ is cycle-free for every proper subset E' of E.*

A variable is needed iff it possesses at least two distinct occurrences in E. A variable α is cyclic iff α is needed and $V(\alpha)$ belongs to some cycle. A non-variable subterm is needed iff it contains at least one occurrence of a needed variable. A vertex is needed iff it contains at least one needed variable. If $\mathcal{G}_E$ is a dag, so is $\mathcal{G}_{E'}$ for E' a linearization of E. Linearization stepwise removes the cycles. Our first result is a separability lemma for positive occur-checks.

Theorem 3.1 *Let E be an elementary cyclic set of equations, then $\mathcal{G}_E$ contains a unique cycle. Let c be the cycle of $\mathcal{G}_E$, then each vertex of c contains a unique needed non-variable term.*

The result is immediate if $\mathcal{G}_E$ has no initial vertices. Otherwise, there exists an equation $k : \phi = C[\psi]$ such that ψ occurs in its vertex according to k by a non-cyclic edge e, and ψ is needed. Then the graph $\mathcal{G}_{E-\{k\}}$ is a dag, we assume that k is the last selected equation in unification. Let i be the iteration such that G_{i+1} is cyclic while G_i is a dag. We prove that there exists a unique path p from v to v', v, v' the vertices merged at iteration i. This creates a cycle. It is easily seen that the graphs under v and v' are disjoint trees, hence the unicity of the cycle. The second statement is proved by first building a sequence of chains. We first show that v' is non-empty. By Proposition 2.3, there exists $\phi \in v'$ that occurs by the last edge of p. Let $k : \psi = C[\phi]$ be some associated equation. Let $p' = V(\psi), \ldots, v'$. If p does not suffix p', we consider the vertex v'', first vertex of the maximal common suffix of both p and p'. If $V(\psi) = v''$, then we have $\psi = \phi'$ for some variable ϕ' by Lemma 2.2 that occurs by an edge. We form a chain between this edge and the edge e in p incident to v''. And we iterate this construction with the variable of the chain that occurs by e. Then, the unicity of the sequence is established by contradiction.

Let $\mathcal{E}$ be a unification problem. As the powerset of $\mathcal{E}$ is finite and there is a finite number of possible linearizations from a given set, the effectiveness of the base of elementary cyclic sets follows easily. Therefore, we have proved that to a set of equations is canonically associated a finite set of elementary cyclic sets. Intuitively, each cyclic set is a basic cause of non-unifiability. In lifting the equations to higher-order, we must resolve each cyclic set. The following sections provide tools for such a resolution.

4 Equational Deductions

Under the *axioms* $\mathcal{E}$ and equational inference rules, an equational deduction $\mathcal{D} \vdash \tau = \tau'$ will be associated to each pair of distinct terms τ, τ' in a vertex of $\mathcal{G}_\mathcal{E}$. To any cycle c will be associated a set of equational deductions: $\mathcal{D} \vdash \phi = C[\phi]$, $C[\_]$ a non-trivial context, $\phi \in \mathcal{S}_c$, $O_C = O(C[\phi], c)$. The set of axioms of $\mathcal{D}$ is noted $\mathcal{A}(\mathcal{D})$. We introduce inference rules of symmetry, transitivity, simplification and substitution; ϕ, ψ denote variables, the other greek letters denote terms.

$$(s)\ \frac{\tau = \rho}{\rho = \tau} \qquad (t)\ \frac{\tau = \phi \quad \phi = \rho}{\tau = \rho} \qquad (su)\ \frac{\phi = \tau \quad \psi = C[\phi]}{\psi = C[\tau]}$$

$$(sl)\ \frac{\rho \rightarrow \sigma = \tau \rightarrow \upsilon}{\rho = \tau} \qquad (sr)\ \frac{\rho \rightarrow \sigma = \tau \rightarrow \upsilon}{\sigma = \upsilon}$$

Notice that this set of inference rules is not complete for equational reasoning. We do not need reflexivity nor congruence (or equivalently the full substitution rule). The meaning of the transitivity and symmetry rules is obvious. The simplification ones ((sl) and (sr)) formalize the downward congruence closure, while the substitution rule will allow one to derive a deduction for the concatenation of two paths p_1 and p_2 from associated deductions $\mathcal{D}_1$ and $\mathcal{D}_2$.

Lemma 4.1 *Let τ_1, τ_2 be two distinct terms, then $\mathcal{D} \vdash \tau_1 = \tau_2$, $\mathcal{D}$ (su)-free, iff $V(\tau_1) = V(\tau_2)$ in $\mathcal{G}_{\mathcal{A}(\mathcal{D})}$.*

The proof of adequation is straighforward by structural induction on deductions. The proof of completeness is by induction on the cardinality of $\mathcal{E} = \mathcal{A}(\mathcal{D})$, using Proposition 2.3.

Lemma 4.2 *Let $p = v_0, \ldots, v_n = (v_0, O)$ be a path. For all $\phi \in v_0$, $\psi \in v_n$, there exists a deduction $\mathcal{D} \vdash \phi = C[\psi]$ with $O_C = O$. Reciprocally, for all deductions $\mathcal{D} \vdash \phi = C[\psi]$, there exists a path from $V^{\mathcal{E}}(\phi)$ to $V^{\mathcal{E}}(\psi)$, where $\mathcal{E} = \mathcal{A}(\mathcal{D})$.*

We first establish the result for paths p such that $v_i = \emptyset$ for $0 < i < n$, via the unique incident edge property for empty vertices (Proposition. 2.3) and Lemma 4.1. The deduction obtained in this case are (su)-free. Then we successively apply this elementary case, using the substitution rule. The inference tree has the following form:

$$
(su)\,\dfrac{\begin{array}{c}\mathcal{D}_n\\ \phi_n = C_n[\psi]\end{array} \qquad \begin{array}{c} (su)\,\dfrac{\begin{array}{c}\mathcal{D}_2\\ \phi_2 = C_2[\phi_3]\end{array} \quad (su)\,\dfrac{\begin{array}{cc}\mathcal{D}_1 & \mathcal{D}_0\\ \phi_1 = C_1[\phi_2] & \phi = C_0[\phi_1]\end{array}}{\phi = C_0[C_1[\phi_2]]}}{\phi = C_0[C_1[C_2[\phi_3]]]} \\ \vdots \\ \phi = C_0 \cdots C_{n-1}[\phi_n]\end{array}}{\phi = C_0 \cdots C_n[\psi]}
$$

The (su)-free deductions $\mathcal{D}_i, 0 \le i \le n+1$, are the *auxiliary* deductions of this deduction.

Corollary 4.3 *For each cycle c in $\mathcal{G}_{\mathcal{E}}$ and each ϕ in c, there exists a deduction of a cyclic equation $\mathcal{D} \vdash \phi = C[\phi]$ with $|O_C| = |c|$, $O_C = O(c, C[\phi])$, and reciprocally.*

Hence, we have a first approximation of a deduction associated to a cycle. We will establish that a canonical deduction exists, up to a cyclic permutation of the auxiliary deduction. However, a first step is to have a normal form result for deductions, in the spirit of natural deduction [12]. In fact, we only need deductions of marked equations, an equation being marked iff one and only one among its right-hand side occurrences is marked. Such equations have the form $\phi = C[\psi]$.

Theorem 4.4 *The following inference system is sound and complete for path deductions, where ϕ, ψ denote variables:*

$$
(s)\,\frac{\phi = \psi}{\psi = \phi} \qquad (t)\,\frac{\phi = \psi \quad \psi = \tau}{\phi = \tau}
$$

$$
(d)\,\frac{\phi = C_1[\psi] \quad \phi = C_2[\tau] \quad C_1[\_] \sim C_2[\_]}{\psi = \tau} \qquad (su)\,\frac{\phi = \tau \quad \psi = C[\phi]}{\psi = C[\tau]}
$$

The proof proceeds by taking a deduction in the original system, and reducing it according to rewriting rules. The size of an instance of (su) is the size of the right-hand side of its left premiss. Once we have a deduction in the above system, we may apply other reductions. Their effect is: localization of the inference of strict equations, diminution of the number of substitutions, and cancellation of internal 0-sized subsitutions. For (su)-free deductions, we have a subformula property: both sides of the conclusion are subterms of the axioms. Hence the normal form is reminiscent of the normal form for first-order logic in sequent calculus [4]: the hypotheses are first split in auxiliary deductions (elimination rules), then the pieces are collected together (introduction rules).

Definition 4.1 *Let $\mathcal{D} \vdash \phi = C[\psi]$ be a path deduction. We define marked occurrences for terms of $\mathcal{D}$:*

- *The occurrence O_C of the conclusion and the left-hand side are marked.*

- *If in the conclusions, displayed occurrences are marked, then in the premisses:*

$$(s)\ \frac{\psi = \phi}{\phi = \psi} \quad \psi \text{ and } \phi \text{ are marked;}$$

$$(t)\ \frac{\phi = \theta \quad \theta = C[\psi]}{\phi = C[\psi]} \quad \phi \text{ and } \theta,\ \theta \text{ and } O_C \text{ are marked;}$$

$$(d)\ \frac{\theta = C_1[\psi] \quad \theta = C_2[C[\psi]]}{\psi = C[\psi]} \quad \tau \text{ and } O_{C_1},\ \tau \text{ and } O_{C_2 C} \text{ are marked;}$$

$$(su)\ \frac{\theta = C_1[\psi] \quad \phi = C_2[\theta]}{\phi = C_2[C_1[\psi]]} \quad \tau \text{ and } O_{C_1},\ \phi \text{ and } O_{C_2} \text{ are marked.}$$

Therefore, in any path deduction $\mathcal{D}$, every equation $\phi = \tau$ is such that ϕ and one and only one occurrence of τ are marked. Notice also that a deduction corresponds to a traveling of $\mathcal{G}_{\mathcal{A}(\mathcal{D})}$. Such a traveling is shown in Fig. 1. We conclude this section by a description of reduced deductions. First, instances of the symmetry rule are lifted to strict axioms. Next, such a deduction has the form of the deduction in the proof of Lemma 4.2, where for all (su)-rules, except possibly the last one, both right-hand sides of their premiss are of positive size. The auxiliary deductions are such that the right-hand sides of the premisses of (d)-rules are of positive size, and the right premiss of both (t)- and (d)-rules is not the conclusion of a (t)-rule. Hence, right branches of length greater than one in auxiliary deductions are sequences of (d)-rules. The following observation will be useful in the next section: each inference rule (except the symmetry rule) eliminates a variable. If one of the two occurrences of the eliminated variable is extracted from a non-strict right-hand side in the axioms, then this extraction is performed by a sequence (right branch) of consecutive instances of (d)-rules. Two (su)-free deductions in normal form for example $\mathcal{C}$, given at the end of the paper, illustrates this normal form.

5 Minimum Deductions are Deterministic

We now address the problem of effectively finding an equational deduction of an equation $\phi = C[\phi]$ given an elementary cyclic set S so that its cycle is equal to $(V(\phi), O_C)$. We first establish that in a minimal deduction, the auxiliary deductions do not eliminate cyclic variables. Next, we prove unicity properties for chains in vertices of the graph $\mathcal{G}_S$. These two results imply the correctness of a deterministic algorithm finding a minimal deduction. In turn the existence of this algorithm proves that, up to permutation, there exists a minimum deduction.

5.1 Auxiliary Deductions are Cycle-Free

We first establish that a minimal deduction doest not involve unneeded variables. The left-hand side of the conclusion of a cyclic inference is its main variable, the variables that are eliminated by substitutions are its proper variables.

Lemma 5.1 *Let $\mathcal{D}$ be a minimal reduced cyclic deduction from an elementary cyclic set S. All marked variables of $\mathcal{D}$ are needed variables of S.*

Any left-hand side is marked in $\mathcal{D}$. Otherwise, some equation is redundant, which contradicts S an elementary cyclic set. For right-hand side occurrences, according to the normal form of deductions, these occurrences are extracted from their common right-hand side $k : \phi = C_0[\psi]$ by two right branches of consecutive (d)-rules. We prove that given two such deductions $\mathcal{D}_1 \vdash \alpha = C_1[\psi]$ and $\mathcal{D}_2 \vdash \beta = C_2[\psi]$, we can build a third one, say $\mathcal{D}_3 \vdash \alpha = C_3[\beta]$, such that $k \notin \mathcal{A}(\mathcal{D}_3)$, and which is smaller than both $\mathcal{D}_1$ and $\mathcal{D}_2$. The proof then proceeds by case on the rule that eliminates ψ: using $\mathcal{D}_3$ we build a smaller cyclic deduction. If ψ is the main variable of $\mathcal{D}$, the proof is analogous.

Lemma 5.2 *Let $\mathcal{D} \vdash \phi = C[\phi]$ be a minimal reduced deduction from some elementary cyclic set S. Then $\mathcal{D}$ does not eliminate cyclic variables above some (d)-rule (in its auxiliary deductions).*

This Lemma is proved by contradiction. If some cyclic variable is eliminated by a (d)-rule, then its vertex contains two needed terms, which contradicts Theorem 3.1.

Therefore, we know the "external" structure of a minimal deduction. It is in normal form. Further, let $(v_0, \ldots, v_n)$ be the sequence of needed vertices of the unique cycle c of the elementary cyclic set S, v_{i+1} being the first needed vertex above v_i along the cycle. By Proposition 2.3, for each vertex v_i there exists a variable ϕ_i that occurs by the cycle in v_i, this variable may be chosen needed. By Theorem 3.1, this variable is the unique needed variable occurrence of τ_{i+1}, τ_{i+1} the unique needed non-variable term in v_{i+1}. Hence the deductions must prove $\phi_{i+1} = \tau_{i+1} = C_i[\phi_i]$ for each vertex v_{i+1}. Further, the auxiliary deductions are "out of" the cycle.

5.2 Chains in Elementary Cyclic Sets

In this section, all variables are assumed to be needed. Let ϕ be some needed variable of an elementary cyclic set S, and assume that ϕ occurs by an edge e in $\mathcal{G}_S$. Then an occurrence O of ϕ in some non-strict right-hand side $\psi = C[\phi]$ is said to be associated to e iff the edge e is the last edge of the path $p = (V(\psi), O_C)$.

Lemma 5.3 *Let S be an elementary cyclic set and ϕ be some needed variable. If ϕ occurs in $V(\phi)$ of $\mathcal{G}_S$ by an edge e, then there exists a unique associated equation $e' : \psi = C[\phi]$ such that e is the last edge of the path $(V(\psi), O_C)$. The occurrence $O(e, \phi)$ will denote O_C.*

This is proved by contradiction: linearizing one of the two occurrences so defined does not modify the abstract graph, contradicting S elementary. We precise the notion of chain, with the notations of Proposition 2.3:

Definition 5.1 *A chain as defined in Proposition 2.3 is an open chain. A closed chain is a triple (α, c, β) where c is an open chain, $\alpha =_s \gamma$ and $\beta =_s \delta$, where γ (resp. δ) is the first (resp. last) variable of the chain c. We also define in an obvious way left (resp. right) closed and right (resp. left) open chains.*

By extension, a closed chain of length 0 is a pair (α, β) of variables such that $\alpha =_s \beta$. Assume that both needed variables α and β occur by the same edge e in v, and that we need to prove $\alpha = \beta$. By Lemma 5.3, we have two well-defined equations $\phi = C[\alpha]$ and $\psi = D[\beta]$. Now, three cases can occur, according to the relative positions of the paths $V(\phi), \ldots, V(\alpha)$ and $V(\psi), \ldots, V(\beta)$: they are equal, one is suffix of the other, or they share at most a proper suffix. These three cases correspond to the various chains introduced in Definition 5.1. They motivate the propositions below.

Let E be a set of equations. Let v be some vertex in $\mathcal{G}_E$. A block of v is a set B containing at least three edges incident to v so that there exists a $\mathcal{S}$-variable ϕ that occurs by e, for all e in B. Let c be a chain of v, then if c contains $(e_1, \ldots, e_n)$ that forms a block, any permutation of $(e_2, \ldots, e_{n-1})$, any subsequence $(e_1, e_{i_1}, \ldots, e_{i_k}, e_n)$ also defines a chain. We are interested in minimal chains. Notice first that such a chain does not repeat any edge. Further a minimal chain does not contain any subsequence of edges defining a block.

Proposition 5.4 *Let S be an elementary cyclic set and v be a shared vertex of $\mathcal{G}_S$. For all pairs (e_1, e_2) of distinct edges incident to v there exists a minimum open chain between e_1 and e_2.*

Let S be an elementary cyclic set and v be some vertex of $\mathcal{G}_S$ such that e_1 and e_2 are two distinct edges both incident to v. Assume that α, β occur in v by e_1 and α', β' occur in v by e_2. Then $\alpha =_s \alpha'$ and $\beta =_s \beta'$ implies $\alpha \equiv \beta$ and $\alpha' \equiv \beta'$. From this it follows that two open chains in a vertex v sharing sequence of edges are equal. Next, we prove that if c_1 and c_2 are two minimal open chains between e_1 and e_2 with equal sets of edges, then their sequences of edges also are equal. Finally, let c_1 and c_2 be two minimal chains between e_1 and e_2 incident to v, they have the same edges.

Proposition 5.5 *Let S be some elementary cyclic set and α, β be two variables with $V(\alpha) = V(\beta)$. Then there exists a minimum closed chain between α and β.*

By Lemma 2.2, we get two variables γ and δ such that $\alpha =_s \gamma$ and $\beta =_s \delta$, γ and δ occur by two edges e and e'. We apply Proposition 5.4 to these edges. This establishes the existence of such chains. As usual, their unicity is proved by contradiction.

Proposition 5.6 *Let S be an elementary cyclic set. Let $\alpha \in v$ and e being incident to v. Then there exists a minimum left-closed and right-open chain that starts with α and ends with β, for some β that occurs in v by e.*

By Proposition 2.3, there exists a variable β that occurs by e. By Proposition 5.5, there exists a chain between α and β, its unicity is proved by contradiction. These three propositions detail the three cases where we will need the unicity property in the next section. In addition we have the

Proposition 5.7 *Let v be some cyclic needed vertex in $\mathcal{G}_S$, S some elementary cyclic set. There exists a maximum open chain in v.*

This follows from Theorem 3.1 and Proposition 5.4. The various chains of example C are shown in Fig. 2.

5.3 Computing the Minimum Deduction

We now collect our pieces together. First, it is easily seen that if $\alpha =_s \beta$ there exist a minimum (t)-proof of this equality. A cyclic variable ϕ in vertex v is the proper variable of v iff ϕ is the (unique) variable that occurs in v by the edge incident to v belonging to the cycle. We are now in position to state our main result.

Theorem 5.8 *Let ϕ be some proper variable of the elementary cyclic set S. There exists a minimum deduction $\mathcal{D} \vdash \phi = C[\phi]$ of the cyclic equation associated to ϕ. The minimum deductions for other proper variables are obtained from $\mathcal{D}$ by a cyclic permutation of the auxiliary deductions of $\mathcal{D}$.*

We establish the result by giving a deterministic algorithm that searches such a proof. The inference rules are denoted by function symbols of arity 2: SU for the substitution, T for the transitivity and D for the simplification rule. By the normal form of deductions and the above observation, the symmetry rule appears only in proofs for $=_s$. The algorithm includes a main procedure and three mutually recursive functions. The first one *Connect* returns a proof $\phi_{i+1} = C_i[\phi_i]$ where ϕ_{i+1} (resp. ϕ_i) is the proper variable of the cyclic needed vertex v_{i+1} (resp. v_i). The procedure *Chain* takes an open chain from α_0 to β_{n-1} (with the notations of Proposition 2.3) and returns a proof of $\alpha_0 = \beta_{n-1}$. Finally, the procedure *Edge* takes an edge and two (distinct) variables that occur by this edge and returns a proof of their equality. The intuition behind this last procedure has been outlined after Definition 5.1.

CYCLE DEDUCTION

Input: an elementary cyclic set S, its graph $\mathcal{G}_S$, some needed cyclic vertex v_0;
Let $v_0, \ldots, v_n$ be the sequence of needed cyclic vertices of $\mathcal{G}_S$,
v_{i+1} the first needed cyclic vertex above v_i along the cycle, with $v_{n+1} = v_0$;
For $i = 0, \ldots, n$ Let $T_i = Connect(v_i, v_{i+1})$;
Return $(S(T_0, S(\cdots S(T_{n-1}, T_n) \cdots)))$.

Function $Connect(v_1, v_2)$
If v_2 possesses a unique incident edge
Then Let $e : \alpha = C[\beta]$ be the unique non-strict equation of v_2;
Let γ be the variable of v_2 that possesses an occurrence by the cycle;
Let $\mathcal{D}$ be the minimum (t)-proof of $\gamma =_s \alpha$;
Return($T(\mathcal{D}, e)$ or e if $\mathcal{D}$ is void);

```
Else Let c = (e_0, α_0, β_0, e_1, ..., e_n, α_{n-1}, β_{n-1}, e_n) be the maximum chain of v_2
     such that w, the unique needed R-variable of v_2 occurs by e_n,
     and e_0 is the cyclic edge incident to v_2;
     Let D_1 = Chain(v_2, c);
     Let D_2 = Edge(β_{n-1}, e, w);
     Return(T(D_1, D_2)).
```

Function $Chain(e_0, \alpha_0, \beta_0, e_1, \ldots, e_n, \alpha_{n-1}, \beta_{n-1}, e_n)$

```
For i = 0,...,n-1 Let D_i^1 be the minimum (t)-proof of α_i =_s β_i;
For i = 0,...,n-1 Let D_i^2 = Edge(v, β_i, e_{i+1}, α_{i+1});
For i = 0,...,n-1 If D_i^1 is void Then D_i^3 = D_i^2 Else D_i^3 = T(D_i^1, D_i^2);
Let D = D_1^3;
For i = 2,...,n-1 Let D = T(D, D_i^3);
Return(T(D, D_{n-1}^1) or D if D_{n-1}^1 is void).
```

Function $Edge(\alpha, e, \beta)$

```
Let e_1 : φ = C[α] and e_2 : ψ = D[β] be associated to O(α, e) and O(β, e);
Let p be the maximal common suffix of p_1 = (V(φ), O_C) and p_2 = (V(ψ), O_D);
If   p = p_1 = p_2
Then If   φ ≡ ψ
     Then Return(D(e_1, e_2));
     Else Let c = (ψ, e_0, α_0, ..., β_{n-1}, e_n, φ) be the minimum closed chain between ψ and φ;
          Let D_1 = Edge(ψ, e_0, α_0);
          Let D_2 = Chain(e_0, α_0, ..., β_{n-1}, e_n);
          Let D_3 = Edge(β_{n-1}, e_n, ψ);
          Let Tr = T(T(D_1, D_2), D_3);
          Return(D(T(Tr, e_1), e_2));
If   p = p_1
Then Let e_0 be the edge of p_2 incident to V(φ);
     Let w be the R-variable associated to D[β] that occurs by e_0 in V(φ);
     Let c = (e_0, α_0, ..., β_{n-1}, e_n, φ) be the minimum left-open right-closed chain between e_0 and φ;
     Let D_1 = Chain(e_0, α_0, ..., β_{n-1}, e_n);
     Let D_2 = Edge(β_{n-1}, e_n, φ);
     Let D_3 = Edge(α_0, e_0, w);
     Let Tr = T(D_1, D_2);
     Return(D(T(Tr, e_1), D_3));
If   p = p_2
Then Let e_n be the edge of p_1 incident to V(ψ);
     Let w be the R-variable associated to C[α] that occurs by e_n in V(ψ);
     Let c = (ψ, e_0, α_0, ..., β_{n-1}, e_n) be
     the minimum left-closed right-open chain between ψ and e_n;
     Let D_1 = Edge(ψ, e_0, α_0);
     Let D_2 = Chain(e_0, α_0, ..., β_{n-1}, e_n);
     Let D_3 = Edge(β_{n-1}, e_n, w);
     Let Tr = T(D_1, D_2);
     Return(D(T(Tr, D_3), e_2));
Else Let v' be the source of the path p;
     Let e, e' be the two edges of the paths p_1 and p_2 that occur in v';
     Let w_0, w_1 be the two corresponding R-variables;
     Let c = (e_0, α_0, ..., β_{n-1}, e_n) be the minimum open chain between e' and e;
     Let D_1 = Edge(α_0, e_0, w_1);
     Let D_2 = Chain(e_0, α_0, ..., β_{n-1}, e_n);
     Let D_3 = Edge(β_{n-1}, e_n, w_0);
     Return(D(T(D_2, D_3), D_1)).
```

The correction of the algorithm follows from Lemmas in section 5.1: the algorithm terminates and computes a cyclic deduction. This deduction is minimum by Propositions 5.4, 5.5, 5.6 and 5.7.

Turning back to $\mathcal{C}$, the reader will have convinced himself that the needed variables are denoted by greek letters. The minimum cyclic deductions for the two proper variables β and γ are given by the following two auxiliary deductions:

$$\mathcal{D}_1 \left\{ \dfrac{\dfrac{\dfrac{\dfrac{\dfrac{\psi=\mu\to a \quad \psi=\nu\to b}{\mu=\nu} \quad \dfrac{\theta=\nu\to g \quad \theta=\lambda\to h}{\nu=\lambda}}{\mu=\lambda} \quad \dfrac{\omega=\lambda\to m \quad \omega=\phi\to l}{\lambda=\phi}}{\mu=\phi} \quad \phi=\beta\to n}{\mu=\beta\to n} \quad \mu=(o\to\gamma)\to p}{\beta=o\to\gamma} \right.$$

$$\mathcal{D}_2 \left\{ \dfrac{\dfrac{\dfrac{\theta=\lambda\to h \quad \theta=(i\to(j\to\gamma))\to k}{\lambda=i\to(j\to\gamma)} \quad \lambda=q\to(\alpha\to\alpha)}{\gamma=\alpha} \quad \dfrac{\dfrac{\dfrac{\theta=\nu\to g \quad \theta=\lambda\to h}{\nu=\lambda} \quad \lambda=q\to(\alpha\to\alpha)}{\nu=q\to(\alpha\to\alpha)} \quad \dfrac{\psi=\nu\to b \quad \psi=(c\to((\beta\to d)\to e))\to f}{\nu=c\to((\beta\to d)\to e)}}{\alpha=\beta\to d}}{\gamma=\beta\to d} \right.$$

The two minimum deductions are:

$$(su)\ \dfrac{\begin{matrix}\mathcal{D}_2 \\ \gamma=\beta\to d\end{matrix} \quad \begin{matrix}\mathcal{D}_1 \\ \beta=o\to\gamma\end{matrix}}{\beta=o\to(\beta\to d)} \qquad (su)\ \dfrac{\begin{matrix}\mathcal{D}_1 \\ \beta=o\to\gamma\end{matrix} \quad \begin{matrix}\mathcal{D}_2 \\ \gamma=\beta\to d\end{matrix}}{\gamma=(o\to\gamma)\to d}$$

References

[1] Coquand Th. and Huet G. *The Calculus of Constructions.* To appear in Information and Control.

[2] Courcelle B. *Fundamental Properties of Infinite Trees.* Theo. Comp. Sci. 25 (1983) 95–169.

[3] Dwork C., Kanellakis P. and Mitchell J. *On the Sequential Nature of Unification.* J. of Logic Programming 1 (1), 35–50.

[4] G. Gentzen. "The Collected Papers of Gerhard Gentzen." Ed. E. Szabo, North-Holland, Amsterdam (1969).

[5] Girard J.Y. "Interprétation fonctionnelle et élimination des coupures dans l'arithmétique d'ordre supérieure." Thèse d'Etat, Université Paris VII (1972).

[6] Goldfarb W. *The Undecidability of the Second-Order Unification Problem.* Theo. Comp. Sci. 13,2 (1981) 225–230.

[7] Huet G. *A Unification Algorithm for Typed λ-calculus.* Theo. Comp. Sci. 1 (1975) 27–57.

[8] Huet G. *Résolution d'équations dans les langages d'ordre 1,2,...,ω.* These d'Etat, Université Paris VII (1976).

[9] Le Chenadec Ph. *The Finite Automaton of an Elementary Cyclic Set.* INRIA Research Report 824, April 1988.

[10] Martelli A., Montanari U. *An Efficient Unification Algorithm.* ACM Toplas, 4,2 (1982) 258–282.

[11] Paterson M.S., Wegman M.N. *Linear Unification.* JCSS 16 (1978) 158–167.

[12] D. Prawitz. "Natural Deduction." Almqist and Wiskell, Stockolm (1965).

TWO APPLICATIONS OF FÜRER'S COUNTER TO ONE-TAPE NONDETERMINISTIC TMs*

Krzysztof Loryś and Maciej Liśkiewicz

Institute of Computer Science, University of Wrocław
Przesmyckiego 20, 51-151 Wrocław, Poland

1. Introduction.

When we construct a Turing machine (TM) M' which is to simulate an another TM M, we often want M' to count simulated steps and work within the same time as M. There is no problem if M' has more work tapes than M. But if M' and M have the same number of tapes then simple methods of step counting cause a significant increase of simulation time. So far some sophisticated counters have been constructed. For example, Paul in [Pa] has constructed a counter which on an average needs at most $log^* t$ steps per one subtraction of one from it (t is the total number of subtractions), and Fürer in [Fü] has constructed a counter allowing to do t subtractions in time proportional to t. The both counters have been constructed for deterministic TMs with at least two work tapes and cannot be simply applied to one-tape machines. However, we show that the Fürer's counter can be handled by nondeterministic single-tape TM. A single-tape TM has a single two-way read-write tape which initially contains the input word (we assume that the tape is infinite to the right only). Using the counter we solve two problems concerning one-tape machines: single-tape and offline NTMs (offline TMs have input word placed on an additional two-way read-only input tape).

Definition 1.1. We say that TM M is strongly $T(n)$-time bounded if on every input w M does not make more than $T(|w|)$ steps, and M is weakly $T(n)$-time bounded if for every accepted input w there is M's computation on w in which M makes at most $T(|w|)$ steps. Sometimes we will say that M recognizes the language strongly (weakly) in time $T(n)$ instead of M is strongly (weakly, resp.) $T(n)$-time bounded.

The first problem, we deal with, concerns time-space tradeoffs. It is well known that every $T(n)$-time bounded single-tape NTM M can be simulated by a $T^{1/2}(n)$-space bounded single-tape NTM M' ([HoUl], [Pat], [IbMo]). Moreover M' can be easily constructed to be weakly $T(n)$-time bounded. Ibarra and Moran have shown ([IbMo]) that if M is

* This research was supported by the Polish Government under program no. RP.I.09.

strongly $T(n)$-time bounded then M' can be constructed to be strongly $T^{3/2}(n)$-time bounded. We improve this result. Namely, we show that every $T(n)$-time bounded (even weakly) single-tape NTM M can be simulated by a strongly $T(n)$-time bounded single-tape NTM M' working within space $T^{1/2}(n)$. We also point that a similar result holds for offline NTMs.

The second problem concerns time hierarchy for NTMs. Seiferas et al ([SeFiMe]) have proved that if $T_1(n+1) \in o(T(n))$ and T is fully time constructible then multitape NTMs working in time $T(n)$ recognize larger class of languages than multitape NTMs working in time $T_1(n)$. Since every multitape $T(n)$-time bounded NTM can be simulated by a two-tape NTM without any loss of time ([BoGr]), the above result can be considered as the result for two-tape NTMs. Using the Fürer's counter we enforce the proof from [SeFiMe] to yield the time hierarchy for single-tape and offline NTMs. The time hierarchy theorems hold for weak complexity classes as well as for strong ones because for well behaved time bounds weakly and strongly time bounded respective one-tape NTMs recognize the same classes of languages.

2. The counter.

In this section we outline the construction of Fürer's counter (see [Fü]) and show that in many cases this counter can be efficiently handled by single-tape NTMs.

The counter has a form of full binary tree, in which each node contains a B-ary digit (for some fixed B). Let for each node v, $h(v)$ denote the height of v (i.e. the distance from v to the leaves), and $d(v)$ denote the digit stored in v. The <u>content</u> of the counter is the number $\sum_{v \in Tree} d(v) \cdot B^{h(v)}$.

If we want to increase the counter by one, we may add one to any of the leaves. If we have chosen a leaf v already containing $B-1$ then we must find the nearest v's ancestor u such that $d(u)<B-1$, add one to it and put zero to all nodes lying on the path from u to v.

The counter's nodes are stored in inorder in consecutive cells of the tape of single-tape TM. On a separate track below each node (except the root) there is put L or R, depending on whether the node is the left or the right son of its father (see Figure 1).

The <u>length</u> of the counter is the number of nodes in the tree. Thus only the numbers 2^k-1 (for $k \in N$) can be the lengths of the counters. Note, that the counter of length 2^k-1 can be constructed in time $k \cdot (2^k-1)$ by single-tape DTM. We say that the counter is <u>overfull</u> if machine attempts to add one to the root which already contains $B-1$.

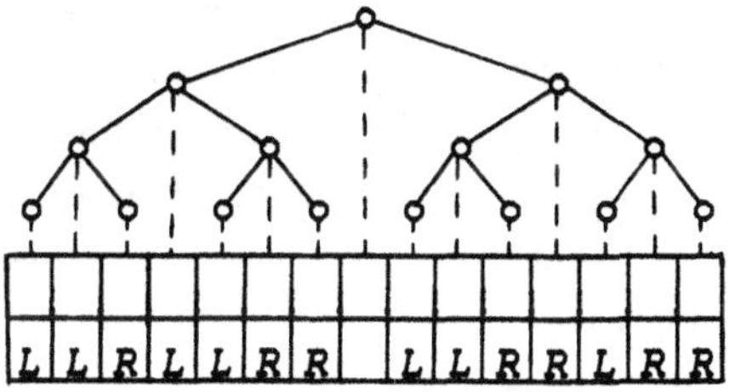

Figure 1.

Lemma 2.1. Let $B=4$.

(a) Full counter (i.e. with all nodes containing 3) of length n contains the number $(3/2)(n+1)n=O(n^2)$.

(b) Let us suppose that we start with the empty counter (i.e. with the content = 0) of length n and after m additions by one the counter is overfull. Then $m \geq (n+1)^2-1$.

(c) m succeeding additions by one to the initially empty counter of length n can be performed by single-tape deterministic TM in $O(m)$ steps.

Proof. (a) and (b) are straightforward.
Let us note that nodes of height h are 2^{h-1} cells from their sons, and at most m/B^h carries are necessary from nodes of height $h-1$ to nodes of height h. It is easy to see that a single carry can be done in $O(h \cdot 2^{h-1})$ steps, so the total time of m additions is at most $O(\sum_{h=0}^{\log_2(n+1)-1} (m/B^h) \cdot h \cdot 2^{h-1}) = O(m)$.

■

Lemma 2.2. Let the counter of length 2^k-1 be written down on the tape of single-tape TM. Then the binary representation of the counter's content can be deterministically computed in time $O(k \cdot (2^k-1))$.

Proof. Let us number from the left to the right all cells occupied by the counter and let $H(i)$ be the least $l \geq 0$ such that $\lfloor i/2^l \rfloor \equiv 1 \bmod 2$. Note that the ith cell stores a node of the height $H(i)$ (for $i=1,\ldots,2^k-1$). Let $T(i)$ denote the content of the part of the counter stored in the first i cells. In order to compute the content of the whole counter the machine moves its head through the tape and being over the ith cell computes

$T(i)=T(i-1)+$"the digit stored in the ith cell"$*4^{H(i)}$.

Since by Lemma 2.1(a) the length of $T(i)$ is $O(k)$ we obtain the stated time complexity.

■

3. Fast simulation of NTMs on short tape.

By a partition of a semiinfinite tape F we mean a sequence $B=(B_0,B_1,B_2,\ldots)$ such that for each i, B_i consists of a finite number of consecutive cells of F, B_{i+1} is directly to the right of B_i, and each cell of F belongs to a unique B_i. The B_i's are called tape segments. If B_0 consists of p cells, and for each $i\geq 1$, B_i consists of s cells, then B is called $\langle p,s\rangle$ partition .

Let M be a single-tape NTM. By crossings of M we mean pairs (d,q), where $d\in\{-1,1\}$ and q is a state of M. Let $B=(B_0,B_1,\ldots)$ be a partition of M's tape, w be a word in the input alphabet and *Comp* be a fixed computation of M on w. For each i, the trace of *Comp* between B_{i-1} and B_i after t steps, denoted *Trace*(*Comp*,i,t) is a finite sequence of crossings defined as follows:

(a) *Trace*(*Comp*,i,0) is the empty sequence,

(b) *Trace*(*Comp*,i,t)=*Trace*(*Comp*,i,$t-1$) if M's head does not cross the boundary between B_{i-1} and B_i during the tth move of *Comp*,

(c) *Trace*(*Comp*,i,t)=*Trace*(*Comp*,i,$t-1$)(d,q) if M in the state q moves its head across the boundary between B_{i-1} and B_i during the tth move of *Comp*; d is -1 if M's head moved left and is 1 otherwise.

Definition 3.1. Let B and *Comp* be as above. The history of *Comp* with respect B after t steps, denoted *History*(*Comp*,B,t), is a finite sequence of crossings defined as follows:

History(*Comp*,B,t)=*Trace*(*Comp*,1,t)#*Trace*(*Comp*,2,t)#...#*Trace*(*Comp*,j_t,t)

where j_t+1 is the number of the last segment visited till then. By length of the history we mean the number of crossings it contains.

Lemma 3.2. Let M be a single-tape NTM of time complexity $T(n)$, let w be a word of length n and s be a natural number. Then for every *Comp*, computation of M on w, there is $p\leq s$ such that for the $\langle p,s\rangle$ partition B *History*(*Comp*,B,$T(n)$) has the length no greater than $T(n)/s$.

Proof. Omitted (see [IbMo]).

Definition 3.3. $S(n)$ is fully space constructible in time $T(n)$ by a single-tape DTM if there is a single-tape DTM which on any input of length n halts within time $T(n)$ and uses exactly $S(n)$ cells.

Let M be $T(n)$-time bounded single-tape NTM and $T^{1/2}(n)$ be fully space constructible in time $T(n)$. One can simply construct a single-tape NTM M' which marks $T^{1/2}(n)$ cells on its tape, guesses a $\langle p,T^{1/2}(n)\rangle$ partition B and a history no longer than $T^{1/2}(n)$ and then simulates M on separate segments. Whenever M tries to move out of the simulated segment M' uses the history to complete the simulation inside this segment. It is easy to see that M' accepts in $O(T(n))$ steps all words accepted by M. On the other hand, one can easily check that if M' accepts a word w then the guessed history corresponds to some accepting computation of M on w. Unfortunately M' can perform infinite computations even if M is strongly $T(n)$-time bounded. We avoid such computations by use of the Fürer's counter.

Theorem 3.4. Let A be accepted by a single-tape NTM M in time $T(n)$, where $T(n) \geq n^2$. Let $T^{1/2}(n)$ be fully space constructible in time $T(n)$. Then A can be accepted strongly by a single-tape NTM M_1 in space $T^{1/2}(n)$ and time $T(n)$.

Proof. Let k satisfy the condition $2^k \geq T^{1/2}(n)+1 > 2^{k-1}$. For $B=4$, M_1 constructs the counter of length 2^k-1. Note that this construction can be done in time $k\cdot(2^k-1)$. Then M_1 simulates M on segments of nondeterministically guessed $\langle p, T^{1/2}(n)\rangle$ partition. When the counter is overfull then M_1 interrupts the simulation and rejects. Thus by Lemma 2.1, M_1 works in time $O(T(n))$. This time can be reduced to $T(n)$ since $T(n) \geq n^2$ and linear time speed-up theorem can be used. Moreover by Lemma 2.1(b) the simulation of some accepting computation of M cannot be interrupted on account of the overfulled counter.

■

In the case of offline NTMs, crossings must contain, apart from a state and a move direction, information about a position of the input head. It causes that the algorithm needs more than $T^{1/2}(n)$ space to store a history. On the other hand, $S(n)=(T(n)\cdot \log n)^{1/2}$ space is sufficient, since by Lemma 3.2 for each accepting M's computation $Comp$ of length $T(n)$ there is a $\langle p, S(n)\rangle$ partition B such that $History(Comp, B, T(n))$ has length no greater than $(T(n)/\log n)^{1/2}$. But this space is unappropriate to use a single counter. The next technical lemma (proved in [LiLo]) shows that we can divide the tape of simulating machine into blocks and count simulated steps in each block separately.

Lemma 3.5. Let H be an offline or a single-tape NTM. Then for each finite computation of H there is a partition of the work tape into blocks $C_1, C_2, \ldots$ of consecutive cells such that for each block

(i) the length n_j of block C_j is equal to $2^{i_j}-1$ for some i_j,

(ii) the number T_j of steps made by H during the computation within C_j satisfy the condition: $(1/4)(n_j+1)^2-1 < T_j \leq (n_j+1)^2-1$.

Theorem 3.6. Let A be accepted by an offline NTM M in time $T(n)$, $T(n) \geq n$. Let $S(n)=(T(n)\cdot \log n)^{1/2}$ be fully space constructible in time $T_1(n)=T(n)+n\cdot(T(n)/\log n)^{1/2}$. Then A can be accepted strongly by an offline NTM M_1 in space $S(n)$ and time $O(T_1(n))$.

Proof(sketch). M_1 nondeterministically divides the tape of length $(T(n)\cdot log\ n)^{1/2}$ into blocks and puts the empty counters into each block. Then M_1 checks if the sum of capacity of these counters does not exceed $6\cdot T(n)$. Note that this condition is fullilled if M_1 has guessed a partition as in Lemma 3.5. Then M_1 simulates M, rejecting if any of the counters is overfull. ■

4. The nondeterministic time hierarchy.

Let $NTIME_1(T(n))$ denote the class of languages recognized weakly in time $O(T(n))$ by single-tape NTMs. Let for NTM M and $w \in L(M)$, $Time_M(w)$ be the number of steps made by M during the shortest accepting computation on w. By convention, we shall designate, that $Time_M(w)=\infty$, for $w \notin L(M)$. Finally, let $L_T(M)=\{w: w \in L(M)$ and $Time_M(w) \leq T(|w|)\}$.

Definition 4.1. We say that a function $T:N \to N$ is <u>fully time constructible</u> if there is a deterministic single-tape machine M recognizing the language $\{1\}^*$ such that $Time_M(1^n)=T(n) \geq n$. M is called a <u>clock</u> for T.

Let us recall first that single-tape deterministic and nondeterministic weakly and strongly $T(n)$-time bounded TMs use in fact $T(n)/log\ T(n)$ space.

Lemma 4.2. ([Ha] and [PaPrRe]). For $T(n) \geq n\cdot log\ n$ every deterministic and nondeterministic single-tape $T(n)$-time bounded TM M is $O(T(n)/log\ T(n))$-space bounded; moreover for nondeterministic machine M time and space bounds are reached on the same computation.

Now we are ready to prove the crucial lemma of this section.

Lemma 4.3. If $T(n) \geq n\cdot log\ n$ is fully time constructible then for every single-tape NTM M, the language $L_T(M)$ can be recognized strongly by a single-tape NTM M_1 in time $O(T(n))$.

Proof. Roughly speaking M_1 simulates M on input w, simultaneously counting the simulated steps. After the simulation of $T(n)$ steps M_1 stops and accepts or rejects, depending on the M's configuration reached at the very end. Of course M_1 can stop and accept earlier if it has earlier reached an M's accepting configuration.

Now we describe M_1's work in detail. At the beginning M_1 computes $T(n)$.

Let N be a clock for $T(n)$ and let the input w has the length n. M_1 acts as N, increasing a counter, described in Section 2, by one after each step of N. Since at the beginning M_1 does not know the required length of the counter, it starts with the counter of length one. Whenever the counter becomes overfull or the N's head tries to go out of the space occupied by the counter, M_1 lenghtens the counter. It is easy to see that having the counter of length 2^i-1 on its tape M_1 can very simply construct the counter of length $2^{i+1}-1$.

When the simulation of N is finished, M_1 computes the binary representation of $T(n)$, marks a space $\lceil T(n)/\log T(n)\rceil$ and next acts like the machine from the proof of Theorem 3.6, i.e. M_1 nondeterministically divides the marked tape into blocks, constructs the empty counter in each block and checks if a total content of all these counters cannot exceed $6\cdot T(n)$. It follows from Lemma 2.1(a) that this condition is fulfilled if M_1 has guessed a partition as in Lemma 3.5. Then M_1 simulates M, rejecting if any of these counters is overfull. If M_1 has reached an accepting state then M_1 accepts if the sum of all counter contents does not exceed $T(n)$.

From Lemma 4.2 we have that M_1 can simulate M on w within space $T(n)/\log T(n)$. Moreover, by Lemma 2.1(b) we have that for the partition of the tape as in Lemma 3.5 there is a computation of M_1 on $w\in L(M)$ without overfulling any counter. So $L(M_1)=L_T(M)$.

We estimate now the time complexity of M_1. Let 2^d-1 be the length of the counter when the simulation of the clock N is finished. Since a counter of length 2^i-1 can be constructed in time $i\cdot(2^i-1)$, the total time for the construction of the counters is $O(\sum_{i=1}^{d} i\cdot(2^i-1))=O(d\cdot(2^d-1))$. By Lemma 4.2 $2^d-1=O(T(n)/\log T(n))$ so the time needed for the constructions of counters is $O(T(n))$.

The total time used for computing binary representations of the counters contents, by Lemma 2.2, is $O(T(n))$ as well.

From Lemma 2.1(c) it follows that $T(n)$ additions to the counters can be also made in time proportional to $T(n)$. ∎

From the above lemma it immediately follows that strong and weak nondeterministic time complexity classes are equal for well-behaved time limits.

Theorem 4.4. For every fully time constructible function $T(n)\geq n\cdot\log n$ the class of languages recognizable strongly in time $O(T(n))$ by single-tape NTMs is equal to $NTIME_1(T(n))$.

The next theorem gives the tight hierarchy for single-tape nondeterministic TMs, completing Seiferas's, Fisher's and Meyer's hierarchy theorem for multi-tape NTMs.

Theorem 4.5 If $T(n)$ is fully time constructible, $n^2 \in o(T(n))$ and $T_1(n+1) \in o(T(n))$ then $NTIME_1(T_1(n)) \subsetneq NTIME_1(T(n))$.

Proof. Let the programs of single-tape NTMs be encoded in such a way that the set $L_{p.c.}$ of all program codes is recognized by deterministic single-tape TM in linear time and no program code is a prefix of another one. Obviously, there is a universal single-tape NTM U such that $L(U)=\{ew:\ e \in L_{p.c.}$ and $w \in L(M_e)\}$ and

$$Time_U(ew) \leq c_e Time_{M_e}(w) + c_e |w|^2 \qquad \text{for } e \in L_{p.c.},\ w \in L(M_e),$$

where the constant c_e depends only on e, and M_e denotes the TM with the program code e.

It follows from Lemma 4.3 that $L_T(U)$ can be recognized by $T(n)$-time bounded single-tape NTMs for fully time constructible functions $T(n) \geq n \cdot log\ n$. So it is sufficient to prove that $L_T(U) \notin NTIME_1(T_1(n))$. To this end we use a translational method from [SeFiMe].

Assume the converse. Let $L_T(U)$ be recognized weakly in time $O(T_1(n))$ by single-tape NTM M_1. Moreover, let M_1^0 denote the machine which on the input w works as M_1 on $w0$. Let L_2 be an arbitrary recursive language over $\{1\}$. Since L_2 is recursive, there is a fully time constructible T_2 and single-tape $T_2(n)$-time bounded NTM M which recognizes L_2.

We define single-tape NTM M' which performs the following algorithm:

1. Check if the input has the form $ex0^k$ for some $e \in L_{p.c.}$ and $x \in \{1\}^*$;
2. Using a clock for T_2 check if $k < T_2(|x|)$;
3. If $k \geq T_2(|x|)$ then work as M on x;
4. If $k < T_2(|x|)$ then work as M_1^0 on the input.

It is easy to see that the steps 1 and 3 can be done in linear time, step 2 in time $O(k \cdot log\ k)$ and step 4 in time $O(T_1(|ex0^{k+1}|))$. Since we can assume that $T_1(n) \geq n \cdot log\ n$ the time complexity of M' is $O(T_1(n+1))$.

Assuming that the method of program coding is so simple that there is a recursive function $f: L_{p.c.} \to L_{p.c.}$ such that $M_{f(e)}$ first writes e on the left of input and thereafter acts as M_e, the following two claims can be proved in the similar way as in [SeFiMe].

Claim 1. There exists an $e_0 \in L_{p.c.}$ and $c>0$ such that $L(M_{e_0})=\{w:\ e_0 w \in L(M')\}$ and $Time_{M_{e_0}}(w) \leq c + Time_{M'}(e_0 w)$ for every $w \in L(M_{e_0})$.

Claim 2. For each sufficiently large l and all $k \geq 0$, $1^l 0^k \in L(M_{e_0}) \leftrightarrow 1^l \in L_2$.

Since in the proof of the Claim 2 we need that $Time_U(e_0 1^l 0^{k+1}) \leq T(|e_0 1^l 0^{k+1}|)$ for sufficiently large l, so the assumption $n^2 \in o(T(n))$ is necessary.

It is easy to see that from machine M_{e_0} one can construct a $T(|e_0|+n)$ time bounded TM which recognizes L_2. But this contradicts the assumption that L_2 is an arbitrary recursive language. ∎

As the class of languages recognizable by strongly $T_1(n)$-time bounded single-tape NTMs is included in $NTIME_1(T_1(n))$ for every function T_1 so combining this with Theorems 4.4 and 4.5 we have

Corollary 4.6. The tight hierarchy theorem holds also for strong time complexity classes.

Remark 4.7. Using a well known translational lemma (see [HoUl]) we can prove that the hierarchy holds beginning from $n \cdot \log n$. But now we must change assumtion $T_1(n+1) \in o(T(n))$ by, for example: $T_1((n+1)^2) \in o(T(n^2))$.

Remark 4.8. However, Lemma 4.2 does not hold for offline TMs, Theorems 4.4 and 4.5 can be enforced for offline NTMs if the function T is such that there exists a deterministic offline TM M which for each input of length n writes on the work tape the binary representation of $T(n)$ in time $T(n)$. Moreover it can be proved that the offline version of Theorem 4.5 holds beginning from the function $n \cdot \log n$.

Acknowledgment. The authors would like to thank professor Leszek Pacholski for illuminating discussions and helpful criticism.

References.

[BoGr] R.V. Book and S.A. Greibach, *Quasi-realtime languages*, Math. Sys. Theory, 4(1970), pp.97-111;

[Fü] M. Fürer, *The tight deterministic time hierarchy*, Proc. 14th Annual ACM Symposium on Theory of Computing, (1982),pp.8-16;

[Ha] J. Hartmanis, *Size arguments in the study of computation speeds*, Proc. Symp. on Computers and Automata, Polytechn. Inst. Brooklyn, (1965);

[HoUl] J.E. Hopcroft and J.D. Ullman, *Relations between time and tape complexities*, J. Assoc. Comp. Mach., 15(1968), pp.414-427;

[IbMo] O.H. Ibarra and S. Moran, *Some time-space tradeoffs results concerning single-tape and offline TMs*, SIAM J. Comput., 12(1983), pp.388-394;

[LiLo] M. Liśkiewicz and K. Loryś, *Fast simulations of time-bounded TMs by space-bounded ones*, Report N-187, Institute of Computer Science, University of Wrocław, Wrocław 1987;

[Pa] W.J. Paul, *On time hierarchies*, J. Comput. Systems Sci., 19(1979), pp.197-202;

[PaPrRe] W.J. Paul, E.J. Prauss and R. Reischuk, *On alternation I*, Acta Informatica, 14(1980), pp.243-255;

[Pat] M.S. Paterson, *Tape bounds for time-bounded Turing machines*, J. Comput. Systems Sci., 6(1972), pp.116-124;

[SeFiMe] J.I. Seiferas, M.J. Fischer and A.R. Meyer, *Separating nondeterministic time complexity classes*, J. Assoc. Comp. Mach., 25(1978), pp.146-167.

Δ_2^p-Complete Lexicographically First Maximal Subgraph Problems

Satoru Miyano

Research Institute of Fundamental Information Science
Kyushu University 33, Fukuoka 812, Japan.

Abstract

The lexicographically first maximal (lfm) induced path problem is shown Δ_2^p-complete. The lfm rooted tree problem is also Δ_2^p-complete. But when restricted to topologically sorted directed acyclic graphs (dags), the lfm rooted tree problem allows a polynomial time algorithm. Moreover, the problem restricted dags with degree 3 is shown in NC^2 while the problem for degree 4 is P-complete.

1. Introduction

Papadimitriou [Pa] is the first who gave a natural problem complete for Δ_2^p, which is the class of problems solvable in polynomial time using oracles in NP. He proved that the uniquely optimum traveling salesman problem is Δ_2^p-complete. Afterwards, Wagner [Wa] has found some Δ_2^p-complete problems related to optimization problems. This paper gives Δ_2^p-complete problems of a new kind. The importance of the Δ_2^p-completeness is not only due to its high complexity but also due to the observation that any Δ_2^p-complete problem is hard to efficiently parallelize even if NP-oracles are available.

For a given hereditary property π on graphs, we consider the problem of finding the lexicographically first maximal (abbreviated to lfm) subset U of vertices of a graph $G = (V, E)$ such that U induces a *connected* subgraph satisfying π, where we assume that V is linearly ordered as $V = \{1, ..., n\}$. Problems of this kind have been extensively studied in [AM], [Ma], [M1], [M2]. In particular, without the connectedness restriction, the P-completeness of the lfm subgraph problem for *any* nontrivial polynomial time testable hereditary property is proved in [M1] as an analogue of the results in [LY], [Y2]. However, since the connectedness is not necessarily inherited by subgraphs, a new analysis is required.

In this paper we are involved in the complexity analysis of problems of this kind. Our main result is that the lfm induced path problem is Δ_2^p-complete. We should here note that this problem is different from the lfm maximal path problem discussed in [AM] which was shown P-complete.

Some of the lfm connected subgraph problems for hereditary properties are polynomial time solvable. For example, the lfm clique problem is obviously in P. In Section 3, we prove a general theorem asserting that the lfm connected subgraph problem for a hereditary property is NP-hard if the property is satisfied by graphs with arbitrarily large diameters and is determined by blocks. Hence the connectedness makes the problem harder.

In Section 4, we concentrate on a special problem, the lfm rooted tree problem. It is also possible to prove that this problem is Δ_2^p-complete even if the instances are directed acyclic graphs (abbreviated to dags). But if vertices of a dag are topologically sorted, it allows a polynomial time algorithm. Moreover, our analysis shows that the problem restricted to topologically sorted dags with degree 4 is P-complete and the degree bound 4 is proved to be optimal in the sense that the problem for degree 3 is, interestingly, solvable in NC^2. Finally, the complexity analysis of the lfm forest problem is given in comparison with the rooted tree problem.

2. The Lexicographically First Maximal Induced Path Problem is Δ_2^p-Complete

The *lfm induced path problem* is to find the lfm subset of vertices that induces a path, a connected graph of degree at most 2 with no cycle. We prove that this is Δ_2^p-complete.

For any graph property π, the lexicographically first maximal subgraph satisfying π is computed by the following greedy algorithm:

begin
  $U \leftarrow \emptyset$;
  for $j = 1$ **to** n **do**
    if $U \cup \{j\}$ can be extended to a subgraph of G satisfying π **then** $U \leftarrow U \cup \{j\}$
end

From the algorithm it is clear that the lfm subgraph problem for π is in Δ_2^p if π is polynomial time testable.

Following [Pa], we give the definition of the *deterministic satisfiability problem* as follows:

Let $x_1, ..., x_{k-1}$ be $k-1$ variables and $Y_1, ..., Y_k$ be k sets of variables. A formula $F(x_1, ..., x_{k-1}, Y_1, ..., Y_k)$ in conjunctive normal form is said to be *deterministic* if F consists of the following clauses:

(1) Either (y) or $(\bar{y})$ is a clause of F for each y in $Y_1 \cup Y_k$.

(2) For each $i = 1, ..., k-1$ and each y in Y_{i+1}, there are sets C_y^i and D_y^i of conjunctions of literals from $Y_i \cup \{x_i\}$ with the following properties:

(i) Exactly one of the conjunctions in $C_y^i \cup D_y^i$ is true for any truth assignment.

(ii) F contains clauses $(\alpha \rightarrow y)$ and $(\beta \rightarrow \bar{y})$ for each $\alpha \in C_y^i$ and each $\beta \in D_y^i$.

DSAT(Deterministic Satisfiability)

Instance: A deterministic formula $F_0(x_1, ..., x_{k-1}, Y_1, ..., Y_k)$ and formulas $F_1(Y_1, Z_1), ...$, $F_{k-1}(Y_{k-1}, Z_{k-1})$ in 3-conjunctive normal form, where $\{x_1, ..., x_{k-1}\}$, $Y_1, ..., Y_k$, $Z_1, ..., Z_{k-1}$ are mutually disjoint sets of variables.

Question: Is there a truth assignment $\hat{x}_1, ..., \hat{x}_{k-1}, \hat{Y}_1, ..., \hat{Y}_k$ satisfying (i) and (ii).

(i) $F_0(\hat{x}_1, ..., \hat{x}_{k-1}, \hat{Y}_1, ..., \hat{Y}_k) = t$.

(ii) $F_i(\hat{Y}_i, Z_i)$ is satisfiable $\iff \hat{x}_i = t$ for $i = 1, ..., k-1$.

Lemma 1 [Pa]. *DSAT is Δ_2^p-complete.*

Lemma 2. *For a formula F in conjunctive normal form, we can construct a graph G_F with specified vertices a, w_0, w_1 of degree 1 such that F is satisfieable (resp. not satisfiable) if and only if the lfm induced path of G_F is a path from a to w_1 (resp. w_0).*

Proof. For simplicity we assume that F is in 3-conjunctive normal form. Let $c_1, ..., c_m$ be the clauses of F and let $x_1, ..., x_n$ be the variables occurring in $c_1, ..., c_m$. For each variable x_i, we use the graph in Fig. 1(a) called the *variable graph*, where $k_i = \max\{|\{c_j : c_j \text{ contains } x_i\}|, |\{c_j : c_j \text{ contains } \bar{x}_i\}|\}$. We call the subgraph induced by $d_i, x_i, \bar{x}_i$ the *value assignment part* for x_i. For each clause $c_j = \alpha_j + \beta_j + \gamma_j$, we use the graph in Fig. 1(b) called the *clause graph* and c_j a *clause vertex*. We call vertices $\alpha_j[c_j]_p$, $\beta_j[c_j]_p$, $\gamma_j[c_j]_p$ $(p = 0, 1)$ *literal vertices*. An example of construction for a formula $F = (x_1 + x_2)(x_1 + \bar{x}_2)(\bar{x}_1 + x_2)(\bar{x}_1 + \bar{x}_2)$ in 2-conjunctive normal form is given in Fig. 2 together with the numbering of vertices, where some edges are not drawn since they make the figure ugly. As shown in Fig. 2, the variable graphs are concatenated in the order of $x_1, ..., x_n$ and the clause graphs are connected using square vertices $z_1, ..., z_m$. It also has special vertices a, b, h_0, h_1, h_2, w_0 and w_1 which are wired as shown. We put edges $\{h_1, z_j\}$ for $j = 1, ..., m$. Due to these edges, $z_1, ..., z_m$ are forbidden to be chosen when h_1 has been chosen before. We also add edges $\{h_0, u\}$ for all literal vertices u. These edges separate the clause vertices from the variable graphs when h_0 is chosen. We connect the vertex x_i (resp. $\bar{x}_i$) to vertices $\bar{x}_i[c_j]_0$, $\bar{x}_i[c_j]_1$ (resp. $x_i[c_j]_0$, $x_i[c_j]_1$) if clause c_j contains the literal $\bar{x}_i$ (resp. $\bar{x}_i$). The vertex x_i (resp. $\bar{x}_i$) is also connected to vertices $\bar{x}_i^{(1)}, \bar{x}_i^{(2)}, \ldots$ (resp. $x_i^{(1)}, x_i^{(2)}, \ldots$) as shown in Fig. 1(a). When x_i (resp. $\bar{x}_i$) has been chosen, these edges prevent the vertices named with the literal x_i (resp. $\bar{x}_i$) from being chosen. The vertices $x_i^{(2k-1)}$ and $x_i^{(2k+1)}$ (resp. $\bar{x}_i^{(2k-1)}$ and $\bar{x}_i^{(2k+1)}$) are connected to $x_i[c_j]_0$ and $x_i[c_j]_1$ (resp. $\bar{x}_i[c_j]_0$ and $\bar{x}_i[c_j]_1$), respectively, if the literal x_i in c_j is the kth occurrence of x_i in $c_1, \ldots, c_m$ counted from left to right. These four vertices are ordered as numbered in Fig. 2 and work to capture the vertex c_j. For the graph G_F with the specified vertex order, the lfm subset U of vertices which induces a path must contain all vertices in $B = \{a, b, c_1, \ldots, c_m, h_2, d_i, e_i, f_i, g_i \ : \ i = 1, \ldots, n\}$ since the set B is obviously extendable to a path. These vertices are colored black in Fig. 2. Moreover, either x_i or $\bar{x}_i$ must be chosen into U since deletion of both vertices raises two vertices d_i, e_i of degree 1 other than the vertex a. Furthermore, either h_0 or h_1 must be chosen. The choice of h_0 or h_1 depends on the satisfiability of the formula.

We show that h_1 (resp. h_0) is chosen into U if and only if F is satisfiable (resp. not satisfiable). Assume that all vertices in B have been chosen. Suppose that h_1 can be chosen. Then none of the square vertices $z_1, \ldots, z_m$ can be chosen. As mentioned before, either x_i or $\bar{x}_i$ must be chosen. If x_i (resp. $\bar{x}_i$) is chosen, then no vertices of the forms $\bar{x}_i^{(k)}$, $\bar{x}_i[c_j]_p$ (resp. $x_i^{(k)}$, $x_i[c_j]_p$) can be chosen. Therefore the choice of h_1 implies that the set $B \cup \{h_1\} \cup \{v_i \ : \ i = 1, \ldots, n\}$ is also extendable to a path for some choice of v_i for $i = 1, \ldots, n$, where v_i is either x_i or $\bar{x}_i$. In this situation, this means that F is satisfiable since each c_j must be connected to some chosen vertex in the variable graph via a literal vertex. Conversely, if F is satisfiable, let $(\hat{x}_1, \ldots, \hat{x}_n)$ be the lexicographically first bit vector which makes the formula true. Then by taking h_1 together with the vertices in the variable graphs corresponding to the bit vector $(\hat{x}_1, \ldots, \hat{x}_n)$ into U, we see that U induces a path from a to w_1. Hence if F is not satisfiable, h_1 cannot be chosen. Therefore h_0 must be chosen. This implies that no literal vertex can be chosen. Therefore z_1 must be chosen to capture $c_1, \ldots, c_m$. Hence w_1 cannot be chosen and all $z_1, \ldots, z_m$ must be chosen into U. In fact $U = B \cup \{x_1, x_1^{(1)}, \ldots\} \cup \ldots \cup \{x_n, x_n^{(1)}, \ldots\} \cup \{h_0\} \cup \{z_1, \ldots, z_m\} \cup \{w_0\}$.□

Theorem 3. *The lfm induced path problem is Δ_2^p-complete.*

Sketch of Proof. We give a reduction from DSAT. Let $F_0(x_1, \ldots, x_{k-1}, Y_1, \ldots, Y_k)$, $F_1(Y_1, Z_1)$, ..., $F_{k-1}(Y_{k-1}, Z_{k-1})$ constitute an instance of DSAT. We construct a graph $G(F_0, \ldots, F_{k-1})$ in the following way (see Fig. 3) and show that $(F_0, \ldots, F_{k-1}) \in$DSAT if and only if the lfm induced path reaches the vertex w_1, where variables are ordered as $Y_1, Z_1, \ldots, Y_{k-1}, Z_{k-1}, Y_k$.

The graph $G(F_0, \ldots, F_{k-1})$ is defined as follows: First we take the graph G_{F_0} that is constructed in Lemma 2 for F_0 but, for a moment, we ignore the variables in $Y_1, \ldots, Y_{k-1}$. We have to decide whether there is a truth assignment $\hat{x}_1, \ldots, \hat{x}_{k-1}, \hat{Y}_1, \ldots, \hat{Y}_k$ such that

(i) $F_0(\hat{x}_1, \ldots, \hat{x}_{k-1}, \hat{Y}_1, \ldots, \hat{Y}_k) = t$.

(ii) $F_i(\hat{Y}_i, Z_i)$ is satisfiable $\Longleftrightarrow \hat{x}_i = t$ for $i = 1, \ldots, k-1$.

Since the condition (ii) must be kept, we replace the value assignment part for the variable x_i by $\tilde{G}_{F_i}$ which will be defined later and connect the variable graphs for Y_i of $\tilde{G}_{F_i}$ to the clause graphs of G_{F_0} as was done in Lemma 2. Then we assign numbers to vertices as in Fig. 2.

$\tilde{G}_{F_i}$ is defined for $F_i(Y_i, Z_i)$ using the construction in Lemma 2 but we need some changes. We just sketch a part of $\tilde{G}_{F_i}$ in Fig. 4, where it is assumed that literal $y_j^{(i)}$ from Y_i appears in clause c_{0l} of F_0 and literals $y_j^{(i)}$ and $\bar{y}_j^{(i)}$ appear in clauses $c_1^{(i)}$ and $c_2^{(i)}$ of $F_i(Y_i, Z_i)$, respectively.

The variable graph for $y_j^{(i)}$ in Y_i has a structure similar to the graph in Fig. 1(a). It consists of two parts as shown in Fig. 4. The upper part is connected to the clause graphs of F_0 as in Fig. 2. The lower part is connected to the clause graphs of F_i in a way that for each literal we use only two vertices which are directly wired to the corresponding clause vertex as shown in Fig. 4. Each vertex on the left (resp. right) side of the lower part is wired to the vertex $y_j^{(i)}$ (resp. $\bar{y}_j^{(i)}$). We assume that all vertices on both sides are connected to some clause vertices of F_i. Therefore the left and right sides may have different numbers of vertices. It may be implicitly understood how these vertices are ordered.

Assume that choices of the vertices in the variable graphs for Y_i have been already done and they define a truth assignment $\hat{Y}_i$. Then by the construction it can be checked that a path can reach the vertex x_i (resp. $\bar{x}_i$) if and only if $F_i(\hat{Y}_i, Z_i)$ is satisfiable.

We show that if the vertex h_1 in Fig. 3 is chosen then $(F_0, ..., F_{k-1})$ is in DSAT and the lfm induced path reaches the vertex w_1. As was seen in Lemma 2, if h_1 is chosen, then no triagle vertex can be chosen. Since F_0 is deterministic, truth values for Y_1 are uniquely determined. Therefore choices of the vertices of the variable graphs for Y_1 are also uniquely determined. By the fact mentioned in the former paragraph, $F_1(\hat{Y}_1, Z_1)$ is satisfiable (resp. not satisfiable) if and only if the vertex x_1 (resp. $\bar{x}_1$) is chosen. If x_1 (resp. $\bar{x}_1$) is chosen, then let $\hat{x}_1 = t$ (resp. f). Since F_0 is deterministic, the truth values for Y_2 are again uniquely determined by $\hat{Y}_1$ and $\hat{x}_1$. By induction, the choice of h_1 determines $\hat{Y}_1$, $\hat{x}_1$,...,$\hat{Y}_{k-1}$, $\hat{x}_{k-1}$ and $\hat{Y}_k$ uniquely and the condition (ii) is kept. Therefore $(F_0, ..., F_{k-1})$ is in DSAT. It can be also shown that the chosen vertices induces a path from a_0 to w_1 via h_1. Conversely, if the conditions (i) and (ii) are satisfied, then the lfm induced path contains h_1 and reaches w_1.□

A *rooted tree* is a directed acyclic graph with a special vertex with indegree 0 called the *root* such that every vertex except the root is reachable from the root. It is also possible to prove the following theorem in a similar way. The reduction is simpler than that for Theorem 3 and we omit it. Unfortunately, we do not have a general result like [M1] for P-complete problems.

Theorem 4. *The lfm rooted tree problem restricted to directed acyclic graphs is Δ_2^p-complete.*

3. The Connectedness Condition Makes the Problems Hard

A graph property π is said to be *hereditary* on induced subgraphs if, whenever a graph G satisfies π, all vertex-induced subgraphs of G also satisfy π. We say that π is *nontrivial* if π is satisfied by infinitely many graphs and there is a graph violating π. We say that π is *determined by the blocks* [Y1] if for any graphs G_1 and G_2 satisfying π the graph formed by identifying a vertex of G_1 and a vertex of G_2 also satisfies π. We define the *diameter* $\delta(\pi)$ by $\sup\{\delta(G) : G \text{ satisfies } \pi\}$, where $\delta(G)$ is the diameter of G.

LFMCSP(π)(the lfm connected subgraph problem for π)
Instance: A graph $G = (V, E)$ and a subset $S \subseteq V$, where $V = \{1, ..., n\}$.
Question: Let U be the lfm subset of V which induces a connected subgraph satisfying π. Then $S \subseteq U$?

Lemma 5 [Be]. *Let G be a connected graph with at least two vertices. Then G has at least two vertices which are not cutpoints. Moreover, G has exactly two such vertices if and only if G is a path.*

Theorem 6. *Let π be a property hereditary on induced subgraphs satisfying the following conditions:*
(i) π is nontrivial on connected graphs.
(ii) $\delta(\pi) = \infty$.
(iii) π is determined by the blocks.
Then LFMCSP(π) is NP-hard.

Proof. Since $\delta(\pi) = \infty$ and π is hereditary, it can be proved by considering the shortest paths of the graphs satisfying π that all paths satisfy π. Let G_3 be a connected graph with minimum number of vetices which violates π. Since all paths satisfy π, G_3 is not a path and therefore contains at least three vertices. Therefore by Lemma 5 G_3 contains at least three vertices a, b, c that are not cutpoints. Let G_0 be the subgraph of G_3, not necessarily connected, obtained by deleting a, b, c from G_3.

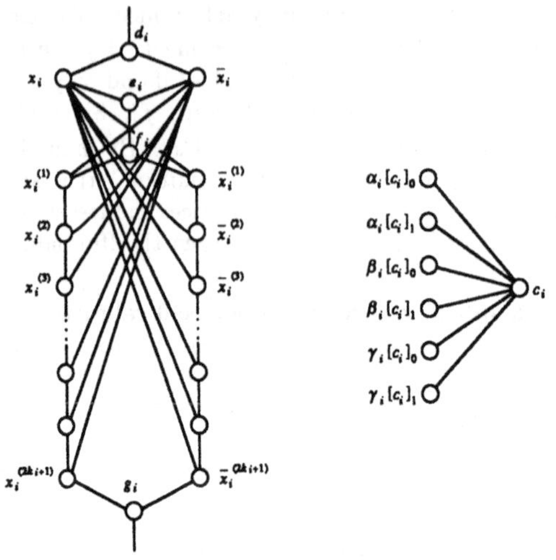

(a) (b)

Fig. 1.

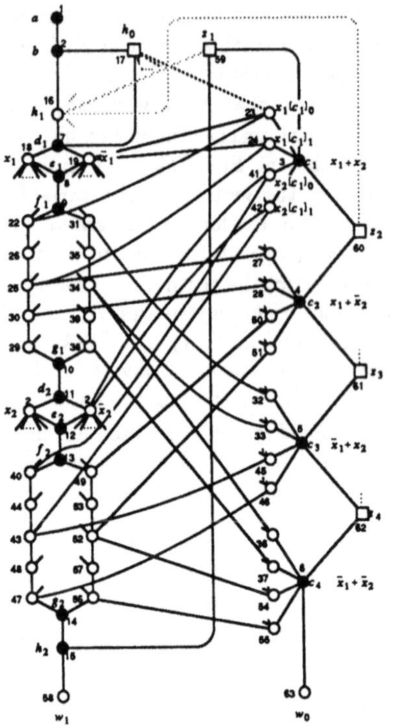

Fig. 2.

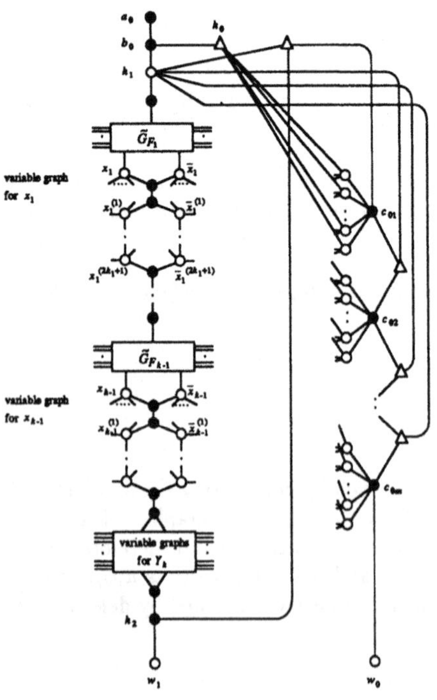

Fig. 3.

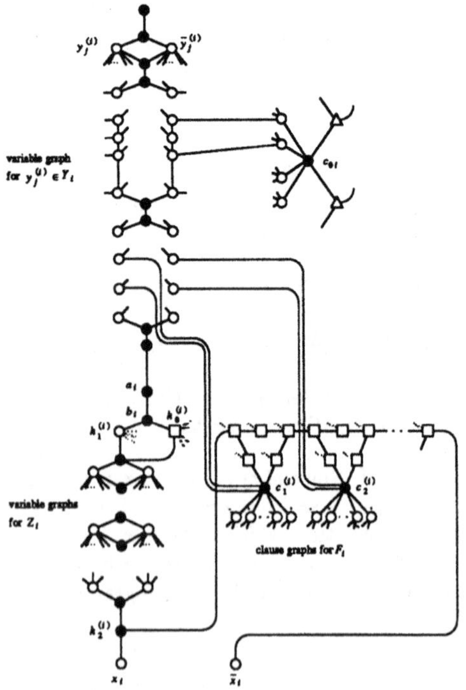

Fig. 4.

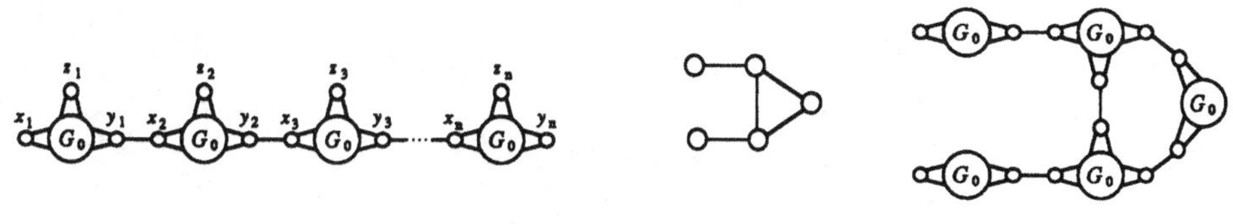

Fig. 5.

It is known that the Hamiltonian path problem restricted to planar graphs with degree at most 3 is NP-complete [GJT]. We shall give a reduction from this problem. Before getting into the detail, we consider the graph in Fig. 5(a), where the graph formed by x_i, y_i, z_i and G_0 is G_3 and x_i, y_i, z_i correspond a, b, c but we do not care the way how x_i, y_i, z_i are identified with a, b, c. By the choice of G_3, the graph obtained by deleting any vertex of a, b, c satisfies π. Therefore, by (iii) the graph obtained by deleting all $z_1, ..., z_m$ from the graph in Fig. 5(a) satisfies π. Moreover, it is connected since a, b, c are not cutpoints. However, adding any of $z_1, ..., z_m$ violates π since G_3 violates π.

Let $G = (V, E)$ be a graph with degree at most 3. Let G_2 be the graph formed by deleting vertex c from G_3. For each vertex v of G with degree 3 (resp. degree 2 or 1), we replace it by G_3 (resp. G_2) (see Fig. 5(b)-(c)). Let $\tilde{G} = (\tilde{V}, \tilde{E})$ be the resulting graph. Let $\tilde{W} \subset \tilde{V}$ be the set of vertices on G_0's. We can give an order on $\tilde{V}$ so that $\tilde{W} < \tilde{V} - \tilde{W}$. Now let $\tilde{U}$ be the lfm subset of vertices of $\tilde{G}$ which induces a connected subgraph satisfying π. Then it is not hard to see that the following statements are equivalent.

(1) G has a Hamiltonian path.

(2) $\tilde{W} \subset \tilde{U}$.

Thus LFMCSP(π) is at least NP-hard.□

Examples of the properties that satisfy the conditions of Theorem 5 are planar, bipartite, cycle-free, etc [Y1]. The reduction in Theorem 6 also shows that if G_3 is chosen to be planar then the problem restricted to planar graphs is also NP-hard. We conjecture that the above result can be extended to Δ_2^p-completeness.

4. The LFM Rooted Tree Problem for Topologically Sorted Dags

We say that a dag $G = (V, A)$ with $V = \{1, ..., n\}$ is *topologically sorted* if each arrow (i, j) in A satisfies $i < j$. In this section we first show that the lfm rooted tree problem for topologically sorted dags can be solved in polynomial time. Then we consider the cases of degree constraints 3 and 4. Our results on the lfm rooted tree problem is summarized in Table I.

	rooted tree	degree	forest	degree
Dags	Δ_2^p-complete		P-complete	3
Topologically	P-complete	4	P-complete	4
sorted dags	NC^2	3	NC^2	3

Table I.

Lemma 7. *The lfm rooted tree problem for topologically sorted dags is in P.*

Proof. Let $G = (V, A)$ be a dag, where $V = \{1, ..., n\}$. The problem can be solved in polynomial time by the following greedy algorithm:

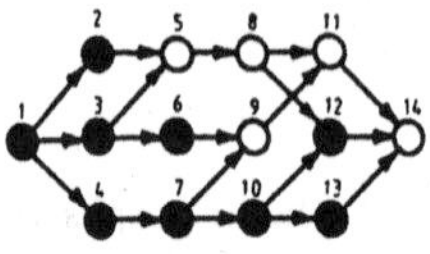

The black (resp. white) vertices are chosen (resp. unchosen) vertices.

Fig. 6.

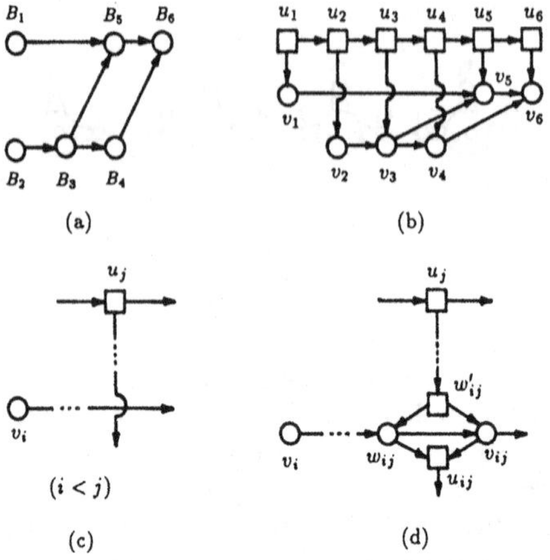

Fig. 7.

begin
  $U \leftarrow \{1\}$;
  for $j \leftarrow 2$ **to** n **do**
    if there is a unique $i \in U$ with $(i,j) \in A$ **then** $U \leftarrow U \cup \{j\}$
end

Before the execution of the j-th step, assume that U is the lfm subset of $\{1, ..., j-1\}$ that can be extended to a rooted tree. Moreover, assume that the subgraph induced by U forms a rooted tree. If j is adjacent to more than two vertices in U, then j has two incoming arrows from U since $i < j$ for any i in U. Therefore j cannot be addend into U. If j is not adjacent to any vertex in U, then there is no rooted tree containing $U \cup \{j\}$ since any i with (i,j) in A must satisfy $i < j$. If j is adjacent to exactly one vertex in U, then the graph induced by $U \cup \{j\}$ is a rooted tree. Hence j can be chosen if and only if it has exactly one incoming arrow from U.□

Theorem 8. *The lfm rooted tree problem for topologically sorted dags with degree at most 3 is in* NC^2.

Proof. Let $G = (V, A)$ be an instance of the problem with degree at most 3, where $V = \{1, ..., n\}$. Without loss of generality, we may assume that every vertex is reachable from the vertex 1 and the vertex 1 is the unique vertex with indegree 0. Let $V_d = \{i \in V : \text{indeg}(i) = d\}$ for $d = 0, ..., 3$. Let i be in V. As the greedy algorithm states, i can be chosen if and only if i has exactly one incoming arrow from a chosen vertex. Since vertices in V_3 have no outgoing arrows, they have no effect on the choices of vertices afterward. Therefore we concentrate on the subgraph G' induced by $V_0 \cup V_1 \cup V_2$. If i is in V_1, the choice of i depends on the unique vertex j with $(j,i) \in A$. Namely, i can be chosen if and only if j is chosen. If i is in V_2, there are exactly two predecessors $j, k < i$. When both j and k are chosen or neither j nor k is chosen, i cannot be chosen. On the other hand, when either j or k is chosen, i can be chosen. From this observation, it is not hard to see that i in $V_1 \cup V_2$ can be chosen if and only if there are odd number of paths from the vertex 1 to i (see Fig. 6). By a method similar to the parallel transitive closure algorithm on adjacency matrices, we can compute in NC^2 the numbers of paths (modulo 2) between vertices in G'. After deciding the choices of the vertices in $V_1 \cup V_2$, the vertices in V_3 are examined. This can be also done in NC^2.□

Theorem 9. *The lfm rooted tree problem for topologically sorted planar dags with degree 4 is P-complete.*

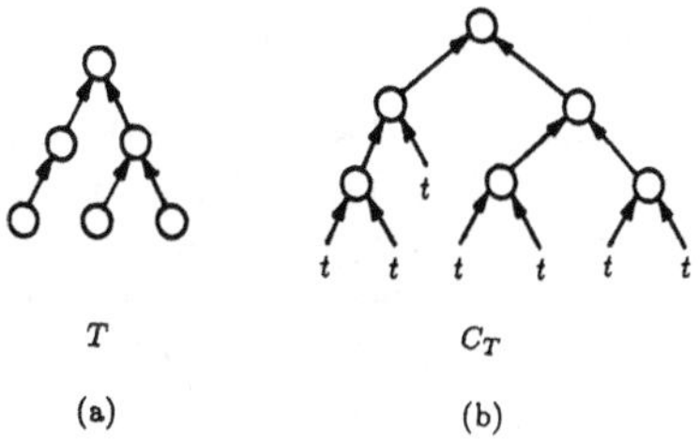

Fig. 8.

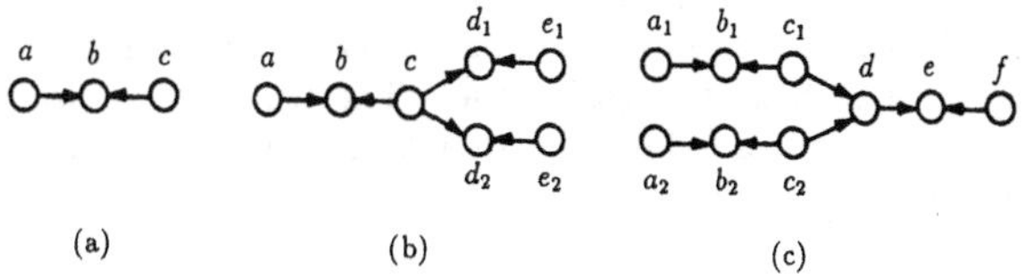

Fig. 9.

Proof. We give a reduction from planar circuits described in [Go]. We may assume that each gate executes one of the operations $t, \neg x, \neg(x \vee y)$ and the fanout of a gate for $\neg(x \vee y)$ (resp. $t, \neg x$) is at most one (resp. two). We describe the reduction by using an example of a circuit in Fig. 7(a) and we omit the formal details. The circuit $B = (B_1, ..., B_6)$ is converted to the graph in Fig. 7(b). The vertices are ordered as $u_1 < v_1 < \cdots < u_6 < v_6$. This graph is not necessarily planar. Let U be the lfm vertex set to be computed. Then it can be easily checked that all u_j are chosen into U and that v_i is chosen into U if and only if value$(B_i) = t$.

The planarity is violated by arrows from u_j crossing the lines of the circuit. This difficulty can be resolved by replacing each such crossing like Fig. 7(c) with the graph in Fig. 7(d), where the vertices are suitably ordered. Then the choice of vertex v_i is the same as that of v_{ij} and there is a path from u_j to u_{ij} via either w_{ij} or v_{ij}. Since the planar circuits in [Go] are very regular, it is easy to compute how the arrows from the square vertices cross the lines of the circuit. The degree of the resulting graph is still 4.□

A *forest* is a collection of disjoint rooted trees. This problem is easily seen to be P-complete since the property *forest* is hereditary [M1]. Therefore we pay attention to the consistency and the vertex degree. It is straightforward to check that the reduction in the proof of Theorem 9 is also valid for the lfm forest problem.

Corollary 10. *The lfm forest problem for topologically sorted planar dags with degree 4 is P-complete.*

The following result asserts that the degree bound 4 in Corollary 8 is optimal.

Theorem 11. *The lfm forest problem restricted to topologically sorted dags with degree at most 3 is in* NC^2.

Proof. We give a sketch of the algorithm. Given a topologically sorted dag $G = (V, A)$, let V_d be the set of the vertices with indegree d for $d = 0, ..., 3$. Let U denote the lfm subset that forms a forest. The following three facts can be easily observed.

(1) All vertices in $V_0 \cup V_1$ can be chosen into U.

(2) The graph obtained by reversing the arrows of the induced subgraph of V_2 is a forest.

(3) A vertex in V_3 can be chosen into U if and only if it is adjacent to at most one chosen vertex.

For each rooted tree T in the forest obtained from V_2, we associate it with a circuit C_T with an operation $\neg(x \wedge y)$ as shown in Fig. 8. Then we can see that a vertex in T can be chosen into U if and only if the value of the corresponding gate is t. Fortunately, the evaluation of such tree-like circuits can be done in NC^2. It is not hard to see that all other necessary computaitons can be also done in NC^2.□

For dags with degree 3 which are not topologically sorted, the problem turns to be P-complete although the lfm forest problem for undirected graphs with degree 3 is not known to be in NC^2 [M1].

Theorem 12. *The lfm forest problem for planar dags with degree 3 is P-complete.*

Proof. We give a reduciton from the planar circuit value problem. We describe how the gates for $f, \neg x$ and $x \wedge y$ can be simulated. We can assume that the fanout of the gates for f and $\neg x$ (resp. $x \wedge y$) is at most two (resp. one). The truth values are simulated by the graph in Fig. 9(a). The order on vertices follows the alphabetical order. When the vertex c is not chosen (resp. chosen), it represents f (resp. t). A gate for $\neg x$ with fanout 2 is simulated by the graph in Fig. 9(b), where (a, b, c) is the input and (c, d_i, e_i) $(i = 1, 2)$ are the outputs. A gate for $x \wedge y$ is simulated by the graph in Fig. 9(c) with the inputs (a_i, b_i, c_i) $(i = 1, 2)$ and the output (d, e, f).□

References

[AM] Anderson, R. and Mayr, E.W., Parallelism and the maximal path problem, Inf. Process. Lett. **24** (1987) 121-124.

[Be] Berge, C., Graphes et hypergraphes, Dunod, 1970.

[GJT] Garey, M.R., Johnson, D.S. and Tarjan, R.E., The planar Hamiltonian circuit problem is NP-complete, SIAM J. Comput. **5** (1976) 704-714.

[Go] Goldschlager, L.M., The monotone and planar circuit value problems are log space complete for P, SIGACT News **9** (1977) 25-29.

[LY] Lewis, J.M. and Yannakakis, M., The node deletion problems for hereditary properties is NP-complete, J. Comput. System Sci. **20** (1980) 219-230.

[Ma] Martel, C.U., Lower bounds on parallel algorithms for finding the first maximal independent set, Inf. Process. Lett. **22** (1986) 81-85.

[M1] Miyano, S., The lexicographically first maximal subgraph problems: P-completeness and NC algorithms, Proc. 14th ICALP (LNCS **267**)(1987) 425-434.

[M2] Miyano, S., A parallelizable lexicographically first maximal edge-induced subgraph problem, Inf. Process. Lett. **29** (1988) 75-78.

[Pa] Papadimitriou, C.H., On the complexity of unique solution, J. Assoc. Comput. Mach. **31** (1984) 392-400.

[Wa] Wagner, K.W., More complicated questions about maxima and minima, and some closure of NP, Proc. 13th ICALP (LNCS **226**)(1986) 434-443.

[Y1] Yannakakis, M., The effect of a connectivity requirement on the complexity of maximum subgraph problems, J. Assoc. Comput. Mach. **26** (1979) 618-630.

[Y2] Yannakakis, M., Node-deletion problems on bipartite graphs, SIAM J. Comput. **10** (1981) 310-327.

PROOF SYSTEM FOR WEAKEST PRESPECIFICATION AND ITS APPLICATIONS

Ewa Orlowska
Polish Academy of Sciences
P.O.Box 22, 00-901 Warsaw, Poland

1. Introduction

The purpose of the present paper is to define a logic based on calculus of binary relations (Tarski 1941) augmented with operations of weakest prespecification and weakest postspecification introduced in Hoare and He Jifeng (1986), to give a deduction method for the logic, and to discuss applications of the logic. Formulas of the logic are intended to represent statements of the form: a pair of objects is a member of a relation. A true formula corresponding to a relation R represents the fact that R coincides with universal relation. Entailment of the form: if relations $R_1,\dots,R_n$ are universal, then a relation R is universal, can also be expressed in the language. Formulas of the language enable us to express several facts which can be formulated in terms of equality or inclusion of relations. The logic is an extension of the system introduced in Orlowska (1986) and investigated in Buszkowski and Orlowska (1986a,b).

2. Weakest prespecification

We consider relational calculus with standard relational operations of union ($\cup$), intersection ($\cap$), complement ($-$), composition (o), and converse ($^{-1}$). Let us consider a family of binary relations in a set OB of objects. Let $1=OB\times OB$ be the universal relation, let 0 be the empty relation, and $I=\{(s,s):s\in OB\}$ be the identity in OB.

Proposition 2.1

(a) $P\subseteq Q$ iff $-P\cup Q=1$

(b) $P=Q$ iff $(-P\cup Q)\cap(-Q\cup P)=1$

(c) $P\neq 1$ iff $1o(-P)o1=1$.

From condition 2.1(c) we obtain the following important lemma.

Proposition 2.2

The following conditions are equivalent:

(a) $R_1=1,\dots,R_n=1$ imply $R=1$

(b) $1o(-(R_1\cap\dots\cap R_n))o1\cup R=1$.

Proposition 2.2 will enable us to use the logic of relations to prove both validity and entailment of relational expressions.

Let relations $Q\subseteq Y\times Z$ and $R\subseteq X\times Z$ be given. The weakest prespecification

$Q\backslash R$ of Q to achieve R is the greatest relation $P \subseteq X \times Y$ such that $P \circ Q \subseteq R$.

Proposition 2.3

The following conditions are equivalent:

(a) $Q\backslash R$ is the weakest prespecification of Q to achieve R

(b) $(x,y) \in Q\backslash R$ iff $(y,z) \in Q$ implies $(x,z) \in R$ for all z.

The following proposition says how the operation of weakest prespecification is related to the standard relational operations.

Proposition 2.4

(a) $(P \cup Q)\backslash R = (P\backslash Q) \cap (Q\backslash R)$

(b) $(Q\backslash R) \cup (Q\backslash S) \subseteq Q\backslash (R \cup S)$

(c) $Q\backslash (R \cap S) = (Q\backslash R) \cap (Q\backslash S)$

(d) $(P\backslash R) \cup (Q\backslash R) \subseteq (P \cap Q)\backslash R$

(e) $(P \circ Q)\backslash R = P\backslash (Q\backslash R)$

(f) $-(Q\backslash R) = (-R\backslash -Q)\backslash -I$

(g) $((P \circ 1) \cap Q)\backslash R = (P\backslash 0) \cup (Q\backslash R)$

(h) $Q^{-1} = -Q\backslash -I$

(i) $Q\backslash R = -((-R) \circ Q^{-1})$.

Proposition 2.5

(a) $P \circ Q \subseteq R$ iff $P \subseteq Q\backslash R$

(b) $R \subseteq S$ implies $Q\backslash R \subseteq Q\backslash S$

(c) $P \subseteq Q$ implies $Q\backslash R \subseteq P\backslash R$

(d) $P \subseteq Q$ iff $-P\backslash -I \subseteq -Q\backslash -I$

(e) $Q\backslash R \subseteq R \circ (-Q\backslash -I) \cup Q\backslash 0$

(f) If $Q \circ (-I) \subseteq -Q$, then $Q\backslash R = R \circ (-Q\backslash -I) \cup Q\backslash 0$

(g) $0\backslash R = 1$, $Q\backslash 1 = 1$, $1\backslash 0 = 0$, $I\backslash R = R$.

3. Weakest postspecification

Let relations $P \subseteq X \times Y$ and $R \subseteq X \times Z$ be given. The weakest postspecification R/P of P to achieve R is the greatest relation $Q \subseteq Y \times Z$ such that $P \circ Q \subseteq R$.

Proposition 3.1

The following conditions are equivalent:

(a) R/P is the weakest postspecification of P to achieve R

(b) $(y,z) \in R/P$ iff $(x,y) \in P$ implies $(x,z) \in R$ for all x.

Proposition 3.2

(a) $R/(P \cup Q) = (R/P) \cap (R/Q)$

(b) $(R \cap S)/P = (R/P) \cap (S/P)$

(c) $(R/P) \cup (S/P) \subseteq (R \cup S)/P$

(d) $(R/P) \cup (R/Q) \subseteq R/(P \cap Q)$

(e) $R/(P \circ Q) = (R/P)/Q$

(f) $R/P = (R\backslash -I)\backslash (P\backslash -I)$

(g) $R/P = -(P^{-1} \circ (-R))$.

Proposition 3.3

(a) $P \circ Q \subseteq R$ iff $Q \subseteq R/P$

(b) $R \subseteq S$ implies $R/P \subseteq S/P$

(c) $P \subseteq Q$ implies $R/Q \subseteq R/P$
(d) $R/P \subseteq (-P\backslash -I) o R \cup (0/P)$.
(e) $R/0=1$, $1/P=1$, $0/1=0$, $R/I=R$.

4. Logic of relations

We define a formal language with expressions of the two kinds: relational expressions, interpreted as binary relations, and formulas, interpreted as schemes of sentences saying that a relation holds for a pair of objects. Expressions of the language are built up from symbols taken from the following pairwise disjoint sets:

VAR a set of object variables
CONREL a set of relational constants such that $1, I \in$ CONREL
$\{\cup, \cap, -, o, ^{-1}, \backslash, /\}$ the set of relational operations.

Set EREL of relational expressions is the smallest set including set CONREL of relational constants and closed with respect to relational operations. Set FORREL of formulas is the set of expressions of the form xPy for $x, y \in$ VAR and $P \in$ EREL.

We define semantics of the language by means of notions of model and satisfiability of formulas in a model. By model we mean a system of the form $M=(OB, \{r_P\}_{P \in CONREL}, m)$, where OB is a nonempty set of objects, for each $P \in$ CONREL r_P is a binary relation in set OB, and m is a meaning function providing interpretation of relational expressions. We assume that function m satisfies the following conditions:

$m(P)=r_P$ for any $P \in$ CONREL,
$m(1)=OB \times OB=1_M$, $m(I)=\{(s,s): s \in OB\}=I_M$,
$m(-P)=-m(P)$, $m(P^{-1})=(m(P))^{-1}$,
$m(P \cup Q)=m(P) \cup m(Q)$, $m(P \cap Q)=m(P) \cap m(Q)$, $m(PoQ)=m(P) o m(Q)$,
$m(Q\backslash R)=m(Q)\backslash m(R)$, $m(R/P)=m(R)/m(P)$.

By valuation we mean a function $v: VAR \rightarrow OB$ which assigns objects to object variables. We say that in model M valuation v satisfies formula xPy whenever objects v(x) and v(y) stand in relation m(P):

M,v sat xPy iff $(v(x),v(y)) \in m(P)$.

We say that a formula F is true in a model M ($\models_M F$) iff M,v sat F for all valuations v. A formula F is valid iff it is true in all models. We say that formulas $F_1, \ldots, F_n$ imply a formula F iff for any model M if $F_1, \ldots, F_n$ are true in M then F is true in M.

Below are listed examples of properties expressible in the language.

Proposition 4.1

(a) $\models_M xPy$ iff $m(P)=1_M$
(b) $\models_M x(1o-Po1)y$ iff $m(P) \neq 1_M$
(c) $\models_M x(-P \cup R)y$ iff $m(P) \subseteq m(R)$
(d) $\models_M x((-P \cup R) \cap (-R \cup P))y$ iff $m(P)=m(R)$
(e) $\models_M x(1o(-(R_1 \cap \ldots \cap R_n))o1 \cup R)y$ iff $m(R_1)=1_M, \ldots, m(R_n)=1_M$ imply $m(R)=1_M$.

Proposition 4.2

(a) $\models_M x(-I\cup P)y$ iff m(P) is reflexive

(b) $\models_M x(-(I\cap P))y$ iff m(P) is irreflexive

(c) $\models_M x(-P\cup P^{-1})y$ iff m(P) is symmetric

(d) $\models_M x(-P\cup -(P^{-1})\cup I)y$ iff m(P) is antysymmetric

(e) $\models_M x(-(P\circ P)\cup P)y$ iff m(P) is transitive

(f) $\models_M x(P\cup P^{-1}\cup I)y$ iff m(P) is connective

(g) $\models_M x(P\circ 1)y$ iff m(P) is a total relation

(h) $\models_M x(-(P^{-1}\circ P)\cup I)y$ iff m(P) is a function.

Proposition 4.3

(a) $\models_M x(1\circ(I\cap -P)\circ 1\cup -R\cup P\circ R)y$ iff m(P) reflexive implies $m(R)\subseteq m(P)\circ m(R)$

(b) $\models_M x(1\circ(I\cap R)\circ 1\cup -(R/1))y$ iff m(R) irreflexive implies $m(R)/1_M=0$.

5. Deduction system

In the present section we define deduction rules for the presented language. We follow the method developed in Rasiowa and Sikorski (1963) for the classical predicate calculus. The rules apply to finite sequences of formulas, and they enable us to decompose formulas in a sequence into some simpler formulas. As a result of decomposition we obtain a single sequence or a pair of sequences. We admit the following rules:

$(\cup)\quad \dfrac{K,\ x(P\cup Q)y,\ H}{K,\ xPy,\ xQy,\ H}$ $\qquad (-\cup)\quad \dfrac{K,\ x(-(P\cup Q))y,\ H}{K,\ x(-P)y,\ H \qquad K,\ x(-Q)y,\ H}$

$(\cap)\quad \dfrac{K,\ x(P\cap Q)y,\ H}{K,\ xPy,\ H \qquad K,\ xQy,\ H}$ $\qquad (-\cap)\quad \dfrac{K,\ x(-(P\cap Q))y,\ H}{K,\ x(-P)y,\ x(-Q)y,\ H}$

$(--)\quad \dfrac{K,\ x(--P)y,\ H}{K,\ xPy,\ H}$

$(^{-1})\quad \dfrac{K,\ xP^{-1}y,\ H}{K,\ yPx,\ H}$ $\qquad (-^{-1})\quad \dfrac{K,\ x(-(P^{-1}))y,\ H}{K,\ y(-P)x,\ H}$

$(\circ)\quad \dfrac{K,\ x(P\circ Q)y,\ H}{K,\ xPz,\ H,\ x(P\circ Q)y \qquad K,\ zQy,\ H,\ x(P\circ Q)y}$

where z is an arbitrary variable

$(-\circ)\quad \dfrac{K,\ x(-(P\circ Q))y,\ H}{K,\ x(-P)z,\ z(-Q)y,\ H}$

where z is a variable which does not appear in any formula above the line

(\\) $$\frac{K,\ xQ\backslash Ry,\ H}{K,\ y(-Q)z,\ xRz,\ H}$$
where z is a variable which does not appear in any formula above the line

(-\\) $$\frac{K,\ x(-(Q\backslash R))y,\ H}{K,\ yQz,\ H,\ x(-(Q\backslash R))y \qquad K,\ x(-R)z,\ H,\ x(-Q\backslash R))y}$$
where z is an arbitrary variable

(/) $$\frac{K,\ xR/Py,\ H}{K,\ z(-P)x,\ zRy,\ H}$$
where z is a variable which does not appear in any formula above the line

(-/) $$\frac{K,\ x(-(R/P))y,\ H}{K,\ zPx,\ H,\ x(-(R/P))y \qquad K,\ z(-R)y,\ H,\ x(-(R/P))y}$$
where z is an arbitrary variable

(symI) $$\frac{K,\ xIy,\ H}{K,\ yIx,\ xIy,\ H}$$

(tranI) $$\frac{K,\ xIy,\ H}{K,\ xIz,\ xIy,\ H \qquad K,\ zIy,\ xIy,\ H}$$
where z is an arbitrary variable

In all the above rules K and H denote finite or empty sequences of formulas.

A formula is said to be indecomposable if it is of the form xPy or x(-P)y for some P∈CONREL and x,y∈VAR. A sequence of formulas is indecomposable if every its element is an indecomposable formula. Otherwise the sequence is said to be decomposable. A sequence of formulas is said to be fundamental if it contains formulas of at least one of the following forms:

(f1) xPy, x(-P)y for some P∈EREL and some x,y∈VAR

(f2) x1y for some x,y∈VAR

(f3) xIx for some x∈VAR.

A sequence K of formulas is said to be valid if for every model M and for every valuation v there is a formula F occurring in K such that M,v sat F.

Proposition 5.1

(a) Every fundamental sequence is valid

(b) Empty sequence is no valid.

Proposition 5.2

(a) If a sequence K is decomposed into a sequence H by means of application of one of the rules (∪),(-∩),(-o),(--),($^{-1}$),($-^{-1}$), (symI),(/),(\), then K is valid iff H is valid

(b) If a sequence K is decomposed into a pair H,H' of sequences by means of application of one of the rules (-∪),(∩),(o),(-/), (-\),(tranI), then K is valid iff both H and H' are valid.

Proofs of these lemmas can be easily obtained from definition of validity, properties of relational operations, reflexivity, symmetry, and transitivity of I.

6. Completeness

Given a formula of the form xPy, where P is a compound relational expression, we can decompose it by successive application of the rules. In the process of decomposition we form a tree whose vertices consist of finite sequences of formulas. We assume that sequences are read from left to right, and the first formula with a compound relational expression is a basis of decomposition. Each vertex of the decomposition tree has at most two successors. We stop decomposing formulas in a vertex after obtaining a fundamental or indecomposable sequence. Sequences satisfying these conditions are called end sequences of the tree. An immediate consequence of propositions 5.1 and 5.2 is the following lemma.

Proposition 6.1
If the decomposition tree of a formula F is finite, then F is valid iff all the end sequences in the tree are fundamental.

Proposition 6.2
If the decomposition tree of a formula F is infinite, then F is not valid.

The proof is similar to that presented in Rasiowa and Sikorski (1963) for the predicate logic. Propositions 6.1 and 6.2 lead to the following completeness theorem.

Proposition 6.3
The following conditions are equivalent:

(a) A formula F is valid

(b) The decomposition tree of F is finite and all its end sequences are fundamental.

Proposition 6.4
(a) The logic of relations does not possess the finite model property

(b) The validity problem for the logic of relations is undecidable.

We say that a relational expression P is positive (negative) if every occurrence of operation o in P is within the scope of an even (odd) number of occurrences of complement operation -, and every occurrence of operations / and \ is within the scope of an odd (even) number of occurrences of -.

Proposition 6.5
The class of formulas xPy such that P is a positive or negative relational expression possesses the finite model property.

Proofs of these propositions can be found in Buszkowski and Orlowska (1986b).

In the following sections we discuss some applications of the relational logic.

7. Proving database dependencies

Let a relational database model be given (Codd 1970), and a relation R from the model. For a subset X of the set AT of attributes in R we consider indiscernibility relation ind(X) in the set T of all the tuples of R. A pair (t,t') of tuples is a member of ind(X) iff the tuples agree in all the columns labelled by the attributes from X. It was shown in Orlowska (1987) that several database dependencies can be expressed in terms of inclusion of relations generated be indiscermibility relations. For example: For $X,Y \subseteq AT$ the functional dependency $X \to Y$ holds iff $ind(X) \subseteq ind(Y)$; The multivalued dependency $X \to\to Y$ holds iff $ind(X) \subseteq ind(X \cup Y) o ind(AT-(X \cup Y))$; The decomposition (X,Y) holds iff $ind(X \cap Y) \subseteq ind(X) o ind(Y)$. Relational representation of dependencies enables us to use the proof system of logic LREL to prove them. The detailed presentation of the subject can be found in Buszkowski and Orlowska (1986b).

8. Proving contractions and equivalence of attributes in information systems

Let an information system (Pawlak 1981) $S=(OB,AT,\{VAL_a\}_{a \in AT},f)$ be given, where OB is a nonempty set of objects, AT is a nonempty set of attributes, for each $a \in AT$ set VAL_a consists of values of attribute a, and f: $OB \times AT \to VAL = \bigcup\{VAL_a : a \in AT\}$ is an information function such that $f(o,a) \in VAL_a$ for any $a \in AT$. We define a family of indiscernibility relations $ind(A) \subseteq OB \times OB$ for $A \subseteq AT$:

$(o,o') \in ind(A)$ iff $f(o,a)=f(o',a)$ for all $a \in A$, $ind(\emptyset)=OB \times OB$.

Observe that $ind(A \cup B)=ind(A) \cap ind(B)$. We can treat attributes as binary relations $a \subseteq OB \times VAL_a$ such that $(o,v) \in a$ iff $f(o,a)=v$. For any $a \in AT$ indiscernibility relation ind(a) equals $a o a^{-1}$.

We say that attribute b is a contraction of attribute a (Iwinski 1987) iff there is a function $h: VAL_a \to VAL_b$ such that aoh=b. Attributes a and b are equivalent iff ind(a)=ind(b). Clearly, both contractions and equivalences of attributes can be proved in logic LREL.

9. Proving control specifications.

Let a universe ST of states of a certain system be given. By a control of the system we mean a binary relation in set ST. A pair (s,s') of states is a member of control S whenever the control S transforms state s into state s'. For example, if states are described in terms of values of some parameters, then elements of control relations are interpreted as pieces of information of the form: if parameters $a_1,\ldots,a_n$ assume values $v_1,\ldots,v_n$, respectively, then after applying control S parameters $b_1,\ldots,b_m$ assume values $u_1,\ldots,u_m$, respectively.

The following problem was posed by Mrozek (Mrozek 1986). Given an actual control S_a and a goal control S_g, find a control R such that (*)$RoS_a=S_g$. Clearly, we can use the proof system of LREL to check whether a relation R satisfies condition (*). It seems that some heuristics could be obtained of solving relational equation (*) by examining the decomposition tree of the formula $x((-S_a\cup S_g)\cap(-S_g\cup S_a))y$ corresponding to equality $S_a=S_g$.

10. Proving theorems of modal logics

Logic LREL can be used as a metasystem for multimodal logics. Consider a propositional modal language with family [R] of necessity operators, where R is an accessibility relation expression constructed with accessibility relation constants by means of relational operations $-,\cup,\cap,o,^{-1}$, and with classical propositional operations of negation ($\neg$), disjunction ($\vee$), conjunction ($\wedge$), implication ($\rightarrow$). Semantics of the modal language is defined in the usual way. Classical operations are interpreted in the standard way, and formula [R]F is satisfied in model M by state s iff for any state s' if $(s,s')\in R$ then F is satisfied in M by s'. A formula F is true in M iff it is satisfied by all the states from M. A formula F is satisfiable iff there are a model M and a state s such that F is satisfied by s in M. A formula F is unsatisfiable iff if is not satisfiable. A formula F is valid iff it is true in all models.

We translate the modal language into relational language as follows. Let a one-to-one mapping t' be given which assigns relational constants to accessibility relation constants and propositional variables, and preserves constants 1 and I. We define translation function t which assigns relational expressions to accessibility relation expressions and modal formulas:

$t(R)=t'(R)$ for any accessibility relation constant R,

$t(-R)=-t(R)$, $t(R^{-1})=t(R)^{-1}$,

$t(R\cup S)=t(R)\cup t(S)$, $t(R\cap S)=t(R)\cap t(S)$, $t(RoS)=t(R)ot(S)$,

$t(p)=t'(p)o1$ for any propositional variable p,

$t(\neg F)=-t(F)$,

$t(F\vee G)=t(F)\cup t(G)$, $t(F\wedge G)=t(F)\cap t(G)$, $t(F\rightarrow G)=t(\neg F\vee G)$,

$t([R]F)=t(F)/t(R)^{-1}$.

The following theorem provides semantic relationship between formulas of logic LREL and modal formulas.

Proposition 10.1

For any model M of modal logic there is a model M' of logic LREL such that a modal formula F is true in M iff $xt(F)y$ is true in M'.

Proposition 10.2

(a) A modal formula F is valid iff xt(F)y is valid in LREL

(b) A modal formula F is unsatisfiable iff x(-t(F))y is valid

(c) $F_1,\ldots,F_n$ imply F in modal logic iff $x(1o-(t(F_1)\cap\ldots\cap t(F_n))o1\cup t(F))y$ is valid in LREL.

Proofs of the above theorems can be found in Orlowska (1987).

References

[1] Buszkowski,W. and Orlowska,E. (1986a) On the logic of database dependencies. Bulletin of the PAS 34, Mathematics, 345-354.

[2] Buszkowski,W. and Orlowska,E. (1986b) Relational calculus and data dependencies. ICS PAS Reports 578, Warsaw.

[3] Codd,E.F. (1970) A relational model for large shared data banks. Communications of ACM 13, 377-387.

[4] Hoare,C.A.R. and He Jifeng (1986) The weakest prespecification. Fundamenta Informaticae IX, Part I 51-84, Part II 217-252.

[5] Iwinski,T. (1987) Contraction of attributes. Bulletin of the PAS, Mathematics, to appear.

[6] Mrozek,A. (1986) private communication.

[7] Orlowska,E. (1984) Reasoning about database constraints. ICS PAS Reports 543, Warsaw.

[8] Orlowska,E. (1987) Algebraic approach to database constraints. Fundamenta Informaticae X, 57-68.

[9] Orlowska,E. (1987) Relational interpretation of modal logics. Bulletin of the Section of Logic, to appear.

[10] Pawlak,Z. (1981) Information systems-theoretical foundations. Information Systems 6, 205-218.

[11] Rasiowa,H. and Sikorski,R. (1963) Mathematics of metamathematics. Polish Scientific Publishers, Warsaw.

[12] Tarski,A. (1941) On the calculus of relations. Journal of Symbolic Logic 6, 73-89.

ON COMPLEXITY OF COUNTING

Marek Piotrów*
Institute of Computer Science, University of Wrocław
Przesmyckiego 20, 51-151 Wrocław, Poland

ABSTRACT. Let $l,u:\mathbb{N}\to\mathbb{N}$, $l<u$. We give a full characterization of intervals $[l,u]$ such that a polynomial-time ATM of a constant numer of alternations can verify the number of words of a given length and in a given (as its oracle) set A, provided that A's density function is in $[l,u]$. We prove also a new lower bound on the approximate counting: there is a recursive set A whose elements cannot be approximate counted in $\Sigma_2^{p,A} \cup \Pi_2^{p,A}$.

1. INTRODUCTION AND OVERVIEW OF THE RESULTS

In many combinatorial problems we have to count the number of objects having a certain property. Abstractly, this can be described as a problem of computing, for a given set $A\subseteq\Sigma^*$, $\Sigma = \{0,1\}$, the values of a function $c_A(n) = |A^n|$, where $A^n = A\cap\Sigma^n$. The corresponding decision problem is to recognize a language $\mathrm{COUNT}(A) = \{1^n\#l \mid l = c_A(n)\}$.

Let M^A denote a Turing machine M with an associated oracle A. Let $l,u:\mathbb{N}\to\mathbb{N}$ be such that $l(n) < u(n) \le 2^n$, for all $n\in\mathbb{N}$. We say that M solves the counting problem in an interval $[l,u]$ if for all $A\subseteq\Sigma^*$:

$$\forall n\in\mathbb{N}(l(n) \le c_A(n) \le u(n)) \quad \text{implies} \quad \mathrm{COUNT}(A) = L(M^A).$$

For $l(n) = 0$ and $u(n) = 2^n$, we say simply that M solves the counting problem. We consider also a slightly simplified problem, namely, a p modulo-counting problem, where $\mathrm{COUNT}_p(A) = \{1^n\#l \mid l = c_A(n) \bmod p\}$ replaces $\mathrm{COUNT}(A)$.

It is clear that a deterministic TM is unlikely to solve such a problem much more faster than in exponential time. But if we consider

---

* This research was supported by the grant RP.I.09 from the Institute of Informatics, University of Warsaw and the grant CPBP 01.01 from the Institute of Mathematics, Polish Academy of Science.

alternating TMs of a constant number of alternations (Σ_{const}ATMs, in short), one might expect that this can be done in polynomial time.

Several authors have investigated the complexity of counting (c.f. [2,6,10]). Balcazar *et al* [2] proved that sparse sets A can be enumerated in the class $\Delta_2^{p,A}$. A certain example of modulo-counting problems, namely, the PARITY problem, has been used to find an oracle that separates the polynomial-time hierarchy from PSPACE. Furst, Saxe and Sipser [3] have reduced the problem of constructing such an oracle to the problem of proving an exponential superpolylog lower bound on the size of fixed depth, unbounded fan-in Boolean circuits that compute PARITY. They gave a superpolynomial lower bound, then Aitai [1] improved it to $\Omega(n^{\log n})$, but Yao [11] was the first whose lower bound was sufficient to get the result.

Restating the result in our terms: it has been proved that none of polynomial-time Σ_{const}-ATMs can solve the counting problem. In [7], we have conjectured that such machines can only solve the problem in intervals of the form $[0,q]$, where q is a polynomial, provided that we consider only sets A such that $|A^n|\le 2^{n-1}$. We have proved there that for each $k\ge 1$ and for each $u(n)\le 2^{n-1}$ there is a Σ_{2k+2}-ATM that can solve the counting problem in the interval $[0,u]$ in time $O(n+u^{1/k}(n)\cdot \log u(n))$. In other words, using a constant number of alternation we can reduce polynomially the amount of time required to solve the counting problem. An interesting question remains whether a superpolynomial reduction is possible.

In Section 2, we prove firstly that for each interval $[0,q]$, where q is a polynomial, there exists a D^p-machine M that solves the counting decision problem in this interval. Recall that D^p-machine M is a pair (N_1,N_2), where N_1 and N_2 are NP-machines and $L(M) = L(N_1)-L(N_2)$ (c.f. [5]). Then, using the method of Furst *et al* [3], we reduce the question about a superpolynomial reduction to the question about the existance of "small" fixed depth, unbounded fan-in Boolean circuits that compute, so called, pseudo-majority functions.

In Section 3, we follow the method of Hastad [4] to establish an exponential lower bound on the size of such circuits, giving in this way negative answer to that question and proving our conjecture of [7]. To be more precise, none of polynomial-time Σ_{const}-ATMs can solve a modulo-counting problem in any interval that contains a function f

such that $\min(f(n), 2^n - f(n))$ is superpolynomial (i.e. not bounded by a polynomial).

Since exact counting is not feasible, one might look for some approximation of $c_A(n)$. Let us recall that a function $g:\mathbb{N}\to\mathbb{N}$ approximates a function $f:\mathbb{N}\to\mathbb{N}$ within a factor $r:\mathbb{N}\to(1,+\infty)$ if for any $n\in\mathbb{N}$:

$$f(n)/r(n) \le g(n) \le f(n)\cdot r(n).$$

Stockmeyer [9] has proved that for each $\varepsilon, d>0$ there is a Δ_3^p-machine M that, for each A, can compute an approximation of $c_A(n)$ within a factor $r(n) = 1+\varepsilon n^{-d}$ and then he has shown that Δ_3^p cannot be replaced by Δ_2^p in this statement. Recall that a Δ_3^p-machine is a pair (D,N), where D (resp. N) is a polynomial-time deterministic TM (resp. Σ_2-ATM) and $M^A = D^{L(N^A)}$. To compute the approximation D makes $O(\log n)$ oracle queries. In Section 4, we improve this lower bound. First, one can easily observe that, in the case of proving lower bounds, we can replace the problem of computing $g(x)$ by a decision problem DP, on condition that for each instance I of DP there is a word x such that x can be easily computed from I and $g(x)$ suffices to decide I. Our decision problem is to check whether $c_A(n)/r(n) \le l \le c_A(n)\cdot r(n)$ holds, for a fixed factor $r:\mathbb{N}\to(1,+\infty)$, for all $A\subseteq\Sigma^*$ and for all inputs $1^n\#l$ such that:

$$l \notin [c_A(n)/r^{3/2}(n), c_A(n)/r^{1/2}(n)) \cup (c_A(n)r^{1/2}(n), c_A(n)r^{3/2}(n)].$$

We prove that for each polynomial factor r there is a recursive set A such that none of Σ_2^p-machines and Π_2^p-machines can solve this decision problem for A. It is also proved that our problem is a proper one, that is, it can be easily solved provided that we can compute an approximation of $c_A(n)$ within a factor $r^{1/2}$.

At the end of this section, let us notice that a language $\mathrm{lecount}(A) = \{1^n\#l \mid l \le c_A(n)\}$ can be used as an oracle be a deterministic TM that, by a binary search, computes values of $c_A(n)$. Since

$$1^n\#l \in \mathrm{lecount}(A) \text{ if and only if } \exists k\le 2^n (1^n\#(l+k) \in \mathrm{COUNT}(A)),$$

the results of this paper can be easily translate to the case of lecount(A) languages.

2. COUNTING IN THE POLYNOMIAL HIERARCHY

THEOREM 2.1 *For any polynomial q there is a D-machine M such that , for all* $A \subseteq \Sigma^*$ *with*

(i) $$\min(c_A(n), 2^n - c_A(n)) \le q(n),$$

M^A *accepts* COUNT(A).

Proof. Let n_0 be a constant such that for all $n \ge n_0$ we have $q(n) < 2^{n-1}$. Let A be such that (i) holds. Clearly, it suffices to prove that

$$C(A) = COUNT(A) \cap \{1^n\#l \mid n \ge n_0\}$$

is in the class D^A since COUNT(A)-C(A) is a P^A-language and D^A is clesed under sumation with P^A-languages. Let

$$LE(A) = \{1^n\#l \mid n \ge n_0 \wedge [(l \le q(n) \wedge l \le c_A(n)) \vee (l \ge 2^n - q(n) \wedge l \ge c_A(n))]\}$$

$$LT(A) = \{1^n\#l \mid (l > q(n) \text{ or } l < c_A(n)) \text{ and } (l < 2^n - q(n) \text{ or } l > c_A(n))\}.$$

It is easy to see that $C(A) = LE(A) - LT(A)$.

Both $LE(A)$ and $LT(A)$ are $NP(A)$-languages. To prove this we describe a nondeterministic TM M that accept $LT(A)$ ($LE(A)$ is accepted in a similiar way). Given an input $1^n\#l$, M performs the following algorithm:

(1) if $l > q(n)$ then go to (3);
(2) guess l+1 words of length n and verify whether all of them belong to A; if not, REJECT otherwise go to (3);
(3) if $l < 2^n - q(n)$ then ACCEPT otherwise guess $2^n - l + 1$ words of length n and ACCEPT if and only if none of them belongs to A.

Obviously, M spends a polynomial amount of time performing this algorithm.

□

We say that $f\colon \Sigma^n \to \Sigma$ is an n-ary pseudo-majority (pM, for short) function if $f(x) = 0$ for all x containning exactly $[n/2]-1$ ones, $f(x) = 1$ for all x containning exactly $[n/2]$ ones and for other x's the value of $f(n)$ can be arbitrary.

We consider unbounded fan-in Boolean circuits. Let $\{x_1, x_2, \ldots, x_n\}$ be a set of input variables, let $\bar{x}_k$ denote the negation of x_k and let 0 and 1 be constant circuits. Σ_0-circuits and Π_0-circuits are elements of $\{x_1,\dots,x_n,\bar{x}_1,\dots,\bar{x}_n,0,1\}$. A Σ_{i+1}-circuit (resp. a Π_{i+1}-circuit) is a nonempty set of Π_i-circuits (resp. Σ_i-circuits). The set is also called as OR gate (resp. AND gate) and the number of its elements is called fan-in. i is the depth of a $\Sigma_i(\Pi_i)$-circuit.

We say that a depth k circuit c is a subcircuit of a depth i circuit C ($k < i$) if $c \in C$ or there is a circuit $C' \in C$ such that c is a subcircuit of C'. The size of a circuit is the total number of its different subcircuits. In a standard way, n variable circuits compute functions from Σ^n into Σ.

LEMMA 2.2. *Let f: $\mathbb{N} \to \mathbb{N}$ be a function such that $f(n) \le 2^n$ and let $g(n) = \min(f(n), 2^n - f(n)+1)$. Let M be a polynomial time Σ_i-ATM and suppose that for some $n,k \in \mathbb{N}$, $l = f(n) \bmod k$, and all sets A^n such that*

$$f(n)-1 \le |A^n| \le f(n),$$

$1^n\#l$ is accepted by M^A if and only if $|A^n| = l \bmod k$. Then for some polynomial $p(n)$ (depending on M) there exists a depth $i+1$, $2^{p(n)}$-size circuit that computes a $2g(n)$-ary pseudo-majority function.

Proof (sketch). Repeating the construction of [3], we can obtain from M a depth $i+1$, $2^{p(n)}$-size circuit of 2^n variables that gives the output value 0 for all inputs containning exactly $f(n)-1$ ones and the value 1 for all inputs containning exactly $f(n)$ ones.

If $f(n) \le 2^{n-1}$ (that is, if $g(n) = f(n)$) then, by replacing $2^n - 2f(n)$ variables with 0, we obtain a circuit computing a $2g(n)$-ary pM function. If $f(n) > 2^{n-1}$ then, by replacing $2f(n)-2^n-2$ variables with 1 and negating the circuit (that is, by replacing x_k with $\bar{x}_k$, 0 with 1, OR with AND and vice versa), we obtain a circuit of $2g(n) = 2(2^n-f(n)+1)$ variables to compute a pM function.

□

3. PSEUDO-MAJORITY LOWER BOUND

A restriction ρ of a set of variables $X = \{x_1,\dots,x_n\}$ is a assignment $X \to \{0,1,*\}$, where $\rho(x_i) = *$ means that x_i remains a variable. Applying ρ to a circuit G of variables X we obtain a simplified circuit $G_{|\rho}$ with the set $\{x_i \mid \rho(x_i) = *\}$ as input variables. Let the bottom fan-in of a circuit G be the maximum fan-in for any depth 1 subcircuit of G.

Let $0 < p < 1$ be a real number. We consider a probability distribution R_p that independently assigns, for each i, the probabilities:

$$Pr[\rho(x_i) = *] = p$$

$$Pr[\rho(x_i) = 0] = Pr[\rho(x_i) = 1] = (1-p)/2.$$

The following is the main theorem of this section. Its proof follows the ideas of the proof of the Hastad's theorem stating the the lower bound on the size of fixed depth, unbounded fan-in Boolean circuits computing the parity function and his comments concerning the majority function [4].

THEOREM 3.1. *Let* D_i $(i = 2,3,\ldots)$ *be a sequence of positive real numbers such that* $D_2 \le 1$ *and* $D_{k+1} \le D_k/(D_k+1)$, *for* $k \ge 2$. *Let*

$$p_k(n) = n^{-D_k}, \quad b_k(n) = \tfrac{1}{10}\, p_k^{-1}(n), \quad s_k(n) = 2^{b_k(n)},$$

and let $\mathbb{C}_k$ *be a set of depth* k *circuits G such that G contains* $\le s_k(n)$ *subcircuits of depth at least 2 and has bottom fan-in* $\le b_k(n)$. *Then for each* $k > 1$ *there exist a constant* n_k *such that, for all* $n > n_k$, *no circuit from* $\mathbb{C}_k$ *can compute an* n*-ary pseudo-majority function.*

Proof. We proceed by induction on k.

For $k = 2$ we only need to observe that n-ary pM function cannot be computed by a depth 2 circuit with bottom fan-in $\le \frac{1}{10}\, n$.

Suppose now that the statement is true for all depth k-1 circuits. Let $G_n \in \mathbb{C}_k$ compute an n-ary pM function. To arrive at a contradiction we shall show that for all sufficiently large n there exists a restriction ρ such that $G_{n|\rho}$ computes an m-ary pM function (for some $m > n_{k-1}$) and it can be converted into a circuit from $\mathbb{C}_{k-1}$.

We use a restriction ρ chosen at random from the distributin R_p, where $p = p_k(n)$. The restriction ρ we look for should fulfil the following:

(A) it assigns the same number of zeroes and ones, and at least $m = p_k(n)\circ n$ stars;

(B) every depth 2 subcircuit of $G_{n|\rho}$ can be reversed from an AND of ORs to an OR of ANDs (or from an OR of ANDs to an AND of ORs) with bottom fan-in still bounded by $b_{k-1}(m)$.

The same number of zeroes and ones guarantees that $G_{n|\rho}$ still computes an pM function. Now we are going to establish the probabilities at which (A) and (B) hold.

$$Pr(A) = \sum_{i=0}^{(n-np)/2} \frac{n!}{i!i!(n-2i)} p^{n-2i} \left(\frac{1-p}{2}\right)^{2i} = \sum_{i=0}^{(n-np)/2} \frac{\binom{2i}{i}}{2^{2i}} \binom{n}{2i} p^{n-2i}(1-p)^{2i} \geq$$

$$\geq \sum_{i=np/2}^{n/2} \frac{1}{2i} \binom{n}{2i} p^{2i}(1-p)^{n-2i} \geq \frac{1}{2n} \sum_{i=np}^{n} \binom{n}{i} p^{i}(1-p)^{n-i} \geq \frac{1}{6n}$$

The first inequality follows from the fact that $2i\binom{2i}{i} \geq 2^{2i}$, the second is true since the terms $\binom{n}{i}p^{i}(1-p)^{n-i}$ decrease for $i = np,\ldots,n$, and the last one holds for large n since the last sum approximates $\frac{1}{2}$.

To evaluate the probability of (B) we need the lemma of Hastad.

LEMMA 3.2 (Hastad) [4]. *Let* G *be an* n *variable AND of ORs (resp. OR of ANDs) all of size* $\leq t$ *and* ρ *be a random restriction from* R_p. *Then the probability that* $G_{|\rho}$ *cannot be written as an OR od ANDs (resp. AND of ORs) all of size* $\leq s$ *is bounded by* α^s, *where* $\alpha < 5pt$ *for sufficiently large* n, *provided* $p = p(n)$ *is* $o(1)$.

In our case $t = s = b_k(n)$ therefore $\alpha < 5p_k(n)\frac{1}{10}p_k^{-1}(n) = \frac{1}{2}$ and

$$1-Pr(B) \leq s_k(n)\cdot\alpha^{b_k(n)} = (2\alpha)^{b_k(n)},$$

$$Pr(A\cap B) \geq Pr(A) - (1-Pr(B)) = \frac{1}{6n} - (2\alpha)^{\frac{1}{10}n^{D_k}}.$$

The last expression is positive for sufficiently large n, thus the restriction exists. In $G_{n|\rho}$, we can merge depth 2 and 3 gates obtainning a depth k-1 circuit. It has at least m input variables, its bottom fan-in is bounded by

$$b_k(n) = \tfrac{1}{10}\, n^{D_k} \leq \tfrac{1}{10}\, n^{(1-D_k)D_{k-1}} = \tfrac{1}{10}\, m^{D_{k-1}} = b_{k-1}(m),$$

and the number of its depth 2 subcircuits is not greater than

$$s_k(n) = 2^{b_k(n)} \leq 2^{b_{k-1}(m)} = s_{k-1}(m).$$

So, for sufficiently large n, $G_{n|\rho} \in \mathbb{C}_{k-1}$ and it computes an m-ary pM function, for $m > n_{k-1}$, and this contradicts the induction hypothesis. □

COROLLARY 3.3. *For each $k > 1$ there exists a real constant $D > 0$ such that, all sufficiently large n, any depth k circuit of n variables which computes an pseudo-majority function must have its size at least 2^{n^D}.*

THEOREM 3.4. *Let $f:\mathbb{N}\to\mathbb{N}$ be such that $f(n) \le 2^n$, for all $n\in\mathbb{N}$, and $g(n) = \min(f(n),2^n-f(n))$ is superpolynomial. Then there exists a set $A\subseteq\Sigma^*$ with $f(n)-1 \le c_A(n) \le f(n)$ such that none of polynomial time Σ_{const}-ATMs can accept a language $\mathrm{COUNT}_k(A)$, for any $k > 1$.*

Proof (sketch). Note that, for any $D > 0$, $(2g)^D$ is also a superpolynomial function. Using this, Corollary 3.3 and Lemma 2.2, by a simply diagonalization over all polynomial time Σ_{const}-ATMs, we can get the result. □

It is easy to see that if f is computable then a recursive A can be obtain.

4. AN LOWER BOUND ON APPROXIMATE COUNTING

Let $r_1,r_2:\mathbb{N}\to\mathbb{N}$ be such that $r_1 > r_2$ and let $r = r_1/r_2$ be an approximation factor. We define a relation $Appr^r \subseteq \mathbb{N}^3$ as follows:

$$Appr^r(n,l,k) \text{ if and only if } k/r(n) \le l \le k\cdot r(n),$$

which can be read as l approximates k within a factor $r(n)$. It is obvious that $Appr^r$ is checkable in deterministic polynomial time, providing r_1 and r_2 are computable in P. We say that a function $g:\mathbb{N}\to\mathbb{N}$ approximates a function $f:\mathbb{N}\to\mathbb{N}$ within a factor r (c.f. [9]; in symbol $g\in ApprFun(f,r)$) if for all $n\in\mathbb{N}$, $Appr^r(n,g(n),f(n))$ holds.

We define $Q\subseteq\mathbb{N}^2$ to be an approximation relation of a function $f:\mathbb{N}\to\mathbb{N}$ and for a factor r (in symbol $Q\in ApprRel(f,r)$) if

$$(1)\quad Q(n,l) = \begin{cases} 1 & \text{if } l \in [f(n)/r^{1/2}(n),\ f(n)\cdot r^{1/2}(n)], \\ 0 & \text{if } l \notin [f(n)/r^{3/2}(n),\ f(n)\cdot r^{3/2}(n)], \\ \text{arbitrary} & \text{otherwise.} \end{cases}$$

This definition might at first look strange, but the main idea which leads to such a definition is that checking $Appr^r(n,l,f(n))$ on l placed closely to $f(n)/r(n)$ or $f(n)\cdot r(n)$ is nearly as difficult as computing the value of $f(n)$.

The first lemma states that a lower bound on $ApprFun(f,r)$ can be derived from a lower bound on $ApprRel(f,r)$.

LEMMA 4.1. *For every $g \in ApprFun(f,r^{1/2})$ the relation Q_g defined as $Q_g(n,l) \equiv Appr^r(n,l,g(n))$ is an element of $ApprRel(f,r)$.*

Proof. Obvious. □

We say that $L \subseteq \{1^n\#l \mid n,l\in\mathbb{N}\}$ is an approximate counting language of a set A and for a factor $r>1$ (in symbol $L\in APPROX(A,r)$) if, for some $Q \in ApprRel(c_A,r)$, $L = \{1^n\#l \mid Q(n.l)\}$.

The following is the main theorem of this section.

THEOREM 4.2. *There exists a recursive set A such that for any polynomial factor r we have*

$$APPROX(A,r) \cap (\Sigma_2^{p,A} \cup \Pi_2^{p,A}) = \emptyset.$$

To prove this we need two lemmas.

LEMMA 4.3. *Let $s: \mathbb{N}\text{->}\mathbb{N}$ be a superpolynomial function that for almost all n fulfils $s(n) < 2^{n/4}$. Let*

$$L(A) = \{x \mid c_A(|x|) > s(|x|)\}.$$

Then for any finite set $B\subseteq\Sigma^*$ and any $\Sigma_2^{p,()}$-machine M there exists an arbitrarily large number n and a set $D \subseteq \Sigma^n$ such that

$$(4)\qquad s(n)/2 \le |D| \le s(n) \quad \text{or} \quad |D| = s^2(n);$$

$$(5)\qquad L(B\cup D) \cap \Sigma^n \ne L(M^{B\cup D}) \cap \Sigma^n.$$

This is a crucial lemma of this section. Due to the space limitation its proof will appear in the full version of the paper.

LEMMA 4.4. *Let s be as in Lemma 4.3. Then there exists a recursive oracle A such that*

(11) $$\forall n\ c_A(n) \in [s(n)/2; s(n)] \cup \{0, s^2(n)\},$$

(12) $$L(A) \notin \Sigma_2^{p,A}.$$

Proof. Using Lemma 4.3 and a simply diagonalization. □

Proof of Theorem 4.2. Let $s(n) = n^{\log n}$ and let A be as in Lemma 4.4. Suppose that for some polynomial factor r there is a language $L \in APPROX(A,r) \cap (\Pi_2^{p,A} \cup \Sigma_2^{p,A})$. To arrive at a contradiction we shall describe a $\Pi_2^{p,A}$-predicate that defines $L'(A) = \Sigma^*-L(A) = \{x \mid c_A(|x|) \le s(|x|)\}$ or a $\Sigma_2^{p,A}$-predicate that defines $L(A)$. Let n_0 be such that $\forall n \ge n_0\ r^2(n) < s(n)$.

Case 1. $L \in \Pi_2^{p,A}$. Then $1^n\#l \in L$ if and only if $\forall^P y\ \exists^P z\ P^A(1^n\#l, y, z)$, where $P^{()}$ is accepted by a deterministic polynomial-time oracle TM. We define a predicate $R^A(x)$

$$R^A(x) \equiv [|x| < n_0 \wedge c_A(|x|) \le s(|x|)] \vee$$

$$\vee [|x| \ge n_0 \wedge (Q^A(x) \vee \forall^P l\ Q_1^A(x,l) \Rightarrow Q_2^A(x,l))],$$

$$Q^A(x) \equiv \forall^P u(|u| = |x| \Rightarrow u \notin A),$$

$$Q_1^A(x,l) \equiv s(|x|)/r^{1/2}(|x|) \le l \le s(|x|)\cdot r^{1/2}(|x|)/2,$$

$$Q_2^A(x,l) \equiv \forall^P y\ \exists^P z\ P^A(1^{|x|}\#l, y, z).$$

It is obvious that $R^A(x)$ is a $\Pi_2^{p,A}$-predicate and one can check that it defines $L'(A)$.

Case 2. $L \in \Sigma_2^{p,A}$. Then $1^n\#l \in L$ if and only if $\exists^P y\ \forall^P z\ P^A(1^n\#l, y, z)$. Let $R^A(x)$ denote the following predicate:

$$[|x| < n_0 \wedge c_A(|x|) > s(|x|)] \vee [|x| \ge n_0 \wedge \exists^P y\ \forall^P z\ P^A(1^{|x|}\#s^2(|x|), y, z)].$$

This is $\Sigma_2^{p,A}$-predicate and one can check that it defines $L(A)$.

□

A careful analysis of the proof of the approximate counting upper bound [9] allows us to observe that the approximation of $c_A(n)$ can be obtained by $\Delta_3^{p,A}$-machine making $O(\log n)$ queries to an oracle from $\Sigma_2^{p,A}$. Our decision problem needs the same number of queries. So a natural question arises: Is it possible to construct a set A such that one query, or more generally, a constant number of queries is not sufficient to compute an approximation of c_A? The following theorem can help to deal with the question.

THEOREM 4.5. (i) *If L is accepted by a $\Delta_3^{p,A}$-machine that makes only one oracle query then $L = L_1 - L_2$, where $L_1, L_2 \in \Sigma_2^{p,A}$.*
(ii) *The class of languages accepted by $\Delta_3^{p,A}$-machines that makes no more than a constant number oracle queries is equal to the Boolean closure of $\Sigma_2^{p,A}$-languages.*

Proof. Straightforward. □

Acknowledgement. The author would like to express his gratitude to Prof. Leszek Pacholski, for his constant encouragement and inspiration, without which this task would be impossible.

REFERENCES

[1] M. Ajtai, Σ_1^1 formulas on finite structures, *Annals of Pure and Applied Logic* 24(1983), 1-48.

[2] J. Balcazar, R. V. Book and U. Shònning, On bounded query machines, *Theoret. Comp. Sci.* 40(1985), 237-243.

[3] M. Furst, J. B. Saxe and M. Sipser, Parity, Circuits and the Polynomial-Time Hierarchy, *Proc. 22nd FOCS*(1981), 260-270.

[4] J. Hastad, Almost optimal lower bounds for small depth circuits, *Proc. 18th ACM STOC*(1986), 6-20.

[5] C. H. Papadimitriou and M. Yannakakis, The complexity of facets (and some facets of complexity), *J. Comput. Syst. Sci.* 28(1984), 244-259.

[6] J. Paris and A. Wilkie, Counting problems in bounded arithmetic, Springer Lecture Notes in Mathematics 1130, *Methods in Mathematical Logic, Proc. Caracas*(1983), 317-340.

[7] M. Piotrów, On complexity of counting in polynomial hierarchy, *TR N-166, Ins. Comp. Sci., Univ. of Wrocław, Poland.*

[8] L. J. Stockmeyer, The polynomial time hierarchy, *Theoret. Comp. Sci.* 3(1977),1-22.

[9] L. J. Stockmeyer, The complexity of approximate counting, *Proc. 15th ACM STOC* (1983), 118-126.

[10] L. G. Valiant, The complexity of computing the permanent, *Theoret. Comp. Sci.* 8(1979), 189-201.

[11] A. C. C. Yao, Separating the polynomial time hierarchy by oracles, *Proc. 26th FOCS* (1985), 1-10.

DESIGN, PROOF AND ANALYSIS OF NEW EFFICIENT ALGORITHMS FOR INCREMENTAL ATTRIBUTE EVALUATION

Qi Lu and Jiahua Qian
Department of Computer Science
Fudan University
Shanghai, P.R.China

1.INTRODUCTION

Introduced by Knuth[6,7], attribute grammars are a good tool for specifying semantics of programming languages and have been successfully used in producing compilers and other software tools and environments[5,8,11]. The most difficult problem of incremental attribute evaluation is the heavy cost of space and low time efficiency. By introducing the multi-dependency relation among attributes, we define a restricted class of attribute grammars NCMD-AG, which has enough expressability. A space saving as well as time efficient incremental evaluation algorithm for NCMD-AG has been designed. In addition, correctness proof and time and space complexity analysis have also been given. Different from previous work[2,4,12], we further generalize the algorithm to deal with ordinary attribute grammars. The generalized algorithm retains the complexity of time and space.

2.ATTRIBUTE GRAMMAR AND ITS INCREMENTAL EVALUATION

An attribute grammar is a context-free grammar extended by attaching attributes to the symbols of the grammar and it allows the semantics of a language to be specified along with its syntax. Formally, an attribute grammar is a 5-tuple $G=(V_T,V_N,V_{att},P,S)$, where V_T , V_N , V_{att} , P and S represent the set of terminal, the set of nonterminal, the set of attribute declaration, the set of production and the start symbol respectively. Each attribute declaration of V_{att} attaches several attributes to certain symbol X of G, i.e., $X \in V_T \cup V_N$. The attributes of X are divided into two finite disjoint sets, one set of synthesized attributes denoted as S(X), and one set of inherited attributes denoted as I(X). We use A(X) to stand for $S(X) \cup I(X)$. Each production of G is attached to a set of semantic functions which is the rule for defining value of attributes.

A derivation tree node labeled X defines a set of attribute

instances corresponding to A(X). For attribute a of A(X), we denote its instance as X.a. A semantic tree is a derivation tree together with an assignment of either a value or a special token null to each attribute instance of the tree. The set of all the arguments of the semantic function computing attribute instance X.a in semantic tree T is denoted as $ARG_T(X.a)$. The set of attribute instance that depends on X.a in T is denoted $DEP_T(X.a)$. For each Y.b in $ARG_T(X.a)$, we call X.a depends on Y.b and express it as DP(Y.b, X.a). We use DPT(Y.b, X.a) to indicate that X.a depends or transitively depends on Y.b. A directed graph that represents functional dependencies among the attribute instances of semantic tree T is denoted as D(T). This paper deals with only attribute grammars that are in normal form, well-formed as well as noncircular.

Incremental attribute evaluation is the fundamental mechanism of generating language-based environment. The basic idea is to represent a program by a semantic tree. Thus the process of developing a program becomes a process of modifying the semantic tree by editing operations. Incremental attribute evaluation is just to reestablish consistent attribute values throughout the tree when a modification to the semantic tree is made.

To discuss the time complexity of incremental attribute evaluation algorithm, we use semantic function application as the unit step. In addition, we introduce the notion of AFFECTED. Let T' denote the inconsistent tree resulting from a subtree replacement, and let T" denote T' after it has been updated. AFFECTED is defined to be the set of attribute instances that have different values in the two trees. Much excellent work has been done on algorithms for incremental attribute evaluation[1,3,9,10]. Although our approach is not theoretically optimal, it's practically efficient.

3.NCMD-AG AND THE CORRESPONDING ALGORITHM

The main approach to incremental attribute evaluation is to propagate changes of attribute value along the dependencies of the semantic tree T until the reevaluated values of attribute instances which can be affected by the subtree replacement equal their old ones. The key issue of it is to schedule a sequence in which attribute instances are evaluated. The time complexity of algorithm relies to a great extent on that sequence.

Consider the propagation of change of value of attribute instances in A(X) along the dependencies of D(T) where X is in T, it is easy to see that the necessary condition for an attribute instance b to be evaluated more than once is that : if b is not in A(X), there are at least two members of $ARG_T(b)$, say a_1 and a_2, such that a_1 and a_2 depend or transitively depend on some member of A(X), i.e., DPT(A(X),a_1) and DPT(A(X),a_2); if b is in A(X), there is at least one member of A(X) a such that DPT(a,b). This brings our important concept, the multi-dependency. We define that attribute instance b multi-depends on A(X) in T if b satisfies the above condition, which is written as MDP(A(X),b). We use $MD_T(X)$ to stand for the set of attribute instances that multi-depend on A(X) in T. So finding a suitable evaluation order for members of $MD_T(X)$ is the key problem we have to solve. To cope with it, there are two basic approaches. One is to put restrictions on attribute grammar and obtain necessary information through static analysis. Another is to dynamically establish the dependencies among members of $MD_T(X)$ in D(T). In this section we discuss the former approach which leads to the NCMD-AG and the corresponding algorithm. In the next section we will adopt the latter approach, which give rise to a generalized algorithm.

We can design an algorithm Find-Multi-Dependency that creates a directed graph MDG(X) to reflect all the transitive dependencies over MD(X) in any context of X, where MD(X) is a set of attributes such that for any attribute instance b and any semantic tree T containing X, if MDP(A(X),b) then the attribute corresponding to b is in MD(X). An attribute grammar is defined to be a NCMD-AG if for each symbol X of G,MDG(X) is acyclic.

Now we take up the design work of an incremental attribute evaluation algorithm for NCMD-AG. It is easy to see that for any semantic tree T, attribute instances of $MD_T(X)$ can be evaluated in an order that satisfies the partial order determined by MDG(X). So we topologically sort MD(X) according to the partial order of MGD(X) and number the members of MD(X) with natural number in decreasing order. We give a NUM value for any attribute instance b of T. If the attribute corresponding to b is in MD(X), we call it b in MD(X) for short, then NUM(b) is the number value of that attribute; if b is not in MD(X), then NUM(b) is set to zero. Supposing MD(X)={a_1,a_2,...,a_n}, all we have to store is a list L(X)=((a_1,NUM(a_1)),...,(a_n,NUM(a_n))). The algorithm is given as follows.

Algorithm 1. NCMD-AG-Incremental-Evaluation(T,r)
<u>declare</u> T:a fully attributed semantic tree,

```
            r:node of T with all the inconsisten attribute instances,
            X:symbol of G labeling r,
            S:a work list,
            b,c:attribute instance,
            oldvalue,newvalue:attribute value;
begin       S:=A(X);  sort(S);
            while S <> ∅ do
                 remove b from the head of S;
                 oldvalue:=value of b;
                 evaluate b;
                 newvalue:=value of b;
                 if oldvalue<>newvalue then
                        for each c of DEP_T(b) do
                            insert(S,c)
                        od
                 fi
            od
end
```

Note that insert(S,c) involves the following work. It first looks up c in L(X). If c is in L(X), then NUM(c) is fetched, otherwise NUM(c) is set to zero. If c is not in S, insert(S,c) puts (c,NUM(c)) into S such that the NUM value of the elements of S is in increasing order. The procedure sort(S) sorts the elements of S according to the NUM value in increasing order. For the newly inserted element, insert(S,c) puts it before any element of S with an equal to or greater than NUM value. We have the following result.

Theorem 1. Algorithm 1 can correctly reestablish consistent attribute value for a modified semantic tree.

Proof: First, we use mathematical induction on the order of evaluation of attribute instances to prove the proposition P. P states that for any attribute instance a, when a is evaluated, all the members of $ARG_T(a)$ have received a consistent final value and will no longer be evaluated. Here final value is the value that will not change in the subsequent evaluation process. As base step, consider the attribute instance a that is first evaluated by algorithm 1. Assume that b is any member of $ARG_T(a)$. If b can not be affected by A(X), i.e., DPT(A(X),b) does not hold in D(T), b has the consistent and final value and will not be evaluated any longer. If DPT(A(X),b) holds in D(T), there must exist a member c of A(X) such that DPT(c,b), which is contrary to the fact that a is at the head of S. So P is true for the first evaluated attribute instance. Consider the general situation when attribute instance a is evaluated. If a is not in L(X), there is exactly one member b of $ARG_T(a)$ such that DPT(A(X),b) holds in D(T). It is clear that a being inserted into S results from finding out that b changed value after b had been evaluated. From the induction assumption, b got the consistent and final value and will no longer be evaluated. Such condition is also true for any other member of $ARG_T(a)$. Consider the case when a is not in L(X). If member b of $ARG_T(a)$ has already been evaluated, then b satisfies P by induction assumption. If b has not been evaluated and DPT(A(X),b) holds in D(T), we first show that it will never be evaluated. If b will be evaluated later on, there must exist an attribute instance c such that DPT(c,b) holds in D(T) and c is in S, thus contrary to the fact that NUM(a)<=NUM(c). If b will no longer be evaluated, we can infer that all member of $ARG_T(b)$ do not change their value. It can be similarly proved that they will not be evaluted any more. Since the semantic tree is consistent before its modification, so b has the consistent and final value. In summary, attribute instance a evaluated in general case also makes P true, which proves the induction step. Therefore proposition P is valid.

The correctness of algorithm 1 can be infered directly from P.

Theorem 2. The time and space complexity of algorithm 1 is O(|AFFECTED|*log|AFFECTED|) and O(|AFFECTED|) respectively.

Proof: Because S is expanded only after the finding of a new element of AFFECTED and the attribute instances put into S at one time has the constant upper bound, and the book keeping for each attribute instance is O(log|AFFECTED|), so the time complexity of algorithm 1 is O(|AFFECTED|*log|AFFECTED|).

Since the space needed to store a L(X) and an element of S has constant upper bounds, we can conclude that the space complexity of algorithm 1 is O(|AFFECTED|).

4.A GENERALIZED ALGORITHM

In order to make the use of the multi-dependency approach widely applicable, we generalize algorithm 1 to be able to treat any attribute grammar, and retain the time and space complexity at the same time.

We adopt the following approach after trading off between time and space. We first statically establish a rough partial order determined by MDG*(X), which can be obtained by algorithm Find-Multi-Dependency. MDG*(X) reflects all the direct dependencies in any context of X among all the attributes which are depend or transitively depend on A(X) when they appear as attribute instance in some context of X. Clearly, the strongly connected components of MDG*(X) have a partial order determined by MDG*(X) itself. We topologically sort these components and number them in decreasing order with natural numbers. For any b in MD(X), NUM(b) is the number assigned of the component containing b. For any b not in MD(X), we set NUM(b) to zero as before. So, if b and c are two arbitrary attribute instance and NUM(b) is smaller than NUM(c), then b can be evaluated before c in any context of X. For each symbol X of grammar G, we similarly store a list $L(X) = ((a_1, NUM(a_1)), \ldots, (a_n, NUM(a_n)))$, where $MD(X) = \{a_1, \ldots, a_n\}$.

It's not difficult to see that if we still use algorithm 1, the only case that requires special treatment is when there is more than one attribute instances at the head of S with the same nonzero NUM value. Suppose $S' = \{a_1, \ldots, a_k\}$ is the set of such attribute instances and n is their NUM value. Obviously, they are in the same strongly connected component of MDG*(X), and we denote the attribute set of that component as DL(n). The dependency relation among $a_1, \ldots, a_k$ is a partial order in D(T) and we use PAR(S') to refer to it. Without loss of generality, we can assume that $\{a_1, \ldots, a_m\}$ is the set of maximum element of partial order PAR(S'), where 1<=m<=k. We can show that for any i, 1<=i<=m, a_i is evaluable in the sense that the value of any member of $ARG_T(a_i)$ will not change. For any b in $ARG_T(a_i)$, if the value of b will change, then b will be evaluated again, there must exist an attribute instance c such that c is in S, DPT(c,b) holds in D(T). Since a_i is the maximum element of PAR(S'), so c is not in S', therefore NUM(c)<NUM(b), which is impossible for the sorted S.

An algorithm Find-Maximum-Element is designed to find the maximum element of PAR(S') dynamically. Let's establish the condition for such a maximum element first. If b is in $ARG_T(a_i)$ and not in DL(n), then $NUM(b) < NUM(a_i)$. It's easy to show that b will no longer be evaluated, hence receive the final value. So the condition for a_i in S' to be a maximum element is that any member of $ARG_T(a_i)$ is either evaluated(the algorithm evaluates an attibute instance only once and assign it a consistent final value) or not in DL(n) and evaluated as discussed above. Any attribute instance satisfying the above condition is called a stopper. To speed up the searching of maximum element, we will store DL(n) for any possible n of MDG*(X) and use another work list S* to take account of all the attribute instances that have already been evaluated. For the sake of reducing redundant searching, our strategy for deciding that a_i in S' is a maximum element is to traverse a tree T(S') rooted at a_i, in which each node is either a stopper or in S' or in DL(n); and each edge is obtained by inverting the direction of the corresponding edge of D(T). We start from a_i and traverse along the opposite direction of the dependencies of D(T) until all the leaf nodes of T(S') are either a stopper or in S'. If T(S') contains some elements of S', say $a_{i_1},\ldots,a_{i_k}$, then a_i is not a maximum element and S should be rearranged such that a_i is put after any one of $a_{i_1},\ldots,a_{i_k}$ in S, otherwise a_i is a maximum element. We propose a searching algorithm as follows.

```
Algorithm 2. Find-Maximum-Element(ai,n,S',S*,S)
declare     S',S*,S:set of attribute instance,
            L,L':worklist,
            ai,b,c:attribute instance,
            n:NUM value;
begin       L:={ai};    L':=∅;    mark ai;
            while L<>∅ do
               remove b from L;
               if b∈S' & b<>ai then L':=L'∪{b} fi;
               for each c in (DL(n)∩ARG_T(b)-S*) do
                       L:=L∪{c}
               od;
               if L'<>∅ then  rearrange S by putting ai
                              after any member of L' in S;
                              return (ai is not maximum element)
               else return (ai is maximum element) fi
end
```

Now the generalized algorithm can be given as:

```
Algorithm 3. Generalized-Incremental-Evaluation(T,r)
declare     T:a fully attributed semantic tree,
            r:node of T containing all the inconsistent attribute
              instances,
            X:symbol of G labeling r,
            S,S',S*:worklist,
```

```
            b,c:attribute instance,
            oldvalue,newvalue:attribute value,
            ok:bool variable,
            HEAD(S):attribute instance at the head of S;
begin       S:=A(X);  S*:=∅;  sort(S);
            while S<>∅ do
                ok:=false;
                remove b from the head of S;
                if b∉L(X) or b∈L(X)&NUM(b)<NUM(HEAD(S))
                     or b is marked by algorithm 2 then ok:=true
                else
                    S':=the set of elements of S with the same
                    nonzero NUM value as b;
                    Find-Maximum-element(b,NUM(b),S',S*);
                    if b is maximum element then
                       ok:=true
                    fi
                fi
                if ok then oldvalue:=value of b; evaluate b;
                           newvalue:=value of b;
                           S*:=s*∪{b};
                           if oldvalue<>newvalue then
                             for each c in DEP_T(b) do
                                 insert(S,c)
                             od
                           fi
                fi
            od
end
```

We can have the following results.

Theorem 3. Algorithm 3 can correctly reestablish consistent attribute value for a modified semantic tree.

Theorem 4. The time and space complexity of algorithm 3 is is O(|AFFECTED|*log|AFFECTED|) and O(|AFFECTED|) respectively.

The proof of theorem 3 and theorem 4 is analogous to that of theorem 1 and theorem 2 respectively.

REFERENCES

[1] R. Hoover, "Dynamically Bypassing Copy Rule Chains in Attribute Grammars", Conference Record of the 13th ACM Symposium on Principles of Programming Languages, St. Petersburg, Florid, Jan. 1986.

[2] X. Jia & J. Qian, "Incremental Evaluation of Attribute Grammars for Incremental Programming Environments", Proceeding of COMPSAC'85, Chicago, Illinois, Oct. 1985.

[3] G. Johnson, "An Approach to Incremental Semantics", Ph.D Thesis, University of Wisconsin, 1983.

[4] U. Kastens, "Ordered Attribute Grammar", Acta Informatica, Vol.13, Fasc.3, 1980.

[5] U. Kastens, B. Hutt & E. Zimmermann, "GAG : A Practical Compiler Generator", Lecture Notes in Computer Science, Springer-verlag, Berlin-Heidelberg-New York, 1982.

[6] E. Knuth, "Semantics of Context-Free languages", Mathematical System Theory 2, 2 (June, 1968), 127-145.

[7] E. Knuth, "Semantics of Context-Free Languages : Correction", Mathematical System of Theory 5, 1 (March, 1971), 95-96.

[8] T. Reps, "Generating Language-Based Environment", Technical Report, Department of Computer Science, Cornell University, TR 82-514, Aug. 1982.

[9] T. Reps, C. Marceau & T. Teitelbaum, "Remote Attribute Updating for Language-Based Editors", Conference record of the 13th ACM Symposium on Principles of Programming Languages, St.Petersburg, Florid, Jan. 1986.

[10] T. Reps, T. Teitelbaum & A.Demers, "Incremental Context-Dependent analysis for Language-Based Editors", ACM TOPLAS, Vol.5, No.3, 1983.

[11] T. Teitelbaum & T. Reps, "The Cornell Program Synthesizer : A Syntax-Directed Programming Environment", CACM Vol.24, No.9, September 1981.

[12] D. Yeh, "On Incremental Evaluation of Ordered Attribute Grammar", BIT, Vol.23, No.3, 1983.

ON EFFICIENCY OF INTERVAL ROUTING ALGORITHMS

Peter Ružička
VUSEI-AR, Dúbravská 3
842 21 Bratislava, Czechoslovakia

1. Introduction

The routing problem for any network and any pair of nodes /called sender and destination/ is to route messages along the shortest possible path from the sender node to the destination node.

Various routing algorithms have been proposed based on a routing table of size O(n) at each node, where n is the number of nodes in the network /see Tajibnapis, 1977/. The table contains the link to be traversed for each destination node.

Recently, Santoro and Khatib /1985/ and van Leeuwen and Tan /1987/ proposed a general method, called the interval routing scheme, where the routing is provided by compact node routing tables of size O(d), where d is the degree of a node. Optimal interval routing algorithms are known for networks with regular topology /such as trees, various types of rings and grids, complete bipartite networks, hypercubes and some combinations of them/. For a non-regular case there is an interval routing algorithm optimal for cycle-free networks and at most within the factor of two from optimality for networks with arbitrary topology.

In this paper we show that the interval routing algorithm cannot be optimal in networks with arbitrary topology. We prove that in the worst case the interval routing algorithm chooses a route of the length at least 3/2 of the network diameter. This answered the question posed by van Leeuwen and Tan /1987/.

2. Definitions and Notation

A network G is an undirected graph $\langle V,E \rangle$ with a finite set V of vertices and a finite set $E \subseteq V \times V$ of edges. For exclusively technical reason each edge in the graph will be replaced by two edges /oriented in opposite directions/.

The interval labelling of the graph G=<V,E> is the labelling of vertices and edges of G satisfying two conditions:

1. the vertex label is an integer from <1,|V|> such that labels of vertices in V are supposed to be all distinct.
2. the label of an edge in E, directed from a vertex v, is
   i. an interval label of the form <i,j> for vertex labels i,j /all vertex labels are considered to be cyclically ordered/, where all intervals for edges in G directed from the vertex v are pairwise disjoint; or
   ii. a complement label δ , where at most one edge in G among edges directed from the vertex v is assigned by this label; or
   iii. a null label λ , which means that the edge assigned by this label is unsignificant with respect to the routing.

A set of all interval labellings of a graph G is called the interval labelling scheme of G.

Given a graph G, a pair of nodes in G and an interval labelling $\mathcal{L}$ of G, one can define an interval routing algorithm $\mathcal{A}(\mathcal{L})$ in the following way:

ALGORITHM $\mathcal{A}(\mathcal{L})$

```
begin
   comment  according to a fixed interval labelling ℒ a current vertex
            label is  i  and a destination vertex label is  j ;
   if  i = j
      then  the destination vertex has been successfully reached;
   if  j belongs to an interval label of some edge directed from the
       vertex with the label  i
      then  route to the new current vertex through this edge
      else  route to the new current vertex through the edge with the
            complement label
end
```

It is obvious that the interval routing algorithm based on any interval labelling $\mathcal{L}$ for a graph G can fail in finding the route between two vertices of G due to a cycle in the route. An interval labelling $\mathcal{L}$ of a graph G is valid /according to the routing algorithm $\mathcal{A}(\mathcal{L})$/, if for two arbitrary vertices u,v of G the algorithm $\mathcal{A}(\mathcal{L})$ successfully reaches v from u if and only if there is a path in the graph G between u and v.

For a given graph G it is decidable in $O(|V|^2)$ whether an interval labelling of G is valid or not. Furthermore, for every graph G there exists a valid interval labelling of G .

We note that the valid interval labelling scheme as defined by van Leeuwen and Tan /1987/ is a special case of the valid interval labelling defined in this paper and thus lower bound results proved in the next section are also valid for their interval routing model.

We need the following notions:

distance (u,v,G) denotes the number of edges in the shortest path between vertices u and v in the graph G.
diameter (G)= maximum $\{\text{distance}(u,v,G) \mid u,v \in V\}$
distance ($\mathcal{A}(\mathcal{L})$,u,v,G) denotes the number of edges in the path routed by $\mathcal{A}(\mathcal{L})$ between vertices u and v in the graph G.
distance ($\mathcal{A}(\mathcal{L})$,G)= maximum $\{\text{distance}(\mathcal{A}(\mathcal{L}),u,v,G) \mid u,v \in V\}$
name (v) denotes the label of the vertex v.

Finally we introduce two notions which enable us to relate the efficiency of routing algorithms.

An interval routing algorithm $\mathcal{A}(\mathcal{L})$ is optimal on $G=\langle V,E\rangle$, if for all $u,v \in V$ it holds

$$\text{distance}(\mathcal{A}(\mathcal{L}),u,v,G)= \text{distance}(u,v,G).$$

An interval routing algorithm $\mathcal{A}(\mathcal{L})$ is α-efficient on G, $\alpha \geq 1$, if it holds

$$\text{distance}(\mathcal{A}(\mathcal{L}),G) \leq \alpha \,.\, \text{diameter}(G).$$

3. Main result

We show that the interval routing algorithm is not optimal, i.e. there is a graph G such that the interval routing algorithm $\mathcal{A}(\mathcal{L})$ is not optimal on G for any valid interval labelling $\mathcal{L}$. In fact we prove much stronger result, namely that the interval routing algorithm cannot be 3/2-efficient.

THEOREM 1

There is a graph G such that for any valid interval labelling $\mathscr{L}$ and for any rational number $\alpha \in <1,3/2>$ the interval routing algorithm $\mathscr{A}(\mathscr{L})$ is not α-efficient on G.

Proof:

We investigate the graph $G_{s,k}$, sketched in Fig. 1, of the size $2ks-s+2$ and of the diameter $2k$ for $k>2$ and $s \geqslant 14$. Every edge in $G_{s,k}$ is considered to be replaced by two edges oriented in opposite directions. We shall consider an arbitrary valid interval labelling $\mathscr{L}$ for the graph $G_{s,k}$. We determine the pair of vertices w_1 and w_2 in $G_{s,k}$ such that the following property is satisfied:

the interval routing algorithm $\mathscr{A}(\mathscr{L})$ finds a path between vertices w_1 and w_2 of the length at least $3/2.\text{diameter}\ (G_{s,k}) + 1/2$. (1)

Consider vertices $v_{i,k}$ for $1 \leqslant i \leqslant s$, $s \geqslant 14$. From the definition of interval labelling it is evident that at least one edge directed from the vertex $v_{i,k}$ must contain an interval label. The graph $G_{s,k}$ is symmetrical according to the "axis vertices" $v_{i,k}$ for $1 \leqslant i \leqslant s$. Hence, without loss of generality we suppose that there are at least s/2 edges of the form $(v_{i,k}, v_{i,k-1})$ containing interval labels. In $\mathscr{L}$ we denote these edges as $(v_{i,k}, v_{i,k-1})$ for $1 \leqslant i \leqslant s/2$. Furthermore, at least s/2-2 pairs of edges $(u, v_{i,1})$ and $(w, v_{i,2k-1})$ for $1 \leqslant i \leqslant s/2$ contain interval labels. In $\mathscr{L}$ we denote these pairs as $(u, v_{i,1})$ and $(w, v_{i,2k-1})$ for $1 \leqslant i \leqslant s/2-2$.

The interval label of the edge $(u, v_{i,1})$ for $1 \leqslant i \leqslant s/2-2$ must contain names of vertices $v_{i,1}, \ldots, v_{i,k-1}$. If this interval does not contain, let us say, the name of the vertex $v_{i,t}$ for some t satisfying $1 \leqslant t \leqslant k-1$, then the property (1) is fulfilled because the shortest path between vertices u and $v_{i,t}$, not containing the edge $(u, v_{i,1})$, is of the length at least $3/2.\text{diameter}\ (G_{s,k}) + 1/2$.

If I_p is the smallest interval containing names of all vertices $v_{p,1}, \ldots, v_{p,k-1}$ for $1 \leqslant p \leqslant s/2-2$, then in $\mathscr{L}$ the following relation holds:

$$I_i \cap I_j = \emptyset \quad \text{for} \quad 1 \leqslant i \neq j \leqslant s/2-2 \qquad (2)$$

If name $(v_{j,t})$ for some t satisfying $1 \leqslant t \leqslant k-1$ belongs to I_i for $i \neq j$, $1 \leqslant i \leqslant s/2-2$, then the interval routing algorithm $\mathscr{A}(\mathscr{L})$

finds the path between vertices u and $v_{j,t}$, containing the edge $(u,v_{i,1})$, of the length at least $3/2.\text{diameter}\ (G_{s,k}) + 1/2$ and the property (1) is fulfilled.

By analogy, if Y_p is the smallest interval containing names of all vertices $v_{p,k+1},\dots,v_{p,2k-1}$ for $1 \leqslant p \leqslant s/2-2$, then in $\mathcal{L}$ the following relation holds

$$Y_i \cap Y_j = \emptyset \quad \text{for} \quad 1 \leqslant i \neq j \leqslant s/2-2 \qquad (3)$$

If K_i is the interval label of the edge $(v_{i,k},v_{i,k-1})$ for $1 \leqslant i \leqslant s/2-2$ in $\mathcal{L}$, then K_i must contain names of all vertices $v_{i,2},\dots,v_{i,k-1}$ and also names of all vertices $v_{1,1},\dots,v_{s/2-2,1}$. On the other hand, K_i cannot contain names of vertices $v_{i,k+1},\dots,v_{i,2k-1}$. Let x and y be two vertices with the following property:

$$\text{name}\ (x) = \text{minimum}\ \{\text{name}\ (v_{j,1}) \mid 1 \leqslant j \leqslant s/2-2\}$$

and

$$\text{name}\ (y) = \text{maximum}\ \{\text{name}\ (v_{j,1}) \mid 1 \leqslant j \leqslant s/2-2\}.$$

Without loss of generality, suppose that in $\mathcal{L}$ it holds $x = v_{s/2-2,1}$ and $y = v_{s/2-3,1}$. For an arbitrary integer i satisfying $1 \leqslant i \leqslant s/2-4$ it follows that K_i contains names of all vertices $v_{j,t}$ for $1 \leqslant j \leqslant s/2-4$, $1 \leqslant t \leqslant k-1$ but that K_i does not contain names of vertices $v_{m,r}$ for $1 \leqslant m \leqslant s/2-4$, $k+1 \leqslant r \leqslant 2k-1$. Hence, if I denotes the smallest interval containing $I_1 \cup \dots \cup I_{s/2-4}$, then the following equation holds

$$I \cap (Y_1 \cup \dots \cup Y_{s/2-4}) = \emptyset \qquad (4)$$

Note that $s/2-4 \geqslant 3$. By the equation (4) there are two indices m_1 and m_2 satisfying $1 \leqslant m_1 \neq m_2 \leqslant s/2-4$ such that there does not exist a vertex x from the set $\{v_{i,j} \mid 1 \leqslant i \leqslant s/2-4,\ 1 \leqslant j \leqslant k-1\}$ whose name is between the name of a vertex from the set $\{v_{m_p,j} \mid k+1 \leqslant j \leqslant 2k-1\}$ and the name of a vertex from the set $\{v_{m_q,j} \mid k+1 \leqslant j \leqslant 2k-1\}$ for $p = 1$, $q = 2$ and $q = 1$, $p = 2$.

In particular consider the following case.

$$\text{name}\ (v_{1,1}) < \text{name}\ (v_{m_1,k+1}) < \text{name}\ (v_{m_2,k+1}) \qquad (5)$$

If name $(v_{m_2,k+1})$ belong to the interval I_{m_2}, then by the inequality (5) there are two vertices u and $v_{m_1,k+1}$ such that $\mathcal{A}(\mathcal{L})$ finds the path between them of the length at least $3/2.\text{diameter}\ (G_{s,k}) + 1/2$ and the property (1) holds. We consider next that name $(v_{m_2,k+1})$ does not belong to the interval I_{m_2}.

By the equality (2) there are two vertices u and $v_{m_2,k+1}$ such that $\mathcal{A}(\mathcal{L})$ finds the path between them of the length at least $3/2.\text{diameter}\ (G_{s,k}) + 1/2$ and the property (1) is satisfied.

Evidently the foregoing argument can apply also in the case dual to (5).

This completes the proof of Theorem 1 .

COROLLARY 1

There is a graph G such that for an arbitrary valid interval labelling $\mathcal{L}$ of G the routing algorithm $\mathcal{A}(\mathcal{L})$ satisfies the lower bound

$$\text{distance}\ (\mathcal{A}(\mathcal{L}),G) \geqslant 3/2.\text{diameter}\ (G) + 1/2\ .$$

Santoro and Khatib /1985/ described a valid interval labelling for an arbitrary graph G such that the interval routing algorithm $\mathcal{A}(\mathcal{L})$ satisfies the upper bound

$$\text{distance}\ (\mathcal{A}(\mathcal{L}),G) \leqslant 2.\text{diameter}\ (G).$$

We remark that on the graph $G_{s,k}$ given in Fig. 1 the interval routing algorithm is tight with respect to the lower bound given in Theorem 1.

Moreover, from the proof of Theorem 1 it holds:

COROLLARY 2

There is a graph G and there are vertices u and v in G such that for an arbitrary valid interval labelling $\mathcal{L}$ the routing algorithm $\mathcal{A}(\mathcal{L})$ on the graph G fulfils the bound

$$\text{distance}\ (\mathcal{A}(\mathcal{L}),u,v,G) \geqslant 3.\text{distance}\ (u,v,G).$$

4. Related results

We show that the technique used in the proof of Theorem 1 can also be applied in proving lower bounds for related problems.

An interval labelling of a graph is called LTI labelling if conditions 2ii and 2iii are omitted in the interval labelling definition.
A k-labelled LTI labelling of a graph G is an LTI labelling where

i. each edge in G may receive up to k interval labels;
ii. at every vertex v in G all interval labels for all edges directed from v are pairwise disjoint.

An LTI labelling $\mathcal{L}$ of a graph G is neighbourly LTI labelling if it is valid and for all edges (u,v) in G it holds $\mathrm{distance}(\mathcal{A}(\mathcal{L}),u,v) = 1$.

Van Leeuwen and Tan /1987/ proved that there exists a 2-labelled neighbourly LTI labelling for any arbitrary graph. The question remains whether such a labelling can be optimal. Using similar technique as in the proof of Theorem 1 we show that the answer to this question is negative.

THEOREM 2

There is a graph G such that for arbitrary 2-labelled LTI labelling the interval routing algorithm is not optimal on G.

We present only the idea of the proof. Theorem 2 follows from the sequence of facts. Suppose that on $G_{s,k}$ there exists a 2-labelled LTI labelling $\mathcal{L}$ such that the interval routing algorithm is optimal on $G_{s,k}$.

Fact 1. For any $i \in \langle 1,s \rangle$ labels of the edge $(v_{i,k},v_{i,k-1})$ in $\mathcal{L}$ contain names of vertices $u,v_{1,1},\dots,v_{s,1},\dots,v_{s,k-1}$ and labels of the edge $(v_{i,k},v_{i,k+1})$ in $\mathcal{L}$ contain names of vertices $w,v_{1,k+1},\dots,v_{1,2k-1},\dots,v_{s,k+1},\dots,v_{s,2k-1}$.

Fact 2. For any $i \in \langle 1,s \rangle$ labels of edges $(u,v_{i,1})$ and $(w,v_{i,2k-1})$ in $\mathcal{L}$ contain names of vertices $v_{i,1},\dots,v_{i,2k-1}$.

Fact 3. There are at most four indices $m_1,\dots,m_4$ such that for any $i \in \{1,2,\dots,s\} - \{m_1,\dots,m_4\}$ it holds: names of vertices $v_{i,k+1},\dots,v_{i,2k-1}$ belong to a label of the edge $(w,v_{i,2k-1})$ in $\mathcal{L}$ and names of vertices $v_{i,1},\dots,v_{i,k-1}$ belong to a label of the edge $(u,v_{i,1})$ in $\mathcal{L}$. Suppose in $\mathcal{L}$ it holds $m_i = s-4+i$ for $i = 1,\dots,4$.

Fact 4. For any $i \in \langle 1,s-4 \rangle$ labels of the edge $(v_{i,k+2},v_{i,k+3})$ contain names of vertices w, $v_{p,r}$ for $1 \leqslant p \leqslant s-4$, $k+1 \leqslant r \leqslant 2k-1$ minus $v_{i,k-1},\dots,v_{i,k+2}$ and do not contain names of vertices $u,v_{p,r}$ for $1 \leqslant p \leqslant s-4$, $1 \leqslant r \leqslant k-2$ plus $v_{i,k-1},\dots,v_{i,k+1}$.

Fact 5. There exists $i \in \langle 1,s-4\rangle$ such that in order to satisfy the optimality of routing algorithm on $G_{s,k}$ the edge $(v_{i,k+2}, v_{i,k+3})$ must contain at least three interval labels in $\mathcal{L}$.

The idea can be generalized in order to prove that for any integer k there is a graph G such that for arbitrary k-labelled LTI labelling the interval routing algorithm is not optimal on G.

Another unresolved problem mentioned by van Leeuwen and Tan /1987/ is whether there is an optimal interval routing algorithm for grids with row and column wrap-around, i.e. grids with each row and column extended to be a ring. The following result holds.

THEOREM 3

The interval routing algorithm is not optimal for row-column wrap-around grids.

5. Final remarks

The question whether there is an optimal interval routing algorithm for any arbitrary network is answered in a negative way. It is shown that for certain networks the interval routing algorithm finds a route of the length at least 3/2 of the network diameter. It means that in the worst case the interval routing algorithms are at least "3/2 worse" with respect to the length complexity than the optimal routing algorithms based on the routing tables of linear size. This fact presents a limitation factor in implementing the interval routing algorithms in large sparse communications networks.

Another problems concerning interval routing remain unresolved. The question is whether there is an interval routing algorithm reaching the lower bound presented in Theorem 1. Another interesting issue concerns the "average" complexity analysis of routing in terms of the sum of distances between all pairs of vertices.

References

N. Santoro and R. Khatib: Labelling and Implicit Routing in Network. The Computer Journal, Vol. 28, No. 1, 5-8, 1985

W.D. Tajibnapis: A Correctness Proof of a Topology Information Maintenance Protocol for a Distributed Computer Network. CACM, Vol. 20, No. 7, 477-485, 1977

J. van Leeuwen and R. B. Tan: Interval Routing. The Computer Journal, Vol. 30, No. 4, 298-307, 1987

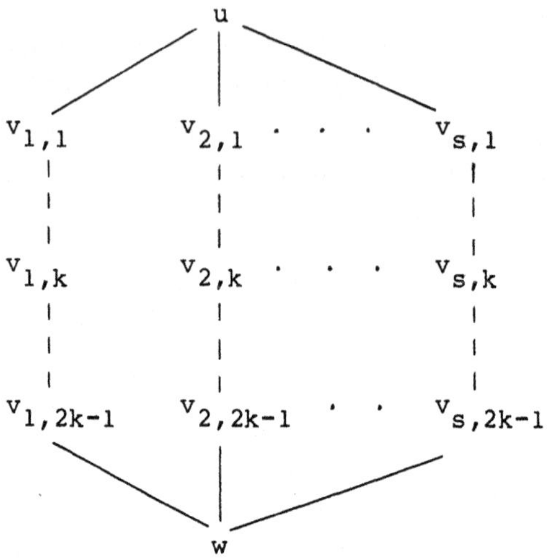

Fig. 1

$G_{s,k}$

AN ALMOST LINEAR ROBINSON UNIFICATION ALGORITHM

Peter Ružička, Igor Prívara
VUSEI-AR, Dúbravská 3
842 21 Bratislava, Czechoslovakia

ABSTRACT: Further asymptotical improvement of original Robinson's unification idea is presented. By postponing the so-called occur-check in Corbin and Bidoit's quadratic rehabilitation of the Robinson algorithm at the end of unification an almost linear unification algorithm is obtained. In the worst case, the resulting algorithm has the time complexity O(p.A(p)), where p is the size of input terms and A is the inverse to the Ackermann function. Moreover, the practical experiments are summarized comparing Corbin and Bidoit's quadratic algorithm with the resulting almost linear unification algorithm based on Robinson's principle.

1. Introduction

The aim of the unification problem is to answer the question whether for two given input terms there is a substitution /an assignment of some terms for variables/ mapping the input terms into the same term. In the case of the positive answer the input terms are said to be unified and the appropriate substitution is called a unifier.

The unification problem plays an important role in many fields of symbolic computations. Well-known are applications in resolution theorem proving, logic programming, term rewriting and, nowadays, also in type inference.

The unification problem has been defined and solved by Robinson [1965]. Robinson's original unification algorithm is inefficient since it requires time exponential in the size of the input terms. The following years brought several improvements in unification problem solutions, culminating with the linear time unification algorithm by Paterson and Wegman [1976] and almost linear but practically very efficient algorithm proposed by Martelli and Montanari [1982].

Due to its conceptual simplicity the original Robinson unification algorithm is very popular in practical applications, in particular in the implementations of the programming language PROLOG. The main drawback of Robinson's idea, its inefficiency due to exponential time complexity, has been eliminated by Corbin and Bidoit [1983]. Their rehabilitation of the Robinson algorithm is based on a suitable choice of data structure to represent terms. Using directed acyclic graphs to represent terms they improved the exponential time complexity of the Robinson unification algorithm down to quadratic time complexity. Furthermore, they showed that modification of the Robinson unification algorithm turns out to be more efficient in practice than the practically best known algorithm described in [Martelli, Montanari 82].

In this paper further asymptotical improvement of original Robinson's idea is presented. In the worst case, the resulting algorithm has almost linear time complexity, more exactly the complexity O(p.A(p)), where p is the sum of input terms sizes and A is an extremely slowly growing function /the inverse to the Ackermann function/. Moreover, the theoretical result has been completed with practical experiments validating the hypothesis that the presented unification algorithm is at least comparable with the algorithm by Corbin and Bidoit from the viewpoint of practical efficiency.

2. Basic notions and results

Let VAR be a countable set of variable symbols and FUN be a countable set of function symbols /$VAR \cap FUN = \emptyset$/ with $arity(f) \geqslant 0$ for $f \in FUN$. Constants are function symbols with arity equal to 0.

Let TERM be a set of terms, recursively defined in the following way:
- if $x \in VAR$, then $x \in TERM$,
- if $f \in FUN$, $arity(f) = n$ and $t_1,\dots,t_n \in TERM$, then $f(t_1,\dots,t_n) \in TERM$.

The size of an arbitrary term $t \in TERM$ is defined as the number of function symbols in the term t.

The substitution σ is a mapping $\sigma: VAR \rightarrow TERM$ such that $\sigma(x) = x$ holds except for a finite subset of VAR. The substitution σ can therefore be described as a finite set $\sigma = \{x_i \rightarrow t_i \mid x_i \in VAR,\ t_i \in TERM\}$ of the variable replacements. Each substitution can be naturally extended to a morphism $TERM \rightarrow TERM$. To apply a substitution σ to a term t one has to replace all occurrences of each variable x_i in t by the corresponding term t_i.

The unifier of the given two terms t_1 and t_2 is a substitution σ such that $\sigma(t_1) = \sigma(t_2)$ holds. The unifier σ is called the most general unifier /mg-unifier/ of two terms if and only if for each unifier τ of the given terms there is a substitution ϕ such that $\tau = \phi.\sigma$ holds. /The symbol . denotes the standard mapping composition./ For any pair of unifiable terms there exists a mg-unifier which is unique up to a permutation of variables. The goal of the unification problem solution is to find a mg-unifier of a given pair of input terms.

The efficiency of unification algorithms depends heavily on the suitable choice of a data structure to represent terms. In the most efficient unification algorithms the terms are represented as directed acyclic graphs /term-dags/ and a substitution /and a variable replacement/ is applied as a simple operation on vertices of those graphs. In the unification algorithm presented in the next section we take advantage of a more general data structure for term representation, namely of the directed graphs /term-digraphs/.

The term-digraph is a directed graph with vertices labelled by symbols from VAR $\cup$ FUN. The label of an arbitrary vertex v is denoted as label(v). The out-degree of a vertex v with label(v) ε VAR is 0. These vertices are further called "variable vertices". The variable vertices are shared, i.e. for each variable occurring in input terms there is exactly one vertex labelled with this variable symbol. The out-degree of a vertex labelled by a symbol f ε FUN is exactly arity(f). These vertices are further called "functional vertices". The term-digraph is a multigraph, i.e. there can be more than one edge connecting a given pair of vertices. The outgoing edges of each vertex of a term-digraph are ordered /in order to distinquish e.g. between representation of the terms f(x,y) and f(y,x)/. To reference the k-th successor of a vertex v in the term-digraph G we use the notation successor(G,v,k).

The term-dag is an acyclic term-digraph. The one-to-one correspondence between term-dags and terms follows easily from the definitions. Thus with each vertex of a term-dag G one can associate a term of the form term(G,v), recursively defined as follows:

```
if v is a variable vertex
then term(G,v) = label(v)
else (*  let f = label(v); n = arity(f);
         v_k = successor (G,v,k) for k = 1,2,...,n *)
     term(G,v) = f (term(G,v_1),...,term(G,v_n))
```

The variable replacement $x_i \to t_i$ on term-digraphs is performed by means of the operation replace(G,v,v´), where v,v´ are two distinct vertices in the term-digraph G. The result of the operation replace(G,v,v´) is the graph G´ satisfying the following properties:

- G´ has the same vertices as G with the same labels;
- G´ has the same edges as G except for those edges in G which lead to the vertex v; these edges are replaced in G´ by edges going to the vertex v´ /the order of the outgoing edges is of course preserved/.

The replace operation can transform an acyclic term-digraph into the term-digraph with cycles. However, the following properties hold:

LEMMA 1 [Corbin, Bidoit 1983]: Let G be a term-dag and there is no path in G from v´ to v.

(1) Then G´ is term-dag.

(2) If v is a variable vertex and σ is a variable replacement label (v) $\rightarrow$ term (G,v´), then for each vertex w it holds term(replace(G,v,v´),w) = if w = v then v else σ(term(G,w)).

Fact (2) in Lemma 1 states that, if there is no path in G from v´ to v, the operation replace(G,v,v´) simulates the variable replacement /substitution/ label(v) $\rightarrow$ term(G,v´). In the term-digraph G´ the vertex v is isolated. This property corresponds to the fact that the variable label(v) does not occur in the term after the variable replacement.

We shall write successor(v,k), term(v), replace(v,v´) instead of successor(G,v,k), term(G,v), replace(G,v,v´) if it is evident which term-digraph G is taken into account.

3. Modification of Robinson´s unification algorithm

In their famous article Corbin and Bidoit [1983] described a modification RG2 of the original Robinson algorithm and proved that in the worst case this modification works in the time complexity $O(p^2)$, where p is the total number of symbols in the input terms. In this paper we present further improvement of Robinson´s unification principle having the time complexity O(p.A(p)), where A is an extremely slowly growing function /the inverse to the Ackermann function/.

The unique source of the quadratic time complexity of the RG2 is the so-called occur-check. The answer to the occur-check is positive iff a given term t contains an occurrence of a given variable x. From the analysis of the example P1 /see Table 1/ it follows that for the depth-first-search unification strategy /which is the pinpoint of Robinson´s idea/ employing the occur-check, the subquadratic time complexity cannot be obtained even if terms are represented as term-graphs.

The main idea of our modification is to omit the occur-check during the unifying depth-first-search. However, without the occur-check an operation replace(G,v,w) /line 3 of the UNIFY procedure/ can create a cycle in the term-digraph G. This is also the reason why we use term-digraphs to represent terms. The presence of cycles in term-digraphs can cause either nontermination or an incorrect answer of the unification algorithm. In the ALMOST-LINEAR-UNIFY algorithm /precisely in the UNIFY procedure/ the first possible drawback is prevented by means of the suitable marking during the term-digraph search. The cycles in term--digraphs are detected in two places. Some of them can be detected already during the term-digraph search /line 11 of the UNIFY procedure/, however, a definite answer can be given only by the "post-occur-check" /line 3 of the ALMOST-LINEAR-UNIFY procedure/ indicating whether the resulting term-digraph contains a cycle or not. The first situation takes place in the example P3 while the second one in the example P5 /Table 1/.

<u>ALGORITHM</u> ALMOST-LINEAR-UNIFY(u1,u2):bool

Input: A pair of vertices (u1,u2) in the term-dag such that term(u1) and term(u2) are terms to be unified.

Output: Bool such that bool=true if and only if two input terms term(u1) and term(u2) are unifiable, otherwise bool=false.

Method:

```
1    begin (*  each vertex of the term-dag is marked as unvisited *)
2          bool: = UNIFY(u1,u2);
3          if bool then bool: = POST-OCCUR-CHECK(u1,u2)
4          fi
5    end
```

RECURSIVE PROCEDURE UNIFY(v1,v2):bool

```
1 begin
2   if one of the input vertices, say v, is a variable vertex
       and the other one is w
3   then replace(v,w); bool: = true
4   else
5      if label(v1) ≠ label(v2)
6      then bool: = false
7      else (*  let n be the number of successors of v1 resp. v2 *)
8           k: = 0; bool: = true;
9           while k < n and bool
10          do k: = k + 1;w1: = successor(v1,k);w2:= successor(v2,k);
11             if w1 or w2 is visited
12             then bool: = false
13             else if w1 ≠ w2
14                  then w1 /w2/ is marked as visited;
15                       bool: = UNIFY(w1,w2);
16                       w1 /w2/ is marked as unvisited;
17                  fi
18             fi
19          od;
20          if bool
21          then replace(v1,v2)
22          fi
23     fi
24  fi
25end
```

The goal of the POST-OCCUR-CHECK procedure is to determine whether, after the UNIFY procedure, the resulting term-digraph contains a cycle or not /suppose that the result of POST-OCCUR-CHECK procedure is true if the given term-digraph is acyclic/. This check can be performed using some of the well-known acyclicity tests for directed graphs /e.g. the topological sort or tests based on the depth-first-search/.

The main properties of the ALMOST-LINEAR-UNIFY algorithm i.e. correctness and asymptotical time complexity, are summarized in two next results.

THEOREM 1: The algorithm ALMOST-LINEAR-UNIFY is correct /in the sense of the described input-output relation/.

Proof: At first suppose that before each call of the operation replace(v,w) /line 3 of the UNIFY procedure/ there is no path from w to v. Then the algorithms ALMOST-LINEAR-UNIFY and RG2, respectively, behave identically and their correctness follows directly from Lemma 1.

On the other hand, if there is a path from w to v before some call of replace(v,w), then after replacement the term-digraph contains a cycle. Therefore in this case two properties have to be proved, the termination of the UNIFY procedure and the correctness of the ALMOST-LINEAR-UNIFY result /bool=false/.

The termination property of the UNIFY procedure is guaranteed by the used marking strategy /lines 14 and 16 of the UNIFY procedure/. In this marking strategy a path from the root vertex u1 /u2/ to the currently processed vertex v1 /v2/ in the UNIFY procedure is marked as visited. If the successor w1 /w2/ of the vertex v1 /v2/ in UNIFY is already marked as visited /test in the line 11 of the UNIFY procedure/ then a term-digraph cycle has been detected. This conclusion is trivial in the case when the path from the root u1 /u2/ to the vertex v1 /v2/ has been encountered. On the other hand, if the vertex w2 /w1/ belongs to the path leading from the root u1 /u2/ to the vertex v1 /v2/ then the homogeneous terms term(w1) and term(w2) have to be unified where w2 /w1/ is an ancestor of the vertex w1 /w2/. Since during such unification a cycling term-digraph is always constructed the termination proof is completed.

To prove the correctness of the result two cases have to be distinguished:

- A cycle is detected during the search of the term-digraph /reported in the line 11 of the UNIFY procedure/. Then computation terminates immediately with the proper result.
- A cycle is not detected during the search of the term-digraph. Then the cycle is /in the worst case/ detected by the POST-OCCUR-CHECK procedure on the resulting term-digraph /line 3 of the ALMOST-LINEAR-UNIFY algorithm/.

The time complexity of the ALMOST-LINEAR-UNIFY algorithm equals the sum of time complexity of the recursive UNIFY procedure and the time necessary to test whether the resulting term-digraph contains a cycle or not /POST-OCCUR-CHECK procedure/. This test can be performed by means of the topological sorting of vertices in term-digraph which requires the time linear to the sum of digraph edges and vertices. Thus the UNIFY time complexity dominates in the time complexity of the ALMOST-LINEAR-UNIFY algorithm.

THEOREM 2: The worst case time complexity of the UNIFY procedure is O(p.A(p)), where p is the total number of symbols in the input terms and A is the inverse to the Ackermann function.

Proof: Let n be a total number of distinct variables, p be a total number of symbols and q be a total size of input terms.

During unification no new vertex is created and the number of edges is not increased /the upper bound is p-2/. Each call of the replace operation isolates one variable or functional vertex in the term-digraph, that means replace is called at most p times. The number of successor operations performed by the UNIFY procedure is upper bounded by 2p. Since each call of the UNIFY procedure isolates a variable or a functional vertex given as an argument of UNIFY, the total number of UNIFY calls is less than n+q and therefore upper bounded by p.

For the efficient implementation of the replace and successor operations one can take advantage of the well-known UNION-FIND problem solution. To exploit this solution the term-digraph can be implemented in the following manner. A vertex consists of a fixed part /a vertex label and a sequence of the outgoing edges/ and of a variable-length part /a set of the ingoing edges/. The replace operation with two vertex arguments u, v can be realized as UNION of two variable-length parts of the vertices u, v and the fixed part of the vertex u is assigned to the result, if u is a functional vertex and v is a variable vertex, otherwise the fixed part of the vertex v is assigned to the result. The successor operation with two arguments /a vertex v and an index k/ can be carried out as FIND which for an edge h /outgoing from the vertex v into the k-th son/ returns the fixed part of a vertex whose variable--length part contains the edge h.

Since the sequence of O(p) operations UNION and FIND can be realized in the time complexity O(p.A(p)), the time complexity of the UNIFY procedure is O(p.A(p)) in the worst case, too.

4. Experimental results

The practical efficiency of the ALMOST-LINEAR-UNIFY algorithm /ALU/ has been analysed by comparing it with the RG2 algorithm presented in [Corbin, Bidoit 83]. The RG2 algorithm has been chosen as a "reference" algorithm for two reasons:
- according to [Corbin, Bidoit 83] RG2 is one of the best unification algorithms from the viewpoint of practical performance,
- since both algorithms RG2 and ALU are based on the same principles and use the same basic operations, their comparison is not too sensible to the implementation details or even tricks.

The experimental comparison of the RG2 and ALU algorithms is based on their uniform implementation in the PROGRESS project environment [Prívara 88]. The standard functions of the PROGRESS system are used for terms representation and manipulation. The Modula-like language of the programming environment BPS /on the SM 52/11 computers/ has been used for implementation.

As a starting point of the experiments three main cases have been specified characterizing different behaviour of both algorithms:
- the input terms are unifiable,
- the input terms are not unifiable due to non-homogeneous terms,
- the input terms are not unifiable due to the positive occur-check.

In addition to them some other properties have been taken into account from which the most important one is the amount of the occur-checks performed during the RG2 unification. Other properties /i.e. when the positive occur-check is encountered or in which phase the ALU algorithm detects the cycle in the data structure/ are important only for the third of the main cases.

Example P1:	t_1: $f(f(\ldots f(f(a,x_1),x_2),\ldots),x_n)$
	t_2: $f(x_n,f(\ldots,f(x_1,a)\ldots))$
Example P2:	t_1: $f(z,g^n(x))$
	t_2: $f(g(z),g^n(y))$
Example P3:	t_1: $f(x,g(x,g(x,\ldots,g(x,g(x,x))\ldots)),x)$
	t_2: $f(g(y,\ldots,g(y,g(y,y))\ldots),y,y)$
Example P4:	t_1: $f(f(\ldots f(f(a,x_1),x_2),\ldots),x_n)$
	t_2: $f(x_n,f(\ldots,f(x_1,b)\ldots))$
Example P5:	t_1: $f(x,g^n(x),x)$
	t_2: $f(g^n(y),y,y)$
Example P6:	t_1: $f(g^n(x))$
	t_2: $f(g^n(y))$
Example P7:	t_1: $f(f(f(\ldots f(f(a,x_1),x_2),\ldots),x_n),z)$
	t_2: $f(f(x_n,f(\ldots,f(x_1,a)\ldots)),g(z))$

Table 1

On the basis of the case analysis the pairs of input terms have been chosen /see Table 1/ representing the most interesting extreme cases, when the behaviour of both algorithms differs. The results of practical performance of both algorithms for the terms with the growing size are summarized in Table 2. The time unit is the number of the system watch "ticks". The table contains an average number of ticks from about 20 control runs.

The experimental comparison of both algorithms for the given input terms is supported by a simple complexity analysis /see Table 3/ in which the number of edges passed during the unification is estimated. In almost all cases the difference in practical performance of both algorithms can be explained using this complexity analysis.

The experimental results are briefly summarized in the following lines:

Case 1: The input terms are unifiable.

The number of the occur-checks performed during the RG2 unification is important for the comparison. If such checks occur frequently, then the ALU algorithm is more efficient. In the extreme case /RG2 passes the quadratic number of edges - see the example P1/ the difference between the performance of both algorithms is significant. The small number of occur-checks during RG2 computation is always compensated by the post--occur-check in the ALU algorithm. In the other extreme case, when there are practically no occur-checks during RG2 unification, the ALU algorithm is slightly worse due to the post-occur-check /see the example P6/.

Case 2: The input terms are not unifiable since the terms are non-homogeneous.

Also for this case the number of the occur-checks performed by RG2 is important. In the extreme case, when RG2 needs to pass a quadratic number of edges, the ALU algorithm is again significantly more efficient

	n =	1	3	5	7	9	11	13	15
P1	RG2	1.5	3.5	6	10	14.5	20	25	32
	ALU	1.5	3	5	7	8.5	10.5	12	14
P2	RG2	1	1	1	1	1	1	1	1
	ALU	2	2.5	3.5	4.5	5	6	7	8
P3	RG2	1.5	1.5	2	2.5	3	3	3.5	4
	ALU	1.5	1.5	1.5	1.5	2	2	2	2
P4	RG2	1	3	5.5	9	13	17.5	23	29
	ALU	1	2	3.5	4.5	5.5	7	8	9
P5	RG2	1	1.5	2	3	3	3.5	4	5
	ALU	1.5	2	2.5	3	3	3.5	4	5.5
P6	RG2	1	2	3	3.5	4.5	5.5	6.5	7
	ALU	1.5	2.5	3.5	4.5	5.5	6.5	7.5	8.5
P7	RG2	2	4	7	11	15	20	26	32
	ALU	2.5	4	6	8	10	11.5	13.5	15

Table 2

	RG2	ALU
P1	$2n^2-2n+4$	$8n$
P2	3	$2n+10$
P3	$8n+3$	$2n+8$
P4	$2n^2+4n$	$6n$
P5	$3n+6$	$2n+10$
P6	$4n+4$	$6n+6$
P7	$2n^2-2n+7$	$8n+4$

Table 3

/see the example P4/. If RG2 asks for occur-check rarely or not at all, both algorithms have approximately the same practical performance.

Case 3: The input terms are not unifiable due to the positive occur--check in the RG2 procedure /resp. due to the cycle in the ALU algorithm/

In addition to the number of occur-checks performed during RG2 computation the following circumstances are now of the interest:
- whether the positive occur-check is encountered early or later,
- whether the presence of the cycle in the constructed digraph is detected during the digraph search /the visited-test in the UNIFY procedure/ or only by the ALU post-occur-check,
- the length of the digraph cycle, detected through the visited-test.

The most disadvantageous case for the ALU algorithm is when the positive occur-check is encountered /almost/ immediately while the corresponding digraph cycle is detected only during the ALU post-occur-check. In this extreme case /see the example P2/ RG2 has constant while ALU has almost linear running time. The second extreme case, when the occur-check gives the positive answer only "at the end" of the RG2 unification and a lot of occur-checks had to be performed before, is advantageous to ALU /see the example P7/. In principle, the later the positive occur-check takes place, the worse is comparison for RG2.
If a cycle is detected already during the UNIFY digraph search the ALU algorithm gains against RG2. If the detected cycle is short and RG2 performs some occur-checks, the ALU algorithm is even better than RG2 /see the example P3/. If the detected cycle is long /see the example P5/, RG2 is more efficient. This is the only case when the number of passed edges does not give a true picture of both algorithms time complexity. RG2 performs 3n "simple" edge passes during the necessary occur-checks and ALU performs only 2n edge passes but the ALU edge passes are more time consuming /more complex operations are performed on each edge/.

The detailed analysis of practical performance of both algorithms indicates that in the first two cases the ALU algorithm is, "on average", more efficient. On the other hand, it is rather difficult to formulate an explicit conclusion in the third case. In this main case many subcases can be distinguished in which the comparison of both algorithms differs diametrically. One can imagine an application/a class of input terms/ for which the RG2 algorithm is better but also applications where the ALU algorithm is preferable. Nevertheless, in this case it also seems that the ALU algorithm is, "on average", at least as efficient as the RG2 algorithm.

5. Conclusions

The known unification algorithms can be classified according to the searching strategies traversing the term-graphs. In the Robinson algorithm and its modifications the straightforward depth-first-search strategy is used. The ALMOST-LINEAR-UNIFY algorithm is asymptotically the best known unification algorithm employing this strategy. Due to its effective implementation Robinson´s unification principle was made comparable with known linear or almost linear unification algorithms using other strategies to search term-graphs.

The experiments showed that from the viewpoint of practical efficiency the ALMOST-LINEAR-UNIFY algorithm is at least comparable with the quadratic RG2 algorithm. The ALMOST-LINEAR-UNIFY algorithm is practically more efficient than the algorithm of Corbin and Bidoit, if the input terms are unifiable or the input terms are not unifiable due to the negative test for homogeneity and is practically as efficient as RG2 if the input terms are not unifiable due to the positive occur-check test.

The practical experiments also validated the hypothesis that the occur-check test in the Robinson´s algorithm can be "correctly" omitted without the loss of efficiency.

6. References

J. CORBIN - M. BIDOIT : A Rehabilitation of Robinson´s Unification Algorithm. IFIP´83, Elsevier Science Publishers, North-Holland, p. 909 - 914, 1983.

A. MARTELLI - V. MONTANARI: An Efficient Unification Algorithm. Transactions on Programming Languages and Systems, Vol. 4, No. 2, p. 258 - 282, 1982.

M.S. PATERSON - M.N. WEGMAN: Linear Unification. Journal of Computer and System Sciences, Vol. 16, p. 158 - 167, 1978.

I. PRÍVARA: PROGRESS - A System Supporting Design and Prototyping of Algebraic Specifications. Technical Report OPS-6-88, VUSEI-AR Bratislava, 1988.

J.A. ROBINSON: A Machine-Oriented Logic Based on the Resolution Principle. Journal of the ACM, Vol. 12, No. 1, p. 23 - 41, 1965.

Random Boolean Formulas Representing any Boolean Function with Asymptotically Equal Probability

(extended abstract)

Petr Savický
Faculty of Mathematics and Physics, Charles University,
Malostranské nám. 25, Praha 1, Czechoslovakia

1. Introduction

The formula size complexity of a Boolean function f depends on the existence or nonexistence of formulas of a given size representing the function f. It might be interesting to study also the number of such formulas. In this case it seems to be natural to choose a model of Boolean formulas which is polynomially equivalent to general formulas and satisfies the following regularity condition: the relative number of very large formulas representing a given Boolean function is nearly the same for all Boolean functions. We construct such a model of formulas. For this purpose we use the method of random formulas with independent subformulas used also in [2], [5] and [1].

Let α be a fixed Boolean connective, i.e. a symbol denoting a function of the type $\{0,1\}^k \to \{0,1\}$, where $k \geq 2$. Let $n \geq 2$ be a fixed natural number.

Definition 1.1 Let x_j for $j=1,2, \dots ,n$ be symbols for Boolean variables and $\neg x_j$ denote the negation of x_j. For any $i \geq 0$ let H_i be the set of formulas defined by

$$H_0 = \{0,1,x_1, \dots ,x_n, \neg x_1, \dots , \neg x_n\}$$
$$H_{i+1} = \{\alpha(\varphi_1,\dots,\varphi_k) \; ; \; \varphi_j \in H_i \text{ for } j=1,2, \dots ,k\}.$$

Notation Let M_α denote the union of H_i for all i and n.

Let T_2^3 be the threshold function "at least two from three", i.e. $T_2^3(x,y,z) = xy \vee yz \vee xz$ and let the selection function $sel(x,y,z)$ be defined by $sel(0,y,z) = y$ and $sel(1,y,z) = z$ for all $y,z \in \{0,1\}$. Using well-known results, see e.g. [6], it can be easily proved that any Boolean formula in an arbitrary but fixed complete basis (for instance $\&, \vee, \neg$) can be transformed into an equivalent formula from M_α with only polynomial increase of the size, if for instance $\alpha = T_2^3$, $\alpha = sel$ or $\alpha(x,y,z) = x \oplus yz$.

Definition 1.2

(a) Let $\tilde{\varphi}_i$ be a random variable denoting a formula chosen randomly from the uniform distribution on H_i. Let $F(\tilde{\varphi}_i)$ denote the Boolean function represented by the formula $\tilde{\varphi}_i$.

(b) For any $f:\{0,1\}^n \to \{0,1\}$ let $p_i(f) = P(F(\tilde{\varphi}_i)=f)$.

Thus $p_i(f)$ is the relative number of formulas in H_i representing the function f. The probabilistic formulation is used in order to simplify the computations.

Now we state the regularity condition mentioned at the beginning more exactly. We require that the limit of $p_i(f)$ when $i \to \infty$ is equal for all f. Hence we study the asymptotic behaviour of $p_i(f)$. The following lemma allows us to study the properties of $\tilde{\varphi}_i$ by induction on i and is used in section 4.

Lemma 1.3 The formula $\tilde{\varphi}_{i+1}$ has the same distribution as the formula $\alpha(\tilde{\varphi}_{i,1}, \dots, \tilde{\varphi}_{i,k})$, where $\tilde{\varphi}_{i,j}$ are independent realizations of $\tilde{\varphi}_i$.

Proof It is easy to see that under the assumptions on $\tilde{\varphi}_{i,j}$, the formula $\alpha(\tilde{\varphi}_{i,1}, \dots, \tilde{\varphi}_{i,k})$ has the uniform distribution on H_{i+1}. □

2. Notation

For any $s \geq 0$ let $B_s = \{0,1\}^s$. Let $0_s \in B_s$ be the element consisting only of zeros. For any $u,v \in B_s$ let $|u|$ be the number of indices j satisfying $v_j=1$ and $u \leq v$ mean $u_j \leq v_j$ for $j=1,2,\dots,s$. Let $u < v$ mean $u \leq v$ and $u \neq v$.

Further let $F_n = \{0,1\}^{B_n}$. Let the meaning of $|u|$, $u \leq v$ for $u, v \in F_n$ be analogous to the meaning for $u,v \in B_s$ with $u(a), v(a)$ for $a \in B_n$ instead of u_j, v_j.

For simplicity of notation we abbreviate 2^n as d and also we use the notation 0_d for the zero function in F_n although F_n is not exactly B_d.

3. Results

Definition 3.1 We say that the connective α is

(a) balanced, if $|\{t \in B_k \; ; \; \alpha(t)=1\}| = 2^{k-1}$
(b) linear, if $\alpha(t) \equiv c_0 \oplus c_1 t_1 \oplus \dots \oplus c_k t_k$ for some $c_0, c_1, \dots, c_k \in \{0,1\}$.

Theorem 3.2 The following two statements are equivalent
(a) α is balanced and nonlinear
(b) for all $f \in F_n$ the following holds $\lim_{i\to\infty} p_i(f) = (1/2)^d$.

Remark There is no binary connective α satisfying the two conditions in (a) from Theorem 3.2 simultaneously. Examples of such ternary connectives may be T_2^3, sel and $x \oplus yz$. Any other ternary balanced and nonlinear connective can be obtained from these ones by permuting and negating variables.

Further, for a particular connective, namely T_2^3, we prove the following estimate.

Definition 3.3 For any $x \in (-1,1)$ let $\beta(x) =_{df} \lim_{i\to\infty} (\frac{4}{3})^i t_i$, where $t_0 = x$ and $t_{i+1} = \frac{3}{4} t_i + \frac{1}{4}(t_i)^3$ for $i \geq 1$.

Theorem 3.4 Let $\alpha = T_2^3$. Then for all $f \in F_n$ the following holds

$$p_i(f) = (1/2)^d (1 + c_f (3/4)^i + o((3/4)^{2i})),$$

where

$$c_f = \sum_{\substack{\{a,b\} \subseteq B_n \\ a \neq b}} \beta(1 - 2\,\frac{h(a,b)}{n+1})(-1)^{f(a) \oplus f(b)},$$

where $h(a,b) = |a \oplus b|$ is the Hamming distance of a,b.

Remark This theorem implies that for $\alpha = T_2^3$ the convergence of $p_i(f)$ is of the first order. There are connectives (with at least four arguments) for which the convergence is of higher order.

Some weaker results obtained by another method were announced in [3].

4. Proofs

Proof of (b)$\Rightarrow$(a) in Theorem 3.2 Suppose (b) is satisfied. If α is linear then all formulas in H_i for all $i \geq 0$ represent linear functions. This is a contradiction. Hence α is nonlinear.

Further, let $N = |\{t \in B_k \; ; \; \alpha(t) = 1\}|$ and $a \in B_n$. By Lemma 1.3, if $X_{i+1} = \widetilde{\varphi}_{i+1}(a)$, $X_i = \widetilde{\varphi}_i(a)$ and $X_{i,j}$ are independent realizations of X_i, then $X_{i+1} = \alpha(X_{i,j}, \dots, X_{i,k})$. If the probability $P(X_i = 1)$ is near to 1/2 then the probability $P(X_{i+1} = 1)$ is near to $N/2^k$. It is easy to see that (b) implies $\lim_{i\to\infty} P(X_i = 1) = 1/2$ and hence (b) implies that α is balanced. □

We mention only basic lemmas and only the main idea of the proof of (a)⇒(b) in Theorem 3.2 and of Theorem 3.4. The complete proof can be found in [4]. It requires very technical computations which are not presented here.

We want to study the distribution of $F(\widetilde{\varphi}_i)$ for increasing i. The distribution of $F(\widetilde{\varphi}_0)$ can be described explicitely from Definitions 1.1 and 1.2. Further we use induction on i.

<u>Lemma 4.1</u> $p_{i+1}(f) = \sum_{\alpha(f_1, \dots, f_k)=f} p_i(f_1) \cdot \dots \cdot p_i(f_k)$

<u>Proof</u> Using Lemma 1.3 we can write $P(F(\widetilde{\varphi}_{i+1}) = f) = P(\alpha(F(\widetilde{\varphi}_{i,1}), \dots, F(\widetilde{\varphi}_{i,k})) = f)$. The random event in the right hand side of this equality is a disjoint union of events

$$F(\widetilde{\varphi}_{i,1}) = f_1 \,\&\, \dots \,\&\, F(\widetilde{\varphi}_{i,k}) = f_k$$

for all k-tuples $\langle f_1, \dots, f_k\rangle$ satisfying $\alpha(f_1, \dots, f_k) = f$. Using independency of $\widetilde{\varphi}_{i,j}$ for $j=1,2, \dots, k$ we get the statement of the lemma. □

If we use Lemma 4.1 in a direct way, we should study the asymptotic behaviour of sequences $\{p_i(f)\}_{i=0}^{\infty}$ in parallel for all Boolean functions f. It appears that it is possible to simplify the situation if we use the followig transformation. The method is a generalization of the method used in [2].

<u>Definition 4.2</u> For any $g, v \in F_n$ and $r, t \in B_k$ let $\langle g,v\rangle$ denote $\bigoplus_{a \in B_n} g(a)v(a)$ and $\langle r,t\rangle$ denote $\bigoplus_{j=1}^{k} r_j t_j$.

<u>Definition 4.3</u> For any $v \in F_n$ and $i \geq 0$ let $\Delta_i(v)$ be defined as follows

$$\Delta_i(v) = \sum_{g \in F_n} p_i(g)(-1)^{\langle g,v\rangle}$$

<u>Lemma 4.4</u> For any $f \in F_n$ and $i \geq 0$ the following holds

$$p_i(f) = (1/2)^d \sum_{v \in F_n} \Delta_i(v)(-1)^{\langle f,v\rangle}$$

<u>Proof</u> We substitute for $\Delta_i(v)$ from Definition 4.3 and simplify the resulting formula. See also [2]. □

<u>Lemma 4.5</u> The following two statements are equivalent

(a) for all $f \in F_n$ $\lim_{i\to\infty} p_i(f) = (1/2)^d$

(b) for all $w \in F_n$, $w \neq 0_d$ $\lim_{i\to\infty} \Delta_i(w) = 0$.

Proof It is a simple consequence of Definition 4.3, Lemma 4.4 and the fact that $\Delta_i(0_d) = 1$. □

Hence for the proof of (a)⇒(b) in Theorem 3.2 it is sufficient to prove (b) from Lemma 4.5 under the assumption that α is balanced and nonlinear. For this purpose we use the following theorem. It is a reformulation of Lemma 4.1 in terms of $\Delta_i(v)$.

Theorem 4.6 For any $r \in B_k$ let

$$S_\alpha(r) = (1/2)^k \sum_{t \in B_k} (-1)^{\langle t,r\rangle \oplus \alpha(t)}.$$

Then for any $w \in F_n$ and $i \geq 0$ the following holds

$$\Delta_{i+1}(w) = \sum_{\substack{\vec{v} \in (F_n)^k \\ v_j \leq w}} \left(\prod_{\substack{a \in B_n \\ w(a)=1}} S_\alpha(\vec{v}(a)) \right) \Delta_i(v_1). \;\ldots\; .\Delta_i(v_k) .$$

Sketch of the proof We express $\Delta_{i+1}(w)$ in terms of $p_{i+1}(f)$ using Definition 4.3. Further, we substitute for $p_{i+1}(f)$ from Lemma 4.1. Then we express all the ocurrences of $p_i(f_j)$ in terms of $\Delta_i(v_j)$ from Lemma 4.4 and at last we simplify the resulting formula.□

Sketch of the proof of (a)⇒(b) in Theorem 3.2 We prove (b) from Lemma 4.5. We proceed by induction on w . In the formula from Theorem 4.6 $\Delta_{i+1}(w)$ depends only on $\Delta_i(w)$ and $\Delta_i(v)$ for $v < w$. Using the induction hypothesis on $\Delta_i(v)$ we get $\Delta_{i+1}(w) = \omega_s(\Delta_i(w)) + \mathcal{E}_i$, where $s = |w|$, ω_s is a polynomial of order k and $\mathcal{E}_i = o(1)$. The case $s = 1$ must be handled separately. For $s \geq 2$ we estimate the coefficients in ω_s and study the properties of iterations of ω_s . The case $s = 2$ is slightly different from $s \geq 3$. For the required estimates of the coefficients in ω_s we use the following representation of $S_\alpha(r)$.

Definition 4.7 Let $e_\alpha \in E^{B_k}$ (E denotes the set of real numbers) and $e_r \in E^{B_k}$ for any $r \in B_k$ be vectors defined as follows

for all $t \in B_k$ $e_\alpha(t) = (1/2)^{k/2}(-1)^{\alpha(t)}$
and $e_r(t) = (1/2)^{k/2}(-1)^{\langle t,r\rangle}$.

It is easy to see that $S_\alpha(r) = e_\alpha e_r$, i.e. the scalar product of e_α and e_r, and that the vectors e_r for $r \in B_k$ form an orthonormal basis of E^{B_k}. In the case $s = 2$ it implies for instance that the sum of the coefficients of ω_s is equal to one, because it is $\sum S_\alpha(r)^2$. The most important consequence of this considerations is that the linear coefficient of ω_s for $s \geq 2$ is less than one if α is not identically equal to any of its arguments nor its negation. □

<u>Sketch of the proof of Theorem 3.4</u> Assume $\alpha = T_2^3$. By more carefull computations we get

(a) $|w|$ is odd $\Rightarrow$ $\Delta_i(w) = \emptyset$

(b) $|w|$ is even $\Rightarrow$ $\Delta_i(w) = O((3/4)^{i|w|/2})$

In particular, if $|w| = 2$ then $\Delta_{i+1}(w) = \frac{3}{4}\Delta_i(w) + \frac{1}{4}\Delta_i(w)^3$.

Using these facts we can get Theorem 3.4 if we restrict the sum in Lemma 4.4 to $v \in F_n$ satisfying $|v| \leq 2$. □

5. Acknowledgement

The author is deeply indebted to P.Pudlák for a lot of helpful discussion and valuable remarks concerning this paper.

[1] Boppana,R.B.: Amplification of Probabilistic Boolean Formulas, Proceedings of the 26th Annual Symposium on Foundations of Computer Science, 1985, pp. 20 - 29.

[2] Razborov,A.A.: Formulas of Bounded Depth in Basis $\{\&,\oplus\}$ and some Combinatorial Problems (Russian), to appear in Složnosť algoritmov i prikladnaja matěmatičeskaja logika, S.I.Adjan editor

[3] Savický,P.: Boolean Functions Represented by Random Formulas, announcement,Commentationes Mathematicea Universitatis Carolinae, 28,2,1987

[4] Savický,P.:Random Boolean Formulas Representing any Boolean Function with Asymptotically Equal Probability,TR Dept. of Comp. Science,Charles Univ.,Prague,1987,to appear in Discrete Mathematics

[5] Valiant,L.G.:Short Monotone Formulae for the Majority Function, Journal of Algorithms 5,pp.363-366,1984

[6] Wegener,I.:The Complexity of Boolean Functions,Stuttgart:B.G. Teubner/New York:Wiley 1987

ON THE POWER OF COMMUNICATION IN ALTERNATING MACHINES

A. Slobodová
Dept. of Theoretical Cybernetics, Comenius University
CS - 842 15 Bratislava, Czechoslovakia

Abstract. The synchronized alternating devices are introduced as a generalization of alternating devices. The synchronization enables the communication among parallel processes in alternating computations. A new complexity measure - synchronization complexity is introduced to measure the amount of communication among processes. The basic results covering the reduction theorem for synchronization complexity and simulations among nondeterministic, alternating and synchronized alternating devices are established. There are found very simple devices that, adding synchronized alternation, are as powerful as Turing machines. As opposed to the fact that two-way alternating finite automata recognize only regular languages it is proved that NLOG is exactly the family of languages recognized by two-way synchronized alternating finite automata with parallel complexity 1. Already one-way synchronized alternating finite automata are more powerful than finite automata. However, the log n synchronization adds nothing to any multihead alternating device. Several further results for different types of devices are established. Using simulation through synchronized alternating devices a new simulation result of nondeterministic devices by alternating ones are obtained.

1. Introduction

Recently many parallel models have been investigated. One of them - alternation - was introduced in Chandra et al. /1981/ as a generalization of nondeterminism. In related papers [3, 5 - 14] the investigations of alternating machines continued.

As a general model of an alternating device a so-called k - head t - tape alternating machine, am /k, t/, is considered. As outlined in Fig. 1 an am /k, t/ N has an input tape with left and right end-markers ¢ and $, and t semi-infinite storage tapes with the left end-marker. Then N has k read-only input tape heads and t read-write storage tape heads.

A *step* of M consists of reading one symbol from each tape, writing one symbol on each storage tape, moving the input and storage heads in specified directions and entering a new state from a finite control, in accordance with the next move relation. The state set is partitioned into accepting, rejecting, existential and universal states.

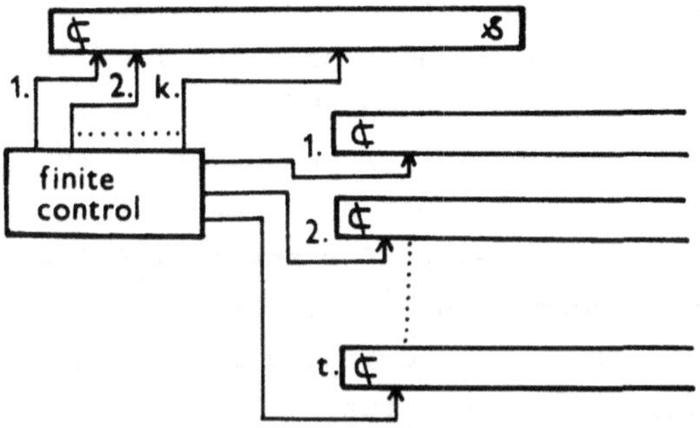

The *synchronized alternating machine* sam /k, t/ M is an am /k, t/, some states of which have a sync element from some given finite set. These states and the configurations associated with them are called sync states and sync configurations, respectively. When a process enters a sync state, it stops and waits until all parallel processes either enter the states with the same sync element or stop in final states.

A *configuration* of M is given by the input, the contents of the storage-tapes, the positions of the input and storage tape heads, and the current state. The *initial configuration* of M on input x is

$$I_M/x/ = /x, \underbrace{\varepsilon, \ldots, \varepsilon}_{t}, \underbrace{1, \ldots, 1}_{k+t}, q_o/$$

where q_o is an initial state and ε is the empty string. A configuration is called existential, universal, accepting, or rejecting, respectively if the corresponding state is existential, universal, accepting, or rejecting, respectively.

Given M, we write $\alpha \vdash_M \alpha'$ and say α' is *successor* of α if the configuration α' follows from the configuration α in one step of M . $\vdash^*_M$ denotes the reflexive transitive closure of relation $\vdash_M$.

A *sequential computation* of M on input x is a sequence

$I_M/x/ = \alpha_1 \vdash_{\overline{M}} \ldots \vdash_{\overline{M}} \alpha_m$. Any subsequence $\alpha_i \vdash_{\overline{M}} \ldots \vdash_{\overline{M}} \alpha_m$, for any i; $1 \leq i \leq m$, is a process computed by M.

Let c be a process computed by M and $\alpha_1 \vdash_{\overline{M}}^{*} \ldots \vdash_{\overline{M}}^{*} \alpha_r$ be a subsequence of c that consists of all sync configurations of c. Suppose for all j; $1 \leq j \leq r$, S_j is the sync element of α_j. Then $S_1, \ldots, S_r$ is called a sync sequence of c.

A computation of M is a finite, nonempty labelled tree V with the following properties:

1. Each node u of V is labelled with a configuration l/u/.
2. If u is an internal /non-leaf/ node of V and l/u/ is existential, then u has exactly one child v such that $l/u/ \vdash_{\overline{M}} l/v/$.
3. If u is an internal node of V, l/u/ is universal and $\{\alpha \mid l/u/ \vdash_{\overline{M}} \alpha\} = \{\alpha_1, \ldots, \alpha_n\}$, then u has exactly n children $v_1, \ldots, v_n$ such that $l/v_i/ = \alpha_i$, for any i; $1 \leq i \leq n$.
4. For any two sync sequences $S^1 = S_1^1, \ldots, S_p^1$; $S^2 = S_1^2, \ldots, S_r^2$, corresponding with two paths of V beginning in the root $S_i^1 = S_i^2$ for all i; $1 \leq i < \min\{p, r\}$ must be true.

An accepting computation of M on x is a computation of M the root of which is labelled with $I_M/x/$, the leaves are labelled with accepting configurations and 4. is true for all i; $1 \leq i \leq \min\{p, r\}$.

We define the language recognized by an sam /k, t/ M as $L/M/ = \{x \mid \text{there is an accepting computation of M on } x\}$, in natural way.

The longest sync sequence over all the sequential computations in an accepting computation V is called a sync sequence of V.

For the well-known classes of languages the same abbreviations are used as in [4]. The devices used in this paper are the same as mentioned in [16]. Of course, sam /k, t/ is a general synchronized alternating model and all well-known deterministic, nondeterministic, alternating and other synchonized alternating devices can easily be derived from it. To represent the differ kinds of devices systematically we use the notation j XY /k, t/ where

j: 1-one-way
   2 or absent - two-way

X: sa - synchronized alternating
   a - alternating
   n - nondeterministic
   d - deterministic

Y: fa - finite automaton
   cm - multicounter machine

bm - multicounter machine with blind counters

A bm is a cm which knows nothing about the contents of its blind counters during the computation, but it can accept only if its blind counters are empty.

pdm - pushdown automaton

tm - Turing machine

k /positive integer, $k \geq 1$/: the number of input tape heads

t /non-negative integer/: the number of storage media /those are tapes, pushdown stores, counters etc./. When $t = 0$ we can leave it out.

If k and t are arbitrary, we shall say that such a device is multihead and multitape.

The class of languages recognized by some kind of devices is denoted by the same but capital letters as the respective device.

Synchronization is introduced as a new complexity measure. Time, space and parallelism are also investigated. A computational complexity is understood as the greatest complexity over all accepting computations of the machine on all inputs with the same length. Suppose M is a sam /k, t/ and V is an accepting computation of M.

For any configuration α let space /α/ denote the sum of the lengths of the nonblank storage-tapes contents in α. Then the space of V is $\mathcal{S}/V/ = \max \{\text{space } /\alpha/ \mid \alpha \text{ accurs in } V\}$. The function $S_M/n/ : N \to N$ is called a space complexity of M if for all positive integers n

$S_M/n/ = \max / \{\mathcal{S}/W/ \mid W$ is an accepting computation of M on $x \in L/M/$ and $|x| = n$, where $|x|$ denotes the length of $x\} \cup \{1\}$ /.

Let $S_1, \ldots, S_m$ be a sync sequence of V and let time $/S_i/$ denote the maximum number of steps of M from the /i-1/-th sync configuration /from the initial configuration if i = 1/ either to the i-th sync configuration or to an accepting one, if no other sync configuration appears. The maximum is brought over all the sequential computations in V. From the above it follows that time $/S_i/$ is generally time between /i-1/-th and i-th synchronization. The time of V is

$\mathcal{T}/V/ = \sum_{i=1}^{m} \text{time } /S_i/$

$T_M/n/ = \max (\{\mathcal{T}/W/ \mid W$ is an accepting computation of M on $x \in L/M/$, and $|x| = n\} \cup \{0\})$ defined on positive integers is called a time complexity of M.

Parallelism of an accepting computation V of M is defined as in [7]. That is, $\mathcal{P}/V/$ is a number of universal configurations in V. The parallel complexity of M is a mapping defined on positive integers as follows.

$P_M/n/ = \max \left(\{\mathcal{P}/W/ \quad W \text{ is an accepting computation of } M \text{ on } x \in L/M/, \text{ and } |x| = n\} \cup \{0\}\right)$.

The length of the sync sequence of V is called a synchronization of V. We denote it by $\mathcal{S}yn/V/$. The <u>synchronization /sync/ complexity</u> of M is a function defined on positive integers as follows.
$Syn_M/n/ = \max \left(\{\mathcal{S}yn/W/ \mid W \text{ is an accepting computation of } M \text{ on } x \in L/M/ \text{ and } |x| = n\} \cup \{0\}\right)$.

<u>Notations for the complexity classes:</u>

The class of languges recognized by satm with the time (space) complexity f/n/ is denoted by SA-TIME /f/n// (SA-SPACE /f/n/). Similarly the alternating, nondeterministic and deterministic classes: A-TIME /f/n//, A-SPACE /f/n//, N-TIME /f/n//, N-SPACE /f/n//, D-TIME /f/n//, and D-SPACE /f/n//; can be defined. For the well-known classes: $\bigcup_{c>0}$ D-TIME $/n^c/$, $\bigcup_{c>1}$ N-SPACE $/\log_c n/$ and $\bigcup_{c>1}$ D-SPACE $/\log_c n/$ we use the abbreviations: P, NLOG and DLOG, respectively.

Since synchronization as a new complexity measure has been introduced, we investigate its constant reduction.

<u>Theorem 1.1</u>

Let K be a positive integer and M be a sam /k, t/ accepting L/M/ with the sync, time, space and parallel complexity $Syn_M/n/$, $T_M/n/$, $S_M/n/$ and $P_M/n/$, respectively.

Then there exists a sam /k, t/ N such that:

1. L/M/ = L/N/
2. $Syn_N/n/ = \lceil Syn_M/n/ / K \rceil$
3. $T_N/n/ \leq 2T_M/n/ + 2$, $S_N/n/ = S_M/n/$, $P_N/n/ = P_M/n/$.

The idea of the proof is based on the fact that in one element of a sync sequence of an accepting computation of N K elements from the sync sequence of M are coded.

2. Nondeterminism versus synchronized alternation

This section discusses the power of alternation and synchronization vis-a'-vis nondeterminism. The addition of these abilities to nondeterministic devices enables us to simplify them by diminishing the number of their input heads and storage tapes, without the loss of their power. The below-mentioned simulation requests only one uni-

versal configuration in any accepting computation.
On the other hand any sam /k, t/ that computes with the parallel complexity 1 can be simulated by some nm /k', t'/. These two results have several interesting consequences. It is shown that alternation and synchronization strenghten currently simple devices, for instance a multicounter machine 1 ncm/1/ /or a finite automaton 1 nfa/1//, just enough to recognize so much as a Turing machine /or nondeterministic Turing nachine in log n space, respectively/.

Theorem 2.1

Let k and t be positive integers and M be a nm /k, t/ accepting L/M/ with time /space, sync and parallel/ complexity $T_M/n/$ $/S_M/n/$, $Syn_M/n/$ and $P_M/n/$, respectively/.

Then there is a sam /1,1/ N such that:
1. L/M/ = L/N/
2. $T_N/n/ = 2T_M/n/ + 2$, $S_N/n/ = S_M/n/$, $P_N/n/ = 1$, $Syn_N/n/ = 2T_M/n/$.

Proof: Let M be a nm /k, t/, where k and t are arbitrary positive integers. Assume that M has k input-tape heads $H_1, \ldots, H_k$ and t storage--tape heads $H_{k+1}, \ldots, H_{k+t}$. Now the behaviour of a sam /1,1/ N simulating M will be described.

A single input-tape head of N simulated $H_1, \ldots, H_k$, and a single storage tape works up t storage-tapes of M. An initial configuration is the only universal configuration in a computation. The computation branches from it in k + t parallel processes. In the i-th process $/1 \leq i \leq k + t/$, N simulated the work of H_i. For i; $1 \leq i \leq k$ the storage--tape head of N remains in the i'th process without movement all the time. Similarly the N's input-tape head in the j-th process, for j; $k + 1 \leq j \leq k + t$, are without movement. Hence, each of the processes operates with one head only. At the same time, each of them must know what is read by the other M's heads. That is why the processes cannot run independently and they must communicate with each other. This communication is mediated by the sync states. All of the configurations are the sync ones.

Now we show how N simulates one step of M. Each of M's configurations corresponds to two configurations in each of the parallel passing sequential computations of N. The first configuration from these ones in the i'th process is given by the same input as M's configuration, by the same position of an "active" head as H_i' s one and by a state. This state has two elements. The first element represents the current state of M. The second one is a sync element. It contains the string of k + t symbols which are guessed by N. These elements will be read by all of M's heads in the next step. Without the conformity between the i-th symbol in the string and the symbol really scanned by an active head, the i-th process cannot continue. According to this fact and to the basis of the synchronization, too, N is able to continue only if it has guessed all the symbols correct in all parallel sequential computations.

Since M is nondeterministic, the next step of N, which is given by the choice of M, must also be synchronized. N passes without both heads movement and writing down, to a sync state. Its sync element represents a choice of M, i. e. a new state of M, symbols that will be written and movements of all its heads. After the successful synchronization N passes to a new state and operates with its heads, according to the sync element.

The fact that N accepts an input iff M does is evident. Moreover: $T_N/n/ = 2T_M/n/ + 2$, $S_N/n/ \le S_M/n/$ (if all of the M's storage-tapes use the same space, then $S_N/n/ = \frac{S_M/n/}{t}$), $P_N/n/ = 1$ (only initial configuration is a universal one), and $Syn_N/n/ = 2T_M/n/$ (because all of the configurations except for the first two are sync configurations). This completes the proof of the theorem.

□

Theorem 2.2

Let k and t be positive integers and M be a sam /k, t/ that accepts L/M/ with parallel complexity $P_M/n/ = 1$.

Then there is an equivalent nm /d.k, d.t/, where d is an upper bound on the branching from the universal configuration of M. Moreover if $T_M/n/$ and $S_M/n/$ denote the time and space complexity of M, respectively, then for the time and space complexity of N holds:

$T_N/n/ \le T_M/n/$, $S_N/n/ = S_M/n/$.

Notation: The class of languages recognized with the unique parallel complexity we denote by the upper index 1.

As a consequences of the last two theorems we quote the next two assertions.

Theorem 2.3: $RE = 1\ SACM^1/1/$

Theorem 2.4: $NLOG = 2\ SAFA^1\ /1/ = \bigcup_{k \in N} 2\ SAFA^1\ /k/$

Corollary 2.4.1: $2\ AFA\ /1/ \subsetneq 2\ SAFA\ /1/$

Proposition 2.4.2:

a/ $NLOG \neq P \Leftrightarrow \bigcup_{k \in N} 2\ AFA\ /k/ \neq 2\ SAFA^1\ /1/$

b/ $NLOG = P \Leftrightarrow \bigcup_{k \in N} 2\ AFA\ /k/ \subseteq \bigcup_{k \in N} 2\ SAFA^1\ /k/$

Lemma 2.5: $\forall k \in N$: 1 SACM /k/ = 1 SABM /k/

Theorem 2.6: RE = 1 SABM /1/

3. One-way synchronized alternating finite automata

With regard to the Theorem 2.6 we are interested now in more simple devices.

Theorem 3.1

Any one-way k-head alternating finite automaton /where k > 1/ can be simulated by a one-way /k - 1/-head synchronized alternating finite automaton.

Corollary 3.1.1: 1 AFA /1/ $\subsetneq$ 1 SAFA /1/

Corollary 3.1.2: $\forall k \in N$, $k > 1$: 1 NFA /k/ $\subsetneq$ 1 SAFA /k - 1/

Corollary 3.1.3: $CFL_{1in} \subseteq$ 1 SAFA /1/

Corollary 3.1.4: CFL $\subsetneq$ 1 SAFA /2/

Propositions 3.2:

$1\ SAFA\ /1/ \subseteq \bigcup_{k \in N} 2\ DFA\ /k/ \Rightarrow P = NLOG = DLOG$

$1\ SAFA\ /1/ \subseteq \bigcup_{k \in N} 2\ NFA\ /k/ \Rightarrow P = NLOG$

$1\ SAFA\ /1/ \subseteq \bigcup_{k \in N} 2\ SAFA^1\ /k/ \Rightarrow P = NLOG$

$1\ SAFA^1\ /1/ \subseteq \bigcup_{k \in N} 2\ DFA\ /k/ \Rightarrow NLOG = DLOG$

Theorem 3.3: $\forall k \in N$: 1 $SAFA^1$ /k/ $\subsetneq$ 1 SAFA /k/

4. Alternation versus synchronized alternation

This section considers the capability of alternating devices to simulate synchronization. First we discuss this problem generally /Theorema 4.1/. Since RE = 1 SABM /1/ as was shown in Section 2, we will be interested then in more simple devices-synchromized alternating finite automata. As was shown in the last section, the addition of the synchronization to alternating finite automata makes them more powerful. It is an interesting question, what will happen when we restrict, in some way, the synchronization?

The unigue but essential disadvantage of alternating devices is that the parallel processes run independently, i. e. they cannot communicate. The simplest idea of how to simulate the synchronization is that the alternating device nondeterministically guesses what processes will communicate about. That means /in the terms of synchronized devices/ that a simulating alternating device guesses and remembers a sync sequence of an accepting computation say S. Then it can check during the computation whether or not this guessed sync sequence agrees with the real sync sequence of simulated device, i. e. if a sync sequence of any sequential computation is an initial substring of S. Otherwise, the simulated device could not accept the input. This idea is a base of the proof of the following theorems. The proofs differ only in how a device remembers the guessed sync sequence.

One way is that the simulating device has one storage medium more than the simulated device /Theorem 4.1/. It is also shown that with an appropriate restriction on a sync complexity, either the states /the proof of Theorem 4.2/ or the addition of several heads /the proof of Theorem 4.3/ are sufficient to remember the guessed sync sequence.

Theorem 4.1

Any /one-/ two-way k-head t-tape synchronized alternating machine M can be simulated by a /one-/ two-way k-head /t + 1/-tape alternating machine N. Moreover, one N's tape is an auxiliary pushdown store using one reversal only and

1. $T_N/n/ = T_M/n/ + Syn_M/n/ \leq 2\ T_M/n/$
2. $S_N/n/ = \max \{S_M/n/, Syn_M/n/\}$
3. $P_N/n/ = P_M/n/$.

Corollary 4.1.1: SA-TIME /f/n// $\subseteq$ A-TIME /2 f/n// holds for any function f/n/: N $\rightarrow$ R.

Corollary 4.1.2: SA-SPACE /f/n// $\subseteq \bigcup_{c>0}$ D-TIME $/2^{2^{c.S/n/}}/$ holds for any function f/n/: N $\rightarrow$ R such that f/n/ $\geq$ log n

Corollary 4.1.3: 2 SAFA /1/ $\subsetneq$ 2 $APDA_1$ /1/ $\subseteq$ A-SPACE /n/, where index 1 denotes that pushdown store uses one reversal only.

A constant synchronization addes nothing to any alternating device. The next theorem formulates this result for the finite automata.

Theorem 4.2

The class of languages recognized by /one-/ two-way synchronized alternating finite automata with a constant sync complexity is equivalent to the class of languages recognized by /one-/ two-way k-head alternating finite automata, for any positive integer k.

Theorem 4.3

Any two-way multihead synchronized alternating finite automaton which operates with a sync complexity at most $\log_2 n$ can be simulated by a multihead alternating finite automaton.

Corollary 4.3.1: $\bigcup_{k \in N} 2\ SAFA_{log}\ /k/ = P$

where index log means $\log_2 n$ sync complexity.

Theorem 4.4

Any /one-/ two-way multihead multitape nondeterministic machine M can be simulated by a /one-/ two-way 1-head 1-tape alternating machine N with an auxiliary pushdown store using one reversal only. Moreover, $T_N/n/ = T_M/n/$ and $P_N/n/ = 1$.

Acknowledgments: I would like to thank Juraj Hromkovič for his comments to this paper.

References

1 A. K. Chandra, D. C. Kozen and L. J. Stockmeyer, Alternation, J. of ACM 28 /1988/ 114 - 133.
2 S. Ginsburg, Algebraic and automata-theoretic properties of formal languages /North Holland, Amsterdam, 1975/.
3 E. M. Gurari and O. H. Ibarra, /Semi-/ alternating stack automata, Math. System Theory 15 /1982/ 211 - 224.
4 J. E. Hopcroft and J. D. Ullman, Formal languages and their relation to automata /Addison - Wesley, Reading, MA, 1969/.
5 J. Hromkovič, Alternating multicounter machine with constant number of reversals, Information Processing Letters 21 /1985/ 7 - 9.
6 J. Hromkovič, On the power of alternation in automata theory, J. of Comp. and Sys. Sci. 31 /1985/ 28 - 39.
7 J. Hromkovič, Tradeoffs for language recognition on parallel computing models, Proc. 13th ICALP'86, Lecture Notes in Computer Science 226 /1986/ 157 - 166.
8 K. Inoue, A. Ito, I. Takanami, H. Taniguchi, A space-hierarchy result on two-dimensional alternating Turing machines with only universal states, Information Sciences 35 /1985/ 79 - 90.
9 K. Inoue, A. Ito, I. Takanami, H. Taniguchi, Two-dimensional alternating Turing machines with only universal states, Inform. and Control 55 /1982/ 193 - 221.
10 K. Inoue, H. Matsuno, I. Takanami, H. Taniguchi, Alternating simple multihead finite automata, Theoret. Comp. Sci. 36 /1985/ 291 - 308.
11 K. N. King, Alternating multihead finite automata, Proc. 8th ICALP'81, Lecture Notes in Computer Science 115 /1981/ 506 - 520.

12 R. J. Ladner, R. J. Lipton and L. J. Stockmeyer, Alternating pushdown and stack automata, SIAM J. Comput. 13 /1984/ 135 - 155.

13 W. J. Paul, E. J. Prauss and R. Reischuk, On alternation, Acta Informatica 14 /1980/ 243 - 255.

14 W. J. Paul, R. Reischuk, On alternation II., Acta Informatica 14 /1980/ 391 - 403.

15 A. Slobodová, Výpočtová sila alternujúcich zariadení s komunikáciou. Comenius University Bratislava, Czechoslovakia, April1987 /in Slovac/.

16 K. Wagner, G. Wechsung, Computational complexity, Mathematische Monographien 19 /VEG Deutscher Verlag der Wissenschaften, Berlin, 1986/.

CLASSES OF CNF-FORMULAS WITH BACKTRACKING TREES OF EXPONENTIAL OR LINEAR AVERAGE ORDER FOR EXACT-SATISFIABILITY

Ewald Speckenmeyer
Abteilung Informatik, Universität Dortmund
Postfach 500 500, D-4600 Dortmund 50

Abstract

We analyse the average case behaviour of a simple backtracking algorithm for determining all exact-satisfying truth assignments of CNF-formulas over n variables with r clauses of length s. A truth assignment exact-satisfies a formula, if in every clause exactly one literal is set to true.

1. For the class of formulas given by the parameters n, r, and s a formula computable in polynomial time is derived, by which the average number of nodes in backtracking trees can be determined under the uniform instance distribution.
2. In case where all clauses have length $s = 3$, it is shown that the average number of nodes in backtracking trees is growing exponentially in n, if $r = 0(n)$, and it is at most n, if $r \geq \frac{37}{40} n^2$.

1 Introduction

The exact-satisfiability problem is to decide whether a boolean formula F in conjunctive normal form (CNF) has a satisfying truth assignment t of the variables occuring in F s.t. every clause c of F (a clause is a disjunction of literals and a literal is a boolean variable a or the negation $\overline{a}$ of a) contains exactly one literal x set to true under t. In this case t is called an exact-satisfying (x-satisfying) truth assignment. The problem is known to be NP-complete, see e.g. [3], problem $LO4$, even if all clauses have exactly three literals and if no negated variables occur.
In case of the exact-satisfiability problem without negated variables, we deal with an alternative formulation of the exact cover problem, namely the problem whether a collection $\mathcal{M} = \{M_1, ..., M_n\}$ of subsets over the universe $U = \cup\ \mathcal{M} = \{u_1, ..., u_r\}$ contains a subcollection $\mathcal{M}' \subseteq \mathcal{M}$ s.t. $\cup\ \mathcal{M}' = U$ and every $u \in U$ belongs to exactly one set in $\mathcal{M}'$. Then $\mathcal{M}'$ is called an exact cover of $\mathcal{M}$. An instance $\mathcal{M}$ of exact cover is transformed into an instance F of exact-satisfiability by associating with each set $M \in \mathcal{M}$ exactly one variable a and with each element $u \in U$ exactly one clause c s.t. a occurs in c iff $u \in M$. Then it is easy to see that an x-satisfying truth assignment of F corresponds to an exact cover of $\mathcal{M}$ and vice versa.
The exact cover problem with weights $w_1, ..., w_n \in \Re$ for the sets $M_1, ..., M_n \in \mathcal{M}$, where for an exact cover of minimal (maximal) cost is asked, is called the set partitioning problem. In their survey paper of set partitioning Balas and Padberg rank set partitioning among all special structures of integer programming to be "a likely candidate for number one", because of its

widespread applications, see [1]. An extensive list of references concerning applications of this problem can be found there, too.
Now it is not hard to see that the exact satisfiability problem with weights from $\Re$ on the variables, where for minimal (maximal) x-satisfying truth assignments is asked (the weights of the variables set to true are added), is a natural extension of the set partitioning problem. In order to determine a minimal (maximal) x-satisfying truth assignment of some formula F we have to find out all x-satisfying truth assignments of F in general and then have to choose an optimal one among them. We therefore consider in this paper a simple backtracking algorithm for determining all x-satisfying truth assignments of formulas and we will estimate its average running time applied to formulas over n variables with r clauses, all of lenght s, under the uniform instance distribution.
Before formulating our results we first introduce some notations and definitions.
Let $L = \{a_1, \overline{a_1}, ..., a_n, \overline{a_n}\}$ be the set of literals over the set $V = \{a_1, ..., a_n\}$ of boolean variables and let *cl (n,s)* $:= \{x_{i_1} + ... + x_{i_s} | 1 \leq i_1 < ... < i_s \leq n, x_{i_j} \in \{a_{i_j}, \overline{a_{i_j}}\}\}$ be the set of clauses (= disjunctions of literals) of length s over V. A clause $c = x_{i_1} + ... + x_{i_s}$ is represented by the set $\{x_{i_1}, ... x_{i_s}\}$ of its literals.
By $cl\ (n,s)^r$ the set of formulas in CNF consisting of r clauses from *cl (n,s)* is denoted. A formula $F \in cl(n,s)^r$ is represented by an ordered multiset of clauses.
A (partial) truth assignment t defined on V is a partial function $t : V \rightarrow L$, where $t(a_i) \in \{a_i, \overline{a}_i\}(t(a_i) = a_i(\overline{a}_i)$ means a_i is set true (false)). We will identify t with the set $\{t(a_i) | t(a_i)$ is defined, $a_i \in V\}$ and we denote by $\overline{t} := \{\overline{t(a_i)} | t(a_i) \in t\}$, as usual $\overline{\overline{a}}_i = a_i$.
Let $c = \{x_{i_1}, ..., x_{i_s}\} \in cl(n,s)$, then t $\underline{x - satisfies}$ c and we write $t_x(c) =$ true iff $|t \cap c| = 1$ and $|\overline{t} \cap c| = |c| - 1$. If $|t \cap c| \geq 2$ or $c \subseteq \overline{t}$ then t $\underline{x - falsifies}$ c and we write $t_x(c) =$ false. $t_x(c)$ is undefined iff either $|t \cap c| = \emptyset$ and $c \not\subseteq \overline{t}$ or $|t \cap c| = 1$ and $|t \cap c| \leq |c| - 2$.
Let $F \in cl(n,s)^r$ then t $\underline{x - satisfies}$ F ($t_x(F) =$ true) iff $\forall c \in F : t_x(c)=$ true, and if there is some $c \in F$ s.t. $t_x(c) =$ false then t $\underline{x - falsifies}$ $F(t_x(F) =$ false). Otherwise $t_x(F)$ is undefined.
F is called $\underline{x - satisfiable}$ iff there is some truth assignment t s.t. $t_x(F) =$ true. A $\underline{x - satisfiable}$ truth assignment t of F with $|t| = |V|$ is called a *solution* of F.
The following simple backtracking algorithm determines all solutions t of $F \in cl(n,s)^r$. The algorithm uses a stack, which stores (partial) truth assignments t of V satisfying $t_x(F) \neq$ false.

Algorithm XSAT

1. read input formula F;
2. push $t = \emptyset$ on the stack;
3. repeat
4. pop top-assignment $t = \{x_i | n \geq i \geq n - j + 1\}, j \geq 0$, from the stack;
5. *if* $t_x(F) =$ true *and* $|t| = n$ *then* output "t is a solution"
6. *else if* $|t| < n$ *then*
7. *begin*
8. $t_1 := t \cup \{a_{n-j}\}; t_2 := t \cup \{\overline{a}_{n-j}\}$;
9. *for* $i := 1$ *to* 2 *do*

10. $\underline{if}$ $t_{i,x}(F)$ is not false $\underline{then}$ push t_i on the stack;

11. $\underline{end}$

12. $\underline{until}$ stack is empty;

It es easy to see that XSAT solves our problem. In order to analyse XSAT it is convenient to identify the computation of XSAT applied to $F \in cl(n,s)^r$ with a unique subtree $T(F)$ of the complete binary tree T_n of depth n. $T(F)$ is node-valued and is called the *backtracking tree of F*. The value at a node of $T(F)$ at depth $k, 0 \leq k \leq n$, is a (partial) truth assignment $t = \{x_n, ..., x_{n-k+1}\}$, reflecting the order in which F is processed by XSAT.
I.e. the value at the root node of $T(F)$ is the empty truth assignment. If v is a node at depth k with the value $t = \{x_n, ..., x_{n-k+1}\}, 0 \leq k < n$, then $t_x(F) \neq$ false always holds. If $|t| = n$ then t is a solution of F, and if $|t| = k < n$ then in $T(F)$ the left (right) son of v exists and its value is $t_2 = t \cup \{\overline{a}_{n-j}\} (t_1 = t \cup \{a_{n-j}\})$ if $t_{2,x}(F) \neq$ false ($t_{1,x}(F) \neq$ false).
Denote by $|T(F)|$ the number of nodes of $T(F)$. Then the following result is obvious.

Lemma 1:
XSAT determines all solutions of a formula $F \in cl(n,s)^r$ in $0((n+|F|) \cdot |T(F)|)$ steps. □
If XSAT is applied to formulas F over n variables with r clauses, where the clauses of F are generated independently and each variable $a_i \in V$ occurs in a clause c either unnegated with probability p or negated with probability q or not at all with probability $1-p-q$, for $p, q > 0$ s.t. $p+q \leq 1$, then XSAT produces backtracking trees with $0(1)$ nodes in the average, if $r \cdot \geq (pq)^{-1} \cdot ln2$. This result is shown in [7] and it implies that the subset of formulas, which are x-satisfiable, is sparse under this random generation procedure.
In this paper we study the average size of backtracking trees, if XSAT is applied to formulas from the uniformly distributed class $cl(n,s)^r$.
We first derive in chapter 2 a relation between the parameters n,r and s s.t. the subset of x-satisfiable formulas in the class $cl(n,s)^r$, whose instances are distributed uniformly, is sparse, too. We show

Theorem 1:
Let $c > (s - \log s)^{-1}$. Then the probability that a randomly chosen formula from $cl(n,s)^r$ is x-satisfiable is going down to 0, for growing values of n, if $r \geq c \cdot n$. □
Next a formula is derived in chapter 2, by which the average number of nodes in backtracking trees of XSAT applied to $cl(n,s)^r$ can be determined in time polynomial in n, r, and s.

Theorem 2:
The average number of nodes in the backtracking trees $T(F)$ of formulas $F \in cl(n,s)^r$ according to XSAT is

$$1 + \sum_{k=1}^{n} 2^k \left[\frac{\sum_{i=0}^{s-1} \binom{k}{i} \cdot 2^{-i} \left[\binom{n-k}{s-i} + \frac{k-i}{2} \binom{n-k}{s-i-1} \right]}{\binom{n}{s}} \right]^r \qquad (1)$$

where we define $\binom{l}{m} = 0$, if $m > l$. □

Unfortunately we obtain no immediate knowledge about the growth of formula (1), whether it is polynomial or exponential, for certain nontrivial relations between n,r, and s. We solve this problem in chapter 3 for the classes $cl(n,3)^{0(n)}$, i.e. for the classes of formulas with clauses of length $s = 3$ and with the number of clauses growing at most linearly in n. We show

Theorem 3:
The average number of nodes in the backtracking trees $T(F)$ of formulas $F \in cl(n,3)^r$, for $r = 0(n)$, according to XSAT is growing exponentially in n. □
From the proof of this theorem we immediatly obtain.

Corollary 1:
The average number of nodes in the backtracking trees of formulas from $cl(n,3)^r$, for $r \geq \frac{37}{40}n^2$ according to XSAT, is bounded by n. □
The result of corollary 1 should be compared with the $e^{0(\sqrt{n})})$ average running time of a comparable backtracking algorithm for determing all satisfying truth asignments for formulas from the class $cl(n,3)^{n^2}$, see [2].
We believe that results similar to theorem 3 and corollary 1 can be shown for different values of $s \geq 4$, too, by the same approach, which we have used in case of $s = 3$. The formulas to be manipulated however then will be more complicated.
In chapter 4 some remarks on further research and on possible extensions of our results are made.
Average case analysis for the related satisfiability problem can be found in [4], [2], [6], e.g. In [5] a more sophisticated backtracking algorithm for deciding whether an arbitrany CNF formula F over n variables with r clauses is x-satisfiable, is designed and its worst case running time is shown to be bounded by $0(r \cdot 2^{n/4})$.

2 Average Order of Backtracking Trees of $cl(n,s)^r$

We shall prove the theorems 1 and 2. We will first determine the average number of x-satisfying truth assignments of formulas from $cl(n,s)^r$.
Let $c = x_{i_1} + ... + x_{i_s} \in cl(n,s)$ Then c is x-satisfied by s of all 2^s
possible truth assignments of the variables in c. So the probability that a random truth assignment $t : V \rightarrow L$ x-satisfies c is $s/2^s$, and because the clauses in formulas from $cl(n,s)^r$ are chosen independently, the probability that t x-satisfies F is $(s/2^s)^r$. From this we obtain the average number of x-satisfying truth assignments of formulas from $cl(n,s)^r$ to be

$$2^n(\frac{s}{2^s})^r \tag{2}$$

We will next determine a relation between the parameters n,r and s s.t. the subset of x-satisfiable fromulas from a class of formulas, whose parameters satisfy this relation, is sparse.
We make the approach of setting $r = c \cdot n$, for some constant $c > 0$. Then we determine c s.t. formula (2) becomes 1, for all n.

$$\begin{array}{lcl} & 2^n(\frac{s}{2^s})^{c \cdot n} & = 1 \\ \Leftrightarrow & (\frac{s}{2^s})^c & = \frac{1}{2} \\ \Leftrightarrow & c(\log s - s) & = -1 \\ \Leftrightarrow & c & = (s - \log s)^{-1} \end{array}$$

I.e. if $c > (s - \log s)^{-1}$ then the average number of solutions of formulas from $cl(n,s)^{c \cdot n}$ goes to 0, if n is growing arbitrarily, thus implying theorem 1.
The following table contains some values of $c = c(s)$ for different values of s

s	3	4	5	10	50
$c(s)$	0.7067	0.5	0.3734	0.14974	0.022544

.

We will next derive a general formula determining the average number of nodes in backtracking trees under XSAT for the class $cl(n,s)^r$. We use a general technique proposed in [2].
Let $t = \{x_n, ..., x_{n-k+1}\}$ be a partial truth assignment having assigned values already to the variables $a_n, ...a_{n-k+1}$. Let $c \in cl(n,s)$.
Then t x-falsifies c, iff either (i) $c \subseteq \bar{t}$ or (ii) $|c \cap t| \geq 2$.
We determine the number of clauses $c \in cl(n,s)$, which are x-falsified by t. Let $C_o = \{c \in cl(n,s) || c \subseteq \bar{t}\}$ be the set of clauses satisfying (i).
Then $|C_o| = \binom{k}{s}$. The set of clauses satisfying (ii) is
$cl(n,s) - \{c \in cl(n,s,)| \; |c \cap t| \leq 1\} = cl(n,s,) - (|C_o' \cup C_1'|)$,
where $C_o' = \{c \in cl(n,s) | c \cap t = \emptyset\}$ and $C_1' = \{c \in cl(n,s,)| \; |c \cap t| = 1\}$.
By elementary combinatorial reasoning we obtain

$$|C_o'| = \sum_{i=0}^{s} \binom{k}{i} \cdot 2^{s-i} \binom{n-k}{s-i} \text{ and} |C_1'| = k \sum_{i=0}^{s-1} \binom{k-1}{i} \cdot 2^{s-1-i} \binom{n-k}{s-1-i}.$$

Because $C_o' \cap C_1' = \emptyset$ these formulas imply

$$|C_o' \cup C_1'| = \binom{k}{s} + \sum_{i=0}^{s-1} \binom{k}{i} 2^{s-i} \left[\binom{n-k}{s-i} + \frac{k-i}{2} \binom{n-k}{s-i-1} \right].$$

Let C be the set of clauses $c \in cl(n,s,)$, which are not x-falsified by t, i.e. for which neither property (i) nor (ii) holds.
Then $C = cl(n,s,) - [C_o \cup (cl(n,s,) - (C_o' \cup C_1'))]$ and because the sets of clauses satisfying (i), (ii) , resp., are disjoint, we can deduce from this formula and the above determined cardinalities.

$$|C| = \sum_{i=0}^{s-1} \binom{k}{i} 2^{s-i} \left[\binom{n-k}{s-i} + \frac{k-i}{2} \binom{n-k}{s-i-1} \right]. \tag{3}$$

A formula $F \in cl(n,s,)^r$, which is not x-falisfied by t must belong to C^r. Because the clauses of F have been chosen independently from $cl(n,s)$, the probability that a randomly chosen formula $F \in cl(n,s,)^r$ is not x-falsified by t is

$$\left[\frac{|C|}{|cl(n,s)|} \right]^r$$

The value of this expression at the same time is equal to the expectation, that the node at depth k of T_n corresponding to t belongs to the backtracking tree $T(F)$ of $F \in cl(n,s)^r$ according to XSAT. Because this expression does not depend on the individual choice of t but only on the number k of assigned variables and - obviously - on n,r, and s, we obtain the following expression for the average number of nodes at depth k of the backtracking trees of formulas from the class $cl(n,s)^r$ under XSAT, for $1 \leq k \leq n$,

$$2^k \left[\frac{\sum_{i=0}^{s-1} \binom{k}{i} \cdot 2^{-i} \left[\binom{n-k}{s-i} + \frac{k-i}{2} \binom{n-k}{s-i-1} \right]}{\binom{n}{s}} \right]^r$$

Because the root is present in any backtracking tree, theorem 2 follows by summing this last formula for $1 \leq k \leq n$.
We have used MAPLE to determine the average number of nodes in backtracking trees according to XSAT from (1) for the classes $cl(25,3)^r$, $cl(50,3)^r$, and $cl(50,4)^r$ for different values of r.

table

r	formula (1) for $cl(25,3)^r$	$cl(50,3)^r$	$cl(50,4)^r$
0	$6.711 * 10^7$	$2.252 * 10^{15}$	$2.252 * 10^{15}$
10	$4.577 * 10^4$	$3.286 * 10^{11}$	$1.067 * 10^{10}$
20	$1.489 * 10^3$	$3.235 * 10^8$	$3.127 * 10^6$
30	$3.062 * 10^2$	$4.339 * 10^6$	$5.078 * 10^4$
40	$1.249 * 10^2$	$2.905 * 10^5$	$5.403 * 10^3$
50	$6.988 * 10^1$	$4.700 * 10^4$	$1.381 * 10^3$
60	$4.638 * 10^1$	$1.281 * 10^4$	$5.551 * 10^2$
70	$3.411 * 10^1$	$4.855 * 10^3$	$2.892 * 10^2$
80	$2.683 * 10^1$	$2.291 * 10^3$	$1.770 * 10^2$
90	$2.210 * 10^1$	$1.260 * 10^3$	$1.206 * 10^2$
100	$1.882 * 10^1$	$7.731 * 10^2$	$8.843 * 10^1$

For the class $cl(25,3)^{100}$ we obtained an average number of nodes in backtracking trees under XSAT of 48.44. This number should be compared with 50341.52, the average number of nodes in backtracking trees under a comparable algorithm for finding all satisfying truth assignments of formulas from the same class, see [8]. I.e. backtracking trees for the exact satisfiability problem are much smaller in the average than for the satisfiability problem.
In the next chapter we will show, however, that backtracking trees under XSAT are still growing exponentially in n for the classes $cl(n,3)^{0(n)}$.

3 On the Growth of the Order of Backtracking Trees for $cl(n,3)^r$

In this chapter we concentrate on classes of CNF-formulas with clauses of length 3 and we will investigate formula (1) of theorem 2. Formula (3) states the number of clauses from *cl(n,s)*, which are not x-falsified by a fixed truth assignment of k variables. By *f'(n,k)* we will denote formula (3) in case of $s = 3$, and $f(n,k) := 2^{-3} \cdot f'(n,k)$. Then a straightforward calculation yields

$$\begin{aligned} f(n,k) = & \tfrac{1}{6}(n-k)(n-k-1)(n-k-2) + \tfrac{k}{2}(n-k)(n-k-1) + \tfrac{3}{8}k(k-1)(n-k) \\ & + \tfrac{1}{16}k(k-1)(k-2) \\ = & \tfrac{1}{6}[n^3 - 3n^2 - \tfrac{3}{4}nk^2 + \tfrac{3}{4}nk + 2n + \tfrac{1}{8}k^3 + \tfrac{9}{8}k^2 - \tfrac{5}{4}k] \quad . \end{aligned}$$

We will show now that XSAT applied to $cl(n,3)^r$, where $r = O(n)$, produces backtracking trees with an exponential number of nodes in the average.

Choose some fixed $\ell \geq 1 s.t. \frac{n}{\ell}$ is an integer greater or equal 1 for infinite many n. Then the following holds

$$\frac{f(n,\frac{n}{\ell})}{\binom{n}{3}} = 1 - \frac{3}{4}\ell^{-2} + \frac{1}{8}\ell^{-3} - 0(\frac{1}{n}).$$

Let $r = c \cdot n$. A necessary condition that formula (1) does not grow exponentially in n is that especially the $\frac{n}{\ell} - th$ terms

$$2^{\frac{n}{\ell}} \cdot \left[\frac{f(n,\frac{n}{\ell})}{\binom{n}{3}}\right]^{c \cdot n} = 2^{\frac{n}{\ell}}\left[1 - \frac{3}{4}\ell^{-2} + \frac{1}{8}\ell^{-3} - 0(\frac{1}{n})\right]^{c \cdot n} \tag{4}$$

of the sum in (1) do not grow exponentially in n. They do not grow exponentially in n, iff

$2^{\frac{1}{\ell}} \cdot \left[1 - \frac{3}{4}\ell^{-2} + \frac{1}{8}\ell^{-3} - 0(\frac{1}{n})\right]^{c} \leq 1$

iff $2^{\frac{1}{\ell}} \leq \left[1 - \frac{3}{4}\ell^{-2} + \frac{1}{8}\ell^{-3} - 0(\frac{1}{n})\right]^{-c}$

iff $c \geq - \left[\ell \cdot \log(1 - \frac{3}{4}\ell^{-2} + \frac{1}{8}\ell^{-3} - 0(\frac{1}{n}))\right]^{-1}$

I.e. the lower bound on c depends on ℓ and n so we will study the function

$$c(\ell, n) = - \left[\ell \cdot log(1 - \frac{3}{4}\ell^{-2} + \frac{1}{8}\ell^{-3} - 0(\frac{1}{n}))\right]^{-1}$$

In order to determine the growth of $c(\ell, n)$ in ℓ, we will calculate

$\lim_{\ell \to \infty} \frac{c(\ell,n)}{\ell^t}$, for $t > 0$

$$\begin{aligned} \frac{c(\ell,n)}{\ell^t} &= -ln2\left[\ell^{1+t} ln(1 - \tfrac{3}{4}\ell^{-2} + \tfrac{1}{8}\ell^{-3} - 0(\tfrac{1}{n}))\right]^{-1} \\ &= -ln2 \frac{\ell^{-(1+t)}}{ln(1-\frac{3}{4}\ell^{-2}+\frac{1}{8}\ell^{-3}-0(\frac{1}{n}))} \end{aligned}$$

and the limit of this formula for growing values of ℓ is of type $(\frac{0}{0})$. So by applying l' Hospital's rule we obtain

$$\lim_{\ell \to \infty} \frac{c(\ell, n)}{\ell^t} = \lim_{\ell \to \infty} ln2 \cdot \frac{(1+t)\left[(1 - 0(\frac{1}{n}))\ell^{-2-t} - \frac{3}{4}\ell^{-4-t} + \frac{1}{8}\ell^{-5-t}\right]}{\frac{3}{2}\ell^{-3} - \frac{3}{8}\ell^{-4}}$$

$$= \begin{cases} \infty & \text{for } 0 < t < 1 \\ 0.92419624 \cdot (1 - 0(\frac{1}{n})) & \text{for } t = 1 \\ 0 & \text{for } t < 1 \end{cases}$$

We only consider values of n and ℓ s.t. $\frac{n}{\ell}$ is a positive integer so we are only interested in the case where $n \geq \ell$, and we just have proved

Lemma 2:
There is some $\ell_0 \geq 1$ s.t. for all $n \geq \ell \geq \ell_0$ the following holds

$$0.924\ \ell \leq c(\ell, n) \leq 0.925\ \ell. \quad \square$$

We now conclude the proof of theorem 3.
The subexpression in squarebrackets of fomula (1), theorem 2, is at most 1. This formula (1) is not increasing in r and so it is sufficient to restrict to the classes of $cl(n,3)^{dn}$ for some $d \geq c(\ell_0, \ell_0)$, where ℓ_0 is taken from lemma 2.

Determine some ℓ' s.t. $c(\ell', n) \geq 2d$, for all $n \geq \ell'$, and $\frac{n}{\ell'}$, is an integer for infinite many values of n. Such a ℓ' exists because of lemma 2.

Consider the growth of the $\frac{n}{l'}$-th terms in the sum of (1), which are

$$\left[2^{\frac{1}{\ell'}}(1 - \frac{3}{4}\ell'^{-2} + \frac{1}{8}\ell'^{-3} - 0(\frac{1}{n}))^d\right]^n .$$

The expression in square brackets is strictly greater than 1, because of the definition of $c(\ell', n)$, for

$$\begin{aligned} 1 = \; & 2^{\frac{1}{l'}}(1 - \tfrac{3}{4}\ell'^{-2} + \tfrac{1}{8}\ell'^{-3} - 0(\tfrac{1}{n}))^{c(\ell',n)} \\ \leq \; & 2^{\frac{1}{l'}}(1 - \tfrac{3}{4}\ell'^{-2} + \tfrac{1}{8}\ell'^{-3} - 0(\tfrac{1}{n}))^{2d} \\ < \; & 2^{\frac{1}{l'}}(1 - \tfrac{3}{4}\ell'^{-2} + \tfrac{1}{8}\ell'^{-3} - 0(\tfrac{1}{n}))^{d} = 1 + \epsilon \end{aligned}$$

for some $\epsilon > 0$, depending on l', but not on n.
I.e. the $\frac{n}{l'}, -th$ terms are growing exponentially in n. Because $d \geq c(\ell_0, \ell_0)$ was chosen arbitrarily theorem 3 follows.
In order to prove corollary 1 we consider the classes of $cl(n,3)^{\frac{37}{40}n^2}$, where $\frac{37}{40} = 0.925$.

By definition of $c(l, n)$ holds

$$\frac{1}{2^\ell}\left[\frac{f(n,\frac{n}{l})}{\binom{n}{3}}\right]^{c(l,n)} = 1, \text{for } 1 \leq \ell \leq n \; .$$

For $n \geq \ell_0$ sufficiently large $c(\ell, n) \leq \frac{37}{40}n$, for all $1 \leq \ell \leq n$, holds because of lemma 2, for $l \geq l_o$, and for $l < l_o$ it is easy to see.
So the value of the $\frac{n}{l} - th$ term in the sum of (1) is

$$\left[\frac{1}{2^\ell}\left(\frac{f(n,\frac{n}{l})}{\binom{n}{3}}\right)^{\frac{37}{40}n}\right]^n \leq \left[\frac{1}{2^\ell}\left(\frac{f(n,\frac{n}{l})}{\binom{n}{3}}\right)^{c(\ell,n)}\right]^n = 1 \; .$$

Thus we have proved corollary 1.

4 Concluding Remarks

Chapter 3 leaves the following question open. For which values of r between $0(n)$ and $\frac{37}{40}n^2$ the average number of nodes in backtracking trees of $cl(n,3)^r$ under XSAT is growing exponentionally and for which it is not? We don't know the answer.

The algorithm XSAT whose average case behaviour we have studied, even if correct, does not exploit all possible problem-depending logical implications. E.g. if a literal x occuring in a clause c is set true, then in order to x-satisfy c, all literals $y \epsilon c - \{x\}$ must be set false. For more sophisticated implications concerning this problem see [5]. At the moment however we do not see a way how to incorporate such heuristics into the average case analysis. Concerning this problem we refer to the related satisfiability problem, where only limited success has been achieved, analysing more clever versions of rigid backtracking strategies. In [6] the pure literal rule is studied. But the authors were not able to incorporate the pure literal rule into the average case analysis of backtracking. It should be mentioned however that in case of finding x-satisfying truth assignments the pure literal rule is not a correct rule.
Besides the correspondence between "set partitioning" and "exact satisfiability", and the obvious correspondence between "set cover" and "satisfiability" there exist similar correspondences 1. between "set splittting" and "not-all-equal satisfiability" and 2. between "set packing" and "at-most-one satisfiability". For these last two problems from logic an average case analysis similar to the analysis in this paper is possible.
The "at-most-one satisfiability" problem however is not NP-complete and can be reduced to the wellknown 2-satisfiability problem. For a truth assignment t and a clause $c = \{x_1, \ldots, x_k\}$ have the following property:
$| t \cap c | \leq 1$ iff $t \cap \{\overline{x_i}, \overline{x_j}\} \neq \phi$ for all $1 \leq i < j \leq k$.
I.e. a truth assignment t setting in each clause at most one literal true can be determined by solving the corresponding 2-satisfiability problem, which is known to be solvable in linear time. For the unexplained notions the reader is referred to [3].

References

[1] E. Balas and M.W. Padberg, Set partitioning - A survey, in: N. Christophides et.al., eds., Combinatorial Optimization, Wiley, Chichester (1979)

[2] C.A.Brown and P.W. Purdom, An average time analysis of backtracking, SIAM J. Comput. 10 (1981) 583-593.

[3] M.R. Garey and D.S. Johnson, Computers and Intractability: A guide to the theory of NP-completeness, Freeman, San Francisco/Calif. (1979)

[4] A. Goldberg, Average case complexity of the satisfiability problem, Proc. 4th Workshop on Automated Deduction, Austin/TX, (1979) 1-6.

[5] B. Monien, E. Speckenmeyer and O. Vornberger, Upper bounds for covering problems, Methods of Operations Research 43 (Verlagsgruppe Athenäum et.al., 1983) 419-431

[6] P.W. Purdom and C.A. Brown, The pure literal rule and polynomial average time, SIAM J.Comput. 14 (1985), 943-953.

[7] E. Speckenmeyer, On the average case complexity of backtracking for the exact satisfiability problem, to appear in: Proc. Kolloquium "Logik in Informatik", Karlsruhe, Oct. 12-16, 1987, Börger/Kleine Büning/Richter, eds., Springer-Verlag (LNCS)

[8] E. Speckenmeyer, B. Monien and O. Vornberger, Superlinear Speedup for parallel backtracking, to appear in: Proc. of the Int. Conf. on Supercomputing, Atheens, June 8-12, 1987, C. Polychrononopoulos, ed., Springer-Verlag (LNCS).

BISECTIONS OF FREE MONOIDS AND A NEW UNAVOIDABLE REGULARITY

Stefano Varricchio
Dipartimento di Matematica, Università "La Sapienza",
Piazzale Aldo Moro 2, 00185 Roma, Italy.

INTRODUCTION

A classical problem in combinatorics on words is searching the "unavoidable regularities", namely those properties defined on free monoids which are always verified by "sufficiently long" words.

In this paper the existence of a new unavoidable regularity will be shown.

Recently C. Reutenauer in [2] has proved the existence of a function N(k,q), such that any word w in A^*, with $|A| = k$ and $|w| \geq N(k,q)$, has a factor of the kind $l_1 l_2 \ldots l_q$ where the l_i's are Lyndon words and $l_1 \geq l_2 \geq \ldots \geq l_q$. In other therms any "sufficiently long" word contains factors which have a "quite high" index with respect to the Lyndon factorization.

We naturally would like to generalize this result. Let $(X_i)_{i \in I}$ be a factorization of a free monoid: is there a function N(q) such that any $w \in A^+$, with $|w| \geq q$, contains a word of index q with respect to $(X_i)_{i \in I}$?

This property will be proved for a particular class of factorizations, the bisections: the proof will be based on the Ramsey theorem .

However the problem is still open for the general case, even in the case of Viennot factorizations which are a first generalization of Lyndon factorizations.

PRELIMINARIES

Let A^* (resp. A^+) be the free monoid (resp. the free semigroup) generated by a non-empty finite set A called <u>alphabet.</u> The elements of A are called <u>letters</u> and those of A^* <u>words</u>. The identity element of A^* denoted by 1 is also called <u>empty word</u>. For any word v in A^*, |v| denotes the <u>length</u> of v, namely the number of its letters. A word v is said to be a <u>factor</u> of w, if w = xvy for some x,y in A^*. If x = 1 then v is a <u>prefix</u> of w, if y = 1 then v is a <u>suffix</u> of w.

A word w is called <u>primitive</u> if $w = z^p$ implies p = 1 . Two words u and w are said to be <u>conjugate</u> if there exist words x, y in A^* such that u = xy and w = yx.

Finally we write $u \leq w$ if u is less than or equal to w with respect to the lexicographic ordering.

RESULTS

In this section we will introduce the factorizations of free monoids. In particular we will consider the most important properties of Lyndon factorizations and bisections. (For a deeper analisys see [1], chapter 5). Finally a new unavoidable regularity will be proved for the bisections.

Definition 1. A factorization of the free monoid A^* is a family $(X_i)_{i \in I}$ indexed by a totally ordered set I, such that any word $w \in A^+$ may be written uniquely as:

$$w = x_1 x_2 \dots x_n$$

with $n \geq 1$ $x_i \in X_{j_i}$ and $j_1 \geq j_2 \geq \dots \geq j_n$. Moreover we call index of w the integer $i(w) = n$.

Definition 2. Let $w \in A^+$, w is said Lyndon word if it is a primitive word that is minimal in its coniugate class. The set of Lyndon words will be denoted by **L**.

Theorem 1. *(Chen, Fox, Lyndon). Any word* $w \in A^+$ *can be written uniquely as :*

$$w = l_1 l_2 \dots l_n$$

with $l_i \in \mathbf{L}$ *and* $l_1 \geq l_2 \geq \dots \geq l_n$.

Thus the family of Lyndon words with respect to the lexicographic ordering is a factorization of the free monoid, usually called Lyndon factorization. The following theorem says that, the property of containing a word of fixed index with respect to the Lyndon factorization is an unavoidable regularity.

Theorem 2. *(Reutenauer). For any* $k, q \in \mathbf{N}$, *there exists an integer* $N(k,q)$ *such that any word* $w \in A^*$, *with* $|A| = k$ *and* $|w| \geq N(k,q)$, *can be written as:*

$$w = u l_1 l_2 \dots l_q v$$

with $l_i \in \mathbf{L}$, $u, v \in A^*$ and $l_1 \geq l_2 \geq \dots \geq l_n$.

Now we consider another important class of factorizations. If in definition 1 the set I has just two elements then we have a bisection, therefore:

Definition 3. A bisection of A^* is a pair (X, Y) of subsets of A^+, such that any word $w \in A^*$ may be uniquely written as:

$$w = x_1 \dots x_n y_1 \dots y_m$$

with $x_i \in X$ and $y_j \in Y$. In this case one has:

$$i(w) = n + m.$$

We now consider a property of the function $i(w)$ that will be used in the following.

Proposition 3. *Let* $w_1, w_2 \in A^*$ *such that* $w_1 = x_1 \dots x_n y_1 \dots y_m$, $w_2 = x'_1 \dots x'_n y'_1 \dots y'_m$, *with* $x_i, x'_i \in X$ *and* $y_j, y'_j \in Y$. *Then* $i(w_1 w_2) > n + m$.

Proof. Evidently

$$w_1 w_2 = x_1 \dots x_n w' y'_1 \dots y'_m$$

with

$$w' = y_1 \dots y_m x'_1 \dots x'_n \in A^+,$$

therefore

$$i(w_1 w_2) = n + i(w') + m > n + m \quad \square$$

In order to extend theorem 2 to the bisections we need to remind a result on repetitive mappings that is proved in [1] (Chapter 4).

Theorem 4. *Let E be a finite set with* $|E| = n$. *Let* $\varphi: A^+ \longrightarrow E$ *be a mapping. Then there is a function* $\psi(k,n)$, *such that any word* $w \in A^+$, *with* $|w| \geq \psi(k,n)$, *can be written as:*

$$w = u w_1 \dots w_k v$$

with $w_i \in A^+$ *and* $\varphi(w_i \dots w_j) = \varphi(w_{i'} \dots w_{j'})$, *for every* i, j, i', j' *such that* $1 \leq i \leq j \leq k$ *and* $1 \leq i' \leq j' \leq k$.

The previous theorem is an application of the Ramsey theorem when $\psi(k,n) = R(2,k+1,n)$ and R is the Ramsey function.

Theorem 5. *Let* (X, Y) *be a bisection of* A^*. *Then there is a function* $N(q)$ *such that any* $w \in A^+$, *with* $|w| \geq N(q)$, *can be written as:*

$$w = u x_1 \dots x_n y_1 \dots y_m v$$

with $x_i \in X$, $y_j \in Y$ *and* $n + m = q$.

Proof. Let $E = \{ (n,m) \in \mathbf{N}_0 \times \mathbf{N}_0 \,/\, 0 \leq n + m \leq q \}$, clearly $|E|$ depends only on q, so that we can write

$$|E| = n(q).$$

Let us consider the mapping

$$\varphi: A^+ \longrightarrow E$$

defined by

$$\varphi(w) = \begin{cases} (n,m), & \text{if } w = x_1 \dots x_n y_1 \dots y_m \text{ with } x_i \in X, y_j \in Y \text{ and } n + m < q \\ (0,0), & \text{otherwise} \end{cases}$$

Let

$$N(q) = \psi(2,n(q))$$

where ψ is the function of theorem 4.

If $w \in A^+$ and $|w| \geq N(q)$, then by theorem 4 one can write:

$$w = uw_1w_2v$$

with $\varphi(w_1) = \varphi(w_2) = \varphi(w_1w_2)$.

Let us prove that $i(w_1) \geq q$. Indeed if $i(w_1) < q$, then we would have

$$\varphi(w_1) = \varphi(w_2) = \varphi(w_1w_2) = (n,m)$$

with

$$1 \leq n + m < q \ ;$$

therefore we can write

$$w_1 = x_1 \ldots x_n y_1 \ldots y_m \ , \quad w_2 = x'_1 \ldots x'_n y'_1 \ldots y'_m,$$

thus, by proposition 3,

$$i(w_1w_2) > n + m \quad \text{and} \quad \varphi(w_1w_2) \neq (n,m),$$

that is a contradiction.

Finally from $i(w_1) \geq q$ it follows that w_1 contains as a factor a word of index q.

□

REFERENCES

[1] Lothaire M., Combinatorics on words,Addison-Wesley(1983)

[2] Christophe Reutenauer, Mots de Lyndon et un théorème de Shirshov, Preprint (1986)

Failures Semantics and Deadlocking of Modular Petri Nets

Walter Vogler
TU München *)

Extended Abstract

Abstract:

One can construct labelled P/T-nets in a modular fashion by exchanging subnets such that the behaviour of the whole net remains the same. We investigate which subnets can be exchanged such that deadlock-freeness is preserved and show that some variations of the failures semantics, which has been developed for TCSP, are useful in this context.

1.Introduction

Concurrent systems can be described or specified with the help of Petri nets. Besides mathematical precision Petri nets have the advantage that they can be graphically represented. But large Petri nets are difficult to handle, i.e. it is difficult to determine their behaviour or prove anything about them, and their graphical representation can loose most of its clarity. Therefore there is quite an interest in the modular construction of Petri nets [An1, An2, An3, Bau, Be, DDS, Go, Mü, SuMu, Va, Vog1, Vog2, Vos]. One can distinguish two approaches to modular construction. One way is to combine nets with known behaviour and the aim is to calculate the behaviour of the composed net. Operators for the composition of nets can be motivated e.g. by the operators of TCSP or CCS, compare [Tau, Go]. Or the construction consists in exchanging subnets and the aim is to preserve the behaviour of the whole net. In this approach one can refine one transition [Va, SuMu, Vog1, Vog2] or several transitions [Mü] or replace subnets with a richer structure [An1, An2, An3, Bau, Vos, DDS]. In any case one removes a subnet from the given net and combines the remainder with the new subnet. This composition can be done by identifying transitions of the two nets [e.g. An1], places of the two nets [e.g. Vog1] or both [Vos] or one can prescribe how the two nets are to be connected by new arcs [e.g. Bau]. Here we use an operator motivated by the parallel composition with synchronisation of TCSP, which works by merging transitions, but we can also capture the replacement technique of [Bau]. It turns out that the two approaches we distinguished above are closely connected.

There are several possibilities what kind of behaviour one wants to preserve: The behaviour might depend on the occurrence sequences, on the markings reached or on deadlocking or liveness properties. In each case we get an external equivalence of nets as follows: Let $\|$ be the operator on nets we use. Then nets N_1 and N_2 are externally equivalent if and only if for all (suitable) nets N $N\|N_1$ and $N\|N_2$ have the same behaviour. Such an external equivalence is what is needed in

*) This work was partially supported by ESPRIT-project No.283

practice for composing nets, but it is difficult to decide since its definition involves infinitely many context nets N. Thus we are looking for an internal equivalence, i.e. one that does not involve those other nets N, that is sufficient or even necessary and sufficient for the external equivalence. (The notions external and internal equivalence were introduced in [Bau]). Even though such an internal equivalence might be undecidable in general, it is of course easier to work with.

There are several possibilities for internal equivalences; some of them are discussed in [Po]. We are especially interested in the failures equivalence. It has been developed for TCSP [BrHoRo] to deal with deadlocking and translated to C/E-nets in [Po].In this paper we will show that this failures equivalence indeed is useful in the setting of labelled Petri nets, when the investigated behaviour is the ability to deadlock. (Note that by a deadlock we throughout mean a situation where no visible transition can occur, we do not mean a set of places as in [BeFe].)

Later on it was refined to capture divergence, too [BrRo,OlHo], where divergence corresponds to looping, an infinite behaviour without visible effects. In this refined semantics divergence is modelled in such a way that if divergence is possible every other behaviour is possible, too. The reason for this is mainly technical. In section 5 and 6 we take as behaviour the set of maximal occurrence sequences, i.e. those that are infinite or lead to a deadlock. Consequently we have to consider divergence, too, but here we model it in a different way, which seems to be more natural - and this way is not a question of design, but we can prove its adequacy.

We demonstrate that in the case of divergence infinite occurrence sequences cannot be calculated from the finite ones and prove that without divergence they can. (Note that we deal with labelled Petri nets.) In the course of our considerations we will solve an open problem from [Bau]. Nearly all proofs had to be omitted.

2.Preliminaries

We will deal with labelled P/T-nets $N = (S_N, T_N, F_N, M_N, l_N)$ where S_N, T_N, F_N, M_N have the usual meaning [BeFe] and $l_N : T_N \rightarrow \Sigma \cup \{\lambda\}$ is a labelling of the transitions with labels from a fixed infinite alphabet Σ or with the empty string λ. Finite capacities can be implemented with complementary places, hence we assume all capicities to be infinite and omit them. For simplicity we further assume that all arc weights are 1, but all definitions and results can be easily transferred to nets with variable arc weights. We use the usual notations $[M_N\rangle$, ${}^{\bullet}x, x^{\bullet}$ for $x \in S_N \cup T_N$, and $M_1[t\rangle, M_1[t\rangle M_2, M_1[w\rangle, M_1[w\rangle M_2$ for $t \in T_N, w \in T_N^*$. $L(N) = \{w \in T^* \mid M_N[w\rangle\}$ is the set of (finite) occurrence sequences of N, $L^\omega(N)$ is the set of infinite occurrence sequences of N, $L^\infty(N) = L(N) \cup L^\omega(N)$. Analogously for a set A A^* is the set of finite sequences, A^ω the set of infinite sequences over A and $A^\infty = A^* \cup A^\omega$. For $w \in L(N)$ we denote the marking reached after the occurrence of w by $M(w)$. We define the following image firing rule:

For $a \in \Sigma$ ($v \in \Sigma^*$ resp.) and markings M_1, M_2 we write $M_1[a\rangle\rangle M_2$ ($M_1[v\rangle\rangle M_2$ resp.), if there is a $w \in T_N^*$ with $M_1[w\rangle M_2$ and $l_N(w) = a$ ($l_N(w) = v$ resp.). $M_1[a\rangle\rangle$ and $M_1[v\rangle\rangle$ are defined analogously.

3. Composition of Nets

To compose nets we use an operator for parallel composition with synchronization as in TCSP (compare e.g. [Go], [Po]). Let $N_i = (S_i, T_i, F_i, M_i, l_i)$, $i = 1, 2$, be nets, $A \subseteq \Sigma$. Then $N_1 \parallel_A N_2 = (S, T, F, M, l)$ is defined by

$$
\begin{aligned}
S &= S_1 \dot{\cup} S_2 \\
T &= \{(t_1,t_2) | t_1 \in T_1 \wedge l_1(t_1) \notin A \wedge t_2 = \lambda\} \\
&\quad \cup \{(t_1,t_2) | t_2 \in T_2 \wedge l_2(t_2) \notin A \wedge t_1 = \lambda\} \\
&\quad \cup \{(t_1,t_2) | t_1 \in T_1 \wedge t_2 \in T_2 \wedge l_1(t_1) = l_2(t_2) \in A\} \\
F &= \{(s,(t_1,t_2)) | s \in S \wedge (t_1,t_2) \in T \wedge [(s,t_1) \in F_1 \vee (s,t_2) \in F_2]\} \\
&\quad \cup \{((t_1,t_2),s) | s \in S \wedge (t_1,t_2) \in T \wedge [(t_1,s) \in F_1 \vee (t_2,s) \in F_2]\} \\
M &= M_1 \dot{\cup} M_2 \qquad \text{(Consider markings as multi-sets)}
\end{aligned}
$$

$$
l(t_1,t_2) = \begin{cases} l_1(t_1) & \text{if} \quad t_1 \neq \lambda \\ l_2(t_2) & \text{if} \quad t_2 \neq \lambda \end{cases}
$$

In other words $N_1 \parallel_A N_2$ is the disjoint union of N_1 and N_2 except for transitions with labels from A: For each $a \in A$ we combine each transition from N_1 labelled a with each transition from N_2 labelled a. If we have the special case that each label from A appears at most once in N_1, N_2 resp., this simply means that equally labelled transitions are merged, as e.g. in [An1].

In [Bau] a building block B and an environment U (both are nets) are composed as follows: U has an injective labelling of transitions without λ's, B has an arbitrary labelling which is only used for the connection of both nets. (The labels of U are different from the labels of B.) For each place s of U subsets $z(s)$, $v(s)$ of Σ are given and the compound net is contructed from the disjoint union of the two nets by adding arcs from each place s of U to each transition of B with a label from $z(s)$ and from each transition with a label from $v(s)$ to s. We can do the same with our operator: Let A be the set of labels appearing in any $z(s)$ or $v(s)$. Then we add to U for each $a \in A$ a transition with label a and connect it to the places according to z and v, getting the net U'. Now we obtain the compound net from above as $B \parallel_A U'$ with the exception that in [Bau] the transitions of B are unobservable in the compound net. Therefore we define for a net N the hiding of $A \subseteq \Sigma$, $N \setminus A$, and for nets $N_1, N_2, A \subseteq \Sigma$ we define $N_1 \parallel \setminus_A N_2$ such that $B \parallel \setminus_A U'$ is the net constructed in [Bau].

$N \setminus A := (S_N, T_N, F_N, M_N, l_{N\setminus A})$, where

$$
l_{N\setminus A}(t) = \begin{cases} l_N(t) & \text{if} \quad l_N(t) \notin A \\ \lambda & \text{if} \quad l_N(t) \in A \end{cases}
$$

$N_1 \parallel \setminus_A N_2 = (N_1 \parallel_A N_2) \setminus A$

The latter reminds of the synchronization in CCS, where synchronized actions are hidden [Mi]. To formulate our first results we need an operator $\parallel_A$ for strings, too, which for $A = \emptyset$ is the well-known shuffle operator. For $u, v \in \Sigma^*$, $A \subseteq \Sigma$ define

$$
\begin{aligned}
u \parallel_A v \;=\; \{ w = w_1 \ldots w_n \mid \exists\, u_i, v_i \in \Sigma \cup \{\lambda\} : u = u_1 \ldots u_n, v = v_1 \ldots v_n, \\
\forall\, i \in \{1, \ldots, n\} : w_i = u_i v_i \in \Sigma \setminus A \vee w_i = u_i = v_i \in A \}
\end{aligned}
$$

and analogously for $u, v \in \Sigma^* \cup \Sigma^\omega$, but not both $u, v \in \Sigma^*$

$$
\begin{aligned}
u \parallel_A v \;=\; \{ w = w_1 \ldots \in \Sigma^\omega \mid \exists\, u_i, v_i \in \Sigma \cup \{\lambda\} : u = u_1 \ldots, v = v_1 \ldots, \\
\forall\, i \in \mathbb{N} : w_i = u_i v_i \in \Sigma \setminus A \vee w_i = u_i = v_i \in A \}
\end{aligned}
$$

Furthermore $v \setminus A$ for $v \in \Sigma^\infty$ is the sequence one gets from v by eliminating all symbols belonging to A, and $u \parallel \setminus_A v = \{w \mid \exists\, w' \in u \parallel_A v : w' \setminus A = w\}$

Lemma 1: Let $N = N_1 \|_A N_2$.

(i) Let $(t_1,t_1')\dots(t_n,t_n') \in T_N^*$, M_1, M_2 markings of N_1, M_1', M_2' markings of N_2. Then $M_1 \dot\cup M_1'[(t_1,t_1')\dots(t_n,t_n')\rangle M_2 \dot\cup M_2'$ if and only if $M_1[t_1\dots t_n\rangle M_2$ and $M_1'[t_1'\dots t_n'\rangle M_2'$.

(ii) Let $(t_1,t_1')\dots \in T_N^\omega$ and M_1, M_1' be markings of N_1, N_2 resp. Then $M_1 \dot\cup M_1'[(t_1,t_1')\dots\rangle$ if and only if $M_1[t_1\dots\rangle$ and $M_1'[t_1'\dots\rangle$.

Proposition 1: For nets N_1, N_2 and $A \subseteq \Sigma$ we have

(i) For $v \in \Sigma^*$ $\quad v \in l(L(N_1 \|_A N_2))$ $\quad$ if and only if
$\exists\, v_1 \in l_1(L(N_1)),\ v_2 \in l_2(L(N_2)) :\ v \in v_1 \|_A v_2$

(ii) For $v \in \Sigma^\infty$ $\quad v \in l(L^\omega(N_1 \|_A N_2))$ $\quad$ if and only if
$\exists\, v_1 \in l_1(L^\omega(N_1)),\ v_2 \in l_2(L^\infty(N_2)) :\ v \in v_1 \|_A v_2$
or $\exists\, v_1 \in l_1(L^\infty(N_1)),\ v_2 \in l_2(L^\omega(N_2)) :\ v \in v_1 \|_A v_2$

4. Deadlocking And Failures Semantics

We will take the ability to deadlock as the behaviour that defines our first external equivalence: Nets are deadlocking-equivalent if we can exchange them in any context without changing the ability to deadlock, i.e. the deadlock-freeness of the whole net.

Definition: A net N can deadlock if there is $M \in [M_N\rangle$, such that for all $a \in \Sigma$ $\neg M[a\rangle\rangle$. Nets N_1, N_2 are deadlock-equivalent if for all nets N and $A \subseteq \Sigma$: $N \|_A N_1$ can deadlock iff $N \|_A N_2$ can deadlock.

In [BrHoRo] the failures semantics was developed for TCSP to treat deadlocks, failures-equivalence was translated to safe Petri nets in [Po].

Definition: The failures semantics of a net N is
$\mathcal{F}(N) = \{(v,X) \mid \exists\, w \in L(N)\ :\ l_N(w) = v \wedge\ \ \forall\, a \in X : \neg M(w)[a\rangle\rangle\}$. If $(v,X) \in \mathcal{F}(N)$, X is called a refusal set. Nets N_1 and N_2 are $\mathcal{F}$-equivalent if $\mathcal{F}(N_1) = \mathcal{F}(N_2)$.

Example:

Note that for $(v,X) \in \mathcal{F}(N)$ X does not necessarily contain all visible actions that may be refused after v. Therefore the following two nets are $\mathcal{F}$-equivalent, although in the first net if b can occur then a can, too, whereas in the second net there is a marking where only b can occur. This difference is concealed since in both cases a λ-transition can block any visible action.

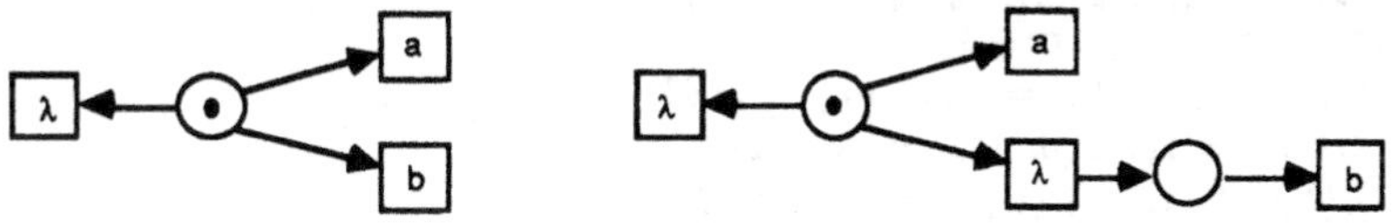

Figure 1

We have that from $(v,X) \in \mathcal{F}(N)$ and $Y \subseteq X$ $\quad (v,Y) \in \mathcal{F}(N)$ follows, furthermore $l(L(N)) = \{v \mid (v,\emptyset) \in \mathcal{F}(N)\}$.

Proposition 2: A net N can deadlock if and only if there is $v \in \Sigma^*$ with $(v,\Sigma) \in \mathcal{F}(N)$.

The following theorem partly corresponds to the definition of the failures semantics of $P_1 \|_A P_2$ in TCSP [OlHo].

Theorem 2: For nets N_1, N_2 and $A \subseteq \Sigma$

$$\mathcal{F}(N_1 \parallel_A N_2) = \{(v,X) \mid \exists\, (v_i,X_i) \in \mathcal{F}(N_i),\ i=1,2 : v \in v_1 \parallel_A v_2 \ \wedge\ X_1 \cap X_2 \supseteq X \setminus A \ \wedge\ X_1 \cup X_2 \supseteq X \cap A\}$$

Now we will see that this theorem, which allows to calculate the behaviour (in some sense) of the compound net from the behaviour of its components, is useful to prove the equality of the external and the internal equivalence given above. In other words, we can prove that failures equivalence allows to handle deadlocking when constructing Petri nets in a modular fashion, and maybe more surprisingly, we can prove that it is necessary for this purpose.

Theorem 3: Let N_1, N_2 be nets. Then N_1 deadlock-equivalent to N_2 if and only if N_1 $\mathcal{F}$-equivalent to N_2.

Proof: "$\Leftarrow$" Follows from Proposition 2 and Theorem 2.
"$\Rightarrow$" Let $l_1(T_1) \cup l_2(T_2) \setminus \{\lambda\} =: A$, $(v,X) \in \mathcal{F}(N_1)$, $v = v_1, \ldots, v_m$. Consider the following net N

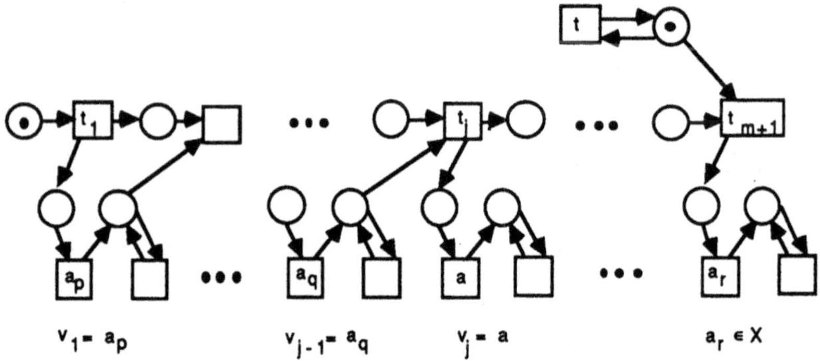

Figure 2

$$S = \{s_a, s'_a, s_j, s \mid a \in A,\ j = 1, \ldots, m+1\}$$

$$T = \{t_a, t'_a, t_j, t \mid a \in A,\ j = 1, \ldots, m+1\}$$

$$\begin{aligned} F = &\ \{(s_a,t_a),(t_a,s'_a),(s'_a,t'_a),(t'_a,s'_a) \mid a \in A\} \\ \cup &\ \{(s_j,t_j) \mid j = 1,\ldots,m+1\} \\ \cup &\ \{(t_j,s_{j+1}),(t_j,s_a) \mid j = 1,\ldots,m,\ v_j = a\} \\ \cup &\ \{(s'_a,t_j) \mid j = 2,\ldots,m+1,\ v_{j-1} = a\} \\ \cup &\ \{(s,t),(t,s),(s,t_{m+1}),(t_{m+1},s_a) \mid a \in X\} \end{aligned}$$

$M(s_1) = M(s) = 1$, $M(s') = 0$ for $s' \in S$, $s \neq s' \neq s_1$.
$l(t_a) = a$ for $a \in A$ and l is injective and λ-free.

The only way to create a deadlock in $N_i \parallel_A N$ is to block t via $t_1 \ldots t_{m+1}$ and in between we must have an occurrence sequence from N_i with image v. Now if after the occurrence of t_{m+1} some $a \in X$ can occur under the image firing rule then t'_a cannot be blocked. Therefore $N_1 \parallel_A N$ can deadlock, thus by assumption $N_2 \parallel_A N$ can deadlock and we must have an occurrence sequence of N_2 that gives $(v,X) \in \mathcal{F}(N_2)$. Therefore $\mathcal{F}(N_1) \subseteq \mathcal{F}(N_2)$ and by symmetry the result follows. □

Remark: [Bau] compares only nets with $l_1(T_1)\backslash\{\lambda\} = l_2(T_2)\backslash\{\lambda\}$ and allows only environments, i.e. nets N in our notation, with injective, λ-free labelling and $l(N) \supseteq l_1(T_1)\backslash\{\lambda\}$. Note that our if-part is more general, i.e. gives a stronger result, whereas the test-nets N we use for the only-if-part are of the required type, thus our result carries over to a restricted approach as in [Bau]. We will have the same situation in the next two sections.

Corollary 1: If N_1 is deadlock-equivalent to N_2, then for all nets N and $A \subseteq \Sigma$ we have $l(L(N \|_A N_1)) = l(L(N \|_A N_2))$.

5. Maximal Sequences and Divergence

To take the ability to deadlock as the behaviour of a net seems to be quite a restricted view, although Theorem 3 and Corollary 1 show its strength. One could take this as a satisfactory result.

The starting point of [Bau] was simply to take $l(L(N))$ as behaviour and to base an external equivalence on this. The related internal equivalence is weaker than the one we obtained and consequently deadlock-freeness is not preserved, see [Bau], also for examples. Therefore a combination of the language and the ability to deadlock is suggested in [Bau]:

Definition: $L_{mf}(N) := \{w \mid w \in L(N)$ and no transition is enabled under $M(w)\}$ (maximal occurence sequences)

$L_{mc}(N) := L^{\omega}(N) \cup L_{mf}(N)$ (maximal countable occurence sequences)

Nets N_1, N_2 are mc-equivalent if for all nets N and $A \subseteq \Sigma$ $l(L_{mc}(N \|_A N_1)) = l(L_{mc}(N \|_A N_2))$.

Remark : This is not exactly the external mc-equivalence defined in [Bau], since we used the operator $\|_A$. In the next section we will define mc'-equivalence using $\| \backslash_A$.

Consider the following example which admittedly is very pathological, but it shows with minimal effort a problem that you can encounter with inconspicious nets as well: N_1 is empty, N_2 consists of a transition labelled λ, N of a transition labelled a. Now $N \|_\emptyset N_1 = N$ and $N \|_\emptyset N_2 = N \dot\cup N_2$ cannot deadlock and have the same occurrence sequences, but $l(L_{mc}(N)) = \{a^\omega\}$ and $l(L_{mc}(N \dot\cup N_2)) = a^* \cup \{a^\omega\}$, since in the latter case after some a's the λ-transition can occur infinitely often. Such an infinite looping is called divergence.

Definition: A net N can diverge if there are $M \in [M_N\rangle$, $w \in T_N^\omega$ such that $M[w\rangle$ and $l_N(w) = \lambda$.

In order to give an internal characterization of mc-equivalence we will add to our failures semantics a set of divergence strings as it was done for TCSP [BrRo,OlHo]. But there are differences: In the improved failures model of TCSP every elongation of a divergence string is a divergence string. The reason for this seems to be mainly technical and it will not be the case here. On the other hand, all strings, also the divergence strings in the failures model of TCSP are finite. This is not sufficient for us. Look at the following example:

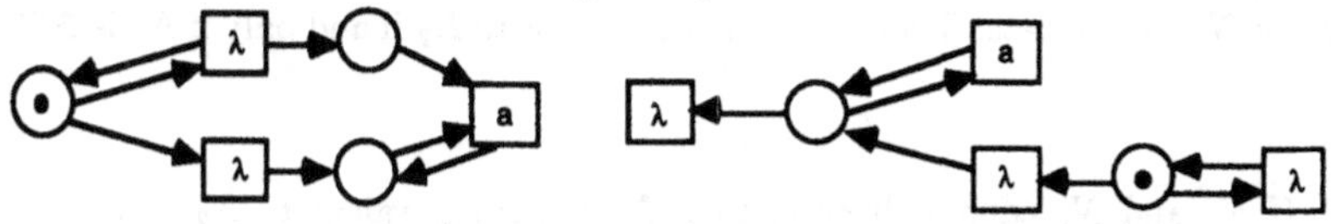

Figure 3

We have $L(N_1) = L(N_2)$, divergence can only occur in the very beginning for both nets, and the finite images of sequences from L_{mc} are equal. But $a^\omega \in l_2(L_{mc}(N_2)) \setminus l_1(L_{mc}(N_1))$. As a consequence of this observation we will add the images of all infinite occurrence sequences to our semantics. Also the failures-part has to be changed: If a net diverges it fails to show any observable action, therefore we add all pairs (v, X) with v a finite image of an infinite occurrence sequence.

Definition: The failures/divergence semantics of a net N is $\mathcal{FD}(N) = (F(N), D(N))$ with
$D(N) = l(L^\omega(N))$,
$F(N) = \mathcal{F}(N) \cup \{(v, X) \mid v \in D(N) \cap \Sigma^*, X \subseteq \Sigma\}$.
Nets N_1, N_2 are $\mathcal{FD}$-equivalent if $\mathcal{FD}(N_1) = \mathcal{FD}(N_2)$.

Again we have $(v, X) \in F(N) \wedge Y \subseteq X \Rightarrow (v, Y) \in F(N)$ and $l(L(N)) = \{v \mid (v, \emptyset) \in F(N)\}$.

Proposition 3: A net N cannot diverge if and only if $D(N) \cap \Sigma^* = \emptyset$.

Proposition 4: If N cannot diverge then $\mathcal{F}(N) = F(N)$.

Before going on let us note that the problem we encountered in the last example cannot arise if the net cannot diverge. The following theorem together with Proposition 4 tells us that for non-divergent nets N $\mathcal{F}(N)$ contains the same information as $\mathcal{FD}(N)$.

Theorem 4: Let N be a net that cannot diverge, $a = a_1 a_2 \ldots \in \Sigma^\omega$. Then $a \in l(L^\omega(N))$ if and only if for all $n \in \mathbb{N}$ $a_1 \ldots a_n \in l(L(N))$.

The next theorem corresponds directly to the definition of the failures semantics for the TCSP-operator $\|_A$ [OlHo].

Theorem 5: For nets N_1, N_2 and $A \subseteq \Sigma$, $N = N_1 \|_A N_2$ we have

$$\begin{aligned} F(N) = & \{(v, X) \mid \exists (v_i, X_i) \in F(N_i),\ i = 1,2 : \\ & \quad v \in v_1 \|_A v_2 \wedge X_1 \cap X_2 \supseteq X \setminus A \wedge X_1 \cup X_2 \supseteq X \cap A\} \\ \cup & \{(v, X) \mid v \in D(N) \cap \Sigma^*, X \subseteq \Sigma\} \end{aligned}$$

$$\begin{aligned} D(N) = & \{v \mid \exists v_1 \in D(N_1), (v_2, \emptyset) \in F(N_2) : v \in v_1 \|_A v_2\} \\ \cup & \{v \mid \exists v_2 \in D(N_2), (v_1, \emptyset) \in F(N_1) : v \in v_1 \|_A v_2\} \\ \cup & \{v \mid \exists v_i \in D(N_i), i = 1,2 : v \in v_1 \|_A v_2\} \end{aligned}$$

Lemma 2: For all nets N $l(L_{mc}(N)) = D(N) \cup \{v \mid (v, \Sigma) \in F(N)\}$

Theorem 6: Let N_1, N_2 be nets. Then N_1 is mc-equivalent to N_2 if and only if N_1 is $\mathcal{FD}$-equivalent to N_2.

Corollary 2: If N_1 and N_2 cannot diverge, then N_1 is mc-equivalent to N_2 if and only if N_1 is $\mathcal{F}$-equivalent to N_2.

6. Hiding the Synchronized Actions

As remarked above [Bau] regards all transitions of the exchangable subnets as internal, i.e. we have to use the operator $\| \setminus_A$ to label the merged transitions with λ. To keep our results compatible to the situation in [Bau] we restrict ourselves to subnets whose label-alphabet is a fixed set A. The mc'-equivalence we define next is quite the same as the external mc-equivalence of [Bau], the difference is that we do not require anything about the labelling of the environments N. But as above, the nets we need in the proof of Theorem 9 have an injective labelling with $l(T) \supseteq A$ and thus Theorem 9 solves the problem of [Bau] how to characterize the external mc-equivalence as defined there with an internal equivalence. (Note that Theorem 6A in the original version of [Bau] contains a mistake, while in the revised version it only gives a sufficient condition for a restricted class of nets.)

Definition: Let N_1, N_2 be nets with $l_i(T_i)\setminus\{\lambda\} = A$, $i = 1,2$. Then N_1 is mc'-equivalent to N_2 if for all nets N $l(L_{mc}(N \| \setminus_A N_1)) = l(L_{mc}(N \| \setminus_A N_2))$.

Accordingly we have to modify the failures-divergence semantics.

Definition: Let N be a net with $l(T)\setminus\{\lambda\} = A$. Then $\mathcal{FD}'(N) = (F'(N), D'(N))$ with
$D'(N) = D(N)$,
$F'(N) = \{(v, X) \mid v \in \Sigma^*, \exists X_1, X_2 \subseteq \Sigma : X = X_1 \cup X_2 \land (v, X_1) \in F(N) \land \forall x \in X_2 : vx_2 \in D(N)\}$.
Nets N_1, N_2 with $l_i(T_i)\setminus\{\lambda\} = A, i = 1,2$, are $\mathcal{FD}'$-equivalent if $\mathcal{FD}'(N_1) = \mathcal{FD}'(N_2)$.

As in the case of $F(N)$ we have that from $(v, X) \in F'(N)$ and $Y \subseteq X$ it follows that $(v, Y) \in F'(N)$.

Proposition 5: Let N_1, N_2 be nets with $l_i(T_i)\setminus\{\lambda\} = A$, $i = 1,2$.
(i) N_1 $\mathcal{FD}$-equivalent $N_2 \Rightarrow N_1$ $\mathcal{FD}'$-equivalent N_2
(ii) If N_1 cannot diverge then $\mathcal{FD}'(N_1) = \mathcal{FD}(N_1)$ and $F'(N_1) = \mathcal{F}(N_1)$.

Note that the reverse implication of (i) does not hold in general.

Before giving the result about the semantics of $N_1 \| \setminus_A N_2$ the reader might expect by now, we give a result on $\mathcal{FD}(N\setminus A)$.

Theorem 7: Let N be a net, $A \subseteq \Sigma$. Then

$$F(N\setminus A) = \{(v, X) \mid \exists (u, X \cup A) \in F(N) : u\setminus A = v\} \cup \{(v, X) \mid v \in D(N\setminus A) \cap \Sigma^*, X \subseteq \Sigma\}$$

$$D(N\setminus A) = \{v \mid \exists u \in D(N) : u\setminus A = v\}$$

Theorem 8: Let N_1, N_2 be nets and $l_2(T_2)\setminus\{\lambda\} = A$, $N = N_1 \| \setminus_A N_2$. Then

$$F(N) = \{(v, X) \mid \exists (v_1, X_1) \in F(N_1), (v_2, X_2) \in F'(N_2) : v \in v_1 \| \setminus_A v_2 \land X_1 \supseteq X\setminus A \land X_1 \cup X_2 \supseteq A\} \cup \{(v, X) \mid v \in D(N) \cap \Sigma^*, X \subseteq \Sigma\}$$

$$D(N) = \{v \mid \exists v_1 \in D(N_1), (v_2, \emptyset) \in F'(N_2) : v \in v_1 \| \setminus_A v_2\} \cup \{v \mid \exists v_2 \in D'(N_2), (v_1, \emptyset) \in F(N_1) : v \in v_1 \| \setminus_A v_2\} \cup \{v \mid \exists v_1 \in D(N_1), v_2 \in D'(N_2) : v \in v_1 \| \setminus_A v_2\}$$

Finally we come to the solution of the problem posed in [Bau]:

Theorem 9: Let N_1, N_2 be nets with $l_i(T_i)\backslash\{\lambda\} = A$, $i = 1, 2$. Then N_1 is mc'-equivalent to N_2 if and only if N_1 is $\mathcal{FD}'$-equivalent to N_2.

We conclude this section with a corollary which closely corresponds to Theorem 6A of [Bau, revised version] (non-divergent building blocks are called fair there), but we have a necessary and sufficient condition.

Corollary 3: If nets N_1, N_2 with $l_i(T_i)\backslash\{\lambda\} = A$, $i = 1,2$, are non-divergent, then N_1 mc'-equivalent to N_2 if and only if N_1 and N_2 are $\mathcal{F}$-equivalent.

7. Decidability Questions

The following theorem shows that subnets one wants to exchange should be taken from some restricted class of Petri nets, since in general the equivalences discussed in this paper are undecidable. Just as an example we show, that $\mathcal{F}$-equivalence for bounded nets is decidable.

Theorem 10: a) For general Petri nets $\mathcal{F}$-, $\mathcal{FD}$- and $\mathcal{FD}'$-equivalence are undecidable.
b) For bounded Petri nets $\mathcal{F}$-equivalence is decidable.

Proof: a) The proof uses reduction from the equality problem for reachability sets, which is undecidable [Ha]. Details will appear in the full paper. □

References

[An1] André, C.: Use of the behaviour equivalence in place-transition net analysis. In: Girault/Reisig (eds.): Application and theory of Petri nets. Informatik Fachberichte 52, Springer 1982, p. 241-250

[An2] André, C.: Structural transformations giving B-equivalent PT-nets. In: Pagnoni/Rozenberg (eds.): Application and theory of Petri nets. Informatik Fachberichte 66, Springer 1983, p.14-28

[An3] André, C.: The behaviour of a Petri net on a subset of transitions. RAIRO Autom. 17, 1983, p. 5-21

[Bau] Baumgarten, B.: On internal and external characterizations of PT-net building block behaviour. Proc. 7th European workshop on application and theory of Petri nets, Oxford, 1986. A revised version is to appear in: G.Rozenberg (ed.): Advances in Petri Nets, and has appeared as Arbeitspapiere der GMD 254, 1987.

[Be] Berthelot, G.: Transformations of Petri nets. Proc. 5th European workshop on appl. and theory of Petri nets, Aarhus, 1984, p. 310-328

[BeFe] Best, E., Fernández, C.: Notations and terminology on Petri net theory, Arbeitspapiere GMD 195, 1986

[BrHoRo] Brookes, S.D., Hoare, C.A.R., Roscoe, A.W.: A theory of communicating sequential processes, JACM 31 (1984), p. 560-599

[BrRo] Brookes, S.D., Roscoe, A.W.: An improved failures model for communicating processes. In: S.D.Brookes, A.W.Roscoe, G. Winskel (eds.): Seminar on Concurrency (1984), LNCS 197, p. 281-305

[DDS] De Cindio, F., De Michelis, G., Simone, C.: GAMERU: A language for the analysis and design of human communication pragmatics within organizational systems. In: Proc. 7th European workshop on application and theory of Petri nets, 1986, p. 343-366

[Go] Goltz, U.: An exercise in building structured nets. In: Proc. 7th European workshop on application and theory of Petri nets, 1986, p. 73-99

[Ha] Hack, M.: The equality problem for vector addition systems is undecidable. TCS 2 (1976), p. 77-95

[Mi] Milner, R.: Lectures on a calculus for communicating systems. In: S.D.Brookes, A.W.Roscoe, G. Winskel: Seminar on Concurrency, LNCS 197, p. 197-230

[Mü] Müller, K.: Constructable Petri nets. EIK 21 (1985), p. 171-199

[OlHo] Olderog, E.R., Hoare, C.A.R.: Specification-oriented semantics for communicating processes, Acta Informatica 23 (1986), p. 9-66

[Po] Pomello, L.: Some equivalence notions for concurrent systems - an overview. Arbeitspapiere der GMD Nr. 103, 1984

[SuMu] Suzuki, I., Murata, T.: A method for stepwise refinement and abstraction of Petri nets. J. Comp. Syst. Sciences 27, 1983, p. 51-76

[Tau] Taubner, D.: Two net-oriented semantics for TCSP. Univ. Hamburg, Bericht FBI-HH-B-116/85, 1985

[Va] Valette, R.: Analysis of Petri nets by stepwise refinements. J. Comp. Syst. Sciences 18, 1979, p. 35-46

[Vog1] Vogler, W.: Behaviour preserving refinements of Petri nets. Proc. 12th Int. workshop on graph theoretic concepts in computer science, Bernried/München, 1986, LNCS 246, p. 82-93

[Vog2] Vogler, W.: Behaviour and life preserving refinements of Petri nets (submitted)

[Vos] Voss, K.: System specification with labelled nets and the notion of interface equivalence. Arbeitspapiere der GMD Nr. 211, 1986

A Decomposition Theorem for Finite-Valued Transducers and an Application to the Equivalence Problem

by *Andreas Weber*

Fachbereich Informatik, J.W. Goethe-Universität,
Postfach 111 932, D-6000 Frankfurt am Main, West Germany.

Abstract: We show: A finite-valued generalized sequential machine (GSM) M can be effectively decomposed into finitely many single-valued GSM's $M_1,\ldots,M_N$ such that the relation realized by M is the union of the relations realized by $M_1,\ldots,M_N$. As an application of this decomposition we get a DTIME($2^{2^{poly}}$)-algorithm deciding the equivalence of finite-valued GSM's. By reduction, both results can be easily generalized to normalized finite transducers.

Acknowledgement: I gratefully thank Helmut Seidl for fruitful discussions and a lot of help.

0. Introduction

Let x be an input string of a normalized finite transducer (NFT) M [1]. The valuedness of x in M is defined by the number of all different output strings on the accepting paths with input x in M. The valuedness of M is the maximal valuedness of an input string of M or is infinite, depending on whether or not a maximum exists. A NFT is called finite-valued (single-valued), if its valuedness is finite (at most 1).

The valuedness is a structural parameter of the relation realized by a finite transducer, which received attention in connection with the equivalence problem: The equivalence of generalized sequential machines (GSM's; a GSM is a NFT without ε-input moves) is undecidable ([Gr68], [I78]). The equivalence of finite-valued NFT's is decidable [CuKa86]. The equivalence problem for single-valued NFT's is PSPACE-complete (see [Sch76], [BHe77], [GuI83]).

It is decidable in polynomial time whether or not a NFT is finite-valued ([We87], see also [WeSe86]). Given any fixed integer d, it can be tested in polynomial time whether or not the valuedness of a NFT is greater than d [GuI83].

In section 2 of this paper we present a decomposition theorem for finite-valued GSM's:

(1) A finite-valued GSM can be effectively decomposed into finitely many single-valued GSM's $M_1,\ldots,M_N$ such that the relation realized by M is the union of the relations realized by $M_1,\ldots,M_N$.

This theorem directly implies two results proved in [We87] (see also [WeSe86]), that is, an upper bound for the valuedness of a finite-valued GSM and a characterization of the infinite valuedness of a GSM, which can be tested in polynomial time.

In section 3 we apply the decomposition theorem to the equivalence problem for finite-valued GSM's. The application is based on a combinatorial word lemma and leads to the following results:

---

[1] In this paper we consider finite transducers only in their normalized form.

(2) Non-inclusion of relations realized by finite-valued GSM's (and hence, non-equivalence of finite-valued GSM's) can be detected by a witness of length $O(2^{2^{poly}})$.

(3) The inclusion of relations realized by finite-valued GSM's (and hence, the equivalence of finite-valued GSM's) is decidable in DTIME$(2^{2^{poly}})$.

By reduction, the results (1)-(3) can be generalized to NFT's (see sections 2 and 3). A noneffective version of (1) was stated in [Sch76] without complete proof. The proof methods used here differ from those in [Sch76]. Note that the algorithm underlying (3) is quite different from the procedure by Culik and Karhumäki [CuKa86] deciding the equivalence of finite-valued NFT's. As far as I know a time analysis for this procedure does not exist. The above mentioned word lemma generalizes a lemma by Schützenberger [Sch76] and may be of own interest. In order to derive (2) and (3) from (1) this word lemma can be replaced by a "machine oriented" approach due to Gurari and Ibarra [GuI81].

The proof of the decomposition theorem is based on a classification of accepting paths: To each accepting path in a GSM M we attach a finite set of specifications. Given any such specification we effectively construct a GSM realizing nothing but the input/output pairs on all accepting paths in M which have the given specification. If M is finite-valued, then the constructed GSM's turn out to be single-valued, and the relations realized by them fill out the relation realized by M. In order to prove this we use methods developed in [We87].

In the first section we summarize some definitions and notations.

1. Definitions and Notations

1.1 NFT's and GSM's

A nondeterministic normalized finite transducer (short form: NFT) is a 6-tuple $M=(Q,\Sigma,\Delta,\delta,Q_I,Q_F)$ whose components have the following meaning:
- Q is a nonempty, finite set of states.
- Σ is a nonempty, finite set of input symbols (called the input alphabet of M).
- Δ is a nonempty, finite set of output symbols (called the output alphabet of M).
- δ is a finite subset of $Q\times(\Sigma\cup\{\varepsilon\})\times\Delta^*\times Q$ (called the transition relation of M).
- $Q_I \subseteq Q$ is the set of initial states.
- $Q_F \subseteq Q$ is the set of final (or accepting) states.

M is called a nondeterministic generalized sequential machine (short form: GSM), if δ is a finite subset of $Q\times\Sigma\times\Delta^*\times Q$. In this paper we mainly deal with GSM's.

A path of length m with input x and output z (short form: for x|z) from p to q in M is a string $\pi = (q_1,x_1,z_1)....(q_m,x_m,z_m)q_{m+1} \in (Q\times(\Sigma\cup\{\varepsilon\})\times\Delta^*)^m\cdot Q$ so that $x = x_1...x_m \in \Sigma^*$, $z = z_1...z_m \in \Delta^*$, $p = q_1 \in Q$, $q = q_{m+1} \in Q$, and for all $i=1,...,m$ $(q_i,x_i,z_i,q_{i+1}) \in \delta$. We define $\hat{\delta} := \{(p,x,z,q) \in Q\times\Sigma^*\times\Delta^*\times Q \mid$ there is a path for x|z from p to q in M$\}$. If M is a GSM, then $\delta = \hat{\delta}\cap(Q\times\Sigma\times\Delta^*\times Q)$. In this case we rename $\hat{\delta}$ by δ.

Let $\pi = (q_1,x_1,z_1)....(q_m,x_m,z_m)q_{m+1}$ and $\tilde{\pi} = (\tilde{q}_1,\tilde{x}_1,\tilde{z}_1)....(\tilde{q}_l,\tilde{x}_l,\tilde{z}_l)\tilde{q}_{l+1}$ be paths in M. If $q_{m+1} = \tilde{q}_1$, then we define the path $\pi\bullet\tilde{\pi} := (q_1,x_1,z_1)....(q_m,x_m,z_m)(\tilde{q}_1,\tilde{x}_1,\tilde{z}_1)....(\tilde{q}_l,\tilde{x}_l,\tilde{z}_l)\tilde{q}_{l+1}$ in M. Let π_1,π_2,π_3,π_4 be paths in M: If $\pi_1\bullet\pi_2$ and $\pi_2\bullet\pi_3$ are defined, then $(\pi_1\bullet\pi_2)\bullet\pi_3 = \pi_1\bullet(\pi_2\bullet\pi_3)$ (i.e., "$\bullet$" is associative). If $\pi_1\bullet\pi_2 = \pi_3\bullet\pi_4$ and $|\pi_1| = |\pi_3|$, then $\pi_1 = \pi_3$ and $\pi_2 = \pi_4$.

A path π from p to q in M is called accepting path, if p is an initial state and q is a final state. The transduction (or relation) realized by M (short form: T(M)) is the set $\{(x,z) \in \Sigma^*\times\Delta^* \mid \hat{\delta}\cap(Q_I\times\{x\}\times\{z\}\times Q_F) \neq \phi\}$. If $(x,z) \in T(M)$, then z is called a value for x in M. The language accepted by M (short form: L(M)) is the set $\{x\in\Sigma^* \mid \exists z\in\Delta^*: (x,z) \in T(M)\}$. Let M' be another NFT: M and M' are equivalent, if T(M) = T(M').

The valuedness of $x\in\Sigma^*$ in M (short form: $val_M(x)$) is the number of all different values for x in M. The valuedness of M (short form: val(M)) is the supremum of the set $\{val_M(x) \mid x\in\Sigma^*\}$. M is called infinite-valued (finite-valued, single-valued), if $\mathrm{val}(M) = \infty$ ($< \infty$, ≤ 1, respectively).

The state $q \in Q$ is called useless, if it is on no accepting path in M. Useless states are irrelevant to the valuedness in M. If no state of M is useless, then M is called reduced. A state $p \in Q$ is said to be connected with a state $q \in Q$ (short form: $p \underset{M}{\longleftrightarrow} q$), if paths from p to q and from q to p in M exist. Note that "$\underset{M}{\longleftrightarrow}$" is an equivalence relation on Q.

We define the criteria (IV2) and (IV3) introduced in [We87] [2] :

(IV2): $\exists\, q_I \in Q_I\ \exists\, p,q \in Q\ \exists\, q_F \in Q_F\ \exists\, u,v,w \in \Sigma^*\ \exists\, \tilde{u},\tilde{v}_1,\tilde{v}_2,\tilde{v}_3,\tilde{v}_4,\tilde{w} \in \Delta^*$:
$\tilde{v}_3\tilde{v}_4 \neq \varepsilon\ \&\ \neg(\tilde{v}_1 \in \mathrm{pref}(\tilde{v}_2)),\ \neg(\tilde{v}_2 \in \mathrm{pref}(\tilde{v}_1))$ [3] $\&\ (q_I,u,\tilde{u},p) \in \hat{\delta}$
$\&\ (p,v,\tilde{v}_3,p),(p,v,\tilde{v}_1,q),(p,v,\tilde{v}_2,q),(q,v,\tilde{v}_4,q) \in \hat{\delta}\ \&\ (q,w,\tilde{w},q_F) \in \hat{\delta}$.

(IV3): $\exists\, q_I \in Q_I\ \exists\, p,q_1,q_2,q_3,q \in Q\ \exists\, q_F \in Q_F\ \exists\, u,v_1,v_2,v_3,w \in \Sigma^*\ \exists\, \tilde{u},\tilde{v}_1,\ldots,\tilde{v}_9,\tilde{w} \in \Delta^*$:
$|\tilde{v}_2| \neq |\tilde{v}_5|\ \&\ (q_I,u,\tilde{u},p) \in \hat{\delta}\ \&$
$(p,v_1,\tilde{v}_1,q_1),(q_1,v_2,\tilde{v}_2,q_1),(q_1,v_3,\tilde{v}_3,p) \in \hat{\delta}\ \&$
$(p,v_1,\tilde{v}_4,q_2),(q_2,v_2,\tilde{v}_5,q_2),(q_2,v_3,\tilde{v}_6,q) \in \hat{\delta}\ \&$
$(q,v_1,\tilde{v}_7,q_3),(q_3,v_2,\tilde{v}_8,q_3),(q_3,v_3,\tilde{v}_9,q) \in \hat{\delta}\ \&\ (q,w,\tilde{w},q_F) \in \hat{\delta}$.

In the rest of section 1.1 let M be a GSM. We define:

$\mathrm{val}_1(\delta) := \max(\{1\} \cup \{\, \#\{z \in \Delta^* \mid (p,a,z,q) \in \delta\} \mid p,q \in Q,\ a \in \Sigma\,\})$,
$\mathrm{im}(\delta) := \{z \in \Delta^* \mid \exists\, p,q \in Q\ \exists\, a \in \Sigma\colon\ (p,a,z,q) \in \delta\}$,
$\mathrm{val}_2(\delta) := \max\{1, \#\mathrm{im}(\delta)\}$,
$\mathrm{diff}(\delta) := \max(\{0\} \cup \{\,||z_1|-|z_2|| \mid \exists a \in \Sigma\colon z_1,z_2 \in \{z \in \Delta^* \mid \delta \cap (Q \times \{a\} \times \{z\} \times Q) \neq \phi\}\})$,
$\mathrm{length}(\delta) := \min\{l \in \mathbb{N} \mid \delta \cap (Q \times \Sigma \times \Delta^* \times Q) \subseteq Q \times \Sigma \times \Delta^{\leq l} \times Q\}$ [4] [5] .

Note that $\mathrm{val}_1(\delta) \leq \mathrm{val}_2(\delta) \leq \#(\Delta^{\leq \mathrm{length}(\delta)})$ and $\mathrm{diff}(\delta) \leq \mathrm{length}(\delta)$.

Let $x = x_1 \ldots x_m \in \Sigma^*$ ($x_1,\ldots,x_m \in \Sigma$). Let $\pi = (q_1,x_1,z_1)\ldots(q_m,x_m,z_m)q_{m+1}$ and $\tilde{\pi} = (\tilde{q}_1,x_1,\tilde{z}_1)\ldots(\tilde{q}_m,x_m,\tilde{z}_m)\tilde{q}_{m+1}$ be paths with input x in M. The difference between π and $\tilde{\pi}$ (short form: $\mathrm{diff}(\pi,\tilde{\pi})$) is defined to be the maximum of the set $\{\,||z_1 \ldots z_l|-|\tilde{z}_1 \ldots \tilde{z}_l|| \mid 0 \leq l \leq m\}$.

Let $x = x_1 \ldots x_m \in \Sigma^*$ ($x_1,\ldots,x_m \in \Sigma$). The graph of accepting paths with input x in M (short form: $G_M(x)$) is the directed graph (V,E) where

$V := \{(q,j) \in Q \times \{0,\ldots,m\} \mid \exists\, q_I \in Q_I\ \exists\, q_F \in Q_F\ \exists\, z_1,z_2 \in \Delta^*\colon\ (q_I,x_1 \ldots x_j,z_1,q) \in \delta\ \&$
$(q,x_{j+1} \ldots x_m,z_2,q_F) \in \delta\}$,
$E := \{((p,j-1),(q,j)) \in V^2 \mid j \in \{1,\ldots,m\}\ \&\ \exists\, z \in \Delta^*\colon\ (p,x_j,z,q) \in \delta\}$.

1.2 NFA's

A nondeterministic finite automaton (short form: NFA) is a 5-tuple $M=(Q,\Sigma,\delta,Q_I,Q_F)$ whose components Q,Σ,δ,Q_I and Q_F have the same meaning as for a GSM $(Q,\Sigma,\Delta,\delta,Q_I,Q_F)$ except that δ is a subset of $Q \times \Sigma \times Q$.

A path of length m for x from p to q in M is a string $\pi = (q_1,x_1)\ldots(q_m,x_m)q_{m+1} \in (Q \times (\Sigma \cup \{\varepsilon\}))^m \cdot Q$ so that $x = x_1 \ldots x_m \in \Sigma^*$, $p = q_1 \in Q$, $q = q_{m+1} \in Q$, and for all $i=1,\ldots,m$ $(q_i,x_i,q_{i+1}) \in \delta$. A path π from p to q in M is called accepting path, if p is an initial state and q is a final state. The language accepted by M (short form: L(M)) is the set $\{x \in \Sigma^* \mid$ there is an accepting path for x in M$\}$.

Let $\pi = (q_1,x_1)\ldots(q_m,x_m)q_{m+1}$ and $\tilde{\pi} = (\tilde{q}_1,\tilde{x}_1)\ldots(\tilde{q}_l,\tilde{x}_l)\tilde{q}_{l+1}$ be paths in M. If $q_{m+1} = \tilde{q}_1$, then we define the path $\pi \bullet \tilde{\pi} := (q_1,x_1)\ldots(q_m,x_m)(\tilde{q}_1,\tilde{x}_1)\ldots(\tilde{q}_l,\tilde{x}_l)\tilde{q}_{l+1}$ in M. Let π_1,π_2,π_3,π_4 be paths in M: If $\pi_1 \bullet \pi_2$ and $\pi_2 \bullet \pi_3$ are defined, then $(\pi_1 \bullet \pi_2) \bullet \pi_3 = \pi_1 \bullet (\pi_2 \bullet \pi_3)$. If $\pi_1 \bullet \pi_2 = \pi_3 \bullet \pi_4$ and $|\pi_1| = |\pi_3|$, then $\pi_1 = \pi_3$ and $\pi_2 = \pi_4$.

---

[2] The notation corresponds to those in [We87]. The criterion (IV1) is not used here.

[3] Let $z \in \Delta^*$: pref(z) denotes the set $\{z_1 \in \Delta^* \mid \exists\, z_2 \in \Delta^*\colon\ z_1 z_2 = z\}$.

[4] $\Delta^{\leq l}$ denotes the set $\bigcup_{i=0}^{l} \Delta^i$.

[5] $\mathbb{N}$ denotes the set of all nonnegative integers.

2. A Decomposition Theorem for Finite-Valued GSM's

In this section we prove the following theorem:

Theorem 1: (Decomposition Theorem for Finite-Valued GSM's)
Let $M=(Q,\Sigma,\Delta,\delta,Q_I,Q_F)$ be a finite-valued GSM with n states [6]. Then, GSM's $M_1,\dots,M_N$ effectively exist such that the following assertions are true:

(i) $T(M) = \bigcup_{i=1}^{N} T(M_i)$.

(ii) $\forall\, i=1,\dots,N$: $\mathrm{val}(M_i) \leq 1$.

(iii) If $\#\Delta > 1$, then $N \leq 5^{n} \cdot 2^{(n+3)\cdot(n-1)} \cdot n^{4\cdot(n-1)} \cdot \mathrm{val}_2(\delta)^{n-1} \cdot (1+\mathrm{diff}(\delta))^{n-1} \cdot \#\Delta^{2\cdot(n^3-1)\cdot\mathrm{diff}(\delta)}$.
If $\#\Delta = 1$, then $N \leq 5^{3n/2} \cdot 2^{(n+2)\cdot(n-1)} \cdot n^{6\cdot(n-1)} \cdot \mathrm{val}_2(\delta)^{n-1} \cdot (1+\mathrm{diff}(\delta))^{2\cdot(n-1)}$.

Intuitively, theorem 1 states that a finite-valued GSM can be effectively decomposed into finitely many single-valued GSM's. By reduction, the theorem can be generalized to NFT's (in fact, in assertion (iii) we have to replace $\mathrm{val}_2(\delta)$ by $1+\mathrm{val}_2(\delta)$ and $\mathrm{diff}(\delta)$ by $\mathrm{length}(\delta)$; see [We87], chapter 13).

In section 3 we apply theorem 1 to the equivalence problem for finite-valued GSM's. Here, we state the following immediate corollaries (for corollary 2 we moreover need lemma A in the appendix):

Corollary 1: Let M be a GSM. M is finite-valued, if and only if finitely many single-valued GSM's $M_1,\dots,M_N$ effectively exist such that $T(M) = \bigcup_{i=1}^{N} T(M_i)$.

Corollary 2: (theorem 10.2 in [We87])
Let M be a GSM. M is infinite-valued, if and only if M complies with at least one of the criteria (IV2),(IV3).

Corollary 3: (see theorem 10.1 in [We87], see also [WeSe86])
Let $M=(Q,\Sigma,\Delta,\delta,Q_I,Q_F)$ be a finite-valued GSM with n states. Then, the valuedness of M is not greater than the upper bound for N stated in assertion (iii) of theorem 1.

It is decidable in polynomial time whether or not a GSM complies with (IV2) or (IV3) (this follows from [Gul81], a direct polynomial-time algorithm is presented in [We87], chapter 11). Therefore, corollary 2 implies that it is decidable in polynomial time whether or not a GSM is finite-valued (theorem 11.1 in [We87], see also [WeSe86]).

Note: The upper bound for the valuedness of a finite-valued GSM stated in [We87], theorem 10.1, is for almost every n better (i.e., smaller) than the upper bound of corollary 3. If $\#\Delta > 1$, theorem 12.1 in [We87] implies that the upper bound in assertion (iii) of theorem 1 as well as those in [We87], theorem 10.1, and in corollary 3 must be at least $\#\Delta^{n^3\cdot\mathrm{diff}(\delta)/343}$. Thus, if $\#\Delta > 1$ and $\mathrm{diff}(\delta) > 0$, these bounds are assymptotically optimal apart from a constant factor in the exponent.

Proof of theorem 1: Let $M=(Q,\Sigma,\Delta,\delta,Q_I,Q_F)$ be a finite-valued, reduced GSM with n states. By lemma A, M does not comply with the criteria (IV2) and (IV3). We define:

$P := \{\pi \mid \pi \text{ is an accepting path in } M\}$.

Let $Q_1,\dots,Q_k \subseteq Q$ be the equivalence classes w.r.t. " $\underset{M}{\longleftrightarrow}$ ". We can number $Q_1,\dots,Q_k$ so that for all $i,j\in\{1,\dots,k\}$ the following holds:

---

[6] In fact, it suffices to assume that M does not comply with the criteria (IV2) and (IV3), which is (according to lemma A in the appendix) a direct consequence of the finite valuedness of M.

$$\delta \cap (Q_i \times \Sigma^* \times \Delta^* \times Q_j) \neq \phi \implies i \leq j .$$

Let $n_i := \#Q_i$ $(i=1,\ldots,k)$.

We prove the theorem according to the following strategy:

(1) We define a set $\mathbf{S}$ of path specifications, and we show:
If $\#\Delta > 1$, then $\#\mathbf{S} \leq 5^n \cdot 2^{(n+3)\cdot(n-1)} \cdot n^{4\cdot(n-1)} \cdot \mathrm{val}_2(\delta)^{n-1} \cdot (1+\mathrm{diff}(\delta))^{n-1} \cdot \#\Delta^{2\cdot(n^3-1)\cdot\mathrm{diff}(\delta)}$.
If $\#\Delta = 1$, then $\#\mathbf{S} \leq 5^{3n/2} \cdot 2^{(n+2)\cdot(n-1)} \cdot n^{6\cdot(n-1)} \cdot \mathrm{val}_2(\delta)^{n-1} \cdot (1+\mathrm{diff}(\delta))^{2\cdot(n-1)}$.

(2) We define a mapping $g: P \to (\mathrm{pot}(\mathbf{S}))\setminus\{\phi\}$ such that the following holds:
$\forall S \in \mathbf{S}\ \forall x \in \Sigma^*\ \forall \pi,\pi' \in P\ \forall z,z' \in \Delta^*$:
π is a path for $x|z$ & π' is a path for $x|z'$ & $S \in g(\pi) \cap g(\pi') \implies z = z'$.

(3) For all $S \in \mathbf{S}$ we effectively construct a GSM $\overline{M}_S$ which realizes the transduction $\{(x,z) \in \Sigma^* \times \Delta^* \mid \exists \pi \in P$: π is a path for $x|z$ & $S \in g(\pi)\}$.

From (1)-(3) follows:

$$T(M) = \bigcup_{S \in \mathbf{S}} T(\overline{M}_S) \quad \& \quad \forall S \in \mathbf{S}:\ \mathrm{val}(\overline{M}_S) \leq 1 .$$

Therefore, steps (1)-(3) prove the theorem.

<u>Execution of step (1):</u>
We define a set $\mathbf{S}$ of path specifications:

$$\mathbf{S} := \bigcup_{l \geq 0}\ \bigcup_{1 \leq i_0 < \ldots < i_l \leq k}\ \bigcup_{1 \leq j_1 < \ldots < j_l \leq 2^{n+1}-3} (Q_I \cap Q_{i_0}) \times$$
$$\prod_{\lambda=1}^{l} [\ \{j_\lambda\} \times Q_{i_{\lambda-1}} \times$$
$$(\ \{z \in \Delta^* \mid \exists p,q \in Q\ \exists a \in \Sigma: (p,a,z,q) \in \delta\} \cup \{z \in \Delta^* \mid\ |z| \leq (n^2 \cdot \sum_{i=i_{\lambda-1}}^{i_\lambda} n_i - 1)\cdot \mathrm{diff}(\delta)\} \cup$$
$$\{(d,p,q) \in \mathbb{Z} \times Q^2 \mid\ |d| \leq (n^2 \cdot \sum_{i=i_{\lambda-1}}^{i_\lambda} n_i - 1)\cdot \mathrm{diff}(\delta) \ \ \&\ \ p \underset{M}{\longleftrightarrow} q\}\ ) \times Q_{i_\lambda}\ ]$$
$$\times (Q_F \cap Q_{i_l}) .$$

We omit the proof of the announced upper bound for $\#\mathbf{S}$; this proof is contained in [We88].

<u>Execution of step (2):</u>
Let $x = x_1 \ldots x_m \in L(M)$ $(x_1,\ldots,x_m \in \Sigma)$. Consider $G_M(x) = (V,E)$. Let $\mu \in \{0,\ldots,m\}$: We define $\mathrm{set}(x,\mu) := \{q \in Q \mid (q,\mu) \in V\}$. $\mathrm{set}(x,\mu)$ denotes the set of states at column μ in $G_M(x)$. Consider the uniquely determined decomposition $x = y_1 \ldots y_d$ and the subsets $A_1,\ldots,A_{d+1}$ of Q such that d is odd and the following holds:

$\forall j=1,\ldots,d+1$: $A_j = \mathrm{set}(x,|y_1 \ldots y_{j-1}|)$,
$\forall j=1,\ldots,d$: j odd $\implies |y_1 \ldots y_j| = \max\{0 \leq \mu \leq m \mid A_j = \mathrm{set}(x,\mu)\}$,
$\forall j=1,\ldots,d$: j even $\implies y_j \in \Sigma$.

Thus, for each odd $j \in \{1,\ldots,d\}$, A_{j+1} "is the last occurence" of A_j in the sequence $\mathrm{set}(x,1)$, $\mathrm{set}(x,2),\ldots,\mathrm{set}(x,m)$ [7]. We observe: $d \leq 2\cdot(2^n-1)-1 = 2^{n+1}-3$.

Let $\pi \in P$ be an accepting path for $x|z$ in M. We shall define $g(\pi) \in \mathrm{pot}(\mathbf{S})$ and we shall show that $g(\pi) \neq \phi$. Consider the uniquely determined decompositions $\pi = \pi_1 \bullet \ldots \bullet \pi_d$ and $z = z_1 \ldots z_d$ and the states $p'_1,q'_1,\ldots,p'_d,q'_d \in Q$ such that for each $j=1,\ldots,d$ π_j is a path for $y_j|z_j$ from p'_j to q'_j in M. By construction: $p'_1 \in A_1 \subseteq Q_I$; $\forall j=2,\ldots,d$: $q'_{j-1} = p'_j \in A_j$; $q'_d \in A_{d+1} \subseteq Q_F$; $\forall j=1,\ldots,d$: j even $\implies z_j \in \mathrm{im}(\delta)$. We define:

$$J := \{1 \leq j \leq 2^{n+1}-3 \mid j \leq d \ \ \&\ \ \neg(p'_j \underset{M}{\longleftrightarrow} q'_j)\} .$$

Let $l := \#J \in \{0,\ldots,k-1\}$ and $1 \leq j_1 < \ldots < j_l \leq 2^{n+1}-3$ such that $J = \{j_1,\ldots,j_l\}$. Let $1 \leq i_0 < i_1 < \ldots < i_l \leq k$ such that $p'_1, p'_{j_1} \in Q_{i_0}$, $q'_{j_\lambda}, p'_{j_{\lambda+1}} \in Q_{i_\lambda}$ $(\lambda=1,\ldots,l-1)$ and $q'_{j_l}, q'_d \in Q_{i_l}$.

---

[7] Clearly, if $\neg(x \in L(M))$, then $d = 1$, $y_1 = x$ and $A_1 = A_2 = \phi$.

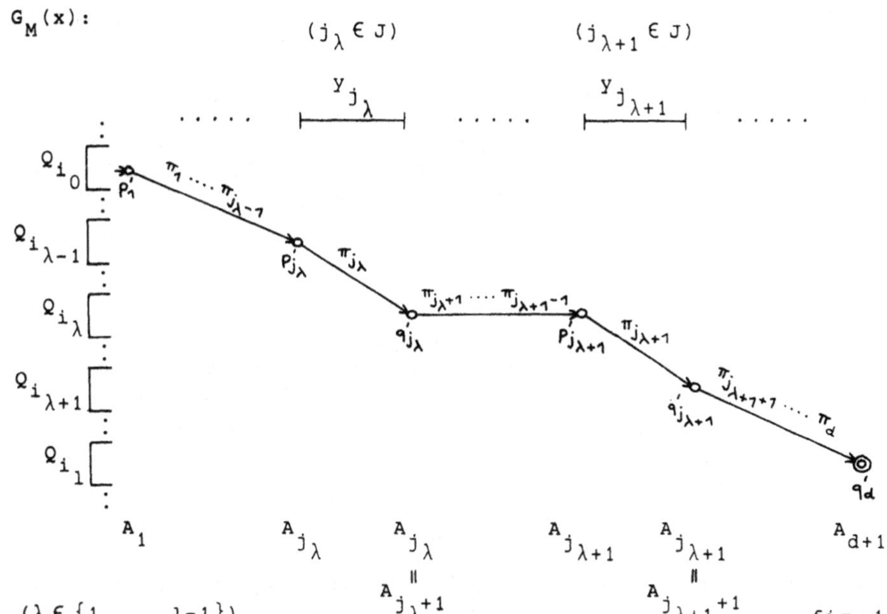

$(\lambda \in \{1,...,l-1\})$ fig. 1

Definition of $g(\pi)$:

$g(\pi) := \{p_1'\} \times \prod_{\lambda=1}^{l} [\{j_\lambda\}\times\{p'_{j_\lambda}\}\times g_{j_\lambda}(\pi_{j_\lambda})\times\{q'_{j_\lambda}\}] \times \{q'_d\}$ where for all $\lambda=1,...,l$,

if j_λ is even: $g_{j_\lambda}(\pi_{j_\lambda}) := \{z_{j_\lambda}\}$,

if j_λ is odd: $g_{j_\lambda}(\pi_{j_\lambda}) := (\{z_{j_\lambda}\} \cap \Delta^{\leq(n^2\cdot \sum_{i=i_{\lambda-1}}^{i_\lambda} n_i - 1)\cdot \mathrm{diff}(\delta)}) \cup$
$\{(d,\tilde{p}_1,\tilde{p}_2) \in \mathbb{Z}\times Q^2 \mid \tilde{p}_1 \underset{M}{\leftrightarrow} \tilde{p}_2$ & $\exists \tilde{z}\in\Delta^*$ $\exists$ a path $\tilde{\pi}$ for $y_{j_\lambda}|\tilde{z}$ from $\tilde{p}_1$ to $\tilde{p}_2$ in M:
$d = |\tilde{z}| - |z_{j_\lambda}|$ & $|d| \leq (n^2\cdot \sum_{i=i_{\lambda-1}}^{i_\lambda} n_i - 1)\cdot\mathrm{diff}(\delta)$ & $\mathrm{diff}(\tilde{\pi},\pi_{j_\lambda}) \leq (n^3-1)\cdot\mathrm{diff}(\delta)\}$.

We prove that $g(\pi)$ is nonempty (i.e., we have to show that for all $j\in J$ $g_j(\pi_j) \neq \phi$): Let $\lambda\in\{1,...,l\}$ such that $\neg(z_{j_\lambda} \in g_{j_\lambda}(\pi_{j_\lambda}))$. Then, j_λ is odd and $|z_{j_\lambda}| > (n^2\cdot \sum_{i=i_{\lambda-1}}^{i_\lambda} n_i - 1)\cdot\mathrm{diff}(\delta)$. Since j_λ is odd and $y_{j_\lambda} \neq \varepsilon$, we can apply lemma B in the appendix to $A := A_{j_\lambda} = A_{j_\lambda+1}$, $y := y_{j_\lambda}$, $p' := p'_{j_\lambda} \in A$ and $q' := q'_{j_\lambda} \in A$. Lemma B implies:

(*) $\exists\, p,q\in Q$ $\exists\, p_1,p_2,p_3,p_4\in Q$ $\exists\, l_1,l_2\in\mathbb{N}$ $\exists\, z_1^{(1)},...,z_4^{(1)},z_6^{(1)},...,z_9^{(1)}\in\Delta^*$:
$(p,y^{l_1},z_1^{(1)},p_1)$, $(p_1,y,z_2^{(1)},p_2)$, $(p_2,y^{l_2},z_3^{(1)},p) \in \delta$ &
$(p,y^{l_1},z_4^{(1)},p') \in \delta$ & $(q',y^{l_2},z_6^{(1)},q) \in \delta$ &
$(q,y^{l_1},z_7^{(1)},p_3)$, $(p_3,y,z_8^{(1)},p_4)$, $(p_4,y^{l_2},z_9^{(1)},q) \in \delta$.

Recall that M does not comply with the criterion (IV3). Recall: π_{j_λ} is a path for $y|z_{j_\lambda}$ from p' to q' in M & $\neg(p' \underset{M}{\leftrightarrow} q')$. Select $\tilde{p}_1 := p_1$, $\tilde{p}_2 := p_2$, $\tilde{z} := z_2^{(1)}$ and $d := |\tilde{z}| - |z_{j_\lambda}|$. Let $\tilde{\pi}$ be an arbitrary path for $y|\tilde{z}$ from $\tilde{p}_1$ to $\tilde{p}_2$ in M. We apply lemma C in the appendix to $p' \in Q_{i_{\lambda-1}}$, $q' \in Q_{i_\lambda}$, $y \in \Sigma^+$, the assertion (*), π_{j_λ}, $\tilde{\pi}$ and a suitable partition of Q. Lemma C implies: $\mathrm{diff}(\tilde{\pi},\pi_{j_\lambda}) \leq (n^2\cdot \sum_{i=i_{\lambda-1}}^{i_\lambda} n_i - 1)\cdot\mathrm{diff}(\delta)$. Thus, $(d,\tilde{p}_1,\tilde{p}_2)$ belongs to $g_{j_\lambda}(\pi_{j_\lambda})$.

Let $S\in\boldsymbol{S}$, $\pi,\pi'\in\boldsymbol{P}$ and $z,z'\in\Delta^*$ such that π is a path for $x|z$, π' is a path for $x|z'$, and $S \in g(\pi)\cap g(\pi')$. We shall show that $z = z'$. Consider the uniquely determined decompositions $\pi = \pi_1\bullet...\bullet\pi_d$, $\pi' =$

$\pi'_1 \bullet \ldots \bullet \pi'_d$ and $z = z_1 \ldots z_d$, $z' = z'_1 \ldots z'_d$ and the states $p_j^{(1)}, q_j^{(1)}, p_j^{(2)}, q_j^{(2)} \in Q$ $(j=1,\ldots,d)$ such that for each $j=1,\ldots,d$ π_j is a path for $y_j|z_j$ from $p_j^{(1)}$ to $q_j^{(1)}$ and π'_j is a path for $y_j|z'_j$ from $p_j^{(2)}$ to $q_j^{(2)}$ in M. We define:

$$J := \{1 \leq j \leq 2^{n+1}-3 \mid j \leq d \ \& \ \neg(p_j^{(1)} \underset{M}{\longleftrightarrow} q_j^{(1)})\}, \quad J' := \{1 \leq j \leq 2^{n+1}-3 \mid j \leq d \ \& \ \neg(p_j^{(2)} \underset{M}{\longleftrightarrow} q_j^{(2)})\}.$$

Since $g(\pi) \cap g(\pi') \neq \phi$, we know: $J = J'$, $p_1^{(1)} = p_1^{(2)} =: p'_1$, $\forall j \in J$: $p_j^{(1)} = p_j^{(2)} =: p'_j$ & $q_j^{(1)} = q_j^{(2)} =: q'_j$ & $g_j(\pi_j) \cap g_j(\pi'_j) \neq \phi$, $q_d^{(1)} = q_d^{(2)} =: q'_d$. Let $l := \#J \in \{0,\ldots,k-1\}$ and $1 \leq j_1 < \ldots < j_l \leq 2^{n+1}-3$ such that $J = \{j_1,\ldots,j_l\}$. Let $1 \leq i_0 < i_1 < \ldots < i_l \leq k$ such that $p'_{j_1} \in Q_{i_0}$ and $q'_{j_\lambda} \in Q_{i_\lambda}$ $(\lambda=1,\ldots,l)$. (see figure 1)

Since M does not comply with the criteria (IV2) and (IV3), it is single-valued inside each Q_i $(i=1,\ldots,k)$. Hence, we know:

$$z_1 \ldots z_{j_1-1} = z'_1 \ldots z'_{j_1-1}, \quad \forall \lambda=1,\ldots,l-1: \ z_{j_\lambda+1} \ldots z_{j_{\lambda+1}-1} = z'_{j_\lambda+1} \ldots z'_{j_{\lambda+1}-1}, \quad z_{j_l+1} \ldots z_d = z'_{j_l+1} \ldots z'_d .$$

Let $\lambda \in \{1,\ldots,l\}$: If $(g_{j_\lambda}(\pi_{j_\lambda}) \cap g_{j_\lambda}(\pi'_{j_\lambda})) \cap \Delta^* \neq \phi$, then $\{z_{j_\lambda}\} = g_{j_\lambda}(\pi_{j_\lambda}) \cap \Delta^* = g_{j_\lambda}(\pi'_{j_\lambda}) \cap \Delta^* = \{z'_{j_\lambda}\}$, i.e., $z_{j_\lambda} = z'_{j_\lambda}$. Otherwise, consider $(d, \tilde{p}_1, \tilde{p}_2) \in \mathbb{Z} \times Q^2$ so that $(d, \tilde{p}_1, \tilde{p}_2) \in g_{j_\lambda}(\pi_{j_\lambda}) \cap g_{j_\lambda}(\pi'_{j_\lambda})$. Since $\tilde{p}_1 \underset{M}{\longleftrightarrow} \tilde{p}_2$, there is exactly one $\tilde{z} \in \Delta^*$ such that $(\tilde{p}_1, y_{j_\lambda}, \tilde{z}, \tilde{p}_2) \in \delta$. Hence, we know: $d = |\tilde{z}| - |z_{j_\lambda}| = |\tilde{z}| - |z'_{j_\lambda}|$, i.e., $|z_{j_\lambda}| = |z'_{j_\lambda}|$. Since j_λ is odd and $y_{j_\lambda} \neq \varepsilon$, we can apply lemma B to $A := A_{j_\lambda} = A_{j_\lambda+1}$, $y := y_{j_\lambda}$, $p' := p'_{j_\lambda} \in A$ and $q' := q'_{j_\lambda} \in A$. Lemma B implies (*). Since $(p', y, z_{j_\lambda}, q') \in \delta$, lemma C implies: $\left||z_{j_\lambda}| - |z_2^{(1)}|\right| \leq (n^2 \cdot \sum_{i=i_{\lambda-1}}^{i_\lambda} n_i - 1) \cdot \mathrm{diff}(\delta)$. Thus, we know in addition to (*):

$$(p', y, z_{j_\lambda}, q'), (p', y, z'_{j_\lambda}, q') \in \delta \ \& \ |z_{j_\lambda}| = |z'_{j_\lambda}| \ \& \ z_2^{(1)} \neq \varepsilon .$$

Since M does not comply with the criterion (IV2), this implies: $z_{j_\lambda} = z'_{j_\lambda}$. In summary, we have shown that $z = z'$.

<u>Execution of step (3):</u>

Let $S \in \mathcal{S}$. We will effectively construct a NFT $M_S = (Q_S, \Sigma, \Delta, \delta_S, Q_{I,S}, Q_{F,S})$ which realizes the transduction $\{(x,z) \in \Sigma^* \times \Delta^* \mid \exists \pi \in P\text{: } \pi$ is a path for $x|z$ & $S \in g(\pi)\}$ such that each path with input ε in M_S has output ε and length at most 2. M_S can be easily transformed into an equivalent GSM $\overline{M}_S$.

Let $S = (q_I, (j_1, p'_{j_1}, \sigma_{j_1}, q'_{j_1}), \ldots, (j_\lambda, p'_{j_\lambda}, \sigma_{j_\lambda}, q'_{j_\lambda}), \ldots, (j_l, p'_{j_l}, \sigma_{j_l}, q'_{j_l}), q_F)$. We know: $l \geq 0$; $1 \leq j_1 < \ldots < j_l \leq 2^{n+1}-3$; $\forall \lambda=1,\ldots,l$: $p'_{j_\lambda}, q'_{j_\lambda} \in Q$ & $\neg(p'_{j_\lambda} \underset{M}{\longleftrightarrow} q'_{j_\lambda})$; $q_I \in Q_I$, $q_F \in Q_F$. Define $J := \{j_1,\ldots,j_l\}$; let $J = J_1 \dot{\cup} J_2$ such that for all $j \in J$,

if $j \in J_1$: $\sigma_j = z_j$ $(\in \Delta^*)$,
if $j \in J_2$: $\sigma_j = (d_j, \tilde{p}_j, \tilde{q}_j)$ $(\in \mathbb{Z} \times Q^2)$,

where for all $j \in J_1$ $z_j \in \mathrm{im}(\delta)$ or $|z_j| \leq (n^3-1) \cdot \mathrm{diff}(\delta)$, and for all $j \in J_2$ $|d_j| \leq (n^3-1) \cdot \mathrm{diff}(\delta)$ and $\tilde{p}_j \underset{M}{\longleftrightarrow} \tilde{q}_j$.

We omit the formal construction of M_S, which is performed in [We88]. Instead, we will explain the desired mode of operation of M_S:

Let $x = x_1 \ldots x_m \in L(M)$ $(x_1,\ldots,x_m \in \Sigma)$. Consider $G_M(x) = (V,E)$. Let $\mu \in \{0,\ldots,m\}$: We define

$$\mathrm{att}(x,\mu) := \{s \in Q \mid \exists r \in Q_I \ \exists z \in \Delta^*\text{: } (r, x_1 \ldots x_\mu, z, s) \in \delta\},$$
$$\mathrm{der}(x,\mu) := \{r \in Q \mid \exists s \in Q_F \ \exists z \in \Delta^*\text{: } (r, x_{\mu+1} \ldots x_m, z, s) \in \delta\}.$$

$\mathrm{att}(x,\mu)$ and $\mathrm{der}(x,\mu)$ denote the set of states attainable from Q_I with $x_1 \ldots x_\mu$ and the set of states derivable to Q_F with $x_{\mu+1} \ldots x_m$, respectively. Recall:

$$\mathrm{set}(x,\mu) = \{q \in Q \mid (q,\mu) \in V\} = \mathrm{att}(x,\mu) \cap \mathrm{der}(x,\mu).$$

Moreover, recall the definition of the decomposition $x = y_1 \ldots y_d$ and of the subsets $A_1,\ldots,A_{d+1}$ of Q (where d is odd) in the execution of step (2).

An accepting path π_S with input x in M_S consists of four components (according to four components of Q_S). The first three components of π_S drive a process which constructs $A_1,\ldots,A_{d+1} \in \mathrm{pot}(Q)$. Let $\mu \in \{0,\ldots,m\}$: After input $x_1 \ldots x_\mu$ the first component of π_S contains $\mathrm{att}(x,\mu)$, the second component contains $\mathrm{der}(x,\mu)$, and the third component contains all $A_1,\ldots,A_j \in \mathrm{pot}(Q)$ fixed up to this point and controls the correctness of their construction. The fourth component of π_S contains a nondeterministically selected path π with input x in M such that π_S and π have the same output $z \in \Delta^*$, and it controls that $S \in g(\pi)$. Consider the uniquely determined decompositions $\pi = \pi_1 \bullet \ldots \bullet \pi_d$ and $z = z'_1 \ldots z'_d$ such that for all $j=1,\ldots,d$ π_j is a path for $y_j|z'_j$. The fourth component of π_S precisely controls the following:

- π is a path from q_I to q_F.
- For all $j \in J$: π_j is a path from p'_j to q'_j.
- For all $j \in J$: $\sigma_j \in g_j(\pi_j)$, in particular:
  - for all even $j \in J$: $j \in J_1$ & $z_j = z'_j$ (in this case: $\sigma_j = z_j$ & $\{z'_j\} = g_j(\pi_j)$).
  - for all odd $j \in J_1$: $z_j = \tilde{z}'_j$ (in this case: $\sigma_j = z_j$ & $\{z'_j\} = g_j(\pi_j) \cap \Delta^*$).
  - for all odd $j \in J_2$: $(d_j, \tilde{p}_j, \tilde{q}_j) \in g_j(\pi_j)$ (in this case: $\sigma_j = (d_j, \tilde{p}_j, \tilde{q}_j)$).

This completes the proof of theorem 1. □

We conclude this section with two additions to theorem 1: Consider $S \in \mathbf{S}$ in the proof of theorem 1. Let M_S and $\overline{M}_S$ be constructed as in the execution of step (3) in this proof.

Addition 1: $\overline{M}_S$ has at most $16 \cdot n^2 \cdot 2^{n \cdot 2^{n+1}} \cdot (1 + \max\{\text{length}(\delta), n^3 \cdot \text{diff}(\delta)\})$ states.

Addition 2: A NFA $\overline{M}'_S$ effectively exists such that the following assertions are true:

(i) $L(\overline{M}'_S) = \Sigma^* \setminus L(\overline{M}_S) = \{x \in \Sigma^* \mid \forall \pi \in P\text{: } \pi \text{ is a path with input } x \Rightarrow \neg(S \in g(\pi))\}$.

(ii) $\overline{M}'_S$ has at most $16 \cdot 2^{n \cdot 2^{n+1}} \cdot 2^{2n^2 \cdot (1+\max\{\text{length}(\delta), n^3 \cdot \text{diff}(\delta)\})}$ states.

Proofs of the additions are given in [We88].

3. Equivalence of Finite-Valued GSM's

Let M_0 and M be finite-valued GSM's with alphabets Σ (input) and Δ (output). Applying theorem 1 and its additions to M one can construct in DTIME($2^{2^{poly}}$) a nondeterministic 2N-counter machine (see [Gul81]) of size $O(2^{2^{poly}})$ (where $N = O(2^{poly})$) which accepts the language $L_0 := \{x \in \Sigma^* \mid \exists z \in \Delta^*\text{: } (x,z) \in T(M_0) \setminus T(M)\}$. [Gul81] implies:

(1) $\neg(T(M_0) \subset T(M)) \Rightarrow \exists x \in L_0\text{: } |x| = O(2^{2^{poly}})$.

(2) It is decidable in DTIME($2^{2^{poly}}$) whether or not $T(M_0) \subset T(M)$.

(1) means: Non-inclusion of $T(M_0)$ in $T(M)$ can be detected by a witness of length $O(2^{2^{poly}})$. We remark that the bounds in (1) and (2) are rather "machine oriented". It seems lengthy to analyse them exactly.

In this section we present a combinatorial word lemma which yields - as an application of theorem 1 - an exact version of (1) (see theorem 2). From this and from theorem 1 a proof of (2) can be easily derived (see theorem 3). The above mentioned word lemma generalizes a lemma by Schützenberger [Sch76] and may be of own interest.

The main result of this section is the following theorem:

Theorem 2: ("a witness for non-inclusion")
Let $M_0 = (Q_0, \Sigma, \Delta, \delta_0, Q_{I,0}, Q_{F,0})$ and $M = (Q, \Sigma, \Delta, \delta, Q_I, Q_F)$ be finite-valued GSM's with n_0 and n states, respectively. If $\neg(T(M_0) \subset T(M))$, then an $(x,z) \in T(M_0) \setminus T(M)$ exists such that $|x| < 3 \cdot N! \cdot n_0 \cdot (\overline{n})^N$ where,

if $\#\Delta > 1$: $N \leq 5^n \cdot 2^{(n+3)\cdot(n-1)} \cdot n^{4\cdot(n-1)} \cdot \text{val}_2(\delta)^{n-1} \cdot (1+\text{diff}(\delta))^{n-1} \cdot \#\Delta^{2\cdot(n^3-1)\cdot\text{diff}(\delta)}$,

if $\#\Delta = 1$: $N \leq 5^{3n/2} \cdot 2^{(n+2)\cdot(n-1)} \cdot n^{6\cdot(n-1)} \cdot \text{val}_2(\delta)^{n-1} \cdot (1+\text{diff}(\delta))^{2\cdot(n-1)}$,

and $\overline{n} \leq 16 \cdot 2^{n \cdot 2^{n+1}} \cdot 2^{2n^2 \cdot (1+\max\{\text{length}(\delta), n^3 \cdot \text{diff}(\delta)\})}$.

From theorems 1 and 2 follows:

Theorem 3: Let M_0 and M be finite-valued GSM's. It is decidable in DTIME($2^{2^{poly}}$) whether or not $T(M_0) \subseteq T(M)$.

Note that theorem 2 alone implies a DTIME($2^{2^{2^{poly}}}$)-algorithm for the decision problem in theorem 3.

By reduction, theorems 2 and 3 can be generalized to NFT's (in fact, in the upper bounds (for N and $\bar{n}$) of theorem 2 we have to replace n by $n \cdot \max\{n, n_0\}$, $val_2(\delta)$ by $1+val_2(\delta)$, and $diff(\delta)$ by $length(\delta)$). Going with the title of this section we state the following immediate corollary to theorem 3:

Corollary 4: (see [CuKa86])
Let M_0 and M be finite-valued GSM's. It is decidable in DTIME($2^{2^{poly}}$) whether or not M_0 and M are equivalent.

The equivalence problem for finite-valued GSM's was proved to be decidable by Culik and Karhumäki [CuKa86]. Their decision procedure uses an algorithm by Makanin as a "subroutine"; it is proved to be recursive by employing a generalization of the (recently confirmed) Ehrenfeucht Conjecture. As far as I know a time analysis for this procedure does not exist.

We omit the proof of theorem 3. The proof of theorem 2 is based on theorem 1 and on the two following word lemmas:

Lemma 1: (Schützenberger [Sch76])
Let Δ be some alphabet. Let $z_0, z_1, z_2, z_3, z_0', z_1', z_2', z_3' \in \Delta^*$ such that $z_0 z_3 = z_0' z_3'$, $z_0 z_1 z_3 = z_0' z_1' z_3'$ and $z_0 z_2 z_3 = z_0' z_2' z_3'$. Then, $z_0 z_1 z_2 z_3 = z_0' z_1' z_2' z_3'$.

Proof: Let w.l.o.g. $|z_0| \geq |z_0'|$. $z_0 z_3 = z_0' z_3'$ implies that for some $z \in \Delta^*$ $z_0 = z_0' z$ and $z z_3 = z_3'$. Thus, $z z_1 = z_1' z$ and $z z_2 = z_2' z$. In summary, we know: $z_0 z_1 z_2 z_3 = z_0' z z_1 z_2 z_3 = z_0' z_1' z z_2 z_3 = z_0' z_1' z_2' z z_3 = z_0' z_1' z_2' z_3'$. ▫

Lemma 2: Let Δ be some alphabet. Define $l_1 := 2$, $l_\nu := 1 + \nu \cdot l_{\nu-1}$ ($\nu = 2,3,\ldots.$). Let I be a nonempty, finite subset of $\mathbb{N}$. Let $l \geq l_{\#I}$, let φ: $\{0,\ldots,l\} \times \{0,\ldots,l\} \to I$, and let $z_{i,j} \in \Delta^*$ ($i \in I \cup \{0\}$, $j \in \{0,\ldots,l+1\}$) such that the following holds:

$$\forall\, 0 \leq j_1 < j_2 \leq l: \quad i := \varphi(j_1, j_2) \implies z_{0,0} z_{0,1} \ldots z_{0,j_1} z_{0,j_2+1} \ldots z_{0,l} z_{0,l+1} = z_{i,0} z_{i,1} \ldots z_{i,j_1} z_{i,j_2+1} \ldots z_{i,l} z_{i,l+1}.$$

Then, there is an $i_0 \in I$ such that

$$z_{0,0} z_{0,1} \ldots z_{0,l} z_{0,l+1} = z_{i_0,0} z_{i_0,1} \ldots z_{i_0,l} z_{i_0,l+1}.$$

Proof: We prove the lemma by induction on #I.
Base of induction: #I = 1, let $I = \{i_0\}$. Since $l > 1$, we can apply lemma 1 to $z_0 := z_{0,0}$, $z_1 := z_{0,1}$, $z_2 := z_{0,2} \ldots z_{0,l}$, $z_3 := z_{0,l+1}$, $z_0' := z_{i_0,0}$, $z_1' := z_{i_0,1}$, $z_2' := z_{i_0,2} \ldots z_{i_0,l}$, $z_3' := z_{i_0,l+1}$. Lemma 1 implies: $z_{0,0} \ldots z_{0,l+1} = z_0 z_1 z_2 z_3 = z_0' z_1' z_2' z_3' = z_{i_0,0} \ldots z_{i_0,l+1}$.
Induction step: #I > 1. Since $l \geq 1 + \#I \cdot l_{\#I-1}$, there is an $i_0 \in I$ such that $\#\{1 \leq j \leq l \mid \varphi(0,j) = i_0\} \geq 1 + l_{\#I-1}$. We define $J := \{1 \leq j \leq l \mid \varphi(0,j) = i_0\}$.
Case 1: $\exists\, j_1, j_2 \in J$: $j_1 < j_2$ & $\varphi(j_1, j_2) = i_0$.
Since $0 < j_1 < j_2$ and $\varphi(0,j_1) = \varphi(0,j_2) = \varphi(j_1,j_2) = i_0$, we can apply lemma 1 to $z_0 := z_{0,0}$, $z_1 := z_{0,1} \ldots z_{0,j_1}$, $z_2 := z_{0,j_1+1} \ldots z_{0,j_2}$, $z_3 := z_{0,j_2+1} \ldots z_{0,l+1}$, $z_0' := z_{i_0,0}$, $z_1' := z_{i_0,1} \ldots z_{i_0,j_1}$, $z_2' := z_{i_0,j_1+1} \ldots z_{i_0,j_2}$, $z_3' := z_{i_0,j_2+1} \ldots z_{i_0,l+1}$. Lemma 1 implies: $z_{0,0} \ldots z_{0,l+1} = z_0 z_1 z_2 z_3 = z_0' z_1' z_2' z_3' = z_{i_0,0} \ldots z_{i_0,l+1}$.
Case 2: $\forall\, j_1, j_2 \in J$: $j_1 < j_2 \implies \varphi(j_1, j_2) \neq i_0$.
Define $I' := I \setminus \{i_0\}$. Let $0 \leq j_0 < j_1 < \ldots < j_{l'} \leq l$ such that $J = \{j_0, \ldots, j_{l'}\}$ where $l' := \#J - 1 \geq l_{\#I'}$. We can apply the induction hypothesis to $\tilde{z}_{i,\lambda} \in \Delta^*$ where for all $i \in I' \cup \{0\}$ $\tilde{z}_{i,0} := z_{i,0} \ldots z_{i,j_0}$, $\tilde{z}_{i,\lambda} := z_{i,j_{\lambda-1}+1} \ldots z_{i,j_\lambda}$ ($\lambda = 1,\ldots,l'$), $\tilde{z}_{i,l'+1} := z_{i,j_{l'}+1} \ldots z_{i,l+1}$. By the induction hypothesis there is an $i_1 \in I'$ such that $z_{0,0} \ldots z_{0,l+1} = \tilde{z}_{0,0} \ldots \tilde{z}_{0,l'+1} = \tilde{z}_{i_1,0} \ldots \tilde{z}_{i_1,l'+1} = z_{i_1,0} \ldots z_{i_1,l+1}$. ▫

Proof of theorem 2: We apply theorem 1 to M: Let $M_1, \ldots, M_N$ be single-valued GSM's constructed as in theorem 1 such that $T(M) = \bigcup_{i=1}^{N} T(M_i)$ and N is bounded as in assertion (iii) of this theorem.

Let $M'_1,\ldots,M'_N$ be NFA's constructed as in addition 2 to theorem 1 such that for all $i=1,\ldots,N$ $L(M'_i) = \Sigma^*\backslash L(M_i)$. Let $M_i = (Q_i,\Sigma,\Delta,\delta_i,Q_{I,i},Q_{F,i})$, $n_i := \#Q_i$, $M'_i = (Q'_i,\Sigma,\delta'_i,Q'_{I,i},Q'_{F,i})$, $n'_i := \#Q'_i$, $\bar{n}_i := \max\{n_i, n'_i\}$ $(i=1,\ldots,N)$. Define $\bar{n} := \max_{i=1}^{N} \bar{n}_i$. Additions 1 and 2 to theorem 1 imply:

$$\bar{n} \leq 16 \cdot 2^{n \cdot 2^{n+1}} \cdot 2^{2n^8 \cdot (1+\max\{\mathrm{length}(\delta), n^3 \cdot \mathrm{diff}(\delta)\})} .$$

We define as in lemma 2: $l_1 := 2$, $l_\nu := 1 + \nu \cdot l_{\nu-1}$ $(\nu=2,3,\ldots)$. Clearly, for all $\nu \in \mathbb{N}$: $l_\nu = \nu! + \nu! \cdot \sum_{i=1}^{\nu} (1/i!) < 3 \cdot \nu!$. We will show:

(*) Let $(x,z) \in T(M_0)\backslash(\bigcup_{i=1}^{N} T(M_i))$ such that $|x|$ is minimal. Then, $|x| < l_N \cdot n_0 \cdot \prod_{i=1}^{N} \bar{n}_i < 3 \cdot N! \cdot n_0 \cdot (\bar{n})^N$.

Thus, the theorem follows from (*).

Proof of (*): We assume that $|x| \geq l_N \cdot n_0 \cdot \prod_{i=1}^{N} \bar{n}_i$. Let $I := \{1 \leq i \leq N \mid x \in L(M_i)\}$ and $I' := \{1,\ldots,N\}\backslash I$. For all $i \in I$ select $z_i \in \Delta^*\backslash\{z\}$ such that $(x,z_i) \in T(M_i)$. Let π_0 be an accepting path for $x|z$ in M_0. For all $i=1,\ldots,N$ let π_i and π'_i be accepting paths for $x|z_i$ in M_i (if $i \in I$) and for x in M'_i (if $i \in I'$), respectively. Since $|x| \geq l_N \cdot n_0 \cdot \prod_{i=1}^{N} \bar{n}_i$, there are states $q_0 \in Q_0$, $q_i \in Q_i$ $(i \in I)$, $q'_i \in Q'_i$ $(i \in I')$ and decompositions $x = y_0 \ldots y_{l+1}$ (where $l \geq l_N$ and $y_1,\ldots,y_l \neq \varepsilon$), $\pi_i = \pi_{i,0} \bullet \ldots \bullet \pi_{i,l+1}$, $z_i = z_{i,0} \ldots z_{i,l+1}$ $(i \in I \cup \{0\}$, $z_0 := z)$, $\pi'_i = \pi'_{i,0} \bullet \ldots \bullet \pi'_{i,l+1}$ $(i \in I')$ such that the following holds:

- For all $i \in I \cup \{0\}$: $\pi_{i,0}$ is a path for $y_0|z_{i,0}$, $\pi_{i,j}$ is a path for $y_j|z_{i,j}$ from q_i to q_i $(j=1,\ldots,l)$, $\pi_{i,l+1}$ is a path for $y_{l+1}|z_{i,l+1}$.
- For all $i \in I'$: $\pi'_{i,0}$ is a path for y_0, $\pi'_{i,j}$ is a path for y_j from q'_i to q'_i $(j=1,\ldots,l)$, $\pi'_{i,l+1}$ is a path for y_{l+1}.

Since $|x|$ is minimal and $M_1,\ldots,M_N$ are single-valued, we can apply lemma 2 to I, l, a suitable mapping φ: $\{0,\ldots,l\}\times\{0,\ldots,l\} \to I$ and to $z_{i,j} \in \Delta^*$ $(i \in I \cup \{0\}$, $j \in \{0,\ldots,l+1\})$. Lemma 2 implies:

$\exists\, i_0 \in I$: $(x,z) = (x,z_{i_0}) \in T(M_{i_0})$. ↯

Therefore, $|x| < l_N \cdot n_0 \cdot \prod_{i=1}^{N} \bar{n}_i$. □

Appendix

Lemma A: (lemma 10.1 in [We87])
Let M be a GSM. If M complies with at least one of the criteria (IV2),(IV3), then M is infinite-valued.

Lemma B: (see lemma 10.4 in [We87])
Let $M=(Q,\Sigma,\Delta,\delta,Q_I,Q_F)$ be a GSM. Let $A \in (\mathrm{pot}(Q))\backslash\{\phi\}$ and $y \in \Sigma^+$ such that the following holds:

$\forall\, r \in A\ \exists\, s \in A\ \exists\, z \in \Delta^*$: $(r,y,z,s) \in \delta$ & $\forall\, s \in A\ \exists\, r \in A\ \exists\, z \in \Delta^*$: $(r,y,z,s) \in \delta$.

Let $p',q' \in A$. Then, the following assertion is true:

$\exists\, p,q \in Q$ [8] $\exists\, p_1,p_2,p_3,p_4 \in Q\ \exists\, l_1,l_2 \in \mathbb{N}\ \exists\, z_1,\ldots,z_4,z_6,\ldots,z_9 \in \Delta^*$:
$(p,y^{l_1},z_1,p_1), (p_1,y,z_2,p_2), (p_2,y^{l_2},z_3,p) \in \delta$ &
$(p,y^{l_1},z_4,p') \in \delta$ & $(q',y^{l_2},z_6,q) \in \delta$ &
$(q,y^{l_1},z_7,p_3), (p_3,y,z_8,p_4), (p_4,y^{l_2},z_9,q) \in \delta$.

Lemma C: (see lemma 10.4 in [We87])
Let $M=(Q,\Sigma,\Delta,\delta,Q_I,Q_F)$ be a reduced GSM with n states which does not comply with the criterion (IV3). Let $Q = Q_1 \cup Q_2 \cup Q_3 \cup Q_4$ be a partition of Q such that for all $1 \leq i < j \leq 4$ $\delta \cap (Q_j \times \Sigma^* \times \Delta^* \times Q_i) = \phi$. Define $n_i := \#Q_i$ $(i=1,2,3,4)$. Let $p' \in Q_2$, $q' \in Q_3$ and $y \in \Sigma^+$ such that the assertion of lemma B is

---

[8] In fact, $p,q \in A$.

true. Let $p_1, p_2 \in Q$ be taken from this assertion. Then, for each path π with input y from p' to q' in M and for each path $\tilde{\pi}$ with input y from p_1 to p_2 in M the following holds:

$$\mathrm{diff}(\pi,\tilde{\pi}) \leq ((n_1+n_2)\cdot(n_2+n_3)\cdot(n_3+n_4) - 1)\cdot \mathrm{diff}(\delta) .$$

(Note: If z and $\tilde{z}$ are the outputs of π and $\tilde{\pi}$, respectively, then $||z| - |\tilde{z}|| \leq \mathrm{diff}(\pi,\tilde{\pi})$).

Lemma A is proved in [We87] as lemma 10.1. Lemma B claims an intermediate result in the first part of the proof of lemma 10.4 in [We87]. A proof of lemma C can be easily derived from the second part of the above mentioned proof.

References:

[BHe77] M. Blattner, T. Head: Single-Valued a-Transducers. JCSS 15 (1977), pp. 310-327.

[CuKa86] K. Culik II, J. Karhumäki: The Equivalence of Finite Valued Transducers (on HDTOL Languages) is Decidable. TCS 47 (1986), pp. 71-84.

[Gr68] T. Griffiths: The Unsolvability of the Equivalence Problem for Λ-Free Non-deterministic Generalized Machines. JACM 15 (1968), pp. 409-413.

[GuI81] E. Gurari, O. Ibarra: The Complexity of Decision Problems for Finite-Turn Multi-counter Machines. JCSS 22 (1981), pp. 220-229.

[GuI83] E. Gurari, O. Ibarra: A Note on Finite-Valued and Finitely Ambiguous Transducers. Math. Systems Theory 16 (1983), pp. 61-66.

[Hs78] M. Harrison: Introduction to Formal Language Theory. Addison-Wesley, Reading, MA, 1978.

[HoU79] J. Hopcroft, J. Ullman: Introduction to Automata Theory, Languages and Computation. Addison-Wesley, Reading, MA, 1979.

[I78] O. Ibarra: The Unsolvability of the Equivalence Problem for ε-Free NGSM's with Unary Input (Output) Alphabet and Applications. SIAM J. Comput. 7 (1978), pp. 524-532.

[Ka86] J. Karhumäki: The Equivalence of Mappings on Languages. Manuscript, 1986.

[Ka87] J. Karhumäki: On Recent Trends in Formal Language Theory. Proc. ICALP 1987, in: LNCS 267 (Springer-Verlag), pp. 136-162.

[Sch76] M. Schützenberger: Sur les relations rationnelles entre monoïdes libres. TCS 3 (1976), pp. 243-259.

[WeSe86] A. Weber, H. Seidl: On the Degree of Ambiguity of Finite Automata. Proc. MFCS 1986, in: LNCS 233 (Springer-Verlag), pp. 620-629.

[We87] A. Weber: Über die Mehrdeutigkeit und Wertigkeit von endlichen Automaten und Transducern. Dissertation, Goethe-Universität Frankfurt am Main, 1987.

[We88] A. Weber: A Decomposition Theorem for Finite-Valued Transducers and an Application to the Equivalence Problem. Interner Bericht 1/88, Fb. Informatik, Goethe-Universität Frankfurt am Main, 1988.

Vol. 270: E. Börger (Ed.), Computation Theory and Logic. IX, 442 pages. 1987.

Vol. 271: D. Snyers, A. Thayse, From Logic Design to Logic Programming. IV, 125 pages. 1987.

Vol. 272: P. Treleaven, M. Vanneschi (Eds.), Future Parallel Computers. Proceedings, 1986. V, 492 pages. 1987.

Vol. 273: J.S. Royer, A Connotational Theory of Program Structure. V, 186 pages. 1987.

Vol. 274: G. Kahn (Ed.), Functional Programming Languages and Computer Architecture. Proceedings. VI, 470 pages. 1987.

Vol. 275: A.N. Habermann, U. Montanari (Eds.), System Development and Ada. Proceedings, 1986. V, 305 pages. 1987.

Vol. 276: J. Bézivin, J.-M. Hullot, P. Cointe, H. Lieberman (Eds.), ECOOP '87. European Conference on Object-Oriented Programming. Proceedings. VI, 273 pages. 1987.

Vol. 277: B. Benninghofen, S. Kemmerich, M.M. Richter, Systems of Reductions. X, 265 pages. 1987.

Vol. 278: L. Budach, R.G. Bukharajev, O.B. Lupanov (Eds.), Fundamentals of Computation Theory. Proceedings, 1987. XIV, 505 pages. 1987.

Vol. 279: J.H. Fasel, R.M. Keller (Eds.), Graph Reduction. Proceedings, 1986. XVI, 450 pages. 1987.

Vol. 280: M. Venturini Zilli (Ed.), Mathematical Models for the Semantics of Parallelism. Proceedings, 1986. V, 231 pages. 1987.

Vol. 281: A. Kelemenová, J. Kelemen (Eds.), Trends, Techniques, and Problems in Theoretical Computer Science. Proceedings, 1986. VI, 213 pages. 1987.

Vol. 282: P. Gorny, M.J. Tauber (Eds.), Visualization in Programming. Proceedings, 1986. VII, 210 pages. 1987.

Vol. 283: D.H. Pitt, A. Poigné, D.E. Rydeheard (Eds.), Category Theory and Computer Science. Proceedings, 1987. V, 300 pages. 1987.

Vol. 284: A. Kündig, R.E. Bührer, J. Dähler (Eds.), Embedded Systems. Proceedings, 1986. V, 207 pages. 1987.

Vol. 285: C. Delgado Kloos, Semantics of Digital Circuits. IX, 124 pages. 1987.

Vol. 286: B. Bouchon, R.R. Yager (Eds.), Uncertainty in Knowledge-Based Systems. Proceedings, 1986. VII, 405 pages. 1987.

Vol. 287: K.V. Nori (Ed.), Foundations of Software Technology and Theoretical Computer Science. Proceedings, 1987. IX, 540 pages. 1987.

Vol. 288: A. Blikle, MetaSoft Primer. XIII, 140 pages. 1987.

Vol. 289: H.K. Nichols, D. Simpson (Eds.), ESEC '87. 1st European Software Engineering Conference. Proceedings, 1987. XII, 404 pages. 1987.

Vol. 290: T.X. Bui, Co-oP A Group Decision Support System for Cooperative Multiple Criteria Group Decision Making. XIII, 250 pages. 1987.

Vol. 291: H. Ehrig, M. Nagl, G. Rozenberg, A. Rosenfeld (Eds.), Graph-Grammars and Their Application to Computer Science. VIII, 609 pages. 1987.

Vol. 292: The Munich Project CIP. Volume II: The Program Transformation System CIP-S. By the CIP System Group. VIII, 522 pages. 1987.

Vol. 293: C. Pomerance (Ed.), Advances in Cryptology – CRYPTO '87. Proceedings. X, 463 pages. 1988.

Vol. 294: R. Cori, M. Wirsing (Eds.), STACS 88. Proceedings, 1988. IX, 404 pages. 1988.

Vol. 295: R. Dierstein, D. Müller-Wichards, H.-M. Wacker (Eds.), Parallel Computing in Science and Engineering. Proceedings, 1987. V, 185 pages. 1988.

Vol. 296: R. Janßen (Ed.), Trends in Computer Algebra. Proceedings, 1987. V, 197 pages. 1988.

Vol. 297: E.N. Houstis, T.S. Papatheodorou, C.D. Polychronopoulos (Eds.), Supercomputing. Proceedings, 1987. X, 1093 pages. 1988.

Vol. 298: M. Main, A. Melton, M. Mislove, D. Schmidt (Eds.), Mathematical Foundations of Programming Language Semantics. Proceedings, 1987. VIII, 637 pages. 1988.

Vol. 299: M. Dauchet, M. Nivat (Eds.), CAAP '88. Proceedings, 1988. VI, 304 pages. 1988.

Vol. 300: H. Ganzinger (Ed.), ESOP '88. Proceedings, 1988. VI, 381 pages. 1988.

Vol. 301: J. Kittler (Ed.), Pattern Recognition. Proceedings, 1988. VII, 668 pages. 1988.

Vol. 302: D.M. Yellin, Attribute Grammar Inversion and Source-to-source Translation. VIII, 176 pages. 1988.

Vol. 303: J.W. Schmidt, S. Ceri, M. Missikoff (Eds.), Advances in Database Technology – EDBT '88. X, 620 pages. 1988.

Vol. 304: W.L. Price, D. Chaum (Eds.), Advances in Cryptology – EUROCRYPT '87. Proceedings, 1987. VII, 314 pages. 1988.

Vol. 305: J. Biskup, J. Demetrovics, J. Paredaens, B. Thalheim (Eds.), MFDBS 87. Proceedings, 1987. V, 247 pages. 1988.

Vol. 306: M. Boscarol, L. Carlucci Aiello, G. Levi (Eds.), Foundations of Logic and Functional Programming. Proceedings, 1986. V, 218 pages. 1988.

Vol. 307: Th. Beth, M. Clausen (Eds.), Applicable Algebra, Error-Correcting Codes, Combinatorics and Computer Algebra. Proceedings, 1986. VI, 215 pages. 1988.

Vol. 308: S. Kaplan, J.-P. Jouannaud (Eds.), Conditional Term Rewriting Systems. Proceedings, 1987. VI, 278 pages. 1988.

Vol. 309: J. Nehmer (Ed.), Experiences with Distributed Systems. Proceedings, 1987. VI, 292 pages. 1988.

Vol. 310: E. Lusk, R. Overbeek (Eds.), 9th International Conference on Automated Deduction. Proceedings, 1988. X, 775 pages. 1988.

Vol. 311: G. Cohen, P. Godlewski (Eds.), Coding Theory and Applications 1986. Proceedings, 1986. XIV, 196 pages. 1988.

Vol. 312: J. van Leeuwen (Ed.), Distributed Algorithms 1987. Proceedings, 1987. VII, 430 pages. 1988.

Vol. 313: B. Bouchon, L. Saitta, R.R. Yager (Eds.), Uncertainty and Intelligent Systems. IPMU '88. Proceedings, 1988. VIII, 408 pages. 1988.

Vol. 314: H. Göttler, H.J. Schneider (Eds.), Graph-Theoretic Concepts in Computer Science. Proceedings, 1987. VI, 254 pages. 1988.

Vol. 315: K. Furukawa, H. Tanaka, T. Fujisaki (Eds.), Logic Programming '87. Proceedings, 1987. VI, 327 pages. 1988.

Vol. 316: C. Choffrut (Ed.), Automata Networks. Proceedings, 1986. VII, 125 pages. 1988.

Vol. 317: T. Lepistö, A. Salomaa (Eds.), Automata, Languages and Programming. Proceedings, 1988. XI, 741 pages. 1988.

Vol. 318: R. Karlsson, A. Lingas (Eds.), SWAT 88. Proceedings, 1988. VI, 262 pages. 1988.

Vol. 319: J.H. Reif (Ed.), VLSI Algorithms and Architectures – AWOC 88. Proceedings, 1988. X, 476 pages. 1988.

Vol. 320: A. Blaser (Ed)., Natural Language at the Computer. Proceedings, 1988. III, 176 pages. 1988.

Vol. 322: S. Gjessing, K. Nygaard (Eds.), ECOOP '88. European Conference on Object-Oriented Programming. Proceedings, 1988. VI, 410 pages. 1988.

Vol. 323: P. Deransart, M. Jourdan, B. Lorho, Attribute Grammars. IX, 232 pages. 1988.

Vol. 324: M.P. Chytil, L. Janiga, V. Koubek (Eds.), Mathematical Foundations of Computer Science 1988. Proceedings. IX, 562 pages. 1988.

Vol. 325: G. Brassard, Modern Cryptology. VI, 107 pages. 1988.

Vol. 326: M. Gyssens, J. Paredaens, D. Van Gucht (Eds.), ICDT '88. 2nd International Conference on Database Theory. Proceedings, 1988. VI, 409 pages. 1988.